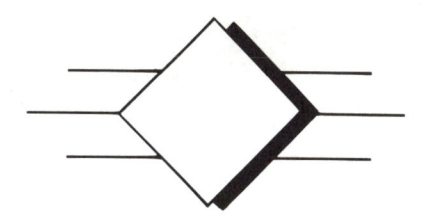

THE NEW YORK PUBLIC LIBRARY DESK REFERENCE

Second Edition

A STONESONG PRESS BOOK

Prentice Hall General Reference

New York   London   Toronto   Sydney   Tokyo   Singapore

Prentice Hall General Reference
15 Columbus Circle
New York, New York 10023

Copyright © 1989, 1993 by The New York Public Library and The Stonesong Press, Inc.

All rights reserved, including the right of reproduction in whole or in part in any form.

The name "*The New York Public Library*" and the representation
of the lion appearing in this Work are trademarks and the property of
The New York Public Library, Astor, Lenox, and Tilden Foundations.

Library of Congress Cataloging-in-Publication Data

The New York Public Library desk reference.—2nd ed.
   p.   cm.
  "A Stonesong Press Book."
  Includes bibliographical references and index.
  ISBN 0-671-85014-8
  1. Encyclopedia and dictionaries.   I. New York Public Library.
AG6.N49   1933
031—dc20   93-18299
                                                                    CIP

Printed in the United States of America on acid-free paper.

10 9 8 7 6 5 4 3 2 1

Second Edition

New York Public Library Project Sponsors

John Masten, *Executive Vice President & Chief Operating Officer*
Paul Fasana, *Senior Vice President and the Andrew W. Mellon Director of The Research Libraries*
Edwin Holmgren, *Senior Vice President and Director of The Branch Libraries*
Elizabeth Kirkland Cahill, *Director of External Relations*
Karen Van Westering, *Manager of Publications*

Editorial Directors

Paul Fargis
Sheree Bykofsky

Managing Editor, Second Edition

Sarah Gold

Associate Editors

Lanie Lee
Robert Lipton
Frances McLaughlin
Gregory W. Tuleja

Contributing Editors

Kenneth Anderson
John Banta
Eugene Brown
Bree Burns
Susan Elliott
Liza Featherstone
Don Gabor
Paul Heacock
Lester Hoffman
Alyssa Katz
Roslyn Kramer
Shelagh Masline
Stephen A. Michaels
Myron Myerson
Andree Nolen
Louise Quayle
Rachel Schwartz
Tad Tuleja

To Alison

A Note from the Editors

Every attempt has been made to ensure that this publication is as accurate as possible and as comprehensive as space would allow. We are grateful to the many researchers, librarians, teachers, reference editors, and friends who contributed facts, figures, time, energy, ideas, and opinions. Our choice of what to include was aided by their advice and their voices of experience. The contents, however, remain subjective to some extent, because we could not possibly cover everything that one might look for in basic information. If errors or omissions are discovered, we would appreciate hearing from you, the user, as we prepare future editions. Please address suggestions and comments to The Stonesong Press in care of Prentice Hall, 15 Columbus Circle, 16th floor, New York, NY 10023.

We hope you find our work useful.

Contents

Preface / xi

1. Time and Dates / 1

Reckoning Days and Hours / 2
Standard Time Around the World / 3
Clocks—Measuring Time / 4
Divisions of Time / 8
The Lunar Calendar / 9
Perpetual Calendar, 1775–2076 / 11
Major U.S. Holidays / 15
Major Canadian Holidays / 15
Major Foreign Holidays / 16
Additional Sources of Information / 19

2. Weights and Measures / 20

U.S. System of Weights and Measures / 21
Customary and Metric Systems of Measurement / 22
Eleven Quick Ways to Measure When You Don't Have a Ruler / 24
Special Weights and Measures / 25
Temperature / 26
Converting Household Measures / 28
Historic Weights and Measures / 29
Common Fractions and Their Decimal Equivalents / 30
Metric Prefixes / 30
Mile-to-Kilometer and Kilometer-to-Mile Conversions / 31
Additional Sources of Information / 31

3. Symbols and Signs / 32

Symbols Used in Astronomy, Biology, Chemistry, Physics, Medicine and Pharmacology, and Mathematics / 33
Electrical Symbols / 36
Map and Chart Symbols / 37
Cultural, Historical, and Recreational Symbols / 38
Weather Symbols / 38
Business and Monetary Symbols / 40
Musical Symbols / 40
Proofreaders' Marks / 41
Diacritical Marks / 42
Religious Symbols / 42
Zodiac Signs / 43
International Road Signs and Travel Symbols / 46
Semaphore Code / 47
International Radio Alphabet and Morse Code / 48
Manual Alphabet (Sign Language) / 48
Braille Alphabet and Braille Numbers / 49
Foreign Alphabets / 49
Roman Numerals / 51
Distress Signals / 52
Ship's Bell Time Signals / 52
Birthstones and Flowers / 53
Additional Sources of Information / 53

4. The Animal World / 54

The Science of Taxonomy / 55
The Biological Classification (*Taxonomy*) *of Modern Humans* / 55
The Orders of Mammals / 56
Invertebrates / 59
Animal First Aid / 60
Extinct Animals / 65
Major U.S. and Canadian Zoos / 68
Additional Sources of Information / 76

5. Math and Science Basics / 77

Decimal and Percent Equivalents of Common Fractions / 78

v

Basic Rules of Mathematics and
  Mathematical Formulas / 78
Basic Formulas of Physics / 80
Heating and Electrical Terms / 81
Alphabetical List of the Elements / 82
Geological Time Chart / 84
Phases of the Moon / 86
Diagram of the Solar System, with Facts About
  the Planets / 87
Brightest Stars / 89
Common Terms in Science and Engineering / 90
Common Computer Terms / 98
Additional Sources of Information / 102

6. Inventions and Scientific Discoveries / 104

Significant Inventions, Technological Advances
  and Discoveries / 105
The Kite / 105
Leonardo da Vinci / 107
Quarks / 123
Additional Sources of Information / 126

7. The Arts / 127

Major Composers of Classical Music / 128
Major Jazz Composers and Performers / 140
Music Terms / 143
The Makeup of a Symphony Orchestra / 151
Major Dancers and Choreographers / 156
Dance Terms / 162
Major Painters and Sculptors / 165
Art Terms / 178
Art Movements and Periods / 180
Major Playwrights / 183
Major Architects / 190
Architectural Terms / 196
Illustrations of Architectural Styles and
  Elements / 200
The Academy Awards, 1927–1992 / 202
Additional Sources of Information / 205

8. Literature / 206

Important U.S. and Canadian Authors / 207
Important British, European, and Russian
  Authors / 214
Important Asian, African, and Latin American
  Authors / 220
Literary Terms / 221
Pseudonyms of Famous Authors / 224
Poet Laureates / 225
Book Awards and Their Recipients / 226
Additional Sources of Information / 229

9. Religions / 230

The World's Major Religions / 231
Significant Dates in the History of Religion / 240
Major Religious Holidays in the United
  States / 241
Roman Catholic Patron Saints / 243
Holy Books of the World / 246
The Greek and Roman Deities / 248
The Roman Catholic Popes / 250
"The Seven . . ." and Other Numbers / 252
The Books of the Bible / 258
The Ten Commandments / 259
Additional Sources of Information / 260

10. Philosophy / 261

Major World Philosophers / 262
Proofs for the Existence of God / 264
Arguments Against God's Existence / 266
Famous Quotes / 269
Philosophical Terms / 270
How to Argue Logically / 273
More Than Just Philosophers / 278
Additional Sources of Information / 282

11. Libraries and Museums / 283

Major Libraries of the United States and Canada
  and Their Special Collections / 284
Major Museums of the United States and Canada
  and Their Special Collections / 293
Reference Works for General Information / 303
The Dewey Decimal System and How to
  Use It / 315
The Library of Congress Subject Headings / 316
Cataloging in Publication Data / 317
Getting Started in Genealogy / 318
Additional Sources of Information / 319

12. Words / 322

Common Abbreviations / 323
U.S. Postal Service Abbreviations / 328
Common Crossword Puzzle Words / 330
Commonly Misspelled Words / 338
Common Phrases: Major European Languages / 339
Frequently Used Foreign Words and Phrases / 340
94 Acceptable Two-Letter Scrabble® Words / 345
Recurrent Letters of the Alphabet / 346
Oxymoron: A Pairing of Contradictory or Incongruous Words / 346
Acronyms / 346
Palindromes / 349
Greek Prefixes / 349
Greek Suffixes / 352
Latin Prefixes / 353
Latin Suffixes / 354
Additional Sources of Information / 355

13. Grammar and Punctuation / 356

The Parts of Speech / 357
Turning Words into Sentences / 358
Punctuation / 360
Spelling Guidelines / 364
Alphabetization / 364
American English and British English / 365
Commonly Misused Words / 367
Four Common Grammatical Problems / 368
Additional Sources of Information / 369

14. Etiquette / 370

Wedding Etiquette / 371
Division of Wedding Expenses / 375
Business Etiquette / 376
How to Prepare a Résumé / 379
Personal Letters / 380
Parties / 381
Deaths and Funerals / 383
Additional Sources of Information / 385

15. Forms of Address / 386

Spoken and Written Forms of Address for U.S. Government Officials, Military Personnel, Foreign Officials, Nobility, and Religious Officials / 387
Order of British Peerage / 391
Abbreviated Titles That Follow Names / 392
Additional Sources of Information / 393

16. Legal Information / 394

Federal Judicial System / 395
Supreme Court Justices / 395
Forms and Contracts / 397
Statute of Limitations / 421
Copyrights / 421
Patents / 422
Legal Terms / 424
Supreme Court Decisions / 431
The Death Penalty / 432
Additional Sources of Information / 433

17. Personal Finances / 434

Tables of Common Interest / 435
Making a Budget / 436
Insurance / 437
Credit and Loans / 441
Real Estate and Mortgages / 443
Investments and Retirement / 446
Investment Terms / 448
Real Estate Terms / 450
Calculating Your Net Worth / 451
Tipping / 452
Additional Sources of Information / 453

18. Useful Addresses / 455

Aging / 456
Alcoholism and Drug Abuse / 461
Children / 462
Better Business Bureaus / 463
State, County, and City Government Consumer Protection Offices / 469
Domestic Violence Resources / 494
Family Planning / 496
Genealogy / 497
Government Agencies and Bureaus / 498
Disabled / 501
Health and Nutrition / 502
Hotlines and Information Services / 503
ZIP Codes / 504
Magazines / 511

Newspapers / 515
Parenting / 519
Radio and Television Networks / 520
Sports Organizations and Halls of Fame / 521
Where to Write Your Senators and
    Representatives / 522
Additional Sources of Information / 523

19. Travel / 524

Travelers' Checklist / 525
Toll-Free Numbers for Rental Cars and Hotels/
    Motels / 526
Airline Codes and Toll-Free Airline
    Numbers / 526
Airport Codes / 527
National Weather Service Average Temperatures—
    North America / 527
National Weather Service Average Temperatures—
    Outside North America / 528
Air Mileage from New York City—
    Domestic / 529
Air Mileage from New York City—Foreign / 529
Foreign Currencies / 530
Foreign Visa Requirements / 532
Passports / 532
Visas / 532
Immunizations / 533
Customs Information / 553
State Tourism Offices / 553
Government Tourist Information Centers / 556
Best Vacation Bets / 558
Theme Parks / 559
Traveling Tips for the Disabled / 559
Traveling with Pets / 560
Travelers' First-Aid Kit / 561
International Auto Registration Marks / 562
Additional Sources of Information / 563

20. Household Tips / 564

Washing Fabrics / 565
Wash-Water Temperatures / 567
Stain Removal / 568
Cooking Equivalents and Substitutions / 580
Cooking Times and Serving Sizes / 584
Refrigeration Food Storage / 589

How to Store Coffee / 589
Temperature of Food for Control of Bacteria / 590
Herbs and Spices / 591
Herbal Salt Substitutes / 591
Chemical Additives / 592
Alcoholic Drink Recipes / 600
Champagne Bottle Sizes / 605
Wines and Their Service / 606
Clothing Size Conversion Tables / 607
Standard Sizes Chart / 608
Additional Sources of Information / 610

21. The Outdoors / 613

Poisonous Cultivated and Wild Plants / 614
Frost Dates for Spring / 616
Frost Dates for Autumn / 617
Germination Tables / 618
Ground Covers / 619
Vines for Special Uses / 619
Botanical Names of Plants / 620
National Park Directory / 624
National Wildlife Refuges / 629
Cloud Nomenclature / 643
Earthquakes / 646
Lunar and Solar Eclipses / 646
Constellations / 650
Additional Sources of Information / 651

22. Sports and Games / 653

Baseball / 654
Basketball / 657
Bowling / 660
Football / 661
Official Football Signals / 663
Golf / 664
Ice Hockey / 666
Soccer / 668
Tennis / 669
Volleyball / 672
Horse Racing / 673
Auto Racing / 674
Olympic Games / 675
Board Games / 678
*The Most Landed-On Spaces on the Monopoly®
    Game Board* / 681

Card Games / 682
Additional Sources of Information / 685

23. Health / 688

Anatomical Drawings with Parts of the Body Labeled / 689
Height and Weight Charts for Adults and Children / 693
Table of Approximate Dates of Childbirth / 696
Life Expectancy Tables / 697
Deaths and Death Rates / 699
Home Remedies / 701
Shelf Life of Medicine / 702
Infectious Diseases and How They Are Spread / 703
Combining Forms of Medical Terms / 704
Breast Self-Examination (BSE) / 705
Recommended Daily Dietary Allowances (RDAs) / 708
Nutritive Values of Foods / 710
Vitamin Food Chart / 732
Vaccines / 736
Activities and the Calories They Consume / 736
Safe Alcohol Consumption / 737
Additional Sources of Information / 739

24. First Aid / 741

Lifesaving Procedures / 742
Mouth-to-Mouth Breathing / 743
Pressure Points / 746
Treatment for Health Emergencies / 749
First-Aid Kits / 758
Directory of Poison Control Centers / 759
The Signs and Signals of Heart Attacks and Strokes / 763
Additional Sources of Information / 763

25. The United States / 765

United States Map / 767
Population / 768

Immigration Statistics / 771
Economic Statistics / 777
Federal Government Finances and Employment / 782
State Government / 788
Territories and Commonwealths / 789
State Flowers, Birds, Mottos, and Nicknames / 790
State Name Origins / 792
Admission of the 13 Original States / 794
Secession of American States / 794
Readmission of American States / 794
The Declaration of Independence / 795
The Constitution of the United States of America / 799
The Emancipation Proclamation / 814
The Monroe Doctrine / 816
The Pledge of Allegiance / 816
The U.S. Flag / 817
Presidents of the United States / 819
The Sequence of Presidential Succession / 822
The Electoral College / 822
Vice-Presidents of the United States / 823
Weather Charts / 824
Important Dates in American History / 829
Government Benefits / 840
Crime Rates / 844
Government Structure / 848
How a Bill Becomes Law / 850
Additional Sources of Information / 851

26. The World / 852

Countries of the World / 853
Great Events in World History / 871
World Exploration and Discovery / 878
Major World Cities / 884
The United Nations / 891
International Organizations / 893
International Conversions / 895
Foreign Dialing Codes / 896
Seven Wonders of the Ancient World / 898
Royal Rulers of Europe and Asia / 899
The Six Wives of Henry VIII / 900
Additional Sources of Information / 901

Index / 903

Preface

> "Knowledge is of two kinds. We know a subject ourselves, or we know where we can find information on it."
> —Samuel Johnson

Most of the information we need today we need quickly. We need ready access to standard facts and a place to verify what we think to be true or false or somehow in question. Until publication of the original edition of *The New York Public Library Desk Reference*, locating the simple, everyday fact required research in various encyclopedias, almanacs, and other basic references. When *The New York Public Library Desk Reference* was first promoted with a touch of hyperbole as "the ultimate one-volume collection of the most frequently sought information," the Staff of the Library firmly believed that this was a book that would be popular with a wide range of readers and useful in homes, offices, and libraries, including this one.

When the editors of The Stonesong Press and the staff of the library originally set out to create and develop this book, we all wanted to achieve three things: to provide a wide-ranging source of information to the most frequently asked reference questions; to provide a great deal of information that would be of perennial interest to the general public; and to organize the information so that one could find answers efficiently and easily. The result would be a practical and useful book that served the widest possible audience.

The subjects chosen for coverage were reviewed by reference librarians who were most familiar with the questions asked over and over again by the public. In addition to librarians, booksellers, and editors, other reference experts were surveyed for ideas about which categories of information would be most frequently sought.

The resulting book seems to have pleased everyone. In fact, the enthusiastic response from the reading public has been overwhelming—far exceeding our original expectations. Even in a world where we are constantly bombarded with information, there is an obvious need for an easy-to-use basic reference. Judging from the letters we have received, a cross section of readers—students of all ages, business people, writers, housewives, lawyers, teachers, clergy, even librarians—have all found it an incomparable resource. It is gratifying to know that the book remains a popular and reliable means for many people to find the information they need.

Knowledge refuses to stand still; there is always more to know and learn. As a result, to maintain the *Desk Reference* as the useful tool we intended it to be, work on the revised edition began almost as soon as the book was published. Amending and updating a book such as this is a complex process involving many people, but we particularly appreciate the help of readers who took the time to write to us about errors or omissions that they discovered in the first edition. All their comments have been reviewed and their suggestions incorporated where appropriate. Every section has been carefully checked for accuracy and continued relevance.

With this new edition, we trust that *The New York Public Library Desk Reference* remains the standard one-volume reference on a wide variety of popular subjects, with quick answers to questions both simple and complex.

We hope our efforts have made the book accurate, browsable, attractive, and easy to use—in short, like the New York Public Library.

The Editorial Board
The New York Public Library

1 Time and Dates

Reckoning Days and Hours / 2
Standard Time Around the World / 3
Clocks—Measuring Time / 4
Divisions of Time / 8
The Lunar Calendar / 9
Perpetual Calendar, 1775–2076 / 11
Major U.S. Holidays / 15
Major Canadian Holidays / 15
Major Foreign Holidays / 16
Additional Sources of Information / 19

Reckoning Days and Hours

The Day

The mean solar day is the average length of a day as determined by noting one passage of the sun across the meridian of an observer and calculating the time that it takes for the sun to cross the same point in the sky a second time. Because the sun's time in making such a circuit varies seasonally, the uniform length of our day is based on a fictional average rather than on what is actually seen on any given day (called the apparent solar day). The mean solar day is the basis of our 24-hour calendar day. It is actually 24 hours, 3 minutes, 56.55 seconds long in sidereal time.

The mean sidereal day is determined by a procedure similar to that of fixing the solar day; however, this procedure uses a star's passage across a reference point on the celestial sphere (that point now being the vernal equinox) instead of the sun's passage. The mean sidereal day is 23 hours, 56 minutes, 4.10 seconds long in solar time. That means that the solar day appears to be about 4 minutes longer than the sidereal day because Earth in its solar orbit has to move a little farther to get back to the point at which the sun crosses the same meridian.

Names of the Days

The names of the days in English derive from either ancient Latin or Saxon systems of naming days after gods or astrological planets.

English	Latin	Saxon
Sunday	Dies Solis (Sun)	Sun's Day
Monday	Dies Lunae (Moon)	Moon's Day
Tuesday	Dies Martis (Mars)	Tiw's Day
Wednesday	Dies Mercurii (Mercury)	Woden's Day
Thursday	Dies Jovis (Jupiter)	Thor's Day
Friday	Dies Veneris (Venus)	Frigg's Day
Saturday	Dies Saturni (Saturn)	Saterne's Day

The Hours

1 mean solar day	=	24 mean solar hours
1 mean solar hour	=	60 mean solar minutes
1 mean solar minute	=	60 mean solar seconds
1 mean solar day	=	86,400 mean solar seconds

When Does a Day Begin?

The standard measurement of the day is from midnight to midnight. This is accepted for civil purposes throughout most of the world, but it has not always been so. Some ancient peoples counted the day from dawn to dawn; others, for instance certain Germanic tribes, counted nights and then grouped them into units of 14—our fortnight; still others, such as Jews, count their days from sunset to sunset.

The 12-Hour System of Counting Hours

Midnight = 12 A.M. or 12 M
Noon = 12 P.M. or 12 N

A.M. (*ante meridiem*) = before noon
P.M. (*post meridiem*) = after noon

The 24-Hour System of Counting Hours

Because the 24-hour system does not repeat numbers and clearly distinguishes between midnight and noon, it is less confusing than the 12-hour system. It is the official system of the U.S. military and it is also used generally throughout Europe. In the 24-hour system, midnight can be designated by 2400 of one day or 0000 of the day following.

How Is the Day Subdivided?

The length of the day is determined by the rotation of Earth. But the division of the day into hours is an arbitrary standard, as is the uniform length of the hour. Before the invention of mechanical clocks, hours were usually of unequal length. Different cultures divided their days in different ways. The Greeks, the Egyptians, and the Romans had a 24-hour day. But they divided it into 12 hours of light and 12 of dark, which meant that the length of the hours depended on the seasons. Only after the invention of mechanical clocks in the late Middle Ages did there develop a need for an hour of uniform length.

Standard Time Around the World

Standard time was fixed in 1883 to prevent the myriad of short time differences that would result if every locality determined the mean solar time by different meridians, depending on the longitude of the particular place. Lines at every 15° longitude were drawn down a map of Earth to create 24 international time zones differing from each preceding and following zone by one hour. Because of political boundaries, such lines often depart from the strict 15° rule and sometimes zigzag or demarcate areas that differ by half an hour only.

The continental United States has four meridians designated to determine standard times: 75°, 90°, 105°, and 120° west of Greenwich, England. Alaska Standard Time is determined by the meridian at 135° west of Greenwich and Hawaii–Aleutian Standard Time is set at the 150° meridian.

Canada has a total of six time zones: the four that apply in the continental United States and an additional two in the east. Atlantic Standard Time is based on 60° west of Greenwich and is one hour ahead of Eastern Standard Time; Newfoundland Standard Time, based on 52° 30′ west, is 30 minutes ahead of Atlantic Standard Time.

Puerto Rico is in the Atlantic Standard Time zone.

Greenwich Mean Time and the Prime Meridian

The mean solar time determined by the meridian that runs through Greenwich, England (Greenwich Mean Time), is called Universal Time. It is used all over the world in navigation, both air and sea, and for scientific purposes, as in astronomy. From Greenwich, too, longitudes are measured around the world, Greenwich being 0°, called the prime meridian.

CLOCKS—MEASURING TIME

The sundial may be the oldest device for measuring time, going back to the Fertile Crescent of about 2000 B.C. Its operation is based on the fact that the shadow of a fixed object will move around it from one side to the other as the sun moves from east to west. Naturally, the duration of the hours marked off by a sundial changes according to the seasons of the year. Along with sundials, ancient peoples used water clocks that measured time by a constant rate of flow of water through a bowl-like device with an outlet. Sand flowing from one compartment into another also was used in late medieval Europe to measure time. These last two methods could be used at night; they also counted more uniform units of time.

With the invention of mechanical clocks, the hours became uniform. The first mechanical clocks appeared in Europe in the fourteenth century (mechanical timepieces existed in China at least two centuries earlier, though the Chinese never developed them highly). The earliest ones were driven by weights strung around a drum. As the weight fell, the mechanism was activated. Next came spring-driven clocks, though they had the disadvantage of running differently when the spring was just wound and at its most tense position and after it had unwound somewhat. The workings of all clocks depend on a motion or vibration that is constant and regular.

Circa 1581 the great Italian physicist Galileo (1564–1642) observed that the time it took for a pendulum to complete one total swing (called the period of oscillation) was almost independent of its magnitude, that is, how far it swung from side to side. He understood that this could be used as a frequency mechanism for regulating a clock. In 1656 a Dutch inventor, Christian Huygens (1629–95), working independently, constructed the first pendulum clock. Pendulum clocks remained the most precise means of measuring time into the twentieth century. Pendulums could be constructed to oscillate at specified frequencies once such factors as latitude, the pull of gravity, and weather and its effect on the materials out of which the clock was made had been compensated for.

Quartz clocks, introduced in the 1930s, improved on the pendulum, though only after years of development. By controlling the frequency of an electric circuit through the regular mechanical vibration of the quartz crystal, high degrees of constancy in vibration can be achieved, making a quartz clock even more accurate than a pendulum.

In the 1940s atomic clocks were introduced. Their frequencies are based on the vibrations of certain atoms and molecules that vibrate the same number of times per second. Atomic clocks are constant to within a few seconds every 100,000 years.

A sundial showing 2:45 P.M.

With each swing of the pendulum, the escape wheel moves one notch as the pallet moves back and forth. Notch by notch, the escapement moves the clock's mechanism to a regular rhythm.

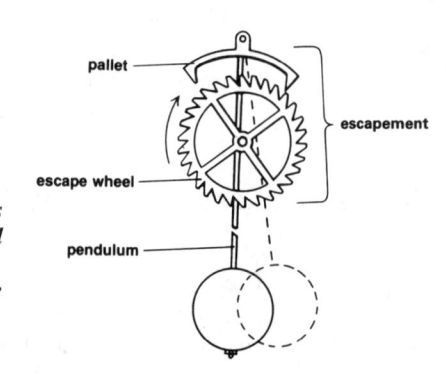

Time Zones: International

The following list gives the time in cities around the world when it is 12 noon Eastern Standard Time. An asterisk (*) indicates the morning of the following day.

Addis Ababa	8 P.M.	Lisbon	5 P.M.
Alexandria	7 P.M.	Liverpool	4 P.M.
Amsterdam	6 P.M.	London	5 P.M.
Athens	7 P.M.	Madrid	5 P.M.
Baghdad	8 P.M.	Managua	11 A.M.
Bangkok	12 M	Manila	1 A.M.*
Barcelona	5 P.M.	Marseilles	6 P.M.
Beijing	1 A.M.*	Mecca	8 P.M.
Belfast	5 P.M.	Melbourne	4 A.M.*
Belgrade	6 P.M.	Mexico City	11 A.M.
Berlin	6 P.M.	Montreal	12 N
Bogotá	12 N	Moscow	8 P.M.
Bombay	10:30 P.M.	Munich	6 P.M.
Brasília	2 P.M.	Naples	6 P.M.
Brussels	6 P.M.	Oslo	6 P.M.
Bucharest	7 P.M.	Ottawa	12 N
Budapest	6 P.M.	Panama	12 N
Buenos Aires	2 P.M.	Paris	6 P.M.
Cairo	7 P.M.	Prague	6 P.M.
Calcutta	10:30 P.M.	Quebec	12 N
Calgary	10 A.M.	Rio de Janeiro	2 P.M.
Cape Town	7 P.M.	Riyadh	8 P.M.
Caracas	1 P.M.	Rome	6 P.M.
Casablanca	5 P.M.	St. Petersburg	8 P.M.
Copenhagen	6 P.M.	San Juan	1 P.M.
Delhi	10:30 P.M.	Santiago	1 P.M.
Dublin	5 P.M.	Seoul	2 A.M.*
Edinburgh	5 P.M.	Shanghai	1 A.M.*
Florence	6 P.M.	Stockholm	6 P.M.
Frankfurt	6 P.M.	Sydney	4 A.M.*
Geneva	6 P.M.	Tangiers	5 P.M.
Glasgow	5 P.M.	Teheran	8:30 P.M.
Halifax	1 P.M.	Tel Aviv	7 P.M.
Hanoi	1 A.M.*	Tokyo	2 A.M.*
Havana	12 N	Toronto	12 N
Helsinki	7 P.M.	Tripoli	7 P.M.
Ho Chi Minh City	1 A.M.*	Vancouver	9 A.M.
Hong Kong	1 A.M.*	Venice	6 P.M.
Istanbul	7 P.M.	Vienna	6 P.M.
Jakarta	12 M	Vladivostock	3 A.M.*
Jerusalem	7 P.M.	Warsaw	6 P.M.
Johannesburg	7 P.M.	Winnipeg	11 A.M.
Karachi	10 P.M.	Yangon	11:30 P.M.
Kuala Lumpur	1 A.M.*	Yokohama	2 A.M.*
Lima	12 N	Zurich	6 P.M.

6 *The New York Public Library Desk Reference*

Standard Time Zones in the United States

Time Zones: United States

The "lower 48" U.S. states and Washington, D.C., are divided into four time zones: Eastern, Central, Mountain, and Pacific. The time in each zone is one hour earlier than in the zone to its east and one hour later than in the zone to its west. The basic pattern of time zones in states is given below.

Eastern (12N)	Central (11 A.M.)	Mountain (10 A.M.)	Pacific (9 A.M.)
Connecticut	Alabama	Arizona	California
Delaware	Arkansas	Colorado	Idaho*
District of Columbia	Florida*	Idaho*	Nevada
	Illinois	Kansas*	Oregon*
Florida*	Indiana*	Montana	Washington
Georgia	Iowa	Nebraska*	
Indiana*	Kansas*	New Mexico	
Kentucky*	Kentucky*	North Dakota*	
Maine	Louisiana		
Maryland	Michigan*	Oregon*	
Massachusetts	Minnesota	South Dakota*	
Michigan*	Mississippi		
New Hampshire	Missouri	Texas*	
New Jersey	Nebraska*	Utah	
New York	North Dakota*	Wyoming	
North Carolina			
Ohio	Oklahoma		
Pennsylvania	South Dakota*		
Rhode Island			
South Carolina	Tennessee*		
Tennessee*	Texas*		
Vermont	Wisconsin		
Virginia			
West Virginia			

* These states fall into two time zones.

Daylight Saving Time in the United States

Daylight Saving Time is attained by advancing the clock one hour. In 1967 the Uniform Time Act went into effect in the United States. It proclaimed that all states, the District of Columbia, and U.S. possessions were to observe Daylight Saving Time starting at 2 A.M. on the last Sunday in April and ending at 2 A.M. on the last Sunday in October. Any state could exempt itself by law and a 1972 amendment to the act authorized the states split by time zones to consider that split in exempting themselves. Arizona, Hawaii, part of Indiana, Puerto Rico, the Virgin Islands, and American Samoa are now exempt. The Department of Transportation, which oversees the act, has modified some local zone boundaries in Alaska, Florida, Kansas, Michigan, and Texas over the last several years. Daylight Saving Time was extended by Congress during 1974 and 1975 to conserve energy, but the country then returned to the previous end-of-April to end-of-October system until 1987, when new legislation went into effect. The new bill, signed by President Reagan on July 8, 1986, moved the start of Daylight Saving Time up to the first Sunday in April, but it did not change the end from the last Sunday in October.

International Time Adjustments

It is common throughout the world for clock time to be adjusted to use added daylight during summer.

Generally, Western Europe goes on daylight time on the last Sunday in March and changes back on the last Sunday in September. Most regions of the Commonwealth of Independent States stay on "advanced time" year-round. China, by government order, operates as one time zone even though it should, geographically, be in five different zones. For religious reasons, Israel is approximately two hours behind the rest of its time zone. Thus, the sun may be setting there as early as 3:30 P.M.

Paraguay, Ireland, and the Dominican Republic adjust their clock time in winter instead of summer. Thus, their time is aptly known as winter time.

International Date Line

An imaginary line set at 180° longitude runs down the Earth. When someone crosses the line traveling to the west, one day is added—that is, Sunday on the east side of the line becomes Monday as one crosses westward. The line, of course, was fixed at the longitude exactly opposite Greenwich, England, on the other side of the Earth, but it zigzags for political reasons so that parts of countries do not find themselves on the wrong side—for instance, all of Siberia is in the Asian system and all of Alaska is in the American system.

Divisions of Time

Unit	Duration	Abbreviation
second		sec., s., "
minute	60 seconds	min., m., '
hour	60 minutes	hr., h., hrs.
day	24 hours	da., d.
week	7 days	wk., w., wks.
fortnight	2 weeks	
month	30 days (generally)	mo., m., mos.
year	12 months	yr., yrs.
olympiad	4 years	
decade	10 years	
century	100 years	cen., c.
millennium	1,000 years	

Year: 365 days; 52 weeks; 12 months.

Calendar year: The civil or legal year from January 1 through December 31.

Fiscal year: A financial year; an accounting period of 12 months. The U.S. government's fiscal year ends September 30, but a fiscal year may end on the last day of any month.

Leap year: A span of 366 days occurring in years divisible by four, such as 1976 and 1984. Even century years, such as 1600, must be divisible by 400. Dates in ordinary years move forward a single day each year, but during leap year, they "leap" forward two days following the last day of February, the 29th.

THE LUNAR CALENDAR

Calendars based on the movements of the moon and sun have been used since ancient times. Whereas today most calendars are based on the solar year of 365.25 days, in ancient times the lunar calendar was the one most commonly used. Notches in bones dating back to 15,000 to 10,000 B.C. have been discovered in what are now Israel and Jordan; their recordings of number sequences are thought to be the first lunar calendars.

In the lunar system, time is based on the number of days between two moons, or 29.5306 days, resulting in a lunar year of 354.3672 days. The lunar year is thus approximately 11 days shorter than the solar year.

The ancient Chinese synchronized their lunar calendar with the solar year by intercalating, or adding, extra months at fixed intervals on a 60-year cycle. This calendar, along with the modern Western one, is still used today in China.

The ancient Hebrews also intercalated months into the lunar calendar to keep it in agreement with the solar year. This calendar of 12 lunar months, with an intercalary month added seven times in every 19-year cycle, is used today in Israel and by Jews throughout the world for religious purposes.

The traditional lunar calendar, without regard to the solar year, is still employed today by Muslims. In order to establish agreement between lunar and civil, or calendar, months, they intercalate 11 days in each 30 years.

Equinox: The day the sun crosses the equator; day and night are equal in length everywhere.

Vernal equinox: In the Northern Hemisphere, about March 21, the first day of spring.

Autumnal equinox: In the Northern Hemisphere, about September 22, the first day of autumn.

Solstice: The day the sun is farthest from the equator.

Summer solstice: In the Northern Hemisphere, June 21, the first day of summer; the longest day of the year.

Winter solstice: In the Northern Hemisphere, December 21, the first day of winter; the shortest day of the year.

Words Describing Periods of Time

annual	yearly
biannual	twice a year (at unequally spaced intervals)
bicentennial	relating to a period of 200 years
biennial	relating to a period of 2 years
bimonthly	every 2 months; twice a month
biweekly	every 2 weeks; twice a week
centennial	relating to a period of 100 years
decennial	relating to a period of 10 years
diurnal	daily; of a day
duodecennial	relating to a period of 12 years
millennial	relating to a period of 1,000 years
novennial	relating to a period of 9 years
octennial	relating to a period of 8 years
perennial	occurring year after year
quadrennial	relating to a period of 4 years
quadricentennial	relating to a period of 400 years
quincentennial	relating to a period of 500 years
quindecennial	relating to a period of 15 years
quinquennial	relating to a period of 5 years
semiannual	every 6 months (at equally spaced intervals)
semicentennial	relating to a period of 50 years
semidiurnal	twice a day
semimonthly	twice a month
semiweekly	twice a week
septennial	relating to a period of 7 years
sesquicentennial	relating to a period of 150 years
sexennial	relating to a period of 6 years
thrice weekly	three times a week
tricennial	relating to a period of 30 years
triennial	relating to a period of 3 years
trimonthly	every 3 months
triweekly	every 3 weeks; three times a week
undecennial	relating to a period of 11 years
vicennial	relating to a period of 20 years

Perpetual Calendar, 1775–2076

Look for the year you want in the following list. The number opposite each year is the number of the calendar on pages 13–14 to use for that year.

Year	#	Year	#	Year	#	Year	#
1775	1	1817	4	1859	7	1901	3
1776	9	1818	5	1860	8	1902	4
1777	4	1819	6	1861	3	1903	5
1778	5	1820	14	1862	4	1904	13
1779	6	1821	2	1863	5	1905	1
1780	14	1822	3	1864	13	1906	2
1781	2	1823	4	1865	1	1907	3
1782	3	1824	12	1866	2	1908	11
1783	4	1825	7	1867	3	1909	6
1784	12	1826	1	1868	11	1910	7
1785	7	1827	2	1869	6	1911	1
1786	1	1828	10	1870	7	1912	9
1787	2	1829	5	1871	1	1913	4
1788	10	1830	6	1872	9	1914	5
1789	5	1831	7	1873	4	1915	6
1790	6	1832	8	1874	5	1916	14
1791	7	1833	3	1875	6	1917	2
1792	8	1834	4	1876	14	1918	3
1793	3	1835	5	1877	2	1919	4
1794	4	1836	13	1878	3	1920	12
1795	5	1837	1	1879	4	1921	7
1796	13	1838	2	1880	12	1922	1
1797	1	1839	3	1881	7	1923	2
1798	2	1840	11	1882	1	1924	10
1799	3	1841	6	1883	2	1925	5
1800	4	1842	7	1884	10	1926	6
1801	5	1843	1	1885	5	1927	7
1802	6	1844	9	1886	6	1928	8
1803	7	1845	4	1887	7	1929	3
1804	8	1846	5	1888	8	1930	4
1805	3	1847	6	1889	3	1931	5
1806	4	1848	14	1890	4	1932	13
1807	5	1849	2	1891	5	1933	1
1808	13	1850	3	1892	13	1934	2
1809	1	1851	4	1893	1	1935	3
1810	2	1852	12	1894	2	1936	11
1811	3	1853	7	1895	3	1937	6
1812	11	1854	1	1896	11	1938	7
1813	6	1855	2	1897	6	1939	1
1814	7	1856	10	1898	7	1940	9
1815	1	1857	5	1899	1	1941	4
1816	9	1858	6	1900	2	1942	5

Year		Year		Year		Year	
1943	6	1977	7	2011	7	2044	13
1944	14	1978	1	2012	8	2045	1
1945	2	1979	2	2013	3	2046	2
1946	3	1980	10	2014	4	2047	3
1947	4	1981	5	2015	5	2048	11
1948	12	1982	6	2016	13	2049	6
1949	7	1983	7	2017	1	2050	7
1950	1	1984	8	2018	2	2051	1
1951	2	1985	3	2019	3	2052	9
1952	10	1986	4	2020	11	2053	4
1953	5	1987	5	2021	6	2054	5
1954	6	1988	13	2022	7	2055	6
1955	7	1989	1	2023	1	2056	14
1956	8	1990	2	2024	9	2057	2
1957	3	1991	3	2025	4	2058	3
1958	4	1992	11	2026	5	2059	4
1959	5	1993	6	2027	6	2060	12
1960	13	1994	7	2028	14	2061	7
1961	1	1995	1	2029	2	2062	1
1962	2	1996	9	2030	3	2063	2
1963	3	1997	4	2031	4	2064	10
1964	11	1998	5	2032	12	2065	5
1965	6	1999	6	2033	7	2066	6
1966	7	2000	14	2034	1	2067	7
1967	1	2001	2	2035	2	2068	8
1968	9	2002	3	2036	10	2069	3
1969	4	2003	4	2037	5	2070	4
1970	5	2004	12	2038	6	2071	5
1971	6	2005	7	2039	7	2072	13
1972	14	2006	1	2040	8	2073	1
1973	2	2007	2	2041	3	2074	2
1974	3	2008	10	2042	4	2075	3
1975	4	2009	5	2043	5	2076	11
1976	12	2010	6				

Time and Dates

14 *The New York Public Library Desk Reference*

Major U.S. Holidays

*January 1	New Year's Day	*Last Monday in May	Memorial Day (observed)
January 15	Martin Luther King, Jr.'s, Birthday	June 3	Jefferson Davis's Birthday (Southern states)
Third Monday in January	Martin Luther King, Jr.'s, Birthday (observed)	June 14	Flag Day
January 19	Robert E. Lee's Birthday (Southern states)	Third Sunday in June	Father's Day
		*July 4	Independence Day
		*First Monday in September	Labor Day
January 20	Inauguration Day	September 17	Citizenship Day
February 2	Groundhog Day	Fourth Friday in September	Native American Day
February 12	Lincoln's Birthday		
February 14	Valentine's Day		
February 22	Washington's Birthday	October 12	Columbus Day
Third Monday in February	Washington's Birthday (observed) (Presidents' Day)	*Second Monday in October	Columbus Day (observed)
March 17	St. Patrick's Day	October 24	United Nations Day
March or April	Easter Sunday	October 31	Halloween
April 1	April Fools' Day	First Tuesday after the first Monday in November	Election Day
April 14	Pan American Day		
May 1	May Day		
Second Sunday in May	Mother's Day	*November 11	Veterans' Day
Third Saturday in May	Armed Forces Day	*Fourth Thursday in November	Thanksgiving Day
May 30	Memorial Day	*December 25	Christmas Day

* These are the officially designated national holidays.

Major Canadian Holidays

January 1	New Year's Day
March or April	Good Friday
	Easter Monday
Last Monday before May 25	Victoria Day
July 1	Canada Day
First Monday in September	Labour Day
Second Monday in October	Thanksgiving Day
November 11	Remembrance Day
December 25	Christmas Day
December 26	Boxing Day

Major Foreign Holidays

January	Australia Day on the last Monday in Australia
January 1	New Year's Day throughout the Western world and in India, Indonesia, Japan, Korea, the Philippines, Singapore, Taiwan, and Thailand; founding of Republic of China (Taiwan)
January 2	Berchtoldstag in Switzerland
January 3	Genshi-Sai (First Beginning) in Japan
January 5	Twelfth Night (Wassail Eve or Eve of Epiphany) in England
January 6	Epiphany, observed by Catholics throughout Europe and Latin America
mid-January	Martin Luther King, Jr.'s, birthday on the third Monday in the Virgin Islands
January 15	Adults' Day in Japan
January 20	St. Agnes Eve in Great Britain
January 26	Republic Day in India
January–February	Chinese New Year and Vietnamese New Year (Tet)
February	Hamstrom on the first Sunday in Switzerland
February 3	Setsubun (Bean-throwing Festival) in Japan
February 5	Promulgation of the Constitution Day in Mexico
February 6	New Zealand Day in New Zealand
February 11	National Foundation Day in Japan
February 27	Independence Day in the Dominican Republic
March 1	Independence Movement Day in Korea; Constitution Day in Panama
March 8	International Women's Day in U.N. member nations
March 17	St. Patrick's Day in Ireland and Northern Ireland
March 19	St. Joseph's Day in Colombia, Costa Rica, Italy, and Spain
March 21	Benito Juarez's Birthday in Mexico
March 22	Arab League Day in Arab League countries
March 23	Pakistan Day in Pakistan
March 25	Independence Day in Greece; Lady Day (Quarter Day) in Great Britain
March 26	Fiesta del Arbol (Arbor Day) in Spain
March 29	Youth and Martyrs' Day in Taiwan
March 30	Muslim New Year in Indonesia
March–April	Carnival/Lent/Easter: The pre-Lenten celebration of Carnival (Mardi Gras) and the post-Lenten celebration of Easter are movable feasts widely observed in Christian countries.
April 1	Victory Day in Spain; April Fools' Day (All Fools' Day) in Great Britain
April 5	Arbor Day in Korea
April 6	Van Riebeeck Day in South Africa
April 7	World Health Day in U.N. member nations
April 8	Buddha's Birthday in Korea and Japan; Hana Matsuri (Flower Festival) in Japan
April 14	Pan American Day in the Americas
April 19	Declaration of Independence Day in Venezuela
April 22	Queen Isabella Day in Spain
April 23	St. George's Day in England
April 25	Liberation Day in Italy; ANZAC Day in Australia and New Zealand
April 26	Union Day in Tanzania
April 29	Emperor's Birthday in Japan
April 30	Queen's Birthday in The Netherlands; Walpurgis Night in Germany and Scandinavia
April–May	Independence Day in Israel

May	Constitution Day on first Monday in Japan
May 1	May Day–Labor Day in the Commonwealth of Independent States and most of Europe and Latin America
May 5	Children's Day in Japan and Korea; Victory of General Zaragosa Day in Mexico; Liberation Day in The Netherlands
May 8	V-E Day in Europe
May 9	Victory over Fascism Day in the Commonwealth of Independent States
May 14	Independence Day in Paraguay
May 31	Republic Day in South Africa
June 2	Founding of the Republic Day in Italy
June 5	Constitution Day in Denmark; World Environment Day in U.N. member nations
June 6	Memorial Day in Korea; Flag Day in Sweden
June 8	Muhammad's Birthday in Indonesia
June 10	Portugal Day in Portugal
June 12	Republic Day in the Commonwealth of Independent States; Independence Day in the Philippines
mid-June	Queen's Official Birthday on second Saturday in Great Britain; Midsummer Celebrations in Sweden
June 16	Soweto Day in U.N. member nations
June 20	Flag Day in Argentina
June 29	Feast of Saints Peter and Paul in Chile, Colombia, Costa Rica, Italy, Peru, Spain, Vatican City, and Venezuela
July 1	Half-year Holiday in Hong Kong; Bank Holiday in Taiwan; Dominion Day in Canada
July 5	Independence Day in Venezuela
July 9	Independence Day in Argentina
July 10	Bon (Feast of Fortune) in Japan
July 12	Orangemen's Day in Northern Ireland
July 14	Bastille Day in France
mid-July	Feria de San Fermin during second week in Spain
July 17	Constitution Day in Korea
July 18	National Day in Spain
July 20	Independence Day in Colombia
July 21–22	National Holiday in Belgium
July 22	National Liberation Day in Poland
July 24	Simon Bolivar's Birthday in Ecuador and Venezuela
July 25	St. James Day in Spain
July 28–29	Independence Day in Peru
August	Bank Holiday on first Monday in Fiji, Grenada, Guyana, Hong Kong, Ireland, and Malawi; Discovery Day on first Monday in Trinidad and Tobago; Independence Day on first Tuesday in Jamaica
August 1	Lammas Day in England; National Day in Switzerland
August 9	National Day in Singapore
August 10	Independence Day in Ecuador
August 14	Independence Day in Pakistan
August 15	Independence Day in India and Korea; Assumption Day in Catholic countries
August 16	National Restoration Day in the Dominican Republic
August 17	Independence Day in Indonesia
August 31	Independence Day in Trinidad and Tobago
September	Rose of Tralee Festival in Ireland

September 7	Independence Day in Brazil
September 9	Choxo-no-Sekku (Chrysanthemum Day) in Japan
September 14	Battle of San Jacinto Day in Nicaragua
mid-September	Sherry Wine Harvest in Spain
September 15	Independence Day in Costa Rica, Guatemala, and Nicaragua; Respect for the Aged Day in Japan
September 16	Independence Day in Mexico and Papua New Guinea
September 18–19	Independence Day in Chile
September 28	Confucius' Birthday in Taiwan
October	Thanksgiving Day in Canada on second Monday; Kruger Day in South Africa during second week
October 1	National Day in People's Republic of China; Armed Forces Day in Korea; National Holiday in Nigeria
October 2	National Day in People's Republic of China; Mahatma Gandhi's Birthday in India
October 3	National Day in the Federal Republic of Germany; National Foundation Day in Korea
October 5	Republic Day in Portugal
October 9	Korean Alphabet Day in Korea
October 10	Founding of Republic of China in Taiwan
October 12	Columbus Day in Spain and widely throughout Latin America
October 19	Ascension of Muhammad Day in Indonesia
October 20	Revolution Day in Guatemala; Kenyatta Day in Kenya
October 24	United Nations Day in U.N. member nations
October 26	National Holiday in Australia
October 28	Greek National Day in Greece
November 1	All Saints' Day, observed by Catholics in most countries
November 2	All Souls' Day in Ecuador, El Salvador, Luxembourg, Macao, Mexico, San Marino, Uruguay, and Vatican City
November 3	Culture Day in Japan
November 4	National Unity Day in Italy
November 5	Guy Fawkes Day in Great Britain
November 11	Armistice Day in Belgium, French Guiana, and Tahiti; Veterans Day in France; Remembrance Day in Canada and Bermuda
November 12	Sun Yat-sen's Birthday in Taiwan
November 15	Proclamation of the Republic Day in Brazil
November 19	National Holiday in Monaco
November 20	Anniversary of the Revolution in Mexico
November 23	Kinro-Kansha-No-Hi (Labor Thanksgiving Day) in Japan
November 30	National Heroes' Day in the Philippines
December 5	Discovery by Columbus Day in Haiti
December 6	Independence Day in Finland
December 8	Feast of the Immaculate Conception, widely observed in Catholic countries
December 10	Constitution Day in Thailand; Human Rights Day in U.N. member nations
mid-December	Nine Days of Posada during third week in Mexico
December 25	Christmas Day, widely observed in all Christian countries
December 26	St. Stephen's Day in Austria, Ireland, Italy, Liechtenstein, San Marino, and Switzerland; Boxing Day in Great Britain and Northern Ireland
December 28	National Day in Nepal
December 31	New Year's Eve throughout the world; Omisoka (Grand Last Day) in Japan; Hogmanay Day in Scotland

Additional Sources of Information

Chase, William D., and Helen M. Chase. *Chase's Annual Events.* Contemporary Books, annual.

Fitzpatrick, Gary L. *International Time Tables.* Scarecrow Press, 1990.

Gregory, Ruth W. *Anniversaries & Holidays*, 4th ed. American Library Association, 1983.

Harland, W. B., et al. *A Geologic Time Scale.* Cambridge University Press, 1990.

Hood, Peter. *How Time Is Measured.* Oxford University Press, 1969.

Landes, Davis S. *Revolution in Time: Clocks and the Making of the Modern World.* Harvard University Press, 1983.

Parise, Frank, ed. *Book of Calendars.* Facts on File, 1982.

Urdang, Laurence, and Christina N. Donohue, eds. *Holidays & Anniversaries of the World.* Gale Research, 1985.

Van Straalen, Alice. *The Book of Holidays Around the World.* Dutton, 1986.

Zerubavel, Eviator. *The Seven Day Cycle: The History and Meaning of the Week.* Free Press, 1985.

2 Weights and Measures

U.S. System of Weights and Measures / *21*

Customary and Metric Systems of Measurement / *22*

Eleven Quick Ways to Measure When You Don't Have a Ruler / *24*

Special Weights and Measures / *25*

Temperature / *26*

Converting Household Measures / *28*

Historic Weights and Measures / *29*

Common Fractions and Their Decimal Equivalents / *30*

Metric Prefixes / *30*

Mile-to-Kilometer and Kilometer-to-Mile Conversions / *31*

Additional Sources of Information / *31*

U.S. System of Weights and Measures

Linear Measures

1 inch	= 2.54 centimeters	
1 nail (cloth)	= 2.25 inches	
1 palm	= 3 inches	
1 hand	= 4 inches	
1 span	= 6 inches	
1 quarter (cloth)	= 9 inches	
1 foot	= 12 inches	
*1 cubit	= 18 inches	= 1.5 feet
1 pace	= 30 inches	= 2.5 feet
1 yard	= 36 inches	= 3 feet
1 fathom	= 6 feet	= 2 yards
1 rod	= 16.5 feet	= 5.5 yards
1 furlong	= 660 feet	= 220 yards
1 mile	= 5,280 feet	= 1,760 yards
1 nautical mile	= 6,076.1155 feet	

Square (Area) Measures

1 square inch	= 6.4516 square centimeters	
1 square foot	= 144 square inches	
1 square yard	= 9 square feet	
1 rood	= 10,890 square feet	= 40 square rods
1 acre	= 43,560 square feet	= 4 roods
1 square mile	= 640 acres	

Cubic (Volume) Measures

1 cubic inch = 16.387064 cubic centimeters
1 cubic foot = 1,728 cubic inches
1 cubic yard = 27 cubic feet

Cubic (Volume) Measures (Dry)

1 pint	= 33.6003125 cubic inches	
1 quart	= 67.200625 cubic inches	= 2 pints
1 gallon	= 268.8025 cubic inches	= 4 quarts
1 peck	= 537.605 cubic inches	= 2 gallons
1 bushel	= 2,150.42 cubic inches	= 4 pecks
1 cranberry barrel	= 5,876 cubic inches	
1 barrel	= 7,056 cubic inches	
1 cord-foot (wood)	= 16 cubic feet	
1 cord (wood)	= 128 cubic feet	= 8 cord-feet
1 freight ton	= 40 cubic feet	
1 register ton	= 100 cubic feet	

Cubic (Volume) Measures (Liquid)

1 fluid dram	= 60 minims	
1 teaspoon	= 80 minims	
1 tablespoon	= 240 minims	= 3 teaspoons
1 fluid ounce	= 480 minims	= 2 tablespoons
1 gill	= 4 fluid ounces	
1 cup	= 8 fluid ounces	= 2 gills
1 pint	= 16 fluid ounces	= 2 cups
1 quart	= 32 fluid ounces	= 2 pints
1 gallon	= 128 fluid ounces	= 4 quarts = 231 cubic inches
1 barrel	= 31.5 gallons	= 7,276.5 cubic inches
1 petroleum barrel	= 42 gallons	= 9,702 cubic inches

Avoirdupois Weights

1 dram	= 27.34375 grains	
1 ounce	= 16 drams	
1 pound	= 16 ounces	
1 hundredweight	= 100 pounds	
1 ton	= 2,000 pounds	= 20 hundredweights

Troy and Apothecaries' Weights

1 scruple	= 20 grains	
1 pennyweight	= 24 grains	
1 dram	= 60 grains	= 3 scruples
1 ounce	= 480 grains	= 8 drams
1 pound	= 12 ounces	

Angular Measures

1 minute	= 60 seconds
1 degree	= 60 minutes
1 sign	= 30 degrees
1 octant	= 45 degrees
1 sextant	= 60 degrees
1 quadrant	= 90 degrees
1 semicircle	= 180 degrees
1 circle	= 360 degrees

Customary and Metric Systems of Measurement

On December 23, 1975, the U.S. Metric Conversion Act was signed, declaring a national policy of encouraging the voluntary use of the metric system. Federal agencies are in the process of making a transition to the metric system for their business-related activities.

Today, the metric system, or SI system (for Système International d'Unités), exists side by side with the U.S. customary system, which dates back to colonial days but is different from the British Imperial System. The debate on whether the United States should adopt the metric system has been going on for nearly 200 years. Today the United States is the only country in the world not totally committed to adopting the system.

The metric system is often considered a simpler form of measurement in that it includes only seven base units for different types of measurement:

The unit of length is the *meter*.
The unit of mass is the *kilogram*.
The unit of temperature is the *kelvin*.
The unit of time is the *second*.

The unit of electric current is the *ampere*.
The unit of light intensity is the *candela*.
The unit of substance amount is the *mole*.

All other metric units are derived from these units. For example, a newton, the unit of force, involves meters, kilograms, and seconds. A pascal, the unit of pressure, is one newton per square meter. Although the metric system was designed to fill all the needs of scientists and engineers, laypeople need know and use only a few simple parts of it.

The metric system is based on the decimal system and follows a consistent name scheme using prefixes. Multiples and submultiples are always related to powers of 10. For example, *deka* means ten times, *hecto* means a hundred times, *kilo* means a thousand times, *mega* means a million times, and so on; *deci* means a tenth of, *centi* means a hundredth of, *milli* means a thousandth of, *micro* means a millionth of, and so on.

Tables of Metric Weights and Measures

Linear Measure

10 millimeters (mm) = 1 centimeter (cm)
10 centimeters = 1 decimeter (dm)
10 decimeters = 1 meter (m)
10 meters = 1 dekameter (dam)
10 dekameters = 1 hectometer (hm)
10 hectometers = 1 kilometer (km)
10 kilometers = 1 myriameter (mym)

Fluid Volume Measure

10 milliliters (ml) = 1 centiliter (cl)
10 centiliters = 1 deciliter (dl)
10 deciliters = 1 liter (l)
10 liters = 1 dekaliter (dal)
10 dekaliters = 1 hectoliter (hl)
10 hectoliters = 1 kiloliter (kl)

Cubic Measure

1,000 cu. millimeters (mm^3) = 1 cu. centimeter (cm^3)
1,000 cu. centimeters = 1 cu. decimeter (dm^3)
1,000 cu. decimeters = 1 cu. meter (m^3) = 1 stere

Area Measure

100 sq. millimeters (mm^2) = 1 sq. centimeter (cm^2)
10,000 sq. centimeters = 1 sq. meter (m^2)
100 sq. meters = 1 are (a)
100 ares = 1 hectare (ha)
100 hectares = 1 sq. kilometer (km^2)

Mass

10 milligrams (mg) = 1 centigram (cg)
10 centigrams = 1 decigram (dg)
10 decigrams = 1 gram (g)
10 grams = 1 dekagram (dag)
10 dekagrams = 1 hectogram (hg)
10 hectograms = 1 kilogram (kg)
1,000 kilograms = 1 metric ton (t)

Comparing the Most Common Measurement Units
Approximate conversions from customary to metric units and vice versa.

	When you know:	You can find:	If you multiply by:
LENGTH	inches	millimeters	25.4
	feet	centimeters	30
	yards	meters	0.9
	miles	kilometers	1.6
	millimeters	inches	0.04
	centimeters	inches	0.4
	meters	yards	1.1
	kilometers	miles	0.62
AREA	square inches	square centimeters	6.5
	square feet	square meters	0.09
	square yards	square meters	0.8
	square miles	square kilometers	2.6
	acres	square hectometers (hectares)	0.4
	square centimeters	square inches	0.16
	square meters	square yards	1.2
	square kilometers	square miles	0.4
	square hectometers (hectares)	acres	2.5
MASS AND WEIGHT	fluid ounces	grams	28
	pounds	kilograms	0.45
	short tons	megagrams (metric tons)	0.9
	grams	fluid ounces	0.035
	kilograms	pounds	2.2
	megagrams (metric tons)	short tons	1.1
LIQUID VOLUME	ounces	milliliters	30
	pints	liters	0.47
	quarts	liters	0.95
	gallons	liters	3.8
	milliliters	ounces	0.034
	liters	pints	2.1
	liters	quarts	1.06
	liters	gallons	0.26

ELEVEN QUICK WAYS TO MEASURE WHEN YOU DON'T HAVE A RULER

1. Most credit cards are 3³/₈ inches by 2¹/₈ inches.
2. Standard business cards are printed 3¹/₂ inches wide by 2 inches long.
3. Floor tiles are usually manufactured in 12-inch by 12-inch squares.
4. U.S. paper currency is 6¹/₈ inches wide by 2⁵/₈ inches long.
5. The diameter of a quarter is approximately 1 inch, and the diameter of a penny is approximately ³/₄ inch.
6. A standard sheet of paper is 8¹/₂ inches wide by 11 inches long.

> Each of the following five items can be used as a measuring device by multiplying its length by the number of times it is used to measure an area in question.
>
> 7. A shoelace
> 8. A tie
> 9. A belt
> 10. Your feet—placing one in front of the other to measure floor area
> 11. Your outstretched arms from fingertip to fingertip

Special Weights and Measures

acre 43,560 square feet. It originally referred to the area a yoke of oxen could plow daily (about 70 yards square).

ampere A unit of electric current. A potential difference of one volt across a resistance of one ohm produces a current of one ampere.

astronomical unit (AU) The unit of length used in astronomy equal to the mean distance of Earth from the sun, or about 93 million miles.

bale A large bundle of goods. In the United States the approximate weight of a bale of cotton is 500 pounds.

board foot (fbm) A measurement used in lumber: 144 cubic inches (12 inches by 12 inches by 1 inch).

bolt Used in measuring cloth: 40 yards.

British thermal unit (Btu) The amount of heat needed to increase the temperature of one pound of water by 1° F.

bundle Two reams of paper.

caliber The diameter of a bore of a gun, usually expressed in modern U.S. and British usage in hundredths or thousandths of an inch and typically written as a decimal fraction.

carat Originally the weight of a seed of the carob tree in the Mediterranean region, today it has two separate meanings: (1) 200 milligrams, or 3.086 grains troy, used for measuring the weight of gemstones, and (2) a measure of the amount of gold per 24 parts of gold alloy; also spelled *karat*. Thus, 24-carat gold is pure, and 18-carat gold is ³/₄ gold and ¹/₄ other metal.

case Four bundles of paper.

chain (ch) A unit of length equal to 66 feet and usually divided into 100 links. Used in surveying.

decibel A unit of relative loudness. The smallest amount of change that can be detected by the human ear is one decibel. A 20-decibel sound is 10 times as loud as a 10-decibel sound; a 30-decibel sound is 100 times as loud.

> 10 decibels—a light whisper
> 20 decibels—quiet conversation
> 30 decibels—normal conversation
> 40 decibels—light traffic
> 50 decibels—a typewriter; loud conversation
> 60 decibels—a noisy office
> 70 decibels—normal traffic; a quiet train
> 80 decibels—raucous music; the subway
> 90 decibels—heavy traffic; thunder
> 100 decibels—a plane at takeoff

The speed of sound is usually placed at 1,088 feet per second at 32° F at sea level.

ell (English) 1¹/₄ yards or ¹/₃₂ bolt. Used for measuring cloth.

em A printer's measure designating the square width of any given type size. The em of 10-point type is 10 points. An en is one-half of an em.

freight ton (measurement ton) 40 cubic feet of merchandise. Used for cargo freight.

gauge A measure of shotgun bore diameter. Gauge numbers originally referred to the number of lead balls of the gun barrel diameter in a pound. Today an international agreement assigns millimeter measures to each gauge.

Gauge	Bore Diameter in mm
6	23.34
10	19.67
12	18.52
14	17.60
16	16.81
20	15.90

great gross 12 gross, or 1,728.

gross 12 dozen, or 144.

hand A unit of measure equal to 4 inches. Used especially to measure the height of horses.

hertz A unit of electromagnetic wave frequency equal to one cycle per second.

hogshead (hhd) Two liquid barrels.

horsepower The power needed to lift 33,000 pounds a distance of 1 foot in 1 minute (about 1½ times the power an average horse can exert) or to lift 550 pounds 1 foot in 1 second. Used to measure the power of steam engines, etc.

knot A unit for measuring the speed of ships. One knot is one nautical mile per hour; ten knots is ten nautical miles per hour, and so on.

league Any of various units of distance from about 2.4 to 4.6 statute miles.

light-year A unit of length in interstellar astronomy equal to the distance that light travels in one year in a vacuum, or about 5,878,000,000,000 miles.

magnum A large bottle of wine holding about $2/5$ gallon.

ohm The unit of electrical resistance in which a potential difference of one volt produces a current of one ampere.

parsec The unit of measure for interstellar space equal to a distance having a heliocentric parallax of one second, or to 206,265 times the radius of Earth's orbit, or to 3.26 light-years, or to 19.2 trillion miles.

pi The ratio of the circumference of a circle to its diameter. A transcendental number having a value to eight places of 3.14159265. For practical purposes, the value is 3.1416.

pica One-sixth inch, or 12 points. Used to measure typographical material.

pipe Two hogsheads. Used to measure wine and other liquids.

point .013836 (approximately $1/72$) inch or $1/12$ pica. Used in printing to measure type size.

quintal 100,000 grams, or 220.46 pounds avoirdupois.

quire 24 or 25 sheets of paper.

ream 480 or 500 sheets of paper, or 20 quires.

Temperature

Prefixes are not as commonly used with temperature measurements as they are with those for weight, length, and volume. The following can be used as general guidelines to tell the weather in both Celsius and Fahrenheit.

0° C	Freezing point of water (32° F)
10° C	A warm winter day (50° F)
20° C	A mild spring day (68° F)
30° C	Quite warm—almost hot (86° F)
37° C	Normal body temperature (98.6° F)
40° C	Heat wave conditions (104° F)
100° C	Boiling point of water (212° F)

Weights and Measures

To convert degrees Fahrenheit to degrees Celsius, multiply by five-ninths after subtracting 32; to convert Celsius to Fahrenheit, multiply by nine-fifths and then add 32.

(Absolute zero = −273° C = −459.4° F)

Deg. C	°F or °C	Deg. F	Deg. C	°F or °C	Deg. F	Deg. C	°F or °C	Deg. F
−17.8	0	32.0	−11.7	11	51.8	−6.1	21	69.8
−17.2	1	33.8	−11.1	12	53.6	−5.6	22	71.6
−16.7	2	35.6	−10.6	13	55.4	−5.0	23	73.4
−16.1	3	37.4	−10.0	14	57.2	−4.4	24	75.2
−15.6	4	39.2	−9.4	15	59.0	−3.9	25	77.0
−15.0	5	41.0						
−14.4	6	42.8	−8.9	16	60.8	−3.3	26	78.8
−13.9	7	44.6	−8.3	17	62.6	−2.8	27	80.6
−13.3	8	46.6	−7.8	18	64.4	−2.2	28	82.4
−12.8	9	48.2	−7.2	19	66.2	−1.7	29	84.2
−12.2	10	50.0	−6.7	20	68.0	−1.1	30	86.0
−0.6	31	87.8	24.4	76	168.8	49.4	121	249.8
0.0	32	89.6	25.0	77	170.6	50.0	122	251.6
0.6	33	91.4	25.6	78	172.4	50.6	123	253.4
1.1	34	93.2	26.1	79	174.2	51.1	124	255.2
1.7	35	95.0	26.7	80	176.0	51.7	125	257.0
2.2	36	96.8	27.2	81	177.8	52.2	126	258.8
2.8	37	98.6	27.8	82	179.6	52.8	127	260.6
3.3	38	100.4	28.3	83	181.4	53.3	128	262.4
3.9	39	102.2	28.9	84	183.2	53.9	129	264.2
4.4	40	104.0	29.4	85	185.0	54.4	130	266.0
5.0	41	105.8	30.0	86	186.8	55.0	131	267.8
5.6	42	107.6	30.6	87	188.6	55.6	132	269.6
6.1	43	109.4	31.1	88	190.4	56.1	133	271.4
6.7	44	111.2	31.7	89	192.2	56.7	134	273.2
7.2	45	113.0	32.2	90	194.0	57.2	135	275.0
7.8	46	114.8	32.8	91	195.8	57.8	136	276.8
8.3	47	116.6	33.3	92	197.6	58.3	137	278.6
8.9	48	118.4	33.9	93	199.4	58.9	138	280.4
9.4	49	120.2	34.4	94	201.2	59.4	139	282.2
10.0	50	122.0	35.0	95	203.0	60.0	140	284.0
10.6	51	123.8	35.6	96	204.8	60.6	141	285.8
11.1	52	125.6	36.1	97	206.6	61.1	142	287.6
11.7	53	127.4	36.7	98	208.4	61.7	143	289.4
12.2	54	129.2	37.2	99	210.2	62.2	144	291.2
12.8	55	131.0	37.8	100	212.0	62.8	145	293.0
13.3	56	132.8	38.3	101	213.8	63.3	146	294.8
13.9	57	134.6	38.9	102	215.6	63.9	147	296.6

14.4	58	136.4	39.4	103	217.4	64.4	148	298.4	
15.0	59	138.2	40.0	104	219.2	65.0	149	300.2	
15.6	60	140.0	40.6	105	221.0	65.6	150	302.0	
16.1	61	141.8	41.1	106	222.8	66.1	151	303.8	
16.7	62	143.6	41.7	107	224.6	66.7	152	305.6	
17.2	63	145.4	42.2	108	226.4	67.2	153	307.4	
17.8	64	147.2	42.8	109	228.2	67.8	154	309.2	
18.3	65	149.0	43.3	110	230.0	68.3	155	311.0	
18.9	66	150.8	43.9	111	231.8	68.9	156	312.8	
19.4	67	152.6	44.4	112	233.6	69.4	157	314.6	
20.0	68	154.4	45.0	113	235.4	70.0	158	316.4	
20.6	69	156.2	45.6	114	237.2	70.6	159	318.2	
21.1	70	158.0	46.1	115	239.0	71.1	160	320.0	
21.7	71	159.8	46.7	116	240.8	71.7	161	321.8	
22.2	72	161.6	47.2	117	242.6	72.2	162	323.6	
22.8	73	163.4	47.8	118	244.4	72.8	163	325.4	
23.3	74	165.2	48.3	119	246.2	73.3	164	327.2	
23.9	75	167.0	48.9	120	248.0	73.9	165	329.0	
74.4	166	330.8	83.3	182	359.6	92.2	198	388.4	
75.0	167	332.6	83.9	183	361.4	92.8	199	390.2	
75.6	168	334.4	84.4	184	363.2	93.3	200	392.0	
76.1	169	336.2	85.0	185	365.0	93.9	201	393.8	
76.7	170	338.0	85.6	186	366.8	94.4	202	395.6	
77.2	171	339.8	86.1	187	368.6	95.0	203	397.4	
77.8	172	341.6	86.7	188	370.4	95.6	204	399.2	
78.3	173	343.4	87.2	189	372.2	96.1	205	401.0	
78.9	174	345.2	87.8	190	374.0	96.7	206	402.8	
79.4	175	347.0	88.3	191	375.8	97.2	207	404.6	
80.0	176	348.8	88.9	192	377.6	97.8	208	406.4	
80.6	177	350.6	89.4	193	379.4	98.3	209	408.2	
81.1	178	352.4	90.0	194	381.2	98.9	210	410.0	
81.7	179	354.2	90.6	195	383.0	99.4	211	411.8	
82.2	180	356.0	91.1	196	384.8	100.0	212	413.6	
82.8	181	357.8	91.7	197	386.6				

CONVERTING HOUSEHOLD MEASURES

From	To	Multiply by
dozens	units	12
baker's dozens	units	13
teaspoons	milliliters	4.93
teaspoons	tablespoons	0.33
tablespoons	milliliters	14.79
tablespoons	teaspoons	3

From	To	Multiply by
cups	liters	0.24
cups	pints	0.50
cups	quarts	0.25
pints	cups	2
pints	liters	0.47
pints	quarts	0.50
quarts	cups	4
quarts	gallons	0.25
quarts	liters	0.95
quarts	pints	2
gallons	liters	3.79
gallons	quarts	4

HISTORIC WEIGHTS AND MEASURES

Units of Volume	Location	Customary	Metric
amphora	Greece	10.3 gal.	38.8 ℓ
	Rome	6.84 gal.	26 ℓ
bath	Israel	2.250 cu. in.	37 ℓ
ephah	Israel	1.1 bu.	40 ℓ
gallon, beer	England	282 cu. in.	4.62 ℓ
hekat	Israel	291 cu. in.	4.77 ℓ
tun	England	252 gal.	954 ℓ

Units of Weight	Location	Customary	Metric
carat	England, U.S.	3 1/6 grains	206 mg
denarius	Rome	0.17 oz.	4.6 g
dinar	Arabia	0.15 oz.	4.2 g
drachma	Greece	0.154 oz.	4.36 g
livre	France	1.08 lb.	490 g
livre (demikilo)	France	1.10 lb.	500 g
mite	England	0.05 grain	3.24 mg
obol	Greece	11.2 grains	0.73 g
pfund	Germany	1.1 lb.	500 g
pound, tower:	England		
12 oz.		5,400 grains	350 g
15 oz.		6.750 grains	437 g
16 oz.		7,200 grains	467 g
shekel	Israel	0.5 oz.	14.1 g
shekel, trade	Babylonia	0.3 oz.	8.37 g

Units of Length	Location	Customary	Metric
cubit	Greece	18.3 in.	46.5 cm
	Israel	21.8 in.	38.2 cm
	Rome	17.5 in.	44.4 cm
hand	England, U.S.	4 in.	10.2 cm
stadion	Greece	622 ft.	190 m
stadium	Rome	606 ft.	185 m

COMMON FRACTIONS AND THEIR DECIMAL EQUIVALENTS

1/2	.5000	1/10	.1000	2/7	.2857	3/11	.2727	5/9	.5556	7/11	.6364
1/3	.3333	1/11	.0909	2/9	.2222	4/5	.8000	5/11	.4545	7/12	.5833
1/4	.2500	1/12	.0833	2/11	.1818	4/7	.5714	5/12	.4167	8/9	.8889
1/5	.2000	1/16	.0625	3/4	.7500	4/9	.4444	6/7	.8571	8/11	.7273
1/6	.1667	1/32	.0313	3/5	.6000	4/11	.3636	6/11	.5455	9/10	.9000
1/7	.1429	1/64	.0156	3/7	.4286	5/6	.8333	7/8	.8750	9/11	.8182
1/8	.1250	2/3	.6667	3/8	.3750	5/7	.7143	7/9	.7778	10/11	.9091
1/9	.1111	2/5	.4000	3/10	.3000	5/8	.6250	7/10	.7000	11/12	.9167

Metric Prefixes

The prefixes below, in combination with the basic metric units such as meter, gram, and liter, provide the multiples and submultiples in the International System. For example, centi + meter = centimeter, meaning one one-hundredth of a meter.

Prefix	Symbol	Multiples	Equivalent
exa	E	10^{18}	quintillionfold
peta	P	10^{15}	quadrillionfold
tera	T	10^{12}	trillionfold
giga	G	10^9	billionfold
mega	M	10^6	millionfold
kilo	k	10^3	thousandfold
hecto	h	10^2	hundredfold
deka	da	10	tenfold

Prefix	Symbol	Submultiples	Equivalent
deci	d	10^{-1}	tenth part
centi	c	10^{-2}	hundredth part
milli	m	10^{-3}	thousandth part
micro	μ	10^{-6}	millionth part
nano	n	10^{-9}	billionth part
pico	p	10^{-12}	trillionth part
femto	f	10^{-15}	quadrillionth part
atto	a	10^{-18}	quintillionth part

MILE-TO-KILOMETER AND KILOMETER-TO-MILE CONVERSIONS

| Miles to Kilometers || Kilometers to Miles ||
Miles	Kilometers	Kilometers	Miles
1	1.6	1	0.6
2	3.2	2	1.2
3	4.8	3	1.9
4	6.4	4	2.5
5	8.0	5	3.1
6	9.7	6	3.7
7	11.3	7	4.3
8	12.9	8	5.0
9	14.5	9	5.6
10	16.1	10	6.2
20	32.2	20	12.4
30	48.3	30	18.6
40	64.4	40	24.9
50	80.5	50	31.1
60	96.6	60	37.3
70	112.7	70	43.5
80	128.7	80	49.7
90	144.8	90	55.9
100	160.9	100	62.1
1,000	1,609.3	1,000	621.4

Additional Sources of Information

Dresner, Stephen. *Units of Measurement: An Encyclopaedic Dictionary of Units, Both Scientific and Popular, and the Quantities They Measure.* Books on Demand UMI.

Gerolde, Steven. *Universal Conversion Factors.* Penwell Books, 1971.

Johnstone, William D. *For a Good Measure.* Avon, 1977.

Kula, Witolde. *Measures and Men.* Princeton University Press, 1985.

Lowe, D. Armstrong. *Guide to International Recommendations on Names and Symbols for Quantities and on Units of Measurement* (WHO supplement, vol. 52). World Health, 1975.

3

Symbols and Signs

Symbols Used in Astronomy, Biology, Chemistry, Physics, Medicine and Pharmacology, and Mathematics / *33–36*

Electrical Symbols / *36*

Map and Chart Symbols / *37*

Cultural, Historical, and Recreational Symbols / *38*

Weather Symbols / *38*

Business and Monetary Symbols / *40*

Musical Symbols / *40*

Proofreaders' Marks / *41*

Diacritical Marks / *42*

Religious Symbols / *42*

Zodiac Signs / *43*

International Road Signs and Travel Symbols / *46*

Semaphore Code / *47*

International Radio Alphabet and Morse Code / *48*

Manual Alphabet (Sign Language) / *48*

Braille Alphabet and Braille Numbers / *49*

Foreign Alphabets / *49*

Roman Numerals / *51*

Distress Signals / *52*

Ship's Bell Time Signals / *52*

Birthstones and Flowers / *53*

Additional Sources of Information / *53*

Symbols Used in Astronomy

⊖ ☾	center	☾, ☽, ☾, ☽	last quarter
☄	comet	Ψ or ♆	Neptune
⊕, ⊖, or ♁	Earth	♇	Pluto
♃	Jupiter	♄	Saturn
☉ ☾	lower limb	☆	star
♂	Mars	☆-P	star–planet altitude correction
☿	Mercury	☉	sun
●, ☾, or ☽	the moon	☉ ☾	upper limb
●	new moon	♅ or ♅	Uranus
☽, ☾, ☽, ☽	first quarter	♀	Venus
○ or ☺	full moon		

Aspects and Nodes

☌	conjunction (0°)	☍	opposition (180°)
✱	sextile (60°)	☊	ascending node
□	quadrature (90°)	☋	descending node
△	trine (120°)		

Symbols Used in Biology

♃	perennial herb	∞	indefinite number
♂, ♂	male organism or cell; staminate plant or flower	×	crossed with; hybrid
		+	wild type
♀	female organism or cell; pistillate plant or flower	P	parental generation
		F	filial generation; offspring
☿	perfect, or hermaphroditic, plant or flower	F_1, F_2, F_3, etc. offspring of the first, second, third, etc., filial generation
○	individual, especially female, organism		
□	individual, especially male, organism		

Symbols Used in Chemistry

+   "and," "plus," "together with," used between the symbols of reacting substances in chemical equations; when placed above a symbol or to its right as a superscript, the plus sign indicates a unit charge of positive electricity; the sign also indicates dextrorotation

—   single bond, used between the symbols of elements or groups that form a compound; when placed above a symbol or to its right as a superscript, the dash indicates a

	unit charge of negative electricity; it also signifies levorotation or the removal of a part from a compound	[ ]	with parentheses, shows certain radicals; in coordination formulas, it shows relationship to the central atom
•	single bond; a unit of positive charge of electricity; separates parts of a compound considered loosely joined	⌒ or ⌣	unites attached atoms or groups in structural formulas for cyclic compounds
⌬	benzene ring	→	gives, passes over to, or leads to
=	"forms" or "results in," used between the symbols of reacting substances in chemical equations; a double bond; two unit charges of negative electricity when placed above a symbol or to its right as a superscript	⇌	is in equilibrium with; forms and is formed from
		↓	precipitation of a substance
		↑	a substance as a gas
		≡, ≈	is equivalent to; used in equations to show how much of one substance will react with a given amount of another so that no excess of either remains
≡	triple bond or triple negative charge		
:	unshared pair of electrons; sometimes, a double bond	<	bivalent element
⋮	triple bond	>	bivalent radical
( )	groups or radicals within a compound		

Symbols Used in Physics

α	alpha particle	e	electronic charge of electron
Å	angstrom unit	E	electric field
β	beta ray	G	conductance; weight
γ	gamma radiation	h	Planck's constant
ε	electromotive force	H	enthalpy
η	efficiency	L	inductance
Λ	equivalent conductivity; permeance	n	index of refraction
λ	wavelength	P	momentum of a particle
μ	magnetic moment	R	universal gas constant
ν	frequency	S	entropy
ρ	density; specific resistance	T	absolute temperature; period
σ	conductivity; cross section; surface tension	V	electrical potential; frequency
φ	luminous flux; magnetic flux	W	energy
φ	fluidity	X	magnification; reactance
Ω	ohm	Y	admittance
B	magnetic induction; magnetic field	Z	impedance
c	speed of light		

Symbols Used in Medicine and Pharmacology

Å angstrom unit
Ā, ĀĀ, āā, āa   of each
a.c.   before meals
ad   up to; so as to make
add.   let there be added; add
ad lib.   at pleasure; as needed or desired
agit.   shake
aq.   water
b. (i.) d.   twice daily
c̄   with
cap.   take; capsule
coch.   a spoonful
d.   give
dil.   dilute *or* dissolve
Dx   diagnosis
fldxt.   fluid extract
ft.   make
ft. mist.   let a mixture be made
ft. pulv.   let a powder be made
gr.   a grain
gtt.   drops
H.   hour
haust.   a draft
Hx   history
in d.   daily
lot.   a lotion
ⓜ   heart murmur
m, ℳ   minim
μ   micron
μμ   micromicron
mod. praesc.   in the manner prescribed
O., o.   a pint
ol.   oil

oz.   ounce
p.c.   after meals
pil.   pill(s)
p.r.n.   as circumstances may require
pulv.   powder
Px   past history
q. (i.) d.   four times daily
q.l.   as much as you please
q.s.   as much as will suffice
q.v.   as much as you like
℞   take: used at the beginning of a prescription
rep.   let it be repeated
Rh+   positive blood factor
RH−   negative blood factor
ð   ¹/₁₀₀₀ of a second
s̄   without
S, Sig.   write: used in prescriptions to indicate the directions to be placed on the label of the medicine
sol.   solution
s.o.s.   if necessary
s̄s̄   one half
tab.   tablet
t. (i.) d.   three times daily
ut dict.   as directed
w/v   weight in volume
℥   ounce
f℥   fluidounce
ʒ   dram
fʒ   fluidram
℈   scruple

Symbols Used in Mathematics

+   plus; positive
−   minus; negative
×   multiplied by

÷   divided by
=   equal to
±   plus or minus

∓	minus or plus	□	square
≠ or ≄	not equal to	▭	rectangle
≡	identical with	⊞	cube
≈	nearly equal to	▱	rhomboid
~	difference	√	square root
≃	congruent to	∛	cube root
>	greater than	∜	fourth root
≫	much greater than	ⁿ√	nth root
<	less than	( )	parentheses ⎫ indicate that the quan-
≪	much less than	[ ]	brackets ⎬ tities enclosed by
≧ or ≥	greater than or equal to	{ }	braces ⎭ them are to be taken together
≦ or ≤	less than or equal to		
≯	not greater than	Σ	summation of
≮	not less than	Π	product
∝	varies directly as; is proportional to	π	pi (3.1416)
:	is to; the ratio of	∪	union
∴	therefore	∩	intersection
∵	since	!	factorial
::	proportion	Λ or φ	empty set; null set
∺	geometrical proportion	∈	is an element of
∞	infinity	∉	is not an element of
∠	angle	e	base (2.718) of natural logarithms
∟	right angle	⊢	is deducible from
⊥	perpendicular	∂	partial differential
∥	parallel	∫	integral
⊙ or ○	circle	∮	contour integral
⌒	arc of a circle	′	minute
○	ellipse	″	second
⌀	diameter	°	degree
△	triangle	%	percent

Electrical Symbols

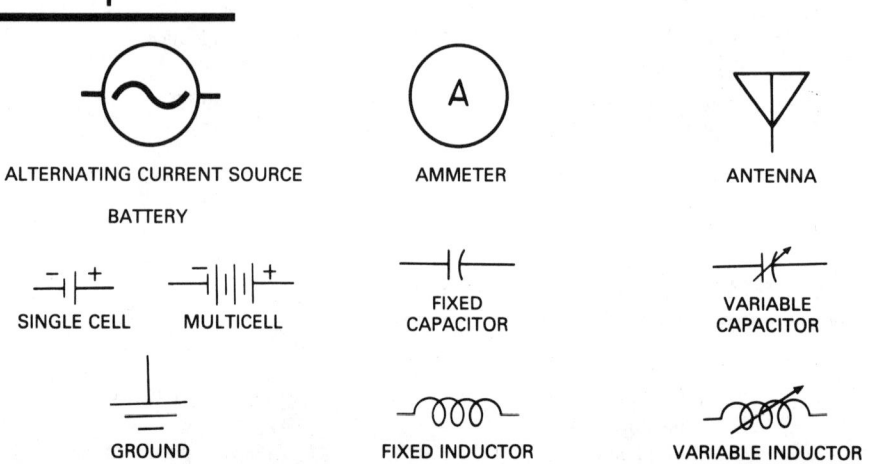

ALTERNATING CURRENT SOURCE

AMMETER

ANTENNA

BATTERY

SINGLE CELL

MULTICELL

FIXED CAPACITOR

VARIABLE CAPACITOR

GROUND

FIXED INDUCTOR

VARIABLE INDUCTOR

Symbols and Signs **37**

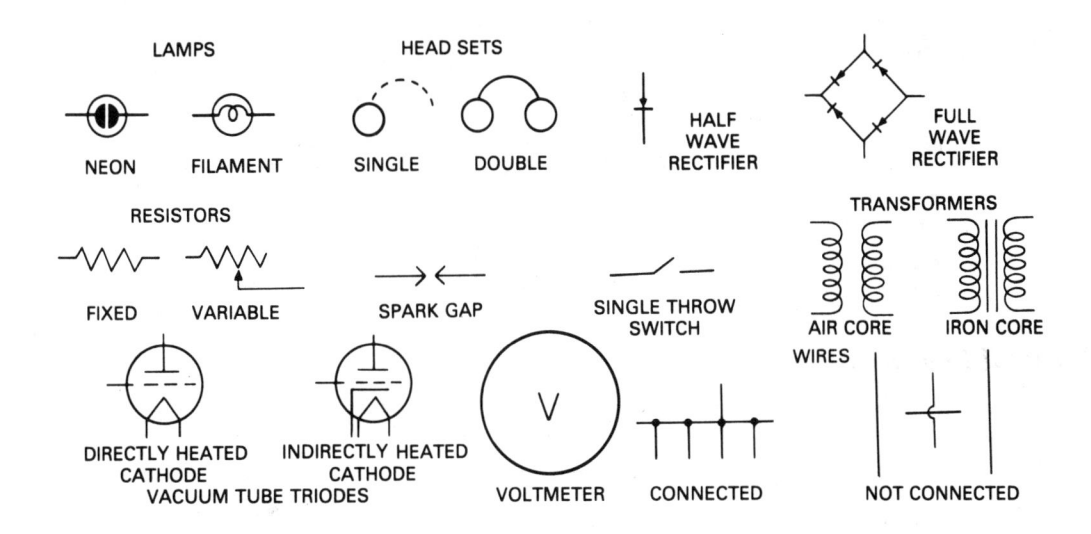

Lamps
- NEON
- FILAMENT

Head Sets
- SINGLE
- DOUBLE

HALF WAVE RECTIFIER

FULL WAVE RECTIFIER

Resistors
- FIXED
- VARIABLE

SPARK GAP

SINGLE THROW SWITCH

Transformers
- AIR CORE
- IRON CORE

Vacuum Tube Triodes
- DIRECTLY HEATED CATHODE
- INDIRECTLY HEATED CATHODE

VOLTMETER

Wires
- CONNECTED
- NOT CONNECTED

Map and Chart Symbols

Boundaries

| INTERNATIONAL | PROVINCIAL OR STATE | COUNTY | TOWNSHIP | INCORPORATED VILLAGE |

Cities and Towns

- CAPITAL CITY
- URBAN AREA
- TOWN OR VILLAGE

Roads and Railroads

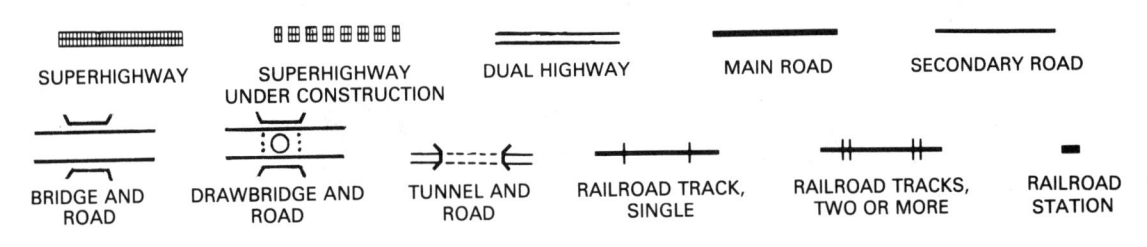

- SUPERHIGHWAY
- SUPERHIGHWAY UNDER CONSTRUCTION
- DUAL HIGHWAY
- MAIN ROAD
- SECONDARY ROAD
- BRIDGE AND ROAD
- DRAWBRIDGE AND ROAD
- TUNNEL AND ROAD
- RAILROAD TRACK, SINGLE
- RAILROAD TRACKS, TWO OR MORE
- RAILROAD STATION

Hydrographic Features

INTERMITTENT RIVER

INTERMITTENT LAKE

FRESHWATER LAKE: RESERVOIR

MARSH: SWAMP

DAMS

FALLS

Natural Features

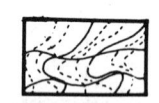

GLACIERS AND ICE SHELVES

PASSES

ELEVATION ABOVE SEA LEVEL

Cultural, Historical, and Recreational Symbols

POINTS OF INTEREST

CAMPSITES

WINTER SPORTS AREAS

STATE MONUMENTS, MEMORIALS, AND HISTORIC SITES

RUINS

NATIONAL WILDLIFE REFUGE

RANGER STATION

Weather Symbols

Weather Conditions

CLEAR SKY

CLOUDY (PARTLY)

CLOUDY (COMPLETELY OVERCAST)

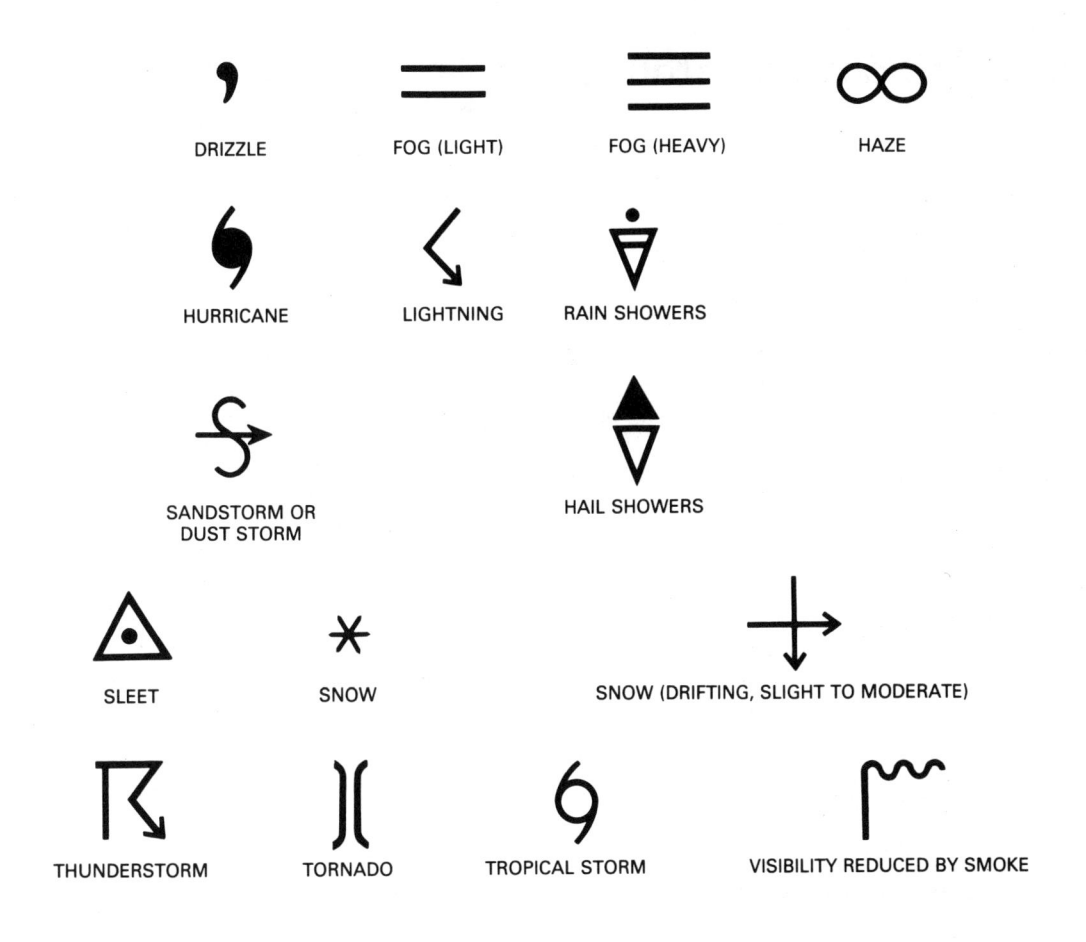

Symbols and Signs

,	DRIZZLE
=	FOG (LIGHT)
≡	FOG (HEAVY)
∞	HAZE
🌀	HURRICANE
<	LIGHTNING
▽̇	RAIN SHOWERS
↯	SANDSTORM OR DUST STORM
▲▽	HAIL SHOWERS
△	SLEET
✴	SNOW
┼→↓	SNOW (DRIFTING, SLIGHT TO MODERATE)
⌐↓	THUNDERSTORM
)(	TORNADO
𝟔	TROPICAL STORM
⌇	VISIBILITY REDUCED BY SMOKE

Wind Speeds

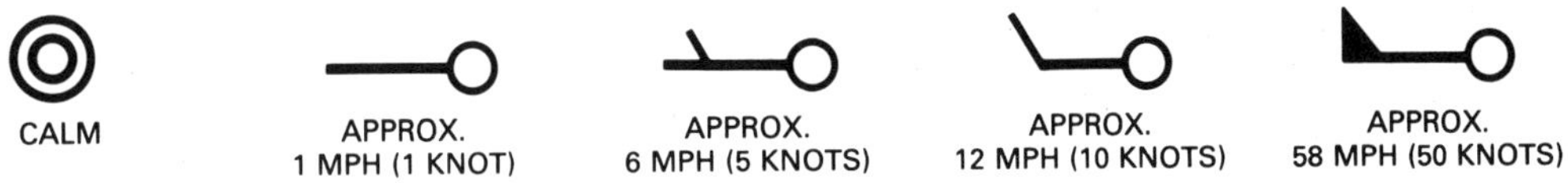

◎	CALM
—○	APPROX. 1 MPH (1 KNOT)
⊢○	APPROX. 6 MPH (5 KNOTS)
╲○	APPROX. 12 MPH (10 KNOTS)
◣○	APPROX. 58 MPH (50 KNOTS)

Weather Fronts

▰▰▰	WARM
▼▼▼	COLD
▲▲▲	OCCLUDED
▲▰▲	STATIONARY

Business and Monetary Symbols

A/C, a/c	account; account current	O/S	out of stock
A/O, a/o	account of	P/A	power of attorney
B/D	bank draft	P/C, p/c	prices current; petty cash
B/E	bill of exchange	P/N	promissory note
B/L	bill of lading	w/	with
B/P	bills payable	W/B	waybill
B/R	bills receivable	w/o	without
B/V	book value	@	at/per/priced at
C/D	carried down; certificate of deposit	#	number, pounds
		%	percent/per hundred
C/N	circular note; credit note	¢	cent
C/O	care of; carried over; cash order	$	dollar
d/d	delivered	DM	deutsche mark
D/O	delivery order	F	franc
G/A	general average	L	lira
L/C, l/c	letter of credit	£	pound
M/D, m/d	month's date	R	ruble
N/S, n/s	not sufficient funds	₨	rupee
o/c	overcharge	Y, ¥	yen

Musical Symbols

𝄞	treble, or G, clef	𝐂	4/4 time	𝄫	double flat
𝄢	bass, or F, clef	𝄵	2/2 time	♮	natural
𝄡	alto, or C, clef	6/8	6/8 time	𝅝	whole note
	measure	♯	sharp	𝅗𝅥	half note
	final bar	X	double sharp	𝅘𝅥	quarter note
3/4	3/4 time	♭	flat	𝅘𝅥𝅮	eighth note

Symbols and Signs

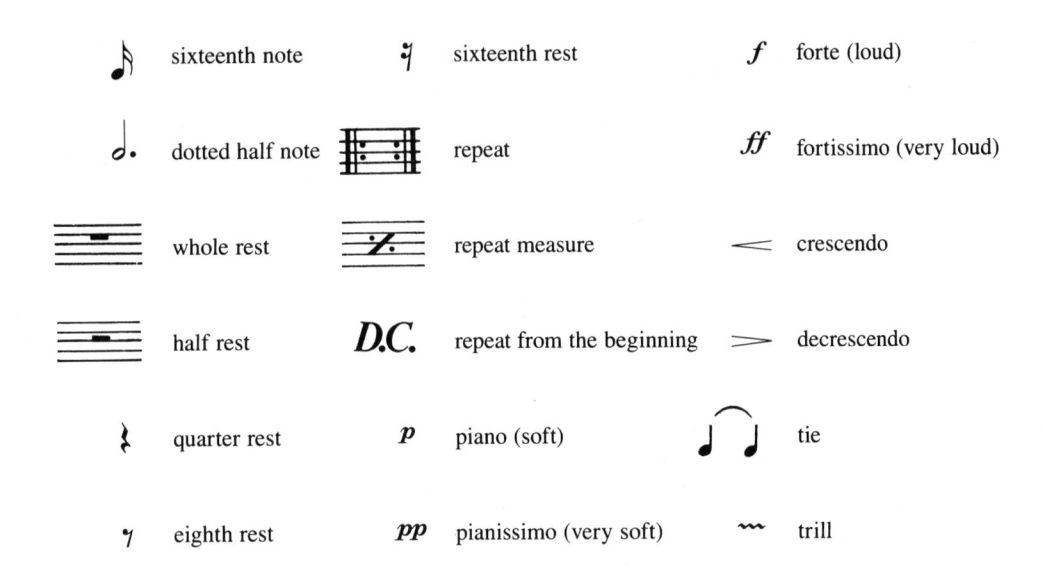

♪	sixteenth note	𝄿	sixteenth rest	*f*	forte (loud)
♩.	dotted half note	𝄈	repeat	*ff*	fortissimo (very loud)
𝄻	whole rest	𝄎	repeat measure	<	crescendo
𝄼	half rest	*D.C.*	repeat from the beginning	>	decrescendo
𝄽	quarter rest	*p*	piano (soft)	♩‿♩	tie
𝄾	eighth rest	*pp*	pianissimo (very soft)	∿	trill

Proofreaders' Marks

∧	Insert material as indicated in margin	no ¶	Do not begin a new paragraph; run paragraphs together
ℐ	Delete	(/)	Insert parentheses
stet	Restore deleted material; let it stand (in text, use dots to indicate what is to be restored)	[/]	Insert brackets
⌒	Close up; print as one word	⌃	Insert comma
ℐ̂	Delete and close up	;/	Insert semicolon
tr	Transpose (in text, indicate by ∩ or ∪ to change order of)	:/	Insert colon
ⓈⓅ	Spell out	⊙	Insert period
#	Insert space	?	Insert question mark
eq #	Space evenly	|·|·|·|	Insert ellipses
hr #	Insert hair space	⌄	Insert apostrophe (or single quotation mark)
◻	Insert or indent one em space	⌵ ⌵	Insert quotation marks
⊓	Move up	|=|	Insert hyphen
⊔	Move down	⊥/M	Insert em dash
⊐	Move to the right	⊥/N	Insert en dash
⊏	Move to the left	∨	Insert superscript or superior
⊐⊏	Center	∧	Insert subscript or inferior
=	Align vertically	*cap*	Capitalize lowercase letter
‖	Align horizontally; straighten type	*lc*	Lowercase capital letter
ꝑ	Turn over inverted letter	*s.c.*	Set SMALL CAPITALS (in text, indicated by double underline)
wf	Wrong font	*rom*	Set in roman type
×	Broken type; reset	*bf*	Set in **boldface** type
¶	Begin a new paragraph	*ital*	Set in *italic* type

Diacritical Marks

- ´   acute accent (as in *café*)
- ˘   breve (pronunciation symbol that indicates a short vowel)
- ¸   cedilla (as in *François*)
- ˆ   circumflex (as in *château*)
- ¨   diaeresis or umlaut (as in *Köln*)
- `   grave accent (as in *à la carte*)
- ¯   macron (pronunciation symbol that indicates a long vowel)
- ~   tilde (as in *São Tomé*)

Religious Symbols

Buddhism

- BUDDHA
- LOTUS 
- THE WHEEL 

Christianity

- CELTIC CROSS
- LATIN CROSS 
- ORTHODOX CROSS 
- AGNUS DEI 
- CHI RHO 
- DESCENDING DOVE; HOLY SPIRIT 

Hinduism

- MANDALA
- OM 
- SHIVA 

Islam

- STAR AND CRESCENT

Judaism

MENORAH STAR OF DAVID TEN COMMANDMENTS

Shinto

TORII

Taoism

WATER: LIFE-GIVING SOURCE YIN-YANG

Zodiac Signs

	Planet	*Element*	*Personality Traits*
Aries — The Ram — Mar. 21–Apr. 19	Mars	fire	bold, impulsive, confident, independent
Taurus — The Bull — Apr. 20–May 20	Venus	earth	patient, determined, stubborn, devoted

			Planet	*Element*	*Personality Traits*
Gemini The Twins May 21–June 21	or	♊	Mercury	air	ambitious, alert, intelligent, temperamental
Cancer The Crab June 22–July 22	or	♋	Moon	water	moody, sensitive, impressionable, sympathetic
Leo The Lion July 23–Aug. 22	or	♌	Sun	fire	noble, generous, enthusiastic, temperamental
Virgo The Virgin Aug. 23–Sept. 22	or	♍	Mercury	earth	intellectual, methodical, placid, tactless
Libra The Scales Sept. 23–Oct. 23	or	♎	Venus	air	just, sympathetic, orderly, persuasive, sociable

Symbols and Signs **45**

		Planet	*Element*	*Personality Traits*
Scorpio The Scorpion Oct. 24–Nov. 21	or ♏	Mars	water	loyal, philosophical, willful, domineering
Sagittarius The Archer Nov. 22–Dec. 21	or ♐	Jupiter	fire	practical, imaginative, mature, just
Capricorn The Goat Dec. 22–Jan. 19	or ♑	Saturn	earth	ambitious, blunt, loyal, persistent
Aquarius The Water Carrier Jan. 20–Feb. 18	or ♒	Uranus	air	unselfish, generous, idealistic, original
Pisces The Fishes Feb. 19–Mar. 20	or ♓	Neptune	water	sympathetic, sensitive, timid, methodical

International Road Signs and Travel Symbols

Danger Signs

CURVE  INTERSECTION  OPENING BRIDGE  ROAD WORKS  TUNNEL  PEDESTRIAN CROSSING

WATCH OUT FOR CHILDREN  ANIMALS CROSSING  ROAD NARROWS  SLIPPERY ROAD  DANGER

Regulatory Signs

NO ENTRY  ROAD CLOSED  CLOSED TO MOTOR VEHICLES  CLOSED TO MOTORCYCLES  CLOSED TO PEDESTRIANS

NO LEFT TURNS  NO U TURNS  OVERTAKING PROHIBITED  SPEED LIMIT  END OF ALL RESTRICTIONS

YIELD  STOP  DIRECTION TO FOLLOW  TRAFFIC CIRCLE

Symbols and Signs

Information Signs

P PARKING	**H** HOSPITAL	MECHANICAL HELP	TELEPHONE
FILLING STATION	CAMPING SITE	CARAVAN SITE	YOUTH HOSTEL

Semaphore Code

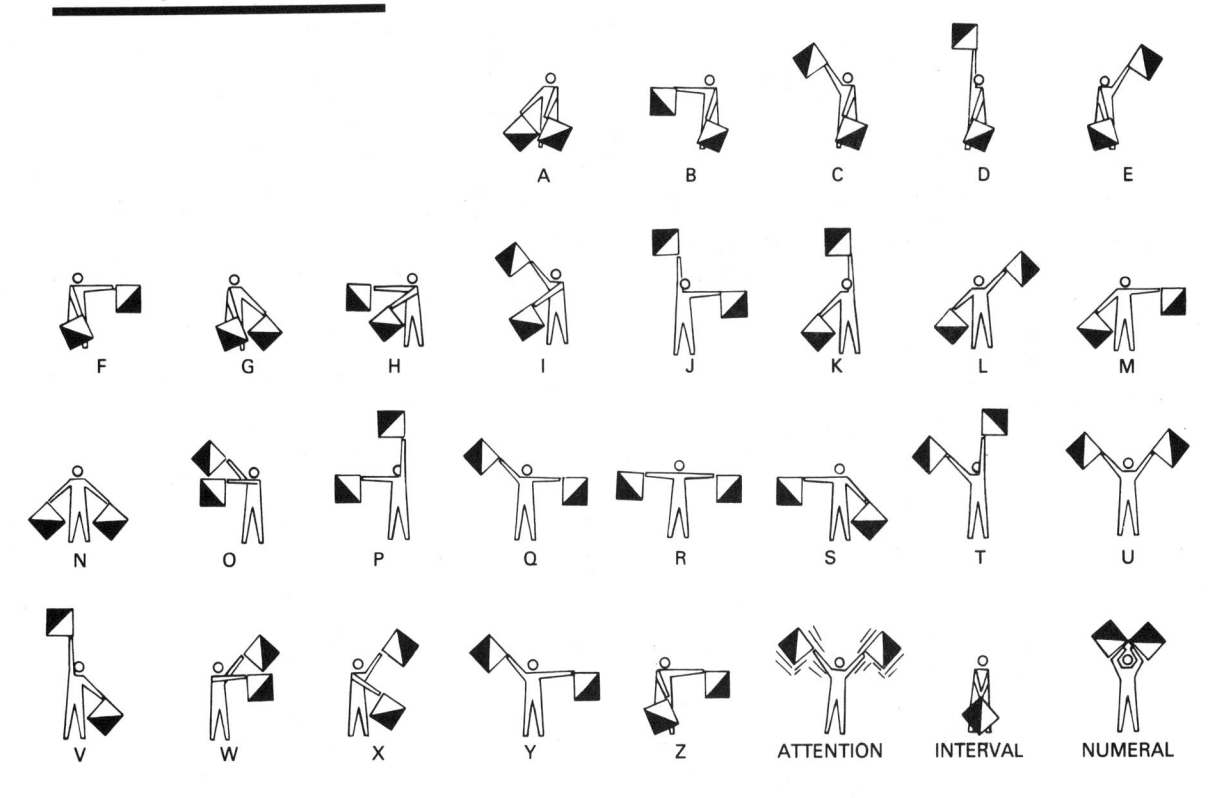

A B C D E
F G H I J K L M
N O P Q R S T U
V W X Y Z ATTENTION INTERVAL NUMERAL

International Radio Alphabet and Morse Code

A: Alpha · —	P: Papa · — — ·	4: · · · · —
B: Bravo — · · ·	Q: Quebec (kaybec) — — · —	5: · · · · ·
C: Charlie — · — ·	R: Romeo · — ·	6: — · · · ·
D: Delta — · ·	S: Sierra · · ·	7: — — · · ·
E: Echo ·	T: Tango —	8: — — — · ·
F: Foxtrot · · — ·	U: Uniform · · —	9: — — — — ·
G: Golf — — ·	V: Victor · · · —	10: — — — — —
H: Hotel · · · ·	W: Whiskey · — —	period: · — · — · —
I: India · ·	X: X-ray — · · —	comma: — — · · — —
J: Juliet · — — —	Y: Yankee — · — —	question mark: · · — — · ·
K: Kilo — · —	Z: Zulu — — · ·	semicolon: — · — · — ·
L: Lima (leema) · — · ·	1: · — — — —	colon: — — — · · ·
M: Mike — —	2: · · — — —	hyphen — · · · · —
N: November — ·	3: · · · — —	apostrophe · — — — — ·
O: Oscar — — —		

Manual Alphabet (Sign Language)

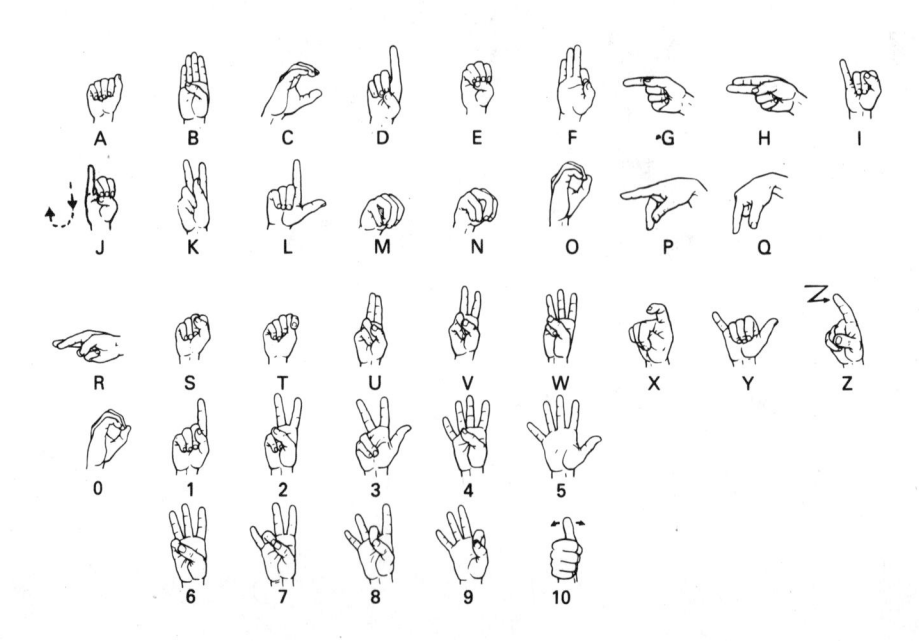

Braille Alphabet and Braille Numbers

a 1	b 2	c 3	d 4	e 5	f 6	g 7	h 8	i 9	j 0
k	l	m	n	o	p	q	r	s	t
u	v	w	x	y	z	Capital Sign	Numeral Sign		

Foreign Alphabets

Arabic

Letters	Names	English Sounds	Letters	Names	English Sounds
ا	alif	a	ض ض ض ض	dad	d
ب ب ب ب	ba	b	ط ط ط ط	ta	t
ت ت ت ت	ta	t	ظ ظ ظ ظ	za	z
ث ث ث ث	tha	th	ع ع ع ع	'ayn	n.a.
ج ج ج ج	jim	j	غ غ غ غ	ghayn	gh
ح ح ح ح	ha	h	ف ف ف ف	fa	f
خ خ خ خ	kha	kh	ق ق ق ق	qaf	q
د د	dal	d	ك ك ك ك	kaf	k
ذ ذ	dhal	dh	ل ل ل ل	lam	l
ر ر	rā	r	م م م م	mim	m
ز ز	zay	z	ن ن ن ن	nun	n
س س س س	sin	s	ة ة ه	ha	h
ش ش ش ش	shin	sh	و و	waw	w
ص ص ص ص	sad	s	ى ى ى ى	ya	y

The Arabic alphabet is comprised primarily of consonants. The use of each of the four consonant forms shown above depends on whether the letter stands alone (first form), is joined to the preceding letter (second form), is joined to both the preceding and following letters (third form), or is joined only to the following letter (fourth form). In Arabic, long vowels are indicated by the consonants *alif* (for *a*), *waw* (for *u*), and *ya* (for *i*). Although short vowels are not usually written, they can be indicated by ´ *fatha* (for *a*), ˎ *kesra* (for *i*), and ˒ *damma* (for *u*). When *ha* (third letter form from bottom) has two dots over it, a new letter is made and is pronounced *t*. *'Ayn* (eleventh from bottom) cannot be represented in English transliteration. Arabic is read from right to left.

Greek

Letters	Names	English Sounds	Letters	Names	English Sounds
A α	alpha	a	N ν	nu	n
B β	beta	b	Ξ ξ	xi	x
Γ γ	gamma	g	O o	omicron	o
Δ δ	delta	d	Π π	pi	p
E ε	epsilon	e	P ρ	rho	r, rh
Z ζ	zeta	z	Σ σ ς	sigma	s
H η	eta	ē	T τ	tau	t
Θ θ	theta	th	Υ υ	upsilon	y, u
I ι	iota	i	Φ φ	phi	ph
K κ	kappa	k	X χ	chi	ch
Λ λ	lambda	l	Ψ ψ	psi	ps
M μ	mu	m	Ω ω	omega	ō

Hebrew

Letters	Names	English Sounds	Letters	Names	English Sounds
א	aleph	n.a.	ל	lamed	l
ב	beth	b,v	מ ם	mem	m
ג	gimel	g	נ ן	nun	n
ד	daleth	d	ס	samekh	s
ה	he	h	ע	ayin	n.a.
ו	vav	v	פ ף	pe	p,f
ז	zayin	z	צ ץ	sadhe	ts
ח	het	h	ק	koph	q
ט	teth	t	ר	resh	r
י	yod	y	ש	shin, sin	sh, s
כ ך	kaf	K, kh	ת	tav	t

Like the Arabic alphabet, the Hebrew alphabet is made up mainly of consonants. Vowels usually do not appear in Hebrew writing, but for educational purposes they are indicated by vowel points—dots or strokes—that are used with a consonant, such as ד , which would read *day*. Five of the consonants—*kaf, mem, nun, pe*, and *sadhe*—become different (the second consonant form in the first column) when they appear at the end of a word. By themselves, the consonants *aleph* and *ayin* are silent. *Bet, Kaf,* and *pe* have alternate pronunciations depending on whether or not a dot, called *dagesh*, appears in the letter; *shin* carries a dot above right, while *sin* carries a dot above left. Hebrew, like Arabic, is read from right to left.

Russian

Letters	English Sounds	Letters	English Sounds
А а	a	С с	s
Б б	b	Т т	t
В в	v	У у	u
Г г	g	Ф ф	f
Д д	d	Х х	kh
Е е	e	Ц ц	ts
Ж ж	zh	Ч ч	ch
З з	z	Ш ш	sh
И и Й й	i, y	Щ щ	shch
К к	k	Ъ ъ	n.a.
Л л	l	Ы ы	y
М м	m	Ь ь	n.a.
Н н	n	Э э	e
О о	o	Ю ю	yu
П п	p	Я я	ya
Р р	r		

The Russian, or Cyrillic, alphabet is based largely on the Greek alphabet. In modern Russian, the ъ is rare. It signifies that the preceding consonant remains hard even when followed by a palatal vowel. The ь signifies that the preceding consonant is palatalized even if it is not immediately followed by a palatal vowel.

Roman Numerals

1	I	70	LXX	1,910	MCMX
2	II	80	LXXX	1,920	MCMXX
3	III	90	XC	1,930	MCMXXX
4	IV	100	C	1,940	MCMXL
5	V	150	CL	1,950	MCML
6	VI	200	CC	1,960	MCMLX
7	VII	300	CCC	1,970	MCMLXX
8	VIII	400	CD	1,980	MCMLXXX
9	IX	500	D	1,990	MCMXC
10	X	600	DC	2,000	MM
15	XV	700	DCC	3,000	MMM
20	XX	800	DCCC	4,000	MMMM or M$\overline{V}$
25	XXV	900	CM	5,000	$\overline{V}$
30	XXX	1,000	M	10,000	$\overline{X}$
40	XL	1,500	MD	50,000	$\overline{L}$
50	L	1,900	MCM or MDCCCC	100,000	$\overline{C}$
60	LX			1,000,000	$\overline{M}$

Distress Signals

I	NEED DOCTOR
II	NEED MEDICINE
X	CANNOT PROCEED
F	NEED FOOD AND WATER
⋙	NEED WEAPONS
K	INDICATE DIRECTION
↑	GOING THIS WAY
D	AIRCRAFT DAMAGED
⌐⌐	ATTEMPTING TAKE OFF
△	SAFE TO LAND
LL	ALL WELL
L	NEED FUEL AND OIL
N	NO
Y	YES
JL	DON'T UNDERSTAND
W	NEED ENGINEER
□	NEED COMPASS AND MAP
!	NEED SIGNAL LAMP

Ship's Bell Time Signals

On most ships, a day consists of six 4-hour watches. The watches change at 8 A.M., noon, 4 P.M., 8 P.M., midnight, and 4 A.M. A chime indicates each half-hour. During a four hour watch, one bell chimes at the first half-hour, two bells at the second, and so on up to eight, when the next watch begins and the sequence starts over again.

1 bell	12:30 or	4:30 or	8:30 A.M. or P.M.
2 bells	1:00	5:00	9:00
3 bells	1:30	5:30	9:30
4 bells	2:00	6:00	10:00
5 bells	2:30	6:30	10:30
6 bells	3:00	7:00	11:00
7 bells	3:30	7:30	11:30
8 bells	4:00	8:00	12:00

On many vessels the ship's whistle is blown at noon. On some ships a lightly struck 1 bell announces 15 minutes before the change of watch.

Birthstones and Flowers

Month	Birthstone	Flower
January	garnet	snowdrop
February	amethyst	primrose
March	aquamarine or bloodstone	violet
April	diamond	daisy
May	emerald	hawthorn
June	pearl, alexandrite, or moonstone	rose
July	ruby	water lily
August	sardonyx or peridot	poppy
September	sapphire	morning glory
October	opal or tourmaline	hops
November	topaz	chrysanthemum
December	turquoise or lapis lazuli	holly

Additional Sources of Information

Adkins, Jan. *Symbols: A Silent Language.* Walker and Company, 1984.

Campbell, Joseph, and M. J. Abadie. *The Mythic Image.* Princeton University Press, 1981.

Cirlot, J. E. *A Dictionary of Symbols.* Philosophy Library, 1972.

Cooper, J. C. *An Illustrated Encyclopaedia of Traditional Symbols.* Thames and Hudson, 1987.

Dreyfuss, Henry, ed. *Symbol Sourcebook: An Authoritative Guide to International Graphic Symbols.* Van Nostrand Reinhold, 1984.

Modley, Rudolf, and William R. Meyers. *Handbook of Pictorial Symbols.* Dover, 1976.

4

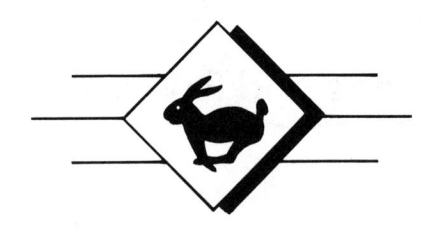

The Animal World

The Science of Taxonomy / 55
The Biological Classification (Taxonomy) of Modern Humans / 55
The Orders of Mammals / 56
Invertebrates / 59
Animal First Aid / 60
Extinct Animals / 65
Major U.S. and Canadian Zoos / 68
Additional Sources of Information / 76

The Science of Taxonomy

Although some modern scientists have divided the natural world into six kingdoms, traditionally three kingdoms are used: the animal kingdom, the mineral kingdom, and the plant kingdom. All animals are made up of a cell or cells, with a nucleus containing the cell's genetic specifications. The animal kingdom is divided into main groups of related animals called *phyla* (singular, *phylum*).

Taxonomy, more recently known as systematics, is the science of naming organisms in these kingdoms in a way that reflects their natural relationships. Although taxonomy dates back to the days of Aristotle, modern taxonomy was developed in the 1700s by Carolus Linnaeus, whose system of binomial nomenclature is still in use. According to this system, each organism is assigned a two-word Latin name designating its genus and species. *Homo sapiens*, for example, are the genus and species of human beings.

Each phylum, the largest grouping of related animals, contains several *classes*. Each of these classes is divided into *orders*, which themselves are further divided into *families, genera,* and *species*. There are more than one million different species of animals in the world, including about 4,000 species of mammals.

THE BIOLOGICAL CLASSIFICATION (TAXONOMY) OF MODERN HUMANS

Biologists classify life on Earth into a hierarchy of groups of related organisms. These groups are called *taxa* (singular, *taxon*). From most inclusive to least inclusive, the taxa are called *kingdom, phylum* (plural, *phyla*), *class, order, family, genus* (plural, *genera*), and *species*. Intermediate taxonomic levels are occasionally created at any level by using the prefixes *super-, sub-,* and *infra-*. The following table shows the taxonomy of modern humans.

Taxonomic Level	Name	Distinguishing Feature
Kingdom	Animalia	Animal
Phylum	Chordata	Spinal cord
Subphylum	Vertebrata	Segmented backbone
Superclass	Tetrapoda	Four limbs
Class	Mammalia	Suckle young
Subclass	Theria	Live birth
Infraclass	Eutheria	Placenta
Order	Primates	Most highly developed
Superfamily	Hominoidea	Human-like
Family	Hominidae	Two-legged
Genus	*Homo*	Human
Species	*sapiens*	Modern human

The Orders of Mammals

All animals with backbones, including humans, are chordates. That is, in the language of taxonomy, they belong to the phylum Chordata. Their subphylum is Vertebrata, meaning that their backbones are segmented. Mammals, members of the class Mammalia of vertebrate animals that includes humans, are the most highly advanced organisms on Earth. They are warm-blooded, hairy, have four-chambered hearts, relatively large brains, and they suckle their young.

There are 19 orders of mammals in the world. Ten of these live in North America. Some orders include a wide range of animals; for example, shrews, lemurs, marmosets, monkeys, apes, and humans are all primates, one order of the class of mammals. Other orders are made up of only one sort of creature; Order Chiroptera, for example, consists of 18 families of bats.

The Latin names of the orders of mammals given here are followed by their common names and the families that make up each order. Examples of the various types of animals included in each family also are given.

Order Artiodactyla (even-toed hoofed animals)

Hoofed animals with an even number of toes include those that ruminate, or digest their food in four-chamber stomachs and chew cuds, and those that do not ruminate. Those that ruminate are the families *Girrafidae* (giraffes), *Cervidae* (deer, moose, reindeer, elk), *Antilocapridae* (pronghorn antelope), and *Bovidae* (cattle, bison, yaks, waterbucks, wildebeest, gazelles, springboks, sheep, musk oxen, goats). Nonruminators include the families *Suidae* (pigs), *Tayassuidae* (peccaries), *Hippopotamidae* (hippopotamuses), and *Camelidae* (camels, llamas).

Order Carnivora (meat-eaters)

There are two suborders of these toe-footed creatures. They include the *Canidae* (wolves, dogs, jackals, foxes), *Ursidae* (bears, giant pandas), *Procyonidae* (coatis, raccoons, lesser pandas), and *Mustelidae* (martens, weasels, skunks, otters), all part of one superfamily that is characterized by long snouts and unretractable claws; and *Felidae* (cats, lions, cheetahs, leopards), *Hyaenidae* (hyenas), and *Viverridae* (mongooses, civets), all of which have retractable claws.

Order Cetacea (whales and porpoises)

Two suborders of Order *Cetacea* are the toothed whales, which have regular conical teeth, and the baleen, or whalebone, whales, which have irregular whalebone surfaces instead of teeth. Toothed whales include the families *Physeteridae* (sperm whales), *Monodontidae* (narwhals, belugas), *Phocoenidae* (porpoises), and *Delphinidae* (dolphins, killer whales). Baleens are in the Family *Eschrichtiidae* (gray whales), *Balaenidae* (right whales), or *Balaenoptridae* (fin-backed whales, hump-backed whales).

Order Chiroptera (bats)

There are two suborders of bats, the only mammals that can fly. Suborder *Megachiroptera* contains one family, the *Pteropodidae* (flying foxes, Old World fruit bats). Suborder *Microchiroptera* contains 17 families, including: *Rhinopomatidae* (mouse-tailed bats), *Emballonuridae* (sheath-tailed bats), *Craseonycteridae* (hog-nosed or butterfly bats), *Noctilionidae* (bulldog or fisherman bats), *Nycteridae* (slit-faced bats), *Megadermatidae* (false vampire bats), and *Rhinolophidae* (horseshoe bats).

Order Dermoptera (colugos or flying lemurs)

These gliding tree mammals from Asia do not fly and are not lemurs, but they are known as flying lemurs, or Family *Cynocephalidae*.

Order Edentata (toothless mammals)

Three families of mammals get by without teeth: *Dasypodidae* (armadillos), *Bradypodidae* (sloths), and *Myrmecophagidae* (hairy anteaters).

Order Hyracoidae (hyraxes, dassies)

Order *Hyracoidae* is one of three orders that has only one modern family remaining. *Procavia capensis* (the African rock hyrax) is one of nine living species in the Family *Procaviidae*.

Order Insectivora (insect-eaters)

The three members are the families *Talpidae* (moles), *Soricidae* (shrews), and *Erinaceidae* (hedgehogs).

Order Lagomorpha (pikas, hares, and rabbits)

Two families make up this order: *Ochotonidae* (pikas) and *Leporidae* (hares and rabbits of all sorts).

Order Marsupialia (pouched mammals)

Included among these are the families *Caenolestidae* (rat opossums), *Diddeelphidae* (true opossums), *Dasyuridae* (native cats, native mice), *Notoryctidae* (marsupial moles), *Myrmecobiidae* (numbats), *Peramelidae* (bandicoots), *Phalangeridae* (koalas), *Vombatidae* (wombats), and *Macropodidae* (kangaroos and wallabies).

Order Monotremata (egg-laying mammals)

These more primitive mammals make up the families *Tachyglossidae* (echidnas, also called spiny anteaters) and *Ornithorhynchidae* (platypuses).

Order Perissodactyla (odd-toed hoofed animals)

The two suborders, Hippomorpha and Ceratomorpha, include creatures that have an odd number of toes. Families in this order are the *Equidae* (horses, donkeys, zebras), the *Tapiridae* (tapirs), and the *Rhinocerotidae* (rhinoceroses).

Order Pholidata

Family *Manidae* (pangolins) is the sole family in this order.

Order Pinnipedia (seals and walruses)

In the fin-footed order there are *Otariidae* (eared seals, sea lions), *Odobenidae* (walruses), and *Phocidae* (earless seals).

Order Primates (primates)

The order to which people belong is divided into two suborders: the *Prosimii*, who have longer snouts than their relatives, and the *Anthropoidae*. The first group includes the families *Tupalidae* (tree shrew), *Lemuridae* (lemurs), *Daubentonlidae* (aye-ayes), *Lorisidae* (lorises, pottos), and *Tarsiidae* (tarsiers). The anthropoids include the families *Callitrichidae* (marmosets), *Cebidae* (New World monkeys), *Cercopithecidae* (baboons, Old World monkeys), *Hylobatidae* (gibbons), *Pongidae* (gorillas, chimpanzees, orangutans), and *Hominidae* (human beings).

Order Proboscidea (elephants)

Large enough to have an order all to itself is Family *Elephantidae*.

Order Rodentia (gnawing mammals)

The most prolific mammals, Order *Rodentia* includes three suborders. It takes in the families *Aplodontidae* (mountain beavers), *Sciuridae* (chipmunks, squirrels, marmots), *Cricetidae* (field mice, lemmings, muskrats, hamsters, gerbils), *Muridae* (Old World mice, rats), *Heteromyidae* (New World mice), *Geomyidae* (gophers), and *Dipodidae* (jerboas).

Order Sirenia (dugongs and manatees)

The families *Trichechidae* (manatees) and *Dugongidae* (dugongs and other sea cows) make up the Order *Sirenia*.

Order Tubulidentata (aardvarks)

Another mammal in an order by itself is Family *Orycteropodidae*.

Invertebrates

Invertebrates are members of the animal kingdom with no spinal column, or backbone. They make up about 95 percent of all animal species. There are 20 phyla of invertebrates, the two largest being Arthropoda and Mollusca. Following are some of the phyla of invertebrates, and descriptions of their members.

Phylum Annelida (segmented worms)

Also called annelid worms, this phylum includes earthworms, leeches, and marine worms. Annelid worms have soft bodies, are symmetrical, and can be anywhere from $1/32$ of an inch (half a millimeter) to 10 feet (3 meters) in length.

Phylum Arthropoda (arthropods)

This is the largest phylum of invertebrates, as well as the one comprising the most creatures; almost 80 percent of all animal species are arthropods. Arthropods have segmented bodies covered by external skeletons, called *exoskeletons*, which are molted from time to time to allow for growth. Their appendages ("arms" and "legs") are paired. Among the animals in this phylum are spiders, horseshoe crabs, crustaceans, insects, and centipedes.

Phylum Coelenterata (coelenterates)

Mostly marine invertebrates, coelenterates have three-layered body walls, tentacles, primitive nervous systems, and special stinger cells to protect themselves. Animals in this phylum include jellyfish, sea anemones, and corals.

Phylum Echinodermata (echinoderms)

Another marine invertebrate, the echinoderm, lives on the floor of the sea. Echinoderms have no heads, tube feet, and external skeletons just below the surface of the skin. They can regenerate virtually any part of their bodies. Starfish, sea urchins, sand dollars, and sea cucumbers are some of the members of this phylum.

Phylum Platyhelminthes (flatworms)

As their name implies, these organisms are basically flat, soft-bodied, and symmetrical. These very primitive creatures come in two varieties: an aquatic group that includes planarians and a parasitic one that counts flukes and tapeworms among its members.

Phylum Mollusca (mollusks)

Most mollusks live inside shells and reside in the water. They have soft, unsegmented bodies and a powerful foot that enables them to move around. Clams, oysters, scallops, bivalves, octopuses, and squid are mollusks.

Phylum Nematoda (roundworms)

These wormlike animals have an outer coat made of noncellular material and a fluid-filled chamber that separates their body walls from their insides. They live both in water and on land. Among their number are rotifers, nematodes, and horsehair worms.

Phylum Porifera (sponges)

Porifera is the most primitive multicellular phylum. Sponges live mostly in colonies in the water, attached to rocks. They are basically sacs taking in water through small holes; their skeletons are formed from hard substances that become stuck in their body walls.

Animal First Aid

Animals, like people, suffer medical problems. Emergency and nonemergency ailments and traumas require quick attention to prevent serious situations from turning into life-threatening ones.

Some problems—bleeding that cannot be stopped or convulsions, for instance—require the immediate attention of an expert in veterinary medicine. Many other problems, however, can be treated by the animal's owner.

The following are some common animal ailments and injuries. The symptoms and treatments for each are described. As with any medical condition, if the symptoms persist or the animal's owner is unsure about the nature of the problem, professional assistance should be sought.

Broken Bones

Symptoms. Some bone breaks show obvious symptoms: twisted or distorted limbs, or in the case of a compound fracture, bone fragments sticking through the skin. Less apparent breaks cause great pain and discomfort. The animal will cry or bite when the affected area is touched; will lie around, often on the affected area; and will usually not walk, although in some cases it will walk despite the break, notably when the pelvis is broken. The fracture will not bear weight. Swelling of the affected area within 24 hours can be expected from any sort of fracture.

Treatment. Treatment of compound fractures by a veterinarian should be sought as soon as possible. Other breaks should be treated by a veterinarian within 24 hours. Apply an ice pack or cold wet compress to the affected area; change regularly. Protect the animal from further injury by confining it to a small room. Apply a temporary splint to broken limbs to avoid further dislocation.

Burns

Symptoms. All burns are painful to the touch. *Electrical burns* are the most serious and can cause heart attacks and death. The burned area will show seared flesh, reddened skin, lesions, and blisters. The animal may suffer respiratory distress; paleness or blueness, especially in lips, gums, and eyelid linings; rigidity in limbs; glassy stare; collapse; and shock. *Thermal burns* cause a singed or charred area; the exposed skin is reddened or inflamed; the wound is warm or hot to the touch. *Friction burns* are similar in appearance to thermal burns, but the skin is chafed or scraped and has bare spots; bare skin is rubbed raw, is reddish in color, and is irritated or inflamed; the trauma causing the burn may leave cuts, lacerations, or embedded foreign matter.

Treatment. Depending on the type and extent of the burn, it can often be treated at home. Electrical burns can stop an animal's heart and must be treated immediately by a veterinarian; if shock occurs, keep the animal warm with heating pads or hot water bottles and a blanket or heavy coat and seek veterinary treatment immediately. Thermal burns can be treated topically by applying the jellylike substance from an aloe plant, a solution made from Domeboro® (available at most pharmacies), or vitamin E oil. Friction burns can be treated in the same way as thermal burns; however, if foreign matter is embedded, or the burn does not respond to treatment, the animal should be taken to a veterinarian.

Cat Diseases

Symptoms. Four major diseases affect the well-being of cats. *Cat distemper* induces high fever, lethargy, vomiting, and diarrhea; young kittens can develop distemper very quickly and will often die of it without exhibiting symptoms. *Rhinotracheitis* causes fever, sneezing, loss of appetite, and dehydration; additional symptoms can include discharge from eyes and nose, congestion, and swelling of membranes in the respiratory tract. *Calici virus* is characterized by sneezing and discharge from the eyes and nose; it may cause fever, lethargy, loss of appetite, dehydration, and ulcers on the tongue. *Pneumonitis* usually causes labored breathing, sneezing, coughing, snorting, wheezing, and listlessness; it may induce a loss of body fluids and very high temperatures.

Treatment. Three of these diseases—cat distemper, rhinotracheitis, and calici virus—can be prevented by annual vaccinations. All four must be treated as quickly as possible by a veterinarian if symptoms are present; professional treatment will, in most cases, effect a cure.

Constipation

Symptoms. The animal struggles or strains during a bowel movement without passing a stool; avoids food; becomes nervous or irritated.

Treatment. Feed the animal brans, cereal foods, vegetables (peas, carrots, corn), kibble; use infant-size glycerine suppositories or soap suppositories; give an enema if the animal will allow it; add a small amount of stool softener, such as Metamucil,® to food; give mineral oil or milk of magnesia, but dosages should depend on size and type of animal (consult a veterinarian).

Dental Disorders

Symptoms. Tartar, a brown crust, appears on teeth, starting at the gum line; tooth enamel erodes, especially on cats; bone fragments, foreign matter, food particles, or hair accumulate on teeth; bad breath is present. *Throat* or *mouth infections* cause coughing and discharges from mouth or nose. *Gingivitis* develops when tartar or dirty teeth are untreated. *Uremia* can cause blackish tartar, bad breath, and extraordinary thirst.

Treatment. Clean the animal's teeth monthly with a mixture of one teaspoon salt or hydrogen peroxide to half a cup of water; apply to teeth with a cotton swab or soft toothbrush. Include hard food, such as kibble, in the animal's diet; provide hard things for the animal to chew on. Infections, gingivitis, or uremia should be treated by a veterinarian.

Diarrhea

Symptoms. The animal passes liquid stool during bowel movement; there may be abnormal coloration of stool.

Treatment. Remove grease, oils, and milk from the animal's diet; avoid high-fiber foods, kibble, and dry catmeal; feed the animal a mix of one part cooked hamburger, drained of grease, and one part rice. If diarrhea results from ingestion of foreign matter (from teething or eating plants, soap, or other household materials), treat it with small doses of Pepto-Bismol® or Kaopectate®. If symptoms persist for more than 24 hours, or if blood is present in stool, consult a veterinarian.

Dog Diseases

Symptoms. A number of conditions affect only dogs. *Canine distemper* causes severe diarrhea and may cause high fever, discharge from eyes and nose, thickening of foot pads, coughing, muscle contractions, convulsions, and pneumonia. *Infectious canine hepatitis* usually results in fever, lethargy, and congestion of the mucous membranes; it also can cause loss of appetite and insatiable thirst. *Leptospirosis* is characterized by high fever, lethargy, loss of appetite, congestion in the whites of the eyes, and possibly pain in walking, jaundice, vomiting, and diarrhea. *Infectious canine tracheobronchitis (kennel cough)* causes high fever and severe dry coughing spasms.

Treatment. All four of these diseases can be prevented by annual vaccinations. If a dog is not vaccinated, early diagnosis of the symptoms of each disease is imperative. None of these diseases can be treated at home; bring the dog to a veterinarian as soon as possible.

External Parasites

Symptoms. Fleas, ticks, lice, maggots, and mites are common external parasites that prey on animals. All cause animals to scratch excessively, which can lead to hair loss. *Fleas* are tiny brown insects that move through the animal's coat. *Ticks* are small, round, dark-colored insects with hard shells that attach themselves to an animal's skin. *Lice* are small, dark-gray insects that remain in one place on an animal's body.

Maggots look like small worms. *Mites,* which are invisible to the unaided eye, characteristically cause skin and ear irritation.

Treatment. External parasites can be readily eliminated and controlled with commercially available powders, baths, sprays, and dips. Check the labels of such treatments carefully to be sure they are appropriate for use on your animal and that they will control the parasite in question. Fleas can be controlled with flea collars, sprays, powders, baths, or dips; treat animal and surrounding furniture and carpets to eliminate infestations. Ticks can be pulled off by hand; the animal should then be treated with spray, powder, or bath to eliminate unseen ticks; treat surrounding furniture and carpets to eliminate infestations. Lyme disease, which is spread by ticks, can be prevented by vaccination. Lice can be treated with the same potions that work on fleas and ticks. Maggots are an increasingly rare parasite that, if present, should be treated by a veterinarian. Mites can cause recurring mange in dogs, or other recurring skin conditions in other animals; any recurring condition should be treated by a veterinarian.

Internal Parasites

Symptoms. All internal parasites drain an animal's natural defenses, leaving it susceptible to infections and diseases. All are likely to cause loss of appetite and lethargy. *Tapeworms* leave visible, light-colored segments that look like rice kernels in stools, around sleeping areas, under the animal's tail, or near its anus. *Roundworms* look like spaghetti; they are light yellow, two to four inches long, have slightly pointed ends, and can be seen in stools or vomit. *Hookworms* are almost invisible to the naked eye, but can cause diarrhea (often with blood present), cramps, pale gums and lips, a dry coat, a slight cough, and noticeable weight loss. *Whipworms* cause symptoms similar to those caused by hookworms, as well as possible inflammation of the colon. *Heartworms* block an animal's arteries, causing tiredness, listlessness, a poor coat, weight loss, and constant panting and coughing. *Coccidia,* one-celled protozoa, cause diarrhea, emaciation, and discharges from the animal's eyes and nose. *Toxoplasmosis* is a parasite that afflicts mostly cats; it frequently presents no symptoms at all.

Treatment. An infestation of internal parasites is a debilitating condition that should be dealt with by a veterinarian. Preventive medications for heartworm are available.

Rabies

Symptoms. Fever, loss of appetite, inability to swallow that results in drooling; can cause encephalitis, convulsions, or paralysis. One type of rabies causes animals to attack anything that moves (cars, animals, people); another type causes only the other symptoms.

Treatment. Prevention of rabies is possible through regular vaccinations. Once contracted, however, there is no effective treatment for rabies and the animal will have to be destroyed.

Respiratory Infections

Symptoms. Sneezing, coughing, runny eyes, swollen glands, difficulty swallowing, labored breathing, fever.

Treatment. If symptoms such as sneezing, coughing, and runny eyes are present but the animal remains active and eats normally, the condition is probably not serious and no treatment is needed. A veterinarian should examine the animal if symptoms continue for a while; if the animal becomes lethargic and loses appetite; if there are discharges of pus from its nose; if congestion becomes heavy or labored breathing is continued; or if fever of more than 102° is present.

Shock

Symptoms. Weakness, collapse, pale or muddy-colored gums, fast heartbeat, difficulty breathing, no breathing, dilated pupils, low body temperature.

Treatment. Keep the animal warm by applying heating pads or hot water bottles and wrapping the animal in heavy blankets or coats. Bring the animal to a veterinarian at once.

Skin Problems

Symptoms. Localized skin conditions cause inflammation or irritation and may cause bald spots of red, raw, or discolored skin. More serious disorders such as moist eczema, wet dermatitis, or acute pruritis cause raw, oozing bald spots that may be damp to the touch or oozing pus. A lump on the animal's skin that does not go away within a few days may be a tumor. Other skin problems can cause dry, flaky skin, an oily coat, and constant biting, licking, or scratching. Symmetrical skin disorders affect both sides of an animal's body equally; a generalized condition affects the animal's whole body.

Treatment. Bald patches of red or raw skin and damp, oozing hot areas should be treated by a veterinarian. Localized inflammation can be treated with soothing topical sprays and lotions. Dry skin or coat can be soaked several times a day with water or a solution made from Domeboro® tablets (available at most pharmacies); small quantities of oil added to the animal's food also will help. Itchiness can be corrected with a solution of one part Alpha-Keri® (available from most pharmacies) to 20 or 30 parts water applied with a spray bottle; repeat as needed. A well-balanced diet, with appropriate levels of vitamins, can maintain healthy skin. Any skin condition that does not go away, or that reappears after treatment, should be treated by a veterinarian.

Sprains

Symptoms. Sprains usually occur in the joints of an animal's limbs, causing rapid swelling. The affected area will be hot to the touch. The animal will not walk normally, if it walks at all.

Treatment. Apply cold compresses or ice packs gently to the swollen area; keep the area cool for a day or two, changing the compress or ice when necessary. Wrap the affected area snugly with cloth, gauze, or athletic bandages; secure the wrapping to be sure the animal does not scratch or bite it off. Keep the animal quiet; discourage activity; avoid stairs. For sprains that heal and reoccur, apply hot towels or compresses; keep the injured area moist and warm for several days. If a sprain does not heal, or pain and swelling continue or are severe, see a veterinarian.

Wounds

Symptoms. *Cuts* can be recognized by the presence of smoothly separated tissue and possible bleeding. *Lacerations* result in jaggedly torn skin, bleeding, swelling, irritation, and black or blue discoloration of the skin. *Abrasions* rub or scrape away the outer layers of skin, causing pain, swelling, redness, and heat. *Bruises* or *contusions* leave black-and-blue tissue and swelling.

Treatment. Any serious wound should be treated by a veterinarian if the bleeding will not stop, if blood is gushing out, or if shock is present. Cuts that are bleeding can be dealt with by applying a pressure bandage (clean gauze or cloth wrapped around some padding) pressed firmly but gently against the wound; an ice bag, pressed firmly but gently on the area; or a tourniquet. After the bleeding has been controlled, clean the wound with hydrogen peroxide or Bactine,® then dry it; keep skin from wrinkling or bunching, then apply an antiseptic or antibiotic to a gauze square and wrap snugly in place; change the dressing daily and keep the animal from removing it. Lacerations can be treated in the same way as cuts, but an ice bag must be used to reduce swelling and prevent further inflammation. Abrasions require the application of a soothing cream, ointment, or lotion (Solarcaine,® Nupercainal,® Unguentine® ointment, or calamine lotion); a bandage is not needed, but the animal must be kept from licking the treated area. Bruises and contusions are best treated with cold compresses or ice packs.

Extinct Animals

Extinction has happened to species and subspecies throughout the time creatures have lived on this planet. The most well-known cases involved the "great dying" of the dinosaurs some 50 to 75 million years ago.

If creatures great and small have in fact been dying off throughout the ages, why is there suddenly concern about animals becoming extinct? Isn't extinction part of the natural order of things?

The answer is no, at least not on the scale it has occurred in recent times. Over most of the last 300 years the rate of extinction of species was about one per year. At present the human-caused rate of species extinction is at least a thousand times as great as that. This biodepletion is most rapid in tropical forests, which, though they cover only 6 percent of the Earth's land surface, shelter at least 50 percent of all species.

The cause of this rapid acceleration in the rate of extinctions is human activity. With some species, like the dodo, the extinction was unintentional: people introduced predators to the dodo's island home where previously there had been none. Other creatures, such as the Eastern buffalo, were purposefully killed off by human beings who wanted to "make room" for themselves.

In the late twentieth century, extinctions are more likely to be a result of human activity. Rural landfills take in urban garbage, open land is blacktopped, factories produce toxins as by-products, and engineers alter waterways. These activities all have a direct impact on the ecosystems that support animal life.

A major cause of the extinction of species in tropical forests is the number of impoverished farmers who are moving into and clearing the forests. Species also suffer from climatic change: the planetary warming from the buildup of carbon dioxide and other greenhouse gases in the global atmosphere.

Increased awareness of the fragile links of interdependence among all of Earth's creatures, and of the impact that human activities can have on those creatures, have led some to hope that the latest era of "great dying" may soon stop. It remains to be seen, however, if the forces already in motion can be stopped in time to save the hundreds of species that teeter on the brink of extinction.

The following lists comprise the number of different animals thought to be extinct as of the early 1990s and the popular names of those animals. Exact figures are difficult to determine, since endangered species often make the transition to extinction quickly and without notice. Occasionally populations of animals thought to be extinct are discovered to be extant. In these lists, numbers of varieties are in parentheses.

Birds

Akioloa (4)	Great auk
Alauwahio (2)	Grosbeak (2)
Amazon (3)	Guadalupe flicker
Bonin night heron	Guadeloupe rufous-sided towhee
Caracara	Heath hen
Chatham Island bellbird	Huia
Chatham Island fernbird	Ivory-billed woodpecker
Conure (2)	Jamaican pauraqué
Courser	Kioea
Delalande's coucal	Laysan apapane
Dodo (2)	Laysan millerbird
Duck (2)	Lord Howe Island blackbird
Elephant bird	Lord Howe Island fantail
Emu (2)	Macaw (4)
Eskimo curlew	Mamo (2)
Finch (5)	Merganser
Flycatcher (2)	Moas (15)
Gadwall	New Caledonian lorikeet
Great amakihi	Norfolk Island kaka

Nukupuu (3)
O-O (3)
Oahu akepa
Omao (3)
Ostrich, Arabian
Owl (10)
Painted vulture
Parakeet (8)
Parrot (3)
Petrel
Pigeon (7)
Quail (2)
Quelili
Rail (17)
Réunion fody
Ryukyu kingfisher

Saint Kitts Puerto Rican bullfinch
Sandpiper (2)
São Tomé grosbeak
Serpent eagle
Shelduck
Solitaire (2)
Sparrow (3)
Spectacled cormorant
Starling (6)
Tanna dove
Thrush (2)
Towhee
Ula-ai-hawane
White eye (2)
White gallinule
Wren (6)

Fish

Cisco (2)
Killifish (2)
Lake Titicaca orestias
Minnow (2)
New Zealand grayling
Pupfish (2)

Speckled dace
Spinedace (2)
Sucker (4)
Thicktail chub
Utah Lake sculpin

Mammals

Agouti (2)
Arizona jaguar
Aurochs
Badlands bighorn sheep
Bali tiger
Bandicoot (4)
Bat (6)
Bear (3)
Blue buck
Buffalo (2)
Burchell's zebra
Caribbean monk seal
Caucasian wisent
Christmas Island musk shrew
Dawson's caribou
Elk (2)
Greenland tundra reindeer
Hartebeest (2)
Hispaniolan hexolobodon
Hutia (5)

Ibex (2)
Isolobodon (2)
Lion (2)
Nesophont (6)
Potoroo (3)
Puerto Rican caviomorph
Quagga
Quemi (2)
Rat (12)
Rufous gazelle
Schomburgk's deer
Sea mink
Shamanu
Steller's sea cow
Syrian onager
Tarpan
Wallaby (2)
Warrah
Wolf (10)

Reptiles

Ameiva (2)	Racer snake (2)
Galliwasp	Round Island boa
Gecko (2)	Skink (3)
Iguana (2)	Tortoise (11)
Lizard (4)	Tree snake (2)

Amphibians

Palestinian painted frog   Vegas Valley leopard frog

Major U.S. and Canadian Zoos

Zoos, or zoological gardens, are private or public parks where animals of all sorts are exhibited and studied. Zoos have existed in one form or another for thousands of years, dating back to ancient China, Egypt, and Rome.

Most major cities throughout the world have zoos. The scale and type of zoo varies widely, from petting zoos that allow contact between children and animals to primate research centers to amusement parks that put on shows with trained porpoises.

The following list of major zoos is arranged by state. The name, address, and phone number of each zoo is given, as well as the number of species and specimens and, where available, the zoo's specialty.

United States

Alabama

Birmingham Zoo
2630 Cahaba Road
Birmingham, AL 35223
205-879-0409
223 species, 793 specimens

Arizona

Arizona-Sonora Desert Museum
2021 North Kinney Road
Tucson, AZ 85743
602-883-1380
289 species, 4,792 specimens
Specialty: Natural history of the Arizona-Sonora desert

Phoenix Zoo
P.O. Box 52191
Phoenix, AZ 85072-2191
602-273-1341
302 species, 1,315 specimens
Specialty: Arabian oryx

Arkansas

Little Rock Zoological Gardens
1 Jonesboro Drive
Little Rock, AR 72205
501-666-2406
216 species, 629 specimens

California

Fresno Zoo
894 West Belmont Avenue
Fresno, CA 93728
209-488-1549
203 species, 616 specimens

The Los Angeles Zoo
5333 Zoo Drive
Los Angeles, CA 90027
213-666-4650
530 species, 1,857 specimens

Marine World Africa USA
2001 Marine World Parkway
Vallejo, CA 94589
707-644-4000
324 species, 2,361 specimens

Oakland Zoo
9777 Golf Links Road
Oakland, CA 94605
415-632-9525
82 species, 331 specimens
Specialty: baby animals

San Diego Zoo
P.O. Box 551
San Diego, CA 92112
619-231-1515
845 species, 3,888 specimens
Specialties: lemurs, tortoises, marsupials

San Francisco Zoological Gardens
1 Zoo Road
San Francisco, CA 94132
415-753-7080
351 species, 6,867 specimens
Specialties: apes, cats

Santa Ana Zoo
1801 E. Chestnut Avenue
Santa Ana, CA 92701
714-836-4000
96 species, 267 specimens
Specialty: primates

Sea World of California
1720 South Shores Road
San Diego, CA 92109
619-222-6363
572 species, 18,367 specimens
Specialties: trained marine mammals, waterfowl, fish

Steinhart Aquarium at California Academy of Sciences
Golden Gate Park
San Francisco, CA 94118
415-750-7145

T. Wayland Vaughan Aquarium-Museum
Scripps Institute of Oceanography
University of California
La Jolla, CA 92093
619-452-4086
203 species, 1,402 specimens
Specialties: marine fish and invertebrates of Southern California

Colorado

Cheyenne Mountain Zoological Park
4250 Cheyenne Mountain Zoo Road
Colorado Springs, CO 80906
132 species, 502 specimens
Specialties: Primates, large felids, hoofed mammals

Denver Zoological Gardens
City Park
Denver, CO 80205
303-331-4100
304 species, 1,300 specimens
Specialties: waterfowl, North American hoofed mammals

Connecticut

Beardsley Zoological Gardens
Noble Avenue
Bridgeport, CT 06610
203-576-8126
101 species, 301 specimens
Specialty: fauna of North and South America

Mystic Marinelife Aquarium
55 Coogan Blvd.
Mystic, CT 06355-1997
203-536-3323

District of Columbia

National Zoological Park
3000 Block of Connecticut Avenue, N.W.
Washington, DC 20008
202-673-4721
491 species, 4,746 specimens

Florida

Busch Gardens
P.O. Box 9158
Tampa, FL 33674
813-988-5171
369 species, 3,381 specimens
Specialties: African hoofed mammals, parrots

Dreher Park Zoo
1301 Summit Boulevard
West Palm Beach, FL 33405-2494
407-533-0887
100 species, 400 specimens
Specialties: South American and South Floridian animals

Jacksonville Zoological Park
8605 Zoo Road
Jacksonville, FL 32218
904-757-4463
210 species, 703 specimens

Marineland of Florida
RFD 1, Box 122
St. Augustine, FL 32086
904-471-1111
106 species, 613 specimens
Specialties: marine mammals, marine theme displays

Miami Metrozoo
12400 S.W. 152nd Street
Miami, FL 33177
305-251-0401
270 species, 3,148 specimens

Georgia

Zoo Atlanta
800 Cherokee Avenue, SE
Atlanta, GA 30315
404-624-5600
278 species, 998 specimens
Specialties: amphibians, reptiles, giant apes

Hawaii

Honolulu Zoo
151 Kapahulu Avenue
Honolulu, HI 96815-4096
808-971-7175
207 species, 766 specimens
Specialty: Galapagos tortoise

Waikiki Aquarium
University of Hawaii
2777 Kalakaua Ave.
Honolulu, HI 96815
808-923-9741

Illinois

Chicago Zoological Park (Brookfield Zoo)
3300 Golf Road
Brookfield, IL 60513
411 species, 2,176 specimens
Specialties: Tropic World, Seven Seas

John G. Shedd Aquarium
1200 South Lake Shore Drive
Chicago, IL 60605
312-939-2426
772 species, 6,662 specimens

Lincoln Park Zoological Gardens
2200 North Cannon Drive
Chicago, IL 60614
312-294-4662
423 species, 1,758 specimens
Specialties: primates, South American mammals

Indiana

Fort Wayne Children's Zoo
3411 Sherman Boulevard
Fort Wayne, IN 46808
219-482-4610

Indianapolis Zoo
1200 West Washington Street
Indianapolis, IN 46222
316 species, 3,044 specimens

Mesker Park Zoo
Bement Avenue
Evansville, IN 47712
812-428-0715
203 species, 644 specimens
Specialty: large geographic exhibits

Kansas

Topeka Zoological Park
635 S.W. Gage Boulevard
Topeka, KS 66606-2066
126 species, 367 specimens

Kentucky

Louisville Zoological Garden
1100 Trevilian Way
Louisville, KY 40213
502-459-2181
292 species, 1,287 specimens

Louisiana

Aquarium of the Americas
Woldenberg Riverfront Park
New Orleans, LA 70130
504-861-2537

Audubon Park & Zoological Garden
P.O. Box 4327
New Orleans, LA 70178
504-861-2537
401 species, 1,535 specimens

Greater Baton Rouge Zoo
P.O. Box 60
Baker, LA 70704
504-775-3877
212 species, 993 specimens

Maryland

Baltimore Zoo
Druid Hill Park
Mansion House
Baltimore, MD 21217
301-396-7102
241 species, 1,086 specimens
Specialty: black-footed penguins

National Aquarium in Baltimore
Pier 3, 501 E. Pratt Street
Baltimore, MD 21202
301-659-4233
474 species, 7,472 specimens

Massachusetts

Franklin Park Zoo
Franklin Park
Boston, MA 02121
617-442-2002

New England Aquarium
Central Wharf
Boston, MA 02110
412 species, 7,606 specimens
Specialties: marine fish, invertebrates of the world

Michigan

Detroit Zoological Park
8450 West 10 Mile Road
P.O. Box 39
Royal Oak, MI 48068
313-398-0903
282 species, 1,287 specimens
Specialties: polar bears, penguins

Potter Park Zoological Gardens
1301 South Pennsylvania Avenue
Lansing, MI 48912
517-483-4221
124 species, 342 specimens

Saginaw Children's Zoo
1435 South Washington Avenue
Saginaw, MI 48601
517-776-1657
85 species, 326 specimens

Minnesota

Lake Superior Zoological Gardens
7210 Fremont Street
Duluth, MN 55807
125 species, 491 specimens

Minnesota Zoological Garden
13000 Zoo Boulevard
Apple Valley, MN 55124
612-431-9200
311 species, 1,818 specimens

St. Paul's Como Zoo
Midway Parkway and Kaufman Drive
St. Paul, MN 55103
612-488-4041
103 species, 335 specimens
Specialties: large mammals

Mississippi

Jackson Zoological Park
2918 West Capitol Street
Jackson, MS 39209
601-352-2585
140 species, 426 specimens

Missouri

Kansas City Zoological Gardens
6700 Zoo Drive
Kansas City, MO 64132
816-333-7406
162 species, 586 specimens

St. Louis Zoological Park
Forest Park
St. Louis, MO 63110
314-781-0900
720 species, 3,408 specimens

Nebraska

Folsom Children's Zoo
2800 A Street
Lincoln, NE 86502
402-475-6741
50 species, 173 specimens

Omaha's Henry Doorly Zoo
3701 South 10th Street
Omaha, NE 68107-2200
402-773-8401
400 species, 7,211 specimens
Specialties: largest cat complex in North America

New Jersey

Turtle Back Zoo
560 Northfield Avenue
South Mountain Reservation, NJ 07052
201-731-5800
171 species, 647 specimens
Specialty: turtles

New Mexico

Rio Grande Zoological Park
903 10th Street, S.W.
Albuquerque, NM 87102
505-843-7413
292 species, 1,204 specimens
Specialty: hoofed mammals

New York

Buffalo Zoological Gardens
Delaware Park
Buffalo, NY 14214
716-837-3900
237 species, 1,424 specimens

**Central Park Wildlife Conservation Center
(formerly Central Park Zoo)**
830 Fifth Avenue
New York, NY 10021
212-439-6500
108 species, 10,717 specimens

**Aquarium for Wildlife Conservation
(formerly New York Aquarium)**
West 8th Street and Surf Avenue
Brooklyn, NY 11224
718-265-3400
287 species, 23,107 specimens

**International Wildlife Conservation Park
(formerly Bronx Zoo)**
185th Street and Southern Boulevard
Bronx, NY 10460
718-220-5100
681 species, 4,756 specimens

Staten Island Zoo
614 Broadway
Staten Island, NY 10310
718-442-3101
187 species, 422 specimens
Specialty: reptiles

North Dakota

Dakota Zoo
Dakota Zoological Society
P.O. Box 711
Bismarck, ND 58502
701-223-7543
142 species, 657 specimens
Specialty: North American fauna

Ohio

Cincinnati Zoo & Botanical Gardens
3400 Vine Street
Cincinnati, OH 45220
513-281-4701
702 species, 427,547 specimens
(425,000 invertebrates)
Specialties: insects, amphibians, great apes, cats

Cleveland Aquarium
Gordon Park
601 East 72nd Street
Cleveland, OH 44103

Cleveland Metroparks Zoological Park
3900 Brookside Park Drive
Cleveland, OH 44109
216-661-6500
506 species, 3,279 specimens
Specialties: Geoffroy's tamarin, white stork

Columbus Zoological Gardens
Box 400
Powell, OH 43065
680 species, 8,260 specimens
Specialties: gorillas, reptiles, cichlids

Toledo Zoological Gardens
P.O. Box 4010
Toledo, OH 43609
419-385-5721
433 species, 2,364 specimens

Oklahoma

Oklahoma City Zoological Park
2101 NE 50th Street
Oklahoma City, OK 73112
520 species, 1,879 specimens

Tulsa Zoological Park
5701 East 36th Street North
Tulsa, OK 74115
918-596-2401
267 species, 1,148 specimens
Specialties: North American animals, plants, earth sciences

Oregon

Metro Washington Park Zoo
4001 S.W. Canyon Road
Portland, OR 97221
503-226-1561
171 species, 715 specimens
Specialties: elephants, chimpanzees

Pennsylvania

Philadelphia Zoological Garden
34th Street and Girard Avenue
Philadelphia, PA 19104
215-243-1100
497 species, 1,824 specimens
Specialties: waterfowl, great apes, reptiles

Pittsburgh Zoo
P.O. Box 5250
Pittsburgh, PA 15206
412-665-3639
369 species, 3,945 specimens

Rhode Island

Roger Williams Park Zoo
Roger Williams Park
Providence, RI 02905
401-785-9450
143 species, 464 specimens

South Carolina

Riverbanks Zoological Park
P.O. Box 1060
Columbia, SC 29202
803-779-8717
439 species, 2,117 specimens

South Dakota

Great Plains Zoo and Museum
805 South Kiwanis
Sioux Falls, SD 57104
605-339-7059
Specialty: animals of the North American Great Plains

Tennessee

Knoxville Zoological Gardens
P.O. Box 6040
Knoxville, TN 37914
615-637-5331
241 species, 879 specimens
Specialties: large cats, African elephants, red pandas, Southern white rhinoceros

Memphis Zoological Garden and Aquarium
2000 Galloway Avenue
Memphis, TN 38112
901-726-4787
403 species, 2,847 specimens
Specialties: aquatic animals, rare ruminants

Texas

Abilene Zoological Gardens
Box 60
Abilene, TX 79604
915-672-9771
153 species, 498 specimens

Caldwell Zoo
P.O. Box 4280
Tyler, TX 75712
214-593-0121
221 species, 1,020 specimens

Dallas Aquarium
P.O. Box 26113
Dallas, TX 75226
214-670-8453
226 species, 1,778 specimens

Dallas Zoo
621 East Clarendon Drive
Dallas, TX 75203
214-670-6825
330 species, 1,454 specimens

Forth Worth Zoological Park
2727 Zoological Park Drive
Fort Worth, TX 76110
817-870-7050
758 species, 4,408 specimens

Gladys Porter Zoo
500 Ringgold Street
Brownsville, TX 78520
512-546-7187
381 species, 1,765 specimens

Houston Zoological Gardens
1513 MacGregor
Houston, TX 77030
713-525-3300
724 species, 3,159 specimens

San Antonio Zoological Garden and Aquarium
3903 North St. Mary's Street
San Antonio, TX 78212
512-734-7184
738 species, 3,401 specimens
Specialties: antelope, waterfowl, whooping cranes

Utah

Hogle Zoological Garden
P.O. Box 8475
Salt Lake City, UT 84108
801-582-1632
311 species, 1,164 specimens

Virginia

Virginia Zoological Park
3500 Granby Street
Norfolk, VA 23504
804-441-2374
110 species, 331 specimens

Washington

Seattle Aquarium
Pier 59, Waterfront Park
Seattle, WA 98010
206-386-4320

Woodland Park Zoological Gardens
5500 Phinney Avenue North
Seattle, WA 98103
206-684-4880
258 species, 2,411 specimens

Wisconsin

Henry Vilas Zoo
500 South Randall Avenue
Madison, WI 53715
608-266-4732
182 species, 618 specimens

Milwaukee County Zoological Gardens
10001 West Bluemound Road
Milwaukee, WI 53226
414-771-3040
321 species, 3,054 specimens

Racine Zoological Garden
2131 North Main Street
Racine, WI 53402
414-636-9189
101 species, 281 specimens

Canada

Alberta

Calgary Zoo, Botanical Garden & Prehistoric Park
P.O. Box 3036, Station B
Calgary, Alberta T2M 4R8
403-232-9300
307 species, 1,295 specimens
Specialty: northern fauna

British Columbia

Stanley Park Zoological Gardens
Stanley Park
Vancouver, British Columbia V6G 1Z4
604-683-1040
94 species, 298 specimens
Specialties: North American mammals and birds

Vancouver Public Aquarium
Stanley Park
P.O. Box 3232
604-685-3364
Vancouver 3, British Columbia V6B 3X8
638 species, 9,499 specimens
Specialties: marine mammals, fishes and invertebrates of the Northeast Pacific

Manitoba

Assiniboine Park Zoo
2355 Corydon Avenue
Winnipeg, Manitoba R3P 0R5
204-888-3634
296 species, 1,156 specimens
Specialty: Nearctic animals

Ontario

Metropolitan Toronto Zoo
P.O. Box 280
West Hill
Toronto, Ontario M1E 4R5
416-392-5900
517 species, 3,489 specimens

Quebec

Aquarium de Quebec
Ministère du Loisir, de la Chasse et de la Pêche
1675 avenue du Parc
Sainte Foy, PQ
Canada G1W 4S3
418-659-5264
234 species, 1,390 specimens

Jardin Zoologique de Quebec
8191 avenue du Zoo
Charlesbourg, PQ
Canada G1G 4G4
418-622-0313
233 species, 794 specimens
Specialty: North American fauna

Montreal Aquarium
La Ronde
St. Helen's Island
Montreal, PQ
Quebec H3C 1A9
514-872-4656
319 species, 2,088 specimens

Société Zoologique de Granby
347 rue Bourget
Case Postale 514
Granby, PQ
Quebec J2G 1E8
514-372-9113
201 species, 720 specimens

Additional Sources of Information

American Kennel Club Staff. *The Complete Dog Book*, 17th ed. Howell, 1985.

Animal Medical Center Staff, and William J. Kay. *Complete Book of Cat Health*. Macmillan, 1985.

Animal Medical Center Staff et al. *The Complete Book of Dog Health*. Howell, 1990.

Day, David. *The Doomsday Book of Animals: A Natural History of Vanished Species*. Viking Penguin, 1983.

Ehrlich, Paul R., David S. Dobkin, and Darryl Wheye. *Birds in Jeopardy: The Imperiled and Extinct Birds of the United States and Canada, Including Hawaii and Puerto Rico*. Stanford University Press, 1992.

Grzimek, Bernhard, ed. *Encyclopedia of Animals*, 15 vols. McGraw-Hill, 1990.

Hahn, Emily. *Animal Gardens: Zoos Around the World*. Begos & Rosenberg, 1991.

Macdonald, David, ed. *The Encyclopedia of Mammals*. Facts On File, 1984.

Margulis, Lynn, and Karlene V. Schwartz. *Five Kingdoms: An Illustrated Guide to the Phyla of Life on Earth*, 2nd ed. Freeman, 1988.

McClung, Robert M. *Lost Wild Worlds*. William Morrow, 1976.

The New International Wildlife Encyclopedia, vols. 1–21. Purnell Reference Books, 1980.

Perrins, Christopher M., and Alex L. A. Middleton, eds. *The Encyclopedia of Birds*. Facts On File, 1985.

Scott, Peter, ed. *The Amazing World of Animals*. Praeger, 1976.

Spaulding, C. E. *A Veterinary Guide for Animal Owners*. Rodale Press, 1976.

West, Geoffrey, ed. *Black's Veterinary Dictionary*, 15th ed. B and N Imports, 1985.

West, Geoffrey, ed. *Encyclopedia of Animal Care*, 12th ed. Williams & Wilkins, 1977.

Whitfield, Philip. *Macmillan Illustrated Animal Encyclopedia*. Macmillan, 1984.

Zoological Parks and Aquariums in the Americas. American Association of Zoological Parks and Aquariums, biannual.

5

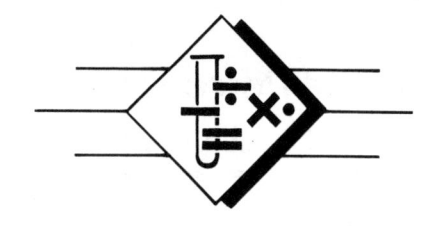

Math and Science Basics

Decimal and Percent Equivalents of Common Fractions / *78*

Basic Rules of Mathematics and Mathematical Formulas / *78*

Basic Formulas of Physics / *80*

Heating and Electrical Terms / *81*

Alphabetical List of the Elements / *82*

Geological Time Chart / *84*

Phases of the Moon / *86*

Diagram of the Solar System, with Facts About the Planets / *87*

Brightest Stars / *89*

Common Terms in Science and Engineering / *90*

Common Computer Terms / *98*

Additional Sources of Information / *102*

Decimal and Percent Equivalents of Common Fractions

Fraction	Decimal	Percent (%)	Fraction	Decimal	Percent (%)
1/32	0.03125	3.125	17/32	0.53125	53.125
1/16	0.0625	6.25	9/16	0.5625	56.25
3/32	0.09375	9.375	19/32	0.59375	59.375
1/10	0.1	10	3/5	0.6	60
1/8	0.125	12.5	5/8	0.625	62.5
5/32	0.15625	15.625	21/32	0.65625	65.625
3/16	0.1875	18.75	2/3	0.66666+	66.666+
1/5	0.2	20	11/16	0.6875	68.75
7/32	0.21875	21.875	7/10	0.7	70
1/4	0.25	25	23/32	0.71875	71.875
9/32	0.28125	28.125	3/4	0.75	75
3/10	0.3	30	25/32	0.78125	78.125
5/16	0.3125	31.25	4/5	0.8	80
1/3	0.33333+	33.333+	13/16	0.8125	81.25
11/32	0.34375	34.375	27/32	0.84375	84.375
3/8	0.375	37.5	7/8	0.875	87.5
2/5	0.4	40	9/10	0.9	90
13/32	0.40625	40.625	29/32	0.90625	90.625
7/16	0.4375	43.75	15/16	0.9375	93.75
15/32	0.46875	46.875	31/32	0.96875	96.875
1/2	0.5	50			

Basic Rules of Mathematics and Mathematical Formulas

Addition and subtraction of fractions:
(Start with a common denominator)

$$\frac{2}{3} + \frac{4}{5} = \frac{10}{15} + \frac{12}{15} = \frac{22}{15} = 1\frac{7}{15}$$

$$\frac{4}{5} - \frac{2}{3} = \frac{12}{15} - \frac{10}{15} = \frac{2}{15}$$

Multiplication of fractions:

$$\frac{2}{5} \times \frac{7}{4} = \frac{14}{20} = \frac{7}{10}$$

Division of fractions:

$$\frac{1}{2} \div 2 = \frac{1}{2} \times \frac{1}{2} = \frac{1}{4}$$

Fractions to decimals:

$$\frac{3}{10} = 0.3; \frac{3}{100} = 0.03; \frac{3}{1,000} = 0.003$$

Unknown multiplied by a number:

$$5x = 10; \frac{5x}{5} = \frac{10}{5}; x = 2$$

Number added to an unknown:

$$y + 7 = 10; y + 7 - 7 = 10 - 7; y =$$

An unknown in a fraction:

$$\frac{a}{5} = \frac{3}{8}; a \times 8 = 5 \times 3; 8a = 15; a = 1$$

Numbers with exponents:

$$\frac{2^3}{3^2} = \frac{2 \times 2 \times 2}{3 \times 3} = \frac{8}{9}$$

$$10^2 \times 10^3 = 10^{2+3} = 10^5$$

$$10^6 \div 10^4 = 10^{6-4} = 10^2$$

$$10^{-3} = \frac{1}{10^3} = \frac{1}{1,000}$$

Area, Circumference, and Volume Equations and Formulas

Area of a square:
  Area = length × width, or length of one side (x) squared (x^2)

Area of a rectangle:
  Area = length × width

Area of a triangle:
  Area = $\frac{1}{2}$ × base × perpendicular height

Area of a regular pentagon (5 sides):
  Area = square of the length of one side × 1.720

Area of a regular hexagon (6 sides):
  Area = square of the length of one side × 2.598

Area of a regular octagon (8 sides):
  Area = square of the length of one side × 4.828

Area of a cube:
  Area = square of the length of one side × 6

Area of a sphere:
  Area = square of the diameter × pi (3.1416)

Area of a circle:
  Area = square of the radius × pi (3.1416)

Area of an ellipse:
  Area = long diameter × short diameter × 0.7854

Circumference of a circle:
  Circumference = diameter × pi (3.1416)

Volume of a cube:
  Volume = cube (x^3) of the length (x) of one side

Volume of a right rectangular pyramid:
  Volume = area of the base × height × $\frac{1}{3}$

Volume of a circular cylinder:
  Volume = square of the radius (r^2) of the base × pi (3.1416) × height

Volume of a sphere:
  Volume = cube of the radius (r^3) × pi (3.1416) × $\frac{4}{3}$

Volume of a right circular cone:
Volume = square of the radius (r^2) of the base × pi (3.1416) × height × $\frac{1}{3}$

Volume of a rectangular solid:
Volume = length × width × height

Basic Solutions to Triangles

Pythagorean theorem:
The square of the hypotenuse of a right-angled triangle is equal to the sum of the squares of the other two sides.

A table of trigonometric functions is required for the following formulas.

Law of Sines:
In any triangle, $a/\sin A = b/\sin B = c/\sin C$

Right triangles:
$a = c \sin A = b \tan A$
$b = c \cos A = a \cot A$
$c = a \operatorname{cosec} A = b \sec A$

For all triangles:
The sum of the angles of a triangle = 180 degrees.
Given two sides (b and c) and one angle (A),
$a = (b^2 + c^2 - 2bc \cos A)$
$\sin B = b/a \sin A$.
Given two angles (A and B) and one side (b),
$a = b \times \sin A/\sin B$
$c = b \times \sin C/\sin B$.
Given three sides (a, b, and c),
$\cos A = (b^2 + c^2 - a^2)/2bc$
$\sin B = b/a \times \sin A$.

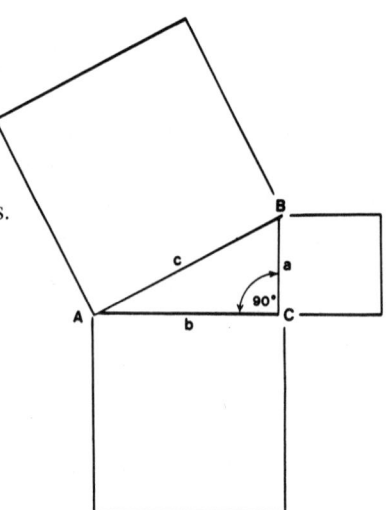

Basic Formulas of Physics

acceleration $a = (v_f - v_0)/t$, where v_f represents the final velocity and v_0 represents the initial velocity.

acceleration of gravity $W = mg$, where W represents the force of weight, m represents the mass of the object, and g represents gravity.

centrifugal force $F = mv^2/gr$, where F represents force, m represents the mass of a moving object, v represents its velocity, g represents the acceleration due to gravity (32.2 ft/sec^2), and r represents the radius of the orbit of the mass.

Coulomb's law $F = k \times Q_a Q_b/d^2$, where F represents the electrostatic force, k represents a constant of proportionality, Q_a and Q_b represent quantities of electrostatic charge, and d represents the distance between the charges.

electrical power $P = IV$, where P represents power, I represents electrical current, and V represents electrical potential.

energy–matter relationship $E = mc^2$, where E represents energy, m represents mass, and c represents the velocity of light.

gravity inverse square law $F = g \times Mm/r^2$, where F represents force, g represents the pull of gravity, M and m represent the masses of two objects, and r represents the distance between the masses.

kinetic energy $KE = \frac{1}{2}mv^2$, where KE represents kinetic energy, m represents the mass of a moving object, and v represents the velocity.

light inverse square law $I_1/I_2 = (d_2/d_1)^2$, where I_1 represents the light intensity at distance d_1 from the source and I_2 represents the intensity of light at distanced d_2 from the source.

mass and weight relationship $m_1/m_2 = W_1/W_2$, where m_1 and m_2 represent two masses and W_1 and W_2 represent their respective weights.

momentum $p = mv$, where p represents momentum, m represents the mass of the object, and v represents velocity.

Newton's second law $F = ma$, where F represents force, m represents mass of the object, and a represents the acceleration.

Ohm's law $R = V/I$, where R represents electrical resistance, V represents electrical potential, and I represents electrical current.

potential energy $E = mgh$, where E represents potential energy, m represents the mass of an object, g represents the acceleration of gravity, and h represents the distance to be traveled by m.

power $P = W/t$, where P represents power, W represents work, and t represents the time required to perform the indicated work.

velocity $v = d/t$, where d represents the distance traveled in time t.

wave equation $V = f\lambda$, where V represents the velocity of the wave, f represents its frequency, and λ represents the wavelength.

weight $W = mg$, where W represents the weight of an object, m represents its mass, and g represents the pull of gravity.

work $W = fd$, where W represents work, f represents the applied force, and d represents the distance over which it is applied.

Heating and Electrical Terms

ampere (amp or **A)** A unit of electrical current, or flow of electrons, that is equal to a charge of 1 coulomb moving through or across a conductor in 1 second. It is named for André M. Ampère, French physicist (1775–1836).

British thermal unit (Btu) A unit of heat energy measured as the amount of heat required to raise the temperature of 1 pound of water from 60° to 61° F at a constant pressure of 1 standard atmosphere (the weight of the atmosphere at mean sea level). One Btu is equal to 1054.5 joules in the meter-kilogram-second system of measurements.

coulomb (coul or **C)** The amount of electric charge that crosses a surface in 1 second when a steady current of 1 ampere is flowing across the surface. It is also equivalent to 6.3×10^{18} electron charges. Named for Charles A. Coulomb, French physicist (1736–1806).

joule (J) A unit of energy or work equal to the force of 1 newton when the point at which the force is applied is displaced 1 meter in the direction of the force. Named for James P. Joule, English physicist (1818–1889).

newton (N) A unit of force equal to the force that will cause an acceleration of 1 meter per second squared to a mass of 1 kilogram. Named for Sir Isaac Newton, English mathematician (1642–1727).

ohm (Ω) A unit of electrical resistance through which a current of 1 ampere will flow when there is a potential difference of 1 volt across it. Named for George S. Ohm, German physicist (1787–1854).

volt (V) A unit of electromotive force equal to the potential difference between two points for which 1 coulomb of electricity will do 1 joule of work in going from one point to the other. Named for Count Alesandro Volta (1745–1827).

watt (W) A unit of electrical power equal to 1 joule per second. It is also the product of the amperes multiplied by the volts. Named for James Watt, Scottish inventor (1736–1819).

Alphabetical List of the Elements

Element*	Symbol	Valence	Atomic number	Atomic weight†
Actinium	Ac	3	89	227.028
Aluminum	Al	3	13	26.981539
Americium	Am	3, 4, 5, 6	95	(243)
Antimony	Sb	3, 5	51	121.75
Argon	Ar	0	18	39.948
Arsenic	As	3, 5	33	74.92159
Astatine	At	1, 3, 5, 7	85	(210)
Barium	Ba	2	56	137.327
Berkelium	Bk	3, 4	97	(247)
Beryllium	Be	2	4	9.012182
Bismuth	Bi	3, 5	83	208.98037
Boron	B	3	5	10.81
Bromine	Br	1, 3, 5, 7	35	79.904
Cadmium	Cd	2	48	112.411
Calcium	Ca	2	20	40.078
Californium	Cf	3	98	(251)
Carbon	C	2, 4	6	12.011
Cerium	Ce	3, 4	58	140.115
Cesium	Cs	1	55	132.90543
Chlorine	Cl	1, 3, 5, 7	17	35.4527
Chromium	Cr	2, 3, 6	24	51.9961
Cobalt	Co	2, 3	27	58.93320
Columbium	(see Niobium)			
Copper	Cu	1, 2	29	63.546
Curium	Cm	3	96	(247)
Dysprosium	Dy	3	66	162.50
Einsteinium	Es	3	99	(252)
Erbium	Er	3	68	167.26
Europium	Eu	2, 3	63	151.965
Fermium	Fm	3	100	(257)
Fluorine	F	1	9	18.9984032
Francium	Fr	1	87	(223)
Gadolinium	Gd	3	64	157.25
Gallium	Ga	2, 3	31	69.723
Germanium	Ge	2, 4	32	72.61
Gold	Au	1, 3	79	196.96654
Hafnium	Hf	4	72	178.49
Helium	He	0	2	4.002602
Holmium	Ho	3	67	164.93032
Hydrogen	H	1	1	1.00794
Indium	In	3	49	114.82
Iodine	I	1, 3, 5, 7	53	126.90447
Iridium	Ir	3, 4	77	192.22
Iron	Fe	2, 3	26	55.847
Krypton	Kr	0	36	83.80
Lanthanum	La	3	57	138.9055
Lawrencium	Lr	3	103	(260)
Lead	Pb	2, 4	82	207.2
Lithium	Li	1	3	6.941
Lutetium	Lu	3	71	174.967
Magnesium	Mg	2	12	24.3050
Manganese	Mn	1, 2, 3, 4, 6, 7	25	54.93805
Mendelevium	Md	2, 3	101	(258)
Mercury	Hg	1, 2	80	200.59

Element*	Symbol	Valence	Atomic number	Atomic weight†
Molybdenum	Mo	2, 3, 6	42	95.94
Neodymium	Nd	3	60	144.24
Neon	Ne	0	10	20.1797
Neptunium	Np	3, 4, 5, 6	93	237.048
Nickel	Ni	2, 3	28	58.69
Niobium	Nb	3, 5	41	92.90638
Nitrogen	N	3, 5	7	14.0067
Nobelium	No	2, 3	102	(259)
Osmium	Os	2, 3, 4, 6	76	190.2
Oxygen	O	2	8	15.9994
Palladium	Pd	2, 3, 4	46	106.42
Phosphorus	P	3, 5	15	30.973762
Platinum	Pt	2, 4	78	195.08
Plutonium	Pu	3, 4, 5, 6	94	(244)
Polonium	Po	2, 4	84	(209)
Potassium	K	1	19	39.0983
Praseodymium	Pr	3	59	140.90765
Promethium	Pm	3	61	(145)
Protactinium	Pa	4, 5	91	231.0359
Radium	Ra	2	88	226.025
Radon	Rn	0	86	(222)
Rhenium	Re	1, 2, 3, 4, 5, 6, 7	75	186.207
Rhodium	Rh	3	45	102.90550
Rubidium	Rb	1	37	85.4678
Ruthenium	Ru	1, 2, 3, 4, 5, 6, 7	44	101.07
Samarium	Sm	2, 3	62	150.36
Scandium	Sc	3	21	44.955910
Selenium	Se	2, 4, 6	34	78.96
Silicon	Si	4	14	28.086
Silver	Ag	1	47	107.8682
Sodium	Na	1	11	22.989768
Strontium	Sr	2	38	87.62
Sulfur	S	2, 4, 6	16	32.066
Tantalum	Ta	5	73	180.9479
Technetium	Tc	2, 4, 5, 6, 7	43	(98)
Tellurium	Te	2, 4, 6	52	127.60
Terbium	Tb	3	65	158.92534
Thallium	Tl	1, 3	81	204.3833
Thorium	Th	4	90	232.0381
Thulium	Tm	3	69	168.93421
Tin	Sn	2, 4	50	118.710
Titanium	Ti	2, 3, 4	22	47.88
Tungsten	W	6	74	183.85
Uranium	U	2, 3, 4, 5, 6	92	238.0289
Vanadium	V	2, 3, 4, 5	23	50.9415
Xenon	Xe	0	54	131.29
Ytterbium	Yb	2, 3	70	173.04
Yttrium	Y	3	39	88.90585
Zinc	Zn	2	30	65.39
Zirconium	Zr	4	40	91.224

* The 103 chemical elements known at present are included in this table. Some of those recently discovered have been obtained only as unstable isotopes.

† Based on Carbon-12. Figures enclosed in parentheses represent the mass number of the most stable isotope.

Geological Time Chart

Age in Millions of Years	Era	Period or Epoch	Important Physical Events	Animal Life
.01 ±.5	CENOZOIC	Holocene	Repeated extensions of ice caps in arctic and north temperate areas	modern human beings
		Pleistocene	Continents generally elevated, mountains high, deserts widespread	primitive man
13 ±1		Pliocene	Mountain building in northwestern North America. Deformation of Tethys geosyncline; Alps and Himalayas rise	gorillas
25 ±1		Miocene	Extensive erosion surfaces cut on Appalachians and Rockies. Cool, dry climates over much of world	whales, sabertooths
36 ±2		Oligocene	Initiation of mountain building in Tethys geosyncline. River and floodplain deposits begin on Great Plains	apes, bats
58 ±2		Eocene	Climates warm and uniform; widespread jungles and forests	alligators
65 ±2		Paleocene	Basins develop between ranges along Pacific Coast and Rockies	Kangaroos, birds, horses, camels, monkeys, elephants
135 ±5	MESOZOIC	Cretaceous	Mountain building in Rockies; seas invade much of western North America and cover Atlantic and Gulf coastal plains	ancient birds, snakes, modern fish
180 ±5		Jurassic	Widespread mild, uniform climates. Mountain building along Pacific Coast of North America. Extensive marine invasions of southern and central Europe	flying reptiles
		Triassic	Fault basins in eastern North America. Extensive deserts and dead seas develop in North America and Eurasia	ichthyosaurs, tyrannosaurs

MILLIONS OF YEARS BEFORE THE PRESENT

Age in Millions of Years	Era	Period or Epoch	Important Physical Events	Animal Life
230 ±10 ▶	PALEOZOIC	Permian	Continents generally elevated; Appalachian and Ural mountains complete their development Tethys geosyncline from Spain to India	ammonites, finbacked reptiles
280 ±10 ▶		Carboniferous	Mountain building in southern North America and central Europe Extensive seas over much of interior North America	amphibians, clams, lungfish
310 ±10 ▶		Devonian	Catskill delta built from New England mountains into New York and Pennsylvania Mountain building in northeastern North America Extensive submergence of geosynclines and interior of North America	starfish
405 ±10 ▶		Silurian	Formation of Caledonian mountains in northwestern Europe Dead seas in Michigan, New York, Ohio, southeastern Canada Deltas and gravel beaches along eastern edge of Appalachian geosyncline	sea scorpions, corals, sharks
425 ±10 ▶		Ordovician	Mountain building in northeastern North America Over 60 percent of North American continent covered by seas	snails, jawless fish, echinoids
500 ±10 ▶		Cambrian	Climates generally mild and uniform Seas invade North American continent Geosynclines develop around edge of North America	protozoans, trilobites
?600 ▶ 1,000 ▶ 2,000 ▶ 3,000 ▶ 4,000 ▶		Precambrian	Fault basins in Lake Superior region Deformation and mountain building through central North America Geosynclines develop throughout central North America Extensive mountain building in Lake Superior region Oldest dated rocks Probable origin of Earth from solar dust cloud	jellyfish, flagellates, amoebas, worms, sponges

MILLIONS OF YEARS BEFORE THE PRESENT

Phases of the Moon

The moon is the closest natural body to the Earth. Eight phases of the moon are visible because the moon has no light of its own. Its daylight side reflects the light of the sun. As pictured above, in (1) the new moon, the dark side of the moon is turned toward the Earth and the moon cannot be seen. The second phase is a crescent moon (2), followed by (3), a half moon, or first quarter. A gibbous moon (4) is then succeeded by a full moon (5). The moon then begins to wane, through gibbous (6), half, or last quarter (7), crescent (8), and back to new again. The cycle takes 27.3 days to complete.

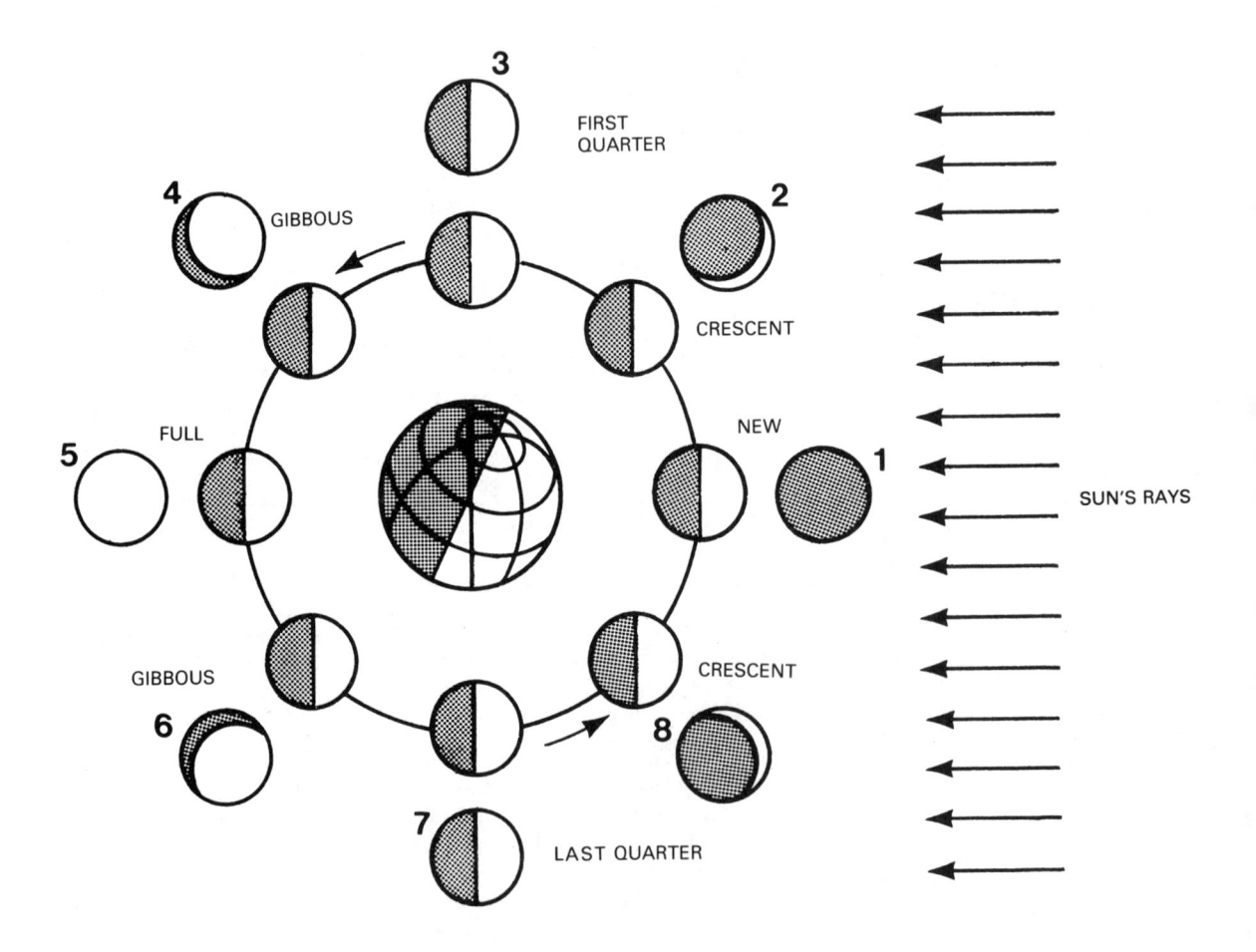

Diagram of the Solar System, with Facts About the Planets

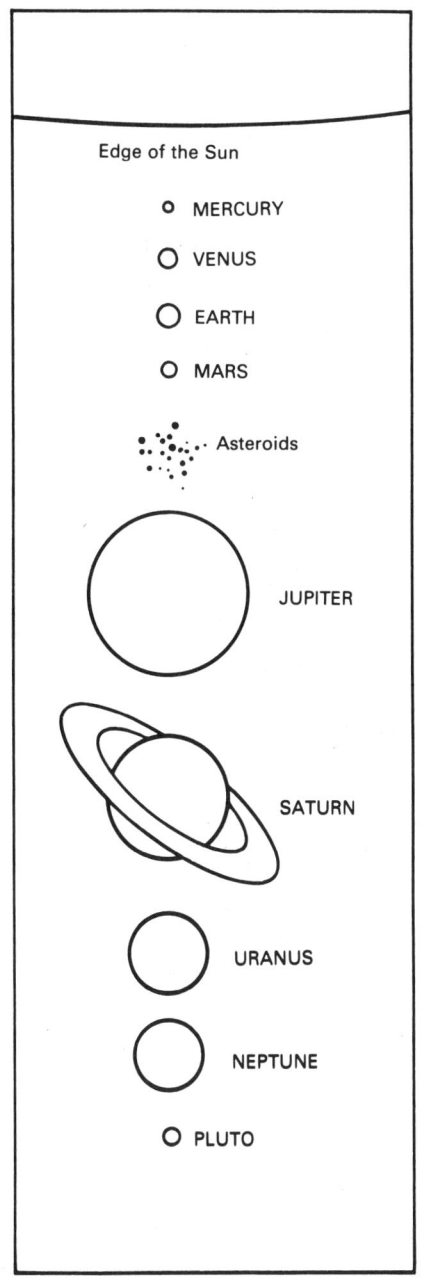

Edge of the Sun

o MERCURY

O VENUS

O EARTH

O MARS

· Asteroids

JUPITER

SATURN

URANUS

NEPTUNE

O PLUTO

Relative size of the planets

The Planets

Mercury Diameter, 3,100 miles; distance from the sun, 36 million miles; orbits the sun every 88 days; rotates on its axis in 59 days.

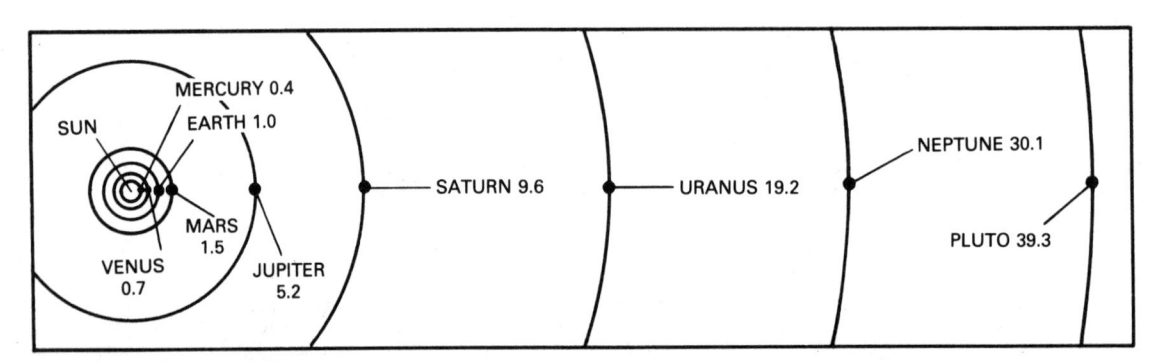

Venus Diameter, 7,700 miles; distance from the sun, 67 million miles; orbits the sun every 225 days; rotates on its axis in 244 days.

Earth Diameter, 7,920 miles; distance from the sun, 93 million miles; orbits the sun every 365 days; rotates on its axis in 24 hours.

Mars Diameter, 4,200 miles; distance from the sun, 141 million miles; orbits the sun every 687 days; rotates on its axis in 24 hours 24 minutes.

Jupiter Diameter, 88,640 miles; distance from the sun, 483 million miles; orbits the sun every 11.9 years; rotates on its axis in 9 hours 50 minutes.

Saturn Diameter, 74,500 miles (diameter of rings, 165,000 miles); distance from the sun, 886 million miles; orbits the sun every 29.5 years; rotates on its axis in 10 hours 39 minutes.

Uranus Diameter, 32,000 miles; distance from the sun, 1,782 million miles; orbits the sun every 84 years; rotates on its axis in 23 hours.

Neptune Diameter, 31,000 miles; distance from the sun, 2,793 million miles; orbits the sun every 165 years; rotates on its axis in 15 hours 48 minutes.

Pluto Diameter, 1,500 miles; distance from the sun, 3,670 million miles; orbits the sun every 248 years; rotates on its axis in 6 days 7 hours.

The average distance of the planets from the sun. The numbers in the diagram give the distances in terms of the astronomical unit (A.U.), or average distance between Earth and the sun. One A.U. is 9.30×10^7 miles, or 1.50×10^8 kilometers.

Math and Science Basics

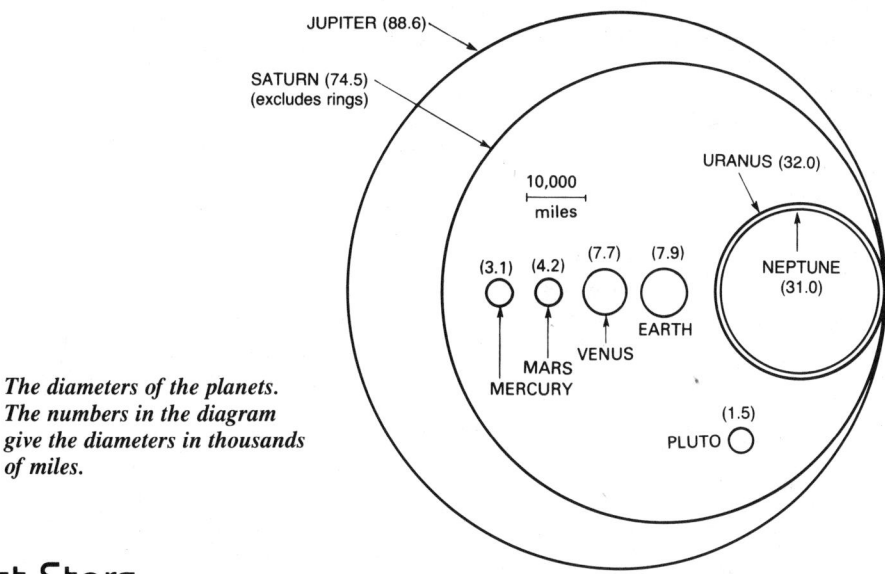

The diameters of the planets. The numbers in the diagram give the diameters in thousands of miles.

JUPITER (88.6)
SATURN (74.5) (excludes rings)
URANUS (32.0)
NEPTUNE (31.0)
10,000 miles
(3.1) MERCURY
(4.2) MARS
(7.7) VENUS
(7.9) EARTH
(1.5) PLUTO

Brightest Stars

Popular Name	Magnitude*	Distance from Earth (light-years)	Astronomical Designation
Sirius	−1.4	9	Canis Majoris
Canopus	−0.7	98	Carinae
Arcturus	−0.1	36	Boötes
Vega	0.0	26	Lyrae
Alpha Centauri	0.0	4	Centauri
Caella	+0.1	45	Aurigae
Rigel	+0.1	900	Orionis
Procyon	+0.4	11	Canis Minoris
Betelgeuse	+0.4	520	Orionis
Achernar	+0.5	118	Eridani
Beta Centauri	+0.6	490	Centauri
Alpha Crucis	+0.79	370	Crucis
Altair	+0.8	16	Aquilae
Aldebaran	+0.9	68	Tauri
Antares	+0.9	520	Scorpii
Spica	+0.9	220	Virginis
Fomalhaut	+1.2	23	Piscis Austrini
Pollux	+1.2	35	Geminorum
Deneb	+1.3	1600	Cygni
Beta Crucis	+1.3	490	Crucis
Regulus	+1.4	84	Leonis
Adhara	+1.5	680	Canis Majoris
Shaula	+1.6	310	Scorpii
Bellatrix	+1.6	470	Orionis
Castor	+2.0	45	Geminorum

* The magnitude astronomers assign to a star depends on the amount of light it gives off and its distance from Earth.

Common Terms in Science and Engineering

Astronomy

aberration The apparent displacement of a star owing to the orbital motion of Earth and the bending of light rays from the star. As Earth travels around the sun, the aberration causes the star to appear to trace an ellipse about its true position.

albedo The proportion of light reflected from a celestial body. The moon reflects only about 7 percent of the sunlight falling on it, while the albedo of Venus is more than 70 percent owing to its heavy cloud cover, which reflects a greater proportion of light.

big bang model A theory that describes the beginning of our universe as a titanic explosion. This explosion did not occur at a particular point in space, according to the theory, but rather was a transition from enormous density and temperature throughout all space to conditions of even lower density and lower temperature as space itself expanded. After the hypothetical explosion, the universe was swamped with energy in the form of radiant energy and various atomic particles. This phase was followed by a cooling and thinning out of the universe. It is believed that the universe is still expanding at this time.

black hole An ultimate state of gravitational collapse. Stars with a mass greater than two solar masses can expect to evolve into this condition, a concentration of matter so dense that even photons (light particles) cannot escape when the pressure of thermonuclear reactions are unable to counteract the force of self-gravitation. Black holes are believed to be associated with certain X-ray-emitting binary star systems, such as Cygnus X-1.

corona The outer envelope, or "atmosphere," of gas surrounding the sun, possibly extending to the orbit of Earth. During an eclipse of the sun, the corona may be visible around the edges of the moon. It has a density that is about one-millionth that of the atmosphere of Earth.

cosmology The study of the universe at large, of the distribution and behavior of the matter and energy in it, of the laws governing these factors, and of its origin and evolution.

critical density or **closure density** The density (in mass equivalents of matter and radiant energy distributed about the universe) above which the expansion of the universe will eventually slow down, stop, and reverse. Below this density, the universe will expand forever.

curved space A concept of Einstein's theory of general relativity that space-time is "warped" by the presence of massive bodies. A ray of light passing near the sun will be deflected, or bent, from a perfectly straight path. As applied to cosmology, the current expansion of the universe will proceed differently according to the type of curvature. If the mass density of the universe is above critical density, it is assumed that the curvature of space is spherical; below critical density, the curvature is considered to be hyperbolic.

galaxy A large system of stars, usually containing between one million and one trillion stars, along with clouds of gas and dust. Galaxies are sometimes classified according to their shapes as spiral, elliptical, or irregular.

gravitational collapse The contraction of a star when the pressure of thermonuclear reactions can no longer sustain the force of self-gravitation. Collapse occurs at the end of a star's life when its fuel of hydrogen and other elements is depleted. Depending on its original mass, the star may evolve into a white dwarf, a neutron star, or a black hole, or it may explode as a supernova.

Hubble flow The mutual recession of celestial objects from each other by virtue of the expansion of the universe.

light-year The distance light travels in one year, approximately 9.5×10^{15} meters, or 6 trillion miles.

matter era A period in the evolution of the universe beginning about 100,000 years after the big bang and continuing to the present time. During this period, the temperature of the universe had cooled to about 3,000° F, making it possible for electrons and protons to form neutral hydrogen atoms in a process of recombination. The atoms, in turn, accumulated in the clouds, stars, and galaxies that we observe today.

Milky Way The spiral galaxy in which our solar system is located. It contains about 150 billion stars, has a diameter of 500,000 light-years, and is about 12 billion years old.

neutron star A tiny star, usually a shrunken remnant of a once larger star, whose thermonuclear reactions could no longer uphold the bulk of the star's mass against the force of self-gravitation. A neutron star is only a few kilometers in diameter, midway between a white dwarf and a black hole.

perturbation The influence of one celestial body on another.

pulsar An object that emits radio waves in preferred directions and in periodic bursts. First discovered in 1967, pulsars are thought to be rapidly spinning neutron stars.

quark An elementary electrical particle that is believed to be the "building block" from which subatomic particles such as protons and neutrons are constructed. It is believed that quarks formed early in the creation of the universe, when the temperature was around a thousand billion degrees and physical forces were roughly equivalent.

quasar A contraction of the word *quasistellar*, used to describe celestial objects with a starlike appearance. Quasars are the most distant objects known. They have large red shifts indicating great recessional velocities and emit energy that is more than a thousand times that of an average galaxy.

radiation era A period early in the age of the universe when the temperature fell from about 10 billion degrees F to 3,000 degrees F, allowing the formation of simple nuclei, such as deuterium and helium. The radiation era was followed by the matter era.

red shift The shift of a spectrum of light toward long, red wavelengths owing to the Doppler effect of recession of a star. The faster an object recedes from Earth, the greater the shift of its light toward the red end of the spectrum. A quasar with a large red shift is moving away from Earth at a velocity of 91 percent the speed of light.

sidereal time Time that is measured by the rotation of Earth with respect to the stars, as distinguished from solar time, which is based on the rotation of Earth with respect to the sun.

supernova A gigantic explosion in which a star undergoing gravitational collapse ejects into space a large portion of its mass. This is accompanied by an immense outburst of light and charged particles.

white star A tiny star, about the size of Earth, which is the shrunken remnant of a once larger star whose thermonuclear reactions could no longer uphold the bulk of the star's mass against the force of self-gravitation. Further gravitational collapse is prevented by a condition in which the atoms are crushed very close together.

Biology

abaxial Facing away from the stem or central axis of a plant or animal.

abiogenesis A theory that living things can develop from nonliving material, as in spontaneous generation.

adaptation The modification of an organism or part of an organism to adjust to new conditions or a new environment, as in adjustment of the eyes to bright light.

adenosine triphosphate (ATP) A chemical compound present in all living cells that provides energy derived from food or sunlight for processes that require activity, such as contraction of a muscle or conduction of a nerve impulse.

appendage A structure attached to a larger structure or part of an organism, such as an arm or leg or other projection of a body area.

ATP *See* adenosine triphosphate.

bacteria Tiny, one-celled plant organisms that are generally parasitic and lacking in chlorophyll. They are commonly involved in processes of fermentation and decay, and many species are the cause of diseases in humans and animals.

bladder A saclike organ with a membranous wall that serves to collect or hold a fluid or gas, such as the urinary bladder or the air bladder of marine animals.

blastula A stage in the development of an embryo after the early phase of cell division when the cells form a hollow ball. The wall of the sphere is a single layer of cells, the blastoderm. The various organs, such as the gut, nervous system, and appendages, eventually evolve from cells of the blastula.

bud An undeveloped appendage of an organism. A plant bud may develop into flowers or leaves while the bud of an animal embryo may become an arm, leg, or wing. Some bacteria and yeast cells reproduce by issuing buds, each of which becomes a new organism.

bug Any of a large number of creeping or flying insects, mainly of the order Hemiptera. Examples of "true bugs" include bed bugs, cinch bugs, squash bugs, and giant water bugs.

calyx A cuplike portion of a plant or animal organ. Examples include the sepals, or outermost parts of a flower, and the funnel-shaped part of a kidney that collects urine as it drains toward the bladder.

carnivore Any meat-eating animal, particularly a member of the order Carnivora, which includes wolves, coyotes, bears, dogs, and cats.

cell The basic structural unit of living things. It usually consists of a membranous wall containing protoplasm, a souplike mixture of proteins, enzymes, and other organic chemicals needed for survival and reproduction. Most cells also contain a nucleus that in turn holds the DNA molecules, or genetic material, that control the various cell functions.

chlorophyll Any of nearly a dozen kinds of green pigments present in most plant cells. Chlorophylls are able to convert the energy from sunlight into carbohydrates, which plants form from carbon dioxide and water present in the environment. The carbohydrates in turn become a source of energy for animals and humans after the plant material is eaten.

chromosome A rod-shaped unit of DNA present in the nucleus of a cell that is capable of reproducing itself. It contains a portion of the genetic or hereditary traits of the species it represents. The number of chromosomes and their shapes and sizes vary among different species and sexes within a species. Human males, for example, possess a Y-shaped chromosome that is not normally present in female cells and that governs masculine physical traits.

deoxyribonucleic acid (DNA) A large molecule of nucleic acid found in the nuclei, usually in the chromosomes, of living cells. It controls such functions as the production of protein molecules in the cell and carries the template for reproduction of all the inherited characteristics of its particular species.

DNA *See* deoxyribonucleic acid.

embryo The young of a species at a very early stage of development, as the rudimentary plant that bursts forth from a seed when it germinates or the bird that has not yet hatched from its egg. In mammals, the embryo stage occurs after the cells of the blastula begin to specialize for the development of the fetus.

endogenous Pertaining to factors influencing an organism that originate within that organism, as distinguished from exogenous factors, such as environmental influences, that originate on the outside.

evolution The process by which a species of plants or animals gradually develops over a period of many generations from a simpler to a more complex form of organism. The traits of the simpler organism are often continued into the more complex form of the same organism, as can be observed in the brain and other structures of the human body.

exogenous *See* endogenous.

fauna The animal life of a region or period of history.

female The sex of an animal that produces ova and bears offspring.

fermentation A process whereby complex carbohydrates or other organic substances are converted to other chemicals by the action of enzymes produced by molds, yeasts, or bacteria. An example is the conversion of sugars to alcohol.

fertilization The union of a male and a female reproductive cell resulting in the formation of a new organism. The term is also used to describe the process or enrichment of the soil for growing crops.

flora The plant life of a region or period of history.

genitalia The reproductive sex organs of a male or female of the species, particularly structures on the outside of the body.

genotype *See* phenotype.

genus A subdivision of a biological family. It is composed of a group of related species, such as the genus *Canis*, which includes various species of dogs.

gonads The male and female reproductive organs.

haploid Half the number of chromosomes ordinarily present in the nucleus of a cell. During reproduction, the offspring receives a haploid number of chromosomes from each parent, making a full, or diploid, set.

herbaceous Herblike, usually used to describe a plant in which persistent woody tissue does not develop.

herbivore An animal that feeds entirely or mainly on plant materials.

hormone A chemical secretion of a gland or other tissue that triggers an action in another gland or tissue in a different part of the body.

immunity A quality of being able to resist an infectious disease.

inbreeding The mating of closely related individuals, as in self-pollinating plants or animals that are brothers and sisters.

joint An area between two parts or segments of an organism, such as the junction of two separate bones of an animal or the node of a plant.

karyotype The general appearance of a set of chromosomes of an individual. Karyotype may be used to determine sex, genetic defects, and other chromosome-related factors.

kernel The entire grain or seed of a cereal plant.

larva The young, immature form of an organism that undergoes a change in structure to become an adult, as a caterpillar or maggot.

leaf An outgrowth of a stem of a plant, usually green, in which many living functions, such as photosynthesis, respiration, and food and water storage, take place.

lipid Any of a group of fatty substances, including oils and waxes, produced by plant or animal tissues. Lipids generally are insoluble in water but they can be dissolved in alcohol, benzene, or similar organic solvents.

male The sex of an animal that produces spermatozoa or of a plant that produces pollen.

mammal A warm-blooded, air-breathing vertebrate of the class Mammalia, possessing hair and mammary glands.

Mendel's laws A series of natural principles of heredity discovered by Gregor Mendel (1822–1884). They govern such factors as dominant and recessive traits resulting from the interaction of genes that are inherited in pairs.

metabolism The chemical and energy changes associated with the consumption of food and oxygen, the production of heat, and the calories used in physical activity.

natural selection A principle proposed by Charles Darwin (1809–1882) to explain the ability of various species to adapt to changes in the environment. Called "survival of the fittest," the theory offered an explanation for the survival of some species and extinction of others.

neuron The structural and functional unit of a nerve, including the cell body and its axon and dendrite fibers.

nucleus A structure present in most plant and animal cells. It contains the chromosomes and ribonucleic acid (RNA) molecules that direct the cell's life functions.

osmosis The diffusion of water through a semipermeable membrane from the side with a greater concentration of a solution to the side with a lesser concentration.

osseous Pertaining to bones, as something composed of bone or resembling bone.

phenotype The physical features or appearance of an individual, as distinguished from the genotype, or genetic composition of his or her cells. Two or more people with the same physical appearance may belong to the same phenotype.

pistil The female sex structure of a plant, usually containing the ovary.

Protozoa A phylum, or large group, of one-celled animals.

receptor Any cell or group of cells that is the target of a stimulus, such as the retina of the eye.

regeneration The ability of some plants and animals to restore or replace lost tissues or structures, such as a claw or feather.

stamen The pollen-producing structure of a plant. It usually consists of an anther, the actual pollen producer, on the tip of a flower filament.

stimulus An environmental influence, such as a chemical or physical irritant, that induces or brings about a response in a cell or organism.

symbiosis A relationship in which two organisms live together for the mutual benefit of each.

terrestrial Pertaining to plant or animal life on land rather than in water.

tissue A group of cells with similar structures and functions.

tropism The involuntary response of an organism to a stimulus, such as the response of a plant to gravity or sunlight.

vacuole Any of the spaces scattered about the protoplasm of a cell, usually containing fluid.

zygote The fertilized egg cell of a plant or animal.

Chemistry

acid A substance that, in liquid form, will turn blue litmus paper red, react with alkalis (bases) to form salts, and dissolve metals to form salts. On the pH scale of 0 to 14, acids register in numbers less than 7.

alcohol Any of a group of organic compounds that contains a hydroxyl (OH) group. A common example is ethyl alcohol (C_2H_5OH).

alkali Any compound that has chemical qualities of a base, such as reacting with acids to form salts. On the pH scale, alkalis register in numbers larger than 7.

anion An ion with a negative electrical charge.

base An alkaline substance, either in molecular or ionic form, that will accept or receive a proton from another chemical unit. An example is a hydroxyl ion.

benzene ring A common organic molecule structure consisting of a ring of six carbon atoms with an equal number of attached hydrogen atoms (C_6H_6). Many organic chemicals occur in a benzene ring format with various atoms or radicals substituted for one or more hydrogen atoms, as in toluene and xylene as variations of benzene.

bond A strong electrical force that holds atoms together in molecules, crystals, and other combinations. A molecular bond may depend on the attractive force of an electron whose orbit spans the outer shells of two or more component atoms. In double bonds, two pairs of electrons may be shared equally by adjacent atoms.

catalyst A substance that accelerates a chemical reaction without becoming a part of the end product of the reaction. A catalyst can generally be recovered in its original form following the reaction.

cation An ion, atom, or group of atoms with a positive electrical charge.

compound A substance formed by the combination of two or more chemical elements that cannot be separated from the combination by physical means. The constituent atoms, however, can usually be separated by means of chemical reactions.

electrolyte Any chemical, such as a mineral, that when melted or dissolved in water will show an electrical attraction or conduct an electric current.

electron A negatively charged particle that moves in an orbit about the nucleus of an atom.

element A substance composed of atoms with the same atomic number or the same number of protons in their nuclei. Examples include oxygen, hydrogen, carbon, and gold.

hydrocarbon Any of a large group of chemical compounds consisting primarily of carbon and hydrogen atoms, usually associated with current or past life processes.

hydroxyl Pertaining to the negatively charged OH (oxygen + hydrogen) radical in an organic compound.

inorganic chemistry A branch of chemical science that deals primarily with elements and compounds that do not include hydrocarbons.

isotope One of two or more atoms having the same atomic number but a different mass number. An example is zinc, which has isotopes with five different mass numbers ranging from 64 to 70. However, all of the isotopes have equal nuclear charges, orbital electrons, and chemical properties.

mass number The atomic weight of an isotope, calculated from the numbers of protons and neutrons in the nucleus.

matter Anything that has weight or fills space, such as a solid, liquid, or gas.

organic chemistry A branch of chemistry that specializes in the composition, properties, and reactions of hydrocarbon compounds.

oxidation Any chemical reaction that increases the number of oxygen atoms in a compound, or in which the positive valence is increased by a loss of electrons.

pH A symbol for hydrogen ion activity of a substance as an expression of the negative logarithm of the concentration of hydrogen ions in moles per liter. Values of pH range from 0 to 14, with a pH of 7 representing acid-base neutrality. The degree of acidity increases as the number progresses toward zero, while alkalinity increases as the pH number approaches 14.

polymer A huge molecule composed of repeating units of the same molecule. An example is polyethylene, formed by linking ethylene molecules into a giant chain.

reduction A chemical reaction in which a substance gains electrons or loses part of its positive valence. Reduction generally occurs in a reaction that also involves oxidation.

solute A substance that is dissolved in a solution.

solvent The substance that represents the greatest proportion of parts of a solution when two or more substances, such as a solid and liquid, are mixed.

valence A number that represents the combining power of an element, ion, or radical. The valence of hydrogen is $+1$, while the valence of oxygen is -2.

Physics

acceleration The rate of change of velocity with respect to time. It is calculated by subtracting the initial or starting velocity from the final velocity and dividing the difference by the time required to reach that velocity. It may be expressed by the formula $a = v_f - v_0/t$.

achromatic An optical system that will transmit light without breaking it down into its component colors.

acoustics The science of the production, transmission, and effect of sound waves.

adiabetic Pertaining to any activity that is not accompanied by a gain or loss of heat.

anode The positive terminal of an electrical current flow. In a vacuum tube, electrons flow from a cathode toward the anode.

Bohr theory A commonly accepted concept of the atom introduced by Niels Bohr in 1913. It holds that each atom consists of a small, dense, positively charged nucleus surrounded by negatively charged electrons that move in fixed, defined orbits about the nucleus, the total number of electrons normally balancing the total positive charge of particles in the nucleus.

Boyle's law The principle that the volume of a gas times its pressure is constant at a fixed temperature.

cathode The negative terminal of an electric current system. In a vacuum tube, the filament serves as the cathode or source of electrons that are emitted.

conduction The transfer of heat by molecular motion from a source of high temperature to a region of lower temperature, tending toward a result of equalized temperatures.

convection The mechanical transfer of heated molecules of a gas or liquid from a source to another area, as when a room is warmed by the movement of air molecules heated by a radiator.

Coulomb's law The principle that an electrostatic force of attraction or repulsion between electrical charges is directly proportional to the product of the electrical charges and inversely proportional to the square of the distance between them.

electromotive force The force that causes the movement of electrons through an electrical circuit.

energy The ability to perform work. Energy may be changed from one form to another, as from heat into light, but it normally cannot be created or destroyed.

force The influence on a body that causes it to accelerate, as expressed by the formula $F = ma$.

heat A form of energy that results from the disordered motion of molecules. As the motion becomes more rapid and disordered, the amount of heat is increased.

kinetic energy Energy that is associated with the motion of an object as expressed by the formula $KE = \frac{1}{2}mv^2$.

mechanics A branch of physics that deals with the motion of objects.

momentum The mathematical product of the mass of a moving object and its velocity, as expressed by the formula $p = mv$.

potential energy Energy that is stored because of position or configuration, such as the gravitational energy of a weight that is positioned on the roof of a building.

power The rate at which work is performed, as expressed by the formula $P = W/t$.

velocity The speed with which an object travels over a specified distance during a measured amount of time. It may be expressed by the formula $v = d/t$.

weight The force on a body produced by the downward pull of gravity on it. It may be expressed by the formula $W = mg$, where m represents the mass of the object and g represents the acceleration of gravity.

work The force applied to an object times the distance over which it is applied, as expressed by the formula $W = Fd$. Work may be independent of the energy expended.

Engineering

absorbing dynamometer A device that absorbs and dissipates the power it measures. An example is the common rope brake.

abutment Any point or surface designed to withstand thrust, as the end supports of an arch or bridge.

aggregate The sand, broken stone, and similar materials that are added to cement and water to form concrete.

apomecometer A surveying instrument used to calculate the height of structures by coincident light reflected from the top and bottom of the structure when the location of the instrument is the same distance from the base of the structure as its height.

balance crane A crane with two arms, one arranged to balance the load on the other.

bearing pile In civil engineering, a column that is sunk into the ground to support a vertical load. It transmits the load to a firmer foundation at a lower depth, or it may consolidate the soil to increase its ability to bear the load.

block gauge A block of hardened steel with opposite faces ground flat and parallel and separated by a specific distance. It is used to check the accuracy of other gauges.

cable way A system of suspending cables between two towers so that a skip suspended from the cables can be raised, lowered, or otherwise maneuvered to any position along the cables.

caisson A watertight compartment built to surround a structure, such as a bridge foundation, that would otherwise be beneath the surface of the water.

camber An upwardly convex curvature applied to a structure or part of a structure for a specific purpose. Examples include the camber added to girders to allow for deflection caused by loading or to the surface of a road to facilitate drainage.

cantilever A beam or girder that is firmly attached at one end but free at the other. A bridge may be started as two cantilevered, or self-supporting, projecting arms, built inward from piers and eventually connected at the center of the span.

differential motion A mechanical movement in which the speed of a driven part is equal to the difference in the speeds of the parts connected to it.

dog Any of a variety of gripping devices, such as a steel securing piece used to fasten a pair of timbers used for shoring.

electromechanical brake A braking device in which the force is obtained partly by the attraction of two magnetized surfaces and partly by mechanical means. It is controlled by a solenoid.

engine Any machine in which power is applied to perform work. Examples include devices that convert thermal, or heat, energy into mechanical work, such as a locomotive.

engineer's chain A surveying device consisting of a chain that is 100 feet in length with each link 1 foot long.

expansion joint A joint between two parts of a structure designed so the two parts can expand when the temperature increases, as on a hot summer day, without causing distortion or damage to the structure. Examples include joints between lengths of rail in a railroad line and sliding socket joints in pipelines.

gasket A flat sheet of asbestos, cotton rope impregnated with graphite, or similar material, used to form a gastight joint between parts of engines, pumps, or other devices.

girder A beam, usually made of steel, used to bridge an open space.

grid In electrical engineering, a network of electrical power lines connecting various generating stations.

helical gears Gear wheels in which the teeth are set at an angle to the axis rather than parallel to the wheel axis.

impeller The rotating part of a centrifugal pump. It imparts kinetic energy to the fluid being moved.

mechanical advantage The ratio of the resistance or load to the applied force or effort of a machine.

skip A bucket, box, or similar device used to transport building materials, spoils, or mining products to or from a work site. It usually is suspended from a crane or cable way.

theodolite A surveying instrument used for measuring horizontal and vertical angles.

Geology/Geography

abyssal zone A region of greatest ocean depth, generally greater than 1,000 meters, including the deep-sea trenches. Biological activity is rare in the abyssal zone; light does not penetrate the water, as the depth and pressure are tremendous. The region represents about 250 million square kilometers of Earth's surface.

age An interval of geological time that indicates when a body of rock was formed in the surface of Earth. A group of ages forms an epoch.

alluvium The sediment carried by rivers, including deposits from estuaries, lakes, and other freshwater bodies draining into a river. The particles of sediment are generally smaller than 0.02 millimeter, depending on such factors as valleyside slopes in the watershed, the distance carried downstream, and progressive wear on the particles as they move downstream.

anthropomorphic soil Soil that is distinctive in composition and contour from the surrounding environment as a result of human activity. An example is soil that has been used for farming.

barrier beach An accumulation of sand, rock, and other material lying parallel to the coast but separated from it by a channel; it measures from a few meters to a few kilometers in width. Large barrier beaches may be identified as barrier islands. They are formed by the action of waves but are usually vulnerable to overwashing or breaching during severe storms.

bathyal zone A zone of ocean water ranging from about 200 meters to 1,000 meters in depth, generally located along continental slopes. Unlike the abyssal zone, light reaches the upper layer of the bathyal zone and there is abundant biological activity in the water. The bathyal zone of the world covers a total of about 40 million square kilometers.

bed The smallest division of stratified sedimentary rock, usually occurring as a relatively thin sheet of sedimentary material separating distinctively different layers above and below it. A bed often marks a particular event in geologic history, such as a volcanic eruption, and it may contain fossils that help identify its age.

Cambrian The earliest period of the Paleozoic era, about 600 million years ago. Rocks formed at this period contain the earliest fossil remains of invertebrate animals.

chronostratigraphy A system of classifying the major divisions of geologic time. According to the system, the smallest segment is a chron; groups of chrons form an age; a group of ages forms an epoch; epochs form periods; periods form eras; and eras form eons. There is no uniform time scale applied to the divisions. For example, the Miocene epoch spans 17 million years but the following Pliocene epoch lasted only 3.7 million years.

continental drift The shifting of continental landmasses from one location to another on the face of Earth owing to seafloor spreading. Evidence supporting the concept is based on comparison of flora, fauna, rock types, and geologic formations. It indicates that until about 250 million years ago, there were just two continents—Pangaea and Gondwanaland—from which the present continents were formed.

Coriolis effect A force produced on objects moving on a north–south line on the surface of Earth because of the angular velocity of Earth as it rotates from west to east. Thus, a projectile fired directly southward from the North Pole would be deviated to the west. The Coriolis force affects mainly the flow of air in the atmosphere.

creep The slow movement of rocks and soil down slopes of hills owing to the pull of gravity. It is believed the movement involves a sliding of the entire Earth mantle over the underlying bedrock rather than changes within the mantle itself. The effect can be observed in the tendency of telephone poles and other objects to alter positions on gentle slopes over a period of years.

diagenesis The process whereby sedimentary rock is formed from sediment because of compaction, reduced pore space between particles, and chemical reactions between molecules of the compressed particles and dissolved substances in moisture between the particles.

doldrums A region between the equator and the trade wind zones where winds are light and variable, storms are frequent and severe, and navigation is difficult.

equinox A date that occurs twice each year when the sun is overhead at local solar time at the equator and day and night are both 12 hours long. It occurs on or about March 21 and September 21.

era An interval of geological time composed of a group of periods. An example is the Paleozoic era, which spans a series of six periods of geological time.

estuary The portion of a river that is affected by ocean tides above the mouth, with a resulting mixture of salt water and fresh water. Most estuaries are former valleys that were flooded by rising ocean levels after the last glacial event. The Hudson River is an example of an estuary.

fjord A narrow sea inlet between mountain slopes. Most fjords were once glaciated valleys that became flooded by rising sea water after the last ice age. In some cases, the bottom of the fjord may be lower than the bottom of the sea at its opening into the fjord.

floodplain A relatively level area alongside a river that is subject to flooding periodically. It usually is composed of sediment that has been deposited over the surface of an original rock-cut valley.

frost hollow An area where cold air, which has a greater density than warm air, tends to collect because there is no free air outlet from the low-lying hollow. As a result, the area is more likely than the surrounding landscape to experience frost on cold days.

geology The science of the structure and composition of Earth.

glacier An accumulation of ice formed in turn by compaction of accumulated snow moving downslope from a source area because of the force of gravity. A glacier is usually confined within the limited space of a valley or basin. It may be gaining ice at the source while losing ice at a point where it melts while moving into warmer temperatures or a body of water.

induration The hardening of porous rocks or soils owing to weather conditions and the chemical actions of dissolved minerals, which form a cement. The concrete-like rock formed by induration usually consists of combinations of calcium, silicon, or iron with carbon and oxygen.

leaching The action of water draining through soil layers carrying dissolved minerals or organic matter from the upper layers. Because leaching tends to remove alkaline substances, the soils eventually become acidic.

Mercator projection A map in which the spherical Earth is projected as a cylinder onto a flat surface. It results in straight-line bearings that are correct and is most commonly used for navigation charts, although the projection distorts the areas toward the North and South poles.

Common Computer Terms

address A location in the computer memory where a particular unit of data is stored. The address may be in the form of an identifying label, name, or number.

ALGOL An algorithmic computer programming language, used mainly by mathematicians and scientists.

algorithm A defined set of instructions or procedural steps that will lead to a logical conclusion for a specific problem.

analog computer A computer that measures a function or behavior involving continuously variable signals, such as signals representing current, voltage, or other factors. An analog computer is also able to respond immediately to changes in input. The output may be presented in the form of a tracing on a graph or a design on a TV picture tube.

analog-to-digital computer A device that is able to convert continuous analog signals into digital data, or discrete numbers.

architecture The design of a computer so that hardware and software interface effectively.

arithmetic/logic unit The part of a computer that performs calculations and comparisons.

array An arrangement of data in which each item may be identified by a key or subscript so that a computer program can be designed to examine and extract specific data. An example is a calendar array in which a particular day of the year can be identified.

ASCII Acronym for *American Standard Code for Information Interchange*, a uniform character code used by many computer systems so that data can be exchanged directly between various types of central and remote units and peripheral devices. Each alphabetic and numeric character requires a full byte.

assembler A computer program designed to assemble machine code from symbolic code or source language.

assembly language A machine-oriented computer-programming language that can be translated directly into machine instructions.

BASIC Acronym for *Beginner's All-purpose Symbolic Instruction Code*, a program that is a standard language for most personal computers. It is designed for developing programs in a "conversational mode" for on-line use.

batch A group of records or collection of transactions that may be processed together.

baud rate The rate at which information is transmitted serially from a computer. It is expressed in terms of bits per second.

BCD *See* binary coded decimal.

binary A numbering system based on twos (2's) rather than decimals (10's). Each element has a digit value of either zero (0) or one (1) and is known as a bit.

binary coded decimal (BCD) A method of encoding four bits of binary computer code to represent the 10 decimal digits. For example, 0 = 0000; 1 = 0001; 2 = 0010; and so on through 9 = 1001.

bit An acronym constructed from the words *bi*nary digi*t*. It refers to a single digit of a binary number.

bootstrap (boot) The process of initializing or loading the basic operating instructions into a computer.

buffer A temporary storage area for data that helps compensate for differences in the speed of operations of two or more parts of a computer system, such as the central processing unit and a printer.

bug Any error or malfunction in a computer operation or program.

byte A set or unit of binary digits, usually eight bits, such as a division of a word. The storage capacity of a disk is usually given in megabytes.

cathode ray tube (CRT) An electronic tube, similar to a television picture tube, on which a computer output is displayed (also called a visual display terminal).

CD-ROM An acronym for *C*ompact *D*isk-*R*ead *O*nly *M*emory, a large-storage compact disk that resembles a music CD and holds information that can be viewed on the computer screen but cannot be altered.

central processing unit (CPU) The part of the computer circuitry that actually handles the data processing and controls the storage, movement, and other basic computer functions.

channel A path through which computer data flow.

character Any digit, letter, punctuation, or symbol, usually represented by a single byte of eight bits.

clock An electronic device that monitors, measures, or synchronizes various functions of a computer system.

COBOL An acronym formed from the words *CO*mmon *B*usiness *O*riented *L*anguage.

command A part of a computer code that gives input/output instructions to the computer.

compiler A set of programs that compiles or converts a program into the machine language instructions used by a particular computer.

console The part of the central processing unit from which the computer operator manually directs activities of the system, as through a keyboard.

control data Computer information that helps organize data in key categories, such as sorting sequences.

control unit The part of the central processing unit that manipulates the sequences of operations according to the program instructions.

CPU *See* central processing unit.

CRT *See* cathode ray tube.

cursor A symbol appearing on a video display indicating the position where a user can add or delete characters.

data acquisition system A system in which data from computers in remote locations can be transmitted to a central computer unit. The flow of data is usually governed by a program control that buffers signal inputs from the various peripheral units.

database A large file of organized information that may be updated and manipulated as needed.

data management system A set of commands used to search and retrieve content and update and reference information from a database.

diagnostic routine A program designed to trace the source of program errors or the cause of a computer malfunction.

digital computer A computer in which discrete numbers are used to express data and instructions.

digitalization rate The speed with which digitalization occurs in an analog-to-digital converter.

direct access *See* random access.

disk (diskette) A circular plate coated with magnetic material that can be used to store computer data.

disk drive A device that is able to "read" data stored in magnetic material on a disk or to "write" data onto such a disk.

disk operating system A program that controls how the various parts of a computer interact; also known by its acronym, DOS.

DOS *See* disk operating system

downtime A period of time during which a computer system is out of operation.

dynamic range The range of voltage or input signals that results in a digital output in an analog-to-digital converter.

error message A message output by the computer, triggered by a program, indicating failure to follow a correct input/output routine, a hardware malfunction, or another problem that may cause the operation to discontinue.

execute Performance of an operation specified by a program routine or instruction.

file A collection of related data or information that is stored as a unit.

floppy disk *See* disk.

FORTRAN An acronym formed from the words *FOR*mula *TRAN*slator. It is a programming language used for mathematical and scientific operations.

garbage A popular term for meaningless data, usually the result of erroneous input/output operations or the result of data left in the computer memory from a previous unrelated project.

generation Pertaining to a group of computers developed within the same time period based on the model of an earlier product.

generator A routine designed to produce a program that will perform a specific version of a general operation, usually by filling in certain details within a predetermined framework.

GUI An acronym for *G*raphical *U*ser *I*nterface, a system through which the user can interact with the computer by means of pictures and symbols called icons.

hard copy A copy of the output of a computer that has been produced on paper, as distinguished from the electronic copy of the same data on disk or tape.

hardware The physical equipment or devices, such as the central processing unit, of a computer system. *See also* software.

hexadecimal A system of whole numbers with a base of 16 used in certain computer operations. Hexadecimal coding uses numerals 0 to 16 with the first 10 digits represented by 0 through 9 and the next 6 digits represented by the letters A through F.

high-level language Any computer language in which each instruction corresponds to a group of machine code instructions. Examples include BASIC and COBOL.

housekeeping Standard computer routines, such as deleting garbage or preliminary input/output functions, that are not directly related to a particular job.

hybrid computer A computer that is able to perform both analog and digital computing functions.

icon The graphic representation of a computer command.

input The information a computer receives from a keyboard, tape, or disk.

input/output (I/O) terminal A computer device that is capable of both receiving and retrieving data.

instruction A part of a program that directs a computer to perform a single specific function as part of a sequence of functions.

interface A device that serves as a link or common surface boundary between two different parts of a computer system.

interrupt A temporary suspension of processing by a computer, caused by input or other activity by another part of the system.

I/O *See* input/output.

joystick A lever that is connected to a computer for use in moving the cursor from one point to another on a video display terminal.

K An abbreviation for kilo and a symbol for 1,000 (actually 2^{10}, or 1,024); it is commonly used to indicate the storage capacity of a computer memory. For example, a 64K memory has a theoretical capacity of 64 × 1,024, or 65,536, bytes or data storage locations.

keyboard A device that encodes characters for a computer function by depressing keys. Pressing the keys may punch holes in punched cards or provide a direct input of data to the computer.

label A group of computer characters used to identify a file, record, or memory storage area.

language A set of characters that can be used to form a meaningful set of words and symbols in writing instructions for a computer. Examples include ALGOL, BASIC, COBOL, and FORTRAN.

light pen A photoelectric device connected to the cathode ray tube of a display unit. It can be used by the operator to activate the computer to change or modify an image displayed by touching the pen to the screen.

machine language A language composed of a set of numbers and symbols that can direct computer operations without the need for translation.

magnetic memory A memory device that uses magnetic fields for storing data.

mainframe computer A large professional computer system used by a major industry or government agency, as distinguished from a smaller minicomputer or microcomputer.

memory The ability of a computer to store and retrieve data.

message A combination of characters or symbols used to communicate information between points of a computer system. *See also* error message.

microcomputer A small personal computer or word processor.

microprocessor A single large-scale integrated circuit on a fingernail-size silicon chip. It contains thousands of individual circuit elements and is the heart of the central processing unit.

minicomputer A computer that is larger in capacity, flexibility, and cost than a microcomputer. It may commonly be used to control industrial processes.

MODEM An acronym formed from the words *MOd*ulator *DEM*odulator. It is an electronic device that allows computer data to be carried over telephone lines.

mouse A movable device attached to a computer that permits the operator to reposition the cursor on the video display terminal. Manipulating the device moves the cursor vertically or horizontally on the screen.

multiprogramming The performance of two or more different computer functions at the same time.

off-line Pertaining to computer functions that are not under the direct control of a central processing unit or computer operator. The term is sometimes applied to hard copy or stored data.

on-line Computer operations that are under the direct control of the central processing unit or operator.

operating system (OS) Any program that controls how the various parts of a computer interact.

optical scanner An electronic device that scans direct or reflected light from a surface, such as a printed page, and converts the signals to machine-readable inputs.

OS *See* operating system.

output The results of a computer operation, which may appear in the form of a printout or visual display.

peripheral Any device that is separate from but connected to the computer for the purpose of supplying input or output functions, such as a modem or printer.

primary memory The part of the computer used as the main storage area for data or programs.

RAM *See* random access memory.

random access The direct retrieval of data from a location in the computer memory without the need for sorting through sequential information.

random access memory (RAM) A computer storage device that permits direct access to data independent of its location in the computer memory.

read only memory (ROM) A type of computer memory that can be used to retrieve data for output only; new data cannot be written into it.

real time Computer operations that permit rapid analyses of data so that decisions can be made immediately.

register A part of the computer's central processing unit that stores information for future use. It may have specific uses, such as arithmetic functions or word processing. A computer may contain several different registers.

response time The amount of time between the input of information into a computer and its output, or response to the input.

ROM *See* read only memory.

serial processing A type of computer function in which two or more programs are run in sequence rather than simultaneously.

software The programs or instructions used to operate a computer system, as distinguished from the hardware.

storage capacity The amount of data that can be stored in a computer memory. *See also* K.

streaming mode A removable magnetic-tape backup system for hard disk drives. It permits copying data from the hard disk so that it can be preserved in the event of a hard drive failure.

terminal An input/output device that allows an operator to control a computer. It may consist of a keyboard and video display screen.

time sharing A computer function of handling two or more tasks simultaneously, as when a mainframe computer is used to process operations of several remote terminals at the same time. Such a system depends on buffering and switching inputs and outputs for each terminal. This is done at such a high rate of speed that operators of individual terminals are unaware that others are sharing the same central processing unit.

track A segment of a disk or other magnetic storage device that stores a fixed amount of data in a designated address for rapid retrieval.

Winchester disk drive A type of hard disk drive capable of transferring data, detecting errors, and making corrections at a high rate of speed.

word A fixed number of bits processed by a computer as a single basic unit.

write The process of recording data in a computer memory.

write-protected disk A computer disk designed to prevent altering the data stored on it.

X-Y digitizer An electronic device that allows a cursor or light pen to produce the X and Y coordinates of a graph on a video display terminal.

Additional Sources of Information

Organizations and Services

Academy of Natural Sciences
19th Street and the Parkway
Philadelphia, PA 19103

American Association for the Advancement of Science
1333 H Street, N.W.
Washington, DC 20005

American Astronomical Society
200 Florida Avenue, N.W.
Washington, DC 20009

American Geological Institute
4220 King Street
Alexandria, VA 22302

American Institute of Physics
335 East 45th Street
New York, NY 10017

American Museum of Natural History
Central Park West and 79th Street
New York, NY 10024

Hale Observatories
813 Santa Barbara Street
Pasadena, CA 91101

Institute for Scientific Information
325 Chestnut Street
Philadelphia, PA 19106

National Academy of Sciences
2101 Constitution Avenue, NW
Washington, DC 20418

National Bureau of Standards
Gaithersburg, MD 20899

National Oceanic and Atmospheric Administration
Department of Commerce
Washington, DC 20230

National Science Foundation
1800 G Street, N.W.
Washington, DC 20550

National Technical Information Service
Department of Commerce
5285 Port Royal Road
Springfield, VA 22161

New York Academy of Sciences
2 East 63rd Street
New York, NY 10021

Scientists Institute for Public Information
355 Lexington Avenue
New York, NY 10017

Smithsonian Institution
1000 Jefferson Drive, S.W.
Washington, DC 20560

Books

Asimov, Isaac. *Asimov's New Guide to Science.* Basic Books, 1984.

Brown, Stanley. *The Realm of Science,* 21 vols. Touchstone, 1972.

Bunch, Bryan, and Alexander Hellemans. *Timetables of Science: A Chronology of the Most Important People and Events in the History of Science.* Simon & Schuster, 1988.

Considine, Douglas. *Van Nostrand's Scientific Encyclopedia,* 7th ed., 2 vols. Van Nostrand Reinhold, 1989.

CRC Handbook of Chemistry and Physics, CRC Press, annual.

Curtis, Anthony R. *Space Almanac.* ARCsoft Publishers, 1990.

Dean, John A. *Lange's Handbook of Chemistry,* 13th ed. McGraw-Hill, 1985.

McGraw-Hill Encyclopedia of Engineering, McGraw-Hill, 1983.

McGraw-Hill Encyclopedia of Science and Technology, 6th ed., 20 vols. McGraw-Hill, 1988.

Runcorn, S. K. *Earth Science,* 3 vols. Elsevier Science, 1971.

6

INVENTIONS AND SCIENTIFIC DISCOVERIES

Significant Inventions, Technological Advances, and Discoveries / *105*

The Kite / *105*

Leonardo da Vinci / *107*

Quarks / *123*

Additional Sources of Information / *126*

Significant Inventions, Technological Advances, and Discoveries

Date	Invention/Discovery	Inventor/Origin
B.C.		
c. 12,000	Fire	Unknown
c. 5000	Woven cloth	Mesopotamia, Egypt
	Copper working	Rudna Glava, Yugoslavia
c. 3500	Wheeled vehicles	Sumeria, Syria
	Potter's wheel	Middle East
	Gold mining	Mesopotamia, Africa
	Sundial	Middle East
c. 3150	Irrigation	China, Egypt
c. 3000	Ox-drawn plow	Egypt
c. 2780	First step pyramid	Imhotep
c. 2700	Great Pyramid of Cheops	Cheops
c. 2640	Silk production	Si-ling Chi
c. 2500	Kite	China
	Cotton production	China, India

THE KITE

The kite is not only the earliest form of flying machine, it is also one of the few ancient technological objects to be used continuously into modern times. There is evidence that kites were known in China as early as 2500 B.C., and they eventually came to be used for recreational, religious, and military purposes throughout Asia and the Pacific islands. Kites served a ceremonial function, for example, in Polynesian myth, in which gods were personified in kite form.

One of the first references to kites in Europe is found in the 1300s: a German book contains an illustration of soldiers using a kite to drop a bomb over the walls of an enemy castle. By the 1600s kites had lost their military overtones, growing popular as toys for children. In 1752 Benjamin Franklin used a kite to show the electrical nature of lightning. During the nineteenth century, kites saved lives—shipwrecked boats would use them to carry lines to potential rescuers on shore.

Also in the 1800s, kites were important in early studies of aeronautics. Lawrence Hargrave of Australia was one of the first to try to make the kite into a flying machine, a forerunner of our modern glider.

c. 1350	22-letter alphabet	Phoenicians
c. 1300	Musical notation	Ugarit, Syria
c. 700	First aqueduct	Sennacherib
c. 570	Geographical and star charts	Anaximander of Miletus
c. 430	Concept of atomic structure	Democritus
c. 400	Profession of medicine	Hippocrates
c. 300	Deductive system of mathematics	Euclid
	Abacus	Asia, Middle East

c. 260	Theory that sun is the center of the solar system	Aristarchus
c. 250	Principles of the lever and other simple machines	Archimedes
c. 221	Beginning of the Great Wall of China	Shih Hwang-ti
c. 190	Ellipse and hyperbola	Appollonius
c. 140	Trigonometry	Hipparchus
c. 100	Stone bridge	Roman engineers, Tiber River, Rome
	Wheel bearings	On a wagon found at Dejbjerg, Jutland
c. 85	Seed-planting machine	China
c. 40	Rotary winnowing machine	China

A.D.

c. 80	Magnetism	China
c. 100	Paper making	China
c. 170	Function of the arteries	Galen
c. 180	Rotary fan	China
c. 230	Wheelbarrow	China
c. 500	Algebra	India
	Decimal system	India, Mesopotamia
c. 550	Water mill	Greece
580	Iron-chain suspension bridge	China
c. 600	Zero	India
640	Windmill	Persia
c. 700	Porcelain	T'ang dynasty
886	24-hour-day measurement system	Alfred the Great
c. 900	Moldboard plow	China
980	Canal locks	Ciao Wei-Yo
c. 1100	Rocket	China
1150	Paper mill	Spain
c. 1150	Gunpowder	China
1250	Magnifying glass	Roger Bacon
1260	Gun/cannon	Konstantin Anklitzen
1269	360° compass	Petrus Peregrinus de Maricourt
1280	Belt-driven spinning wheel	Hans Speyer
1285	Eyeglasses	Alessandro de Spina
1287	Nitric acid	Raymond Lully
1326	Metal cannon	Rinaldo di Villamagna
1335	Public striking clock	Palace Chapel of the Visconti, Milan, Italy
1360	Mechanical clock	Henri de Vick of Wurttemburg for King Charles V of France
1410	Wire	Rodolph of Nuremberg
1450	Printing press with movable type	Johann Gutenberg
1455	Cast-iron pipe	Castle of Dillenburgh, Germany
1474	Lunar nautical navigation	Regiomontanus
1489	(+) and (−) signs in mathematics	Johann Widman
1493	Drawing of a flying machine	Leonardo da Vinci

LEONARDO DA VINCI

Modern science has its roots in the Italian Renaissance, and perhaps the most striking example of "the Renaissance Man" is Leonardo da Vinci (1452–1519). While he is best known for his work as an artist, Leonardo's scientific contributions may rival his renowned *Mona Lisa*. In 1493 Leonardo sketched a design for a hovering machine that he called a "helix pteron," an early version of our modern helicopter. He designed and built the first swinging miter lock gates for canals. And, in a forerunner of modern road systems, he sketched the separation of traffic on two levels. In his scientific contributions, Leonardo was a precursor of two other Renaissance greats, Copernicus and Galileo.

1500	Portable clock	Peter Henlein
1520	Spirally grooved rifle barrel	August Kotter
1525	Portable shotgun (harquebus)	Marquis of Pescara
c. 1535	Heliocentric planetary model	Copernicus
1538	Optic nerve	Constanzo Varolio
1540	Artificial limbs	Ambroise Paré
	Pistol	Camillo Vettelli
1550	Screwdriver	Gunsmiths and armorers (location unknown)
	Wrench	Unknown
	Ligature to stop bleeding during surgery	Ambroise Paré
1557	Enamel	Bernard Palissy
	Platinum	Julius Caesar Scaliger
1561	Dredger	Pieter Breughel
1565	Graphite pencil	Konrad Gesner
1569	Screw-cutting machine and ornamental turning lathe	Jacques Besson
1581	Pendulum motion	Galileo Galilei
1582	Modern calendar	Pope Gregory XIII and Christoph Clavius
1585	Time bomb	Dutch siege of Antwerp
1589	Hosiery-knitting machine	Rev. William Lee
1590	Compound microscope	Zacharias Jannsen
	Law of falling bodies	Galileo Galilei
1592	Wind-powered sawmill	Cornelius Corneliszoon
	Thermoscope (primitive thermometer)	Galileo Galilei
1597	Proportional compass (sector)	Galileo Galilei
1599	Silk-knitting machine	Rev. William Lee
1600	Wind-driven land vehicle	Simon Stevin
1603	Pantograph	Christoph Scheiner
1606	Surveying chain	Edmund Gunter
1609	Astronomical telescope	Galileo Galilei
	Laws of planetary motion	Johannes Kepler
1611	Coke	Simon Sturtevant
	Rainbow theory	Johannes Kepler
1611	Double convex microscope	Johannes Kepler
1614	Logarithms	John Napier
1615	Solar-powered motor	Salomon de Caux

	Surveying by triangulation	Willebrord Snell von Roigen
1616	Function of the heart and complete circulation of the blood	William Harvey
	Medical thermometer	Santorio Santorio
1621	Rectilinear slide rule	William Oughtred
1630	Circular slide rule	Richard Delamain
1631	Multiplication (×) sign	William Oughtred
	Vernier scale	Pierre Vernier
1637	Analytic geometry	René Descartes
1638	Micrometer	William Gascoigne
1642	Calculating machine	Blaise Pascal
1643	Barometer (Torricellian tube)	Evangelista Torricelli and Vincenzo Viviani
1647	Map of moon and star catalog	Helvius (Johannes Hewelcke)
1648	Hydrochloric acid	Johann Rudolph Glauber
	Concept of air pressure in barometers	Blaise Pascal
1650	Lymph glands	Olof Rudbeck
1654	Air vacuum pump	Otto von Guericke
	Basic laws of probability	Blaise Pascal and Pierre de Fermat
1656	Pendulum clock	Christiaan Huygens
1658	Clock balance spring	Robert Hooke
	Red blood cells	Jan Swammerdam
1661	Wood (methyl) alcohol	Robert Boyle
1662	Boyle's law/gas pressure laws	Robert Boyle
	Statistical mathematics	Sir William Petty
1664	Hygrometer	Francesco Folli
1666	Principles of integral calculus	Isaac Newton
1667	Blood transfusion (lamb to boy)	Jean-Baptiste Denis, France
	Wind gauge	Christian Forner
1668	Reflecting telescope	Isaac Newton
1669	Phosphorus	Hennig Brand
1671	Silk-spinning machine	Edmund Blood
	Binary number system	Gottfried Wilhelm Leibnitz
1674	Tourniquet	Morel, France
1675	Calibrated foot ruler	Unknown
1676	Artificial water filtration	William Woolcott
1679	Pressure cooker	Denis Papin
1682	Halley's comet	Edmond Halley
1683	Bacteria	Anton van Leeuwenhoek
	Spermatozoa	Anton van Leeuwenhoek
1684	Theory of gravity	Isaac Newton
1690	Speed of light	Ole Römer
1694	Plant pollen	Rudolph Jakob Camerarius
1695	Epsom salts	Nehemiah Grew
1699	Portable fire pump	Dumaurier Duperrier
1701	Machine seed drill	Jethro Tull
1702	Tidal pump	George Sorocold
	Boron/borax	Guillaume Homberg
1709	Coke smelting (iron)	Abraham Derby

	Anemometer	Wolfius
	Alcohol thermometer	Gabriel Fahrenheit
1711	Tuning fork	John Shore
1712	Steam engine	Thomas Newcomen
1716	True porcelain (Meissen)	Johann Friedrich Bottger
1717	Fahrenheit temperature scale	Gabriel Fahrenheit
1718	Mercury thermometer	Gabriel Fahrenheit
1719	Color printing	Jakob Christof Le Blon
1729	Aberration of light	Rev. James Bradley
1731	Octant (Hadley's quadrant)	John Hadley
1732	Copper-zinc alloy	Christopher Pinchbeck
	Threshing machine	Michael Menzies
1733	Arsenic	George Brandt
	Flint-glass lens	Chester Moor Hall
	Flying shuttle	John Kay
1735	Plant classification system	Carl Linnaeus
1736	Scarlet fever	William Douglass
1740	Curare (drug)	Charles Marie de Lacondamine
1742	Crucible steel production	Benjamin Huntsman
	Celsium temperature scale	Anders Celsius
1743	Wool carding machine	David Bourne
	Compound lever	John Wyatt
1746	Leyden jar (prototype of electrical condenser)	Pieter van Musschenbroeck and E. G. von Kleist
1747	Scurvy cure	James Lind
1748	Sea quadrant	B. Cole
1750	Dyanometer	Gaspard de Prony
1751	Nickel	Axel Frederik Cronstedt
1752	Lightning conductor	Benjamin Franklin
1755	Iron-girder bridge	M. Garvin
1756	Carbon dioxide	Joseph Black
1757	Sextant	John Campbell
1758	Achromatic lens (for eyeglasses)	John Dolland
	Refracting telescope	John Dolland
1760	Screw manufacturing machine	Job and William Wyatt
	Cast-iron cog wheel	Carron Iron Works, Scotland
1761	Mass production of steel scissors	Robert Hinchliffe
	Medical percussion method (diagnostic technique)	Joseph Leopold Avenbrugger
1762	Fire extinguisher	Dr. Godfrey
1764	Spinning jenny	James Hargreaves
1766	Hydrogen	Henry Cavendish
1768	Aerometer	Antoine Baumé
1769	Steam automobile	Joseph Cugnot
	Steam tractor	Joseph Cugnot
	Hydraulic spinning machine	Richard Arkwright
1770	Sulfur dioxide	Joseph Priestley
	Electric battery	John Cuthbertson
1772	Nitrogen	Daniel Rutherford

1774	Oxygen	Karl Wilhelm Scheele, Joseph Priestley, and Antoine-Laurent Lavoisier
	Ammonia	Joseph Priestley
	Barium	Karl Wilhelm Scheele
	Chlorine	Karl Wilhelm Scheele
	Manganese	Karl Wilhelm Scheele
1775	Chain-driven machine	Crane (England)
	Digitalis (as drug)	William Withering
1776	One-person submarine	David Bushnell
1777	Circular saw	Samuel Miller
	Iron boat	Yorkshire, England
1778	Mortise tumbler (lock)	Robert Barron
	Flush toilet	Joseph Bramah
	Molybdenum	Karl Wilhelm Scheele
1779	Glycerine	Karl Wilhelm Scheele
1780	Artificial insemination	Lazzaro Spallanzani
1781	Uranus	William Herschel
1782	Tellurium	Franz Joseph Müller
	Hot-air balloon	Joseph-Michel and Jacques-Étienne Montgolfier
1783	Hydrogen balloon	Jacques Alexandre Charles and the Robert brothers
	Tungsten	Don Fausto d'Elhuyar and Juan José d'Elhuyar
1784	Bifocal lenses	Benjamin Franklin
	Model helicopter	Launoy (France)
	Rope-spinning machine	Robert March
1785	Automatic grist mill	Oliver Evans
	Methane and ethylene	Claude Louis Berthollet
	Rule of electrical forces	Charles Coulomb
1786	Steamboat	John Fitch
1787	Roller bearings	John Garnett
	Power loom	Edmund Cartwright
1789	Uranium	Martin Heinrich Klaproth
	Zirconium	Martin Heinrich Klaproth
	Table of 31 chemical elements	Antoine Lavoisier
1790	Semaphore (visual telegraph)	Claude Chappé
	Cotton spinning and weaving machine (first U.S. patent)	William Pollard
1793	Cotton gin	Eli Whitney
	Astigmatism	Thomas Young
	Strontium	Thomas Charles Hope
	Daltonism (color blindness)	John Dalton
1794	Ball bearings	Philip Vaughan
1795	Hydraulic press	Joseph Bramah
1796	Lithography	Aloys Senefelder
	Smallpox vaccine	Edward Jenner
1797	Chromium	Louis Nicolas Vaquelin
	First parachute jump	André Jacques Garnerin

Year	Invention/Discovery	Person
1798	Process of mass production	Eli Whitney
1799	Metric system	French Academy of Sciences
1800	Infrared light	William Herschel
	Method for storing electricity	Alessandro Volta
	Submarine (metal clad)	Robert Fulton
1801	Asteroids	Giuseppe Piazzi
	Niobium	Charles Hatchett
	Wave theory of light	Thomas Young
	Ultraviolet light	Johann Wilhelm Ritter (and William Hyde Wollaston)
1803	Modern atomic theory	John Dalton
	Iridium	Smithson Tennant
	Palladium and rhodium	William Hyde Wollaston
	Spray gun (aerosol medication)	Alan de Vilbiss
1804	Fishnet-making machine	Joseph Marie Charles Jacquard
	Food canning process	Nicolas Appert
1805	Mechanical silk loom	Joseph Marie Charles Jacquard
	Amphibious vehicle	Oliver Evans
	Morphine	Friedrich Wilhelm Adam Serturner
1806	Beaufort wind scale	Francis Beaufort
	Carbon paper	Ralph Wedgwood
1807	Patent for gas-driven automobile	Isaac de Rivez
	Long-distance steamboat	Robert Fulton
	Potassium	Humphrey Davy
	Sodium	Humphrey Davy
	Sensory-motor nerve system	Charles Bell
1810	Homeopathy	Samuel Hahnemann
	Ammonia-soda reaction	Augustin Jean Fresnel
	Metronome	Dietrich Nikolaus Winkel
	Mowing machine	Peter Gaillard
1811	Avogadro's law	Amedeo de Quaregna e di Ceretto
	Iodine	Bernard Courteois
1813	Gun cartridge	Samuel Pauly
	Gas meter	Samuel Clegg
	Mine safety lamp	Humphrey Davy and George Stephenson
1814	Steam locomotive	George Stephenson
1816	Stethoscope	René Théophile Hyacinthe Laënnec
	Phosphorus match	François Derosne
1817	Parkinson's disease	James Parkinson
	Lithium	John August Arfwedson
	Dental plate	Anthony A. Plantson
1818	Cadmium	Friedrich Strohmeyer
	Selenium	Johan Jakob Berzelius
	Hydrogen peroxide	Baron Louis-Jacques Thénard
	Strychnine	Pierre-Joseph Pelletier and Joseph Biènaimé Caventou
	Geothermal energy experiment	F. de Larderel
1819	Dental amalgam	Charles Bell
	Dioptric system (for lighthouses)	Augustin Jean Fresnel

1820	Diphtheria	Pierre Fidèle Bretonneau
	Quinine	Pierre-Joseph Pelletier and Joseph Bièmaimé Caventou
	Electromagnetism	Hans Christian Oersted
1821	Caffeine	Pierre Joseph Pelletier
	Electric motor principle	Michael Faraday
	Heliotrope	Carl Friedrich Gauss
1822	Thermocouple	Thomas Johann Seebeck
1823	Electromagnet	William Sturgeon
1824	Galvanometer	André-Marie Ampère
	Magnetic pull	François Jean Dominique of Arago
1825	Binocular telescope	J. P. Lemière
1826	Gas stove	James Sharp
1827	Aluminum	Friedrich Wohler
	Electrical resistance	George Simon Ohm
	Astigmatic lens	George Biddell Airy
	Microphone	Charles Wheatstone
	Trifocal lens	John Isaac Hawkins
	Water turbine	Benoît Fourneyron
1828	Differential gear	Onésiphore Pecqueur
	Stethoscope with earpiece	Pierre Adolphe Poirry
	Cocoa	Conrad van Houten
	Beryllium	Friedrich Wohler
	Thorium	Johan Jakob Berzelius
1830	Vanadium	Nils Gabriel Sefstrom
	Thermostat	André Ure
	Friction match	Charles Sauria
	Lawn mower	Edwin Beard Budding
	Paraffin	Karl, Baron von Reichenbach
1831	Electric bell	Joseph Henry
	Reaping machine	Cyrus McCormick
	Electromagnetic induction	Michael Faraday
	Electromagnetic balance	Antoine César Becquerel
	Magnetic north pole	James Clark Ross
1833	Differential calculating machine	Charles Babbage
	Creosote	Karl, Baron von Reichenbach
	Nervous reflex	Marshall Hall
1834	Galvanic cells (continuous electric light)	James Bowman Lindsay
1835	Automatic revolver	Samuel Colt
1836	Steam shovel	William Smith Otis
	Stroboscope	Joseph Antoine Ferdinand Plateau
	Combine harvester	H. Hoare and J. Hascall
	Acetylene	Edmund Davy
1837	Braille reading system	Louis Braille
	Daguerreotype	Louis Jacques Mandé Daguerre
	Electric telegraph	William Fothergill Cooke and Charles Wheatstone
	Electric motor	Thomas Davenport
	Morse code	Samuel F. B. Morse

1838	Plant cells	Matthias Jakob Schleiden
	Stereoscope	Charles Wheatstone
1839	Animal cells	Theodore Schwann
	Protoplasm	Jan Evangelista Purkinje
	Vulcanization of rubber	Charles Goodyear
	First fuel cell	William Robert Grove
1840	Ozone	Christian Friedrich Schonbein
	Chronoscope	Charles Wheatstone
	Electroplating	John Wright
1841	Incandescent lamp	Frederick de Moleyne
1842	Carbon electrode battery	Robert Wilhelm Eberhard von Bunsen
	Underwater telegraph cable	Samuel F. B. Morse
	Ether anesthesia	Crawford Williamson Long
1844	Nitrous oxide anesthesia	Horace Wells and Gardner Q. Colton
1845	Rotary printing press	Richard M. Hoe
	Giant telescope	William Parsons
1846	Sewing machine	Elias Howe
	Use of anesthetic gases in surgery	William Morton
	Neptune	Johann Gottfield Galle and Heinrich Ludwig d'Arrest
1847	Nitroglycerine	Ascanio Sobrero
	Chloroform anesthesia	Jacob Bell and James Young Simpson
1849	Schrapnel shell	Edward Boxer
1850	Foucault's pendulum (proving Earth's rotation)	Jean Bernard Léon Foucault
1851	Doppler principle	Christian Doppler
	Absolute zero	Lord Kelvin (William Thompson)
	Odometer	William Grayson
	Ophthalmoscope	Herman von Helmholtz
	Flash photography	Henry F. Talbot
1852	Steam-powered airship	Henri Giffard
	Piloted glider	George Cayley
	Microfilm	John Benjamin Dancer
	Fluorescence	George Gabriel Stokes
1853	Hypodermic syringe	Charles Gabriel Pravaz and Alexander Wood
1854	Paleozoic fossils	Adam Sedgwick
1855	Spinal anesthesia	J. L. Corning, U.S.
	Bunsen burner	Robert Wilhelm Eberhard von Bunsen
	Stopwatch	Edward Daniel Johnson
	Safety match	Johan Edvard Lundstrom
	Battlefield nursing care	Florence Nightingale
1857	Passenger elevator	Elisha G. Otis
1858	Cell replication theory	Rudolf Virchow
	Mobius band	August Mobius
	Atomic and molecular weights	Stanislao Cannizzaro
1859	Cathode rays	Julius Plucker
	Theory of evolution through natural selection	Charles Darwin

	Internal combustion engine (coal gas)	Jean-Joseph-Etienne Lenoir
	Technique for drilling oil wells	Edwin Drake
	Ironclad ship	France (*La Gloire*)
1860	Linoleum	Frederick Walton
	Snap button	John Newnham
	Cesium	Robert Wilhelm Eberhard von Bunsen and Gustav Robert Kirchoff
1861	Pneumatic drill	Germain Sommelier
	Speech center of brain	Pierre Paul Broca
1862	Machine gun	Richard Jordan Gatling
1863	Phonograph (machine that wrote down what was played on a piano)	Fenby, U.S.
	TNT	J. Wilbrand
	Sodium carbonate process	Ernest Solvay
1864	Electromagnetic wave transmission	Mahlon Loomis
	Pasteurization	Louis Pasteur
	Refutation of spontaneous generation	Louis Pasteur
	Nitroglycerine and dynamite explosives	Alfred Nobel
	Railroad sleeping car	George Pullman
1865	Electric arc welding	Henry Wilde
	Reinforced concrete	W. B. Wilkinson
	Yale cylinder lock	Linus Yale, Jr.
	Offset printing (web press)	William Bullock
	Genetics	Gregor Johann Mendel
1866	Transatlantic cable	Cyrus West Field, Samuel Canning, and Daniel Gooch
	Lip reading	Alexander Melville Bell
1867	Formaldehyde	August Wilhelm von Hofmann
	Barbed wire	Lucien B. Smith
	Introduction of antiseptic practices in hospitals	Joseph Lister
	Bicycle	Ernest Michaux
	Typewriter	Christopher Latham Sholes
1868	Margarine	Hippolyte Megé-Mouries
	Stapler	Charles Henry Gould
	Plywood	John K. Mayo
	Helium (in sun's chromosphere)	Edward Frankland and Joseph Normal Lockyer
1869	Periodic law	Dmitri Ivanovitch Mendeleyev
	Color photography	Charles Cros and Louis Ducos du Hauron
	Celluloid	John Wesley Hyatt and Isaiah Smith Hyatt
1872	Hydroplane	Rev. Charles Meade Ramus
	Solar water distillation	Charles Wilson
1873	Direct current electric motor	Zénobe Théophile Gramme
	Electromagnetic radiation	James Clerk-Maxwell
1875	Mimeograph	Thomas Alva Edison
1876	Articulating telephone	Alexander Graham Bell

Inventions and Scientific Discoveries **115**

	Dewey decimal system	Melvil Dewey
	Carburetor (surface type)	Gottlieb Daimler
	Refrigerator	Karl Paul Gottfried von Linde
1877	Differential gear	James Starley
	Switchboard	Edwin T. Holmes
	Four-cycle internal combustion engine	Nikolaus August Otto
	Phonograph	Thomas Alva Edison
	Liquid oxygen	Louis-Paul Cailletet and Raoul Pictet
1878	Cathode ray tube	William Crookes
	Milking machine	L. O. Colvin
	Electric alternator	Zénobe Théophile Gramme and Hippolyte Fontaine
	Carbon filament	Joseph Wilson Swann
1879	Arc lighting system	Edwin James Houston and Elihu Thomson
	Cash register	James J. Ritty
	Saccharin	Constantin Fahlberg and Ira Remsen
	Incandescent bulb patent	Thomas Alva Edison
1880	Hearing aid	R. G. Rhodes
	First successful roll film	George Eastman
	Inoculation	Louis Pasteur
1881	Interferometer	Albert A. Michelson
	Rechargeable battery	Camille Fauré
	Telephotography	Shelford Bidwell
1882	Induction coil	Lucien Gaulard and John Gibbs
	Commercial electric fan	Schuyler Skaats Wheeler
	Skyscraper	William Le Baron Jenny
	Three-wire system for transporting electrical power	Thomas Alva Edison
	Fountain pen	Lewis Edson Waterman
	Carburetor (float-feed spray)	Edward Butler
	Tuberculosis and cholera germs	Robert Koch
1883	Long-span suspension bridge (Brooklyn Bridge)	John Augustus Roebling
1884	Steam turbine	Charles Parsons
	Local anesthesia (cocaine)	K. Koller
	Gram bacteria test	Hans Christian Joachim Gram
1885	Ammonium picrate (explosive)	Eugène Turpin
	Gas-engine automobile	Gottlieb Daimler, Wilhelm Maybach, and Karl Friedrich Benz
1886	Aluminum electrolysis process	Paul Louis Toussaint Héroult and Charles Martin Hall
	Railway car brake	George Westinghouse
	Comptometer	Dorr Eugene Felt
	Linotype machine	Ottmar Mergenthaler
1887	Mach supersonic scale	Ernst Mach
	Contact lens	Eugen A. Frick
	Electrocardiogram	Augustus Desire Walker
1888	Alternating current motor	Nikola Tesla

	Cellulose photographic film	John Carbutt
	Monorail	Charles Lartigue
	Monotype	Tolbert Lanston
	Hand camera	George Eastman
	Gas-engine farm tractor	Charter Engine Co., U.S.
	Cotton picker	Angus Campbell
	Data-processing computer	Herman Hollerith
1889	Active molecules	Svante August Arrhenius
	Cordite	James Dewar and Frederick Augustus Abel
	Lysine (amino acid)	Edmund Drechsel
1890	Motion pictures	William Friese-Greene
	Electric subway train	London, England
1891	Electric motor car	William Morrison
	Silicon carbide	Eduard Goodrich Acheson
	Flashlight	Bristol Electric Lamp Co., England
	Aluminum boat	Escher Wyss & Co., Switzerland
	Zipper	Whitcomb L. Judson
	Diphtheria antitoxin	Emil Adolf von Behring and Shibasaburo Kitasato
1892	Cholera vaccine	Waldemar Mordecai Wolff Haffkine
	Phagocytes	Illya Mechnikov
	Vacuum flask (early thermos)	Sir James Dewar
	Viruses	Dmitri Iosifovich Ivanovsky
	Viscose rayon	C. F. Cross and E. J. Bevan
1893	Photoelectric cell	Julius Elster and Hans F. Geitel
	Electric toaster	Crompton & Co., England
	Diesel engine	Rudolf Diesel
1894	Argon gas	John William Strutt and William Ramsay
	Helium	William Ramsay
	Escalator	Jesse W. Reno
1895	X-rays	Wilhelm Konrad von Roentgen
	Electric hand drill	Wilhelm Fein
	Photographic typesetting	William Friese-Greene
	First public motion picture showing with on-screen projection	Louis Lumière and Auguste Lumière
	Wireless telegraph	Guglielmo Marconi
	Gas-engine motorcycle	Count Albert de Dion and Georges Bouton
1896	Electron	Joseph John Thomas
	Histidine (amino acid)	Albrecht Kossel and Sven A. Hedin
	Science of radioactivity	Henri Becquerel
1897	Conditioned reflexes	Ivan Petrovic Pavlov
	Cause of malaria (mosquito)	Ronald Ross
	Digestion physiology	Ivan Petrovic Pavlov
	Plasticine	William Harbutt
	Worm gear	Frederick W. Lanchester
1898	Antineuritic vitamin B	Christiaan Eijkman
	Krypton	William Ramsay and Morris William Travers

Inventions and Scientific Discoveries 117

	Neon	William Ramsay and Morris William Travers
	Xenon	William Ramsay and Morris William Travers
	Vitamin-deficiency diseases	Christiaan Eijkman
	Loudspeaker	Horace Short
1899	Aspirin	Felix Hoffman
1900	Radon	Friedrich Ernst Dorn
	Tryptophan (amino acid)	Frederick Gowland Hopkins
	Paper clip	Johann Vaaler
	Alkaline battery	Thomas Alva Edison
	Tractor	Benjamin Holt
1901	Blood groups	Karl Landsteiner
	Valine and proline (amino acids)	Emil Hermann Fischer
	Electric typewriter	Thaddeus Cahill
	Vacuum cleaner	H. Cecil Booth
	Quantum theory	Max Karl Ernst Planck
1902	Hormones	William Maddock Bayliss and Ernest H. Starling
	Ionosphere	Arthur Edwin Kennelly and Oliver Heaviside
	Radium	Pierre Curie and Marie Curie
	Air conditioning	Willis H. Carrier
	Disc brakes	Frederick W. Lanchester
1903	First successful airplane flight	Orville Wright and Wilbur Wright
	Barbiturates	Emil Herman Fischer and Emil Adolf von Bering
1904	Diode vacuum tube	John Ambrose Fleming
1905	Theory of relativity	Albert Einstein
	Silicones	Frederic S. Kipping
	Chemical foam fire extinguisher	Alexander Laurent
	Hydraulic centrifugal clutch	Hermann Fottinger
1906	Crystal radio apparatus	H. H. C. Dunwoody
	Animated cartoon film	James S. Blackton and Walter Booth
	Motion picture sound	Eugen Augustin Lauste
	Wasserman test (for syphilis)	August von Wasserman
1907	Detergents (household)	Henkel et Cié., Germany
	Upright vacuum cleaner (attached dust bag)	J. Murray Spangler
	Modern color photography	Louis Lumière
1908	Bakelite	Leo Henrik Baekeland
	Cellophane	Jacques E. Brandenberger
1909	Synthetic ammonia	Fritz Haber
	Typhus fever body louse	Charles Jules Henri Nicolle
	IUD (intrauterine device)	R. Richter
1910	Tumor virus	Francis Peyton Rous
	Gene theory of heredity	Thomas Morgan
	Neon lighting	Georges Claude
1911	Cosmic rays	Victor Franz Hess
	Theory of atomic structure	Ernest Rutherford and Niels Bohr

	Concept of black hole	John Archibald Wheeler
	Superconductivity	Heike Kamerlingh Onnes
	Binet intelligence test	Alfred Binet
	Calculating machine (full automatic multiplication and division)	Jay. R. Monroe
	Monoplane	Léon Levasseur
1912	Diffraction of X-rays	Max Theodor Felix von Laue
	Thiamine (vitamin B_1)	Casimir Funk
	Diesel locomotive	North British Locomotive Co., England
	Cabin biplane (airliner forerunner)	Igor Sikorsky
1913	Stainless steel	Harry Brearley
	Vitamin A	Thomas B. Osborne, Lafayette B. Mendel, Elmer V. McCollum, and M. Davis
	Isotope labeling	Georg von Hevesy and Friedrich A. Paneth
	Moving assembly line for mass production	Henry Ford
1914	Brassiere	Mary Phelps Jacob
	Leica 35mm camera	Oskar Barnack
	Tear gas	Dr. von Tappen
1915	Amplitude modulation (AM) radio	Hendrick Johannes van der Bijl and Raymond A. Heising
	British army tank	Walter Wilson and William Tritton
1917	VHF electromagnetic waves	Guglielmo Marconi
	SONAR detection system	Paul Langevin and Robert Boyle
1918	Vitamin D	Edward Mellanby
	Electric food mixer	Universal Co., U.S.
	Domestic refrigerator	Nathaniel Wales and E. J. Copeland
1920	Commercial radio broadcasts	Station KDKA, Pittsburgh, PA
1921	Insulin	Frederick G. Banting and Charles H. Best
	Hydraulic four-wheel brakes	Duesenberg Motor Co., U.S.
	Lie detector	John Larsen
	Wirephoto	Western Union Cables, U.S.
1922	Vitamin E	Herbert McLean Evans
	Three-dimensional movies	Perfect Pictures, U.S.
1924	Spin dryer	Savage Arms Corp., U.S.
1925	Quantum mechanics	Max Born and Werner Karl Heisenberg
	Technetium and rhenium	Ida Eva Noddack and Walter Karl Friedrich Noddack
	Wave mechanics	Erwin Schrödinger
	Hi-fi radio loudspeaker	C. W. Rice and E. W. Kellogg
1926	Aerosol can	Erik Rotheim
	Synthetic rubber	I. G. Farben, Germany
	Liquid-fueled rocket	Robert H. Goddard
	Television	John Logie Baird, C. F. Jenkins, and D. Mihaly
1927	Iron lung	Philip Drinker and Louis Shaw

Inventions and Scientific Discoveries

	Pop-up toaster	Charles Strite
	First solo, nonstop transatlantic flight	Charles Lindbergh
	Uncertainty principle in physics	Werner Heisenberg
	Sex hormones	Bernhard Zondek and Selmar Ascheim
1928	Penicillin	Alexander Fleming
	Vitamin C	Albert von Nagyrapolt Szent-Györgyi
	Particles in visible light	Chandrasekhara Raman
	Geiger counter	Hans Geiger
	Teletype	Edward Ernst Kleinschmidt
	PVC (polyvinylchloride)	Carbide Corp., Carbon Chemical Corp., and Du Pont, U.S.
	Tomography	André Bocage
1929	Electron microscope	Max Knoll and Ernst Ruska
	Coaxial cable	Bell Telephone Laboratories, U.S.
	Brain-wave electroencephalograph	Hans Berger
	Frozen food	Clarence Birdseye
	First color television image transmission	Bell Telephone Laboratories, U.S.
1930	Pluto	Clyde Tombaugh
	Pepsin	John Howard Northrop
	Cyclotron	Ernest O. Lawrence and N. E. Edlesfsen
	Polystyrene	I. G. Farben, Germany
	TV electronic scanning suitable for the home	Philo T. Pharnsworth
1931	Neutrino	Wolfgang Pauli
	Radio astronomy	Karl Jansky
	Photographic exposure meter	J. Thomas Rhamstine
	Fiberglass	Owens Illinois Glass Co., U.S.
	Blood bank	Sergei Sergeivitch
	TWX (teletypewriter exchange)	Bell Telephone & Telegraph, U.S.
	Electric razor	Jacob Schick
	Cathode-ray tube for television transmission	Vladimir Zworykin
1932	Neutron	James Chadwick
	Proton bombardment (lithium disintegration)	John Douglas Cockcroft and Ernest Thomas Sinton Walton
	Positron	Carl David Anderson and Patrick M. Stuart Blackett
	Deuterium (heavy hydrogen)	Harold Urey
	Defibrillator	William Bennett Kouwenhoven
	Wind tunnel	Ford Motor Co., U.S.
	Nylon and neoprene	Wallace Carothers and Arnold Collins
1933	Riboflavin (vitamin B$_2$)	Richard Kuhn
	Pantothenic acid	Roger J. Williams
	Frequency modulation (FM)	Edwin H. Armstrong
	Polyethylene	Reginald Gibson and E. W. Fawcett
1934	Cerenkov effect	Pavel Alekseevich Cerenkov
	Vitamin K	Carl Peter Henrik Dam and Edward Adelbert Doisy
	Progesterone	Adolf Friedrich Johann Butenandt

	Vitamin B$_6$	Albert von Nagyrapolt Szent-Györgyi
1935	Meson	Hideki Yakawa
	Electronic hearing aid	Edwin A. Steven
	Richter earthquake scale	Charles Francis Richter
1936	Jet engine	Frank Whittle and Hans von Ohain
	Helicopter (contra-rotating rotors)	Henrich Focke
	Plexiglas	I. G. Farben, Germany
1937	Citric acid cycle	Hans Adolf Krebs
	Niacin	Conrad A. Elvehjem
	Radio telescope	Grote Reber
1938	Cortisone	Edward C. Kendall, Philip S. Hench, and Tadeus Reichstein
	Folic acid	P. L. Day
	Teflon	Roy Plunkett
	LSD	Albert Hofman and Arthur Stoll
	Pressurized airplane cabin	Transcontinental Airways, Boeing 307 Stratoliner
	Ballpoint pen	Lázló J. Biro and Georg Biro
	Fluorescent lighting	Arthur H. Compton and George Inman
	Photocopy machine	Chester Carlson
	First clear plastic contact lens	T. Obrig and F. Muller
1939	Jet aircraft	Hans von Ohain
	Binary calculator	John Atanasoff and George R. Stibitz
	DDT	Paul Hermann Müller
	Microfilm camera	Elgin G. Fassel
	Betatron	Donald W. Kerst
1940	Plutonium	Glenn Theodore Seaborg and Edwin Mattison McMillan
	Radar	Robert M. Page (word coined by S. M. Tucker)
	Automatic transmission	General Motors, U.S.
	Cavity magnetron (radar tube)	John Randall
1941	Microwave radar	U.S. Radiation Laboratory
	Dacron	John R. Whinfield
	First color television system	Peter Goldmark
1942	Humanmade atomic reaction (Manhattan Project)	Enrico Fermi and team
	Vitamin H (biotin)	Vincent du Vigneaud
1943	Streptomycin	Selman A. Waksman
	Electronic computer	Max Newman and T. H. Flowers
1944	Americium	Glenn T. Seaborg and Albert Ghiorso
	Curium	Glenn T. Seaborg and Albert Ghiorso
	Sequence-controlled calculator	Howard Aiken
1945	Artificial kidney	Willem J. Kolff
	Atomic bomb	J. R. Oppenheimer and team
	Tupperware	Earl W. Tupper
	Vinyl floor covering	Du Pont, U.S.
1946	Electronic vacuum tube computer (ENIAC)	John W. Mauchly and J. Presper Eckert

1947	Coenzyme A	Fritz A. Lipman
	Vitamin B$_{12}$ as cure for pernicious anemia	Karl A. Folkers
	Radiocarbon dating	Willard Frank Libby
	Holography	Dennis Gabor
	Supersonic aircraft	Bell XS-1, U.S.
	First supersonic flight	Chuck Yeager
1948	Transistor	William Shockley, John Bardeen, and Walter H. Brattain
	Atomic clock	William F. Libby
	Cybernetics	Norbert Wiener
	Long-playing phonographic record (microgroove record)	Peter Goldmark
	Solid electric guitar	Leo (Clarence) Fender, "Doc" Kauffman, and George Fullerton
	Velcro	Georges de Mestral
	Corneal contact lenses	Kevin Tuohy
1949	Berkelium	Glenn T. Seaborg and Stanley G. Thompson
	Jet airliner	R. E. Bishop and team
1950	Chlorpromazine (tranquilizer)	Paul Charpentier
	Radioimmunoassay	Rosalyn Sussman Yalow
	Xerographic copying machine	Haloid Co., U.S.
1951	Oral contraceptive pill	Gregory Goodwin Pincus, Min Chuch Chang, John Rock, and Carl Djerassi
1952	Artificial heart valve	Charles A. Hufnagel
	Hydrogen bomb	Edward Teller and team
	Experimental videotape	John Mullin and Wayne Johnson
	Transistor radio	Sony, Japan
1953	DNA (deoxyribonucleic acid)	Francis H. Compton Crick and James D. Watson
	Fermium	Albert Ghiorso and Stanley G. Thompason
	Measles vaccine	John F. Enders and Thomas Peebles
	Reperine (antidepressant drug)	Nathan S. Kline
	Reserpine (antihypertensive)	Nathan S. Kline
	Heart-lung machine	John H. Gibbon
1954	Regular broadcast of color television	National Television System Committee, U.S.
1955	Fiber optics	Narinder S. Kapany
	Mendelevium	Albert Ghiorso
	RNA synthesis	Severo Ochoa
	Ultrasound (to observe heart)	Leskell, U.S.
	Polio vaccine (killed-virus)	Jonas Salk
	Felt-tip pen	Esterbrook, England
	Stereo tape recording	EMI Stereosonic Tapes
	Hovercraft	Christopher S. Cockerell
1956	Amniocentesis	St. Mary's Hospital, England

	Human growth hormone	Choh Hao Li
	DNA synthesis with enzymes, nucleotides	Arthur Kornberg
	Plastic contact lens	Norman Bier
1957	BCS theory (superconductivity)	John Bardeen, Leon N. Cooper, and J. Robert Schrieffer
	Interferon (protein)	Alick Isascs and Jean Lindeman
	Mossbauer effect (gamma radiation)	Rudolph Ludwig Mossbauer
	Polio vaccine (live virus)	Albert S. Sabin
	Sputnik (artificial satellite)	USSR
	FORTRAN (computer language)	John Backus and team for IBM, U.S.
	Intercontinental ballistic missile	USSR
	Laser theory	Gordon Gould
	Artificial-heart pacemaker	Clarence Lillehie
1958	Laser	Charles A. Townes and Arthur L. Schawlow
	Communications satellite	SCORE, U.S.
	ALGOL computer language	Switzerland
	Nobelium	Albert Ghiorso
	Van Allen radiation belts	James A. Van Allen
1959	Tunnel diode	Sony, Japan, based on work by Leo Esaki
	Integrated circuit	Jack S. Kilby, Texas Instruments, U.S.
	Microwave radio system	Pacific Great Eastern Railway between Vancouver and Dawson Creek–Fort St. John, British Columbia, Canada
	COBOL computer language	Grace Murray Hopper
	Ion engine	Alvin T. Forrester
1960	Argon ion laser	D. R. Herriott, A. Javan, and W. R. Bennett, Bell Laboratories, U.S.
	Vertical takeoff and landing aircraft	Frank Taylor and team at Short Brothers & Harland, Northern Ireland
	Weather satellite	NASA, U.S.
	Muonium	Vernon W. Hughes and co-workers
1961	Manned spaceflight	*Vostok 1*, U.S.S.R.
	Stereophonic radio broadcast	Zenith and General Electric Companies, U.S.
	Valium	Hoffman-LaRoche Laboratories, Switzerland
	Kenyapithecus wickeri (hominid)	Louis S. B. Leakey
1962	Minicomputer	Digital Corp., U.S.
	Robotics	Rand Corp. and IBM, U.S.
	X-ray sources in the constellations	Riccardo Giacconi
	Muon neutrino	Leon Max Lederman, Melvin Schwartz, and Jack Steinberger
1963	Cassette tapes	Philips Co., The Netherlands
	Anti-xi-zero (atomic particle)	Unknown
	Quarks	Murray Gell-Mann and George Zweig
	Quasars	Marten Schmidt

QUARKS

Murray Gell-Mann and George Zweig formulated the concept of quarks in 1963 to explain the large variety of new elementary particles, called hadrons, that were being discovered. (Protons and neutrons are two types of hadrons.) Quarks are hypothetical particles presumed to be the basic constituents of hadrons. Quarks come in various "flavors," such as up, down, strange, and charmed.

But Gell-Mann and Zweig's theory left unanswered the question of why no one had ever observed isolated quarks. One theory stated that hadrons are composed of strings of quarks that are bound together so tightly that an infinite amount of energy would be required to break the bonds.

The search for quarks continued, and in 1969 strong evidence of their existence was discovered at the Stanford Linear Accelerator Center (SLAC). Richard E. Taylor of SLAC, Henry W. Kendall of MIT, and Jerome I. Friedman of MIT shared the 1990 Nobel prize for this work.

Year	Invention/Discovery	Inventor/Discoverer
1964	BASIC computer language	Thomas E. Kurtz and John G. Kemeny
	Carbon fiber	RAF Farnborough, England
	Home-use transistor videotape recorder	Sony, Japan
	Laser eye surgery	H. Vernon Ingram
1965	Word processor	IBM, U.S.
	Rubella vaccine	Paul D. Parkman and Harry M. Meyer, Jr.
1966	Integrated radio circuit	Sony, Japan
	Noise reduction system for audio tapes	Ray M. Dolby
1967	Bubble memory prototype (computers)	A. H. Bobeck and team at Bell Telephone Laboratories, U.S.
	Pulsars	Jocelyn Bell Burnell
1968	Holographic storage technique	Bell Telephone Laboratories, U.S.
	Hemoglobin molecule structure (complete)	Max Ferdinand Perutz
1969	Moon landing	NASA, U.S.
	PASCAL computer language	Niklaus Wirth
	Videotape cassette	Sony, Japan
	Jumbo jet airliner	Joe Sutherland and team at Boeing, U.S.
	Antibody chemical and molecular structure	Rodney Robert Porter
1970	Bar code system	Monarch Marking, U.S., and Plessey Telecommunications, England
	Computer floppy disk	IBM, U.S.
	Remote-controlled lunar vehicle	USSR
1971	Earth-orbiting space station	USSR
	Liquid crystal display (LCD)	Hoffmann-LaRoche Laboratories, Switzerland
	Quartz digital watch	George Theiss and Willy Crabtree
1972	Video disk	Philips Co., The Netherlands
	Video game	Noland Bushnel
	Artificial hip	John Charnley

	Enkephalin (brain chemical)	John Hughes
	Antimatter particles	Yuri Dmitriyevich Prokoshkin and co-workers
	Black holes	Robert L. F. Boyd
1973	Computerized axial tomography (CAT scan)	Allan Macleod Cormack and Godfrey N. Hounsfield
	Earth-orbiting space station	NASA, U.S.
	Microcomputer	Trong Truong
	Recombinant DNA	Paul Berg
1974	Nonimpact printing	Honeywell, U.S.
	J/psi atomic particle	Burton Richter and Samuel Chao Chung Ting
1975	Hybrid cells	Jack Lucy and Ted Cocking
	Monoclonal antibodies	César Milstein
	Betamax videotaping system	Sony, Japan
	Video home system (VHS)	Matsushita/JVC, Japan
1976	Charm subatomic particle	Stanford Linear Accelerator Center, U.S.
	Mars space probes	NASA's *Viking I* and *Viking II*
1977	Upsilon particle	Leon Lederman
	Neutron bomb	U.S. military
	Space shuttle	NASA, U.S.
	Alkyd paint	Winsor & Newton Ltd., England
1978	Cyclosporin A	Tony Allison and Roy Calne
	Human insulin	Genentech, U.S.
	Charon (Pluto's moon)	James Walter Christy and Robert S. Harrington
	Test-tube baby	Patrick C. Steptoe and Robert G. Edwards
1979	Single-cell protein process	ICI Agricultural Division, England
1980	Solar-powered aircraft	Paul Macready
1981	Anti-interferon	Medical Research Council's Molecular Biology Laboratory, England
	First official recognition of AIDS (acquired immune deficiency syndrome)	U.S. Centers for Disease Control
	Silicon 32-bit chip	Hewlett-Packard, U.S.
	Nuclear magnetic resonance (NMR) scanner	Thorn-EMI Research Laboratories and Nottingham University, England
1982	Abnormal cancer-causing genes	Robert Weinberg and Mariano Barbacid
	Artificial heart	Robert Jarvik
	Airborne observatory	NASA, U.S.
1983	W and Z particles	Carlo Rubbia and Simon van der Meer
	Biopol (biodegradable plastic)	ICI Agricultural Division, England
	Biosensors	Cambridge Life Sciences, England
	Carbon-fiber aircraft wing	Great Britain
	512K dynamic access memory chip	IBM, U.S.
1984	Gene cloning	National Institutes of Health, U.S.; Transgene, France; and Otago University, New Zealand

	Genetically engineered blood-clotting factor	Genentech, U.S.
	Compact disk player	Sony and Fujitsu Companies, Japan, and Philips Co., The Netherlands
	Megabit computer chip	IBM, U.S.
	Isolation of virus believed to cause AIDS	Robert C. Gallo, U.S. National Cancer Institute; Luc Montagnier, Pasteur Institute, France; Myron Essex, Harvard School of Public Health, U.S. (the three were awarded the Albert Lasker Award for Public Service in 1986)
1985	Cloned leprosy genes (for vaccines)	Ron Davis and co-workers
	Anxiety chemical (human brain)	Alessandro Guidotti and Erminio Costa
	CD-ROM (compact disk read-only memory)	Hitachi, Japan
	Image digitizer	Optronics, England
	Polymer electric conductor	Terje Skotheim and team, Brookhaven National Laboratory, U.S.
	Soft bifocal contact lens	Sofsite Contact Lens Laboratory, U.S.
	Positron emission tomography	Michael Phelps
	Publication of the first image from a positron transmission microscope	James Van House and Arthur Rich
	First baby born from frozen embryo	Australia
1986	DNA fingerprinting	Alec Jeffreys
	Diminished ozone shield	Susan Solomon, National Oceanic and Atmospheric Administration, U.S.
	High-temperature superconductivity	Georg Bednorz and Karl Alex Müller
	Synthetic skin	G. Gregory Gallico, III
1987	Higher-temperature superconductivity	C. W. Chu, M. K. Wu, and co-workers
	Alzheimer's disease gene	National Institutes of Health, U.S.; University of Cologne, Germany
	Gene-altered bacteria	Advanced Genetic Sciences, U.S.
1988	Galaxy 12 billion light-years away	Simon J. Lilly
	Patented animal life	Philip Leder and Timothy Stewart
1989	Introduction of foreign gene into human patient	Steven A. Rosenberg and co-workers at National Institutes of Health, U.S.
1991	Controlled nuclear fusion	Joint European Torus (Jet), Oxfordshire, England
	X-ray research showing first photographs of the human brain recalling a word	Dr. Marcus Raichle and co-workers

Additional Sources of Information

Boyer, Carl. *History of Mathematics.* John Wiley & Sons, Inc., 1991.

Concise Biographical Dictionary of Scientists. Charles Scribner's Sons, 1981.

Biographical Dictionary of Mathematicians. Charles Scribner's Sons, 1991.

Biographical Dictionary of Scientists. Charles Scribner's Sons, 1981.

Clarke, Donald. *Encyclopedia of How It Works.* Marshall Cavendish Ltd., 1977.

Encyclopedia of Food Science and Technology. John Wiley & Sons, Inc., 1992.

Encyclopedia of Modern Technology. G. K. Hall, 1987.

Scientists and Inventors, Facts On File, 1979.

Foods and Food Production Encyclopedia. Van Nostrand Reinhold Co., Inc., 1982.

Hall, A. R., E. J. Holyard, Charles Singer, and Trevor Williams. *A History of Technology.* Oxford University Press, 1984.

Macaulay, David. *The Way Things Work.* Houghton-Mifflin, 1988.

McGraw-Hill Concise Encyclopedia of Science and Technology. McGraw-Hill, 1987.

McNeil, Ian. *Encyclopedia of the History of Technology.* Routledge, 1990.

Newman, James. *World of Mathematics.* Simon and Schuster, 1956.

Pacey, Arnold. *Technology in World Civilization: A Thousand-Year History.* The M.I.T. Press, 1990.

Strandh, Sigvard. *The History of the Machine.* A&W Publishers Inc., 1979.

Williams, Trevor. *A Short History of Twentieth-Century Technology.* Oxford University Press, 1982.

7

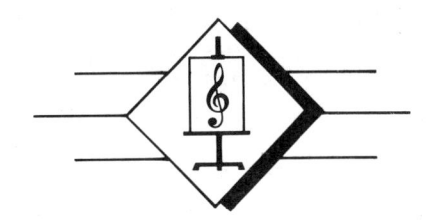

The Arts

Major Composers of Classical Music / *128*
Major Jazz Composers and Performers / *140*
Music Terms / *143*
The Makeup of a Symphony Orchestra / *151*
Major Dancers and Choreographers / *156*
Dance Terms / *162*
Major Painters and Sculptors / *165*
Art Terms / *178*
Art Movements and Periods / *180*
Major Playwrights / *183*
Major Architects / *190*
Architectural Terms / *196*
Illustrations of Architectural Styles and Elements / *200*
The Academy Awards, 1927–1992 / *202*
Additional Sources of Information / *205*

Major Composers of Classical Music

American

Amram, David (1930–), b. Pennsylvania. Composer and musical director of the New York Shakespeare Festival (1956–68) and the Lincoln Center Repertory Theater (1963–65). He has composed incidental music for plays, orchestra, opera, choral works, and jazz concerts.

Barber, Samuel (1910–81), b. Pennsylvania. Winner, Pulitzer prize, for the opera *Vanessa* (1958), and *Piano Concerto No. 1* (1963). Known for their romantic style, his works also include two symphonies, the overture to *The School for Scandal* (1932) and the popular *Adagio for Strings* (1938).

Beach, Amy Marcy (1867–1944), b. New Hampshire. Composer whose symphonies, Mass, and concerto were widely performed in the United States and abroad, particularly between 1893 and 1914. She is one of the first U.S. women composers to have achieved wide respect and popularity. Her works include *Gaelic Symphony in E Minor, op. 32* (1896), *Piano Concerto in C Sharp Minor* (1899), and *Scottish Legend op. 54* (1903).

Bernstein, Leonard (1918–90), b. Massachusetts. Conductor and music director of the New York Philharmonic (1958–69). He composed symphonies, songs, ballets, and is best known for his musicals, including *West Side Story* (1957). His world renown also stemmed from his ability to discuss music vividly and in a way intelligible to the musically uneducated person.

Blitzstein, Marc (1905–64), b. Pennsylvania. Pianist, composer, librettist. He was a student of Schoenberg. Among his most important works are orchestral variations; a piano concerto; operas, including the choral opera *The Cradle Will Rock* (1937); ballets; and film music.

Bloch, Ernest (1880–1959), b. Switzerland. Director of the Cleveland Institute of Music (1920–25) and the San Francisco Conservatory (1925–30). Influenced by his Jewish heritage, his works include symphonies, such as *Hivers-Printemps* (1905), *Israel* (1912–17), *America* (1926), *Voice in the Wilderness,* and *Evocations*; opera; chamber music; choral works; a piano sonata; songs; and *Avodath Hakodesh* (1933), a sacred service for Reformed Judaism.

Cage, John (1912–1992), b. California. Originator of controversial and experimental theories, performances, and compositions. He is best known for his experiments with random chance music and introducing performances with prepared piano. His works include the *Music of Changes* for piano (1951), derived from the ideas of *I Ching; Imaginary Landscape No. 4* for 12 radios tuned randomly (1951); and *4'33"* (1952), in which no sound is called for. Cage has collaborated with dancer Merce Cunningham, artist Marcel Duchamp, and others.

Copland, Aaron (1900–90), b. New York. Composer of three symphonies, a piano concerto, other orchestral works, chamber music, and ballets, including *Billy the Kid* (1938) and *Rodeo* (1942). The creator of a distinctly American music, Copland received the Pulitzer prize in 1945 for *Appalachian Spring* (1944).

Corigliano, John (1938–), b. New York. Composer whose lyrical and rhythmical expression is in the tradition of Bartók and Prokofiev. His works include *Kaleidoscope* (1959) for two pianos, *Violin Sonata* (1963), and the score for the film *Altered States* (1981).

Cowell, Henry Dixon (1897–1965), b. California. Pianist and composer of symphonies, an opera, and a piano concerto, *Tales of Our Countryside* (1939). Cowell founded the New Musical

Society (1927); he invented (with Leon Thoremin) the "rhythmicon," an electronic instrument, and a method of playing the piano with forearm, elbow, and fist. His books on music include *New Musical Resources* (1930) and *Charles Ives and His Music* (1955).

Dello Joio, Norman (1913–   ), b. New York. Concert pianist, organist, and award-winning composer whose style reflects the influence of American jazz, Italian opera, and the neoclassicism of the early 1900s. His works include piano sonatas, chamber music, orchestral and choral pieces, and ballets. He won the 1957 Pulitzer prize in music for his *Meditations on Ecclesiastes* for orchestra.

Gershwin, George (1898–1937), b. New York. Composer of music in a distinct blend of classical, popular, and jazz styles. Gershwin's works include numerous popular songs and musical comedies and more ambitious concert pieces: *Rhapsody in Blue* (1924), *An American in Paris* (1928), and the jazz opera *Porgy and Bess* (1935).

Hanson, Howard (1896–1981), b. Nebraska. Conductor and composer of romantic works, including symphonies, piano music, and the opera *Merry Mount* (1934). He served as director of the Eastman School of Music (1924–64) in Rochester, New York, and received the 1944 Pulitzer prize in music for his Symphony No. 3, *The Requiem* (1943).

Ives, Charles (1874–1954), b. Connecticut. Composer of advanced and innovative works and winner of the Pulitzer prize in 1947 for his *Symphony No. 3*. His compositions—including four symphonies, chamber and choral music, songs, and piano works—stressed American folk and popular music, jazz, military marches, patriotic songs, and revival hymns.

MacDowell, Edward (1860–1908), b. New York. Best known as a composer of piano works; MacDowell also wrote orchestral works, symphonic poems, and a suite that appropriates melodies of northern Native Americans. He was the first head of the department of music at Columbia University (1896–1904).

Menotti, Gian Carlo (1911–   ), b. Italy. Composer of ballets, a piano concerto, and some of the most popular operas of the mid–twentieth century. He won the 1950 Pulitzer prize for *The Consul* and the 1955 Pulitzer prize for *The Saint of Bleecker Street*. He founded the Festival of Two Worlds in Spoleto, Italy.

Moore, Douglas (1893–1969), b. New York. Composer of works noted for their use of the American vernacular, including the operas *The Devil and Daniel Webster* (1939) and *The Ballad of Baby Doe* (1956). He was the author of *Listening to Music* (1931) and *From Madrigal to Modern Music* (1942), and won the 1951 Pulitzer prize for *Giants of the Earth* (1951).

Piston, Walter (1894–1976), b. Maine. Professor at Harvard and neoclassical composer of orchestral works, string quartets, sonatas, chamber music, and the ballet *The Incredible Flautist* (1938). Piston wrote studies of harmony and counterpoint. He won the Pulitzer prize in 1948 for his *Symphony No. 3* and in 1961 for his *Symphony No. 7*.

Schoenberg, Arnold (1874–1951), b. Austria. Originator of the revolutionary 12-tone system. The theory is exemplified in his works of 1921–33, including the *Five Pieces* (1923) for piano and the *Serenade* (1923) for seven instruments and bass baritone.

Schuman, William (1910–92), b. New York. President of the Julliard School of Music (1945–61) and Lincoln Center (1962–69). Schuman composed ballets, concertos, and chamber, orchestral, and choral works that featured energetic melodies, lively rhythms, and brilliant orchestrations. He was the winner of the first Pulitzer prize for music in 1943 for *A Free Song*.

Sessions, Roger (1896–1985), b. New York. Composer of intense, intellectual works, including eight symphonies, a violin concerto, piano works, organ pieces, and songs. His books include *Questions About Music* (1970). Sessions's most popular work is the orchestral suite *The Black Maskers* (1923), and he won the 1982 Pulitzer prize for *Concerto for Orchestra*.

Thomson, Virgil (1896–1989), b. Missouri. Music critic and composer. Based on early American hymns and folk songs, his works include two operas (with librettos by Gertrude Stein), a ballet, choral and chamber music, pieces for theater and film (among them *The River*, 1937), keyboard music, and songs. He wrote several books, including *The State of Music* (1939) and *Music, Right and Left* (1951). He won the 1949 Pulitzer prize for the documentary *Louisiana Story*.

Varèse, Edgar (1883–1965), b. France. Founder and conductor of the New Symphony Orchestra, New York (1919) and founder of the International Composers Guild (1921). Varèse was a leading experimental composer of the early 1920s and wrote nontraditional works for orchestra with electronic music. His *Poème Electronique* (1958) is considered a major work in this field.

Zwilich, Ellen Taaffe (1939–   ), b. Florida. Composer and first woman to receive the Pulitzer prize in music composition, in 1983, for her *Symphony No. 1* Her works have been characterized as romantic with a lush Straussian flavor. Among her other works is *Trio for Piano, Violin, and Cello* (1987).

Austrian

Berg, Alban (1885–1935). Composer in Arnold Schoenberg's 12-tone system. Principal works are the opera *Wozzeck* (1925) and the unfinished opera *Lulu* (1937), orchestral pieces, concertos, string quartets, *Lyric Suite* (1926–28), and a piano sonata.

Bruckner, Anton (1824–96). Organist and composer of romantic music. Much revised by his friends, his original compositions were published in 1929. Principal works include nine symphonies, choral works, and chamber music for string quintet.

Czerny, Karl (1791–1857). Virtuoso pianist and composer of many works for piano. Best known for his technical studies, Czerny was a pupil of Beethoven and a teacher of Liszt.

Haydn, Franz Joseph (1732–1809). Consummate artist of the classical style in music, who has been called the "father of the symphony." Among his works are more than 100 symphonies, numerous concertos, 20 operas (five are lost), marionette operas, church music, string quartets, piano trios, keyboard sonatas and variations, songs, and 377 arrangements of Scottish and Welsh airs. His most famous works include *The Bird* quartet (1781), the oratorios *The Creation* (1798) and *The Seasons* (1801), and the *Surprise Symphony* (1791).

Haydn, Johann Michael (1737–1806). Brother of Franz Joseph Haydn; composer of oratorios and church music, symphonies, concertos, divertimenti, quintets, and other instrumental works.

Mahler, Gustav (1860–1911). Conductor of the Hamburg and Vienna operas and the Metropolitan Opera in New York. He composed nine symphonies, as well as songs, in a late romantic style, including *Resurrection Symphony* (1894) and *Symphony of a Thousand* (1907).

Mozart, Wolfgang Amadeus (1756–91). Master of the classical style in all its forms of his time. Mozart began to compose and perform at age 6; at age 11 he had composed three symphonies and 30 other works and arranged some piano concertos of J. S. Bach. His principal works include the operas *The Marriage of Figaro* (1786), *Don Giovanni* (1787), and *The Magic Flute* (1791); chamber music; piano sonatas and fantasias; 50 symphonies; and church music, including the *Requiem* (1791). One of his most popular compositions is *A Little Night Music* (1787). Mozart's works are noted for their lyrical charm.

Schubert, Frans Seraph Peter (1797–1828). Composer of numerous symphonies, masses, quartets, and sonatas, but most notably of songs in the spirit of early romantic poetry. His works after 1823 consummate his lyrical, melodic style, as in the *No. 9 C Major Symphony* ("The Great") (1828), 22 piano sonatas, including the *Wanderer Fantasie* (1822), and the *Trios in B-flat* (1827) and *E-flat* (1827).

Strauss, family of Viennese musicians. *Johann I* (1804–49) was the composer of waltzes famous throughout Europe. He was the father of *Johann II* (1825–99), who became his rival, composer of more than 400 waltzes, including *The Blue Danube* (1866) and *Tales from the Vienna Woods* (1868), as well as operettas. His brothers, *Josef* (1827–70) and *Eduard I* (1835–1916), were also successful composers and conductors.

Webern, Anton von (1883–1945). Editor, conductor, and composer in the 12-tone system of Arnold Schoenberg. Webern wrote a symphony for small orchestra, three cantatas, a string quartet, a concerto for nine instruments, songs, and other works. His major choral works include *Das Augenlicht* (1935), *First Cantata* (1939), and *Second Cantata* (1943).

British

Britten, (Edward) Benjamin (1913–76). Major twentieth-century composer famous for his vocal music and operas. The latter include *Peter Grimes* (1945), *The Rape of Lucretia* (1946), *Billy Budd* (1951), *The Turn of the Screw* (1954), and *A Midsummer Night's Dream* (1960). Among his most popular works are *A Ceremony of Carols* (1942), *A Young Person's Guide to the Orchestra* (1945), and the *War Requiem* (1962).

Byrd, William (1543–1623). Organist and composer. A master of sixteenth-century polyphony, Byrd excelled in the composition of church music, including *Gradualia* (1605–07).

Delius, Frederick (1862–1934). Composer of orchestral works, including *Paris* (1899), *Appalachia* (1896), and *Brigg Fair* (1907); choral works, including *Sea Drift*; and the operas *A Village Romeo and Juliet* (1901) and *Fennimore and Gerda* (1910).

Dowland, John (c. 1563–1626). Lutenist and composer of the most important English collection of songs for lute. His most famous work is *Lachrymae* (1605), a collection of dance pieces.

Elgar, Sir Edward (1857–1934). Composer best known for *Pomp and Circumstance,* a set of five marches; an adaptation of *Pomp and Circumstance* (1902) for the coronation of King Edward VII; *The Dream of Gerontius* (1900); *The Enigma Variations* for orchestra (1899); and *Introduction and Allegro for Strings* (1905).

Gibbons, Orlando (1583–1625). Organist and composer of anthems, madrigals, chamber music, and keyboard pieces.

Holst, Gustav (1874–1934). Composer who combined an interest in folk music with a knowledge of Hindu scales and Sanskrit literature. His later music experimented with harmony and polytonality. Principal works include the operas *Savitri* (1908) and *The Perfect Fool* (1923); for orchestra, *The Planets* (1914–16) and *Egdon Heath* (1927); and for chorus, *Hymns from the Rig-Veda* (1910) and *Hymn for Jesus* (1917).

Morley, Thomas (1557–1602). Composer, theorist, and organist at St. Paul's Cathedral. Morley was granted a monopoly on music printing (1598) and wrote the first comprehensive treatise on composition in English (1597). He became known for his light songs, including canzonets, airs, and madrigals.

Purcell, Henry (c. 1659–95). Organist at Westminster Abbey and composer of music for more than 40 plays, including the first important English opera, *Dido and Aeneas* (1689), *The Fairy Queen* (1692), and *The Tempest* (1695); and odes, songs, cantatas, church music, chamber music, and keyboard works.

Sullivan, Sir Arthur (1842–1900). Conductor, organist, and composer. His works include the grand opera *Ivanhoe* (1891); ballads; oratorios; cantatas, including *The Golden Legend*; church music; a symphony; songs, and works for piano. He is best known for light operas to librettos by W. S. Gilbert.

Tallis, Thomas (c. 1505–85). Organist and composer. He was granted a monopoly in music printing with William Byrd (1575). Tallis's works include church music and secular pieces for vocals and keyboard.

Vaughan Williams, Ralph (1872–1958). Composer noted for his adaptations of English folk music and Tudor church music. Principal compositions include *A London Symphony* (1913), *Norfolk Rhapsodies* (1906), and *The Lark Ascending* (1914), all for orchestra; *A Sea Symphony* (1910) and *Five Mystical Songs* (1911) for chorus; the operas *Hugh the Drover* (1914), *Riders to the Sea* (1937), and *The Pilgrim's Progress* (1951); and works for stage, chamber music, and songs.

French

Berlioz, Hector (1803–69). Conductor and composer of romantic works. Berlioz is best known for his genius with orchestration and his way of relating musical works to story ideas, as in the *Symphonie Fantastique* (1830). He also wrote the symphonic work *Harold in Italy* (1834), the opera *Damnation of Faust* (1846), and the oratorio *Childhood of Christ* (1850–54).

Bizet, Georges (1838–75). Composer best known for the operas *Carmen* (1875), *The Pearlfishers* (1863), *The Young Maid of Perth* (1867), and *Djmileh* (1872). His *Symphony in C Major* (1868) is highly regarded. His music is melodic and tightly organized, with uncomplicated orchestral accompaniment.

Boulanger, Lili (1893–1918). Composer in an impressionist style. She composed over 50 works in the genres of secular and sacred music, chorus with and without orchestra, cantatas, chamber music, songs, and an uncompleted opera. Boulanger is best known for her cantata *Faust et Hélène* (1913), for which she was awarded the Prix de Rome.

Boulez, Pierre (1925–   ). Composer of experimental works using the serial technique, including *Pli selon pli (1962)* and *Memoriales* (1975). Many of his compositions contain unusual rhythms with separate sounds, reflecting his interest in Asian music. He served as music director of the New York Philharmonic (1971–77).

Couperin, François (1668–1733). Member of a family of distinguished organists. Organist to the king at Versailles, he composed music for organ and harpsichord, instrumental ensembles, secular songs, and church music. He wrote a well-known textbook, *The Art of Playing the Harpsichord*.

Debussy, Claude (1862–1918). Composer noted for his impressionist style. Orchestral works include *La Mer* (1903–05) and *Nocturnes* (1893–99); piano works include *Clair de lune* (1890), preludes, études, arabesques, and *The Children's Corner* (1906–08). Debussy also wrote choral works, an opera, and the well-known tone poem *Prelude to the Afternoon of a Faun* (1894).

Delibes, (Clément Philibert) Léo (1836–91). Composer of operas, including *Le Roi l'a dit* (1873) and *Lakmé* (1883), and ballets, including *Coppélia* (1870) and *Sylvia* (1876).

Dukas, Paul (1865–1935). Composer best known for his orchestral scherzo *Sorcerer's Apprentice* (1897), the opera *Ariane et barbe-Bleue* (1907), and the ballet *La Peri* (1912).

Fauré, Gabriel (1845–1924). Organist and composer who excelled in song writing and an adventurous use of harmony. He wrote the operas *Prométhée* (1900) and *Pénélope* (1913), orchestral music, chamber works, and piano and church music. Fauré was the teacher of Maurice Ravel.

Franck, César (1822–90). A teacher who influenced an entire generation of composers. Distinctive compositions include *Symphony in D Minor* (1888), the *Symphonic Variations* (1885) for piano and orchestra, *Prelude, Chorale, and Fugue* (1884), and the opera *Hulda* (1894).

Gounod, Charles (1818–93). Composer of the operas *Faust* (1859) and *Romeo and Juliet* (1867). Gounod also wrote church music, symphonies, and cantatas. His music includes elements of seriousness, melodrama, and sentimentality.

Honegger, Arthur (1892–1955). Founding member of the Parisian group "The Six" in 1916 with Erik Satie, Darius Milhaud, and Jean Cocteau. Rejecting romanticism and impressionism, Honegger is best known for the oratorio *King David* (1921), and *Pacific 231* (1923) and *Joan of Arc at the Stake* (1935) for orchestra.

Ibert, Jacques François Antoine (1890–1962). Ibert's colorful works include a suite for orchestra, *Escales* (1922); *Divertissement* (1930); music for theater and film; chamber music; and works for piano and organ. He served as director of the Académie de France in Rome (1937) and the Paris Opera (1955).

Lully, Jean-Baptiste (orig. Lulli, Giambattista) (1632–87). Lully composed for the comedy ballets of Molière and was the founder of the French opera (tragédie lyrique). He also composed court ballets, divertissements, church music, and two instrumental suites. His best-known works include *Cadmus and Hermione* (1673), *Amadis de Gaule* (1684), and *Roland* (1685).

Massenet, Jules Emile Frédéric (1842–1912). Best known for his pop operas *Le Roi de Lahore* (1877), *Manon* (1884), *Werther* (1892), and *Le Jongleur de Notre-Dame* (1902). Massenet also wrote oratorios, orchestral works, concertos, and songs.

Messiaen, Olivier Eugène Prosper Charles (1908–92). Organist and composer of symphonic poems and works for piano, organ, and vocals. He became known for using bird calls, electronic sounds, religious songs, and oriental themes in his compositions. Messiaen helped form *Le Jeune France* in 1936 and wrote a treatise on composition. His works include the 10-movement symphony *Turangalila* (1949).

Milhaud, Darius (1892–1974). A member of the Parisian group "The Six," Milhaud composed works that combine jazz, polytonality, and Brazilian elements. He is well known for the opera *Christophe Colomb* (1930) and for ballets, including *Creation of the World* (1923).

Offenbach, Jacques (1819–80). Composer of 90 operettas, including the popular *Orpheus in the Underworld* (1858), *La Belle Hélène* (1864), and *La Vie Parisienne* (1866). His best work is thought to be *The Tales of Hoffmann*, which was unfinished at his death, and later completed by Ernest Guiraud.

Poulenc, Francis (1899–1963). Member of the Parisian circle "The Six," Poulenc composed ballets, including *Les Biches* (1924); chamber music; a concerto for two pianos; songs; choral works; a cantata; and operas, among them *Dialogues of the Carmelites* (1957). He was noted for his vocal music featuring beautiful melodies and sensitive lyrics.

Rameau, Jean-Philippe (1683–1764). Theorist and important composer of French opera. His works include the operas *Castor et Pollux* (1737) and *Dardanus* (1739), the opera-ballet *Les Indes galantes* (1735), and the ballet-bouffon *Platée* (1745). His *Treatise of Harmony* (1722) laid the foundation for the modern theory of harmony.

Ravel, Maurice (1875–1937). Leading exponent of impressionism, who relied on the strong melodies and rich textures of nineteenth-century classical music. Ravel's principal works include *Rhapsodie espagnole* (1908), *Daphnis and Chloe* (1912), and *Bolero* (1928), for orchestra, and *Valses nobles et sentimentales* (1911) and *Gaspard de la nuit* (1908), for piano.

Saint-Saëns, Charles Camille (1835–1921). Pianist and composer. Saint-Saëns began performing at age 10 and later composed symphonic poems under the influence of Franz Liszt; operas, including *Samson et Dalila* (1877); and concertos.

Satie, Erik (1866–1925). Composer noted for his ironic, humorous style and ranked as a leader in the development of modern music. Satie composed three ballets, including *Parade* (1917); operettas; a symphonic drama, *Socrates*; songs; and piano pieces.

German

Bach, Johann Sebastian (1685–1750). Baroque organist and composer, and one of the greatest creators of Western music. Among his religious works are more than 200 cantatas, the *Mass in B Minor* (1733–49), and the *St. Matthew Passion* (1727). His other works include the *Well-Tempered Clavier* (1722) (preludes and fugues), the Brandenburg concertos (1721), and many sonatas and suites. He had 20 children, 10 of whom survived, including **Wilhelm Friedemann** (1710–84), organist and composer; **Carl Philipp Emanuel** (1714–88), composer of religious music, symphonies, concertos, sonatas, and chamber music; **Johann Christoph Friedrich** (1732–95), composer; and **Johann Christian** (1735–82), composer of operas, chamber music, and church music.

Beethoven, Ludwig van (1770–1827). Considered one of the greatest composers of instrumental works, particularly symphonies, he is regarded as one of the founding fathers of musical romanticism. Beethoven was a student of Haydn, whose influence permeates his early works. By 1824 he had lost his hearing, but he continued to compose under the sponsorship of aristocratic patrons. His works include *Fidelio* (1805), an opera; a violin concerto and five piano concertos; the *Egmont* overture (1810); 32 piano sonatas, including the *Appassionata* (1804–05); 16 string quartets; the *Mass in D* (*Missa Solemnis*) (1818–23); and nine symphonies, the best known of which are the *Third* (*Eroica*) (1802), the *Fifth* (*Victory*), the *Sixth* (*Pastoral*) (1809), and the *Ninth* (*Choral*). The *Ninth*, completed in 1823, is considered the greatest of his works.

Brahms, Johannes (1833–97). Developer of a romantic style that was both lyrical and classical. His principal works include four symphonies, two overtures, and two serenades for orchestra; two piano concertos, one violin concerto, one concerto for violin and cello; *A German Requiem* (1857–68), his best-known choral work; piano solos, including variations on themes by Paganini, Handel, and Schumann; chamber music; rhapsodies; ballades; piano duets; waltzes; Hungarian dances; songs; folk song arrangements; and 11 choral preludes for organ.

Bruch, Max (1838–1920). Famous for his setting of the melody to the Jewish prayer *Kol Nidre* (1880), for cello and orchestra. His works also include three symphonies, three operas, an operetta, choral works, and chamber music.

Gluck, Christoph Willibald von (1714–87). Composer of more than 100 operas, among them *Orfeo ed Euridice* (1762) and *Alceste* (1767), which established a new style of Italian opera;

11 symphonies; instrumental trios; seven odes by Friedrich Klopstock for solo voice and keyboard; and a flute concerto.

Handel, George Frideric (1685–1759). Baroque composer most famous for the oratorio *Messiah* (1742). Trained in law and music in Germany, Handel produced his operas in Italy and London, incorporating German, Italian, and English styles. Among his works are many operas, including *Almira* (1705), *Ottone* (1723), and *Orlando* (1733); *Music for the Royal Fireworks* (1749) and the *Water Music* (1717); suites for harpsichord; chamber music; and many Italian cantatas.

Hindemith, Paul (1895–1963). Composer, teacher, theorist, performer, and conductor who brought a neoclassical element to contemporary music. Early works, such as the opera *Murder, Hope of Women* (1921), reflect the expressionism of the period. Later works, including *Ludus Tonalis* (1942), exemplify his new theory of tonality expounded in *The Craft of Musical Composition* (1941, 1945). Hindemith was banned by the Nazis for his modernity. His best-known work is a symphony from his opera *Mathis the Painter* (1938).

Humperdinck, Engelbert (1854–1921). Composer of six operas, including the popular *Hansel and Gretel* (1893); incidental music; vocal works; and songs.

Mendelssohn, Felix (1809–47). Pianist, conductor, and composer of orchestral works, including five symphonies and the overture *A Midsummer Night's Dream* (1826); choral works, including the oratorios *St. Paul* (1836) and *Elija* (1846); operas; incidental music; an eight-book collection of piano works; *Songs Without Words* (1830–45); and songs. His music contains smooth progressions in harmony accompanying melodies that are easy to sing.

Meyerbeer, Giacomo (1791–1864). Composer of operas in a spectacular style that influenced Richard Wagner. His works include *Robert le Diable* (1831), *Les Huguenots* (1836), and *Le Prophète* (1849).

Orff, Carl (1895–1982). Composer of stage works that combined instrumental singing, gestures, and dance, including the cantata *Carmina Burana* (1937); the opera *Der Mond* (1939); and musical plays. Orff developed a widely used system for teaching music to children.

Schumann, Clara Josephine née Wieck (1819–96). Pianist and composer of piano works and songs. She was a renowned interpreter of music, particularly the works of her husband, Robert Schumann.

Schumann, Robert (1810–56). Composer of piano music, including sonatas and impromptus, and of orchestral works. His compositions include *Symphonic Etudes* (1834), *Fantasia in C Major* (1836), *Album for the Young* (1848), and *Piano Concerto in A Minor* (1845). The *Rhenish Symphony* (1850) combined classical and romantic elements.

Strauss, Richard (1864–1949). Composer of numerous operas, many with librettos by Hugo von Hoffmansthal, including the famous *Der Rosenkavalier* (1911); two ballets; tone poems for orchestra, including *Also sprach Zarathustra* (1896); concertos; *Metamorphosen* (1945) for 23 solo strings; chamber music; songs; and piano works.

Wagner, Richard (1813–83). Composer of operas and architect of a theory of the "total" work of art, in which drama, spectacle, and music are fused. Principal works include *Der Ring des Nibelungen* (1853–74), which was made up of four operas: *Das Rheingold* (1854), *Die Walküre* (1856), *Siegfried* (1857–69), and *Götterdämmerung* (1874); *Tristan and Isolde* (1859); and *Parsifal* (1882). Exiled for his role in the revolution of 1848, Wagner resettled in Bavaria in 1864, where he constructed his theater at Bayreuth.

Weber, Carl Maria von (1786–1826). Composer, conductor, pianist, critic, and virtual creator of Romantic German opera. Principal works include the operas *Der Freischütz* (1821) and *Oberon* (1826), choral and orchestral pieces, piano sonatas, concertos, dances, and songs.

Italian

Bellini, Vincenzo (1801–35). Composer of emotional and technically challenging operas, including *La Straniera* (1829), *La Sonnambula* (1831), *Norma* (1831), and *I Puritani* (1835).

Boccherini, Luigi (1743–1805). Cellist and composer. His principal compositions are for chamber music; he also wrote symphonies, concertos, and vocal music. His most popular works are his *Concerto in B-flat* (1770) for cello and the minuet from his *String Quartet No. 3* (1771).

Boito, Arrigo (1842–1918). Poet and composer of operas, including *Mefistofele* (1868) and *Nerone* (1918). Boito is known chiefly for his librettos, notably for *Otello* (1887) and *Falstaff* (1893) by Giuseppe Verdi.

Cherubini, Maria Luigi (1760–1842). Composer of about 30 operas, among them the classic "rescue" opera *The Water Carrier* (1800); church music; string quartets; and piano sonatas. He served as director of the Paris Conservatory (1822).

Clementi, Muzio (1752–1832). Pianist and composer of symphonies, piano sonatas, and piano studies, including *Gradus ad Parnassum* (1817).

Corelli, Arcangelo (1653–1713). Violinist and composer. His trio sonatas, solo violin sonatas, and concerti grossi established a style of composition for the violin.

Dallapiccola, Luigi (1904–75). Composer of 12-tone atonal music characterized by delicate counterpoint, lyrical line and textures, and subtle tone colors. He is most noted for his operas *The Prisoner* (1944) and *Odysseus* (1968), the oratorio *Job* (1950), and the *Christmas Concerto* (1956).

Donizetti, Gaetano (1797–1848). Prolific composer of operas. His best-known works included *Lucrezia Borgia* (1833), *La Favorite* (1840), and the comic operas *L'Elisir d'amore* (1832) and *Don Pasquale* (1843).

Leoncavallo, Ruggiero (1858–1919). Composer of operas. His most successful was *Pagliacci* (1892). He wrote his own librettos, a ballet, and a symphonic poem.

Mascagni, Pietro (1863–1945). Opera composer and conductor. His most famous work is *Cavalleria Rusticana* (1890).

Monteverdi, Claudio (1567–1643). Ordained priest and composer of church music, including masses, vespers, and madrigals. He also wrote secular vocal music, at least 12 operas, and ballets. His works helped change the strict style of Renaissance music to the emotional style of the baroque movement. His *Orfeo* (1607) is called the first modern opera.

Palestrina, Giovanni Pierluigi da (Johannes Praenestinus) (c. 1525–94). Organist, choirmaster, and composer of church music, including masses, motets, and lamentations. He also wrote both sacred and secular madrigals.

Pergolesi, Giovanni Battista (1710–36). Composer of operas and comic intermezzos that became the prototype of the *opera buffa;* church music, including his renowned *Stabat Mater* (1736); and sonatas, which contributed to the development of the form.

Puccini, Giacomo (1858–1924). Composer of many operas with highly emotional melodies and orchestral brilliance. Best known are *La Bohème* (1896), *Tosca* (1900), and *Madame Butterfly* (1904). *Turandot* was completed after his death by Franco Alfano.

Respighi, Ottorino (1879–1936). Composer of operas, tone poems, and other orchestral works, chamber music, concertos, and songs. Among his most popular works are *The Fountains of Rome* (1917) and *The Pines of Rome* (1924), both symphonic poems.

Rossini, Gioacchino (1792–1868). Composer of operas. The best known are *William Tell*

(1829) and *The Barber of Seville* (1816). Rossini also wrote cantatas, songs, piano pieces, and woodwind quintets.

Scarlatti, Alessandro (1660–1725). Conductor and the most prolific composer of Italian operas of his time. Besides about 80 operas, he wrote 20 oratorios, some 600 cantatas, 10 masses, a passion, motets, and other church music, chamber pieces, concertos, and works for harpsichord.

Scarlatti, (Giuseppe) Domenico (1685–1757). Son of Alessandro Scarlatti and greatest Italian composer for harpsichord of his time. He wrote 550 pieces, now called sonatas, as well as concertos, operas, cantatas, masses, a *Stabat Mater*, and two *Salve Reginas*.

Tartini, Giuseppe (1692–1770). Violinist, teacher, composer, and theorist. He composed over 100 violin concertos and symphonies, solo sonatas, trio sonatas, and church music; published treatises on violin playing and acoustics; and established a violin school in Padua (1728).

Verdi, Giuseppe (1813–1901). Foremost composer of operas; his works are performed more often today than those of any other opera composer. They include *Rigoletto* (1851), *La Traviata* (1853), and the supreme *Otello* (1887) and *Falstaff* (1893). Verdi also composed church music, including the *Requiem* (1874), *Ave Maria* (1880), *Stabat Mater* (1898), and *Te Deum* (1898).

Vivaldi, Antonio (1678–1741). Violinist, composer, and ordained priest. Master of the Italian baroque, Vivaldi is best known for his instrumental music and the concertos *The Four Seasons* (1725). He also wrote church music, an oratorio, and nearly 50 operas.

Russian

Borodin, Aleksandr (1833–87). Composer and scientist. His works include three symphonies; *In the Steppes of Central Asia* (1880) for orchestra; string quartets; and the opera *Prince Igor* (1887), completed after his death by Nicolai Rimsky-Korsakov and Aleksandr Glazunov (1890).

Glinka, Mikhail (1804–57). Composer of two operas and other works. *A Life for the Czar* (1836) and *Russian and Ludmilla* (1842) established a Russian style against the conventions of Italian opera. Glinka introduced folk song into instrumental composition in the orchestral fantasia *Kamarinskaya*.

Khachaturian, Aram (1903–78). Armenian composer whose works are distinguished for their incorporation of oriental folk elements. He is best known for the ballet *Gavané* (1942) and its popular *Sabre Dance*.

Mussorgsky, Modest (1839–81). Composer of operas and orchestral works. Mussorgsky is best known for his operas *Boris Godunov* (1868, 1874) and *Khovanschina* (1886), as well as for *Pictures at an Exhibition* (1874) for piano and *Night on Bald Mountain* (1860–66) for orchestra.

Prokofiev, Sergei (1891–1953). Composer, pianist, and conductor. His principal compositions are the operas *Love for Three Oranges* (1921) and *War and Peace* (1942); *Peter and the Wolf* (1936) and *Classical Symphony* (1918), for orchestra and narrator; and seven symphonies, piano concertos, ballets, and piano sonatas.

Rachmaninoff, Sergei (1873–1943). Composer, pianist, and conductor whose works are filled with passion, power, and a feeling of melancholy. Rachmaninoff emigrated to the United States at age 17. His compositions include three operas; orchestral works, including the tone poem *Isle of the Dead* (1909); four concertos, including the *Second Piano Concerto* (1901); choral works; chamber music; and songs.

Rimsky-Korsakov, Nicolai (1844–1908). Composer of operas and orchestral works, including the popular symphonic suite *Scheherazade* (1888). His greatest works are the operas *Mlada* (1892), *Christmas Eve* (1895), *Sadko* (1898), and *The Golden Cockerel* (1907). His orchestration influenced the work of Igor Stravinsky and others.

Rubinstein, Anton (1829–94). Pianist and composer; founder of the Conservatory in St. Petersburg (1862). A representative of traditional Western ideas against the current of nationalism, he composed *Musical Portraits (Faust, Ivan the Terrible, Don Quixote)* for orchestra, 19 operas, six symphonies (including *The Ocean*), chamber music, five piano concertos, and other works.

Scriabin, Aleksandr (1872–1915). Composer and pianist. Scriabin experimented with esoteric harmonies related to theosophical ideas in *The Divine Poem* (1905) and *Poem of Ecstasy* for orchestra; he wrote sonatas, preludes, and *Prometheus* (1909–10), which includes the use of a "color organ" for slide projection.

Shostakovich, Dmitri (1906–75). Composer of chamber and symphonic works characterized by a bold, expressive modern style. Shostakovich alternated between political and satirical composition, later trying to bring his work closer to official prescriptions. His works include 15 symphonies, among them *May the First* (1930) and the outstanding *Ninth Symphony* (1940); operas; ballets, including *Lady Macbeth of Mtsensk* (1934) and revised in 1962 as *Katerina Ismailova*; piano works; sonatas; and 15 string quartets.

Stravinsky, Igor (1882–1971). Composer of the epochal ballets *The Firebird* (1910), *Petrouchka* (1911), and *Rite of Spring* (1913). Later works, such as *The Soldier's Tale* (1918), for narrator and instruments, and the ballet suite *Apollon Musagète* (1928), are more austere and neoclassical. Stravinsky settled in the United States in 1941, where he experimented with 12-tone composition, as in *Requiem Canticles* (1966).

Tchaikovsky, Peter Ilyich (1840–93). One of the most important Russian composers. His music is characterized by masterful orchestration and spirited yet often melancholy melodies. Tchaikovsky is best known for his ballet music, including *Swan Lake* (1876), *The Sleeping Beauty* (1889), and *The Nutcracker* (1892); and for his operas *Eugene Onegin* (1878) and *Queen of Spades* (1890). He also wrote symphonies, including the popular *Symphony No. 5* (1888), chamber music, and choral works, and published books on harmony, autobiographical essays, and translations.

Other

Albéniz, Isaac (1860–1909). Spanish composer and pianist. Albéniz is known for his later piano works, notably *Iberia* (1906–09); he also wrote operas, including *The Magic Opal* (1893).

Bartók, Béla (1881–1945). Hungarian pianist and composer who studied and collected Hungarian folk music and developed a musical style that emphasized energetic rhythm, folk song scales, dissonance, and highly personal forms. His principal works include orchestral pieces; the opera *Duke Bluebeard's Castle* (1918); the ballet *The Wooden Prince* (1914–16); the pantomime *The Miraculous Mandarin* (1919, 1924, 1935); chamber music; piano works, including the *Mikrokosmos* (1926–37); and arrangements of folk songs. He emigrated to the United States in 1940.

Chávez, Carlos (1899–1978). Mexican composer of works using the idioms of Indian folk music, including *Xochipilli Macuilxochitl* (1940). Well-known works are the symphonic ode *Clio* (1969) and *Discovery* (1969).

Chopin, Frédéric François (1810–49). Polish composer and pianist. Called "the poet of the piano," he composed hundreds of pieces for that instrument, most notably two piano concertos, and other pieces including *Fantaisie-Impromptu* (1834).

Dvořák, Antonín (1841–1904). Czech composer of symphonies, operas, dances, and choral works in a nationalistic spirit and neo-Romantic style. His works include the *Symphonic Variations*, *Slavonic Rhapsodies*, and the opera *The Peasant Rogue* (1877). His best-known work, the *Symphony from the New World* (1893), contains elements of both Czech and American music.

Falla, Manuel de (1876–1946). Spanish composer and pianist. He published little but was the outstanding Spanish composer of his time. Principal works are the operas *La Vida Breve* (1905) and *El Retablo de Maese Pedro* (1923), the ballets *El Amor Brujo* (1915) and *The Three-Cornered Hat* (1919), and the *Fantasia Béticu* (1919) for piano.

Grainger, Percy Aldridge (1882–1961). Australian pianist and composer who settled in the United States in 1914. Head of the music department at New York University, he was known for his arrangements of traditional tunes from a variety of sources and for his interpretation of Edvard Grieg's piano music. His choral works include *Marching Song of Democracy* (1917) and *Tribute to Foster* (1930).

Granados, Enrique (1867–1916). Spanish pianist and composer, born in Cuba. Granados founded and directed the Academía Granados (1901) and composed seven operas, orchestral works, chamber music, a collection of *Tonadillas*, and *Goyescas* (1916), based on the paintings of Goya.

Grieg, Edvard (1843–1907). Norwegian composer, conductor, and pianist. Principal works include the overture *I Host* (1866), two suites from *Peer Gynt* (1876, 1888, 1891), *At a Southern Convent Gate* (1871) for chorus, and the 10-volume *Lyric Pieces* for piano.

Janáček, Leoš (1854–1928). Czech composer. Janáček wrote 10 operas, including *Jenufa* (1904); orchestral, choral, and piano works; chamber music; and songs. He published collections of Moravian folk music and a treatise on harmony.

Kodǎly, Zoltǎn (1882–1967). Hungarian composer and music educator whose works are distinguished by the influence of native folk music. His best-known works are the suites from *Háry János* (1927) and *Psalmus Hungaricus* (1923). Kodály developed a widely used method of teaching music.

Lasso, Orlando di (Roland de Lassus) (1532–94). Belgian composer. Among his many works are masses, motets, magnificats, and other church music. The complete edition of his nearly 2,000 works comprises 60 volumes.

Liszt, Franz (1811–86). Hungarian composer who spent time in Paris and Rome and is credited with developing the rhapsody as a form of serious music and employing the term *symphonic poem* for a composition. He was an unsurpassed virtuoso pianist and a composer of symphonies, including *Faust* (1857); piano concertos, études, and 19 *Hungarian Rhapsodies* (1839–85); choral pieces; fantasia and fugues for organ; and songs.

Nielsen, Carl (1865–1931). Danish composer of operas, symphonies, string quartets, piano pieces, and songs, including *Hymns amoris* (1896). Nielsen served as director of the Copenhagen Conservatory (1915–27).

Paderewski, Ignace (1860–1941). Polish pianist and composer. One of the most renowned pianists of modern times, in 1919 Paderewski was prime minister of Poland. He composed many piano works, the opera *Manru* (1901), a symphony, a concerto, and songs.

Sibelius, Jean (1865–1957). Finnish composer. Sibelius attempted a national music, as in *En Saga* (1892) and *Lemminkäinen's Homecoming* (1895), based on the Finnish epic the *Kalevala*. Notable works include *The Swan of Tuonela* (1893), *Finlandia* (1900), and *The Oceanides* (1914).

Smetana, Bedřich (1824–84). Czech composer whose nationalist music was based on folk songs and dances, as in the opera *The Bartered Bride* (1866). Smetana wrote his best instrumental works despite deafness, especially *The Moldau*, which is part of *My Country* (1879), and the string quartets *From My Life* (1876).

Villa-Lobos, Heitor (1887–1959). Brazilian composer and educator. His works show the influence of Indian music and Brazilian folk songs; they include five operas, six symphonies, symphonic poems, serenades, choral music, piano solos, and songs.

Wieniawski, Henri (1835–80). Polish violinist and composer. Among Wieniawski's compositions are two concertos and popular pieces, including *Légende*.

Major Jazz Composers and Performers

Armstrong, Louis "Satchmo" (c. 1890–1971), b. Louisiana. Trumpeter and singer, and first internationally known jazz soloist. He introduced the music of New Orleans to the world, inaugurated the style of improvisation, and was the first to record scat singing. His most influential recording may be "West End Blues" (1939), but his most famous is "Hello, Dolly" (1969).

Basie, William "Count" (1904–84), b. New Jersey. Pianist and bandleader. His brand of Kansas City jazz became the classic swing band style, featuring spare keyboard playing with a precise four-beat rhythm section. He started The Barons of Rhythm in Kansas City, Missouri, in 1935 and then moved to New York in 1936. His hits include "Jumpin' at the Woodside" (1938) and "Stay Cool" (1946).

Beiderbecke, Bix (1903–31), b. Iowa. Cornetist, pianist, and composer. Famous for his solos, he was known as the first great white jazz musician. He advanced simple jazz into a more complex form built around improvisation and extended chords. His improvisations on "Singin' the Blues" (1927) were much admired and imitated.

Carter, Betty (1930–   ) b. Michigan. Vocalist noted for her scat singing, humming, moaning, and extraordinary technique. She performed with the bands of Max Roach, Charlie Parker, Miles Davis, and others from the late 1940s through the late 1950s.

Christian, Charlie (c. 1916–42), b. Texas. A major contributor to the bebop movement, he was also among the first to capitalize on the sound of the electric guitar. He was admired for his innovative use of harmonic inversions, dissonance, and long strings of uninflected eighth notes. Major works include "Seven Come Eleven," (1939) "Gone With What Wind," (1940) and "Breakfast Feud" (1941).

Coleman, Ornette (1930–   ), b. Texas. Saxophonist and composer. He was a major influence on the avant-garde or "free-jazz" movement of the late 1950s and early 1960s, with a revolutionary style of breaking the restrictions of chords, ordinary harmony, bar lines, and tempered scales. Major recordings include "Something Else" (1958), "Congeniality" (1959), and "A Dedication to Poets and Writers" (1962).

Coltrane, John (1926–67), b. North Carolina. Tenor/soprano saxophonist, composer, and bandleader. His explosive style and angular melodic lines have influenced jazz musicians. He is credited with developing polytonality in modern jazz, and his quartet, which performed from 1960 to 1965, ranks among the best. His masterworks include "Giant Steps" (1959) and "A Love Supreme" (1964).

Davis, Miles (1926–91), b. Illinois. Trumpeter, composer, and bandleader. His lyrical and inventive playing made him a trendsetter for more than four decades. A major contributor to the bebop and cool forms of jazz, he pioneered the jazz-rock movement in the 1960s. His influential recordings include "Steamin' " (1956), "Kind of Blue" (1959), and "Bitches Brew" (1969).

Ellington, Edward Kennedy "Duke" (1899–1974), b. Washington, D.C. Pianist, composer, and bandleader. Nominated for a Pulitzer prize, he is considered the most important composer of big-band music. He wrote and arranged many jazz classics, popular songs, and blues or "mood" pieces. "Mood Indigo" (1930), "It Don't Mean a Thing (If It Ain't Got That Swing)" (1932), "Sophisticated Lady" (1933), and "In a Sentimental Mood" (1935) are among his many great recordings.

Evans, Bill (1929–80), b. New Jersey. Pianist, arranger, and composer whose soft harmonies, intricate voicing, and melodic improvising changed the sound of the piano in jazz. He earned national recognition for his playing in "Kind of Blue" (1959) with the Miles Davis Sextet.

Fitzgerald, Ella (1918–   ), b. Virginia. Vocalist acclaimed for her pure tone, voice control, improvisation, and interpretation of ballads. Her first hit was "A Tisket, A Tasket" (1938) and she became world famous in 1946 when she sang with the *Jazz at the Philharmonic* concert series.

Gillespie, John Birks "Dizzy" (1917–1993) b. South Carolina. Trumpeter and bandleader who pioneered the bebop movement in 1945 along with Charlie Parker. His Latin-influenced sound and virtuosity in upper-register playing are evident in his compositions "Salt Peanuts" (1945) and "A Night in Tunisia" (1946).

Goodman, Benny (1909–86), b. Illinois. Clarinetist and bandleader known as the "Pied Piper of Swing." He played with symphony orchestras and pioneered interracial bands. His best-known recordings include "After You've Gone" (1935) and "Moonglow" (1936).

Hancock, Herbie (1940–   ) b. Illinois. Pianist and composer whose highly individual keyboard style blends blues and bebop. He joined the Miles Davis Quintet in 1963 and helped expand the traditional jazz concept of the rhythm section and its relationship to the soloist. He contributed to the rock-jazz movement of the late 1960s and 1970s with his composition "Maiden Voyage" (1965).

Hawkins, Coleman (1904–69), b. Missouri. His powerful, original style and rich tone made him the dominant tenor saxophonist during the late 1930s and early 1940s. He played with Fletcher Henderson's orchestra (1923–43). His most celebrated recording is "Body and Soul" (1939).

Henderson, Fletcher (c. 1897–1952), b. Georgia. Bandleader, arranger, and trumpeter who pioneered the concept of the big band in the swing era. His best works include "Down South Camp Meeting" (1934), "Wrappin' It Up" (1934), and "King Porter Stomp" (1935).

Hines, Earl "Fatha" (c. 1903–83), b. Pennsylvania. Pianist and bandleader. He is known for his innovative "trumpet-style" single-note solos coupled with powerful rhythm and bass patterns. His best recordings include "A Monday Date" (1928) and "Skip the Gutter" (1928) with Louis Armstrong.

Holiday, Billie "Lady Day" (1915–59), b. Maryland. Vocalist famous for her melancholy improvisations of ballads and popular songs. She was discovered by record producer and critic John Hammond in 1933 and sang with Benny Goodman, Lester Young, Count Basie, and other great jazz musicians. She developed a large public following with her recordings of "Strange Fruit" (1939) and "Lover Man" (1944).

Joplin, Scott (1868–1917), b. Texas. Composer and pianist who popularized the early jazz form of ragtime. His composition "The Maple Leaf Rag" (c. 1899) became an instant hit. His works include 33 rags, about two dozen songs, and a ragtime opera.

Lewis, John A. (1920–   ), b. Illinois. Pianist and composer known for applying classical forms to jazz based on improvisation and carefully worked-out changes of tempo, key, meter, and instrumentation. He was one of the pioneers of cool jazz and founded the Modern Jazz Quartet. His noted works include "Bluesology" (1956) and "Between the Devil and the Deep Blue Sea" (1957).

Miller, Glenn (1904–44), b. Iowa. Trombonist, arranger, and star bandleader during the big-band swing era. His distinctive sound combined a clarinet and four saxophones. "In the Mood" (1939) and "String of Pearls" (1941) were among his many hit songs.

Mingus, Charlie (1922–79) b. Arizona. Double bassist, pianist, composer, arranger, and bandleader. He combined gospel and jazz forms to create the funky sound. He was the dominant bassist of the late 1950s and early 1960s. Best compositions include "Goodbye pork pie hat" (1959) and "Better git it in your soul" (1959).

Monk, Thelonious (1917–82), b. North Carolina. Pianist and composer noted for his spare style, slow tempo, and distinctive phrasing. Monk was a major contributor to bebop. " 'Round About Midnight" (1947) and "Criss Cross" (1951) are among his many important compositions.

Morton, Ferdinand "Jelly Roll" (c. 1890–1941) b. Louisiana. Pianist, composer, and preeminent soloist who recorded about 175 sides and piano rolls between 1923 and 1929. Combining blues, rags, and marches, he is considered the first important jazz composer. His influential works included "The Pearls" (1919), "Wolverine Blues" (1923), "Grandpa's Spells" (1923), and "Smoke-house Blues" (1926).

Parker, Charlie "Bird" (1920–55) b. Kansas. Alto saxophonist and composer whose virtuosity and inventive melodic lines made him a major influence in bebop. "Groovin' High" (1945) and "Out of Nowhere" (1948) are among his most innovative solos.

Reinhardt, Django (1910–53) b. Belgium. Considered the most important jazz guitarist. His swing style of playing was characterized by a full sound, strong rhythms, salvos of sixteenth notes, vibrato, and surprising melodic lines. Notable works include "Tiger Rag" (1934) and "Stardust" (1935).

Smith, Bessie (1894–1937) b. Tennessee. Vocalist considered the greatest of all the classic blues singers. She achieved the height of her fame in the 1920s pioneering jazz-oriented blues. Her best recordings include "Down-hearted Blues" (1923) and "Cold in Hand Blues" (1925).

Tatum, Art (1910–56) b. Ohio. Pianist known for his dazzling high-speed arpeggios and elaborate runs stretching the length of the keyboard. Tatum was the premier pianist of New York's Swing Street clubs from the 1930s through the 1950s. "Tea for Two" (1923), "Tiger Rag" (1933), and "Stompin' at the Savoy" (1953) are among his many great recordings.

Vaughan, Sarah "Sassy" (1924–90) b. New Jersey. Vocalist renowned for her operatic power, elegant phrasing, and extraordinarily wide range. She became popular while singing with Billy Eckstine's band in the mid-1940s. "Lover Man" (1945), recorded with Charlie Parker and Dizzy Gillespie, established her reputation.

Waller, Thomas "Fats" (1904–43), b. New York. Pianist, songwriter, and entertainer. Waller's jazz ragtime style of playing in the 1920s and 1930s made many of his songs jazz standards. His notable works, "Honeysuckle Rose" (1929) and "Ain't Misbehavin' " (1929), brought him fame as a satirical songwriter and entertainer.

Williams, Mary Lou (1910–81), b. Georgia. Pianist, arranger, and composer. Known as "the first great female instrumentalist in jazz," she created harmonically innovative arrangements ranging from swing to avant-garde. She arranged scores for the bands of Earl Hines, Benny Goodman, and Duke Ellington. Her most famous composition is "Zodiac Suite" (1945).

Young, Lester "Prez" (1909–59), b. Mississippi. Tenor saxophonist and premier soloist credited with transforming the "hot" jazz of the 1930s into the "cool" jazz of the 1940s and 1950s. His influential recordings include "Shoe Shine Boy" (1936), "Lady Be Good" (1936), and "Lester leaps in" (1939).

Music Terms

a cappella   Choral music without accompaniment (literally, "in the church style").

accelerando   A direction to gradually increase the tempo.

accent   The emphasis given to one tone over another.

accidental   A sign used to indicate chromatic alteration; a sharp, double sharp, flat, double flat, or natural prefixed to single notes.

accompaniment   Secondary instrument or background vocal added to the principal instrument or soloist.

acoustics   The science of sound, which deals with intensity, quality, resonance, pitch, tone, and other qualities of sound.

adagietto   A direction to play slightly faster than adagio.

adagio   A direction to play slowly; between andante and largo.

adagissimo   A direction to play very slowly.

ad libitum   A direction to interpret, improvise, or omit, according to the player's preference.

affetuoso   A direction to play affectionately, with warmth.

agitato   A direction to play in an agitated, restless, hurried manner.

air   A tune or melody. The French eighteenth-century term for song; also, an instrumental piece whose melodic style is similar to that of a solo song.

alla breve   A direction to play twice as fast as the notation signifies; $2/2$ instead of $4/4$.

allargando   A direction to play slower, louder.

allegretto A direction to play with moderately quick movement; between andante and allegro.

allegro A direction to play quickly, briskly.

allemande A moderately slow dance of German origin.

allentando A direction to slow down.

alto The highest adult male voice, or lowest female voice; also, a tenor violin or viola.

andante A direction to play in moderate tempo; "walking" speed; between allegretto and adagio.

andantino A direction to play in tempo slightly quicker than andante.

animato A direction to play with animation.

answer In a fugue, the second or fourth statement of the subject.

anthem A choral piece for use in church services.

appassionato A direction to play passionately.

appoggiatura An inharmonious note preceding a principal note, marked with a diagonal line through it, of short or long duration.

arabesque A lyrical piece in a fanciful style; a term used first by Schumann and later by Debussy.

aria An extended vocal solo in an opera or oratorio.

arioso A piece of recitative song, but more songlike.

arpeggio The technique of playing the notes of a chord successively rather than simultaneously.

ascending Moving upward on a musical scale.

assai A direction to play very quickly.

a tempo A direction to play in time, following a deviation from the regular tempo.

atonal Having no recognized tonal center or key.

aubade Morning music, in contrast to *serenade*, or evening music.

augmentation Presentation of a theme in notes of doubled value; the opposite of *diminution*.

auxiliary note Usually, a grace note one degree above or below a principal note.

ballad A narrative song, originally accompanied by dancing; also, an instrumental piece in ballad style.

bar line A line drawn vertically across the staff to divide into measures.

baritone The male voice between bass and tenor; also, any musical instrument intermediary between bass and tenor.

baroque A term signifying the music composed between 1600 and 1750, characterized by homophonic texture with the uppermost part carrying the melody over the bass line, a search for affective expression, the development of new styles for various functions and new techniques, such as dissonance and tonality.

bass The lowest male voice, or lowest part in a musical composition; also, short for the double bass or bass tuba.

beat A unit of rhythm or time in a composition as indicated by the conductor's gesture; each unit of a measure with respect to accent.

bebop (bop) One of the principal styles of jazz developed in the early 1940s, characterized by complicated melody lines and chord patterns played at exceptional speed.

bel canto The Italian vocal techniques of the eighteenth century with an emphasis on beauty of sound and brilliance of performance rather than dramatic expression or romantic emotion.

berceuse A cradle song.

binary Musical form in which both main sections are repeated and where the first section characteristically is tonally not self-contained but demands a resolution in the second part (AB).

bolero A Spanish dance accompanied by castanets.

bowing A method of using the bow on stringed instruments as indicated by signs for down bow (⊓) or up bow (∨).

brace A vertical line used to join two or more staves.

buffa In the comic style.

buffo The singer of a comic part.

cadence A progression of chords that seems to move to a harmonic close or point of rest.

cadenza An ornamental passage near the end of a composition.

canon A contrapuntal composition in which the same melody is imitated by one or more voices overlapping in time in the same or related key.

cantata A vocal form from the baroque period that consists of arias, recitatives, duets, and choruses. The term now refers to secular or sacred choral works accompanied by orchestra, similar to the oratorio but shorter.

canticle Religious song or chant.

canzona A form of Italian lyric poetry corresponding to the ode, set to music in a style similar to a madrigal, though simpler; also, an instrumental piece in the style of a song.

canzonet A vocal piece in a light vein, somewhat like a dance song, usually with instrumental accompaniment; a short instrumental piece.

capriccio A short composition in free form.

castrato A male singer castrated as a boy to maintain a soprano or alto voice range.

catch A humorous round for three or more voices.

chaconne A musical form based on a reiterated harmonic pattern.

chamber music Instrumental compositions performed by a small ensemble, with one player for each part.

chanson A song for solo voice or vocal ensemble; also, an instrumental piece of vocal character.

chant A sacred song, usually monophonic and in free rhythm and used in accordance with prescribed ritual. It is the oldest form of choral music.

chorale A psalm or hymn tune sung in church; also, a harmonization of a chorale melody.

chord The combination of three or more tones played at once. A *diatonic chord* uses only notes proper to the key. A *triad* is a chord of three notes in which the lowest is combined with the third and fifth above it. A *common chord* is a triad in root position. A *dominant chord* is founded on the dominant of the key. An *inverted chord* uses a tone other than the root as its lowest tone.

chromatic scale Consecutive series of notes that employ only a progression of semitones.

classical Term for the period and style of music from about 1700 to about 1830, characterized by regular, short, clearly articulated phrases combined with symmetrical patterns and textures. Haydn, Mozart, and Beethoven are its chief representatives.

clef A character that indicates the pitch of a particular line on a staff.

coda A passage that brings a piece or movement to a conclusion.

comma The small difference in pitch that occurs in the same note when obtained through different combinations of octaves, perfect fifths, and pure thirds.

common time Four-four (4/4) time—that is, four quarter notes to a measure.

compound interval An interval that extends beyond an octave.

compound time Time in which each beat of the bar is divisible into three, in contrast to *simple time*, in which each is divisible into two.

concertmaster The leader of the first violins, next in rank to the conductor.

concerto A composition for solo instrument, usually with orchestral accompaniment.

concerto grosso A style of composition developed during the Baroque period (1600–1750) in which two groups of musicians, one large and one small, alternate in an echo effect.

concert pitch Pitch at which the piano and other nontransposing instruments play.

console The part of the organ from which the player controls the instrument—the keyboard, pedals, and so on—as distinguished from the pipes.

consonance Combination of pitches that produce little tension and are generally considered pleasing; opposite of dissonance.

consort A chamber ensemble; also, music written for such a group.

con spirito A direction to play in a lively manner.

continuo The bass, or lowest, line of a composition.

contralto The range of a low female voice; alto.

cool Style of modern jazz pioneered in the 1950s and 1960s, characterized by understated and emotionally subdued arrangements played by small ensembles.

counterpoint Music consisting of two or more melodic lines that are played simultaneously.

countersubject The contrasting motif to the subject of a fugue.

countertenor The male alto voice.

couplet Two lines having the same meter.

courante A lively dance in triple time; also, the second part of a suite.

crescendo A direction to increase the volume.

cut time Another term for 2/2 meter.

da capo A direction to repeat from the beginning.

decrescendo A direction to decrease the volume.

descant A different melody sung in a higher pitch and simultaneously with the main melodic line. It is the earliest form of polyphony, with contrasting motions between the parts.

descending Moving downward on a musical scale.

development The extension of a theme through contrapuntal elaboration, modulation, rhythmical variation, etc.

diatonic Referring to minor and major scales that employ a particular combination of whole tones and half tones; the harmony and melodies that employ only the pitches of a particular diatonic scale.

diminished chord A chord in which the highest and lowest tones form a diminished interval.

diminished interval A perfect or minor interval reduced by a semitone.

diminuendo Diminishing; getting softer.

diminution The breaking up of the notes in a melody into quick figures, as is done in variations.

dissonance A combination of tones that are unresolved, jarring.

divertimento An eighteenth-century form of instrumental chamber music having several short movements.

divertissement A fantasia on well-known tunes.

divisi In orchestral music, an indication that a group of players who play the same parts are to play two or more separate parts.

do The first tone of a diatonic scale.

dolce A direction to play softly, sweetly.

dolente, doloroso Sorrowful.

dominant The fifth tone of the major or minor diatonic scale.

dominant chord A chord with the fifth pitch of a scale as its root.

doppio movimento Twice as fast.

Dorian mode A church mode represented on the white keys of a keyboard instrument by an ascending scale from D to D.

dot Written after a note, an indication of the prolongation of its length by one-half; the double dot indicates by three-fourths. Above or below the note, the dot indicates staccato.

double stop A chord of two notes played on a bowed string instrument, obtaining a two-part harmony.

doxology In Christian worship, a hymn of praise to God.

duet A composition for two players or two voices, with or without accompaniment.

duple Two units to the measure, such as $2/2$, $2/4$, or $2/8$.

duration The length of a tone.

dynamics Varying and contrasting degrees of intensitiy or loudness.

eighth A note whose value is one-eighth of a whole note.

enharmonic Tones that have the same pitch when played on tempered instruments but that are different in notation, such as C (♯) and D (♭).

episode The section of a fugue in which the main melody is not heard.

estinto So soft that it can hardly be heard.

étude A study; an exercise in technique.

exposition The statement of the musical material on which a movement is based.

expression marks Marks used to help the interpretation of a work; they are concerned with dynamics, tempo, and mood and indicate forte, allegro, con spirito, etc.

fa The fourth note of a diatonic scale.

falsetto The false voice; an adult male voice in the alto and treble range.

fantasia A piece in which the composition follows the fancy rather than any conventional form; of an improvisational character.

fermata A symbol (𝄐) placed over the note to show that it is to be played longer than its normal duration.

fifth The interval between the tonic and the fifth tone above it. In the key of C major, C to G is a fifth.

figuration The extended use of a particular melodic or harmonic figure; the ornamental treatment of a passage.

finale The last movement of a work of several movements; for example, the conclusion of a concerto or the last act of an opera.

flat The sign (♭), indicating the pitch is to be lowered by one semitone.

form The pattern of design of a work; its basic elements are repetition, variation, and contrast in the areas of harmony, rhythm, and tone.

forte A direction to play loudly.

fortissimo A direction to play very loudly.

forza A direction to play with force.

forzando Strongly accenting.

fourth The interval between the tonic and the fourth diatonic tone above it; in the key of C major, C to F is a fourth.

fugue A composition in which three or more voices enter at different times and imitate the main melody in different ways according to a set pattern.

fundamental Also called the tonic; the lowest tone of a chord when the chord is founded on that tone; also, the lowest note in the harmonic series.

funk (funky) Style of African American music popular in the mid-1960s that combines soul and jazz. It is characterized by complex interlocking syncopated rhythm patterns in duple meter.

galop A quick dance in $^2/_4$ time popular in the nineteenth century.

giocoso Jocose; merry.

glee A simple part song, generally for male voices.

glissando The execution of rapid scales by sliding the finger rapidly across keys or strings.

grace note An ornamental note not essential to the melody and not counted as part of the measure.

grandezza Grandeur.

grave A direction to play slowly, solemnly.

grazioso A direction to play gracefully.

Gregorian chant A style of church music for unaccompanied voices, without definite rhythm, in one of the eight church modes.

half note A note having half the time value of a whole note and twice that of a quarter note.

harmonic A tone whose frequency is an integral multiple of a single frequency known as the fundamental tone.

harmony The simultaneous sounded pitches, as in chords.

homophonic Single-voiced; music in which one melody or part is supported by chords; the opposite of *polyphonic*.

imitation The use of the same or similar melodic material in different voices successively.

impresario The conductor or manager of an opera or concert company.

impromptu An improvised composition without fixed form.

incidental music Music for performance during the action of a play.

interlude A short piece played between the acts of a drama; the verses of a song, parts of a church service, or sections of a cantata.

intermezzo A play with music performed between the acts of an opera or drama that gave rise to opera buffa; an interlude; a short movement in a symphony.

interval The distance in pitch between two notes, harmonic if they are played together, melodic if they are played in succession. *Perfect i.:* the prime, fourth, fifth, and octave. *Major i:* the second, third, sixth, and seventh of the major scale. *Minor i:* a chromatic half step smaller than a major interval. *Augmented i.:* a chromatic half step larger than perfect and major. *Diminished:* A chromatic half step smaller than perfect and minor.

intonation The degree of accuracy with which pitches are produced.

inversion The transposition of the lower and upper notes of an interval. In an inverted chord, the lowest tone is not its root; an inverted melody is one in which its intervals are inverted.

Ionian mode A mode of church music represented on the white keys of a keyboard by an ascending scale from C to C.

key The main pitch or tonal center to which all of the composition's pitches are related.

key signature Sharps or flats placed at the beginning of a composition to indicate its key.

la The sixth tone of a diatonic scale.

largo A direction to play broadly, more slowly than adagio but not as slowly as grave.

leading tone The seventh degree or tone of the scale; a semitone below the tonic.

legato A direction to play smoothly and continuously.

lento A direction to play slowly, but not as slowly as largo.

libretto The text of an opera or oratorio.

litany A song of invocation to God.

madrigal An unaccompanied song for three or more voices using counterpoint and imitation.

maestoso A direction to play in a majestic, stately manner.

magnificat Canticle of the Virgin Mary sung as part of the evening service in Reformed churches and at vespers in the Catholic church.

major Applied to chords, intervals, scales, and keys; a standard in contrast to diminished, augmented, or minor.

major scale A diatonic scale in which the half steps occur between the third and fourth and the seventh and eighth tones.

march A composition usually in duple meter and in simple, strongly marked rhythms and regular phrases for a procession or parade.

mass A musical setting of the liturgy of the Eucharist.

mazurka A polka-like Polish folk dance in triple time with strong accents on the normally weak second and third beats.

measure A unit of rhythm or musical time, indicated by bar lines.

mediant The third tone of a diatonic scale.

melody A rhythmically organized succession of single tones that form a musical idea.

mensural music A medieval term for music with definite note values, as distinguished from plainsong.

meter A scheme of accents; a grouping of beats into units of measure.

mezzo Medium, half; moderate.

mezzo-forte A direction to play moderately loudly.

mezzo-soprano The female voice between soprano and alto.

mi The third tone in the diatonic scale.

middle C The pitch represented by the first ledger line below the treble clef or the first above the bass clef.

minor Intervals, scales, keys, and chords having intervals a semitone less than major.

minor scale A diatonic scale having a minor third between the first and third tones and having several forms with different intervals above the fifth.

minuet A slow, graceful dance of French origin in triple time; a composition in this rhythm.

mode A selection of tones arranged in a scale that form the basic tonal substance of a composition.

modulation The change from one key to another through a succession of chords.

molto Very.

monophony Music consisting of a single melodic line without additional parts or accompaniment, as in plainsong or folk song.

mordent An ornament played by quickly alternating a note with the note below it.

morendo A fading away.

motet An unaccompanied vocal composition with sacred lyrics from the thirteenth century.

motif A short, significant melodic and/or rhythmic figure that recurs throughout a composition or section as a unifying element.

motion The pattern of changing pitch levels in a melody.

natural A musical symbol indicating the removal of a sharp or flat from a particular pitch.

nocturne A Romantic musical composition, usually for piano, with an expressive melody over a broken-chord accompaniment.

note A symbol used to express the relative time value of tones.

obbligato An added melody, usually played by a solo instrument to enhance a vocal line.

octave The distance between two pitches having the same name and located 12 half steps apart.

octet A composition of eight parts or voices; also, the group of its performers.

opera A drama set to music, in which words are sung in the form of recitatives, arias, and ensembles, usually accompanied by orchestra and generally performed with sets and costumes.

operetta A light opera, usually humorous, with spoken dialogue, dances, and almost unfailingly, a happy ending.

opus A numbered musical work or composition.

oratorio A musical setting of scriptural text set without costumes, scenery, or action.

orchestra A large group of musicians who play together on various musical instruments, including strings, woodwinds, brass, and percussion.

overture An introduction to a large composition such as an opera or oratorio; however, it can be independent or the predecessor of a symphonic poem.

parallel motion The relative changes of pitches in two or more simultaneous voice-parts when the intervals separating them remain the same.

part In orchestral or chamber music, the music or melodic line for a particular series of notes for voice or instrument.

partita A set of related instrumental pieces; a series of variations or a suite.

part song A nineteenth-century choral composition in the homophonic style in which the top part is the only carrier of the melody.

passion music A musical setting for the story of the suffering and death of Christ.

THE MAKEUP OF A SYMPHONY ORCHESTRA

Strings: 12 to 14 first violins, 10 to 12 second violins, 8 to 10 violas, 6 to 8 cellos, 4 to 6 double basses.

Woodwinds: 2 flutes, 2 oboes, 2 clarinets, 2 bassoons.

Brass: 2 trumpets, 2 or 4 horns, 2 or 3 trombones, 1 tuba.

Percussion: 2 or 3 kettledrums and various instruments of definite pitch (glockenspiel, bells, xylophone) and indefinite pitch (snare drum, bass drum, cymbals, triangle).

Harps: 1 or 2 (2 are called for more often than 1).

A larger orchestra would have this typical composition:

Strings: 16 first violins, 14 second violins, 12 violas, 10 cellos, 8 double basses.

Woodwinds: 2 flutes and piccolo, 2 oboes and English horn, 2 clarinets and bass clarinet, 2 bassoons and contrabassoon.

Brass: 3 trumpets, 4 horns, 3 trombones, 1 tuba.

Percussion and harps: As above.

pasticcio An operatic medley of the eighteenth century made up of contributions of two or more composers.

pastorale A musical composition suggestive of rural life.

pentatonic scale A five-toned scale without semitones; the diatonic scale with fourth and seventh tones omitted.

phrase A complete musical idea.

pianissimo A direction to play very softly.

piano A direction to play softly.

piano quartet A term usually applied to quartets for piano, violin, viola, and cello.

piano quintet A combination of piano with string quartet.

pitch The perceived highness or lowness of a sound.

pizzicato For violins and other bowed instruments, a direction that the string is to be picked with the finger.

plainsong A nonmetrical chant in one of the church modes.

poco Little.

polka A lively dance in ²/₄ time that originated in Bohemia c. 1830.

polonaise A Polish dance in ³/₄ time adopted as a musical form by Chopin.

polyphony Contrapuntal music; a style in which two or more melodies are interwoven; the opposite of *homophony*.

prelude An introductory movement complete in itself, as opposed to an introduction, which leads directly into the principal section; a short piano piece in one movement.

program music Music intended to depict a story or image.

progression *Melodic:* the passage from tone to tone; *harmonic:* the passage from chord to chord.

quartet A composition of four parts or voices; also, the performers of a four-part composition.

quintet A composition of five voices or instruments; also, the performers of a five-part composition.

ragtime Style of American music popular from about 1890 to the beginning of World War I, characterized by syncopated melodies set against a rhythmically strong bass.

re The second tone of a diatonic scale.

recitative A style of singing resembling dramatic speech.

refrain Repeated lines that occur at the end of each stanza of a song or poem.

register The range of a voice or instrument; a portion of the range of an instrument, as in upper register or lower register.

requiem A mass for the dead; also, a musical setting for such a mass.

resolution The progression from a dissonant tone or harmony to one that is consonant.

rest A symbol indicating pause or silence.

rinforzando A sudden accent on a single note or chord.

ritardando A direction to gradually slow the tempo.

ritenuto Immediate reduction in tempo.

romance   A short vocal or instrumental composition of a romantic character without fixed form.

rondo   A form of instrumental composition with a refrain that occurs at least three times in its original key between contrasting couplets.

root   The tonic of a triad or chord; the lowest tone, unless the chord is inverted.

round   A canon for three or more voices; common name for a circle canon in which each singer returns from the conclusion of the melody to its beginning, repeating it.

scale   A series of tones arranged according to rising pitches.

scat   Technique of jazz singing that utilizes nonsense syllables for improvising vocal solos.

scherzo   A playful, humorous instrumental composition, usually in a rapid 3/4 meter.

second   The interval between the tonic and the second tone of a diatonic scale; in the key of C major, C to D is a second.

semitone   One-half of a whole tone.

septet   A composition for seven voices or instruments.

sequence   Repetition of a short musical phrase at a different pitch.

serenade   An impromptu or unsolicited vocal or instrumental performance, often outdoors; an instrumental composition in several movements for a small group, between the symphony and the suite.

seventh   The interval between the tonic and the seventh tone of a diatonic scale; in the key of C major, C to B is a seventh.

si (or **ti**)   The seventh tone in a diatonic scale.

signature   A symbol placed on the staff at the beginning of a piece that shows the key and the meter.

sixth   The interval between the tonic and the sixth tone of a diatonic scale; in the key of C major, C to A is a sixth.

slur   A curved line over a series of notes that are to be played smoothly and continuously.

sol   The fifth tone of a diatonic scale.

solo   A piece performed either alone or with accompaniment.

sonata   An instrumental composition of three or four independent movements varying in mood, character, and tempo.

sonatina   A short, simple sonata.

soprano   The highest female or boy's voice; the treble.

sostenuto   Sustaining the tone to or beyond the nominal value.

sotto voce   In a low voice.

staccato   Direction to play notes in a distinct, detached manner.

staff   The five horizontal lines on and between which notes are written.

stretto   Compressed; in a fugue, the overlapping of subject and answer.

subdominant   The dominant below; the fourth tone of the diatonic scale, in the same relation to the key note from below as the dominant is from above.

subito Suddenly.

subject A melody or melody fragment that, because of its character, design, position, or treatment, is used in the basic musical form of a composition.

submediant The sixth tone of a diatonic scale.

subtonic The seventh tone of a diatonic scale.

suite An instrumental composition consisting of a series of movements or distinct compositions; originally, a cycle of dance tunes.

supertonic The second tone of a diatonic scale.

symphonic poem Originated by Franz Liszt, a large narrative orchestral work in one movement based on a nonmusical idea, either poetic or realistic.

symphony A sonata for orchestra, usually in four contrasting movements.

syncopation A rhythmic pattern that places emphasis on beats that are not normally accented, thus creating a catchy, lilting sound.

tempo The speed at which a composition is played.

tenor The highest natural adult male voice; also, the instrument of corresponding range.

ternary form The form of a composition in three parts with repetition following one contrast (ABA).

texture The way in which melody and harmony are combined to create layers of sound.

theme and variation A musical form in which the theme is repeated and varied.

third The interval between the tonic and the third tone of a diatonic scale; in the key of C major, C to E is a third.

ti (or **si**) The seventh tone in a diatonic scale.

tie A curved line that combines the duration of two notes of the same pitch.

time Used synonymously with measure or rhythm.

time signature The meter of a composition, shown by two numbers, one above the other; the lower tells the kind of note that represents one beat; the upper tells the number of these notes that make up a measure.

toccata A composition popular in the sixteenth century, for organ or harpsichord, and resembling the capriccio.

tonal center The tonic pitch around which a composition or scale is centered.

tone A sound of definite duration and pitch; a note.

tone cluster A group of notes played simultaneously with forearm, elbow, and fist in a method introduced by Henry Cowell.

tonic The first tone of a diatonic scale; also called fundamental. In the key of C major, C is the tonic.

transposition The rewriting or playing of a composition in a key other than the original one.

treble clef G clef; indicates that the pitch G is located on the second line above middle C.

tremolo Rapid repetition of a note to resemble trembling.

triad A chord composed of a fundamental tone and the third and fifth above it.

trio A composition for three parts or voices; the second part of a minuet or march.

triplet A group of three notes played in the time value of two.

triple time Time in which there are three beats to a measure.

turn An embellishment consisting of a group of four or five notes that turn around the principal note.

tutti Indications for passages for the whole orchestra as distinguished from those of the soloist.

twelve-tone music A method of composition based on a chromatic scale of 12, rather than 8, tones, developed by Arnold Schoenberg.

unison Equal pitch; performance of the same part by all voices.

variation Development of a theme through a variety of forms; differences in rhythm, key, harmony, etc.

vivace A direction to play in a lively manner.

voice Vocal or instrumental part of a composition.

waltz A dance in triple time performed by couples, which reached its peak of popularity during the nineteenth century; also, music in this rhythm.

whole note The longest note in common use.

whole tone An interval of a major second; the interval of two semitones.

Musical Notes

Name	Note	Rest
whole note	𝅝	𝄻
half note	𝅗𝅥	𝄼
quarter note	𝅘𝅥	𝄽
eighth note	𝅘𝅥𝅮	𝄾
sixteenth note	𝅘𝅥𝅯	𝄿
thirty-second note	𝅘𝅥𝅰	𝅀
sixty-fourth note	𝅘𝅥𝅱	𝅁

Major Dancers and Choreographers

American

Ailey, Alvin (1931–89). American choreographer noted for blending African, modern, and jazz elements, as seen in works such as *Revelations* (1960) and *Cry* (1971). His Alvin Ailey American Dance Theater was formed in 1958.

Arpino, Gerald (1928–   ). American choreographer. Principal choreographer of the Joffrey Ballet, he became its artistic director in 1988. His sometimes trendy, energetic works include *Viva Vivaldi!* (1965) and *Trinity* (1970).

Astaire, Fred (1899–1987). American actor and dancer in musical comedies on Broadway, such as *The Band Wagon*, and films, including *Top Hat* (1935) and *Shall We Dance?* (1937). Having started in vaudeville with his sister, Adele, Astaire later costarred with Judy Garland, Rita Hayworth, and Ginger Rogers, and was distinguished by his original and graceful tap dancing.

Balanchine, George (1904–83). Russian-born American choreographer. Balanchine worked with Diaghilev's Ballets Russes (1924–29), then came to America, founding the School of American Ballet in 1934. The New York City Ballet was created in 1948, with Balanchine as artistic director. He was an avatar of neoclassicism and the plotless ballet. Some of his major works, such as *Apollo* (1928) and *Agon* (1957), use the music of Stravinsky; other important works include *Serenade* (1934) and *Jewels* (1967).

Castle, Vernon (1887–1918) and **Irene** (1893–1969). Exhibition ballroom dancers whose elegance and style contributed to the spread of ballroom dancing before World War I. They created the Castle Walk and popularized the tango and other dances.

Cunningham, Merce (1919–   ). American choreographer. He danced with Martha Graham's company, forming his own troupe in 1953, collaborating often with John Cage. His avant-garde and abstract works use isolated movements and the random ordering of dance movements. His works include *Summerspace* (1958) and the consecutively numbered *Events* (begun in 1964).

d'Amboise, Jacques (1934–   ). American dancer and leading interpreter of the works of Balanchine during his years with the New York City Ballet (1949–79). He founded the National Dance Institute, which brings dance to New York City schoolchildren.

de Mille, Agnes (1909–   ). American choreographer. De Mille created ballets rooted in American folklore, such as *Rodeo* (1942) and *Fall River Legend* (1948). She also choreographed musicals for Broadway, including *Oklahoma!* (1943), and wrote *Dance to the Piper* (1952) and other books on dance.

Duncan, Isadora (1877–1927). American dancer, one of the first figures in modern dance. Turning to ancient Greece for inspiration, she rejected the rigid system of ballet and created an expressive form of dance, which she performed dressed in a flowing tunic. Her works include *Marseillaise* (1915) and *Marche Slave* (1917).

Dunham, Katherine (1912–   ). American choreographer and teacher. Through such works as the *Tropical Revues*, she was one of the first to bring African and Caribbean dance to the American stage. She also choreographed *Cabin in the Sky* (1940) for Broadway.

Farrell, Suzanne (1945–   ). American dancer with the New York City Ballet (1961–69, 1975–89) and Ballet of the 20th Century (1970–75). One of the leading interpreters of the works of Balanchine, Farrell created important roles in such ballets as *Don Quixote* (1965).

Feld, Eliot (1943–   ). American choreographer. He joined the American Ballet Theater in 1963, choreographing his first works, *Harbinger* and *At Midnight* (both 1967), there. In 1968 he formed the American Ballet company and in 1974 the Feld Ballet.

Graham, Martha (1894–1991). American choreographer. A leader of modern dance, she created a rigorous technique, which includes the contraction, a dramatic percussive movement based on the body's movement during intake and release of breath. Her works such as *Appalachian Spring* (1944) explore American roots; others, such as *Night Journey* (1947) and *Clytemnestra* (1958), draw on Greek mythology, exploring the psychology and passions of their protagonists.

Gregory, Cynthia (1946–   ) American dancer. Noted for her virtuoso technique and majestic presence, she joined the San Francisco Ballet in 1961 and American Ballet Theater in 1965, where she was a principal dancer until 1991.

Holm, Hanya (1898–1992) German-born choreographer and teacher. A protégée of Mary Wigman, she started choreographing her own modern dance works in America, including *Trend* (1937). She also choreographed *Kiss Me Kate* (1948) and *My Fair Lady* (1956) for Broadway.

Humphrey, Doris (1895–1958) A dancer with Denishawn, she left in 1927 to start a company with Charles Weidman. Her choreography is based on the principle of fall and recovery, which caters to the range of movement from balance to unbalance. Her works include *The Shakers* (1930) and *With My Red Fires* (1936).

Horton, Lester (1906–53) American dancer, choreographer, and teacher. A leader in modern dance and influenced by Native American dance, he formed the Lester Horton Dancers in 1934. Among his notable students was Alvin Ailey.

Joffrey, Robert (1930–88). American choreographer. He formed his first company in 1954, and in 1956 he founded what became the Robert Joffrey Ballet. Joffrey's works include *Pas de Déesses* (1954) and *Astarte* (1967).

Kelly, Gene (1912–   ). American actor, dancer, choreographer. In films such as *An American in Paris* (1952) and *Invitation to the Dance* (1956) he tried to make the choreography integral to the story and explored cinematic techniques for filming dance.

Kirstein, Lincoln (1907–   ). A promoter of American ballet, he brought Balanchine to America and cofounded with him the School of American Ballet. He was general director of the New York City Ballet (1948–89) and wrote *Dance: A Short History of Classic Theatrical Dancing* (1935) and other books.

Martins, Peter (1946–   ) b. Denmark. After dancing with the Royal Danish Ballet (1965–1969), Martins joined the New York City Ballet in 1970, becoming co-ballet master in chief in 1983 and ballet master in chief in 1990. Among his works, which follow in Balanchine's neoclassical tradition, are *Calcium Night Light* (1977), *Eight Easy Pieces* (1979), *Ecstatic Orange* (1987), and *Jazz* (1993).

Mitchell, Arthur (1934–   ). American dancer with the New York City Ballet from 1955. In 1968 he founded the Dance Theater of Harlem, the first black classical dance company.

Nikolais, Alwin (1912–1993). American choreographer and founder of the Nikolais Dance Theater; his works, such as *Kaleidoscope* (1956), are theatrical productions in which dance, lighting, and sound play equal roles, forming abstract yet evocative patterns.

Robbins, Jerome (1918–). American dancer and choreographer for the Ballet Theater (1941–44), where he choreographed *Fancy Free* (1944), and the New York City Ballet, where he was associate artistic director (1949–56) and later codirector (1983–90). His ballets combine the classical idiom with influences from jazz, modern, and social dance. Among his important works are *Goldberg Variations* (1971) and *Dances at a Gathering* (1969). His choreography for Broadway includes *West Side Story* (1957) and *Fiddler on the Roof* (1964).

Robinson, Bill (Bojangles) (1878–1949). American tap dancer who brought a new lightness to tap. Gaining renown with his appearance in the revue *Blackbirds* in 1928, he appeared in movies, including *The Little Colonel* with Shirley Temple.

St. Denis, Ruth (1879–1968). American dancer. Inspired by the Orient, her dances, such as *Radha* (1904) and *The Cobras* (1906), were both exotic and spiritual. In 1915, St. Denis founded Denishawn—the first school of modern dance—with her husband, Ted Shawn.

Shawn, Ted (1891–1972). American founder of Denishawn with Ruth St. Denis. In the 1930s he started Men Dancers; with works such as *The Kinetic Molpai* (1935) he focused attention on male dancing. Shawn also founded the Jacob's Pillow Dance Festival.

Tallchief, Maria (1925–). American dancer with the Ballet Russe de Monte Carlo (1942–47) and the New York City Ballet (1948–1965). She founded the Chicago City Ballet, and is currently artistic director of the Lyric Opera of Chicago Ballet.

Taylor, Paul (1930–). American choreographer. He formed his own company in 1954, and his imaginative modern dance works are often characterized by their humor. His works include *Arden Court* (1981) and *Company B* (1991).

Tharp, Twyla (1942–). American choreographer of idiosyncratic works that use ballet idiom to novel effect. She had her own modern dance company (1965–88), then served as artistic associate with the American Ballet Theater (1988–91). Her works include *Deuce Coupe* (1973) and *Push Comes to Shove* (1976). She also choreographed the films *Hair* (1979) and *Amadeus* (1984), and directed *Singing in the Rain* (1985) on Broadway.

Villella, Edward (1936–). American dancer. As a member of the New York City Ballet (1957–79), he was noted for his virile dancing. He has been artistic director of the Miami City Ballet since 1985.

Weidman, Charles (1901–75). American dancer and choreographer. After dancing with Denishawn, he founded a company with Doris Humphrey in 1927 and later began his own company. His works, known for their humor, include *Flickers* and *And Daddy Was a Fireman*.

British

Ashton, Sir Frederick (1904–88). A pioneer of British ballet, he was chief choreographer of the Sadler's Wells (now Royal) Ballet from 1935 and its director from 1963 to 1970. His works, noted for their lyrical classicism, include *Symphonic Variations* (1946), *Les Patineurs* (1937), and *Ondine* (1958).

Dolin, Anton (1904–83). English dancer with Diaghilev's Ballets Russes (1924–29) and Ballet Theater. One of Britain's first danseurs nobles, in 1949 he founded the London Festival Ballet with Alicia Markova and served as artistic director.

Fonteyn, Dame Margot (1919–91). English dancer and prima ballerina assoluta of the Royal Ballet, which she joined in 1934 when it was the Vic Wells Ballet. Known for her musicality and refinement, she was the partner of Rudolf Nureyev after 1962; her major roles include Aurora in *Sleeping Beauty* and Juliet in *Romeo and Juliet*.

Markova, Dame Alicia (1910–). English dancer with the Ballets Russes (1925–29), Ballet Theater (1941–45), and other companies. Markova was one of the leading interpreters of *Giselle* and the first British ballerina of international renown.

Rambert, Dame Marie (1888–1982). Polish-born dancer, teacher, and ballet director. She advised Nijinsky on rhythm when he was choreographing *Le Sacre du printemps* and later became one of the pioneers of modern British ballet, founding her Ballet Rambert in 1935.

Tudor, Antony (1908–87). English choreographer of ballets of psychological drama. He was associated with the American Ballet Theater (1939–49), then known as Ballet Theater, later serving as associate artistic director (1974–80). Among the ballets that exemplify his use of gesture to express character are *Lilac Garden* (1936) and *Pillar of Fire* (1942).

Valois, Dame Ninette de (1898–). A founder of modern British ballet. After dancing with the Ballets Russes (1923–26), she founded a school in London, and in 1931 a company, the Vic-Wells Ballet, which became the Sadler's Wells Ballet and then the Royal Ballet. Her works include *The Rake's Progress* (1935) and *The Haunted Ballroom* (1934).

French

Béjart, Maurice (1927–). French choreographer. He founded the Ballet de l'Etoile in 1953, and later the Ballet of the 20th Century. In 1988, his troupe moved to Lausanne, Switzerland. Béjart's controversial works are highly theatrical and sometimes mystical; they include *Symphony for a Lonely Man* (1955) and *Ring Around the Ring* to Wagner (1991).

Camargo, Marie (1710–70). French dancer at the Paris Opera and rival of Marie Sallé, Camargo shortened the dancer's skirt to show her brilliant entrechats and other beats and eliminated the heels from her shoes for greater freedom of movement.

Noverre, Jean Georges (1727–1810). French choreographer and ballet reformer who tried with the *ballet d'action* to highlight the expressiveness of the ballet and integrate dance with drama. He wrote down his ideas in his *Letters sur la danse et sur les ballets*.

Perrot, Jules (1810–1892). French dancer and ballet master of the Imperial Theater in St. Petersburg (1851–58). A leading dancer and choreographer of the Romantic era, he choreographed *La Esmeralda* and parts of *Giselle* (1841).

Petit, Roland (1924–). French founder of the Ballets de Paris de Roland Petit (1948) and director of the Ballet National de Marseilles since 1972. His story ballets combine high and popular art; his works include *Le Jeune homme et la mort* (1946) and *Le Loup* (1953).

Sallé, Marie (1707–1756). French dancer with the Paris Opera (1727–40) and rival of Camargo. An advocate of the use of pantomime in ballet, Sallé was noted for her expressiveness and intelligence.

Vestris, Auguste (1760–1842). French dancer and teacher, illegitimate son of Gaetano. As premier danseur of the Paris Opera, he was noted for his exceptional elevation and virtuosity.

Vestris, Gaetano (1728–1808). Italian-born dancer and choreographer. Known as "the god of the dance," he became premier danseur of the Paris Opera in 1751 and co-choreographer in 1761. He was the first to discard the mask worn by dancers in performance.

Russian

Baryshnikov, Mikhail (1948–). A principal with the Kirov Ballet (1968–74), the Russian dancer defected to the West in 1974, joining the American Ballet Theater and serving as its director (1980–89). He then formed the White Oak Dance Project. His virtuosity and purity of classical style make him one of the leading male dancers of the period.

Danilova, Alexandra (1904–). Russian-born dancer. Noted for her charm and elegance, she was a ballerina with the Ballet Russes (1927–29) and prima ballerina with the Ballet Russe de Monte Carlo (1938–52). She taught at the School of American Ballet (1964–89) and appeared in the film *The Turning Point* (1977).

Diaghilev, Sergei Pavlovich (1872–1929). Russian impresario and founder of the Ballets Russes (1909). He brought together leading choreographers, composers, and artists, from Fokine and Balanchine to Stravinsky and Picasso, whose collaborations revolutionized the ballet.

Eglevsky, Andre (1917–77). Russian-born dancer. A leading dancer with the Ballet Russe de Monte Carlo (1939–42), Ballet Theater (1942–43) and New York City Ballet (1951–58). He founded the Eglevsky Ballet Company in 1961.

Fokine, Michel (1880–1942). Russian-born choreographer for the Ballets Russes (1909–12, 1914–15). His emphasis on dramatic coherence and on the unity of the style of dance and decor with the subject matter revolutionized the ballet. His important works include *The Firebird* (1910) and *Petrouchka* (1911).

Ivanov, Lev (1834–1901). Russian choreographer. His most important ballets were *The Nutcracker* (1892) and the second and fourth acts of *Swan Lake* (1894).

Karsavina, Tamara (1885–1978). Russian dancer with the Ballets Russes and partner of Nijinsky. She created important roles in *The Firebird* and *Petrouchka* and wrote her autobiography, *Theatre Street*.

Lifar, Serge (1905–86). Russian dancer with the Ballets Russes (1923–29), where he created the title role in Balanchine's *Prodigal Son*. As director of the Paris Opera Ballet (1929–45, 1947–58), he reinvigorated French ballet, choreographing many works including *Icare* (1935) and *Suite en blanc* (1943).

Makarova, Natalia (1940–). Russian dancer. A leading member of the Kirov Ballet (1959–70), she defected to the West, where she danced with the American Ballet Theater, the Royal Ballet, and other companies. She won a Tony for her performance in the musical *On Your Toes*.

Massine, Léonide (1895–1979). Russian-born dancer and choreographer with the Ballets Russes (1914–21, 1925–28) and the Ballet Russe de Monte Carlo (1932–42). His works include *Parade* (1917) and *Gaîté Parisienne* (1938).

Nijinska, Bronislava (1891–1972). The sister of Vaslav Nijinsky, she also worked with the Ballets Russes as a dancer and innovative choreographer, incorporating sport and satire into ballet. Among her important ballets are *Les Noces* (1923) and *Les Biches* (1924).

Nijinsky, Vaslav (1889–1950). Polish-Russian dancer and choreographer with the Ballets Russes, creating important roles in Fokine's ballets, such as *Petrouchka*. Considered by many to be the greatest dancer of the twentieth century, he also choreographed works such as *L'Après-midi d'un faune* (1912) and *Le Sacre du printemps* (1913), which were radical breaks with ballet tradition.

Nureyev, Rudolf (1938–93). Russian dancer with the Kirov Ballet, he defected to the West in 1961, where he often partnered Dame Margot Fonteyn with the Royal Ballet. A leading dancer of his time, he was noted for his virtuosity and animal sensuality. He was director of the Paris Opera from 1983 to 1989.

Pavlova, Anna Matveyevna (1881–1931). Russian ballerina. She danced briefly with the Ballets Russes, then toured with her own company, introducing ballet to people all over the world. An outstanding ballerina, she was known for her grace and lightness and the spiritual quality of her dancing.

Petipa, Marius (1818–1910). French dancer who became first ballet master of the Imperial Theater of St. Petersburg in 1862. Russian ballet reached its apogee under his direction. One of the leading choreographers in ballet history, his works include *La Bayadère* (1877) and *The Sleeping Beauty* (1890).

Plisetskaya, Maya (1925–   ). Leading Russian ballerina with the Bolshoi Ballet, which she joined in 1945. She is noted for her virtuosity and dramatic presence, and for the pliancy of her arms.

Ulanova, Galina Sergeyevna (1910–   ). Russian dancer and teacher noted for her dramatic projection and lyricism. After joining the Kirov Ballet in 1928, she left to dance with the Bolshoi Ballet (1944–61), becoming the prima ballerina of Soviet ballet.

Youskevitch, Igor (1912–   ). Russian-born dancer with the Ballet Russe de Monte Carlo (1938–44) and the Ballet Theater (1946–55). He was admired for his nobility and elegance, and for his partnership with Alicia Alonso.

Other

Alonso, Alicia (1921–   ). Cuban dancer known for the purity of her classical style, particularly in the role of Giselle. After dancing with the American Ballet Theater and other companies, she founded the National Ballet of Cuba in 1959.

Bournonville, Auguste (1805–79). Danish choreographer. His Romantic works, such as *Napoli* (1842), form the core of the repertory of the Royal Danish Ballet.

Bruhn, Erik (1928–86). Danish-born dancer noted for his immaculate technique and nobility of style. After dancing with the American Ballet Theater and other companies, he was artistic director of the National Ballet of Canada (1983–86).

Cerrito, Fanny (1817–1909). Italian dancer, one of the leading ballerinas of the Romantic era. Noted for her strength and sensuous appeal, she created the leading role in *Ondine* (1843).

Elssler, Fanny (1810–84). Austrian daughter of an assistant to Franz Joseph Haydn, Elssler was one of the great ballerinas of the Romantic era, noted for her dramatic projection and earthiness. Her most famous dance was the Cachucha in *Le Diable boiteux* (1836).

Grisi, Carlotta (1819–99). Italian dancer with the Paris Opera. One of the great Romantic ballerinas, she created the title role in *Giselle*, whose libretto was written for her by Théophile Gautier.

Jooss, Kurt (1901–79). German choreographer whose theatrical works combined classical and modern modes of dance. His important works include *The Green Table*, a scathing indictment of war, and *Big City* (1932).

Taglioni, Marie (1804–84). Italian ballerina, the incarnation of the spiritual and lyrical ideal of the Romantic era. In the title role of *La Sylphide* (1832), she brought toe dancing to a new artistic level.

Wigman, Mary (1886–1973). German dancer and choreographer. The first major European modern dancer, Wigman choreographed somber works in an expressionist mode. Her works include *Totenmal* (1930).

Dance Terms

abstract dance A plotless work composed of pure dance movements, although the composition may suggest a mood or subject.

adagio Any dance to slow music; also, part of the classical pas de deux in ballet.

air, en l' In ballet, a step done off the ground—for instance, tour en l'air, rond de jambe en l'air. It is the opposite of *par terre*.

allegro A dance with a fast or moderate tempo.

allongé In ballet, an elongated line; in particular, the horizontal line of an arabesque with one arm stretched front and the other back.

arabesque In ballet, the extension of one leg straight in back at 90 degrees, with shoulders square; the position of the arms may vary.

assemblé In ballet, a jump from one to both feet, usually landing in fifth position.

attitude In ballet, a pose in which one leg is raised in back or in front with knee bent, usually with one arm raised.

balancé A step that rocks from one foot to the other, usually in ³/₄ time.

ballet From the Italian *balletto*, diminutive of *ballo*, "dance." Classical theatrical dancing based on the *danse d'école*, the rules and vocabulary that were codified around 1700 in France.

ballet blanc A ballet in which the women wear white tutus, such as the second and fourth acts of *Swan Lake*.

ballet d'action A ballet with a plot, usually tragic, advocated by reformer Jean Georges Noverre, ballet master of the Paris Opera, to bring dramatic coherence to the performance of ballet.

ballet de cour, le (court ballet) Spectacles for entertainment, usually with allegorical or mythological themes, performed by the aristocracy in the sixteenth and seventeenth centuries, combining music, recitatives, and mime.

ballo Standard Italian dances and their music of the fifteenth and sixteenth centuries.

ballon In ballet, the ability of a dancer to remain suspended in air during a jump; elasticity in jumping.

ballroom dances Social dances usually performed by couples, including the fox-trot, waltz, tango, rumba, and cha cha.

bas, en In ballet, low, as in placement of arms.

basic movement In ballroom dance, a characteristic figure that remains constant.

basse danse A solemn court dance usually in duple time, popular in the fifteenth and sixteenth centuries.

battement A beating movement of the legs.

bourrée, pas de A series of small, fast steps executed with the feet very close together.

brisé In ballet, a jump off one foot that is "broken" by a beating of the legs in the air.

cabriole In ballet, a leap in which the lower leg beats against the upper one at an angle, before the dancer lands again on the lower leg.

cachucha A Spanish dance in ¾ or ⅜ time with castanets.

cakewalk An African-American dance in which couples strut and compete with high kicks and fast steps.

cambré In ballet, a bend from the waist to the side or to the back.

cancan Originating around 1830 as a social dance, by 1844 it had become a raucous dance performed in French music halls.

chassé A sliding step in which one foot "chases" and displaces the other.

chat, pas de Catlike leap in which one foot follows the other into the air, knees bent; the landing is in the fifth position.

ciseaux A jump in which the legs open in second position in the air, resembling a scissors.

coda In ballet, the third and final part of the classical pas de deux.

contraction A basic movement in the technique of Martha Graham, based on breath inhalation and exhalation.

contredanse Popular social dance during the eighteenth century; done in rows or circles, it may have derived from English country dancing.

corps de ballet The members of a ballet company who do not perform solo.

country dance Traditional English dance in which dancers form two facing lines.

croisée In ballet, a position with the body at an oblique angle and the working leg crossing the line of the body.

danseur noble A male dancer who performs the "princely" roles of the classical ballet, such as the Prince in *Swan Lake*.

dégagé In ballet, shifting weight from one foot to the other.

développé An unfolding of the leg in the air.

écarté In ballet, a position with one leg extended at an oblique angle while the body is also at an oblique angle.

effacé In ballet, a position of the body at an oblique angle and partly hidden.

entrechat A ballet movement in which the dancer repeatedly crosses his or her legs in the air.

épaulement In ballet, the position of the torso from the waist up.

fandango A lively Spanish dance in triple time performed with castanets or tambourines.

fermé In ballet, a closed position of the feet.

five positions In ballet, the basic positions of the feet. First position: feet in a straight line, heels touching. Second position: feet in a straight line, heels apart. Third position: one foot in front of the other, parallel to it, with heel of front foot in hollow instep of back foot. Fourth position: one foot in front of the other, parallel, but apart. Fifth position: One foot in front of the other, parallel, with heel in front foot touching toe of back foot.

flamenco A Sevillian gypsy dance, possibly originating in India, also with Moorish and Arabian influences, originally accompanied by songs and clapping and later by the guitar, and characterized by its heelwork (*taconeo*).

fondu In ballet, a lowering of the body by bending the knee.

fouetté en tournant A spectacular movement in which the dancer propels himself or herself around a supporting leg with rapid circular movements of the other leg while remaining in a fixed spot.

fox-trot A social dance of American origin in duple time.

glissade In ballet, a gliding step which usually connects two steps.

haut, en In ballet, a position of the arms above the head.

jeté A leap from one leg to the other in which one leg is thrown to the side, front, or back. *Grand jeté*: a large leap forward.

jitterbug A lively social dance popular during the 1930s; it originated at the Savoy Ballroom in Harlem in 1928, where it was known as the Lindy.

kabuki A Japanese dance drama featuring stylized narrative choreographic movements

mazurka A Polish national dance in triple time with an accent on the second beat, characterized by proud bearing, clicking of heels, and *holubria*, a special turning step.

minuet A slow and graceful dance, the most popular dance of the eighteenth century, characterized by symmetrical figures and elaborate curtsys and bows.

morris dance An English folk dance that appeared in the fifteenth century, in which dancers wore bells on their legs and characters included a fool, a boy on a hobby horse, and a man in blackface.

ouvert In ballet, an open position of the feet.

par terre Steps performed on the floor. It is the opposite of *en l'air*.

pas de deux A dance for two, usually a woman and a man. In its traditional form, it begins with an entrée and adagio, followed by solo variations for each dancer, and a coda.

pavane A grave, processional court dance popular in the sixteenth and seventeenth centuries.

penché In ballet, leaning forward.

piqué Stepping directly onto the point of a foot.

pirouette A turn on one leg, with the toe of the other leg touching the knee of the turning leg.

plié A bending of the knees in any of the five positions. *Demi plié*: a half bending of the knees, with heels on the floor. *Grand plié*: a full bending of the knees.

point A position on the tip of the toes. *Demi-point*: a position on the balls of the feet.

polka A Bohemian folk dance in duple time with a hop on the fourth beat. It became a popular ballroom dance in the mid-nineteenth century.

port de bras In ballet, the positions of the arms.

premier danseur Principal male dancer.

promenade In ballet, a slow turn of the body on the whole foot.

quadrille A social dance popular in the nineteenth century. It was a square dance in five sections, each in a different time.

reel Popular in Britain, Ireland, and Scotland, it is a lively dance for two or more couples; also, the second part of the Virginia reel. The Highland fling is a variant.

relevé In ballet, a rising with a spring movement to point or demi-point.

révérence A ballet bow or curtsy in which one foot is pointed in front and the body leans forward.

spotting A fixing of the eyes on one spot as long as possible during turns to avoid dizziness and to keep one's orientation.

square dance An American folk dance with an even number of couples forming a square, two lines, or a circle. The dance is comprised of figures announced by a caller.

tango A social dance in 2/4 time, which after originating in Spain, developed in Argentina, where it was influenced by black dance style and rhythm.

tour en l'air A turn while jumping straight up in the air.

variation Any solo performance in a ballet.

waltz A social dance in 3/4 time that became widely popular in the nineteenth century. It developed from the Landler, a German-Austrian turning dance.

Major Painters and Sculptors

American

Albers, Josef (1888–1976), b. Germany. Painter and designer, teacher at the Bauhaus, and director of the Yale School of Art. Best known for his *Homage to the Square* series (begun 1949) and for his widely studied color theories.

Calder, Alexander (1898–1976), b. Pennsylvania. Best known for his mobiles and playful wire constructions of circuses, begun in 1926. Much of his later work is large, heavy sculpture, often for public areas.

Cassatt, Mary (1845–1926), b. Pennsylvania. Spent much of her life in Paris, where she was allied with the impressionists. She is best known for paintings of women with children, such as *The Bath* (1892), and etchings, such as *The Letter* (1891).

Cornell, Joseph (1903–72), b. New York. His surrealist-influenced constructions are boxes filled with found objects and collaged images, arranged in privately symbolic ways. Some of the best-known examples are *Medici Slot Machine* (1942) and *Hôtel du Nord* (1953).

Davies, Arthur Bowen (1862–1928), b. New York. Member of The Eight and an organizer of the historic 1913 Armory Show. His symbolic, idyllic paintings include landscapes such as *Unicorns* (1906).

Davis, Stuart (1894–1964), b. Pennsylvania. Davis developed a distinctly American interpretation of cubism in his brightly colored paintings, such as *Hot Still-Scape for Six Colors* (1940) and *Colonial Cubism* (1954).

de Kooning, Willem (1904–   ), b. The Netherlands. A leader of abstract expressionism in the United States, de Kooning is best known for his monumental, violently painted *Woman* series, begun in the early 1950s.

Demuth, Charles (1883–1935), b. Pennsylvania. One of the first to incorporate geometric shapes of modern technology into painting. His best-known work is *I Saw the Figure 5 in Gold* (1928).

Dove, Arthur Garfield (1880–1946), b. New York. In his paintings of abstracted natural forms, such as *Waterfall* (1925) and *Rise of the Full Moon* (1937), Dove was a forerunner of abstract expressionism.

Eakins, Thomas (1844–1916), b. Pennsylvania. An important portraitist, Eakins was criticized for innovations such as working from live nude models. His best-known works include *The Gross Clinic* (1875), which shows an operation in progress, and *Max Schmitt in a Single Scull* (1871).

Feininger, Lyonel (1871–1956), b. New York. Feininger, who taught at the Bauhaus (1919–32), developed a style of delicate architectural forms fractured by rays of light, as in *Church at Gelmeroda* (1936).

Frankenthaler, Helen (1928–   ), b. New York. Frankenthaler developed a technique of staining canvases with paint, creating sensuous abstract works such as *Mountains and Sea* (1952), a seminal work in this style, and *Arden* (1961).

Gorky, Arshile (1904–48), b. Armenia. An influence on abstract expressionism, Gorky painted abstract but often biomorphic forms in brilliant, glowing colors, as in *The Liver Is the Cock's Comb* (1944).

Henri, Robert (1865–1929), b. Ohio. Painter and influential teacher. As a member of The Eight, he was a leader in the rebellion against academic art. Henri is best known for his dramatic portraits, such as *Woman in Manteau* (1898), *Himself* (1913), and *Herself* (1913).

Hofmann, Hans (1880–1966), b. Germany. Founder of two U.S. art schools important in the development of abstract expressionism. Hofmann boldly manipulated violent, clashing colors, as in *Effervescence* (1944) and *The Gate* (1959).

Homer, Winslow (1836–1910), b. Massachusetts. One of the most prominent nineteenth-century American painters, Homer is best known for his dramatic seascapes, such as *West Point, Prout's Neck, Maine* and *On a Lee Shore* (both 1900).

Hopper, Edward (1882–1967), b. New York. Hopper painted lonely street scenes, buildings, and interiors, giving careful attention to light and shade, as in *Nighthawks* (1942) and *Early Sunday Morning* (1930).

Indiana, Robert (1928–   ), b. Indiana. Pop artist best known for his bold and vivid signlike paintings and sculpture, such as the *Love* series (begun 1966).

Johns, Jasper (1930–   ), b. Georgia. A founder of pop art, Johns uses everyday signs, symbols, and objects in his paintings and sculptures, such as flags, targets, and beer cans. An example is the painting *Three Flags* (1958).

Kline, Franz (1910–62), b. Pennsylvania. He painted large canvases with dynamic black and white brush strokes, as in *White Forms* (1955) and *Mahoning* (1956). His work exemplifies abstract expressionism.

Lichtenstein, Roy (1923–   ), b. New York. Pop artist known for his paintings based on comic strips, such as *Masterpiece* (1962) and *Good Morning, Darling* (1964).

Louis, Morris (1912–62), b. Maryland. He used a technique of soaking poured paint through canvases, so that the canvas essentially became dyed by the paint. His work includes the *Veil* series (1954, 1958) and the *Unfurled* series (1960–61).

Moses, Grandma (Anna Mary Robertson Moses) (1860–1961), b. New York. A farmer's wife who began painting in her 70s. Her primitive, colorful works of farm life, such as *Sugaring-Off* (1943), achieved wide popularity.

Motherwell, Robert (1915–91), b. Washington. Painter, writer, and important theoretician of abstract expressionism. His works are characterized by amorphous shapes in austere colors; best known is the series *Elegy for the Spanish Republic*, begun in 1949.

Nevelson, Louise (1900–88), b. Russia. Sculptor known for her large works of painted wood, metal, and found objects, such as *Sky Cathedral* (1958) and *World* (1966).

Newman, Barnett (1905–71), b. New York. Painter whose works bridged abstract expressionism and the color field movement. His canvases are typically large planes of flat color with thin vertical stripes, such as *Onement I* (1948) and *Concord* (1949). He also produced sculpture.

Noguchi, Isamu (1904–88), b. California. Sculptor well known for his abstract works designed for architectural spaces, such as the sculpture garden for the UNESCO building in Paris (1958) and the entrance for the Museum of Modern Art in Tokyo (1969).

O'Keeffe, Georgia (1887–1987), b. Wisconsin. Painter whose most characteristic images are sculptural, organic forms such as bones and flowers. She lived in New Mexico and often used elements of the southwestern landscape, as in *Cow's Skull, Red, White, and Blue* (1931).

Oldenburg, Claes (1929–   ), b. Sweden. Leader of the pop art movement, known for his giant sculptures of common objects, such as *Dual Hamburger* (1962) and *Lipstick* (1969).

Parrish, Maxfield (1870–1966), b. Pennsylvania. Creator of posters, magazine covers, and book illustrations in a distinctive, decorative style.

Pollock, Jackson (1912–56), b. Wyoming. A pioneer of abstract expressionism, Pollock developed a method called action painting. His canvases are typically large, with paint dripped, poured, and thrown in complex, dense rhythms, as in *Number 1* (1948), *Number 32* (1950), and *Blue Poles* (1953).

Prendergast, Maurice Brazil (1859–1924), b. Canada. Member of The Eight. He painted landscapes and figures in a colorful, decorative style influenced by the Nabis, as in *The Promenade* (1913).

Rauschenberg, Robert (1925–   ), b. Texas. His collage-like "combine paintings" appropriating everyday images and objects represent a transition between abstract expressionism and pop art. His work includes *Bed* (1955) and *Monogram* (1959).

Reinhardt, Ad (Adolph) (1913–67), b. New York. Associated with minimalism, Reinhardt began painting monochrome canvases by 1953. He is best known for his *Black Paintings*, begun in 1960.

Remington, Frederic (1861–1909), b. New York. Painter, sculptor, illustrator, and writer whose subject was life on the western plains. His works include the sculpture *Bronco Buster* (1895) and the painting *Evening on a Canadian Lake* (1905).

Rivers, Larry (1923–   ), b. New York. In his use of popular images from sources such as artworks and advertising, Rivers was a forerunner of pop art. His paintings include *Washington Crossing the Delaware* (1953) and the *Dutch Masters* series (1963). He has also done sculpture.

Rockwell, Norman (1894–1978), b. New York. Illustrator best known for his *Saturday Evening Post* covers (1916–63). His realistically drawn, popular works portray anecdotal scenes of small-town America. *The Four Freedoms* (1943) are among his most famous paintings.

Rothko, Mark (1903–70), b. Russia. Important figure in abstract expressionism. His canvases contain soft-edged, luminously colored rectangular forms. His work includes *No. 10* (1950) and a series of murals for an ecumenical chapel in Houston (1967–69).

Sargent, John Singer (1856–1925), b. Italy. Painter known for his vivid portraits of high society, such as *The Daughters of Edward D. Boit* (1882) and *Madame X* (1884). He also produced impressionistic watercolor landscapes.

Segal, George (1924–   ), b. New York. Sculptor known for his life-size plaster human figures in everyday environments, such as *Woman in Restaurant Booth* (1961) and *Cinema* (1963). Segal is associated with pop art.

Shahn, Ben (1898–1969), b. Lithuania. Versatile artist of social-realistic work that often tells a story without preaching. In the early 1930s he did a series of 23 paintings based on the Sacco-Vanzetti trial.

Sheeler, Charles (1883–1965), b. Pennsylvania. Photographer and painter known for his depictions of industrial forms reduced to cool, formal simplification, such as the paintings *Ballardvale Revisited* (1949) and *Steel-Croton* (1953).

Smith, David (1906–65), b. Indiana. Renowned abstract sculptor of welded metal forms. He worked on his large *Cubi* series from the late 1950s until his death.

Stella, Frank (1936–   ), b. Massachusetts. Abstract painter of large, colorful works on irregularly shaped canvases. Works such as *Empress of India* (1965) use series of angular stripes; later works such as *Guadalupe Island* (1979) exhibit sweeping arched forms and wildly exuberant colors.

Sully, Thomas (1783–1872), b. England. A leading portraitist, especially of national figures. His most famous work is the historical painting *Washington's Passage of the Delaware* (1819).

Warhol, Andy (1930–87), b. Pennsylvania. Leader of the pop art movement. His works are notable for the repetition of everyday images, such as Campbell's soup cans, or figures from popular culture, such as Marilyn Monroe (both series begun 1962).

West, Benjamin (1738–1820), b. Pennsylvania. Working in both Neoclassical and Romantic styles, he produced paintings such as *The Death of General Wolfe* (1770) and *Death on a Pale Horse* (1802). West worked mainly in England and was a founder and president of the Royal Academy of Arts there.

Whistler, James Abbott McNeill (1834–1903), b. Massachusetts. Painter and graphic artist whose works show a brilliant sense of color and design. His paintings include *The White Girl: Symphony in White No. 1* (1862) and *The Artist's Mother: Arrangement in Gray and Black* (1871). His series of *Nocturnes* foreshadowed abstract art.

Wood, Grant (1891–1942), b. Iowa. Painter best known for his stern figures and stylized landscapes of the rural Midwest. *American Gothic* (1930) is a quintessential American work.

Wyeth, Andrew (1917–   ), b. Pennsylvania. Popular painter of rural landscapes and portraits in a meticulous, naturalistic style. His best-known work is *Christina's World* (1948). In 1986, Wyeth astonished the public with the appearance of a previously secret series, the *Helga* paintings.

Belgian

See Flemish, Belgian.

British

Bacon, Francis (1909–1992), b. Ireland. Painter of disturbing, hallucinatory images, as in *Three Studies at the Base of a Crucifixion* (1944) and his series based on Velázquez's *Pope Innocent X* portrait, begun in the 1950s.

Blake, William (1757–1827). Painter, engraver, and poet. Blake, a mystic and visionary, illustrated the Book of Job (1818–20), Dante's *Divine Comedy* (1824–27), and his own poetic works in an unearthly, highly personal style.

Constable, John (1776–1837). Leading English landscape painter. In works such as *The White Horse* (1819), *The Hay Wain* (1821), and *Salisbury Cathedral* (1827), he carefully observed natural phenomena and changes.

Gainsborough, Thomas (1727–88). Portraitist and landscape painter. His well-known works include *Mr. and Mrs. Robert Andrews* (1748), *Mrs. Siddons* (1785), and his most famous painting, *The Blue Boy* (1770).

Hogarth, William (1697–1764). Painter and engraver of satirical works, often on moral themes and told in a series of scenes, such as *The Rake's Progress* (1733–35) and *Marriage à la Mode* (1743–45).

Moore, Henry (1898–1986). Sculptor whose abstract and figurative works are characterized by smooth organic shapes and hollows. His many public commissions include works for the Time-Life building in London (1952–53) and for Lincoln Center for the Performing Arts in New York City (1962–65).

Reynolds, Sir Joshua (1723–92). Reynolds, first president of the Royal Academy of Arts, painted portraits of nearly every important figure of his day with great versatility. His works include *Commodore Keppel* (1753) and *Mrs. Siddons as the Tragic Muse* (1784).

Rossetti, Dante Gabriel (1828–82). Painter and poet; one of the founders of the Pre-Raphaelite Brotherhood in 1848. His sensual and symbolic works include *The Annunciation* (1850) and *Beata Beatrix* (1864).

Turner, Joseph Mallord William (1775–1851). A foremost English landscape painter. Turner depicted atmospheric effects with a style of shimmering light and luminous colors, as in *Calais Pier* (1803) and *The Grand Canal* (1835).

Dutch

Bosch, Hieronymus (Jerom Bos) (c. 1450–1516). Painter of bizarre and colorful religious allegories, filled with grotesque figures and animals and obscure symbolism. His works include *The Garden of Earthly Delights* (c. 1505–10) and *The Temptation of St. Anthony* (c. 1500).

Hals, Frans (c. 1580–1666). He painted lively and naturalistic portraits and genre scenes in vivid, sparkling colors. His works include *The Banquet of the Officers of the St. George Militia* (1616) and *The Laughing Cavalier* (1624).

Mondrian, Piet (1872–1944). A founder of the Stijl group and the magazine *iDe Stijl*. Mondrian developed a geometric style, "neoplasticism"; typical works consist of primary-color squares bounded by black outlines, as in *Composition in Yellow and Blue* (1929) and *Red, Yellow, and Blue Composition* (1930).

Rembrandt Harmenszoon van Rijn (1606–69). A master of the Dutch school, he produced some 600 paintings distinguished by their profound humanity, including *The Anatomy Lesson of Dr. Tulp* (1632), *The Blinding of Samson* (1636), and *The Night Watch* (1642). Rembrandt also painted nearly 100 self-portraits, dating from the 1620s to his last years.

Van Gogh, Vincent (1853–90). One of the most influential nineteenth-century artists. Many of Van Gogh's vibrant, expressive paintings were produced in a 29-month period preceding his suicide. Among his most famous works are *The Potato Eaters* (1885), *The Night Café* (1888), *Starry Night* (1889), and a number of self-portraits.

Vermeer, Jan (Johannes) (1632–75). Vermeer mainly painted intimate interiors, often with solitary figures, depicting them with clarity and luminous, subtle colors. His work includes *Head of a Girl* (c. 1665), *Woman Weighing Pearls* (c. 1665), and *The Letter* (1666).

Flemish, Belgian

Bruegel, Pieter, the Elder (c. 1525–69). Flemish painter of peasants at work and play, genre scenes, landscapes, and illustrations of proverbs. His paintings include *The Corn Harvest* (1565) and *The Peasant Wedding* (c. 1567).

Ensor, James (Baron) (1860–1949). Belgian painter and etcher. Ensor created innovative and grotesque compositions, such as *The Temptation of St. Anthony* (1887) and *The Entry of Christ into Brussels* (1888), opening the way for the surrealist movement.

Limbourg, Herman, Jean, and **Pol** (active 1380–1416). Flemish brothers who worked in France for the Duke of Berry. Their *Les Très Riches Heures du Duc de Berry* (1413–16) is an exquisite, colorful, illuminated manuscript, showing activities of daily life.

Magritte, René (1898–1967). A leading Belgian surrealist painter. His works, such as *The Key of Dreams* (1930) and *The Human Condition* (1934), are odd fantasies based on everyday situations, or plays on relationships between pictures and words.

Rubens, Peter Paul (1577–1640). A foremost Flemish artist and a major baroque figure. Working with great freedom and vitality, Rubens produced dynamic, monumental paintings. His works include *The Raising of the Cross* (1610–11), a series of allegorical paintings on the life of Marie de Médici (1622–25), and *The Judgment of Paris* (1638–39).

Van der Weyden, Rogier (c. 1400–64). Flemish painter. His religious works, such as *The Descent from the Cross* (1435) and *The Last Judgment* (c. 1450), combine monumentality with a profound sense of emotion. His penetrating portraits include *Francesco d'Este* (c. 1455).

Van Dyck, Sir Anthony (1599–1641). A major Flemish baroque artist. Van Dyck's many portraits of the aristocracy include a number of Charles I of England, his royal patron from 1632 on, such as *Portrait of Charles I Hunting* (c. 1635). He also painted religious works, such as the *Lamentation* (1635).

Van Eyck, Jan (c. 1390–1441). A master of Flemish painting. In works such as the church altarpiece in Ghent (1426–32) and the *Arnolfini Wedding Portrait* (1434), Van Eyck achieved an unprecedented luminosity, intensity of color, and detail.

French

Arp, Jean (Hans) (1887–1966). Creator of abstract paintings, sculptures, and collages using organic forms, such as *Squares Arranged According to the Laws of Chance* (1916–17) and *Navel, Shirt, and Head* (1926). Arp was associated with dadaism and surrealism.

Bonnard, Pierre (1867–1947). A founder of the Nabis, Bonnard was a painter, lithographer, and illustrator. He excelled at domestic interiors with subtle lighting effects. His work includes *Bowl of Fruit* (1933).

Braque, Georges (1882–1963). A figure in fauvism and, with Picasso, a founder of cubism. His works include the *Large Nude* (1907–08) and *Woman with a Mandolin* (1937).

Cézanne, Paul (1839–1906). Postimpressionist painter. His works include *The Card Players* (1890–92), *Bathers* (1898–1905), and a series of increasingly abstracted, geometric landscapes of Mont Sainte-Victoire. Cézanne had a profound influence on modern art, especially cubism.

Chardin, Jean-Baptiste-Siméon (1699–1779). Painter of genre scenes and still lifes in a subtle, delicate, unsentimental style. His works include *Return from Market* (1739) and *Saying Grace* (c. 1740).

Corot, Jean-Baptiste Camille. Influential landscape painter whose delicately lit, carefully observed works include *View of the Forest of Fontainebleau* (1831) and *View of Avray* (c. 1840).

Courbet, Gustave (1819–77). The foremost realist painter, Courbet was a revolutionary at odds with political authority and visual idealization. His works include *The Stone Breakers* (1849) and *The Artist's Studio* (1854–55).

Daumier, Honoré (1808–79). Painter, lithographer, and sculptor. A great social satirist, Daumier produced some 4,000 lithographs, such as *Rue Transnonain, 14 April, 1834* (1834), and *The Legislative Belly*.

David, Jacques-Louis (1748–1825). The leading neoclassical painter. David's work reflects his passion for the ideas of the French Revolution and for classical art. His paintings include *The Oath of the Horatii* (1784) and *The Death of Marat* (1793).

Degas, Edgar (1834–1917). Painter and sculptor; he exhibited with the impressionists, although his approach differed from theirs. His paintings, such as *The Bellini Family* (1858–59) and *The Glass of Absinthe* (1876), often use daring spatial innovations.

Delacroix, Eugène (1798–1863). Foremost French romantic painter. His exuberant, freely painted, and richly colored works include *The Death of Sardanapalus* (1827) and *Liberty Leading the People* (1830).

Dubuffet, Jean (1901–85). Painter and sculptor of semiabstract, primitive works. He often used mixed media such as asphalt, pebbles, and glass to enrich his paintings' surface. His works include the *Topographies* and *Texturologies* series (1957–59).

Duchamp, Marcel (1887–1968). Painter and sculptor; he created cubist works and also cofounded dadaism. His "ready-mades" are everyday objects exhibited as art. His works include the painting *Nude Descending a Staircase* (1912), the ready-made *Fountain* (1917), and the construction *The Bride Stripped Bare by Her Bachelors, Even* (1915–23).

Dufy, Raoul (1877–1953). Painter, illustrator, and decorator known for his fauvist landscapes, seascapes, and portraits of society, including *Riders in the Wood* (1931) and *Cowes Regatta* (1934).

Fragonard, Jean-Honoré (1732–1806). Rococo painter of playful, erotic scenes, done in delicate colors and free brushwork. His works include *The Swing* (1769) and four *Progress of Love* paintings (1771–73).

Gauguin, Paul (1848–1903). Postimpressionist painter. At age 35, he left his career and family to devote himself to painting; he developed a style called synthetism. His best-known works, using flat planes, solid figures, and bright colors, were done in Tahiti and include *Nevermore* (1897) and *Where Do We Come From? What Are We? Where Are We Going?* (1897).

Géricault, Théodore (Jean Louis André Théodore) (1791–1824). A founder of romanticism. His works, based on contemporary events, were done in a powerful, spontaneous style. They include *A Cavalry Officer* (1812) and *The Raft of the Medusa* (1819).

Ingres, Jean-Auguste Dominique (1780–1867). A leading neoclassic painter, Ingres was also deeply influenced by Raphael. His works, including *La Grande Odalisque* (1814), *La Comtesse* *d'Haussonville* (1845), and *The Turkish Bath* (1859–62), are both rigidly academic and richly sensual.

Léger, Fernand (1881–1955). He created a distinctive style, characterized by flat planes of color and simplified forms based on the surfaces of machines. His paintings include *The City* (1919) and *Le Grand Déjeuner* (1921).

Lorrain, Claude (Claude Gellée, called Claude) (1600–82). In his influential landscape paintings, such as *The Embarkation of the Queen of Sheba* (1648) and *The Expulsion of Hagar* (1668), he depicted atmospheric and lighting variations in a lyrical, sensitive style.

Maillol, Aristide (1861–1944). Sculptor, painter, and woodcut artist. His best-known works are his calm, monumental female nudes, such as *The Mediterranean* (c. 1901).

Manet, Édouard (1832–83). He introduced extraordinary thematic and technical innovations. His *Luncheon on the Grass* and *Olympia* (both 1863), both paintings of contemporary women, nude and unidealized, shocked viewers of the time. His works also include *A Bar at the Folies-Bergères* (1881).

Matisse, Henri (1869–1954). Painter, sculptor, and lithographer. Matisse, a leader of the Fauves, was a master of vivid color and line used in decorative, sensual patterns. His paintings include *La Joie de Vivre* (1905–06) and *The Dance* (1910).

Millet, Jean-François (1814–75). Realist painter associated with the Barbizon School. His unidealized scenes of peasant life include *The Sower* (1850) and *The Angelus* (1855–57).

Monet, Claude (1840–1926). A founder of impressionism and a major landscape painter. His works include many series of the same subject seen under different atmospheric and lighting conditions, such as haystacks (1891), the Rouen Cathedral (1892–94), and water lilies (1899–1926).

Morisot, Berthe (1841–95). The first woman to join the impressionists. Morisot's paintings have a delicate, luminous style and smooth brushwork. Her works include *The Cradle* (1873) and *Young Woman at the Dance* (1880).

Pissarro, Camille (1830–1903), b. Virgin Islands. Impressionist painter; he was also influenced by pointillism. His works include *Red Roofs* (1877) and *The Boulevard Montmartre at Night* (1897).

Poussin, Nicolas (1594–1665). Painter who developed the standard for French classical art, though he spent most of his life in Italy. His contemplative, precise works include *The Rape of the Sabine Women* (1636–37) and *The Holy Family on the Steps* (1648).

Renoir, Pierre Auguste (1841–1919). Impressionist painter of sensuous, joyous, light-filled works, such as *Moulin de la Galette* (1876), *The Bathers* (1884–87), and *Luncheon of the Boating Party* (1881).

Rodin, Auguste (1840–1917). Sculptor of unusual power and expression. Many of his most famous works, such as *The Thinker* (1879–1900) and *The Kiss* (1886–98), are enlarged figures from his great unfinished *Gates of Hell* (begun 1880). Other well-known works include *The Burghers of Calais* (1884–86) and *Balzac* (1892–97).

Rouault, Georges (1871–1958). Expressionist; also associated with the Fauves. His subjects, in paintings such as *Little Olympia* (1906), *Three Judges* (1913), and *Christ Mocked* (1932), were prostitutes, corrupt judges, and Christ.

Rousseau, Henri (1844–1910). Self-taught painter of naive, stylized, colorful works, often of jungle scenes, including *Sleeping Gypsy* (1897) and *The Dream* (1910).

Rousseau, Théodore (1812–67). A leading figure of the Barbizon School. His landscapes, such as *Descent of the Cattle* (1835), are full of gravity and intensity.

Seurat, Georges (1859–91). Painter who developed the pointillist or neoimpressionist technique of using small dots of pure color. His works include *Bathing at Asnières* (1883–84) and *A Sunday Afternoon on the Island of La Grande Jatte* (1885–86).

Toulouse-Lautrec, Henri de (1864–1901). Painter and lithographer. He depicted music halls, cabarets, and brothels in an unidealized, vivid way, as in *At the Moulin de la Galette* (1892) and *In the Parlor at the Rue des Moulins* (1894).

Vuillard, Édouard (1868–1940). Painter, lithographer, and member of the Nabis, known for his intimate interiors and interest in flat patterns, as in *Mother and Sister of the Artist* (c. 1893) and *Sitting Room with Three Lamps* (1899).

Watteau, Jean-Antoine (1684–1721). Rococo painter. In works such as *A Pilgrimage to Cythera* (1717) and *La Toilette* (1720), he depicted delicate, sensuous scenes in an exquisitely colored, lyrical manner.

German

Beckmann, Max (1884–1950). Expressionist painter. His highly personal style reflected the misery of contemporary events in Germany. His works include *The Night* (1918–19), and a series of nine triptychs, including *Departure* (1932–35).

Dürer, Albrecht (1471–1528). Painter, engraver, and most influential artist of the German school. Durer is known for his technical mastery and his adoption of the principles of the Italian Renaissance. His works include the *Apocalypse* woodcuts (1498), the engraving *St. Jerome in His Study* (1514), and the painting *Four Apostles* (1526).

Ernst, Max (1891–1976). A founder of dadaism and surrealism. His grotesque, sometimes whimsical paintings include *Two Children Are Threatened by a Nightingale* (1924) and *The Temptation of St. Anthony* (1945).

Grosz, George (1893–1959). Painter known for his savage caricatures of post–World War I bourgeois society, such as *The Suicide* (1916) and *Eclipse of the Sun* (1926). He left Germany for the United States in 1933.

Grünewald, Mathias (Mathis Gothardt Neithardt) (c. 1475–1528). Religious painter of unusually expressive works, most frequently of the crucifixion of Christ. His masterpiece is the Isenheim altarpiece (1515).

Holbein, Hans, the Younger (c. 1497–1543). Outstanding portrait and religious painter of the Northern Renaissance. His works include *Sir Thomas More* (1527) and the *Madonna of the Burgomeister Meyer* (c. 1528).

Kollwitz, Käthe Schmidt (1867–1945). Graphic artist and sculptor whose works reflect her socialist and pacifist views. They include the etching series *Peasants' War* (1902–08) and the lithography series *The War* (1923) and *Death* (1934–35).

Italian

Angelico, Fra (Guido or **Guidolino di Pietro**, also known as **Giovanni da Fiesole)** (c. 1400–55). Religious painter of great expressiveness; a master of graceful line and color. His works include the frescoes for San Marco in Florence, including *The Annunciation* (c. 1447), and scenes from the lives of saints Stephen and Lawrence in the Vatican (c. 1447–49).

Bellini, family of Renaissance painters. **Jacopo** (c. 1400–70) ran a workshop in Venice with his sons **Gentile** (1429–1507) and **Giovanni** (c. 1430–1516). Jacopo's work includes *The Madonna and Child with Lionello d'Este* (c. 1441). Gentile excelled at depicting contemporary Venetian ceremonies, as in *The Procession in the Piazza San Marco* (1496). Giovanni, probably the most talented, produced expressive works such as *St. Francis in Ecstasy* (c. 1475) and the San Zaccaria altarpiece (1505).

Bernini, Giovanni Lorenzo (Gianlorenzo) (1598–1680). Sculptor, architect, painter, and leading baroque artist. His dramatic, masterful sculptures include *David* (1623) and *The Ecstasy of St. Theresa* (1645–52). Among his paintings is *Saints Andrew and Thomas* (1627).

Boccioni, Umberto (1882–1916). Painter, sculptor, and major figure of futurist art. His works include the painting *The City Rises* (1910) and the sculpture *Unique Forms of Continuity in Space* (1913).

Botticelli, Sandro (Alessandro di Mariano Filipepi) (c. 1444–1510). A favorite of the Medici, this Renaissance painter was a supreme colorist and master of the rhythmic line. He is known for his mythological scenes, such as *Primavera* (c. 1478) and *The Birth of Venus* (c. 1482). His religious works include *Madonna of the Magnificat* (c. 1485).

Canova, Antonio (1757–1822). Neoclassical sculptor. His graceful, polished works include the tomb of Pope Clement XIV (1783–87) and *Pauline Borghese as Venus* (1805–07).

Caravaggio, Michelangelo Merisi da (c. 1573–1610). An influential painter whose bold works are masterpieces of dramatic light and shadow featuring figures with strong physical presence. They include *The Calling of St. Matthew* (c. 1598) and *The Conversion of St. Paul* (1600–01).

Carracci, family of painters. The brothers **Annibale** (1560–1609) and **Agostino** (1557–1602) and their cousin **Ludovico** (1555–1619) established an important academy of painting in Bologna. Annibale, the most talented, and Agostino painted richly sculptural, decorative frescoes for the Farnese Palace in Rome (1597–1600). Annibale also did landscape paintings, such as *Landscape with the Flight into Egypt* (1604).

Cellini, Benvenuto (1500–71). Sculptor, metalsmith, and author. His works include the gold and enamel saltcellar of Francis I (1540) and his masterpiece, the Mannerist *Perseus with the Head of Medusa* (1545–54).

Chirico, Giorgio de (1888–1978), b. Greece. Forerunner of surrealism. His best-known paintings are characterized by deep perspective, solitary figures, and objects used out of context. They include *Mystery and Melancholy of a Street* (1914) and *Disquieting Muses* (1916–17).

Correggio (Antonio Allegri) (c. 1494–1534). He painted graceful, delicately lit works, especially on mythological themes, such as *Jupiter and Io* (c. 1530), and illusionistic ceiling frescoes, such as *The Assumption of the Virgin* for the cathedral in Parma (1526–30).

da Vinci, Leonardo. *See* **Leonardo da Vinci**.

della Robbia, Florentine family of sculptors and ceramicists known for their enameled terracotta. **Luca** (c. 1400–82) founded a workshop; his works include *The Resurrection* and *The Ascension* (both late 1440s), for the Florence Cathedral. His nephew **Andrea** (1435–1525), best known for his medallions for the Foundling Hospital in Florence, continued the workshop with his sons, **Luca II, Giovanni,** and **Girolamo**.

Donatello (Donato di Niccolo di Betto Bardi) (c. 1386–1466). An innovative Renaissance artist, he developed a technique of shallow relief, *schiacciato*. Donatello's powerful and expressive sculptures include *David* (c. 1408), *St. George* (c. 1415), and *Mary Magdelene* (c. 1456).

Ghiberti, Lorenzo   (1378–1455). Major early Renaissance sculptor. His two pairs of bronze doors for the Florence Baptistery, with their finely modeled scenes, are his masterpieces (1403–24 and 1425–52). His life-size bronzes include *St. John the Baptist* (1412–16) and *St. Matthew* (1419).

Giorgione (Giorgione da Castelfranco)   (c. 1476–1510). His poetic and warmly colored works had a major influence on Venetian painting. They include *The Tempest* (c. 1500–10), *The Three Philosophers* (c. 1505–10), and *Sleeping Venus*, which was completed by Titian (c. 1510).

Giotto (Giotto di Bondone)   (c. 1266–1337). Most important early Italian painter. His monumental figures and realistic treatment of pictorial space were major innovations. His works include the *Ognissanti Madonna* (c. 1310), frescoes in the Arena Chapel, Padua (finished 1313), and frescoes in the Bardi and Peruzzi chapels, Santa Croce, Florence (1320s).

Leonardo da Vinci   (1425–1519). Painter, sculptor, architect, engineer, and scientist. His balanced, beautifully painted designs embody the High Renaissance; his studies of perspective and anatomy were also highly influential. His paintings include *The Virgin of the Rocks* (1483–85), *The Last Supper* (1495–98), and the *Mona Lisa* (1503–06).

Lippi,   family of Florentine painters. **Fra Filippo** (c. 1406–69) was a foremost early Renaissance artist whose works include *The Coronation of the Virgin* (1441) and the frescoes for the Prato cathedral (1452–65). His son, **Filippino** (c. 1457–1504), painted a fresco cycle for the Strozzi Chapel, Santa Maria Novella, Florence (1495–1502).

Mantegna, Andrea   (1431–1506). Early Renaissance painter and engraver. His works show monumental forms and an interest in perspective. They include frescoes for the Ovetari Chapel, Church of the Eremitani, Padua (1448–57), and the San Zeno altarpiece (1456–59).

Michelangelo Buonarroti   (1475–1564). Sculptor, painter, architect, poet. The influence of this foremost Renaissance figure on Western art was supreme. His works, all in a heroic style, include the sculptures *Pietà* (1499), *David* (1501–04), *Moses* (1513–16), and the tombs of Lorenzo and Giuliano de Medici (1519–34); the *Sistine Chapel*'s ceiling (1508–12) and its *Last Judgment* fresco (1534–41).

Modigliani, Amedeo   (1884–1920). Painter and sculptor. His style is characterized by an elongated, smooth line. Most of his works are portraits and female nudes, such as the paintings *Jeanne Hébuterne* (1919) and *Reclining Nude* (1919).

Piero della Francesca   (c. 1420–92). Major Renaissance painter. His works are characterized by strong symmetricality and angularity and an interest in precise ratios of perspective. They include frescoes of *The Legend of the True Cross* in the Church of San Francesco, Arezzo (1452–64), and *The Flagellation of Christ* (c. 1456).

Pisano,   family of sculptors. **Nicola** (c. 1220–1284) worked in an elaborate, architectural style; his works include pulpits for the Pisa Baptistery (finished 1260) and Siena Cathedral (1265–68). His son, **Giovanni** (c. 1250–1314), created the decorative facade, Siena Cathedral (1284–96), and the pulpit, Pisa Cathedral (1302–10).

Raphael (Santi or **Sanzio)**   (1483–1520). His exquisitely balanced paintings epitomize the High Renaissance. They include frescoes for the Vatican's Stanza della Segnatura, including *The School of Athens* (finished 1511); *Calatea* (c. 1512) and *The Sistine Madonna* (1512).

Tintoretto (Jacopo Robusti)   (1518–94). A great Venetian mannerist who employed dramatic lighting, coloring, and foreshortening. His paintings include a cycle in the Scuola di San Rocco, Venice, including an enormous *Crucifixion* (1564–87), and *The Last Supper* (1592–94).

Titian (Tiziano Vecellio) (c. 1490–1576). High Renaissance painter whose innovations, especially his expressive use of color, were influential. His works include *The Assumption of the Virgin* (1516–18), *Pope Paul III and His Grandsons* (1546), and the *Pietà* (1576).

Uccello, Paolo (c. 1396–1475). Florentine painter; early master of perspective. His colorful, decorative works, including three panels of *The Battle of San Romano* (c. 1455) and a cycle of frescoes for Santa Maria Novella, Florence (c. 1445), are notable for their foreshortening.

Veronese, Paolo (Paolo Caliari) (1528–88). Venetian painter whose large works depicting scenes of sumptuous ceremonies are distinguished by opulent colors. They include *The Marriage at Cana* (1562), *The Feast in the House of Levi* (1573), and decorative paintings for the Ducal Palace, Venice (1577–82).

Verrocchio, Andrea del (Andrea di Michele di Francesco di Cioni) (1435–88). Leading early Renaissance sculptor and painter. His sculptures include *The Doubting of Thomas* (1465); among his paintings is *The Baptism of Christ* (1472), in which he was assisted by his pupil, Leonardo da Vinci.

Mexican

Kahlo, Frida (1907–54). Painter of vivid works, especially self-portraits, conveying intense psychic and physical pain. They include *Frida and Diego Rivera* (1931) and *The Love Embrace of the Universe, the Earth (Mexico), Diego, Me and Señor Xolotl* (1949).

Orozco, José Clemente (1883–1949). Muralist whose monumental scenes contain humanitarian symbolism. His murals are in the New School for Social Research, New York City (1931), and Dartmouth College, New Hampshire (1932–34).

Rivera, Diego (1886–1957). A founder of the Mexican mural Renaissance. His works pay homage to Mexico's history and workers. They include *The History of Mexico*, National Palace of Mexico City (1929–36), and a series at the Detroit Institute of Arts (1933).

Siqueiros, David Alfaro (1896–1974). One of the three great Mexican muralists. His dynamic brushwork reflects revolutionary themes. Siqueiros's murals include a series at the Plaza Art Center, Los Angeles (1932) and *The Liberation of Chile* at the Mexican School, Chillán, Chile (1942).

Tamayo, Rufino (1899–1991). A leading Mexican painter; his decorative works are influenced by cubism, fauvism, and themes from Mexican folklore. They include *Sleeping Musicians* (1950) and a series of murals at Smith College, Massachusetts (1943).

Spanish

Dalí, Salvador (1904–89). Surrealist painter who worked in a precise style. His hallucinatory images can be seen in *The Persistence of Memory* (1931), *Crucifixion* (1951), and *The Last Supper* (1955).

El Greco. *See* Greco, El.

Goya y Lucientes, Francisco Jose de (1746–1828). Highly original painter and graphic artist; his expressive works are often telling social satires. They include the paintings *Nude Maja* and *Clothed Maja* (both c. 1804), and *Charles IV and His Family* (1800); and etching series, such as *Los Caprichos* (1799) and *Disasters of War* (1810–14).

Greco, El (Domenikos Theotokopoulos) (1541–1614), b. Crete. Painter of dynamic scenes, often of religious ecstasy. His works, distinguished by elongated figures and vivid highlights, include *The Disrobing of Christ* (1577–79), *The Burial of Count Orgaz* (1586), and *View of Toledo* (1600).

Gris, Juan (José Victoriano González) (1887–1927). A developer of synthetic cubism, he used simple forms and a rhythmic style in his paintings and collages. His works include *Homage to Picasso* (1911–12), *The Violin* (1916), and *Violin and Fruit Dish* (1924).

Miró, Joan (1893–1983). Surrealist painter; he worked in a playful, lyrical style, with colorful, amoebic shapes. His works include *Harlequin's Carnival* (1924–25), *Dog Barking at the Moon* (1926), and ceramic murals for the UNESCO building, Paris (1955–58).

Murillo, Bartolemé Estéban (1618–82). Religious and portrait painter. Among his important works are a series for the Charity Hospital in Seville (1671–73) and many depictions of the Immaculate Conception and portraits.

Picasso, Pablo (Pablo Ruiz y Picasso) (1881–1973). Painter, sculptor, graphic artist, ceramicist; an enormously versatile, original, and prolific artist. His *Les Desmoiselles d'Avignon* (1907) is a seminal cubist work. Other important paintings include *The Three Musicians* (1921) and *Guernica* (1937).

Ribera, Jusepe de (1591–1652). Baroque painter, mainly of religious scenes. His naturalistic yet mystical works include *The Martyrdom of St. Bartholomew* (c. 1630) and *The Mystic Marriage of St. Catherine* (1648).

Velázquez, Diego Rodríguez de Silva y (1599–1660). One of the greatest of Spanish painters. He is a master of shimmering tones and brilliant colors. His expressive works include *The Surrender of Breda* (1634–35), *Pope Innocent X* (1650), and *The Maids of Honor* (1656).

Zurbarán, Francisco de (1598–1664). Baroque painter. His works, mostly religious, combine severity with spiritual intensity. They include *The Apotheosis of St. Thomas Aquinas* (1631) and *St. Serapion* (1628).

Other

Brancusi, Constantin (1876–1957). Romanian sculptor whose economical, simple style was radically innovative. His works include *Bird in Space* (1919) and the immense *Endless Column*, erected in a park near his birthplace (1937).

Chagall, Marc (1887–1985). Russian painter who lived mainly in France. His poetic, colorful, and symbolic works are often based on Jewish folklore. They include *I and the Village* (1911), *Self-Portrait with Seven Fingers* (1911), and murals for the Metropolitan Opera House, New York City (installed 1966).

Gabo, Naum (Naum Neemia Pevsner) (1890–1977). Russian constructivist sculptor and theorist. His works include *Column* (1923) and *Kinetic Construction* (1920), a sculptor with a motor. In his *Realist Manifesto* he proposed that concepts of time and space be included in art.

Giacometti, Alberto (1901–66). Swiss sculptor and painter, known especially for his sculptures of elongated figures, such as *The Forest* (1950) and *Walking Man* (1960).

Kandinsky, Wassily (1866–1944). Russian painter, a founder of the avant-garde *Blaue Reiter* group and a teacher at the Bauhaus. His series of *Compositions, Improvisations,* and *Impressions,* beginning in 1910, are often seen as the first purely abstract works.

Klee, Paul (1879–1940). Swiss painter whose works, such as *Twittering Machine* (1922) and *Park Near L(ucerne)* (1938), combine theories of abstraction with playful childlike inventiveness. Klee was associated with the *Blaue Reiter* group.

Klimt, Gustav (1862–1918). Austrian painter; a founder of the Vienna Secession group and a figure of the art nouveau movement. His exotic, erotic, symbolic works include *Judith* (1909) and *The Kiss* (1907–08).

Kokoschka, Oskar (1886–1980). Austrian expressionist painter. He produced many portraits and landscapes, such as *Le Marquis de Montesquiou* (1909–10) and *Jerusalem* (1929–30), as well as a series of self-portraits.

Malevich, Kasimir Severinovich (1878–1935). Russian painter, founder of suprematism. He is known for his sparse geometric paintings, including *Black Square* (1915) and the *White on White* series (c. 1918). He described his theories in the book *The Non-Objective World* (1915).

Munch, Edvard (1863–1944). Leading Norwegian painter and graphic artist. He foreshadowed expressionism with his charged images of terror, despair, and isolation, as in the paintings *The Scream* (1893) and *Vampire* (1895).

Phidias (Pheidias) (c. 500–432 B.C.). One of the greatest of ancient Greek sculptors, although none of his original works survive. He sculpted the enormous *Athena Parthenos*, Athens (c. 447–439 B.C.), and the *Zeus*, Olympia, one of the Seven Wonders of the Ancient World (c. 435 B.C.).

Praxiteles (c. 370–330 B.C.). He was considered the greatest Greek sculptor of his time. His *Hermes with the Infant Dionysus* (c. 350–330 B.C.) is the only existing original work by an ancient master. He also sculpted the *Aphrodite of Cnidus* (c. 350–330 B.C.).

Schiele, Egon (1890–1918). Austrian expressionist painter and graphic artist who developed an angular, linear style. Many of his works are nudes, often in disturbing, erotic poses. His paintings include *The Embrace* (1917) and *Paris von Gütersloh* (1918).

Tatlin, Vladimir Evgrafovich (1885–1953). Russian artist, a founder of constructivism. His works include the *Relief Constructions* series (begun 1913) and the *Corner Reliefs* (begun 1915).

Art Terms

acrylic Water-soluble paint made from pigments and a plastic binder.

aquatint An etching technique in which a solution of asphalt or resin is used on the plate. It produces prints with rich, gray tones.

caricature An artwork humorously exaggerating the qualities, defects, or peculiarities of a person or idea.

cartoon A humorous sketch or drawing usually telling a story or caricaturing some person or action. In fine arts, a preparatory sketch or design for a picture or ornamental motif to be transferred to a fresco or tapestry.

carving In sculpture, the cutting of a form from a solid, hard material such as stone or wood, in contrast to the technique of modeling.

casting In sculpture, a technique of reproducing a work by pouring into a mold a substance such as plaster or molten metal, which then hardens.

chiaroscuro The rendering of light and shade in painting; the subtle gradations and marked variations of light and shade for dramatic effect.

collage A composition made of cut and pasted pieces of materials, sometimes with images added by the artist.

colors, complementary Two colors at opposite points on the color scale, for example, orange and blue, green and red.

colors, primary Red, yellow, and blue, the mixture of which will yield all other colors in the spectrum but which themselves cannot be produced through a mixture of other colors.

colors, secondary Orange, green, and purple, colors produced by mixing two primary colors.

composition The organization of forms and colors within an artwork.

drypoint A technique of engraving, using a sharp-pointed needle, that produces a furrowed edge resulting in a print with soft, velvety lines.

encaustic Painting technique using pigments dissolved in hot wax.

engraving The art of producing printed designs through various methods of incising on wood or metal blocks, which are then inked and printed.

etching The technique of producing printed designs through incising onto a coated metal plate, which is then bathed in corrosive acid, inked, and printed.

figure A representation of a human or an animal form.

foreshortening Reducing or distorting in order to represent three-dimensional space as perceived by the eye, according to the rules of perspective.

fresco Meaning "fresh" in Italian. The technique of painting on moist lime plaster with colors ground in water.

frieze A band of painted or sculpted decoration, often at the top of a wall.

genre painting A realistic style of painting in which everyday life forms the subject matter, as distinguished from religious or historical painting.

gesso Ground chalk or plaster mixed with glue, used as a base coat for tempera and oil painting.

gouache A method of watercolor painting, but prepared with a more gluey base, producing a less transparent effect.

highlight On a represented form, a point of most intense light.

impasto Paint applied very thickly. It often projects from the picture surface.

landscape Painting in which natural scenery is the subject.

lithography A printing process in which ink impressions are taken from a flat stone or metal plate prepared with a greasy substance, such as an oily crayon.

modeling In sculpture, the building up of form using a soft medium such as clay or wax, as distinguished from carving. In painting and drawing, using color and lighting variations to produce a three-dimensional effect.

monochrome A painting or drawing executed in a single color.

monotype A single print made from a metal or glass plate on which an image has been represented in paint, ink, etc.

mural A large painting or decoration done on a wall.

oil A method of painting with pigments mixed with oil. It can produce a vast range of effects of light and color.

palette A flat board used by a painter to mix and hold colors, traditionally oblong, with a hole for the thumb; also, a range of colors used by a particular painter.

pastel A soft, subdued color; a drawing stick made of ground pigments, chalk, and gum water.

perspective A method of representing three-dimensional volumes and spatial relationships on a flat surface to produce an effect similar to what is seen by the eye.

polychrome Of many or various colors.

polyptych In painting, a work made of several panels or scenes joined together. A diptych has two panels; a triptych, three.

primary colors *See* **colors, primary**.

relief In sculpture, the projection of an image or form from its background. Sculpture formed in this manner is described as high relief or low relief (bas-relief), depending on the degree of projection. In painting or drawing, the apparent projection of parts conveying the illusion of three dimensions.

secondary colors *See* **colors, secondary**.

stenciling A method of producing images or letters from sheets of cardboard, metal, or other materials from which forms have been cut away.

still life The representation of inanimate objects in painting, drawing, or photography.

tempera A painting technique using pigments mixed with egg yolk and water. It produces clear, pure colors.

texture The visual and tactile quality of a work of art based on the particular way the materials are handled; also, the distribution of tones or shades of a single color.

tone The effect of the harmony of color and values in a work.

trompe l'oeil Meaning "fool the eye" in French. In painting, the fine, detailed rendering of objects to convey the illusion that the painted forms are real and three-dimensional.

values In painting, the degree of lightness or darkness in a color.

wash In painting, a thin layer of translucent color.

watercolor Painting in pigments suspended in water. It can produce brilliant colors and effects of transparency.

woodcut A print made by carving on a wood block, which is then inked and printed.

Art Movements and Periods

abstract expressionism Movement in painting, originating in New York City in the 1940s. It emphasized spontaneous personal expression, freedom from accepted artistic values, surface qualities of paint, and the act of painting itself. Pollock, de Kooning, Motherwell, and Kline, are important abstract expressionists.

art deco Design style prevalent during the 1920s and 1930s, characterized by a sleek use of straight lines and slender forms.

art nouveau A decorative art movement that emerged in the late nineteenth century. Characterized by dense asymmetrical ornamentation in sinuous forms, it is often symbolic and of an erotic nature. Klimt worked in an art nouveau style.

Ash Can School   Group of American artists active from 1908 to 1918. It included members of The Eight such as Henri and Davies; Hopper was also part of the Ash Can group. Their work featured scenes of urban realism.

Barbizon School   An association of French landscape painters, c. 1840–70, who lived in the village of Barbizon and who painted directly from nature. Théodore Rousseau was a leader; Corot and Millet were also associated with the group.

baroque   A movement in European painting in the seventeenth and early eighteenth centuries, characterized by violent movement, strong emotion, and dramatic lighting and coloring. Bernini, Caravaggio, and Rubens were among important baroque artists.

Byzantine   A style of the Byzantine Empire and its provinces, c. 330–1450. Appearing mostly in religious mosaics, manuscript illuminations, and panel paintings, it is characterized by rigid, monumental, stylized forms with gold backgrounds.

classicism   Referring to the principles of Greek and Roman art of antiquity with its emphasis on harmony, proportion, balance, and simplicity. In a general sense, it refers to art based on accepted standards of beauty.

color field painting   A technique in abstract painting developed in the 1950s. It focuses on the lyrical effects of large areas of color, often poured or stained onto the canvas. Newman, Rothko, and Frankenthaler painted in this manner.

conceptual art   A movement of the 1960s and 1970s that emphasized the artistic idea over the art object. It attempted to free art from the confines of the gallery and the pedestal.

constructivism   A Russian abstract movement founded by Tatlin, Gabo, and Antoine Pevsner, c. 1915. It focused on art for the industrial age. Tatlin believed in art with a utilitarian purpose.

cubism   A revolutionary movement begun by Picasso and Braque in the early twentieth century. It employs an analytic vision based on fragmentation and multiple viewpoints.

dadaism   A movement, c. 1915–23, that rejected accepted aesthetic standards. It aimed to create antiart and nonart, often employing a sense of the absurd.

The Eight   A group of American painters who united out of opposition to academic standards in the early twentieth century. Members of the group were Robert Henri, Arthur Davies, Maurice Prendergast, William James Glackens, Ernest Lawson, Everett Shinn, John Sloan, and George Luks.

expressionism   Refers to art that uses emphasis and distortion to communicate emotion. More specifically, it refers to early twentieth-century northern European art, especially in Germany c. 1905–25. Artists such as Rouault, Kokoschka, and Schiele painted in this manner.

fauvism   From the French word *fauve*, meaning "wild beast." A style adopted by artists associated with Matisse, c. 1905–08. They painted in a spontaneous manner, using bold colors.

folk art   Works of a culturally homogeneous people without formal training, generally according to regional traditions and involving crafts.

futurism   An Italian movement c. 1909–19. It attempted to integrate the dynamism of the machine age into art. Boccioni was a futurist artist.

Gothic   A European movement beginning in France. Gothic sculpture emerged c. 1200, Gothic painting later in the thirteenth century. The artworks are characterized by a linear, graceful, elegant style more naturalistic than that which had existed previously in Europe.

impressionism   A late-nineteenth-century French school of painting. It focused on transitory visual impressions, often painted directly from nature, with an emphasis on the changing effects of light and color. Monet, Renoir, and Pissarro were important impressionists.

mannerism A style, c. 1520–1600, that arose in reaction to the harmony and proportion of the High Renaissance. It featured elongated, contorted poses, crowded canvases, and harsh lighting and coloring.

minimalism A movement in American painting and sculpture that originated in the late 1950s. It emphasized pure, reduced forms and strict, systematic compositions.

Nabis From the Hebrew word for "prophet." A group of French painters active in the 1890s who worked in a subjective, sometimes mystical style, stressing flat areas of color and pattern. Bonnard and Vuillard were members.

naive art Artwork, usually paintings, characterized by a simplified style, nonscientific perspective, and bold colors. The artists are generally not professionally trained. Henri Rousseau and Grandma Moses worked in this style.

neoclassicism A European style of the late eighteenth and early nineteenth centuries. Its elegant, balanced works revived the order and harmony of ancient Greek and Roman art. David and Canova are examples of neoclassicists.

op art An abstract movement in Europe and the United States, begun in the mid-1950s, based on the effects of optical patterns. Albers worked in this style.

photorealism A figurative movement that emerged in the United States and Britain in the late 1960s and 1970s. The subject matter, usually everyday scenes, is portrayed in an extremely detailed, exacting style. It is also called superrealism, especially when referring to sculpture.

pointillism A method of painting developed by Seurat and Paul Signac in the 1880s. It used dabs of pure color that were intended to mix in the eyes of viewers rather than on the canvas. It is also called divisionism or neoimpressionism.

pop art A movement that began in Britain and the United States in the 1950s. It used the images and techniques of mass media, advertising, and popular culture, often in an ironic way. Works of Warhol, Lichtenstein, and Oldenburg exemplify this style.

postimpressionism A term coined by British art critic Roger Fry to refer to a group of nineteenth-century painters, including Cézanne, Van Gogh, and Gauguin, who were dissatisfied with the limitations of impressionism. It has since been used to refer to various reactions against impressionism, such as fauvism and expressionism.

Pre-Raphaelite Brotherhood A group of English painters formed in 1848. These artists attempted to recapture the style of painting preceding Raphael. They rejected industrialized England and focused on painting from nature, producing detailed, colorful works. Rossetti was a founding member.

realism In a general sense, refers to objective representation. More specifically, a nineteenth-century movement, especially in France, that rejected idealized academic styles in favor of everyday subjects. Daumier, Millet, and Courbet were realists.

Renaissance Meaning "rebirth" in French. Refers to Europe c. 1400–1600. Renaissance art, which began in Italy, stressed the forms of classical antiquity, a realistic representation of space based on scientific perspective, and secular subjects. The works of Leonardo, Michelangelo, and Raphael exemplify the balance and harmony of the High Renaissance (c. 1495–1520).

rococo An eighteenth-century European style, originating in France. In reaction to the grandeur and massiveness of the baroque, rococo employed refined, elegant, highly decorative forms. Fragonard worked in this style.

Romanesque A European style developed in France in the late eleventh century. Its sculpture is ornamental, stylized, and complex. Some Romanesque frescoes survive, painted in a monumental, active manner.

romanticism   A European movement of the late eighteenth to mid-nineteenth century. In reaction to neoclassicism, it focused on emotion over reason, and on spontaneous expression. The subject matter was invested with drama and usually painted energetically in brilliant colors. Delacroix, Géricault, Turner, and Blake were Romantic artists.

suprematism   A Russian abstract movement originated by Malevich c. 1913. It was characterized by flat geometric shapes on plain backgrounds and emphasized the spiritual qualities of pure form.

surrealism   A movement of the 1920s and 1930s that began in France. It explored the unconscious, often using images from dreams. It used spontaneous techniques and featured unexpected juxtapositions of objects. Magritte, Dali, Miró, and Ernst painted surrealist works.

symbolism   A painting movement that flourished in France in the 1880s and 1890s in which subject matter was suggested rather than directly presented. It featured decorative, stylized, and evocative images.

Major Playwrights

American

Albee, Edward   (1928–   ). Playwright, producer, director. His masterpiece, *Who's Afraid of Virginia Woolf* (1962), concerns the illusions with which we try to fill our lives. Other works include *The Zoo Story* (1959) and *A Delicate Balance* (1966).

Barry, Philip   (1896–1949). His most successful plays are witty and elegant comedies about the social elite. They deal with the true nature of love and marriage and with a quest for personal fulfillment. His works include *Holiday* (1929), *The Animal Kingdom* (1932), and *The Philadelphia Story* (1939).

Chayesfky, Paddy (Sidney)   (1923–   ). Playwright and television and screen writer. His most notable television plays, such as *Marty* (1953), and stage plays, such as *The Tenth Man* (1959), are about the search for love as a source of spiritual redemption. His screenplays include *Network* (1976).

Hellman, Lillian   (1905–84). Dramatist. Her tightly constructed plays skillfully depict human perversity and evil. Among her best are *The Children's Hour* (1934), *The Little Foxes* (1939), and *Watch on the Rhine* (1941).

Inge, William   (1913–1973). Playwright. His tightly constructed realistic dramas deal with small-town life in the American Midwest, giving form to the yearnings and the guilt of simple people. Among his best plays are *Come Back, Little Sheba* (1950), *Picnic* (1953), *Bus Stop* (1955), and *Dark at the Top of the Stairs* (1957).

Mamet, David   (1947–   ). Dramatist, best known for *American Buffalo* (1975), which depicts the sinister forces pervading American business.

Miller, Arthur   (1915–   ). Outstanding contemporary dramatist. His concern with the moral problems of American society led him to probe the psychological causes of behavior. His classic *Death of a Salesman* (1949) won the Pulitzer prize; other plays include *The Crucible* (1953) and *A View from the Bridge* (1955).

Odets, Clifford (1906–63). Leading playwright of the Group Theatre, and the most important of the American social dramatists of the 1930s. His plays of social and political protest include *Waiting for Lefty* (1935) and *Awake and Sing* (1935). Among his other works are *Golden Boy* (1937), *The Big Knife* (1949), and *The Country Girl* (1951).

O'Neill, Eugene (1888–1953). Probably the greatest American dramatist; also one of the bleakest and most pessimistic. He essayed almost every modern dramatic form. His later, naturalistic plays deal with the inevitability of fate: *The Iceman Cometh* (1939), *Long Day's Journey into Night* (1941), and *A Moon for the Misbegotten* (1943). Other significant works include *Anna Christie* (1920), *Desire Under the Elms* (1924), and *Ah, Wilderness!* (1933). He won the Pulitzer prize four times and, in 1936, the Nobel prize for literature.

Saroyan, William (1908–81). Playwright and novelist. His essential theme is the triumph of childlike goodness over the corruption of a materialistic society. He won the Pulitzer prize for his classic *The Time of Your Life* (1939), but refused the award.

Shepard, Sam (1943–). Playwright and actor. Myth and reality clash in his plays, which explore the disintegration of American values and the chaos beneath. His works include *Operation Sidewinder* (1970), *Buried Child* (1978), which won a Pulitzer prize and *Fool for Love* (1984).

Sherwood, Robert (1896–1955). Dramatist and biographer. His plays deal with the conflict between man's civilized values and his frequent descent into savagery. Among his best works are *The Petrified Forest* (1935), *Idiot's Delight* (1936), and *There Shall Be No Night* (1940).

Wilder, Thornton (1897–1975). Playwright, novelist, and essayist. His work is a celebration of human existence; he sees man and the universe as intimately related. His major plays are *Our Town* (1938), *The Skin of Our Teeth* (1942), which both won Pulitzer prizes, and *The Matchmaker* (1953).

Williams, Tennessee (1911–1983). Probably the greatest American dramatist since O'Neill. His essential theme is the vulnerability of beauty to time and to a society dominated by violence. Among his most significant plays are *The Glass Menagerie* (1945), *A Streetcar Named Desire* (1947), which won a Pulitzer prize, *Summer and Smoke* (1948), *Cat on a Hot Tin Roof* (1955), which also won a Pulitzer, and *Night of the Iguana* (1961).

British

Beaumont, Francis (c. 1584–1616). Jacobean dramatist, best known for his collaborations with John Fletcher. They developed a new form called "tragicomedy," which allowed for the treatment of serious themes without a tragic resolution. Their works include *Philaster* (1610) and *The Maid's Tragedy* (c. 1611). Beaumont alone wrote *The Knight of the Burning Pestle* (c. 1607), a burlesque of the historical romances of the time.

Coward, Noël (1899–1973). Playwright, actor, composer, and director. His comedies present witty, stylish people acting in accordance with their unconventional morality and in league against more banal types. His best plays are *Private Lives* (1930), *Design for Living* (1930), and *Blithe Spirit* (1933).

Dekker, Thomas (c. 1572–1632). Dramatist and pamphleteer. He centered his plays on contemporary life and merged Elizabethan romance with everyday realism, exhibiting sympathy for society's outcasts. His best plays are *The Shoemaker's Holiday* (1600), *The Honest Whore, Part*

I (with Thomas Middleton, 1604; Part II, 1630), *Westward Ho!* (with John Webster, 1604), *The Roaring Girl* (with Middleton, 1607–08) and *The Witch of Edmonton* (with William Rowley and John Ford, 1621).

Eliot, Thomas Stearns (T.S.) (1888–1965). Poet, critic, and playwright, born in America. He spearheaded a new interest in formal verse drama. His most admired play, *Murder in the Cathedral* (1935), derived its form from Greek tragedy, medieval morality plays, and church ritual. Other plays include *The Cocktail Party* (1949).

Fletcher, John (1579–1625). Prolific and immensely popular playwright who collaborated with Francis Beaumont and many others, apparently including Shakespeare (*The Two Noble Kinsmen* [1613] and *Henry VIII* [1613]). Alone, Fletcher wrote two early tragedies, *Valentinian* (1610–14) and *Bonduca* (1609–14), and the comedies *Wit Without Money* (c. 1614) and *Rule a Wife and Have a Wife* (1624). He helped to lay the basis for the Restoration "comedy of manners."

Goldsmith, Oliver (c. 1728–74). Irish-born essayist, poet, novelist, and comic playwright. He ridiculed the sentimental comedy of the time and promoted what he called "laughing comedy," designed to make us smile at our own follies. His comic masterpiece is *She Stoops to Conquer* (1773).

Jonson, Ben (1527–1637). Dramatist, poet, and literary critic. He developed the "comedy of humours," which featured characters dominated by one overruling passion. His masterpieces are *Volpone* (1605–06), *Epicoene* (1610), *The Alchemist* (1610), and *Bartholomew Fair* (1614).

Kyd, Thomas (1558–1594). Author of *The Spanish Tragedy* (1592), which introduced the theme of vengeance into Elizabethan drama; the "tragedy of revenge" became popular throughout the period. Kyd drew his inspiration from the Roman tragedies of Seneca.

Marlowe, Christopher (1564–93). Poet and playwright who ushered in the great age of Elizabethan drama. His distinctive blank verse—called "Marlowe's mighty line"—established this verse style as a basic tool of Elizabethan playwrights. His masterpieces are *Tamburlaine the Great: Part I* (c. 1586–87; *Part II*, 1587), *Dr. Faustus* (c. 1588), *The Jew of Malta* (c. 1589), and *Edward II* (1591). Marlowe, often in trouble with the law, was murdered in 1593.

Middleton, Thomas (c. 1570–1627). Jacobean dramatist with a dark and pessimistic vision of human corruption. In his comedies, the manners of the age are held up to scathing ridicule; his tragedies are remarkable for their penetrating psychological realism. His plays include *A Trick to Catch the Old One* (c. 1607), *A Chaste Maid in Cheapside* (1611), *The Changeling* (with William Rowley, 1622), and *Women Beware Women* (c. 1625).

Osborne, John (1929–   ). His work was fueled by a disgust for the quality of life in contemporary Britain. In the opening of his most famous play, *Look Back in Anger* (1956), his protagonist, Jimmy Porter, a working-class intellectual rebel, opens fire on the establishment. Among Osborne's other works are *The Entertainer* (1957), *Luther* (1961), and *Inadmissible Evidence* (1964).

Pinter, Harold (1930–   ). Dramatist and actor. The motivation for the action in his plays is typically omitted; the characters evade real communication. The central motif is often two people in a room, involved in a seemingly commonplace situation that is gradually invested with menace, dread, and mystery. Pinter's language reproduces the inflections and rambling irrelevancy of everyday speech. His best plays include *The Birthday Party* (1958), *The Dumb Waiter* (1959), *The Homecoming* (1965), and *Betrayal* (1978).

Shakespeare, William (1564–1616). Elizabethan poet and dramatist. The most influential writer in English literature and perhaps the greatest dramatist of all time. His plays resonate with the full range of human emotion and experience. In his dramatic poetry, the English language reached perfection. As Ben Jonson wrote in his great tribute, "He was not of an age, but for all time!" Shakespeare wrote tragedies, comedies, and histories. His tragedies are: *Titus Andronicus* (1594), *Romeo and Juliet* (c. 1595–96), *Julius Caesar* (1599), *Hamlet* (1602), *Othello* (1602–03), *Timon of Athens* (1604–05), *King Lear* (1605–06), *Macbeth* (1605–06), *Antony and Cleopatra* (1606–07), and *Coriolanus* (1607–10). His comedies are: *The Comedy of Errors* (1591–94), *The Taming of the Shrew* (1593–94), *The Two Gentlemen of Verona* (1594–95), *Love's Labour's Lost* (1593–1650), *A Midsummer Night's Dream* (1595–96), *The Merchant of Venice* (1596–97), *Much Ado About Nothing* (1598–99), *The Merry Wives of Windsor* (1598–99), *As You Like It* (1599–1600), *Twelfth Night* (1599–1600), *Troilus and Cressida* (1601–02), *All's Well That Ends Well* (1602–03), *Measure for Measure* (1603–04), *Pericles* (1606–08), *Cymbeline* (1609–10), *The Winter's Tale* (1610–11), and *The Tempest* (1611). The histories are: *Henry VI: Part I* (1589–91), *Henry VI: Part II* (1590–91), *Henry VI: Part III* (1590–91), *Richard III* (1593), *Richard II* (1595), *King John* (1596–97), *Henry IV: Part I* (1597–98), *Henry IV: Part II* (1597–98), *Henry V* (1598–99), and *Henry VIII* (1612).

Shaw, George Bernard   (1856–1950). Irish-born dramatist, journalist, critic and Fabian socialist. His plays combine brilliant, incisive wit with a moral purpose: to expose the follies of the contemporary social order. He created a "drama of ideas," in which philosophical discussion becomes a theatrical event. Among his best-known works are *Arms and the Man* (1894), *Man and Superman* (1905), *Major Barbara* (1905), *Pygmalion* (1912), *Heartbreak House* (1913–19), and *Saint Joan* (1923).

Sheridan, Richard Brinsley   (1751–1816). Irish-born comic playwright, theatrical manager, and politician. Sheridan sought to restore a comedy of wit to the post-Restoration theater, which had been engulfed by middle-class moralizing. His masterpieces are *The Rivals* (1775) and *The School for Scandal* (1777).

Stoppard, Tom   (1937–   ). Playwright, born in Czechoslovakia. Heavily influenced by Beckett and the Theatre of the Absurd, he is best known for *Rosencrantz and Guildenstern Are Dead* (1967) and *The Real Inspector Hound* (1968).

Tourneur, Cyril   (1575–1626). Jacobean dramatist, author of two famous tragedies of revenge, both based on Senecan drama: *The Revenger's Tragedy* (1606–07: the authorship of this play is in dispute but is generally ascribed to Tourneur) and *The Atheist's Tragedy* (1607–11).

Webster, John   (c. 1580–1634). Jacobean dramatist, creator of two outstanding tragedies, *The White Devil* (1609–12) and *The Duchess of Malfi* (1613–14). His vision was one of dark, brooding pessimism.

Wilde, Oscar   (1854–1900). Irish-born playwright, novelist, poet, and aesthete. Famous for his epigrammatic wit and for his eccentricity in dress and lifestyle, Wilde used his satirical gifts to expose the shallowness and hypocrisy of Victorian society. His comic masterpiece is *The Importance of Being Earnest* (1895).

French

Anouilh, Jean   (1910–   ). Dramatist and screenwriter. His plays, which are laced with humor, deal with the impossibility of purity surviving in a world dominated by compromise. Among his best-known works are *Thieves' Carnival* (1932), *Antigone* (1944), *The Waltz of the Toreadors* (1952), and *The Lark* (1953).

Beckett, Samuel   (1906–   ). Playwright and novelist, born in Ireland. One of the originators of the Theatre of the Absurd, he mixes comedy with existential anguish to express the dilemma of twentieth-century man, beset by an undefined sense of guilt and a loss of purpose. His major works include *Waiting for Godot* (1952) and *Endgame* (1957).

Corneille, Pierre (1606–84). The first of the great French neoclassic dramatists. His early masterpiece, *Le Cid* (1637), was harshly criticized by the French Academy because it did not adhere to the "classical unities." All his later tragedies followed the rules. Other works include *Horace* (1640), *Cinna* (1640–41), and *Polyeuctes* (1641–42).

Genet, Jean (1919–86). Novelist and preeminent dramatist of the Theatre of the Absurd. In the face of the void, his deeply alienated characters assume inauthentic roles, which become ritualized. Genet's best plays include *The Maids* (1947), *The Balcony* (1956), and *The Blacks* (1959).

Giraudoux, Jean (1882–1944). Novelist and dramatist. Many of his plays are reinterpretations of Greek myth. Among his best works are *Tiger at the Gates* (1935) and *The Madwoman of Chaillot* (1946).

Hugo, Victor Marie (1802–85). Poet, novelist, playwright, and politician; he was the acknowledged leader of French romanticism. The famous "battle" that disrupted the premiere of his tragedy *Hernani* (1830) marked a watershed in the history of the romantic movement. Other plays include *The King Amuses Himself* (1832—the source for Verdi's *Rigoletto*), *Ruy Blas* (1838), and *The Burgraves* (1843).

Ionesco, Eugene (1912–   ). Dramatist, born in Romania. One of the leading exponents of the Theatre of the Absurd. At the core of his work is the idea that human existence, language, and effort are essentially meaningless. His most famous plays are *The Bald Soprano* (1950), *The Lesson* (1951), and *Rhinoceros* (1959).

Molière (Jean Baptiste Poquelin) (1622–73). Actor, director, theater manager. He took the stylized comic archetypes of the commedia dell'arte and made them human, while retaining the "flaw" that always led them to folly. The result was a new genre, "character comedy." His satires caused great controversy. His greatest plays are *The School for Wives* (1662), *Tartuffe* (1664), *The Misanthrope* (1666), *The Miser* (1668), and *The Bourgeois Gentleman* (1670).

Racine, Jean (1639–99). Exemplar of French classicism and master of the Alexandrine line. The classical unities of time, place, and action provided an ideal framework for the concise action of his tragedies. His protagonists are usually driven by a single, dominant passion. His greatest works are *Andromache* (1667), *Bérénice* (1670), *Phèdre* (1676), and *Athalie* (1691).

Rostand, Edmund (1868–1918). Poet and dramatist, responsible for the brief revival of the romantic spirit in the era of naturalism. His one masterpiece, *Cyrano de Bergerac* (1897), is a tour de force of dramatic poetry.

Sartre, Jean-Paul (1905–80). Philosopher, novelist, essayist, and playwright. His dramas expound his existential philosophy: that man is essentially free, in a universe without God; and that he is defined by his own acts and is obliged to choose responsibly. Among his best-known works are *No Exit* (1944) and *Dirty Hands* (1948). Sartre won the Nobel prize for literature in 1964.

German

Brecht, Bertolt (1895–1956). Playwright, poet, stage director, and theorist. He created "epic theatre," the purpose of which was to make people first *think*, and only later feel, about what they were seeing. The technique he used was alienation—the creation of emotional distance between the spectator and the event. Paradoxically, his ironic dramas are deeply moving. Among his greatest plays are *In the Jungle of Cities* (1923), *The Threepenny Opera* (1928), *Galileo* (1938–39), *Mother Courage and Her Children* (1941), and *The Good Woman of Setzuan* (1943).

Buchner, Georg (1813–37). Three plays established Buchner as a seminal figure. His themes were distinctly modern: man's loneliness, his helplessness before the events of history and the conditions of society, and the absurdity of a world without God. Works by Buchner include *Danton's Death* (1835) and *Woyzeck* (1836).

Greek

Aeschylus (525–456 B.C.). The originator of Greek tragedy as we know it. He added a second actor to the drama (thus making true stage dialogue possible), and he raised tragic diction to the level of grandeur. He explored themes of the transmission of evil from generation to generation, and cosmic justice. He probably wrote some 90 plays, of which 7 survive complete, including *Prometheus Bound* (466–459 B.C.) and the trilogy *The Oresteia* (458 B.C.).

Aristophanes (c. 445–385 B.C.). The only surviving (and probably greatest) writer of attic old comedy. His freewheeling and joyous plays blend political satire, personal lampoon, portraits of domestic life, dance, music, and fantasy. Only 11 of his more than 40 plays survive, including *The Acharnians* (425 B.C.), *The Clouds* (423 B.C.), *The Wasps* (422 B.C.), *Peace* (422 B.C.), *The Birds* (414 B.C.), *Lysistrata* (411 B.C.), and *The Frogs* (405 B.C.).

Euripides (480–406 B.C.). Last of the great Greek tragedians. Influenced by the rationalism of the sophists, Euripides was distinctively modern. The depth of his characterization was new to the attic stage, prefiguring psychological realism. His hatred of war was the mainspring of some of his best dramas. He wrote 92 plays, of which 19 survive, including *Alcestis* (438), *Medea* (431), *The Trojan Women* (415), *Electra* (413), *Iphegenia in Tauris* (412), *Orestes* (408), and *The Bacchae* (405).

Sophocles (c. 496–406 B.C.). The second of the great Greek tragedians. He introduced a third speaking actor, thus making possible more complex dramatic interactions. By creating self-contained works rather than the customary trilogies, he narrowed the focus to one solitary individual at the critical moment of his life, refusing to yield to time or circumstance. He wrote approximately 123 plays, of which 7 survive, including *Antigone* (c. 442–441 B.C.), *Oedipus Rex* (c. 430–426 B.C.), *Electra* (c. 409 B.C.), and *Oedipus at Colonus* (c. 404–401 B.C.).

Irish

O'Casey, Sean (1880–1964). His plays present an antiheroic view of life, alternately tragic and comic: He mocks sentimental patriotism by looking at the brutality of war through the eyes of working-class Irish women. Among his best works are *The Shadow of a Gunman* (1923), *Juno and the Paycock* (1924), and *The Plough and the Stars* (1926).

Synge, John Millington (1871–1909). Poet and dramatist. His Irish peasant characters aspire to a wild life of freedom and fantasy, which they achieve in imagination as expressed through their powerful and poetic Irish idiom. Among his works are *In the Shadow of the Glen* (1903), *Riders to the Sea* (1904), and *The Playboy of the Western World* (1907). Synge was cofounder of the Abbey Theatre, with William Butler Yeats and Lady Gregory.

Roman

Plautus (c. 251–184 B.C.). Popular comic playwright. His plays were based on Greek comedy and performed in Greek dress. A typical plot presents a young lover kept from his beloved by a stubborn father, a greedy pimp, or lack of money. A clever slave contrives an elaborate intrigue to unite the lovers, and the play follows the ups and downs of the scheme. Among his surviving works are *Pseudolus* (191 B.C.) and *The Menaechmi* (date unknown).

Seneca (4 B.C.–A.D. 65). Tragic playwright, stoic philosopher, and statesman. The form of his plays follows the conventions of Greek tragedy; but the content reflects his concern with the stoic absolutes of passion and reason. His plays deal with the triumph of evil in a single human soul and its devastating impact on the outer world. Nine of his plays survive, including *Agamemnon*, *Medea*, and *Phaedre* (dates unknown).

Russian

Chekhov, Anton Pavlovich (1860–1904). Great modern dramatist and short-story writer. He depicts the provincial aristocracy before the revolution, trapped in a stultifying environment and paralyzed by a lack of will. Stanislavsky's production at the Moscow Art Theatre of Chekhov's greatest plays—*The Seagull* (1896), *Uncle Vanya* (1899), *The Three Sisters* (1901), and *The Cherry Orchard* (1904)—made the Russian theater famous throughout the world.

Gorky, Maxim (Alexei Maximovich Peshkov) (1868–1936). Russian novelist, short-story writer, and playwright. Writing out of his own experience of poverty, he won international fame for his drama of the slums, *The Lower Depths* (1902).

Spanish

Calderón de la Barca, Pedro (1600–81). Poet and last great playwright of the Spanish Golden Age. He wrote more than 200 full-length plays, as well as more than 70 one-act sacramental dramas, called "autos." In a time when the Spanish Empire was crumbling, his essential themes were faith and honor. Among his best-known plays are *The Phantom Lady* (1629), *Life Is a Dream* (1631–32), *Devotion to the Cross* (1633), *Secret Vengeance for Secret Insult* (1635), and *The Mayor of Zalamea* (1640–44).

García Lorca, Federico (1899–1936). Spanish poet and playwright, executed by Franco's soldiers soon after the outbreak of the Spanish Civil War. His poetic tragedies deal with the conflict between the individual and society—a conflict particularly bitter in Spain, where life was tightly regulated by an unyielding conservative moral code. His most famous plays are *Blood Wedding* (1933), *Yerma* (1934), and *The House of Bernarda Alba* (1936).

Molina, Tirso de (Gabriel Tellez) (c. 1571–1648). A disciple of Lope de Vega, and the second great dramatist of the Spanish Golden Age. His most famous play is *The Trickster of Seville* (c. 1625), in which he created the great modern myth of Don Juan.

Vega Carpio, Lope de (1562–1635). Member of the Spanish Armada and the first great dramatist of the Spanish Golden Age. He established the *commedia* (new comedy) as the principal dramatic form in the Spain of his time. His works include *Fuenteovejuna* (1612), *The Peasant in his Nook* (1611–15), *The King's the Best Magistrate* (1620–23), and *The Knight from Olmedo* (1620–25).

Other

Ibsen, Henrik (1828–1906). Norwegian playwright. Generally credited with being the "father of modern drama," he demonstrated the power of psychological realism. His plays often present individuals in bitter conflict with the norms of society. His masterpieces include *Peer Gynt* (1867), *A Doll's House* (1879), *Ghosts* (1881), *An Enemy of the People* (1883), *The Wild Duck* (1884), and *Hedda Gabler* (1891).

Pirandello, Luigi (1867–1936). Italian dramatist and novelist, winner of the 1934 Nobel prize for literature. The playwright par excellence of the conflict between illusion and reality, he depicts with eloquence the isolation of the individual from society and from himself. Among his best-known plays are *Right You Are—If You Think You Are* (1917), *Six Characters in Search of an Author* (1921), and *The Man with the Flower in His Mouth* (1923).

Strindberg, Johan August (1849–1912). Swedish playwright and seminal modern dramatist, best known for his intensely psychological plays about tormented male-female relationships. His later plays prefigure expressionism. Among his best-known works are *The Father* (1887), *Miss Julie* (1889), *The Dance of Death* (*Part I* and *Part II*—1900), and *A Dream Play* (1902).

Major Architects

American

Bulfinch, Charles (1763–1844), b. Massachusetts. He designed the first theater in New England, the Federal Street Theater (1794), the Massachusetts State House (1795–97), and the Massachusetts General Hospital (1818–23), all in Boston. In his completion of the design of the Capitol building, Washington, D.C. (1818–30), he achieved a model for state capitols throughout the country.

Burnham, Daniel Hudson (1846–1912), b. New York. Architect and city planner. With his partner, John Root, he designed the first major skeleton skyscraper, the Masonic Temple Building, Chicago (1892). Alone, Burnham designed the Flatiron Building, New York City (1903), and Union Station, Washington, D.C. (1903–07).

Fuller, (Richard) Buckminster (1895–1983), b. Massachusetts. Architect and engineer. His revolutionary designs, such as the geodesic dome, aimed at achieving the maximum effect with a minimal investment of materials.

Graves, Michael (1934–   ), b. Indiana. Postmodern architect. His influences range from classical Greece and Rome to the work of Le Corbusier. Graves' designs are known for their use of color and mix of delicacy and strength. They include the Fargo-Moorhead Cultural Center Bridge, Fargo, North Dakota, and Moorhead, Minnesota (1977), and the Public Services Building, Portland, Oregon (1980–82).

Gropius, Walter (1883–1969), b. Germany. A great modern functionalist. In 1919, he reorganized the Weimar School of Art into the Bauhaus. He designed the glass Fagus Factory,

Alfeld (1911–12) and the Bauhaus buildings, Dessau (1925–26). His U.S. work includes the Pan American Building, New York City (1957). In 1946, he and young associates formed The Architects Collaborative (TAC), working together on buildings such as the United States Embassy, Athens (1956).

Hunt, Richard Morris (1827–95), b. Vermont. Architect. His work, which closely follows historical styles, exemplifies nineteenth-century eclecticism. He designed the Lenox Library (1870–77) and the Tribune Building (1873–76), both in New York City, and various mansions, such as those for the Vanderbilts in New York City and Newport, Rhode Island.

Jefferson, Thomas (1743–1826), b. Virginia. President, statesman, architect, and scientist. Jefferson, a self-taught architect, designed Monticello, his house near Charlottesville, Virginia (1768–82), the Virginia State Capitol in Richmond (1785–99), and the University of Virginia, Charlottesville (1817–26).

Jenney, William Le Baron (1832–1907), b. Massachusetts. Architect and engineer. His Home Insurance Building in Chicago, 10 stories high (1884–85), is often considered to have been the first skyscraper. It was the first steel-framed office building.

Johnson, Philip Cortelyou (1906–   ), b. Ohio. Architect. He is noted for his glass-walled house in New Canaan, Connecticut (1949), the New York State Theater at Lincoln Center (1964), his collaboration with Mies van der Rohe on the Seagram Building (1958), and the American Telephone and Telegraph Building (1978–84), all in New York City. Johnson's writings include *The International Style* (1932), which he coauthored.

Kahn, Louis Isadore (1901–74), b. Estonia. Kahn designed the Yale University Art Gallery, New Haven (1951–53), the Kimbell Art Museum, Fort Worth (1966–72), and many housing projects, such as Carver Court Housing, Coatesville, Pennsylvania (1941–43). The Richards Medical Research Building, University of Pennsylvania (1957–64), has been admired for its integration of form and function.

Latrobe, Benjamin Henry (1764–1820), b. England. Considered the first professional architect in the United States, Latrobe produced some of the best monumental architecture of his time in classic revival style. His works include the Bank of Pennsylvania, Philadelphia (1799), and the Roman Catholic Cathedral, Baltimore, the first cathedral built in the United States (1805–18). He also worked on the Capitol, Washington, D.C. (1803–17).

Mies van der Rohe, Ludwig (1886–1969), b. Germany. A director of the Bauhaus (1930–33) and a founder of modern architecture. His U.S. buildings, mainly unornamented skyscrapers, include Chicago's Lake Shore Drive Apartments (1948–51), the Chicago Federal Center (1959–73), and, with Philip Johnson, the Seagram Building, New York City (1958).

Pei, I(eoh) M(ing) (1917–   ), b. China. He carefully integrates his expressive works with their surrounding environment. His buildings include the Mile High Center, Denver (1955), the John Hancock Tower, Boston (1973), the East Wing of the National Gallery of Art, Washington, D.C. (1978), and a pyramidal addition to the Louvre Museum, Paris (1989).

Richardson, Henry Hobson (1838–86), b. Louisiana. His monumental building, Trinity Church, Boston (1872–77), exemplifies the "Richardson romanesque" style. His work also includes the Marshall Field store, Chicago (1885–87).

Mills, Robert (1781–1855), b. South Carolina. Mills, a classic revivalist, was appointed architect of public buildings in Washington, D.C. There, he built the Patent Office (1836–40), the Treasury (1836–42), and the Post Office (1839–42). In 1833, he designed the Washington Monument (built 1848–84).

Saarinen, Eero (1910–61), b. Finland. Son of Eliel. His works, especially his domed constructions, are innovative. His projects include the Kresge Auditorium, Massachusetts Institute of Technology, Cambridge, Massachusetts (1953–56); Dulles International Airport, Chantilly, Virginia (1958–62); and the Gateway Arch, St. Louis (1959–64). He also designed furniture, especially chairs.

Saarinen, (Gottlieb) Eliel (1873–1950), b. Finland. Architect and city planner. He designed the National Museum (1902–04) in Helsinki, Finland. His work in the United States includes several buildings at the Cranbrook Foundation, where he was president of the Academy of Art, and, with his son, Eero, performance halls at the Berkshire Music Center in Tanglewood, Massachusetts (late 1930s–early 1940s). Saarinen's writings include *The City: Its Growth, Its Decay, Its Future* (1943).

Strickland, William (1788–1854), b. New Jersey. Classic revivalist architect. His most original work is the Merchants' Exchange, Philadelphia (1832–34). Also in Philadelphia, he built the Second Bank of the United States (1818–24) and the U.S. Mint (1829–33). He was a founder and first president of the American Institution of Architects.

Sullivan, Louis Henry (1856–1924), b. Massachusetts. Prominent in the development of modern architecture, Sullivan propounded the theory that form should follow function. He designed the Wainwright Building, St. Louis (1890–91), the Transportation Building at the World's Columbian Exposition, Chicago (1893), and the Stock Exchange (1893–94) in Chicago.

Venturi, Robert (1925–   ), b. Pennsylvania. Venturi uses architectural elements from popular culture in his work, which includes Guild House, Philadelphia (1962–66), the Humanities and Social Sciences Building, State University of New York, Purchase (1968–70), and the new building for the Seattle Art Museum (1991). His writings include *Complexity and Contradiction in Architecture* (1966).

Walter, Thomas Ustick (1804–87), b. Pennsylvania. As government architect in Washington, D.C., from 1851 to 1865, he added the Senate and House wings to the Capitol, built its central dome, and designed the interior of the Library of Congress. Walter was a founder and president of the American Institute of Architects.

White, Stanford (1853–1906), b. New York. Architect. He worked in partnership with Charles Follen McKim and William Rutherford Mead. White's accomplishments include the first Madison Square Garden (1887–91), Washington Memorial Arch (1889–92), and the New York Herald Building (1890–95), all in New York City. White's buildings reflect his passion for graceful, decorative elements and rich ornamentation.

Wright, Frank Lloyd (1867–1959), b. Wisconsin. Architect. His innovative approach integrated modern technology into architectural aesthetics. He is especially known for his dramatic interior spaces. His buildings include the Larkin Building, Buffalo (1904); the Imperial Hotel, Tokyo (1915–22); the Kaufmann house, "Falling Water," Bear Run, Pennsylvania (1936–39); a Unitarian church, Madison, Wisconsin (1947); and the Guggenheim Museum, New York City (1959).

British

Chambers, Sir William (1723–96), b. Sweden. His *Treatise on the Decorative Part of Civil Architecture* (1759) was a classic design text. He is known for Somerset House, London (begun 1776), and for decorative architecture in Kew Gardens, Surrey, England, especially the Chinese Pagoda (1763).

Jones, Inigo (1573–1652). One of the first great English architects. He broke from the Jacobean style, thus beginning the Renaissance and the Georgian periods in English architecture. His works include the Queen's House, Greenwich Palace, Kent (1616–35), and the royal banqueting hall, Whitehall Palace, London (1619–22), both employing Palladian principles.

Lutyens, Sir Edwin Landseer (1869–1944). The leading English architect of his time, Lutyens combined romantic and classical styles. His outstanding achievement is the plan of New Delhi, India, centering on the Viceroy's House (1912–31). Other works include war memorials, such as the Cenotaph in London (1919–20), and the British Embassy in Washington, D.C. (1927–28).

Paxton, Sir Joseph (1803–65). Architect and horticulturist. His Great Conservatory, a greenhouse in Chatsworth, England (1836–40), served as a model for the glass Crystal Palace, which he built for the Great Exhibition of 1851 in London. Paxton's use of glass and iron in this building was a great technological innovation.

Pugin, Augustus Welby Northmore (1812–52). Architect, designer, and author. Pugin, a Gothic revivalist, worked on the interior and ornamentation of the Houses of Parliament (1844–52) and designed more than 65 churches, including Saint George's, London (1840–48). His writings, however, were more influential than his buildings.

Nash, John (1752–1835). Architect and city planner. Nash, a leader in the neoclassic Regency style, planned the layout of Regent Street and Regent's Park in London (built c. 1818), remodeled Buckingham Palace (1824–30), and worked on the "Indian"-style Royal Pavilion in Brighton (1815–21).

Smirke, Sir Robert (1781–1867). Classic revival architect. His best-known work is the main facade of the British Museum, London (1823–47). Other achievements include the Royal College of Physicians (1822–25) and the General Post Office (1823–29), also in London. Upon his retirement, his brother Sydney Smirke (1798–1877) continued work on the British Museum (1854–57).

Soane, Sir John (1753–1837). Soane, a classic revivalist, developed a complicated and highly personal style. His works in London include the Bank of England (begun 1788), the Dulwich College Art Gallery (1811–14), and his own eccentric house at Lincoln's Inn Fields (1812–13), now a museum.

Vanbrugh, Sir John (1664–1726). Architect and dramatist. His buildings include Blenheim Palace, Oxfordshire (1705–16), which epitomizes the English baroque, and the Queen's Theatre in the Haymarket, London (1704–05). He designed theatrical, picturesque country houses, such as Seaton Delaval, Northumberland (begun 1720).

Wren, Sir Christopher (1632–1723). Astronomer, architect, and mathematician; his elegant and dignified designs were highly influential. He designed St. Paul's Cathedral, London (1675–1710), and 52 other London churches, including St. Mary-le-Bow (1671–80). Other works include the Sheldonian Theatre, Oxford (1664–69), and Trinity College Library, Cambridge (1679–84).

French

Garnier, Jean Louis Charles (1825–98). His principal work is the ornate Opéra in Paris, with its grand staircase (1861–75). He also built the Casino at Monte Carlo (1878–81) and Bischofsheim's Observatory, Nice (1880–88).

Hardouin Mansart, Jules (1646–1708). Baroque architect. In 1699, he became chief architect of the royal buildings. Some of his major works are at the Palace of Versailles, including the Galerie des Glaces and the Grand Trianon (both 1678–89). In Paris, he designed the Church of the Invalides (1679–91) and the Place Vendôme (1698).

Labrouste, Henri (Pierre François Henri) (1801–75). He was one of the first to successfully use metal construction in architecture, as in the reading room of the Bibliothèque Sainte-Geneviève, Paris (1843–50). He also worked extensively on the Bibliothèque Nationale (1854–75).

Le Corbusier (Charles Édouard Jeanneret) (1887–1965). b. Switzerland. His innovative buildings and writings express a revolutionary approach toward aesthetic and technological architectural problems. His works, reflecting industrial as well as sculptural influences, include the Villa Savoye, Poissy, France (1928–31), collaboration on the United Nations buildings, New York City (1947–53), and buildings for the new capital of the Punjab, Chandigarh, India (1951–65).

Ledoux, Claude Nicolas (1736–1806). This imaginative neoclassicist's buildings include the Pavilion de Louveciennes and the theater at Besançon in France (both 1771–73). He is known for his architectural treatise of 1804 and for his plans for Chaux, an ideal city for the workers of the salt mines of Arc-et-Senans, France.

Italian

Alberti, Leone Battista (1404–72). Architect and painter. His treatise, *De Re Aedificatoria* (c. 1450), established architecture as an intellectual field. His works include the exteriors of the churches of San Francesco in Rimini (c. 1450–61) and Sant'Andrea in Mantua (c. 1470–72).

Bernini, Giovanni Lorenzo (Gianlorenzo) (1598–1680). Major Italian baroque architect and sculptor. As architect of St. Peter's in Rome, he designed the ornate tabernacle under the dome (1624–33) and the monument for St. Peter's chair (1657–66). From 1656 to 1667, he worked on the piazza and colonnade in front of St. Peter's. His Cornaro Chapel, in the church of Santa Maria della Vittoria, Rome (1647–51), is a dynamic melding of sculpture and architecture.

Borromini, Francesco (1599–1667). Italian baroque architect. His influential designs for churches and palaces were complex and extravagant. His works include the churches of San Carlo alle Quattro Fontane (1634–41) and Sant'Ivo alla Sapienza (1642–60), and the completion of the church of Sant'Agnese, Piazza Navona (1653–57), all in Rome.

Bramante (Donato di Angelo di Antonio) (1444–1514). Leading Italian High Renaissance architect. He designed much of the church of Santa Maria presso San Satiro (c. 1480) and the east end of Santa Maria delle Grazie (c. 1492), both in Milan. His plans for St. Peter's, Rome (1505–06), though not fully carried out, were influential.

Brunelleschi, Filippo (1377–1446). The first great architect of the Italian Renaissance. His masterpiece is the celebrated ribbed octagonal dome for the Florence Cathedral (1420–36). His other works include the Foundling Hospital (1419) and the churches of San Lorenzo (begun c. 1420) and Santo Spirito (begun 1436), all in Florence.

Da Vinci, Leonardo. *See* **Leonardo da Vinci**.

Giotto (Giotto di Bondone) (c. 1266–1337). Florentine architect and painter. In 1334 he was appointed architect of the Florence Cathedral. His main accomplishment is the multicolored bell tower called Giotto's Tower (begun 1334).

Leonardo da Vinci (1452–1519). Painter, sculptor, architect, engineer, and scientist. Around 1488, Leonardo did architectural work for the Milan Cathedral; he later worked on the reconstructions of cathedrals in Pavia and Piacenza. Beginning in 1506, he served as architect and engineer in Milan for Louis XII. In Rome, from 1513 to about 1515, he worked on several projects for the Vatican. Although most of Leonardo's designs were not executed, his architectural studies are of great historic importance.

Michelangelo Buonarroti (1475–1564). Italian Renaissance sculptor, painter, architect, and poet. Michelangelo's designs include the Medici Chapel (1520–34), where he powerfully combined architecture and sculpture, and the Laurentian Library (begun 1524), both at San Lorenzo, Florence. His work includes designs for St. Peter's (1546–64); its monumental dome, completed after Michelangelo's death, is based largely on his ideas.

Palladio, Andrea (1508–80). Italian Renaissance architect; a leading figure in Western architecture. Classical models were of extreme importance to him. He published a famous treatise in 1570. His works include rebuilding the Basilica at Vicenza, Italy (1549–80); many houses, including the Villa Barbaro, Maser, Italy (1554–58); and the Villa Rotunda, Vicenza (1567–70). In Venice, he built the churches of San Giorgio Maggiore (1560–80) and Il Redentore (1576–80).

Piranesi, Giovanni Battista (1720–1778). Architect and designer. Although he constructed few buildings—among them Santa Maria del Priorato (1764) in Rome—his imaginative designs and theoretical writings were a major influence on European neoclassicism. His *Antichità Romane* (176) and *Parere su l'Architettura* presented classical Rome as the creative foundation for a contemporary architecture.

Other

Aalto, Alvar (1898–1976). Finnish architect and furniture designer. The works of this leading twentieth-century architect combine Finnish building traditions with modern techniques. They include the Municipal Library, Viipuri, Finland (1933–35), the Finnish Pavilion for the World's Fair, New York City (1939), and the undulating Baker House, Massachusetts Institute of Technology, Cambridge, Massachusetts (1946–49).

Adam, Robert (1728–92). Scottish architect. He designed, with his brother James, numerous public and private buildings in England and Scotland in a distinctive and decorative style that combines Palladian, Renaissance, and classical elements. Notable examples are Osterley Park (1761–80) and Syon House (1762–69), both in Middlesex, England.

Behrens, Peter (1868–1940). German architect and industrial designer. His factory buildings, such as the A. E. G. Turbine Factory, Berlin (1908–09), show a simple, utilitarian approach. He is also known for the German Embassy, Leningrad (1911–12). Le Corbusier, Mies van der Rohe, and Gropius were his students.

Berlage, Hendrik Petrus (1856–1934). Pioneering modern Dutch architect. He is known for the redbrick Stock Exchange (1897–1903) and the Diamond Workers' Union Building (1899–1901), both in Amsterdam. He was also active in urban planning and furniture design.

Gaudí y Cornet, Antonio (1852–1926). Spanish architect whose colorful, sculptural, undulating style has similarities to art nouveau as well as surrealism. His masterpiece is the unfinished Expiatory Church of the Holy Family, Barcelona (begun 1883; work still in progress). Other examples of his work are Parc Güell (1900–14) and Casa Battló (1904–06) in Barcelona.

Hoffmann, Josef Franz Maria (1870–1956). Austrian architect and decorator; a leader of the early-twentieth-century Viennese style. He is known for his use of rectilinear forms with delicate ornamentation, as in the Palais Stoclet, Brussels (1905–11).

Loos, Adolf (1870–1933). Austrian architect. His purity of form influenced the development of the modern functional style. His best-known works include the office and store building on Michaelerplatz and the Steiner House, both in Vienna (both 1910).

Mackintosh, Charles Rennie (1868–1928). Scottish architect, artist, and furniture designer. His interiors, such as those for four Glasgow tearooms (1896–1919), display a sumptuous art nouveau style. His buildings, such as the Glasgow School of Art (1896–99), are subtly proportioned.

Mendelsohn, Erich (1887–1953). German architect. In Germany, he built the Herman and Co. hat factory, Luckenwalde (1921–23), and the sculptural Einstein Tower Observatory, Potsdam (1919–24). He designed several buildings in Israel, including the Hebrew University on Mount Scopus, Jerusalem (1937–39), and four synagogues in the United States.

Niemeyer, Oscar (1907–   ). Brazilian architect. Influenced by Le Corbusier, Niemeyer is a daring and original designer. He collaborated on the United Nations buildings, New York City (1947–53), directed the building of Brazil's new capital, Brasília (1950–60), and designed the Mondadori Headquarters in Milan (1968–75).

Wagner, Otto (1841–1918). Austrian architect. The most significant work by this pioneer of modern architecture is the Postal Savings Bank Office, Vienna (1904–12). He also designed stations for the Vienna Municipal Railway (1894–1901) and the church at Steinhof (1905–07). His writings, including *Modern Architecture* (1895), were influential.

Architectural Terms

abacus   A stone slab at the top of a classical column aiding the support of the architrave.

acropolis   The elevated stronghold in ancient Greek cities.

adobe   Sun-dried brick used in places with warm, dry climates, such as Egypt and Mexico; also, the structures built out of adobe bricks.

aisle   A passageway of a Christian church or a Roman basilica running parallel to the nave, separated from it by an arcade or colonnade.

ambulatory   A continuous aisle in a building, especially around the apse in a church.

apse   A semicircular area at the end of a church; in most churches it contains the altar.

arcade   A series of arches supported by columns or piers, or a passageway formed by these arches.

arch   A curved structure used to span an opening.

architrave   The lowest part of an entablature resting on the capital of a column.

ashlar   Stones hewn, squared, and smoothed for use in building, as distinguished from rough building stones.

atrium   In an ancient Roman house, a central room open to the sky, usually having a pool for the collection of rainwater. In churches, a front courtyard.

attic   The story above the cornice of a building.

baldachin An ornamented canopy over an altar, tomb, or throne.

baptistery A part of a church or a separate building, often octagonal or round, in which baptisms take place.

baroque A style that flourished in the seventeenth and early eighteenth centuries, characterized by exuberant decoration, curvaceous forms, and a grand scale generating a sense of movement; later developments within the movement show more restraint.

basilica In ancient Roman architecture, a large oblong building, generally with double columns and a semicircular apse at one end. In Christian architecture, a church with a nave, apse, and aisles.

Bauhaus The style of the Bauhaus School, founded in Germany by Walter Gropius in 1919, emphasizing simplicity, functionalism, and craftsmanship.

buttress A projecting support built into or against the external wall of a building, typically used in Gothic buildings. A flying buttress is an arch that transfers the thrust of a vault to a lower support.

Byzantine A style of the Byzantine Empire, dating from the fifth century. Its churches are characterized by masonry construction around a central plan, with domes; foliage patterns on stone capitals; and interiors decorated with mosaics and frescoes.

campanile A bell tower, usually not actually attached to a church.

cantilever A horizontal projection, such as a balcony or beam, supported at one end only.

choir A square or rectangular area in a church between the apse and the crossing.

classical revival Movement in England and the United States in the late eighteenth and nineteenth centuries that looked to the traditions of Greek and Roman antiquity.

classicism The architecture of Greek and Roman antiquity, distinguished by the qualities of simplicity, harmony, and balance; also, a later style that emphasizes these values.

clerestory A row of windows in the upper part of a wall, especially in a church, to admit light below.

cloister In religious institutions, a courtyard with covered walks.

colonnade A row of columns, usually equidistant, supporting a beam or entablature.

column A cylindrical vertical support usually consisting of a base, shaft, and capital.

Composite Order A Roman order; its capital combines the Corinthian acanthus leaf decoration with volutes from the Ionic Order.

Corinthian Order The latest of the three Greek orders, similar to the Ionic, but with the capital decorated with carvings of the acanthus leaf.

cornice The upper part of an entablature, extending beyond the frieze; also, ornamental molding projecting along the top of a building or wall.

crossing In a church, the area where the transept and the nave intersect, usually emphasized by a dome or tower.

dome A vaulted roof of circular or polygonal shape.

Doric Order The first and simplest of the three Greek orders and the only one that normally has no base.

entablature The upper horizontal part of a classical order, between a capital and the roof; it consists of the architrave, frieze, and cornice.

facade Any important face of a building, usually the principal front with the main entrance.

forum The main public square of an ancient Roman city.

frieze The middle part of an entablature, often decorated with sculpture.

gargoyle A spout placed on the roof gutter of a Gothic building to carry away rainwater, usually carved in the shapes of fanciful animals and grotesque beasts.

Georgian The prevailing style of English architecture during the reigns of George I, II, and III (1714–1820), based on the principles of the Italian Renaissance architect Andrea Palladio.

Gothic A style employed in Europe during the thirteenth, fourteenth, and fifteenth centuries. It is characterized by the use of pointed arches and ribbed vaults, piers, and buttresses in the support of its stone construction. The style is exemplified in France by the Cathedral of Notre Dame in Paris and the cathedrals in Amiens and Chartres.

Gothic revival A movement in the United States and Britain in the late eighteenth and nineteenth centuries that returned to building styles of the Gothic period.

international style A movement that developed in the 1920s, characterized by a regularized surface, a lightening of mass, and, often, large expanses of glass. Gropius, Mies van der Rohe, and Le Corbusier worked in this style.

Ionic Order Second of the three Greek orders. Its capital is decorated with spiral scrolls (volutes).

lantern A small structure on top of a dome, tower, or roof, often open to admit light below.

lintel *See* **post and lintel**.

loggia A roofed gallery with an open arcade or colonnade on at least one side.

minaret A slender, lofty tower with balconies, attached to a Muslim mosque.

module The measurement by which parts of a building are related to one another, for example, the diameter of a column.

narthex The transverse entrance hall of a church.

nave In a Roman basilica, the central aisle. In a church, the main section extending from the entrance to the crossing.

Norman A style of buildings erected by the Normans (1066–1154) based on the Italian romanesque and characterized by sparsely decorated masonry and the use of the round arch. The style was used principally in castles, churches, and abbeys of massive proportions.

obelisk A tall, tapering, four-sided stone shaft with a pyramidal top.

ogive The pointed arch used in Gothic architecture.

order A term applied to the three styles of Greek columns and entablatures, the Doric, Ionic, and Corinthian, and to the Roman Composite and Tuscan orders, developed from the original three orders.

pagoda A multistoried building, typically Asian, forming a tower with upward curving roofs over the individual stories.

pediment In a classical building, the triangular gable between the horizontal entablature and the sloping roof; in general, an architectural feature over a door or window.

pendentive A curved triangle at the corners of a square or polygonal room, used at the opening of a dome.

pier An upright masonry support.

pilaster A flattened, shallow column or pier projecting from a wall. It usually has a base, shaft, and capital but is decorative rather than structural.

portico A structure usually attached to a building, such as a porch, consisting of a roof supported by piers or columns.

post and lintel A method of construction in which vertical beams (posts) are used to support a horizontal beam (lintel).

postmodernism A style that emerged in the 1970s characterized by references to and evocations of past architectural styles, particularly the classical tradition. It is frequently colorful and wittily ornamentative.

pyramid A quadrilateral masonry mass with steeply sloping sides meeting at an apex; in ancient Egypt, pyramids were used as royal tombs.

relief Moldings and ornamentation projecting from the surface of a wall.

Renaissance A European style of the fifteenth and sixteenth centuries, beginning in Italy. Ancient Roman elements were adapted to contemporary uses, with attention to the principles of the architect Vitruvius and to existing ruins. Symmetry, simplicity, and exact mathematical relationships were emphasized.

rococo A style originating in France c. 1720, developed out of baroque types and characterized by elegant, delicate ornamentation and refined use of different materials, such as stucco, metal, or wood, for a delicate effect.

Romanesque A style developed in Europe c. 1050, characterized by heavy masonry and the use of the round arch, barrel and groin vaults, narrow openings, and the vaulting rib, the vaulting shaft, and central and western towers.

spandrel The triangular area between the sides of two adjacent arches.

spire A tall, tapering, pointed roof on a tower, as in the top of a steeple.

tracery Ornament of ribs, bars, etc., in panels or screens, as in the upper part of a Gothic window.

transept A structure that forms the arms of a cross-shaped church.

Tudor A style of English architecture prevalent during the reigns of the Tudors (1485–1558), transitional between Gothic and Palladian, with emphasis on country manors.

turret A small tower, usually starting at some distance from the ground, attached to a building such as a castle or fortress.

Tuscan Order A Roman order resembling the Doric, but with a base and an unfluted shaft.

vault An arched brick or stone ceiling or roof. The simplest form is the **barrel vault**, a single continuous arch; the **groined vault** consists of two barrel vaults joined at right angles; a **ribbed vault** has a web of ribs added to the groins.

volute A spiral scroll used on Ionic and Corinthian capitals.

westwork In German Romanesque, a monumental entrance to a church consisting of towers, with a chapel above.

ziggurat In ancient Assyria and Babylonia, a tower in the shape of a stepped pyramid. It formed the base of a temple.

Illustrations of Architectural Styles and Elements

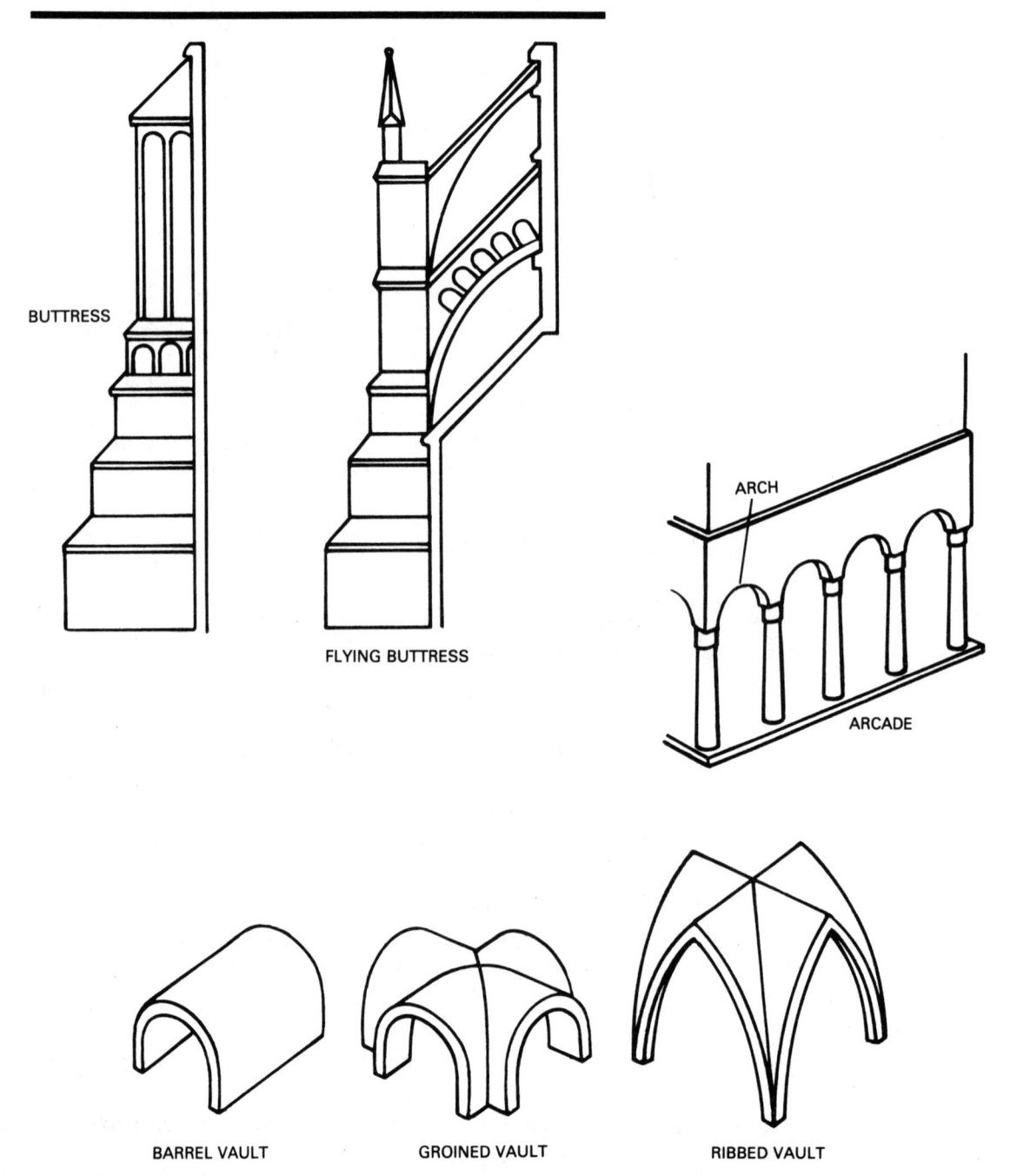

BUTTRESS

FLYING BUTTRESS

ARCH

ARCADE

BARREL VAULT

GROINED VAULT

RIBBED VAULT

The Arts **201**

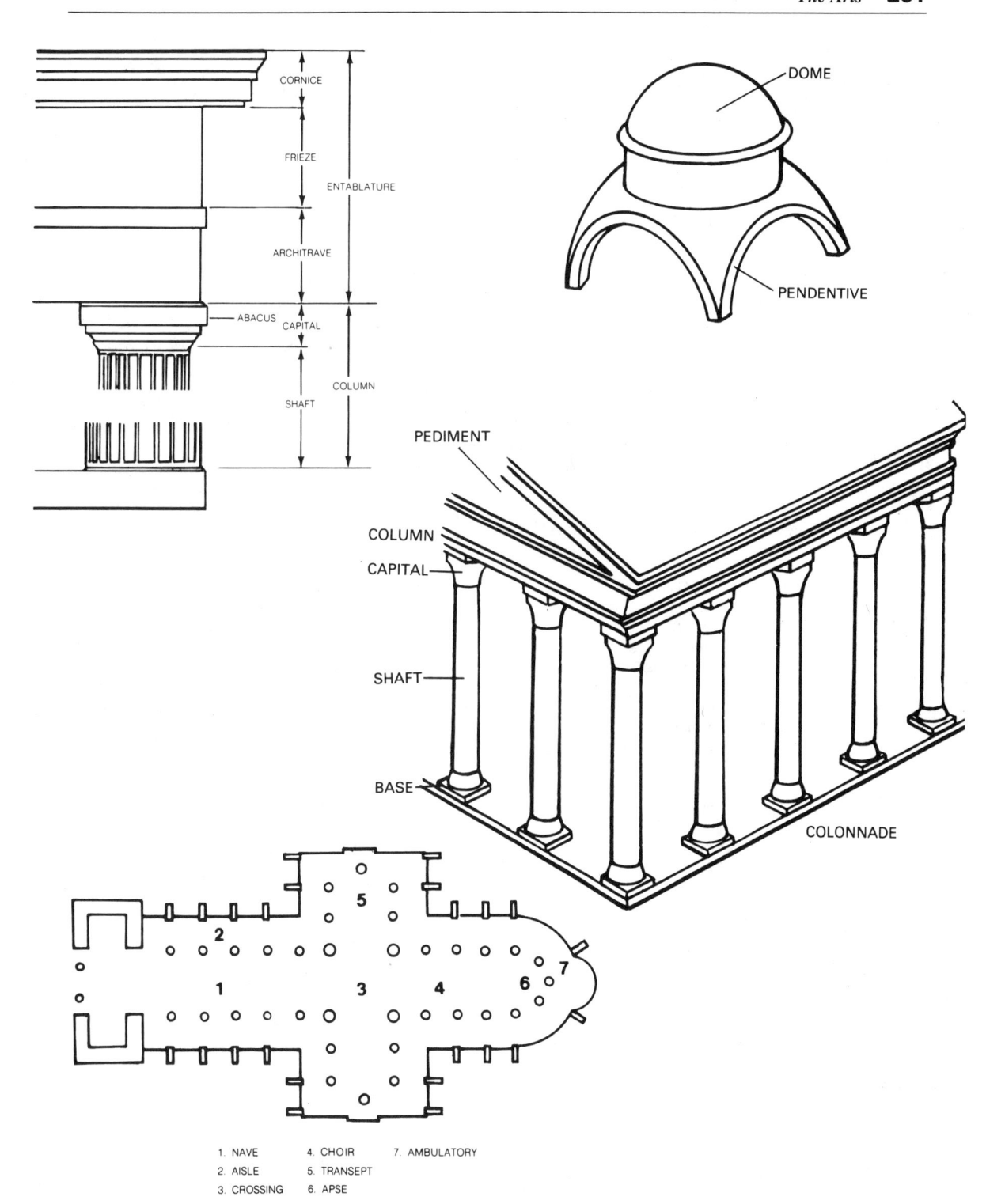

- CORNICE
- FRIEZE
- ENTABLATURE
- ARCHITRAVE
- ABACUS
- CAPITAL
- COLUMN
- SHAFT

- DOME
- PENDENTIVE

- PEDIMENT
- COLUMN
- CAPITAL
- SHAFT
- BASE
- COLONNADE

1. NAVE
2. AISLE
3. CROSSING
4. CHOIR
5. TRANSEPT
6. APSE
7. AMBULATORY

The Academy Awards

	Best actor	Best actress	Best director	Best picture
1927–28	Emil Jannings (*The Way of All Flesh*)	Janet Gaynor (*Seventh Heaven*)	Frank Borzage (*Seventh Heaven*) Lewis Milestone (*Two Arabian Knights*)	*Wings*
1928–29	Warner Baxter (*In Old Arizona*)	Mary Pickford (*Coquette*)	Frank Lloyd (*The Divine Lady*)	*Broadway Melody*
1929–30	George Arliss (*Disraeli*)	Norma Shearer (*The Divorcee*)	Lewis Milestone (*All Quiet on the Western Front*)	*All Quiet on the Western Front*
1930–31	Lionel Barrymore (*A Free Soul*)	Marie Dressler (*Min and Bill*)	Norma Taurog (*Skippy*)	*Cimarron*
1931–32	Frederic March (*Dr. Jekyll and Mr. Hyde*) Wallace Berry (*The Champ*)	Helen Hayes (*The Sin of Madelon Claudet*)	Frank Borzage (*Bad Girl*)	*Grand Hotel*
1932–33	Charles Laughton (*The Private Life of Henry VIII*)	Katharine Hepburn (*Morning Glory*)	Frank Lloyd (*Cavalcade*)	*Cavalcade*
1934	Clark Gable (*It Happened One Night*)	Claudette Colbert (*It Happened One Night*)	Frank Capra (*It Happened One Night*)	*It Happened One Night*
1935	Victor McLaglen (*The Informer*)	Bette Davis (*Dangerous*)	John Ford (*The Informer*)	*Mutiny on the Bounty*
1936	Paul Muni (*The Story of Louis Pasteur*)	Luise Rainer (*The Great Ziegfeld*)	Frank Capra (*Mr. Deeds Goes to Town*)	*The Great Ziegfeld*
1937	Spencer Tracy (*Captains Courageous*)	Luise Rainer (*The Good Earth*)	Leo McCarey (*The Awful Truth*)	*The Life of Emile Zola*
1938	Spencer Tracy (*Boys Town*)	Bette Davis (*Jezebel*)	Frank Capra (*You Can't Take It with You*)	*You Can't Take It with You*
1939	Robert Donat (*Goodbye Mr. Chips*)	Vivien Leigh (*Gone with the Wind*)	Victor Fleming (*Gone with the Wind*)	*Gone with the Wind*
1940	James Stewart (*The Philadelphia Story*)	Ginger Rogers (*Kitty Foyle*)	John Ford (*The Grapes of Wrath*)	*Rebecca*
1941	Gary Cooper (*Sergeant York*)	Joan Fontaine (*Suspicion*)	John Ford (*How Green Was My Valley*)	*How Green Was My Valley*
1942	James Cagney (*Yankee Doodle Dandy*)	Greer Garson (*Mrs. Miniver*)	William Wyler (*Mrs. Miniver*)	*Mrs. Miniver*
1943	Paul Lukas (*Watch on the Rhine*)	Jennifer Jones (*The Song of Bernadette*)	Michael Curtiz (*Casablanca*)	*Casablanca*
1944	Bing Crosby (*Going My Way*)	Ingrid Bergman (*Gaslight*)	Leo McCarey (*Going My Way*)	*Going My Way*
1945	Ray Milland (*The Lost Weekend*)	Joan Crawford (*Mildred Pierce*)	Billy Wilder (*The Lost Weekend*)	*The Lost Weekend*

The Arts

	Best actor	Best actress	Best director	Best picture
1946	Frederic March (*The Best Years of Our Lives*)	Olivia de Havilland (*To Each His Own*)	William Wyler (*The Best Years of Our Lives*)	*The Best Years of Our Lives*
1947	Ronald Coleman (*A Double Life*)	Loretta Young (*The Farmer's Daughter*)	Elia Kazan (*Gentleman's Agreement*)	*Gentleman's Agreement*
1948	Laurence Olivier (*Hamlet*)	Jane Wyman (*Johnny Belinda*)	John Huston (*The Treasure of the Sierra Madre*)	*Hamlet*
1949	Broderick Crawford (*All the King's Men*)	Olivia de Havilland (*The Heiress*)	Joseph L. Mankiewicz (*A Letter to Three Wives*)	*All the King's Men*
1950	Jose Ferrer (*Cyrano de Bergerac*)	Judy Holliday (*Born Yesterday*)	Joseph L. Mankiewicz (*All About Eve*)	*All About Eve*
1951	Humphrey Bogart (*The African Queen*)	Vivien Leigh (*A Streetcar Named Desire*)	George Stevens (*A Place in the Sun*)	*An American in Paris*
1952	Gary Cooper (*High Noon*)	Shirley Booth (*Come Back, Little Sheba*)	John Ford (*The Quiet Man*)	*The Greatest Show on Earth*
1953	William Holden (*Stalag 17*)	Audrey Hepburn (*Roman Holiday*)	Fred Zinnemann (*From Here to Eternity*)	*From Here to Eternity*
1954	Marlon Brando (*On the Waterfront*)	Grace Kelly (*The Country Girl*)	Elia Kazan (*On the Waterfront*)	*On the Waterfront*
1955	Ernest Borgnine (*Marty*)	Anna Magnani (*The Rose Tattoo*)	Delbert Mann (*Marty*)	*Marty*
1956	Yul Brynner (*The King and I*)	Ingrid Bergman (*Anastasia*)	George Stevens (*Giant*)	*Around the World in Eighty Days*
1957	Alec Guinness (*The Bridge on the River Kwai*)	Joanne Woodward (*The Three Faces of Eve*)	David Lean (*The Bridge on the River Kwai*)	*The Bridge on the River Kwai*
1958	David Niven (*Separate Tables*)	Susan Hayward (*I Want to Live*)	Vincente Minnelli (*Gigi*)	*Gigi*
1959	Charlton Heston (*Ben-Hur*)	Simone Signoret (*Room at the Top*)	William Wyler (*Ben-Hur*)	*Ben-Hur*
1960	Burt Lancaster (*Elmer Gantry*)	Elizabeth Taylor (*Butterfield 8*)	Billy Wilder (*The Apartment*)	*The Apartment*
1961	Maximillian Schell (*Judgment at Nuremberg*)	Sophia Loren (*Two Women*)	Jerome Robbins, Robert Wise (*West Side Story*)	*West Side Story*
1962	Gregory Peck (*To Kill a Mockingbird*)	Anne Bancroft (*The Miracle Worker*)	David Lean (*Lawrence of Arabia*)	*Lawrence of Arabia*
1963	Sidney Poitier (*Lilies of the Field*)	Patricia Neal (*Hud*)	Tony Richardson (*Tom Jones*)	*Tom Jones*
1964	Rex Harrison (*My Fair Lady*)	Julie Andrews (*Mary Poppins*)	George Cukor (*My Fair Lady*)	*My Fair Lady*
1965	Lee Marvin (*Cat Ballou*)	Julie Christie (*Darling*)	Robert Wise (*The Sound of Music*)	*The Sound of Music*
1966	Paul Scofield (*A Man for All Seasons*)	Elizabeth Taylor (*Who's Afraid of Virginia Woolf?*)	Fred Zinnemann (*A Man for All Seasons*)	*A Man for All Seasons*
1967	Rod Steiger (*In the Heat of the Night*)	Katharine Hepburn (*Guess Who's Coming to Dinner*)	Mike Nichols (*The Graduate*)	*In the Heat of the Night*

	Best actor	Best actress	Best director	Best picture
1968	Cliff Robertson (*Charly*)	Katharine Hepburn (*The Lion in Winter*); Barbra Streisand (*Funny Girl*)	Sir Carol Reed (*Oliver!*)	*Oliver!*
1969	John Wayne (*True Grit*)	Maggie Smith (*The Prime of Miss Jean Brodie*)	John Schlesinger (*Midnight Cowboy*)	*Midnight Cowboy*
1970	George C. Scott (*Patton;* refused)	Glenda Jackson (*Women in Love*)	Franklin Schaffner, Frank McCarthy (*Patton*)	*Patton*
1971	Gene Hackman (*The French Connection*)	Jane Fonda (*Klute*)	William Friedkin (*The French Connection*)	*The French Connection*
1972	Marlon Brando (*The Godfather*; refused)	Liza Minnelli (*Cabaret*)	Bob Fosse (*Cabaret*)	*The Godfather*
1973	Jack Lemmon (*Save the Tiger*)	Glenda Jackson (*A Touch of Class*)	George Roy Hill (*The Sting*)	*The Sting*
1974	Art Carney (*Harry and Tonto*)	Ellen Burstyn (*Alice Doesn't Live Here Anymore*)	Francis Ford Coppola (*The Godfather, Part II*)	*The Godfather, Part II*
1975	Jack Nicholson (*One Flew over the Cuckoo's Nest*)	Louise Fletcher (*One Flew over the Cuckoo's Nest*)	Milos Forman (*One Flew over the Cuckoo's Nest*)	*One Flew over the Cuckoo's Nest*
1976	Peter Finch (*Network*)	Faye Dunaway (*Network*)	John G. Avildsen (*Rocky*)	*Rocky*
1977	Richard Dreyfuss (*The Goodbye Girl*)	Diane Keaton (*Annie Hall*)	Woody Allen (*Annie Hall*)	*Annie Hall*
1978	Jon Voight (*Coming Home*)	Jane Fonda (*Coming Home*)	Michael Cimino (*The Deer Hunter*)	*The Deer Hunter*
1979	Dustin Hoffman (*Kramer vs. Kramer*)	Sally Field (*Norma Rae*)	Robert Benton (*Kramer vs. Kramer*)	*Kramer vs. Kramer*
1980	Robert De Niro (*Raging Bull*)	Sissy Spacek (*Coal Miner's Daughter*)	Robert Redford (*Ordinary People*)	*Ordinary People*
1981	Henry Fonda (*On Golden Pond*)	Katharine Hepburn (*On Golden Pond*)	Warren Beatty (*Reds*)	*Chariots of Fire*
1982	Ben Kingsley (*Gandhi*)	Meryl Streep (*Sophie's Choice*)	Richard Attenborough (*Gandhi*)	*Gandhi*
1983	Robert Duvall (*Tender Mercies*)	Shirley MacLaine (*Terms of Endearment*)	James L. Brooks (*Terms of Endearment*)	*Terms of Endearment*
1984	F. Murray Abraham (*Amadeus*)	Sally Field (*Places in the Heart*)	Milos Forman (*Amadeus*)	*Amadeus*
1985	William Hurt (*Kiss of the Spider Woman*)	Geraldine Page (*The Trip to Bountiful*)	Sydney Pollack (*Out of Africa*)	*Out of Africa*
1986	Paul Newman (*The Color of Money*)	Marlee Matlin (*Children of a Lesser God*)	Oliver Stone (*Platoon*)	*Platoon*
1987	Michael Douglas (*Wall Street*)	Cher (*Moonstruck*)	Bernardo Bertolucci (*The Last Emperor*)	*The Last Emperor*
1988	Dustin Hoffman (*Rain Man*)	Jody Foster (*The Accused*)	Barry Levinson (*Rain Man*)	*Rain Man*
1989	Daniel Day-Lewis (*My Left Foot*)	Jessica Tandy (*Driving Miss Daisy*)	Oliver Stone (*Born on the Fourth of July*)	*Driving Miss Daisy*

	Best actor	Best actress	Best director	Best picture
1990	Jeremy Irons (*Reversal of Fortune*)	Kathy Bates (*Misery*)	Kevin Costner (*Dances with Wolves*)	*Dances with Wolves*
1991	Anthony Hopkins (*The Silence of the Lambs*)	Jodie Foster (*The Silence of the Lambs*)	Jonathan Demme (*The Silence of the Lambs*)	*The Silence of the Lambs*
1992	Al Pacino (*Scent of a Women*)	Emma Thompson (*Howard's End*)	Clint Eastwood (*Unforgiven*)	*Unforgiven*

Additional Sources of Information

Apel, Willi, ed. *The Harvard Dictionary of Music,* rev., enl. Harvard University Press, 1969.
Arnold, Denis, ed. *The New Oxford Companion to Music,* 2 vol. Oxford University Press, 1983.
Boorstin, Daniel J. *The Creators: A History of Heroes of the Imagination.* Random House, 1992.
Chujoy, Anatole, and P. W. Manchester, eds. *The Dance Encyclopedia.* Simon & Schuster, 1967.
Collier, James L. *The Making of Jazz: A Comprehensive History.* Dell, 1979.
Corey, Melinda and George Ochoa. *A Cast of Thousands.* Facts on File, 1992.
Fleming, John et al. *Penguin Dictionary of Architecture,* 4th ed. Viking Penguin, 1991.
Gassner, John, and Edward Quinn, eds. *The Reader's Encyclopedia of World Drama.* Crowell, 1969.
Hartnoll, Phyllis, ed. *The Oxford Companion to the Theatre,* 4th ed. Oxford University Press, 1983.
Hunt, William D., Jr. *Encyclopedia of American Architects.* McGraw-Hill, 1980.
Janson, Horst W. *History of Art,* 4th ed. Abrams, 1991.
Jezic, Diane Peacock. *Women Composers: The Lost Tradition Found.* Feministi Press, 1989.
Kennedy, Michael. *The Oxford Dictionary of Music.* Oxford University Press, 1985.
Kerfeld, Barry. *The New Grove Dictionary of Jazz.* Macmillan, 1988.
Kirstein, Lincoln. *Dance: A Short History of Classic Theatrical Dancing.* Princeton Book Co., 1987.
Kobbe, Gustave. *The Definitive Kobbe's Opera Book.* Putnam, 1987.
Koegler, Horst. *Concise Oxford Dictionary of Ballet.* Oxford University Press, 1982.
Kostof, Spiro. *A History of Architecture: Settings and Rituals.* Oxford University Press, 1985.
Marks, Claude. *World Artists, 1950–1980.* H. W. Wilson Co., 1984.
McGraw-Hill Encyclopedia of World Drama, 5 vols. McGraw-Hill, 1972.
McDonagh, Don. *The Rise and Fall and Rise of Modern Dance.* Chicago Review, 1990.
Musgrove, John, ed. *A History of Architecture: Sir Banister-Fletcher's,* 19th ed. Butterworth, 1987.
Phaidon Encyclopedia of Art and Artists. Phaidon Press Ltd., 1978.
Random House Library of Painting and Sculpture. Random House, 1981.
Sadie, Stanley, ed. *The New Grove Dictionary of Music and Musicians,* 20 vols. Macmillan, 1980.
Sadie, Stanley, ed. *The New Grove Dictionary of Opera,* 4 vols. Macmillan, 1992.
Shipley, Joseph T. *Crown Guide to the World's Great Plays,* rev. ed. Crown, 1984.
Stephenson, Richard M. and Joseph Iaccarino. *The Complete Book of Ballroom Dancing.* Doubleday, 1980.
Vinson, James, ed. *Contemporary Dramatists.* St. Martin's Press, 1973.

8 Literature

Important U.S. and Canadian Authors / *207*

Important British, European, and Russian Authors / *214*

Important Asian, African, and Latin American Authors / *220*

Literary Terms / *221*

Pseudonyms for Famous Authors / *224*

Poet Laureates / *225*

Book Awards and Their Recipients / *226*

Additional Sources of Information / *229*

Important U.S. and Canadian Authors

Any list of "important" authors is subject to debate. The following list includes writers who have had a substantial impact on American and Canadian literature, whether as a result of a single work or an entire oeuvre. This list is not all-inclusive, but it does contain most of the authors who are generally considered to have made a substantial contribution to American and Canadian literature.

The titles and dates of first publication of each author's major works are given. An asterisk (*) designates a book that was awarded a Pulitzer prize in literature; a plus sign (+) indicates that the work was awarded a National Book Award; a dagger (†) indicates that the author was awarded a Nobel prize in literature; a (C) indicates the author is Canadian. In those instances where an author is known by a pseudonym, he or she is listed by that pseudonym with the real name in brackets.

Note: *See also* Chapter 7 for major playwrights.

Agee, James (1909–55): *Let Us Now Praise Famous Men* (1941), **A Death in the Family* (1957), *Agee on Film* (1958)

Aiken, Conrad (1889–1973): *The House of Dust: A Symphony* (1920), **Selected Poems* (1929), *Conversation; or, Pilgrim's Progress* (1940), *The Soldier* (1944), *The Kid* (1947), *Ushant: An Essay* (1952)

Alcott, Louisa May (1832–88): *Little Women* (1868–69), *Little Men* (1871), *Silver Pitchers and Independence* (1876), *Spinning-Wheel Stories* (1884)

Algren, Nelson (1909–81): *The Man with the Golden Arm* (1949), *A Walk on the Wild Side* (1956)

Anderson, Sherwood (1876–1941): *Winesburg, Ohio* (1919), *The Triumph of the Egg* (1921), *A Story Teller's Story* (1924), *Dark Laughter* (1925), *Beyond Desire* (1932)

Asimov, Isaac (1920–92): *Foundation* (1951), *Foundation and Empire* (1952), *Second Foundation* (1953), *Opus 200* (1979), *Foundation and Earth* (1986)

Atwood, Margaret (C) (1939–): *The Circle Game* (1966), *Surfacing* (1972), *Selected Poems* (1976), *Dancing Girls* (1977), *Life Before Man* (1979), *Bodily Harm* (1981), *The Handmaid's Tale* (1985), *Cat's Eye* (1988)

Auchincloss, Louis [Stanton] (1917–): *Portrait in Brownstone* (1962), *The Winthrop Covenant* (1976), *Life, Law and Letters* (1979), *Diary of a Yuppie* (1987)

Auden, W(ystan) H(ugh) (1907–73): *Spain* (1937), *For the Time Being* (1945), **The Age of Anxiety: A Baroque Eclogue* (1948), *Collected Shorter Poems, 1930–44* (1950), *Making, Knowing and Judging* (1956), *The Dyer's Hand* (1962), *Collected Poems* (1976)

Audubon, John James (1785–1851): *The Birds of America* (1827–38)

Austin, Mary (1868–1934): *Isidro* (1905), *A Woman of Genius* (1912), *The Ford* (1917), *Earth Horizon* (1932)

Baldwin, James (1924–87): *Go Tell It on the Mountain* (1953), *Notes of a Native Son* (1955), *Nobody Knows My Name* (1961), *Another Country* (1962), *Just Above My Head* (1979)

Baraka, Imamu Amiri (formerly LeRoi Jones, 1934–   ): *Dutchman* (1964), *The Slave* (1964), *The Toilet* (1964), *Black Music* (1967), *Black Magic . . .* (1969), *Selected Plays and Prose* (1979), *Selected Poetry* (1979)

Barth, John [Simmons] (1930–   ): *The Sot-Weed Factor* (1960), *Giles Goat-Boy* (1966), *Chimera* (1972), *The Last Voyage of Somebody the Sailor* (1991)

Barthelme, Donald (1931–89): *Come Back, Dr. Caligari* (1964), *Snow White* (1967), *City Life* (1970), *Sixty Stories* (1982)

Bartlett, John (1820–1905): *Familiar Quotations* (1855)

Baum, Lyman Frank (1856–1919): *The Wonderful Wizard of Oz* (1900)

Beattie, Ann (1947–   ): *Distortions* (1976), *Chilly Scenes of Winter* (1976), *Where You'll Find Me* (1986), *Picturing Will* (1990)

Bellow, Saul (1915–   )†: *Dangling Man* (1944), +*The Adventures of Augie March* (1953), *Henderson the Rain King* (1959), *Herzog* (1964), +*Mr. Sammler's Planet* (1971), *Humboldt's Gift* (1975), *The Dean's December* (1982), *More Die of Heartbreak* (1987)

Benchley, Robert (1889–1945): *Love Conquers All* (1922), *My Ten Years in a Quandary* (1936), *Benchley Beside Himself* (1943)

Benét, Stephen Vincent (1898–1943): *John Brown's Body* (1928), *Ballads and Poems, 1915–30* (1931), *Thirteen O'Clock* (1937), *Western Star* (1943)

Benét, William Rose (1886–1950): *Oxford Anthology of American Literature* (editor, 1938), *The Dust Which Is God* (1941)

Bierce, Ambrose (c. 1842–1914): *Tales of Soldiers and Civilians* (1891), *Can Such Things Be?* (1893), *The Devil's Dictionary* (1911)

Bontemps, Arna (1902–73): *God Sends Sunday* (1931), *Drums at Dusk* (1939), *Sam Patch* (1951), *One Hundred Years of Negro Freedom* (1961)

Boyle, Kay (1903–   ): *Wedding Day* (1930), *Plagued by the Nightingale* (1931), *Death of a Man* (1936), *Thirty Stories* (1946), *The Underground Woman* (1975), *Fifty Stories* (1980)

Bradbury, Ray (1920–   ): *The Martian Chronicles* (1950), *The Illustrated Man* (1951), *Fahrenheit 451* (1953), *Something Wicked This Way Comes* (1962), *I Sing the Body Electric* (1969)

Bradstreet, Anne (c. 1612–72): *The Tenth Muse Lately Sprung Up in America* (1650)

Brooks, Gwendolyn (1917–   ): *Annie Allen* (1949), *In the Mecca* (1968), *Family Pictures* (1970)

Buck, Pearl (1892–1973)†: *The Good Earth* (1931), *My Several Worlds* (1954), *Imperial Woman* (1956), *Command the Morning* (1959), *A Bridge for Passing* (1962)

Burroughs, Edgar Rice (1875–1950): *Tarzan of the Apes* (1914)

Burroughs, William S. (1914–   ): *The Naked Lunch* (1959), *Nova Express* (1964), *Cities of the Red Night* (1981)

Capote, Truman (1924–84): *Other Voices, Other Rooms* (1948), *The Grass Harp* (1951), *Breakfast at Tiffany's* (1958), *In Cold Blood* (1966)

Cather, Willa (1873–1947): *O Pioneers!* (1913), *The Song of the Lark* (1915), *My Antonia* (1918), *One of Ours* (1922), *Shadows on the Rock* (1931)

Chandler, Raymond (1888–1959): *The Big Sleep* (1939), *Farewell, My Lovely* (1940), *The Long Goodbye* (1954)

Cheever, John (1912–82): +*The Wapshot Chronicle* (1957), *The Wapshot Scandal* (1964), *Falconer* (1977), **The Stories of John Cheever* (1978)

Chopin, Kate (1851–1904): *Bayou Folk* (1894), *the Awakening* (1899)

Connor, Ralph [Charles William Gordon] (C) (1860–1937): *Black Rock: A Tale of the Selkirks* (1898), *The Sky Pilot: A Tale of the Foothills* (1899), *The Men from Glengarry: A Tale of the Ottawa* (1901), *Glengarry School Days: A Story of Early Days in Glengarry* (1902), *The Foreigner: A Tale of Saskatchewan* (1909), *The Sky Pilot in No Man's Land* (1919)

Cooper, James Fenimore (1789–1851): *The Spy* (1821), *The Pioneers* (1823), *The Pilot* (1823), *The Last of the Mohicans* (1826), *The Prairie* (1827), *The American Democrat* (1838), *The Pathfinder* (1840), *The Deerslayer* (1841)

Crane, Stephen (1871–1900): *Maggie: A Girl of the Streets* (1893), *The Red Badge of Courage* (1895), *The Black Riders* (1895), *The Open Boat* (1898), *The Monster* (1899)

cummings, e.e. [Edward Estlin] (1894–1962): *The Enormous Room* (1922), *&* (1925), *is 5* (1926), *50 Poems* (1940), *I + I* (1944), *95 Poems* (1958), +*Poems 1923–1954* (1955)

Davies, Robertson (C) (1913–   ): *A Mixture of Frailties* (1958), *Fifth Business* (1970), *The Rebel Angels* (1981), *What's Bred in the Bone* (1985), *The Lyre of Orpheus* (1990)

Dickinson, Emily (1830–86): *Poems* (1890), *Poems: Second Series* (1891), *Poems: Third Series* (1896), *The Single Hound* (1914)

Didion, Joan (1934–   ): *Slouching Towards Bethlehem* (1968), *The White Album* (1979), *Play It As It Lays* (1970), *Democracy* (1984)

Dillard, Annie (1945–   ): **Pilgrim at Tinker Creek* (1974), *Teaching a Stone To Talk* (1982), *The Living* (1992)

Doctorow, E(dgar) L(awrence) (1931–   ): *The Book of Daniel* (1971), *Ragtime* (1975), *Loon Lake* (1980), *World's Fair* (1986), *Billy Bathgate* (1989)

Dos Passos, John (1896–1970): *Manhattan Transfer* (1925), *The 42nd Parallel* (1930), *1919* (1932), *The Big Money* (1936)

Dreiser, Theodore (1871–1945): *Sister Carrie* (1900), *The Financier* (1912), *The Titan* (1914), *The Genius* (1915), *An American Tragedy* (1925)

Edel, Leon (1907–   ): * +*Henry James: A Life* (5 vols, 1953–1972), *Bloomsbury, A House of Lions* (1979), *Stuff of Sleep and Dreams* (1982)

Eliot, T(homas) S(tearns) (1888–1965)†: *Prufrock and Other Observations* (1917), *The Waste Land* (1922), *Murder in the Cathedral* (1935), *Four Quartets* (1943)

Ellison, Ralph (1914–   ): +*Invisible Man* (1952)

Emerson, Ralph Waldo (1803–82): *Nature* (1836), "The American Scholar" (1837), *Essays: First Series* (1841), *Essays: Second Series* (1844), *Conduct of Life* (1860), *Society and Solitude* (1870)

Faulkner, William (1897–1962)†: *Soldier's Pay* (1926), *Sartoris* (1929), *The Sound and the Fury* (1929), *As I Lay Dying* (1930), *Absalom, Absalom!* (1936), *The Hamlet* (1940), *A Fable (1954), *The Reivers (1962)

Fitzgerald, F. Scott (1896–1940): *Tales of the Jazz Age* (1922), *The Great Gatsby* (1925), *Tender Is the Night* (1934), *The Last Tycoon* (1941)

Franklin, Benjamin (1706–90): *Poor Richard's Almanack* (1733–58), *Autobiography* (1771–88)

Frost, Robert (1874–1963): *North of Boston* (1914), *Mountain Interval* (1916), **New Hampshire* (1923), **Collected Poems* (1930), **A Further Range* (1936), **A Witness Tree* (1942), *In the Clearing* (1962)

Gardner, John (1933–82): *Grendel* (1971), *October Light* (1976), *Freddy's Book* (1980)

Ginsberg, Allen (1926–   ): *Howl and Other Poems* (1956), *Kaddish and Other Poems* (1961), **The Fall of America: Poems of These States* (1973)

Hammett, Dashiell (1894–1961): *The Maltese Falcon* (1930), *The Thin Man* (1932)

Hawkes, John Clendennin Burne, Jr. (1925–   ): *The Lime Twig* (1961), *The Blood Oranges* (1971), *Death, Sleep and the Traveler* (1974)

Hawthorne, Nathaniel (1804–64): *Twice-Told Tales* (1837; enlarged 1842), *The Scarlet Letter* (1850), *The House of the Seven Gables* (1851)

Heinlein, Robert A. (1907–   ): *Stranger in a Strange Land* (1961), *Time Enough for Love* (1973)

Heller, Joseph (1923–   ): *Catch-22* (1961), *Something Happened* (1974), *Good as Gold* (1979)

Hellman, Lillian (1905–84): *An Unfinished Woman* (1969), *Pentimento* (1973), *Scoundrel Time* (1976)

Hemingway, Ernest (1899–1961)†: *The Sun Also Rises* (1926), *A Farewell to Arms* (1929), *To Have and Have Not* (1937), *For Whom the Bell Tolls* (1940), **The Old Man and the Sea* (1952), *A Moveable Feast* (1964)

Henry, O. [William Sydney Porter] (1862–1910): *Cabbages and Kings* (1904), *The Four Million* (1906), *The Trimmed Lamp* (1907), *The Voice of the City* (1908), *Whirligigs* (1910), *Strictly Business* (1910), *Sixes and Sevens* (1911), *Rolling Stones* (1913), *Postscripts* (1923)

Hersey, John [Richard] (1914–   ): **A Bell for Adano* (1944), *Hiroshima* (1946), *The Wall* (1950)

Howells, William Dean (1837–1920): *The Rise of Silas Lapham* (1885), *A Traveler from Altruria* (1894)

Hughes, Langston (1902–67): *The Weary Blues* (1926), *The Ways of White Folks* (1934), *Shakespeare in Harlem* (1941), *Ask Your Mama* (1961)

Hurston, Zora Neale (1891–1960): *Mules and Men* (1935), *Their Eyes Were Watching God* (1937), *Dust Tracks on a Road* (1942)

Irving, Washington (1783–1859): *History of New York* (1809), *The Sketch Book* (1819–20), *The Crayon Miscellany* (3 vols., 1835)

Jackson, Shirley (1919–65): *The Lottery* (1949), *The Bird's Nest* (1954), *The Haunting of Hill House* (1959), *We Have Always Lived in the Castle* (1962)

James, Henry (1843–1916): *The American* (1877), *The Europeans* (1878), *Daisy Miller* (1879), *The Portrait of a Lady* (1881), *The Bostonians* (1886), *Embarrassments* (1896), *The Two Magics* (1898), *The Awkward Age* (1899), *The Ambassadors* (1903), *The Golden Bowl* (1904)

Jarrell, Randall (1914–1965): *Selected Poems* (1955), +*The Woman at the Washington Zoo* (1960)

Jong, Erica (1942–   ): *Fear of Flying* (1973), *Fanny* (1980)

Kerouac, Jack (1922–69): *On the Road* (1957), *The Dharma Bums* (1958), *Desolation Angels* (1965)

Kosinski, Jerzy (1933–91): *The Painted Bird* (1965), +*Steps* (1968), *Being There* (1971), *Cockpit* (1975), *Passion Play* (1979), *Pinball* (1982), *The Hermit of 69th Street* (1988)

Lardner, Ring (1885–1933): *You Know Me, Al: A Bushar's Letters* (1916), *How to Write Short Stories* (1924), *The Love Nest and Other Stories* (1926)

Leacock, Stephen (C) (1869–1944): *Literary Lapses* (1910), *Nonsense Novels* (1911), *Sunshine Sketches of a Little Town* (1912), *Arcadian Adventures with the Idle Rich* (1914), *My Discovery of the West* (1937)

Lewis, Sinclair (1885–1951)†: *Main Street* (1920), *Babbitt* (1922), *Arrowsmith* (1925), *Dodsworth* (1929)

London, Jack (1876–1916): *The Call of the Wild* (1903), *The Sea-Wolf* (1904), *White Fang* (1906), *The Iron Heel* (1908), *Martin Eden* (1909)

Longfellow, Henry Wadsworth (1807–82): *Voices of the Night* (1839), *Ballads and Other Poems* (1841), *Hiawatha* (1855), *The Courtship of Miles Standish* (1858), *The Tales of a Wayside Inn* (1863)

Lowell, James Russell (1819–91): *A Fable for Critics* (1848), *The Vision of Sir Launfal* (1848), *The Cathedral* (1869)

Lowell, Robert (1917–77): *Land of Unlikeness* (1944), *Lord Weary's Castle* (1946), *The Mill of the Kavanaughs* (1951), *Old Glory* (1964), *Dolphin* (1973)

Lowry, Malcolm (1909–57): *Ultramarine* (1933), *Under the Volcano* (1947), *Hear Us O Lord from Heaven Thy Dwelling Place* (1961)

Mailer, Norman (1923–): *The Naked and the Dead* (1948), *An American Dream* (1965), *The Armies of the Night* (1968), *The Executioner's Song* (1979), *Ancient Evenings* (1983), *Tough Guys Don't Dance* (1987), *Harlot's Ghost* (1990)

Malamud, Bernard (1914–86): *+The Fixer* (1967), +*The Magic Barrel* (1958), *The Tenants* (1971), *God's Grace* (1982)

McCarthy, Mary (1912–89): *The Groves of Academe* (1952), *Memories of a Catholic Girlhood* (1957), *The Group* (1963), *Cannibals and Missionaries* (1979), *Intellectual Memoirs: New York, 1936–1938* (1992)

McCullers, Carson (1917–67): *The Heart Is a Lonely Hunter* (1940), *Member of the Wedding* (1946), *Clock Without Hands* (1961)

Melville, Herman (1819–91): *Typee* (1846), *Omoo* (1847), *White-Jacket* (1850), *Moby-Dick* (1851)

Mencken, H(enry) L(ouis) (1880–1956): *The American Language* (1919, rev. 1921, 1923, 1936; suppl. 1945, 1948)

Michener, James (1907–): *Tales of the South Pacific* (1947), *Hawaii* (1959), *The Source* (1965), *The Drifters* (1971), *Chesapeake* (1978), *Caribbean* (1979), *Texas* (1985), *Alaska* (1988), *Mexico* (1992)

Miller, Henry (1891–1980): *Tropic of Cancer* (1934), *Tropic of Capricorn* (1939)

Mitchell, Margaret (1900–49): *Gone with the Wind* (1936)

Montgomery, Lucy Maude (C) (1874–1942): *Anne of Green Gables* (1908), *Emily of New Moon* (1923), *The Blue Castle* (1926), *A Tangled Web* (1931), *Jane of Lantern Hill* (1937)

Morrison, Toni [Chloe Anthony Wofford] (1931–): *The Bluest Eye* (1970), *Sula* (1973), +*Song of Solomon* (1977), *Tar Baby* (1981), *Beloved* (1987), *Jazz* (1992)

Munro, Alice (C) (1931–): *Dance of the Happy Shades* (1968), *Lives of the Girls and Women* (1971), *Who Do You Think You Are* (1978), *The Progress of Love* (1986)

Oates, Joyce Carol (1938–): *A Garden of Earthly Delights* (1967), *Expensive People* (1968), +*them* (1969), *Bellefleur* (1980), *On Boxing* (1987), *You Must Remember This* (1988), *American Appetites* (1989), *Black Water* (1992)

Paine, Thomas (1737–1809): *Common Sense* (1776), *The Age of Reason* (1794–95)

Parker, Dorothy (1893–1967): *Men I'm Not Married To* (1922), *Women I'm Not Married To* (1922), *Laments for the Living* (1930), *After Such Pleasures* (1933), *Here Lies* (1942), *Collected Poems: Not So Deep as a Well* (1937)

Percy, Walker (1916–): +*The Moviegoer* (1961), *The Last Gentleman* (1966), *Love in the Ruins* (1971), *The Thanatos Syndrome* (1987)

Plath, Sylvia (1932–63): *The Colossus* (1960), *The Bell Jar* (1963), *Ariel* (1965), *Collected Poems* (1981)

Poe, Edgar Allan (1809–49): *Poems by Edgar A. Poe* (1831), *Tales of the Grotesque and Arabesque* (1840), *Tales* (1845), *The Raven and Other Poems* (1845)

Porter, Katherine Anne (1890–1980): *Flowering Judas* (1930), *Pale Horse, rPale Rider* (1939), *The Leaning Tower* (1944), *Ship of Fools* (1962), *Collected Stories* (1965)

Pound, Ezra (1885–1972): *Cantos* (1970)

Pratt, E. J. (C) (1882–1964): *The Witches' Brew* (1925), *Titans: Two Poems* (1926), *The Fable of the Goats and Other Poems* (1932), *The Titanic* (1935), *Brebeuf and His Brethren* (1940), *Towards the Last Spike* (1952), *The Collected Poems of E. J. Pratt* (1958)

Pynchon, Thomas (1937–): *V* (1963), +*Gravity's Rainbow* (1973) *Vineland* (1990)

Rand, Ayn (1905–82): *The Fountainhead* (1943), *Atlas Shrugged* (1957)

Richler, Mordecai (C) (1931–): *A Choice of Enemies* (1957), *The Apprenticeship of Duddy Kravitz* (1959), *Cocksure* (1968), *St. Urbain's Horseman* (1971), *Solomon Gursky Was Here* (1989)

Roberts, Sir Charles G. D. (C) (1860–1943): *Orion, and Other Poems* (1880), *In Divers Tones* (1887), *Songs of the Common Day* (1893), *Earth's Enigmas* (1896), *The Vagrant of Time* (1927), *The Iceberg, and Other Poems* (1934), *Further Animal Stories* (1936)

Ross, Sinclair (C) (1908–): *As for Me and My House* (1941), *The Well* (1958), *The Lamp at Noon and Other Stories* (1968), *Whir of Gold* (1970), *Sawbones Memorial* (1974)

Roth, Philip (1933–): +*Goodbye, Columbus* (1959), *Letting Go* (1962), *Portnoy's Complaint* (1969), *The Great American Novel* (1973), *The Ghost Writer* (1979), *The Counterlife* (1986), *The Facts: A Novelist's Autobiography* (1988), *Deception* (1990), *Patrimony: A True Story* (1991)

Salinger, J. D. (1919–): *The Catcher in the Rye* (1951), *Franny and Zooey* (1961)

Sandburg, Carl (1878–1967): *Chicago Poems* (1916), *Cornhuskers* (1918), *Complete Poems* (1950)

Saroyan, William (1908–81): *The Daring Young Man on the Flying Trapeze* (1934), *The Human Comedy* (1943), *One Day in the Afternoon of the World* (1964)

Sexton, Anne (1928–74): *Live or Die* (1966), *Love Poems* (1969)

Singer, Isaac Bashevis (1904–91)†: *Satan in Goray* (1935), *The Family Moskat* (1950), *Gimpel the Fool* (1957), *The Spinoza of Market Street* (1961), *Old Love* (1979), *The King of the Fields* (1988)

Stein, Gertrude (1874–1946): *Three Lives* (1909), *The Autobiography of Alice B. Toklas* (1933), *Yes Is for a Very Young Man* (1946)

Steinbeck, John (1902–68)†: *Tortilla Flat* (1935), *Of Mice and Men* (1937), *The Long Valley* (1938), **The Grapes of Wrath* (1939), *East of Eden* (1952)

Stowe, Harriet Beecher (1811–96): *Uncle Tom's Cabin* (1852)

Styron, William (1925–   ): *Lie Down in Darkness* (1951), **The Confessions of Nat Turner* (1967), *Sophie's Choice* (1979)

Thoreau, Henry David (1817–62): *Civil Disobedience* (1849), *Walden* (1854), *The Maine Woods* (1864)

Twain, Mark [Samuel Langhorne Clemens] (1835–1910): *The Innocents Abroad* (1869), *Roughing It* (1872), *The Adventures of Tom Sawyer* (1876), *The Adventures of Huckleberry Finn* (1884), *Following the Equator* (1897)

Tyler, Anne (1941–   ): *A Slipping-Down Life* (1970), *Searching for Caleb* (1976), *Morgan's Passing* (1980), *Dinner at the Homesick Restaurant* (1982), *The Accidental Tourist* (1985), **Breathing Lessons* (1988), *Saint Maybe* (1991)

Updike, John (1932–   ): *Rabbit, Run* (1960), *Couples* (1968), **Rabbit Is Rich* (1981), *The Witches of Eastwick* (1984), *Rabbit at Rest* (1990)

Vonnegut, Kurt Jr., (1922–   ): *Cat's Cradle* (1963), *Slaughterhouse-Five; or The Children's Crusade* (1969), *Breakfast of Champions* (1973), *Bluebeard* (1987)

Walker, Alice (1944–   ): *Meridian* (1976), **The Color Purple* (1982), *The Temple of My Familiar* (1988)

Warren, Robert Penn (1905–   ): **All the King's Men* (1946), **Promises* (1957), *The Cave* (1959)

Webster, Noah (1758–1843): *An American Dictionary of the English Language* (2 vols., 1828)

Welty, Eudora (1909–   ): *The Bride of the Innisfallen* (1955), *Thirteen Stories* (1965), **The Optimist's Daughter* (1970), *The Collected Stories of Eudora Welty* (1980), *One Writer's Beginnings* (1984)

Wharton, Edith (1862–1937): *Ethan Frome* (1911), *Xingu and Other Stories* (1916), **The Age of Innocence* (1920)

White, E. B. (1899–1985): *One Man's Meat* (1942), *Here Is New York* (1949), *Charlotte's Web* (1952), *The Elements of Style* (1959)

Whitman, Walt (1819–92): *Leaves of Grass* (1855), *Drum-Taps* (1865), *Passage to India* (1871), *Two Rivulets* (1876), *November Boughs* (1888)

Wilson, Edmund (1895–1972): *Axel's Castle* (1931), *The Wound and the Bow* (1941), *Patriotic Gore* (1962)

Wolfe, Thomas (1900–38): *Look Homeward, Angel* (1929), *Of Time and the River* (1935), *The Web and the Rock* (1939)

Wolfe, Tom [Thomas Kennerly Wolfe, Jr.] (1931–   ): *The Pump House Gang* (1968), *The Electric Kool-Aid Acid Test* (1968), *The Right Stuff* (1975), *The Bonfire of the Vanities* (1988)

Wouk, Herman (1915–   ): **The Caine Mutiny* (1951), *Marjorie Morningstar* (1955), *The Winds of War* (1971), *War and Remembrance* (1978)

Wright, Richard (1908–60): *Native Son* (1940), *Black Boy* (1945), *The Outsider* (1953)

Important British, European, and Russian Authors

This list of important European authors is not meant to be comprehensive. It includes most European writers who have made substantial contributions to the literature of their countries, their continent, and the world at large. Some of their most significant works appear here. A dagger (†) indicates that the author was awarded a Nobel prize in literature.

The years of first publication are given in parentheses. Authors known by their pseudonyms are so listed, with their real names given in brackets.

Note: *See also* Chapter 7 for major playwrights.

Amis, Kingsley (English, 1922–): *Lucky Jim* (1954), *One Fat Englishman* (1963), *Jake's Thing* (1978), *Stanley and the Women* (1984), *Old Devils* (1986), *Difficulties with Girls* (1988)

Andersen, Hans Christian (Danish, 1805–75): *Fairy Tales for Children* (1835–42), *Tales and Stories* (1839), *New Fairy Tales* (1843–47), *New Tales and Stories* (1858–67)

Austen, Jane (English, 1775–1817): *Sense and Sensibility* (1811), *Pride and Prejudice* (1813), *Emma* (1816), *Persuasion* (1818)

Balzac, Honoré de (French, 1799–1850): *Droll Tales* (1832–37), *The Human Comedy* (1842–53)

Baudelaire, Charles Pierre (French, 1821–67): *Les fleurs du mal* (1857), *Les paradis artificiels* (1860), *Les épaves* (1861), *Nouvelles fleurs du mal* (1866), *Petits poèmes en prose* (1869)

Belloc, Joseph Hilaire Peter (English, 1870–1953): *The Bad Child's Book of Beasts* (1896), *On Nothing* (1908), *Cautionary Tales for Children* (1908), *On Everything* (1909), *On Anything* (1910)

Blake, William (English, 1757–1827): *Poetical Sketches* (1783), *Songs of Innocence* (1789), *The Marriage of Heaven and Hell* (1793), *The Visions of the Daughters of Albion* (1793), *Songs of Experience* (1794), *Milton* (1804)

Blasco Ibañez, Vicente (Spanish 1867–1928): *The Fruit of the Vine* (1896), *Blood and Sand* (1898), *The Mayflower* (1902), *The Cabin* (1905), *Reeds and Mud* (1908)

Blok, Alexander Alexandrovich (Russian, 1880–1921): *Verses About the Beautiful Lady* (1904), *The Puppet Show* (1906), *A Frightful World* (c. 1910), *Dances of Death* (c. 1910), *Black Blood* (c. 1910), *The Twelve* (1918)

Boccaccio, Giovanni (Italian, 1313–75): *Decameron* (1351–53)

Böll, Heinrich (German, 1917–): *Traveler, If You Come to Spa* (1950), *Adam, Where Art Thou?* (1951), *Billiards at Half-past Nine* (1959), *The Clown* (1963), *Group Portrait with Lady* (1971), *The Lost Honor of Katharina Blum* (1974), *The Safety Net* (1982)

Boswell, James (English, 1740–95): *The Life of Samuel Johnson* (1791)

Brontë, Charlotte (English, 1816–55): *Jane Eyre* (1847)

Brontë, Emily (English, 1818–48): *Wuthering Heights* (1847)

Browning, Elizabeth Barrett (English, 1806–61): *The Seraphim and Other Poems* (1838), *Sonnets from the Portuguese* (1850), *Aurora Leigh* (1857), *Last Poems* (1862)

Browning, Robert (English, 1812–89): *Bells and Pomegranates* (1841–46), *Dramatic Lyrics* (1842), *Dramatic Romances and Lyrics* (1845), *Christmas Eve and Easter Day* (1850), *Men and Women* (1855), *Dramatis Personae* (1864)

Bulgakov, Mikhail (Russian, 1891–1940): *The Master and Margarita* (1967), *The Heart of a Dog* (1968)

Burgess, Anthony (English, 1917–   ): *A Clockwork Orange* (1962), *Napoleon Symphony: A Novel in Four Movements* (1974), *Earthly Powers* (1980), *Enderby's Dark Lady* (1984)

Burns, Robert (Scottish, 1759–96): *Poems, Chiefly in the Scottish Dialect* (1786), *The Scots Musical Museum* (1787–96)

Byron, Lord [George Gordon] (English, 1788–1824): *Childe Harold's Pilgrimage*, Cantos I and II (1812), *Childe Harold*, Cantos III and IV (1816, 1817), *The Prisoner of Chillon* (1816), *Manfred* (1817), *Don Juan* (1819–24)

Calvino, Italo (Italian, 1923–85): *The Path of the Nest of Spiders* (1947), *The Watcher and Other Stories* (1958), *Cosmicomics* (1965), *T Zero* (1967), *Invisible Cities* (1972), *If on a Winter's Night a Traveler* (1979), *Mr. Palomar* (1985)

Camus, Albert (French, 1913–60)†: *The Stranger* (1942, revised 1953), *The Myth of Sisyphus and Other Essays* (1942), *Caligula* (1944), *The Plague* (1947), *The Rebel* (1951), *The Fall* (1956), *Exile and the Kingdom* (1957)

Canetti, Elias (German, 1905–   )†: *Auto-da-Fé* (1936), *Crowds and Power* (1960)

Capek, Karel (Czech, 1890–1938): *R.U.R.* (1921), *Tales from One Pocket* (1929), *Tales from the Other Pocket* (1929), *Hordubal* (1933), *Meteor* (1934), *An Ordinary Life* (1934)

Carroll, Lewis [Charles Lutwidge Dodgson] (English, 1832–98): *Alice's Adventures in Wonderland* (1865), *Through the Looking Glass* (1871)

Catullus (Roman, c. 84 B.C.–54 B.C.): verse

Cervantes Saavedra, Miguel de (Spanish, 1547–1616): *Don Quixote* (1605–15), *Exemplary Novels* (1613)

Chaucer, Geoffrey (English, c. 1340–1400): *The Canterbury Tales* (after 1387)

Chekhov, Anton Pavlovich (Russian, 1860–1904): *Motley Tales* (1886), *The Duel* (1892), *Uncle Vanya* (1896), *The Seagull* (1896), *Three Sisters* (1900), *The Cherry Orchard* (1904)

Christie, Agatha (English, 1891–1976): *The Murder of Roger Ackroyd* (1926), *Murder on the Orient Express* (1934), *Death on the Nile* (1937), *And Then There Were None* (1940), *The Pale Horse* (1961)

Coleridge, Samuel Taylor (English, 1772–1834): *Lyrical Ballads* (1798), *Sybilline Leaves* (1817), *Biographia Literaria* (1817), *The Poetical Works* (1834)

Colette [Sidonie-Gabrielle Colette] (French, 1873–1954): *Claudine* (1900–03), *The Vagrant* (1910), *Mitsou* (1918), *Chéri* (1920), *A Lesson in Love* (1928), *Gigi* (1944)

Conrad, Joseph (English, 1857–1924): *The Nigger of the "Narcissus"* (1897), *Lord Jim* (1900), *Typhoon* (1902), *Nostromo* (1904), *Chance* (1914), *Victory* (1915)

Dante Alighieri (Italian, 1265–1321): *Divine Comedy* (c. 1310–20)

Defoe, Daniel (English, 1660–1731): *Robinson Crusoe* (1719), *Moll Flanders* (1722), *Roxanna* (1724)

Dickens, Charles (English, 1812–70): *Oliver Twist* (1838), *Nicholas Nickleby* (1839), *A Christmas Carol* (1843), *David Copperfield* (1850), *Bleak House* (1853), *A Tale of Two Cities* (1859), *Great Expectations* (1861), *Edwin Drood* (1870)

Dinesen, Isak [Karen Christence Dinesen, Baroness Blixen-Finecke] (Danish, 1885–1962): *Seven Gothic Tales* (1934), *Out of Africa* (1937), *Winter's Tales* (1942), *Last Tales* (1957)

Donne, John (English, 1572–1631): *The Anniversaries* (1611, 1612), *Songs and Sonnets* (1633)

Dostoyevsky, Fyodor Mikhaylovich (Russian, 1821–81): *Notes from the Underground* (1864), *Crime and Punishment* (1866), *The Idiot* (1869), *The Possessed* (1871–72), *The Brothers Karamazov* (1880)

Doyle, Sir Arthur Conan (English, 1859–1930): *Study in Scarlet* (1887), *The Sign of the Four* (1890), *The Adventures of Sherlock Holmes* (1892), *The Valley of Fear* (1915), *The Case Book of Sherlock Holmes* (1927)

Dryden, John (English, 1631–1700): *All for Love* (1678), *Absalom and Achitophel* (1681), *The Medal* (1682), *MacFlecknoe* (1682)

Dumas, Alexandre, père (French, 1802–70): *The Count of Monte-Cristo* (1844–45), *The Three Musketeers* (1844), *The Corsican Brothers* (1844)

Durrell, Lawrence (English, 1912–90): *The Alexandria Quartet* (1957–60)

Eliot, George [Mary Ann Evans] (English, 1819–80): *Silas Marner* (1861), *Middlemarch* (1871–72)

Fielding, Henry (English, 1707–54): *The Tragedy of Tragedies; or, The Life and Death of Tom Thumb the Great* (1731), *Joseph Andrews* (1742), *Tom Jones* (1749)

Flaubert, Gustave (French, 1821–80): *Madame Bovary* (1857), *Sentimental Education* (1869)

Forster, E. M. (English, 1879–1970): *A Room with a View* (1908), *Howard's End* (1910), *A Passage to India* (1924)

García Lorca, Federico (Spanish, 1898–1936): *Canciones* (1927), *Ode to Walt Whitman* (1933), *Lament for the Death of Ignacio Sanchez Mejias* (1935), *Poet in New York* (1940)

Gide, André (French, 1869–1951)†: *The Immoralist* (1902), *Straight is the Gate* (1909), *The Pastoral Symphony* (1919), *The Counterfeiters* (1926)

Goethe, Johann Wolfgang von (German, 1749–1832): *Wilhelm Meister's Apprenticeship* (1795–96), *Faust*, Part I (1819), Part II (1821)

Gogol, Nikolai (Russian, 1809–52): *Arabesques* (1835), *Mirgorod* (1835), *The Inspector General* (1836), *Dead Souls* (1842), *Collected Works* (1842)

Golding, William (English, 1911–   )†: *Lord of the Flies* (1954), *Free Fall* (1959), *Rites of Passage* (1980)

Gombrowicz, Witold (Polish, 1904–69): *Memoir from Adolescence* (1933), *Ferdydurke* (1937), *Pornografia* (1960)

Gorky, Maxim (Russian, 1868–1936): *Foma Gordeyev* (1899), *Twenty-Six Men and a Girl and Other Stories* (1902), *The Lower Depths* (1902), *Mother* (1906)

Grass, Günter   (German, 1927–   ): *The Tin Drum* (1959), *The Flounder* (1977), *The Rat* (1986)

Grimm, Wilhelm   (German, 1786–1859): **Grimm, Jakob**   (German, 1785–1863): *Grimm's Fairy Tales* (1812–15)

Hamsun, Knut   (Norwegian, 1859–1952)†: *Hunger* (1890), *Mysteries* (1892), *The Growth of the Soil* (1917)

Hardy, Thomas   (English, 1840–1928): *Far from the Madding Crowd* (1874), *The Return of the Native* (1878), *Tess of the D'Urbervilles* (1891), *Jude the Obscure* (1896)

Hasek, Jaroslav   (Czech, 1883–1923): *The Good Soldier Svejk and Other Strange Stories* (1912), *The Good Soldier Svejk and His Fortunes in the World War* (4 vols., 1921–23)

Hesse, Hermann   (German, 1877–1962)†: *Demian* (1919), *Siddhartha* (1922), *Steppenwolf* (1927)

Homer   (Greek, c. 700 B.C.): *The Iliad, The Odyssey*

Hopkins, Gerard Manley   (English, 1844–89): *Poems* (1918)

Hugo, Victor Marie   (French, 1802–85): *The Hunchback of Notre-Dame* (1831), *Lucretia Borgia* (1833), *Les Misérables* (1862)

Johnson, Samuel   (English, 1709–84): *A Dictionary of the English Language* (1755)

Joyce, James   (Irish, 1882–1941): *Dubliners* (1914), *Portrait of the Artist as a Young Man* (1916), *Ulysses* (1922), *Finnegan's Wake* (1939)

Kafka, Franz   (German, 1883–1924): *Metamorphosis* (1915), *The Judgment* (1916), *In the Penal Colony* (1919), *The Trial* (1925), *The Castle* (1926), *Amerika* (1927)

Keats, John   (English, 1795–1821): *The Poems of John Keats* (1817), *Endymion* (1818), *Lamia, Isabella, and The Eve of St. Agnes and Other Poems* (1820)

Kipling, Rudyard   (English, 1865–1936)†: *Plain Tales from the Hills* (1888), *The Phantom Rickshaw* (1889), *Barrack-Room Ballads* (1892), *The Jungle Book* (1894), *The Second Jungle Book* (1895), *Captains Courageous* (1897), *Kim* (1901), *Just So Stories* (1902)

Lawrence, D(avid) H(erbert)   (English, 1885–1930): *Sons and Lovers* (1913), *Women in Love* (1920), *Lady Chatterley's Lover* (1928)

Lessing, Doris   (British, 1919–   ): *The Grass Is Singing* (1950), *Martha Quest* (1952), *The Golden Notebook* (1962), *Briefing for a Descent into Hell* (1971), *Shikasta* (1979), *The Good Terrorist* (1985), *The Fifth Child* (1988)

Malory, Sir Thomas   (English, ?–1471): *Le Morte d'Arthur* (1485)

Malraux, André   (French, 1901–76): *Man's Fate* (1933), *Man's Hope* (1937)

Mandelstam, Osip Emilevich   (Russian, 1891–1938): *Kamen* (1913), *Tristia* (1922), *Journey to Armenia* (1933)

Mann, Thomas   (German, 1875–1955)†: *Buddenbrooks* (1900), *Death in Venice* (1912), *The Magic Mountain* (1924)

Manzoni, Alessandro   (Italian, 1785–1873): *The Betrothed* (1827)

Marvell, Andrew   (English, 1621–78): *Miscellaneous Poems* (1681)

Maugham, William Somerset   (English, 1874–1965): *Of Human Bondage* (1915), *Cakes and Ale* (1930), *The Summing Up* (1938), *The Razor's Edge* (1944)

Maupassant, Henri René Albert Guy de   (French, 1850–93): *Boule de suif* (1880), *La Maison Tellier* (1881), *Bel-Ami* (1885), *Pierre et Jean* (1888), *Yvette* (1885)

Mauriac, François Charles   (French, 1885–1970)†: *Genetrix* (1923), *Thérèse* (1927), *The Desert of Love* (1929), *A Woman of the Pharisees* (1941)

Milton, John   (English, 1608–74): *Paradise Lost* (1667), *Paradise Regained* (1671)

Montaigne, Michel de   (French, 1533–92): *Essais* (1580)

Nabokov, Vladimir Vladimirovich   (Russian, 1889–1977): *Lolita* (1955), *Invitation to a Beheading* (1959), *Pale Fire* (1962), *Speak, Memory* (1967)

Orwell, George [Eric Blair]   (English, 1903–50): *Animal Farm* (1945), *1984* (1949)

Ovid   (Roman, 43 B.C.–A.D. 17): *Amores* (c. 16 B.C.), *Heroines*, *Metamorphoses*

Pasternak, Boris Leonidovich   (Russian, 1890–1960)†: *My Sister—Life* (1922), *Doctor Zhivago* (1957)

Petrarch   (Italian, 1304–74): *Collected Works* (1544)

Petronius   (Roman, ?–66): *Satyricon* (c. 50)

Plutarch   (Greek, c. 46–120): *Moralia*, *Parallel Lives*

Pope, Alexander   (English, 1688–1744): *An Essay on Criticism* (1711), *The Rape of the Lock* (1714)

Proust, Marcel   (French, 1871–1922): *Remembrance of Things Past* (7 vols., 1913–27)

Pushkin, Alexander Sergeevich   (Russian, 1789–1837): *Eugene Onegin* (1831)

Rabelais, François   (French, c. 1494–1553): *Gargantua and Pantagruel* (1532–64)

Rilke, Rainer Maria   (German, 1875–1926): *Poems from the Book of Hours* (1905), *New Poems* (2 vols., 1907–08), *Duino Elegies* (1923), *Sonnets to Orpheus* (1923)

Rimbaud, Arthur   (French, 1854–91): *A Season in Hell* (1873), *Illuminations* (1886)

Rostand, Edmond   (French, 1868–1918): *The Princess Faraway* (1895), *Cyrano de Bergerac* (1897)

Sand, George [Amandine Aurore Lucie Dupin]   (French 1804–76): *Indiana* (1832), *Lelia* (1833), *The Companion of the Tour of France* (1841), *Consuelo* (1842–43), *He and She* (1859), *The Marquis of Villemer* (1860–61)

Sappho   (Greek, c. 612 B.C.–?): verse

Sartre, Jean-Paul   (French, 1905–80)†: *Nausea* (1938), *The Flies* (1943), *Being and Nothingness* (1943), *No Exit* (1944), *The Condemned of Altona* (1959)

Scott, Sir Walter   (Scottish, 1771–1832): *The Heart of Midlothian* (1818), *The Bride of Lammermoor* (1819), *Ivanhoe* (1819), *Kenilworth* (1821)

Shelley, Mary Wollstonecraft   (English, 1797–1851): *Frankenstein, or the Modern Prometheus* (1818)

Shelley, Percy Bysshe   (English, 1792–1822): *Prometheus Unbound* (1820), *Adonais* (1821)

Solzhenitsyn, Aleksandr I.   (Russian, 1918–   )†: *One Day in the Life of Ivan Denisovich* (1962), *The Cancer Ward* (1968), *The Gulag Archipelago* (1973–76)

Spenser, Edmund   (English, c. 1552–99): *The Faerie Queene* (1590)

Stendhal [Marie-Henri Beyle] (French, 1788–1842): *The Red and the Black* (1830), *The Charterhouse of Parma* (1839)

Stevenson, Robert Louis (Scottish, 1850–94): *Treasure Island* (1883), *The Strange Case of Dr. Jekyll and Mr. Hyde* (1886)

Swift, Jonathan (Irish, 1667–1745): *Gulliver's Travels* (1726)

Swinburne, Algernon Charles (English, 1837–1909): *Atalanta in Calydon* (1865), *Poems and Ballads: First Series* (1866), *Poems and Ballads: Second Series* (1878), *Astrophel* (1894), *A Tale of Balen* (1896)

Tennyson, Alfred (Lord) (English, 1809–92): *Poems, Chiefly Lyrical* (1830), *Poems* (1832), *Poems* (1842), *Locksley Hall* (1842), *In Memoriam* (1833–50), *Maud, and Other Poems* (1855), *Idylls of the King* (1859–85)

Thackeray, William Makepeace (English, 1811–63): *Barry Lyndon* (1844), *Vanity Fair* (1847–48)

Thomas, Dylan Marlais (English-Welsh, 1914–53): *Eighteen Poems* (1934), *Twenty-five Poems* (1936), *A Child's Christmas in Wales* (1952), *Under Milk Wood* (1954), *Adventures in the Skin Trade* (1955)

Tocqueville, Alexis de (1805–1859): *Democracy in America* (2 vols., 1835; 2 supplementary vols., 1840), *The Old Regime and the Revolution* (1856)

Tolstoy, Leo [Count Lev Nikolayevich] (Russian, 1828–1910): *War and Peace* (1863–69), *Anna Karenina* (1875–77)

Trollope, Anthony (English, 1815–82): *The Warden* (1855), *Barchester Towers* (1857)

Turgenev, Ivan (Russian, 1818–83): *A Month in the Country* (1855), *A Sportsman's Sketches* (1852), *A Nest of Gentlefolk* (1859), *On the Eve* (1860), *Fathers and Sons* (1862), *Smoke* (1867)

Undset, Sigrid (Norwegian, 1882–1949): *Kristin Lavransdatter* (1920–22), *Olaf Andunsson* (1925–27)

Valéry, Paul (French, 1871–1945): *Charmes* (1922)

Verne, Jules (French, 1828–1905): *A Voyage to the Center of the Earth* (1864), *Twenty Thousand Leagues Under the Sea* (1870), *Around the World in Eighty Days* (1873)

Virgil [Publius Vergilius Maro] (Roman, 70–19 B.C.): *Georgics* (37–30 B.C.), *Bucolics* (37 B.C.), *Aeneid* (30–19 B.C.)

Voltaire [François-Marie Arouet] (French, 1694–1778): *Candide* (1759)

Wilde, Oscar (Irish, 1854–1900): *The Portrait of Dorian Gray* (1891), *Salome* (1893), *The Importance of Being Earnest* (1899)

Woolf, Virginia (English, 1882–1941): *Mrs. Dalloway* (1925), *To the Lighthouse* (1927), *A Room of One's Own* (1929)

Wordsworth, William (English, 1770–1850): *Lyrical Ballads* (1798), *Poems Chiefly of Early and Late Years* (1842)

Yeats, William Butler (Irish, 1865–1939)†: *The Wind Among the Reeds* (1899), *The Wild Swans at Coole* (1919), *The Winding Stair* (1929), *Collected Poems* (1933)

Zola, Emile (French, 1840–1902): *Thérèse Raquin* (1867), *Nana* (1880), *Germinal* (1885)

Important Asian, African, and Latin American Authors

Armah, Ayi Kweh (Ghanaian, 1939–): *The Beautiful Ones Are Not Yet Born* (1968), *Why Are We So Blest?* (1972)

Bashō [Matsuo Munefusa] (Japanese, 1644–94): *The Narrow Road to the Deep North* (1689)

Beti, Mongo [Alexandre Biyidi] (Cameroonian, 1932–): *Le pauvre Christ de Bomba* (1956), *Mission terminée* (1957), *Le roi miraculé* (1958)

Borges, Jorge Luis (Argentinian, 1899–1986): *A Universal History of Infamy* (1935), *Six Problems for Don Isidro Parodi* (1942), *Ficciones* (1944), *The Aleph and Other Stories* (1949), *Labyrinthe* (1960), *The Book of Sand* (1975)

Cavafy, C. P. (Egyptian, 1863–1933): *Poems* (1935)

Cesaire, Aimé (West Indian, 1913–): *Return to My Native Land* (1939), *State of the Union* (1946), *The Tragedy of King Christophe* (1963)

Chatterje, Bankim-Chandra (Indian, 1838–94): *The Chieftain's Daughter* (1880), *Kopal-Kundala: A Tale of Bengali Life* (1885), *Krishna Kante's Will* (1895)

Confucius (Chinese, c. 551–479 B.C.): *The Analects of Confucius*

Fuentes, Carlos (Mexican, 1928–): *The Death of Artemio Cruz* (1962), *Distant Relations* (1981), *The Old Gringo* (1986), *Christopher Unborn* (1989), *The Campaigo* (1990)

García Márquez, Gabriel (Colombian, 1928–)†: *One Hundred Years of Solitude* (1967), *The Autumn of the Patriarch* (1975), *Love in the Time of Cholera* (1988), *The General in His Labyrinth* (1989)

Gordimer, Nadine (South African, 1923–): *Occasion for Loving* (1963), *A Guest of Honor* (1970), *Burgher's Daughter* (1979), *Something Out There* (1984), *My Son's Story* (1991)

Guzmán, Martín Luis (Mexican, 1887–1976): *The Eagle and the Serpent* (1928), *Memorias de Pancho Villa* (4 vols., 1938–40)

Kawabata, Yasunari (Japanese, 1899–1972)†: *Snow Country* (1948), *Thousand Cranes* (1952), *Beauty and Sadness* (1965)

Lao-tzu (Chinese, c. 6th century B.C.): *Tao-te-ching*

Laye, Camara (Guinean, 1928–80): *The African Child* (1953), *The Radiance of the King* (1954), *The Guardian of the Word* (1978)

Li Po (Chinese, 701–762): *Complete Works*

Machado de Assis, Joaquim Maria (Brazilian, 1839–1908): *The Posthumous Memoirs of Braz Cubas* (1881), *Philosopher or Dog?* (1891), *Dom Casmurro* (1899)

Mahfouz, Naguib (Egyptian, c. 1911–)†: *New Cairo* (1946), *Midag Alley* (1947), *Between the Two Palaces* (1956), *The Palace of Desire* (1957), *The Sugar Bowl* (1957), *Miramar* (1967), *Respected Sir* (1987), *Wedding Song* (1987)

Márquez, Gabriel García. See García Márquez, Gabriel.

Mishima, Yukio (Japanese, 1925–70): *Confession of a Mask* (1949), *Forbidden Colors* (2 vols., 1951–53), *The Sailor Who Fell from Grace with the Sea* (1963), *The Sea of Fertility* (4 vols., 1969–71)

Murasaki, Shikibu (Japanese, c. 978–1015): *The Tale of the Genji* (c. 1010)

Naipaul, V. S.   (Trinidadian, 1932–   ): *The Mystic Masseur* (1957), *A House for Mr. Biswas* (1961), *The Middle Passage* (1962), *In a Free State* (1971)

Natsume Sōseki   (Japanese, 1867–1916): *I Am a Cat* (1905–07), *The Three-Cornered World* (1907), *And Then* (1910)

Neruda, Pablo [Neftali Ricardo Reyes Basoalto]   (Chilean, 1904–73)†: *Twenty Love Poems and a Story of Despair* (1924), *Canto General* (1950), *Elementary Odes* (3 vols., 1954–57), *We Are Many* (1967), *End of the World* (1969)

Omar Khayyam   (Persian, 1048–1131): *Rubaiyat* (1859)

Paton, Alan Stewart   (South African, 1903–88): *Cry the Beloved Country* (1948)

Paz, Octavio   (Mexican, 1914–   ): *The Labyrinth of Solitude* (1950), *Sun-Stone* (1957), *Salamandra (1958–1961* (1962), *Ladera esta 1962–1968* (1969), *Vuelta* (1976)

Rushdie, Salman   (Indian, 1947–   ): *Grimus* (1975), *Midnight's Children* (1981), *Shame* (1983), *The Satanic Verses* (1989), *Haroun and the Sea of Stories* (1991)

Sembene, Ousmane   (Senegalese, 1923–   ): *The Black Docker* (1956), *The Storm* (1964), *The Money Order* (1965)

Senghor, Léopold Sédar   (Senegalese, 1906–   ): *Chants d'ombre* (1945), *Nocturnes* (1961), *Liberté I. Negritude et Humanisme* (1964)

Soyinka, Wole   (Nigerian 1934–   )†: *Three Plays* (1963), *The Road* (1965), *The Forest of a Thousand Daemons* (1968), *Aké* (1981)

Tagore, Rabindranath   (Indian, 1861–1941)†: *Gitanjali: Song Offering* (1912), *King of the Dark Chamber* (1914), *Gora* (1924)

Tanizaki Jun'ichiro   (Japanese, 1886–1965): *Tattoo* (1911), *The Secret History of the Lord Musashi* (1935), *The Key* (1956), *Seven Japanese Tales* (1963)

Ts'ao Hsueh-ch'in   (Chinese, c. 1715–63): *The Dream of Red Chamber* (c. 1763)

Vargas Llosa, Mario   (Peruvian, 1936–   ): *The Green House* (1966), *Conversations in the Cathedral* (1969), *The War of the End of the World* (1984), *The Real Life of Alejandro Mayta* (1986)

Literary Terms

allegory   A story with an underlying meaning symbolized by the characters and action.

alliteration   The repetition of the same sounds—usually initial consonants of words or of stressed syllables—in any sequence of neighboring words.

allusion   Reference to a familiar person or event, often from literature.

anachronism   A chronological error in literature that places a person, event, or object in an impossible historical context.

anagram   A word created by transposing the letters of another word.

analogy   The relation of one thing to something familiar.

antagonist   The major character opposing a hero or a protagonist.

anthropomorphism   The assigning of human characteristics and feelings to animals and nonhuman things.

anticlimax   Something that works against a climax, such as humor; a sudden descent from the lofty to the trivial.

antihero A protagonist lacking in heroic qualities like courage, idealism, and honesty.

antithesis A rhetorical figure in which sharply opposing ideas are expressed within a balanced grammatical structure.

assonance The close repetition of similiar vowel sounds.

autobiography The story of one's life as written by oneself.

ballad A poem, often meant to be sung, that tells a story.

bathos A sudden descent from the lofty to the ordinary or ridiculous.

belles-lettres Literature. Currently, lighter writings or appreciative essays on the beauties of literature.

bibliography A list of books on a similar subject or by a given author or authors.

biography The story of someone's life as written by another.

blank verse Unrhymed poetry, especially poetry written in iambic pentameter.

cacophony Discordant sounds, sometimes used in poetry for effect.

cadence The natural rhythm of language determined by its inherent alternation of stressed or unstressed syllables.

caesura A pause or break in a line of verse.

climax The point of high emotional intensity at which a story or play reaches its peak.

conceit A fanciful image, especially an elaborate or startling analogy.

couplet Two successive lines of poetry, usually rhymed.

denouement Literally, the "unknotting": the final unraveling of the plot following the climax.

diction The choice and arrangement of words in a literary work.

doggerel Crudely written poetry.

elegy A poetic lament.

epic An extended narrative poem, exalted in style and heroic in theme.

epistolary novel A novel written in the form of correspondence.

essay A short written work of nonfiction, usually on one topic.

euphony Harmonious sounds, often used in poetry for effect.

fable A prose or poetic story that illustrates a moral.

fiction Narrative writing drawn from the imagination of the author rather than from history or fact.

foot A group of syllables forming a metrical unit.

free verse A poem without regular meter or line length.

genre A literary type or class.

haiku An unrhymed poem form, originated by the Japanese, consisting of three lines of five, seven, and five syllables that record the essence of a moment.

hero A character, often the protagonist, who exhibits qualities such as courage, idealism, and honesty.

high comedy Comedy that is characterized by intellect or wit.

historical novel A narrative that places fictional characters or events in historically accurate surroundings.

hyperbole A deliberate overstatement.

iamb A metrical foot that contains one short or unstressed syllable preceding one long or stressed syllable.

iambic pentameter Poetry consisting of five parts per line, each part having one short or unstressed syllable and one long or stressed syllable.

imagery Figurative language used to evoke particular mental pictures.

irony An expression of a meaning that contradicts the literal meaning.

literature Novels, stories, poems, and plays of high standards that entertain, inform, stimulate, or provide aesthetic pleasure.

low comedy Humorous material that employs physical actions or jokes of questionable taste.

malapropism A mistaken substitution of one word for another that sounds similar, generally with humorous effect.

metaphor A figure of speech in which two unlikely objects are compared by identification or by the substitution of one for the other.

meter The pattern of stressed and unstressed syllables in poetry.

motif A theme, character, or verbal pattern that recurs in literature or folklore.

myth A legend, usually made up in part of historical events, that helps define the beliefs of a people and that often has evolved as an explanation for rituals and natural phenomena.

nonfiction A historically accurate narrative.

novel A long work of fictional prose.

novella A short novel; also, the early tales or short stories of French and Italian writers.

ode A lyric poem marked by strong feelings and an involved style.

onomatopoeia Formation of a word by imitating the natural sound associated with the object or action involved; the use of words that are so named.

oxymoron A figure of speech that employs two contradictory terms.

palindrome A word, a sentence, or a group of sentences (sometimes in verse) that reads the same backward and forward.

parable A short story that illustrates a moral.

paradox An apparently contradictory statement that contains a truth that reconciles the contradiction.

parody A humorous, often exaggerated, imitation of a serious literary work.

pathetic fallacy The assigning of human attributes to nature.

pathos An element that evokes feelings of pity, tenderness, and sympathy.

personification The assigning of human attributes to abstractions, objects, and other nonhuman things.

plot The orginization of individual incidents in a narrative or play.

poem A rhythmic expression of feelings or ideas, often using metaphor, meter, and rhyme.

poetic license The practice of violating rules, expectations, or conventions to achieve a desired effect.

prologue An introductory speech or monologue, given by an actor or actress before a play, which helps to set the stage for what is to come.

prose Literary expression not marked by rhyme or metrical regularity.

protagonist The main character of a play, novel, or story, usually the hero.

pun A humorous and often clever play on words in which one word evokes another with a similar sound but a different meaning.

refrain A phrase or verse that is repeated throughout a poem or song.

rhetorical question A question put forth to achieve an effect or make a point, to which an answer is not expected.

rhyme The repetition of similar or identical sounds at the ends of lines of verse.

rhythm The pattern of stressed and unstressed syllables in a line of poetry or prose.

satire Ridicule of a subject; the work in which it is contained.

short story A brief work of narrative prose.

simile A comparison of two unlike things that usually employs *like* or *as*.

soliloquy A dramatic monologue meant to convey the thoughts of a character in a play.

sonnet A poem consisting of fourteen iambic pentameter lines with a rigidly prescribed rhyming scheme.

spondee A type of metrical foot with two stressed syllables.

spoonerism The transposition of the initial sounds of two or more words, often with humorous results. Named for a Professor Spooner of Oxford, who was famous for such transpositions.

style An author's individual method and tone.

subplot A secondary plot in a story.

symbol In literature, something that stands for, or means, something else.

theme The central idea or thesis of a work.

trochee A metrical foot that contains one long or stressed syllable preceding one short or unstressed syllable.

verse Lines of writing arranged in metrical patterns, or a single such line.

Pseudonyms of Famous Authors

Real Name	Pseudonym or Pen Name
Kingsley Amis	Robert Markham
Hans Christian Andersen	Villiam Christian Walter
Isaac Asimov	Dr. A., Paul French
Louis Auchincloss	Andrew Lee
L. Frank Baum	Edith Van Dyne
Robert Benchley	Guy Fawkes
Ambrose Bierce	Dod Grile
Eric Arthur Blair	George Orwell
Anne Brontë	Acton Bell, Lady Geralda, Olivia Vernon, Alexandria Zenobia
Charlotte Brontë	C. B., Currer Bell, Marquis of Douro, Genius, Lord Charles Wellesley
Emily Jane Brontë	R. Alcon, Ellis Bell
William S. Burroughs	William Lee
Barbara Cartland	Barbara Hamilton McCorquodale
Agatha Christie	Agatha Christie Mallowen, Mary Westmacott
Samuel Langhorne Clemens	Mark Twain
Howard Fast	E. V. Cunningham
Erle Stanley Gardner	A. A. Fair, Charles M. Green, Carleton Kendrake, Charles J. Kenny
Theodor Seuss Geisel	Theo Lesieg, Dr. Seuss
Edward St. John Gorey	Eduard Blutig, Mrs. Regera Dowdy, Redway Grode, O. Mude, Hyacinthe Phypps, Ogdred Weary, Dreary Wodge
Dashiell Hammett	Peter Collinson
Robert A. Heinlein	Anson MacDonald
Eleanor Alice Burford Hibbert	Eleanor Burford, Philippa Carr, Elbur Ford, Victoria Holt, Kathleen Kellow, Jean Plaidy, Ellalice Tate
L. Ron Hubbard	Elron, Tom Esterbrook, Rene La Fayette, Capt. B. A. Northrop, Kurt von Rachen
Ford Madox Hueffer	Ford Madox Ford
E. Howard Hunt	John Baxter, Gordon Davis, Robert Dietrich, David St. John
Salvatore A. Lombino	Hunt Collins, Evan Hunter, Richard Marsten, Ed McBain
LeRoi Jones	Imamu Amiri Baraka
Teodor Jozef Konrad Korzeniowski	Joseph Conrad
Louis LaMoore	Louis L'Amour, Tex Burns
T. E. Lawrence	J. H. Ross, T. E. Shaw
Manfred Lee and Frederic Dannay	Ellery Queen, Barnaby Ross
Kenneth Millar	John Ross Macdonald, Ross Macdonald
Edna St. Vincent Millay	Nancy Boyd
Mystery Writers of America, California chapter	Theo Durrant
Conor Cruise O'Brien	Donat O'Donnell
Dorothy Parker	Constant Reader

Real Name	Pseudonym or Pen Name
Eric Partridge	Vigilans
William Sydney Porter	O. Henry
William Saroyan	Sirak Goryan
Terry Southern	Maxwell Kenton
Irving Stone	Irving Tannenbaum
Gore Vidal	Edgar Box
Nathan Wallenstein Weinstein	Nathanael West
J. A. Wight	James Herriot
John Burgess Wilson	Anthony Burgess, Joseph Kell
Willard Huntington Wright	S. S. Van Dine

Poet Laureates

English

In 1616 Ben Jonson was named England's first poet laureate; however, the title did not become an official royal office until 1668, when John Dryden assumed the honored post. Since that time, the office has been awarded for life. The poet laureate is responsible for composing poems for court and national occasions. At the time of each laureate's death, it is the duty of the prime minister to nominate successors from which the reigning sovereign will choose. It is the Lord Chamberlain who appoints the poet laureate by issuing a warrant to the laureate-elect. The life appointment is always announced in the *London Gazette*.

Laureateship	Poet	Birth and Death Dates
1668–88	John Dryden	1631–1700
1689–92	Thomas Shadwell	1643?–92
1692–1715	Nahum Tate	1652–1715
1715–18	Nicholas Rowe	1674–1718
1718–30	Laurence Eusden	1688–1730
1730–57	Colley Cibber	1671–1757
*1757–85	William Whitehead	1715–85
1785–90	Thomas Warton	1728–90
1790–1813	Henry James Pye	1745–1813
1813–43	Robert Southey	1774–1843
1843–50	William Wordsworth	1770–1850
†1850–92	Alfred, Lord Tennyson	1809–92
1896–1913	Alfred Austin	1835–1913
1913–30	Robert Bridges	1844–1930
1930–67	John Masefield	1878–1967
1968–72	Cecil Day-Lewis	1904–72
1972–84	Sir John Betjeman	1906–84
1984–	Ted Hughes	(b. 1930)

* The 1757 appointment was declined by Thomas Gray.
† The 1850 appointment was declined by Samuel Rogers.

American

Laureateship	Poet	Birth and Death Dates
1986	Robert Penn Warren	1905–1989
1987	Richard Wilbur	1921–
1988	Howard Nemerov	1920–1991
1990	Mark Strand	1934–
1991	Joseph Brodsksy	1940–
1992	Mona Van Duyn	1921–
1993	Rita Dove	1952–

Book Awards and Their Recipients

Nobel Prize in Literature

1901	René F.A. Sully-Prudhomme, France	1931	Erik A. Karlfeldt, Sweden
1902	Theodor Mommsen, Germany	1932	John Galsworthy, Great Britain
1903	Bjornsterne Björnson, Norway	1933	Ivan A. Bunin, Russia
1904	Frederic Mistral, France	1934	Luigi Pirandello, Italy
	José Echegaray, Spain	1935	*No award*
1905	Henryk Sienkiewicz, Poland	1936	Eugene O'Neill, U.S.
1906	Giosue Carducci, Italy	1937	Roger Martin du Gard, France
1907	Rudyard Kipling, Great Britain	1938	Peal S. Buck, U.S.
1908	Rudolph C. Eueken, Germany	1939	Frans E. Sillanpää, Finland
1909	Selma Lagerlöf, Sweden	1940	*No award*
1910	Paul J.L. von Heyse, Germany	1941	*No award*
1911	Maurice Maeterlinck, Belgium	1942	*No award*
1912	Gerhart Hauptmann, Germany	1943	*No award*
1913	Rabindranath Tagore, India	1944	Johannes V. Jensen, Denmark
1914	*No award*	1945	Gabriela Mistral, Chile
1915	Romain Rolland, France	1946	Hermann Hesse, Switzerland
1916	Verner von Heidenstamm, Sweden	1947	André Gide, France
1917	Karl A. Gjellerup, Denmark	1948	T.S. Eliot, Great Britain
	Henrik Pontoppidan, Denmark	1949	William Faulkner, U.S.
1918	*No award*	1950	Bertrand Russell, Great Britain
1919	Carl F. G. Spitteler, Switzerland	1951	Pär F. Lagerkvist, Sweden
1920	Knut Hamsun, Norway	1952	François Mauriac, France
1921	Anatole France, France	1953	Sir Winston Churchull, Great Britain
1922	Jacinto Benavente y Martinez, Spain	1954	Ernest Hemingway, U.S.
1923	William Butler Yeats, Ireland	1955	Halldor K. Laxness, Iceland
1924	Wladyslaw S. Reymont, Poland	1956	Juan Ramón Jiménez, Puerto Rico
1925	George Bernard Shaw, Great Britain	1957	Albert Camus, France
1926	Grazia Deledda, Italy	1958	Boris L. Pasternak, U.S.S.R. (prize declined)
1927	Henri Bergson, France		
1928	Sigrid Undset, Norway	1959	Salvatore Quasimodo, Italy
1929	Thomas Mann, Germany	1960	Saint-John Perse, France
1930	Sinclair Lewis, U.S.	1961	Ivo Andric, Yugoslavia

1962 John Steinbeck, U.S.
1963 Giorgos Seferis, Greece
1964 Jean-Paul Sartre, France (prize declined)
1965 Mikhail Sholokhov, U.S.S.R.
1966 Samuel Joseph Agnon, Israel
 Nelly Sachs, Sweden
1967 Miguel Angel Asturias, Guatemala
1968 Yasunari Kawabata, Japan
1969 Samuel Beckett, Ireland
1970 Aleksandr I. Solzhenitsyn, U.S.S.R.
1971 Pablo Neruda, Chile
1972 Henrich Böll, Federal Republic of Germany
1973 Patrick White, Australia
1974 Eyvind Johnson, Sweden
 Harry Edmund Martinson, Sweden
1975 Eugenio Montale, Italy
1976 Saul Bellow, U.S.
1977 Vicente Aleixandre, Spain
1978 Isaac Bashevis Singer, U.S.
1979 Odysseus Elytis, Greece
1980 Czeslaw Milosz, Poland-U.S.
1981 Elias Canetti, Bulgaria-Great Britain
1982 Gabriel García Márquez, Colombia-Mexico
1983 William Golding, Great Britain
1984 Jaroslav Siefert, Czechoslovakia
1985 Claude Simon, France
1986 Wole Soyinka, Nigeria
1987 Joseph Brodsky, U.S.
1988 Naguib Mahfouz, Egypt
1989 Camilo José Cela, Spain
1990 Octavio Paz, Mexico
1991 Nadine Gordimer, South Africa
1992 Derek Walcott, Trinidad-U.S.

Pulitzer Prize in Letters

Fiction

1918 Ernest Poole, *His Family*
1919 Booth Tarkington, *The Magnificent Ambersons*
1920 *No award*
1921 Edith Wharton, *The Age of Innocence*
1922 Booth Tarkington, *Alice Adams*
1923 Willa Cather, *One of Ours*
1924 Margaret Wilson, *The Able McLaughlins*
1925 Edna Ferber, *So Big*
1926 Sinclair Lewis, *Arrowsmith* (prize declined)
1927 Louis Bromfield, *Early Autumn*
1928 Thornton Wilder, *The Bridge of San Luis Rey*
1929 Julia M. Peterkin, *Scarlet Sister Mary*
1930 Oliver LaFarge, *Laughing Boy*
1931 Margaret Ayer Barnes, *Years of Grace*
1932 Pearl S. Buck, *The Good Earth*
1933 T.S. Stribling, *The Store*
1934 Caroline Miller, *Lamb in His Bosom*
1935 Josephine W. Johnson, *Now in November*
1936 Harold L. Davis, *Honey in the Horn*
1937 Margaret Mitchell, *Gone with the Wind*
1938 John P. Marquand, *The Late George Apley*
1939 Marjorie Kinnan Rawlings, *The Yearling*
1940 John Steinbeck, *The Grapes of Wrath*
1941 *No award*
1942 Ellen Glasgow, *In This Our Life*
1943 Upton Sinclair, *Dragon's Teeth*
1944 Martin Flavin, *Journey in the Dark*
1945 John Hersey, *A Bell for Adano*
1946 *No award*
1947 Robert Penn Warren, *All the King's Men*
1948 James A. Michener, *Tales of the South Pacific*
1949 James Gould Cozzens, *Guard of Honor*
1950 A.B. Guthrie, Jr., *The Way West*
1951 Conrad Richter, *The Town*
1952 Herman Wouk, *The Caine Mutiny*
1953 Ernest Hemingway, *The Old Man and the Sea*
1954 *No award*
1955 William Faulkner, *A Fable*
1956 MacKinlay Kantor, *Andersonville*
1957 *No award*
1958 James Agee, *A Death in the Family*
1959 Robert Lewis Taylor, *The Travels of Jaimie McPheeters*
1960 Allen Drury, *Advise and Consent*
1961 Harper Lee, *To Kill a Mockingbird*

1962 Edwin O'Connor, *The Edge of Sadness*
1963 William Faulkner, *The Reivers*
1964 No award
1965 Shirley Ann Grau, *The Keepers of the House*
1966 Katherine Anne Porter, *The Collected Stories of Katherine Anne Porter*
1967 Bernard Malamud, *The Fixer*
1968 William Styron, *The Confessions of Nat Turner*
1969 N. Scott Momaday, *House Made of Dawn*
1970 Jean Stafford, *Collected Stories*
1971 No award
1972 Wallace Stegner, *Angle of Repose*
1973 Eudora Welty, *The Optimist's Daughter*
1974 No award
1975 Michael Shaara, *The Killer Angels*
1976 Saul Bellow, *Humboldt's Gift*
1977 No award
1978 James Alan McPherson, *Elbow Room*
1979 John Cheever, *The Stories of John Cheever*
1980 Norman Mailer, *The Executioner's Song*
1981 John Kennedy Toole, *A Confederacy of Dunces*
1982 John Updike, *Rabbit Is Rich*
1983 Alice Walker, *The Color Purple*
1984 William Kennedy, *Ironweed*
1985 Alison Lurie, *Foreign Affairs*
1986 Larry McMurtry, *Lonesome Dove*
1987 Peter Taylor, *A Summons to Memphis*
1988 Toni Morrison, *Beloved*
1989 Anne Tyler, *Breathing Lessons*
1990 Oscar Hijuelos, *The Mambo Kings Play Songs of Love*
1991 John Updike, *Rabbit at Rest*

General Nonfiction

1962 Theodore White, *The Making of the President 1960*
1963 Barbara W. Tuchman, *The Guns of August*
1964 Richard Hofstadter, *Anti-Intellectualism in American Life*
1965 Howard Mumford Jones, *O Strange New World*
1966 Edwin Way Teale, *Wandering Through Winter*
1967 David Brion Davis, *The Problem of Slavery in Western Culture*
1968 Will and Ariel Durant, *Rousseau and Revolution*
1969 Norman Mailer, *The Armies of the Night*
    René Jules Dubois, *So Human an Animal: How We are Shaped by Surroundings and Events*
1970 Eric H. Erikson, *Gandhi's Truth*
1971 John Toland, *The Rising Sun*
1972 Barbara W. Tuchman, *Stilwell and the American Experience in China, 1911–1945*
1973 Frances FitzGerald, *Fire in the Lake*
    Robert Coles, *Children of Crisis* (vols. 2 and 3)
1974 Ernest Becker, *The Denial of death*
1975 Annie Dillard, *Pilgrim at Tinker Creek*
1976 Robert N. Butler, *Why Survive? Being Old in America*
1977 William W. Warner, *Beautiful Swimmers*
1978 Carl Sagan, *The Dragons of Eden*
1979 Edward O. Wilson, *On Human Nature*
1980 Douglas R. Hofstadter, *Gödel, Escher, Bach: An Eternal Golden Braid*
1981 Carl E. Schorske, *Fin-de-Siecle Vienna: Politics and Culture*
1982 Tracy Kidder, *The Soul of a New Machine*
1983 Susan Sheehan, *Is There No Place on Earth for Me?*
1984 Paul Starr, *Social Transformation of American Medicine*
1985 Studs Terkel, *The Good War*
1986 Joseph Lelyveld, *Move Your Shadow*
    J. Anthony Lukas, *Common Ground*
1987 David K. Shipler, *Arab and Jew*
1988 Richard Rhodes, *The Making of the Atomic Bomb*
1989 Neal Sheehan, *A Bright Shining Lie: John Paul Vann and America in Vietnam*
1990 Dale Maharidge and Michael Williamson, *And Their Children After Them*
1991 Bert Holldobler and Edward O. Wilson, *The Ants*

Additional Sources of Information

Atkinson, Frank, *Dictionary of Literary Pseudonyms,* 4th ed. American Library Association, 1986.

Baldick, Chris. *The Concise Oxford Dictionary of Literary Terms.* Oxford University Press, 1991.

Bauer, Andrew. *The Hawthorn Dictionary of Pseudonyms.* Hawthorn Books, 1971.

Beckson, Karl, and Arthur Ganz. *Literary Terms: A Dictionary.* Farrar, Straus & Giroux, 1989.

Bede, Jean-Albert, and William B. Edgerton. eds. *Columbia Dictionary of Modern European Literature.* Columbia University Press, 1980.

Drabble, Margaret, ed. *The Oxford Companion to English Literature,* 5th ed. Oxford University Press, 1985.

Foster, David, and Virginia R. Foster. *Modern Latin American Literature,* 2 vols. Frederick Ungar, 1975.

Frye, Northrop, Sheridan Baker, and George Perkins. *The Harper Handbook to Literature.* Harper & Row, 1985.

Hart, James D. *The Oxford Companion to American Literature.* Oxford University Press, 1986.

Herdeck, Donald E. *African Authors: A Companion to Black African Writing.* Black Orpheus Press, 1973.

Holman, Clarence Hugh. *A Handbook to Literature,* 5th ed. Macmillan, 1986.

Perkins, George, et al. *Benet's Reader's Encyclopedia of American Literature.* Harper Collins, 1991.

Toye, William, ed. *The Oxford Companion to Canadian Literature.* Oxford University Press, 1983.

9

Religions

The World's Major Religions / 231
Significant Dates in the History of Religion / 240
Major Religious Holidays in the United States / 241
Roman Catholic Patron Saints / 243
Holy Books of the World / 246
The Greek and Roman Deities / 248
The Roman Catholic Popes / 250
"The Seven . . ." and Other Numbers / 252
The Books of the Bible / 258
The Ten Commandments / 259
Additional Sources of Information / 260

The World's Major Religions

Religious beliefs of one sort or another are an intrinsic aspect of virtually every society that has ever existed on this planet. Many of these beliefs are organized and codified, often based on the teachings and writings of one or more founders. Other belief systems are less rigid in their external structures and may be transmitted orally from one generation to the next, whether by family members or by religious leaders within the community.

While all religious beliefs are of vital importance to those who hold them, the less formalistic belief systems—variously referred to as animist or tribal religions, and adhered to by peoples all over the world—have proven somewhat enigmatic to Western minds. This section, therefore, deals only with those religions that are recognizable as such to Westerners, ones that employ certain readily identifiable tenets, beliefs, and doctrines.

Baha'i

Baha'i has more than 5 million followers. It was founded by Mirza Husayn 'Ali Nuri, who took the name Bahá'u'lláh (Glory of God) while in exile in Baghdad. Bahá'u'lláh's coming had been foretold by Mirza Ali Mohammad, known as al-Bab, who founded Babism in 1844, from which the Baha'i faith grew. The central tenets of the Baha'i faith are the oneness of God, the oneness of humanity, and the common foundation of all religion. Baha'ists also believe in the equality of men and women, universal education, world peace, and the creation of a world federal system of government.

Buddhism

Buddhism has 307 million followers. It was founded by Siddhartha Gautama, known as the Buddha (Enlightened One), in southern Nepal in the sixth and fifth centuries B.C. The Buddha achieved enlightenment through meditation and gathered a community of monks to carry on his teachings. Buddhism teaches that meditation and the practice of good religious and moral behavior can lead to Nirvana, the state of enlightenment, although before achieving Nirvana one is subject to repeated lifetimes that are good or bad depending on one's actions (*karma*). The doctrines of the Buddha describe temporal life as featuring "four noble truths": Existence is a realm of suffering; desire, along with the belief in the importance of one's self, causes suffering; achievement of Nirvana ends suffering; and Nirvana is attained only by meditation and by following the path of righteousness in action, thought, and attitude.

Confucianism

A faith with 5.6 million followers, Confucianism was founded by Confucius, a Chinese philosopher, in the sixth and fifth centuries B.C. Confucius's sayings and dialogues, known collectively as the *Analects*, were written down by his followers. Confucianism, which grew out of a strife-ridden time in Chinese history, stresses the relationship between individuals, their families, and society, based on *li* (proper behavior) and *jen* (sympathetic attitude). Its practical, socially oriented philosophy was challenged by the more mystical precepts of Taoism and Buddhism, which were partially incorporated to create neo-Confucianism during the Sung dynasty (A.D. 960–1279). The overthrow of the Chinese monarchy and the Communist revolution during the twentieth century have severely lessened the influence of Confucianism on modern Chinese culture.

Ethical Culture

Ethical Culture, which has 7,000 followers, was founded as the Society for Ethical Culture in 1876 in New York City by Felix Adler. The International Union of Ethical Societies was formed in 1896. It joined other humanist organizations in 1952 to form the International Humanist and Ethical Union, based in Utrecht, The Netherlands. The Ethical Culture movement stresses the importance of ethics and morality in human interaction, although it offers no system of ethics or other religious beliefs of its own.

Hinduism

A religion with 648 million followers, Hinduism developed from indigenous religions of India in combination with Aryan religions brought to India c. 1500 B.C. and codified in the Veda and the Upanishads, the sacred scriptures of Hinduism. Hinduism is a term used to broadly describe a vast array of sects to which most Indians belong. Although many Hindus reject the caste system—in which people are born into a particular subgroup that determines their religious, social, and work-related duties—it is widely accepted and classifies society at large into four groups: the Brahmins or priests, the rulers and warriors, the farmers and merchants, and the peasants and laborers. The goals of Hinduism are release from repeated reincarnation through the practice of yoga, adherence to Vedic scriptures, and devotion to a personal guru. Various deities are worshiped at shrines; the divine trinity, representing the cyclical nature of the universe, are Brahma the creator, Vishnu the preserver, and Shiva the destroyer.

Islam

Islam has 840 million followers. It was founded by the prophet Muhammad, who received the holy scriptures of Islam, the Koran, from Allah (God) c. A.D. 610. Islam (Arabic for "submission to God") maintains that Muhammad is the last in a long line of holy prophets, preceded by Adam, Abraham, Moses, and Jesus. In addition to being devoted to the Koran, followers of Islam (Muslims) are devoted to the worship of Allah through the Five Pillars: the statement "There is no god but God, and Muhammad is his prophet"; prayer, conducted five times a day while facing Mecca; the giving of alms; the keeping of the fast of Ramadan during the ninth month of the Muslim year; and the making of a pilgrimage at least once to Mecca, if possible. The two main divisions of Islam are the Sunni and the Shiite; the Wahabis are the most important Sunni sect, while the Shiite sects include the Assassins, the Druses, and the Fatimids, among countless others.

Judaism

Stemming from the descendants of Judah in Judea, Judaism was founded c. 2000 B.C. by Abraham, Isaac, and Jacob and has 18 million followers. Judaism espouses belief in a monotheistic God, who is creator of the universe and who leads His people, the Jews, by speaking through prophets. His word is revealed in the Hebrew Bible (or Old Testament), especially in that part known as the Torah. The Torah also contains, according to rabbinic tradition, a total of 613 biblical commandments, including the Ten Commandments, which are explicated in the Talmud. Jews believe that the human condition can be improved, that the letter and the spirit of the Torah must be followed, and that a Messiah will eventually bring the world to a state of paradise. Judaism promotes community among all people of Jewish faith, dedication to a synagogue or temple (the basic social unit of a group of Jews, led by a rabbi), and the importance of family life. Religious observance takes place both at home and in temple. Judaism is divided into three main groups who vary in their interpretation of those parts of the Torah that deal with personal, communal, international, and religious activities: the Orthodox community, which views the Torah as derived from God, and therefore absolutely binding; the Reform movement, which follows primarily its ethical content; and the Conservative Jews, who follow most of the observances set out in the Torah but allow for change in the face of modern life. A fourth group, Reconstructionist Jews, rejects the concept of the Jews as God's chosen people, yet maintains rituals as part of the Judaic cultural heritage.

Orthodox Eastern Church

With 158 million followers, the Orthodox Eastern Church is the second largest Christian community in the world. It began its split from the Roman Catholic Church in the fifth century; the break was finalized in 1054. The followers of the Orthodox Church are in fact members of many different denominations, including the Church of Greece, the Church of Cyprus, and the Russian Orthodox Church. Orthodox religion holds biblical Scripture and tradition, guided by the Holy Spirit as expressed in the consciousness of the entire Orthodox community, to be the source of Christian truth. It rejects doctrine developed by the Western churches. Doctrine was established by seven ecumenical councils held between 325 and 787 and amended by other councils in the late Byzantine period. Relations between the Orthodox churches and Roman Catholicism have improved since Vatican Council II (1962–65).

Protestantism

Major Protestant Denominations in the United States

Name	Founder	Followers	Tenets
Amish Mennonites	Founded in Switzerland in the 1500s after secession from the Zurich state church; the followers of Jacob Ammann broke from the other Mennonites in Switzerland and Alsace in 1693; most Amish Mennonites emigrated to Pennsylvania in the eighteenth century when others rejoined the main Mennonite group.	40,000 Amish Mennonites; 180,000 Mennonites	The Bible is the sole rule of faith; beliefs are outlined in the *Dordrecht Confession of Faith* (1632); Mennonites shun worldly ways and modern innovation (education and technology); the sacraments are adult baptism and communion.
Baptists	Founded by John Smyth in England in 1609 and Rogert Williams in Rhode Island in 1638.	31 million	No creed; authority stems from the Bible; most Baptists oppose the use of alcohol and tobacco; baptism is by total immersion.
Church of Christ	Organized by Presbyterians in Kentucky in 1804 and in Pennsylvania in 1809.	1.6 million	The New Testament is believed in and what is written in the Bible is followed without elaboration; rites are not ornate; baptism is of adults.
Church of England	King Henry VIII of England broke with the Roman Catholic Church; he issued the Act of Supremacy in 1534, which declared the king of England to be the head of the Church of England.	6,000 in Anglican Orthodox Church in the United States	Supremacy of the Bible is the test of doctrine; emphasis is on the most essential Christian doctrines and creeds; the *Book of Common Prayer* is used; the Church of England is part of the Anglican community, which is represented in the United States mainly by the Episcopal Church.

Name	Founder	Followers	Tenets
Episcopal Church	U.S. offshoot of the Church of England; it installed Samuel Seabury as its first bishop in 1784 and held its first General Convention in 1789; the Church of England, headed by King Henry VIII, broke with the Roman Catholic Church in 1534.	2.7 million	Worship is based on the *Book of Common Prayer* and interpretation of the Bible using a modified version of the Thirty-Nine Articles (originally written for the Church of England in 1563); services range from spartan to ornate, from liberal to conservative; baptism is of infants.
Lutheran Church	Based on the writings of Martin Luther, who broke (1517–21) with the Roman Catholic Church and led the Protestant Reformation; the first Lutheran congregation in North America was founded in 1638 in Wilmington, Delaware; the first North American regional synod was founded in 1748 by Heinrich Melchior Mühlenberg.	8 million	Faith is based on the Bible and the Augsburg Confession (written in 1530); salvation comes through faith alone; services include the Lord's Supper (communion); Lutherans are mostly conservative in religious and social ethics; infants are baptized, the church is organized in synods; the two largest synods in the United States are the Evangelical Lutheran Church in America and the Lutheran Church-Missouri Synod.
Mennonites. *See* Amish Mennonites.			
Methodist Church	Reverend John Wesley began evangelistic preaching within the Church of England in 1738; a separate Wesleyan Methodist Church was established in 1791; the Methodist Episcopal Church was founded in the United States in 1784.	13.5 million	The name derives from the founders' desire to study religion "by rule and method" and follow the Bible interpreted by tradition and reason; worship varies by denomination within Methodism (the United Methodist Church is the largest congregation); the church is perfectionist in social dealings; communion and the baptism of infants and adults are practiced.

Name	Founder	Followers	Tenets
Pentecostal churches	The churches grew out of the "holiness movement" that developed among Methodists and other Protestants in the first decade of the twentieth century.	3.5 million	Baptism in the Holy Spirit, speaking in tongues, faith healing, and the second coming of Jesus are believed in; of the various Pentecostal churches, the Assemblies of God is the largest; a perfectionist attitude toward secular affairs is common; services feature enthusiastic sermons and hymns; adult baptism and communion are practiced.
Presbyterian Church	Grew out of Calvinist churches of Switzerland and France; John Knox founded the first Presbyterian church in Scotland in 1557; the first presbytery in North America was established by Irish missionary Francis Makemie in 1706.	3.2 million	Faith is in the Bible; the sacraments are infant baptism and communion; the church is organized as a system of courts in which clergy and lay members (presbyters) participate at local, regional, and national levels; services are simple, with emphasis on the sermon.
Seventh-Day Adventist Church	Grew out of the teachings of William Miller in the 1840s; formally founded in North America in 1863.	734,527	The Bible is the only creed; the second coming of Jesus is emphasized; members abstain from alcoholic beverages and tobacco; baptism and communion are practiced.
United Church of Christ	Formed in 1957 by the union of the General Council of Congregational Christian Churches with the Evangelical and Reformed Churches.	1.7 million	Belief in the Bible is guided by the *Statement of Faith* (written in 1959); the church is organized by congregations, which are represented at a general synod that sets policy; services are simple, with emphasis on the sermon; infant baptism and communion are practiced.

Other Christian-Based Organizations

Name	Founder	Followers	Tenets
The Church of Jesus Christ of Latter-Day Saints (Mormons)	Joseph Smith, in the 1820s, found golden tablets with *The Book of Mormon* inscribed on them; church headquarters were established in upstate New York in 1830, then in Ohio in 1831; after two more attempts to establish a permanent home for the church (the second resulting in Smith's death at the hands of a mob), Salt Lake City, Utah, was founded in 1847 under the leadership of Brigham Young.	4.5 million	Faith is based on the Bible, *The Book of Mormon*, *The Doctrine and Covenants,* and *The Pearl of Great Price,* all of which are considered scripture; stress is placed on revelation through the connection of spiritual and physical worlds and through proselytizing; members abstain from alcohol and tobacco and believe in community self-reliance; public services are conservative; there is baptism, laying on of hands, and communion; a secret temple holds other ceremonies, including baptism for the dead.
Jehovah's Witnesses	Founded by Charles T. Russell in the United States in the late nineteenth century.	893,000	Belief is in the imminent second coming of Christ and the potential salvation of mortal souls during the millennium; all members are ministers who proselytize their faith with door-to-door missionary work; members refuse service in the armed forces, will not salute national flags or participate in politics, will not accept blood transfusions (but will accept all other forms of medical treatment), and discourage smoking, drunkenness, and gambling.

Name	Founder	Followers	Tenets
Religious Society of Friends (Quakers)	George Fox in England in the seventeenth century began preaching against organized churches, professing a doctrine of the Inner Light.	113,000	Reliance is on the Inner Light, the voice of God's Holy Spirit experienced within each person; meetings are characterized by quiet meditation without ritual or sermon; Quakers are active in peace, education, and social welfare movements; they refuse to bear arms or take oaths; earlier schisms are still reflected in three main affiliations of Friends.
Unitarian Universalist Association	The denomination resulted from the merger of the Universalist Church of America (organized in 1779) and the American Unitarian Association (founded in 1825).	171,000	Members profess no creed; strong social, ethical, and humanitarian concerns are manifest in the search for religious truth through freedom of belief; theists, humanists, and agnostics are accepted in religious fellowship; efforts are aimed at the creation of a worldwide interfaith religious community; many members come from other denominations and religions.

Roman Catholicism

The Roman Catholic Church, with 900 million followers, is the largest Christian church in the world. It claims direct historical descent from the church founded by the apostle Peter. The Pope in Rome is the spiritual leader of all Roman Catholics. He administers church affairs through bishops and priests. Members accept the gospel of Jesus Christ and the teachings of the Bible, as well as the church's interpretations of these. God's grace is conveyed through the seven sacraments, especially the Eucharist or communion that is celebrated at mass, the regular service of worship. The other six sacraments are baptism, confirmation, penance, holy orders, matrimony, and anointing of the sick. Redemption through Jesus Christ is professed as the sole method of obtaining salvation, which is necessary to ensure a place in heaven after life on earth.

Rosicrucianism

Rosicrucianism is a modern movement begun in 1868 by R. W. Little that claims ties to an older Society of the Rose and Cross that was founded in Germany in 1413 by Christian Rosencreuz. The number of its followers is uncertain. The Ancient Mystical Order Rosae Crusis (AMORC) was founded in San Jose, California, in 1915 by H. Spencer Lewis. The Rosicrucian Brotherhood was established in Quakertown, Pennsylvania, by Reuben Swinburne Clymer in 1902. Both sects could be classified as either fraternal or religious organizations, although they claim to empower members with cosmic forces by unveiling secret wisdom regarding the laws of nature.

Shinto

Shinto, with 3.5 million followers, is the ancient native religion of Japan, established long before the introduction of writing to Japan in the fifth century A.D. The origins of its beliefs and rituals are unknown. Shinto stresses belief in a great many spiritual beings and gods, known as *kami*, who are paid tribute at shrines and honored by festivals, and reverence for ancestors. While there is no overall dogma, adherents of Shinto are expected to remember and celebrate the *kami*, support the societies of which the *kami* are patrons, remain pure and sincere, and enjoy life.

Taoism

Both a philosophy and a religion, Taoism was founded in China by Lao-tzu, who is traditionally said to have been born in 604 B.C. Its number of followers is uncertain. It derives primarily from the *Tao-te-ching*, which claims that an ever-changing universe follows the Tao, or path. The Tao can be known only by emulating its quietude and effortless simplicity; Taoism prescribes that people live simply, spontaneously, and in close touch with nature and that they meditate to achieve contact with the Tao. Temples and monasteries, maintained by Taoist priests, are important in some Taoist sects. Since the Communist revolution, Taoism has been actively discouraged in the People's Republic of China, although it continues to flourish in Taiwan.

Significant Dates in the History of Religion

B.C.

c. 2000?	Abraham, founder of Judaism, is alive.
c. 13th century	Moses, Hebrew lawgiver, is alive.
c. 1100–c. 500	The *Veda,* sacred texts of the Hindus, are compiled.
604	Traditional birth date of Lao-tzu, founder of Taoism.
588	Traditional date of Zoroaster's revelation.
c. 563–c. 483	Buddha, founder of Buddhism, is alive.
551–479	Confucius, founder of Confucianism, is alive.
c. 540–c. 468	Mahavira, founder of the Jains, is alive.
c. 200	The *Bhagavad Gita,* important Hindu text, is written.
6 or 4–c. A.D. 30	Jesus of Nazareth, founder of Christianity, is alive.

A.D.

33?	The Crucifixion and death of Jesus Christ.
64?	Peter, disciple of Jesus and, according to tradition, first bishop of Rome, dies.
c. 70–c. 100	First four books of the New Testament—Matthew, Mark, Luke, and John—are written.
5th century	Two Buddhist sects—Zen and Pure Land (or Amidism)—are established.
c. 570–632	Muhammad the prophet—whose teachings, recorded in the Koran, form the basis of Islam—is alive.
622	Muhammad flees persecution in Mecca and settles in Yathrib (later Medina); the first day of the lunar year in which this event, known as the Hegira, takes place marks the start of the Muslim era.
936	Traditional date of the arrival from Iran of the first Parsis (followers of Zoroastrianism) in India.
1054	Catholic Pope Leo IX condemns the patriarch of Constantinople, finalizing the split between the Eastern Orthodox Church and the Roman Catholic Church.
c. 1224–74	Saint Thomas Aquinas, Italian philosopher and Roman Catholic theologian, is alive.
1309–77	The Roman Catholic papacy is seated in Avignon, France.
1483–1546	Martin Luther, leader of the Protestant Reformation in Germany and author of "95 Theses" (1517) is alive.
1491–1556	Ignatius Loyola, founder of the Jesuit Order of Roman Catholic priests, is alive.
1509–64	John Calvin, leader of the Protestant Reformation in France, is alive.
1549	The first Christian mission in Japan is established.
1582	Jesuit Matteo Ricci is the first missionary to be sent to China.
1620	Plymouth Colony in North America is founded in December by 102 English Puritan separatists, known as Pilgrims.
1624–91	George Fox, English founder of the Protestant Society of Friends (the Quakers) is alive.

1703–91	John Wesley, English founder of the Protestant movement that later became the Methodist Church, is alive.
1859	Charles Darwin, English naturalist, publishes *Origin of Species,* which elucidates his theory of organic evolution.
1869–70	The first Roman Catholic Vatican Council, at which the dogma of papal infallibility is promulgated, is convened by Pope Piux IX.
1869–1948	Mohandas K. Gandhi, Indian spiritual and political leader who helped his country achieve independence from Britain and sought rapprochement between Hindus and Muslims, is alive.
1933–45	The systematic persecution and attempted extermination of European Jews, known as the Holocaust, by Adolf Hitler's Nazi party takes place.
1948	The independent Jewish state of Israel is declared.
1962–65	The second Roman Catholic Vatican Council, at which changes were made in the liturgy and greater participation in services by lay church members was encouraged, is convened by Pope John XXIII and concluded by Pope Paul VI.

Major Religious Holidays in the United States

January 6	*Feast of the Epiphany* (Christian) marks the arrival of the Three Wise Men who sought the newborn baby Jesus and the Twelfth Night, or end, of the Christmas season.
February 2	*Candlemas* (Christian) celebrates the presentation of the Christ child in the temple and the purification of the Blessed Virgin Mary 40 days after she gave birth to Jesus; mostly observed in Roman Catholic, Orthodox Eastern, and Anglican churches.
February 14	*St. Valentine's Day* (Roman Catholic) celebrates the feast day of the patron saint of lovers, engaged couples, and anyone wishing to marry; it has, by tradition, become an ecumenical day celebrating love and affection.
February or March	*Purim* (Jewish), the Feast of Lots, memorializes Queen Esther's prevention of the annihilation of the Persian Jews with a celebratory festival of food, entertainment, and costumes; held on the 14th day of the lunar month of Adar or Adar II.
	Shrove Tuesday (Christian), or Mardi Gras, is the last day before Lent; it is celebrated by eating rich foods forbidden during Lent and by carnivals in such cities as New Orleans, Rio de Janeiro, and Nice.
February, March, or April	*Lent* (Christian) is a 40-day period of fasting and penitence in preparation for Easter that begins on Ash Wednesday in Western churches and on the Monday 41 days before Easter in the Orthodox Eastern Church.
March 17	*St. Patrick's Day* (Roman Catholic) celebrates the feast day of the patron saint of Ireland; by tradition, it has become a day to celebrate the Irish and their contributions to U.S. culture.

March or April	*Passover* (Jewish), or Pesach, commemorates the time when Moses led the Jews out of Egypt; it is celebrated for seven days by Reform and Israeli Jews and for eight days by Orthodox and Conservative Jews, starting on the fourteenth day of the lunar month Nisan with a meal of remembrance called a seder.
	Palm Sunday (Christian) celebrates Jesus's triumphal ride into Jerusalem and the start of Holy Week; it is observed the Sunday before Easter.
	Maundy Thursday (Christian), the Thursday before Easter, marks the Last Supper, the Agony in the Garden, and the arrest of Jesus.
	Good Friday (Christian), the Friday before Easter, commemorates Jesus's Crucifixion.
	Holy Saturday (Christian), the Saturday before Easter, is observed primarily in Roman Catholic, Orthodox Eastern, and Anglican churches.
	Easter Sunday (Christian) celebrates the day Jesus Christ rose from the dead.
May or June	*Ascension Day* (Christian) celebrates Christ's ascent to heaven; it is held 40 days after Easter.
	Shavuot (Jewish) celebrates the harvest of grain while also observing the receipt of the Ten Commandments by Israel; it is held for one day by Reform and Israeli Jews or for two days by Orthodox and Conservative Jews, starting the sixth day of the lunar month of Sivan.
	Pentecost (Christian), or Whitsunday, marks the descent of the Holy Spirit on the Apostles; it is held 50 days after Easter.
August 15	*The Assumption of the Blessed Virgin Mary* (Roman Catholic and Orthodox Eastern) is the principal feast day in honor of Mary, celebrating her assumption, body and soul, into heaven after her death.
September or October	*Rosh Hashanah* (Jewish) marks the start of the new year with solemn prayer and the blowing of the shofar, a ram's horn; it is observed for one day by Reform and Israeli Jews or for two days by Orthodox and Conservative Jews, starting the first day of the lunar month of Tishri.
	Yom Kippur (Jewish), the Day of Atonement, is a day of fasting and repentance for the previous year's sins; it concludes the 10 days of penitence that began on Rosh Hashanah; it is observed on the 10th day of the lunar month of Tishri.
	Sukkoth (Jewish), the Feast of the Tabernacles, is an autumn harvest festival that recalls the wandering of the Jews in the wilderness; it is celebrated for eight days (seven in Israel) starting on the 15th day of the lunar month of Tishri.
Sunday nearest October 31	*Reformation Sunday* (Protestant) celebrates the day Martin Luther nailed his "95 Theses" to a church door, heralding the start of the Protestant Reformation.
November 1	*All Saints' Day* (Christian) is the feast day honoring all martyrs and the Virgin Mary; it is celebrated by Roman Catholic, Orthodox Eastern, and Anglican churches; it is also known as

	All Hallow's Day and is preceded by Halloween on October 31.
Sunday nearest November 30 through Christmas Eve	*Advent* (Christian) is the period of repentance in preparation for the anniversary of the birth of Christ.
December	*Hanukkah* (Jewish), the Festival of Lights, is marked by the lighting of eight candles in a menorah; it commemorates the restoration of traditional worship and the rededication of the temple in Jerusalem after the victory of the Jews over the troops of the Syrian emperor Antiochus; it is held for eight days beginning on the 25th day of the lunar month of Kislev.
December 8	*Feast of the Immaculate Conception* (Roman Catholic) honors the Virgin Mary's state of freedom from original sin from the time of her conception.
December 9	*Feast of the Conception of St. Anne* (Orthodox Eastern) celebrates the conception of the Virgin Mary.
December 25	*Christmas Day* (Christian) celebrates the birth of Jesus Christ; in many Western countries it has become a nonsectarian winter holiday.
———*	*Id al-Adha* (Islamic), the Feast of Sacrifice, is the culmination of the pilgrimage to Mecca.
———*	*Ramadan* (Islamic) is a month of fasting to celebrate the revelation of the Koran.

* The Islamic calendar works on a lunar cycle; annual holidays thus advance about 10 days a year on the solar calendar. It takes Ramadan, for example, 36 years to move around the entire solar year.

Roman Catholic Patron Saints

Protector of	*Saint*
Accountants	Matthew
Actors	Genesius
Air travelers	Joseph of Cupertino
Altar boys	John Berchmans
Architects	Barbara
Art	Catherine of Bologna
Artists	Luke
Astronomers	Dominic
Athletes	Sebastian
Authors	Francis de Sales
Bakers	Elizabeth of Hungary
Bankers	Matthew
Barren women	Antony of Padua
Beggars	Alexius, Giles
Blind	Raphael

Protector of	*Saint*
Bookbinders	Peter Celestine
Bookkeepers	Matthew
Booksellers	John of God
Boy Scouts	George
Bricklayers	Stephen
Brides	Nicholas of Myra
Broadcasters	Archangel Gabriel
Builders	Vincent Ferrer
Cab drivers	Fiacre
Cancer victims	Peregrine Laziosi
Carpenters	Joseph
Charitable societies	Vincent de Paul
Childbirth	Gerard Majella
Children	Nicholas of Myra
Church	Joseph
Comedians	Vitus
Cooks	Martha
Cripples	Giles
Dancers	Vitus
Deaf	Francis de Sales
Dentists	Apollonia
Desperate situations	Jude
Domestic animals	Antony
Dying	Joseph
Ecologists	Francis of Assisi
Editors	John Bosco
Emigrants	Frances Xavier Cabrini
Falsely accused	Raymund Nonnatus
Farmers	Isidore the Farmer
Fathers	Joseph
Fire fighters	Florian
Fire prevention	Catherine of Siena
Fishermen	Andrew, Peter
Foundlings	Holy Innocents
Funeral directors	Joseph of Arimathea
Gardeners	Adelard
Girls	Agnes
Glassworkers	Luke
Gravediggers	Antony the Abbot
Grocers	Michael
Hairdressers	Martin de Porres
Heart patients	John of God
Hospitals	Camillus de Lellis, John of God
Hotelkeepers	Amand
Invalids	Roch
Jewelers	Eligius
Journalists	Francis de Sales
Laborers	Isidore

Protector of	*Saint*
Lawyers	Thomas More, Yves
Learning	Ambrose
Librarians	Jerome
Lost articles	Antony of Padua
Lovers	Valentine
Mariners	Nicholas of Tolentine
Married women	Monica
Mentally ill	Dympna
Messengers	Gabriel
Midwives	Raymund Nonnatus
Missions	Francis Xavier, Thérèse of Lisieux, Leonard of Port Maurice
Mothers	Monica
Musicians	Cecelia, Gregory
Nurses	Agatha, Camillus de Lellis, John of God
Orators	John Chrysostom
Orphans	Jerome Emiliani
Painters	Luke
Pawnbrokers	Nicholas of Myra
Philosophers	Catherine of Alexandria, Justin
Physicians	Cosmas and Damian, Luke
Plasterers	Bartholomew
Poets	David
Police officers	Michael
Poor	Antony of Padua
Postal workers	Gabriel
Preachers	Catherine of Alexandria, John Chrysostom
Pregnant women	Gerard Majella
Priests	John Vianney
Printers	Augustine, Genesius, John of God
Prisoners	Dismas
Radio workers	Gabriel
Rheumatism	James the Greater
Sailors	Brendan, Erasmus
Scholars	Brigid
Scientists	Albert the Great
Sculptors	Claude
Secretaries	Genesius
Servants	Martha
Sick	John of God, Camillus de Lellis
Skaters	Lidwina
Skiers	Bernard
Social justice	Joseph
Social workers	Louise de Marillac
Soldiers	George, Martin of Tours
Students	Catherine of Alexandria, Thomas Aquinas
Surgeons	Cosmas and Damian, Luke
Tax collectors	Matthew
Teachers	Gregory, John Baptist de la Salle

Protector of	Saint
Television	Clare of Assisi
Theologians	Alphonsus Liguori, Augustine
Throat ailments	Blaise
Travelers	Christopher
Vintners	Amand, Morand, Vincent
Vocations	Alphonsus
Widows	Paula
Women in labor	Anne
Writers	Francis de Sales
Youth	Aloysius Gonzaga

Holy Books of the World

The Analects A collection of Confucius' teachings thought to have been recorded by his students. They are considered the only sayings that can safely be attributed to him.

Bhagavad Gita A Sanskrit poem that is part of the Indian epic known as the *Mahabharata*. It describes, in a dialogue between Lord Krishna and Prince Arjuna, the Hindu path to spiritual wisdom and the unity with God that can be achieved through *karma* (action), *bhakti* (devotion), and *jnana* (knowledge). The *Bhagavad-Gita* was probably written sometime between 200 B.C. and A.D. 200.

Five Classics Five works traditionally attributed to Confucius that form the basic texts of Confucianism. They are the *Spring and Autumn Annals*, a history of Confucius's native district; the *I Ching* (or *Book of Changes*), a system of divining the future; the *Book of Rites*, which outlines ceremonies and describes the ideal government; the *Book of History*; and the *Book of Songs*, a collection of poetry. Together they promulgate a system of ethics for managing society based on sympathy for others, etiquette, and ritual. Although the dates of these books are uncertain, they were probably written before the third century B.C.

Koran (Arabic, **al-Qur'ân**) The primary holy book of Islam. It is made up of 114 *suras*, or chapters, which contain impassioned appeals for belief in God, encouragement to lead a moral life, portrayals of damnation and beatitude, stories of Islamic prophets, and rules governing the social and religious life of Muslims. Believers maintain that the Koran contains the verbatim word of God, revealed to the prophet Muhammad through the Angel Gabriel. Some of the *suras* were written during Muhammad's lifetime, but an authoritative text was not produced until c. A.D. 650.

New Testament The second portion of the Christian Bible, which contains 27 books that form the basis of Christian belief. These books include the sayings of Jesus, the story of his life and work, the death and resurrection of Jesus now celebrated as Easter, the teachings and writings of the apostles, and instruction for converting nonbelievers and for performing baptisms, blessings, and other rituals. The New Testament is believed to have been written c. A.D. 100, some 70 to 90 years after the death of Jesus.

Old Testament The Christian name for the Hebrew Bible. It is the sacred scripture of Judaism and the first portion of the Christian Bible. According to Jewish teachings, it is made up of three parts: *the Law* (also known as the Torah or Pentateuch), comprising the first five books (Genesis,

Exodus, Leviticus, Numbers, and Deuteronomy), which describes the origins of the world, the covenant between the Lord and Israel, the exodus and entry into the promised land, and the various rules governing social and religious behavior; *the Prophets*, including the former prophets (Joshua, Judges, Samuel 1–2, Kings 1–2) and the latter prophets (Isaiah, Jeremiah, Ezekiel, and the 12 minor prophets), which describes the history of the Israelites, the stories of heroes, kings, judges, and wars, and the choosing of David as leader of the Israelites; and *the Writings* (including Psalms, Job, Song of Solomon, and Ruth, among others), which describes the reactions of the people to the laws and covenants, as well as prayers and praises of the covenant. Some books of the Old Testament regarded as sacred by the Jews are not accepted as such by Christians; among Christians there are differences between Roman Catholics and Protestants about the inclusion of some books, the order of the books, and the original sources used in translating them. Scholars generally agree that the Old Testament was compiled from c. 1000 B.C. to c. 100 B.C.

THE FOUR HORSEMEN OF THE APOCALYPSE

The Book of Revelation, attributed to John the Apostle, refers to four horsemen who will ride forth to the detriment of humankind.

Pestilence: Rides a white horse, carrying a bow and a crown.
War: Rides a red horse and swings a great sword.
Famine: Rides a black horse and carries scales.
Death: Rides a pale horse and has Hades close behind.

Talmud A compilation of Jewish oral law and rabbinical teachings that is separate from the scriptures of the Hebrew Bible, or Old Testament. It is made up of two parts: the *Mishna*, which is the oral law itself, and the *Gemara*, a commentary on the *Mishna*. The Talmud contains both a legal section (the *Halakah*) and a portion devoted to legends and stories (the *Aggada*). The authoritative Babylonian Talmud was compiled in the sixth century.

Tao-te-ching (The Way and Its Power) The basic text of the Chinese philosophy and religion known as Taoism. It is made up of 81 short chapters or poems that describe a way of life marked by quiet effortlessness and freedom from desire. This is thought to be achieved by following the creative, spontaneous life force of the universe, called the Tao. The book is attributed to Lao-tzu, but it was probably a compilation by a number of writers over a long period of time.

Upanishads The basis of Hindu religion and philosophy that form the final portion of the *Veda*. The 112 Upanishads describe the relationship of the *Brahman*, or universal soul, to the *atman*, or individual soul; they also provide information about Vedic sacrifice and yoga. The original texts of the Upanishads come from various sources and were written beginning c. 900 B.C.

Veda The sacred scripture of Hinduism. Four Vedas make up the *Samhita*, a collection of prayers and hymns that are considered to be revelations of eternal truth written by seer-poets inspired by the gods. The *Rig-Veda*, the *Sama-Veda*, and the *Yajur-Veda* are books of hymns; the *Atharva-Veda* compiles magic spells. These writings maintain that the *Brahman*, or Absolute Self, underlies all reality and can be known by invoking gods through the use of hymns or mantras. The Vedic texts were compiled between c. 1000 B.C. and c. 500 B.C., making them the oldest known group of religious writings.

The Greek and Roman Deities

The gods and goddesses of ancient Greece and Rome have had a lasting impact on Western religious thought. They have also played an important part in the development of the arts, philosophy, and psychology. The following lists give the names of these ancient deities as well as the spheres of influence ascribed to them.

Greek	Roman*	
Adonis	—	Symbolizes the death of nature each autumn and its rebirth in the spring
Aeolus	—	God of the winds
Aphrodite	Venus	Goddess of love and beauty
Apollo	—	God of beauty, youth, poetry, music, prophesy, and archery
Ares	Mars	God of war
Artemis	Diana	Goddess of the hunt, the moon, and nature
Asclepius	Aesculapius	God of medicine
Athena	Minerva	Goddess of wisdom
Chaos	—	God of the shapeless void that preceded creation of the Earth
Cronus	Saturn	Leader of the Titans who ruled the heavens after overthrowing his father, Uranus
Demeter	Ceres	Goddess of the earth, grain, and harvests
Dionysus	Bacchus (Liber)	God of wine
Dis (Hades)	Pluto	God of the underworld
Eos	Aurora	Goddess of dawn
Eris	Discordia	Goddess of strife and discord
Eros	Cupid (Amor)	God of love
Fates	Fates	Three sisters—Clotho, Lachesis, and Atropis (called Nona, Decuma, and Morta by the Romans)—who spun the thread of human destiny and cut it with their shears when they pleased
	Flora	Goddess of flowers
Furies (Eumenides)	Furies	Three goddesses, their heads topped by serpents, who punished those who escaped human justice
Gorgons	—	Three winged sisters—Euryale, Medusa, and Stheno—the sight of whom turned mortals to stone
Graces	Graces	Three sisters—Aglaia, Euphrosyne, and Thalia—who were goddesses of banquets, dances, social enjoyments, and the arts
Hebe	Juventas	Goddess of youth
Hephaestus	Vulcan	God of fire
Hera	Juno	Sister and wife of Zeus; queen of the goddesses
Herakles	Hercules	Son of Zeus; greatest of Greek heroes, who performed 12 labors and was eventually granted immortality
Hermaphroditus	—	Son of Hermes and Aphrodite who was joined forever to the nymph of the fountain of Salmacis, creating one body with the sexual characteristics of both males and females
Hermes	Mercury	Messenger of the gods; patron of thieves

Greek	*Roman**	
Hestia	Vesta	Goddess of the hearth
Hygeia	———	Goddess of health
Hymen	———	God of marriage
Hypnus	Somnus	God of sleep
	Janus	Porter of heaven, who opens the year; also god of gates and doors, with two opposing faces
	Lares	Spirits of ancestors who watch over homes and cities
	Lemures	Spirits of the dead, both good and bad
Metis	Prudence	First wife of Zeus, who helped him become king of gods; personification of prudence
Morpheus	———	God of dreams
Muses	Camenae	Nine sisters, daughters of Zeus, who are goddesses of the arts and sciences: Clio (history), Euterpe (lyric poetry), Thalia (comedy), Melpomene (tragedy), Terpsichore (dance), Erato (erotic poetry), Polyhymnia (sacred poetry), Urania (astronomy), and Calliope (epic poetry; chief of the Muses)
Nemesis	———	Goddess of vengeance
Nike	Victoria	Goddess of victory
Nymphs	———	Nature spirits who oversee water, trees, mountains, valleys, and particular locations
Nyx	Nox	Goddess of night
Pan	Faunus	God of flocks and shepherds
Persepshone	Proserpine	Goddess of the underworld; symbol of the death of nature each autumn and its rebirth each spring
Plutus	———	God of wealth
	Pomona	Goddess of fruit trees and gardens
Poseidon	Neptune	God of the oceans
Priapus	———	God of fertility
Psyche	Psyche	Goddess of the soul, who was united with Eros, or Cupid
Rhea	Ops	Wife of Cronus; mother of the Olympian gods and goddesses Demeter, Hades, Hera, Hestia, Poseidon, and Zeus
	Romulus	Founder of the city of Rome; raised by a wolf with his twin brother, Remus
Satyrs	Satyrs	Field and forest gods with goats' feet and horns who represent nature's bounty
Selene	Luna	Goddess of the moon
Sirens	———	Sea nymphs whose singing enchanted those who heard it
Thanatos	Mors	God of death
Titans	Titans	Sons and daughters of Uranus, who took power when Cronus overthrew their father: Atlas, Coeus, Crius, Dione, Epimetheus, Eurynome, Hyperion, Iapetus, Leto, Maia, Mnemosyne, Oceanus, Ophion, Pallas, Phoebe, Prometheus, Rhea, Tethys, Themis, and Thia
Tyche	Fortuna	Goddess of fortune or fate
Uranus	———	God of heaven; father of the Titans
Zeus	Jupiter (Jove)	Chief god of Olympus; ruler of heaven, who wielded thunder and lightning.

* ——— indicates no corresponding Roman deity.

The Roman Catholic Popes

The religious head of the Roman Catholic Church is known as the pope or the bishop of Rome. He is elected by the College of Cardinals, who as a group rank next to the pope in ecclesiastical authority. New popes are elected upon the death or retirement of a current pope. To be elected, a new pope must be named on two-thirds of the ballots cast, and each member of the College of Cardinals must vote. Once elected, a pope must be asked by the dean of cardinals if he accepts the post. If he does, he is then asked to choose a name. The custom of a pope changing his name upon election originated shortly before the year 1000.

The following list includes all the popes of the Roman Catholic Church, beginning with St. Peter the Apostle, who is traditionally considered to be the first pope because of his appointment by Jesus and his role in organizing the church. Also included in this list are the so-called antipopes, those who were elected or claimed to be pope at various times during church history but whose positions were later invalidated; their names appear in brackets. The list gives the names of the popes, the years of their papacies, and the original names of those who changed their names upon election. Alternate spellings of names are given in parentheses.

Pope	Reign	Original Name
St. Peter the Apostle	died c. 64	Symeon (Simon)
St. Linus	c. 66–c. 78	
St. Anacletus (Cletus)	c. 79–c. 91	
St. Clement I	c. 91–c. 100	
St. Evaristus	c. 100–c. 109	
St. Alexander I	c. 109–c. 116	
St. Sixtus I	c. 116–c. 125	
St. Telesphorus	c. 125–c. 136	
St. Hyginus	c. 136–c. 142	
St. Pius I	c. 142–c. 155	
St. Anicetus	c. 155–c. 166	
St. Soter	c. 166–c. 174	
St. Eleutherius (Eleutherus)	c. 174–189	
St. Victor I	189–198	
St. Zephyrinus	198–217	
St. Callistus (Calixtus) I	217–222	
[St. Hippolytus]	217–235	
St. Urban I	222–230	
St. Pontianus (Pontian)	July 21, 230–September 29, 235	
St. Anterus	November 21, 235–January 3, 236	
St. Fabian	January 10, 236–January 20, 250	

Pope	Reign	Original Name
St. Cornelius	March 251–June 253	
[Novatian]	March 251–c. 258	
St. Lucius I	June 25, 253–March 5, 254	
St. Stephen I	May 12, 254–August 2, 257	
St. Sixtus II	August 30, 257–August 6, 258	
St. Dionysius	July 22, 260–December 26, 268	
St. Felix I	January 3, 269–December 30, 274	
St. Eutychian	January 4, 275–December 7, 283	
St. Gaius (Caius)	December 17, 283–April 22, 296	
St. Marcellinus	June 30, 296–c. 304	
St. Marcellus I	November/December, 306–January 16, 308	
St. Eusebius	April 18, 310–October 21, 310	
St. Miltiades (Melchiades)	July 2, 311–January 11, 314	
St. Silvester I	January 31, 314–December 31, 335	
St. Mark	January 18, 336–October 7, 336	
St. Julius I	February 6, 337–April 12, 352	
Liberius	May 17, 352–September 24, 366	
[Felix II]	c. 355–November 22, 365	
St. Damasus I	October 1, 366–December 11, 384	
[Ursinus]	September 366–November 367	
St. Siricius	December 384–November 26, 399	
St. Anastasius I	November 27, 399–December 19, 401	
St. Innocent I	December 22, 401–March 12, 417	
St. Zosimus	March 18, 417–December 26, 418	
St. Boniface I	December 28, 418–September 4, 422	
[Eulalius]	December 27, 418–April 3, 419	
St. Celestine I	September 10, 422–July 27, 432	
St. Sixtus III	July 31, 432–August 19, 440	
St. Leo I	August/September, 440–November 10, 461	
St. Hilary (Hilarus)	November 19, 461–February 29, 468	
St. Simplicius	March 3, 468–March 10, 483	
St. Felix III (II)	March 13, 483–March 1, 492	
St. Gelasius I	March 1, 492–November 21, 496	
Anastasius II	November 24, 496–November 19, 498	
St. Symmachus	November 22, 498–July 19, 514	
[Lawrence]	November 22, 498–February 499; 501–506	
St. Hormisdas	July 20, 514–August 6, 523	
St. John I	August 13, 523–May 18, 526	
St. Felix IV (III)	July 12, 526–September 22, 530	
Boniface II	September 22, 530–October 17, 532	
[Dioscorus]	September 22, 530–October 14, 530	
John II	January 2, 533–May 8, 535	Mercury
St. Agapitus I	May 13, 535–April 22, 536	

Pope	Reign	Original Name
St. Silverius	June 8, 536–November 11, 537	
Vigilius	c. 538–June 7, 555	
Pelagius I	April 16, 556–March 3, 561	
John III	July 17, 561–July 13, 574	Catelinus
Benedict I	June 2, 575–July 30, 579	
Pelagius II	November 26, 579–February 7, 590	
St. Gregory I	September 3, 590–March 12, 604	
sabinian	September 13, 604–February 22, 606	
Boniface III	February 19, 607–November 12, 607	
St. Boniface IV	September 15, 608–May 8, 615	
St. deusdedit I	October 19, 615–November 8, 618	
Boniface V	December 23, 619–October 25, 625	
Honorius I	October 27, 625–October 12, 638	
Severinus	May 28, 640–August 2, 640	
John IV	December 24, 640–October 12, 642	
Theodore I	November 24, 642–May 14, 649	

THE SEVEN CANONICAL HOURS

Psalms 118:164 states: "Seven times a day I praise you." These hours were designated as follows: Matins and lauds, prime, tierce, sext, nones, vespers, and compline.

Pope	Reign	Original Name
St. Martin I	July 5, 649–June 17, 653	
St. Eugene I	August 10, 654–June 2, 657	
St. Vitalian	July 30, 657–January 27, 672	
Deusdedit III (Adeodatus II)	April 11, 672–June 17, 676	
Donus	November 2, 676–April 11, 678	
St. Agatho	June 27, 678–January 10, 681	
St. Leo II	August 17, 682–July 3, 683	
St. Benedict II	June 26, 684–May 8, 685	
John V	July 23, 685–August 2, 686	
Conon	October 21, 686–September 21, 687	
[Theodore]	687	
[Paschal]	687	
St. Sergius I	December 15, 687–September 9, 701	
John VI	October 30, 701–January 11, 705	
John VII	March 1, 705–October 18, 707	
Sisinnius	January 15, 708–February 4, 708	
Constantine	March 25, 708–April 9, 715	
St. Gregory II	May 19, 715–February 11, 731	
St. Gregory III	March 18, 731–November 28, 741	
St. Zachary (St. Zacharius)	December 3, 741–March 15, 752	
Stephen	March 22 or 23, 752–March 25 or 26, 752	

Pope	Reign	Original Name
Stephen II (III)	March 26, 752–April 26, 757	
St. Paul I	May 29, 757–June 28, 767	
[Constantine]	July 5, 767–August 6, 768	
[Philip]	July 31, 768	
Stephen III (IV)	August 7, 768–January 24, 772	
Adrian I (Hadrian I)	February 1, 772–December 25, 795	
St. Leo III	December 26, 795–June 12, 816	
Stephen IV (V)	June 22, 816–January 24, 817	
St. Paschal I	January 24, 817–February 11, 824	
Eugene II	February 824–August 827	
Valentine	August 827–September 827	
Gregory IV	827–January 25, 844	
[John]	January 844	
Sergius II	January 844–January 27, 847	
St. Leo IV	April 10, 847–July 17, 855	
Benedict III	September 29, 855–April 17, 858	
[Anastasius (Bibliothecarius)]	August 855–September 855	
St. Nicholas I	April 24, 858–November 13, 867	
Adrian II (Hadrian II)	December 14, 867–November or December 872	
John VIII	December 14, 872–December 16, 882	
Marinus I	December 16, 882–May 15, 884	
St. Adrian III (St. Hadrian III)	May 17, 884–September 885	
Stephen V (VI)	September 885–September 14, 891	
Formosus	October 6, 891–April 4, 896	
Boniface VI	April 896	
Stephen VI (VII)	May 896–August 897	
Romanus	August 897–November 897	
Theodore II	November 897	
John IX	January 898–January 900	
Benedict IV	May/June 900–August 903	
Leo V	August 903–September 903	
[Christopher]	September 903–January 904	
Sergius III	January 29, 904–April 14, 911	
Anastasius III	c. June 911–c. August 913	
Lando	c. August 913–c. March 914	
John X	March 914–May 928	
Leo VI	May 928–December 928	
Stephen VII (VIII)	December 928–February 931	
John XI	February or March 931–December 935 or January 936	
Leo VII	January 3, 936–July 13, 939	
Stephen VIII (IX)	July 14, 939–October 942	
Marinus II	October 30, 942–May 946	
Agapetus (Agapitus) II	May 10, 946–December 955	

Pope	Reign	Original Name
John XII	December 16, 955–May 14, 964	Octavian
Leo VIII	December 4, 963–March 1, 965	
Benedict V	May 22, 964–June 23, 964	
John XIII	October 1, 965–September 6, 972	
Benedict VI	January 19, 973–July 974	
[Boniface VII]	June 974–July 974; August 984–July 20, 985	Franco
Benedict VII	October 974–July 10, 983	
John XIV	December 983–August 20, 984	Peter Canepanova
John XV	August 985–March 996	
Gregory V	May 3, 996–February 18, 999	Bruno
[John XVI]	February 997–May 998	John Philagathos
Silvester II	April 2, 999–May 12, 1003	Gerbert
John XVII	May 16, 1003–November 6, 1003	John Sicco
John XVIII	December 25, 1003–July 1009	John Fasanus
Sergius IV	July 31, 1009–May 12, 1012	Peter
Benedict VIII	May 17, 1012–April 9, 1024	Theophylact
[Gregory]	1012	
John XIX	April 19, 1024–October 20, 1032	Romanus
Benedict IX	October 21, 1032–September 1044; March 10, 1045–May 1, 1045; November 8, 1047–July 16, 1048	Theophylact
Silvester III	January 20, 1045–March 10, 1045	John of Sabina
Gregory VI	May 1, 1045–December 20, 1046	John Gratian
Clement II	December 24, 1046–October 9, 1047	Suidger
Damasus II	July 17, 1048–August 9, 1048	Poppo
St. Leo IX	February 12, 1049–April 19, 1054	Bruno
Victor II	April 13, 1055–July 28, 1057	Gebhard
Stephen IX (X)	August 2, 1057–March 29, 1058	Frederick of Lorraine
[Benedict X]	April 5, 1058–January 24, 1059	John Mincius
Nicholas II	December 6, 1058–July 19 or 26, 1061	Gerard
Alexander II	September 30, 1061–April 21, 1073	Anselm
[Honorius II]	October 28, 1061–May 31, 1064	Peter Cadalus
St. Gregory VII	April 22, 1073–May 25, 1085	Hildebrand
[Clement III]	June 25, 1080; March 24, 1084–September 8, 1100	Guibert
Victor III	May 24, 1086; May 9, 1087–September 16, 1087	Daufer (Daufari)
Urban II	March 12, 1088–July 29, 1099	Odo (Eudes)
Paschal II	August 13, 1099–January 21, 1118	Rainerius
[Theodoric]	September 1100–January 1101	
[Albert (Adalbert)]	1101	
[Silvester IV]	November 18, 1105–April 12, 1111	Maginulf
Gelasius II	January 24, 1118–January 29, 1119	John of Gaeta
[Gregory VIII]	March 8, 1118–April 1121	Maurice Burdinus
Calistus II	February 2, 1119–December 14, 1124	Guido
Honorius II	December 21, 1124–February 13, 1130	Lamberto of Ostia

Pope	*Reign*	*Original Name*
[Celestine II]	December 15–16, 1124	Teobaldo Boccapecci
Innocent II	February 14, 1130–September 24, 1143	Gregorio Papareschi
[Anacletus II]	February 14, 1130–January 25, 1138	Pietro Pierleoni
[Victor IV]	March 1138–May 29, 1138	Gregorio Conti
Celestine II	September 26, 1143–May 8, 1144	Guido of Citta di Castello
Lucius II	March 12, 1144–February 15, 1145	Gherardo Caccianemici
Eugene III	February 15, 1145–July 8, 1153	Bernardo Pignatelli
Anastasius IV	July 8, 1153–December 3, 1154	Corrado
Adrian IV (Hadrian IV)	December 4, 1154–September 1, 1159	Nicholas Breakspear
Alexander III	September 7, 1159–August 30, 1181	Orlando (Roland) Bandinelli
[Victor IV]	September 7, 1159–April 20, 1164	Ottaviano
[Paschal III]	April 22, 1164–September 20, 1168	Guido of Crema
[Calistus III]	September 1168–August 29, 1178	Giovanni
[Innocent III]	September 29, 1179–January 1180	Lando
Luicius III	September 1, 1181–November 25, 1185	Ubaldo Allucingoli
Urban III	October 25, 1185–October 20, 1187	Umberto Crivelli
Gregory VIII	October 21, 1187–December 17, 1187	Alberto de Morra
Clement III	December 19, 1187–March 1191	Paolo Scolari
Celestine III	March/April 1191–January 8, 1198	Giacinto Bobo
Innocent III	January 8, 1198–July 16, 1216	Lotario
Honorius III	July 18, 1216–March 18, 1227	Cencio Savelli
Gregory IX	March 19, 1227–August 22, 1241	Ugo (Ugolino)
Celestine IV	October 25, 1241–November 10, 1241	Goffredo da Castiglione
Innocent IV Sinibaldo Fieschi	June 25, 1243–	7, 1254
Alexander IV	December 12, 1254–May 25, 1261	Rinaldo, Count of Segni
Urban IV	August 29, 1261–October 2, 1264	Jacques Pantaléon
Clement IV	February 5, 1265–November 29, 1268	Guy Foulques
Gregory X	September 1, 1271–January 10, 1276	Tedaldo Visconti
Innocent V	January 21, 1276–June 22, 1276	Pierre of Tarentaise
Adrian V (Hadrian V)	July 11, 1276–August 18, 1276	Ottobono Fieschi
John XXI	September 8, 1276–May 20, 1277	Pedro Julião (Peter of Spain)
Nicholas III	November 25, 1277–August 22, 1280	Giovanni Gaetano
Martin IV	February 22, 1281–March 28, 1285	Simon de Brie (Brion)
Honorius IV	April 2, 1285–April 3, 1287	Giacomo Savelli
Nicholas IV	February 22, 1288–April 4, 1292	Girolamo Masci
St. Celestine V	July 5, 1294–December 13, 1294	Pietro del Morrone
Boniface VIII	December 24, 1294–October 11, 1303	Benedetto Caetani
Benedict XI	October 22, 1303–July 7, 1304	Niccolò Boccasino
Clement V	June 5, 1305–April 20, 1314	Bertrand de Got
John XXII	August 7, 1316–December 4, 1334	Jacques Duèse
[Nicholas V]	May 12, 1328–July 25, 1330	Pietro Rainalducci
Benedict XII	December 20, 1334–April 25, 1342	Jacques Fournier
Clement VI	May 7, 1342–December 6, 1352	Pierre of Rosier d'Egleton

Pope	Reign	Original Name
Innocent VI	December 18, 1352–September 12, 1362	Étienne Aubert
Urban V	September 28, 1362–December 19, 1370f	Guillaume de Grimoard
Gregory XI	December 30, 1370–March 27, 1378	Pierre Roger de Beaufort
Urban VI	April 8, 1378–October 15, 1389	Bartolomeo Prignano
[Clement VII]	September 20, 1378–September 16, 1394	Robert of Cambrai
Boniface IX	November 2, 1389–October 1, 1404	Pietro Tomacelli
[Benedict XIII]	September 28, 1394–July 26, 1417	Pedro de Luna
Innocent VII	October 17, 1404–November 6, 1406	Cosimo Gentile de'Migliorati
Gregory XII	November 30, 1406–July 4, 1415	Angelo Correr
[Alexander V]	June 26, 1409–May 3, 1410	Pietro Philarghi (Peter of Candia)
[John XXIII]	May 17, 1410–May 29, 1415	Baldassare Cossa
Martin V	November 11, 1417–February 20, 1431	Oddo Colonna
[Clement VIII]	June 10, 1423–July 26, 1429	Gil Sanchez Muñoz
[Benedict XIV]	November 12, 1425–?	Bernard Garnier
Eugene IV	March 3, 1431–February 23, 1447	Gabriele Condulmaro
[Felix V]	November 5, 1439–April 7, 1449	Amadeus VIII, Duke of Savoy
Nicholas V	March 6, 1447–March 24, 1455	Tommaso Parentucelli
Callistus III	April 8, 1455–August 6, 1458	Alfonso de Borja (Borgia)
Pius II	August 19, 1458–August 15, 1464	Enea Silvo
Piccolomini (Paul II)	August 30, 1464–July 26, 1471	Pietro Barbo
Sixtus IV	August 9, 1471–August 12, 1484	Francesco della Rovere
Innocent VIII	August 29, 1484–July 25, 1492	Giovanni Battista Cibò
Alexander VI	August 11, 1492–August 18, 1503	Rodrigo de Borja y Borja (Borgia)
Pius III	September 22, 1503–October 18, 1503	Francesco Todeschini
Julius II	November 1, 1503–February 21, 1513	Giuliano dell Rovere
Leo X	March 11, 1513–December 1, 1521	Giovanni de' Medici
Adrian VI (Hadrian VI)	January 9, 1522–September 14, 1523	Adrian Florensz Dedal
Clement VII	November 19, 1523–September 25, 1534	Giulio de' Medici
Paul III	October 13, 1534–November 10, 1549	Alessandro Farnese
Julius III	February 8, 1550–March 23, 1555	Giovanni Maria Ciocchi del Monte
Marcellus II	April 9, 1555–May 1, 1555	Marcello Cervini
Paul IV	May 23, 1555–August 18, 1559	Giampietro Carafa
Pius IV	December 25, 1559–December 9, 1565	Giovanni Angelo Medici
St. Pius V	January 7, 1566–May 1, 1572	Michele Ghislieri
Gregory XIII	May 14, 1572–April 10, 1585	Ugo Boncompagni
Sixtus V	April 24, 1585–August 27, 1590	Felice Peretti
Urban VII	September 15, 1590–September 27, 1590	Giambattista Castagna
Gregory XIV	December 5, 1590–October 16, 1591	Niccolò Sfondrati
Innocent IX	October 29, 1591–December 30, 1591	Giovanni Antonio Fachinetti
Clement VIII	January 30, 1592–March 5, 1605	Ippolito Aldobrandini

THE TWELVE APOSTLES

The twelve men who were chosen to be the missionaries of Christ's word were: Peter, Andrew, James (the Greater), John, Thomas, James (the Less), Jude (or Thaddaeus), Philip, Bartholomew, Matthew, Simon, and Judas Iscariot (who was replaced by Matthias). St. Paul is also considered an apostle.

Pope	Reign	Original Name
Leo XI	April 1, 1605–April 27, 1605	Alessandro Ottaviano de' Medici
Paul V	May 16, 1605–January 28, 1621	Camillo Borghese
Gregory XV	February 9, 1621–July 8, 1623	Alessandro Ludovisi
Urban VIII	August 6, 1623–July 29, 1644	Mafeo Barberini
Innocent X	September 15, 1644–January 1, 1655	Giambattista Pamfili
Alexander VII	April 7, 1655–May 22, 1667	Fabio Chigi
Clement IX	June 20, 1667–December 9, 1669	Giulio Rospigliosi
Clement X	April 29, 1670–July 22, 1676	Emilio Altieri
Innocent XI	September 21, 1676–August 12, 1689	Benedetto Odescalchi
Alexander VIII	October 6, 1689–February 1, 1691	Pietro Ottoboni
Innocent XII	July 12, 1691–September 27, 1700	Antonio Pignatelli
Clement XI	November 23, 1700–March 19, 1721	Giovanni Francesco Albani
Innocent XIII	May 8, 1721–March 7, 1724	Michelangelo dei Conti
Benedict XIII	May 29, 1724–February 21, 1730	Pietro Francesco Orsini
Clement XII	July 12, 1730–February 6, 1740	Lorenzo Corsini
Benedict XIV	August 17, 1740–May 3, 1758	Prospero Lorenzo Lambertini
Clement XIII	July 6, 1758–February 2, 1769	Carlo della Torre Rezzonico
Clement XIV	May 18, 1769–September 22, 1774	Lorenzo Ganganelli
Pius VI	February 15, 1775–August 29, 1799	Giovanni Angelo Brachi
Pius VII	March 14, 1800–July 20, 1823	Luigi Barnabà Chiaramonte
Leo XII	September 28, 1823–February 10, 1829	Annibale Sermattei della Genga
Pius VIII	March 31, 1829–November 30, 1830	Francesco Saverio Castiglione
Gregory XVI	February 2, 1831–June 1, 1846	Bartolomeo Albert Cappellari
Pius IX	June 16, 1846–February 7, 1878	Giovanni Maria Mastai-Ferretti
Leo XIII	February 20, 1878–July 20, 1903	Gioacchino Vincenzo Pecci
St. Pius X	August 4, 1903–August 20, 1914	Giuseppe Melchiorre Sarto
Benedict XV	September 3, 1914–January 22, 1922	Giacomo Della Chiesa
Pius XI	February 6, 1922–February 10, 1939	Ambrogio Damiano Achille Ratti

Pius XII	March 2, 1939–October 9, 1958	Eugenio Maria Giuseppe Giovanni Pacelli
John XXIII	October 28, 1958–June 3, 1963	Angelo Giuseppe Roncalli
Paul VI	June 21, 1963–August 6, 1978	Giovanni Battista Montini
John Paul I	August 26, 1978–September 28, 1978	Albino Luciani
John Paul II	October 16, 1978–	Karol Wojtyla

THE BOOKS OF THE BIBLE

The Old Testament

Genesis
Exodus
Leviticus
Numbers
Deuteronomy
Joshua
Judges
I Samuel
II Samuel
I Kings
II Kings
Isaiah
Jeremiah
Ezekiel
Hosea
Joel
Amos
Obadiah
Jonah
Micah
Nahum
Habakkuk
Zephaniah
Haggai
Zachariah
Malachi
Psalms
Proverbs
Job
The Song of Songs
Ruth
Lamentations
Ecclesiastes
Esther
Daniel
Ezra
Nehemiah
I Chronicles
II Chronicles

The New Testament

Matthew
Mark
Luke
John
Acts
Romans
I Corinthians
II Corinthians
Galatians
Ephesians
Philippians
Colossians
I Thessalonians
II Thessalonians
I Timothy
II Timothy
Titus
Philemon
Hebrew
James
I Peter
II Peter
I John
II John
III John
Jude
Revelation

THE TEN COMMANDMENTS

During their exodus from the land of Egypt, Moses led the people of Israel to Mount Sinai, where God issued to Moses the Ten Commandments. These commandments form the foundation of both Jewish and Christian morality. The following is from Exodus, chapter 20; the bold numbers indicate the verse number (the Ten Commandments also appear, with slightly different wording, in Deuteronomy 5:6–21).

1. **2** I am the Lord thy God, which have brought thee out of the land of Egypt, out of the house of bondage.
2. **3** Thou shalt have no other gods before me.
   4 Thou shalt not make unto thee any graven image, or any likeness of any thing that is in heaven above, or that is in the earth beneath, or that is in the water under the earth.
   5 Thou shalt not bow down thyself to them, nor serve them; for I the Lord thy God am a jealous God, visiting the iniquity of the fathers upon the children unto the third and fourth generation of them that hate me; **6** And shewing mercy unto thousands of them that love me, and keep my commandments.
3. **7** Thou shalt not take the name of the Lord thy God in vain; for the Lord will not hold him guiltless that taketh his name in vain.
4. **8** Remember the sabbath day, to keep it holy. **9** Six days shalt thou labour, and do all thy work; **10** But the seventh day is the sabbath of the Lord thy God; in it thou shalt not do any work, thou, nor thy son, nor thy daughter, thy manservant, nor thy maidservant, nor thy cattle, nor thy stranger that is within thy gates; **11** For in six days the Lord made heaven and earth, the sea, and all that in them is, and rested the seventh day; wherefore the Lord blessed the sabbath day, and hallowed it.
5. **12** Honour thy father and thy mother; that thy days may be long upon the land which the Lord thy God giveth thee.
6. **13** Thou shalt not kill.
7. **14** Thou shalt not commit adultery.
8. **15** Thou shalt not steal.
9. **16** Thou shalt not bear false witness against thy neighbour.
10. **17** Thou shalt not covet they neighbour's house, thou shalt not covey thy neighbour's wife, nor his manservant, nor his maidservant, nor his ox, nor his ass, nor anything that is thy neighbour's.

Additional Sources of Information

Cavendish, Richard, ed. *Man, Myth and Magic: The Illustrated Encyclopedia of Mythology, Religion and the Unknown*, 2nd ed. Marshall Cavendish, 1983.

Glasse, Cyril. *The Concise Encyclopedia of Islam.* Harper & Row, 1991.

Holy Days in the United States, History, Theology, Celebration. U.S. Catholic Conference, 1984.

Kelly, J. N. D. *The Oxford Dictionary of Popes.* Oxford University Press, 1986.

Kolatch, Alfred J. *The Jewish Book of Why.* David Publications, 1981.

Martin, Richard P., ed. Bulfinch's Mythology: The Age of Fable, the Age of Chivalry, Legends of Charlemagne. HarperCollins, 1991.

Meagher, Paul Kevin, Thomas C. O'Brien, and Sister Consuelo Maria Aherne, eds. *Encyclopedic Dictionary of Religion*, 3 vols. Catholic University Press, 1979.

New Catholic Encyclopedia. McGraw-Hill, 1967.

Parrinder, Geoffrey. *The Wisdom of the Early Buddhists.* New Directions, 1977.

Parrinder, Geoffrey, ed. *World Religions: From Ancient History to the Present.* Facts On File, 1984.

Powers, Mala. *Follow the Year: A Family Celebration of Christian Holidays.* Harper & Row, 1985.

Suzuki, Shunryu. *Zen Mind, Beginner's Mind.* John Weatherhill, 1986.

Telushkin, Joseph. *Jewish Literacy: The Most Important Things to Know About the Jewish Religion, Its People, Its History.* William Morrow, 1991.

Walsh, Michael, ed. *Butler's Lives of the Saints*, concise ed. HarperCollins, 1991.

10

Philosophy

Major World Philosophers / 262
Proofs for the Existence of God / 264
Arguments Against God's Existence / 266
Famous Quotes / 269
Philosophical Terms / 270
How to Argue Logically / 273
More Than Just Philosophers / 278
Additional Sources of Information / 282

Major World Philosophers

Abelard, Peter (1079–1142). French philosopher. One of the most influential medieval logicians and theologians. Around 1113, while teaching theology in Paris, Abelard fell in love with his student Heloise, whom he secretly married; he was condemned for heresy a few years later because of his nominalist views. He wrote *Sic et Non*.

Anaxagoras (c. 500–428 B.C.). Greek pre-Socratic philosopher who is said to have made Athens the center of philosophy and to have been Socrates' teacher; he rejected the four elements theory of Empedocles and posited instead an infinite number of unique particles of which all objects are composed.

Anaximander (c. 611–547 B.C.). Greek pre-Socratic thinker who believed the universal substance to be "the boundless" or "the indefinite," rather than something resembling familiar objects. Unlike Thales (his teacher) and Anaximenes, he did not believe that a single element underlies all things.

Anaximenes (6th century B.C.). One of the pre-Socratics and an associate of Anaximander. He agreed with Thales that one type of substance underlies the diversity of observable things. Anaximenes believed that air was that universal substance and that all things are made of air in different degrees of density.

Anselm, St. (1033–1109). Italian monk and Scholastic theologian who became archbishop of Canterbury. St. Anselm founded Scholasticism, integrated Aristotelian logic into theology, and believed that reason and revelation are compatible. He is most famous for his influential ontological argument for God's existence.

Aquinas, St. Thomas (1225–74). The greatest thinker of the Scholastic School. His ideas, in 1879, made the official Catholic philosophy. He incorporated Greek ideas into Christianity by showing Aristotle's thought to be compatible with church doctrine. In his system, reason and faith (revelation) form two separate but harmonious realms whose truths complement rather than oppose one another. He presented influential philosophical proofs for the existence of God. His works include *Summa Theologica* and *On Being and Essence*.

Aristotle (384–322 B.C.). Greek philosopher, scientist, logician, and student of many disciplines. Aristotle studied under Plato and became the tutor of Alexander the Great. In 335 he opened the Lyceum, a major philosophical and scientific school in Athens. Aristotle emphasized the observation of nature and analyzed all things in terms of "the four causes." In ethics, he stressed that virtue is a mean between extremes and that man's highest goal should be the use of his intellect. Most of Aristotle's works were lost to Christian civilization from the fifth through the twelfth centuries. Among his writings are *Metaphysics*, *Politics*, and *Rhetoric*.

Augustine of Hippo, St. (354–430). The greatest of the Latin church fathers and possibly the most influential Christian thinker after St. Paul. St. Augustine emphasized man's need for grace. His *Confessions* and *The City of God* were highly influential.

Averroes (1126–98). Spanish-born Arabian philosopher, lawyer, and physician whose detailed commentaries on Aristotle were influential for over 300 years. He emphasized the compatibility of faith and reason but believed philosophical knowledge to be derived from reason. The church condemned his views.

Avicenna (980–1037). Islamic medieval philosopher born in Persia. His Neoplatoist interpretation of Aristotle greatly influenced medieval philosophers, including St. Thomas Aquinas. Avicenna was also a physician; his writings on medicine were important for nearly 500 years.

Bacon, Sir Francis (1561–1626). English statesman, essayist, and philosopher, one of the great precursors of the tradition of British empiricism and of belief in the importance of scientific method. He emphasized the use of inductive reasoning in the pursuit of knowledge.

Bentham, Jeremy (1748–1832). English philosopher and lawyer, and one of the founders of utilitarianism. Bentham was a highly influential reformer of the British legal, judicial, and prison systems. He is the author of *Introduction to the Principles of Morals and Legislation*.

Berkeley, George (1685–1753). Irish philosopher and an Anglican bishop, one of the British empiricists. Berkeley held to a "subjective idealism." He believed that everything that exists is dependent on being perceived by a mind. According to this view, material objects are simply collections of sensations or "ideas" in the mind of a person or of God. His works include *Essay Toward a New Theory of Vision* and *A Treatise Concerning the Principles of Human Knowledge*.

Boethius (c. 475–535). Roman statesman, philosopher, and translator of Aristotle, whose *Consolation of Philosophy* (written in prison) was widely read throughout the Middle Ages; it showed reason's role in the face of misfortune and was the link between the ancient philosophers and the Scholastics.

Buber, Martin (1878–1965). German-Israeli philosopher influenced by Jewish mysticism and existentialism, a major force in twentieth-century Jewish thought and philosophy of religion. His *I and Thou* held that God and man can have a direct and mutual "dialogue."

Comte, Auguste (1798–1857). French founder of positivism and social reformer. Comte put forth a "religion of humanity" that replaced the notion of God with the notion of humankind as a whole. He invented the term *sociology*.

Democritus (c. 460–370 B.C.). Greek philosopher who proposed a mechanistic theory of the world that required no supernatural forces, only the constant motion of the indestructible atoms of which everything is composed. He held that perception is an unreliable source of knowledge and knowledge can be obtained through reason only.

Descartes, René (1596–1650). French philosopher and scientist, considered the father of modern philosophical inquiry. Descartes tried to extend mathematical method to all knowledge in his search for certainty. Discarding the medieval appeal to authority, he began with "universal doubt," finding that the only thing that could not be doubted was his own thinking. The result was his famous "*Cogito, ergo sum*," or "I think, therefore I am." His major works are the *Discourse on Method* and *Meditations*.

Dewey, John (1859–1952). Leading American philosopher, psychologist, and educational theorist. Dewey developed the views of Charles S. Peirce (1839–1914) and William James into his own version of pragmatism. He emphasized the importance of inquiry in gaining knowledge and attacked the view that knowledge is passive.

Diderot, Denis (1713–84). Materialist thinker of the French Enlightenment and originator of the *Encyclopédie*.

Diogenes (c. 400–325 B.C.). Greek founder of cynicism who rejected social conventions and supposedly lived in a tub in defiance of conventional comforts.

Empedocles (c. 495–435 B.C.). Greek pre-Socratic philosopher who believed the universe to consist of the four elements, air, fire, water, and earth. Empedocles held that the interaction between love and hate causes the mixing of the elements.

Engels, Friedrich (1820–95). German socialist thinker and historian, and the cofounder of Marxism; Marx's lifelong collaborator and coauthor of the *Communist Manifesto*; and an originator of the philosophy of dialectical materialism.

PROOFS FOR THE EXISTENCE OF GOD

While theology may take God's existence as absolutely necessary on the basis of authority, faith, or revelation, many philosophers—and some theologians—have thought it possible to demonstrate by reason that there must be a God.

St. Thomas Aquinas, in the thirteenth century, formulated the famous "five ways" by which God's existence can be demonstrated philosophically:

1. *The "unmoved mover" argument.* We know that there is motion in the world; whatever is in motion is moved by another thing; this other thing also must be moved by something; to avoid an infinite regression, we must posit a "first mover," which is God.
2. *The "nothing is caused by itself" argument.* For example, a table is brought into being by a carpenter, who is caused by his parents. Again, we cannot go on to infinity, so there must be a first cause, which is God.
3. *The cosmological argument.* All physical things, even mountains, boulders, and rivers, come into being and go out of existence, no matter how long they last. Therefore, since time is infinite, there must be some time at which none of these things existed. But if there were nothing at that point in time, how could there be anything at all now, since nothing cannot cause anything? Thus, there must always have been at least one necessary thing that is eternal, which is God.
4. *Objects in the world have differing degrees of qualities such as goodness.* But speaking of more or less goodness makes sense only by comparison with what is the maximum goodness, which is God.
5. *The teleological argument (argument from design).* Things in the world move toward goals, just as the arrow does not move toward its goal except by the archer's directing it. Thus, there must be an intelligent designer who directs all things to their goals, and this is God.

Two other historically important "proofs" are the ontological argument and the moral argument. The former, made famous by St. Anselm in the eleventh century and defended in another form by Descartes, holds that it would be logically contradictory to deny God's existence. St. Anselm began by defining God as "that [being] than which nothing greater can be conceived." If God existed only in the mind, He then would not be the greatest conceivable being, for we could imagine another being that is greater because it would exist both in the mind and in reality, and that being would then be God. Therefore, to imagine God as existing only in the mind but not in reality leads to a logical contradiction; this proves the existence of God both in the mind and in reality.

Immanuel Kant rejected not only the ontological argument but the teleological and cosmological arguments as well, based on his theory that reason is too limited to know anything beyond human experience. However, he did argue that religion could be established as presupposed by the workings of morality in the human mind ("practical reason"). God's existence is a necessary presupposition of there being any moral judgments that are objective, that go beyond mere relativistic moral preferences; such judgments require standards external to any human mind—that is, they presume God's mind.

Epictetus (c. 50–138). Stoic moral philosopher who established a school of philosophy after being freed as a slave. His *Manual* teaches that only by detaching ourselves from what is not in our power can we attain inward freedom.

Epicurus (341–270 B.C.). Founder of the Epicurean philosophy and a follower of Democritus, founder of atomism. Virtually all of Epicurus's writings are lost.

Hegel, Georg Wilhelm Friedrich (1770–1831). German philosopher whose idealistic system of metaphysics was highly influential; it was based on a concept of the world as a single organism developing by its own inner logic through trios of stages called "thesis, antithesis, and synthesis" and gradually coming to embody reason. Hegel held the monarchy to be the highest development of the state. His works include *Logic* and *Phenomenology of Mind*.

Heidegger, Martin (1889–1976). German philosopher who studied with Husserl. Heidegger's own philosophy, which was influenced by Kierkegaard, emphasized the need to understand "being," especially the unique ways that humans act in and relate to the world. He wrote *Being and Time*.

Heraclitus (c. 535–475 B.C.). Pre-Socratic philosopher opposed to the idea of a single ultimate reality. Heraclitus believed that all things are in a constant state of change.

Hobbes, Thomas (1588–1679). English materialist and empiricist, one of the founders of modern political philosophy. In the *Leviathan*, Hobbes argued that because men are selfish by nature, a powerful absolute ruler is necessary. In a "social contract," men agree to give up many personal liberties and accept such rule.

Hume, David (1711–76). British empiricist whose arguments against the proofs for God's existence are still influential. In his *Treatise of Human Nature*, Hume held that moral beliefs have no basis in reason, but are based solely on custom.

Husserl, Edmund (1859–1938). German philosopher who founded the phenomenology movement. He aimed at a completely accurate description of consciousness and conscious experience. His works include *Logical Investigations* and *Ideas for a Pure Phenomenology*.

James, William (1842–1910). American philosopher and psychologist, one of the founders of pragmatism, and one of the most influential thinkers of his era. James viewed consciousness as actively shaping reality, defined truth as "the expedient" way of thinking, and held that ideas are tools for guiding our future actions rather than reproductions of our past experiences. His writings include *The Will to Believe* and *Pragmatism*.

Kant, Immanuel (1724–1804). German philosopher, possibly the most influential of modern times. He synthesized Leibniz's rationalism and Hume's skepticism into his "critical philosophy": in *The Critique of Pure Reason*, he wrote that ideas do not conform to the external world, but rather the world can be known only insofar as it conforms to the mind's own structure. In *The Critique of Practical Reason*, Kant claimed that morality requires a belief in God, freedom, and immortality, although these can be proved neither scientifically nor by metaphysics. Finally, in his *Metaphysic of Morals*, he presented the concept of the categorical imperative.

Kierkegaard, Søren (1813–55). Danish philosopher, religious thinker, and extraordinarily influential founder of existentialism. Kierkegaard held that "truth is subjectivity," that religion is an individual matter, and that man's relationship to God requires suffering. He wrote *Either/Or* and *Fear and Trembling*.

Leibniz, Gottfried Wilhelm (1646–1716). German philosopher, diplomat, and mathematician, one of the great minds of all time. Leibniz was an inventor (with Sir Isaac Newton) of the calculus and a forefather of modern mathematical logic. He held that the entire universe is one large system expressing God's plan. His writings include *New Essays on Human Understanding*.

Locke, John (1632–1704). Highly influential founder of British empiricism. In his *Essay Concerning Human Understanding*, Locke wrote that all ideas come to mind from experience and that none are innate. He also held that authority derives solely from the consent of the governed, a view that deeply influenced the American Revolution and the writing of the U.S. Constitution. His two *Treatises on Government* express his political thought.

Lucretius (c. 99–55 B.C.). Roman Epicurean philosopher and poet. In *De Rerum Natura* (On the Nature of Things), Lucretius depicted the entire world, including the soul, as composed of atoms.

Machiavelli, Niccolò (1469–1527). Italian Renaissance statesman and political writer. In *The Prince*, one of the most influential political books of modern times, Machiavelli argues that any act of a ruler designed to gain and hold power is permissible. The term *Machiavellian* is used to refer to any political tactics that are cunning and power-oriented.

ARGUMENTS AGAINST GOD'S EXISTENCE

Arguments against God's existence have been given by philosophers, atheists, and agnostics. Some of these arguments find God's existence incompatible with observed facts; some are arguments that God does not exist because the concept of God is incoherent or confused. Others are criticisms of the proofs offered *for* God's existence.

One of the most influential and powerful "proofs" that there is no God proceeds from "The Problem from Evil." This argument claims that the following three statements cannot *all* be true: (a) evil exists; (b) God is omnipotent; and (c) God is all-loving. The argument is as follows:

- If God can prevent evil, but *doesn't*, then He isn't all-loving.
- If God intends to prevent evil, but *cannot*, then He isn't omnipotent.
- If God *both* intends to prevent evil and is capable of doing so, then how can evil exist?

Another argument claims that the existence of an all-knowing God is incompatible with the fact of free will—that humans do make choices. If God is omniscient, He must know beforehand exactly what a person will do in a given situation. In that case, a person is not in fact free to do the alternative to what God knows he or she will do, and free will must be an illusion. To take this one step further, if one chooses to commit a sin, how can it then be said that one sinned freely?

Hume provided powerful critiques of the main arguments for God's existence. Against the cosmological argument (Aquinas's third argument), he argued that the idea of a necessarily existing being is absurd. Hume stated, "Whatever we can conceive as existent, we can also conceive as nonexistent." He also asked why the ultimate source of the universe could not be the entire universe itself, eternal and uncaused, without a God?

Hume also criticized the argument from design (Aquinas's fifth argument). In particular, he emphasized that there is no legitimate way we can infer the properties of God as the creator of the world from the qualities of His creation. For instance, Hume questioned how we can be sure that the world was not created by a team; or that this is not one of many attempts at creations, the first few having been botched; or, on the other hand, that our world is not a poor first attempt "of an infant deity who afterwards abandoned it, ashamed of his lame performance."

Maimonides (1135–1204). Spanish-born medieval Jewish philosopher and thinker. Maimonides tried to synthesize Aristotelian and Judaic thought. His works, such as *Guide to the Perplexed*, had enormous influence on Jewish and Christian thought.

Marcus Aurelius (121–180). Roman emperor from A.D. 161, and a proponent of the Stoic philosophy. His *Meditations* held that death is as natural as birth and that the world is rational and orderly. Although a great humanitarian, Marcus Aurelius persecuted the Christians of his time.

Marx, Karl (1818–83). German revolutionary thinker, social philosopher, and economist. His ideas, formulated with Engels, laid the foundation for nineteenth-century socialism and twentieth-century communism. Although Marx was initially influenced by Hegel, he soon rejected Hegel's idealism in favor of materialism. His *Communist Manifesto* and *Das Kapital* are among the most important writings of the last 200 years.

Mill, John Stuart (1806–73). English empiricist philosopher, logician, economist, and social reformer. His *System of Logic* described the basic rules for all scientific reasoning. As a student of Jeremy Bentham, he elaborated on utilitarian ethics; in *On Liberty*, he presented a plea for the sanctity of individual rights against the power of any government.

Montesquieu, Baron de (Charles-Louis de Secondat) (1689–1755). French political philosopher, influenced by Locke. In *Spirit of the Laws*, Montesquieu put forth the theory of separation of powers that strongly influenced the writing of the U.S. Constitution.

Moore, G. E. (George Edward) (1873–1958). British philosopher who emphasized the "common sense" view of the reality of material objects. In ethics, Moore held that goodness is a quality known directly by moral intuition and that it is a fallacy to try to define it in terms of anything else.

More, Sir Thomas (1478–1535). A leading Renaissance humanist and statesman, Lord Chancellor of England. More was beheaded for refusing to accept the king as head of the church. Influenced by Greek thinking, he believed in social reform and drew a picture of an ideal peaceful state in his *Utopia*.

Nietzsche, Friedrich Wilhelm (1844–1900). German philosopher, philologist, and poet. As a moralist, he rejected Christian values and championed a "Superman" who would create a new, life-affirming, heroic ethic by his "will to power." His works include *Thus Spake Zarathustra* and *Beyond Good and Evil*.

Parmenides (b. c. 515 B.C.). The founder of Western metaphysics. This pre-Socratic thinker held that "being" is the basic substance and ultimate reality of which all things are composed and that motion, change, time, difference, and reality are illusions of the senses.

Pascal, Blaise (1623–62). French philosopher, mathematician, scientist, and theologian. His posthumous *"Pensées"* ("Thoughts") argues that reason is by itself inadequate for man's spiritual needs and cannot bring man to God, who can be known only through mystic understanding.

Plato (c. 428–348 B.C.). Athenian father of Western philosophy and student of Socrates, after whose death he traveled widely. Upon returning to Athens, he founded an academy, where he taught until he died. His writings are in the form of dialogues between Socrates and other Athenians. Many of Plato's views are set forth in *The Republic*, where an ideal state postulates philosopher kings, specially trained at the highest levels of moral and mathematical knowledge. Plato's other works analyzed moral virtues, the nature of knowledge, and the immortality of the soul. His views on cosmology strongly influenced the next two thousand years of scientific thinking.

Plotinus (205–270). Egyptian-born founder of Neoplatonism, who synthesized the ideas of Plato and other Greek philosophers. Plotinus believed all reality is caused by a series of outpourings (called emanations) from the divine source. Although not himself a Christian, he was a major influence on Christianity.

Pythagoras (c. 582–507 B.C.). Greek philosopher, mathematician, and mystic, founder of a religious brotherhood that believed in the immortality and the transmigration of the soul. Pythagoras may have been the first thinker to assert that numbers constitute the true nature of all things; he also may have coined the term *philosophy*.

Rousseau, Jean Jacques (1712–78). Swiss-French thinker, born in Geneva. Rousseau has been enormously influential in political philosophy, educational theory, and the romantic movement. In *The Social Contract* (1762), he viewed governments as being expressions of the people's "general will," or rational men's choice for the common good. Rousseau emphasized man's natural goodness.

Russell, Bertrand (1872–1970). English philosopher and logician influential as an agnostic and a pacifist. Early work with Alfred North Whitehead gave birth to modern logic; they coauthored *Principia Mathematica*. Russell changed his views numerous times but always sought to establish philosophy, especially epistemology, as a science.

Santayana, George (1863–1952). Spanish-born American philosopher and poet; a student of William James. Santayana attempted to reconcile Platonism and materialism, studied how reason works, and found "animal faith," or impulse, to be the basis of reason and belief. Among his works are *The Sense of Beauty* and *The Life of Reason*.

Sartre, Jean-Paul (1905–80). French philosopher, novelist, and dramatist; one of the founders of existentialism. Sartre was a Marxist through much of his life. He held that man is "condemned to be free" and to bear the responsibility of making free choices. His primary philosophical work was *Being and Nothingness*.

Schopenhauer, Arthur (1788–1860). German post-Kantian philosopher who held that although irrational will is the driving force in human affairs, it is doomed not to be satisfied. He believed that only art and contemplation could offer escape from determinism and pessimism. Schopenhauer strongly influenced Nietzsche, Freud, Tolstoy, Proust, and Thomas Mann. He wrote *The World as Will and Representation*.

Scotus, John Duns (c. 1266–1308). Scottish-born Scholastic philosopher who tried to integrate Aristotelian ideas into Christian theology. Scotus emphasized that all things depend not just on God's intellect but on divine will as well. He wrote *On the First Principle*.

Smith, Adam (1723–1790). Scottish philosopher and economist. The author of *The Wealth of Nations*, he believed that if government left the marketplace to its own devices, an "invisible hand" would guarantee that the results would benefit the populace. Smith has had enormous influence on economists into the present day.

Socrates (c. 470–399 B.C.). Athenian philosopher who allegedly wrote down none of his views, supposedly from his belief that writing distorts ideas. His chief student, Plato, is the major source of knowledge about his life. Socrates questioned Athenians about their moral, political, and religious beliefs, as depicted in Plato's dialogues; his questioning technique, called dialectic, has greatly influenced Western philosophy. Socrates is alleged to have said that "the unexamined life is not worth living." In 399 B.C., he was brought to trial on charges of corrupting the youth and religious heresy. Sentenced to die, he drank poison.

Spinoza, Benedict (Baruch) (1623–77). Dutch-born philosopher expelled from the Amsterdam Jewish community for heresy in 1656; he was attacked by Christian theologians 14 years later. In *Ethics*, Spinoza presents his views in a mathematical system of deductive reasoning. A proponent of monism, he held—in contrast to Descartes—that mind and body are aspects of a single substance, which he called God or nature.

FAMOUS QUOTES

Aristotle (384–322 B.C.): "Man is by nature a political animal."
Sir Francis Bacon (1561–1626): "Knowledge is power."
Jeremy Bentham (1748–1832): "The greatest happiness of the greatest number is the foundation of morals and legislation."
Confucius (551–479 B.C.): "Hold faithfulness and sincerity as first principles."
René Descartes (1596–1650): "Cogito, ergo sum" (Latin for "I think, therefore I am").
Ralph Waldo Emerson (1803–82): "Nature is a mutual cloud, which is always and never the same."
Friedrich Engels (1820–95): "The state is not 'abolished,' it withers away."
Georg Hegel (1770–1831): "What experience and history teach us is this—that people and governments have never learned anything from history, or acted on principles deduced from it."
Thomas Hobbes (1588–1679): "The life of man [in a state of nature is], solitary, poor, nasty, brutish, and short."
Immanuel Kant (1724–1804): "Happiness is not an ideal of reason but of imagination."
John Locke (1632–1704): "No man's knowledge here can go beyond his experience."
Niccolò Machiavelli (1469–1527): "God is not willing to do everything, and thus take away our free will and that share of glory which belongs to us."
Karl Marx (1818–83): "The proletarians have nothing to lose [in this revolution] but their chains. They have a world to win. Workers of the world, unite!"
"Religion is the opium of the people."
"The class struggle necessarily leads to the dictatorship of the proletariat."
John Stuart Mill (1806–73): "Liberty consists in doing what one desires."
Friedrich Nietzsche (1844–1900): "I teach you the Superman. Man is something to be surpassed."
Thomas Paine (1737–1809): "Suspicion is the companion of mean souls, and the bane of all good society."
Plato (428–348 B.C.): "The life which is unexamined is not worth living."
Jean Jacques Rousseau (1712–78): "Man was born free, and everywhere he is in chains."
Bertrand Russell (1872–1970): "It is undesirable to believe a proposition when there is no ground whatever for supposing it true."
Seneca (c. 4 B.C.–A.D. 65): "Even while they teach, men learn."
Socrates (c. 470–399 B.C.): "There is only one good, knowledge, and one evil, ignorance."
Voltaire (1694–1778): "If God did not exist, it would be necessary to invent Him."

Thales of Miletus (c. 636–546 B.C.). Regarded as the first Western philosopher, this pre-Socratic monist thinker is said to have believed that the fundamental principle of all things, or universal substance, is water. All of his writings are lost.

Unamuno, Miguel de (1864–1936). The major Spanish philosophical thinker of his time. Unamuno criticized philosophical abstractions such as "man" for ignoring concrete men. He held that reason by itself is virtually useless and cannot reveal the basic fact of human immortality. He wrote *The Tragic Sense of Life in Men and Nations*.

Voltaire (François Marie Arouet) (1694–1778). French philosopher, essayist, and historian; one of the major thinkers of the Enlightenment. A Deist who was anti-Christian, Voltaire widely advocated tolerance of liberal ideas and called for positive social action. His novel *Candide* is a parody of the optimism of Leibniz.

Whitehead, Alfred North (1861–1947). British philosopher and mathematician who worked with Bertrand Russell. Whitehead tried to integrate twentieth-century physics into a metaphysics of nature.

William of Ockham (Occam) (c. 1285–1349). Franciscan monk and important English theologian and philosopher. In his nominalism, he opposed much of the thought of St. Thomas Aquinas and of medieval Aristotelianism; he also rejected the pope's power in the secular realm.

Wittgenstein, Ludwig (1889–1951). Austrian-born philosopher who spent the last 20 years of his life in England. Wittgenstein was one of the most influential philosophers of the century, primarily through his emphasis on the importance of the study of language. His *Tractatus Logico-Philosophicus* influenced analytic philosophy. His later views emphasized that philosophic problems are often caused by linguistic confusions.

Zeno of Elea (c. 490–430 B.C.). Pre-Socratic philosopher and disciple of Parmenides. Zeno argued that motion, change, and plurality are logical absurdities and that only an unchanging being is real. His four arguments against motion (Zeno's paradoxes) attempted to demonstrate logically that the notions of time and motion are erroneous.

Zeno (of Citium) the Stoic (c. 334–262 B.C.). Greek philosopher born in Cyprus; the founder of Stoicism.

Philosophical Terms

Entries in this glossary include terms used by philosophers (for instance, a priori); "isms" that describe philosophical viewpoints or positions (for example, pantheism); and specific historical movements (such as existentialism) and schools (Cartesianism). Names of philosophers referred to in the glossary who are listed under "Major World Philosophers" are marked with an asterisk*.

absolutism The doctrine that there is one explanation of all reality—the absolute—that is unchanging and objectively true. Absolutists (such as G. W. F. Hegel*) hold that this absolute, such as God or mind, is eternal and that in it all seeming differences are reconciled.

aesthetics (esthetics) The philosophical study of art, or of beauty in general. It attempts to systematically answer such questions as, What is beauty? How do we evaluate works of art? Are aesthetic judgments objective or subjective? How does art embody truth and convey knowledge? How does beauty in art relate to beauty in nature?

agnosticism The belief that it is impossible to know whether God exists, or to have any other theological knowledge. English thinkers T. H. Huxley (1825–95) and Bertrand Russell* were influential agnostics.

altruism The ethical theory that morality consists of concern for and the active promotion of the interests of others. Altruists strongly disagree with the doctrine of egoism, which states that individuals act only in their own self-interest.

analytical philosophy An influential twentieth-century movement whose major proponents include Bertrand Russell,* Ludwig Wittgenstein,* and such logical positivists as Rudolph Carnap (1891–1970) and Willard Van Orman Quine (1908–   ). This school of thought emphasizes restating philosophical problems in highly structured terms based on modern logic.

analytic statement A statement true by definition, such as "All triangles have three sides."

anarchism A political philosophy that advocates the abolition of an organized state as the ruling government. Its advocates believe that individuals should be free to organize themselves in the ways that best enable them to fulfill their needs and ideals. The Russian thinker Mikhail Bakunin (1814–76) was an influential anarchist.

angst A German word meaning anxiety, anguish, or dread. The term was used by Heidegger* and other adherents of existentialism to express their belief that anxiety characterizes the human condition and that dread arises from our realization that we are totally responsible for all of our choices.

anthroposophy The philosophy of Rudolf Steiner (1861–1925), an Austrian-born thinker who held that cultivating man's spiritual development is humanity's most important task. His followers founded a large number of schools worldwide based on his philosophy.

a posteriori knowledge Knowledge based on or derived from sensory experience.

a priori knowledge Knowledge acquired by the mind or reasoning alone, without any specific basis in experience—for instance, $2+2=4$.

argument An attempt to relate one set of statements, called the premises or the starting point, to another set, called the conclusion or the end point, by valid means. Arguments are either inductive or deductive. *See also* **syllogism.**

Aristotelianism The thinking and writings of Aristotle,* influential until the fall of Rome, when all but his writings on logic were lost to Christian civilization in Europe. However, his works were preserved in Syrian and Arabic cultures and were revived at the end of the twelfth century.

asceticism The view that attention to the body's needs is evil, an obstacle to moral and spiritual development, and displeasing to God. According to this view, humans are urged to withdraw into an inner spiritual world to reach the good life.

associationism A philosophical theory of the mind that holds that all mental states can be analyzed as separate component items and that all mental activity can be explained by the combining and recombining of these items, often called ideas. David Hume* and John Stuart Mill* were prominent advocates of this view. *See also* **association of ideas.**

association of ideas (laws of association) The principles by which the mind connects ideas. Aristotle* included similarity, contrast, and closeness; David Hume* held the basic laws to be resemblance, closeness in time or place, and causality. Hume and John Stuart Mill* are the two most prominent philosophers who emphasized association as the basic principle of the mind. *See also* **associationism.**

atheism The rejection of the belief in God. Some atheists have held that there is nothing in the world that requires a God in order to be explained. Atheism is not the same as agnosticism, which holds that we can have knowledge neither of the existence nor of the nonexistence of God.

atomism The theory that reality is composed of simple and indivisible units (atoms) that are completely separate from and independent of one another. Philosophers have differed as to the nature of atoms; for instance, the Greek thinkers Leucippus and Democritus* (fifth century B.C.) held that the atoms are different-shaped bits of matter.

bad faith Term used by Jean-Paul Sartre* for self-deception and the deception of others caused by denying one's freedom of choice and one's responsibility for making decisions.

becoming That which changes from one form to another, or, in Plato,* that which is known only by experience and exists only temporarily. *See also* **being.**

being Frequently used in metaphysics to contrast with appearance or nonexistence; often synonymous with unchanging substance, ultimate reality, God, infinity, or all that exists. Aristotle held that being is the subject matter of metaphysics. *See also* **becoming.**

bioethics A branch of philosophy that studies ethical issues that arise from conflicts between human rights and medical and biological research and the technology they use. Areas of concern are genetic manipulation, euthanasia, and brain control.

British empiricism The empiricism of Locke,* Berkeley,* and Hume* in the seventeenth and eighteenth centuries. They share the axiom that our knowledge of the world derives from experience or sensation rather than from reason. This view is opposed to rationalism, as well as to the Platonic notion of Forms as the source of knowledge.

British idealism (neo-Hegelianism) The philosophy of Hegel* as revived in England and Scotland in the mid-nineteenth century. The most prominent members of this school were T. H. Green (1836–82), Bernard Bosanquet (1848–1923), and F. H. Bradley (1846–1924). They were united in their opposition to empiricism and utilitarianism and in their emphasis on mind and spirit as primary.

Buridan's ass A story, falsely attributed to the fourteenth-century thinker John Buridan, in which an ass, faced with two equally desirable bales of hay, starves to death because he cannot find a good reason for preferring one bale to the other.

Cambridge Platonists A group of seventeenth-century English philosophers and theologians who tried to provide Christian theology with a philosophical defense based on Platonic and Neoplatonic theories. Ralph Cudworth (1617–88) was the most prominent member.

Cartesianism The views of Descartes* as interpreted by rationalistic, dualistic, and theistic philosophers. Nicolas Malebranche (1638–1715) was the most prominent of the group.

categorical imperative Kant's* term for the binding moral law, which dictates that one should act only according to a maxim that could serve as a universal law, for instance, to treat humanity as an end and never only as a means.

cause Whatever is responsible for change, action, or motion. Historically, Aristotle's* analysis of cause falls into four types: material cause, the substance a thing is made of; formal cause, the design of the thing; efficient cause, the maker of the thing; and final cause, its purpose or function. Hume* argued that all knowledge of cause comes from our actual experience of observed regularities.

certainty According to Descartes,* a condition of knowing that anything is true; various types of statements that are certain, for example, $1+1=2$, or all widows are female.

chain of being An idea, originating with Plato* and very influential in Western thought into the Renaissance, that all possible things are realized in the world in an ordered chain of diminishing complexity and richness, from God down to the tiniest, humblest bit of matter. The view captures the concept of the universe as an ordered hierarchy.

conceptualism The theory that general ideas, such as the idea of man or of redness, exist as entities produced by the human mind and that they can exist in the minds of all men. This view is typically contrasted with nominalism and realism.

cosmogony A theory or story about the origin of the universe, either scientific or mythological. Cosmogonies are also called creation myths.

cosmology The systematic study of the origin and structure of the universe as a whole. In such philosophers as Plato,* Aristotle,* and Kant,* cosmology was based on metaphysical speculation; today cosmology is a branch of the physical sciences.

counterexample A specific fact that refutes or negates a generalization; for instance, a black swan is a counterexample to the statement "All swans are white."

Cynics A school of Greek philosophers founded by Diogenes.* According to legend, Diogenes walked around night and day with a lighted lantern seeking an honest man but could not find one. The Cynics held that men should live in a simple state of nature with as few desires and needs as possible. They advocated moderation, self-discipline, and training of the mind as well as the body.

Cyrenaics A school of philosophy of the fourth century B.C. in Athens founded by Cyrene, a disciple of Socrates. Cyrenaics believed that only momentary feelings of pleasure or pain can be known; they held that the good life is one that maximizes pleasure derived from satisfying one's bodily desires. *See also* **hedonism**.

deductive reasoning Reasoning from a general statement to a particular or specific example; for example, "All cats are mortal; William is a cat; therefore, William is mortal." *See also* **syllogism**.

deism A philosophical viewpoint appearing in England in the seventeenth and eighteenth centuries and in France in the eighteenth century. Deists hold that although God created the universe and its laws, He then removed Himself from any ongoing interaction with the material world.

deontology The ethical philosophy that makes duty the basis of all morality. According to deontological theorists, such as Kant,* some acts—such as keeping a promise or telling the truth—are moral obligations regardless of their consequences.

determinism The view that every event has a cause and that everything in the universe is absolutely dependent on and governed by causal laws. Since determinists believe that all events, including human actions, are predetermined, determinism is typically thought to be incompatible with free will.

dialectic A term with different meanings for different philosophers. It derives from the Greek word meaning "to converse" and is used to describe Socrates'* method of teaching by question-and-answer technique. Plato* used the word to mean the study of the Forms. In Kant,* it refers to a method of criticizing claims of knowledge going beyond experience. Hegel* means by it the necessary pattern of thinking.

dialectical materialism The philosophy of Karl Marx* and many of his followers. It holds that matter is the primary reality and that it obeys the dynamic laws of change. The most fundamental of these laws is that progress occurs through conflict and struggle between opposing forces, such as between different classes and between capitalism and communism. *See also* **Marxism**.

HOW TO ARGUE LOGICALLY

We like to think that we speak logically all the time, but we are aware that we sometimes use illogical means to persuade others of our point of view. In the heat of an impassioned argument, or when we are afraid our disputant has a stronger case, or when we don't quite have all the facts we'd like to have, we are prone to engage in faulty processes of reasoning, using arguments we hope will appear sound.

Such defective arguments are called *fallacies* by philosophers who, starting with Aristotle, have catalogued and classified these fallacious arguments. There are now over 125 separate fallacies, most with their own impressive-sounding names, many of them in Latin.

Some arguments have easily recognizable defects. For instance, in the *argument ad hominem*, a person's views are criticized because of a logically irrelevant personal defect: "You can't take Smith's advice on the stock market; he's a known philanderer." In the *genetic fallacy*, something is mistakenly reduced to its origins: "We know that emotions are nothing more than physiology; after all, medical research has shown emotions involve the secretion of hormones." Another illogical argument is named for the erroneous thinking a wagering person may fall prey to, the *gambler's fallacy* (also called the *Monte Carlo fallacy*): "I'm betting on heads; it's got to come up since we've just had nine straight tails."

Some fallacies may not be recognized as erroneous reasoning because they are such commonly used forms of argument. For instance, if we say, "I'm sure my cold is due to the weather; I started sneezing right after it went from 60 degrees to 31 degrees in three hours," we are committing the fallacy with the Latin name of *post hoc ergo propter hoc* ("after this, therefore because of this"). Many a political argument exemplifies the fallacy of *arguing in a circle*; for instance: "Only wealthy men are capable of leading the country; after all, leadership can be learned only if you have had money to exercise power." Many prejudicial or stereotypical arguments commit the *fallacy of division*, or of applying to the part what may be true of the whole: "North Dakota has wide-open spaces; since Jack's farm is there, it must be quite large." The converse of this is the *fallacy of composition*, where properties of the parts are erroneously attributed to the whole: "Every apple on this tree is rotten; therefore, the tree itself is hopelessly diseased."

It may be a surprise to realize that some widely accepted forms of argument are just as fallacious as the most logically defective reasoning. When we appeal to the beliefs or behavior of the majority to prove the truth of something, we are committing the *fallacy of consensus gentium*: "Imbibing alcohol cannot be bad for people, since all cultures studied have used alcohol." Or consider the person who argues that "Tragedy is the highest form of literature; after all, didn't Aristotle consider it such?" This is a form of the *fallacy of arguing from authority*. There is also the *fallacy of ignoratio elenchus*, which has nothing to do with ignorance; its name means that the point made is irrelevant to the issue at hand, as in the untenable view of a lawyer who says, "Ladies and gentlemen of the jury, you cannot convict my client of manslaughter while driving under the influence; after all, advertisements for alcohol exist everywhere in our culture."

doubt According to Descartes,* the argument that nothing can be considered true unless it can never be doubted under any conditions. Descartes doubted everything "systematically" to find out if anything is indubitable; his "Cogito, ergo sum" ("I think, therefore I am") survived his test.

dualism Any philosophical theory holding that the universe consists of, or can only be explained by, two independent and separate forces, such as matter and spirit, the forces of good and evil, or the supernatural and natural. *See also* **mind-body problem.**

duty According to many ethical theories, the basis of the virtuous life. The Stoics held that man has a duty to live virtuously and according to reason; and Kant* held that his categorical imperative is the highest law of duty, no matter what the consequences.

egocentric predicament The belief that each of us is limited to, and by, our unique pattern of perceptions. Any knowledge of the world outside our minds would thus be colored by our perceptions. *See also* **solipsism.**

egoism The ethical theory that each person should forward his or her own self-interest. Egoists sometimes argue that this is not selfishness, but that self-interest is compatible with helping others as well. Some egoists also argue that, psychologically speaking, human beings always in fact seek their own well-being.

élan vital *See* **vitalism.**

Eleatics A school of pre-Socratic philosophers from Elea in southern Italy, of whom Parmenides* and Zeno of Elea* are the best known. The Eleatics denied the reality of what is known to the senses, holding that the ultimate reality is an undifferentiated and unchanging "being."

empirical Based on experience, observation, or facts—in short, describing any knowledge derived from or validated by sensory experience.

empiricism The view that all knowledge of the world derives solely from sensory experience, using observation and experimentation if needed; empiricism also holds that reason on its own can never provide knowledge of reality unless it also utilizes experience. *See also* **British empiricism.**

Encyclopedists A group of eighteenth-century French writers who combined to produce an encyclopedia of philosophy, art, and science (1751–65) edited by Diderot* and D'Alembert. The work was skeptical about religion and advocated liberal, democratic political views. At the time, it was the largest compendium of human knowledge that had ever been produced.

Enlightenment (Age of Reason) A period that stretched from the early seventeenth to the early nineteenth century, especially in France, England, and Germany. Its thinkers strove to make reason the ruler of human life; they believed that all men could gain knowledge and liberation. Major Enlightenment figures include Voltaire,* Rousseau,* Diderot,* and Montesquieu* in France; Bacon*, Hobbes,* and Locke* in England; and Leibniz,* Lessing (1729–81), and Herder (1744–1803) in Germany.

Epicureanism A school founded by Epicurus* about 306 B.C. that taught that pleasure and happiness should be man's supreme goals. Epicureans sought mental pleasures over bodily ones.

epistemology The branch of philosophy that studies how knowledge is gained, how much we can know, and what justification there is for what is known.

eschatology In theology, the study of "final things," such as death, resurrection, immortality, the second coming of Christ, and the day of judgment.

essence That which makes a specific thing what it is and not something else; its nature. While the Greek philosophers viewed essence and substance as basically the same, St. Thomas Aquinas* and the philosophy of Scholasticism held that even nonexistent things have natures or essences distinguishable from the fact of their existence.

esthetics *See* **aesthetics.**

euthanasia The act of allowing a terminally ill person to freely choose when and how he or she will die; mercy killing.

existentialism A philosophy of the nineteenth and twentieth centuries. The dogma holds that since there are no universal values, man's essence is not predetermined but is based only on free choice; man is in a state of anxiety because of his realization of free will; and there is no objective truth. Major existentialists were Kierkegaard,* Nietzsche,* Sartre,* Heidegger,* Karl Jaspers (1883–1969), and the religious existentialists Martin Buber* and Gabriel Marcel (1889–1973).

fatalism The belief that "what will be will be," since all past, present, and future events have already been predetermined by God or another all-powerful force. In religion, this view may be called predestination; it holds that whether our souls go to heaven or hell is determined before we are born and is independent of our good deeds.

Forms According to Plato,* the eternal, unchanging, immaterial, and perfect archetypes of which all existing things are merely imperfect copies; also called Ideas.

four elements According to many early Greek philosophers, the four basic constituents of the physical world: earth, air, fire, and water.

free will The theory that human beings have freedom of choice or self-determination; that is, that given a situation, a person could have done other than what he did. Philosophers have argued that free will is incompatible with determinism. *See also* **indeterminism.**

golden mean The ethical doctrine, originating with Aristotle, that virtuous actions fall exactly between too much of some quality, such as impulsive behavior, and too little of it, such as timidity. It is associated with ethics calling for moderation.

golden rule The fundamental moral rule of most religions, especially Christianity, that states, "Do unto others as you would have others do unto you."

greatest happiness principle *See* **principle of utility; utilitarianism.**

hedonism A philosophy of ethics holding that pleasure is the highest or the only good in life, and that men should strive for pleasure and the avoidance of pain. Among the chief proponents of hedonism were the Epicureans and the utilitarians.

Hegelianism (neo-Hegelianism) A school of thought associated with Hegel* in the nineteenth and early twentieth centuries, especially in England, America, France, and Italy. F. G. Bradley (1846–1924), Josiah Royce (1855–1916), and Benedetto Croce (1866–1952) were prominent members; they emphasized the importance of spirit and the belief that ideas and moral ideals are fundamental.

Hobson's choice A choice offered without any real alternative—therefore, not really a choice at all.

humanism Any philosophic view that holds that humankind's well-being and happiness in this lifetime are primary and that the good of all humanity is the highest ethical goal. Twentieth-century humanists tend to reject all beliefs in the supernatural, relying instead on scientific methods and reason. The term is also used to refer to Renaissance thinkers, especially in the fifteenth century in Italy, who emphasized knowledge and learning not based on religious sources.

idealism A term applied to any philosophy holding that mind or spiritual values, rather than material things or matter, are primary in the universe. *See also* **British idealism.**

immortality The view that the individual soul is eternal, and thus survives the death of the body it resides in. *See also* **transmigration of souls.**

indeterminism The view that there are events that do not have any cause; many proponents of free will believe that acts of choice are capable of not being determined by any physiological or psychological cause.

inductive reasoning Any process of reasoning from something particular to something general, or from a part to a whole. Inductive reasoning can be valid or invalid.

innate ideas Ideas that are inborn and part of the mind at birth, rather than based on specific experiences. Descartes* believed there are "clear and distinct" ideas that are innate and that form the basis of all knowledge. Plato* believed that knowledge of the Forms derives from innate ideas.

instrumentalism A theory that holds that ideas and concepts should be regarded as tools or instruments to be used in specific situations. As such, they cannot be described as true or false, but only as effective or ineffective. This theory was first put forth by John Dewey.*

intuitionism Any philosophy holding that intuition is the basis of knowledge or of philosophy. French philosopher Henri Bergson (1859–1941) was a prominent advocate. In particular, intuitionism refers to a British school of thought that maintains that all ethical knowledge rests on moral intuition.

justice According to most philosophers, starting with Plato,* the harmonious balance between the rights of the various members of a society. Justice is usually understood as including such social virtues as fairness, equality, and correct and impartial treatment.

language *See* **philosophy of language.**

language game A concept introduced by Ludwig Wittgenstein,* who drew an analogy between how we use language and how we play games: both have rules and moves that make sense only in the context of a particular game. Wittgenstein and his followers used this concept to point out that philosophers frequently try to make moves in one context that make sense only in another, as when they try to verify religious statements as if they were a part of science.

linguistic philosophy (linguistic analysis) The twentieth-century school of thought whose key tenet is that philosophical problems are best approached by asking questions about the use of words and by analyzing how language works in specific social contexts.

logic The study of the rules and the nature of reasoning and of valid or sound patterns of thought. Aristotle* classified many of the rules of reasoning. In the late nineteenth and early twentieth centuries, logic was advanced into a branch of mathematics. Currently, mathematical logic is a growing field independent of philosophy. *See also* **syllogism**.

logical positivism A twentieth-century school founded in the 1920s in Europe that was extremely influential for American and English philosophers. It advocated the principle of verifiability, according to which all statements that could not be validated empirically were meaningless. Logical positivism held that this principle showed that all of metaphysics, religion, and ethics was incapable of being proved either true or false. *See also* **Vienna Circle**.

Manichaeanism A religious-philosophical doctrine that originated in Persia in the third century and reappeared throughout the next 1300 years. It holds that the entire universe, especially human life, is a struggle between the opposing forces of good and evil (light and darkness).

Marxism The political, economic, and philosophical theories developed by Karl Marx* and Friedrich Engels* in the second half of the nineteenth century. The philosophical side of Marxism is called dialectical materialism; it emphasizes economic determinism. *See also* **dialectical materialism**.

materialism The theory that holds that the nature of the world is dependent on matter, or that matter is the only fundamental substance; thus, spirit and mind either do not exist or are manifestations of matter.

mathematical logic *See* **logic**.

mathematics *See* **philosophy of mathematics**.

mechanism The philosophical theory that states that living organisms, including humans, are complex machines, since they are composed of matter.

metaethics A branch of philosophy that analyzes ethics. It is concerned with such issues as, How are moral decisions justified? What is the foundation of any ethical view? What language is used to state moral beliefs?

metaphysics The branch of philosophy concerned with the ultimate nature of reality and existence as a whole. Metaphysics also includes the study of cosmology and philosophical theology. Aristotle* produced the first "system" of metaphysics.

metempsychosis *See* **transmigration of souls**.

Miletian School The pre-Socratics from Miletus in Greece—Thales* and his two best-known pupils, Anaximander* and Anaximenes.*

mind *See* **philosophy of mind**.

mind-body problem A central problem of modern philosophy that originated with Descartes.* It asks how the mind and the body are related.

monad According to Leibniz,* the ultimate and indivisible units of all existence. Monads are not material, like atoms; each monad is self-activating, a unique center of force. All monads are in a "preestablished harmony" with each other and with God, the supreme monad.

monism The theory that everything in the universe is composed of, or can be explained by or reduced to, one fundamental substance, energy, or force.

mysticism Any philosophy whose roots are in mystical experiences, intuitions, or direct experiences of the divine. In such experiences, the mystic believes that his or her soul has temporarily achieved union with God. Mystics believe reality can be known only in this manner, not through reasoning or everyday experience.

myth of Er A parable at the end of Plato's *Republic* about the fate of souls after bodily death; according to Plato,* the soul must choose wisdom in the afterlife to guarantee a good life in its next cycle of incarnation.

naturalism A philosophic view stating that all there is in reality is what the physical and human sciences (for example, physics or psychology) study and that there is no need to posit any supernatural forces or being, such as God, mind, or spirit.

naturalistic fallacy A belief of many twentieth-century philosophers in England and America that it is invalid to infer any statements of morality (for example, "Men ought to act kindly") from factual statements (for example, "Kindness is a natural quality"). The notion tries to derive *ought* from *is* and was first described by Hume.*

natural law The theory that there is a higher law than the manmade laws put forth by specific governments. This law is universal, unchanging, and a fundamental part of human nature. Advocates of this view believe that natural law can be discovered by reason alone. The theory originated with the Stoics and was elaborated on by St. Thomas Aquinas,* among others.

natural rights Certain freedoms or privileges that are held to be an innate part of the nature of being a human being and that cannot be denied by society. These are different from civil rights, which are granted by a specific nation or government. Philosophers have differed on which rights are natural, but usually included are life, liberty, equality, equal treatment under the law, the pursuit of happiness, and equality of opportunity. Locke's* influential views on natural rights inspired the writers of the American Constitution.

necessary and contingent truth Terms used by philosophers to contrast two types of statements, such as "All widowers are male," which is necessarily true, and "All widowers are over 20 years old," which may be true but is not necessarily true.

Neoplatonism A school of philosophy that flourished from the second to the fifth centuries A.D. It was founded by Plotinus* and was influential for the next thousand years.

nihilism A term first used in *Fathers and Sons* (1862) by the Russian novelist Turgenev. *Ethical nihilism* is the theory that morality cannot be justified in any way and that all moral values are, therefore, meaningless and irrational. *Political nihilism* is the social philosophy that society and its institutions are so corrupt that their complete destruction is desirable. Nihilists may, therefore, advocate violence and even terrorism in the name of overthrowing what they believe to be a corrupt social order.

nominalism The view that general terms, such as "table," do not refer to essences, concepts, abstract ideas, or anything else; "table" makes sense only because all tables resemble each other. According to this view, such general terms do not have any independent existence.

non sequitur A Latin phrase meaning "it does not follow"; any argument where the conclusion drawn has not even the slightest connection to the premises offered.

objectivism The view that there are moral truths that are valid universally and that it is wrong to knowingly gain pleasure from causing another pain.

obligation In ethics, a moral necessity to do a specific deed. Some ethicists, following Kant,* hold that moral obligations are absolute. *See also* **categorical imperative.**

Ockham's razor A principle attributed to the fourteenth-century English philosopher William of Ockham.* It states that entities should not be multiplied beyond necessity, or that one should choose the simplest explanation, the one requiring the fewest assumptions and principles.

ontology A branch of metaphysics that studies the nature of existence or reality, as such, as opposed to specific types of existing entities.

operationalism (operationism) A philosophy of science according to which any scientific concept must be definable in terms of concrete, observable activities or the operations to which it refers.

optimism The philosophic attitude that this is the best of all possible worlds, that hope and joy are justified, and that all things are ordered for the best. According to optimists, such as Leibniz,* evil either is an illusion or will be compensated for by an even greater good.

Ordinary Language Philosophy The twentieth-century school advocating that we can best understand and resolve philosophic problems by analyzing how people other than philosophers ordinarily use language and the presuppositions underlying such use; the school holds that everyday language is adequate for philosophy. Wittgenstein,* Gilbert Ryle (1900–76), and John L. Austin (1911–60) were the most influential members of this school.

pantheism The belief that God and the universe are identical; among modern philosophers, Spinoza* is considered to be a pantheist.

particulars *See* **universals.**

Pascal's wager An argument made by Blaise Pascal* for believing in God. Pascal said that either the tenets of Roman Catholicism are true or they are not. If they are true, and we wager that they are true, then we have won an eternity of bliss; if they are false, and death is final, what has the bettor lost? On the other hand, if one wagers against God's existence and turns out to be wrong, there is eternal damnation.

personalism A term applied to any philosophy that makes personality (whether of people, God, or spirit) the supreme value or the source of reality. Personalism as a movement flourished in England and America in the nineteenth and twentieth centuries. Personalists are usually idealists.

pessimism The philosophic attitude holding that hope is unreasonable, that man is born to sorrow, and that this is the worst of all possible worlds. Schopenhauer's* philosophy is an example of extreme pessimism.

phenomenalism The doctrine that the only knowledge we can ever have is of appearances, and thus that we can never know the nature of ultimate reality. Major adherents of the philosophy were John Stuart Mill* and some members of the Vienna Circle.

Phenomenology A school founded by Edmund Husserl,* and an important influence on existentialism. This school developed its own philosophical "method" of using intuition for describing consciousness and experience. Phenomenologists claim that this method can be used to study the inherent qualities of phenomena as they appear to the mind.

philosopher king In Plato's* *Republic*, a philosopher trained by formal study in disciplines including mathematics and philosophy. Plato emphasized that philosopher kings' leadership would be shown by their ability to see the Forms, or universal ideals. *See also* **Forms**.

philosophes Term applied to eighteenth-century French Enlightenment thinkers such as Rousseau,* Diderot,* and Voltaire.*

philosophy of language The area of philosophic study whose subject matter is the nature and workings of language. Detailed discussions of such topics as meaning, reference, grammar, and symbols infuse this branch of philosophy.

philosophy of mathematics A branch of philosophy that studies such questions as, What are mathematical statements about? Why is mathematics true? How do we come to have mathematical knowledge? Why is mathematics so useful in studying reality?

MORE THAN JUST PHILOSOPHERS

Before knowledge was as specialized as it is today, many of the greatest philosophers followed their other interests while creating or studying philosophical systems. They did groundbreaking work in areas as far afield from philosophy proper as geometry, zoology, literary criticism, and calculus.

Perhaps Aristotle was the model for some of these thinkers, since he was regarded not only in his own time but throughout most of the Middle Ages as a universal genius whose knowledge on any subject he had written on could hardly be questioned. His nonphilosophical writings were astonishingly broad; even a partial list of his subjects, which include physics, zoology, botany, sociology, political theory, and economics, is testimony to one of the greatest minds of all time.

Even medicine and the law were not too far afield for some of the great philosophers. Avicenna, Averroes, and John Locke were trained in medicine; Avicenna's *Canon of Medicine* was the most influential medieval medical treatise. And Jeremy Bentham, a founder of utilitarianism, was one of the most influential jurists and lawyers of the nineteenth century; his work deeply influenced reform of the British penal, judicial, and parliamentary systems.

History, too, is a philosopher's domain. *History of England*, not his philosophy books, brought David Hume success and renown in mid-eighteenth-century England.

Both mathematics and logic were fruitfully developed by philosophers when they were not writing philosophical works. Leibniz is the coinventor of calculus, along with Sir Isaac Newton; Pascal is one of the fathers of the modern theory of probability; and Descartes invented analytical geometry almost single-handedly.

Logic, although now a separate discipline, was a part of philosophy until a hundred years ago. Aristotle was the founder of logic, but many other philosophers have invented or organized entire sections of the field. Mill formulated the "rules" of scientific experimentation that are now called Mill's methods; and Russell and Whitehead wrote *Principia Mathematica*, probably the most important work in modern logic.

The list of philosophers engaged in other fields is seemingly endless. Examples include Nietzsche, whose *On the Birth of Tragedy* is a classic in Greek studies and literary criticism; William James, whose *Principles of Psychology* deeply influenced decades of thinking in that field; and John Dewey, the father of the American progressive education movement.

philosophy of mind The area of philosophy that studies the mind, consciousness, and mental functions such as thinking, intention, imagination, and emotion. It is not one specific branch of philosophy, but rather an aspect of most traditional branches, such as metaphysics, epistemology, and aesthetics.

philosophy of religion A branch of philosophy concerned with such questions as, What is religion? What is God? Can God's existence be proved? Is there immortality? What is the relationship between faith, reason, and revelation? Is there a divine purpose in the world?

philosophy of science The branch of philosophy that studies the nature of science. It is particularly concerned with the methods, concepts, and assumptions of science, as well as with analyzing scientific concepts such as space, time, cause, scientific law, and verification.

physicalism A theory about knowledge that originated within the Vienna Circle. It holds that all factual statements can be reduced to observations of physical objects and events. *See also* **operationalism.**

Platonism Thoughts and writings developed in the fifth century B.C. in Athens by Plato,* the greatest student of Socrates.* Platonism's chief tenet is that the ultimate reality consists of unchanging, absolute, eternal entities called Ideas or Forms; all earthly objects are not truly real but merely partake in the Forms.

Plato's cave An analogy in Plato's* *Republic* between reality and illusion. The main image is of men who see on the walls of a cave only the shadows of the real objects moving around outside the cave. When these men leave the cave and see the real objects, they cannot, upon returning to the cave, convince those who have never left of the reality of the objects.

pluralism The view that there are more than two kinds of fundamental, irreducible realities in the universe, or that there are many separate and independent levels of reality.

political philosophy The branch of philosophy that studies man as a political animal. It is concerned with such questions as, What obligations do I have to my government? How is political power justified? Under what conditions is war justified? It also studies the nature of property, justice, freedom, liberty, and political rights.

positivism A theory originated by French philosopher Auguste Comte.* It holds that all knowledge is defined by the limits of scientific investigation; thus, philosophy must abandon any quest for knowledge of an ultimate reality or any knowledge beyond that offered by science. *See also* **logical positivism.**

pragmatism An American philosophy developed in the nineteenth century by Charles Sanders Peirce (1839–1914) and William James,* and elaborated on in the twentieth century by John Dewey.* Its central precepts are that thinking is primarily a guide to action and that the truth of any idea lies in its practical consequences.

predestination *See* **fatalism.**

premises *See* **argument.**

Presocratics Name given to all Greek "theorists of nature" or philosophers who lived before Socrates. Among the pre-Socratics are Anaximander,* Pythagoras,* and Thales.*

principle (or law) of noncontradiction Dating back to Aristotle, this universally accepted "law of thought" has two parts: A statement cannot be both true and false; nothing can both have a quality, like red, and not have it, at the same time.

principle of sufficient reason The philosophical doctrine of Leibniz* that asserts that for every fact there is a reason for its being the way it is rather than another way, even though we may not know that reason.

principle of utility (greatest happiness principle) The basic tenet of utilitarianism. It states that the highest ethical good provides the greatest happiness for the greatest number of people.

psychologism A view of philosophy holding that all philosophic concepts and problems are explainable based on psychological principles and that they should be treated by some form of psychological analysis. Advocates of this view may disagree on the type of psychological approach that is appropriate.

Pythagoreans Followers of Pythagoras.* The group flourished until about 400 B.C. and were influential in philosophy, religion, mathematics, and science. They strongly influenced the thinking of Plato* and Neoplatonists.

QED Latin for *quod erat demonstrandum* ("that which was to be demonstrated"). This abbreviation is often used right before or after stating a conclusion, as a synonym for *therefore, thus*, or *as was to be shown.*

rationalism The philosophic approach that holds that reality is knowable by the use of reason or thinking alone, without recourse to observation or experience. *See also* **seventeenth-century rationalists.**

realism The major medieval and modern view on the problem of universals other than nominalism. *Extreme realism*, which is close to Plato's* theory of Forms, holds that universals exist independently of both particular things and the human mind; *moderate realism* holds that they exist as ideas in God's mind, through which He creates things.

reincarnation *See* **transmigration of souls.**

relativism The precept that people's ideas of right and wrong vary considerably from place to place and time to time; therefore, there are no universally valid ethical standards.

religion *See* **philosophy of religion.**

Scholasticism A general term referring to the Christian philosophy of the Middle Ages, especially at the medieval universities. The Scholastics basically followed Aristotle's* empiricism, using highly analytical logical and linguistic methods of argumentation, especially with respect to the problem of universals.

science *See* **philosophy of science.**

sensationalism An empiricist theory of knowledge that holds that sensations are both the source of all knowledge and the ultimate verification of any statements. Hobbes* originated the view; Étienne Condillac (1715–1880) and Ernst Mach (1838–1916) developed it.

sense data The sensory qualities or feelings we experience directly, such as shapes, colors, and smells, without any interpretation of the material objects that may be causing them. Some empiricists and sensationalist philosophers make sense data the foundation of all factual knowledge.

seventeenth-century rationalists A broad term referring to the rationalism shared by Descartes,* Leibniz,* and Spinoza.* It held that reason and deduction could provide knowledge of the world independent of experience.

skepticism The philosophic theory that no certain knowledge can be attained by man. Broadly speaking, skepticism states that all knowledge should be questioned and tested, for instance, by the scientific method.

social contract That concept of an agreement between people, or between people and government or ruler, in which it is agreed that some personal liberties will be given up in exchange for the security of stable political rule. The term is used in the political philosophy of Hobbes,* Locke,* and Rousseau* to justify a form of political authority.

solipsism The theory that one cannot know anything other than his or her own thoughts, feelings, or perceptions; therefore, other people and the real world must be projections of one's own mind with no existence in and of themselves. *See also* **egocentric predicament.**

Sophists Wandering teachers in the fourth and fifth centuries in ancient Greece who taught any subjects that their paying students wished to learn, from grammar to public speaking. They were strongly ridiculed by Plato,* who held that they were less interested in truth than in pleasing their students for a fee.

spiritism A term referring to the belief that spirits of the dead communicate with the living, for instance, at seances or through a medium.

spiritualism The view that the ultimate reality in the universe is the spirit. Advocates of this view may disagree about the nature of the spirit.

state of nature A term used by seventeenth- and eighteenth-century social philosophers such as Hobbes,* Locke,* and Rousseau.* It referred to the condition of man without political organization, or before government.

Stoicism A Greek school founded by Zeno* in the third century B.C. Stoics held that men should submit to natural law and that a man's chief duty is to conform to his destiny. They also believed the soul to be another form of matter, and thus not immortal.

subjectivism The theory that all moral values are completely dependent on the personal tastes, feelings, or inclinations of the individual and have no source of validity outside of such human subjective states of mind.

substance A changeless, self-subsistent entity, not dependent on anything else, that underlies being in all its forms. It has been identified with God, mind, matter, and self-contained ultimate realities. *See also* **monad.**

supernaturalism The belief that there are forces, energies, or beings beyond the material world—such as God, spirit, or occult forces—that affect events in our world.

syllogism A kind of deductive reasoning or argument. As defined by Aristotle, it was considered the basis of reasoning for over two thousand years. In every syllogism, there are two statements (premises) from which a conclusion follows necessarily. Syllogisms are of three basic logical types, as illustrated by these examples:

1. If a broom is new, it sweeps clean; the broom is new; therefore, it sweeps clean.
2. Either the horse is male or female; the horse is not female; therefore, it is male.
3. All philosophers are men; all men are mortal; therefore, all philosophers are mortal.

synthetic statement A factual statement describing a state of affairs, such as "Triangles are used in architectural studios."

tabula rasa A Latin phrase meaning "blank slate," used by Locke* to describe the state of the human mind at birth. Locke believed there are no innate ideas and that the mind gets all of its ideas from experience.

tautology Any statement that is necessarily true merely because of its meaning, such as "Bachelors are unmarried males," or "Every green object is colored." *See also* **necessary and contingent truth.**

teleoligical ethics In contrast with deontological ethics, this moral theory holds that whether an action is morally right depends solely on its expected consequences. *See also* **utilitarianism.**

Thomism The philosophical and theological system developed by St. Thomas Aquinas* in the thirteenth century. One of its chief principles is that philosophy seeks truth through reason while theology seeks it through revelation from God; therefore, the two are compatible.

transcendent Beyond the realm of sense experience. In many religious views, God is held to be transcendent.

transcendentalism A nineteenth-century movement developed in New England and expounded by Ralph Waldo Emerson (1803–82) and Henry David Thoreau (1817–62). It maintains that beyond our material world of experience is an ideal spiritual reality that can be grasped intuitively.

transmigration of souls (metempsychosis; reincarnation) The belief that the same soul can, in different lifetimes (incarnations), reside in different bodies, human or animal. While typically a part of most Eastern religions, the doctrine came into Western philosophy from Pythagoras* and his contemporaries in the sixth century B.C. and especially through Plato.

universals The properties, or the abstract or general words, that apply to many individual things, called particulars. Redness, for instance, is a universal that applies to all red things.

utilitarianism A theory of morality holding that all actions should be judged for rightness or wrongness in terms of their consequences; thus, the amount of pleasure people derive from those consequences becomes the measure of moral goodness. Jeremy Bentham* and John Stuart Mill,* in the nineteenth century, were the chief proponents of this view. *See also* **principle of utility.**

utopianism The belief in the possibility or desirability of not just a better but a perfect society. The term derives from Sir Thomas More's* *Utopia* (1516), which depicts an ideal state. Utopian states also appear in the writings of Plato* and Bacon.*

verifiability *See* **logical positivism.**

Vienna Circle A major school of logical positivism founded by Moritz Schlick (1882–1936) in the 1920s. It was known for its hostility to metaphysics and theology and for its belief that physics is the model for all knowledge of the world. Other leading members of the school were Rudolph Carnap (1891–1970) and Otto Neurath (1882–1945).

vitalism The theory that living organisms are inherently different from inanimate bodies; thus, life cannot be explained fully by materialistic theories as it is based on a vital force that is unlike other physical forces. Aristotle,* Hans Driesch (1867–1941), and Henri Bergson (1859–1941) were prominent vitalists. In Bergson's view, the élan vital is the evolutionary force in organisms that propels life to achieve higher levels of structure.

will to believe A phrase made famous by William James.* He held that in the absence of decisive evidence, the mind may create belief in order to act, often resulting in discovery. He also maintained that believing in such situations is a human right that should not be backed away from.

will to power The view, expounded by Nietzsche,* that power is the chief motivating force in human nature. The view was influential in twentieth-century psychology and social science.

Young Hegelians A group of thinkers in Germany in the first half of the nineteenth century whose views strongly influenced Karl Marx.* They were followers of Hegel* who believed that the political conditions under which they lived were irrational. They held that the goal of philosophy should be to promote a revolution of ideas and critical thinking about the world. Ludwig Feuerbach (1804–72) was the most important of the Young Hegelians.

Additional Sources of Information

Organizations and Services

The Philosophy Documentation Center is a key source of information. Its publications include U.S. and international directories of philosophers and *The Philosopher's Index*, a bibliographic journal and a series of cumulative bibliographies dating to 1940, arranged by author and subject.

Philosophy Documentation Center
Bowling Green State University
Bowling Green, OH 43403

Books

Copleston, Frederick C. *History of Philosophy*, 9 vols. Doubleday, 1985.

deGeorge, Richard T. *The Philospher's Guide to Sources, Research Tools, Professional Life, and Related Fields*. Regents Press of Kansas, 1980.

Durant, Will. *The Story of Philosophy*. Pocket Books, 1983.

Edwards, Paul, ed. *The Encyclopedia of Philosophy*, 4 vols. Free Press, 1973.

Ferm, Vergilius. *A History of Philosophical Systems*. Philosophical Library, 1950.

Lacey, A. R. *A Dictionary of Philosophy*. Routledge, Chapman & Hall, 1990.

Magill, Frank N., ed. *Masterpieces of World Philosophy*. HarperCollins, 1990.

O'Connor, D. J. *A Critical History of Western Philosophy*. Free Press, 1985.

Reese, William L., ed. *Dictionary of Philosophy and Religion: Eastern and Western Thought*. Humanities Press, 1981.

Runes, Dagobert D., ed. *Dictionary of Philosophy*. Rowman & Allanhead, 1984.

Russell, Bertrand. *A History of Western Philosophy.*

Urmson, James O. *A Concise Encyclopedia of Western Philosophy and Philosophers*, 3rd ed. Hyman, 1990.

Weiner, Philip P., ed. *Dictionary of the History of Ideas: Studies of Selected Pivotal Ideas*, 5 vols. Scribner's, 1985.

11

Libraries and Museums

Major Libraries of the United States and Canada and Their Special Collections / *284*

Major Museums of the United States and Canada and Their Special Collections / *293*

Reference Works for General Information / *303*

The Dewey Decimal System and How to Use It / *315*

The Library of Congress Subject Headings / *316*

Cataloging in Publication Data / *317*

Getting Started in Genealogy / *318*

Additional Sources of Information / *319*

Major Libraries of the United States and Canada and Their Special Collections

United States

Arizona

University of Arizona Library
Tucson, AZ 85721
602-621-2101

Established in 1891, the University of Arizona has more than 2.7 million volumes, with special collections on photography as an art form, fine arts, drama, private presses, Southwestern Americana, Arizona, science history, science fiction, and Mexican colonial history.

California

South State Cooperative Library System
7400 East Imperial Highways
Downey, CA 90241
213-940-8465

Founded in 1912, this library system contains more than 5.1 million volumes, with special collections on Afro-American studies, Asian-Pacific studies, California, multimedia, mountaineering, Hispanic-Americans, Native Americans, and poetry. The collection is dispersed among 114 community, mobile, and institutional libraries.

Los Angeles Public Library System
630 W. Fifth Street
Los Angeles, CA 90071
213-612-3200

Founded in 1872, this public library system has 62 branches with more than 5.3 million volumes. Its special collections are on California studies, children's literature, cooking, genealogy, Native American studies, modern languages, orchestral scores, U.S. patents, and standards and specifications.

Stanford University Libraries
Stanford, CA 94305
415-723-9108

Founded in 1892, Stanford's libraries contain 5.4 million volumes. Its special collections cover transportation, music, science, California, Irish literature, engineering mechanics, children's literature, Chicano studies, theater, and Hebraica and Judaica.

University of California, Berkeley
Berkeley, CA 94720
415-642-3773

Founded in 1871, this library contains more than 7.5 million volumes. Special collections include the letters, literary manuscripts, and scrapbooks of Samuel Clemens (Mark Twain Collection) and Recollections of Persons Who Have Contributed to the Development of the West (Regional Oral History Office).

University of California Los Angeles Library
405 Hilgard Avenue
Los Angeles, CA 90024
213-825-1201

Founded in 1919, the University of California Los Angeles Library has holdings of more than 5.4 million books. It has special collections on British Commonwealth history, contemporary Western writers, early English children's books, folklore, Latin American studies, Mazarinades, mountaineering, and Western Americana.

University of Southern California
Edward L. Doheny Memorial Library
University Park
Los Angeles, CA 90089
213-740-2928

Founded in 1880, the University of Southern California has more than 2.4 million volumes, with a number of independent departmental libraries whose subject matter ranges from architecture and fine arts to gerontology. Its special collections include Native American ethnopharmacology, American literature, cinema, dentistry, international relations, Latin American studies, and philosophy.

Colorado

University of Colorado, Boulder
University Libraries Campus Box 184
Boulder, CA 80309
303-492-7511

Founded in 1876, the University of Colorado maintains holdings of more than 2 million volumes, with special collections on juvenile literature, the history of silver, mountaineering, and Western U.S. history.

Connecticut

Yale University Library
120 High Street
P.O. Box 1603A, Yale Station
New Haven, CT 06520
203-432-1775

The second largest university library in the United States, Yale has 8.8 million volumes in its collection. Its rare books total more than 500,000. Yale's special collections are numerous; they include works by James Boswell, the Aaron Burr family, Daniel Defoe, John Dryden, James Joyce, D. H. Lawrence, the Lindbergh family, Marcus Aurelius, H. L. Mencken, Napoleon, Mark Twain, and Edith Wharton. The *American Library Directory* lists more than 50 subjects of special strength for Yale, including Babylonian tablets, futurism, legal thought, playing cards, sporting books, urban and regional planning, and Western Americana. Founded in 1701.

District of Columbia

The Library of Congress
Washington, DC 20540
202-707-5000

The nation's largest single library, the Library of Congress, established in 1800, contains over 80 million items, including about 20 million books and pamphlets. Its collections include over 1 million volumes on Hispanic and Portuguese culture and the largest collection of Russian literature outside the Soviet Union. Special collections include books for the blind and physically handicapped, cartography, folk music, law books, manuscripts, microforms, motion pictures, music, the Orient, prints and photographs, and more than half a million rare books. The library's first priority is service to the Congress of the United States. It also registers creative work for copyright and provides services to both the public and libraries throughout the country.

Florida

University of Florida Libraries
210 Library West
Gainesville, FL 32611
904-392-0342

Founded in 1905, this system contains more than 2.5 million volumes, with special collections on Florida history, Latin America, Judaica, aerial photographs, coastal engineering, New England literature, Brazilian law, and Florida newspapers.

Georgia

University of Georgia Libraries
Athens, GA 30602
404-542-0621

Founded in 1800, this library system contains more than 2.4 million volumes, with special collections on music, theater, Georgia, Confederate imprints, Georgia authors, nineteenth- and twentieth-century politics, and Georgia newspapers.

Hawaii

Hawaii State Library System
Office of the State Librarian
465 South King Street
Honolulu, HI 96813
808-548-5596

Founded in 1852, Hawaii's libraries contain more than 2.1 million volumes, with a special collection devoted to Hawaiian history.

Illinois

Chicago Public Library
1224 W. Van Buren Street
Chicago, IL 60610
312-269-2900

Founded in 1872, Chicago's libraries offer more than 4.3 million volumes with special collections of national, U.S., foreign, and trade bibliographies;

Chicago information; foreign-language encyclopedias; Abraham Lincoln papers; miniature books; early American newspapers; and World War I and II posters.

Northwestern University Library
1935 Sheridan Road
Evanston, IL 60208
708-491-7658

Founded in 1856, Northwestern holds more than 2.4 million volumes and bound periodicals, with special collections on Africa, architecture, contemporary music scores, feminism, German classics, Italian futurism, manuscripts, and printing.

University of Chicago Libraries
1100 East 57th Street
Chicago, IL 60637
312-702-8740

The University of Chicago, founded in 1891, contains more than 4.6 million volumes. It maintains special collections of English Bibles, Lincolniana, modern poetry, anatomical illustrations, and Kentucky and Ohio River Valley history; children's books; early theology and Bible criticism; German fiction, 1790–1850, and books on ophthalmology.

University of Illinois Library at Urbana–Champaign
1408 West Gregory Drive
Urbana, IL 61801
217-333-0790

This library's collection includes more than 7 million volumes, with special collections on American humor and folklore, freedom of expression, sixteenth- and seventeenth-century Italian drama, nineteenth-century publishing, Carl Sandburg, and H. G. Wells. Founded 1868.

Indiana

Indiana University at Bloomington
Tenth Street and Jordan Avenue
Bloomington, IN 47405
812-855-3403

Founded in 1824, Indiana University has amassed a collection of more than 4.2 million volumes, with special collections of English and American literature, nineteenth-century British plays, English history, scientific and medical history, the works of Aristotle, and nineteenth-century French opera.

Iowa

University of Iowa Libraries
Iowa City, IA 52242
319-353-5867

Established in 1855, Iowa's libraries contain more than 2.5 million volumes, with special collections on Leigh Hunt and his friends, Abraham Lincoln, American Indians, Iowa authors, typography, the Union Pacific Railroad, editorial cartoons, the French Revolution, and the history of medicine.

Kansas

University of Kansas Libraries
Watson Library
Lawrence, KS 66045
913-864-3956

Established in 1866, Kansas' libraries contain in excess of 2.4 million volumes, with special collections on Anglo-Saxons, botany, children's books, Chinese classics, Colombia, the Continental Renaissance, economics, historical cartography, Irish history and literature, Kansas history, poetry, opera, ornithology, sound recordings, travel, and women.

Maryland

Enoch Pratt Free Library
400 Cathedral Street
Baltimore, MD 21201
301-396-5856

Founded in 1886, Enoch Pratt's 1.9 million-volume collection has a special H. L. Mencken section and a Maryland history collection.

Johns Hopkins University
Milton S. Eisenhower Library
Baltimore, MD 21218
301-338-8325

Established in 1876, Johns Hopkins has more than 2.4 million volumes, with special collections on economics, Lord Byron, French drama, modern German drama, German literature, sheet music, slavery, and trade unions.

Massachusetts

Boston Public Library
Copley Square
Boston, MA 02117
617-536-5400

Founded in 1852, the Boston library system is believed to be the oldest free municipal library system supported by taxation anywhere in the world. It has 4.1 million volumes, with the following special collections: the library of John Quincy Adams; military science, history, and the Civil War; astronomy, mathematics, and navigation; Robert and Elizabeth Browning; Daniel Defoe; drama; genealogy; government documents; heraldry; music; patents; Christian Science; the Sacco-Vanzetti papers; Walt Whitman; and World War I.

Harvard University Library
Wadsworth House
Cambridge, MA 02138
617-495-3650

With more than 11 million volumes, the Harvard Library, founded in 1638, is the largest university library in the United States. Its special collections are numerous. They include the Trotsky archive; the Theodore Roosevelt Collection; and works by such authors as Dante, T. S. Eliot, Faulkner, Goethe, Kipling, Longfellow, Milton, Petrarch, Rousseau, Shakespeare, Steinbeck, and Thomas Wolfe. Some of its branches are located outside of Massachusetts, such as the Harvard Library in New York and the Dumbarton Oaks Research Library and Collection in Washington, DC. Others specialize in topics ranging from music to divinity and include Harvard's famed law library and the fine arts library at the Fogg Art Museum.

Massachusetts Institute of Technology (MIT) Libraries
Room 14S-216
Cambridge, MA 02139
617-253-5651

Founded in 1862, MIT's library holdings total approximately 2 million volumes, with special collections devoted to the early history of aeronautics, architecture and planning, civil engineering, nineteenth-century U.S. glass manufacturers, early works in mathematics and physics, shipbuilding and naval history, and spectroscopy.

University of Massachusetts at Amherst Library
Amherst, MA 01003
508-545-0284

Founded in 1865, this university system maintains holdings in excess of 2 million volumes, with special collections on slavery and antislavery pamphlets; county atlases of New England, New York, and New Jersey; and the French Revolution.

Michigan

Detroit Public Library
5201 Woodward Avenue
Detroit, MI 48202
313-833-1000

Founded in 1865, Detroit's library contains more than 2.5 million volumes, with special collections on automotive history, labor history, and black music, dance, and drama.

Michigan State University Library
East Lansing, MI 48824
517-355-2344

Established in 1855, Michigan State has holdings of more than 3 million volumes, with special collections on American popular culture, American radical history, apiculture, cookery, criminology, fencing, illuminated manuscripts in facsimile, natural science, and veterinary history.

University of Michigan Libraries
Ann Arbor, MI 48109
313-764-8584

Founded in 1817, the University of Michigan's libraries contain nearly 6 million volumes, the fifth largest collection in the country. The system comprises 18 collections located around campus. Major facilities include a medical and a fine arts library. Separately administered are a library of Americana, a law library, a business administration library, and the Gerald R. Ford Presidential Library.

Wayne State University Libraries
Detroit, MI 48202
313-577-4020

Wayne State has more than 2 million volumes, with special collections on nineteenth-century Spanish history, social studies, women and the law, law, and children and young people.

Minnesota

University of Minnesota Libraries–Twin Cities
499 O. Meredith Wilson Library
309 19th Avenue South
Minneapolis, MN 55455
612-624-4520

Founded in 1851, this university system contains more than 3.6 million volumes, with special collections on American and English literature, the history of quantum physics, ballooning, dime novels, information processing, Sherlock Holmes, children's literature, performing arts, private presses, August Strindberg, and the history of biology and medicine.

Missouri

Kansas City Public Library
311 East 12th Street
Kansas City, MO 64106
816-221-2685

Founded in 1873, this library's collection numbers more than 2 million volumes, with special collections on black history and Missouri Valley history and genealogy.

St. Louis University Libraries
St. Louis University
St. Louis, MO 63103
314-658-3100

Founded in 1818, this system contains more than 1.2 million bound volumes and government documents. Libraries on campus include a divinity library, a library of the School of Social Service, a law library, and a medical library.

University of Missouri-Columbia
Elmer Ellis Library
Columbia, MO 65201
314-882-4701

Established in 1839, this library holds more than 2.2 million volumes, with special collections devoted to American best-sellers, criminal law, philosophy, World War I and II posters, cartoons, and Fourth of July orations.

Washington University Libraries
Skinker and Lindell Boulevards
St. Louis, MO 63130
314-889-5400

Founded in 1853, this system maintains more than 2 million volumes, with special collections on German language and literature, Romance languages and literature, classical archeology and numismatics, architecture, musicology, history of the Russian Revolution and the Soviet Union, American and New York Stock Exchange reports, printing, and early history of communications-semantics.

New Jersey

Princeton University Library
Princeton, NJ 08544
609-258-3180

Founded as the College of New Jersey, Elizabeth, in 1746, the library's principal building is the Harvey S. Firestone Memorial Library, constructed in 1948. Princeton has approximately 4 million volumes, with special collections devoted to the Brontës, Disraeli, aeronautics, American historical manuscripts, chess, civil rights, coins, Emily Dickinson, emblem books, fishing and angling, graphic arts, Mormon history, mountaineering, papyrus manuscripts, publishing, sports, women, and famous individuals.

Rutgers, The State University of New Jersey
University Libraries
169 College Avenue
New Brunswick, NJ 08903
908-932-7505

Established in 1766, this venerable library contains more than 2.2 million volumes. It has a special collection of New Jersey public-sector collective bargaining contracts.

New York

Brooklyn Public Library System
Grand Army Plaza
Brooklyn, NY 11238
718-780-7700

Founded in 1896 and consolidated with the Brooklyn Library in 1902, the library system now has 58 branches with a total of more than 4.1 million books. Special collections cover Brooklyn history, chess and checkers, the Civil War, costumes, fire protection, and Walt Whitman.

Columbia University
University Libraries
535 West 114th Street
New York, NY 10027
212-854-2247

Founded in 1761, Columbia offers more than 5.4 million volumes, with special collections on anatomy, architecture, cancer research, fine arts, physiology, and plastic surgery.

Cornell University Libraries
Ithaca, NY 14853
607-255-4144

With approximately 5 million volumes, the Cornell libraries include special collections on Southeast Asia, civil engineering, medical dissertations, field recordings, early sixteenth-century music, beekeeping, food and beverages, and labor history.

New York Public Library
Astor, Lenox & Tilden Foundations Library
Fifth Avenue at 42nd Street
New York, NY 10018
212-930-0800

Established in 1895 by the consolidation of the Astor and Lenox libraries and the Tilden Trust, the New York Public Library contains more than 30 million catalogued items: books, manuscripts, microfilm, prints, maps, recordings, photographs, and sheet music. It has special collections on black history and culture, performing arts, English and American literature, bindings and illustrated books, Japanese prints, tobacco, early Bibles including the Gutenberg, voyages and travels, and Jewish, Oriental, Slavonic, and local history and genealogy. The library's 82 branches have 3.2 million circulating volumes and 5 million nonbook items.

New York State Library
State Education Department, Cultural Education Center
Empire State Plaza
Albany, NY 12230
518-474-5930

Founded in 1818, New York State's library contains more than 1.9 million volumes, with special collections on Dutch colonial records, New York State political and social history, and the Shakers.

New York University
Elmer Holmes Bobst Library
70 Washington Square South
New York, NY 10012
212-998-2440

Established in 1831, New York University's holdings total approximately 2 million volumes, with special collections on Lewis Carroll, Robert Frost, rare Judaica and Hebraica, mathematics, and the history of dentistry.

Queens Borough Public Library System
89-11 Merrick Boulevard
Jamaica, NY 11432
718-990-0700

Organized in 1896, this library system contains more than 4.6 million volumes and has 59 branches. It maintains special collections of Long Island history and genealogy and a collection of over 1.5 million pictures.

State University of New York at Buffalo
University Libraries
432 Capen Hall
Buffalo, NY 14260
716-636-2965

Founded in 1922, the State University libraries hold more than 1.8 million volumes, with special collections of poetry, the works of J. Frank Dobie, New York State governors' autographs, and books on science and engineering and the history of medicine.

Syracuse University Libraries
E. S. Bird Library
222 Waverly Avenue
Syracuse, NY 13244
315-443-3725

Established in 1871, Syracuse University has holdings of more than 1.3 million volumes, with special collections on Stephen Crane, Loyalists in the American Revolution, economic history, Margaret Bourke-White, Rudyard Kipling, and cartoonists; science fiction books and manuscripts; and the papers of Averell Harriman, Dorothy Thompson, and Benjamin Spock.

University of Rochester
Rush Rhees Library
Rochester, NY 14627
716-275-4461

Founded in 1850, the Rochester library's holdings include more than 2 million volumes, with special collections on nineteenth- and twentieth-century public affairs, nineteenth-century botany and horticulture, American literature, regional history, and Leonardo da Vinci.

North Carolina

Duke University
William R. Perkins Library
Durham, NC 27706
919-684-2034

Founded in 1838, Duke's library contains more than 2.9 million volumes, with special collections on American almanacs, architecture, city directories, Samuel Taylor Coleridge, Confederate imprints, Ralpho Waldo Emerson, Latin American history, manuscripts, the Methodist Church, newspapers, the Philippines, utopias, and Wesleyana.

University of North Carolina at Chapel Hill
Walter Royal Davis Library
Chapel Hill, NC 27599
919-962-0454

Founded in 1795, North Carolina's library contains more than 3.1 million volumes, with special collections on North Carolina and Southern history.

Ohio

Cleveland Public Library
325 Superior Avenue
Cleveland, OH 44114
216-623-2800

Founded in 1869, the Cleveland Public Library contains 2.5 million volumes. Its special collections are devoted to folklore, the Orient, and chess.

Ohio State University Libraries
William Oxley Thompson Memorial Library
1858 Neil Avenue Mall
Columbus, OH 43210
614-292-6151

Established in 1873, Ohio State offers approximately 4 million volumes and bound periodicals. Special collections include those on the American Association of Editorial Cartoonists, American fiction to 1925, American sheet music, Australia, daguerreotypes and ambrotypes, dance notation, Reformation history, and science fiction magazines.

Public Library of Cincinnati and Hamilton County
800 Vine Street
Library Square
Cincinnati, OH 45202
513-369-6900

Founded in 1853, Cincinnati's library has more than 3.5 million volumes, with 139,337 maps and special collections on local history, genealogy, theology, art, music, theater, and oral history.

Oklahoma

University of Oklahoma
University Libraries
410 West Brooks
Norman, OK 73019
405-325-6422

Founded in 1895, the University of Oklahoma's library holds more than 2.2 million volumes, with special collections devoted to early science, Western history, Native American papers, political speeches, theater, film, and dance.

Pennsylvania

Carnegie Library of Pittsburgh
4400 Forbes Avenue
Pittsburgh, PA 15213
412-622-3100

Founded in 1895, the Carnegie Library collection contains more than 2.4 million volumes, with approximately 69,000 in foreign languages. It maintains special collections on architecture and design, the Atomic Energy Commission, cartoons, local history, U.S. patents, World War I, and nineteenth-century American and German music journals.

Free Library of Philadelphia
Logan Square
Philadelphia, PA 19103
215-686-5360

Founded in 1891, the Free Library contains 3.1 million volumes, with special collections on orchestral music, common law, automobile history, Americana, cuneiform tablets, Charles Dickens, Edgar Allan Poe, Beatrix Potter, Arthur Rackham, theater, and maps (including over 130,000 single-sheet maps, atlases, and geographies).

Pennsylvania State University
Fred Lewis Pattee Library
University Park, PA 16802
814-865-3665

Established in 1857, Penn State's library has approximately 2 million volumes, with special collections on American sociology, anthropology, art, architecture, Australia, Bibles, black literature, the Columbus family papers, English literature, photography, Pennsylvania, science fiction, surrealism, and the United Steelworkers of America.

University of Pennsylvania Libraries
Van Pelt Library
3420 Walnut Street
Philadelphia, PA 19104
215-898-7558

Founded in 1749, the University of Pennsylvania's libraries hold more than 3.2 million volumes, with special collections on church history, the Spanish Inquisition, canon law, witchcraft, Shakespeare, alchemy and chemistry, Aristotle, Bibles, Jonathan Swift, Sanskrit manuscripts, Theodore Dreiser, Washington Irving, and the Spanish Golden Age of literature, as well as Benjamin Franklin imprints.

University of Pittsburgh
University Libraries
Pittsburgh, PA 15260
412-648-7710

Founded in 1873, the University of Pittsburgh has holdings of more than 2.5 million volumes, with special collections on ballet, nineteenth- and twentieth-century American and English theater, popular culture, early history and travel, children's literature, "Mr. Rogers' Neighborhood" videos, and ethnic organizations.

South Carolina

University of South Carolina
Thomas Cooper Library
Columbia, SC 29208
803-777-3142

Founded in 1801, South Carolina's system contains more than 1.8 million volumes, with special collections on archeology, ornithology, aerial photography, and rare medical books.

Texas

Dallas Public Library
1515 Young Street
Dallas, TX 75201
214-670-1400

Founded in 1901, Dallas's library contains over 3 million volumes. Special collections cover business histories, children's literature, classical literature, classical recordings, Dallas black history, diaries and manuscripts on dance, fashion, genealogy, grants, printing, and Texas.

Houston Public Library
500 McKinney Avenue
Houston, TX 77002
713-247-2700

Founded in 1901, the Houston Public Library has more than 3.1 million volumes, with special collections of Bibles; books on the Civil War, genealogy, Texas, and petroleum; Salvation Army posters; early Houston photographs; early printing and illuminated manuscripts; juvenile literature; and sheet music.

University of Texas Libraries
P.O. Box P
Austin, TX 78713
512-471-3811

Founded in 1883, this university library system serves a student body of more than 46,000. With more than 5.5 million volumes, its holdings are divided among individual libraries devoted to Asia; film; the Middle East; Latin America; public affairs; architecture and planning; chemistry; classics; engineering; fine arts; geology; physics, math, and astronomy; science; business research; humanities; population research; and law. Its special collections cover Southern history, Canada, British Commonwealth literature, the U.S. Volleyball Association, and oral histories.

Utah

University of Utah
Marriott Library
Salt Lake City, UT 84112
801-581-7200

Founded in 1850, Utah's library contains in excess of 2 million volumes, with special collections on the Middle East, Western Americana, and the history of medicine.

Virginia

University of Virginia
Alderman Library
Charlottesville, VA 22903
804-924-3026

Established in 1819, Virginia's library holds more than 2.6 million volumes, with special collections devoted to American literature, the American Revolution, Americana, the Civil War and Reconstruction, political cartoons, Ceylon, classical studies, Stephen Crane, Oliver Cromwell, John Dos Passos, evolution, William Faulkner, finance, Rober Frost, Gothic novels, Bret Harte, Nathaniel Hawthorne, international law, Washington Irving, Thomas Jefferson, modern art, Mark Twain, typography and printing, Virginia, voyages and travels, and Walt Whitman.

Washington

University of Washington Libraries
FM-25
Seattle, WA 98195
206-543-1760

Founded in 1862, this university's holdings exceed 4.3 million volumes, with special collections devoted to East Asia, fisheries, forest resources, oceanography, and the Pacific Northwest.

Wisconsin

Milwaukee Public Library
814 West Wisconsin Avenue
Milwaukee, WI 53233
414-278-3000

Founded in 1878, the Milwaukee Public Library has more than 2.3 million volumes, with special collections on the Great Lakes, H. G. Wells, British and American authors, genealogy, and cookbooks.

University of Wisconsin–Madison
General Library System and Memorial Library
728 State Street
Madison, WI 53706
608-262-3193

The University of Wisconsin has amassed a collection of more than 4.5 million volumes since its founding in 1850. Special collections include those on alchemy, American gifts, book plates, Brazilian positivism, Buddhism, children's literature, C. S. Lewis's letters, Calvinist theology and Dutch history, chess, Early American women authors, history of chemistry, medieval history, Mexican pamphlets, Polish literature and history, Tibetan studies, Mark Twain, and Welsh theology.

Canada

Alberta

University of Alberta
University Library
Edmonton, Alberta T6G 2J8
403-492-4327

Established in 1909, Alberta's university system contains more than 2.8 million volumes, with special collections on literature, Native Americans, Victorian book arts, western Canada, and theology and canon law.

Ontario

University of Toronto Library System
Toronto, Ontario M5S 1A5
416-978-2282

Founded in 1827, the University of Toronto has holdings of more than 6.3 million volumes, with extensive sections of sheet music, films, slides, maps, and photographs. Its special collections include those on Shakespeare, the history of science, Darwin, Victorian natural history, ornithology, medical and related sciences, Italian plays, juvenile drama, Canada, and Canadian authors.

British Columbia

University of British Columbia Library
1956 Main Mall
Vancouver, British Columbia V6T 1Y3
604-228-3871

Established in 1915, British Columbia's library holds more than 2.4 million volumes, with special collections on Pacific Northwest history, Canada, the Orient, the history of science, English literature, and Canadian and Japanese maps.

Quebec

McGill University Libraries
3459 McTavish Street
Montreal, Quebec H3A 1Y1
514-398-4677

Founded in 1821, this university system serves an enrollment of about 24,000 students and has holdings of 1.3 million volumes. Its special collections cover architecture, William Blake, Canada, entomology, early geology, the history of science and medicine, natural history and ornithology, printing, Shakespeare, and sixteenth- and seventeenth-century tracts.

Major Museums of the United States and Canada and Their Special Collections

United States

Arizona

University Art Museum, Arizona State University Art Collections
Nelson Fine Arts Center and Matthews Center,
Arizona State University
Tempe, AZ 85287
602-965-ARTS

Founded in 1950, Arizona State's collection includes American paintings of the eighteenth and nineteenth centuries; a fine print collection with Rembrandts, Whistlers, and Dürers; fine Americana and decorative arts, particularly pottery; European painting and sculpture; Latin American arts; and crafts.

California

California Palace of the Legion of Honor
Lincoln Park
San Francisco, CA 94121
415-221-4811

The Fine Arts Museums of San Francisco
M. H. deYoung Museum
Lincoln Park
San Francisco, CA 94121
415-750-3600

These museums are run by a joint administration, although they are not located near each other. Founded in 1924 and 1895, respectively, each museum has extensive collections. The deYoung includes the Hearst collection of Flemish Gothic tapestries; fine primitive pre-Columbian artifacts; Northwest Coast Native American, African, and Oceanic arts collections; and Renaissance and Baroque art. The California Palace is noted for its eighteenth-century French furniture and decorative arts; its French paintings, including those of Monet, Renoir, Fragonard, Boucher, Manet, and Corot; Rodin sculptures; and an extraordinary collection of prints and drawings of all periods.

J. Paul Getty Museum
17985 Pacific Coast Highway,
Malibu, CA 90265
310-458-2003

The world's best-endowed museum, the Getty was created in 1953. This popular museum is housed in a re-creation of the first-century B.C. Villa dei Paryri at Herculaneum, complete with elaborate gardens. The Getty has acquired extraordinary classical collections, including illuminated manuscripts and French decorative arts.

Huntington Library, Art Collections, and Botanical Garden
1151 Oxford Road
San Marino, CA 91108
818-405-2100

In the Huntington complex, established in 1919, a beautiful garden setting enhances the extraordinary collections of eighteenth-century British paintings, including Gainsborough's *Blue Boy* and Lawrence's *Pinkie*; Renaissance bronzes and eighteenth-century marbles; early editions of Shakespeare and Chaucer in the extensive library; and prints and drawings. The setting includes a Japanese garden and sixteenth-century samurai's house.

Los Angeles County Museum of Art
5905 Wilshire Boulevard
Los Angeles, CA 90036
213-857-6111

Established in 1910, this museum houses a general collection in three pavilions surrounded by a sculpture garden with works from Rodin's time to the present. Its acquisitions include early Near and Middle Eastern antiquities; Roman, Greek, Western, and modern art; Far Eastern collections; textiles; costumes; Indian arts; pottery; Italian mosaics; pre-Columbian, African, and Oceanic arts; and nineteenth- and twentieth-century American and European paintings.

Norton Simon Museum
411 W. Colorado Boulevard
Pasadena, CA 91105
213-449-6840

Established in 1924 as the Pasadena Museum of Modern Art, this museum has developed worldwide prominence through the loans of collector Norton Simon. His collections include European art from the Renaissance to recent times, with Old Masters of the highest quality.

Colorado

The Denver Art Museum
100 West 14th Avenue Parkway
Denver, CO 80204
303-640-2295

The Denver Art Museum is noted for its collection of primitive African, Oceanic, American, Native American, and Northwest Indian arts; its Peruvian art; its collection of the arts of China, Japan, Korea, India, Southeast Asia, Tibet, and the Middle and Near East; period rooms; Impressionist, post-Impressionist, and modern paintings; prints, drawings, and photographs; and the Neusteter Institute of Fashion, Costume, and Textiles.

Connecticut

The New Britain Museum of American Art
56 Lexington Street
New Britain, CT 06052
203-229-0257

The New Britain Collection, established in 1903, focuses on outstanding American paintings from colonial times to the present. It includes Hudson River School painters and the Low memorial collection of American illustration, with N. C. Wyeth classics.

Yale Center for British Art
1080 Chapel Street
Box 2120
New Haven, CT 06520
203-432-2800

This collection of British watercolors, drawings, paintings, books, and prints is the largest of its kind outside of Great Britain. Established in 1977, the center was the gift of Paul Mellon, a lifelong collector of British art.

Yale University Art Gallery
1111 Chapel Street
New Haven, CT 06520
203-432-0600

This outstanding world art collection has been built up since the gallery's founding in 1832. It includes the Jarves collection of early Italian paintings; collections of American silver, painting, and decorative arts; modern art; Greek and Roman vases; manuscripts; prints and drawings; and primitive arts.

Delaware

Delaware Art Museum
2301 Kentmere Parkway
Wilmington, DE 19806
302-571-9590

The Delaware Art Museum, founded in 1912, specializes in American paintings, with examples by Hudson River School painters such as John Sloan, Howard Pyle, and the Wyeth family. There is an extensive collection of English pre-Raphaelites; a research library on American arts; and prints and drawings.

Henry Francis Du Pont Winterthur Museum
Route 52
Winterthur, DE 19735
302-888-4600

Founded in 1930, Winterthur has an outstanding collection of American furniture, furnishings, and decorative arts from the colonial period to the mid-nineteenth century. Period rooms display extensive collections of ceramics, glass, Chinese porcelain, fabrics, lighting fixtures, and carpets.

District of Columbia

Arthur M. Sackler Gallery, Smithsonian Institution
1050 Independence Avenue, SW
Washington, DC 20560
202-357-2700

This gallery contains a permanent collection of Asian art, including ancient works from China, the Indian subcontinent, and Southeast Asia as well as scrolls and other work by notable twentieth-century painters.

Freer Gallery of Art, Smithsonian Institution
12th Street at Jefferson Drive, SW
Washington, DC 20560
202-357-2104

Established in 1906, the Freer has one of the world's best collections of Oriental art and a comprehensive collection of Whistler paintings (his close friend Charles Freer gathered the collection and donated it).

Hirshhorn Museum and Sculpture Garden, Smithsonian Institution
Independence Avenue at 7th Street, SW
Washington, DC 20560
202-357-3091

Created in 1966 to specialize in modern art, the Hirshhorn's collection is so vast that only a small portion can be displayed at any time.

National Air and Space Museum, Smithsonian Institution
Sixth Street and Independence Avenue, SW
Washington, DC 20560
203-357-2700

Founded in 1946, this museum houses a definitive collection of aeronautical and astronautical items; air and space craft; and instruments, equipment, art, uniforms, and personal memorabilia related to air and space.

National Gallery of Art
Constitution Avenue and 4th Street, NW
Washington, DC 20565
202-737-4215

The National Gallery was endowed by Andrew Mellon in 1937 and continues to benefit from his children's donations. It includes paintings and sculptures of all schools of Western art, decorative arts, and drawings and prints, with all the classic masters represented.

National Museum of American Art, The Smithsonian Institution
8th and G Streets, NW
Washington, DC 20560
202-357-2700

Housed in the historic Greek Revival Old Patent Office, the museum has a definitive collection of American arts, including graphic and decorative arts, from colonial times to the present.

Hawaii

Honolulu Academy of Arts
900 South Beretania Street
Honolulu, HI 96814
808-538-3693

The academy, founded in 1927, has a general collection representing everything from ancient Near Eastern and Mediterranean arts to European and American arts. Medieval art, the Michener Collection of Japanese prints, Monet's *Water Lilies*, and the arts of Africa, Oceania, and the Americas are also included.

Illinois

The Art Institute of Chicago
Michigan Avenue at Adams Street
Chicago, IL 60603
312-443-3600

Founded in 1879, the Art Institute of Chicago has excellent collections in all areas of art. It is noted for the works of Old Masters, Impressionists, and American and Far Eastern artists; graphics; and Thorne miniature rooms. Famed works include Seurat's *Sunday Afternoon on the Island of la Grande Jatte*, Rembrandt's *Young Girl at an Open Half-Door*, and Mary Cassatt's *The Bath*.

The Field Museum of Natural History
Roosevelt Road at Lake Shore Drive
Chicago, IL 60605
312-922-9410

Founded in 1893, the Field Museum contains definitive collections on anatomy, anthropology, costumes, ethnology, geology, Native American artifacts, science, textiles, and zoology. Among its highlights are a full-scale replica of a Pawnee Earth Lodge and a herbarium.

Oriental Institute Museum, University of Chicago
1155 East 58th Street
Chicago, IL 60637
312-962-9520

Founded in 1919, the Oriental Institute houses a top collection of archeology and art of the ancient Near East, Babylonia, Egypt, early Christian cultures, and Islamic civilization.

Indiana

Indiana University Art Museum
Fine Arts Building
Bloomington, IN 47405
812-855-5445

This fine general collection, founded in 1941, includes everything from ancient to contemporary art, with Egyptian, Greek, and Roman sculpture; coins and glass; Western fine and decorative arts from the fourteenth to the twentieth centuries; and Far Eastern arts.

Indianapolis Museum of Art
1200 West 38th Street
Indianapolis, IN 46208
317-923-1331

Noted for its Chinese, primitive, and American art, this museum, founded in 1883, has an outstanding general collection of Old Masters, Turner watercolors, and European and American decorative arts.

Kansas

Wichita Art Museum
619 Stackman Drive
Wichita, KS 67203
316-268-4921

Established in 1935, this museum's outstanding collection ranges from art of the Old West by Charles M. Russell to Eakins' *Starting Out After Rail*. It is noted for its American paintings, sculptures, prints, and drawings.

Kentucky

J. B. Speed Art Museum
2035 South Third Street
Louisville, KY 40208
502-636-2893

This extensive collection, founded in 1925, includes European painting, sculpture, and decorative arts from the Middle Ages to the present; French and Flemish tapestries; and Kentuckiana.

Maryland

The Baltimore Museum of Art
Art Museum Drive
Baltimore, MD 21218
301-396-7101

Best known for its classic modern collections, this outstanding museum, established in 1914, displays contemporary drawings, period rooms illustrating stylistic development in Maryland, Old Masters paintings, and Far Eastern art.

Walters Art Gallery
600 North Charles Street
Baltimore, MD 21201
301-547-9000

Assembled by father and son, the Walters Art Gallery opened in 1931 with exquisite medieval treasures and Byzantine and Islamic art; early Christian liturgical vessels, Renaissance enamels, and jewelry; paintings from various periods; and Greek, Roman, and Etruscan art.

Massachusetts

Fogg Art Museum
32 Quincy Street
Harvard University
Cambridge, MA 02138
617-495-9400

With the largest and most extensive art collection of any university in the United States, the Fogg, opened in 1895, is particularly noted for its drawings and prints of all periods. It also has a fine collection of Chinese sculptures, stones and bronzes, jades, and ceramics.

Isabella Stewart Gardner Museum
280 The Fenway
Boston, MA 02115
617-566-1401

This personal collection, founded in 1900, covers a wide range of world art, with masterpieces such as Titian's *The Rape of Europa*, Giotto's *Presentation of the Child Jesus in the Temple*, and Botticelli's *Madonna of the Eucharist*.

Museum of Fine Arts
465 Huntington Avenue
Boston, MA 02115
617-267-9300

This collection, founded in 1870, includes masterpieces from around the world. It is noted for its Far Eastern, ancient, Egyptian, Greek, and Roman collections, as well as Old Masters, Impressionist, and post-Impressionist works, and American paintings and decorative arts. It also has American silver, prints and drawings, ancient musical instruments, and ship models. Famed works include Paul Revere's Liberty Bowl, Renoir's *Le Bal à Bougival*, and a Greek marble *Head of Aphrodite*.

Museum of Science
Science Park
Boston, MA 02114
617-589-0100

Founded in 1830, this science and technology museum includes collections of mineral and plant specimens, mounted animals, and exhibits on human physiology. Interactive exhibits demonstrate the principles of electricity as well as the inner workings of computers. The planetarium features rotating shows relating to space.

Old Sturbridge Village
Sturbridge, MA 01566
508-347-3362

Set up in 1938 as a living history museum, Old Sturbridge has a considerable collection of tools, crafts, arts and artifacts, decorative arts, and more than 100 period buildings of the eighteenth and nineteenth centuries.

Michigan

The Detroit Institute of Arts
5200 Woodward Avenue
Detroit, MI 48202
313-833-7900

Founded in 1885, this institute is renowned for its comprehensive collection of world arts, especially its Old Master paintings of northern Europe, French eighteenth-century decorative arts, art of the ancient world, period rooms, prints and drawings, and American arts since colonial times.

Henry Ford Museum and Greenfield Village
20900 Oakwood Boulevard
Dearborn, MI 48121
313-271-1620

Described as a "Disneyland of Americana," the indoor/outdoor facilities, established in 1929, of the museum and village offer demonstrations of crafts and manufacturing techniques that complement its extensive collections of arts, crafts, artifacts, and technology. Activities include everything from antique car rallies to country fairs on its 14 acres.

Minnesota

The Minneapolis Institute of Arts
2400 Third Avenue South
South Minneapolis, MN 55404
612-870-3000

This outstanding general collection is strongest in European paintings from Old Masters to the present. Founded in 1912, the institute also houses the Pillsbury Collection of Chinese bronzes, Japanese prints and paintings, textiles, and photographs.

Walker Art Center
Vineland Place
Minneapolis, MN 55403
612-375-7600

Founded in 1879, this museum contains contemporary art, including paintings, sculpture, drawings, and prints. Its renowned Minneapolis Sculpture Garden is a 7$\frac{1}{2}$-acre urban garden featuring 40 sculptures and a conservatory with horticultural displays.

Missouri

Nelson-Atkins Museum of Art
4525 Oak Street
Kansas City, MO 64111
816-561-4000

This museum contains prestigious collections of European and American art. Its renowned Oriental Collection is comprised of the Chinese Temple Room, galleries displaying furniture and porcelain, a specially humidified gallery of delicate scroll paintings, a sculpture gallery, and a display of glazed T'ang dynasty tomb figures.

The St. Louis Art Museum
Forest Park
St. Louis, MO 63110
314-721-0067

Founded in 1881, the St. Louis Art Museum contains a comprehensive collection of art from all eras of civilization. Among its more than 35,000 works are important pre-Columbian and German Expressionist collections.

New Jersey

The Art Museum
Princeton University
Princeton, NJ 08544
609-258-3788

Opened in 1882, this comprehensive collection contains a wide spectrum of world art, including Chinese paintings and bronzes, classical antiquities, and French paintings and sculptures.

New Mexico

The University of New Mexico Art Museum
Fine Arts Center
Albuquerque, NM 87131
505-277-7315

Established in 1963, the museum has important collections of nineteenth- and twentieth-century prints and photographs and American painting of the twentieth century, with emphasis on artists who worked in New Mexico.

New York

Albany Institute of History and Art
125 Washington Avenue
Albany, NY 12210
518-462-1522

Founded in 1791, the institute's collection focuses on the fine and decorative arts of Albany and Hudson River artists, with portraits, silver, furniture, and period rooms.

American Museum of Natural History
Central Park West at 79th Street
New York, NY 10024
212-873-1300

One of the world's largest natural history museums, opened in 1869, it has exceptional collections on Native Americans, Eskimos, dinosaurs, wildlife, minerals, and fossil specimens.

The Brooklyn Museum
200 Eastern Parkway
Brooklyn, NY 11238
718-638-5000

The Brooklyn Museum was founded in 1823 and has amassed comprehensive collections of Egyptian and classical arts; American arts; European and American graphics; and pre-Columbian, African, Native American, and other primitive arts.

The Cloisters
Fort Tryon Park, NY 10040
212-923-3700

A branch of the Metropolitan Museum devoted exclusively to medieval art, the Cloisters was built on a 4½-acre site overlooking the Hudson. It was opened in 1938 and incorporates four medieval cloisters, an arcade, a chapel, and exhibition rooms. The museum features twelfth- and thirteenth-century Byzantine and Romanesque art from France and Spain.

Cooper-Hewitt National Museum of Design, The Smithsonian Institution
2 East 91st Street
New York, NY 10128
212-860-6868

Established in 1897, the Cooper-Hewitt is housed in the Carnegie mansion. Its excellent collection of decorative arts includes furniture, fabrics, wallpaper, ceramics, drawings, prints, architecture and design publications, and metalwork. It boasts the world's largest collection of Winslow Homer drawings and sketches by other late nineteenth-century artists.

The Frick Collection
1 East 70th Street
New York, NY 10021
212-288-0700

The former home of Henry Clay Frick, built in 1914 as an eighteenth-century model, still has most of its original furnishings intact, including excellent European paintings from the fourteenth through the eighteenth centuries.

Guggenheim Museum
See **Solomon R. Guggenheim Museum**.

The Jewish Museum
1109 Fifth Avenue
New York, NY 10128
212-399-3344

This preeminent U.S. collection numbers over 23,000 objects spanning 4 millennia, ranging from ancient Eastern Mediterranean archeological artifacts to contemporary art and including paintings, sculpture, ceramics, textiles, wood, metalwork, photography, drawings, prints, coins, medals, and broadcast materials. A permanent exhibit, The Jewish Experience, spans 4,000 years of history and culture.

The Metropolitan Museum of Art
Fifth Avenue at 82nd Street
New York, NY 10028
212-879-5500

One of the world's major museums, founded in 1870, the Metropolitan houses definitive collections covering about 5,000 years of art. A few of the highlights include medieval armor collections, Tiffany stained-glass windows, the complete Temple of Dendur (an early Christian structure from Egypt), extensive painting collections, sculpture, decorative arts, and a re-creation of a classic Ming dynasty Chinese garden court.

Museum of American Folk Art
2 Lincoln Square
New York, NY 10023
212-977-7170

This museum, established in 1961, elevates the crafts of the past to fine-art status. It includes collections of quilts, weathervanes, folk paintings, sculptures, weavings, and needlework from the colonial period to the early twentieth century.

The Museum of Modern Art
11 West 53rd Street
New York, NY 10019
212-708-9400

Begun in 1929, this exceptional collection traces the evolution of art from the Impressionist period forward. It represents a variety of disciplines, including drawings and prints, industrial design, architecture, paintings, sculpture, and decorative arts.

The Solomon R. Guggenheim Museum
1071 Fifth Avenue
New York, NY 10128
212-727-6200

Founded in 1937, this excellent collection of modern drawings, prints, paintings, and sculpture emphasizes abstract and nonobjective subjects. It is housed in a stunning Frank Lloyd Wright Building.

Whitney Museum of American Art
945 Madison Avenue
New York, NY 10021
212-570-3600

Opened in 1966, the Whitney houses New York's largest collection of twentieth-century art, with changing exhibitions of drawings, paintings, sculpture, and architecture. It shows contemporary avant-garde film and video and holds the Biennial of Contemporary American Art, a major showcase of the best recent work.

Ohio

Cincinnati Art Museum
Eden Park
Cincinnati, OH 45202
513-721-5204

Founded in 1886, this major museum has an excellent, comprehensive general collection noted for its Near Eastern and American arts, Old Masters, medieval art, musical instruments, and drawings and prints. It includes works by Corot, Titian, Grant Wood, Gainsborough, Goya, and Velazquez.

Cleveland Museum of Art
11150 East Boulevard
Cleveland, OH 44106
216-421-7340

This excellent museum, founded in 1913, has a wide-ranging collection representing the artistic accomplishments of cultures throughout the world. It is recognized for one of the best Far Eastern collections and for its medieval art, Old Masters, classical antiquities, and American arts from the colonial time forward.

The Toledo Museum of Art
2445 Monroe Street at Scottwood Avenue
Box 1013
Toledo, OH 43697
419-255-8000

This museum is a renowned cultural center for art and music, featuring extensive collections of glass, European and American paintings, sculpture and decorative arts. Collections range from ancient Egypt, Greece, and Rome through the Middle Ages and the Renaissance to contemporary Europe and America.

Oklahoma

Thomas Gilcrease Institute of American History and Art
1400 Gilcrease Museum Road
Tulsa, OK 74127
918-582-3122

This exceptional art collection, founded in 1942, captures the saga of America from prehistoric to modern times; the Gilcrease's art of the Old West is rivaled only by that of the Smithsonian. The institute also has maps, books, documents, artifacts, and manuscripts.

Oregon

Portland Art Museum
1219 South West Park Avenue
Portland, OR 97205
503-226-2811

The Portland, founded in 1892, focuses on Native American arts of the Northwest. It also includes a unique collection of Cameroon art, pre-Columbian arts, Renaissance painting and sculpture, Ethiopian crosses, and European and American painting and sculpture.

Pennsylvania

Franklin Institute Science Museum and Planetarium
20th and the Benjamin Franklin Parkway
Philadelphia, PA 19103
215-448-1200

Founded in 1824, this comprehensive museum offers collections featuring science, history, industry, technology, aeronautics, astronomy, space exploration, and stamps and coins.

Museum of Art, The Carnegie
4400 Forbes Avenue
Pittsburgh, PA 15213
412-622-1975

This museum, founded in 1896, displays art from around the world, including American art since the colonial period; ancient and classical art; African, pre-Columbian, and Native American art; and European painting, sculpture, and decorative arts from the Renaissance forward. Works by Van Gogh, Cézanne, and Monet are included.

Pennsylvania Academy of the Fine Arts
118 N. Broad Street
Philadelphia, PA 19102
215-972-7600

Founded in 1805, the Pennsylvania Academy offers an excellent collection of American art from the eighteenth century to the present, with major works by Thomas Eakins, Charles Willson Peale, and William Rush.

Philadelphia Museum of Art
26th Street and Benjamin Franklin Parkway
Philadelphia, PA 19101
215-763-8100

This museum, established in 1876, is noted for its masterpieces from the twelfth to the nineteenth centuries; Barberini tapestries designed by Rubens; arms and armor; glass; European and American period rooms; folk, decorative, and primitive art; and the Stieglitz Center collection of photographs.

The University Museum of Archaeology and Anthropology, University of Pennsylvania
33rd and Spruce Streets
Philadelphia, PA 19104
215-898-4000

Founded in 1887, the museum is renowned for its worldwide acquisitions of ancient and primitive art, its collection of Native American gold, and the largest grouping of West African art in the Americas. It has sponsored more than 275 expeditions to gather outstanding artifacts from the ancient Near, Middle, and Far East, Southeast Asia, the Mediterranean, the Pacific, Europe, Africa, and the Americas.

Texas

Amon Carter Museum
3501 Camp Bowie Boulevard
Fort Worth, TX 76107
817-738-1933

Housed in an impressive building designed by Philip Johnson since its founding in 1961, this museum concentrates on American paintings and sculptures from the nineteenth century forward, specializing in the works of the Old West. It also has a fine print collection and excellent Remingtons and Russells.

Kimbell Art Museum
3333 Camp Bowie Boulevard
Box 9440
Fort Worth, TX 76107
817-332-8451

Noted for its masterpieces from around the world, this collection, founded in 1972, ranges from twelfth-century panel paintings to J. M. W. Turner landscapes, Gainsboroughs, and Goyas.

The Museum of Fine Arts
1001 Bissonet
Box 6826
Houston, TX 77265
713-639-7300

This wide-ranging collection of world art, established in 1900, is especially strong in contemporary art; pre-Columbian and Native American art; Old Masters; and later European and American paintings and sculptures.

Virginia

Colonial Williamsburg
Goodwin Building
P.O. Box 1776
Williamsburg, VA 23185
804-229-1000

This village-style museum, founded in 1926, showcases American arts from colonial times forward. Colonial Williamsburg has 88 preserved and restored buildings dating from 1693 to 1837 and 50 reconstructed eighteenth-century buildings surrounded by gardens.

Virginia Museum of Fine Arts
2800 Grove Avenue
Richmond, VA 23221
804-367-0844

This museum, which opened its doors in 1936, features important collections of British sporting art and French Impressionist and post-Impressionist art, American paintings since World War II, and art nouveau and art deco objects; a collection of Russian imperial Easter eggs by Fabergé; and one of the nation's leading collections of art from India, Nepal, and Tibet. Among its holdings are works by Goya and Monet.

Wisconsin

Elvehjem Museum of Art, University of Wisconsin
800 University Avenue
Madison, WI 53706
608-263-2246

Established in 1962, this is one of the three largest university museums in the United States. Its wide-ranging collection of world art dates back to ancient times, with fine examples of classical coins and marbles; American painting, sculpture, and decorative arts from the eighteenth century forward; Indian miniatures; and Socialist Realist (propagandist) paintings from Russia.

Museum of Civilization
Victoria Memorial Museum Building
Metcalfe and McLeod Streets
Ottawa, Ontario K1A 0M8
613-992-3497

Opened in 1845, this museum specializes in history and folk culture, with excellent collections of the arts and crafts of Native Americans, particularly Eskimos and Northwest Coast Indians.

National Gallery of Canada
380 Sussex Drive
Ottawa, Ontario K1N 9N4
613-990-1985

With more than 40,000 works, this museum contains the largest collection of Canadian art in the world and includes painting, sculpture, prints, drawings, photographs, video, film, and Inuit art.

Canada

Alberta

The Glenbow Museum
130 9th Avenue, SE
Calgary, Alberta T26 OP3
403-264-8300

This museum features exhibits on military history, mineralogy, and western Canadian history. These include artifacts from Indian and Inuit peoples as well as the Hudson Bay Company and the Canadian Pacific Railroad, which was built during the nineteenth century. The art gallery features works by historical and contemporary western Canadian artists, including Francis N. Hopkins, Emily Carr, John Hall, Ron Moppett, and Chris Cran.

The Royal Tyrrell Museum
Box 7500
Drumheller, Alberta T0J 0Y0
403-823-7707

Canada's only museum devoted to paleontology features hands-on displays and computer simulations covering 4.5 billion years of Earth's history. Forty full dinosaur skeletons comprise the world's largest exhibit of complete dinosaurs.

British Columbia

The Royal British Columbia Museum of Anthropology
675 Belleville Street
Victoria, British Columbia V8V 1X4
604-387-3701

The Royal British Columbia Museum displays a range of exhibitions depicting the accomplishments of native peoples, the achievements of early explorers and settlers, and British Columbia's natural heritage and archeological past. It includes a 14-foot-high woolly mammoth roaming a barren hilltop 10,000 years ago and a native Indian penitentiary.

Ontario

Art Gallery of Hamilton
123 King Street West
Hamilton, Ontario L8P 4S8
416-527-6610

A major North American museum, this gallery was established in 1914. It is noted for its collection of

Canadian art; twentieth-century British and American painting, sculpture, drawings, and prints; and French Impressionist works.

Royal Ontario Museum
100 Queens Park
Toronto, Ontario M5S 2C6
416-586-5549

From suits of armor to suits by Chanel, totem poles to monstrous dinosaurs, the ROM is the largest museum in Canada. It is one of the world's few multidisciplinary museums combining art, archeology, and science. The museum features a planetarium, as well as a prominent display of historical and contemporary ceramic art.

Children's Museums

There are more than 90 museums located throughout the United States devoted to children. While most museums offer at least a few special programs for children, those listed here focus almost exclusively on young visitors. A representative group is described in detail. For additional information, see the listing "Children's and Junior Museums" in *The Official Museum Directory*, published annually by the American Association of Museums.

Brooklyn Children's Museum
145 Brooklyn Avenue
Brooklyn, NY 11213
718-735-4400

Founded in 1899, this was the world's first children's museum. Its teaching collection includes more than 50,000 items, with exhibits on cultural history, natural history, and technology. It houses a greenhouse, a steam engine, and a gristmill. Children may attend workshops in school classes or groups. A portable loan collection and children's resource library is also available.

Capital Children's Museum
800 Third Street NE
Washington, DC 20002
202-543-8600

Founded in 1974, Capital Children's International Hall has a hands-on exhibit on Mexico where children learn to make their own tortillas, weave, and do other Mexican arts and crafts. Additional facilities include a living room, a metric exhibit, a simple machines display, a computer classroom, a communications exhibit, and a futuristic center.

Children's Museum
Museum Wharf
300 Congress Street
Boston, MA 02210
617-426-6500

Located on Boston's picturesque waterfront, Children's Museum was founded in 1913. It offers special collections of Native American and Japanese art; Americana; games, toys, dolls, and doll houses; and bird, insect, shell, and mineral specimens. The Exhibit Center presents participatory and cased exhibitions on child development, natural history, science and technology, careers, handicaps, and cross-cultural understanding. Its Resource Center makes available over 10,000 books, games, and other items to teachers, parents, students, and visitors.

The Children's Museum of Manhattan
212 West 83rd Street
New York, NY 10024
212-721-1223

Founded in 1979, this museum features hands-on, participatory exhibits related to science, nature, and art. A center for media and performing arts includes a television production and editing studio where children create their own television programs. Other activities include making paper, painting and drawing in an art studio, and creating postage stamps. Children contribute their art, toys, and found objects to the museum's rotating exhibits.

Eugene Field House and Toy Museum
634 South Broadway
St. Louis, MO 63102
314-421-4689

Founded in 1936, this museum is housed in the birthplace of Eugene Field. It contains a collection of antique toys and dolls, along with a library on the works of Field.

The Exploratorium
3601 Lyon Street
San Francisco, CA 94123
415-563-7337

Housed in the Palace of Fine Arts, this science museum offers 500 participatory exhibits and art works illustrating the physical nature of the world and the sensory mechanisms through which we perceive it. Founded in 1969, it hosts field trips, concerts, lectures, and school groups.

Kidspace—A Participatory Museum
390 South El Molino
Pasadena, CA 91101
213-449-9143

Kidspace offers creative learning experiences for children, as in a mock television studio that children operate, a radio booth for broadcasting, and a medical clinic. There is even a robot who talks to visitors. Parents may host birthday parties in the museum.

Los Angeles Children's Museum
310 North Main Street
Los Angeles, CA 90012
213-687-8801

Children participate in a variety of activities at this museum in such places as Sticky City, with giant foam blocks for construction fun; City Streets, with city vehicles and street signs; TV Studios, where children create their own news broadcasts; and Workshop Place, which fosters creativity in arts and crafts.

Please Touch Museum
210 North 21st Street
Philadelphia, PA 19103
215-963-0667

Founded in 1976, the Please Touch Museum issues a children's newspaper and offers special exhibits on cultural artifacts of daily life, folk art and sculpture, natural science, technology, musical instruments, games, registered toys, costumes, masks, foot gear, and hats.

Reference Works for General Information

The following lists are not meant to be comprehensive but are intended to serve as wide-ranging sources for the subjects. A library will provide further reference materials and works on each of the subjects.

General Reference Works

American Reference Books Annual. Libraries Unlimited, 1970—.
    This annual volume covers 1,300 to 1,800 new titles each year, reviewing about 300 categories of reference books. The most recent works in many disciplines are listed.

Bartlett's Familiar Quotations: A Collection of Passages, Phrases and Proverbs Traced to Their Sources in Ancient and Modern Literature, 16th ed. Little Brown, 1992.
    This work lists more than 22,500 familiar and world-famous quotations along with a 600-page keyword subject index.

Books in Print. Bowker, 1947—.
    This annual listing of books now in print or slated for publication by January 31 of the following year currently contains well over 700,000 titles.

Carruth, Gorton, ed. *The Volume Library.* The Southwestern Company, 1917—.
    This two-volume, 2.5-million-word family encyclopedia is revised annually. It covers subjects of interest to students and their families and is illustrated and thoroughly indexed.

Chambers's Biographical Dictionary, rev. ed. Cambridge University Press, 1986.
    Introduced in 1897, *Chambers's* currently lists more than 15,000 biographies spanning the history of the world.

Encyclopaedia Britannica, 15th ed. Encyclopaedia Britannica, 1987.
    A major comprehensive reference tool for any library.

Ethridge, James M., ed. *The Directory of Directories: An Annotated Guide to Business and Industrial Directories, Professional and Scientific Rosters, and Other Lists and Guides of All Kinds*, 2nd ed. Information Enterprises, 1982.
    The work lists 5,200 directories with categories such as business, education, and leisure, providing full details on each publication.

Guinagh, Kevin, ed. *Dictionary of Foreign Phrases and Abbreviations*, 3rd ed. H. W. Wilson, 1982.
    This helpful dictionary defines more than 5,000 French, German, Greek, Italian, Latin, and Spanish abbreviations, phrases, proverbs, and quotations.

Guinness Book of Records. Bantam, 1955—Facts On File, 1991—.
    An annual guide to "the biggest, largest, longest, most" all-time records.

Information Industry Market Place: An International Directory of Information Products and Services. Bowker, 1978–79—.
    This international directory describes information collection centers, database and abstract publishers, information brokers, support services and suppliers, conferences, associations, periodicals, and reference books.

Readers' Guide to Periodical Literature. H. W. Wilson, 1900—.
    The *Readers' Guide* provides a quick overview of current events through indexing of 174 general-interest U.S. magazines in a range of subject areas.

Sheehy, Eugene P., ed. *Guide to Reference Books*. American Library Association, 1986.
    Found on nearly every reference librarian's basic bookshelf, Sheehy's *Guide* is grouped into five main categories: general reference works; humanities; social and behavioral sciences; history and area studies; and science, technology, and medicine.

Who's Who in America. Marquis Who's Who, 1899—.
    The individuals listed in *Who's Who* provide the data to be included, so entries vary in completeness and accuracy. The work includes biographical details on approximately 72,000 Americans and others prominently linked to America.

World Almanac and Book of Facts. Newspaper Enterprise Association, 1868—.
    A handy and easy-to-use reference, the *World Almanac* is updated annually. It provides statistics and factual data on economic, educational, industrial, political, religious, and social issues.

World Book Encyclopedia. World Book-Childcraft International, 1992.
    Easy to use, the *World Book* is targeted at elementary through high school students, providing general reference information.

Anthropology and Ethnology. See also Social Science

Allen, James Paul, and Eugene James Turner. *We the People: An Atlas of America's Ethnic Diversity*. Macmillan, 1988.
    An atlas devoted to ethnic settlement in the United States. Maps show the distribution of ethnic groups in America; the text discusses the immigration history in the United States and migrations of ethnic populations.

Glazer, Nathan, and Daniel P. Moynihan, eds. *Ethnicity: Theory and Experience*. Harvard University Press, 1975.

A classic collection of articles dealing with sociological theory as well as ethnic experience in the United States.

Hunter, David E., and Philip Whitten, eds. *Encyclopedia of Anthropology*. Harper & Row, 1976.
The first English-language encyclopedia in anthropological studies, this volume is compact, comprehensive, and accessible. It includes some 1,400 articles on pertinent topics, supplemented by generous illustrations, maps, diagrams, and photographs.

Thernstrom, Stephan, Ann Orlov and Oscar Handlin, eds. *Harvard Encyclopedia of American Ethnic Groups*. Belknap Press at Harvard University Press, 1980.
Defining *ethnic* in the widest possible way, this book contains substantial articles on American ethnic groups. Origins, migration and settlement, history in America, socioeconomic structure, religion and politics, and many other topics are addressed.

Applied Arts

Boger, Louise A. *The Dictionary of Antiques and Decorative Arts*, rev. ed. Scribner, 1979.
This volume is international in scope, with short articles and illustrations covering furniture, glass, ceramics, styles, terms, and biographies.

Kovel, Ralph, and Terry Kovel. *Kovel's Antiques and Collectibles Price List*. Crown, annual.
This book includes prices for more than 50,000 antiques and collectible items.

Kovel, Ralph, and Terry Kovel. *Kovel's Know Your Antiques*. Crown, 1990.
This guide offers tips on how to recognize and evaluate any antique, large or small, like an expert. It covers pottery, porcelain, silver, pewter, furniture, pressed and cut glass, prints, bottles, ironware, tinware, letters, sheet music, autographs, books, magazines, and more. This volume also provides advice about caring for antiques and recognizing frauds as well as bibliographies for each specialty.

Kovel, Ralph, and Terry Kovel. *Kovel's Know Your Collectibles*. Crown, 1981.
This guide advises on what collectible objects are likely to increase in value and how to preserve, protect, and sell them. It covers ceramics, pottery, furniture, glass, toys, print advertisements, and many other items, with bibliographies for each major specialty.

Liman, Ellen. *The Collecting Book*. Penguin, 1980.
This book thoroughly describes individual collecting areas such as advertising memorabilia, comic books, tobacco items, clothing, boxes and tins, pottery, glass, and toys. It includes chapters on buying, preserving, and displaying collectibles, as well as numerous black-and-white photographs and extensive references to related publications and organizations.

Art and Architecture

American Art Directory. Bowker, 1898—.
A biennial guide to the thousands of art councils, museums, art libraries, and art schools in the United States, Canada, and abroad.

Artist's Market. Writer's Digest, 1974—.
This annual publication details names, addresses, contacts, payments, and other data for 4,000 purchasers of cartoons, illustrations, and photographs. It is considered a standard in its field.

Bell, Doris L. *Contemporary Art Trends: A Guide to Sources, 1960–1980*. Scarecrow Press, 1981.
This work identifies 41 contemporary art trends with listings of appropriate books and museum catalogs. It also contains a listing of 200 contemporary art journals and a bibliography.

Hamlin, Talbot. *Architecture Through the Ages*. Putnam, 1953.
This excellent college text offers a survey history from the social point of view. Indexed and illustrated.

Mayer, Ralph. *A Dictionary of Art Terms and Techniques*. HarperCollins, 1981.
This book defines more than 3,200 terms used in the fields of ceramics, drawing, painting, printmaking, and sculpture.

Musgrove, John, ed. *Sir Bannister Fletcher's A History of Architecture*, 19th ed. Butterworth, 1987.
This comprehensive view of architectural history has been revised and expanded to include worldwide coverage. It is extensively illustrated, with glossary, index, and bibliographies appended to each chapter.

Phaidon Dictionary of Twentieth-Century Art, 2nd ed. Dutton, 1977.
This concise and thorough survey covers international art movements and artists in depth from 1900.

Placzek, Adolph K., ed. *Macmillan Encyclopedia of Architects*, four volumes. Free Press, 1982.
This volume offers a social and historical view of architecture through the ages, from ancient to modern times, in Europe, the Middle East, and North America.

Wilkes, Joseph A., and Robert T. Packard. *Encyclopedia of Architecture: Design, Engineering and Construction*. Wiley, 1988.
This five-volume work addresses the history of Western architecture over the past 200 years and covers 500 different topics, with 3,000 photographs. Each article was prepared by experts in the field.

Astronomy

Moore, Patrick, ed. *The International Encyclopedia of Astronomy*. Orion, 1987.
This popular reference work condenses difficult concepts into readable prose. No prior knowledge of astronomy is assumed. More than 2,500 entries include several major essays by experts in various fields as well as shorter articles. Illustrated in full color.

Muirden, James. *The Amateur Astronomer's Handbook*, 3rd ed. Harper, 1982.
This is an excellent guide for beginners who want to select equipment and set up their own observatories. It includes celestial charts and tables of eclipses and planetary positions.

Pasachoff, Jay M. *Contemporary Astronomy*, 3rd ed. CBS College Publishing, 1985.
This textbook is perfect for beginners who have no background in mathematics or physics, presenting astronomical concepts in clear, colloquial English.

Eicher, David J. *The Universe from Your Backyard: A Guide to Deep Sky Objects from Astronomy Magazine*. Cambridge University Press, 1988.
This is a useful guide for all amateur astronomers.

Communications

Barnouw, Eric, ed. *International Encyclopedia of Communications*. 4 vols. Oxford University Press, 1989.
This comprehensive, illustrated four-volume encyclopedia covers the entire spectrum of communications studies. Most articles are followed by brief bibliographies, and the work is extensively cross-referenced.

Brown, Les. *Les Brown's Encyclopedia of Television*. Zoetrope, 1982.
This reference work covers television terminology, notable television programs, and profiles of important television personalities, including actors, directors, producers, and writers.

Representative American Speeches Series. H. W. Wilson, 1967—.
   This annual publication includes selected major speeches with biographical notes on the speaker.

Writers Market: Where to Sell What You Write. Writer's Digest, 1929—.
   An essential annual reference for freelance writers that gives the pertinent data on more than 4,500 publishers of books, periodicals, audiovisual materials, greeting cards, plays, and other materials. It includes basics of copyright law and authors' rights.

Economics and Business

Brownstone, David M., and Carruth, Gorton. Where to Find Business Information: A World Guide for Everyone Who Needs the Answers to Business Questions (A Hudson Group book), 2nd ed. Wiley, 1982.
   More than 5,000 English-language publications from around the world are listed and briefly described, with concentration on current periodical publications and services, especially magazines, newsletters, computerized data bases, printouts, and microforms. The compendium deals with all subjects of interest to business.

Business Periodicals Index: A Cumulative Subject Index to Periodicals in the Fields of Accounting, Advertising, Banking and Finance, General Business, Insurance, Labor and Management, Marketing and Purchasing, Office Management, Public Administration, Taxation, Specific Businesses, Industries, and Trades. H. W. Wilson, 1958—.
   This monthly index provides data on approximately 250 periodicals and certain U.S. government documents.

Consumers Index to Product Evaluations and Information Sources. Pierian Press, 1973—.
   Quarterly; annual cumulation.
   A quarterly guide to consumer magazine articles in 14 subject areas.

Consumer Reports Buying Guide. Consumers Union, 1936—.
   Issued annually as the December issue of *Consumer Reports*, this guide is a starting point for a comparative analysis of all types of products. It contains test results, brand and model ratings and rankings, and general buying advice on products as diverse as stereos and orange juice. It also provides a subject index to evaluations from the previous five years of *Consumer Reports*.

Dow Jones Irwin Business Almanac. Dow Jones-Irwin, 1977—.
   This annual almanac provides business, financial, and tax statistics. It includes a short business directory and a review of the previous year's significant business news.

Dun and Bradstreet Million Dollar Directory. Dun and Bradstreet, 1959—.
   This annual directory offers alphabetical listing of industries and businesses with a net worth of at least $1 million. It includes the name, address, corporate officers, Standard Industrial Classification (SIC) number, approximate sales, and number of employees for approximately 39,000 U.S. companies.

Dun and Bradstreet's Guide to Your Investments. Crowell, 1973—.
   An introductory guide for amateur stock market investors, this annual explains basic concepts for all types of investments: common and preferred stocks; bonds; real estate; stock options; small business investment companies; and formula investing.

Fortune World Business Directory. Time, Inc., 1957—.
   Taken from the annual listing in the May issue of *Fortune* magazine ranking the 500 largest U.S. industrial corporations, this directory includes the "Fortune 500" plus the 50 largest banks.

Franchise Opportunities Handbook. U.S. Bureau of Industrial Economics and Minority Business Development Agency, 1972—.
   One of the best publications on franchising, this annual guide provides details on equity capital needed to buy specific franchises, available training, and support services.

Help: (Washington): The Useful Almanac. Everest House, 1977—.
   This annual almanac offers up-to-date information for consumers. It is arranged topically, with material on health, real estate, nutrition, energy, education, insurance, and numerous other subjects.

Moody's Handbook of Common Stocks. Moody's Investors Service, 1965—.
   Described as a quick-reference tool, Moody's quarterly publishes data on approximately 1,000 stocks, outlining capitalization, earnings, and projected outlook for each.

Standard and Poor's Register of Corporations, Directors and Executives. Standard and Poor's, 1928—.
   A standard in the field, Standard and Poor's *Register* offers three volumes each year with current information on about 46,000 U.S. and Canadian companies. The volumes include biographies of executives as well as separate listings of newly added individuals and companies, obituaries for the previous year, and complete data on each company.

Standard Directory of Advertisers. National Register Publishing, 1907—.
   This annual directory lists over 17,000 companies that advertise nationally through various media. The directory provides details on officers and sales personnel, product lines, advertising agencies, and media.

Thomas Register of American Manufacturers and Thomas Register Catalog File. Thomas Publications, 1905—.
   This annual authoritative listing of manufacturers is grouped by more than 70,000 product classifications. Its 17 volumes contain lists of products and services; company names, addresses, and phone numbers; names of executives; and ratings, as well as a brand-name index and company catalogs.

U.S. Master Tax Guide. Commerce Clearing House, 1917—.
   Using information on the Internal Revenue Code regulations and court and tax court decisions, this annual handbook covers all aspects of preparing federal income taxes for corporations, estates and trusts, individuals, and partnerships. It is considered a standard in its field.

Education

American Council on Education. *American Universities and Colleges*, 14th ed. Walter de Gruyter, 1992.
   This comprehensive directory provides information about the structure of higher education in the United States, as well as complete details on each of the more than 1,700 institutions granting baccalaureate or higher degrees.

Durnin, Richard G. *American Education: A Guide to Information Sources.* Gale, 1982.
   This bibliography covers books relating to American education, with 107 topical chapters listing works on childhood through higher education. Most works included are recent publications, but classic works also are described.

Good, Carter V. *Dictionary of Education*, 3rd ed. McGraw-Hill, 1973.
   This volume offers definitions of technical and professional terms and concepts in all areas of education.

The World of Learning. Europa Publications, 1947—.
   This annual directory of international institutions includes educational and scientific institutions and organizations listed by country.

Ethnic Studies

See **Anthropology and Ethnology**.

Film

Halliwell, Leslie. *Halliwell's Film Guide*, 8th ed. HarperCollins, 1991.
This regularly revised comprehensive work covers a wide range of popular film lore.

Katz, Ephraim. *The Film Encyclopedia*, Harper, 1979.
This volume covers directors, producers, actors, composers, and screenwriters, as well as major studios and film centers; it does not list individual movies.

Genealogy and Heraldry

Andereck, Paul A., and Richard A. Pence. *Computer Genealogy: A Guide to Research Through High Technology*. Ancestry Publishing, 1991.
This volume will aid researchers in the selection of suitable computer programs and explains complicated technical jargon.

Beard Field, Timothy. *How to Find Your Family Roots*, McGraw-Hill, 1977.
This is a guide to specific genealogical research.

Cerny, Johni, and Wendy Elliot. *The Library: A Guide to the LDS Family History Library*. Ancestry Publishing, 1988.
The book is an explanatory guide to the largest single collection of genealogical works, run by the Church of Jesus Christ of Latter Day Saints.

Doane, Gilbert H., and James B. Bell. *Searching for Your Ancestors: The How and Why of Genealogy*, 5th ed. University of Minnesota Press, 1980.
This introductory guide to genealogical research covers both techniques and sources for locating genealogical data.

Eakle, Arlene, and Johni Cierny. *The Source: A Guidebook of American Genealogy*. Ancestry Publishing, 1984.
The book is a compilation of resources, research tchniques, and record sources.

Kurzweil, Arthur. *From Generation to Generation*. Schocken Books, 1982.
This volume addresses genealogical techniques and subjects particular to Jewish family history, from locating information on European shtetls to Sephardic research.

Geography and Travel Guides

Rand McNally Comprehensive World Atlas. Rand McNally, 2nd ed., 1991.
This atlas includes 350 color maps and map inserts, with individual maps of each U.S. state and Canadian province. It also provides a list of 1980 census totals for about 20,000 U.S. political subdivisions. The main index contains 82,000 entries.

Rand McNally Road Atlas, latest edition. United States, Canada, and Mexico. Rand McNally.
This annual publication offers maps of all 50 states, each Canadian province, Central America, Mexico, and Puerto Rico, plus a 23,000-item place-name index. It also includes information on population, national park areas, mileage, recreational and historical sites, area codes, time zones, and how to compute miles per gallon.

Webster's New Geographical Dictionary, rev. ed. Merriam-Webster, 1984.
This work presents basic geographic, demographic, economic, and historical notes on world countries, regions, cities, and natural features, with maps.

History

Barraclough, Geoffrey, ed. *The Times Concise Atlas of World History,* rev. ed. Hammond, 1986.
Seven sections detail the history of the world, beginning with "The World of Early Man" and concluding with "The Age of Global Civilizations." This work contains approximately 600 maps and illustrations depicting the rise and fall of major civilizations, as well as significant religious and historical events.

Barzun, Jacques, and Henry G. Graff. *The Modern Researcher,* 4th ed. Harcourt Brace Jovanovich, 1985.
This essential reference stresses historical research and provides methodologies useful to those in the humanities and social sciences. New material for the 4th edition covers the use of computers, word processors, and data bases.

Carruth, Gorton. *The Encyclopedia of American Facts & Dates.* Harper & Row, 1987.
This chronologically arranged encyclopedia of American history has become a standard reference book for students and others seeking basic information. It covers explorations, treaties, battles, politics, literature, and science, among other topics.

Law

Black, Henry Campbell, et al. *Black's Law Dictionary: Definitions of the Terms and Phrases of American and English Jurisprudence, Ancient and Modern,* 6th ed. West, 1990.
A standard reference in the field, *Black's* gives detailed definitions in all aspects of law, including criminal procedure, estate planning, accounting, taxes, and commercial transactions.

Cohen, Morris L., and Robert C. Berring. *How to Find the Law,* 9th ed. West, 1989.
A basic text for law students, as well as a helpful tool for the layman investigating resources and methodologies of legal research.

Linguistics

Guinagh, Kevin, ed. *Dictionary of Foreign Phrases and Abbreviations,* 3rd ed. H. W. Wilson, 1982.
This dictionary contains definitions for more than 5,000 French, German, Greek, Italian, Latin, and Spanish abbreviations, phrases, quotations, and proverbs that appear in the English language. Similar expressions are cross-referenced.

Roget's International Thesaurus, 5th ed. HarperCollins, 1992.
Topical listings of more than 250,000 words are provided, with an alphabetical index for easy use.

Strunk, William, Jr., and E. B. White. *The Elements of Style,* 3rd ed. Macmillan, 1979.
A classic book noted for its simplicity and directness, *Elements* consists of only five chapters: "Elementary Rules of Usage," "Elementary Principles of Composition," "A Few Matters of Form," "Words and Expressions Commonly Misused," and "An Approach to Style."

Webster's New World Dictionary, 3rd College Edition. Simon & Schuster, 1988.
This authoritative dictionary provides over 150,000 entries, with in-depth etymologies, pronunciations, foreign expressions, a syllabification system, and over 11,000 Americanisms.

Webster's Ninth New Collegiate Dictionary, 9th ed. G. & C. Merriam, 1989.
Almost 160,000 entries are offered, with pronunciations, functional labels, inflected forms, word histories, usage, and word divisions. Also included are first known date of use for each word. The dictionary contains sections with biographical and geographical entries, foreign words and phrases, degree-granting colleges and universities, signs and symbols, and a style manual.

Literature

Drabble, Margaret, ed. *The Oxford Companion to English Literature*, 5th ed. Oxford University Press, 1985.
Entries on English fiction, authors, and literary schools and movements are presented.

Garland, Henry, and Mary Garland. *The Oxford Companion to German Literature*, 2nd ed. Oxford University Press, 1986.
German writers and their works, with cultural and historical background, are provided.

Gassner, John, and Edward Quinn, eds. *The Reader's Encyclopedia of World Drama*. Crowell, 1969.
The book has entries on playwrights, critics, national dramatic literatures, and histories. Emphasis is on drama as literature.

Granger, Edith. *Granger's Index to Poetry.* Columbia University, 1986.
This standard work is indexed by title, first line, author, and subject.

Hart, James D. *Oxford Companion to American Literature*, 5th ed. Oxford University Press, 1983.
This volume has entries on American fiction, authors, and literary schools and movements.

Harvey, Paul, and J. E. Heseltine. *The Oxford Companion to French Literature.* Oxford University Press, 1969.
This volume covers authors and their works, with survey articles, terms, and movements from the Middle Ages to 1939.

Howatson, M. C. *The Oxford Companion to Classical Literature*, 2nd ed. Oxford University Press, 1989.
This comprehensive guide has entries on authors, characters, plots, literary forms, and cultural and historical background. A chronological table and maps are included.

MLA International Bibliography of Books and Articles on the Modern Languages and Literatures. Modern Language Association of America, 1921—. Annual.
This useful reference covers articles and books in English, French, German, Spanish, Italian, Portuguese, Rumanian, and other languages.

Reader's Adviser, 6 vols. Bowker, 1988.
This basic guide to literature covers the best in English and American fiction, poetry, essays, biographies, and other areas in the fields of reference, history, philosophy, and science.

Medical Science

American Medical Association Encyclopedia of Medicine, Charles B. Clayman, M.D., ed. Random House, 1989.
This clear, systematic account of current medical knowledge and terminology covers a wide range of diseases, their causes, and symptoms.

American Medical Association Family Medical Guide, rev. ed., Jeffrey R. M. Kung and Asher J. Finkel, eds. Random House, 1987.
This layperson's handbook features articles on diseases and disorders, diagnostic charts, and an index of drugs and medications.

American Medical Association Home Medical Advisor, Charles B. Clayman, Jeffrey R. M. Kinz, and Harriet S. Meyer, eds. Random House, 1988.
This is a self-help guide to symptoms, disorders, diseases, and medical emergencies, illustrated with charts.

Physicians' Desk Reference to Pharmaceutical Specialties and Biologicals. Medical Economics, 1947—.
This compendium, commonly referred to as the PDR, is a standard reference work for physicians and other health professionals. It offers details on dosage, contraindications, side effects, precautions, and undesirable interactions of pharmaceutical products.

The Wellness Encyclopedia, staff of the University of California, Berkeley, Wellness Letter, eds. Houghton Mifflin, 1991.
This comprehensive guide focuses on preventive health through good eating, exercise, and risk reduction for disease.

Music

Abraham, Gerald. *The Concise Oxford History of Music*. Oxford University Press, 1979.
This scholarly survey of Western music from ancient to modern times is presented chronologically. It describes the musical styles of each period and region, with extensive bibliographies.

Grout, Donald J. *A History of Western Music*, 4th ed. Norton, 1988.
The standard one-volume history of music is used in thousands of colleges and graduate schools. This illustrated volume contains a bibliography, chronology, and glossary.

Havlice, Patricia Pate. *Popular Song Index*. Scarecrow Press, 1975. Supplement, 1978. Second Supplement, 1984.
More than 300 songbooks from the period 1940 to 1972, including children's songs, folk songs, hymns, and popular music, are anthologized. The supplement includes another 72 anthologies from the period 1970 to 1975.

Randel, Don Michael. *New Harvard Dictionary of Music*. Harvard University Press, 1986.
This comprehensive dictionary includes definitions and brief articles on music history, aesthetics, and theory.

Sadie, Stanley, ed. *The New Grove Dictionary of Music and Musicians,* 6th ed. 20 vols. Grove's Dictionaries of Music, 1980.
This comprehensive dictionary includes entries and articles on composers, performers, theorists, music publishers, scholars, terminology, genres, and orchestras, with exhaustive bibliographies.

Mythology, Folklore, and Popular Customs

Martin, Richard P., ed. *Bulfinch's Mythology: The Age of Fable, the Age of Chivalry, the Legends of Charlemagne*. HarperCollins, 1991.
The classic work on mythology, Bulfinch's summarizes Greek, Roman, Norse, Arthurian, and other myths, with notes on the *Iliad*, the *Odyssey*, and the *Aeneid*.

Mercatante, Anthony. *The Facts On File Encyclopedia of World Mythology and Legend*. Facts On File, 1988.
This comprehensive reference covers world mythologies in thematic, biographical and narrative essays.

Thompson, Stith. *The Folktale*. University of California Press, 1977.
Considered a standard in the field, this work discusses the form and development of folk stories, with summaries of the most popular folk tales of Europe, western Asia, and the Native North Americans. It also covers various methods of researching and studying folk tales and folklore.

Philosophy

Edwards, Paul. *Encyclopedia of Philosophy*. Free Press, 1973.
An excellent scholarly reference, this four-volume encyclopedia contains hundreds of articles relevant to political science as well as biographies of scores of key figures such as Aristotle, Darwin, Hobbes, Jefferson, Locke, Machiavelli, Malthus, Marx, Mill, Plato, and Rousseau.

Magill, Frank N., ed. *Masterpieces of World Philosophy: More Than 100 Classics of the World's Greatest Philosophers Analyzed and Explained.* HarperCollins, 1990.
This book contains more than 100 synopses and commentaries on key figures in Eastern and Western philosophy, including analyses of important influences on their development.

Political Science

Congressional Quarterly's Guide to Congress, latest ed. Congressional Quarterly.
This accurate, nonpartisan guide to the history, power, structure, and workings of Congress includes the texts of the Articles of Confederation, Constitution, Declaration of Independence, and important preconstitutional documents.

Greenstein, F. I., and N. W. Polsby. *The Handbook of Political Science.* Addison-Wesley, 1975.
This is an extremely useful encyclopedic survey of the entire field, including administration, civil rights, civil liberties, elections, and federalism.

Lesko, Mathew. *Information U.S.A.* Viking Penguin, 1986.
This book bills itself as "the ultimate guide to the largest source of information on earth," the U.S. government. It includes names, addresses, and phone numbers to locate information about hundreds of subjects, including consumer products, child care, medical services, educational opportunities, grants and loans, data bases, marketing surveys, and government services.

Robert, Henry M. *Robert's Rules of Order,* 11th rev. ed. HarperCollins, 1991.
This completely revised edition provides the authoritative guide to parliamentary procedure.

Washington Information Directory. Congressional Quarterly, 1975—.
This annual publication describes 5,000 congressional, executive, and nongovernmental agencies, committees, and organizations. It is considered an indispensable guide to both official and unofficial Washington.

Recreation and Sports

McWhirter, Norris. *Guinness Book of Sports Records.* Facts On File, 1991.
A handy reference to record-setting facts and figures for men's and women's sports.

Webster's Sports Dictionary. G. & C. Merriam, 1976.
This authoritative sports reference book defines terms for all popular spectator sports (baseball, basketball, football), international games (cricket, soccer), and recreational pursuits (hunting, mountain climbing). Diagrams and drawings further illuminate the subject.

Religion

Adams, Charles J., ed. *A Reader's Guide to the Great Religions,* 2nd ed. The Free Press, 1977.
Through bibliographic essays, this work covers major religions as well as ancient beliefs, religions of Mexico and Central and South America, the Sikh religion, and the Jains. It includes a subject index and an index of authors, compilers, translators, and editors for the serious researcher.

Attwater, Donald. *The Penguin Dictionary of Saints,* rev. ed. Penguin, 1984.
This book provides brief biographical sketches of 750 of the best-known saints. The selections are worldwide but emphasize those in Great Britain.

Brandon, S. G. F., ed. *Dictionary of Comparative Religions.* Macmillan, 1978.
Thorough and concise, this volume defines anthropology, iconography, philosophy, and the psychology of primitive, ancient, Asian, and Western religions. Articles describe practices and philosophies of specific religions, with terminology for each and pertinent bibliographies.

The Illustrated Bible Dictionary. 3 volumes. Tyndale House, 1980.
>Comprehensive and well organized, this dictionary is based on the revised standard version. It offers definitions from all aspects of books of the Bible; major works and doctrines; and history, geography, customs, and cultures of biblical times. Extensive photographs, charts, diagrams, cross-references, and a useful index are included.

Morrison, Clinton. *An Analytical Concordance to the Revised Standard Version of the New Testament.* Westminster Press, 1979.
>This massive work contains both a concordance and an index-lexicon. Entries give the English word followed by a subtitle line with three elements: definition, Greek word, and an English transliteration of the Greek word. Included are complete listings of each passage in which the subject word appears, with an explanation of its use in context.

Science and Technology

Chambers Science and Technology Dictionary. W. R. Chambers Ltd and Cambridge University Press, 1988.
>A revision and expansion of a classic work, the *Chambers Dictionary* provides 45,000 understandable, alphabetical definitions of terms used in a variety of scientific disciplines.

Chen, Ching-Chih. *Scientific and Technical Information Sources*, 2nd ed. MIT, 1986.
>Although the book is primarily a guide for science and technology librarians, it is a useful guide to relevant sources for the layperson.

McGraw-Hill Encyclopedia of Science and Technology, 6th ed. McGraw-Hill, 1987.
>This 20-volume compendium continues to be the basic reference source covering important topics from earliest times to the present. Annual updates are available.

Social Science

See also **History; Sociology.**

Sills, David L., ed. *International Encyclopedia of the Social Sciences.* Macmillan, 1977. Biographical suppl., 1979.
>This scholarly summary of the social sciences offers articles on specific topics, as well as some 600 biographies.

UNESCO Dictionary of the Social Sciences. Julius Gould and William L. Kolb, eds. The Free Press, 1964.
>This excellent reference includes about 2,000 signed articles defining terminology in anthropology, economics, political science, sociology, and other social science specialties.

Sociology

Barnes, Harry Elmer, and Howard Becker. *Social Thought from Lore to Science*, 3rd ed. Peter Smith, 1982.
>This is a three-volume encyclopedic inventory of the history of sociology.

Directory of Counseling Services. International Association of Counseling Services, 1969— .
>This annual publication lists members of the American Personnel and Guidance Association who offer public and private counseling dealing with education, family, marriage, personal problems, rehabilitation, and vocational guidance.

Statistics and Demography

Bureau of the Census Catalog. U.S. Bureau of the Census, 1946—.
This catalog provides listings of all published and unpublished material (tape, cards, or microform) created ⸍ the Census Bureau during the period covered.

Kotz, Samuel, and Normal L. Johnson, eds. *Encyclopedia of Statistical Sciences.* Wiley, 1987.
Information on many topics in statistical history and application of statistical methods is presented in this nine-volume work, intended primarily for readers who seek more information than general references can offer.

United Nations Statistical Yearbook. United Nations, 1949—.
This annual publication is considered the best source for international statistics. It offers data on such topics as agriculture, balance of payments, communications, construction, energy, population, transport, and wages and prices in 150 countries and territories.

Theater and Performing Arts

Hatnoll, Phyllis, ed. *The Oxford Companion Guide to World Theatre*, 4th ed. Oxford University Press, 1983.
Articles on all aspects of theater are included, from history to theater architecture, technical theater, terminology, and experimental theater. Also included are articles on national dramatic literature, plays, actors, playwrights, and teachers.

Hughes, Catherine. *American Theater Annual.* Gale Research, 1976—.
All plays opening on and off Broadway during the year are listed, with details of cast members, opening and closing dates, plot summaries, and review excerpts.

Koegler, Horst. *The Concise Oxford Dictionary of Ballet*, 2nd ed. Oxford University Press, 1982.
This book contains more than 5,000 alphabetically arranged entries covering all areas of ballet: choreographers, composers, dancers, history, schools and companies, and basic definitions.

Notable Names in the American Theater. James T. White, 1976.
This major work is divided into nine sections: "New York Productions"; "Premieres in America"; "Premieres of American Plays Abroad"; "Theater Group Biographies"; "Theater Building Biographies"; "Awards"; "Bibliographical Biography"; "Necrology"; and, most valuable, "Notable Names in the American Theater." The sections cover administrators, agents, archivists, authors, casting directors, composers, conductors, critics, designers, directors, educators, historians, lyricists, performers, playwrights, producers, and teachers.

Theatre World. Crown, annual.
This theater yearbook gives a complete pictorial and statistical record of each Broadway season from 1944–45 to the present.

The Dewey Decimal System and How to Use It

Melvil Dewey (1851–1931) believed in organization. Even as a child he was busy devising a way to arrange his family's pantry to make it more efficient. Before his system of classifying library books was adopted, many libraries relied on systems that filed books by size or color—cumbersome and not very useful methods at best. While working as a librarian at

Amherst College, Dewey developed a system that is used by most school and small public libraries today. Published anonymously in 1876, his classifications divide nonfiction books into 10 broad categories:

000–099	General works (encyclopedias and similar works)
100–199	Philosophy (how people think and what they believe)
200–299	Religion (including mythology and religions of the world)
300–399	Social sciences (folklore and legends, government, manners and customs, vocations)
400–499	Language (dictionaries, grammars)
500–599	Pure science (mathematics, astronomy, chemistry, nature study)
600–699	Technology (applied sciences—aviation, building, engineering, homemaking)
700–799	Arts (photography, drawing, painting, music, sports)
800–899	Literature (plays, poetry)
900–999	History (ancient and modern, geography, travel)

Each of these sections is further divided for accuracy in classification. For example, the numbers 500–599 cover the pure sciences, such as astronomy, chemistry, mathematics, paleontology, and physics. Each of these areas has its own division and section number. All books on mathematics are assigned numbers in the 510 to 519 range; mathematics is then broken down into types, such as algebra, arithmetic, and geometry. Geometry's specific number is 513, which can be subdivided through the use of decimal points to provide 10 basic categories. Additional digits can be added, creating an ever more precise categorization system.

Books are arranged alphabetically within each classification by the first letters of the author's last name. Therefore, a library that has several books on American history of the colonial period will assign the same basic number (973.2) to all the books and shelve them alphabetically.

Dewey's aim was to create a system that would be simple enough for even casual users to understand, but complex enough to meet a library's expanding needs. His system was developed to meet the needs of many libraries. A second popular system was created to fit the requirements of a specific library, the Library of Congress. This system, now in wide use, is even more detailed and has the advantage of being able to accommodate growth of knowledge in unexpected areas.

The Library of Congress Subject Headings

The Library of Congress Classification System is used in most large public and university libraries today. A Library of Congress (LC) number contains three lines: a letter at the top, a number in the middle, and a letter/number combination at the bottom.

The Library of Congress went through several systems before devising its own method. Because the Library of Congress contains almost every book ever published in the United

States, as well as valuable tapes and research materials, it needs a highly flexible system. The Library of Congress Classification System contains 20 classes:

A:	General works	N:	Fine arts
B:	Philosophy, psychology, and religion	P:	Language and literature
C–F:	History	Q:	Science
G:	Geography, anthropology, recreation	R:	Medicine
H:	Social sciences	S:	Agriculture
J:	Political science	T:	Technology
K:	Law	U:	Military science
L:	Education	V:	Naval science
M:	Music	Z:	Bibliography and library science

Each of these classes can be divided into a subclass with the addition of a second letter. By adding numbers, the category becomes even more specific. The flexibility of the system becomes apparent when one sees that the alphabet permits 26 subdivisions of any one class. Each of the subdivisions can be broken down further by using the numbers 1 to 9999.

Librarians recommend that researchers turn to *Subject Headings Used in the Dictionary Catalog of the Library of Congress* for assistance. Because the LC system groups related topics together, a researcher may discover unexpected, related avenues to pursue.

CATALOGING IN PUBLICATION DATA

On the copyright page of most books, under the heading "Cataloging in Publication Data," are numbers and abbreviations that help librarians to index new acquisitions for the card catalog. These data can be helpful to readers as well. A typical entry is shown below with an explanation of each part of the entry:

Library of Congress Cataloging in Publication Data

[*Author*]　　McLanathan, Richard B.K.
[*Title*]　　　World art in American museums.

[*Possible subject card headings, in order of importance*]　　1. Art—United States—Guide-books.　2. Art museums—United States—Guide-books.　3. Museums—United States—Guide-books.　4. Art—Canada—Guide-books.　5. Art—museums—Guide-books.　6. Museums—Canada—Guide-books.
　　　　　　　　　　1. Title.
[*Library of Congress No.*]　　N510.M34　1983　708.13　(Dewey Decimal No.)
　　　　　　　　　　ISBN 0-385-18515-4 (International Standard Book Number: country number; publisher number; title number; and check digit. The ISBN was started by the British in 1967 and adopted in the United States a year later.)

Cataloging in Publication Data might also include information on a book's illustrator, whether a book has an index or bibliography, and number of pages.

GETTING STARTED IN GENEALOGY

The search for a greater understanding of our ancestors has boomed in the United States since the American Bicentennial celebration and the publication of Alex Haley's immensely popular *Roots*. Genealogists lament that too many of us live in historical vacuums, unable to name more than a generation or two of our closest relatives. To join this search for a history that extends beyond the last few generations, experts offer several tips:

1. Begin with your closest family members, recording basic information that is already known to you and working backward. This part of the investigation can be quite far-reaching if you contact distant relatives and check sources that they suggest. You may be fortunate enough to have access to family Bibles, letters, and diaries. Vital records such as birth and death certificates can yield a wealth of information at this stage.

2. Consult popular references for research techniques. Some of the best follow.

   Andereck, Paul A., and Richard A. Pence. *Computer Genealogy: A Guide to Research Through High Technology.* Ancestry, 1985.
   Crandall, Ralph. *Shaking Your Family Tree.* Yankee Publishing, 1986.
   Doane, Gilbert Harry, and James B. Bell. *Searching for Your Ancestors: The How and Why of Genealogy,* 5th ed. University of Minnesota Press, 1980.
   Jacobus, Donald Lines. *Genealogy as Pastime and Profession,* 2nd ed. Genealogical Publishing Co., 1978.

3. Check out the libraries. Extensive genealogical collections exist at the Library of Congress, the New York Public Library, the Los Angeles Public Library, the Newberry Library in Chicago, and the Allen County Public Library in Fort Wayne, Indiana. Specialized libraries, such as the famed Genealogical Library of the Church of Jesus Christ of Latter-Day Saints in Salt Lake City, Utah, can be extremely helpful. This particular library offers more than 1.3 million reels of microfilm of all types of documents useful to genealogists. Also visit or contact local libraries in areas where your ancestors are known to have lived.

Major Genealogical Libraries

Burton Collection, Detroit Public Library, 5201 Woodward Avenue, Detroit, MI 48202
Dallas Public Library, 1515 Young Street, Dallas, TX 75201
Daughters of the American Revolution Library, 1776 D Street NW, Washington, DC 20006 (to be used with the Library of Congress and National Genealogical Society Library, 4527 17th Street N, Arlington, VA 22207)
Genealogical Society Library, 50 East North Temple Street, Salt Lake City, UT 84150
Los Angeles Public Library, 630 West 5th Street, Los Angeles, CA 90071
Newberry Library, 60 West Walton Street, Chicago, IL 60610
New England Genealogical Society, 101 Newbury Street, Boston, MA 02116
New York Historic Genealogical and Biographical Society, 122-6 East 58th Street, New York, NY 10022
New York Public Library, 5th Avenue and 42nd Street, New York, NY 10018
Allen County Public Library, 301 West Wayne Street, Fort Wayne, IN 46802
State Historical Society of Wisconsin, 816 State Street, Madison, WI 53706
Western Reserve Historical Society, 10825 East Boulevard, Cleveland, OH 44106

4. Consider contacting the American Archives Association if your search involves identifying and locating missing and unknown heirs to estates. The association charges a percentage fee for successful searches. Call any weekday between 8:30 A.M. and 4:30 P.M., EST.

American Archives Association
1350 New York Avenue NW
Washington, DC 20005
202-737-6090

Additional Sources of Information

Organizations and Services

American Crafts Council Library
44 West 53rd Street
New York, NY 10019
212-274-0630

Questions about the history of crafts, or about learning how to pursue a particular craft, such as weaving or pottery, are answered. Calls may be made Tuesday through Friday between 10 A.M. and 5 P.M., EST.

American Film and Video Association
P.O. Box 48659
8050 N. Milwaukee Avenue
Niles, IL 60648
708-698-6440

Information is provided about animation, business films, documentary and educational films, films as art, and independent films. Questions about film schools and film vocabulary can also be answered. The library contains over 1,300 books and has special files on film festivals, library administration, grants, filmmakers, and film centers in the United States. Calls may be made weekdays, from 2 P.M. to 6 P.M., EST.

American Museum of Natural History Library
79th Street and Central Park West
New York, NY 10024
212-769-5400

Founded in 1869, this special library has 400,000 volumes devoted to subjects ranging from anthropology to travel and expedition, with sections on biology, ethology, entomology, geology, herpetology, history of science, ichthyology, living and fossil invertebrates, mammalogy, mineralogy, museology, ornithology, and paleontology. Its special collections are devoted to astronomical instruments, rare books and manuscripts, rare films, and many other areas. The museum's librarians offer assistance in all areas.

Consumer Information Center
Pueblo, CO 81009
719-948-3334

This federal government agency provides a wide selection of free publications such as its monthly *National Consumer Buying Alert* and guides to solar energy, tire buying, nutrition, budgeting, housing, and gardening. Write for a free catalog, or specify your area of interest.

Educational Resources Information Center (ERIC)
1200 19th Street NW
Washington, DC 20208
202-219-2289

The National Institute of Education within the U.S. Department of Education sponsors ERIC, the educational information system, to provide literature pertaining to various aspects of education. General questions about education are also answered. If a computer search is necessary, a charge will be imposed; otherwise, the information is free. ERIC also provides referrals to other organizations, including its own clearinghouses on adult, career, and vocational education; counseling and personnel services; educational management; elementary and early childhood education;

handicapped and gifted children; higher education; information resources; junior colleges; languages and linguistics; reading and communications skills; rural education and small schools; science, mathematics, and environmental education; social studies/social science education; teacher education; tests, measurements, and evaluation; and urban education. Calls are accepted 8 A.M. to 5:30 P.M., EST, weekdays.

Federal Information Center
P.O. Box 600
Cumberland, MD 21502
301-722-9098

This government-sponsored answer center will respond to general information questions or will refer you to a likely source of information. It also provides names, addresses, and telephone numbers of various government agencies and offers a free brochure listing all Federal Information Centers across the country.

Museum of Broadcasting
1 East 53rd Street
New York, NY 10022
212-621-6600

Founded in 1976, this museum has collected more than 10,000 radio and 8,000 TV tapes from the 1920s to the present and 2,400 radio scripts, with 1,600 available on microfiche. Its staff is knowledgeable about all aspects of broadcasting and has access to a thousand-volume library of books and magazines.

The National Archives
Central Reference Service Division
Washington, DC 20408
202-501-5402

This federal government agency is responsible for keeping the permanent records of the U.S. government. Its holdings include maps, photographs, films, U.S. Census records, and all types of correspondence generated and received by government officials. The archives also contain ship passenger records dating as far back as 1820 and military records from the Revolutionary War. Some of its holdings occasionally overlap those of the Library of Congress. Call between 8:45 A.M. and 5:15 P.M., EST, weekdays.

Nutrition Information Center
The New York Hospital–Cornell Medical Center
Room 904
Memorial Sloan-Kettering Cancer Center
515 East 71st Street
New York, NY 10021
212-746-5454

Advice is provided on clinical nutrition, nutrition research, and general nutrition. The staff will also furnish educational materials, make referrals, and assist in program planning. Calls may be made weekdays between 9 A.M. and 5 P.M., EST.

The Performing Arts Library
Roof Terrace Level
John F. Kennedy Center for the Performing Arts
Washington, DC 20566
202-416-8780

Both the public and professional artists may call the library for information and reference assistance on broadcasting, dance, film, music, theater, and related areas. The library is a joint project of the Kennedy Center and the Library of Congress.

United Nations
United Nations Publications
Room 1059
New York, NY 10017
212-963-1234

This international organization's publications cover a wide range of topics, including human rights, public finance, atomic energy, treaties, and international statistics. The UN makes materials available in hardbound and paperback books, pamphlets, bulletins, periodicals, and official records—all in English, and frequently also in Spanish, French, and Russian. Write for a catalog and details of current offerings.

United States Military Academy Library
West Point, NY 10996
914-938-2209

Founded in 1802, the academy's library contains 400,000 volumes pertaining to the history of the military as well as government documents.

Data Banks Available for Computer Research

BRS Information Technologies
1200 Route 7
Latham, NY 12110
800-289-4277   518-783-1161

BRS provides online access to bibliographic and full-text data bases covering diverse subjects, among them agriculture, books in print, chemistry, energy, medicine, dentistry, mental health, and social sciences. Its clients represent Canada, Europe, and the Middle East, as well as the United States.

CompuServe, Inc.
Information Services
P.O. Box 20212
5000 Arlington Centre Boulevard
Columbus, OH 43220
800-848-8199
614-457-0802 in Ohio or Canada

This online system offers forums for users of various computers, with electronic editions of newspapers and computer magazines, an international newswire, conferences, and message boards. CompuServe provides remote computing services, a videotex information service, and a value-added network service, as well as games, entertainment, and personal finance services.

DIALOG Information Services, Inc.
3460 Hillview Avenue
Palo Alto, CA 94304
800-334-2564   415-858-2700

This online system provides access to approximately 280 databases, making it possible to search through thousands of newspapers, general-interest and trade magazines, and other publications in seconds. It includes data bases compiled by Dun & Bradstreet, Moody's Investor's Service, and Standard & Poor's.

Dow Jones News/Retrieval
P.O. Box 300
Princeton, NJ 08534
609-520-4000

This online computer service offers an interactive information service with up-to-the-minute news and information to the business and financial community. Stories from the *Wall Street Journal*, *Barron's*, and the *Dow Jones News Service* appear as quickly as 90 seconds after filing and go back as far as 90 days. Dow Jones also offers online stock trading and portfolio management services.

ORBIT Search Service
800 Westpark Drive
McLean, VA 22102
800-456-7248   703-442-0900

This bibliographic data base provides online services. Users may request copies of full-text documents from any of the available services.

WILSONLINE
The H. W. Wilson Company
950 University Avenue
Bronx, NY 10452
212-588-8400

WILSONLINE provides online access to *The Readers' Guide to Periodical Literature*, the *Business Periodicals Index*, the *Index to Legal Periodicals*, the *Education Index*, and numerous other periodical resources. It is used widely by corporations, government agencies, libraries, schools, and universities. Its database covers more than 3,000 periodicals and 500,000 books.

12

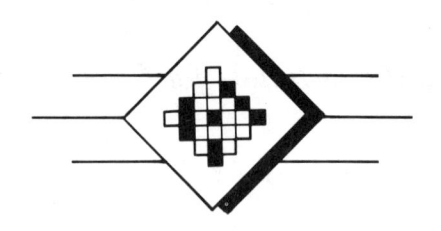

Words

Common Abbreviations / *323*

U.S. Postal Service Abbreviations / *328*

Common Crossword Puzzle Words / *330*

Commonly Misspelled Words / *338*

Common Phrases: Major European Languages / *339*

Frequently Used Foreign Words and Phrases / *340*

94 Acceptable Two-Letter Scrabble® Words / *345*

Recurrent Letters of the Alphabet / *346*

Oxymoron: A Pairing of Contradictory or Incongruous Words / *346*

Acronyms / *346*

Palindromes / *349*

Greek Prefixes / *349*

Greek Suffixes / *352*

Latin Prefixes / *353*

Latin Suffixes / *354*

Additional Sources of Information / *355*

Common Abbreviations

Note: *See also* **Acronyms**, page 346.

An abbreviation is a shortened form of a word or phrase. Some abbreviations, such as Mr. and Mrs., always substitute for the longer form. Abbreviations are not limited to, but frequently are used for, titles, academic degrees, organizations, measurements, and scientific words.

a	acre
AAA	American Automobile Association
A.B.	*arterium baccalaureus* (Latin, bachelor of arts)
ABM	antiballistic missile
A.C.	alternating current
A.D.	*anno domini* (Latin, in the year of our Lord)
ae.	*aetate* (Latin, aged)
AEF	American Expeditionary Force (World War I)
AFL	American Federation of Labor
AIDS	acquired immune deficiency syndrome
A.M.	*ante meridiem* (Latin, before noon)
AMA	American Medical Association
anon.	anonymous
A.R.A.	Associate of the Royal Academy
ASAP	as soon as possible
B.A.	bachelor of arts
Bart., Bt.	baronet
BBB	Better Business Bureau
bbl.	barrel(s)
B.C.	before Christ
B.C.E.	before the Christian era
B.D.	bachelor of divinity
B.P.O.E.	Benevolent and Protective Order of Elks
B.S.	bachelor of sicence
B.S.A.	Boy Scouts of America
bu.	bushel
B.V.M.	Blessed Virgin Mary
C	centigrade, Celsius
c., ca.	*circa* (Latin, about)
CAB	Civil Aeronatuics Board
Cantab.	*Cantabrigiensis* (Latin, of Cambridge)
CARE	Cooperative for American Relief Everywhere
CCC	Civilian Conservation Corps
CEO	chief executive offices
cf.	*confere* (Latin, compare)
CIA	Central Intelligence Agency

CIO	Congress of Industrial Organizations
cm	centimeter
c/o	in care of
COD	cash on delivery
COO	chief operating officer
CORE	Congress of Racial Equality
CP	Communist party
C.P.A.	certified public accountant
CPI	Consumers Price Index
CPR	cardiopulmonary resuscitation
CPU	central processing unit (computers)
C.S.A.	Confederate States of America
CST	Central Standard Time
cu.	cubic
D.A.	district attorney
D.A.R.	Daughters of the American Revolution
DC	District of Columbia
D.C.	district current; doctor of chiropractic
D.D.	doctor of divinity
D.D.S.	doctor of dental surgery
DOA	dead on arrival
doz.	dozen
D.S.M.	Distinguished Service Medal
D.S.O.	Distinguished Service Order
DST	Daylight Savings Time
DTs	delerium tremens
D.V.M.	doctor of veterinary medicine
E.E.O	equal employment opportunity
e.g.	*exempli gratia* (Latin, for example)
EPA	Environmental Protection Agency
Esq.	esquire
EST	eastern standard time
et al.	*et alii, et aliae, et alia* (Latin, and others)
etc.	*et cetera* (Latin, and others)
F	Fahrenheit
FAA	Federal Aviation Administration
ff.	and following
FBI	Federal Bureau of Investigation
FCC	Federal Communications Commission
FDA	Food and Drug Administration
FDIC	Federal Deposit Insurance Corporation
FHA	Federal Housing Administration
f.o.b.	free on board
FRS	Federal Reserve System
f/t	full time
ft.	foot
FTC	Federal Trade Commission

f/x	special effects (movies)
FYI	for your information
GAO	General Accounting Office
G.A.R.	Grand Army of the Republic
GMT	Greenwich mean time
GNP	gross national product
GOP	Grand Old party (Republican party)
GPO	Government Printing Office; general post office
G.S.A.	Girl Scouts of America
H.M.S.	his/her majesty's ship
HQ	headquarters
H.R.	House of Representatives
H.R.H.	his/her royal highness
HUD	(Department of) Housing and Urban Development
ibid.	*ibidem* (Latin, in the same place)
ICBM	intercontinental ballistic missile
ICC	Interstate Commerce Commission
i.e.	*id est* (Latin, in the same place)
IHS	Jesus (Greek contraction)
in.	inch
I.N.R.I.	*Iesus Nazarenus Rex Iudaeorum* (Latin, Jesus of Nazareth, King of the Jews)
INS	Immigration and Naturalization Service
I.O.U.	I owe you
I.Q.	intelligence quotient
IRS	Internal Revenue Service
ISBN	international standard book number
J.D.	*jurum doctor* (Latin, doctor of laws), *juris doctor* (Latin, doctor of jurisprudence, doctor of law)
K	1,000
k.	karat
kg	kilogram
K.G.B.	*Komitet Gosudarstvennoi Bezopasnosti* (Russian, State Security Committee)
km	kilometer
kt.	knight
kw.	kilowatt
kwh.	kilowatt-hour
l	liter
lat.	latitude
lb.	pound
l.c.	lower case (printing)
L.C.	Library of Congress
L.H.D.	*litterarum humaniorum doctor* (Latin, doctor of humane letters)
Litt.D.	*litterarum doctor* (Latin, doctor of literature)

LL.B.	*legum baccalaureus* (Latin, bachelor of laws)
LL.D.	*legum doctor* (Latin, doctor of laws)
long.	longitude
L.P.N.	licensed practical nurses
m	meter
m.	married
M.A.	master of arts
M.B.A.	master of business administration
MC	master of ceremonies
M.D.	*medicinae doctor* (Latin, doctor of medicine)
mg	milligram
mi.	mile
ml	milliliter
mm	millimeter
M.O.	money order; *modus operandi* (Latin, mode of operation)
M.P.	member of Parliament; military police
mph	miles per hour
M.S.	master of science
ms., mss.	manuscript, manuscripts
MSG	monosodium glutamate
N/A	not applicable
N.A.	North America
NAACP	National Association for the Advancement of Colored People
NASA	National Aeronautics and Space Administration
NATO	North Atlantic Treaty Organization
N.B.	*nota bene* (Latin, note well)
NCO	noncommissioned officer
NOW	National Organization for Women
NP	notary public
NRA	National Recovery Administration; National Rifle Association
NRC	National Regulatory Commission
N.S.	New Style (Russian dating)
NSC	National Security Council
O.B.E.	Order of the British Empire
op. cit.	*opere citato* (Latin, in the work cited)
O.S.	Old Style (Russian dating)
OSHA	Occupational Safety and Health Administration
o/t	overtime
Oxon.	*Oxoniensis* (Latin, of Oxford)
oz.	ounce
PA	public address
PC	personal computer
P & I	principal and interest
pk.	peck
P & L	profit and loss
P.M.	*post meridiem* (Latin, after noon); prime minister

pro tem.	*pro tempore* (Latin, for the time being)
P.S.	postscript
p/t	part time
pt.	pint
PTA	Parent-Teacher Association
PX	post exchange (commissary)
Q.E.D.	*quod erat demonstrandum* (Latin, which was to be proved)
qt.	quart
q.v.	*quod vide* (Latin, which see)
R.	*rex, regina* (Latin, king, queen)
R.A.	Royal Academy
rbi	runs batted in (baseball)
R & D	research and development
REM	rapid eye movement
RFD	rural free delivery
RIP	*requiescat in pace* (Latin, rest in peace)
RN	registered nurse
ROTC	Reserve Officers' Training Corps
rpm	revolutions per minute
RR	railroad
R & R	rest and relaxation (military)
R.S.V.	Revised Standard Version (Bible)
R.S.V.P.	*répondez s'il vous plaît* (French, respond if you please)
Rx	prescription
s	seconds
S.A.	South America; Salvation Army
SAC	Strategic Air Command
S.A.S.E.	self-addressed stamped envelope
s.c.	small capitals (printing)
SDI	Strategic Defense Initiative
SDS	Students for a Democratic Society
SEC	Securities and Exchange Commission
Sen.	Senate
seq.	*sequentes* (Latin, the following)
S.J.	Society of Jesus (Jesuits)
SOS	international distress signal, often wrongly though to stand for "Save Our Ship"
SPCA	Society for the Prevention of Cruelty to Animals
SPQR	*Senatus Populusque Romanus* (Latin, the Senate and the Roman people)
sq.	square
SS.	saints
SS	Social Security; steamship
T	ton
TD	touchdown (football)
T.N.T.	trinitrotoluene
TVA	Tennessee Valley Authority

u.c.	upper case (printing)
UFO	unidentified flying object
U.K.	United Kingdom
UN	United Nations
UNESCO	United Nations Educational Scientific, and Cultural Organization
UNICEF	United Nations International Children's Emergency Fund
U.S.	United States
U.S.A.	United States of America; United States Army
U.S.A.F.	United States Air Force
U.S.C.G.	United States Coast Guard
U.S.I.A.	United States Information Agency
U.S.M.C.	United States Marine Corps
U.S.N.	United States Navy
U.S.S.	United States ship
U.S.S.R.	Union of Soviet Socialist Republics
VA	Veterans Administration
V.F.W.	Veterans of Foreign Wars
V.I.P.	very important person
viz.	*videlicet* (Latin, namely)
V.P.	vice-president
w	watt
WAC	Women's Army Corps
WAVES	Women Appointed for Volunteer Emergency Service (U.S. Navy)
W.C.T.U.	Women's Christian Temperance Union
Xmas	Christmas
yd.	yard
Y.M.C.A., Y.W.C.A.	Young Men's (Women's) Christian Association
Y.M.H.A., Y.W.H.A.	Young Men's (Women's) Hebrew Association
yr.	year

U.S. Postal Service Abbreviations

Two-Letter State and Territory Abbreviations

Alabama	AL	Connecticut	CT	Hawaii	HI
Alaska	AK	Delaware	DE	Idaho	ID
American Samoa	AS	District of Columbia	DC	Illinois	IL
Arizona	AZ	Federated States of		Indiana	IN
Arkansas	AR	Micronesia	FM	Iowa	IA
California	AR	Florida	FL	Kansas	KS
California	CA	Georgia	GA	Kentucky	KY
Colorado	CO	Gaum	GU	Louisiana	LA

Maine	ME	New Mexico	NM	South Carolina	SC
Marshall Islands	MH	New York	NY	South Dakota	SD
Maryland	MD	North Carolina	NC	Tennessee	TN
Massachusetts	MA	North Dakota	ND	Texas	TX
Michigan	MI	Northern Mariana Islands	MP	Utah	UT
Minnesota	MN	Ohio	WH	Vermont	VT
Mississippi	MS	Oklahoma	OK	Virginia	VA
Missouri	MO	Oregon	OR	Virgin Islands	VI
Montana	MT	Palau	PW	Washington	WA
Nebraska	NE	Pennsylvania	PA	West Virginia	WV
Nevada	NV	Puerto Rico	PR	Wisconsin	WI
New Hampshire	NH	Rhode Island	RI	Wyoming	WY
New Jersey	NJ				

Geographic Directional Abbreviations

North	N	West	W	Southwest	SW
East	E	Northeast	NE	Northwest	NW
South	S	Southeast	SE		

Street Designators (Street Suffixes)

Word	*Abbreviation*	*Word*	*Abbreviation*	*Word*	*Abbreviation*
Alley	ALY	Court	CT	Gardens	GDNS
Annex	ANX	Courts	CTS	Gateway	GTWY
Arcade	ARC	Cove	CV	Glen	GLN
Avenue	AVE	Creek	CRK	Freen	GRN
Bayou	BYU	Crescent	CRES	Grove	GRV
Beach	BCH	Crossing	XING	Harbor	HBR
Bend	BND	Dale	DL	Haven	HVN
Bluff	BLF	Dam	DM	Heights	HTS
Bottom	BTM	Divide	DV	Highway	HWY
Boulevard	BLVD	Drive	DR	Hill	HL
Branch	BR	Estates	EST	Hills	HLS
Bridge	BRG	Expressway	EXPY	Hollow	HOLW
Brook	BRK	Extension	EXT	Inlet	INLT
Burg	BG	Fall	FL	Island	IS
Bypass	BYP	Falls	FLS	Islands	ISS
Camp	CP	Ferry	FRY	Isle	ISLE
Canyon	CYN	Field	FLD	Junction	JCT
Cape	CPE	Fields	FLDS	Key	KY
Causeway	CSWY	Flats	FLT	Knolls	KNLS
Center	CTR	Ford	FRD	Lake	LK
Circle	CIR	Forest	FRST	Lakes	LKS
Cliffs	CLFS	Forge	FRG	Landing	LNDG
Club	CLB	Fork	FRK	Lane	LN
Corner	COR	Forks	FRKS	Light	LGT
Corners	CORS	Fort	FT	Loaf	LF
Course	CRSE	Freeway	FWY	Locks	LCKS

Words **329**

Lodge	LDG	Plaza	PLZ	Station	STA
Loop	LOOP	Point	PT	Stream	STRM
Mall	MALL	Port	PRT	Street	ST
Manor	MNR	Prairie	PR	Summit	SMT
Meadows	MDWS	Radial	RADL	Terrace	TER
Mill	ML	Ranch	RNCH	Trace	TRCE
Mills	MLS	Rapids	RPDS	Track	TRAK
Mission	MSN	Rest	RST	Trail	TRL
Mount	MT	Ridge	RDG	Trailer	TRLR
Mountain	MTN	River	RIV	Tunnel	TUNL
Neck	NCK	Road	RD	Turnpike	TPKE
Orchard	ORCH	Row	ROW	Union	UN
Oval	OVAL	Run	RUN	Valley	VLY
Park	PARK	Shoal	SHL	Viaduct	VIA
Parkway	PKY	Shoals	SHLS	View	VW
Pass	PASS	Shore	SHR	Village	VLG
Path	PATH	Shores	SHRS	Ville	VL
Pike	PIKE	Spring	SPG	Vista	VIS
Pines	PNES	Springs	SPGS	Walk	WALK
Place	PL	Spur	SPUR	Way	WAY
Plains	PLNS	Square	SQ	Wells	WLS

Common Crossword Puzzle Words

Certain words frequently appear in crossword puzzles. Following is a list of such words, particularly ones not used regularly in everyday speech. Many of these words will be recognized by avid crossword puzzle solvers. People new to crosswords will find familiarity with the list helpful in checking and building a crossword vocabulary.

aalii	tree; wood	Aeolus	Greek god of wind
Aare	Swiss river	aga	Muslim chief
abbé	monk; cleric	agar	moss; culture medium
abele	white poplar	agee	awry; askew
abet	aid; assist	agha	Muslim leader
abou	father (Arabic)	agora	assembly
acer	maple genus	Agra	site of Taj Mahal
Acre	Israeli city	aile	winged (heraldry)
acta	deeds	Aino, Ainu	Japanese aborigine
Adah	wife of Lamech	Aire	French river
Adak	Alaskan island	ait	river island
Adar	Jewish month	alae	winglike part
adit	mine entrance	alar	winged
adze	shaping tool	alef	Hebrew letter

alen	Danish length	aux	French commune
Aleut	Alaskan Indian	avav	Pepper shrub; hummingbird
Alma	Crimean river	avocet	bird; plover
aloe	bitter herb; lily	awn	beard on grain
alop	askew	axil	leaf angle
ama	cup; candlenut	axon	nerve-cell process
amah	Oriental nurse		
ameer	Arab chieftain	Baal	god; idol
amir	Arab chieftain	baft	astern
Amos	biblical prophet	Bahia	Brazilian state; bay
ana	collection; anthology	baht	Siamese coin
anas	duck genus	Baku	Caspian harbor
ani	blackbird; cuckoo	Bali	Indonesian island
anil	indigo shrub	Balt	Lett; Lithuanian
anile	old-womanish; feeble	banc	judge's bench
anion	ion; particle	bane	evil; scourge
anise	fragrant seed	bani	Romanian money
anoa	wild Celebes ox	Bann	Irish river
ans	Belgian commune	Barre	Vermont city
ansa	loop; handle	Baya	Bantu tribe
ante	poker stake; before	Beda	Arabian city
anti	opposed	beka	biblical money; Hebrew weight
A one	first-rate; tops	Belem	Brazilian city
apa	wallaba tree	Benares	Indian city
apis	bee; Egyptian sacred bull	Bera	Arabian city
apod	footless	berm	bank; lodge
Apollo	sun god	Berne	Swiss city
Aral	Soviet sea	bes	ancient Roman weight
Aran	Irish island	besa	Abyssianian money
Ares	Greek god of war	besant	old French money
aria	opera solo	bezant	circle (heraldry)
aril	seed covering	bhar	Indian weight
artel	union; cooperative	bilk	cheat
arum	cuckoopint; flowering plant	binh	Annam weight
Asgard	abode of Norse gods	bisse	snake (heraldry)
Astarte	Phoenician love goddess	Blanc	peak in Alps
atap	palm; nipa	boa	feathered scarf; constrictor
ates	sweetsop	bole	friable clay
Atka	Aleutian tribe	bolo	knife; machete
atle	Tamarisk salt tree	Bonn	West German city
Atli	Norse king	brae	Scottish hillside
Aton	Egyptian solar deity	brut	dry wine
atri	Italian commune		
Attica	Greek district; New York State prison	cabal	secret group; junta
		Caen	French city
Attu	Alaskan island	Caddo	Indian tribe
Aude	French river	cadi	Muslim judge
Auk	diving bird	Cain	Abel's brother
aune	French length	calp	limestone

cam	gear	Ela	highest note; Guido's note
Carib	South American Indian	Elam	biblical kingdom
carr	pool	elan	dash; ardor
cava	pepper shrub; vein	Elbe	German river
Cayuga	Iroquoian tribe	Elia	Lamb pen name; Kazan
cere	wax; wrap	Elul	Jewish month
Ceres	grain goddess	emir	Muslim chieftain
Clare	Irish county	emu	ostrichlike bird
Clio	muse of history	Enna	Sicilian city
Comus	god of mirth	Enns	Austrian river
Coos	Oregon tribe	Enos	Seth's son
copa	Spanish measure	ente	grafted (heraldry)
cor	heart; brightest star	ento	inner (prefix)
corium	dermis; layer	Enyo	Ares' mother
cos	lettuce	Eolus	Colorado mountain
Cree	Indian tribe	epee	fencing blade
Crimea	Russian peninsula	ephah	Hebrew measure
cuir	leather (French)	epi	finial; spire
cull	choose; assort	Erda	Norse earth goddess
cuya	Cuban timber tree	eri	silkworm
		Eris	goddess of discord
dace	carplike fish	Erlau	Hungarian commune
Dade	Florida county	ern	sea eagle
dado	groove	erne	sea eagle; Irish river
Dail	Irish parliament	Erse	Gaelic
daler	Dutch money	esker	glacial ridge
Davos	Swiss resort	esne	serf
Dee	English river	esse	existence; abstract being
dhai	midwife	Este	Italian commune
dhak	East Indian dye tree	Estes	Colorado park
dhal	lentil	estop	prevent by law
dhan	cattle; property	et al	and others (Latin abbreviation)
dhow	Oriental sailing ship	etui	vanity case; needle case
dinar	Bulgarian or Yugoslav money	evoe	bacchanals' cry
dop	diamond holder	ewer	pitcher
dopp	dip	exe	English river
Duma	Russian council		
durn	gatepost	fane	temple
dyad	pair	fanon	cape; orale
Dyak	Borneo tribe	faro	card game
dyne	unit of force	Faroe	Danish islands
		fass	Austrian measure
ebon	black	faun	satyr; Roman half goat
Edda	Icelandic saga; Norse prose	Faunus	rural deity
ede	Dutch commune	fels	Indian money
Eder	German river	fete	festival
Edo	Tokyo	fiat	command; decree
Eger	German river	fief	feudal estate

fils	son (French)	Hilo	Hawaiian city
flak	antiaircraft bursts	hin	Hebrew measure
flan	custard	Hiram	biblical ruler
flay	skin	hiro	Japanese length
fosse	moat; pit	Hler	Norse god
Frey	Norse god	hoar	frost
Frigg	Odin's wife	hod	brick tray; coal scuttle
		Hood	Oregon mountain
gad	rove	hora	Israeli dance
Gael	Celt	Horeb	biblical mountain
gam	mouth; leg	Hosea	biblical prophet
gaol	prison	Hoth	Norse god
gar	needle fish	huk	Philippine guerrilla
gard	French department	hula	Hawaiian dance
gare	railway station (French)	Hun	barbarian; vandal
Gaspé	Canadian peninsula	Hydra	nine-headed monster
gata	shark		
Gaza	biblical city	iamb	verse foot
Gerd	Frey's wife	ibex	wild goat
Geri	Odin's wolf	ibid.	same place (abbreviation)
ghat	range; pass	ibis	wading bird
gila	lizard	Ibo	West African tribe
Gilead	biblical mountain	ici	here (French)
gnu	antelope; wildebeest	icon	religious image
Goa	former Portuguese colony	Ida	Asia Minor range; Crete mountain
Golo	Bantu tribe	Idas	killer of Castor
Goshen	biblical land of plenty	ideo	idea (prefix)
gowl	monster	ides	Roman date
gradus	ancient Roman length	iglu	Eskimo hut
graf	German count	ilex	holly
grao	Portuguese weight	ilia	hip bones
gulden	Dutch money	imam	caliph
		immi	Swiss measure
Hades	Greek underworld	Indus	Indian river
hadj	pilgrimage	inee	arrow poison
haft	handle	Inez	Don Juan's mother
ha ha	laugh; sunken fence	Inga	shrub genus
haka	dance	Iole	Hercules' captive
Hamar	city in Norway	Iona	Scottish isle
Hamite	biblical tribe	Ionia	Asia Minor district
Han	river in China	iota	Greek letter; bit
hart	stag	Irra	Babylonian god
hemo	blood (prefix)	Isar	Bavarian river
Hera	queen goddess	Iser	Czech river
Herat	Afghanistan city	Isere	French river
Hermes	Greek god	Isis	Egyptian goddess; sister and wife of Osiris
Herod	biblical ruler		
Herr	Mister (German)	itea	Virginia willow
Hesse	German state	ixia	iris

jako	parrot	kopek	Russian money
jama	tunic	koss	Indian length
jami	mosque	kraal	enclosure
jann	genie	kris	dagger
jara	palm	Krishna	Hindu god
Jebu	West African tribe	krona	Icelandic money
Jehu	biblical ruler	Kronos	Titan
Jena	German city	kudu	African antelope
jeté	ballet jump	Kurd	Turkish tribe
jhow	Tamarisk shrub	kvas	Russian sour beer
jib	triangular sail		
jilt	cheat; reject	lac	resin
jinn	demon	lact	milk (prefix)
Joad	English philosopher	Lagos	capital of Nigeria
Joshua	biblical ruler	lait	milk (French)
Jove	chief Roman god	lama	Buddhist monk; Tibetan priest
juba	African dance	Lamech	biblical patriarch
Jung	psychiatrist	lar	gibbon
Juno	Roman queen of gods	lath	strip of wood
junu	charm	lave	bathe
jura	French department	lea	meadow
		Leda	Castor's mother; swan
kabul	Indian river	lees	dregs
kadi	judge	Lena	Asian river
Kafir	Bantu tribe	Lenape	Indian tribe
kana	Japanese writing	Leto	Apollo's mother
Kano	Nigerian walled city	Levi	Jacob's son; Hebrew tribe
kaph	Hebrew letter	Leyte	Pacific island
Kara	Arabian sea	libra	Mexican weight
kava	Polynesian beverage	Lido	Adriatic resort
kawa	Pepper shrub	limn	portray
kela	Arabian weight	limu	edible seaweed
keno	lotto; bingolike game	Linz	Austrian city
Kent	English county	liss	fleur-de-lis
kepi	military cap	lobo	timber wolf
kerf	notch	loch	Scottish lake
khat	Turkish length	Loki	Norse god
Kiel	German canal	loup	half-mask (French)
Kiev	Russian city	luff	sail into wind
kil	monk's cell; Irish church; kilometer (abbreviation)	Luna	moon goddess
		Lys	Belgian river
kiln	oven		
Kiowa	Indian tribe	Maas	Dutch river
kipe	basket	mage	magician
kiri	Kaffir war club	Maia	Hermes' mother
kiwi	flightless bird	Main	German river
Kobe	Honshu port	mani	peanut
Koko	Lord High Executioner	mano	hand grinding stone
kola	nut	marl	clayey soil

Maui	Hawaiian island	octo	eight (prefix)
Mayo	Irish county; mayonnaise	oda	harem room
Mede	ancient Persian	odea	music hall
Medusa	Gorgon	Order	Baltic river
mega	great (prefix)	oeuf	egg (French)
meld	declare, in cards	ogee	arch; molding
Melos	Aegean island	Okie	migratory worker
merl	blackbird	okra	gumbo
Metz	French city	ola	palm leaf
mil	wire measure	olay	palm leaf
Milo	Greek Island	olio	medley
Minos	Greek king	olla	jar; meat dish
moa	flightless bird; ostrich	Olor	swan genus
Moab	biblical tribe	Omei	China mountains
moho	honey-eating bird	omni	all (prefix); Atlanta arena
mohr	gazelle	Omsk	Russian city
mojo	voodoo charm	oner	individual; corker
moki	New Zealand raft	onus	burden
Moro	Philippine Muslim	opah	colorful fish
Mors	Roman god of death	ope	unlock (poetic)
Morta	goddess of fate	orca	killer whale
Muir	Alaska glacier	Orel	Russian port
mumm	disguise	orle	heraldic bearing
		Orly	French airport
nacre	mother-of-pearl	orne	French department
nae	no (Scottish)	ort	morsel; leftover
Nahor	biblical patriarch	osier	willow tree
naif	lustrous	Ossa	Greek mountain
Namur	Belgian commune	otic	pertaining to the ear
nard	anoint; spice	Otoe	Oklahoma tribe
neap	tide	oyez	attention; court cry
neb	beak; nose		
Nebo	biblical mountain	paal	Javanese length
nee	born (French)	pac	boot, moccasin
Nene	English river; Hawaiian bird	paca	rodent
nep	catnip	padre	priest; cleric
Nereid	sea nymph	pala	Indian weight
ness	promontory	palp	tentacle; feeler
Nestor	Greek king	Panay	Philippine island
neve	glacier; snow	pard	leopard
newt	eft	parr	young fish
nez	nose (French)	pas	dance step
nimb	halo	pavis	shield; cover
nipa	drink; East Indian palm	Pelée	Martinique volcano
		pelu	hardwood tree
oast	kiln; oven	peri	fairy
obi	Oriental sash	phon	loudness
obit	death notice	phot	light unit
oca	edible tuber	pica	type measure

Pico	Azores volcano	Siva	Hindu god
		skag	part of a ship's keel
rale	rattle; breathing noise	skew	twist
Rama	incarnation of Vishnu	Skye	Hebrides island
rame	branch	sloe	plum; blackthorn
rana	Indian prince	Smee	Captain Hook's assistant; pintail duck
rani	Indian queen		
rati	Indian weight	snee	dirk; knife
Remi	ancient people of Gaul	soir	evening (French)
rena	rockfish	Sol	sun god
ret	soak flax	sora	marsh bird
rete	network	Spad	biplane; nail
Rhea	Titan; Cronos' wife	Spes	Roman goddess of hope
Rhus	Sumac genus	Sri	Hindu goddess
ria	narrow inlet; estuary	SRO	box-office sign
rial	Iranian coin	stere	dry measure
rien	nothing (French)	stet	let it stand
Riga	Baltic city	stile	wall step; set of steps
rime	frost	stoa	portico
ripa	riverbank	suet	hard fat
rom	gypsy husband	Suva	Fiji capital
rood	crucifix		
Rosa	shrub genus	Taal	Afrikaans
Ross	Antartic sea	Tabor	biblical mountain
roti	roasted (French)	tabu	forbidden
rotl	Muslim weight	tace	body armor
Ruhr	German river; industrial area	tael	Oriental weight
rune	mysterious sign; old alphabet character	tamp	pack; ram
		Taos	New Mexico town
rupee	Indian money	tapa	bark cloth
		Tara	Irish capital; plantation in *Gone with the Wind*
Saar	European river		
Sac	Algonquin Indian; pouch	tare	biblical weed; allowance
sago	starch; pudding	tarn	lake; pool
samp	cereal; maize; pudding	taro	edible root
sans	without (French)	tat	make lace; crochet
sari	Indian dress	tec	detective
sego	edible bulb	tela	membrane; tissue
sera	antitoxins; evening (Italian)	tele	from a distance (prefix)
serac	glacial ridge; white cheese	tern	gull
sere	dry; parched	Terra	earth goddess
serif	part of printer's letter	Thalia	one of the Graces
seta	bristle	Thetis	Achilles' mother
Seth	biblical patriarch; Adam's son	tia	aunt (Spanish)
shay	carriage	tic	spasm
Shem	biblical patriarch	tio	uncle (Spanish)
shiv	knife	Tioga	New York county
Sikh	Hindu soldier	toga	Roman cloak
sine	trigonometry function	tole	lacquered metalware
sire	lord; father; beget	Toltec	Mexican tribe

tome	large volume	viz	namely
tong	Chinese secret society	voce	voice (Italian)
tor	craggy hill; pea	vole	rodent
tort	civil wrong		
torte	rich cake	WAC	female GI
tret	waste allowance	Waco	Texas city
Triton	Greek god of sea	wadd	black ocher
Truk	Island in Carolines	wadi	dry river bed
tsar	Russian despot	wale	cloth ridge
tsun	Chinese length	wang	Dutch East Indies weight
tun	vat; cask	weft	web; yarn
tutu	New Zealand shrub, ballet skirt	weir	fish trap
tyro	novice	wen	cyst; old English letter
		woad	dyestuff
über	over (German)	Wodan	Norse god
uca	crab	Woden	Norse god
uke	ukelele	Wotan	Norse god
ule	rubber tree	xema	Arctic gull
ulex	spine shrub	Xenia	Ohio city
Ulm	German city	xeno	foreign (prefix)
ulna	elbow bone	xeres	wine; sherry
unde	wavy; lined (heraldry)	Xosa	Kaffir tribe
ungula	hoof; claw	Xtian	Christian
Ural	Russian river; range		
Urd	Norse goddess of destiny	yaba	cabbage tree
urde	key-shaped (heraldry)	yak	ox
Uri	Swiss commune	Yalu	Korean river
Uria	Bathsheba's husband	yamp	tuber
ursa	bear	yapa	palm-leaf mat
urus	ox; aurochs	yegg	burglar
Ute	Colorado Indian	Yemen	Arabian state
Utu	Babylonian god	yen	Japanese money; urge
uvea	iris layer	yin	Chinese weight
uvic	grapelike	Ymir	Norse giant
		Yser	Belgian river
Vaal	South African river		
vair	heraldic tincture	zak	Dutch measure
vale	valley; glen; farewell	zany	nutty; crazy
vari	diverse (prefix)	Zara	Italian province
vasa	ducts	zee	final letter; zed
Veda	Hindu bible	Zen	Buddhist sect
vega	meadow	zero	nothing; cipher
veld	South African grassland	zeta	Greek letter
Venus	Roman goddess of love	Zeus	chief Olympian god
vert	green	Zion	hill; heaven
Vesta	goddess of hearth	Zulu	Bantu tribe
Vishnu	Hindu god	Zuni	Pueblo Indian
vita	life (Latin)	zwei	two (German)
vite	quick (French)		
vivo	lively (music)		

Commonly Misspelled Words

See also "Commonly Misused Words" on page 367.

abscess	calendar	dessert/desert	glacier
accept/except	cantaloupe	devise	government
accessory	capital/capitol	diaphragm	grammar
accidentally	cashmere	diarrhea	grease
accommodate	caterpillar	dictionary	guarantee
accompany	ceiling	diphtheria	guess
accrue	cellar	disappear	guest
acquaintance	cemetery	disappoint	
acquire	cereal/serial	dispel	handkerchief
address	chamois	dissatisfied	harass
affect/effect	chandelier		height
aisle/isle	changeable	effect/affect	heir
allege	chaperon(e)	eighth	hemorrhage
all right	chauffeur	embarrass	hygiene
already	chief	embezzle	hypocrisy
amateur	cinnamon	environment	
analogous	circuit	equipped	idol/idle
antarctic	circumference	erroneous	incite/insight
antecedent	cocoa	especially	independence
apparent	colonel/kernel	etiquette	indict
arctic	committee	exaggerate	indispensable
argument	compliment/	exceed	infinitesimal
arithmetic	complement	excel	irresistible
asparagus	comptroller	existence	isthmus
asthma	concede	expense	its/it's
athletic	conceive		
attendance	conscientious	familiar	judgment
attorney	conscious	fascinate	
auxiliary	consensus	fatigue	khaki
	consignment	February	
banana	convenient	fiancé	laboratory
baptize	coquette	fiancée	larynx
bargain	corduroy	financier	laugh
battalion	correspondent	foreclosure	league
bazaar	cough	forehead	library
beginning	counterfeit	foreign	license
believe	crucifixion	foreword/forward	licorice
benign		formerly/formally	literature
biscuit	debt	forth/fourth	lose/loose
bizarre	definite	fragile	lying
bookkeeper	dependent	freight	
buoyant	design		mackerel
bureau	desirable	gauge	maintenance
burglar	desperately	gingham	malign

maneuver
manual
mathematics
mattress
minuscule
mischief
missionary
misspell
misstate
molasses
mortgage
mosquitoes

necessary
neighbor
niece
noticeable
nuisance

obedience
occasion
occur
occurred
o'clock
offense
omitted

parallel
parliament
phenomenon
physician
plaid

pneumonia
politically
porcelain
possess
potatoes
prairie
precede/proceed
preferred
principle/principal
privilege
probably
protégé
protégée
pseudonym
psychology
ptomaine

quiet/quite

rarefy
raspberry
receipt
receive
recess
recognize
recommend
reference
remittance
rendezvous
repellent
repentance
reservoir

résumé
reverence
rhythm
ridiculous

sacrilege
sacrilegious
sandwich
satire/satyr
scissors
secretary
seize
separately
siege
sieve
similar
sincerely
soliloquy
special
squirrel
stationary/stationery
straight/strait
strengthen
succeed
success
suit/suite
superintendent
supersede
susceptible
synagogue
syringe

tariff

temperance
tenement
than/then
their/there/they're
threshold
to/too/two
tobacco
tomatoes
tragedy
truly
Tuesday

usually

vaccinate
vacuum
villain
vinegar

warrant
Wednesday
weird
wholly
whose/who's
withhold

yolk
your/you're

zephyr

COMMON PHRASES: MAJOR EUROPEAN LANGUAGES

English	French	German	Italian	Spanish
Hello/good day	Bonjour	Guten Tag	Buon giorno	Buenos días/Hola
Please	Sî'l vous plait	Bitte	Prego/per favore	Con su permiso/ por favor
Thank you	Merci	Danke schön	Grazie	Gracias
Excuse me/ pardon me	Excusez-moi/ pardonnez-moi	Entschuldigen Sie mir	Scusi	Pardóneme
Yes	Oui	Ja	Si	Sí
No	Non	Nein	No	No
Goodbye/so long	Au revoir/ à bientôt	Auf wiedersehen	Arrivederci	Adios/hasta la vista

Frequently Used Foreign Words and Phrases

à bas (F)	down with
ab initio (L)	from the beginning
ab ovo usque ad mala (L)	from soup to nuts (lit., "from the egg to the apples")
ab urbe condita (L)	from the founding of the city (Rome, 753 B.C.)
a cappella (It)	in the church style (vocally)
adagio (It)	slowly
ad astra per aspera (L)	to the stars through difficulties
ad eundum (L)	to the same degree
ad hoc (L)	for a particular purpose (lit., "to this")
ad infinitum (L)	without end
ad libitum (L)	ad lib, freely (lit., "to pleasure")
ad nauseam (L)	to the point of disgust
aere perennius (L)	more durable than bronze
aficionado (Sp)	enthusiast, fan
alea jacta est (L)	the die is cast
alfresco (It)	in the open air
alma mater (L)	old school (lit., "fostering mother")
aloha (Hw)	greeting or farewell
amor con amor se paga (Sp)	one good turn deserves another (lit., "love is repaid with love")
amor vincit omnia (L)	love conquers all
ancien régime (Fr)	the old regime (pre-French revolution)
anno domini; A.D. (L)	in the year of the Lord
annus mirabilis (L)	wonderful year
a posteriori (L)	inductive (lit. "from what comes after")
après moi, le déluge (Fr)	after me, the deluge
a priori (L)	deductive (lit., "from what comes before")
arma virumque cano (L)	I sing of arms and the man (Virgil)
ars gratia artis (L)	art for art's sake
ars longa, vita brevis (L)	art is long, life is short
au contraire (Fr)	on the contrary
au courant (Fr)	up to date, contemporary
au naturel (Fr)	nude, plain
aurea mediocritas (L)	golden mean
autre temps, autre mœurs (Fr)	other times, other customs
avant-garde (Fr)	forward, advanced; vanguard
ave atque vale (L)	hail and farewell
beau geste (Fr)	noble gesture
beau idéal (Fr)	highest ideal
bête noire (Fr)	someone or something strongly detested (lit., "black beast")
biensénce (Fr)	decorum, mannerliness
billet doux (Fr)	love letter
Blitzkreig (Gr)	lightning war

bon marché (Fr)	inexpensive (lit., "good market")
bon mot (Fr)	clever turn of phrase
bonne chance (Fr)	good luck
bon vivant (Fr)	partygoer; one who enjoys life
bon voyage (Fr)	good journey
campesino (Sp)	peasant, farmer
canard (Fr)	insult, hoax (lit., "duck")
carpe diem (L)	seize the day
carte blanche (Fr)	free hand, no restrictions (lit., "white card")
cause célèbre (Fr)	scandal; notorious incident
caveat emptor (L)	let the buyer beware
c'est la vie (Fr)	that's life
ceteris paribus (L)	other things being equal
chacun à son gout (Fr)	each to his own taste
chef d'œuvre (Fr)	masterpiece
cherchez la femme (Fr)	look for the woman
chutzpah (Y)	gall, daring
ciao (It)	goodbye, so long
circa (c., ca.)	about, approximately
cogito ergo sum (L)	I think, therefore I am
cognoscenti (It)	intellectuals; those in the know
comédie de mœurs (Fr)	comedy of manners
comme il faut (Fr)	proper, appropriate
con mucho gusto (Sp)	with pleasure
corpus delicti (L)	evidence (lit., "body of the crime")
coup de grâce (Fr)	final blow
coup d'état (F)	overthrow of government
credo quia absurdum (L)	I believe because it is absurd
cui bono? (L)	to whose benefit?
cul de sac (Fr)	dead end (lit., "end of the bag")
cum grano salis (L)	with a grain of salt
de capo (It)	from the top
déclassé (Fr)	fallen in social standing
décolletage (Fr)	low-cut style
de facto (L)	in fact
de gustibus non est disputandum (L)	there is no arguing about taste
de jure (L)	in law
demi-monde (Fr)	underworld; other side of the tracks
de mortuis nil nisi bonum (L)	of the dead [say nothing] but good
Deo gratias (L)	thanks be to God
Deo volente (L)	God willing
dernier cri (Fr)	the last word
déshabillé (Fr)	carelessly or scantily dressed
deus ex machina (L)	desperate or contrived solution (lit., "god from the machine")
Ding an sich (Gr)	the thing in itself
dolce far niente (It)	sweet idleness
Doppelgänger (Gr)	phantom double

Drang nach Osten (Gr)	drive toward the east
dum spiro spero (L)	while there's life, there's hope
embarras de richesses (Fr)	embarrassment of riches
enfant terrible (Fr)	prodigy
en passant (Fr)	in passing; by the way
entre nous (Fr)	privately, between us
épater le bourgeois (Fr)	shock the middle class
e pluribus unum (L)	from many, one
ersatz (Gr)	fake, imitation
et cetera (etc.) (L)	and others
Eureka! (Gk)	I've found it!
ex cathedra (L)	with high authority (lit., "from the chair")
exempli gratia (e.g.) (L)	by way of example
ex post facto (L)	after the fact
fait accompli (Fr)	accomplished fact
faute de mieux (Fr)	for want of something better
faux pas (Fr)	social error (lit, "false step")
femme fatale (Fr)	alluring, dangerous woman
fin de siècle (Fr)	end of century; decadent
flagrante delicto (L)	caught in the act (lit., "with the crime blazing")
gaudeamus igitur (L)	let us therefore rejoice
glasnost (R)	openness
gnothi seauton (Gk)	know yourself
gonif (Y)	thief
goy	gentile
habeas corpus (L)	writ requiring a court appearance (lit., "[that] you have the body")
haut monde (Fr)	high society
hoi polloi (Gk)	common people, mob
homo lupus homini (L)	man is a wolf to man
honi soi qui mal y pense (Fr)	shame to him who thinks evil of it
hubris (Gk)	overweening pride, arrogance
idée fixe (Fr)	fixed idea, obsession
id est (i.e.) (L)	that is
infra dignitatem (infra dig.) (L)	beneath one's dignity
in loco parentis (L)	in the place of parents
in medias res (L)	in the middle of things
in vino veritas (L)	in wine, truth
ipso facto (L)	by the fact itself
joie de vivre (Fr)	good spirits, exuberance (lit., "joy of living")
jus gentium (L)	law of nations
kamikaze (J)	suicide pilot (lit, "divine wind")
klutz (Y)	clumsy person

kvetch (Y)	complain, carp
la belle dame sans merci (Fr)	the beautiful woman without mercy
laissez-faire (Fr)	noninterference (lit., "let [people] do [as they wish]")
lapsus linguae (L)	slip of the tongue
Lebensraum (Gr)	living room; elbow room
lèse majesté	treason
l'état, c'est moi (Fr)	I am the state
lingua franca (L)	common language (lit., "French tongue")
macher (Y)	big shot
magnum opus (L)	major work
mañana (Sp)	tomorrow
manqué (Fr)	failed
maven (Y)	expert, authority
mazel tov (Y)	congratulations
mea culpa (L)	my fault
memento mori (L)	reminder of death
mens sana in corpore sano (L)	a sound mind in a sound body
meshuggah (Y)	crazy
mirabile dictu (L)	amazingly (lit., "remarkable to say")
modus operandi (M.O.) (L)	method of operation
morituri te salutamus (L)	we who are about to die salute you
mutatis mutandis	with the needed changes made
ne plus ultra (L)	the best
n'est-ce pas? (Fr)	isn't that true?
noblesse oblige (Fr)	the responsibility of noble birth
nom de plume (Fr)	pen name
non sequitur (L)	something that does not follow
nosh (Y)	nibble, eat
nota bene (N.B.) (L)	note well
nunc aut nunquam (L)	now or never
obiter dictum (L)	something said in passing; a peripheral comment
o tempora, o mores! (L)	o the times, o the customs!
panem et circenses (L)	bread and circuses
par excellence (Fr)	above all, preeminently
par exemple (Fr)	for example
pari passu (L)	at an equal pace
parvenu (Fr)	newcomer, upstart; noveau riche
passim (L)	here and there
per diem (L)	by the day
per favore (It)	please
persona non grata (L)	unwanted person
pièce de résistance (Fr)	showpiece item
pied à terre (Fr)	in-town apartment; temporary lodging
plus ça change, plus c'est la même chose (Fr)	the more things change, the more they are the same

pons asinorum (L)	insoluble problem (lit., "bridge of asses")
por favor (Sp)	please
prego (It)	please; you're welcome
prima facie (L)	on the face of it; at first sight
primus inter pares (L)	first among equals
prix fixe (Fr)	fixed price
pro bono publico (L)	for the public good
quid pro quo (L)	fair exchange; tit for tat
quién sabe? (Sp)	who knows?
quod erat demonstrandum (Q.E.D.) (L)	as has been demonstrated
quod vide (q.v.) (L)	which see (used as cross-reference)
raison d'être (Fr)	reason for being
rara avis (L)	rarity (lit., "rare bird")
reductio ad absurdum (L)	reduction to absurdity (in logical argument)
répondez s'il vous plaît (R.S.V.P.) (Fr)	respond if you please
requiescat in pace (R.I.P.)	rest in peace
salaam aleicham (A)	peace
sancta sanctorum (L)	holy of holies
sangfroid (Fr)	aplomb; composure
savoir faire (Fr)	social savvy (lit., "to know what to do")
schadenfreude	pleasure taken in problems of others
schlemiel (Y)	unlucky person, loser
schmaltz (Y)	excessive sentimentality
schtick (Y)	gimmick; a performer's idiosyncracy
semper fidelis (L)	always faithful
shalom (H)	greeting or farewell (lit., "peace")
sic (L)	thus
sic semper tyrannis (L)	thus always to tyrants
sic transit gloria mundi (L)	thus passes the glory of the world
sine qua non (L)	something indispensable (lit., "without which not")
sotto voce (It)	softly (lit., "in a soft voice")
status quo (L)	current state of affairs
Sturm und Drang (Gr)	storm and stress
sui generis (L)	one of a kind, unique
tabula rasa (L)	clean slate (lit., "erased tablet")
tant mieux (Fr)	all the better
tant pis (Fr)	all the worse
tempus fugit (L)	time flies
terra firma (L)	solid ground
terra incognita (L)	unknown territory
tête-à-tête (Fr)	intimate conversation (lit., "head to head")
tout de suite (Fr)	immediately
tout le monde (Fr)	everyone
tovarish (R)	comrade

trompe l'œil (Fr)	illusionary art or decor (lit., "fool the eye")	
vade mecum (L)	handbook, guide (lit., "go with me")	
vaya con Dios (Sp)	go with God	
veni, vedi, vici (L)	I came, I saw, I conquered	
verboten (Gr)	forbidden	
verbum sapienti sat (L)	a word to the wise is enough	
volte-face (Fr)	about face, reversal	
vox clamantis in deserto (L)	a voice crying in the desert	
vox populi, vox Dei (L)	the voice of the people is the voice of God	
Wanderjahre (Gr)	year of travel	
Wanderlust (Gr)	desire to travel	
Weltanschauung (Gr)	philosophy, outlook	
Weltschmerz (Gr)	world-weariness (lit., "world pain")	
Wunderkind (Gr)	prodigy	
yenta (Y)	gossip or busybody	
Zeitgeist (Gr)	spirit of the times	

Key to abbreviations:

A	Arabic	H	Hebrew	lit.	literally
Fr	French	Hw	Hawaiian	Sp	Spanish
Gk	Greek	It	Italian	R	Russian
Gr	German	L	Latin	Y	Yiddish

94 Acceptable Two-Letter Scrabble® Words

aa	ay	er	is	na	ox	un
ad	ba	es	it	ne	oy	up
ae	be	et	jo	no	pa	us
ag	bi	ex	ka	nu	pe	ut
ah	bo	fa	la	od	pi	we
ai	by	go	li	oe	re	wo
al	da	ha	lo	of	sh	xi
am	de	he	ma	oh	si	xu
an	do	hi	me	om	so	ya
ar	ef	hm	mi	on	ta	ye
as	eh	ho	mm	op	ti	
at	el	id	mo	or	to	
aw	em	if	mu	os	uh	
ax	en	in	my	ow	um	

RECURRENT LETTERS OF THE ALPHABET

The normal frequencies with which letters of the alphabet occur from most to least frequent: E, T, A, O, I, N, S, H, R, D, L, U, C, M, P, F, Y, W, G, B, V, K, J, X, Z, Q.

OXYMORON: A PAIRING OF CONTRADICTORY OR INCONGRUOUS WORDS

bittersweet	home office	passively aggressive
clearly confused	jumbo shrimp	randomly organized
cruel kindness	linear curve	same difference
definite maybe	liquid gas	sweet sorrow
eloquent silence	nonalcoholic beer	taped live
idiot savant	nondairy creamer	war games
genuine imitation	old news	working vacation
good grief	open secret	

Acronyms

Acronyms are pronounceable formations made by combining the initial letters or syllables of a string of words.

ACTION	American Council to Improve Our Neighborhoods
AID	Agency for International Devleopment; American Insitute of Decorators; Amy Intelligence Department
AIDS	acquired immune deficiency syndrome
ALCOA	Aluminum Company of America
AMEX	American Express Company; American Stock Exchange
ARC	AIDS-related complex
ARCO	Atlantic Richfield Company
ASCAP	American Society of Composers, Authors and Publishers
AWOL	absent without leave
BAM	Brooklyn Academy of Music; Basic Access Method
BART	Bay Area Rapid Transit
BASE	Bank-Americard Service Exchange
BASIC	Beginner's All-purpose Symbolic Instruction Code (computer language)
BASS	Bass Anglers Sportsman Society
BIB	Bureau of International Broadcasting
BIZNET	American Business Network (database of Chamber of Commerce)
BOLD	Bibliographic On-Line Display (document retrieval system)
CALM	Citizens Against Legalized Murder
CARE	Cooperative for American Relief Everywhere
CAT (scan)	computerized axial tomography
CLASSMATE	Computer Language to Aid and Stimulate Scientific, Mathematical and Technical Education
COBOL	Common Business-Oriented Language

COMEX	Commodity Exchange (New York)
CONOCO	Continental Oil Company
CONUS	Continental United States
CORE	Congress of Racial Equality
CURE	Citizens United for Racial Equality
DAM	Dayton Art Museum; Denver Art Museum
DELCO	Dayton Engineering Laboratory Company
DISCO	Defense Industrial Security Clearing Office
DOS	disk operating system; digital operating system
DYNAMO	Dynamic Action Management Operation
EARS	Electronic Airborn Reaction System; Electronically Agile Radar System; Emergency Airborne Reaction System
ELECTRA	Electrical, Electronics and Communications Trade Association
ENDEX	Environmental Data Index
EPCOT	Experimental Prototype Community of Tomorrow
EXIMBANK	Export-Import Bank of the United States
FEDLINK	Federal Library Information Network
FEW	Federally Employed Women
FICA	Federal Insurance Contributions Act (Social Security)
FLIP	Flexible Loan Insurance Program; floating instrument platform
FORTRAN	formula translator (programming language)
GAG	Graphic Arts Guild
GARB	Garment and Allied Industries Requirements Board
GATT	General Agreement on Tariffs and Trade
GIPSY	General Information Processing
GLAD	Gay and Lesbian Advocates and Defenders
GMAT	Graduate Management Admission Test
GRAD	Graduate Resume Accumulation and Distribution
GUPCO	Gulf Petroleum Corporation
HALF	Human Animal Liberation Front
HART	Honolulu Area Rapid Transit
HEAL	Health Education Assistance Loans
INLAW	infantry laser weapon
INTERMARC	International Machine-Readable Catalog
INTERPOL	International Criminal Police Organization
INTERTELL	International Intelligence Legion
IRA	individual retirement account; Irish Republican Army
JOBS	Job Opportunities in the Business Sector
JUMPS	Joint Uniform Military Pay System
LEAP	Loan and Educational Aid Program
LILCO	Long Island Lighting Company
LORAN	Long-range Aid to Navigation
LSAT	Law School Admission Test
MACOM	major Army command
MAD	mutually assured destruction
MADD	Mothers Against Drunk Driving
MARC	machine-reading cataloging
MASH	mobile Army surgical unit
MOMA	Museum of Modern Art (New York)

NAM	Network access machine; National Association of Manufacturers; National Air Museum
NAPA	National Automoative Parts Association; National Police Officers' Association of America
NARAD	Navy Research and Development
NARCO	United National Narcotics Commission
NASA	National Aeronautics and Space Administration
NASCAR	National Association of Stock Car Auto Racing
NASDAQ	National Association of Securities Dealers Automatic Quotation
NATO	North Atlantic Treaty Organization
NECCO	New England Confectionary Company
NOMAD	Navy oceanographic and meteorological device
NORAD	North American Air Defense
NOW	National Organization for Women
OASIS	Overseas Access Service for Information Systems
ODECO	Ocean Drilling and Exploration Company
ODESY	On-Line Data Entry System
OPEC	Organization of Petroleum Exporting Countries
OXFAM	Oxford Famine Relief
PAC	political action committee; Pacific Air Command
PATCO	Port Authority Transit Corporation
PATH	Port Authority Trans-Hudson
PEN	Poets, Playwrights, Editors, Essayists, and Novelists
PERT	program evaluation and review technique
PET	parent effectiveness training
PIN	personal identification number; Police Information Network
PIRG	public interest research group
QUICKTRAN	Quick FORTRAN (computer language)
RADAR	radio detecting and ranging
RAM	random-access memory
READ	real-time electronic access and display
RIF	Reading Is Fundamental
ROM	read-only memory
ROTC	Reserve Officer's Training Corps
SADD	Students Against Drunk Driving
SAFE	system for automated flight efficiency
SALT	strategic arms limitation talks
START	Strategic Arms Reduction Talks
SUNOCO	Sun Oil Company
SEATO	Southeast Asia Treaty Organization
TAC	Tactical Air Command
UNESCO	United Nations Educational, Social, and Cultural Organization
UNICEF	United Nations International Children's Emergency Fund (now shortened to United Nations Children's Fund)
UNIVAC	universal automatic computer
VISTA	Volunteers in Service to America
WAC	Women's Army Corps
WASP	white Anglo-Saxon Protestant
WAVES	Women Accepted for Volunteer Emergency Service (Navy)
WHO	World Health Organization

WIN	work incentive program
WISE	World Information Systems Exchange
WUDO	Western European Defense Organization
YUPPIE	young urban professional
ZIP	zone improvement plan (U.S. Postal Service)

PALINDROMES

A palindrome can be a single word, a verse, a sentence, a series of sentences, or a number that reads the same forward and backward. People have been creating palindromes in all languages since at least as early as the third century B.C. Palindromic sentences often become jokes when meanings are ascribed to them and when punctuation is added. For example, the two best-known English palindromes are "Able was I ere I saw Elba," which was not written by but could have been uttered by Napoleon, and "Madam, I'm Adam," which is fun to think of as the first introduction. Note that "madam" alone is a palindromic word, but sentences are more amusing:

> Enid and Edna dine.
> A man, a plan, a canal, Panama!
> Draw, O Caesar, erase a coward.
> Al lets Dell call Ed Stella.
> Dennis sinned.
> Ma is a nun, as I am.
> Naomi, did I moan?
> Niagara, O roar again!
> He lived as a devil, eh?

And here is a palindromic conversation between two owls:

> "Too hot to hoot!"
> "Too hot to woo!"
> "Too wot?"
> "Too hot to hoot!"
> "To woo!"
> "Too wot?"
> "To hoot! Too hot to hoot!"

Greek Prefixes

Prefix	Meaning in English	Prefix	Meaning in English
a	not	an	not
acantho	spiny, thorny	ana	again, thorough, thoroughly
acous	hearing		
acro	top, tip	andro	man
adeno	gland	anem(o)	wind
aero	air, gas	anthropo	man
allo	other	anti	against
amphi	both, around	apo	away
amylo	starch	arch(i)	chief

Prefix	Meaning in English	Prefix	Meaning in English
arche(o), archae(o)	old, ancient	dactylo	finger
arthro	joint	deca	ten
aster, astro	star	dendro	tree
atmo	vapor	dermo, dermato	skin
auto	self	deutero	second
azo	nitrogen	di(s)	apart
		dia	through
baro	weight	dino	terrible
batho, bathy	deep	diplo	double
biblio	book	dodeca	twelve
bio	life	dyna, dynamo	force, power
blepharo	eyelid	dys	evil, difficult
bracchio	arm		
brachy	short	echino	spiny
branchio	gills	ecto	outside, external
broncho	throat	ef	out
		ele, em, en	in, into
		encephalo	brain
caco	evil	ennea	nine
cardio	heart	entero	gut
carpo	fruit	ento	inside, interior
cath, cato	down, thorough, thoroughly	entomo	insect
		eo	dawn, early
ceno	common	eph, epi	on
cephalo	head	ergo	work
cero	wax	erythro	red
chilo	lip	ethno	race, nation
chiro	hand	eu	good
chloro	green	ex	out
chole, cholo	bile	exo	outside, external
chondro	cartilage		
choreo	dance	galacto	milk
choro	country	gam(o)	copulation, together
chrom(at)o	color	gastro	stomach
chrono	time	geo	earth, land
chryso	gold	geronto	old age
cleisto	closed	glosso	tongue
clino	slope	gluc, glyc	sweet
cocci	berry-shaped	glypto, glyph	carving
coela	stomach	gnath(o)	jaw
conio	dust	gon(o)	reproduction (sexual)
copro	excrement	grapho	writing
cosmo	universe	gymno	nude, naked
cranio	skull	gynec(o), gynaec(o)	woman
cryo	cold		
crypto	hidden	haemato	blood
cteno	comb, rake	hagio	holy
cymo	wave	halo	salt, sea
cysto	bladder	haplo	simple
cyto	cell	hecto	hundred
		helico	spiral

Prefix	Meaning in English	Prefix	Meaning in English
helio	sun	myo	muscle
hema	blood	necro	dead body
hemi	half	neo	new
hepato	liver	nepho	cloud
hepta	seven	nephro	kidney
hetero	different	neuro	nerve
hexa	six	noso	sickness
histo	tissue	noto	back (of body)
hodo	path, way	nycto	night
holo	whole, complete		
homeo	similar, like	octa, octo	eight
homo	same	odonto	tooth
hydro	water	oligo	few
hyeto	rain	ombro	rain
hygro	wet	oneiro	dream
hylo	matter	onto	being
hymeno	membrane	oo	egg
hyper	above	ophio	snake
hypno	sleep	opthalm(o)	eye
hypo	under	ornitho	bird
hypso	high	oro	mouth
hystero	womb	ortho	straight
		osteo	bone
iatro	medicine	oto	ear
ichthyo	fish	oxy	sharp
iso	equal		
		pachy	thick
		paleo, palaeo	ancient, old
kerato	horn	pan	all
kinesi, kineto	movement	para	close, beside
		patho	suffering, disease
lepto	slender	pedo	child
leuko	white	penta	five
litho	stone	peri	around, very
logo	word, oral	petro	stone
lyo, lysi	dissolving	phago	eating
		phlebo	vein
macro	large	phono	sound
malaco	soft	photo	light
mega, megalo	great	phreno	brain
melano	black	phyco	seaweed
mero	part	phyllo	leaf
meso	middle	phylo	species
meta	beyond, after, changed	physio	nature
metro	measure	phyto	plant
micro	small	picro	bitter
miso	hatred	piezo	pressure
mono	one, single	pleuro	side (of body)
morpho	shape	pluto	riches
myelo	spinal cord	pneumato	breath, spirit
mylo	fungus	pneumo	lung

Words **351**

Prefix	Meaning in English	Prefix	Meaning in English
polio	gray matter	stato	position
poly	many	stauro	cross
pro	before, forward	steno	short, narrow
proto	first	stereo	solid
pseudo	false	stomato	mouth
psycho	mind, spirit, soul	stylo	pillar
psychro	cold	sy, syl, sym, syn	with
ptero	wing		
pyo	pus	tachy	rapid
pyro	fire	tauto	same
		tele	distant
rheo	flow	teleo	final
rhino	nose	telo	distant, final
rhizo	root	thalasso	sea
		thanato	death
sacchro	sugar	theo	god
sapro	decompse	thermo	heat
sarco	flesh	thio	sulfur
scato	excrement	toco	child, birth
schisto, schizo	split	topo	place
sclero	hard	toxico	poison
seleno	moon	trachy	rough
sidero	iron		
somato	body	xeno	foreign
speleo	cave		
spermato	seed	zoo	living
sphygmo	pulse	zygo	double
splanchno	guts		

Greek Suffixes

Suffix	Meaning in English	Prefix	Meaning in English
algia	pain	drome, dromous	run (race)
androus	man		
archy	rule, government	emia	blood
biosis	life	gamy	marriage
blast	bud	gen(ous), geny,	
branch	gills	gony	giving birth to, bearing
		gnathous	jaw
carpous	fruit	gnomy, gnosis	knowledge
cele	hollow	gon	angle
cephalic, cephalous	head	gonium	seed
chrome	color	gram, graph(y)	writing
coccous	berry-shaped		
cracy, crat	rule, government	hedral, hedron	side, sided
dendron	tree	iasis	disease
derm	skin	iatrics, iatry	medical treatment
		itis	inflammation

Prefix	Meaning in English	Prefix	Meaning in English
kinesis	movement	phyllous	leaf
lepsy	seizure, fit	phyte	plant
lith	stone	plasia, plasis	growth
logy	science of, list	plasm	matter
lysise, lyte	dissolving	plast	cell
machy	battle, fight	plegia	paralysis
mancy, mantic	foretelling	plerous	wing
mania(c)	craving		
mere, merous	part	rrhagia, rrhagic,	
meter, metry	measure	rrhea	flow
morphic, morphous	shape		
mycete	fungus	saur	lizard
nomy	science of, law of	scope, scopy	observation
odont	tooth	sect, section	cutting
odynia	pain	soma, some	body
oid	like, similar	sophy	wisdom
oma	tumor	sperm, spermous	seed
opia	eye, sight	stichous	row
opsia	sight	stome, stomous	mouth
opsis	appearance		
pathy	suffering, disease	taxis, taxy	order
phage, phagous	eating	tomy	cutting
phany	manifestation	trophy	feed
phobe, phobia	fear	tropous, tropy	turned
phone, phony	sound		

Latin Prefixes

Prefix	Meaning in English	Prefix	Meaning in English
a, abs	from	cis	near, on the near side of
ac, ad, af, ag, al, an, ap, as, at	to, toward	co, col, com, con, cor	with, thorough, thoroughly
alti, alto	high	contra	against
ambi	both	costo	rib
ante	before	cruci	cross
api	bee	cupro	copper, bronze
aqui	water		
arbori	tree	de	not, down
audio	hearing	deci	tenth
avi	bird	demi	half
		denti	tooth
bacci	berry	di(s)	apart
brevi	short	digit(i)	finger
		dorsi, dorso	back (of body)
calci	lime		
centi	hundred	e, ec, ef	out
cerebro	brain	equi	equal
cervico	neck		
circum	around		
cirro	curl		

Prefix	Meaning in English	Prefix	Meaning in English
extra	outside, external	per	through, very
		pinni	fin, web
febri	fever	pisci	fish
ferri, ferro	iron	plano	flat
fissi	split	plumbo	lead (metal)
fluvio	river	pluvio	rain
		post	after
gemmi	bud	pre	before
		preter	beyond
igni	fire	primi	first
il, im, in	not, against, in, into, on	pro	for, forward
inguino	groin	pulmo	lung
inter	between		
intra, intro	inside, interior	quadri	four
ir	not, against, in, into, on	quinque	five
juxta	close, near, beside	re	again
		recti	straight
labio	lip	reni	kidney
lacto	milk	retro	backward
ligni	wood		
luni	moon	sacro	dedicated
		sangui	blood
magni	great	se	apart
mal(e)	bad, evil	sebi, sebo	fatty
multi	many	septi	seven
		sidero	star
naso	nose	somni	sleep
nati	birth	spiro	breath
nocti	night	stelli	star
		sub, suc, suf,	
ob, oc	against	sum, sup	under
octa, octo	eight	super, supra	above
oculo	eye		
of, op	against	terri	land, earth
oleo	oil	trans	through, on the far
omni	all		side of
oro	mouth		
ossi	bone	ultra	beyond
ovi, ovo	egg	uni	one, single
pari	equal	vari(o)	different

Latin Suffixes

Suffix	Meaning in English	Suffix	Meaning in English
cidal, cide	kill	grade	walking
fid	split	pennale	wing
fugal, fuge	run away from	vorous	eating

Additional Sources of Information

Berlitz, Charles. *Native Tongues.* Putnam Publishing Group, 1984.

Betteridge, Harold T. *Cassell's German Dictionary,* rev. ed. Macmillan, 1978.

Buchanan-Brown, John, et al. *Le Mot Juste: A Dictionary of Classical and Foreign Words and Phrases.* Vintage Books, 1981.

Byrne, Josefa Heifetz. *Mrs. Byrne's Dictionary of Unusual, Obscure and Preposterous Words.* Vintage Books, 1981.

Cassell's Italian Dictionary. Macmillan, 1977.

Chapman, Robert L., ed. *New Dictionary of American Slang.* HarperCollins, 1987.

Chapman, Robert L., ed. *Roget's International Thesaurus,* 5th ed. Harper & Row, 1992.

Ciardi, John. *The Complete Browser's Dictionary: The Best of John Ciardi's Two Browser's Dictionaries in a Single Compendium of Curious Expressions and Intriguing Facts.* Harper & Row, 1988.

De Sola, Ralph. *Abbreviations Dictionary,* 7th ed. Elsevier, 1986.

Ehrlich, Eugene, and Raymond Hand, Jr. *NBC Handbook of Pronunciation.* HarperPerennial, 1991.

Girard, Denis, ed. *Cassell's French Dictionary.* Macmillan, 1977.

Grambs, David. *Random House Dictionary for Writers and Readers.* Random House, 1990.

Laird, Charlton, ed. *Webster's New World Thesaurus,* rev. ed. Simon & Schuster, 1985.

McCrum, Robert, et al. *The Story of English.* Sifton/Viking, 1986.

Oxford English Dictionary, 2nd ed., 20 vols. Oxford University Press, 1989.

Peers, Edgar A., ed. *Cassell's Spanish Dictionary.* Macmillan, 1978.

Random House College Dictionary, rev. ed. Random House, 1991.

Random House Dictionary of the English Language, 2nd ed. Random House, 1987.

Safire, William. *I Stand Corrected: More on Language.* Times Books, 1984.

Safire, William. *You Could Look It Up: More on Language.* Times Books, 1988.

Simpson, D. P., ed. *Cassell's Latin Dictionary.* Macmillan, 1977.

Skillin, Marjorie E., and R. Gay. *Words Into Type,* 3rd ed. Prentice Hall, 1986.

Stein, Jess, and Stuart Berg Flexner, eds. *Random House Thesaurus: College Edition.* Random House, 1984.

Urdang, Laurence. *The Random House Basic Dictionary of Synonyms and Antonyms.* Balantine, 1991.

Urdang, Laurence, ed. *The New York Times Everyday Reader's Dictionary of Misunderstood, Misused and Mispronounced Words,* rev. ed. Times Books, 1985.

Webster's Compact Rhyming Dictionary. Merriam-Webster, 1987.

Webster's Third New International Dictionary, Unabridged. Merriam-Webster, 1986.

Webster's New World Crossword Puzzle Dictionary. Simon & Schuster, 1983.

Webster's New World Dictionary, Third College Ed. Simon & Schuster, 1988.

Webster's Ninth New Collegiate Dictionary. Merriam-Webster, 1985.

Zinsser, William. *On Writing Well: An Informal Guide to Writing Nonfiction,* rev. ed. Harper & Row, 1985.

13

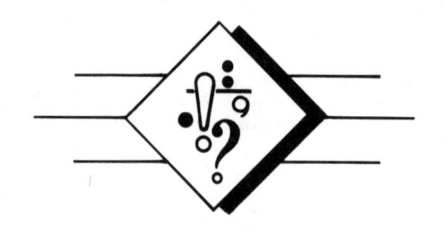

Grammar and Punctuation

The Parts of Speech / *357*

Turning Words into Sentences / *358*

Punctuation / *360*

Spelling Guidelines / *364*

Alphabetization / *364*

American English and British English / *365*

Commonly Misused Words / *367*

Four Common Grammatical Problems / *368*

Additional Sources of Information / *369*

The purpose of language is to communicate thoughts and ideas from one person to another. To do this effectively, all those using a given language must do so in the same way, putting words and sentences together in similar fashion so they are readily understood by anyone familiar with that language.

This is not to say that everyone must write the same sentence to communicate the same concept. On the contrary, American English is so varied that it is possible to express the same basic idea in any number of ways. And each of those ways can be equally correct.

What makes a variety of different sentences equally valid is grammar. Grammar is a set of rules that define the ways words can and cannot be used. These rules are not arbitrarily imposed on the language by English teachers or grammarians; they have, instead, grown out of the language itself and can be observed in action in the everyday speech and writing of those who grew up speaking and writing it.

Much of grammar is intuitive and can be understood by anyone who has spoken American English for any length of time, even without a knowledge of the rules. For instance, the sentence *You be not home go yet* is readily recognized as incorrect even without knowledge of the rules of word order.

But because American English is a complex and difficult language, it is sometimes helpful to have the rules at hand in case logic and intuition fail. What follows, then, are the basics of grammar, spelling, punctuation, and alphabetization for American English. The information presented here is by no means exhaustive, and, because language is a constantly changing thing, there can never be a "final word" as to what is correct and what is incorrect. Still, this guide should help provide a start in understanding grammar, usage, and punctuation.

The Parts of Speech

The parts of speech define the ways words can be used in various contexts. Every word in the English language functions as at least one part of speech; many words can serve, at different times, as two or more parts of speech, depending on the context.

adjective A word or combination of words that modifies a noun *(blue-green, central, half-baked, temporary)*.

adverb A word that modifies a verb, an adjective, or another adverb *(slowly, obstinately, much)*.

article Any of three words used to signal the presence of a noun. *A* and *an* are known as indefinite articles; *the* is the definite article.

conjunction A word that connects other words, phrases, or sentences *(and, but, or, because)*.

interjection A word, phrase, or sound used as an exclamation and capable of standing by itself *(oh, Lord, damn, my goodness)*.

noun A word or phrase that names a person, place, thing, quality, or act *(Fred, New York, table, beauty, execution)*. A noun may be used as the subject of a verb, the object of a verb, an identifying noun, the object of a preposition, or an appositive (an explanatory phrase coupled with a subject or object).

preposition A word or phrase that shows the relationship of a noun to another noun *(at, by, in, to, from, with)*.

pronoun A word that substitutes for a noun and refers to a person, place, thing, idea, or act that was mentioned previously or that can be inferred from the context of the sentence *(he, she, it, that)*.

verb A word or phrase that expresses action, existence, or occurrence *(throw, be, happen)*. Verbs can be transitive, requiring an object (*her* in *I met her*), or intransitive, requiring only a subject (*The sun rises*). Some verbs, like *feel*, are both transitive (*Feel the fabric*) and intransitive (*I feel cold*, in which *cold* is an adjective and not an object).

Turning Words into Sentences

Individual words, even once their parts of speech are identified, do not communicate very much by themselves. They must be combined in such a way that they can convey meaning. This is done by forming sentences that combine words that have meaning in and of themselves (nouns, verbs, adjectives, adverbs, and pronouns) with those that are solely functional (conjunctions, prepositions, interjections, and articles).

There are three main types of sentences that can be constructed from these parts. Statements are sentences that tell of a fact, an occurrence, or an opinion; they provide information (*My daughter is almost three years old*). Questions are sentences that seek out information (*How old is your daughter?*). Commands are sentences that make a demand (*Tell your daughter to keep her hands off the cookies*). In addition, there are exclamations (*You're a fool!*), answers to questions (*Fine, thank you*), sounds or cries (*Yipes!*), and calls to others (*Yoo-hoo, Buzzy!*).

Once the type of sentence has been selected, the subject, verb, and identifying noun or direct and indirect objects of the sentence can be determined. Their placement within the sentence goes along with the function they perform.

Subject

A subject is a noun or pronoun that is generally the doer of the verb's action (*Herb* in the sentence *Herb kicked the ball*) or the thing being described (*The painting* in the sentence *The painting is beautiful*). It usually appears before the verb. In some cases more than one noun appears before the verb. This signifies a compound subject (*Paul and Carol* in the sentence *Paul and Carol argue only about money*).

Verb

Subject–Verb Agreement

The verb generally follows the subject in statements (*are* in the sentence *We are happy*). It is often the first word in commands (*come* in *Come over here,* in which the subject *You* is understood, though not written). The verb precedes the subject in questions (*Am* in *Am I blue?*). The verb and the subject must agree in number if the verb is one that can show number. Verbs that show number are the conjugations of *to be* and the third-person singular present tense form of verbs, which usually end in -*s* (*he shops,* but *they shop* for plural form). Both the subject and verb must be either singular (*I am*) or plural (*we are*).

A few subjects pose particularly tricky problems of subject–verb agreement. *Either* and *neither* are frequently misconstrued as plural subjects, although they should always be paired with singular verbs (*Neither of us is ready*). Other subjects, such as *none* and *pair,* can be used in singular or plural constructions, depending on their meaning. For instance, when *none* means "not one," it is singular (*None of the guests is here*); when it means "not any," it is plural (*None are more beautiful than a rose*).

Compound subjects can also pose agreement difficulties. Most of the time a compound subject is plural (*Paul and Carol are ready for vacation*). But when a compound subject expresses a thought or concept that is definitely singular, it should be followed by a singular verb (*Hitting a ball and driving it over the outfield wall is a skill few can master*).

Tense

Tense is also indicated by the verb; but with the exception of the verb *to be*, past tense forms do not show the number involved. For the verb *to be*, *was* is used for the singular in the first and third person (*I was, she was*) and *were* is employed for plurals (*they were*) and for the second person singular (*you were*). The majority of other verbs are made into past tense forms by adding *-ed*, regardless of whether the verb's action is performed by the subject (*My dog walked*). In past participles (parts of a verb that express completed action, usually in the passive voice), the verb's action is performed on the subject (*My dog was walked*).

However, a number of verbs are made into past tense forms in ways that follow no general rule at all. *Bite* becomes *bit*, *fight* becomes *fought*, *go* becomes *went*, and so on. The only rule that can be applied is the age-old maxim "when in doubt, consult a dictionary."

Objects and Identifying Nouns

There are three types of nouns that can follow the verb in most sentence constructions: direct objects, indirect objects, and identifying nouns. Each operates somewhat differently; again, relative position within the sentence is a determining factor in choosing the appropriate noun.

The most straightforward is the identifying noun. It indicates the same person or thing as the subject of the sentence and generally stands alone, without another noun present on its "side" of the verb. In the sentence *The painting is a watercolor*, *watercolor* is the identifying noun.

When a single noun appears after the verb but does not refer to the same thing as the sentence's subject, it is called the direct object. The direct object is the recipient of the verb's action. In the sentence *She repaired the radio*, *radio* is the direct object.

In sentences with two nouns following the verb, the first is generally the indirect object, the word that tells to whom or for whom the action was done. The second is the direct object, the actual recipient of the action. In the sentence *Carol gives Tyler a bath*, a *bath* is what is given (the direct object) and *Tyler*, recipient of the bath, is the indirect object.

Modifiers

There are two basic types of modifiers: single-word modifiers, which are generally adverbs or adjectives, and phrases, which are usually introduced by prepositions. Once more, position within a sentence goes along with the function of a modifier.

Adjectives, which modify nouns, often precede the nouns they modify. They serve to restrict, characterize, or further define the nouns immediately following. Thus, *great* in the sentence *You did a great job* is an adjective modifying the noun *job*.

Nouns can also be used to modify nouns. They, too, appear immediately before the noun being modified, and only their position in the sentence indicates that they are acting as modifiers rather than nouns. The noun *telephone* works as a modifier of the noun *booth* when it appears in the phrase *a telephone booth*.

When two or more adjectives each modify the noun independently, they are separated by commas (*a silly, cheerful mood*). When the first adjective modifies an idea expressed by the combination of the second adjective and the noun, no comma is used (*a pretty oil painting*). In some cases, two or more adjectives are combined, often with a hyphen, so that they function as a single adjective. In these compound adjectives, the first term modifies the second, which modifies the noun (*a high-flying airplane*).

Adverbs modify verbs, adjectives, or other adverbs or phrases. They can often be recognized by their characteristic *-ly* ending. When modifying verbs, adverbs generally appear immediately after the verbs (*quickly* in the sentence *He walked quickly through the room*). When used to modify an adjective, the adverb will immediately precede the adjective (*a swiftly moving deer*); such compounds are not hyphenated.

Phrases that modify nouns are often introduced by prepositions or pronouns. They immediately follow the nouns they modify and form an entity known as a dependent clause. While useful in defining the nouns to which they are attached, they are not essential to the sentence in the way a subject, verb, and object are. Examples of modifying phrases are *in the corner* in the sentence *The dog in the corner wagged her tail* and *who wants to know* in the sentence *Anyone who wants to know can get the information*.

Punctuation

Punctuation helps to make sense of the various parts constituting a sentence. It shows where to pause or stop, defines possession and contraction, sets off nonessential modifiers and asides, indicates excitement or interrogation, clarifies incompletion or continuation, and denotes dialogue and special terms.

Terminating Punctuation

There are four punctuation marks that signal the end of a sentence: the period (.), the question mark (?), the exclamation point (!), and the ellipsis (. . . .).

Period

The **period** is used at the end of any sentence that is not a question or an exclamation. It shows that a sentence is finished and is followed by a space and a capital letter beginning the next sentence.

Question Mark

The **question mark** is used to terminate a sentence that is a question (*How much do you think this is worth?*), to terminate a question within quoted dialogue (*"Do you like my haircut?" he asked*), or to terminate a question within a sentence (*Will the Orioles lose every game this year? is the question on the minds of fans everywhere*). The question mark is not used to set off indirect questions (*Everyone wants to know whether the Orioles will continue losing*).

Exclamation Point

The **exclamation point** terminates sentences that convey excitement (*What a finish that play has!*) or are emphatic (*Leave me alone!*). It can also be used to terminate individual words used as interjections (*You'll get here today? Terrific!*), even when an interjection is within a sentence (*Take four parts gin, add one part vermouth, and, behold! you have a martini*).

Ellipsis

The **ellipsis** indicates that one or more words are missing. When used at the end of a complete sentence, an ellipsis is made up of four dots (*I had hoped to go. . . .*). Four dots indicate that although what's there makes a complete sentence, one or more words have been omitted from the end of the sentence. A four-dot ellipsis can also indicate the omission of one or more sentences. When the middle portion of a sentence has been omitted, a three-dot ellipsis is used.

Pause Punctuation

The punctuation marks that can indicate a pause are the comma (,), the semicolon (;), the colon (:), the dash (—), and the ellipsis (. . .).

Comma

Commas are used to separate two main clauses set apart by a conjunction (such as *and*, *but*, or *or*) (*I'd hoped to be done this afternoon, but I'm not sure that's possible*). They can separate shorter clauses that do not have a conjunction between them (*I work, I sleep, I work some more*). They are also used to set off all manner of words and phrases, such as adverbial clauses (*When he was finished, he set down his knife*), transitional expressions (*Her remarks, on the other hand, were uncalled for*), conjunctions (*We are often late; however, we must be back by five o'clock*), illustrative expressions (*They were confused; that is, they felt bewildered and afraid*), and nonrestrictive clauses (*Your writing, although it is quite good, is not what we're looking for*).

In addition, commas are employed to separate a series of words or phrases (*Hope, charity, and faith were not enough to sustain her*); to set off direct address (*You know, son, that's a good idea*); to set a direct quotation apart from the speaker (*"Don't quote me," he said*); and to set off a question being asked about the previous part of the sentence (*It was fun, wasn't it?*).

Finally, commas indicate the inference of a word not stated, especially one used earlier in the sentence (*For us it's money; for them, food*); set off the parts of an address, place name, or date (*They went to London, England, to conduct research*); and separate a name from a title following it (*Paul Fargis, President*).

Semicolon

The **semicolon** signals a more complete stop than is indicated by the comma. It is used to separate parts of a sentence that contain commas (*Our organization runs on the dedication, concern, and compassion of its staff; the generosity, moral support, and wisdom of its directors; and the gratitude, hope, and joy expressed by those it serves*). It can also join clauses that are not connected by a coordinating conjunction (*They left for London yesterday; I am leaving today.*) as well as those joined by conjunctive adverbs (*It's easy to lie; however, lying is a bad habit to get into*).

Colon

The **colon** represents the next closest thing to the full stop indicated by a period. It can mark the separation of an enumerated list or extract from the rest of a text (*The Ten Commandments:*) or the introduction of an appositive (*She wanted only one thing: sleep*) or series (*It's easy to list the things money won't buy: love, health, happiness, and peace*). The colon also precedes an illustrative or explanatory phrase; many style guides recommend beginning such phrases with capital letters if they can function as sentences in and of themselves (*His Excellency demands satisfaction: He will expect you on the dueling field at dawn*).

Colons are frequently used in contexts other than sentences. They can separate book titles from their subtitles (*Curious Customs: The Stories Behind 296 Popular American Rituals*), set off the salutation in business correspondence (*Dear Mr. President:*) and the labels in memoranda (*To:*), and separate the elements of time (*8:45*), ratios (*3:5 mix of boys to girls*), and biblical references (*Deuteronomy 1:5*).

Dash

The **dash**, known as the em dash to compositors and editors, represents an abrupt shift within a sentence. It separates a clause or phrase from the rest of the sentence, whether for emphasis (*You want—my god, you need—an expert*) or to introduce a parenthetical remark (*He hopes to turn a profit—something I can't see happening any time soon—within six months*). Dashes also are used to separate quoted material from its author (*"I still find the Strunkian wisdom a comfort"—E. B. White*).

Ellipsis

The **ellipsis** is used in dialogue to indicate faltering speech (*"We want . . . that is, . . ."*).

Brackets and Parentheses

Brackets [] are specialized tools for setting off material from the rest of the text. They can be used with editorial comments: The *main point [emphasis mine] has been missed;* or as parentheses within parentheses: *It is hoped (some might say prayed [even atheists pray sometimes]) that she will pull through.* They should not be employed when simple parentheses will do.

Parentheses () are used to set off explanatory words and phrases that demand more of a break than is shown by commas and less than that indicated by dashes: *We can't bear it (or so we believe)*; to surround numbers when enumerating points in a sentence: *He hopes (1) to be employed, and (2) to make lots of money*; to give abbreviations: *American Telephone & Telegraph (AT&T)*; and to indicate potential plurals or other alternatives: *Please tell us which course (s) of action you wish to take.*

Apostrophes, Single Quotation Marks, and Double Quotation Marks

Apostrophes

Apostrophes are used to indicate a contraction (*didn't*) or a possessive by adding *'s* to most words (*Mr. Marx's humor*); an apostrophe alone is added to form the possessive of plurals (*the kittens' tails*). Apostrophes also appear in shortened forms of the year (*the '80s*) and for plurals of numbers, letters, and terms (*She received two A's and three B's*).

Single Quotation Marks

Single quotation marks are used for quotes within quotes (*" 'I'm not sure,' is what I think he said," she responded*) and for titles and special terms mentioned in dialogue (*"She said she doesn't read the 'His' column anymore," he told his buddy*).

Double Quotation Marks

Double quotation marks are used for direct quotations and dialogue (*"What was she up to?" he asked*); to set off special terms (*soldiers are sometimes called "grunts"*); and to indicate the titles of stories, articles, songs, book chapters, TV and radio shows, poems, and lectures.

Punctuating a sentence that contains quotation marks can be tricky. Commas used to set off quoted material from the speaker are placed within the quotation marks (*"I hope it's finished," she said*). A period is also placed within the quotation marks (*"We're done."*). A question mark or exclamation point ending a sentence that ends in a quotation mark is placed within the quotation marks too (*"Will you marry me?"*). However, when quoted material is used in a question, but is not itself a question, the question mark is placed outside (*Do you think he really meant "till death do us part"?*).

Spelling Guidelines

Many words in American English are spelled just as they sound. That is, a long *a* sound is often spelled with an *a*. Aside from the old saw "*i* before *e* except after *c*, unless sounded as *a* as in *neighbor* and *weigh*," there are few easy ways of remembering the intricacies of correct spelling. The following table shows the ways in which various sounds common in English words can be spelled.

Sound	Spellings
a	s*a*t, m*e*ringue, s*a*lmon, l*au*gh
ah	f*a*ther, *au*nt, c*a*lm, s*e*rgeant, Afrik*aa*ns
aw	s*aw*, c*au*ght, *o*rder, *ough*t, w*a*lk
ay	f*a*de, *a*erobic, pl*ai*n, c*ay*, br*ea*k, n*eigh*, wh*ey*, r*e*gime
ch	*c*ello, *ch*ip, ques*ti*on, na*t*ure
e	*a*ny, g*ue*ss, l*eo*pard, fr*ie*nd, br*ea*d
ee	m*e*, s*ee*, l*ea*, sk*i*, *ei*ther, *Ae*sop, ver*y*, bel*ie*ve, ph*oe*nix
er	*ear*th, j*er*k, st*ir*, t*ur*n, auth*or*, mart*yr*
f	*f*all, tele*ph*one, rou*gh*
ih	h*i*t, *E*nglish, w*o*men, b*u*sy, c*a*bbage, b*ui*ld, c*a*rriage, s*ie*ve
i	*i*ce, sl*y*, g*ey*ser, h*igh*, b*uy*, d*ie*, pap*ay*a, *eye*
j	*j*am, le*dge*, tra*g*edy
k	*k*elp, *ch*aracter, sla*ck*, a*c*re, a*qu*a, a*cc*ount
n	*n*ap, *kn*ow, *pn*eumonia, *gn*aw
oh	b*o*ne, *oa*t, s*ou*l, *oh*, f*o*lk, br*oo*ch, cr*ow*, th*ough*, bur*eau*, l*oa*d
oo	d*o*, l*oo*, bl*ew*, s*ue*, y*ou*, cr*ui*se,
ow	c*ow*, b*ough*, s*au*erkraut, f*ou*nd
sh	pu*sh*, o*ce*an, *ch*auffeur, spe*ci*al, fa*sc*ist, ti*ss*ue, compul*si*on, na*ti*on, vi*ci*ous, no*xi*ous, nau*se*ous, *s*ure
uh	*u*p, *o*ven, tr*ou*ble, w*a*s, d*oe*s
v	lo*v*e, o*f*
z	*x*ylophone, *z*ebra, vi*s*ible
zh	re*g*ime, divi*si*on, bra*z*ier

Alphabetization

There are two ways of alphabetizing a list of words, terms, or names. In both cases, lists can be compiled by comparing the first letter, then the second letter, and so forth. In a word-by-word list, only the first word of each entry is considered; hyphens are ignored. A letter-by-letter list is considered without regard for whether the entry consists of one word or more than one; spaces and hyphens are ignored.

The following list is arranged according to the word-by-word system:

sea	season ticket
sea gull	seasoning
Sea Side Heights	second best
seafood	second name
seal	secondary
seaside	

Now here is the same list compiled under the letter-by-letter system:

sea	seasoning
seafood	season ticket
sea gull	secondary
seal	second best
seaside	second name
Sea Side Heights	

Either method of alphabetization is acceptable, as long as it is scrupulously adhered to. While some lists may be better served by one approach or the other, it is not more correct to use one or the other.

American English and British English

It has been said that the United States and Great Britain are two nations divided by a single language. This is true in a number of ways. In the first place, spellings of the same words can be decidedly different. The following list shows some common examples of the variances between American and British spellings.

American	British	American	British
center	centre	labor	labour
check (money)	cheque	organization	organisation
color	colour	pajamas	pyjamas
curb	kerb	peddler	pedlar
gray	grey	program	programme
honor	honour	realize	realise
inquire	enquire	recognize	recognise
jail	gaol	theater	theatre
jewelry	jewellery		

The two versions of the English language also diverge when it comes to the names for many everyday objects and events. It is easy for a visitor from across the Atlantic to provoke amusement from the natives by calling a cloth used to wipe one's mouth a *napkin* in England, or by asking an American waiter for the *W.C.* The following is a list of some common American terms and their counterparts in the United Kingdom.

American	British	American	British
apartment	flat	line	queue
bathroom	toilet, W.C., or loo	napkin	serviette
candy	sweets	oven	cooker
checkers	draughts	round-trip ticket	return ticket
closet	cupboard	suspenders	braces
corn	maize	truck	lorry
cracker	biscuit	trunk (of car)	boot
diaper	nappy	underpass	subway
drugstore	chemist's	undershirt	vest
faucet	tap	vacation	holiday
gas, gasoline	petrol		
hood (of car)	bonnet		

As if confusion about spelling and word choice were not enough, there are also punctuation differences between American and British English. While American English always uses double quotation marks to indicate speech, British English, especially in older texts, sometimes uses single quotation marks. More recent British publications sometimes use double quotation marks.

In both American and British English, periods and commas at the end of a quote come before the closing quotation marks when the quote is a full sentence (or a full sentence broken up by a connecting phrase such as "He said"):

"When you come to meet me," she explained hastily, "please bring the blue folders."

In American English, the placement of periods and commas remains the same even when the quote is a sentence fragment. But in British English, periods and commas punctuating sentence fragments are placed outside quotation marks.

American English:
She described the party as "a sumptuous affair," and said that she arrived home "long after midnight."

British English:
She described the party as "a sumptuous affair", and said that she arrived home "long after midnight".

Commonly Misused Words

See also "Commonly Misspelled Words" on page 338.

accept   to receive; to answer affirmatively
except   to leave out (verb); with the exclusion of (preposition)

affect   to influence; to pretend
effect   a result, an influence, an impression (noun); to bring about (verb)

antagonist   an adversary
protagonist   the leading character

anxious   worried, uneasy
eager   impatiently desirous

bathos   triteness, sentimentality
pathos   sympathy

brake   to reduce speed
break   to separate; to collapse; to destroy

capital   a city that is a seat of government; money; an uppercase letter
capitol   the building in which a legislature meets

compare   to examine differences and similarities
contrast   to examine differences

diagnosis   the identification of a disease or situation
prognosis   a prediction of the likely course of a disease or situation

dinner   the main meal of the day, at noontime or in the evening
supper   the evening meal

dyeing   coloring with dye
dying   ceasing to live

emigrate   to leave a country to live elsewhere
immigrate   to enter a country to live there

flair   skill, talent
flare   a bright light; an outburst

gorilla   an ape
guerrilla   a member of an irregular military force

hole   a space, a void
whole   complete, intact

illegible   cannot be read because of bad printing or handwriting
unreadable   uninteresting, not worth reading

ingenious   brilliant, clever
ingenuous   simple, naive

its   belonging to it
it's   it is

lay   to put; to set down
lie   to rest in a horizontal position; to make an untrue statement

liable   responsible; likely
libel   a defamatory statement

majority   more than half
plurality   more votes than any other candidate; the margin of victory

notable   worthy, impressive
notorious   widely known and ill-regarded

peace   harmony; the absence of war
piece   part of a whole

personal   intimate; having to do with a specific person
personnel   the employees of a company or organization

pray   to address a deity; to implore
prey   a victim

principal   main (adjective); the person in charge (noun)
principle   a moral rule; a law

put (someone) down   to criticize or disparage someone
put (someone) on   to mislead someone, especially in a joking way

recollect   to remember
re-collect   to collect again

sail   fabric that catches the wind to propel a boat (noun); to ride in a boat, especially one that is wind-powered (verb)
sale   a discounted offering; the act of selling

stationary not moving
stationery writing materials

talk to to address others
talk with to converse together

viral having to do with a virus
virile manly

whose of which; of who
who's who is

your belonging to you
you're you are

FOUR COMMON GRAMMATICAL PROBLEMS

Double Negative: Do not use two negative words to express a single negative statement.

>WRONG: I *don't* owe Amy *no* money.
>RIGHT: I *don't* owe Amy any money.
>RIGHT: I owe Amy *no* money.

Dangling Participial Phrase: A participial phrase modifies the first noun or pronoun following the comma that ends the participial phrase.

>WRONG: Sitting in the living room, a loud *knock* on the door was heard by Ellen.
>RIGHT: Sitting in the living room, *Ellen* heard a loud knock on the door.

Split Infinitive: Do not place an adverb between the parts of an infinitive.

>WRONG: I try *to* often *visit* Laura.
>RIGHT: I try *to visit* Laura often.

Parallel Structure: When parts of a sentence are parallel in meaning, place them in parallel or similar constructions.

>WRONG: Her morning consisted of a leisurely breakfast and strolling downtown.
>RIGHT: Her morning consisted of a leisurely breakfast and a stroll downtown.

Or:

>WRONG: We are responsible for choosing the costumes and that they should all be the correct size.
>RIGHT: We are responsible for choosing the costumes and making sure that they are all the correct size.

Additional Sources of Information

Bernstein, Theodore M. *The Careful Writer: A Modern Guide to English Usage.* Macmillan, 1977.

The Chicago Manual of Style, 13th ed. University of Chicago Press, 1982.

Fowler, H. W. *A Dictionary of Modern English Usage,* 2nd ed. (rev. by Sir Ernest Gowers). Oxford University Press, 1987.

Miller, Casey, and Kate Swift. *The Handbook of Nonsexist Writing: For Writers, Editors and Speakers,* 2nd ed. Harper & Row, 1988.

MLA Handbook for Writers of Research Papers, Theses, and Dissertations. Modern Language Association, 1988.

Morris, William, and Mary Morris. *Harper Dictionary of Contemporary Usage,* 2nd ed. Harper-Reference, 1992.

Shertzer, Margaret. *The Elements of Grammar.* Macmillan, 1986.

Strunk, W., Jr., and E. B. White. *The Elements of Style,* 3rd ed. Macmillan, 1979.

Words into Type, 3rd ed. Prentice-Hall, 1986.

Zinsser, William. *On Writing Well: An Informal Guide to Writing Nonfiction,* rev. ed. Harper & Row, 1985.

14

Etiquette

Wedding Etiquette / *371*
Division of Wedding Expenses / *375*
Business Etiquette / *376*
How to Prepare a Résumé / *379*
Personal Letters / *380*
Parties / *381*
Deaths and Funerals / *383*
Additional Sources of Information / *385*

For most people, etiquette in everyday life has little to do with white gloves and raised pinkies, although this is a common image of what etiquette is all about. In fact, etiquette involves the use of good manners, consideration for others, and adherence to unspoken rules of behavior that are expected to be followed in certain situations.

This chapter explains the basic rules of conduct expected of late-twentieth-century Americans when they engage in a number of common business and social activities. It is hardly exhaustive—a great many books have been written on planning and organizing a wedding, for instance—and it does not cover the moral, psychological, or social implications of etiquette. But it does describe what can be expected to occur when one participates in certain activities and what is expected of those who participate.

Wedding Etiquette

Because weddings vary greatly in their level of formality and style, each component of a wedding—from the invitations to the reception—is flexible. The rule of thumb is that the various elements that make up a wedding should be compatible. That is, if a formal, evening church wedding is held, it should be preceded by formal, engraved invitations and followed by a formal, sit-down dinner; likewise, a wedding held in an open field in the countryside would call for an informal dining arrangement, perhaps a buffet.

Invitations and Announcements

Wedding invitations, like weddings themselves, come in two basic varieties: formal and informal. A formal, traditional invitation is engraved or printed in black ink on high-quality white or ivory paper. The size of the paper is either 5-by-7, folded in half before being put in an envelope, or 4-by-5, inserted into an envelope without folding.

The wording of a formal wedding invitation is written in the third person, and the date and time are written out in full. A typical example might read:

>Mr. and Mrs. Henry Appleton
>request the honor of your presence
>at the marriage of their daughter
>Carol June
>to
>Mr. Alan Hart
>Saturday, the fourth of February
>at eleven o'clock
>St. Albert's Church
>Bayonne, New Jersey

The invitation to the wedding ceremony itself can also invite the recipient to a reception afterward. If all those receiving invitations to the reception are not invited to the ceremony, or vice versa, a separate invitation to the reception is printed and, for those invited to both events, included with the wedding invitation. The reception invitation or the combined invitation should include the instructions "R.S.V.P."

Traditionally, the invitation is covered with a piece of tissue paper and enclosed with the reception invitation (and a response card and its envelope, if desired) in an inner envelope. The names of those invited, including a couple's children if they are also invited, are written out in full on the inner envelope. This inner envelope is then enclosed in an outer envelope that bears the handwritten names of all invited and their address, without abbreviations. Modern custom allows the bride's parents to forgo using an inner envelope altogether when sending out invitations.

Other enclosures that may be sent with the wedding invitation include cards designating reserved pews, "At-Home" cards that announce when the bride and groom will return from their honeymoon and where they will reside, and maps or other travel information.

Nontraditional, informal invitations can be designed and printed or handwritten in whatever style or form the bride and groom desire. They should, however, be in good taste—avoiding garish colors and bad poetry—and in harmony with the style of the wedding itself.

Wedding announcements usually are sent to people who would like to know about the wedding but who would not be expected to attend. They use the same paper and printing as the invitations. The wording is also similar, although the parents of both the bride and the groom are often mentioned and the words *announce the marriage of* replace *request the honor of your presence at the marriage of*. Wedding announcements are sent out the day of, or shortly after, the wedding.

Response to a wedding invitation is dictated by the type of invitation. A formal invitation traditionally is answered with a third-person, handwritten note that might read:

> Mr. and Mrs. Harold Sloane
> accept with pleasure (or regret they will be unable to attend)
> Mr. and Mrs. Appleton's
> kind invitation for
> Saturday, the fourth of February.

Of course, if a response card is enclosed, it may simply be filled out and returned. If the invitation is less formal, a handwritten response in more standard, informal English is correct.

Showers

Bridal or wedding showers can be given by any close friend of the bride. They should not be given by a member of the bride's immediate family.

There is no set rule for the number of showers that can be held before a wedding, although only members of the wedding party are invited to more than one shower. Neither is there a hard-and-fast rule for the types of parties they should be; serving anything from coffee and cake to cocktails to a light supper is appropriate.

Unless it is a surprise shower, the guest list is drawn up by the bride (or the bride and groom if both are to be present). The host for the party should set the limit on the number of guests. Guests invited to the shower should also be invited to the wedding, unless the wedding is to be very small.

Everyone attending a shower is expected to bring a present, which is opened at the party. The host or another friend of the bride should keep a list of who gave what, so that thank-you notes can be sent later on.

Bachelor Dinner

Several days before the wedding, a bachelor dinner can be given for the groom. It is usually held in a private room of a restaurant and hosted by the best man or the ushers, although a groom may give his own bachelor dinner.

Generally, the men drink and eat a great deal. At some point in the evening, the groom toasts his bride-to-be. It is rarely appropriate to break the glasses after such a toast, although this was once the custom. The only important rule regarding bachelor dinners is that they should not be held the night before the wedding, so that there is adequate time for the groom to recover from the festivities.

Ceremony

The wedding ceremony itself can be as formal or informal as the bride and groom wish it to be. Weddings are held in city halls, open fields, private homes, reception halls, restaurants, and churches and synagogues. For most weddings to which guests are invited, and especially church and synagogue weddings, a prescribed series of events will take place.

First comes the processional. In Christian and Reform Jewish weddings, the ushers come down the aisle first, arranged in height order, followed by any junior ushers. They are followed by junior bridesmaids, then bridesmaids, in height order, with the shortest first. Then comes the maid or matron of honor, the flower girls, the ring bearer, and, finally, the bride, holding the right arm of her father. The groom and the best man wait at the front of the room with the clergy.

Orthodox and Conservative Jewish processionals are led by the ushers, who are followed by the bridesmaids. Next come the rabbi and cantor followed by the best man and then the groom, accompanied by his mother and father. The maid of honor is next; she is followed by the bride, who walks between her mother and father.

The guests stand during the processional and remain standing until the clergy has asked them to sit, usually after opening remarks or a prayer. Once at the front of the room, the bride's father (or parents) step back or to one side and the groom steps forward to meet his bride. Bride and groom stand next to each other holding hands or with her hand on his arm, if they wish.

In Protestant ceremonies, the father of the bride gives her away before sitting down in the first pew. In Roman Catholic ceremonies, the father of the bride sits with his wife as soon as the bride is delivered to the groom. Orthodox and Conservative Jewish ceremonies require that the parents of the bride and groom remain at the front of the room; if there is space, they stand under the marriage canopy, known as a *chuppah*.

The actual events of the wedding ceremony differ widely among various denominations. Most Christian services include a blessing of the ring or rings. (If the bride is wearing an engagement ring, she should put it on her right hand for the service, then place it outside the wedding band afterward.) Orthodox Jewish services are mostly in Hebrew, and two glasses of wine are shared by the couple before the groom breaks the goblet at the end of the ceremony.

The recessional for Christian and Reform Jewish weddings is led by the bride and groom. They are followed by the flower girl, the best man and maid or matron of honor, and the ushers and bridesmaids; a line of bridesmaids follows the bride and a line of ushers follows the groom. Orthodox and Conservative Jewish recessionals are led by the bride and groom, followed by the bride's parents, the groom's parents, the maid of honor with the best man, the flower girl, and the rabbi and cantor. Bridesmaids and ushers bring up the rear. In Orthodox ceremonies, all the men are on one side and all the women on the other.

Reception

The style of the reception will follow from the style of the rest of the wedding. Ordinarily, photographs are taken immediately after the ceremony; they are ordered and paid for by the bride's family.

A receiving line, made up of the mothers of the bride and groom, the wedded couple, the maid of honor, and, at the discretion of those involved, the fathers of the couple, the bridesmaids, the best man, and the ushers, greets guests as they enter the room.

Formal receptions have assigned tables for those attending. The bridal party will generally be at the head table, and a parents' table will be nearby. Other guests should be assigned to tables with people whose company they will enjoy.

Almost all receptions include a toast to the bride and groom, which is proposed by the best man. The groom should reply with thanks after the toast has been drunk and offer a toast to his bride; other toasts may be offered as well. The toasts can be followed by dancing or a meal, if one is to be served. The wedding cake is cut just before dessert, or shortly before the bride and groom leave the reception if it is not a formal dinner. The bride cuts the first slice, with the help of her new husband, from the bottom tier of the cake, and the couple offer each other a bite. The top layer of the cake, with its decorations, is removed and saved for the bride and groom, while the remainder is cut up and served to the guests.

At the reception's end, the bride usually will toss her bouquet from stairs or a landing, turning her back and throwing it over her shoulder to her bridesmaids or other female friends; the one who catches it is supposed to marry next. Then the newlyweds change clothes, say goodbye to their families, and, led by the best man, leave in a shower of paper rose petals or rice.

Gifts and Thank-You Notes

Gifts can be sent to the address on the At-Home card, if one is enclosed with the invitation, or to the home of the bride's mother. They also can be brought to the reception. Among some people, money is an appropriate wedding gift; it is usually presented to the bride in an envelope, which she will place in a special purse or in a box or basket put out for this purpose. Envelopes, and usually gifts as well, are not opened until after the reception.

Thank-you notes should be handwritten and should mention the gift that was given. They should be sent shortly after the couple's honeymoon is over.

DIVISION OF WEDDING EXPENSES

Today, the groom and his family often offer to share some of the wedding expenses that traditionally have been borne by the bride's family. This is a significant change of custom, as the costs of traditional weddings have become too prohibitive for many families to absorb. However, if the groom's family does not offer to share expenses, the bride's family should plan a wedding in accordance with their means.

The traditional division of expenses is listed below. In addition to the change noted above, it should be kept in mind that there are numerous exceptions and variations depending on religion, ethnicity, or local custom. Many items may be omitted without diminishing the ceremony in any way.

Expenses Paid by Bride's Family

Bridal consultant, if needed
Invitations and announcements
Flowers for the church and receptions, bouquets for the bridesmaids, bouquet for bride (sometimes given by groom)
Music for the ceremony, including organist or choir fee
Transportation of bridal party to church or synagogue and reception

Bride's presents to her bridesmaids
Bride's present to groom (optional)
Groom's wedding ring
Sexton's fee (church fee)
Accommodations for out-of-town bridesmaids
All expenses of reception, including music

Expenses Paid by Groom's Family

Bride's rings, both engagement and wedding
Groom's present to bride (optional)
Groom's presents to ushers and best man
Groom's boutonniere and boutonnieres for ushers
Ties and gloves for the ushers
Clergy member's fee; tips to altar boys
Corsages for immediate members of both families and bride's going-away corsage

Accommodations for out-of-town ushers
Bachelor dinner (optional, and often given by ushers)
Rehearsal dinner (optional, but becoming more standard)
Honeymoon

Expenses Paid by Bridesmaids

Dress and accessories
Transportation to and from town of wedding

Gift to the couple and contribution to a gift from all bridesmaids to the bride

Expenses Paid by Ushers

Transportation to and from town of wedding
Rental of wedding attire

Gift to the couple and contribution to a gift from all ushers to the groom
Bachelor dinner (optional, and often given by groom)

Expenses Paid by Out-of-Town Guests

Transportation and accommodations

Gift to the couple

Anniversary Gifts

Etiquette authorities differ on the appropriate gifts to be presented on the occasion of individual wedding anniversaries. The following list represents a modern consensus, with the eight oldest and most traditional gifts indicated in *italics*.

1	*Paper* or plastics	9	Pottery	35	Coral or jade
2	Cotton or calico	10	*Tin* or aluminum	40	Rubies or garnets
3	Leather	11	Steel	45	Sapphires or tourmalines
4	Linen, silk, or synthetics (rayon, nylon)	12	Silk or linen	50	*Gold*
		13	Lace	55	Emeralds or turquoise
5	*Wood*	14	Ivory	60	*Diamonds* or gold
6	Iron	15	*Crystal* or glass	75	Diamonds or gold
7	Copper, wool, or brass	20	China		
8	Bronze or electrical appliances	25	*Silver*		
		30	Pearls		

Business Etiquette

The business world is extraordinarily demanding and extremely competitive. In it, there are really only a few criteria on which members will be judged: competence, initiative, leadership, and how well one gets along with others. It is this last area in which manners plays a crucial role, for individuals must be able to present themselves well and deal well with others if they wish to succeed in business.

Appointments

Business life requires that people meet each other face-to-face to conduct transactions or exchange information. To do so, they schedule appointments. The first rule regarding business appointments is that they should be kept if at all possible; failing to show up for an appointment will be taken as a sign of disinterest, carelessness, and lack of professionalism. If an appointment cannot be kept, it should be canceled as far in advance as possible. If an individual is unavoidably delayed, he or she should telephone the host or have someone else make the call.

When guests are shown into the office where the appointment will take place, the host should rise from his or her desk, shake hands, and greet them; if the host and guests have not met before, they should introduce themselves. The guests should be offered seats, and the host should either sit back down at the desk or sit with the visitors. Coffee or tea may be offered by the host but should not be requested by the guests.

Any business meeting should get to the business at hand as quickly as possible. It is just as important to listen as it is to talk, not simply to be polite but to get the most out of the meeting. It is also important not to interrupt others during meetings. Taking notes during a business meeting is acceptable.

The host usually will conclude a business meeting, either by making remarks that sum up the discussion or by suggesting outright that everything pertinent has now been discussed. It is important for guests to pick up on such cues, gather their belongings, thank the host, shake hands, and leave. A follow-up letter, thanking the host for the meeting and outlining whatever was agreed upon at the meeting, should be sent by the next business day.

Entertainment

Business entertaining generally takes place in an office; over breakfast, lunch, or dinner, at a restaurant; or over drinks after work. The purpose of business entertaining is to conduct business in a congenial setting that is less formal than an office.

The person initiating business entertainment acts as the host. That person is responsible for deciding on the setting, making reservations, and paying the bill. The site chosen for entertaining a client or colleague should be appropriate to the person being invited and the nature of the business relationship; a prestigious restaurant would be right for entertaining a major client, while drinks at a clubby bar might be a good choice for entertaining a vendor who regularly sells supplies to the company.

Regardless of setting, it should be kept in mind that business is the main purpose of the get-together. The host should endeavor to bring up the business at hand before the guest becomes impatient. However, business discussions should not interfere with the pleasure of enjoying the meal.

The host should pick up the check when it is brought to the table, look it over, and pay it. Because business entertaining should give both parties more or less equal status, it makes no difference whether the host is a man or a woman. There is no reason for a guest even to show a pretense of wanting to pick up the check; the guest can express his or her thanks to the host as they are leaving.

Gifts

Gift-giving is not at all unusual among people who work together. Bosses often give gifts to employees for birthdays, Christmas, or Secretaries' Day; staff members may give the boss a present for holidays or birthdays; office colleagues sometimes give each other gifts; and executives can give presents to clients or vendors.

Such gifts are generally not lavish, although the type of gift is dictated by the nature of the relationship. Bosses tend to give larger presents to their employees than staff members give to the boss. Gifts to colleagues reflect the degree of friendship between them. Clients or vendors give and receive gifts appropriate to the amount of business transacted and the longevity of the relationship.

Business gifts should be less personal than gifts for a friend. A datebook or similar office accessory, costume jewelry, a tie, or a bottle of wine makes a good, inexpensive business gift. More lavish presents, like theater tickets, food baskets, or a case of wine can be given to longstanding clients or employees.

The Telephone

For many companies, the telephone is an essential tool for conducting business. Proper telephone manners can make it an effective tool.

Many people think that having a secretary or assistant place calls will enhance the image of an executive. In fact, having others place calls for oneself is an inconvenience, both for the secretary or assistant who must place the call and for the person receiving the call, who must wait for the executive to get on the line. People in business should place their own phone calls.

When the call goes through, the caller should identify himself or herself by name and company; if the nature of the call is not readily apparent, the caller should volunteer this information. With some companies, this process will have to be repeated two or three times—with the switchboard operator, a secretary, and the person being called.

A caller should not take offense if asked to identify the reason for the call, although this type of questioning is often a thinly disguised way of keeping a boss insulated from people he or she does not want to receive calls from. Screening phone calls is acceptable, but not if the caller is then asked to hold the line and finally is told that the person being called is not available. As with placing calls, the most convenient and least rude way of dealing with incoming calls is to answer them yourself; if you are too busy to answer the phone yourself, a secretary should keep the interrogation of a caller to a minimum.

People answering business phones should identify themselves and ask if they can help the caller. They should be attentive, organized, and unhurried. If answering someone else's phone, they should be ready to take a message.

Business phones should not be used for personal calls. If a personal call must be made, or if one is received, it should be kept as brief as possible. Similarly, business calls should be kept brief and to the point. Chattiness and rudeness are always to be avoided in business telephone calls.

Letter Writing

Like business phone calls, business letters should be brief and to the point. The first line below the letterhead should bear the date, with the name, company, and address of the recipient appearing two lines below it at the left margin. Two lines below the address, the salutation is given.

If the recipient is known personally, he or she can be greeted by first name ("Dear Fred:"). If the recipient is known casually or not at all, use *Mr.* or *Ms.* ("Dear Mr. Burrows:" or "Dear Ms. Johnston:"). When the addressee is unknown, "Dear Sir or Madam:" or something like "Dear Sales Manager:" can be employed.

The first paragraph of a business letter should clearly explain the purpose of writing. It should be straightforward and concise. If the letter is being written at the suggestion of someone else, this should be stated in the first paragraph along with the reason for writing.

The length of a business letter is determined by what needs to be said. If a reply is desired, the last paragraph should simply state, "I look forward to hearing from you at your earliest convenience." A response by a specific date should not be demanded unless there is a good reason for doing so.

Appropriate closings for a business letter include "Best wishes," "Sincerely," "Sincerely yours," or "Yours truly." Informal closings like "Yours," or "Cheers," should not be used. The signature can either be your full name ("Henry Wiggins") or, if the writer and the recipient are well acquainted, a first name alone ("Henry"). The writer's full name and company title should be typed below the signature unless they appear at the top of the letterhead.

How to Prepare a Résumé

A résumé is a tool that can be used to obtain a job interview. Along with a cover letter, it is the first impression a prospective employee makes on a potential employer. Therefore, it is important that a résumé provide as much relevant information as possible about the person being described in it: you. It is also important that the résumé be kept brief—no more than one full side of a sheet of $8^{1}/_{2}$-by-11-inch paper.

A résumé must be neatly typed, with at least a $^{3}/_{4}$-inch margin on both sides, top, and bottom. Single-space all information in the résumé, leaving one line of space between blocks of information. Use underlining, capital letters, and asterisks to highlight important information.

Begin a résumé with your name, address, and home and business telephone numbers. They can be laid out on the page in any way you find visually pleasing, so far as space allows. Do not include your age, marital status, or other personal facts.

Many résumés then list a career goal, for example, "Career goal: Systems engineer responsible for monitoring, maintaining, and improving plant facilities" or "Objective: Position as illustrator/designer with opportunity to create book jackets from concept through mechanicals." This is a good tactic if you are looking for a specific type of job; however, job-hunters who would consider any of several possible careers are better off omitting any specific career goal.

Most résumés then present a chronological outline of work experience, starting with one's current or most recent job and working backward. For each job listed, the important duties and skills involved should be outlined or described. Depending on how much "real world" experience you have, relevant high school or college employment, internships, and part-time work can be included. Such a portion of a typical résumé might look like this:

WORK EXPERIENCE

1986–present   Vice President, Marketing, *Techno Corp.*

Responsible for developing, implementing, and overseeing marketing of all services provided by this computer firm.

—Created company's first five-year marketing plan

—Developed continuing training program for sales force

—Increased client billings by 25 percent

1983–1986   Marketing Director, *Numbercrunch, Inc.*

This section is followed by one outlining your educational background, again going from your most recent experience backward. List the date, school or course attended, and certificate or diploma obtained. Depending on the extent of your work experience, you may wish to give a more detailed description of your higher education. If you are a college student, you may wish to list your high school and any pertinent coursework or special achievements.

In the last part of your résumé, list any work you have done with civic or charitable organizations and any awards or certificates of recognition you have received. Place these under an appropriate heading, such as "COMMUNITY SERVICE." If you have no such background, leave this section out of your résumé.

Finally, it is unnecessary to write "References available upon request" at the bottom of a résumé. Anyone looking at it will assume you can provide references and will ask for them if and when they are needed.

Personal Letters

The demise of personal letter writing is considered by many to be a sad comment on the overall lack of civility in our society. Many people arrange their lives in such a way that they never need to write a letter outside of business situations. There are, however, several situations in which a note or letter is expected. And there are many other circumstances in which written communication will delight the recipient.

Thank-you notes should always be sent to the host and hostess of an overnight guest, for wedding presents, and for presents of any sort that the giver has not been thanked for personally. Thank-you notes to the host or hostess of a party or to someone who has done a favor are not required, but they will make the writer's gratitude clear and warm the heart of the person who gets them.

Other situations demand notes or letters as well. The death of someone in a friend's family is one such event. This is especially true if you cannot express your condolences personally at a wake or during *shiva*. A letter of condolence need not be long and involved, but it should be a personal, handwritten note, not just a printed sympathy card.

Formal invitations require a written response. For many, wedding invitations are the most common sort of formal invitation received. While response cards are frequently included with wedding invitations, a personal response in addition to or in place of the response card will be greatly appreciated.

When a friend or family member has something important to celebrate—a promotion or graduation, or receipt of an award or other honor—a congratulatory note will make the celebration even happier. Even the briefest of notes adds a warmth that cannot be conveyed by a phone call.

Personal letter writing can also be done for no good reason at all. Or rather, you may write letters to friends and family simply to keep in touch with them and to let them know that you are thinking of them. These are perhaps the most enjoyable letters to receive.

Personal letters, while not requiring a strict format, do have a few guidelines. The date should be written at the top, either in the center or the right-hand corner. The salutation, which may be a bit warmer than it would for a business letter ("My dearest Jeanne,") should be followed by a comma instead of a colon.

The body or text of a personal letter is, of course, a highly personal matter. It should be written with less of an eye to what would be stylistically or grammatically correct and more of an eye to expressing feelings and thoughts. A personal letter should sound like you, and techniques that would be out of place in a business letter, such as using dashes, ellipses, and sentence fragments, can be employed in personal correspondence.

Closings for personal letters are also a matter of choice. "Love," is appropriate for those you do love; "Fondly," or "All my best," or "Affectionately," might be right for friends. As with the rest of the letter, the closing should express your own feelings.

Parties

Parties come in all shapes and sizes. They can be held for holidays, anniversaries, housewarmings, birthdays, weddings, or farewells or just to have some friends over. They range from sit-down dinners in banquet halls to tea and cookies in living rooms. But no matter the size or style of the party, certain aspects need to be tended to make it a success.

Invitations

Invitations can be given in writing, in person, or by telephone, depending on the sort of party they are for. Engraved invitations are sent for formal parties, like weddings and anniversary parties. Less formal events require less formal invitations; handwritten notes on personal stationery or printed invitation cards with blanks that can be filled in can be used. Invitations to small informal parties can be issued by telephone. Invitations should be sent out about three weeks before a party.

R.S.V.P.s

Your invitation should include a request that guests respond if you want to know in advance who will be coming. A formal invitation can include a response card or just "R.S.V.P." Informal invitations can include a statement like, "Unless we hear otherwise, we'll expect you on the third," or "Please let us know if you can make it." Telephone invitations will usually get immediate responses; however, if you are invited by telephone and do not know whether you can attend, it is acceptable to put off a response. In any case, it is important to respond to an invitation as quickly as possible so the hosts can plan accordingly.

Formal Dinner Parties

Seating Arrangements

The host and hostess, as well as any guests of honor, are the people around whom seating arrangements are set at more formal dinner parties. The host and hostess will usually sit at either end of the table; a male guest of honor sits at the hostess' right and a female guest of honor at the host's right. Other guests are told where to sit by the host and hostess, either personally or by using place cards. While it is customary to alternate men and women at a sit-down dinner, this practice can be ignored if there are more members of one sex than of the other. Husbands and wives can be seated together or separated. Obviously, buffet dinner parties, cocktail parties, and other informal get-togethers do not require any sort of specific seating arrangement; guests can be expected to fend for themselves.

Tableware

A place setting at a formal dinner party can be somewhat intimidating to guests unfamiliar with such events. The arrangement of plates, glasses, and utensils is fairly standard, however, and fairly easy to deal with.

The basic setting should be in place when the guests sit down. A service plate is in the center, usually with the napkin on top of it. Flanking the plate will be the flatware: a dessert or salad fork to the immediate left of the plate, a dinner fork to the left of it, and a fish fork, if needed, on the outside. To the right of the plate are, from closest to furthest, the salad knife, the meat knife, the fish knife, a soup or fruit spoon (or both), and, if shellfish is being served, a shellfish fork. Utensils are used in order from the outside in.

Glasses are placed above the knives to the right of the plate. There will be a water goblet and, extending to the right from there, a champagne glass, one or two wine glasses, and a sherry glass.

Formal Place Setting
- a) oyster or shellfish fork
- b) soup spoon
- c) fork and knife for fish
- d) fork and knife for meat
- e) fork and knife for salad and cheese
- f) sherry glass (with soup)
- g) white wine glass (with fish)
- h) red wine glass (with meat)
- i) water goblet
- j) champagne glass (with dessert)

Note: *Always use the outside silver first (after the oyster fork and soup spoon, just remember to use the fork farthest to the left and the knife farthest to the right).*

In addition to the service plate, a butter plate is placed above the forks, to the left of the service plate. The butter knife is set across the butter plate.

Serving

Food at a formal dinner party is usually served by hired help. Guests are served from the left, and plates are cleared from the right. The female guest of honor is served first; if there is no guest of honor, women are served before men or, if this is hard to manage, a woman is served the first plate with the other guests served in order. The hostess is served last. Warmed dinner plates are usually brought out just before the entree is served. A clean service plate should be brought out for each of the other courses.

Deaths and Funerals

Plans for death should be discussed with family and loved ones before such plans are likely to be needed. A person's desires regarding the sort of funeral held, disposal of the body by burial or cremation, donation of organs, and so forth need to be known. Practical matters—where to find insurance papers, the will, bills, bank accounts, safety deposit boxes, or investment holdings—also should be dealt with in advance.

Funeral Arrangements

The details of funeral arrangements are handled by funeral directors. Placement of a death notice in the newspaper; selection of a coffin; travel to church, synagogue, and/or graveyard; and a variety of other services are provided. Many of these arrangements can be made in advance or at the time of death. The death notice would include the deceased's name and date of death, the names of immediate family members who survive, and the place and time of the wake and funeral if the funeral is not private.

Wakes

Traditionally, wakes were held at the dead person's home, but today wakes are usually held at a funeral home. They are strictly a Christian phenomenon; Jews sit *shiva* during a seven-day period of mourning and remembrance immediately after burial. Anyone who wishes to may attend a wake, unless it is kept private. The hours and days are set and usually appear in the death notice in the newspaper. Nonfamily members should sign the guest book provided at the funeral home, stay just long enough to express sympathy to the bereaved family, then leave. Expressions of sympathy are best if they come from the heart; when at a loss for what to say, a simple "I'm sorry" is enough. Standing, kneeling, or praying at the coffin is optional.

Flowers

Sending flowers is a customary way of expressing sympathy, especially if attendance at the wake or funeral is not possible. They can be sent to either the funeral home or the church along with a card. Flowers are not appropriate for Jewish funerals or if the death notice requests donations to charity in lieu of them.

Funeral Services

Unless specified as private in the death notice, funeral services can be attended by anyone. They should be viewed not as an obligation but as an opportunity to publicly bid farewell to the person who died and to show concern for the survivors. Religious affiliation is unimportant; one may attend a funeral service regardless of faith. It is important to speak to the bereaved family at the funeral service; if sympathy has already been expressed at the wake, a positive comment about the service, the eulogy, or the church or synagogue would be appropriate.

Burial

For Jews, burial takes place within 24 hours, or as quickly as possible. Christians are buried two or more days after death. Close friends and family members are generally the only people expected to attend the actual interment.

A reception generally is held after the burial. The funeral director or a family member will invite those present to attend. It can be held at the home of a relative or at a catering hall or restaurant. Food and drink are provided by the bereaved family or arranged for by them.

Letters or Calls of Condolence

These are appropriate in lieu of attendance at a wake or funeral service. They should be brief and should focus on memories of the dead person, sympathy for the survivors, and offers of help to the survivors. Avoid pity in such communications or visits, and make clear that a response is not expected soon.

After Burial

It is important to be available to the grieving family after all ceremonies are over. If the family is Jewish, they will sit shiva seven days; it is appropriate to drop by and bring food but not flowers. If the family is Christian, stop by a few days later to listen and talk. Whatever the religious affiliation, friends who are willing to listen and talk to bereaved family members are highly valued at this time.

Additional Sources of Information

Baldridge, Letitia. *The Amy Vanderbilt Complete Book of Etiquette: A Guide to Contemporary Living,* Doubleday, 1978.

Baldridge, Letitia. *Letitia Baldridge's Complete Guide to the New Manners for the '90s.* Rawson Associates, 1990.

Bryan, Dawn. *The Art and Etiquette of Gift Giving.* Bantam, 1987.

Ford, Charlotte. *Charlotte Ford's Book of Modern Manners.* Crown, 1988.

Gelles-Cole, Sandi, ed. *Letitia Baldridge's Complete Guide to Executive Manners.* Rawson Associates, 1985.

Mark, Lisbeth. *The Book of Hierarchies: A Compendium of Steps, Ranks, Orders, Levels, Classes, Grades, Tiers, Arrays, Degrees, Lines, Divisions, Categories, Precedents, Priorities & Other Distinctions.* William Morrow, 1984.

Martin, Judith. *Miss Manners' Guide to Excruciatingly Correct Behavior.* Galahad Books, 1991.

Martin, Judith. *Miss Manners' Guide to Rearing Perfect Children.* Viking Penguin, 1985.

McCaffree, Maryjane, and Pauline Innis. *Protocol: The Complete Handbook of Diplomatic, Official and Social Usage,* rev. ed. Devon, 1985.

Post, Elizabeth. *Emily Post on Entertaining: Answers to the Most Often Asked Questions About Entertaining at Home and in Business.* Harper & Row, 1987.

Post, Elizabeth. *Emily Post's Etiquette,* 15th ed. Harper & Row, 1992.

Post, Elizabeth. *Emily Post's Wedding Etiquette & Planner,* Harper & Row, 1982.

Rowland, Diana. *Japanese Business Etiquette: A Practical Guide to Business and Social Success with the Japanese.* Warner Books, 1985.

15

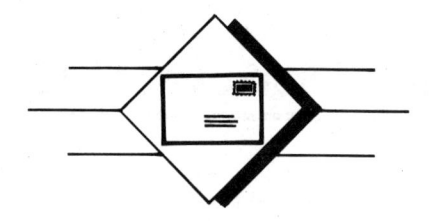

Forms of Address

Spoken and Written Forms of Address for U.S. Government Officials, Military Personnel, Foreign Officials, Nobility, and Religious Officials / *387*

Order of British Peerage / *391*

Abbreviated Titles That Follow Names / *392*

Additional Sources of Information / *393*

Spoken and Written Forms of Address for U.S. Government Officials, Military Personnel, Foreign Officials, Nobility, and Religious Officials

This section gives the correct forms of address for U.S. public officials, diplomats, religious leaders, royalty, the British peerage, and military personnel. For each personage the chart gives the appropriate form or forms to be used in addressing letters, in letter salutations, in direct conversation, and in more formal introductions.

In diplomatic and other public circles, "Sir" is generally considered an acceptable alternative to the formal address in both written and spoken greetings; this does not apply to religious or titled persons. The use of "Madam" or "Ma'am" for a female addressee is less customary but still acceptable, especially for high officeholders ("Madam Governor"). This rule also holds for high officials of foreign countries.

For greetings in which "Mr." is used, the feminine equivalent may be "Madam" or, less formally, "Mrs.," "Miss," or "Ms." Although there is no formal rule for the use of "Ms.," the preference of the addressee should be respected.

Person	*Letter Address*	*Letter Greeting*	*Spoken Greeting*	*Formal Introduction*
President of the United States	The President The White House Washington, DC 20500	Dear Mr. (or Madam) President	Mr. (or Madam) President	The President or the President of the United States
former President	The Honorable John J. Jones Address	Dear Mr. (or Mrs., Ms.) Jones	Mr. (or Mrs., Ms.) Jones	The Honorable John J. Jones
Vice President	The Vice President Executive Office Building Washington, DC 20501	Dear Mr. (or Madam) Vice President	Mr. (or Madam) Vice President	The Vice President or the Vice President of the United States
Cabinet members	The Honorable John (or Jane) Jones The Secretary of _____ or The Attorney General Washington, DC	Dear Mr. (or Madam) Secretary	Mr. (or Madam) Secretary	The Secretary of _____
Chief Justice	The Chief Justice The Supreme Court Washington, DC 20543	Dear Mr. (or Madam) Justice or Dear Mr. (or Madam) Chief Justice	Mr. (or Madam) Chief Justice	The Chief Justice

Person	Letter Address	Letter Greeting	Spoken Greeting	Formal Introduction
Associate Justice	Mr. Justice Jones or Madam Justice Jones The Supreme Court Washington, DC 20543	Dear Mr. (or Madam) Justice	Mr. Justice or Mr. Justice Jones; Madam Justice or Madam Justice Jones	Mr. Justice Jones; Madam Justice Jones
United States Senator	The Honorable John (or Jane) Jones United States Senate Washington, DC 20510	Dear Senator Jones	Senator Jones	Senator Jones from Montana
Speaker of the House	The Honorable John (or Jane) Jones Speaker of the House of Representatives United States House of Representatives Washington, DC 20515	Dear Mr. (or Madam) Speaker	Mr. Speaker; Madam Speaker	The Speaker of the House of Representatives
United States Representative	The Honorable John (or Jane) Jones United States House of Representatives Washington, DC 20515	Dear Mr. (or Mrs., Ms.) Jones	Mr. (or Mrs., Ms.) Jones	Representative Jones from New Jersey
United Nations Ambassador	The Honorable John (or Jane) Jones U.S. Ambassador to the United Nations United Nations Plaza New York, NY 10017	Dear Mr. (or Madam) Ambassador	Mr. (or Madam) Ambassador	The United States Ambassador to the United Nations
Ambassador	The Honorable John (or Jane) Jones Ambassador of the United States American Embassy Address	Dear Mr. (or Madam) Ambassador	Mr. (or Madam) Ambassador	The American Ambassador The Ambassador of The United States of America
Consul-General	The Honorable John (or Jane) Jones American Consul General Address	Dear Mr. (or Mrs., Ms.) Jones	Mr. (or Mrs., Ms.) Jones	Mr. (or Mrs., Ms.) Jones
Foreign Ambassador	His (or Her) Excellency John (or Jean) Johnson The Ambassador of _____ Address	Excellency or Dear Mr. (or Madam) Ambassador	Excellency; or Mr. (or Madam) Ambassador	The Ambassador of _____
Secretary-General of the United Nations	His (or Her) Excellency Milo (or Mara) Jones Secretary-General of the United Nations United Nations Plaza New York, NY 10017	Dear Mr. (or Madam) Secretary-General	Mr. (or Madam) Secretary-General	The Secretary-General of the United Nations

Forms of Address

Person	Letter Address	Letter Greeting	Spoken Greeting	Formal Introduction
Governor	The Honorable John (or Jane) Jones Governor of ——— State Capitol Address	Dear Governor Jones	Governor or Governor Jones	The Governor of Maine: Governor Jones of Maine
State legislators	The Honorable John (or Jane) Jones Address	Dear Mr. (or Mrs., Ms.) Jones	Mr. (or Mrs., Ms.) Jones	Mr. (or Mrs., Ms.) Jones
Judges	The Honorable John J. Jones Justice, Appellate Division Supreme Court of the State of ——— Address	Dear Judge Jones	Justice or Judge Jones; Madam Justice or Judge Jones	The Honorable John (or Jane) Jones; Mr. Justice Jones or Judge Jones; Madam Justice Jones or Judge Jones
Mayor	The Honorable John (or Jane) Jones; His (or Her) Honor the Mayor City Hall Address	Dear Mayor Jones	Mayor Jones; Mr. (or Madam) Mayor; Your Honor	Mayor Jones; The Mayor
The Pope	His Holiness, the Pope or His Holiness, Pope John XII Vatican City Rome, Italy	Your Holiness or Most Holy Father	Your Holiness or Most Holy Father	His Holiness, the Holy Father; the Pope; the Pontiff
Cardinals	His Eminence, John Cardinal Jones, Archbishop of ——— Address	Your Eminence or Dear Cardinal Jones	Your Eminence or Cardinal Jones	His Eminence, Cardinal Jones
Bishops	The Most Reverend John Jones, Bishop (or Archbishop) of ——— Address	Your Excellency or Dear Bishop (Archbishop) Jones	Your Excellency or Bishop (Archbishop) Jones	
Monsignor	The Reverend Monsignor James Harding Address	Reverend Monsignor or Dear Monsignor	Monsignor Harding or Monsignor	Monsignor Harding
Priest	The Reverend John Jones Address	Reverend Father or Dear Father Jones	Father or Father Jones	Father Jones
Brother	Brother John or Brother John Jones Address	Dear Brother John or Dear Brother	Brother John or Brother	Brother John
Sister	Sister Mary Luke Address	Dear Sister Mary Luke or Dear Sister	Sister Mary Luke or Sister	Sister Mary Luke
Protestant Clergy	The Reverend John (or Jane) Jones*	Dear Dr. (or Mr., Ms.) Jones	Dr. (or Mr., Ms.) Jones	The Reverend (or Dr.) John Jones

Person	Letter Address	Letter Greeting	Spoken Greeting	Formal Introduction
Bishop (Episcopal)	The Right Reverend John Jones* Bishop of _____ Address	Dear Bishop Jones	Bishop Jones	The Right Reverend John Jones, Bishop of Detroit
Rabbi	Rabbi Arthur (or Anne) Milgrom Address	Dear Rabbi Milgrom	Rabbi Milgrom or Rabbi	Rabbi Arthur Milgrom
King or Queen	His (Her) Majesty King (Queen) _____ Address (letters traditionally are sent to reigning monarchs not directly but via the private secretary)	Your Majesty; Sir or Madam	Varies depending on titles, holdings, etc.	
Other royalty	His (Her) Royal Highness, the Prince (Princess) of _____ Address	Your Royal Highness	Your Royal Highness; Sir or Madam	His (Her) Royal Highness, the Duke (Duchess) of Gloucester
Duke/Duchess	His/Her Grace, the D_____ of _____	My Lord Duke/Madam or Dear Duke of _____/Dear Duchess	Your Grace or Duke/Duchess	His/Her Grace, the Duke/Duchess of Bridgeport
Marquess/Marchioness	The Most Honorable the M_____ of Bridgeport	My Lord/Madam or Dear Lord/Lady Bridgeport	Lord/Lady Bridgeport	Lord/Lady Bridgeport
Earl	The Right Honorable the Earl of Franklin	My Lord or Dear Lord Franklin	Lord Franklin	Lord Franklin
Countess (wife of an earl)	The Right Honorable the Countess of Franklin	Madam or Dear Lady Franklin	Lady Franklin	Lady Franklin
Viscount/Viscountess	The Right Honorable the V_____ Tyburn	My Lord/Lady or Dear Lord/Lady Tyburn	Lord/Lady Tyburn	Lord/Lady Tyburn
Baron/Baroness	The Right Honorable Lord/Lady Austin	My Lord/Madam or Dear Lord/Lady Austin	Lord/Lady Austin	Lord/Lady Austin
Baronet	Sir John Jones, Bt.	Dear Sir or Dear Sir John	Sir John	Sir John Jones
Wife of Baronet	Lady Jones	Dear Madam or Dear Lady Jones	Lady Jones	Lady Jones
Knight	Sir John Jones	Dear Sir or Dear Sir John	Sir John	Sir John Jones
Wife of knight	Dear Madam or Dear Lady Jones	Lady Jones	Lady Jones	
Military Personnel	For commissioned officers in the U.S. armed services, the full rank is used as a title only in addressing letters and in formal introductions: one writes to Major General Ann Jones, U.S. Army, and introduces her as Major General Jones. In greetings the full rank is shortened to General: "Dear General Jones." Similar acceptable shortened greetings follow:			

	Full Rank	*Greetings*
Army, Air Force, Marines	General of the Army	General
	Lieutenant General	General
	Brigadier General	General
	Lieutenant Colonel	Colonel
	First Lieutenant	Lieutenant
	Second Lieutenant	Lieutenant
Navy, Coast Guard	Fleet Admiral	Admiral
	Vice Admiral	Admiral
	Rear Admiral	Admiral
	Lieutenant Commander	Commander
	Lieutenant, Junior Grade	Lieutenant

For enlisted personnel, a similar principle applies. Sergeants—whether staff sergeants, gunnery sergeants, or first sergeants—are greeted simply as "Sergeant"; privates first class are referred to as "Private"; and, in the Navy and Coast Guard, chief petty officers are referred to as "Chief." Other noncommissioned officers are greeted by their ranks, although, informally, lower grades may be referred to generically as "Soldier" or "Sailor."

The universal terms of respect that lower ranks must use when addressing senior officers are "Sir" and "Madam." These terms are not applied to noncommissioned officers, however; the appropriate affirmative response to a sergeant, for example, is "Yes, Sergeant."

* If the cleric holds a doctorate in divinity, it is customary to add the designation D.D. after his or her name in the letter address.

Order of British Peerage

Titles of nobility, or peerages, are granted by the king or queen of Great Britain upon the recommendation of the prime minister. In most *hereditary peerages*, the title passes on to a peer's oldest son, or to his closest male heir if the peer has no son (the other children are considered commoners). The title becomes extinct if there is no male heir. There are some ancient peerages that allow the title to be passed to a daughter if the holder leaves no male descendant. The last hereditary peerage was granted in 1964.

Life peerages are created each year by the British monarch for several distinguished persons. Life peers hold the rank for their own lives only; the titles do not pass on to their children. Both men and women may be granted life peerages, and the titles given to them are baron or baroness.

The following are the five grades of peers ranked from the highest to the lowest and the dates they were created. (Duke is the highest hereditary rank below that of prince.)

1. duke or duchess (1337)
2. marquess, marquis or marchioness (1385)
3. earl or countess (c. 800–1000)
4. viscount or viscountess (1440)
5. baron or baroness (c. 1066)

Abbreviated Titles That Follow Names

An abbreviated title can tell more about a person than his or her name. It will identify a rank or position, membership in a monastic or secular order, academic degree, or military or civil honor. The following list includes some familiar as well as some obscure abbreviated titles.

Abbreviation	Title
A.B.	*artium baccalaureus* (bachelor of arts)
A.M.	*artium magister* (master of arts)
B.A.	bachelor of arts
B.D.	bachelor of divinity
B.S.	bachelor of science
D.B.	*divinitatis baccalaureus* (bachelor of divinity)
D.C.	doctor of chiropractic
D.D.	*divinitatis doctor* (doctor of divinity)
D.D.S.	doctor of dental surgery
D.O.	doctor of osteopathy
D.S.O.	Distinguished Service Order
D.V.M.	doctor of veterinary medicine
Esq.	esquire
F.R.S.	fellow of the Royal Society
J.D.	*juris doctor* (doctor of law, doctor of jurisprudence), *jurum doctor* (doctor of laws)
J.P.	justice of the peace
Kt.	knight
L.H.D.	*litterarum humaniorum doctor* (doctor of humanities)
Litt.D.	*litterarum doctor* (doctor of letters)
LL.B.	*legum baccalaureus* (bachelor of laws)
M.A.	master of arts
M.B.A.	master of business administration
M.D.	*medicinae doctor* (doctor of medicine)
M.P.	member of Parliament
M.S.	master of science
M.S.W.	master of social work
Ph.B.	*philosophiae baccalaureus* (bachelor of philosophy)
Ph.D.	*philosophiae doctor* (doctor of philosophy)
Ph.G.	graduate in pharmacy
Psy.D.	doctor of psychology
R.N.	registered nurse
S.B.	bachelor of science
S.J.	Society of Jesus
S.M.	master of science
S.T.B.	*sacrae theologiae baccalaureus* (bachelor of sacred theology)

Additional Sources of Information

Baldridge, Letitia. *The Amy Vanderbilt Complete Book of Etiquette: A Guide to Contemporary Living*, rev. ed. Doubleday, 1978.

Blumenthal, Lassor A. *The Art of Letter Writing*. Putnam, 1986.

Crisp, Quentin, and Joseph Hofsess. *Manners from Heaven: A Divine Guide to Good Behavior*. Harper & Row, 1985.

Lott, James E. *Practical Protocol: A Guide to International Courtesies*. Gulf, 1973.

Mark, Lisbeth. *The Book of Hierarchies: A Compendium of Steps, Ranks, Orders, Levels, Classes, Grades, Tiers, Arrays, Degrees, Lines, Divisions, Categories, Precedents, Priorities & Other Distinctions*. William Morrow, 1984.

Martin, Judith. *Miss Manners' Guide to Excruciatingly Correct Behavior*. Galahad Books, 1991.

McCaffree, Maryjane, and Pauline Innis. *Protocol: The Complete Handbook of Diplomatic, Official and Social Usage*, rev. ed. Devon, 1985.

Post, Elizabeth. *Emily Post's Etiquette*, 15th ed. HarperCollins, 1992.

Swartz, Oretha D. *Service Etiquette*, 4th ed. Naval Institute Press, 1988.

16

Legal Information

Federal Judicial System / *395*

Supreme Court Justices / *395*

Forms and Contracts / *397*

Statute of Limitations / *421*

Copyrights / *421*

Patents / *422*

Legal Terms / *424*

Supreme Court Decisions / *431*

The Death Penalty / *432*

Additional Sources of Information / *433*

Federal Judicial System

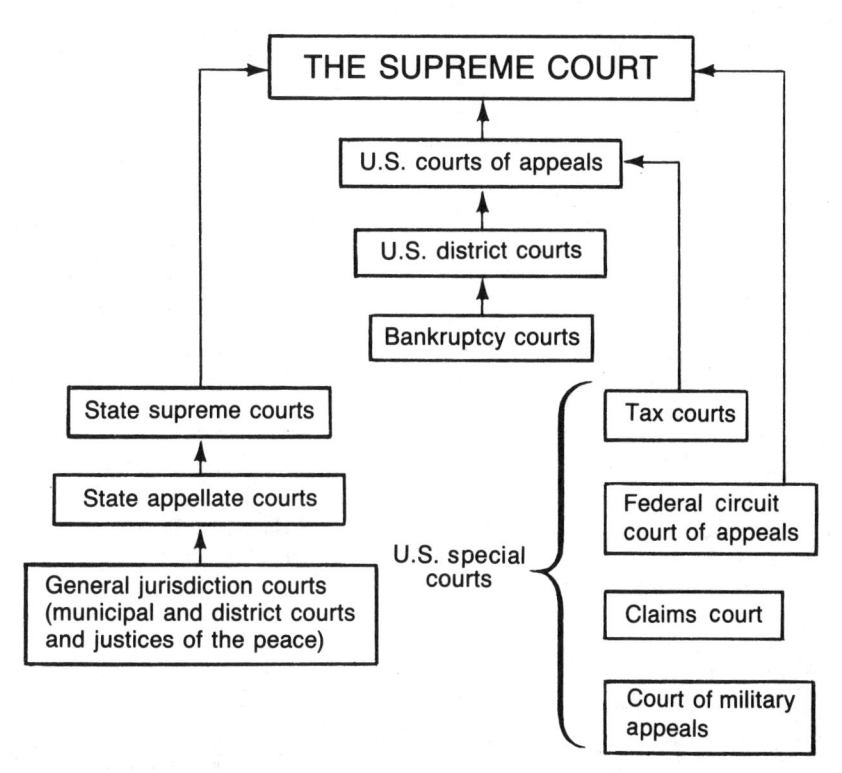

```
                    THE SUPREME COURT
                            ▲
                            |
                    U.S. courts of appeals
                            ▲
                            |
                    U.S. district courts
                            ▲
                            |
                    Bankruptcy courts
```

- State supreme courts
- State appellate courts
- General jurisdiction courts (municipal and district courts and justices of the peace)

U.S. special courts:
- Tax courts
- Federal circuit court of appeals
- Claims court
- Court of military appeals

Supreme Court Justices

Justice	Term	Justice	Term
*John Jay	1789–95	Bushrod Washington	1798–1829
John Blair	1789–96	Alfred Moore	1799–1804
William Cushing	1789–1810	*John Marshall	1801–35
John Rutledge	1789–91	William Johnson	1804–34
James Wilson	1789–98	Brockholst Livingston	1806–23
James Iredell	1790–99	Thomas Todd	1807–26
Thomas Johnson	1791–93	Joseph Story	1811–45
William Paterson	1793–1806	Gabriel Duval	1812–35
*John Rutledge	1795 (Senate rejected his appointment as chief justice)	Smith Thompson	1823–43
		Robert Trimble	1826–28
		John McLean	1829–61
		Henry Baldwin	1830–44
*Oliver Ellsworth	1796–1800	James M. Wayne	1835–67
Samuel Chase	1796–1811	*Roger B. Taney	1836–64

Justice	Term	Justice	Term
Philip P. Barbour	1836–41	Louis D. Brandeis	1916–39
John Catron	1837–65	John H. Clarke	1916–22
John McKinley	1837–52	*William H. Taft	1921–30
Peter V. Daniel	1841–60	Pierce Butler	1922–39
Samuel Nelson	1845–72	George Sutherland	1922–38
Levi Woodbury	1845–51	Edward T. Sanford	1923–30
Robert C. Grier	1846–70	Harlan F. Stone	1925–41
Benjamin R. Curtis	1851–57	*Charles E. Hughes	1930–41
John A. Campbell	1853–61	Owen J. Roberts	1930–45
Nathan Clifford	1858–81	Benjamin N. Cardozo	1932–38
David Davis	1862–77	Hugo L. Black	1937–71
Samuel F. Miller	1862–90	Stanley F. Reed	1938–57
Noah H. Swayne	1862–81	William O. Douglas	1939–75
Stephen J. Field	1863–97	Felix Frankfurter	1939–62
*Salmon P. Chase	1864–73	Frank Murphy	1940–49
Joseph P. Bradley	1870–92	*Harlan F. Stone	1941–46
William Strong	1870–80	James F. Byrnes	1941–42
Ward Hunt	1873–82	Robert H. Jackson	1941–54
*Morrison R. Waite	1874–88	Wiley B. Rutledge	1943–49
John M. Harlan	1877–1911	Harold H. Burton	1945–58
William B. Woods	1881–87	*Fred M. Vinson	1946–53
Stanley Matthews	1881–89	Tom C. Clark	1949–67
Samuel Blatchford	1882–1903	Sherman Minton	1949–56
Horace Gray	1882–1902	*Earl Warren	1953–69
*Melville W. Fuller	1888–1910	John Marshall Harlan	1955–71
Lucius Q. C. Lamar	1888–93	William H. Brennan, Jr.	1956–90
David J. Brewer	1890–1910	Charles E. Whittaker	1957–62
Henry B. Brown	1891–1906	Potter Stewart	1958–81
George Shiras, Jr.	1892–1903	Arthur J. Goldberg	1962–65
Howell E. Jackson	1893–95	Byron R. White	1962–
Edward D. White	1894–1910	Abe Fortas	1965–69
Rufus W. Peckham	1896–1909	Thurgood Marshall	1967–91
Joseph McKenna	1898–1925	*Warren E. Burger	1969–86
Oliver W. Holmes	1902–32	Harry A. Blackmun	1970–
William R. Day	1903–22	Lewis F. Powell, Jr.	1972–87
William H. Moody	1906–10	William H. Rehnquist	1972–86
*Edward D. White	1910–21	John Paul Stevens, III	1975–
Charles E. Hughes	1910–16	Sandra Day O'Connor	1981–
Horace H. Lurton	1910–14	*William H. Rehnquist	1986–
Joseph R. Lamar	1911–16	Antonin Scalia	1986–
Willis Van Devanter	1911–37	Anthony M. Kennedy	1988–
Mahlon Pitney	1912–22	David H. Souter	1990–
James C. McReynolds	1914–41	Clarence Thomas	1991–

* chief justice

Forms and Contracts

The wording of the documents in the following sections are fairly standard versions of simple agreements, requests, or statements. They are meant to demonstrate the content of such documents. Because laws vary from state to state, and because agreements can have their own special circumstances, terms, or other complexities, it is always a good idea to consult with a lawyer before drawing up or signing a contract.

Certificate of Notary

A certificate of notary often accompanies agreements or statements; it may be required in some localities. The certificate of notary might be useful with the following documents in this section:

>Bill of Sale
>Declaration of Gift
>Request for Reason for Adverse Credit Action
>Power of Attorney
>Living Will
>Privacy Act/Freedom of Information Act Request

CERTIFICATE OF NOTARY

STATE OF   )
)   ss:
COUNTY OF   )

On this _____ day of _____, 19___, before me personally came and appeared _____, known, and known to me, to be the individual described in and who executed the foregoing instrument, and who duly acknowledged to me that he/she executed same for the purpose therein contained.

IN WITNESS WHEREOF, I hereunto set my hand and official seal.

_____
Notary Public

My commission expires:_____

Leases

Lease Agreement—Unfurnished Apartment

Landlord _____

_____
                            Address   *Phone*

Managing Agent _____

_____
                            Address   *Phone*

Premises _____
                            Address   *Apt. No.*

Tenant _____

Tenant _____

1. The LANDLORD hereby leases to _____ (and) _____ , hereinafter termed TENANT, the premises described above for a term of beginning and ending _____ , at a monthly rate of $_____ , making a total rental amount payable under this lease of $_____ .

2. The tenant agrees to pay the rent herein provided subject to the terms and conditions set forth herein.

3. Rent shall be payable in equal monthly installments to be paid in advance on the _____ day of each month.

4. Rent shall be payable in the following manner:

(Specify above if payments are to be made by mail, and if so, to what address. If payments are to be made to the landlord or the landlord's agent in person, state the place where, and the person to whom, payments are to be made.)

5. Upon receiving any payment of rent in cash, the landlord agrees to issue a receipt stating the tenant's name, a description of the premises, the amount of rent paid, the date paid and the period for which rent is paid.

6. The landlord covenants that the leased premises are, to the best of his or her knowledge, clean, safe, sound, and healthful and that there exists no violation of any applicable housing code, law or regulation of which he or she is aware.

7. The tenant agrees to comply with all sanitary laws, ordinances, and rules, and all orders of the Board of Health or other authorities affecting the cleanliness, occupancy, and preservation of the premises during the term of this lease.

8. The tenant shall use the leased premises exclusively as a private residence for no more than _____ persons, and the tenant will not make alterations therein without the written consent of the landlord.

9. The tenant shall keep fixtures in said apartment in good order and repair, and the tenant shall cause to be made, at the tenant's expense, all required repairs to heating and air-conditioning apparatus, refrigerator, range, electric and gas fixtures, and plumbing work whenever such damage shall have resulted from misuse, waste, or neglect, it being understood that the landlord is to have same in good order and repair when giving possession.

10. The tenant shall not keep or have in the leased premises any article or thing of a dangerous, inflammable, or explosive nature that might be pronounced "hazardous" or "extra hazardous" by any responsible insurance company.

11. The tenant shall give prompt notice to the landlord of any dangerous, defective, unsafe, or emergency condition in the leased premises, said notice being given by any suitable means. The landlord shall repair and correct said conditions promptly upon receiving notice thereof from the tenant.

12. The landlord covenants that all essential services are now provided and shall be provided at all times during the term of this lease and any extension, renewal, or continuation thereof, except where any interruption of essential services shall be for maintenance or for cause beyond control of the landlord such as strike, storm, civil insurrection, fire, or acts of God. "Essential services" hereunder are defined as heat, hot and cold running water, a properly functioning toilet, light in public areas, and suitable building security.

13. The _____ shall pay for gas and electricity except to the extent otherwise set forth herein.

14. The landlord covenants that consumption of electricity for the public halls and other common areas and use and consumption of gas for heat or hot water in public areas are recorded on separate meters, and that said electricity and gas are and will at all times be billed to and paid by the landlord.

15. The tenant covenants that during the last 30 days of this lease, or any renewal thereof, the landlord or his agents, with reasonable notice, and at reasonable hours, have the privilege of showing the premises to prospective buyers or tenants.

16. The tenant shall, at reasonable times, give access to the landlord or his agents for any reasonable and lawful purpose. Except in situations of compelling emergency, or to show the premises for rental or sale, the landlord agrees to give the tenant 24 hours' notice, stating the time and date when access will be sought, and the reason therefor.

17. The landlord covenants that the tenant and the tenant's family shall have, hold, and enjoy the leased premises for the term of this lease, subject to the provisions and conditions set forth herein.

18. The tenant covenants that he shall not commit nor permit a nuisance in or upon the premises, that he shall not maliciously or by reason of gross negligence damage the premises, and that he shall not engage in conduct so as to interfere substantially with the comfort and safety of occupants of adjacent apartments or buildings.

19. The tenant agrees to place a security deposit with the landlord in the amount of $_____ , to be used by the landlord for the cost of replacing and/or repairing damage, if any, to the premises caused by the intentional or negligent acts of the tenant.

20. The landlord agrees, within 10 days of receiving said security deposit, to deposit same in an interest-bearing account in a banking organization, in which said deposit shall earn interest at a rate which shall be the prevailing rate earned by other such deposits made with banking organizations in such circumstances.

21. The landlord agrees, within 10 days of making such deposit, to notify the tenant, in writing, of the name and address of the banking organization in which the deposit of security money has been made.

22. The landlord shall be entitled to receive, as administrative expenses, an amount equal to one percent per annum upon the security payment so deposited, which shall be in lieu of all other administrative and custodial expenses. The balance of the interest paid by the banking organization shall be the money of the tenant and shall be paid to the tenant on each anniversary of this lease or any extension or renewal thereof.

23. The landlord agrees to return said security deposit to the tenant within 10 days of the tenant's vacating the leased premises subject to the terms and conditions set forth herein.

24. In the event of any breach by the tenant of any of the tenant's covenants or agreements herein, the landlord may give the tenant five days' notice to cure said breach, setting forth in writing which covenants or agreements have been breached. If any breach is not cured within said five-day period, or reasonable steps to effectuate said cure are not commenced and diligently pursued within said five-day period and thereafter until said breach has been cured, the landlord may terminate this lease upon five days' additional notice to the tenant, with said notice being in lieu of a Notice to Quit, which tenant hereby waives. The tenant shall then become liable for the cost of landlord's normal redecorating and cleaning expenses related to preparation of the premises for rental to a succeeding tenant.

Said termination shall be ineffective if the tenant cures said breach or commences and diligently pursues reasonable steps to effectuate such cure at any time prior to the expiration of said five-day termination. Upon terminating this lease as provided herein, the landlord or his agent may commence proceedings against the tenant for his removal as provided for by law.

25. In the event of any breach by the landlord of any of the landlord's covenants or agreements herein, the tenant may give the landlord 10 days' notice to cure said breach, setting forth in writing the manner in which said covenants and agreements have been breached. If said breach is not cured within said 10-day period, or reasonable steps to effectuate said cure are not commenced and diligently pursued within said 10-day period and thereafter until said breach has been cured, rent hereunder shall be fully abated from the time at which said 10 days' notice expired until such time as the landlord has fully cured the breach set forth in the notice provided for in this paragraph.

26. In no case shall any abatement of rent hereunder be effected where the condition set forth in the notice provided for herein was created by the intentional or negligent act of the tenant, but the landlord shall have the burden of proving that rent abatement may not be effected for the foregoing reason.

27. The landlord agrees to deliver possession of the leased premises at the beginning of the term provided for herein. In the event of the landlord's failure to deliver possession at the beginning of said term, the tenant shall have the right to rescind this lease and to recover any consideration paid under terms of this agreement.

28. The tenant agrees that this lease shall be subject to and subordinate to any mortgage or mortgages now on said premises or which any owner of said premises may hereafter at any time elect to place on said premises.

29. Unless otherwise provided for elsewhere in this lease, any notice required or authorized herein shall be given in writing, one copy of said notice mailed via U.S. certified mail, return receipt requested, and one copy of said notice mailed via U.S. first-class mail.

Notice to the tenant shall be mailed to him at the leased premises. Notice to the landlord shall be mailed to him, or to the managing agent, at their respective addresses as set forth herein, or at such new address as to which the tenant has been duly notified.

30. This lease constitutes the entire agreement between the parties hereto. No changes shall be made herein except by writing, signed by each party and dated. The failure to enforce any right or remedy hereunder, and the payment and acceptance of rent hereunder, shall not be deemed a waiver by either party of such right or remedy in the absence of a writing as provided for herein.

31. In the event legal action is required to enforce any provision of this agreement, the prevailing party shall be entitled to recover reasonable attorney's fees and costs.

32. The landlord and tenant agree that this apartment lease, when filled out and signed, is a binding legal obligation.

IN WITNESS WHEREOF, the parties hereto have executed this agreement.

_____
Landlord

By _____

_____
Witness as to landlord

_____
Witness as to landlord

_____
Tenant

_____
Witness as to tenant

_____
Witness as to tenant

_____
Tenant

_____
Witness as to tenant

_____
Witness as to tenant

Dated this _____ day of _____, 19_____.

Seasonal Lease Agreement—Furnished Country/Seashore House

Landlord _____
_____
Address   Phone

Managing Agent _____
_____
Address   Phone

Premises _____
_____

Tenant _____
_____
Address   Phone

Tenant _____
_____
Address   Phone

1. The LANDLORD hereby leases to _____ (and) _____, hereinafter termed TENANT, the premises described above for a term of _____ beginning _____ and ending _____, at a monthly rate of $_____, making a total rental amount payable under this lease of $_____ .

2. The tenant agrees to pay the rent in the following manner:

(Landlord specify if payments are to be made by mail, and if so, to what address. If payments are to be made to the landlord or his agent in person, state the place where, and the person to whom, payments should be made.)

3. The tenant, in addition to rent, agrees to pay all charges for water, gas, fuel oil, and electricity used during the term of the lease, such charges to be paid monthly in addition to rent.

4. Upon receipt of any payment for rent or utilities in cash, the landlord agrees to issue a receipt stating the tenant's name, a description of the premises, the amount paid, the date paid, and the period for which rent or utilities is paid.

5. The tenant agrees to place a security deposit of $_____ , to be used by the landlord at the termination of this lease for the cost of replacing or repairing damage, if any, to the premises or furnishings caused by the intentional or negligent acts of the tenant.

6. The landlord agrees to return said security deposit to the tenant upon the tenant's vacating the premises subject to the terms and conditions herein.

7. The tenant agrees to take good care of the premises and of the furnishings therein, and at the end of the term of this lease to deliver up to the landlord the premises and furnishings in good order, normal wear and tear excepted.

8. The landlord covenants that the leased premises are, to the best of his or her knowledge, clean, safe, sound, and healthful and that there exists no violation of any applicable housing code, law, or regulation of which he or she is aware, and that no such violation will be permitted to exist during the term of this lease or any extension thereof.

9. The tenant shall promptly comply with all laws, orders, ordinances, and regulations pertaining to his or her use of the premises, and the tenant shall not keep therein any article or thing of a dangerous, flammable or explosive nature that might be pronounced "hazardous" or "extra hazardous" by any responsible insurance company.

10. The tenant shall, in case of fire, give immediate notice to the proper authorities and to the landlord who will cause the damage to be promptly repaired; but if the premises be so damaged that the landlord shall decide to terminate this lease, then upon 10 days' personal or written notice to the tenant this lease shall terminate and the accrued rent shall be paid up to the time of the fire.

11. The tenant shall do no cooking in any room used for sleeping purposes, but shall have the right to use jointly with any other tenants a room set aside by the landlord for that purpose.

12. The tenant shall, at reasonable times, give access to the landlord or his agents for any reasonable and lawful purpose. Except in situations of compelling emergency, the landlord shall give the tenant at least 24 hours' notice of intention to seek access, the date and time at which access will be sought, and the reason therefor.

13. In the event of default by the tenant, the tenant shall remain liable for all rent due or to become due during the term of this lease. The landlord shall have the obligation to relet the premises in the landlord's name for the balance of the term, or longer, and will apply proceeds of such reletting toward the reduction of the tenant's obligations enumerated herein.

14. The tenant shall permit the landlord or his agents to show the premises at reasonable hours, to persons desiring to rent or purchase same, 30 days prior to the expiration of this lease, and will permit the notice "To Let" or "For Sale" to be placed on said premises and remain thereon without hindrance or molestation after said date.

15. The tenant shall not assign this lease, nor underlet or underlease the premises, or any part thereof, nor make any alterations to the premises, nor permit same to be used at any time during the term of this lease for any other purpose than a private residence.

16. This lease, and any attached List of Furnishings signed by both parties and dated, and incorporated herein by reference for all purposes, constitutes the entire agreement between the parties hereto. No changes shall be made herein except by writing, signed by each party and dated.

17. In the event legal action is required to enforce any provision of this agreement, the prevailing party shall be entitled to recover reasonable attorney's fees and costs.

18. This lease, when filled out and signed, is a binding legal obligation.

IN WITNESS WHEREOF, the parties hereto have executed this agreement.

_____
Landlord

By _____

_____
Witness as to landlord

_____
Tenant

_____
Tenant

_____
Witness as to tenant

_____
Witness as to tenant

Dated this _____ day of _____ , 19_____ .

"Open" Rental Agreement

THIS AGREEMENT is made this _____ day of _____,

19_____ , between _____ , of

_____ ,

   Street Address   *City*   *State*   *Zip*

hereinafter called "Owner," and _____ , of

_____

   Street Address   *City*   *State*   *Zip*

hereinafter called "Renter."

Property

_____

_____

_____

_____

_____   _____   _____

    Year   *Make*   *Model/Type*

_____   _____   _____

  Capacity   *Horsepower*   *Serial No.*

    The Owner warrants that to the best of his/her knowledge and belief the aforesaid property is free of any known faults or deficiencies which would affect its safe and dependable operation under normal and prudent usage.

Rental Period

The Owner agrees to rent the above-described property to the Renter for a period of _____ beginning _____ and ending _____ .

Use of Property

_____

_____

_____

_____

_____

The Renter further agrees that the rented property (A) shall not be used beyond any rated capacity; (B) shall not be used for any illegal purpose; (C) shall not be used in any manner for which it was not designed, built, or designated by the manufacturer; (D) will not be used in a negligent manner; (E) will not be operated by any other person without the written permission of the Owner; and (F) will not be removed from the designated area of use or operation.

Area of Use or Operation

The Renter agrees to operate/use the above-described property only at the following location or within the following described area(s):

_____

_____

_____

Insurance

The Renter hereby agrees that he/she shall fully indemnify the Owner for any and all damage to or loss of the rented property and any accessories or related equipment during the term of this Agreement whether caused by fire, theft, flood, vandalism, or any other cause, except that which shall be determined to have been caused by a fault or deficiency of the rented property, accessories, or equipment.

Rental Rate

The Renter hereby agrees to pay the Owner at the rate of $_____ per _____ for the use of said property and any accessories/equipment. Any fuel used shall be paid for by the Renter.

Deposit

The Renter further agrees to make a deposit of $_____ with the Owner, said deposit to be used, in the event of loss of or damage to the rented property and any accessories/equipment during the term of this Agreement, to defray fully or partially the cost of necessary repairs or replacement. In the absence of any damage or loss, said deposit shall be credited toward payment of the rental fee and any excess shall be returned to the Renter.

Return of Property to Owner

The Renter hereby agrees to return the rented property and any accessories/equipment to the Owner at _____
_____ no later than _____ .

Termination of Agreement

It is mutually agreed that the Renter shall have the right to terminate this Agreement at any time by payment of one full day's rental for each 24-hour period or any part thereof, during which the Renter has retained possession of the property and any accessories/equipment during the term of this Agreement.

IN WITNESS WHEREOF, the parties hereto hereby execute this Agreement.

(Signed) _____
Renter

(Signed) _____
Owner

Contract

Agreement Between Owner and Contractor

THIS AGREEMENT is hereby entered into this _____ day of _____ , 19_____ , between

_____ , of

| Street Address | City | Street | Zip | Phone |

hereinafter called Owner, and _____ , of

| Street Address | City | Street | Zip | Phone |

hereinafter called the Contractor.

The said parties, for the considerations hereinafter mentioned, hereby agree to the following:

Description of the Work

1. The Contractor shall provide all materials and labor required to perform all of the work for: as shown on the drawing(s), and set forth in the specifications and/or description(s) prepared by _____ , which drawing(s) and specifications and/or description(s) are identified by the signatures of the parties to this agreement, and which form a part of this agreement and are incorporated by reference herein for all purposes.

Payment

2. Under the terms of this agreement, the Owner agrees to pay the Contractor, for materials to be furnished and work to be done, the sum of _____ ($_____), subject to any additions or deductions as hereinafter provided for in this agreement, and to make the following payments:

and that the final payment shall be made subject to the hereinafter stated conditions of this agreement.

It is agreed that no payment made under this agreement shall be considered conclusive evidence of full performance of this contract, either wholly or in part by the Contractor, and that acceptance of payment shall not be considered by the Contractor to be acceptance by the Owner of any defective materials or workmanship.

Liens

3. Final payment shall not be due until such time as the Contractor has provided the Owner with a release of any liens arising from this agreement; or receipts for payment in full for all materials and labor for which a lien could be filed; or a bond satisfactory to the Owner indemnifying the Owner against any lien.

Timely Completion of the Work

4. The Contractor agrees that the various portions of the work shall be completed on or before the following dates:
and the entire work shall be completed on or before the _____ day of _____ , 19 ____ .

In the event the work is not completed by the aforementioned date, the Owner shall be entitled to receive as damages from the Contractor, the sum of _____
_____ ($_____) per _____) , it being agreed that the aforementioned sum is reasonable, taking into account the difficulty in determining the exact amount of damages the Owner would sustain in the event of said delay, and that the agreed sum shall be considered as liquidated damages.

If the Contractor is delayed in the completion of the work by any changes ordered in the work, by acts of God, fire, flood, or any other unavoidable casualties; or by labor strikes, late delivery of materials; or by neglect of the Owner, his agents or representatives; or by any subcontractor employed by the Contractor; the time for completion of the work shall be extended for the same period as the delay occasioned by any of the aforementioned causes.

Surveys and Easements

5. The Owner shall provide and pay for all surveys. All easements for access across the property of another, and for permanent changes, and for the construction or erection of structures shall also be obtained and paid for by the Owner.

Licenses, Permits, and Building Codes

6. The Contractor shall obtain and pay for all permits and licenses required for the prosecution and timely completion of the work. The Contractor shall comply with all appropriate regulations relating to the conduct of the work and shall advise the Owner of any specifications or drawings which are at variance therewith.

Materials and Equipment

7. The Contractor shall provide and pay for all materials, tools, and equipment required for the prosecution and timely completion of the work. Unless otherwise specified in writing, all materials shall be new and of good quality.

Samples

8. Whenever the Owner may require, the Contractor will furnish for approval all samples as directed, and the work shall be in accordance with approved samples.

Labor and Supervision

9. In the prosecution of the work the Contractor shall at all times keep a competent foreman and a sufficient number of workers skilled in their trades to suitably perform the work.

The foreman shall represent the Contractor and, in the absence of the Contractor, all instructions given by the Owner to the foreman shall be binding upon the Contractor as though given to the Contractor. Upon request of the foreman, instructions shall be in writing.

Alterations and Changes

10. All changes and deviations in the work ordered by the Owner must be in writing, the contract sum being increased or decreased accordingly by the Contractor. Any claims for increases in the cost of the work must be presented by the Contractor to the Owner in writing, and written approval of the Owner shall be obtained by the Contractor before proceeding with the ordered change or revision.

In the event that additional work, not shown on the drawings and/or not described in the specifications, is required to comply with laws, regulations, or building codes, such additional work shall be considered as done under the terms of this agreement.

Correction of Deficiencies

11. The Contractor agrees to reexecute any work which does not conform to the drawings and specifications, warrants the work performed, and further agrees that he shall remedy any defects resulting from faulty materials or workmanship which shall become evident during a period of one year after completion of the work. This provision shall apply with equal force to all work performed by subcontractors as to work that is performed by direct employees of the Contractor.

Protection of the Work

12. It shall be the responsibility of the Contractor to reasonably protect the work, the property of the Owner, and adjacent property and the public, and the Contractor shall be responsible for any damage, injury, or death resulting from his negligence or from any intentional act of the Contractor or the Contractor's employees, agents, or subcontractors.

Cleaning Up

13. The Contractor shall keep the premises free from the accumulation of waste and, upon completion of the work, shall remove all waste, equipment, and other materials and leave the premises in broom-clean condition.

Contractor's Liability Insurance

14. The Contractor shall obtain insurance to protect himself against claims for property damage arising out of his or any subcontractor's performance of this contract; and to protect himself against claims under provisions of Workman's Compensation and any similar employee benefit acts, and from claims for bodily injury, including death, due to performance of this contract by the Contractor or any subcontractor employed for the performance of this contract.

Owner's Liability Insurance

15. It shall be the responsibility of the Owner, at the Owner's option, to obtain insurance to protect himself from the contingent liability of claims for property damage and bodily injury, including death, that may arise from the performance of this contract.

Fire Insurance with Extended Coverage

16. The Owner shall obtain fire insurance with extended coverage at 100 percent of the value of the entire structure, including materials and labor related to the work described in this agreement. Certificates of insurance shall be filed with the Contractor if he so requests. The aforesaid fire insurance need not include tools, equipment, scaffolding, or forms owned or rented by the Contractor, any subcontractor, or their respective employees.

Owner's Right to Terminate the Agreement

17. In the event the Contractor shall fail to meet the provisions of this agreement, the Owner shall, after seven (7) days' written notice to the Contractor and his surety, have the right to take possession of the premises in order to complete the work as specified in the agreement. The Owner may deduct the cost thereof from any payment then and thereafter due to the Contractor or may, at his option, terminate the agreement, take possession of any materials, and complete the work as he deems appropriate. If the unpaid balance of the contracted sum exceeds the Owner's expenses of completing the work, such excess shall be paid to the Contractor. If such expense shall exceed the unpaid balance, the Contractor shall pay the difference to the Owner.

Contractor's Right to Terminate the Agreement

18. In the event the Owner shall fail to pay the Contractor within seven (7) days after the date upon which payment shall become due, the Contractor shall have the right, after seven (7) days' written notice to the Owner, to stop work and may, at his option, terminate the agreement and recover from the Owner payment for all work executed, plus any loss sustained, plus a reasonable profit, plus damages.

In the event the work is stopped by any court or other public authority for a period of thirty (30) days through no fault of the Contractor, the Contractor shall have the right to stop work and may, at his option, terminate the agreement and recover from the Owner payment for all work executed, plus any loss sustained, plus a reasonable profit, plus damages.

Assignment of Rights

19. Neither the Owner nor Contractor shall have the right to assign any rights or interest occurring under this agreement without the written consent of the other, nor shall the Contractor assign any sums due, or to become due, to him under the provisions of this agreement.

Access and Inspection

20. The Owner, Owner's representative, and public authorities shall at all times have access to the work.

An appropriately licensed representative of the Owner, whose authority shall be set forth in writing by the Owner, shall have the authority to direct the removal of any materials and the taking down of any portions of the work failing to meet drawings, specifications, laws, regulations, or building codes; the reexecution of said work deemed as being done under the provisions of Article 11 of this agreement.

Any other removal of materials or taking down of any portions of the work as directed by the Owner's representative shall be in writing and at the sole expense of the Owner.

Attorney Fees

21. Attorney fees and court costs shall be paid by the defendant in the event that judgment must be obtained, and is, to enforce this agreement or any breach thereof.

IN WITNESS WHEREOF, the parties hereto set their hands and seals the day and year written above.

_____   _____
Witness as to Owner   *Owner*

_____   _____
Witness as to Contractor   *Contractor*

Bill of Sale

𝔅ill of 𝔖ale
of

_____

STATE OF _____)
) ss:
COUNTY OF _____)

KNOW YE ALL MEN BY THESE PRESENTS,

    That I, _____ , of

_____ ,
   Street Address   *City*   *State*   *Zip*

for and in consideration of payment of the sum of $_____ , the receipt of which is hereby acknowledged, do hereby grant, bargain, sell, and convey to:

_____ , of

_____ ,
   Street Address   *City*   *State*   *Zip*

and his/her heirs, executors, administrators, successors, and assigns the following property:

    I hereby warrant that I am the lawful owner of said property and that I have full legal right, power, and authority to sell said property. I further warrant said property to be free of all encumbrances and that I will warrant and defend said property hereby sold against any and all persons whomsoever.
    IN WITNESS WHEREOF, I, the seller, have hereto set my hand and seal this _____ day of _____ , 19_____ .

                    (Signed) _____
                                                  Seller

Declaration of a Gift

Declaration of Gift

TO ALL TO WHOM THESE PRESENTS SHALL COME OR MAY CONCERN, KNOW THAT on this _____ day of _____, 19_____ I, _____

_____, of _____,
  Street   City   State   Zip

being of sound and disposing mind and memory, do hereby irrevocably give, bestow, and deliver up to

_____,

of _____,
  Street   City   State   Zip

all of my right, title, and interest in the following described property valued at _____

_____ ($_____):

_____

_____

_____

_____

_____

_____

_____

IN WITNESS WHEREOF, I hereunto set my hand and seal on the date above mentioned.

_____

Promissory Note

Promissory Note

$ _____

Date _____

_____ after the above date I promise to pay to the order of _____
(number of days)

_____ the sum of _____
_____ ($_____), together with interest at _____ percent per annum, payable at _____.

 The maker and endorser of this note further agree to waive demand, notice of nonpayment and protest, and in case suit shall be brought for the collection hereof, or the same has to be collected upon demand of an attorney, to pay reasonable attorney's fees for making such collection. Deferred interest payments to bear interest from maturity at _____ percent per annum, payable semiannually.

(Signed) _____
Maker

(Signed) _____
Endorser

Due _____

Security Agreement

Security Agreement

STATE OF _____)
) ss:
COUNTY OF _____)

KNOW YE ALL MEN BY THESE PRESENTS,

That I, _____ , of

_____ ,
Street Address   Apt. No.   City   State   Zip

hereinafter called "Debtor," hereby grant to _____ , of

_____ ,
Street Address   Apt. No.   City   State   Zip

hereinafter called the "Secured Party," a security interest in the following described property as collateral to secure payment of the obligation described herein.

Collateral

_____

_____

_____

_____

Obligation

_____

_____

_____

_____

_____

    Default in the payment of all or any part of the obligation described is a default under this Agreement. Upon such default the Secured Party may declare all of the above-described obligation(s) immediately due and payable and shall have the remedies of a secured party under provisions of the Uniform Commercial Code. In the event legal action is required to enforce any provision of this Agreement, the prevailing party shall be entitled to recover reasonable attorney's fees and costs.

    The Debtor hereby agrees to exercise reasonable caution and care in use of the herein-described collateral; to adequately insure or keep insured the described collateral; not to attempt to sell, assign, or dispose of said collateral or his/her interest therein; not to encumber nor to permit any encumbrance against same; and not to remove said collateral from the county where the Debtor resides without written permission of the Secured Party.

EXECUTED this _____ day of _____ , 19_____ .

(Signed) _____
                                                                Debtor

(Signed) _____
                                                            Secured Party

Request for Reason for Adverse Credit Action

Date: _____

REQUEST FOR REASON FOR ADVERSE CREDIT ACTION

Dear

On _____ , I was notified that my application for credit dated _____ was denied based upon information received by you from a source other than a consumer credit reporting agency.

Pursuant to my right under the Fair Credit Reporting Act, Title 15 USC, Sec. 1681m(b), I hereby request that the nature of the information received by you be disclosed to me.

Please forward such information to me at the above address.

Thank you for your prompt attention to this matter.

                                                        Sincerely,

Power of Attorney

Power of Attorney

STATE OF   )
) ss:
COUNTY OF   )

KNOW YE ALL MEN BY THESE PRESENTS,

That I, _____ , of

_____ ,
Street Address   *Apt. No.*   *City*   *State*   *Zip*

do hereby make, constitute, and appoint_____ , of

_____ ,
Street Address   *City*   *State*   *Zip*

as my true and lawful Attorney-in-Fact, for me and in my name, place, and stead to:

_____

_____

_____

_____

_____

    I further give and grant to my said Attorney-in-Fact full power and authority to do and perform every act necessary and proper to be done in the exercise of any of the foregoing powers as fully as I might or could do if personally present, with full power of substitution and revocation, hereby ratifying and confirming all that my said Attorney-in-Fact shall lawfully do, or cause to be done by virtue hereof.

    This instrument may not be changed orally.

    IN WITNESS WHEREOF, I have hereunto set my hand and seal this _____ day of _____ , 19_____ .

(Signed) _____

Living Will

𝕷𝖎𝖛𝖎𝖓𝖌 𝖂𝖎𝖑𝖑

Directive to Physicians:

I, _____ , of

_____ ,
Street Address   *Apt. No.*   *City*   *State*   *Zip*

being of sound mind, do hereby willfully and voluntarily make known my desire that my life not be prolonged under any of the following conditions, and do hereby further declare:

1. If I should, at any time, have an incurable condition caused by any disease or illness, or by any accident or injury, and be determined by any two or more physicians to be in a terminal condition whereby the use of "heroic measures" or the application of life-sustaining procedures would only serve to delay the moment of my death, and where my attending physician has determined that my death is imminent whether or not such "heroic measures" or life-sustaining measures are employed, I direct that such measures and procedures be withheld or withdrawn and that I be permitted to die naturally.

2. In the event of my inability to give directions regarding the application of life-sustaining procedures or the use of "heroic measures," it is my intention that this directive shall be honored by my family and physicians as my final expression of my right to refuse medical and surgical treatment, and my acceptance of the consequences of such refusal.

3. I am mentally, emotionally, and legally competent to make this directive and I fully understand its import.

4. I reserve the right to revoke this directive at any time.

5. This directive shall remain in force until revoked.

IN WITNESS WHEREOF, I have hereunto set my hand and seal this _____ day of _____, 19_____ .

(Signed) _____

Declaration of Witness

The declarant is personally known to me and I believe him/her to be of sound mind and emotionally and legally competent to make the herein-contained **Directive to Physicians**. I am not related to the declarant by blood or marriage, nor would I be entitled to any portion of the declarant's estate upon his/her decease, nor am I an attending physician of the declarant, nor an employee of the attending physician, nor an employee of a health care facility in which the declarant is a patient, nor a patient in a health care facility in which the declarant is a patient, nor am I a person who has any claim against any portion of the estate of the declarant upon his/her decease.

(Signed) _____
                                                Witness

_____
                                                Address

(Signed) _____
                                                Witness

_____
                                                Address

Privacy Act/Freedom of Information Act Request

Attn:
    This is a request under provisions of Title 5 USC, Sec. 552, the Freedom of Information Act, and Title 5 USC, Sec. 552a, the Privacy Act.
    Please furnish me with copies of all records on me retrievable by the use of an individual identifier and by the use of any combination of identifiers (e.g., name + date of birth + Social Security number, etc.) that are contained in the following systems of records:

    In order to identify myself and to facilitate your search of records systems, I provide the following information:

Last Name	First	Middle

Street	City	State	Zip

Date of Birth	Place of Birth	Sex	Social Security Number

    In the event that any part or all of my records are withheld, I request a complete list of all records being withheld and the specific exemption being claimed for the withholding of each.
    In the event that search and copying fees are estimated to exceed $_____ , I request an opportunity to review such records, or to have a duly authorized representative review such records, in order to select those to be copied.
    If you have any questions regarding this request, please telephone me at _____ weekdays between _____ and _____ or write to me at the above address.
    As provided for by Sec. 552(a)(6)(i) of the Freedom of Information Act, I shall expect to receive a reply within ten (10) business days.

                                     Sincerely,

Statute of Limitations

A statute of limitations defines the time span after an alleged offense during which legal action may be brought. After that time has elapsed, legal proceedings cannot be initiated, regardless of a case's merits.

Federal Statute of Limitations

Capital Offenses

There is no limitation on prosecution in cases punishable by death and in the crime of murder, even when the death penalty is not prescribed.

Noncapital Offenses

The limitation on noncapital offenses is five years, although Congress may make specific exceptions.

State Statute of Limitations

Varies by crime and by state.

Copyrights

The copyright law protects works of authorship, published or unpublished, in any tangible medium of expression. Under this law, creators of, among other things, books, theatrical works, computer programs, videotapes, movies, music, lyrics, choreography, pantomimes, and recordings can secure exclusive rights to perform, display, or reproduce their works. These individuals have a property right in their work and may license it for reproduction or other use.

However, anyone may make "fair use" of copyrighted material. The definition of this term depends on who is using the material, how much is used, the percentage of the entire work that the excerpt used constitutes, the purpose of the use, and the effect such use may have on the ability of the copyright holder to derive income from his or her creation. For example, a teacher may be able to photocopy a few pages of a book for use in a classroom, but an advertising firm may be entitled to quote no more than a few lines from the same book in an ad without obtaining permission from the copyright holder. And while it may be lawful to quote 200 words from a novel without asking permission, the same would not be true in the case of a poem if the 200 words constituted the whole poem.

The most recent version of the copyright law took effect in 1978. Works created before 1978 are protected for 28 years from the time they were first published. The copyright may be renewed for an additional 47 years. Works created since the beginning of 1978 may be copyrighted for the life of the author plus 50 years after his or her death. For works made for hire, and for anonymous and pseudonymous works (unless the author's identity is revealed in Copyright Office records), the term is 100 years from creation or 75 years from first publication, whichever period is shorter.

On March 1, 1989, the United States joined the Berne Convention for the Protection of Literary and Artistic Works, an international copyright treaty. Under this convention, works are copyrighted from the moment they are fixed, or notated in some tangible form, such as in writing or on audiotape.

Works published as of March 1, 1989, need not display a copyright notice, but it is still recommended. Works created but not published before 1978 and works registered with the Copyright Office as unpublished works before 1978 also need not display a copyright notice. Works published or registered before March 1, 1989, are subject to pre-Berne requirements regarding the display of a copyright notice.

This notice includes the word "Copyright," or the abbreviation "Copr.," the year the work was first published, and the name of the owner of the copyright. The copyright symbol, a "C" in a circle (except for recordings, which use a circled "P"), must also be displayed.

Displaying the notice of copyright is sufficient to establish exclusive rights to an original work. However, formal registration of a copyright claim is a prerequisite in many cases to filing suit for infringement for works whose country of origin is the United States. In addition, subject to certain exceptions, the remedies of statutory damages and attorneys' fees are not available for those infringements occurring before registration.

A copy of any work registered for copyright must be deposited with the Library of Congress. Works that are not registered for copyright may also need to be deposited there.

In addition to the Berne Convention, the United States is also a member of the Universal Copyright Convention, another multilateral agreement. Most countries of the world belong to one or both of these conventions, offering international copyright protection to works of American authors. The basic feature of this protection is "national treatment," under which the alien author is treated by a country in the same manner that it treats its own authors.

Filing for copyright registration presently costs $20. For more information and application forms, write to:

Register of Copyrights
The Library of Congress
Washington, DC 20559

Patents

Congressional grants of patents and copyrights are based on Article I, Section 8 of the Constitution, which reads "Congress shall have power . . . to promote the progress of science and useful arts, by securing for limited times to authors and inventors the exclusive rights to their respective writings and discoveries."

A patent is the grant of a property right to an inventor, excluding others from making, using, or selling his or her invention. The invention may consist of "any new and useful process, machine, manufacture, or composition of matter, or any new and useful improvements thereof . . ." It also covers ornamental designs and plants and new forms of animal life. But no one can patent printed matter or a way of doing business.

In addition to being useful, the invention must be new. If the inventor describes the invention in a printed publication or uses the invention publicly, or places it on sale, he or she must apply for a patent before one year has gone by; otherwise, any right to a patent will be lost.

The Patent and Trademark Office currently receives more than 150,000 applications for patents each year, and it has granted more than 5 million since 1790. The agency grants new patents only after a diligent search of the records to make sure that the patent is original. Inventors may use its Search Room (patent research library) in Washington or any of the many Patent Depository Libraries throughout the United States to conduct their own searches before filing.

Although inventors can handle their own applications, the agency advises that the process is complex enough to require a patent attorney—a lawyer who also has a degree in engineering or physical science.

Only the inventor may apply for a patent. If the inventor is dead or incapacitated, legal representatives or a guardian may apply. If two or more persons shared the ideas for the invention, they may apply jointly. But if one person had the idea and the other financed its development, only the person with the original idea may apply. "Small entities"—independent inventors, small businesses, and nonprofit organizations—pay a modest filing fee; others pay a higher one.

The application consists of a written description of the invention, with "claims" relating its distinguishing features—ways in which it does things in an entirely novel manner or improves significantly on previous inventions. If applicable, pen-and-ink or color drawings must accompany the description. Models are usually unnecessary. The Patent Office keeps all documents submitted in application for a patent strictly confidential while the application process runs it course.

It is not uncommon for some or all of the claims to be rejected on the first action by the patent examiner; relatively few applications are allowed as filed. The applicant responds to the examiner's objections with clarification and explanation. If the Patent Office finally rejects the application, the inventor can take the case to the Board of Patent Appeals and Interferences. If the board turns down the application, the inventor has recourse either to the Court of Appeals for the Federal Circuit or to a civil suit in U.S. District Court in Washington, D.C.

In about 1 percent of all applications, two or more applications are filed by different inventors claiming substantially the same patentable invention. Only one can receive a patent, and the procedure to determine that one is called an "interference." Each party to such a proceeding must submit evidence of facts proving when the invention was made. As in the case of the rejection of any other patent, the decision of the examiners can be appealed.

If the patent is granted, it is good for 17 years. The fee for granting a patent is presently $345 for small entities and $690 for large ones. Inventors also must pay maintenance fees after 3½, 7½, and 11½ years. Currently, these fees for small entities are $450, $905, and $1,365; for large ones, they are $900, $1,810, and $2,730.

Once a patent is granted, all documents relating to it become available for public inspection. The Patent Office can, however, keep such information secret if its commissioner decides that such information is vital to the national security.

As with any other property, patents may be sold or assigned in whole or in part to someone else. The patent holder also may license others to use the process or produce the product under specific conditions. The Patent Office cautions that a part owner of a patent, no matter how small his or her interest, may make, use, and sell the invention for his or her own profit without regard to the other owner and may sell the interest or any part of it, or license others to use or make it. Therefore, inventors should be very careful when agreeing to sell a part interest in their patent.

Patented articles must be marked with the word "Patent" and the number of the patent. Some people use "Patent Pending" or "Patent Applied For" to inform others of the status of a patent claim, but such words have no legal effect. To combat infringement of a patent, a patentee may bring a civil suit.

Patents granted by the Patent and Trademark Office protect inventions in the United States only. However, the United States is a signatory of several treaties that facilitate applications for patent protection in other countries. For further information, write to:

Commissioner of Patents and Trademarks
Washington, DC 20231

Legal Terms

accessory An individual who helps another person commit or try to commit a crime before the fact, but who is not present at the commission of the crime. An accessory *during* the fact witnesses a crime but does not do what he or she could do to prevent it; one who helps another avoid arrest for the commission of a crime is an accessory after the fact.

accomplice An individual who joins with another to commit a crime. The accomplice bears equal responsibility under the law.

actus reus A wrongful act, as opposed to *mens rea*, or thoughts and intentions behind the act. For example, in a murder, homicide is the actus reus, and "malice aforethought" is the mens rea.

adjudication A final judgment in a legal proceeding.

affidavit A written statement sworn or affirmed to be true before a person legally authorized to administer an oath.

age of consent The minimum age for marrying without parental consent; also, the minimum age for consensual sexual relations. Sexual intercourse at an earlier age can result in a charge of assault or statutory rape, even if both people participate willingly.

alibi An assertion that someone was not present at the scene of an alleged crime.

amicus curiae Latin for "friend of the court." A person or organization not party to a case who submits information useful to the court in that proceeding. Amicus curiae briefs are generally submitted when the suit involves matters of wide public interest.

amnesty An act of government forgiving members of a group, such as unregistered gun owners or illegal aliens, that would normally be subject to prosecution.

appeal A request to a superior court to reverse the decision of a lower court or government agency or to grant a new trial.

appellate court A court whose jurisdiction is confined to reviewing decisions of lower courts or agencies.

arraignment A court procedure in which formal charges are brought against a defendant, who is advised of his or her constitutional rights and may have the opportunity to offer a plea.

assault A threatened or attempted physical attack in which the attacker appears to have the ability to bring about bodily harm if not stopped; *aggravated assault* involves an attack perpetrated with recklessness and intent to injure seriously, or an assault with a deadly weapon. *Battery* is an assault in which the assailant makes contact.

attachment A court writ authorizing legal authorities to seize property that may be needed for the payment of a judgment in a judicial proceeding.

bail Security provided to ensure the presence of a defendant in court during the course of a case. Defendants raising this security are said to "make bail"; those fleeing and forfeiting the security have "jumped bail." The actual document securing the defendant's release is the bail bond.

bar Collective term for all lawyers practicing in a particular court system.

battery *See* **assault.**

bench warrant A court order authorizing a public official to arrest a person and bring that individual to court.

bequest Personal property bequeathed (given as a gift) in a will. *Devise* is the term for real property handed down through a will.

beyond a reasonable doubt The degree to which jurors must be convinced before they may convict a person of a crime. The jurors must find the prosecution's case proven beyond the point at which a reasonable, average, prudent person would be convinced before returning a verdict of guilty.

bill of particulars The specific events to be dealt with in a criminal trial, presented to the defendant so that he or she may effectively prepare a defense.

binding over Action of a lower court shifting a case to a grand jury or superior court when the inferior court believes that a crime has been committed. Also, a court order to jail a defendant during the course of a proceeding.

boilerplate Language uniformly found in certain types of documents—for instance, the "small print" in a contract that people often neglect to read.

breach of contract Failure to do something required in a contract.

breaking and entering The illegal entrance into premises with criminal intent. Simply pushing a door open and walking in may constitute breaking and entering.

brief A document in which a lawyer makes his or her client's case by raising legal points and citing authorities.

burden of proof In a civil case, the requirement that a plaintiff or defendant must show that the majority of evidence is on his or her side in order to win a suit. In a criminal case, the prosecutor's burden of proof is to prove every fact involved in a charge.

burglary Unlawful presence in a building with the aim of committing a felony or taking something of value. *See also* **robbery.**

capacity The ability to understand the facts and significance of one's behavior. A defendant cannot be convicted of a crime in which he or she did not have the legal capacity to comprehend it.

cease and desist order A legal order preventing a person or organization from continuing a specific activity. A *mandatory injunction*, on the other hand, orders the performance of a specified act.

certiorari A writ in which a superior court commands an inferior court to deliver the records of a proceeding to the superior body so that it may decide whether there is basis for appeal.

character witness *See* **witness.**

chattel Personal, rather than real, property; a *chattel mortgage*, for example, is a loan to buy an expensive item, such as a car, in which the item, or chattel, is security for the debt.

circumstantial evidence Evidence based not on direct observation or knowledge but rather implied from things already known.

class action A lawsuit brought by a group of people with a shared purpose.

clemency A reduction of criminal punishment, often granted to prevent execution of a prisoner.

codicil An addition to a will altering it.

common-law marriage A relationship in which two people live together as husband and wife without formally getting married.

community property Property owned by husband and wife jointly.

competency hearing A procedure to determine legal capacity, for example, of a defendant in a criminal case, to understand the charges, and to cooperate with a lawyer in preparing a defense. *Compos mentis* is a finding of competence to stand trial; *non compos mentis*, a lack of competence to go to trial.

complaint The first statement of facts (in a civil proceeding) or accusation (in a criminal case).

compos mentis See **competency hearing**.

consent decree An agreement between two parties sanctioned by the court, for example, between a company and the government involving alleged violations of antitrust laws. In the consent decree, the company would agree to cease such practices without formally admitting guilt.

conspiracy The plotting by two or more people to break the law.

contempt of court Anything done to hinder the work of the court. *Civil contempt* involves failure to follow a court order benefiting another party in a case, as in the failure to pay court-ordered damages; *criminal contempt* consists of the obstruction of justice.

contract A commitment between two or more parties, enforceable by law.

corpus delicti The object upon which a crime has been committed. The term does not necessarily refer to a body, although a corpse with a knife in its back would be an example in an alleged homicide.

corroborating evidence Additional evidence, or evidence different in kind, that backs up proof already offered in a proceeding.

criminal negligence See **negligence**.

cross-examination The interrogation of a witness to discredit or show in new light testimony already offered by that person in direct examination.

custody In a divorce case, the right to house, care for, and discipline a child.

damages A court-ordered monetary award to someone hurt by another.

decree A court's decision in a case; its judgment.

de facto A practice whose sanction is custom, as opposed to *de jure*, a practice formally backed by law.

defamation The damaging of another person's reputation through writing (libel) or speech (slander).

default judgment A court determination made against a defendant who fails to show up in court or fails to take some other court-required action.

defendant A person or institution in a legal proceeding being sued or accused.

de jure See **de facto**.

deposition A pretrial interrogation of a witness, usually in a lawyer's office.

directed verdict A verdict in a civil trial declared by the court before the jury gets the case. Judges render this verdict when the facts and the law in a case point to a definite conclusion. There cannot be a directed verdict of guilty in a criminal trial, since that would violate a defendant's right to trial by jury.

discovery A pretrial process that enables one side in a litigation to elicit information from the other side relating to facts in the case.

disorderly conduct A broad spectrum of offenses, such as drunkenness or fighting, that disturb the public peace.

district attorney See **prosecutor**.

docket A list of cases to be tried by a court—its calendar; also, a summary of a court's activities.

double jeopardy The condition of being tried a second time for a crime once a first case has been decided. This is prohibited by the Fifth Amendment of the U.S. Constitution.

due process The general doctrine that legislation must promote the legitimate aims of government (substantive due process) and that nobody can be deprived of liberty or property through unfair procedures (procedural due process).

easement A right to use another person's land.

emancipation The parental yielding of authority over, control over, and responsibility for a minor.

eminent domain The right of the state to convert private property to public property.

entrapment A defense in which a defendant seeks to show that he or she would not have committed an unlawful act if not tricked into doing it by law enforcement officials.

equal protection The Fourteenth Amendment requirement that all groups of people be treated equally by the legal system.

estate Everything an individual owns.

eviction The dispossessing of a tenant from land or premises he or she has occupied.

evidence Testimony, documents, and objects used to prove matters of fact at a trial.

exclusionary rule A rule preventing introduction at a criminal trial of evidence obtained in violation of the Constitution's prohibition against unreasonable searches and seizures, even if that evidence would otherwise be admissible. *See also* **search and seizure.**

executor/executrix A man or woman, respectively, appointed to administer the provisions of a will.

eyewitness One who can testify as to what happened because he or she was there when it happened and saw it; technically, one who offers testimony of something overheard is an "earwitness."

fair hearing A special administrative procedure set up to ensure that a person will not be harmed or denied his or her rights without due process of law before a court can intervene; examples of extraordinary circumstances calling for a fair hearing include loss of welfare benefits and deportation.

fair use The conditions under which one can use material copyrighted by another.

false imprisonment *See* **kidnapping.**

false pretenses Taking another's property through trickery. This crime involves intent to secure title to the property through some seemingly legal transaction. *See also* **larceny.**

fee Unencumbered ownership of property; *freehold* is land held in fee.

felony A serious crime, as opposed to a *misdemeanor*; the distinction is often made in terms of the applicable punishment, felonies being punishable by a certain minimum prison term—under federal law, a year.

felony murder Homicide committed in the course of another crime, such as a burglary.

fiduciary A person in a position of trust who acts for the benefit of another person; examples are executors, corporate directors, and infant guardians.

finding The basis in fact or law for a judgment. *See also* **judgment.**

fraud The injury of a person or group of persons through deceit.

freehold *See* **fee.**

frisk *See* **stop and frisk.**

garnishment Legal impoundment of funds owed by C to B to pay off B's debt to A; for example, the seizing of a person's pay at work to pay off a debt owed to another party.

grandfather clause A provision in some laws allowing people who had legally engaged in an activity prior to its restriction by law to continue to engage in that activity.

grand jury A jury of from 12 to 23 people empowered to look into possible criminal activity in an area, report on it, and indict individuals when it finds evidence that they have committed crimes.

guardian A person entrusted to look out for the interests of a minor or an incompetent person. The specific fiduciary relationship is defined by law and court orders.

habeas corpus The order by a judge to have a prisoner brought to court to determine the legality of the imprisonment.

hearsay evidence Statements made outside of court attesting to some fact, where the person making the statements may not be cross-examined or otherwise scrutinized; for example, if A testifies in court that he or she heard B say something, in most cases, B's statement will not be admissible as evidence.

homicide An act in which one person causes the death of another. *See also* **manslaughter; murder.**

hung jury A jury that is unable to reach a verdict.

immunity from prosecution Exemption of a witness from prosecution to thwart a refusal to testify based on constitutional rights. The witness cannot be prosecuted on the basis of anything he or she says while testifying under such immunity.

impanel To select a jury.

in camera A judicial proceeding from which the public is excluded. Although the term literally means "in chambers," the proceeding can be held anywhere outside of open court.

indictment A document, delivered to a grand jury, in which a public prosecutor accuses one or more persons of committing a crime. If the grand jury thinks the evidence submitted is sufficient to warrant a trial, it will endorse the indictment as a true bill.

infant A person who has not reached the age of majority (usually 18), at which he or she enjoys the full rights of citizenship and is legally responsible for his or her acts.

information A prosecuting attorney's written accusation of criminal activity, similar to an indictment but not presented to a grand jury. Information may be used to initiate proceedings against defendants in state, but not federal, courts.

infringement A violation of a law or right.

injunction A court order preventing someone from doing a specific act.

injury The violation of a person's rights to the point where he or she suffers any kind of damage, including financial.

in loco parentis A person or institution acting toward a minor "in place of parents" without a formal adoption procedure; for example, the relationship between a school and a student.

inquest A coroner's investigation of the cause of death.

in rem A proceeding involving property without reference to the claims of people on that property.

insanity A mental state in which one lacks legal responsibility.

intestate Without a will.

judgment A court's final decision in a case.

jury A representative group of people who determine issues of fact at a trial. The Constitution guarantees the right to trial by jury for all crimes punishable by imprisonment for more than six months. In civil trials, juries range in number from 6 to 12 people. State trial juries do not need a unanimous vote to convict (with the exception of 6-person juries), but federal juries do.

kidnapping The illegal seizure and removal of a person without his or her consent. *False imprisonment* involves illegally confining a person against his or her will without moving that person and can be committed by police officers who fail to make arrests properly.

larceny The act of gaining the use or possession of property through an overtly illegal act, as in stealing a car. *Grand larceny* involves the theft of an object worth more than a specified amount. *See also* **robbery**.

leading question A lawyer's question to a witness that predetermines the answer, thus putting words in the witness' mouth. Such questions are legitimate during cross-examination but not during direct examination.

libel *See* **defamation**.

magistrate An official, such as a justice of the peace, who performs low-level judicial functions.

majority, age of *See* **infant**.

malfeasance Wrongful conduct by a public official. *Misfeasance* is the misperforming of a proper act; *nonfeasance*, the nonperformance of an act that a person has agreed to or is duty-bound to do.

malice aforethought An antisocial state of mind, often at issue in a murder trial, marked by cruelty and recklessness for which there is no justification. *See also* **manslaughter**.

malpractice Wrongful conduct by a professional, either through negligence or lack of ethics.

mandamus A writ commanding someone, often a public official, to perform some act. Mandamus is frequently issued when time is of the essence.

mandatory injunction *See* **cease and desist order**.

manslaughter Homicide without malice aforethought. *Voluntary manslaughter* is homicide with mitigating circumstances, for example, a fight in which one person kills another; *involuntary manslaughter*, killing through criminal negligence, as in drunk driving.

material witness *See* **witness**.

mens rea *See* **actus reus**.

Miranda rule The obligation of the police, when interrogating someone after an arrest, to read to that person his or her constitutional rights to a lawyer and to remain silent until advised by counsel, and to inform the suspect that anything he or she says may be used as evidence.

misdemeanor *See* **felony**.

misfeasance *See* **malfeasance**.

mistrial The ending of a trial before the rendering of a verdict. Possible causes include a hung jury or the incapacity of the judge, jurors, or attorneys.

mitigating circumstances Conditions under which a crime was committed that tend to reduce the punishment in a case, for example, the circumstances leading to a crime of passion.

moral turpitude Baseness, depravity, vileness, or extreme antisocial behavior.

murder Homicide with malice aforethought. Murder in the second degree generally involves less premeditation than the same crime in the first degree.

negligence Carelessness, acting without reasonable caution, putting another person at risk of injury, or not performing an act that one is obliged to do, with the same consequences. In *criminal negligence* there is the added element of recklessness.

next of kin Closest blood relatives or, lacking them, the next closest relations, even if they are related only by marriage.

nolo contendere A defendant's statement that the charges in a case will not be contested.

non compos mentis *See* **competency hearing.**

nonfeasance *See* **malfeasance.**

notary public A person with the authority to administer oaths, witness documents, and accept depositions.

on the merits A court judgment resting on the facts in the case rather than on a legal technicality.

open court Judicial proceedings fully accessible to the public.

pardon An act by which a governor or the president can excuse a person from punishment and restore his or her civil rights; however, a pardon usually does not wipe out a conviction.

parole The release of a person from prison under controlled conditions. The parolee must fulfill certain requirements, such as reporting regularly to a parole officer.

perjury The act of lying while under oath.

plaintiff The person who initiates a lawsuit.

plea A defendant's answer to a complaint.

plea bargaining A deal between prosecutor and accused, in which the accused pleads guilty in return for lesser punishment than might be received at the end of a trial.

polling the jury A proceeding in which the judge asks each juror, after the verdict has been rendered, to restate his or her decision in the case.

power of attorney A document in which one person authorizes another to act as an agent on his or her behalf.

preliminary hearing A proceeding held after an arrest but before an indictment to see whether there is sufficient evidence to continue holding the prisoner and proceed with a case.

premeditation Calculation, often a factor in determining the degree of guilt in a murder case.

preponderance of evidence The standard of proof used to settle civil lawsuits, determining which side's evidence has greater weight.

presentment A grand jury's accusation, based not on material presented to it by a prosecutor, but rather on its own investigation.

preventive detention The holding of a prisoner without bail; also accomplished by setting bail so high that the prisoner cannot meet it.

probable cause The rule under which police need to have a reasonable belief that someone has committed a crime before making an arrest, or that the object for which they are searching in connection with a crime is at a specific location before they search for and seize it. *See also* **search and seizure.**

probate The process in which the legitimacy of a will is established.

probation The procedure under which a court, rather than imprisoning a person convicted of a crime, leaves that individual at liberty but under court supervision.

pro bono Designating the taking of a case by an attorney without a fee. Pro bono cases are often defended on behalf of groups backing important causes.

process A writ requiring that a person appear in court.

prosecutor The person responsible for bringing the accused to justice. Depending on the level on which he or she functions, the prosecutor is usually called a district attorney, county prosecutor, federal prosecutor, or, if appointed by a legislature to conduct an investigation, special prosecutor.

protective custody The imprisonment of an individual for his or her own protection.

public defender A lawyer provided by the state to an accused person who cannot afford or who refuses counsel.

reasonable doubt *See* **beyond a reasonable doubt.**

release on one's own recognizance Release of the accused on a promise to appear in court rather than on bail.

restraining order A temporary order granted to prevent some action until a hearing can be held on that action.

robbery The use of violence or intimidation to seize another person's property. *See also* **burglary.**

search and seizure A law enforcement procedure involving the search of a person or premises when police have probable cause to suspect they will find and be able to seize criminal evidence. *See also* **probable cause; search warrant.**

search warrant A court order authorizing law enforcement officials to look for objects or people involved in the commission of a crime and to produce them in court; the order stipulates the places that the officials may search.

self-defense A plea by which a person may justify the use of force to ward off an attack if the attack was unprovoked, retreat was impossible, and the threat of harm seemed imminent.

self-incrimination An act in a legal proceeding by which a person says something that incriminates himself or herself; under the Fifth Amendment, a person cannot be forced to make such a statement.

sequester To prevent a jury from having outside contacts until a trial is finished.

show cause order A court order, issued at the request of one party, requiring a second party to convince the court, usually within a matter of days, that a specific act should not be carried out or allowed.

slander *See* **defamation.**

statute of limitations The time limitation for bringing a legal action.

statutory rape A criminal offense involving sex with a girl under the age of consent; the age differs in various states.

stay A court order preventing some act or proceeding until a specific condition is met or the stay is lifted.

stop and frisk A procedure in which police who believe a suspect may be carrying a weapon with intent to use it can stop that person and search the suspect's outer layer of clothing for a weapon.

subpoena A court writ requiring a person to appear to testify at a judicial proceeding at a specific time and place under penalty of law.

summary judgment A procedure by which a party in a civil dispute, if it believes the other side's argument is without merit, can move to have a case resolved before trial.

summons A notice to appear in court as a defendant in a suit.

testament *See* **will.**

tort A violation of legal duty, not involving a contract, that results in harm to another person or another person's property, for example, an act of libel that damages a person's reputation.

true bill *See* **indictment.**

verdict A judge or jury's finding of fact. The judgment, not the verdict, is the final determination in a case; for example, a judge can declare a jury's verdict "false"—that is, invalid because it is not based on the evidence.

voir dire A term usually applied to the interrogation of people to see whether they qualify as jurors. The term, which is French for "speak the truth," also describes a trial hearing without the jury present to determine a matter of fact or law, such as the validity of a confession.

waiver The conscious forgoing of a legal right.

warrant A court writ directing a public employee to do something, for example, to make an arrest.

will A document specifying the disposition of a person's property after his or her death. Most states require two or three people to witness a will. Although *will* generally means the same thing as *testament*, the latter applies only to the distribution of personal, as opposed to real, property.

witness A person who testifies in court under oath. A *material witness* is one whose testimony is central to a case; a *character witness* testifies to the character of an individual.

writ A written order from a judicial body commanding a law enforcement officer to do something specified.

wrongful death statute A law that enables survivors or the person administering an estate to sue for money damages in a death caused by some person or persons. The law is based on the fact that the death deprives survivors or the estate of the services or income of the deceased.

youthful offender One who, at a judge's discretion, may be sentenced with special consideration given to his or her age. The category applies to defendants older than juveniles (no longer minors) but not yet, in the opinion of the judge, adults.

Supreme Court Decisions

The following Supreme Court decisions are among the most significant in the nineteenth and twentieth centuries.

1803 *Marbury v. Madison.* For the first time, the Supreme Court ruled an act of Congress unconstitutional, establishing the principle of judicial review.

1819 *McCullock v. Maryland.* The Court's ruling upheld the constitutionality of the creation of the Bank of the United States and denied to the states the power to tax such an institution because, as Justice John Marshall put it, "the power to tax is the power to destroy."

1819 *Trustees of Dartmouth College v. Woodward.* The Court ruled that a state could not arbitrarily alter the terms of a contract. Although this case applied to a college, its implications widened in later years when the same principle was used to limit states' ability to interfere with business contracts.

1857 *Dred Scott v. Sanford.* The Missouri Compromise was declared unconstitutional because it deprived a person of his property (a slave) without due process of law. This was only the second time that the Court had asserted the power of judicial review. The decision also stated that slaves are not citizens of any state or of the United States.

1877 *Munn v. Illinois.* States were allowed to regulate businesses when "a public interest" was involved. This principle was weakened by rulings in other cases in the late nineteenth century.

1895 *U.S. v. E. C. Knight Co.* In stating that manufacturing and commerce are not connected, and that the Sherman Anti-Trust Act could not be applied to manufacturers, the Court seriously impaired the government's ability to regulate monopolies.

1896 *Plessy v. Ferguson.* The Supreme Court ruled that state laws enforcing segregation by race are constitutional if accommodations are equal as well as separate. Subsequently overturned by *Brown v. Board of Education of Topeka*.

1904 *Northern Securities Co. v. U.S.* The High Court backed government action against big businesses that restrained trade, in effect, putting teeth in the Sherman Anti-Trust Act.

1908 *Muller v. Oregon.* The Court ruled that a state could legislate maximum working hours based on evidence compiled by attorney Louis Brandeis.

1911 *Standard Oil Co. of New Jersey Et Al. v. U.S.* The Court dissolved the Standard Oil Trust not because of its size but because of its unreasonable restraint of trade. The principle involved is called "the rule of reason."

1919 *Schenck v. U.S.* The Court upheld the World War I Espionage Act. In a landmark decision dealing with free speech, Justice Oliver W. Holmes said that a person who encourages draft resistance during a war is a "clear and present danger."

1935 *Schechter v. U.S.* Invalidating the National Industrial Recovery Act of the New Deal, the Court declared that Congress could not delegate its powers to the president.

1951 *Dennis Et Al. v. U.S.* The Supreme Court ruled the 1946 Smith Act constitutional; the act made it a crime to advocate the overthrow of the government by force. In its 1957 *Yates v. U.S.* decision, the Court tempered this ruling by permitting such advocacy in the abstract if it is not connected to action to achieve this goal.

1954 *Brown v. Board of Education of Topeka.* In an example of sociological jurisprudence, the Court held unconstitutional laws enforcing segregated schools; it called for desegregation of schools "with all deliberate speed."

1957 *Roth v. U.S.* The ruling based obscenity decisions on whether a publication appeals to "prurient interests." The Court also said that obscene material is that which lacks any "redeeming social importance."

1961 *Mapp v. Ohio.* The High Court extended the federal exclusionary rule to the states; this rule prevented prosecutors from using illegally obtained evidence in a criminal trial.

1962 *Baker v. Carr.* The Court held that state legislatures must be apportioned to provide equal protection under the law (Fourteenth Amendment). A follow-up decision applied the same principle to the size of congressional districts, insisting that they be approximately equal in population.

1966 *Miranda v. Arizona.* The case declared that before questioning suspects, police must inform them of their right to remain silent, that any statements they make can be used against them, and that they have the right to remain silent until they have an attorney, which the state will provide if they cannot afford to pay.

1972 *Furman v. Georgia.* The Court found unconstitutional all death penalty statutes then in force in the states, but held out the possibility that if they were rewritten so as to be less subjective and randomly imposed, they might be constitutional (as the Court has subsequently held in many instances).

1973 *Roe v. Wade.* The Court ruled state laws prohibiting abortion unconstitutional, except as they apply to the last trimester of pregnancy, on the basis that the Fourteenth Amendment provides for a woman's freedom to make a private decision about her reproductive practices.

1978 *University of California v. Bakke.* The ruling allowed a university to admit students on the basis of race if the school's aim is to combat discrimination. Subsequent decisions of the Court have filled in the details of how government and business may use quotas to make up for past racism.

1986 *Bowers v. Hardwick.* In a case involving enforcement of Georgia's law against sodomy, the Court ruled that states have the power to regulate sexual relations in private between consenting adults.

1989 *Webster v. Reproductive Health Services.* The Court upheld a Missouri law forbidding public employees to perform most abortions, prohibiting the use of public buildings for abortions, and requiring a fetal viability test prior to abortions after the 20th week of pregnancy. This case set a precedent allowing other states to restrict access to abortions.

THE DEATH PENALTY

States That Have Capital Punishment

Alabama	Nebraska	
Arizona	Nevada	
Arkansas	New Hampshire	
California	New Jersey	
Colorado	New Mexico	
Connecticut	North Carolina	
Delaware	Ohio	
Florida	Oklahoma	
Georgia	Oregon	
Idaho	Pennsylvania	
Illinois	South Carolina	
Indiana	South Dakota	
Kentucky	Tennessee	
Louisiana	Texas	
Maryland	Utah	
Mississippi	Virginia	
Missouri	Washington	
Montana		

States That Do Not Have Capital Punishment

Alaska
Hawaii
Iowa
Kansas
Maine
Massachusetts
Michigan
Minnesota
New York
North Dakota
Rhode Island
Vermont
Washington, D.C.
West Virginia
Wisconsin

Additional Sources of Information

Organizations and Services

American Bar Association (ABA)
750 North Lakeshore Drive
Chicago, IL 60611
312-988-5522

The ABA publishes the *Directory of Lawyer Referral Services*, which lists services located throughout the United States and covers a range of general and special-interest needs. The office is open from 9 A.M. to 5 P.M., CST.

NAACP Legal Defense and Education Fund
99 Hudson Street
16th Floor
New York, NY 10013
212-219-1900

The staff at the NAACP Legal Defense Fund will put individuals or groups who feel that they have been discriminated against in touch with an attorney who can help. The office is open weekdays from 9:30 A.M. to 5 P.M., EST.

National Center for Youth Law
114 Sansome Street
Suite 900
San Francisco, CA 94104
415-543-3307

This organization provides counseling and referrals related to legal matters affecting young people, including juvenile justice and child welfare. The office is open from 9 A.M. to 5 P.M., PST.

National Legal Aid and Defender Association
1625 K Street, NW
8th Floor
Washington, DC 20006
202-452-0620

This association acts as a clearinghouse of organizations providing legal services for those without the means to pay. The office is open from 9 A.M. to 5:30 P.M., EST.

NOW Legal Defense and Education Fund
99 Hudson Street
Suite 1201
New York, NY 10013
212-925-6635

This organization provides referrals for legal issues related to women's rights, such as economic inequality, pregnancy discrimination, and problems with changing one's surname. The office is open weekdays from 9:30 A.M. to 5:30 P.M., EST.

Books

American Bar Association. *The American Lawyer: How and When to Choose One.* ABA, 1986.

American Bar Association. *You and the Law.* Publications International, 1990.

Belli, Melvin, and Allen P. Wilkinson, *Everybody's Guide to the Law.* Outlet Books, 1986.

Black, Henry C. *Black's Law Dictionary*, 6th ed. West, 1990.

Cottrell, Robert Ogen. *Write Your Own Contracts.* Ogden Shepard, 1986.

Everyone's Guide to Copyrights, Trademarks, and Patents. Running Press, 1990.

Gifis, Steven H. *Law Dictionary*, 3rd ed. Barron's Educational Series, 1991.

Kubey, Craig. *You Don't Always Need a Lawyer.* Consumer Reports Books, 1991.

Oran, Daniel. *Law Dictionary for Non-Lawyers.* West, 1985.

Reader's Digest Family Legal Guide: A Complete Encyclopedia of Law for the Layman. Reader's Digest, 1981.

Ross, Martin J., and Jeffrey Ross. *Handbook of Everyday Law*, 4th ed. Harper & Row, 1981.

Yates, Sharon Fass, ed. *The Reader's Digest Legal Question & Answer Book.* Reader's Digest, 1988.

17

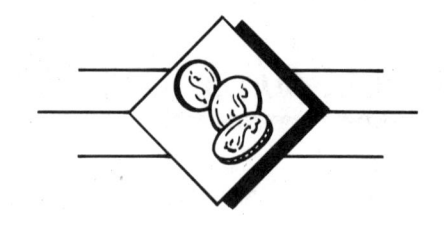

Personal Finances

Tables of Common Interest / *435*

Making a Budget / *436*

Insurance / *437*

Credit and Loans / *441*

Real Estate and Mortgages / *443*

Investments and Retirement / *446*

Investment Terms / *448*

Real Estate Terms / *450*

Calculating Your Net Worth / *451*

Tipping / *452*

Additional Sources of Information / *453*

Personal finances are often a mystifying subject. The objective of making more from your income than just enough to live on is shared by many. But faced with a huge assortment of possible investments, insurance plans, real estate ventures, and retirement plans, how can you, as an individual, decide on the best course of action?

This section provides a starting point. It contains information on making a budget, kinds of insurance available, loans, real estate and mortgages, Social Security and retirement planning, and glossaries of financial and real estate terms. However, consultation with books and periodicals devoted to financial planning or with professional financial planners is recommended before you create a master plan for your own personal finances.

Tables of Common Interest

Simple Interest

Simple interest is computed on the amount of the principal of a loan. That principal is multiplied by the rate of interest; the resulting figure is then multiplied by the time over which the loan will be repaid.

Simple Interest on a $100 Loan

Time	5%	6%	7%	8%	9%	10%	15%	20%
1 month	.4167	.5000	.5833	.6667	.7500	.8333	1.2500	1.6667
6 months	2.5000	3.0000	3.5000	4.0000	4.5000	5.0000	7.5000	10.0000
12 months	5.0000	6.0000	7.0000	8.0000	9.0000	10.0000	15.0000	20.0000
24 months	10.0000	12.0000	14.0000	16.0000	18.0000	20.0000	30.0000	40.0000
36 months	15.0000	18.0000	21.0000	24.0000	27.0000	30.0000	45.0000	60.0000

Annual rate

Compound Interest

Compound interest is computed by multiplying the sum of the principal and the accrued interest by the rate of interest. This calculation must be refigured each time the principal is compounded. To determine the approximate number of years it will take for the principal to double, divide the interest rate percent into 72.

Compound Interest on $100 Principal, Compounded Annually

Time	5%	6%	7%	8%	9%	10%
6 months	2.50	3.00	3.50	4.00	4.50	5.00
1 year	5.00	6.00	7.00	8.00	9.00	10.00
2 years	10.25	12.36	14.49	16.64	18.81	21.00
3 years	15.76	19.10	22.50	25.97	29.50	33.10
4 years	21.55	26.25	31.08	36.05	41.16	46.41
5 years	27.63	33.82	40.26	46.93	53.86	61.05

Annual rate

Making a Budget

The first step in personal financial planning is to get a clear picture of where you now stand. An inventory of expected income and expenses projected on both a monthly and an annual basis will allow individuals and families to create a budget. A budget helps to keep expenses within the boundaries of income while also showing what amount, if any, is available for investments.

Following are outlines of income and expense categories that should be included in any personal budget. Note that expenses include fixed obligations and flexible or discretionary outlays, which can be changed as circumstances and objectives change.

Income

Salaries (total in household)   _____
Bonuses, tips   _____
Investments (interest, dividends, capital gains, real estate income)   _____
TOTAL INCOME   _____

Expenses

Housing (rent or mortgage payments)
_____

Utilities (gas, electric, water, telephone)   _____
Taxes (federal, state, and local income; local real estate; Social Security)   _____
Interest payments (car, bank loan, credit card, other loans)   _____
Principal payments (amounts of borrowed principal repaid)   _____
Insurance (health, life, property)   _____
Education (tuition, supplies, room and board)   _____
Personal expenses   _____
Contributions   _____
Food   _____
Transportation   _____
TOTAL FIXED OUTLAYS   _____
Clothing   _____
Entertainment   _____
Vacations and recreation   _____
Furniture, appliances, and home improvements   _____
Health and beauty   _____
Savings (general or specific for future purchases or objectives)   _____
Miscellaneous   _____
TOTAL VARIABLE OUTLAYS   _____
TOTAL EXPENSES   _____
AMOUNT AVAILABLE FOR INVESTING (total income minus total expenses)   _____

ATLAS

World Time Zones
United States Time Zones
United States
North America
Canada
Mexico
South America
Africa
Europe
Asia
Australia

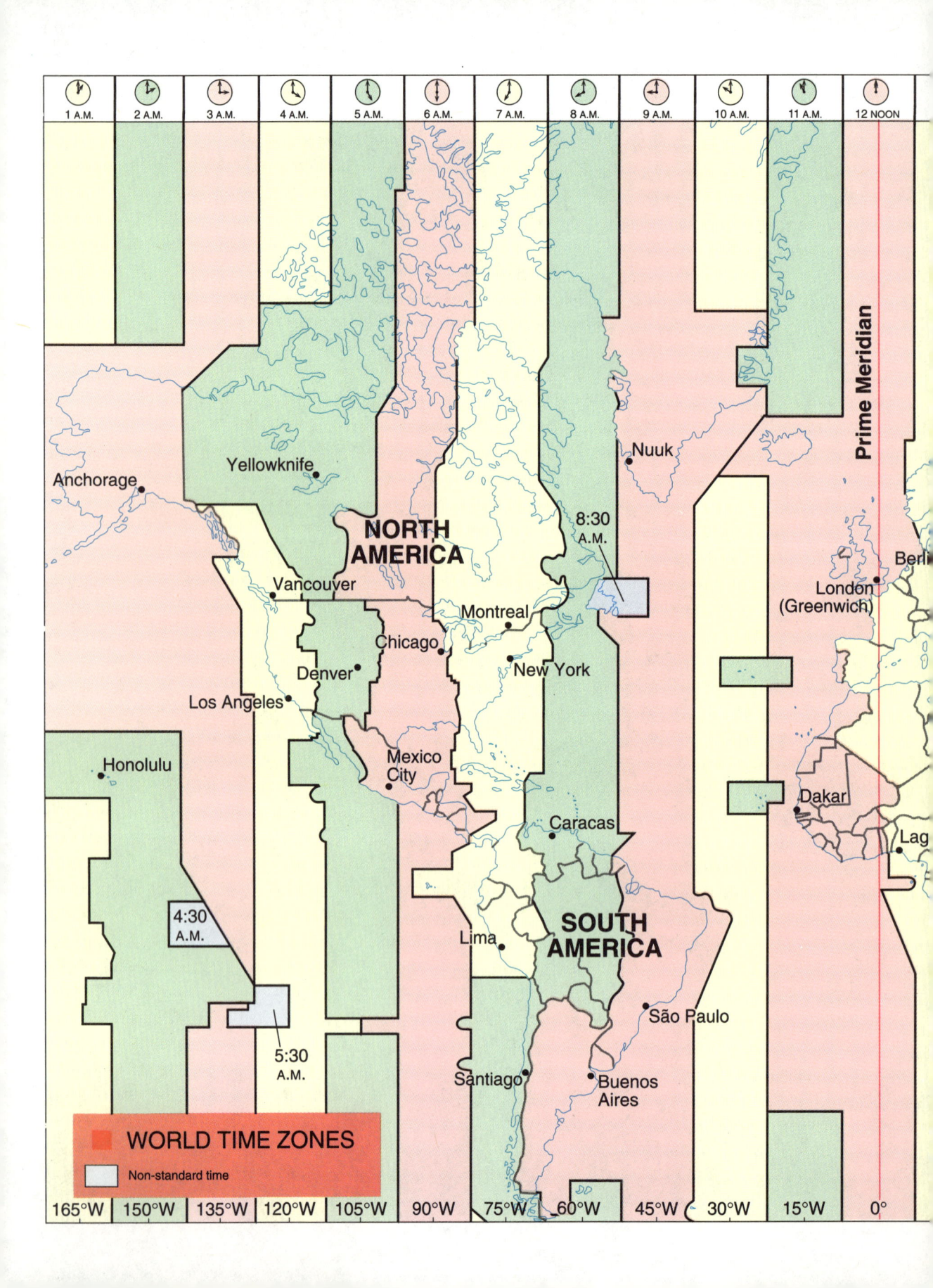

WORLD TIME ZONES

| 1 A.M. | 2 A.M. | 3 A.M. | 4 A.M. | 5 A.M. | 6 A.M. | 7 A.M. | 8 A.M. | 9 A.M. | 10 A.M. | 11 A.M. | 12 NOON |

- Anchorage
- Yellowknife
- Nuuk
- **NORTH AMERICA**
- 8:30 A.M.
- Vancouver
- Montreal
- London (Greenwich)
- Berlin
- Chicago
- Denver
- New York
- Los Angeles
- Honolulu
- Mexico City
- Dakar
- Lagos
- Caracas
- 4:30 A.M.
- Lima
- **SOUTH AMERICA**
- 5:30 A.M.
- São Paulo
- Santiago
- Buenos Aires

Prime Meridian

Non-standard time

165°W | 150°W | 135°W | 120°W | 105°W | 90°W | 75°W | 60°W | 45°W | 30°W | 15°W | 0°

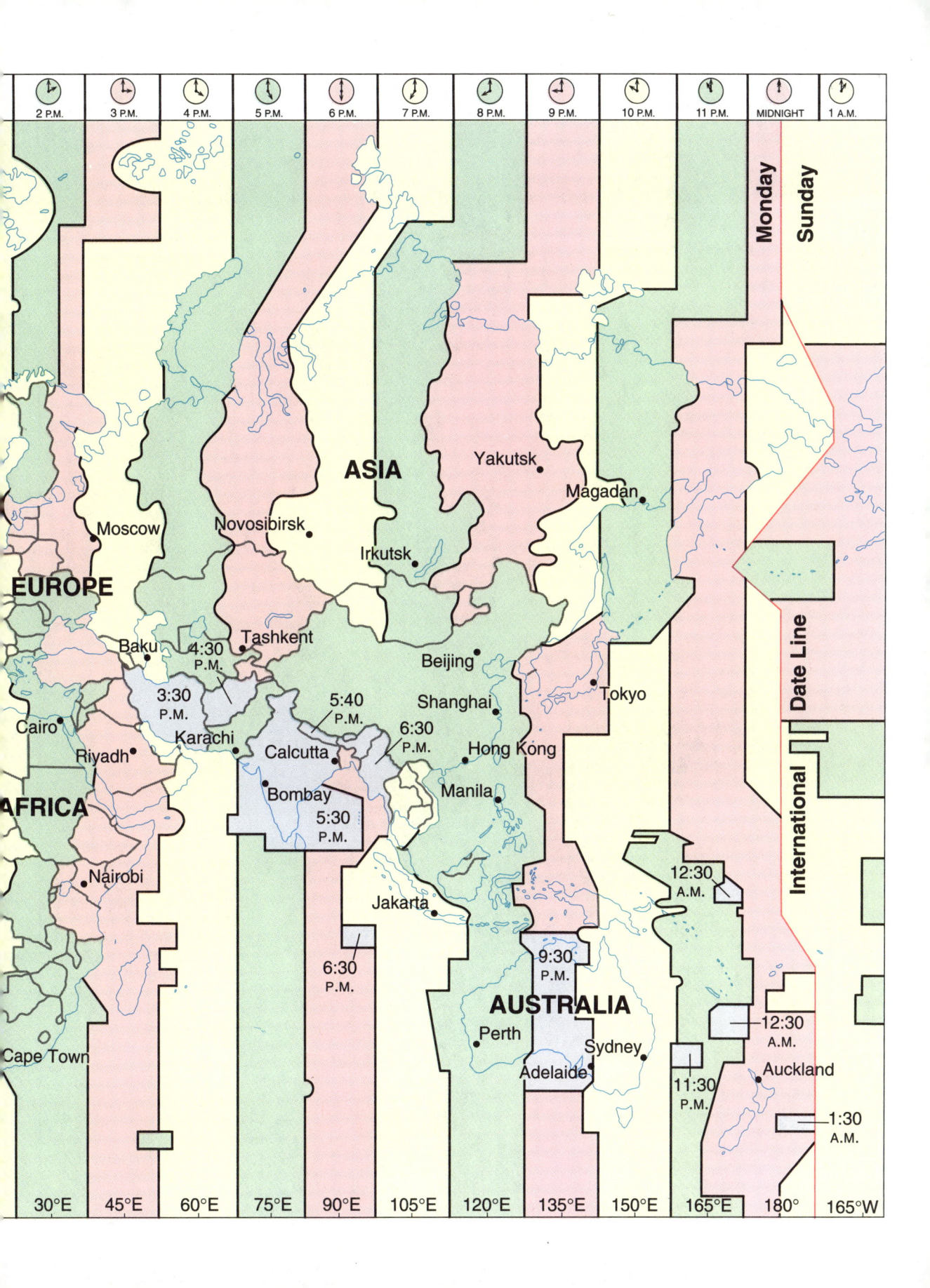

| 2 P.M. | 3 P.M. | 4 P.M. | 5 P.M. | 6 P.M. | 7 P.M. | 8 P.M. | 9 P.M. | 10 P.M. | 11 P.M. | MIDNIGHT | 1 A.M. |

EUROPE

AFRICA

ASIA

AUSTRALIA

Moscow
Novosibirsk
Yakutsk
Magadan
Irkutsk
Baku
Tashkent — 4:30 P.M.
3:30 P.M.
Cairo
Riyadh
Karachi
Calcutta — 5:40 P.M.
Beijing
Shanghai
6:30 P.M.
Hong Kong
Tokyo
Bombay
5:30 P.M.
Manila
Nairobi
Jakarta
6:30 P.M.
12:30 A.M.
Perth
9:30 P.M.
Sydney
Adelaide
11:30 P.M.
12:30 A.M.
Auckland
Cape Town
1:30 A.M.

Monday / Sunday

International Date Line

30°E 45°E 60°E 75°E 90°E 105°E 120°E 135°E 150°E 165°E 180° 165°W

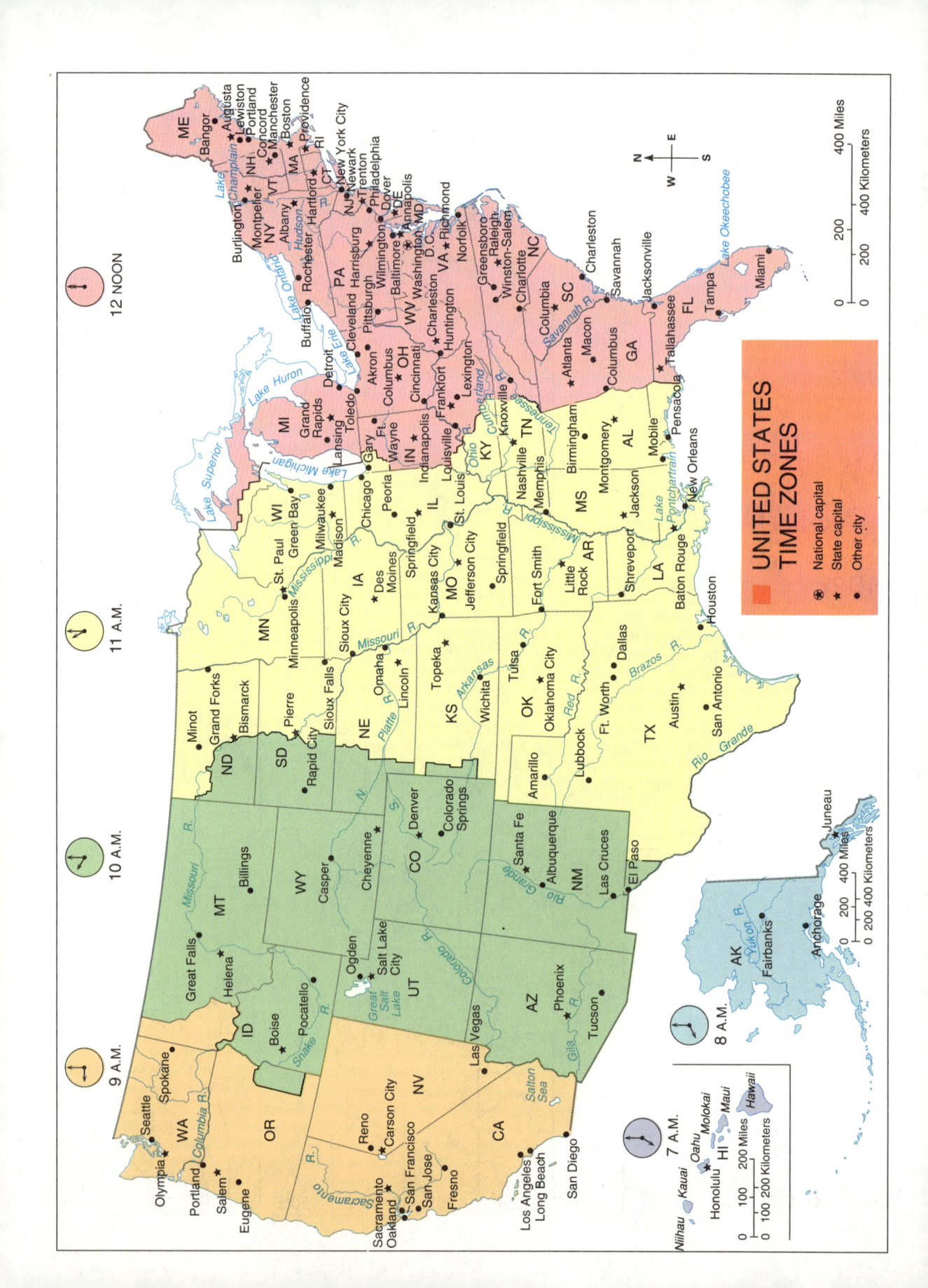

UNITED STATES TIME ZONES

UNITED STATES
National capital
State capital
Other city
WA
OR
CA
NV
ID
MT
WY
UT
CO
AZ
NM
ND
SD
NE
KS
OK
TX
MN
IA
MO
AR
LA
WI
IL
MS
MI
IN
KY
TN
AL
OH
WV
GA
FL
PA
VA
NC
SC
NY
VT
NH
ME
MA
CT
RI
NJ
DE
MD
D.C.
AK
HI
Seattle
Olympia
Spokane
Portland
Salem
Eugene
CASCADE MTS.
Columbia R.
Sacramento R.
Sacramento
Oakland
San Francisco
San Jose
Fresno
SIERRA NEVADA
Reno
Carson City
GREAT BASIN
Los Angeles
Long Beach
San Diego
Salton Sea
Las Vegas
Boise
Pocatello
Snake R.
Great Falls
Helena
Missouri R.
Billings
ROCKY MOUNTAINS
Casper
Ogden
Great Salt Lake
Salt Lake City
Cheyenne
Denver
Colorado Springs
Colorado R.
Rio Grande
Santa Fe
Albuquerque
Phoenix
Gila R.
Tucson
Las Cruces
El Paso
LLANO ESTACADO
Minot
Grand Forks
Bismarck
Pierre
Rapid City
Sioux Falls
GREAT PLAINS
N. Platte R.
S.
Omaha
Lincoln
Topeka
Wichita
Arkansas R.
Amarillo
Lubbock
Tulsa
Oklahoma City
Red R.
OUACHITA MTS.
OZARKS
Ft. Worth
Dallas
Brazos R.
Austin
San Antonio
Houston
Minneapolis
St. Paul
Mississippi R.
Sioux City
Missouri R.
Des Moines
Kansas City
Jefferson City
Springfield
Fort Smith
Little Rock
Shreveport
Baton Rouge
Lake Superior
Green Bay
Milwaukee
Madison
Lake Michigan
Chicago
Peoria
Springfield
St. Louis
Memphis
Jackson
Lake Pontchartrain
New Orleans
Mobile
Pensacola
Grand Rapids
Lansing
Detroit
Lake Huron
Lake Erie
Toledo
Gary
Ft. Wayne
Indianapolis
Louisville
Ohio R.
Cumberland R.
Tennessee R.
Nashville
Knoxville
Lexington
Frankfort
Cincinnati
Columbus
Akron
Cleveland
Birmingham
Montgomery
Atlanta
Macon
Columbus
Tallahassee
Jacksonville
Tampa
Lake Okeechobee
Miami
Savannah
Savannah R.
Charleston
Columbia
Charlotte
Winston-Salem
Greensboro
Raleigh
APPALACHIAN MTS.
Norfolk
Richmond
Huntington
Charleston
Washington
Baltimore
Annapolis
Dover
Wilmington
Philadelphia
Trenton
Newark
New York City
Pittsburgh
Harrisburg
Buffalo
Rochester
Lake Ontario
Hudson R.
Albany
Hartford
Providence
Boston
Manchester
Concord
Portland
Lewiston
Augusta
Bangor
Burlington
Montpelier
Lake Champlain
N
W
E
S
0
200
400 Miles
0
200
400 Kilometers
BROOKS RANGE
Yukon R.
Fairbanks
ALASKA RANGE
Anchorage
Juneau
0
200
400 Miles
0
200
400 Kilometers
Niihau
Kauai
Oahu
Honolulu
Molokai
Maui
Hawaii
0
100
200 Miles
0
100
200 Kilometers

NORTH AMERICA
National capital
ASIA
BERING SEA
Bering Strait
ARCTIC OCEAN
BEAUFORT SEA
Yukon R.
ALASKA
GULF OF ALASKA
Mackenzie R.
GREENLAND (DEN.) (KALAALLIT NUNAAT)
BAFFIN BAY
Arctic Circle
LABRADOR SEA
HUDSON BAY
CANADA
ROCKY MOUNTAINS
Newfoundland
Columbia R.
GREAT PLAINS
L. SUPERIOR
L. MICHIGAN
L. HURON
L. ERIE
L. ONTARIO
St. Lawrence R.
Ottawa
GREAT BASIN
SIERRA NEVADA
Missouri R.
PACIFIC OCEAN
Colorado R.
Washington, D.C.
Ohio R.
UNITED STATES
APPALACHIAN MTS.
ATLANTIC OCEAN
Bermuda (U.K.)
Rio Grande
Mississippi R.
Tropic of Cancer
SIERRA MADRE OCCIDENTAL
GULF OF CALIFORNIA
MEXICO
GULF OF MEXICO
THE BAHAMAS
Nassau
Havana
CUBA
PUERTO RICO (U.S.)
DOMINICAN REPUBLIC
Port-au-Prince
HAITI
Santo Domingo
JAMAICA
Kingston
VIRGIN ISLANDS (U.K. & U.S.)
Mexico City
BELIZE
Belmopan
GUATEMALA
Guatemala City
HONDURAS
Tegucigalpa
San Salvador
EL SALVADOR
NICARAGUA
Managua
CARIBBEAN SEA
Panama Canal
San José
COSTA RICA
Panamá City
PANAMA
SOUTH AMERICA
Equator
N
0 250 500 750 Miles
0 250 500 750 Kilometers

CANADA
National capital
Province/Territory capital
ALASKA
YUKON
Whitehorse
NORTHWEST TERRITORIES
Yellowknife
Victoria Island
Baffin Island
BAFFIN BAY
Arctic Circle
GREAT BEAR L.
GREAT SLAVE L.
ROCKY MOUNTAINS
BRITISH COLUMBIA
Victoria
ALBERTA
Edmonton
GREAT PLAINS
Peace R.
SASKATCHEWAN
Saskatchewan R.
Regina
MANITOBA
L. WINNIPEG
Winnipeg
HUDSON BAY
ONTARIO
Toronto
Ottawa
QUÉBEC
Québec
NEWFOUNDLAND
St. John's
LABRADOR SEA
PRINCE EDWARD ISLAND
Charlottetown
NEW BRUNSWICK
Fredericton
NOVA SCOTIA
Halifax
ATLANTIC OCEAN
UNITED STATES
SUPERIOR
L. MICHIGAN
L. HURON
L. ONTARIO
ERIE
0 300 600 Miles
0 300 600 Kilometers

MEXICO
National capital
State capital
UNITED STATES
Mexicali
BAJA CALIFORNIA NORTE
GULF OF CALIFORNIA
SONORA
Hermosillo
CHIHUAHUA
Chihuahua
SIERRA MADRE OCCIDENTAL
COAHUILA
Saltillo
NUEVO LEON
Monterrey
SIERRA MADRE ORIENTAL
TAMAULIPAS
Ciudad Victoria
BAJA CALIFORNIA SUR
La Paz
SINALOA
Culiacán
DURANGO
Durango
ZACATECAS
Zacatecas
SAN LUIS POTOSÍ
San Luis Potosí
AGUASCALIENTES
Aguascalientes
NAYARIT
Tepic
GUANAJUATO
Guanajuato
QUERÉTARO
Querétaro
HIDALGO
Pachuca
TLAXCALA
Tlaxcala
JALISCO
Guadalajara
COLIMA
Colima
MICHOACÁN
Morelia
MÉXICO
Toluca
Mexico City
DISTRITO FEDERAL
MORELOS
Cuernavaca
PUEBLA
Puebla
VERACRUZ
Jalapa
GUERRERO
Chilpancingo
OAXACA
Oaxaca
TABASCO
Villahermosa
CHIAPAS
Tuxtla Gutiérrez
CAMPECHE
Campeche
YUCATÁN
Mérida
QUINTANA ROO
Chetumal
BELIZE
GUATEMALA
GULF OF MEXICO
PACIFIC OCEAN
Tropic of Cancer
0 100 200 300 Miles
0 100 200 300 Kilometers

SOUTH AMERICA
★ National capital
NORTH AMERICA
CARIBBEAN SEA
PACIFIC OCEAN
ATLANTIC OCEAN
Caracas
VENEZUELA
Orinoco R.
Georgetown
GUYANA
Paramaribo
SURINAME
Cayenne
FRENCH GUIANA
GUIANA HIGHLANDS
Bogotá
COLOMBIA
Galápagos Islands (E.C.)
Quito
ECUADOR
Equator
AMAZON BASIN
Negro R.
Amazon R.
Madeira R.
PERU
Lima
ANDES
Titicaca
La Paz
BOLIVIA
Sucre
MOUNTAINS
BRAZIL
São Francisco R.
Brasília
BRAZILIAN HIGHLANDS
GRAN CHACO
Paraguay R.
PARAGUAY
Asunción
CHILE
Tropic of Capricorn
Paraná R.
ARGENTINA
Santiago
URUGUAY
Montevideo
Buenos Aires
PAMPAS
PATAGONIA
Strait of Magellan
Falkland Islands (U.K.)
Tierra Del Fuego
Cape Horn
South Georgia Island (U.K.)
N
0 200 400 600 Miles
0 200 400 600 Kilometers
20°N
10°N
0°
10°S
20°S
30°S
40°S
50°S
100°W
90°W
80°W
70°W
60°W
50°W
40°W
30°W
20°W

AFRICA
National capital
EUROPE
ASIA
ATLANTIC OCEAN
ATLANTIC OCEAN
INDIAN OCEAN
MEDITERRANEAN SEA
RED SEA
GULF OF ADEN
Suez Canal
Strait of Gibraltar
Azores Islands (PORT.)
Madeira Islands (PORT.)
Canary Islands (SP.)
Ascension (U.K.)
St. Helena (U.K.)
SEYCHELLES
COMOROS
ATLAS MOUNTAINS
S A H A R A
TIBESTI MTS.
KALAHARI DESERT
Tropic of Cancer
Tropic of Capricorn
Equator
40°N
20°N
0°
20°S
40°S
40°W
20°W
0°
20°E
40°E
60°E
MOROCCO
Rabat
ALGERIA
Algiers
TUNISIA
Tunis
LIBYA
Tripoli
EGYPT
Cairo
Nile R.
L. Nasser
WESTERN SAHARA
MAURITANIA
Nouakchott
MALI
Bamako
Niger R.
NIGER
Niamey
CHAD
L. Chad
N'Djamena
SUDAN
Khartoum
Blue Nile R.
White Nile R.
ETHIOPIA
Addis Ababa
DJIBOUTI
Djibouti
SOMALIA
Mogadishu
SENEGAL
Dakar
GAMBIA
Banjul
GUINEA-BISSAU
Bissau
GUINEA
Conakry
SIERRA LEONE
Freetown
LIBERIA
Monrovia
IVORY COAST
Abidjan
BURKINA FASO
Ouagadougou
GHANA
Accra
TOGO
Lomé
BENIN
Porto-Novo
NIGERIA
Lagos
CAMEROON
Yaoundé
CENTRAL AFRICAN REPUBLIC
Bangui
EQUATORIAL GUINEA
Malabo
SÃO TOME & PRINCIPE
GABON
Libreville
CONGO
Brazzaville
ZAIRE
Kinshasa
(Congo) R.
Zaire R.
CABINDA (ANG.)
UGANDA
Kampala
L. Turkana
KENYA
Nairobi
RWANDA
Kigali
BURUNDI
Bujumbura
L. Victoria
L. Tanganyika
TANZANIA
Dar es Salaam
L. Nyasa
ANGOLA
Luanda
ZAMBIA
Lusaka
L. Kariba
Zambezi R.
MALAWI
Lilongwe
MOZAMBIQUE
Maputo
MADAGASCAR
Antananarivo
ZIMBABWE
Harare
NAMIBIA
Windhoek
WALVIS BAY (S. AFR.)
BOTSWANA
Gaborone
VENDA
Thohoyandou
Mmabatho
BOPHUTHATSWANA
Pretoria
Mbabane
SWAZILAND
Maseru
LESOTHO
TRANSKEI
Umtata
CISKEI
Bisho
Orange R.
SOUTH AFRICA
Cape Town
N
0 400 800 Miles
0 400 800 Kilometers

EUROPE
National capital
GREENLAND/
KALAALLIT
NUNAAT
(DENMARK)
ICELAND
Reykjavik
NORWEGIAN SEA
Faroe Islands
(Den.)
Shetland Islands
(U.K.)
Arctic Circle
NORWAY
Oslo
SWEDEN
Stockholm
SCANDINAVIAN PENINSULA
Gulf of Bothnia
FINLAND
Helsinki
Tallinn
ESTONIA
Riga
LATVIA
LITHUANIA
Vilnius
RUSSIA
Moscow
BARENTS SEA
URAL
MOUNTAINS
NORTH SEA
BALTIC SEA
DENMARK
Copenhagen
IRELAND
Dublin
N.
IRELAND
SCOTLAND
United
Kingdom
ENGLAND
WALES
London
ATLANTIC OCEAN
English Channel
NETHERLANDS
Amsterdam
BELGIUM
Brussels
LUXEMBOURG
Paris
FRANCE
Seine
Loire R.
Rhone
Bay of
Biscay
FEDERAL
REPUBLIC
OF
GERMANY
Berlin
Elbe R.
Danube
LIECHTENSTEIN
POLAND
Warsaw
Vistula R.
BELARUS
Minsk
UKRAINE
Kiev
Dnepr R.
CZECH
REPUBLIC
Prague
SLOVAKIA
AUSTRIA
Vienna
Budapest
HUNGARY
SWITZERLAND
Bern
SLOVENIA
CARPATHIAN MTS.
MOLDOVA
Chisinau
ROMANIA
Bucharest
KAZAKHSTAN
Ural R.
Volga R.
CASPIAN SEA
CAUCASUS MTS.
GEORGIA
Tbilisi
Baku
ARMENIA
Yerevan
AZERBAIJAN
BLACK SEA
Bosporus
CROATIA
BOSNIA
AND
HERZEGOVINA
Belgrade
Serbia
YUGOSLAVIA
Montenegro
ALBANIA
Tiranë
MACEDONIA
Sofia
BULGARIA
GREECE
Athens
AEGEAN SEA
Crete
TURKEY
Ankara
CYPRUS
Nicosia
PORTUGAL
Lisbon
SPAIN
Madrid
PYRENEES
IBERIAN PENINSULA
ANDORRA
MONACO
Corsica
(Fr.)
Sardinia
(It.)
Balearic
Islands
(Sp.)
Strait of
Gibraltar
Gibraltar (U.K.)
SAN
MARINO
Po R.
APENNINES
ADRIATIC SEA
Rome
VATICAN
CITY
ITALY
Sicily
MALTA
MEDITERRANEAN SEA
AFRICA
N
0 250 500 Miles
0 250 500 Kilometers
0 500 Miles
0 500 Kilometers
70°N
60°N
50°N
40°N
80°N
20°W
10°W
0°
10°E
20°E
30°E
40°E
50°E
60°E
70°E

ASIA
National capital
ARCTIC OCEAN
PACIFIC OCEAN
INDIAN OCEAN
EAST SIBERIAN SEA
BERING SEA
SEA OF OKHOTSK
SEA OF JAPAN
EAST CHINA SEA
SOUTH CHINA SEA
BAY OF BENGAL
ARABIAN SEA
GULF OF ADEN
RED SEA
PERSIAN GULF
CASPIAN SEA
ARAL SEA
BLACK SEA
MEDITERRANEAN SEA
AFRICA
RUSSIA
SIBERIA
WEST SIBERIAN PLAIN
URAL MOUNTAINS
KOLYMA RANGE
KAMCHATKA PENINSULA
Sakhalin (U.S.R.)
Kuril Islands (U.S.R.)
Aleutian Islands (U.S.)
Ob R.
Yenisey R.
Lena R.
Amur R.
Irtysh R.
Ural R.
L. Baikal
L. Balkhash
KAZAKHSTAN
UZBEKISTAN
TURKMENISTAN
KYRGYZSTAN
TAJIKISTAN
Tashkent
Bishkek
Alma Ata
Ashkhabad
Dushanbe
MONGOLIA
Ulan Bator
GOBI DESERT
ALTAI MTS.
TIEN SHAN
KUN LUN SHAN
TIBETAN PLATEAU
HIMALAYAS
CHINA
Beijing
Huang He R.
Yangtze R.
NORTH KOREA
P'yongyang
SOUTH KOREA
Seoul
JAPAN
Tokyo
TAIWAN
Taipei
HONG KONG (U.K.)
MACAU (PORT.)
PHILIPPINES
Manila
VIETNAM
Hanoi
LAOS
Vientiane
Mekong
THAILAND
Bangkok
CAMBODIA
Phnom Penh
BURMA
Rangoon
Irrawaddy
MALAYSIA
Kuala Lampur
SINGAPORE
BRUNEI (U.K.)
INDONESIA
Sumatra
Jakarta
Java
Borneo
Celebes
Timor
New Guinea
INDIA
New Delhi
DECCAN PLATEAU
NEPAL
Kathmandu
BHUTAN
Thimphu
BANGLADESH
Dhaka
SRI LANKA
Colombo
MALDIVES
PAKISTAN
Islamabad
Indus R.
AFGHANISTAN
Kabul
IRAN
Teheran
ZAGROS MTS.
IRAQ
Baghdad
Tigris R.
Euphrates
TURKEY
Ankara
CYPRUS
SYRIA
Damascus
LEBANON
Beirut
ISRAEL
Jerusalem
JORDAN
Amman
KUWAIT
Kuwait City
BAHRAIN
QATAR
SAUDI ARABIA
Riyadh
ARABIAN PENINSULA
UNITED ARAB EMIRATES
Abu Dhabi
OMAN
Muscat
REPUBLIC OF YEMEN
Sanaa
Socotra (Republic of Yemen)
Arctic Circle
Tropic of Cancer
Equator
N
0 500 1000 Miles
0 500 1000 Kilometers

AUSTRALIA AND THE SOUTH PACIFIC

Budgets are useful only when the amounts specified in each category are not regularly exceeded. If you have trouble keeping a budget, you may want to make sure that your spending targets reflect your actual expenses and that the members of your household understand the ultimate benefits of budgeting income and expenses.

Insurance

Life is full of risks. One means of minimizing the effects of these risks is to obtain insurance. By insuring your health, your life, your property, and your car and getting coverage for loss of income in the event of a disability, you can assure yourself and your family of financial stability even if catastrophe strikes. Additionally, you can use some types of insurance to further your personal financial goals.

Health Insurance

Health insurance covers the costs of medical care. It is available to individuals and families through private insurance companies, Blue Cross-Blue Shield organizations, and health maintenance organizations (HMOs). While many Americans are covered by one of these plans—paid for or organized through employers, unions, or other groups—individual policies can be bought to provide additional coverage or to replace the group benefits. For the self-employed, individual policies are often the only choice available.

Private Insurance

Health insurance obtained from a private company can cover a wide variety of services, paying for them directly or through reimbursements to the insured individual.

Basic coverage usually includes hospital expenses such as room and board, surgeon's fees, diagnostic charges, anesthesia, operating or delivery room fees, drugs, and medical equipment. Also included in some basic policies are reasonable medical expenses for outpatient care, emergency room treatment, nursing care, and even prescription drugs and eyeglasses. The typical basic plan includes an annual deductible, generally around $200 for an individual, which must be spent before coverage begins; the plan then pays a set percentage, usually 80 percent, of covered costs for specified illnesses and conditions. Such plans frequently pay according to a predetermined fee schedule; any amounts in excess of the scheduled fee are considered to be beyond the limits of "reasonable" expenses and will not be reimbursed or paid out. Basic plans without any supplemental insurance are considered insufficient because they often exclude common medical conditions; in addition, the limits of coverage are often too low to provide adequate protection.

Major medical coverage pays only for major medical expenses beyond those covered by basic insurance plans. There is a deductible, a co-insurance provision that requires the insured individuals themselves to pay a set percentage of medical costs up to a set amount, and a high ceiling on liability. There are generally few excluded conditions or fee schedules.

Important provisions to look for in major medical policies include guaranteed renewability to age 65, a reasonable cutoff for the co-insurance provision, and full coverage for acute-care facilities.

Comprehensive medical coverage combines basic and major medical coverage in one package. It provides a set amount of basic coverage after a deductible and then coverage for charges beyond that amount and for other major medical expenses with a co-insurance provision coming into effect.

Blue Cross–Blue Shield

The basic difference between Blue Cross-Blue Shield plans and those offered by private companies is the way payments for covered expenses are handled. Blue Cross usually pays hospital costs directly to the care provider rather than reimbursing the insured individual. Blue Shield plans come in three varieties: full-service coverage that pays health-care providers directly for all covered conditions; indemnity coverage that reimburses the insured individual; and partial service benefits that provide full coverage for those with incomes below a certain level and indemnity coverage for those whose incomes are above that level.

Health Maintenance Organizations (HMOs)

HMOs provide medical care to those who pay a quarterly fee. They are oriented toward preventive health care, and those paying the premium are entitled to medical, surgical, and hospital care; some plans also cover the costs of some prescription medicines and provide partial coverage of dental services. Some HMOs provide the services of several doctors at a single location connected with a hospital. Others allow subscribers to receive care from doctors in their individual offices; the doctors are then reimbursed by the HMO on a fee-for-service basis. Important aspects of an HMO that should be scrutinized are the patient-to-physician ratio, the services for which deductibles or additional fees are charged, the availability of maternity benefits, and the relationship of the HMO or participating doctor to a hospital.

Life Insurance

The purpose of life insurance is to provide future financial security for your family. It provides an immediate estate that will enable your family to maintain their household after you die. Life insurance can also be used to build up cash reserves for future expenses, such as retirement or college tuition.

By purchasing a life insurance policy, you are buying into a risk-sharing group. Although no one can predict with any reliability when any individual is going to die, it is possible to predict with great accuracy the number of nonsmoking 32-year-old women who exercise regularly and are not overweight who will die at any given point over the next 40 years. The costs of premiums for people of different ages in different risk categories can then be calculated on the basis of how much the insurance company will pay out in benefits to each group's beneficiaries.

There are six types of life insurance available.

Term insurance provides a death benefit to beneficiaries for a specified period of time. It can be renewable or convertible to whole life and features a low initial premium that rises with each new term. Term life typically has no cash value.

Whole life insurance offers protection for life at a fixed premium. It provides a fixed death benefit and a cash value that can be borrowed against and that increases over the years.

Universal life insurance offers permanent protection, flexible premiums and death benefits, and a cash value based on premiums paid to date and current interest rates.

Excess interest whole life insurance provides permanent protection, a fixed premium that the insurer may adjust after the policy is issued, a fixed death benefit, a cash value that grows dependent on market conditions, and the possibility that premiums may be reduced or dispensed with for one or more years if investments are sufficiently profitable.

Variable life insurance offers permanent protection, fixed or flexible premiums, policyholder control over the investment of the policy's cash value, and variable death benefits and cash values depending on performance of the investments account.

Adjustable life insurance gives permanent protection that can be reduced to a shorter term if desired, a death benefit that can be raised or lowered, and premiums that can be increased or decreased.

The American Council of Life Insurance recommends that people evaluate their life insurance needs, buy from a company licensed in their state, select a trustworthy insurance agent, compare costs of similar policies, ask about lower premium rates for nonsmokers, and read their policies and understand them. After selecting coverage that is right for you, inform your beneficiaries about the kind and amount of life insurance you own, keep your policy in a safe place at home, keep the company's name and policy number in a safe deposit box, and check your coverage periodically to be sure it meets your current needs.

Disability Insurance

Disability insurance provides coverage for loss of income when an illness or injury prevents you from working. Temporary disability insurance is provided in California, Hawaii, New Jersey, New York, Rhode Island, and Puerto Rico. Social Security also provides disability coverage at varying levels depending on family size and the recipient's age.

In addition, there are three types of disability insurance available through private companies. *Noncancellable policies* protect your income as long as you continue to make premium payments; coverage may be increased as income increases. *Guaranteed renewable policies* are less expensive than noncancellable ones because insurers can increase premium rates. *Optionally renewable policies* can be renewed or not renewed each year, with variable premium rates. They are the least expensive private option.

Property and Liability Insurance

The purchase of a home is the largest investment most individuals will make in their lifetimes. The home also represents the largest portion of their total financial worth. It therefore makes sense to insure against its possible damage or loss. Even renters stand to lose a substantial amount of money if the uninsured contents of their apartments or houses are destroyed.

There is a wide array of homeowners' insurance policies, including coverage for renters and apartment dwellers. The type of coverage most appropriate for you depends on the sort of risks the property is exposed to and the value of the property. Some policies cover only specific causes of damage or loss, while others provide "all-risk" coverage that will pay for any loss or damage except that specifically excluded by the policy. The available homeowners' policies are as follows.

Homeowners' 1 covers fire, lightning, extended perils (such as windstorms, hail, smoke damage, explosions, riots, and vehicular and aircraft damage), vandalism, malicious mischief, theft, and personal liability.

Homeowners' 2 adds extended coverage for a variety of other potential problems, such as broken water pipes, freezing, and building collapse, to the coverage offered in Homeowners' 1.

Homeowners' 3 is an "all risks" policy for buildings that is more extensive than either 1 or 2; it also can cover personal property to a limited extent.

Homeowners' 4 covers personal property only; the extent of coverage is generally the same as in 2, but the policy is designed for renters.

Homeowners' 5 provides the most comprehensive "all risks" coverage for homes and personal property.

Homeowners' 6 is designed for condominium owners; it covers loss of personal property and loss of use of the dwelling.

Homeowners' 8 is more limited than Homeowners' 1; it is for homes that are below the standard underwriters use to determine eligibility for insurance.

Homeowners' policies cover more than just a home and its contents. Most types include the main dwelling, any other structures on the property, personal belongings that are kept either in the dwelling or elsewhere, costs of additional living expenses, and comprehensive personal liability, including medical payments and damage to others' property.

Comprehensive personal liability insurance protects against the loss of your home or property in the event someone is accidentally injured, whether the injury occurs at the home or elsewhere (such as on a golf course or during a softball game). It will pay up to a set amount for each occurrence of personal liability (injury and property damage) and up to set amounts for medical payments to others and damage to others' property. Excluded from comprehensive personal liability insurance provisions of most homeowners' policies are losses resulting from business or professional activities; use of boats, ships, and planes; intentional injury or damage; acts of war, or nuclear accidents; and liabilities covered by other insurance policies, such as workers' compensation. Additional liability insurance is available for these situations.

Automobile Insurance

When you are evaluating the risks to which you are regularly exposed, driving a car is one that must be considered. The possibility of an accident involving your car is so great that many states have made at least limited automobile insurance mandatory.

Automobile insurance covers three broad risk categories.

Liability insurance covers personal injuries and property damage resulting from ownership, maintenance, or use of a vehicle. Separate limits for payments apply to each person involved in an accident and to property damage incurred.

Medical insurance covers the medical costs incurred in an accident up to a set amount per person per accident.

Collision insurance pays the costs of having a car repaired after it has been damaged in an accident.

Additional automobile insurance, such as comprehensive insurance, is also available to pay for damages resulting from fire and theft. Insurance can also be obtained to pay for damages resulting from an uninsured driver, for towing and labor, and for transportation needed while a damaged car is being repaired. Many states mandate the inclusion of no-fault personal injury insurance in any automobile insurance policy; this provides benefits for those injured in an accident regardless of who was responsible for the accident.

The types of coverage and the monetary limits of the policy, the driver's age, the frequency of use of the vehicle, the driver's accident history, and the place where the vehicle is kept are considered in determining the cost of liability insurance. Costs for coverage of damage to a vehicle are calculated on the purchase price of the vehicle and its age. When evaluating insurance policies, it is important to compare what is not covered by a given policy—its exclusions—as well as what is covered and how much it will cost. Comparative shopping and a trustworthy insurance agent can help automobile owners to choose wisely when buying insurance for use of their vehicles.

Credit and Loans

One key to enhancing personal finances is credit. With loans, credit cards, revolving charge plans at department stores, and other methods of delaying payment, people obtain goods and services for which they otherwise would have to wait. Of course, use of credit results in debts and interest charges that must be paid to maintain a good credit rating and ensure the availability of more credit.

Getting credit is a fairly straightforward procedure. You can apply to a bank for a loan or a bank credit card, such as Visa® or MasterCard®, or to a department store or gasoline company for a revolving charge account, by filling out an application form. These companies will ask about your income, employment history, length and type of residence, credit history, and major assets (car, home, etc.) in order to determine your creditworthiness.

A positive credit history—meaning that you have received credit and made payments on time—is one of the strongest recommendations for further credit. If you have never had credit before, a good first step is to obtain a department store or gasoline company credit card, which is often easier to get, or to take out a small loan at a bank where you keep a savings and/or a checking account. Having a reasonably large amount of money in the bank also can help persuade issuers to provide you with credit.

When looking to obtain credit, especially once creditworthiness has been established, comparison shopping is very important. Different states have different limits on the amount of interest that can be charged on consumer loans and bank cards. Interest rates on loans can range from less than 2 percent per month to 36 percent per year or more; credit card rates range from under 11 percent to 22 percent or more per year. You do not need to be a resident of a state to get credit from lending institutions headquartered there, and you can apply by mail.

The amount of indebtedness you should assume is not easy to calculate. The credit-granting institution bases its decision on your gross income and expenses. Your own decision about how much credit you should use is harder to come by. Calculating the amount of money you have available from your income after deducting monthly expenses will give you some idea of what you can afford, although other factors—such as ever-decreasing balances in your checking and savings accounts, use of overdrafts or credit to cover regular expenses, and difficulty making payments on credit lines you already have—may suggest that additional credit is not a good idea.

Problems that can arise from credit, such as billing errors or unfair denial of credit, can be remedied under federal regulations. The Fair Credit Billing Act requires that, if you notify a creditor in writing about an error on a bill, your complaint must be acknowledged within 30 days and resolved within 90 days. The Equal Credit Opportunity Act requires creditors to give a reason if you are denied credit and prohibits discrimination based on race, sex, age, marital status, color, religion, national origin, or receipt of public assistance.

If you are denied credit on the basis of a negative report from a credit bureau, you can obtain the information that agency supplied to the creditor free of charge if you request it within 30 days of being turned down or for a small fee at any time. You can challenge the accuracy of any item in your credit file; this will force the credit bureau to investigate the item and remove it if it cannot be substantiated. Any item in your file also can be amended at your request to include a 100-word explanation that will be added to your file.

Hundreds of credit bureaus exist throughout the United States, but three companies predominate nationally. Contact one of the following for information on your credit rating:

Equifax Credit Information Systems
P.O. Box 740241
Atlanta, GA 30374-0241
404-885-8000

Trans Union Corporation
P.O. Box 7000
North Olmsted, OH 44070
312-645-6000

TRW Information Services
Attention: Consumer Assistance
P.O. Box 749029
Dallas, TX 75374-9029
214-235-1200, ext. 251
714-991-6000 (West Coast)

Real Estate and Mortgages

American society is geared toward home ownership. The desire to own a home, and the labyrinthine process of purchasing one, can have tremendous impact on an individual's or a family's finances. A home represents the single largest financial commitment most people will make in their lifetimes. It therefore requires a careful, reasoned decision based on a thorough examination of the steps involved in the purchase. What follows are some of the basics involved in buying a home and obtaining a mortgage. Potential home buyers are cautioned to seek out as much additional information as is practical from specialized books, real estate professionals, and friends who have made similar purchases.

The Decision to Buy a Home

Owning their own home is something most people believe to be desirable regardless of their financial circumstances. They think that owning a home is a perfect investment, and that renting is akin to throwing money away. This is not always the case. Home ownership often includes a great many hidden expenses, while renters take care of the basic need for shelter at a set monthly cost without having to deal with such headaches as taxes, sewage disposal, or sidewalk repairs.

A number of factors need to be considered when deciding whether you should buy your own home. First among these should be the way you lead your life. Home ownership can provide greater space, a chance to set down roots, the option to make any alterations you choose, the possibility of providing yard space and better schools for your children, and the pride of having a home of your own. Renters have greater flexibility about when they can move, pay less of their income for shelter, avoid the ancillary costs and added work of maintaining a residence, and can use any excess funds for investments that offer a guaranteed rate of return.

Also of great importance in the decision to buy a home is your current financial situation. Home ownership requires enough money to make a down payment (generally at least 10 percent of the purchase price, and often 20 or 25 percent), to obtain a mortgage, and to make payments on that mortgage for many years to come. Renters need to have enough money to pay the rent each month.

Affordability

It is best to shop for a mortgage before you shop for a home so as to know how much money is available to you. A longstanding rule of thumb is that the annual cost of a home should not exceed 25 percent of your gross income. If you can manage monthly payments that do not exceed 25 percent of your income, you will probably have little trouble obtaining a mortgage or making the payments.

But even if mortgage payments come to 25 percent of your income, the cost of a home will be substantially more. Funds to cover utilities, water and sewage costs, taxes, repairs, improvements, and even garbage cans and yard equipment will be needed. Additional costs may include more costly commutation. It is wise to set aside an additional 10 percent of the basic annual costs for unseen expenses.

A careful evaluation of present and projected income and expenses—including money spent on nonessential interests, hobbies, and pastimes—will give you some idea of what you can afford to pay for a home on a monthly basis. From there, you can look at mortgage payment schedules to find out how much of a mortgage you can afford.

One thing to keep in mind when deciding what you can afford is that many experts recommend against buying the most expensive house in a given neighborhood. A lower-priced home in a higher-priced neighborhood offers greater security and a better likelihood of seeing the property value increase.

An Old Home or a New One?

If there is a choice between buying a new home or one that has been occupied before, you must weight the pluses and minuses of each. The value of similar new and used homes in similar neighborhoods will go up about equally, but other aspects of each may make you choose one over the other.

New homes have more modern amenities, are often less likely to suffer system breakdowns (that is, plumbing, heating, and water supply), should not require much upkeep or many repairs, and often can be mortgaged for a greater percentage of the price over a longer term. Older homes frequently are less expensive, have larger rooms, are better built, have finished landscaping, and are closer to the center of town. The individual merits of the actual houses you look at will guide you in making a final choice.

The Down Payment

Among the many decisions to be made in the home-buying process is whether to make a large or small down payment.

While a higher down payment can reduce your monthly payments or the term of the mortgage, there are a number of advantages in making as small a down payment as possible: you retain access to your money; the money you pay in later years will be less valuable, because of inflation, than any spent now; and the interest included in your mortgage payments is tax deductible, so the more you borrow, the more you can deduct.

The Mortgage

At one time the only mortgages widely available in the United States were fixed-rate mortgages that required fixed monthly payments for a specific period, usually 25 or 30 years. Recently, however, a wide variety of different mortgage options have become available.

The *graduated payment mortgage* (GPM) has a fixed rate of interest but varying payments. Payments begin lower and are increased at a fixed rate each year, rising to a level higher than on a fixed-rate mortgage. Initial payments may be lower than the cost of interest, in which case the unpaid interest is added to the principal. This type is good for first-time buyers who expect their incomes to rise during the course of the mortgage.

The *pledged-account mortgage* (PAM) is a variation of the GPM that takes the difference between payments and the accrued interest from a savings account pledged to that purpose by the borrower.

The *adjustable rate mortgage* (ARM) has a flexible interest rate that varies according to a selected interest-rate index. It may go up when the index goes up and most go down when the index goes down; it may contain limitations on the maximum and minimum rates. The changing rate can affect the monthly payment, the term, or the outstanding principal. Some plans change the rate more frequently than they change the payments. This can result in underpayments on interest that are then added to the outstanding balance.

The *graduated-payment adjustable-rate mortgage* (GPARM) combines features of GPMs and ARMs. Some plans defer interest in the early years; others set rising payments during the first several years; and still others fix low payments early on. Countless variations are possible.

The *wraparound mortgage* allows the buyer to assume the balance of a lower-rate mortgage from the seller, making payments to amortize both that original mortgage and the additional amount being borrowed at prevailing rates. This mortgage reduces the overall interest rate on the total amount.

The *shared-appreciation mortgage* (SAM) is available from some lenders. In return for a reduced interest rate, the lender receives a set portion of the amount by which the home has appreciated when it is sold or the loan is paid. Because the final value of the home cannot be determined in advance, additional interest can be due if the value has not appreciated sufficiently.

A *reverse mortgage* really is not a mortgage at all, but a way of getting monthly payments in return for some of the equity in a house. It is advantageous for those over 75 with significant equity and insufficient cash.

In addition to the mortgage payments themselves, many lenders also charge "points." These additional amounts—each point is equal to 1 percent of the loan—are paid by the buyer at the time the mortgage goes into effect, at the closing.

Going to Contract

Anything and everything can and possibly will go wrong when it comes time to draw up a contract and close the deal to buy a home. No list of potential pitfalls could be considered all-inclusive. The best advice is to obtain a lawyer who is familiar with the kind of property purchase you are making and to read every word in every document presented to you with your lawyer.

Investments and Retirement

If you are like most people, your main source of income for the greater part of your life is the salary or fees you earn from working. This income may or may not be adequate to support the life-style you wish to maintain. If you would like to increase your income, you might consider making investments. Even if your earned income is enough for the present, you may want to invest now in order to plan for a secure retirement.

Setting Goals

There is little point in considering investments without developing the goals you hope to reach by making them. Investing is a means to an end. That end generally can be described as financial security—having enough income to live on after you retire. But a more specific set of goals is essential.

Short-term and long-term strategies must be developed. The amounts you have available to invest now, and those you can make available in the future, must be calculated. The rate of return you require from your investments must be figured, taking into account the amount of income you will need them to produce in the future after factoring in inflation. Your need for access to the principal or profit on short notice must be evaluated, too, along with whether you are willing to take greater risks for a potentially higher return or will accept lower profits in return for greater security.

Other aspects that should be considered in creating short- and long-term goals are diversification of your investments to reduce risks; the tax status of the income your investments produce; and the availability of loans using your investments as collateral.

Setting goals is a continual process. Your current goals should be based on how you envision your future.

Choosing Your Investments

Once you have decided on your investment goals, you must answer the most difficult question of all: What should you invest in? The possibilities are almost limitless.

It is unwise to select an investment without close scrutiny. Selecting a stock because someone—even a stockbroker—tells you "it's a good bet" is not a good way to handle your money. You can select the types of investments you believe will be most effective in helping you reach your short- and long-term goals. But professional assistance should then be sought from an appropriate source: bankers for information about money market accounts, individual retirement accounts, or certificates of deposit; or stockbrokers for stock and bonds.

Passbook savings are the first investments most people are exposed to. They are insured by the federal government, require no minimum deposit, offer set interest rates, and can be added to or withdrawn from at any time. *Time deposits* offer higher interest rates, require a minimum deposit of $2,500 in most cases, are available for varying lengths of time, and often provide free checking privileges. They penalize early withdrawals. *Money market accounts* generally require a minimum deposit of $1,000 to $2,500, pay interest rates comparable to those available on larger certificates of deposit, have no requirements for length of time of deposit, and allow withdrawals and transfers at any time.

Certificates of deposit (CDs) are available in varying amounts (usually from $500) for anywhere from one week to two years, pay high interest rates, and penalize early withdrawals. *Long-term certificates* require deposits for two and a half years or more, compound interest for greater yields, and offer high interest rates.

Individual Retirement Accounts (IRAs) have varying minimum deposit requirements, provide interest that will not be taxed until it is withdrawn, have maximum individual deposit limits of $2,000 per year, and sometimes allow depositors to deduct the amounts of their deposits from their taxable income.

Mutual fund accounts come in a variety of types. Your choice will depend on whether your investment needs require growth of capital, substantial current flow of income, or a balance of reasonable capital growth, reasonable current income, and security of the principal. Minimum deposits vary, and deposits can be withdrawn at any time.

Bond funds allow investors to buy into a diversified portfolio of bonds. They can easily be resold but lose value if interest rates rise. Some funds can be exempt from federal income tax. *U.S. savings bonds* require a minimum $25 deposit, mature in 10 years, and provide virtually guaranteed security. *Corporate bonds* require a minimum deposit of $1,000, mature in 1 to 30 years, and can easily be cashed in. They provide the current market rate of return but can lose value if interest rates rise. *Zero-coupon bonds* provide a fixed yield when the bond matures, are sold at a large discount off face value, and mature in six months to 10 years or longer, usually at a value of $1,000.

Stock funds allow investors to diversify their stock holdings, require minimum investments, and change in value according to stock market price changes. *Common stocks* can provide dividend income and long-term growth of capital but require careful management to avoid loss or diminution of capital.

Treasury bills are six-month instruments available in $10,000 denominations. They offer market interest rates with high security, can be easily sold, and are not subject to state and local income taxes.

More detailed information about the common types of investments outlined here—as well as more "exotic" investments ranging from oil drilling ventures and real estate partnerships to precious metals, commodities, or a relative's new business—can be obtained from books, government publications, and the agencies that regulate such activities.

Planning for Retirement

Although few working people require income from their investments to meet routine expenses, most people will require income from outside sources in order to retire in security and comfort. There are three potential providers of retirement income; pension plans funded by an employer; government retirement funds; and an individual's own retirement fund. The best way to assure your own financial security after retirement is to arrange for retirement income from at least two or even all three of these sources.

Employer-funded retirement plans can be pension plans, profit-sharing plans, or a combination of the two. Most pension plans define the benefits due and eligibility qualifications required of each employee in advance. They are designed to provide employees with a guaranteed income after they reach a certain age, generally 65, and retire. Some plans allow for early retirement at reduced benefits. In addition to providing income after retirement, many plans also provide vested benefits for employees who stop working for the company before they reach the minimum retirement age, death benefits, medical benefits, and a pension for surviving spouses. *Profit-sharing plans* differ from pension plans in that an employer's contributions to the fund are dependent on company profits. Profit-sharing plans also may have provisions for vesting at an earlier age and withdrawal and loan privileges.

Social Security is the basic retirement plan provided by the government. More than 90 percent of the workers in the United States are earning benefits under Social Security through contributions they and their employers make in the form of Social Security taxes. Social Security provides monthly payments to qualified workers who retire at age 62 or older, health insurance for the elderly under Medicare, and monthly payments to disabled workers and to spouses and children of workers who retire, become disabled, or die. The dollar amount of benefits is dependent on the rate set by the government as well as on other sources of income the retiree has available. Qualification for Social Security benefits is earned on the basis of "quarters of coverage." Workers earn one credit toward coverage for a set amount of income they earn, up to four credits each calendar year. A worker is eligible for retirement benefits if he or she has earned as many credits as the number of calendar years between age 21 (or since 1950) and retirement.

Individual retirement plans can be created according to needs and financial resources using many of the investments outlined above. The most popular individual plan, the Individual Retirement Account (IRA), allows some individuals to deduct contributions of up to $2,000 a year from their income taxes. Under rules that took effect in 1987, married couples with adjusted gross incomes under $50,000, and single people with gross incomes under $35,000, may deduct up to $2,000 in contributions to their IRAs, with deductions phased out over the next $10,000 of adjusted gross income.

Investment Terms

accrued interest Interest earned by a bond since the last payment was made.

AMEX The American Stock Exchange.

appreciation The increase in value of an investment.

asset Something owned by one or owed to one.

bear market A declining stock market.

bid and asked price The highest price offered for a security at a given time (*bid*) and the lowest price accepted for that security at that time (*asked*).

Big Board The New York Stock Exchange.

blue chip The stock of a top-rated company known for the quality of its products and the security and return on investment of its stock; also the company itself.

bond A corporation's note acknowledging indebtedness for a certain amount and promising to pay interest at a given rate on that amount as well as to pay back the principal on a certain date. *See also* **junk bond; Treasury bond.**

book value The theoretical worth of a share of stock as shown on a company's balance sheet; this has little relationship to the stock's market value.

bull market A rising stock market.

capital gain or capital loss The gain or loss resulting from the sale of an asset.

capitalization All securities issued by a company, including bonds, common and preferred stock, and debentures.

capital stock All shares of stock in a company, both common and preferred.

collateral Property or securities used by a borrower to secure a loan.

convertible securities Securities that can be exchanged by the holder for common stock or another security.

coupon bond A bond with coupons attached that are clipped by the holder and presented for payment of interest due.

current assets The total amount of cash, securities, inventory, and receivables expected during the normal business cycle of a company, usually one year.

current liabilities The total amount of debt and other payments that will be due during the normal business cycle of a company, usually one year.

debenture An unsecured promissory note backed by a company's general credit.

discount The amount of money below the issuing price of a stock or bond by which it sells.

discretionary account A securities account that leaves some or all decisions about purchases and sales to the discretion of a broker.

dividend A payment by a company equally divided among its stockholders. *See also* **stock dividend.**

Dow Jones average The average price of selected stocks, used as an indicator of the stock market's performance.

equity The interest stockholders have in a company, or the amount of property a property holder has actually paid for as opposed to the portion held by a mortgage.

ex-dividend A stock that does not pay a recently declared dividend to its new purchaser.

Federal Deposit Insurance Corporation (FDIC) The federal agency that insures amounts up to $100,000 deposited in qualified banks.

fiduciary Someone who acts on behalf of another in financial matters.

gilt-edged security A high-grade preferred stock or bond issued by a company with a strong performance record.

income fund A mutual fund designed to provide current income.

Individual Retirement Account (IRA) A tax-sheltered and sometimes tax-deductible retirement plan.

interest The money paid by a borrower to a lender for the use of the borrowed money.

investment The use of money to make more money.

junk bond A high-risk, high-yielding corporate bond.

Keogh plan A tax-sheltered retirement plan for self-employed people with no pension plans.

liabilities All claims against and amounts owed by a company.

listed stock Stock traded on a securities exchange.

margin The portion of a stock's price paid by the buyer when the broker arranges for the remainder to be purchased on credit.

market order An order to buy or sell at the current market price of a security.

maturity The date on which a bond or loan is to be paid off.

money market fund A mutual fund that invests in short-term financial securities.

municipal bond A bond issued by a local government.

mutual fund An investment company that continually offers new stock and redeems outstanding shares on demand.

odd lot An amount of stock bought or sold in units other than 10 shares or 100 shares.

offer The price at which someone is willing to sell.

over-the-counter market The arena in which stocks not listed on exchanges are bought and sold.

par The issuing value of a share of common stock.

preferred stock Stock that must receive its share of earnings before payment is made on common stock.

premium The amount over par value by which a preferred stock is sold.

puts and calls Options that give the right to sell or buy a specified number of shares of stock at a specified price within a specified time.

red herring A preliminary prospectus issued to gauge interest in a new stock issue.

Securities and Exchange Commission (SEC) The federal agency that oversees securities trading.

stock Ownership shares in a company.

stock dividend Shares distributed to current shareholders in a company in proportion to those they hold.

stock split The division of currently outstanding shares into a larger number of shares.

tax shelter A way in which taxes on income may be legally decreased, eliminated, or deferred.

tender offer An offer by one company to purchase shares of stock in another company directly from its stockholders.

Treasury bill A short-term U.S. government security sold at discount in competitive bidding.

Treasury bond A long-term U.S. government bond issued in $1,000 denominations.

yield The amount of dividend or interest expressed as a percentage of the selling price.

zero-coupon bonds Bonds that are sold at a discount from their face value but that do not pay interest.

Real Estate Terms

amortization A gradual paying off of a mortgage by periodic installments.

appraisal An estimation of a property's value, often made by lenders before deciding the amount of a mortgage.

assessed valuation A value placed on a property as a basis for taxation.

assumable mortgage A mortgage taken over from the seller of a property by the buyer.

balloon payment The final payment on a loan or mortgage, usually larger than the previous payments.

binder An agreement by the buyer to cover the down payment on the purchase of real estate before a final contract is drawn up.

broker Usually a licensed agent who acts on behalf of the seller of a property, making arrangements for the sale.

closing The meeting of a buyer, a seller, a banker, and attorneys for all parties at which a real estate sale is completed with the writing of checks; it usually takes place 30 to 60 days after signing of the contract.

commission The amount paid to a real estate broker for services rendered.

condominium A form of individual ownership in a multiple-unit dwelling, townhouse, or detached house in which the owner buys title to a single unit and an interest in common areas.

contract A binding agreement between parties to transact real estate under agreed-upon terms.

cooperative apartment A form of individual ownership in a multiple-unit dwelling in which buyers purchase shares in a cooperative corporation that owns the building; the shares entitle the holder to a proprietary lease on an apartment in the building.

deed A written document that conveys ownership of real property.

equity The value of an owner's real property after deducting mortgages and liens.

escrow A written agreement to place money or property with someone else until it is due to be delivered to a designated party; often used for payment of taxes along with mortgage payments.

Fannie Mae The Federal National Mortgage Association, the largest secondary mortgage agency.

Federal Housing Administration (FHA) A division of the federal government's Department of Housing and Urban Development that insures mortgages.

Freddie Mac The Federal Home Loan Mortgage Corporation, which buys mortgages from lenders, allowing the lenders to make new mortgages.

Ginnie Mae The Government National Mortgage Association, which buys FHA-insured loans from lenders.

indexing A means of adjusting the interest rate on a loan or mortgage according to an agreed-upon index or indicator.

interest Money paid to a lender for use of borrowed principal.

lien An interest in a property granted as collateral for a loan or mortgage.

mortgage A written instrument that creates a lien on a given property in return for a loan.

point An amount equal to 1 percent of a loan, charged to the borrower by the lender.

prepayment penalty An additional fee charged for paying off a mortgage before it is due.

principal The amount of money borrowed from a lender for a mortgage, upon which interest is computed.

title A written document that gives evidence of property ownership.

Calculating Your Net Worth

Use the following chart to calculate your current net worth. Be sure to include amounts held individually and jointly to evaluate your family's net worth.

Assets

Cash on hand and liquid assets
    Checking and savings accounts   _____
    Cash value of life insurance   _____
    U.S. savings bonds   _____
    Equity in pension funds   _____
    Money market funds   _____
    Brokerage funds   _____
    Trusts   _____
    Debts owed you   _____
    Other   _____
    TOTAL   _____
Personal holdings
    Car(s) (current value)   _____
    Home(s)   _____
    Boat(s)   _____
    Major appliances   _____
    Furs and jewelry   _____
    Antiques and collectibles   _____
    Art   _____
    Other   _____
    TOTAL   _____

Investments
    Common stocks   _____
    Preferred stocks   _____
    Corporate and municipal bonds   _____
    Mutual funds   _____
    Certificates of deposit   _____
    Business investments   _____
    Real estate investments   _____
    IRAs   _____
    Other   _____
    TOTAL   _____
TOTAL ASSETS   _____

Liabilities

    Bills due   _____
    Revolving charge and bank-card debts   _____
    Taxes due   _____
    Outstanding mortgage   _____
    Outstanding loans (bank, insurance, etc.)   _____
    Stock margin accounts payable   _____
    Other debts   _____
TOTAL LIABILITIES   _____
NET WORTH (Assets minus liabilities)   _____

Tipping

The following list suggests what are generally considered to be adequate amounts to tip various people for services rendered. It should be kept in mind that tips are a way of expressing satisfaction. Larger tips should be left for those who provide extraordinarily good service; smaller tips or no tip at all should be left when service is poor.

Location	*Person*	*Amount*
Restaurant	waiter or waitress	15% of bill
	headwaiter/maitre d'	none, unless special services are provided; then, about $5
	wine steward	15% of wine bill
	bartender	10–15% of bar bill
	busboy	none
	servers at counter	15% of bill
	coat check attendant	$1 for one or two coats
	restroom attendant	50 cents
	car park attendant	50 cents

Location	Person	Amount
Hotel	chambermaid	no tip for one-night stays; $1–$2 a night or $5–$10 a week for longer stays
	room-service waiter	15% of bill
	bellhop	$1 per bag for bringing you to your room with luggage; 50 cents for opening and showing the room
	lobby attendant	none for opening door or calling taxi from stand; $1 or more for help with luggage or finding a taxi on the street
	desk clerk	none unless special service is given during long stay; then, $5
Train	dining car waiter	15% of bill
	stewards/bar-car waiters	15% of bar bill
	redcaps	posted rate plus 50 cents
Airport	skycaps	$1 or more for full baggage cart
	in-flight personnel	none
Cruise ship	cabin steward	2.5% to 4% of total fare
	dining-room steward	2.5% to 4% of total fare
	cabin boy, bath steward, bar steward, wine steward	5% to $7\frac{1}{2}$% of total fare divided proportionately among them, paid at the end of each week
Taxi	driver	15% of fare, no less than 50 cents
Barbershop	haircutter	15% of the cost, generally a minimum of $1
Beauty shop	one operator	15% of bill
	several operators	10% of bill to person who sets hair; 10% divided among others
	manicurist	$1–$2 or more, depending on cost
Sports arena	usher	50 cents to $1 per party if shown to your seat

Additional Sources of Information

Organizations and Services

Consult the following organizations for referrals to reputable financial planners.

Institute of Certified Financial Planners
7600 East Eastman Avenue
Suite 301
Denver, CO 80231-4397
303-751-7600

International Association for Financial Planning
Two Concourse Parkway
Suite 800
Atlanta, GA 30328
404-395-1605

The following publications offer substantial coverage of events and trends that affect personal finances. Addresses are for subscriptions.

Barron's National Business Weekly
200 Burnett Road
Chicopee, MA 01020

Business Week
1221 Avenue of the Americas
New York, NY 10020

Kiplinger's Personal Finance Magazine
The Kiplinger Washington Editors, Inc.
1729 H St., NW
Washington, DC 20006

Money (monthly)
P.O. Box 54429
Boulder, CO 80322

Books

Alperson, Myra, et al. *The Better World Investment Guide.* Prentice Hall, 1991.
Banford, Janet, et al. *The Consumer Reports Money Book 1992.* Consumers Union, 1992.
Brown, Charlene. *The Consumer Guide to Credit.* United Resource Press, 1991.
Dunnan, Nancy. *Dun & Bradstreet Guide to Your Investments.* HarperCollins, 1992.
Klott, Gary L. *The Complete Financial Guide to the 1990s.* Times Books, 1990.
Leonard, Frances. *Women and Money.* Addison Wesley, 1991.
Lerner, Joel J. *Financial Planning for the Utterly Confused*, 3rd ed. McGraw-Hill, 1991.
Loeb, Marshall. *Marshall Loeb's Money Guide.* Little Brown, annual.
Pollan, Stephen M., and Mark Levine. *The Business of Living.* Fireside, 1991.
Porter, Sylvia. *Love and Money.* Avon, 1986.
Shane, Dorlene V. *Be Your Own Financial Planner: The 21-Day Guide to Financial Success.* Wiley, 1987.
Sheen, Brian J. *Nest Egg Investing: The Lifelong Program for Financial Independence.* Putnam, 1987.
Shook, R. J., and Robert L. *The Wall Street Dictionary.* New York Institute of Finance, 1990.
Sloane, Leonard. *The New York Times Book of Personal Finance*, 3rd ed. Times Books, 1992.
Stribling, Catherine. *Growing Up Financially: A Money Management Guide.* Ballantine, 1986.
Tobias, Andrew P. *Still! The Only Investment Guide You'll Ever Need.* Simon & Schuster, 1991.

18

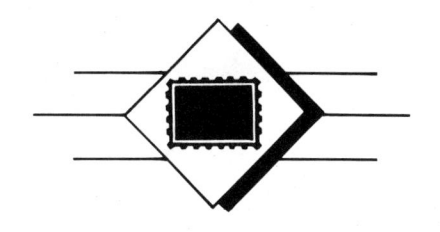

Useful Addresses

Aging / *456*

Alcoholism and Drug Abuse / *461*

Children / *462*

Better Business Bureaus / *463*

State, County, and City Government Consumer Protection Offices / *469*

Domestic Violence Resources / *494*

Family Planning / *496*

Genealogy / *497*

Government Agencies and Bureaus / *498*

Disabled / *501*

Health and Nutrition / *502*

Hotlines and Information Services / *503*

ZIP Codes / *504*

Magazines / *511*

Newspapers / *515*

Parenting / *519*

Radio and Television Networks / *520*

Sports Organizations and Halls of Fame / *521*

Where to Write Your Senators and Representatives / *522*

Additional Sources of Information / *523*

Aging

Private Organizations

American Association of Retired Persons
National Gerontology Resource Center
1909 K Street, NW
Washington, DC 20049
202-872-4700

American Association of Retired Persons
Widowed Persons Service
1909 K Street, NW
Washington, DC 20049
202-872-4700

American Society on Aging
833 Market Street
Suite 512
San Francisco, CA 94103
415-882-2910

Andrus Gerontology Center
University of Southern California
Los Angeles, CA 90089
213-740-8241

Associacion Nacional por Personas Mayores
Library Resource Center
2727 West 6th Street
Suite 270
Los Angeles, CA 90057
203-487-1922

National Senior Citizens Law Center
1052 West 6th Street
Suite 700
Los Angeles, CA 90017
213-482-3550

Rehabilitation Research and Training Center on Aging
University of Southern California
c/o Rancho Los Amigos Hospital
7600 Consuelo Street
Downey, CA 90242
213-722-7402

Self-Help for the Elderly
445 Grant Avenue
San Francisco, CA 94108
415-982-9171

State Commissions and Offices

State commissions and offices on aging are responsible for coordinating services for older Americans. They can provide information on programs, services, and opportunities for the aging.

Alabama

Commission on Aging
136 Catoma Street
Montgomery, AL 36130
205-242-5743
800-243-5463 (Alabama only)

Alaska

Older Alaskans Commission
P.O. Box C
Juneau, AK 99811-0209
907-465-3250

Arizona

Aging and Adult Administration
1400 West Washington, 950A
Phoenix, AZ 85007
602-542-4446

Arkansas

Office of Aging and Adult Services
Department of Human Services
P.O. Box 1437
Little Rock, AR 72203-1437
501-682-2441
800-482-8049 (Arizona only)

California

Department of Aging
1600 K Street
Sacramento, CA 95814
916-322-5290
916-323-8913 (TDD)
800-231-4024 (California only)

Colorado

Colorado Department of Social Services
1575 Sherman Street
Denver, CO 80203-1714
303-866-5700

Connecticut

Department on Aging
175 Main Street
Hartford, CT 06106
203-566-3238
800-443-9946
(voice/TDD in Connecticut)

Delaware

Division of Aging
Department of Health and Social Services
1901 North DuPont Highway
New Castle, DE 19720
302-421-6791
800-223-9074 (Delaware only)

District of Columbia

D.C. Office on Aging
1424 K Street, NW, 2nd Floor
Washington, DC 20005
202-724-5623

Florida

Aging and Adult Services
1321 Winewood Boulevard
Room 323
Tallahassee, FL 32399-0700
904-488-8922

Georgia

Office of Aging
878 Peachtree Street, NE
Suite 632
Atlanta, GA 30309
404-894-5333

Hawaii

Executive Office on Aging
335 Merchant Street, Room 241
Honolulu, HI 96813
808-548-2593
800-468-4644 (Hawaii only)

Idaho

Idaho Office on Aging
Statehouse, Room 108
Boise, ID 83720
208-334-3833

Illinois

Department on Aging
421 East Capitol Avenue
Springfield, IL 62701
217-785-2870
800-252-8966
(voice/TDD)

Indiana

Aging/In-Home Care Services Division
Department of Human Services
P.O. Box 7083
Indianapolis, IN 46207-7083
317-232-7020
800-622-4972
(toll free in IN)

Iowa

Department of Elder Affairs
914 Grand Avenue, Suite 236
Des Moines, IA 50319
515-281-5187
800-532-3213 (Iowa only)

Kansas

Department on Aging
Docking State Office Building
Room 122 South
915 Southwest Harrison Street
Topeka, KS 66612-1500
913-296-4986
800-432-3535 (Kansas only)

Kentucky

Division for Aging Services
Department for Social Services
275 East Main Street
6th Floor West
Frankfort, KY 40621
502-564-6930
502-564-5497 (TDD)
800-372-2991 (Kentucky only)
800-372-2973 (TDD Kentucky only)

Louisiana

Governors Office of Elder Affairs
P.O. Box 80374
Baton Rouge, LA 70898
504-925-1700

Maine

Bureau of Elder and Adult Service
35 Anthony Avenue
Statehouse, Station 11
Augusta, ME 04333-0011
207-626-5335

Maryland

Office on Aging
301 West Preston Street
10th Floor
Baltimore, MD 21201
301-225-1100
301-383-7555 (TDD)
800-243-3425 (Maryland only)

Massachusetts

Executive Office of Elder Affairs
38 Chauncy Street
Boston, MA 02111
617-727-7750
800-882-2003 (Massachusetts only)
800-872-0166 (TDD Massachusetts only)
800-922-2275 (TDD in Massachusetts—Elder Abuse Hotline)

Michigan

Office of Services to the Aging
P.O. Box 30026
Lansing, MI 48909
(517) 373-8230

Minnesota

Minnesota Board on Aging
444 Lafayette Road
St. Paul, MN 55155-3843
612-296-2544
800-652-9747 (Minnesota only)

Mississippi

Council on Aging
Division of Aging and Adult Services
421 West Pascagoula Street
Jackson, MS 39203
601-949-2070
800-345-6347 (Mississippi only)

Missouri

Division of Aging
P.O. Box 1337
Jefferson City, MO 65102
314-751-8535
800-392-0210 (Missouri only)

Montana

Coordinator of Aging Services
Governor's Office
State Capitol
Helena, MT 59620
406-444-4204
800-332-2272 (Montana only)

Nebraska

Nebraska Department on Aging
State Office Building
P.O. Box 95044
Lincoln, NE 68509
402-471-2306

Nevada

Division for Aging Services
Department of Human Resources
340 North 11th Street
Las Vegas, NV 89158
702-486-3545

New Hampshire

Division of Elderly and Adult Services
6 Hazen Drive
Concord, NH 03301
603-271-4680
800-351-1888 (New Hampshire only)

New Jersey

Division on Aging
Department of Community Affairs
101 South Broad Street, CN 807
Trenton, NJ 08625
609-292-4833
800-792-8820 (New Jersey only)

New Mexico

State Agency on Aging
224 East Palace Avenue
4th Floor
Santa Fe, NM 87501
505-827-7640 (voice/TDD)
800-432-2080 (New Mexico only)

New York

New York State Office for the Aging
Agency Building 2, ESP
Albany, NY 12223
518-474-5731
800-342-9871 (New York only)

North Carolina

Division of Aging
Department of Human Resources
Caller Box No. 2953
693 Palmer Drive
Raleigh, NC 27626-0531
919-733-3983
800-662-7030
(voice/TDD in North Carolina only)

North Dakota

Aging Services
Department of Human Service
600 East Boulevard
Bismarck, ND 58505
701-224-2310
800-472-2622 (North Dakota only)

Ohio

Ohio Department of Aging
50 West Broad Street, 9th Floor
Columbus, OH 43266-0501
614-466-5500
614-466-6191 (TDD)
800-282-1206 (Ohio only—nursing home information)

Oklahoma

Special Unit on Aging
P.O. Box 25352
Oklahoma City, OK 73125
405-521-2281
405-521-2827 (TDD)

Oregon

Senior Services Division
Department of Human Resources
State of Oregon
313 Public Service Building
Salem, OR 97310
503-378-4728
800-232-3020
(voice/TDD in Oregon only)

Pennsylvania

Department of Aging
231 State Street
Harrisburg, PA 17101
717-783-1549

Rhode Island

Department of Elderly Affairs
160 Pine Street
Providence, RI 02903
401-277-2880 (voice/TDD)
800-322-2880 (Rhode Island only)

South Carolina

South Carolina Commission on Aging
400 Arbor Lake Drive
Suite B-500
Columbia, SC 29223
803-735-0210
800-868-9095

South Dakota

Office of Adult Services and Aging
700 Governors Drive
Pierre, SD 57501
605-773-3656

Tennessee

Commission on Aging
706 Church Street, Suite 201
Nashville, TN 37243-0860
615-741-2056

Texas

Texas Department on Aging
P.O. Box 12786, Capitol Station
Austin, TX 78711
512-444-2727 (voice/TDD)
800-252-9240 (Texas only)

Utah

Division of Aging and Adult Services
P.O. Box 45500
Salt Lake City, UT 84145-0500
801-538-3910

Vermont

Department of Aging and Disabilities
103 South Main Street
Waterbury, VT 05671-2301
802-241-2400 (voice/TDD)

Virginia

Department for the Aging
700 East Franklin Street
10th Floor
Richmond, VA 23219
804-225-2271 (voice/TDD)
800-552-4464 (Virginia only)
800-552-3402 (Virginia only—Ombudsman Hotline)

Washington

Aging and Adult Services Administration
OB-44A
Olympia, WA 98504
206-493-2509
800-422-3263 (Washington only)

West Virginia

Commission on Aging
State Capitol
Charleston, WV 25305
304-348-3317

Wisconsin

Bureau on Aging
P.O. Box 7851
Madison, WI 53707
608-266-2536

Wyoming

Division on Aging
139 Hathaway Building
Cheyenne, WY 82002-0480
307-777-7986
800-442-2766 (Wyoming only)

American Samoa

Territorial Administration on Aging
Government of American Samoa
Pago Pago, AS 96799
011-684-633-1251

Guam

Office of Aging
Government of Guam
P.O. Box 2816
Agana, GU 96910
011-671-734-2942

Puerto Rico

Office of Elder Affairs
Call Box 563
Old San Juan Station, PR 00902
809-721-4560

Virgin Islands

Department of Human Services
Barbel Plaza South
Charlotte Amalie
St. Thomas, VI 00802
809-774-0930

Alcoholism and Drug Abuse

Al-Anon Family Group Headquarters
P.O. Box 862
Midtown Station
New York, NY 10018

Alcohol and Drug Problems Association of North America
444 North Capitol Street, NW
Washington, DC 20001
202-737-4340

Alcohol, Drug Abuse and Mental Health Administration
U.S. Department of Health and Human Services
Parklawn Building
5600 Fishers Lane
Rockville, MD 20857
303-443-3783

Alcoholics Anonymous World Services
P.O. Box 459
Grand Central Station
New York, NY 10163
212-686-1100

American Council on Alcoholism
8501 La Salle Road
Towson, MD 21204
800-527-5344

American Council on Alcohol Problems
3426 Bridgeland Drive
Bridgton, MO 65044
314-739-5944

Association of Halfway House Alcoholism Programs of North America
786 East 7th Street
St. Paul, MN 55106
612-771-0933

BACCHUS of the U.S. (Boost Alcohol Consciousness Concerning the Health of University Students)
P.O. Box 10430
Denver, CO 80210
303-871-3068

Community Organization for Drug Abuse, Mental Health, and Alcohol
2025 North Central Avenue
Phoenix, AZ 85004-1547
612-234-0096

Do It Now Foundation
P.O. Box 27568
Tempe, AZ 85285
602-491-0393

Families Anonymous
P.O. Box 528
Van Nuys, CA 91408
818-989-7841

Narcotics Anonymous
P.O. Box 9999
Van Nuys, CA 94109
818-780-3951

National Association for Children of Alcoholics
31582 S Coast Highway
South Laguna, CA 92677-3066

National Association of Alcoholism and Drug Abuse Counselors
3717 Columbia Pike
Arlington, VA 22204
703-920-4644

National Association on Drug Abuse Problems
355 Lexington Avenue
New York, NY 10017
212-986-1170

National Cocaine Hotline
800-262-2476

National Council on Alcoholism
12 West 21st Street
New York, NY 10010
800-NCA-CALL

National Families in Action
Drug Information Center
2296 Henderson Mill Road
Atlanta, GA 30345
404-934-6364

National Federation of Parents for Drug-Free Youth
1423 North Jefferson
Springfield, MO 65802
417-836-3709

National Parents Resource Institute for Drug Education
50 Hurt Plaza
Atlanta, GA 30303
404-577-4500

Odyssey Institute Corporation
817 Fairfield Avenue
Bridgeport, CT 06604
212-794-1734

Potsmokers Anonymous
208 West 23rd Street
Apartment 1414
New York, NY 10011
212-254-17777

Therapeutic Communities of America
307 Fourth Avenue
Pittsburgh, PA 15222
412-562-0105

Women in Crisis
133 West 21st Street
New York, NY 10011
212-242-4880

Children

Child Abuse

American Association for Protecting Children
c/o American Humane Association
9725 East Hampton Avenue
Denver, CO 80231
800-227-5242

Clearinghouse on Child Abuse and Neglect Information
Department of Health and Human Services
P.O. Box 1182
Washington, DC 20013
202-251-5157

National Committee for Prevention of Child Abuse
332 South Michigan Avenue
Chicago, IL 60604
312-663-3520

National Network of Youth Advisory Boards
P.O. Box 402036
Ocean View Bridge
Miami Beach, FL 33140
305-532-2607

Parents Anonymous
6733 South Sepulveda
Los Angeles, CA 90046
213-410-9732

Disabled Children

Association for Children with Retarded Mental Development
162 Fifth Avenue
New York, NY 10010
212-741-0100

ERIC Clearinghouse on Handicapped and Gifted Children
Department of Education
1920 Association Drive
Reston, VA 22091
703-620-3660

National Center for Learning Disabilities
99 Park Avenue
New York, NY 10016
212-687-7211

National Information Center for Children and Youth with Handicaps
P.O. Box 1492
Washington, DC 20013
703-893-6061

Runaways

American Youth Work Center
1751 N Street, NW
Washington, DC 20036
202-785-0764

Contact Center
P.O. Box 81826
Lincoln, NE 68501
402-464-0602

National Runaway Switchboard
3080 North Lincoln Avenue
Chicago, IL 60657
800-621-4000

Network of Runaway and Youth Services
1319 F Street, NW
Washington, DC 20004
202-783-7949

Better Business Bureaus

United States

National Headquarters

Council of Better Business Bureaus
4200 Wilson Boulevard
Arlington, VA 22203
703-276-0100

Local Bureaus

Alabama

P.O. Box 55268
Birmingham, AL 35255-5268
205-558-2222

118 Woodburn Street
Dothan, AL 36301
205-792-3804

P.O. Box 383
Huntsville, AL 35804
205-533-1640 (24 hours)

707 Van Antwerp Building
Mobile, AL 36602-3221
205-433-5494/95
800-544-4171 (southern Alabama)

Union Bank Building
Suite 806
Commerce Street
Montgomery, AL 36104-3559
205-262-5606

Alaska

4011 Arctic Boulevard
#206
Anchorage, AK 99503-5701
907-562-0704

Arizona

4428 North 12th Street
Phoenix, AZ 80514-4585
602-264-1721

50 W. Drachman Street
Suite 103
Tucson, AZ 85705-7353
602-622-7651 (inquiries)
602-622-7654 (complaints)
800-696-2827 (S. Arizona)

Arkansas

1415 South University
Little Rock, AR 72204-2605
501-664-7274

California

705 18th Street
Bakersfield, CA 93301-4882
805-322-2074

P.O. Box 970
Conlon, CA 92324-0814
714-825-7280

6101 Ball Road
Suite 309
Cypress, CA 90630-3966
714-527-0680

1398 West Indianapolis
#102
Fresno, CA 93705-0341
209-222-8111

3400 West 6th Street
Suite 403
Los Angeles, CA 90020
213-251-9696

494 Alvarado Street
Suite C
Monterey, CA 93940-2717
408-372-3149

510 16th Street
Suite 550
Oakland, CA 94612-1564
510-238-1000

400 S Street
Sacramento, CA 95814-6997
916-443-6843

3111 Camino del Rio, North
Suite 600
San Diego, CA 92108-1729
619-521-5898

33 New Montgomery Street Tower
#290
San Francisco, CA 94105-4506
415-243-9999

1505 Meridian Avenue
Suite C
San Jose, CA 95125-5316
408-978-8700

P.O. Box 294
San Mateo, CA 94401-0294
415-696-1240

P.O. Box 746
Santa Barbara, CA 93101-0746
805-963-8657

300 B Street
Santa Rosa, CA 95401-8541
707-577-0300

1111 North Center Street
Stockton, CA 95202-1383
209-948-4880/81

Colorado

P.O. Box 7970
Colorado Springs, CO 80907-5454
719-636-1155

1780 South Bellaire
Suite 700
Denver, CO 80222-4350
303-758-2100 (inquiries, 24 hours)
303-758-2212 (complaints)

1730 South College Avenue
Suite 303
Fort Collins, CO 80525-1073
303-484-1348
800-873-3222 (southern Wyoming
    only)

119 West 6th Street
Suite 203
Pueblo, CO 81003-3119
719-542-6464

Connecticut

P.O. Box 1410
Fairfied, CT 06430-1410
203-374-6161

100 South Turnpike Road
Wallingford, CT 06492-4395
203-269-2700 (inquiries)
203-269-4457 (complaints)

Delaware

2055 Limestone Road
Suite 200
Wilmington, DE 19808-5532
302-996-9200

District of Columbia

1012 14th Street, NW
14th floor
Washington, DC 20005-3410
202-393-8000

Florida

P.O. Box 7950
Clearwater, FL 34618-7950
813-535-5522

2976-E Cleveland Avenue
Fort Myers, FL 33901-6003
813-334-7331
813-334-7152

3100 University Boulevard South
Suite 239
Jacksonville, FL 32216-2756
904-721-2288

2605 Maitland Center Parkway
Maitland, FL 32751-7147
407-660-9500

16291 Northwest 57th Avenue
Miami, FL 33014-6709
305-625-0307 (inquiries)
305-625-1302 (complaints)

250 School Road
Suite 11-W
New Port Richey, FL 34652
813-842-5459

P.O. Box 1511
Pensacola, FL 32597-1511
904-433-6111

1950 Port St. Lucie Boulevard
Suite 211
Port St. Lucie, FL 34952
407-878-2010

1111 North Westshore Boulevard
Suite 207
Tampa, FL 33607
813-854-1154

2247 Palm Beach Lakes Boulevard
Suite 211
West Palm Beach, FL 33409
407-686-2200

Georgia

P.O. Box 3241
Albany, GA 31706-3241
912-883-0744

100 Edgewood Avenue
Suite 1012
Atlanta, GA 30303-3075
404-688-4910

P.O. Box 2085
Augusta, GA 30903-2085
404-722-1574

P.O. Box 2587
Columbus, GA 31902-2587
404-324-0712/13

1765 Shurling Drive
Macon, GA 31211-2499
912-742-7999

P.O. Box 13956
Savannah, GA 31416-0956
912-354-7521

Hawaii
1600 Kapiolani Boulevard
Suite 714
Honolulu, HI 96814-3801
808-942-2355

Idaho
1333 West Jefferson
Boise, ID 83702-5320
208-342-4649

1547 South Boulevard
Idaho Falls, ID 83402-5026
208-524-9754

Illinois
211 West Wacker Drive
Chicago, IL 60606
312-444-1188 (inquiries)
312-346-3313 (complaints)

3024 West Lake
Peoria, IL 61615-3770
309-688-3741

810 East State Street
3rd Floor
Rockford, IL 61104
815-963-2222

Indiana
P.O. Box 405
Elkhart, IN 46515-0405
219-262-8996

4004 Morgan Avenue
Suite 201
Evansville, IN 47715-2265
812-473-0202

1203 Webster Street
Fort Wayne, IN 46802-3493
800-552-4631 (Indiana only)

4231 Cleveland Street
Gary, IN 46408-2490
219-980-1511
800-637-2118 (northern Indiana only)

Victoria Centre
22 East Washington Street
Suite 200
Indianapolis, IN 46204-3584
317-488-2222

52303 Emmons Road
Suite 9
South Bend, IN 46637-4200
219-277-9121
800-439-5313 (northern Indiana only)

Iowa
852 Middle Road
Suite 290
Bettendorf, IA 52722-4100
319-355-6344

615 Insurance Exchange Building
Des Moines, IA 50309-2375
515-243-8137

318 Badgerow Building
Sioux City, IA 51101
712-252-4501

Kansas
501 Jefferson
Suite 24
Topeka, KS 66607-1190
913-232-0454

212 South Market Street
#300
Wichita, KS 67202-3857
316-263-3146

Kentucky
311 West Short Street
Lexington, KY 40507-1203
606-259-1008

844 South Fourth Street
Louisville, KY 40203-2186
502-583-6546

Louisiana
1602 Murray Street
Suite 117
Alexandria, LA 71301-6875
318-473-4494

2055 Wooddale Boulevard
Baton Rouge, LA 70806-1546
504-926-3010

501 East Main Street
Houma, LA 70360-4455
504-868-3456

P.O. Box 30297
Lafayette, LA 70593-0297
318-981-3497

P.O. Box 7314
Lake Charles, LA 70606-7314
318-478-6253

141 De Siard Street
Suite 808
Monroe, LA 71201-7380
318-387-4600

1539 Jackson Avenue
#400
New Orleans, LA 70130-5483
504-581-6222 (24 hours)

3612 Youree Drive
Shreveport, LA 71105-2122
318-861-6417

Maine
812 Stevens Avenue
Portland, ME 04103-2648
207-878-2715

Maryland
2100 Huntingdon Avenue
Baltimore, MD 21211-3215
301-347-3990

Massachusetts
20 Park Plaza
Suite 820
Boston, MA 02116-4404
617-426-9000
800-4BBB-811 (801 area code only)

293 Bridge Street, Suite 320
Springfield, MA 01103-1402
413-734-3114

P.O. Box 379
Worcester, MA 01601-0379
508-755-2548

Michigan

620 Trust Building
Grand Rapids, MI 49503-3001
616-774-8236

30555 Southfield Road
Suite 200
Southfield, MI 48076-7751
313-644-1012 (inquiries)
313-644-9136 (complaints)

Minnesota

2706 Gannon Road
Minneapolis-St. Paul, MN
 55116-2600
612-699-1111

Mississippi

460 Briarwood Drive
Suite 340
Jackson, MS 39206-3088
601-956-8282

Missouri

306 East 12th Street
Suite 1024
Kansas City, MO 64106-2418
816-421-7800

5100 Oakland
Suite 200
St. Louis, MO 63110-1400
314-531-3300 (inquiries)

205 Park Central East
Suite 509
Springfield, MO 65806-1326
417-862-9231

Nebraska

719 North 48th Street
Lincoln, NE 68504-3491
402-467-5261

1613 Farnam Street
#417
Omaha, NE 68102-2158
402-346-3033

Nevada

1022 East Sahara Avenue
Las Vegas, NV 89104-1515
702-735-6900/1969

P.O. Box 21269
Reno, NV 89515-1269
702-322-0657

New Hampshire

410 South Main Street
Concord, NH 03301-3459
603-224-1991

New Jersey

494 Broad Street
Newark, NJ 07102-3294
201-642-INFO

2 Forest Avenue
Paramus, NJ 07652-5291
201-845-4044

1300A Route 46, West
#215
Parsippany, NJ 07054
201-334-5990

1721 Route 37 East
Toms River, NJ 08753-8329
908-270-5577

1700 Whitehorse
Hamilton Square
Suite D-5
Trenton, NJ 08690-3596
201-588-0808

P.O. Box 303
Westmont, NJ 08108-0303
609-854-8467

New Mexico

4600-A Montgomery NE
Suite 200
Albuquerque, NM 87109-1292
800-873-2224 (New Mexico only)
505-884-0500

308 North Locke
Farmington, NM 87401-5855
505-326-6501

2407 W. Picacho
Suite B-2
Las Cruces, NM 88005
505-524-3130

New York

346 Delaware Avenue
Buffalo, NY 14202-1899
716-856-7180

266 Main Street
Farmingdale, NY 11735-0009
900-463-6222

257 Park Avenue South
New York, NY 10010-7384
212-533-7500/6200

1122 Sibley Tower
Rochester, NY 14604-1084
716-546-6776

847 James Street
#200
Syracuse, NY 13202-2552
315-479-6635

30 Glenn Street
White Plains, NY 10603-3213
914-428-1230/31

North Carolina

801 BB&T Building
Asheville, NC 28801-3418
704-253-2392

1130 East 3rd Street
Suite 400
Charlotte, NC 28204-2626
704-332-7151 (24 hours)

3305-10 16th Avenue, SE
#303
Conover, NC 28613-9608
704-464-0372

3608 West Friendly Avenue
Greensboro, NC 27410-4895
919-852-4240/41/42

3125 Poplarwood Court
Suite 308
Raleigh, NC 27604-1080
919-872-9240

Useful Addresses **467**

800-222-0950 (eastern North Carolina only)
919-688-6143 (Durham)
919-967-0296 (Chapel Hill)

2110 Cloverdale Avenue
Suite 2-B
Winston-Salem, NC 27103-2516
919-725-8348

Ohio

222 West Market Street
Akron, OH 44303-2111
216-253-4590

1434 Cleveland Avenue, NW
Canton, OH 44703-3135
216-454-9401
800-362-0494 (Ohio only)

898 Walnut Street
Cincinnati, OH 45202-2097
513-421-3015

2217 East 9th Street
#200
Cleveland, OH 44115-1299
216-241-7678

1335 Dublin Street
#30A
Columbus, OH 43215-1000
614-486-6336

40 West Fourth Street
Suite 1250
Dayton, OH 45402-1828
513-222-5825

P.O. Box 269
Lima, OH 45802-0269
419-223-7010

425 Jefferson Avenue
Suite 909
Toledo, OH 43604-1055
419-241-6276

P.O. Box 1495
Youngstown, OH 44501-1495
216-744-3111

Oklahoma

17 South Dewey
Oklahoma City, OK 73102
405-239-6081/6860 (inquiries)
405-239-6083 (complaints)

6711 South Yale
Suite 230
Tulsa, OK 74136-3327
918-492-1266

Oregon

610 Southwest Alder Street
Suite 615
Portland, OR 97205
503-226-3981
800-488-4155 (Oregon and Washington)

Pennsylvania

528 North New Street
Bethlehem, PA 18018-5789
215-866-8780

6 Marion Court
Lancaster, PA 17602
717-291-1151

P.O. Box 2297
Philadelphia, PA 19103-0297
215-488-6100

610 Smithfield Street
Pittsburgh, PA 15222-2578
412-456-2700

P.O. Box 993
Scranton, PA 18501-0993
717-342-9129

Rhode Island

Bureau Park
Box 1300
Warwick, RI 02887-1300
401-785-1212 (inquiries)
401-785-1213 (complaints)

South Carolina

P.O. Box 8326
Columbia, SC 29202-8326
803-254-2525

113 Mills Avenue
Greenville, SC 29605
803-242-5052

1601 Oak Street
#403
Myrtle Beach, SC 29577-1601
803-626-6881

Tennessee

P.O. Box 1178 TCAS
Blountville, TN 37616
615-323-6311

1010 Market Street
#200
Chattanooga, TN 37402-2614
615-266-6144

P.O. Box 10327
Knoxville, TN 37939-0327
615-522-2552

P.O. Box 750704
Memphis, TN 38175-0704
901-795-8771

Nations Bank Plaza
414 Union Street
#1830
Nashville, TN 37219-1778
615-254-5872

Texas

3300 South 14th Street
Suite 307
Abilene, TX 79605-5052
915-691-1533

P.O. Box 1905
Amarillo, TX 79105-1905
806-379-6222

221 West 6th Street
#450
Austin, TX 78701-3403
512-476-1616

P.O. Box 2988
Beaumont, TX 77701-2011
409-835-5348

4346 Carter Creek Parkway
Bryan, TX 77802-4413
409-260-2222

4535 South Padre Island Drive
#28
Corpus Christi, TX 78411-4418
512-854-2892

2001 Bryan Street
Suite 850
Dallas, TX 75201-3093
214-220-2000

5160 Montano Avenue
Lower Level
El Paso, TX 79903-4904
915-772-2727

512 Main Street
#807
Fort Worth, TX 76102-3968
817-332-7585

2707 North Loop West
Suite 900
Houston, TX 77008-1085
713-868-9500

P.O. Box 1178
Lubbock, TX 79408-1178
806-763-0459

P.O. Box 60206
Midland, TX 79711-0206
915-563-1880
800-592-4433 (915 area code only)

P.O. Box 3366
San Angelo, TX 76902-3366
915-949-2989

1800 Northeast Loop 410
Suite 400
San Antonio, TX 78217-5296
512-828-9441

P.O. Box 6652
Tyler, TX 75711-6652
903-581-5704

P.O. Box 7203
Waco, TX 76714-7203
817-772-7530

P.O. Box 69
Weslaco, TX 78596-0069
512-968-3678

1106 Brook Avenue
Wichita Falls, TX 76301-5079
817-723-5526
800-388-1771 (Texas only)

Utah

1588 South Main Street
Salt Lake City, UT 84115-5382
801-487-4656
800-594-8977 (Utah only)

Virginia

4022-B Plank Road
Fredericksburg, VA 22407-4800
703-786-8397

3608 Tidewater Drive
Norfolk, VA 23509-1499
804-627-5651
804-851-9101 (Peninsula area)

701 East Franklin
Suite 712
Richmond, VA 23219-2332
804-648-0016

31 West Campbell Avenue
Roanoke, VA 24011-1301
703-342-3455

Washington

127 West Canal Street
Kennewick, WA 99336-3819
509-582-0222

2200 Sixth Avenue
#828
Seattle, WA 98121-1857
206-448-6222 (24 hours)
206-448-8888

East 123 Indiana
#106
Spokane, WA 99207-2356
509-328-2100

P.O. Box 1274
Tacoma, WA 98401-1274
206-383-5561

P.O. Box 1584
Yakima, WA 98907-1584
509-248-1326

Wisconsin

740 North Plankinton Avenue
Milwaukee, WI 53203-2478
414-273-1600

Puerto Rico

P.O. Box 363488
San Juan, PR 00936-3488
809-756-5400

Canada

National Headquarters

2180 Steeles Avenue West
Suite 219
Concord, Ontario L4K 2Z5
416-699-1248

Local Bureaus

Alberta

7330 Fisher Street, SE
Suite 357
Calgary, Alberta T2H 2H8
403-258-2920

9707 110th Street
Edmonton, Alberta T5K 2L9
403-482-2341

Red Deer, Alberta
Edmonton, Alberta T5K 2L9
403-343-3200

British Columbia
788 Beatty Street
Suite 404
Vancouver, BC V6B 2M1
604-682-2711

201-1005 Langley Street
Victoria, BC V8W 1V7
604-386-6348

Manitoba
365 Hargrave Street
Room 204
Winnipeg, Manitoba R3B 2K3
204-943-1486

Newfoundland
P.O. Box 516
St. John's, Newfoundland A1C 5K4
709-364-2222

Nova Scotia
P.O. Box 2124
Halifax, Nova Scotia B35 3B7
902-422-6581 (inquiries)
902-422-6582 (complaints)

Ontario
50 Bay Street, South
Hamilton, Ontario L8P 4V9
416-527-1111

354 Charles Street, East
Kitchener, Ontario N2G 4L5
519-579-3080

P.O. Box 2153
London, Ontario N6A 4E3
519-673-3222

71 Bank Street
6th floor
Ottawa, Ontario K1P 5N2
613-237-4856

11-101 King Street
St. Catherines, Ontario L2R 3H6
416-687-6686

One St. John's Rd.
Suite 501
Toronto, Ontario M6P 4C7
416-766-5744

500 Riverside Drive West
Windsor, Ontario N9A 5K6
519-258-7222

Quebec
2055 Peel Street
Suite 460
Montreal, Quebec H3A 1V4
514-286-9281

475 rue Richelieu
Quebec City, PQ G1R 1K2
418-523-2555

1601 McAra Street
Regina, Saskatchewan S4N 6H4
306-352-7601

State, County, and City Government Consumer Protection Offices

Listed below are consumer protection offices that are part of state, county, and city governments. Some are located in governors' offices, state attorney generals' offices, or mayors' offices. Check in your state to see which office can help resolve complaints, furnish information or helpful publications, or provide other services. As a general rule, the first place to go for help with a consumer problem is the local office nearest your home. However, if you are having a problem with a business outside your state, contact the consumer office in the state in which you made the purchase. Since most offices require that complaints be in writing, you might save time by writing, rather than calling, with your initial complaint.

Alabama

State Office
Director Consumer Protection Division
Office of Attorney General
11 South Union Street
Montgomery, AL 36130
205-242-7334
800-392-5658 (Alabama only)

Alaska

The Consumer Protection Section in the Office of the Attorney General has been closed. Consumers with complaints are being referred to the Better Business Bureau in Anchorage.

Arizona

State Offices
Chief Counsel
Consumer Protection Office of the Attorney General
1275 West Washington Street, Room 259
Phoenix, AZ 85007
602-542-3702
602-542-5763
800-352-8431 (Arizona only)

Assistant Attorney General
Consumer Protection Office of the Attorney General
402 West Congress Street, Suite 315
Tucson, AZ 85701
602-628-6504

County Offices
County Attorney Apache
County Attorney's Office
P.O. Box 637
St. Johns, AZ 85936
602-337-4364, ext. 240

County Attorney
Cochise County Attorney's Office
P.O. Drawer CA
Bisbee, AZ 85603
602-432-9377

County Attorney
Coconino County Attorney's Office
Coconino County Courthouse
100 East Birch
Flagstaff, AZ 86001
602-779-6518

County Attorney
Gila County Attorney's Office
1400 East Ash Street
Globe, AZ 85501
602-425-3231

County Attorney
Graham County Attorney's Office
Graham County Courthouse
800 West Main
Safford, AZ 85546
602-428-3620

County Attorney
Greenlee County Attorney's Office
P.O. Box 1387
Clifton, AZ 85533
602-865-3842

County Attorney
La Paz County Attorney's Office
1200 Arizona Avenue
P.O. Box 709
Parker, AZ 85344
602-669-6118

County Attorney
Mohave County Attorney's Office
315 North 4th Street
Kingman, AZ 86401
602-753-0719

County Attorney
Navajo County Attorney's Office
Governmental Complex
Holbrook, AZ 86025
602-524-6161

County Attorney
Pima County Attorney's Office
1400 Great American Tower
32 North Stone
Tucson, AZ 85701
602-740-5733

County Attorney
Pinal County Attorney's Office
P.O. Box 887
Florence, AZ 85232
602-868-5801

County Attorney
Santa Cruz County Attorney's Office
2100 North Congress Drive, Suite 201
Nogales, AZ 85621
602-281-4966

County Attorney
Yavapai County Attorney's Office
Yavapai County Courthouse
Prescott, AZ 86301
602-771-3344

County Attorney
Yuma County Attorney's Office
168 South Second Avenue
Yuma, AZ 85364
602-329-2270

City Office
Supervising Attorney
Consumer Affairs Division
Tucson City Attorney's Office
110 East Pennington Street, 2nd Floor
P.O. Box 27210
Tucson, AZ 85726-7210
602-791-4886

Arkansas

State Office
Director
Consumer Protection Division
Office of Attorney General
200 Tower Building
323 Center Street
Little Rock, AR 72201
501-682-2341 (voice/TDD)
800-482-8982
(voice/TDD in Arkansas)

California

State Offices
Director
California Department of Consumer Affairs
400 R Street, Suite 1040
Sacramento, CA 95814
916-445-0660 (complaint assistance)
916-445-1254 (consumer information)
916-522-1700 (TDD)
800-344-9940 (California only)

Office of Attorney General
Public Inquiry Unit
P.O. Box 944255
Sacramento, CA 94244-2550
916-322-3360
800-952-5225 (California only)
800-952-5548 (TDD California only)

Bureau of Automotive Repair
California Department of Consumer Affairs
10240 Systems Parkway
Sacramento, CA 95827
916-366-5100
800-952-5210 (California only)

County Offices
Coordinator Alameda County Consumer Affairs Commission
4400 MacArthur Boulevard
Oakland, CA 94619
415-530-8682

District Attorney
Contra Costa County
District Attorney's Office
725 Court Street, 4th Floor
P.O. Box 670
Martinez, CA 94553
415-646-4500

Senior Deputy District Attorney
Business Affairs
Fresno County District Attorney's Office
2220 Tulare Street, Suite 1000
Fresno, CA 93721
209-488-3156

District Attorney
Consumer and Major Business
Fraud Section
Kern County District Attorney's Office
1215 Truxtun Avenue
Bakersfield, CA 93301
805-861-2421

Director
Los Angeles County Department of Consumer Affairs
500 West Temple Street, Room B-96
Los Angeles, CA 90012
213-974-1452

Director
Citizens Service Office
Marin County Mediation Services
Marin County Civic Center, Room 412
San Rafael, CA 94903
415-499-6190

District Attorney
Marin County
District Attorney's Office
Marin County Civic Center, Room 155
San Rafael, CA 94903
415-499-6482

Deputy District Attorney
Consumer Protection Division
Marin County District Attorney's Office
Hall of Justice, Room 183
San Rafael, CA 94903
415-499-6450

District Attorney
Mendocino County District
Attorney's Office
P.O. Box 1000
Uklah, CA 95482
707-463-4211

Coordinator
Monterey County Office of Consumer Affairs
P.O. Box 1369
Salinas, CA 93902
408-755-5073

**Deputy District Attorney
Consumer Affairs Division
Napa County District Attorney's Office**
931 Parkway Mall
P.O. Box 720
Napa, CA 94559
707-253-4059

**Deputy District Attorney in Charge Major
Fraud Unit Orange County District Attorney's
Office**
801 Civic Center Drive West, Suite 120
Santa Ana, CA 92701
714-541-7600

**Deputy District Attorney in Charge
Consumer and Environmental Protection Unit
Orange County District Attorney's Office**
801 Civic Center Drive West, Suite 120
Santa Ana, CA 92702-0808
714-541-7600

**Deputy District Attorney
Economic Crime Division
Riverside County District Attorney's Office**
4075 Main Street
Riverside, CA 92501
714-275-5400

**Supervising Deputy District Attorney
Consumer and Environmental Protection
Division Sacramento County District
Attorney's Office**
P.O. Box 749
Sacramento, CA 95812-0749
916-440-6174

**Director
Consumer Fraud Division
San Diego County District Attorney's Office**
P.O. Box X-1011
San Diego, CA 92112
619-531-3507 (fraud complaint line)

**Attorney
Consumer and Environmental Protection Unit
San Francisco County District Attorney's Office**
732 Brannan Street
San Francisco, CA 94103
415-552-6400 (public inquiries)
415-553-1814 (complaints)

**Deputy District Attorney
Consumer and Business Affairs Division
San Joaquin County District Attorney's Office**
222 East Weber, Room 202
P.O. Box 990
Stockton, CA 95202
209-468-2419

**Director, Economic Crime Unit
Consumer Fraud Department**
County Government Center
1050 Monterey Street, Room 235
San Luis Obispo, CA 93408
805-549-5800

**Deputy in Charge
Consumer Fraud and Environmental Protection
Unit
San Mateo County District Attorney's Office**
401 Marshall Street
Hall of Justice and Records
Redwood City, CA 94063
415-363-4656

**Deputy District Attorney
Consumer Protection Unit
Santa Barbara County District Attorney's Office**
1105 Santa Barbara Street
Santa Barbara, CA 93101
805-568-2300

**Deputy District Attorney
Consumer Fraud Unit
Santa Clara County District Attorney's Office**
70 West Hedding Street, West Wing
San Jose, CA 95110
408-299-7400

**Director
Santa Clara County Department of Consumer
Affairs**
2175 The Alameda
San Jose, CA 95126
408-299-4211

**Coordinator, Division of Consumer Affairs
Santa Cruz County District Attorney's Office**
701 Ocean Street, Room 200
Santa Cruz, CA 95060
408-425-2054

**Deputy District Attorney
Consumer Affairs Unit
Solano County District Attorney's Office**
600 Union Avenue
Fairfield, CA 94533
707-421-6860

Deputy District Attorney
Consumer Fraud Unit
Stanislaus County District Attorney's Office
P.O. Box 442
Modesto, CA 95353
209-571-5550

Deputy District Attorney
Consumer and Environmental Protection
Division
Ventura County District Attorney's Office
800 South Victoria Avenue
Ventura, CA 93009
805-654-3110

Supervising Deputy District Attorney
Special Services Unit—Consumer/
Environmental
Yolo County District Attorney's Office
P.O. Box 245
Woodland, CA 95695
916-666-8424

City Offices

Supervising Deputy City Attorney
Consumer Protection Division Los Angeles
City Attorney's Office
200 North Main Street
1600 City Hall East
Los Angeles, CA 90012
213-485-4515

Consumer Affairs Specialist
Consumer Division
Santa Monica City Attorney's Office
1685 Main Street, Room 310
Santa Monica, CA 90401
213-458-8336

Colorado

State Offices

Consumer Protection Unit
Office of Attorney General
110 16th Street, 10th Floor
Denver, CO 80202
303-620-4500

Consumer and Food Specialist
Department of Agriculture
700 Kipling Street, Suite 4000
Lakewood, CO 80215-5894
303-239-4114

County Offices

District Attorney
Archuleta, LaPlata and San Juan Counties
District Attorney's Office
P.O. Drawer 3455
Durango, CO 81302
303-247-8850

District Attorney
Boulder County District Attorney's Office
P.O. Box 471
Boulder, CO 80306
303-441-3700

Executive Director
Denver County District Attorney's Consumer
Fraud Office
303 West Colfax Avenue, Suite 1300
Denver, CO 80204
303-640-3555 (inquiries)
303-640-3557 (complaints)

Chief Deputy District Attorney
Economic Crime Division
El Paso and Teller
Counties District Attorney's Office
326 South Tejon
Colorado Springs, CO 80903-2083
719-520-6002

District Attorney
Pueblo County District Attorney's Office
Courthouse
215 West 10th Street
Pueblo, CO 81003
719-546-6030

Consumer Fraud Investigator
Weld County District Attorney's Consumer
Office
P.O. Box 1167
Greeley, CO 80632
303-356-4000 ext. 4735

Connecticut

State Offices

Commissioner
Department of Consumer Protection
State Office Building
165 Capitol Avenue
Hartford, CT 06106
203-566-4999
800-842-2649 (Connecticut only)

Assistant Attorney General
Antitrust/Consumer Protection
Office of Attorney General
110 Sherman Street
Hartford, CT 06105
203-566-5374

City Office
Director
Middletown Office of Consumer Protection
City Hall
Middletown, CT 06457
203-344-3492

Delaware

State Offices
Director
Division of Consumer Affairs
Department of Community Affairs
820 North French Street, 4th Floor
Wilmington, DE 19801
302-577-3250

Deputy Attorney General for Economic Crime and Consumer Protection
Office of Attorney General
820 North French Street
Wilmington, DE 19801
302-577-3250

District of Columbia

Director
Department of Consumer and Regulatory Affairs
614 H Street, NW
Washington, DC 20001
202-727-7000

Florida

State Offices
Assistant Director
Department of Agriculture and Consumer Services
Division of Consumer Services
218 Mayo Building
Tallahassee, FL 32399
904-488-2226
800-342-2176 (TDD Florida only)
800-327-3382 (information and education, Florida only)
800-321-5366 (lemon law, Florida only)

Chief
Consumer Litigation Section
The Capitol
Tallahassee, FL 32399-1050
904-488-9105

Chief
Consumer Division
Office of Attorney General
4000 Hollywood Boulevard
Suite 505 South
Hollywood, FL 33021
305-985-4780

County Offices
Director
Broward County Consumer Affairs Division
115 South Andrews Avenue, Room 119
Fort Lauderdale, FL 33301
305-357-6030

Consumer Advocate
Metropolitan Dade County Consumer Protection Division
140 West Flagler Street, Suite 902
Miami, FL 33130
305-375-4222

Chief
Dade County Economic Crime Unit
Office of State Attorney
1469 Northwest 13th Terrace, Room 600
Miami, FL 33125
305-324-3030

Manager
Hillsborough County Department of Consumer Affairs
412 East Madison Street, Room 1001
Tampa, FL 33602
813-272-6750

Chief
Orange County Consumer Fraud Unit
250 North Orange Avenue
P.O. Box 1673
Orlando, FL 32802
407-836-2490

Citizens Intake
Palm Beach County
Office of State Attorney
P.O. Drawer 2905
West Palm Beach, FL 33402
407-355-3560

Director
Palm Beach County Department of Consumer Affairs
3111 S. Dixie Highway, Suite 128
West Palm Beach, FL 33405
407-355-2670

Administrator
Pasco County Consumer Affairs Division
7530 Little Road
New Port Richey, FL 34654
813-847-8110

Director
Pinellas County Office of Consumer Affairs
P.O. Box 17268
Clearwater, FL 34622-0268
813-530-6200

Coordinator
Seminole Economic Crime Unit
Office of State Attorney
100 East First Street
Sanford, FL 32771
407-322-7534

State Attorney
Consumer Fraud Unit
700 S. Park Avenue
Titusville, FL 32780
407-264-5230

City Offices

Chief of Consumer Affairs
City of Jacksonville
Division of Consumer Affairs
421 W. Church Street, Suite 404
Jacksonville, FL 32202
904-630-3667

Chairman
Lauderhill Consumer Protection Board
1176 Northwest 42nd Way
Lauderhill, FL 33313
305-321-2450

Chairman
Tamarac Board of Consumer Affairs
7525 Northwest 88th Avenue
Tamarac, FL 33321
305-722-5900 (ext. 389 10 A.M.–noon, Tues., Wed., Thurs.)

Georgia

State Office
Administrator
Governors Office of Consumer Affairs
2 Martin Luther King, Jr. Drive, SE
Plaza Level—East Tower
Atlanta, GA 30334
404-651-8600
404-656-3790
800-869-1123 (Georgia only)

Hawaii

State Offices
Director
Office of Consumer Protection
Department of Commerce and Consumer Affairs
828 Fort St. Mall, Suite 600B
P.O. Box 3767
Honolulu, HI 96812-3767
808-586-2630

Investigator
Office of Consumer Protection
Department of Commerce and Consumer Affairs
75 Aupuni Street
Hilo, HI 96720
808-933-4433

Investigator
Office of Consumer Protection
Department of Commerce and Consumer Affairs
3060 Eiwa Street
Lihue, HI 96766
808-241-3365

Investigator
Office of Consumer Protection
Department of Commerce and Consumer Affairs
54 High Street
P.O. Box 3767
Honolulu, HI 96812
808-586-2630

Idaho

State Office
Deputy Attorney General
Office of the Attorney General
Consumer Protection Unit
Statehouse, Room 113A
Boise, ID 83720-1000
208-334-2424
800-432-3545 (Idaho only)

Illinois

State Offices

Director
Governors Office of Citizens Assistance
222 South College
Springfield, IL 62706
217-782-0244
800-642-3112 (Illinois only)

Chief
Consumer Protection Division
Office of Attorney General
100 West Randolph, 12th Floor
Chicago, IL 60601
312-814-3580
312-793-2852 (TDD)

Director
Department of Citizen Rights
100 West Randolph, 13th Floor
Chicago, IL 60601
312-814-3289
312-814-7123 (TDD)

Regional Offices

Assistant Attorney General
Carbondale Regional Office
Office of Attorney General
626A East Walnut Street
Carbondale, IL 62901
618-457-3505
618-457-4421 (TDD)

Assistant Attorney General
Champaign Regional Office
34 East Main Street
Champaign, IL 61820
217-333-7691 (voice/TDD)

Assistant Attorney General
East St. Louis Regional Office
Office of Attorney General
8712 State Street
East St. Louis, IL 62203
618-398-1006
618-398-1009 (TDD)

Assistant Attorney General
Granite City Regional Office
Office of Attorney General
1314 Niedringhaus
Granite City, IL 62040
618-877-0404

Assistant Attorney General
Kankakee Regional Office
Office of Attorney General
1012 North 5th Avenue
Kankakee, IL 60901
815-935-8500

Assistant Attorney General
LaSalle Regional Office
Office of Attorney General
1222 Shooting Park Road, Suite 106
Peru, IL 61354
815-224-4861
815-224-4864 (TDD)

Office of Attorney General
3405 Broadway
Mt. Vernon, IL 62864
618-242-8200 (voice/TDD)

Assistant Attorney General
Peoria Regional Office
Office of Attorney General
323 Main Street
Peoria, IL 61602
309-671-3191
309-671-3089 (TDD)

Quincy Regional Office
Office of Attorney General
523 Main Street
Quincy, IL 62301
217-223-2221 (voice/TDD)

Assistant Attorney General
Rockford Regional Office
Office of Attorney General
119 North Church Street
Rockford, IL 61101
815-987-7580
815-987-7579 (TDD)

Assistant Attorney General
Rock Island Regional Office
Office of Attorney General
1614 Second Avenue
Rock Island, IL 61201
309-793-0950
309-793-0956 (TDD)

**Assistant Attorney General and Chief
Consumer Protection Division
Office of Attorney General**
500 South Second Street
Springfield, IL 62706
217-782-9011
800-252-8666 (Illinois only)

**Assistant Attorney General
Waukegan Regional Office
Office of Attorney General**
12 South County Street
Waukegan, IL 60085
708-336-2207
708-336-2374 (TDD)

**Assistant Attorney General
West Frankfort Regional Office**
Office of Attorney General
222 East Main Street
West Frankfort, IL 62896
618-937-6453

**Assistant Attorney General
West Chicago Regional Office
Office of Attorney General**
122A County Farm Road
Wheaton, IL 60187
708-653-5060 (voice/TDD)

**County Offices
Consumer Fraud Division–303 Cook County
Office of State's Attorney**
303 Daley Center
Chicago, IL 60602
312-443-4600

**State's Attorney
Madison County Office of State's Attorney**
325 E. Vandalia
Edwardsville, IL 62025
618-692-6280

**Director
Consumer Protection Division
Rock Island County State's Attorney's Office**
County Courthouse
Rock Island, IL 61201
309-786-4451, ext. 229

**City Offices
Consumer Fraud**
Wheeling Township
1616 North Arlington Heights Road
Arlington Heights, IL 60004
708-259-7730 (Wed. only)

**Commissioner
Chicago Department of Consumer Services**
121 North LaSalle Street, Room 808
Chicago, IL 60602
312-744-4090
312-744-9385 (TDD)

**Administrator
Des Plaines Consumer Protection Commission**
1420 Miner Street
Des Plaines, IL 60016
708-391-5363

Indiana

**State Office
Chief Counsel and Director Consumer
Protection Division Office of Attorney General**
219 State House
Indianapolis, IN 46204
317-232-6330
800-382-5516 (Indiana only)

**County Offices
Director Consumer Protection
Division Lake County Prosecutors Office**
2293 North Main Street
Crown Point, IN 46307
219-755-3720

Marion County Prosecuting Attorney
560 City-County Building
200 East Washington Street
Indianapolis, IN 46204-3363
317-236-3522

Vanderburgh County Prosecuting Attorney
108 Administration Building
Civic Center Complex
Evansville, IN 47708
812-426-5150

**City Office
Director
Gary Office of Consumer Affairs**
Annex East
1100 Massachusetts Street
Gary, IN 46407
219-886-0145

Iowa

State Office
Assistant Attorney General
Consumer Protection Division
Office of Attorney General
1300 East Walnut Street, 2nd Floor
Des Moines, IA 50319
515-281-5926

Kansas

State Office
Deputy Attorney General
Consumer Protection Division
Office of Attorney General
301 West 10th
Kansas Judicial Center
Topeka, KS 66612-1597
913-296-3751
800-432-2310 (Kansas only)

County Offices
Head
Consumer Fraud Division
Johnson County District Attorney's Office
Johnson County Courthouse
P.O. Box 728
Olathe, KS 66061
913-782-5000

Chief Attorney
Consumer Fraud and Economic Crime Division
Sedgwick County District Attorney's Office
Sedgwick County Courthouse
Wichita, KS 67203
316-268-7921

Assistant District Attorney
Shawnee County District Attorney's Office
Shawnee County Courthouse, Room 212
Topeka, KS 66603-3922
913-291-4330

City Office
Assistant City Attorney
Topeka Consumer Protection Division
City Attorney's Office
215 East 7th Street
Topeka, KS 66603
913-295-3883

Kentucky

State Offices
Director Consumer Protection Division
Office of Attorney General
209 Saint Clair Street
Frankfort, KY 40601-1875
502-564-2200
800-432-9257 (Kentucky only)

Administrator
Consumer Protection Division
Office of Attorney General
107 S. 4th Street
Louisville, KY 40202
502-588-3262
800-432-9257 (Kentucky only)

Louisiana

State Office
Chief Consumer Protection Section
Office of Attorney General
State Capitol Building
P.O. Box 94005
Baton Rouge, LA 70804-9005
504-342-7373

County Office
Chief
Consumer Protection Division
Jefferson Parish District Attorney's Office
200 Huey P. Long Avenue
Gretna, LA 70053
504-364-3644

Maine

State Offices
Superintendent
Bureau of Consumer Credit Protection
State House Station No. 35
Augusta, ME 04333-0035
207-582-8718
800-332-8529

Chief
Consumer and Antitrust Division
Office of Attorney General
State House Station No. 6
Augusta, ME 04333
207-289-3716 (9 A.M.–1 P.M.)

Maryland

State Offices

Chief
Consumer Protection Division
Office of Attorney General
200 St. Paul Place
Baltimore, MD 21202-2021
301-528-8662 (9 A.M.–3 P.M.)
301-576-6372 (TDD in Baltimore area)
301-565-0451 (TDD in DC metro area)
800-969-5766

Director
Licensing & Consumer Services
Motor Vehicle Administration
6601 Ritchie Highway, NE
Glen Burnie, MD 21062
301-768-7420

Consumer Affairs Specialist
Eastern Shore Branch Office
Consumer Protection Division Office of Attorney General
Salisbury District Court/Multiservice Center
201 Baptist Street, Suite 30
Salisbury, MD 21801-4976
301-543-6620

Director
Western Maryland Branch Office
Consumer Protection Division
Office of Attorney General
138 East Antietam Street, Suite 210
Hagerstown, MD 21740-5684
301-791-4780

County Offices

Administrator
Howard County Office of Consumer Affairs
9250 Rumsey Rd.
Columbia, MD 21045
301-313-7220
301-313-7201/2323 (TDD)

Executive Director
Montgomery County Office
of Consumer Affairs
100 Maryland Avenue, 3rd Floor
Rockville, MD 20850
301-217-7373

Executive Director
Prince George's County
Consumer Protection Commission
9201 Basil Court
Landover, MD 20785
301-925-5100
301-925-5167 (TDD)

Massachusetts

State Offices

Chief
Consumer Protection Division
Department of Attorney General
131 Tremont Street
Boston, MA 02111
617-727-8400
(information and referral)

Secretary
Executive Office of Consumer Affairs and Business Regulation
One Ashburton Place, Room 1411
Boston, MA 02108
617-727-7780
(information and referral)

Managing Attorney
Western Massachusetts Consumer Protection Division
Department of Attorney General
436 Dwight Street
Springfield, MA 01103
413-784-1240

County Offices

Complaint Supervisor
Consumer Fraud Prevention
Franklin County District Attorney's Office
238 Main Street
Greenfield, MA 01301
413-774-5102

Director
Consumer Fraud Prevention
Hampshire County District Attorney's Office
1 Court Square
Northhampton, MA 01060
413-586-9225

Project Coordinator
Worcester County Consumer Rights Project
340 Main Street, Room 370
Worcester, MA 01608
508-754-7420 (9:30 A.M.–4 P.M.)

City Offices
Commissioner
Mayor's Office of Consumer Affairs and Licensing
Boston City Hall, Room 613
Boston, MA 02201
617-725-3320

Director
Consumer Information Center
Springfield Action Commission
P.O. Box 1449 Main Office
Springfield, MA 01101
413-737-4376
(Hampton and Hampshire counties)

Michigan

State Offices
Assistant in Charge
Consumer Protection Division
Office of Attorney General
P.O. Box 30213
Lansing, MI 48909
517-373-1140

Executive Director
Michigan Consumers Council
414 Hollister Building
106 West Allegan Street
Lansing, MI 48933
517-373-0947
517-373-0701 (TDD)

Director
Bureau of Automotive Regulation
Michigan Department of State
Lansing, MI 48918
517-373-7858
800-292-4204 (Michigan only)

County Offices
Prosecuting Attorney
Bay County Consumer Protection Unit
Bay County Building
Bay City, MI 48708-5994
517-893-3594

Director
Consumer Protection Department
Macomb County
Office of the Prosecuting Attorney
Macomb Court Building, 6th Floor
Mt. Clemens, MI 48043
313-469-5350

Director
Washtenaw County Consumer Services
4133 Washtenaw Street
P.O. Box 8645
Ann Arbor, MI 48107-8645
313-971-6054

City Office
Director City of Detroit
Department of Consumer Affairs
1600 Cadillac Tower
Detroit, MI 48226
313-224-3508

Minnesota

State Offices
Director
Office of Consumer Services
Office of Attorney General
117 University Avenue
St. Paul, MN 55155
612-296-2331

Consumer Services Division
Office of Attorney General
320 West 2nd Street
Duluth, MN 55802
218-723-4891

County Office
Citizen Protection Unit
Hennepin County Attorney's Office
C2000 County Government Center
Minneapolis, MN 55487
612-348-4528

City Office
Director
Consumer Affairs Division
Minneapolis Department of Licenses & Consumer Services
One C City Hall
Minneapolis, MN 55415
612-348-2080

Mississippi

State Offices
Special Assistant Attorney General
Chief
Consumer Protection Division
Office of Attorney General
P.O. Box 22947
Jackson, MS 39225-2947
601-354-6018

Director
Regulatory Services
Department of Agriculture and Commerce
500 Greymont Avenue
P.O. Box 1609
Jackson, MS 39215
601-354-7063

Consumer Counselor
Gulf Coast Regional Office
of the Attorney General
P.O. Box 1411
Biloxi, MS 39533
601-436-6000

Missouri

State Offices
Office of the Attorney General
Consumer Complaints or Problems
P.O. Box 899
Jefferson City, MO 65102
314-751-3321
800-392-8222 (Missouri only)

Chief Counsel
Trade Offense Division
Office of Attorney General
P.O. Box 899
Jefferson City, MO 65102
314-751-3321
800-392-8222 (Missouri only)

Montana

State Office
Consumer Affairs Unit
Department of Commerce
1424 Ninth Avenue
Helena, MT 59620
406-444-4312

Nebraska

State Office
Assistant Attorney General
Consumer Protection Division
Department of Justice
2115 State Capitol
P.O. Box 98920
Lincoln, NE 68509
402-471-2682

County Office
Douglas County Attorney
County Attorney's Office
428 Hall of Justice
17th and Farnam
Omaha, NE 68183
402-444-7040

Nevada

State Offices
Commissioner of Consumer Affairs
Department of Commerce
State Mail Room Complex
Las Vegas, NV 89158
702-486-7355
800-992-0900 (Nevada only)

Consumer Services Officer
Consumer Affairs Division
Department of Commerce
4600 Kietzke Lane, M-245
Reno, NV 89502
702-688-1800
800-992-0900 (Nevada only)

County Office
Investigator
Consumer Fraud Division
Washoe County District Attorney's Office
P.O. Box 11130
Reno, NV 89520
702-328-3456

New Hampshire

State Office
Chief Consumer Protection and Antitrust
Bureau
Office of Attorney General
State House Annex
Concord, NH 03301
603-271-3641

New Jersey

State Offices
Director
Division of Consumer Affairs
P.O. Box 45027
Newark, NJ 07101
201-648-4010

Commissioner
Department of the Public Advocate
CN 850, Justice Complex
Trenton, NJ 08625
609-292-7087
800-792-8600 (New Jersey only)

Deputy Attorney General
New Jersey Division of Law
1207 Raymond Boulevard
P.O. Box 45029
Newark, NJ 07101
201-648-7579

County Offices
Director
Atlantic County Consumer Affairs
1333 Atlantic Avenue, 8th Floor
Atlantic City, NJ 08401
609-345-6700

Director
Bergen County Division of Consumer Affairs
21 Main Street, Room 101-E
Hackensack, NJ 07601-7000
201-646-2650

Director
Burlington County Office of Consumer Affairs
49 Rancocas Road
Mount Holly, NJ 08060
609-265-5054

Director
Camden County Office of Consumer Affairs
1800 Pavilion West
2101 Ferry Avenue, Suite 609
Camden, NJ 08104
609-757-8397

Director
Cape May County Consumer Affairs
DN-310, Central Mail Room
Cape May Court House
Cape May Court House, NJ 08210
609-465-1076

Director
Cumberland County Department of Consumer Affairs and Weights and Measures
788 East Commerce Street
Bridgeton, NJ 08302
609-453-2202

Director
Essex County Consumer Services
15 Southmunn Avenue, 2nd Floor
East Orange, NJ 07018
201-678-8071/8928

Director
Gloucester County Consumer Affairs
152 North Broad Street
Woodbury, NJ 08096
609-853-3349
609-848-6616 (TDD)

Director
Hudson County Division of Consumer Affairs
595 Newark Avenue
Jersey City, NJ 07306
201-795-6295

Director
Hunterdon County Consumer Affairs
P.O. Box 283
Lebanon, NJ 08833
908-236-2249

Director
Mercer County Consumer Affairs
640 South Broad Street, Room 229
Trenton, NJ 08650-0068
609-989-6671

Director
Middlesex County Consumer Affairs
149 Kearny Avenue
Perth Amboy, NJ 08861
201-324-4600

Director
Monmouth County Consumer Affairs
1 East Main Street
P.O. Box 1255
Freehold, NJ 07728-1255
908-431-7900

Director
Morris County Consumer Affairs
P.O. Box 900
Morristown, NJ 07963-0900
201-285-6070
201-584-9189 (TDD)

Director
Ocean County Consumer Affairs
P.O. Box 2191
County Administration Building
Room 130-1
Toms River, NJ 08754-2191
908-929-2105

Director
Passaic County Consumer Affairs
County Administration Building
309 Pennsylvania Avenue
Paterson, NJ 07503
201-881-4547, 4499

Somerset County Consumer Affairs
County Administration Building
P.O. Box 3000
Somerville, NJ 08876
908-231-7000, ext. 7400

Office Manager
Union County Consumer Affairs
300 North Avenue East
P.O. Box 186
Westfield, NJ 07091
201-654-9840

Director
Warren County Consumer Affairs
Dumont Administration Building Route 519
Belvedere, NJ 07823
908-475-6500

City Offices
Director Brick Consumer Affairs
Municipal Building
401 Chambers Bridge Road
Brick, NJ 08723
908-477-3000, ext. 296

Director
Cinnaminson Consumer Affairs
Municipal Building
1621 Riverton Road
Cinnaminson, NJ 08077
609-829-6000

Director
Clark Consumer Affairs
430 Westfield Avenue
Clark, NJ 07066
908-388-3600

Director
Elizabeth Consumer Affairs
City Hall
60 West Scott Plaza
Elizabeth, NJ 07203
908-820-4183

Director
Fort Lee Consumer Protection Board
Bourough Hall
309 Main Street
Fort Lee, NJ 07024
201-592-3579

Director
Glen Rock Consumer Affairs
Municipal Building, Harding Plaza
Glen Rock, NJ 07452-2100
201-670-3956

Consumer Advocate
City Hall
94 Washington Street
Hoboken, NJ 07030
201-420-2038

Director
Livingston Consumer Affairs
357 South Livingston Avenue
Livingston, NJ 07039
201-535-7976

Director
Middlesex Borough Consumer Affairs
1200 Mountain Avenue
Middlesex, NJ 08846
908-356-8090

Director
Mountainside Consumer Affairs
1455 Coles Avenue
Mountainside, NJ 07092
908-232-6600

Department of Community Services
Municipal Building
North Bergen, NJ 07047
201-330-7292, 91

Director
Nutley Consumer Affairs
City Hall
228 Chestnut Street
Nutley, NJ 07110
201-284-4936

Director
Parsippany Consumer Affairs
Municipal Building, Room 101
1001 Parsippany Boulevard
Parsippany, NJ 07054
201-263-7011

Director
Perth Amboy Consumer Affairs
City Hall
260 High Street
Perth Amboy, NJ 08861
908-826-0290, ext. 61, 62

Director
Plainfield Action Services
510 Watchung Avenue
Plainfield, NJ 07060
908-753-3519

Director
Secaucus Department of Consumer Affairs
Municipal Government Center
Secaucus, NJ 07094
201-330-2019

Director
Union Township Consumer Affairs
Municipal Building
1976 Morris Avenue
Union, NJ 07083
908-688-6763

Director
Wayne Township Consumer Affairs
475 Valley Road
Wayne, NJ 07470
201-694-1800, ext. 290

Director
Weehawken Consumer Affairs
400 Park Avenue
Weehawken, NJ 07087
201-319-6005

Director
West New York Consumer Affairs
428 60th Street
West New York, NJ 07093
201-861-2522

New Mexico

State Office
Consumer Protection Division
Office of Attorney General
P.O. Drawer 1508
Santa Fe, NM 87504
505-827-6060
800-432-2070 (New Mexico only)

New York

State Offices
Chairperson and Executive Director
New York State Consumer Protection Board
99 Washington Avenue
Albany, NY 12210-2891
518-474-8583

Assistant Attorney General
Bureau of Consumer Frauds
and Protection Office of Attorney General
State Capitol
Albany, NY 12224
518-474-5481

Chairperson and Executive Director
New York State Consumer
Protection Board
250 Broadway, 17th Floor
New York, NY 10007-2593
212-417-4908 (complaints)
212-417-4482 (main office)

Assistant Attorney General
Bureau of Consumer Frauds
and Protection Office of Attorney General
120 Broadway
New York, NY 10271
212-341-2345

Regional Offices
Assistant Attorney General in Charge
Binghamton Regional Office
Office of Attorney General
59–61 Court Street, 7th Floor
Binghamton, NY 13901
607-773-7877

Assistant Attorney General in Charge
Buffalo Regional Office
Office of Attorney General
65 Court Street
Buffalo, NY 14202
716-847-7184

Assistant Attorney General in Charge
Plattsburgh Regional Office
Office of Attorney General
70 Clinton Street
Plattsburgh, NY 12901
518-563-8012

Assistant Attorney General in Charge
Poughkeepsie Regional Office
Office of Attorney General
235 Main Street
Poughkeepsie, NY 12601
914-485-3920

Assistant Attorney General in Charge
Rochester Regional Office
Office of Attorney General
144 Exchange Boulevard
Rochester, NY 14614
716-546-7430

Assistant Attorney General in Charge
Suffolk Regional Office
Office of Attorney General
300 Motor Parkway
Hauppauge, NY 11788
516-231-2400

Assistant Attorney General in Charge
Syracuse Regional Office
Office of Attorney General
615 Erie Boulevard West
Syracuse, NY 13204-2465
315-448-4848

Assistant Attorney General in Charge
Utica Regional Office
Office of Attorney General
207 Genesee Street
Utica, NY 13501
315-793-2225

County Offices
Deputy Director of General Services
Broome County Bureau of Consumer Affairs
Governmental Plaza, P.O. Box 1766
Binghamton, NY 13902
607-778-2168

Director
Dutchess County Department of Consumer Affairs
38-A Dutchess Turnpike
Poughkeepsie, NY 12603
914-471-6322

Assistant District Attorney
Consumer Fraud Bureau
Erie County District Attorney's Office
25 Delaware Avenue
Buffalo, NY 14202
716-858-2424

Commissioner
Nassau County Office of Consumer Affairs
160 Old Country Road
Mineola, NY 11501
516-535-2600

Executive Director
New Justice Conflict Resolution Services Inc.
210 East Fayette Street, Suite 700
Syracuse, NY 13202
315-471-4676

Commissioner
Orange County Department of Consumer Affairs and Weights and Measures
99 Main Street
Goshen, NY 10924
914-294-5151, ext. 1762

District Attorney
Orange County District Attorney's Office
255 Main Street
County Government Center
Goshen, NY 10924
914-294-5471

Putnam County Office
Facility Department of Consumer Affairs
Myrtle Avenue
Mahopac Falls, NY 10542-0368
914-621-2317

Director/Coordinator
Rockland County Office of Consumer Protection
County Office Building
18 New Hempstead Road
New City, NY 10956
914-638-5282

Director
Steuben County Department of Weights, Measures and Consumer Affairs
3 East Pulteney Square
Bath, NY 14810
607-776-9631
607-776-9631, ext. 2101 (voice/TDD)

Commissioner
Suffolk County Department of Consumer Affairs
Suffolk County Center
Hauppauge, NY 11788
516-360-4600

Director
Ulster County Consumer Fraud Bureau
285 Wall Street
Kingston, NY 12401
914-339-5680, ext. 240

Chief
Frauds Bureau
Westchester County
District Attorney's Office
111 Grove Street
White Plains, NY 10601
914-285-3303

Director
Westchester County Department of Consumer Affairs
Room 104, Michaelian Office Building
White Plains, NY 10601
914-285-2155

City Offices
Director
Babylon Consumer Protection Board
Town Hall Office Annex
281 Phelps Lane
North Babylon, NY 11703
516-422-7636

Town of Colonie
Consumer Protection
Memorial Town Hall
Newtonville, NY 12128
518-783-2790

Commissioner
Mt. Vernon Office of Consumer Affairs
City Hall
Mt. Vernon, NY 10550
914-665-2433

Commissioner
New York City Department of Consumer Affairs
42 Broadway
New York, NY 10004
212-487-4444

Bronx Neighborhood Office
New York City
Department of Consumer Affairs
1932 Arthur Avenue, Room 104-A
Bronx, NY 10457
212-579-6766

Brooklyn Neighborhood Office
New York City Department of Consumer Affairs
1360 Fulton Street, Room 320
Brooklyn, NY 11216
718-636-7092

Director
Queens Neighborhood Office
New York City Department of Consumer Affairs
120–55 Queens Boulevard, Room 301A
Kew Gardens, NY 11424
718-261-2922

Director
Staten Island Neighborhood Office
New York City Department of Consumer Affairs
Staten Island Borough Hall, Room 422
Staten Island, NY 10301
718-390-5154

Director
City of Oswego
Office of Consumer Affairs
City Hall
West Oneida Street
Oswego, NY 13126
315-342-8150

Chairperson
Ramapo Consumer Protection Board
Ramapo Town Hall
237 Route 59
Suffern, NY 10901-5399
914-357-5100

Schenectady
Bureau of Consumer Protection
City Hall, Room 22
Jay Street
Schenectady, NY 12305
518-382-5061

Director
White Plains Department of Weights and Measures
77 South Lexington Avenue
White Plains, NY 10601-2512
914-422-6359

Director
Yonkers Office of Consumer Protection, Weights and Measures
201 Palisade Avenue
Yonkers, NY 10703
914-377-6807

North Carolina

State Office
Special Deputy Attorney General
Consumer Protection Section
Office of Attorney General
Raney Building
P.O. Box 629
Raleigh, NC 27602
919-733-7741

North Dakota

State Offices
Office of Attorney General
600 East Boulevard
Bismarck, ND 58505
701-224-2210
800-472-2600 (North Dakota only)

Director
Consumer Fraud Section
Office of Attorney General
600 East Boulevard
Bismarck, ND 58505
701-224-3404
800-472-2600 (North Dakota only)

County Office
Executive Director
Quad County Community Action Agency
27 1/2 South 3rd Street
Grand Forks, ND 58201
701-746-5431

Ohio

State Offices
Consumer Frauds and Crimes Section
Office of Attorney General
30 East Broad Street
State Office Tower, 25th Floor
Columbus, OH 43266-0410
614-466-4986 (complaints)
614-466-1393 (TDD)
800-282-0515 (Ohio only)

Office of Consumers' Counsel
77 South High Street, 15th Floor
Columbus, OH 43266-0550
614-466-9605 (voice/TDD)
800-282-9448 (Ohio only)

County Offices
Director
Economic Crime Division
Franklin County Office of Prosecuting Attorney
369 South High Street
Columbus, OH 43215
614-462-3555

County Prosecutor
Consumer Protection Division
Lake County Office of Prosecuting Attorney
Lake County Court House
Painesville, OH 44077
216-357-2683
800-899-5253 (Ohio only)

Assistant Prosecuting Attorney
Montgomery County Fraud Section
301 West 3rd Street
Dayton Montgomery
County Courts Building
Dayton, OH 45402
513-225-5757

Prosecuting Attorney
Portage County Office of Prosecuting Attorney
466 South Chestnut Street
Ravenna, OH 44266-0671
216-296-4593

Prosecuting Attorney
Summit County Office of Prosecuting Attorney
53 University Avenue
Akron, OH 44308-1680
216-379-2800

City Offices
Chief
Cincinnati Office of Consumer Services
Division of Human Services
City Hall, Room 126
Cincinnati, OH 45202
513-352-3971

Director
Youngstown Office of Consumer Affairs and Weights and Measures
26 South Phelps Street
City Hall
Youngstown, OH 44503-1318
216-742-8884

Oklahoma

State Offices
Assistant Attorney General
Office of Attorney General
420 West Main, Suite 550
Oklahoma City, OK 73102
405-521-4274

Administrator
Department of Consumer Credit
4545 Lincoln Boulevard, Suite 104
Oklahoma City, OK 73105-3408
405-521-3653

Oregon

State Office
Attorney in Charge
Financial Fraud Section
Department of Justice
Justice Building
Salem, OR 97310
503-378-4320

Pennsylvania

State Offices
Director
Bureau of Consumer Protection
Office of Attorney General
Strawberry Square, 14th Floor
Harrisburg, PA 17120
717-787-9707
800-441-2555 (Pennsylvania only)

Consumer Advocate
Office of Consumer Advocate–Utilities
Office of Attorney General
1425 Strawberry Square
Harrisburg, PA 17120
717-783-5048 (utilities only)

Deputy Attorney General
Bureau of Consumer Protection
Office of Attorney General
27 North 7th Street
Allentown, PA 18101
215-821-6690

Director
Bureau of Consumer Services
Pennsylvania Public Utility Commission
203 North Office Building
Harrisburg, PA 17120
717-787-4970
800-782-1110 (Pennsylvania only)

Deputy Attorney General
Bureau of Consumer Protection
Office of Attorney General
919 State Street, Room 203
Erie, PA 16501
814-871-4371

Attorney in Charge
Bureau of Consumer Protection
Office of Attorney General
132 Kline Village
Harrisburg, PA 17104
717-787-7109
800-441-2555 (Pennsylvania only)

Deputy Attorney General
Bureau of Consumer Protection
Office of the Attorney General
IGA Building, Route 219 North
P.O. Box 716
Ebensburg, PA 15931
814-949-7900

Deputy Attorney General
Bureau of Consumer Protection
Office of Attorney General
21 South 12th Street, 2nd Floor
Philadelphia, PA 19107
215-560-2414
800-441-2555 (Pennsylvania only)

Deputy Attorney General
Bureau of Consumer Protection
Office of Attorney General
Manor Complex, 5th Floor
564 Forbes Avenue
Pittsburgh, PA 15219
412-565-5394

Deputy Attorney General
Bureau of Consumer Protection
Office of Attorney General
State Office Building, Room 358
100 Lackawanna Avenue
Scranton, PA 18503
717-963-4913

County Offices

Director
Beaver County Alliance for Consumer Protection
699 5th Street
Beaver, PA 15009-1997
412-728-7267

Director/Chief Sealer
Bucks County Consumer Protection, Weights and Measures
50 North Main
Doylestown, PA 18901
215-348-7442

Director
Chester County Bureau of Consumer Protection, Weights and Measures
Courthouse, 5th Floor, North Wing
High and Market Streets
West Chester, PA 19380
215-344-6150

Consumer Mediator
Cumberland County Consumer Affairs
One Courthouse Square
Carlisle, PA 17013-3387
717-240-6180

Director
Delaware County Office of Consumer Affairs, Weights and Measures
Government Center Building
Second and Olive Streets
Media, PA 19063
215-891-4865

Director
Montgomery County Consumer Affairs Department
County Courthouse
Norristown, PA 19404
215-278-3565

City Office

Chief Economic Crime Unit
Philadelphia District Attorney's Office
1421 Arch Street
Philadelphia, PA 19102
215-686-8750

Rhode Island

State Offices
Director
Consumer Protection Division
Department of Attorney General
72 Pine Street
Providence, RI 02903
401-277-2104
401-274-4400 ext. 354 (voice/TDD)
800-852-7776 (Rhode Island only)

Executive Director
Rhode Island Consumers' Council
365 Broadway
Providence, RI 02909
401-277-2764

South Carolina

State Offices
Assistant Attorney General
Consumer Fraud and Antitrust Section
Office of Attorney General
P.O. Box 11549
Columbia, SC 29211
803-734-3970

Administrator
Department of Consumer Affairs
P.O. Box 5757
Columbia, SC 29250-5757
803-734-9452
803-734-9455 (TDD)
800-922-1594 (South Carolina only)

State Ombudsman
Office of Executive Policy and Program
1205 Pendleton Street, Room 308
Columbia, SC 29201
803-734-0457
803-734-1147 (TDD)

South Dakota

State Office
Assistant Attorney General
Division of Consumer Affairs
Office of Attorney General
500 East Capitol
State Capitol Building
Pierre, SD 57501-5070
605-773-4400

Tennessee

State Offices

Deputy Attorney General
Antitrust and Consumer Protection Division
Office of Attorney General
450 James Robertson Parkway
Nashville, TN 37243-0485
615-741-2672

Director
Division of Consumer Affairs
Department of Commerce and Insurance
500 James Robertson Parkway, 5th Floor
Nashville, TN 37243-0600
615-741-4737
800-342-8385 (Tennessee only)
800-422-CLUB (health club hotline, Tennessee only)

Texas

State Offices

Assistant Attorney General and
Chief Consumer Protection Division
Office of Attorney General
P.O. Box 12548
Austin, TX 78711
512-463-2070

Assistant Attorney General
Consumer Protection Division
Office of Attorney General
714 Jackson Street, Suite 700
Dallas, TX 75202-4506
214-742-8944

Assistant Attorney General
Consumer Protection Division
Office of Attorney General
6090 Surety Drive, Room 260
El Paso, TX 79905
915-772-9476

Assistant Attorney General
Consumer Protection Division
Office of Attorney General
1019 Congress Street, Suite 1550
Houston, TX 77002-1702
713-223-5886

Assistant Attorney General
Consumer Protection Division
Office of Attorney General
1208 14th Street, Suite 900
Lubbock, TX 79401-3997
806-747-5238

Assistant Attorney General
Consumer Protection Division
Office of Attorney General
3600 North 23rd Street, Suite 305
McAllen, TX 78501-1685
512-682-4547

Assistant Attorney General
Consumer Protection Division
Office of Attorney General
115 East Travis Street, Suite 925
San Antonio, TX 78205-1607
512-225-4191

Office of Consumer Protection
State Board of Insurance
816 Congress Avenue, Suite 1400
Austin, TX 78701-2430
512-322-4143

County Offices

Assistant District Attorney and Chief
of Dallas County District Attorney's Office
Specialized Crime Division
133 North Industrial Boulevard, LB 19
Dallas, TX 75207-4313
214-653-3820

Assistant District Attorney and Chief
Harris County Consumer Fraud Division
Office of District Attorney
201 Fannin, Suite 200
Houston, TX 77002-1901
713-221-5836

City Office

Director
Dallas Consumer Protection Division
Health and Human Services Department
320 East Jefferson Boulevard, Suite 312
Dallas, TX 75203
214-948-4400

Utah

State Offices

Director
Division of Consumer Protection
Department of Commerce
160 East 3rd South
P.O. Box 45802
Salt Lake City, UT 84145-0802
801-530-6601

Assistant Attorney General
for Consumer Affairs
Office of Attorney General
115 State Capitol
Salt Lake City, UT 84114
801-538-1331

Vermont

State Offices

Assistant Attorney General and Chief
Public Protection Division
Office of Attorney General
109 State Street
Montpelier, VT 05609-1001
802-828-3171

Supervisor
Consumer Assurance Section
Department of Agriculture, Food and Market
120 State Street
Montpelier, VT 05620-2901
802-828-2436

Virginia

State Offices

Chief Antitrust and Consumer Litigation Section
Office of Attorney General
Supreme Court Building
101 North 8th Street
Richmond, VA 23219
804-786-2116
800-451-1525 (Virginia only)

Director
Division of Consumer Affairs
Department of Agriculture and Consumer
Services
Room 101, Washington Building
1100 Bank Street
P.O. Box 1163
Richmond, VA 23219
804-786-2042

Investigator
Northern Virginia Branch
Office of Consumer Affairs
Department of Agriculture and Consumer
Services
100 North Washington St., Suite 412
Falls Church, VA 22046
703-532-1613

County Offices

Section Chief
Office of Citizen and Consumer Affairs
#1 Court House Plaza, Suite 314
2100 Clarendon Boulevard
Arlington, VA 22201
703-358-3260

Director
Fairfax County Department of Consumer Affairs
3959 Pender Drive, Suite 200
Fairfax, VA 22030-6093
703-246-5949
703-591-3260 (TDD)

Administrator
Prince William County
Office of Consumer Affairs
4370 Ridgewood Center Drive
Prince William, VA 22192-9201
703-792-7370

City Offices

Director
Alexandria Office of Citizens Assistance
City Hall
P.O. Box 178
Alexandria, VA 22313
703-838-4350
703-838-5056 (TDD)

Coordinator
Division of Consumer Affairs
City Hall
Norfolk, VA 23501
804-441-2821
804-441-2000 (TDD)

Assistant to the City Manager
Roanoke Consumer Protection Division
364 Municipal Building
215 Church Avenue, SW
Roanoke, VA 24011
703-981-2583

Director, Consumer Affairs Division Office of the
Commonwealth's Attorney
3500 Virginia Beach Boulevard, Suite 304
Virginia Beach, VA 23452
804-431-4610

Washington

State Offices

Investigator Consumer and Business Fair
Practices Division
Office of the Attorney General
111 Olympia Avenue, NE
Olympia, WA 98501
206-753-6210

Director of Consumer Services
Consumer and Business Fair Practices Division
Office of the Attorney General
900 Fourth Avenue, Suite 2000
Seattle, WA 98164
206-464-6431
800-551-4636 (Washington only)

Chief Consumer and Business Fair Practices
Division
Office of the Attorney General
West 1116 Riverside Avenue
Spokane, WA 99201
509-456-3123

Contact Person
Consumer and Business Fair Practices Division
Office of the Attorney General
1019 Pacific Avenue, 3rd Floor
Tacoma, WA 98402-4411
206-593-2904

City Offices

Director
Department of Weights and Measures
3200 Cedar Street
Everett, WA 98201
206-259-8810

Chief Deputy Prosecuting Attorney
Fraud Division
1002 Bank of California
900 4th Avenue
Seattle, WA 98164
206-296-9010

Director
Seattle Department of Licenses and Consumer
Affairs
102 Municipal Building
600 4th Avenue
Seattle, WA 98104-1893
206-684-8484

West Virginia

State Offices

Director
Consumer Protection Division
Office of Attorney General
812 Quarrier Street, 6th Floor
Charleston, WV 25301
304-348-8986
800-368-8808 (West Virginia only)

Director
Division of Weights and Measures
Department of Labor
1800 Washington Street, East
Building 3, Room 319
Charleston, WV 25305
304-348-7890

City Office

Director
Department of Consumer Protection
P.O. Box 2749
Charleston, WV 25330
304-348-8172

Wisconsin

State Offices

Administrator
Division of Trade and Consumer Protection
Department of Agriculture, Trade and
Consumer Protection
801 West Badger Road
P.O. Box 8911
Madison, WI 53708
608-266-9836
800-422-7128 (Wisconsin only)

Regional Supervisor
Division of Trade and Consumer Protection
Department of Agriculture, Trade and
Consumer Protection
927 Loring Street
Altoona, WI 54720
715-839-3848
800-422-7128 (Wisconsin only)

Regional Supervisor
Division of Trade and Consumer Protection
Department of Agriculture, Trade and
Consumer Protection
200 North Jefferson Street, Suite 146A
Green Bay, WI 54301
414-448-5111
800-422-7128 (Wisconsin only)

Regional Supervisor
Consumer Protection Regional Office
Department of Agriculture, Trade and
Consumer Protection
3333 N. Mayfair Rd., Suite 114
Milwaukee, WI 53222-3288
414-257-8956

Assistant Attorney General
Office of Consumer Protection and Citizen
Advocacy
Department of Justice
P.O. Box 7856
Madison, WI 53707-7856
608-266-1852
800-362-8189

Assistant Attorney General
Office of Consumer Protection
Department of Justice
Milwaukee State Office Building
819 North 6th Street, Room 520
Milwaukee, WI 53203-1678
414-227-4948
800-362-8189

County Offices

District Attorney
Marathon County District Attorney's Office
Marathon County Courthouse
Wausau, WI 54401
715-847-5555

Assistant District Attorney
Milwaukee County District Attorney's Office
Consumer Fraud Unit
821 West State Street, Room 412
Milwaukee, WI 53233-1485
414-278-4792

Consumer Fraud Investigator
Racine County Sheriff's Department
717 Wisconsin Avenue
Racine, WI 53403
414-636-3125

Wyoming

State Office
Assistant Attorney General
Office of Attorney General
123 State Capitol Building
Cheyenne, WY 82002
307-777-7874

American Samoa

Assistant Attorney General
Consumer Protection Bureau
P.O. Box 7
Pago Pago, AS 96799
011-684-633-4163/64

Puerto Rico

Secretary
Department of Consumer Affairs (DOCA)
Minillas Station, P.O. Box 41059
Santurce, PR 00940
809-721-0940

Secretary
Department of Justice
P.O. Box 192
San Juan, PR 00902
809-721-2900

Virgin Islands

Commissioner
Department of Licensing and Consumer Affairs
Property and Procurement Building
Subbase #1, Room 205
St. Thomas, VI 00802
809-774-3130

Domestic Violence Resources

Below is a partial listing of domestic violence resources in the United States. Where possible, a statewide, toll-free hotline is listed; for states that do not have one, there is an organization that can refer you to legal assistance, crisis counseling, and shelters in your area.

Alabama

Alabama Coalition Against Domestic Violence
205-832-4842
(8 A.M.–5 P.M. weekdays)

Alaska

Alaska Network on Domestic Violence and Sexual Assault
907-586-3650

Arkansas

Arkansas Coalition Against Violence to Women and Children
800-332-4443 (state hotline, 24 hours)

California

Central California Coalition on Domestic Violence
800-925-3993 (call for referrals)

Northern California Coalition for Battered Women and their Children
415-457-2464
(9 A.M.–5 P.M. weekdays)

Colorado

Colorado Coalition Against Domestic Violence
303-573-9018 (call collect, 9 A.M.–5 P.M.)

Connecticut

Connecticut Coalition Against Domestic Violence
203-524-5890 (call collect, 8:30 A.M.–4:30 P.M. weekdays)

Delaware

Family Violence Program Battered Women's Hotline
302-762-6110 (24 hours)

District of Columbia

DC Coalition Against Domestic Violence
Emergency Domestic Relations Project
202-662-9640
(9 A.M.–5:30 P.M.)

Florida

Florida Coalition Against Domestic Violence
407-628-3885 (call collect, 9 A.M.–5 P.M.)
After business hours, an answering machine gives out a toll-free hotline number.

Georgia

Georgia Advocates for Battered Women and Children
404-524-3847
(9 A.M.–5 P.M.)

Idaho

Idaho Council on Domestic Violence
208-334-5580 (call collect, 8 A.M.–5 P.M. weekdays)

Illinois

Illinois Coalition Against Domestic Violence
217-789-2830
(9 A.M.–5 P.M.)

Indiana

Indiana Coalition Against Domestic Violence
812-882-7900
800-332-7385 (state hotline, 24 hours)

Kansas

Kansas Coalition Against Sexual and Domestic Violence
316-232-2757
316-231-8251 (call collect,
9 A.M.–5 P.M., hours may vary)

Kentucky

Lincoln Trail Domestic Violence Program (Elizabethtown)
800-767-5838

YWCA Spouse Abuse Center (Lexington)
800-544-2022

Louisiana

Project S.A.V.E.
504-523-3755
(9 A.M.–5 P.M.)

Maine

Caring Unlimited
207-324-1957 (call collect, 24-hour hotline)

Maryland

Maryland Network Against Domestic Violence
410-268-4393
(8 A.M.–5 P.M.; no collect calls accepted, but will call victims back if requested)

Massachusetts

Massachusetts Coalition of Battered Women's Services
617-426-8492 (call collect,
9 A.M.–5 P.M.)

Minnesota

Minnesota Coalition for Battered Women
612-646-6177 (call collect, 9 A.M.–5 P.M. weekdays)
612-646-0994 (emergency hotline, call collect 24 hours)

Mississippi

Mississippi Coalition Against Domestic Violence
601-435-1968 (8 A.M.–5 P.M.)

Montana

Montana Coalition Against Domestic Violence
406-586-0263 (eastern Montana, 24 hours)

Violence Free Crisis Line
406-752-7273 (northwestern Montana, 24 hours)

Womensplace
800-543-7606 (western Montana, 24 hours)

Nebraska

Nebraska Domestic Violence and Sexual Assault Coalition
402-476-6256 (8 A.M.–5 P.M. weekdays)

Nevada

Nevada Network Against Domestic Violence
800-992-5757 (state hotline, 24 hours)

New Hampshire

Helpline
800-852-3311 (multi-issue state hotline, 24 hours)

New Jersey

New Jersey Coalition for Battered Women
800-572-7233 (state hotline, 24 hours; bilingual, TTY accessible for the deaf)

New Mexico

New Mexico State Coalition Against Domestic Violence
800-773-3645 (state hotline)

Women's Community Association
505-247-4219 (24 hours)

New York

New York State Coalition Against Domestic Violence
800-942-6906 (English, 24 hours)

Poder
800-942-6908 (Spanish, 7 A.M.–11 P.M.)

North Carolina

North Carolina Coalition Against Domestic Violence
919-490-1467 (9 A.M.–5 P.M. weekdays)

North Dakota

North Dakota Council on Abused Women's Services
800-472-2911 (state hotline, 24 hours)

Ohio

Turning Point
800-232-6505 (state hotline, 24 hours)

Oklahoma

Oklahoma Coalition on Domestic Violence and Sexual Assault
800-522-SAFE (state hotline, 24 hours)

Oregon

Oregon Coalition Against Domestic and Sexual Violence
503-239-4486/87 (9 A.M.–5 P.M.)

Pennsylvania

Pennsylvania Coalition Against Domestic Violence
800-932-4632 (8 A.M.–5 P.M.)

Rhode Island

Rhode Island Council on Domestic Violence
401-723-3051 (call collect, 8:30 A.M.–4:30 P.M.)

South Dakota

South Dakota Coalition Against Domestic Violence and Sexual Assault
605-698-3947
605-226-1212 (hours may vary)

Texas

Women's Advocacy Project
800-777-3247 (legal hotline, daytime)
800-374-4673 (family violence hotline, daytime)

Vermont

Vermont Network Against Domestic Violence and Sexual Assault
802-223-1302 (weekdays, daytime)

Virginia

Virginians Against Domestic Violence
804-780-3505 (call collect, 9 A.M.–3 P.M.)

Washington

Washington State Domestic Violence Hotline
800-562-6025 (24 hours)

West Virginia

Department of Health and Human Resources
800-352-6513 (state multi-issue hotline)

Wisconsin

Wisconsin Coalition Against Domestic Violence
608-255-0539 (9 A.M.–5 P.M. weekdays)

Wyoming

Wyoming Family Violence and Sexual Assault Statewide Referral
800-442-8337 (24 hours)

Family Planning

Association for Voluntary Surgical Contraception
122 East 42nd Street
New York, NY 10168
212-351-2500

Family Life Information Exchange
Health and Human Services Department
P.O. Box 10716
Rockville, MD 20850
301-770-3662

Human Life and Natural Family Planning Foundation
5609 Broadmoor Street
Alexandria, VA 22310
703-836-3377

International Planned Parenthood Foundation
902 Broadway
New York, NY 10010
212-995-8800

National Family Planning and Reproductive Health Association
122 C Street, NW
Washington, DC 20001
202-628-3535

Planned Parenthood Federation of America
810 Seventh Avenue
New York, NY 10019
212-603-4637

Population Institute
110 Maryland Avenue, NW
Washington, DC 20002
202-544-3300

Resolve
5 Water Street
Arlington, MA 02174
617-743-2424

Genealogy

African-American Family History Association
P.O. Box 115268
Atlanta, GA 30310
404-730-1942

American Archives Association
7979 Old Georgetown Road
Washington, DC 20814
202-737-6090

American Family Records Association
P.O. Box 15505
Kansas City, MO 64106
816-373-6570

Jewish Genealogical Society
P.O. Box 6398
New York, NY 10128
212-427-5395

Library of Congress
Local History and Genealogy Reading Room
1st Street and Independence Avenue
Washington, DC 20540
202-707-5000

National Archives and Records Administration
Consultant's Office
7th Street and Pennsylvania Avenue, NW
Washington, DC 20408
202-501-5402

National Genealogical Society
4527 Seventeenth Street N.
Arlington, VA 22207
703-525-0050

National Society, Daughters of Founders and Patriots of America
Park Lane Building, No. 615
2025 I Street, NW
Washington, DC 20006

National Society, Daughters of the American Revolution
1776 D Street, NW
Washington, DC 20006
202-628-1776

National Society of Colonial Dames of America
6723 Whittier Avenue, L-4
McLean, VA 22101
703-556-0881

National Society of the Children of the American Revolution
1776 D Street, NW
Washington, DC 20006

Government Agencies and Bureaus

Here is a selection of federal agencies that offer enforcement and/or complaint-handling services for the general public. Many offices also have telecommunications devices for the deaf (TDDs). Voice users can call 800-877-8339 for the help of a relay operator from the Federal Information Relay Service.

Agriculture Department
Office of the Consumer Advisor
Washington, DC 20250
202-382-9681

Civil Rights Commission
Congressional and Community Relations
1121 Vermont Avenue, NW
Washington, DC 20425
202-376-8312
202-376-8116 (voice/TDD)

Commerce Department
Consumer Affairs
14th Street and Constitution Avenue, NW
Washington, DC 20230
202-377-5001

Commodity Futures Trading Commission
Office of Governmental Affairs
2033 K Street, NW
Washington, DC 20581
202-254-3067 (complaints)
202-254-8630 (information)

Consumer Information Center
Pueblo, CO 81009
719-948-4000

Consumer Product Safety Commission
Product Safety Hotline
Washington, DC 20207
800-638-CPSC (hotline)
800-638-8270 (TDD hotline)

Education Department
Consumer Affairs Staff
Room 3061
Washington, DC 20202
202-401-3679

Energy Department
Office of Consumer and Public Liaison
Washington, DC 20585
202-586-5373

Environmental Protection Agency
Public Information Center
Washington, DC 20460
202-382-2080
202-382-4565 (voice/TDD)
800-426-4791 (safe drinking water hotline)

Federal Communications Commission
Consumer Assistance and Small Business Office
1919 M Street NW
Washington, DC 20554
202-632-7000
202-632-6999 (TDD)

Federal Deposit Insurance Corporation
Office of Consumer Affairs
550 17th Street, NW
Washington, DC 20429
202-898-3536
202-898-3535 (voice/TDD)
800-424-5488
800-442-5488 (TDD)

Federal Home Loan Mortgage Corporation
8200 Jones Branch Drive
McLean, VA 22102
703-903-2039

Federal Maritime Commission
Office of Informal Inquiries and Complaints
1100 L Street, NW
Washington, DC 20573
202-523-5807

Federal Reserve System
Board of Governors
Division of Consumer and Community Affairs
Washington, DC 20551
202-452-3946
202-452-3544 (TDD)

Federal Trade Commission
Public Reference Section
6th Street and Pennsylvania Avenue, NW
Washington, DC 20580
202-326-2222 (publications)

Useful Addresses **499**

Health and Human Services Department
Food and Drug Administration
Consumer Affairs and Information Staff
5600 Fishers Lane
Rockville, MD 20857
301-443-3170

Inspector General's Hotline
800-368-5779

Housing and Urban Development Department
Washington, DC 20410
800-347-3735 (HUD fraud hotline)

Interior Department
Consumer Affairs Administrator
Office of the Secretary
Washington, DC 20240
202-208-5521

Interstate Commerce Commission
Office of Compliance and Consumer Assistance
Washington, DC 20423
202-275-7148

Labor Department
Coordinator of Consumer Affairs
Washington, DC 20210
202-523-6060

National Credit Union Administration
1776 G Street, NW
Washington, DC 20456
202-682-9640

National Health Information Center
P.O. Box 1133
Washington, DC 20013-1133
800-336-4797

National Institute of Standards and Technology
Office of Weights and Measures
Washington, DC 20234
301-975-4004

National Labor Relations Board
1717 Pennsylvania Avenue, NW
Washington, DC 20570
202-632-4950

Nuclear Regulatory Commission
Office of Governmental and Public Affairs
Washington, DC 20555
301-492-0240
301-492-4626 (voice/TDD)

Peace Corps
Recruitment
1990 K Street, NW
Washington, DC 20526
800-424-8580

Postal Rate Commission
Office of the Consumer Advocate
1333 H Street, NW
Washington, DC 20268
202-789-6830

Securities and Exchange Commission
Office of Filings, Information and Consumer Services
450 5th Street, NW
Washington, DC 20549
202-272-7440 (investor complaints)
202-272-5624 (SEC information line)
202-272-2552 (voice/TDD)

Small Business Administration
Office of Consumer Affairs
409 3rd Street, SW
Washington, DC 20416
202-205-6948 (complaints)
800-U-ASK-SBA (information)
202-205-7333 (TDD)

Transportation Department
400 7th Street
Washington, DC 20590
800-FAA-SURE (air safety)
202-366-2220 (airline service complaints)
800-424-9393 (auto safety hotline outside DC)
800-424-9153 (auto safety hotline TDD outside DC)
202-267-0972 (boating safety classes)
800-368-5647 (boating safety hotline)
800-368-5647 (railway safety)

United States Postal Service
Consumer Advocate
United States Postal Service
Washington, DC 20260-6720
202-268-2284
202-268-2310 (voice/TDD)

Veterans Affairs Department
810 Vermont Avenue, NW
Washington, DC 20420
202-233-2411

Federal Information Centers

The Federal Information Center (FIC) offers information about federal government services, programs, and regulations. The FIC can also tell you which federal agency to contact for help with specific problems.

The toll-free numbers listed below can be called only within the states and cities listed. If your area is not listed, call 301-722-9098. The nationwide toll-free TDD number is 800-326-2996.

Alabama
Birmingham, Mobile: 800-366-2998

Alaska
Anchorage: 800-729-8003

Arizona
Phoenix: 800-359-3997

Arkansas
Little Rock: 800-366-2998

California
Los Angeles, San Diego, San Francisco, Santa Ana: 800-726-4995
Sacramento: 916-973-1695

Colorado
Colorado Springs, Denver, Pueblo: 800-359-3997

Connecticut
Hartford, New Haven: 800-347-1997

Florida
Ft. Lauderdale, Jacksonville, Miami, Orlando, St. Petersburg, Tampa, West Palm Beach: 800-347-1997

Georgia
Atlanta: 800-347-1997

Hawaii
Honolulu: 800-733-5996

Illinois
Chicago: 800-366-2998

Indiana
Gary: 800-366-2998
Indianapolis: 800-347-1997

Iowa
All locations: 800-735-8004

Kansas
All locations: 800-735-8004

Kentucky
Louisville: 800-347-1997

Louisiana
New Orleans: 800-366-2998

Maryland
Baltimore: 800-347-1997

Massachusetts
Boston: 800-347-1997

Michigan
Detroit, Grand Rapids: 800-347-1997

Minnesota
Minneapolis: 800-366-2998

Missouri
St. Louis: 800-366-2998
All other locations: 800-735-8004

Nebraska
Omaha: 800-366-2998
All other locations: 800-735-8004

New Jersey
Newark, Trenton: 800-347-1997

New Mexico
Albuquerque: 800-359-3997

New York
Albany, Buffalo, New York, Rochester, Syracuse: 800-347-1997

North Carolina
Charlotte: 800-347-1997

Ohio
Akron, Cincinnati, Cleveland, Columbus, Dayton, Toledo: 800-347-1997

Oklahoma
Oklahoma City, Tulsa: 800-366-2998

Oregon
Portland: 800-726-4995

Pennsylvania
Philadelphia, Pittsburgh: 800-347-1997

Rhode Island
Providence: 800-347-1997

Tennessee
Chattanooga: 800-347-1997
Memphis, Nashville: 800-366-2998

Texas
Austin, Dallas, Forth Worth, Houston, San Antonio: 800-366-2998

Utah
Salt Lake City: 800-359-3997

Virginia
Norfolk, Richmond, Roanoke: 800-347-1997

Washington
Seattle, Tacoma: 800-726-4995

Wisconsin
Milwaukee: 800-366-2998

Disabled

Operator Services

Hearing- and speech-impaired people who use a telecommunications device for the deaf (known as TDD or TTY) can get help with calls made from a TDD to a TDD by using the following service:

TDD/TTY Operator Services
800-855-1155

The TDD operator can help you if you have telecommunications devices for the deaf to make:

- Credit card calls (if you have a telephone credit card)
- Collect calls (calls paid for by the person you are calling)
- Third number telephone calls (calls billed to a number other than the one you are calling to or from)
- Person-to-person calls (calls to a specific person)
- Calls from a hotel or motel
- Calls from a coin phone (credit card, collect, or bill to third number calls only)

The TDD operator can also help you:

- Get the number if you have a problem with a call
- Get assistance for problems with calls
- Get telephone numbers that you cannot find in the telephone book
- Report problems with your telephone

The TDD operator cannot interpret voice to TDD or TDD to voice.
   Remember, most calls made with the help of an operator are more expensive, so dial calls yourself when you can to save money.

Books for Blind and Physically Handicapped Persons

The **Library of Congress** has a free reading program for blind and physically handicapped individuals and offers publications in Braille and recorded books and magazines to persons who cannot hold a book or see well enough to read regular print. Special playback equipment is available on a loan basis from the Library of Congress, and cassettes and recordings on discs can be ordered from about 158 cooperating libraries. Anyone who is medically certified as unable to hold a book or read ordinary print because of a visual handicap can borrow these materials postage-free and return them in the same manner.

For more information, send name and address to:

National Library Service for the Blind and
Physically Handicapped
The Library of Congress
Washington, DC 20542

Recording for the Blind (RFB) is a national nonprofit service organization that provides free cassettes of educational textbooks and other resources to medically certified individuals. Eligibility extends to visually, physically, and perceptually handicapped individuals. One of RFB's special services is a collection of cassettes of a wide variety of consumer publications from the federal government. There is a one-time registration fee.

For more information and an application, contact:

Recording for the Blind
20 Roszel Road
Princeton, NJ 08540
609-452-0606
800-221-4792 (toll free outside New Jersey)

Health and Nutrition

AIDS Hotline
800-342-AIDS

Alzheimer's Association
70 East Lake Street
Chicago, IL 60601
312-853-3060

American Dietetic Association
216 West Jackson Boulevard
Chicago, IL 60606
312-899-0040

American Health Foundation
320 East 43rd Street
New York, NY 10017
212-953-1900

American Institute for Preventive Medicine
24450 Evergreen Road
Southfield, MI 48075
313-352-7666

American Institute of Nutrition
9650 Rockville Pike
Bethesda, MD 20814
301-530-7050

American Medical Association
505 North State Street
Chicago, IL 60610
312-464-5000

Cancer Hotline
800-4-CANCER

Center for Food Safety and Applied Nutrition
Food and Drug Administration
200 C Street, NW
Washington, DC 20204

Center for Medical Consumers
237 Thompson Street
New York, NY 10012
212-674-7105

Centers for Disease Control
Health and Human Services Department
1600 Clifton Road, NE
Atlanta, GA 30333
404-639-3286

Community Nutrition Institute
2001 S Street, NW
Washington, DC 20009
202-462-4700

Health and Human Services Department
U.S. Office of Consumer Affairs
1725 Eye Street, NW
Washington, DC 20201

Health Care Financing Administration
Health and Human Services Department
6325 Security Boulevard
Baltimore, MD 21207
800-638-6833

Human Nutrition Information Service
Agriculture Department
6505 Belcrest Road
Hyattsville, MD 20782
301-436-8617

ODPHP National Health Information Center
P.O. Box 1133
Washington, DC 20013-1133
800-336-4797

Office of Information and Consumer Affairs
Occupational Safety and Health Administration
Labor Department
200 Constitution Avenue
Washington, DC 20210
202-523-8151

Second Surgical Opinion Program
Health and Human Services Department
200 Independence Avenue, SW
Washington, DC 20201
800-838-6833

Society for Nutrition Education
1700 Broadway
Oakland, CA 94612
415-444-7133

HOTLINES AND INFORMATION SERVICES

AIDS Hotline	800-342-AIDS
Air safety hotline	800-FAA-SURE
Alzheimer's Disease and Related Disorders Association	800-621-0379
Auto safety hotline	800-424-9393
	202-426-0123 in Washington, DC
Cancer hotline	800-4-CANCER
Child abuse hotline	800-4-A-CHILD
Child support hotline	800-252-3515
Depression hotline	800-551-0008
Dial-a-hearing screening test	800-222-EARS
	800-345-EARS in Pennsylvania
Drug hotline	800-662-HELP
Gay/lesbian youth hotline	800-347-TEEN
Insurance Information Institute	800-221-4954
Medicare hotline	800-638-6833

HOTLINES AND INFORMATION SERVICES (continued)

National Center for Missing and Exploited Children	800-843-5678
National Runaway Switchboard	800-621-4000
Parents Anonymous/Abuse prevention hotline	800-421-0353
Parents who have kidnapped their children hotline	800-A-WAY-OUT
Product safety hotline Consumer Product Safety Commission	800-638-2772
Rape/sexual abuse hotline	800-551-0008
Shriner's Hospital free children's hospital care referral line	800-237-5055

Zip Codes

Five-digit ZIP (Zone Improvement Plan) Codes were introduced in 1964 to identify each postal delivery area in the United States. In some communities, two cities may share a ZIP Code; in others, such as New York City, one geographic area may have many ZIP Codes, including separate ZIP Codes for each major office building. In this book, the ZIP Codes are representative rather than specific for the larger cities. In New York City, for example, the indicated ZIP Code is 10199, which is technically the ZIP Code for the Manhattan borough postmaster. For the ZIP Code for a specific address in any area served by the U.S. Postal Service, the reader should consult a copy of the *U.S. Postal Service National Five-Digit ZIP Code & Post Office Directory*, available at any local post office and revised yearly.

Aberdeen, SD	57401	Anchorage, AK	99501	Atlanta, GA	30304
Abilene, TX	79604	Anderson, IN	46011	Atlantic City, NJ	08401
Addison, IL	60101	Anderson, SC	29621	Attleboro, MA	02703
Akron, OH	44309	Annapolis, MD	21401	Auburn, AL	36830
Alameda, CA	94501	Ann Arbor, MI	48106	Auburn, NY	13021
Albany, GA	31706	Anniston, AL	36201	Auburn, WA	98002
Albuquerque, NM	87101	Antioch, CA	94509	Augusta, GA	30901
Alexandria, LA	71301	Appleton, WI	54911	Aurora, CO	80010
Alexandria, VA	22313	Arcadia, CA	91006	Aurora, IL	60504
Alhambra, CA	91802	Arlington, TX	76010	Austin, TX	78710
Allen Park, MI	48101	Arlington Heights, IL	60004	Azusa, CA	91702
Allentown, PA	18101	Artesia, CA	90701	Bakersfield, CA	93302
Alton, IL	62002	Arvada, CO	80004	Baldwin Park, CA	91706
Altoona, PA	16601	Asheville, NC	28810	Baltimore, MD	21233
Amarillo, TX	79120	Ashland, KY	41101	Bangor, ME	04401
Ames, IA	50010	Aspen, CO	81611	Barberton, OH	44203
Anaheim, CA	92803	Athens, GA	30601	Bartlesville, OK	74003

City	ZIP	City	ZIP	City	ZIP
Baton Rouge, LA	70821	Brattleboro, VT	05301	Chelsea, MA	02150
Battle Creek, MI	49016	Brea, CA	92621	Chesapeake, VA	23320
Bay City, MI	48706	Bremerton, WA	98310	Chester, PA	19013
Bayonne, NJ	07002	Bridgeport, CT	06602	Cheyenne, WY	82001
Baytown, TX	77520	Bristol, CT	06010	Chicago, IL	60607
Beaumont, TX	77707	Brockton, MA	02401	Chicago Heights, IL	60411
Beavercreek, OH	45434	Broken Arrow, OK	74012	Chico, CA	95926
Beaverton, OR	97005	Brookfield, WI	53045	Chicopee, MA	01020
Bell, CA	90201	Brookline, MA	02146	Chula Vista, CA	91910
Belleville, IL	62220	Brooklyn Center, MN	55429	Cicero, IL	60650
Belleville, NJ	07109	Brooklyn Park, MN	55443	Cincinnati, OH	45234
Bellevue, WA	98009	Brook Park, OH	44142	Claremont, CA	91711
Bellflower, CA	90706	Brownsville, TX	78520	Clarksville, TN	37040
Bell Gardens, CA	90201	Brunswick, OH	44212	Clearwater, FL	34618
Bellingham, WA	98225	Bryan, TX	77801	Cleveland, OH	44101
Beloit, WI	53511	Buena Park, CA	90622	Cleveland, TN	37311
Bergenfield, NJ	07621	Buffalo, NY	14240	Cleveland Heights, OH	44118
Berkeley, CA	94704	Burbank, CA	91505	Clifton, NJ	07015
Berwyn, IL	60402	Burlingame, CA	94010	Clinton, IA	52732
Bessemer, AL	35020	Burlington, IA	52601	Clovis, CA	93612
Bethel Park, PA	15102	Burlington, NC	27215	Clovis, NM	88101
Bethesda, MD	20814	Burlington, VT	05401	Coconut Grove, FL	33233
Bethlehem, PA	18016	Burnsville, MN	55337	College Station, TX	77840
Bettendorf, IA	52722	Burton, MI	48509	Colorado Springs, CO	80901
Beverly, MA	01915	Butte, MT	59701	Columbia, MO	65201
Beverly Hills, CA	90210	Calumet City, IL	60409	Columbia, SC	29292
Billings, MT	59101	Camarillo, CA	93010	Columbia, TN	38401
Biloxi, MS	39530	Cambridge, MA	02140	Columbus, GA	31908
Binghamton, NY	13902	Camden, NJ	08101	Columbus, IN	47201
Birmingham, AL	35203	Campbell, CA	95008	Columbus, MS	39701
Bismarck, ND	58501	Canton, OH	44711	Columbus, OH	43216
Blacksburg, VA	24060	Cape Coral, FL	33910	Compton, CA	90220
Blaine, MN	55434	Cape Girardeau, MO	63701	Concord, CA	94520
Bloomfield, NJ	07003	Carbondale, IL	62901	Concord, NH	03301
Bloomington, IL	61701	Carlsbad, CA	92008	Coon Rapids, MN	55433
Bloomington, IN	47401	Carlsbad, NM	88220	Coral Gables, FL	33114
Bloomington, MN	55420	Carrollton, TX	75006	Coral Springs, FL	33065
Blue Springs, MO	64015	Carson, CA	90745	Corona, CA	91720
Boca Raton, FL	33432	Carson City, NV	89701	Corpus Christi, TX	78469
Boise, ID	83708	Casper, WY	82601	Corvallis, OR	97333
Bolingbrook, IL	60439	Cedar Falls, IA	50613	Costa Mesa, CA	92626
Bossier City, LA	71111	Cedar Rapids, IA	52401	Council Bluffs, IA	51501
Boston, MA	02205	Champaign, IL	61820	Covina, CA	91722
Boulder, CO	80302	Chandler, AZ	85224	Covington, KY	41011
Bountiful, UT	84010	Chapel Hill, NC	27514	Cranston, RI	02910
Bowie, MD	20715	Charleston, SC	29423	Crystal, MN	55428
Bowling Green, KY	42101	Charleston, WV	25301	Culver City, CA	90230
Bowling Green, OH	43402	Charlotte, NC	28228	Cumberland, MD	21502
Boynton Beach, FL	33435	Charlottesville, VA	22906	Cupertino, CA	95014
Bradenton, FL	34206	Chattanooga, TN	37421	Cuyahoga Falls, OH	44222

Cypress, CA	90630	Elmira, NY	14901	Fridley, MN	55432
Dallas, TX	75260	El Monte, CA	91731	Fullerton, CA	92634
Daly City, CA	94015	El Paso, TX	79910	Gadsden, AL	35901
Danbury, CT	06810	Elyria, OH	44035	Gainesville, FL	32608
Danville, IL	61832	Emporia, KS	66801	Gaithersburg, MD	20877
Danville, VA	24541	Englewood, CO	80110	Galesburg, IL	61401
Davenport, IA	52802	Enid, OK	73701	Galveston, TX	77550
Davis, CA	95616	Erie, PA	16515	Gardena, CA	90247
Dayton, OH	45401	Escondido, CA	92025	Garden City, MI	48135
Daytona Beach, FL	32114	Euclid, OH	44112	Garden Grove, CA	92642
Dearborn, MI	48120	Eugene, OR	97401	Garfield, NJ	07026
Dearborn Heights, MI	48127	Evanston, IL	60201	Garfield Heights, OH	44125
Decatur, AL	35602	Evansville, IN	47708	Garland, TX	75040
Decatur, IL	62521	Everett, MA	02149	Gary, IN	46401
Deerfield Beach, FL	33441	Everett, WA	98203	Gastonia, NC	28052
De Kalb, IL	60115	Fairborn, OH	45324	Glendale, AZ	85301
Delray Beach, FL	33444	Fairfield, CA	94533	Glendale, CA	91209
Del Rio, TX	78840	Fairfield, OH	45014	Glendora, CA	91740
Denton, TX	76201	Fair Lawn, NJ	07410	Glenview, IL	60025
Denver, CO	80201	Fall River, MA	02720	Gloucester, MA	01930
Des Moines, IA	50318	Fargo, ND	58102	Goldsboro, NC	27530
Des Plaines, IL	60018	Farmington, NM	87401	Grand Forks, ND	58201
Detroit, MI	48233	Fayetteville, AR	72701	Grand Island, NE	68802
Dothan, AL	36303	Fayetteville, NC	28302	Grand Junction, CO	81501
Downers Grove, IL	60515	Ferndale, MI	48220	Grand Prairie, TX	75051
Downey, CA	90241	Findlay, OH	45839	Grand Rapids, MI	49501
Dubuque, IA	52001	Fitchburg, MA	01420	Granite City, IL	62040
Duluth, MN	55806	Flagstaff, AZ	86001	Great Falls, MT	59401
Duncanville, TX	75138	Flint, MI	48502	Greeley, CO	80631
Dunedin, FL	32132	Florence, AL	35631	Green Bay, WI	54303
Durham, NC	27701	Florence, SC	29501	Greenfield, WI	53220
East Chicago, IN	46312	Florissant, MO	63033	Greensboro, NC	27420
East Cleveland, OH	44112	Fond du Lac, WI	54935	Greenville, MS	38701
East Detroit, MI	48021	Fontana, CA	92335	Greenville, NC	27834
East Lansing, MI	48823	Fort Collins, CO	80521	Greenville, SC	29602
Easton, PA	18042	Fort Dodge, IA	50501	Gresham, OR	97030
East Orange, NJ	07019	Fort Lauderdale, FL	33110	Grosse Pointe, MI	48230
East Providence, RI	02914	Fort Lee, NJ	07024	Gulfport, MS	39503
East St. Louis, IL	62201	Fort Myers, FL	33906	Hackensack, NJ	07602
Eau Claire, WI	54703	Fort Pierce, FL	34981	Hagerstown, MD	21740
Edina, MN	55424	Fort Smith, AR	72901	Hallandale, FL	33009
Edmond, OK	73034	Fort Wayne, IN	46802	Haltom City, TX	76117
Edmonds, WA	98020	Fort Worth, TX	76161	Hamilton, OH	45011
El Cajon, CA	92020	Frankfort, KY	40601	Hammond, IN	46320
El Dorado, AR	71730	Frederick, MD	21701	Hampton, VA	23670
Elgin, IL	60120	Fredericksburg, VA	22404	Hanover Park, IL	60103
Elizabeth, NJ	07207	Freeport, IL	61032	Harlingen, TX	78550
Elk Grove, IL	60007	Freeport, NY	11520	Harrisburg, PA	17107
Elkhart, IN	46515	Fremont, CA	94538	Hartford, CT	06101
Elmhurst, IL	60126	Fresno, CA	93706	Harvey, IL	60426

Hattiesburg, MS	39402	Johnstown, PA	15901	Leominster, MA	01453
Haverhill, MA	01831	Joliet, IL	60436	Lewiston, ID	83501
Hawthorne, CA	90250	Jonesboro, AR	72401	Lewiston, ME	04240
Hayward, CA	94544	Joplin, MO	64801	Lexington, KY	40511
Hazelton, PA	18201	Kalamazoo, MI	49001	Lima, OH	45802
Hempstead, NY	11551	Kankakee, IL	60901	Lincoln, NE	68501
Hialeah, FL	33010	Kansas City, KS	66106	Lincoln Park, MI	48146
Highland, IN	46322	Kansas City, MO	64108	Linden, NJ	07036
Highland Park, IL	60035	Kearny, NJ	07032	Lindenhurst, NY	11757
Highland Park, MI	48203	Kenner, LA	70062	Little Rock, AR	72231
High Point, NC	27260	Kennewick, WA	99336	Littleton, CO	80120
Hillsboro, OR	97123	Kenosha, WI	53140	Livermore, CA	94550
Hilo, HI	96720	Kent, OH	44240	Livonia, MI	48150
Hobbs, NM	88240	Kettering, OH	45429	Lodi, CA	95240
Hoboken, NJ	07030	Killeen, TX	76541	Logan, UT	84321
Hoffman Estates, IL	60195	Kingsport, TN	37660	Lombard, IL	60148
Holland, MI	49423	Kingston, NC	28501	Lompoc, CA	93436
Hollywood, FL	33022	Kingsville, TX	78363	Long Beach, CA	90809
Holyoke, MA	01040	Kirkwood, MO	63122	Long Beach, NY	11561
Honolulu, HI	96820	Knoxville, TN	37950	Long Branch, NJ	07740
Hopkinsville, KY	42240	Kokomo, IN	46902	Longmont, CO	80501
Hot Springs, AR	71901	La Crosse, WI	54601	Longview, TX	75602
Houma, LA	70360	Lafayette, IN	47901	Longview, WA	98632
Houston, TX	77201	Lafayette, LA	70501	Lorain, OH	44052
Huber Heights, OH	45424	La Habra, CA	90631	Los Altos, CA	94022
Huntington, WV	25704	Lake Charles, LA	70601	Los Angeles, CA	90052
Huntington Beach, CA	92647	Lakeland, FL	33805	Los Gatos, CA	95030
Huntington Park, CA	90255	Lakewood, CA	90714	Louisville, KY	40231
Huntsville, AL	35813	Lakewood, CO	80215	Loveland, CO	80538
Hurst, TX	76053	Lakewood, OH	44107	Lowell, MA	01853
Hutchinson, KS	67501	Lake Worth, FL	33461	Lubbock, TX	79402
Idaho Falls, ID	83401	La Mesa, CA	91941	Lufkin, TX	75901
Independence, MO	64050	La Mirada, CA	90638	Lynchburg, VA	24506
Indianapolis, IN	46206	Lancaster, CA	93534	Lynn, MA	01901
Inglewood, CA	90311	Lancaster, OH	43130	Lynwood, CA	90262
Inkster, MI	48141	Lancaster, PA	17604	Macon, GA	31213
Iowa City, IA	52240	Lansing, IL	60438	Madison, WI	53714
Irvine, CA	92713	Lansing, MI	48924	Madison Heights, MI	48071
Irving, TX	75015	La Puente, CA	91747	Malden, MA	02148
Irvington, NJ	07111	Laredo, TX	78041	Manchester, NH	03103
Ithaca, NY	14850	Largo, FL	34640	Manhattan, KS	66502
Jackson, MI	49201	Las Cruces, NM	88001	Manhattan Beach, CA	90266
Jackson, MS	39205	Las Vegas, NV	89199	Manitowoc, WI	54220
Jackson, TN	38301	Lawrence, IN	46226	Mankato, MN	56001
Jacksonville, FL	32203	Lawrence, KS	66044	Mansfield, OH	44901
Jamestown, NY	14701	Lawrence, MA	01842	Maple Heights, OH	44137
Janesville, WI	53545	Lawton, OK	73501	Maplewood, MN	55109
Jefferson City, MO	65101	Leavenworth, KS	66048	Marietta, GA	30060
Jersey City, NJ	07303	Lebanon, PA	17042	Marion, IN	46952
Johnson City, TN	37601	Lee's Summit, MO	64063	Marion, OH	43302

Marlborough, MA	01752	Morgantown, WV	26505	North Miami, FL	33261
Marshalltown, IA	50158	Mountain View, CA	94042	North Miami Beach, FL	33160
Mason City, IA	50401	Mount Prospect, IL	60056	North Olmsted, OH	44070
Massillon, OH	44646	Mount Vernon, NY	10551	North Richland Hills, TX	76180
Maywood, IL	60153	Muncie, IN	47302	North Tonawanda, NY	14120
McAllen, TX	78501	Murfreesboro, TN	37130	Norwalk, CA	90650
McKeesport, PA	15134	Murray, UT	84107	Norwalk, CT	06856
Medford, MA	02155	Muskegon, MI	49440	Norwich, CT	06360
Medford, OR	97501	Muskogee, OK	74401	Norwood, OH	45212
Melbourne, FL	32901	Nacogdoches, TX	75961	Novato, CA	94947
Melrose, MA	02176	Nampa, ID	83651	Nutley, NJ	07110
Memphis, TN	38101	Napa, CA	94558	Oak Forest, IL	60452
Menlo Park, CA	94025	Naperville, IL	60540	Oakland, CA	94615
Menomonee Falls, WI	53051	Nashua, NH	03060	Oak Lawn, IL	60455
Mentor, OH	44060	Nashville, TN	37229	Oak Park, IL	60301
Merced, CA	95340	National City, CA	91950	Oak Park, MI	48237
Meriden, CT	06450	Naugatuck, CT	06770	Oak Ridge, TN	37830
Meridian, MS	39301	New Albany, IN	47150	Ocala, FL	32678
Merrillville, IN	46410	Newark, CA	94560	Oceanside, CA	92054
Mesa, AZ	85201	Newark, DE	19711	Odessa, TX	79761
Mesquite, TX	75149	Newark, NJ	07102	Ogden, UT	84401
Miami, FL	33152	Newark, OH	43055	Oklahoma City, OK	73125
Miami Beach, FL	33139	New Bedford, MA	02740	Olathe, KS	66061
Middletown, CT	06457	New Berlin, WI	53151	Olympia, WA	98501
Middletown, OH	45042	New Britain, CT	06050	Omaha, NE	68108
Midland, MI	48640	New Brunswick, NJ	08901	Ontario, CA	91761
Midland, TX	79711	New Castle, PA	16108	Orange, CA	92613
Midwest City, OK	73130	New Haven, CT	06511	Orange, NJ	07051
Milford, CT	06460	New Iberia, LA	70560	Orem, UT	84057
Milpitas, CA	95035	New London, CT	06320	Orlando, FL	32802
Milwaukee, WI	53203	New Orleans, LA	70113	Oshkosh, WI	54901
Minneapolis, MN	55401	Newport, RI	02840	Ottumwa, IA	52501
Minnetonka, MN	55345	Newport Beach, CA	92660	Overland Park, KS	66204
Minot, ND	58701	Newport News, VA	23607	Owensboro, KY	43201
Mishawaka, IN	46544	New Rochelle, NY	10802	Oxnard, CA	93030
Missoula, MT	59801	Newton, MA	02158	Pacifica, CA	94044
Mobile, AL	36601	New York, NY	10199	Paducah, KY	42001
Modesto, CA	95350	Niagara Falls, NY	14302	Palatine, IL	60067
Moline, IL	61265	Niles, IL	60648	Palm Springs, CA	92263
Monroe, LA	71203	Norfolk, VA	23501	Palo Alto, CA	94303
Monroeville, PA	15146	Normal, IL	61761	Panama City, FL	32401
Monrovia, CA	91016	Norman, OK	73069	Paramount, CA	90723
Montclair, NJ	07042	Norristown, PA	19401	Paramus, NJ	07652
Montebello, CA	90640	Northampton, MA	01060	Paris, TX	75460
Monterey, CA	93940	Northbrook, IL	60062	Parkersburg, WV	26101
Monterey Park, CA	91754	North Charleston, SC	29406	Park Ridge, IL	60068
Montgomery, AL	36119	North Chicago, IL	60064	Parma, OH	44129
Moore, OK	73160	North Las Vegas, NV	89030	Pasadena, CA	91109
Moorhead, MN	56560	North Little Rock, AR	72114	Pasadena, TX	77501

Pascagoula, MS	39567	Raleigh, NC	27611	St. Petersburg, FL	33730
Passaic, NJ	07055	Rancho Cucamonga, CA	91730	Salem, MA	01970
Paterson, NJ	07510	Rancho Palos Verdes, CA	90274	Salem, OR	97301
Pawtucket, RI	02860	Rapid City, SD	57701	Salina, KS	67401
Peabody, MA	01960	Raytown, MO	64133	Salinas, CA	93907
Pembroke Pines, FL	33024	Reading, PA	19612	Salt Lake City, UT	84199
Pensacola, FL	32501	Redding, CA	96001	San Angelo, TX	76902
Peoria, IL	61601	Redlands, CA	92373	San Antonio, TX	78284
Perth Amboy, NJ	08861	Redondo Beach, CA	90277	San Bernardino, CA	92403
Petaluma, CA	94952	Redwood City, CA	94064	San Bruno, CA	94066
Petersburg, VA	23804	Reno, NV	89510	San Buenaventura (Ventura), CA	
Phenix City, AL	36867	Renton, WA	98058		93001
Philadelphia, PA	19104	Revere, MA	02151	San Clemente, CA	92672
Phoenix, AZ	85027	Rialto, CA	92376	San Diego, CA	92199
Pico Rivera, CA	90660	Richardson, TX	75080	Sandusky, OH	44870
Pine Bluff, AR	71601	Richfield, MN	55423	Sandy, UT	84070
Pinellas Park, FL	34665	Richland, WA	99352	San Francisco, CA	94188
Pittsburg, CA	94565	Richmond, CA	94802	San Gabriel, CA	91776
Pittsburgh, PA	15290	Richmond, IN	47374	San Jose, CA	95101
Pittsfield, MA	01201	Richmond, VA	23232	San Leandro, CA	94577
Placentia, CA	92670	Ridgewood, NJ	07450	San Luis Obispo, CA	93401
Plainfield, NJ	07061	Riverside, CA	92507	San Mateo, CA	94402
Plano, TX	75074	Riviera Beach, FL	33404	San Rafael, CA	94901
Plantation, FL	33318	Roanoke, VA	24022	Santa Ana, CA	92799
Pleasant Hill, CA	94523	Rochester, MI	48308	Santa Barbara, CA	93102
Pleasanton, CA	94566	Rochester, MN	55901	Santa Clara, CA	95051
Plum, PA	15239	Rochester, NY	14692	Santa Cruz, CA	95060
Plymouth, MN	55447	Rockford, IL	61125	Santa Fe, NM	87501
Pocatello, ID	83201	Rock Hill, SC	29730	Santa Maria, CA	93454
Pomona, CA	91766	Rock Island, IL	61201	Santa Monica, CA	90406
Pompano Beach, FL	33060	Rockville, MD	20850	Santa Rosa, CA	95402
Ponca City, OK	74601	Rockville Center, NY	11570	Sarasota, FL	34230
Pontiac, MI	48343	Rocky Mount, NC	27801	Saratoga, CA	95070
Portage, IN	46368	Rome, GA	30161	Savannah, GA	31402
Port Arthur, TX	77640	Rome, NY	13440	Sayreville, NJ	08872
Port Huron, MI	48060	Rosemead, CA	91770	Schaumburg, IL	60194
Portland, ME	04101	Roseville, MI	48066	Schenectady, NY	12305
Portland, OR	97208	Roseville, MN	55113	Scottsdale, AZ	85251
Portsmouth, NH	03801	Roswell, NM	88201	Scranton, PA	18505
Portsmouth, OH	45662	Royal Oak, MI	48068	Seal Beach, CA	90740
Portsmouth, VA	23707	Sacramento, CA	95813	Seaside, CA	93955
Poughkeepsie, NY	12601	Saginaw, MI	48065	Seattle, WA	98109
Providence, RI	02904	St. Charles, MO	63301	Selma, AL	36701
Provo, UT	84601	St. Clair Shores, MI	48080	Shaker Heights, OH	44120
Pueblo, CO	81003	St. Cloud, MN	56301	Shawnee Mission, KS	66202
Quincy, IL	62301	St. Joseph, MO	64501	Shawnee, OK	74801
Quincy, MA	02269	St. Louis, MO	63155	Sheboygan, WI	53081
Racine, WI	53403	St. Louis Park, MN	55426	Shelton, CT	06484
Rahway, NJ	07065	St. Paul, MN	55101	Sherman, TX	75090

Shreveport, LA	71102	Thousand Oaks, CA	91360	Waukesha, WI	53186
Silver Spring, MD	20907	Tinley Park, IL	60477	Wausau, WI	54401
Simi Valley, CA	93065	Titusville, FL	32780	Wauwatosa, WI	53213
Sioux City, IA	51101	Toledo, OH	43601	Weirton, WV	26062
Sioux Falls, SD	57101	Topeka, KS	66603	West Allis, WI	53214
Skokie, IL	60076	Torrance, CA	90510	West Covina, CA	91793
Slidell, LA	70458	Torrington, CT	06790	Westfield, MA	01085
Somerville, MA	02143	Trenton, NJ	08650	Westfield, NJ	07090
Somerville, NJ	08876	Troy, MI	48099	West Haven, CT	06516
South Bend, IN	46624	Troy, NY	12180	West Jordan, UT	84084
South Euclid, OH	44121	Tucson, AZ	85726	Westland, MI	48185
Southfield, MI	48037	Tulsa, OK	74103	West Lafayette, IN	47906
South Gate, CA	90280	Turlock, CA	95380	West Memphis, AR	72301
Southgate, MI	48195	Tuscaloosa, AL	35401	West Mifflin, PA	15122
South San Francisco, CA	94080	Tustin, CA	92680	Westminster, CA	92683
Sparks, NV	89431	Twin Falls, ID	83301	Westminster, CO	80030
Spartanburg, SC	29301	Tyler, TX	75712	West New York, NJ	07093
Spokane, WA	99210	Union City, CA	94587	West Orange, NJ	07052
Springfield, IL	62703	Union City, NJ	07087	West Palm Beach, FL	33406
Springfield, MA	01101	University City, MO	63130	Wheaton, IL	60187
Springfield, MO	65801	Upland, CA	91786	Wheat Ridge, CO	80033
Springfield, OH	45501	Upper Arlington, OH	43221	Wheeling, WV	26003
Springfield, OR	97477	Urbana, IL	61801	White Plains, NY	10602
Stamford, CT	06904	Utica, NY	13504	Whittier, CA	90605
State College, PA	16801	Vacaville, CA	95688	Wichita, KS	67276
Sterling Heights, MI	48311	Valdosta, GA	31601	Wichita Falls, TX	76307
Steubenville, OH	43952	Vallejo, CA	94590	Wilkes-Barre, PA	18701
Stillwater, OK	74074	Valley Stream, NY	11580	Williamsport, PA	17701
Stockton, CA	95208	Vancouver, WA	98661	Wilmette, IL	60091
Stow, OH	44224	Vicksburg, MS	39180	Wilmington, DE	19850
Strongsville, OH	44136	Victoria, TX	77901	Wilmington, NC	28402
Suffolk, VA	23434	Vineland, NJ	08360	Wilson, NC	27893
Sunnyvale, CA	94086	Virginia Beach, VA	23450	Winona, MN	55987
Sunrise, FL	33345	Visalia, CA	93277	Winston-Salem, NC	27102
Superior, WI	54880	Vista, CA	92083	Woburn, MA	01801
Syracuse, NY	13220	Waco, TX	76702	Woodland, CA	95695
Tacoma, WA	98413	Walla Walla, WA	99362	Woonsocket, RI	02895
Tallahassee, FL	32301	Walnut Creek, CA	94596	Worcester, MA	01613
Tamarac, FL	33320	Waltham, MA	02154	Wyandotte, MI	48192
Tampa, FL	33630	Warner Robins, GA	31093	Wyoming, MI	49509
Taunton, MA	02780	Warren, MI	48090	Yakima, WA	98903
Taylor, MI	48180	Warren, OH	44481	Yonkers, NY	10702
Tempe, AZ	85282	Warwick, RI	02886	Yorba Linda, CA	92686
Temple, TX	76501	Washington, DC	20013	York, PA	17405
Terre Haute, IN	47808	Waterbury, CT	06701	Youngstown, OH	44501
Texarkana, TX	75501	Waterloo, IA	50701	Ypsilanti, MI	48197
Texas City, TX	75590	Watertown, NY	13601	Yuma, AZ	85364
Thornton, CO	80229	Waukegan, IL	60085	Zanesville, OH	43701

Magazines

Arts and Entertainment

Back Stage
1515 Broadway
New York, NY 10036

Entertainment Weekly
1675 Broadway
New York, NY 10019

National Enquirer
Lantana, FL 33464

Popular Photography
1633 Broadway New York, NY 10019

Premiere
2 Park Avenue
New York, NY 10016

TV Guide Magazine
4 Radnor Corporate Center
Radnor, PA 19088

Business and Personal Finance

Business Week
1221 Avenue of the Americas
New York, NY 10020

Entrepreneur
2392 Morse Avenue
Irvine, CA 92714

Forbes
60 Fifth Avenue
New York, NY 10011

Fortune
1271 Avenue of the Americas
New York, NY 10020

Money
1271 Avenue of the Americas
New York, NY 10020
Subscriptions:
591 North Fairbanks Court
Chicago, IL 60611

Consumerism

Accent on Living
P.O. Box 700
Gilum Road and High Drive
Bloomington, IL 61702

Kiplinger's Personal Finance Magazine
The Kiplinger Washington Editors, Inc.
1729 H St. NW
Washington, DC 20006

Consumer Reports
Consumers Union of the U.S., Inc.
101 Truman Avenue
Yonkers, NY 10703

Consumers Digest
5705 North Lincoln Avenue
Chicago, IL 60659

Gray Panther Network
1424 16th Street, NW
Washington, DC 20036

Modern Maturity
American Association of Retired Persons
3200 East Carson Street
Lakewood, CA 90712

Cooking and Dining

Bon Appetit
5900 Wilshire Boulevard
Los Angeles, CA 90036

Food and Wine
1120 Avenue of the Americas
New York, NY 10036

Gourmet
360 Madison Avenue
New York, NY 10017

General Interest

The Atlantic
745 Boylston Street
Boston, MA 02116

Ebony
820 South Michigan Avenue
Chicago, IL 60605

Harpers
666 Broadway
New York, NY 10012

Life
1271 Avenue of the Americas
New York, NY 10020

National Geographic
17th and M Streets, NW
Washington, DC 20036

The New Yorker
20 West 43rd Street
New York, NY 10036

People
1271 Avenue of the Americas
New York, NY 10020

Psychology Today
24 E. 23rd St.
New York, NY 10010

Reader's Digest
Pleasantville, NY 10570

Saturday Evening Post
1100 Waterway Boulevard
Indianapolis, IN 46202

Smithsonian
900 Jefferson Drive
Washington, DC 20560

Utne Reader
1624 Harmon Place
Minneapolis, MN 55403

Vanity Fair
350 Madison Avenue
New York, NY 10017

Health and Nutrition

East West Journal
17 Station Street
Box 1200
Brookline, MA 02147

Prevention
33 East Minor Street
Emmaus, PA 18098

Self
350 Madison Avenue
New York, NY 10017

Weight Watchers Magazine
360 Lexington Avenue
New York, NY 10017

Home and Gardening

Architectural Digest
5900 Wilshire Boulevard
Los Angeles, CA 90036

Better Homes and Gardens
1716 Locust Street
Des Moines, IA 50336

Country Living
5400 South 60th Street
Box 643
Greendale, WI 53129

The Family Handyman
7900 International Drive
Minneapolis, MN 55425

Horticulture
20 Park Plaza
Boston, MA 02116

House Beautiful
1700 Broadway
New York, NY 10019

Metropolitan Home
750 Third Avenue
New York, NY 10017

Southern Living
2100 Lakeshore Drive
Birmingham, AL 35209

Men's Interests

Details
632 Broadway
New York, NY 10012

Esquire
1700 Broadway
New York, NY 10019

Gentlemen's Quarterly (GQ)
350 Madison Avenue
New York, NY 10017

Playboy
680 North Lake Shore Drive
Chicago, IL 60611

News

Newsweek
444 Madison Avenue
New York, NY 10022

Time
1271 Avenue of the Americas
New York, NY 10020

U.S. News & World Report
2400 N Street, NW
Washington, DC 20037

Parenting

American Baby
475 Park Avenue South
New York, NY 10016

Child Magazine
110 Fifth Avenue
New York, NY 10011

Expecting
685 Third Avenue
New York, NY 10017

Parents Magazine
685 Third Avenue
New York, NY 10017

Public, Social, and Political Affairs

See also **News** section.

Mother Jones
1663 Mission Street
San Francisco, CA 94103

The Nation
72 Fifth Avenue
New York, NY 10011

The New Republic
1220 19th Street, NW
Washington, DC 20036

Science and Mechanics

Discover Magazine
114 Fifth Avenue
New York, NY 10011

Home Mechanix
2 Park Avenue
New York, NY 10016

Popular Mechanics
224 West 57th Street
New York, NY 10019

Popular Science
2 Park Avenue
New York, NY 10016

Scientific American
415 Madison Avenue
New York, NY 10017

Sports and the Outdoors

Backpacker
Rodale Press
33 East Minor Street
Emmaus, PA 18098

Bicycling Magazine
Rodale Press
33 East Minor Street
Emmaus, PA 18098

Boating
1633 Broadway
New York, NY 10019

Camping Magazine
American Camping Association
5000 State Road, 67 N
Martinsville, IN 46151

Car and Driver
1633 Broadway
New York, NY 10019

Field and Stream
2 Park Avenue
New York, NY 10016

Outdoor Life
2 Park Avenue
New York, NY 10016

Sports Illustrated
1271 Avenue of the Americas
New York, NY 10020

Travel

Condé Nast Traveler
360 Madison Avenue
New York, NY 10017

Travel & Leisure
1120 Avenue of the Americas
New York, NY 10036

Women's Interests

Allure
360 Madison Avenue
New York, NY 10017

Bride's
360 Madison Avenue
New York, NY 10017

Cosmopolitan
224 West 57th Street
New York, NY 10019

Elle
1633 Broadway
New York, NY 10019

Essence
1500 Broadway
New York, NY 10036

Family Circle
110 Fifth Avenue
New York, NY 10011

Glamour
360 Madison Avenue
New York, NY 10017

Good Housekeeping
959 Eighth Avenue
New York, NY 10019

Harpers Bazaar
1700 Broadway
New York, NY 10019

Ladies' Home Journal
100 Park Avenue
New York, NY 10017

Lears
655 Madison Avenue
New York, NY 10021

Mademoiselle
360 Madison Avenue
New York, NY 10017

McCall's
110 Fifth Avenue
New York, NY 10011

Mirabella
200 Madison Avenue
New York, NY 10016

Modern Bride
475 Park Ave South
New York, NY 10022

Ms.
230 Park Avenue
New York, NY 10169

New Woman
215 Lexington Avenue
New York, NY 10016

Redbook
224 West 57th Street
New York, NY 10019

Vogue
350 Madison Avenue
New York, NY 10017

Woman's Day
1633 Broadway
New York, NY 10019

Women's Circle
Box 299
Lynnfield, MA 01940-0299

Working Woman
342 Madison Avenue
New York, NY 10173

Newspapers

National

Christian Science Monitor
One Norway Street
Boston, MA 02115-3195

USA Today
1000 Wilson Boulevard
Arlington, VA 22209

Wall Street Journal
200 Liberty Street
New York, NY 10281

Major Daily by State

Alabama

Birmingham News
Box 2553
Birmingham, AL 35202-2553

Birmingham Post-Herald
Box 2553
Birmingham, AL 35202-2553

Montgomery Advertiser
Box 1000
Montgomery, AL 36101-1000

Alaska

Anchorage Daily News
Box 149001
Anchorage, AK 99514-9001

Anchorage Times
Box 100040
Anchorage, AK 99510-0040

Arizona

Arizona Republic
Box 1950
Phoenix, AZ 85001-1950

Arizona Daily Star
Box 26807
Tucson, AZ 85726-6807

Phoenix Gazette
Box 1950
Phoenix, AZ 85001-1950

Arkansas

Arkansas Democrat
Capitol Avenue and Scott
Box 2221
Little Rock, AR 72203

Arkansas Gazette
Box 1821
Little Rock, AR 72203-1821

California

Fresno Bee
1626 E Street
Fresno, CA 93786-0001

Los Angeles Herald Examiner
1111 South Broadway
Los Angeles, CA 90015
213-744-8000

Los Angeles Times
Times Mirror Square
Los Angeles, CA 90053

Oakland Tribune
409 13th Street
Oakland, CA 94612-2601

Sacramento Bee
2100 Q Street
P.O. Box 15779
Sacramento, CA 95852

San Diego Tribune
350 Camino de la Reina
San Diego, CA 92108

San Diego Union
350 Camino de la Reina
San Diego, CA 92108

San Francisco Chronicle
901 Mission Street
San Francisco, CA 94103

San Francisco Examiner
110 Fifth Street
San Francisco, CA 94103

Colorado

Denver Post
1560 Broadway
Denver, CO 80202

Rocky Mountain News
400 West Colfax Avenue
Denver, CO 80204

Connecticut

Hartford Courant
285 Broad Street
Hartford, CT 06115-2510

New Haven Register
40 Sargent Drive
New Haven, CT 06511

Delaware

Journal
831 Orange Street
Wilmington, DE 19801-1709

News-Journal
950 West Basin Road
New Castle, DE 19720

District of Columbia

Washington Post
1150 15th Street, NW
Washington, DC 20071

Florida

Florida Times Union
One Riverside Avenue
Jacksonville, FL 32202-4924

Fort Lauderdale Sun-Sentinel
200 East Lasloas Boulevard
Ft. Lauderdale, FL 33301-2293

Miami Herald
One Herald Plaza
Miami, FL 33132-1693

Orlando Sentinel
633 North Orange Avenue
Orlando, FL 32801

St. Petersburg Times
Box 1121
St. Petersburg, FL 33731

Tampa Tribune
202 S. Parker Street
Tampa, FL 33606-2308

Georgia

Atlanta Constitution
72 Marietta Street, NW
Atlanta, GA 30303

Atlanta Journal
72 Marietta Street, NW
Atlanta, GA 30303

Hawaii

Honolulu Advertiser
605 Kapiolani Boulevard
Honolulu, HI 96813

Honolulu Star Bulletin
Box 3080
Honolulu, HI 96802

Idaho

Idaho Statesman
1200 North Curtis Road
Boise, ID 83707

Illinois

Chicago Sun-Times
401 North Wabash Avenue
Chicago, IL 60611

Chicago Tribune
435 North Michigan Avenue
Chicago, IL 60611

Indiana

Indianapolis News
307 North Pennsylvania Street
Indianapolis, IN 46204-1811

Post-Tribune
1065 Broadway
Gary, IN 46402-2998

South Bend Tribune
225 West Colfax Avenue
South Bend, IN 46626-0001

Iowa

Des Moines Register
Box 957, 50304
Des Moines, IA 50304

Kansas

Topeka Capital-Journal
616 Jefferson Street
Topeka, KS 66607-1197

Wichita Eagle
825 East Douglas Street
Wichita, KS 67202

Kentucky

Courier-Journal
525 West Broadway
Louisville, KY 40202-2137

Herald-Leader
100 Midland Avenue
Lexington, KY 40508

Louisiana

Morning Advocate
525 Lafayette Street
Baton Rouge, LA 70821

Times-Picayune
3800 Howard Avenue
New Orleans, LA 70140

Maine

News
491 Main Street
Bangor, ME 04401

Portland Press Herald
Box 1460
390 Congress Street
Portland, ME 04104

Maryland

The Baltimore Sun
501 North Calvert Street
Baltimore, MD 21278-0001

Massachusetts

Boston Globe
135 Morrissey Boulevard
Boston, MA 02107

Boston Herald
300 Harrison Avenue
Boston, MA 02118-2297

Michigan

Detroit Free Press
321 West Lafayette Boulevard
Detroit, MI 48226

Detroit News
615 West Lafayette Boulevard
Detroit, MI 48226

Minnesota

St. Paul Pioneer Press Dispatch
345 Cedar Street
St. Paul, MN 55101-1057

Star Tribune
425 Portland Avenue
Minneapolis, MN 55488-0001

Mississippi

Clarion Ledger
311 East Pearl Street
Jackson, MS 39202

Missouri

Kansas City Star
1729 Grand Avenue
Kansas City, MO 64108

Kansas City Times
1729 Grand Avenue
Kansas City, MO 64108

Post-Dispatch
900 North Tucker Boulevard
St. Louis, MO 63101

Montana

Billings Gazette
401 North Broadway
Billings, MT 59101-1243

Great Falls Tribune
Box 5468
Great Falls, MT 59403

Nebraska

Lincoln Journal
926 P Street
Lincoln, NE 68501

Lincoln Star
926 P Street
Lincoln, NE 68508

World-Herald
World-Herald Square
Omaha, NE 68102

Nevada

Las Vegas Review-Journal
1111 W. Bonanza
Las Vegas, NV 89125

Las Vegas Sun
121 South Martin Luther King Boulevard
Box 4275
Las Vegas, NV 89106

Reno Gazette Journal
955 Kuenzli Street
Reno, NV 89502-1160

New Hampshire

Union-Leader
Box 9555
Manchester, NH 03108

New Jersey

Asbury Park Press
3601 Highway 66
Neptune, NJ 07754

Record
150 River Street
Hackensack, NJ 07601

Star-Ledger
Star-Ledger Plaza
Newark, NJ 07102-1200

New Mexico

Albuquerque Journal
Drawer J
Albuquerque, NM 87103

Albuquerque Tribune
7777 Jefferson NE
Albuquerque, NM 87109

New York

Buffalo News
One News Plaza
Box 100
Buffalo, NY 14240

Newsday
235 Pinelawn Road
2Melville, NY 11747-4250

New York Daily News
220 East 42nd Street
New York, NY 10017-5806

New York Post
210 South Street
New York, NY 10002-7889

New York Times
229 West 43rd Street
New York, NY 10036-3913

North Carolina

Observer
Box 32188-28232
Charlotte, NC 28232

News & Observer
215 South McDowell Street
Raleigh, NC 27602

North Dakota

Bismarck Tribune
Box 1498
707 East Front Avenue
Bismarck, ND 58502-1498

Ohio

Akron Beacon Journal
44 East Exchange Street
Akron, OH 44328-0001

Blade
541 Superior Street
Toledo, OH 43660-0001

Cincinnati Enquirer
617 Vine Street
Cincinnati, OH 45202-2410

Cincinnati Post
125 East Court Street
Cincinnati, OH 45202-1211

Cleveland Plain Dealer
1801 Superior Avenue
Cleveland, OH 44114-2198

Columbus Dispatch
34 South Third Street
Columbus, OH 43215

Daily News
Fourth and Ludlow Streets
Dayton, OH 45401

Oklahoma

Oklahoman
500 North Broadway
Oklahoma City, OK 73125

Tulsa Tribune
Box 1770
Tulsa, OK 74102

Tulsa World
Box 1770
Tulsa, OK 74102

Oregon

The Oregonian
1320 Southwest Broadway
Portland, OR 97201-3469

Pennsylvania

Philadelphia Daily News
P.O. Box 7788
Philadelphia, PA 19101

Philadelphia Inquirer
400 North Broad Street
Philadelphia, PA 19101

Pittsburgh Post-Gazette
P.O. Box 957
50 Boulevard of Allies
Pittsburgh, PA 15222

Pittsburgh Press
34 Boulevard of Allies
Pittsburgh, PA 15230

Rhode Island

Journal-Bulletin
75 Fountain Street
Providence, RI 02902

South Carolina

Evening Post
134 Columbus Street
Charleston, SC 29403-4800

News & Courier
134 Columbus Street
Charleston, SC 29403-4800

The State
P.O. Box 1333
Columbia, SC 29202

South Dakota

Argus Leader
Box 5034
Sioux Falls, SD 57117-5034

Tennessee

Commercial Appeal
495 Union Avenue
Memphis, TN 38103-3221

Nashville Banner
1100 Broadway
Nashville, TN 37203-3116

News-Sentinel
204 West Church Avenue
Knoxville, TN 37902-1612

Tennessean
1100 Broadway
Nashville, TN 37203-3116

Texas

Austin American-Statesman
Box 670
Austin, TX 78767

Dallas Morning News
Communications Center
Dallas, TX 75265

Dallas Times Herald
1101 Pacific Avenue
Dallas, TX 75202-2745

Express-News
Avenue E and Third Street
San Antonio, TX 78205

Fort Worth Star-Telegram
400 West 7th Street
Fort Worth, TX 76102

Houston Chronicle
801 Texas Avenue
Houston, TX 77002

Houston Post
Box 4747
Houston, TX 77210

San Antonio Light
Box 161
San Antonio, TX 78291

Utah

Desert News
30 East First Street
Salt Lake City, UT 84110

Salt Lake Tribune
P.O. Box 867
Salt Lake City, UT 84110

Vermont

Free Press
191 College Street
Burlington, VT 05401

Virginia

Virginian-Pilot
150 West Brambleton Avenue
Norfolk, VA 23510

Richmond News-Leader
Box C-32333
Richmond, VA 23293-0001

Richmond Times-Dispatch
Box C-32333
Richmond, VA 23293-0001

Washington

Seattle Post-Intelligencer
101 Elliott Avenue, W
Seattle, WA 98119

Seattle Times
Box 70
Seattle, WA 98111-1070

West Virginia

Herald Dispatch
Box 2017
946 Fifth Avenue
Huntington, WV 25720

News-Register
1500 Main Street
Wheeling, WV 26003

Wisconsin

Milwaukee Journal
Box 661
Milwaukee, WI 53201-0661

Milwaukee Sentinel
Box 371
Milwaukee, WI 53201-0371

State Journal
Box 8058
Madison, WI 53708

Wyoming

Wyoming Eagle
702 West Lincolnway
Cheyenne, WY 82001

Wyoming State Tribune
702 West Lincolnway
Cheyenne, WY 82001

Parenting

Adoption

Adoptive Families of America
3333 Highway 100 W
Minneapolis, MN 55422
612-535-4829

Missing Persons International
P.O. Box 1337
Canyon Country, CA 91386
805-251-3536

National Adoption Information Clearinghouse
1400 Eye Street, NW
Washington, DC 20005
202-842-1919

Orphan Voyage
2141 Road 2300
Cedaredge, CO 81413
303-856-3937

Yesterday's Children
P.O. Box 1554
Evanston, IL 60204
312-545-6900

Single-Parent Families

America's Society of Separated and Divorced Men
575 Keep Street
Elgin, IL 60120
312-695-2200

Big Brothers/Big Sisters of America
230 North 13th Street
Philadelphia, PA 19107
215-567-7000

Parents Without Partners
8807 Colesville Road
Silver Springs, MD 20910
301-588-9354

Single Mothers By Choice
P.O. Box 1642
Gracie Square Station
New York, NY 10028
212-988-0993

Radio and Television Networks

ABC, Inc.
77 West 66th Street
New York, NY 10023
    ABC Entertainment
    ABC News
    ABC Sports
    ABC Productions
    ABC Radio Networks
    ABC Television Network Group
    Capital Cities/ABC Broadcast Group
    Capital Cities/ABC Publishing Group

American Movie Classics
150 Crossways Park West
Woodbury, NY 11797

Arts & Entertainment Cable Network (A&E)
555 Fifth Avenue
New York, NY 10017

Associated Press Broadcast Services
1825 K Street, NW
Washington, DC 20006-1253
    AP News Service
    Associated Press Broadcasters Inc.
    Radio Division

Black Entertainment Television
1232 31st Street, NW
Washington, DC 20007

Bravo
150 Crossways Park West
Woodbury, NY 11797

Cable News Network (CNN)
One CNN Center
Box 105366
Atlanta, GA 30348-5366

Cable Public Affairs Network (C-SPAN)
400 North Capitol Street, NW
Washington, DC 20001

CBS, Inc.
51 West 52nd Street
New York, NY 10019
    CBS Affiliate Relations Division
    CBS Entertainment Division
    CBS Marketing Division
    CBS News Division
    CBS Operations and Administration
    CBS Radio Division
    CBS Sports Division
    CBS Television Network Division

Cinemax
1100 Avenue of the Americas
New York, NY 10036

Consumer News and Business Channel
2200 Fletcher Avenue
Fort Lee, NJ 07024

The Discovery Channel
8201 Corporate Drive
Landover, MD 20785

The Disney Channel
3800 West Alameda Avenue
Burbank, CA 91505

Entertainment and Sports Programming Network (ESPN)
ESPN Plaza
Bristol, CT 06010

The Family Channel
1000 Centerville Turnpike
Virginia Beach, VA 23463

Financial News Network
600 Third Avenue
New York, NY 10016

Fox Broadcasting Company
10201 West Pico Boulevard
Los Angeles, CA 90035

Home Shopping Networks
Box 9090
Clearwater, FL 34618-9090

The Learning Channel
1525 Wilson Boulevard
Rosslyn, VA 22208

Madison Square Garden Network
Two Pennsylvania Plaza
New York, NY 10121

MTV Networks, Inc.
1515 Broadway
New York, NY 10036

The Nashville Network
Box 10210
250 Harbor Plaza
Stamford, CT 06904-2210

National Public Radio
2025 M Street, NW
Washington, DC 20036

NBC, Inc.
30 Rockefeller Plaza
New York, NY 10112
   NBC Entertainment
   NBC News
   NBC Sports Division
   NBC Television Network
   NBC Television Stations

Nickelodeon
1775 Broadway
New York, NY 10019

PRISM
225 City Avenue
Bala Cynwyd, PA 19004

Public Broadcasting Service
Headquarters
1320 Braddock Place
Alexandria, VA 22314-1698
   National Press Relations/CA
   4401 Sunset Boulevard
   Los Angeles, CA 90027

   National Press Relations/NY
   1790 Broadway
   New York, NY 10019-1412

Reuters Information Services, Inc.
1700 Broadway
New York, NY 10019

Sheridan Broadcasting Networks
One Times Square Plaza
New York, NY 10036

Turner Network Television
One CNN Center
Box 105366
Atlanta, GA 30348-5366

Unistar Radio Networks
660 Southpointe Court
Colorado Springs, CO 80906

United Press International
1400 Eye Street, NW
Washington, DC 20005
   UPI National Broadcast
   UPI Radio Network

USA Network
1230 Avenue of the Americas
New York, NY 10020

Viewer's Choice
909 Third Avenue
New York, NY 10022

The Weather Channel
2600 Cumberland Parkway
Atlanta, GA 30339

Westwood One Inc.
9540 Washington Boulevard
Culver City, CA 90232
   Mutual Broadcasting System, Inc.
   1755 S. Jefferson Davis Highway
   Arlington, VA 22202

   NBC Radio Network
   1755 S. Jefferson Davis Highway
   Arlington, VA 22202

Sports Organizations and Halls of Fame

American and National Basketball Associations
645 Fifth Avenue
New York, NY 10022

American and National Leagues of Professional Baseball Clubs
350 Park Avenue
New York, NY 10022

American Hockey League
425 Union Street
West Springfield, MA 01089-4108

International Association of Sports Museums and Halls of Fame
101 West Sutton Place
Wilmington, DE 19810

Baseball Hall of SHAME
P.O. Box 31867
Palm Beach Gardens, FL 33420

International Boxing Hall of Fame
P.O. Box 425
Canastota, NY 13032

International Tennis Hall of Fame
100 Park Avenue
New York, NY 10017

Naismith Memorial Basketball Hall of Fame
1150 West Columbus Avenue
Springfield, MA 01105

National Association of Professional Baseball Leagues
(minor league clubs)
P.O. Box A
St. Petersburg, FL 33731

Baseball Hall of Fame/Committee on Baseball Veterans
P.O. Box 590
Cooperstown, NY 13326

National Bowling Association
377 Park Avenue South
7th Floor
New York, NY 10016

National Football Foundation and Hall of Fame
Bell Tower Building
1865 Palmer Avenue
Larchmont, NY 10538

National Football League
410 Park Avenue
New York, NY 10022

National Hockey League
960 Sun Life Building
1155 Metcalfe Street
Montreal, PQ, Canada H3B 2W2

Professional Bowler's Association of America
1720 Merriman Road
P.O. Box 5118
Akron, OH 44313

Professional Golfer's Association of America
100 Avenue of Champions
Palm Beach Gardens, FL 33418

Where to Write Your Senators and Representatives

Senators' and representatives' offices are housed in the Capitol Building as well as in six other buildings listed below. However, constituents can write to their senators and representatives as follows.

Senator's name
United States Senate
Washington, DC 20510

Representative's name
United States House of Representatives
Washington, DC 20515

Most government departments and agencies have their own ZIP Codes; the correct one should be used. The Senate ZIP Code differs from that of the House. All Senate office buildings have the 20510 ZIP Code, and all House office buildings have the 20515 ZIP Code.

Listings of specific addresses of members of Congress are in the more current edition of *The Congressional Staff Directory* or *Congressional Quarterly's Washington Directory*, both of which are available in local libraries. These books also list the home offices of members of Congress. Local telephone directories may also be consulted.

Both the Senate and House have offices in the Capitol Building, but additional offices are housed at the following buildings:

Senate Offices

Dirksen Senate Office Building
Constitution Avenue between 1st and
2nd Streets, NE

Hart Senate Office Building
2nd Street and Constitution Avenue, NE

Russell Senate Office Building
Constitution Avenue between Delaware Avenue and
1st Street, NE

House Offices

Cannon House Office Building
Independence Avenue between C and
First Streets, SE

Longworth House Office Building
Independence Avenue between C and South Capitol
Streets, SE

Rayburn House Office Building
Independence Avenue, between South Capitol and
First Streets, SE

Additional Sources of Information

Brobeck, Stephen. *The Modern Consumer Movement: A Guide to Sources.* G. K. Hall, 1990.

Congressional Directory. U.S. Government Printing Office, biannual.

Consumer Guide Buying Guide. Consumer Guide, annual

Consumer Reports Buying Guide. Consumer Reports, annual.

Consumer Sourcebook. Gale Research, biannual.

Eiler, Andrew. *The Consumer Protection Manual.* Facts On File, 1984.

Kenworthy, William E. *Consumer Handbook: How to Make a Claim When You Have Been Sold a Bill of Goods.* Lawprep Press, 1991.

Post-Purchase Remedies. United States Federal Trade Commission, Office of Policy Planning and Evaluation, 1980.

Shilling, Dana. *Fighting Back: A Consumer's Guide for Getting Satisfaction.* Quill, 1982.

19 Travel

Travelers' Checklist / 525

Toll-Free Numbers for Rental Cars and Hotels/Motels / 526

Airline Codes and Toll-Free Airline Numbers / 526

Airport Codes / 527

National Weather Service Average Temperatures—North America / 527

National Weather Service Average Temperatures—Outside North America / 528

Air Mileage from New York City—Domestic / 529

Air Mileage from New York City—Foreign / 529

Foreign Currencies / 530

Foreign Visa Requirements / 532

Passports / 532

Visas / 532

Immunizations / 533

Customs Information / 553

State Tourism Offices / 553

Government Tourist Information Centers / 556

Best Vacation Bets / 558

Theme Parks / 559

Traveling Tips for the Disabled / 559

Traveling with Pets / 560

Travelers' First-Aid Kit / 561

International Auto Registration Marks / 562

Additional Sources of Information / 563

Travelers' Checklist

Things to Do

Arrange for the post office to hold your mail, or have someone collect it daily.
Stop all deliveries to your home.
Arrange for the care of animals, plants, and lawn.
Put valuables in a safe deposit box.
Notify neighbors and police of absence and let them know how you can be reached.
Leave a key with a neighbor.
Arrange for travelers' insurance coverage, if needed.
Notify travel agent of any special needs you might have, such as the use of an airport wheelchair.
Reconfirm your airline ticket and other reservations.
Tag your luggage with brightly colored stickers or ribbons for easy identification.
Set timers or leave a light on.
Empty refrigerator and turn it on low.
Turn off hot water.
Lock all doors and windows.

Things to Bring

Airline or other tickets and travel documents.
Auto registration, if driving.
Passport, visas, and health certificates.
Medical information and doctor's name and telephone number.
Special prescriptions or prescription medications.
Insurance papers.
Credit cards.
Travelers' checks and personal checks.
Cash, including some in the currency of the country to which you are traveling.
Names and addresses of people to contact in an emergency.
Names, addresses, phone numbers, reservation numbers, and dates for places where you will be staying.
Lightweight fold-up tote bag for purchases.
Addresses of friends and family to whom to send mail.

Toll-free Numbers for Rental Cars and Hotels/Motels

Note: In some areas dialing "1" before the number may be necessary.

Car Rental Agencies

Avis 800-331-1212
Budget 800-527-0700
Hertz 800-654-3131
National 800-CAR-RENT

Rent-a-Wreck 800-421-7253
Thrifty 800-367-2277
Ugly Duckling 800-THE-DUCK
Value 800-327-2501

International Car Rental Agencies

Auto Europe 800-223-5555
Avis 800-3310-2112

Europcar 800-CAR-RENT
Hertz 800-654-3001

Hotels/Motels

Best Western 800-528-1234
Hilton 800-HILTONS
Holiday Inn 800-HOLIDAY
Hotels of the World 800-223-6800
   Atlantic City, Reno, Las Vegas, and Tahoe Hotels 800-255-5722
   Condo Reservations 800-321-2525

Howard Johnson 800-654-2000
Hyatt 800-228-9000
Marriott 800-228-9290
Ramada Inn 800-2-RAMADA
Red Lion 800-547-8010

Airline Codes and Toll-free Airline Numbers

Note: In some areas, dialing "1" before the number may be necessary.

EI	AerLingus 800-223-6537	NW	Northwest Airlines, domestic 800-225-2525
AM	Aeromexico 800-237-6639		Northwest Airlines, international 800-447-4747
AF	Air France 800-237-2747		
AS	Alaska Airlines 800-426-0333		
AZ	Alitalia 800-223-5730	QF	Qantas 800-227-4500
AA	American Airlines 800-433-7300	SA	Scandinavian Air 800-221-2350
BA	British Airways 800-247-9297	SR	Swissair 800-221-4750
CO	Continental Airlines 800-525-0280	TW	TWA, domestic 800-221-2000
DL	Delta Airlines 800-221-1212	TW	TWA, international 800-892-4141
EA	Eastern Airlines 800-EASTERN	UA	United Airlines 800-24106522
JL	Japan Airlines 800-424-9235	AL	US Air 800-428-4322
LH	Lufthansa 800-645-3880		

AIRPORT CODES

ATL	Atlanta International Airport	LAX	Los Angeles International Airport
BOS	Logan International Airport (Boston)	LGA	LaGuardia Airport (New York City)
BWI	Baltimore-Washington International Airport	MCO	Orlando International Airport
		MIA	Miami International Airport
CLT	Charlotte Airport	MSP	Minneapolis-St. Paul International Airport
DFW	Dallas-Ft. Worth Airport		
DTW	Detroit Metro Wayne County Airport	MSY	New Orleans International Airport
HOU	Houston Hobby Airport	ORD	Chicago O'Hare Field
IAD	Dulles International Airport (Washington, D.C.)	PHL	Philadelphia International Airport
		SEA	Seattle International Airport
IAH	Houston Inter-Continental Airport	SFO	San Francisco International Airport
JFK	John F. Kennedy International Airport (New York City)		

National Weather Service Average Temperatures (Fahrenheit) — North America

Location	Jan–Mar (Avg high/low)	Apr–Jun (Avg high/low)	Jul–Sep (Avg high/low)	Oct–Dec (Avg high/low)
Acapulco	88/72	90/77	90/75	90/72
Bermuda	68/57	81/59	85/72	79/60
Boston	43/20	75/38	80/55	62/25
Chicago	43/18	75/40	81/58	88/23
Dallas	67/36	90/55	94/68	78/38
Detroit	42/19	77/37	82/55	60/24
Honolulu	77/67	81/68	83/73	82/69
Houston	72/44	90/60	83/70	81/52
Las Vegas	72/29	99/45	103/57	84/30
Los Angeles	67/46	76/50	82/58	76/47
Mexico City	75/42	78/51	74/53	70/43
Miami	78/61	86/67	88/75	83/62
Nassau	79/64	87/69	89/75	85/67
New Orleans	71/47	88/61	90/73	79/48
New York City	45/24	77/42	82/60	69/29
Oklahoma City	62/28	87/49	92/63	73/30
Philadelphia	49/26	80/43	85/60	66/30
Phoenix	75/39	101/53	104/69	86/40
Port-au-Prince	89/68	92/71	94/73	90/69
St. Lucia	84/69	88/71	88/73	87/70
Salt Lake City	51/17	82/38	92/49	66/22
San Diego	64/47	69/53	74/62	71/52

Location	Jan–Mar (Avg high/low)	Apr–Jun (Avg high/low)	Jul–Sep (Avg high/low)	Oct–Dec (Avg high/low)
San Francisco	61/45	66/49	69/53	68/47
San Juan	80/70	85/72	86/75	85/72
Santa Fe	51/19	78/35	80/49	62/20
Santo Domingo	89/68	92/71	94/73	90/69
Seattle	52/36	69/43	72/52	59/38
Toronto	37/15	73/34	79/51	56/21
Vancouver	50/32	69/40	74/49	57/35
Washington, D.C.	53/27	83/44	87/59	67/29

National Weather Service Average Temperatures (Fahrenheit) — Outside North America

Location	Jan–Mar (Avg high/low)	Apr–Jun (Avg high/low)	Jul–Sep (Avg high/low)	Oct–Dec (Avg high/low)
Athens	60/44	86/52	92/67	75/47
Bangkok	93/68	95/76	90/76	88/68
Berlin	46/26	72/39	75/50	56/29
Bogotá	68/48	67/51	66/49	66/49
Buenos Aires	85/60	72/41	64/42	82/50
Cairo	75/47	95/57	96/68	86/50
Calcutta	93/55	97/75	90/78	89/55
Caracas	79/56	81/60	80/61	79/58
Dublin	51/34	65/39	67/48	57/37
Hong Kong	67/55	85/67	87/77	81/59
Java	86/74	87/74	88/73	87/74
Jerusalem	65/41	85/50	87/62	81/45
Istanbul	51/37	77/45	82/61	68/41
Kathmandu	77/35	86/53	84/66	80/37
Lima	83/66	80/58	68/56	78/58
Lisbon	63/46	77/53	82/62	72/47
London	50/36	69/42	71/52	58/38
Madrid	59/35	80/45	87/57	65/36
Manila	91/69	93/73	88/75	88/70
Montevideo	83/59	71/43	63/43	79/49
Munich	48/23	70/38	74/48	56/26
Nairobi	79/54	75/53	75/51	76/55
Panama	90/71	87/74	87/74	87/73
Paris	54/34	73/43	76/53	60/36
Quito	72/46	71/45	73/44	72/45
Rio de Janeiro	85/72	80/64	76/63	82/66
Rome	59/40	82/50	87/62	71/44
Santiago	85/49	74/37	66/37	83/45

Location	Jan–Mar (Avg high/low)	Apr–Jun (Avg high/low)	Jul–Sep (Avg high/low)	Oct–Dec (Avg high/low)
Seoul	47/15	80/41	87/59	67/20
Singapore	88/73	89/75	88/75	87/74
Taipei	70/53	89/63	92/73	81/57
Tokyo	54/29	76/46	86/66	69/33

Air Mileage from New York City— Domestic

Albuquerque	1,810		Nashville	758
Atlanta	747		New Orleans	1,173
Baltimore	170		Omaha	1,144
Boston	188		Philadelphia	83
Chicago	711		Phoenix	2,142
Denver	1,628		Portland	2,455
Detroit	483		St. Louis	873
Kansas City, MO	1,097		Salt Lake City	1,972
Los Angeles	2,446		San Francisco	2,568
Memphis	953		Seattle	2,419
Miami	1,095		Washington, D.C.	204

Air Mileage from New York City— Foreign

Acapulco	2,260		Lima	3,651
Amsterdam	3,639		Lisbon	3,366
Antigua	1,783		London	3,456
Aruba	1,963		Madrid	3,588
Athens	4,927		Manchester	3,336
Barbados	2,100		Mexico City	2,086
Bermuda	771		Milan	4,004
Bogotá	2,487		Nassau	1,101
Brussels	3,662		Oslo	3,671
Buenos Aires	5,302		Paris	3,628
Caracas	2,123		Reykjavík	2,600
Copenhagen	3,849		Rio de Janeiro	4,816
Curaçao	1,993		Rome	4,280
Frankfurt	3,851		St. Croix	1,680
Geneva	3,859		San Juan	1,609
Glasgow	3,211		Santo Domingo	1,560
Hamburg	3,806		Tel Aviv	5,672
Kingston	1,583		Zurich	3,926

Foreign Currencies

This chart lists the official names for selected currencies around the world. Colonial legacies have made certain names—dollar, peso, franc, and pound, for example—widespread. The traveler should not assume equivalency in value, or transferability, among units sharing a name; that is, one cannot spend Central African *francs* in France or Turkish *lira* in Rome.

Afghanistan	afghani	Cuba	peso
Albania	lek	Cyprus	pound
Algeria	dinar	Czech and Slovak	
Andorra	French franc	Federal Republic	koruna
	Spanish peseta	Denmark	krone
Angola	kwanza	Djibouti	franc
Antigua and Barbuda	East Caribbean dollar	Dominica	East Caribbean dollar
Argentina	austral	Dominican Republic	peso
Australia	dollar	Ecuador	sucre
Austria	schilling	Egypt	pound
Bahamas	dollar	El Salvador	colon
Bahrain	dinar	Equatorial Guinea	ekuele
Bangladesh	taka	Ethiopia	birr
Barbados	dollar	Fiji	dollar
Belgium	franc	Finland	markka
Belize	dollar	France	franc
Benin	franc CFA*	Gabon	franc CFA*
Bhutan	ngultrum	Gambia	dalasi
Bolivia	peso	Germany	mark
Bophuthatswana	South African rand	Ghana	cedi
Botswana	pula	Greece	drachma
Brazil	cruzado	Grenada	East Caribbean dollar
Brunei	dollar	Guatemala	quetzal
Bulgaria	lev	Guinea	syli
Burkina Faso	franc CFA*	Guinea-Bissau	peso
Burundi	franc	Guyana	dollar
Cambodia	riel	Haiti	gourde
Cameroon	franc CFA*	Honduras	lempira
Canada	dollar	Hungary	forint
Cape Verde	escudo	Iceland	krona
Central Africa	franc CFA*	India	rupee
Chad	franc CFA*	Indonesia	rupiah
Chile	peso	Iran	rial
China	yuan	Iraq	dinar
Ciskei	South African rand	Ireland	pound
Colombia	peso	Israel	shekel
Commonwealth of		Italy	lira
Independent States	ruble	Ivory Coast	franc CFA*
Comoros	franc CFA*	Jamaica	dollar
Congo	franc CFA*	Japan	yen
Costa Rica	colon	Jordan	dinar

Kenya	shilling	St. Kitts and Nevis	East Caribbean dollar
Kiribati	Australian dollar	St. Lucia	East Caribbean dollar
Korea, North	won	St. Vincent and the Grenadines	East Caribbean dollar
Korea, South	won	San Marino	Italian lira
Kuwait	dinar	São Tomé and Principe	dobra
Laos	kip	Saudi Arabia	riyal
Lebanon	pound	Senegal	franc CFA*
Lesotho	loti	Seychelles	rupee
Liberia	dollar	Sierra Leone	leone
Libya	dinar	Singapore	dollar
Liechtenstein	Swiss franc	Solomons	dollar
Luxembourg	franc	Somalia	shilling
Madagascar	franc	South Africa	rand
Malawi	ringgit	Spain	peseta
Maldives	rupee	Sri Lanka	rupee
Mali	franc CFA*	Sudan	pound
Malta	pound	Suriname	guilder
Marshalls	dollar	Swaziland	lilangeni
Mauritania	ouguiya	Sweden	krona
Mauritius	rupee	Switzerland	franc
Mexico	peso	Syria	pound
Micronesia	dollar	Taiwan	New Taiwan dollar
Monaco	French franc	Tanzania	shilling
Mongolia	tugrik	Thailand	baht
Morocco	dirham	Togo	franc CFA*
Mozambique	metical	Tonga	dollar
Myanmar	kyat	Transkei	South African rand
Namibia	South African rand	Trinidad and Tobago	dollar
Nauru	Australian dollar	Tunisia	dinar
Nepal	rupee	Turkey	lira
Netherlands	guilder	Tuvalu	Australian dollar
New Zealand	dollar	Uganda	shilling
Nicaragua	cordoba	United Arab Emirates	dirham
Niger	franc CFA*	United Kingdom	pound sterling
Nigeria	naira	United States	dollar
Norway	krone	Uruguay	peso
Oman	rial	Vanuatu	vatu
Pakistan	rupee	Vatican City	lira
Palau	dollar	Venda	South African rand
Panama	balboa	Venezuela	bolivar
Papua New Guinea	kina	Vietnam	dong
Paraguay	guarani	Western Samoa	tala
Peru	inti	Yemen, North	rial
Philippines	peso	Yemen, South	dinar
Poland	zloty	Yugoslavia	dinar
Portugal	escudo	Zaire	zaire
Qatar	riyal	Zambia	kwacha
Romania	leu	Zimbabwe	dollar
Rwanda	franc		

* Communauté financière africaine (African Financial Community)

Foreign Visa Requirements

This listing is prepared solely for the information of U.S. citizens traveling as tourists and does not apply to persons planning to immigrate to foreign countries. A visa is generally an endorsement or stamp placed by officials of a foreign country on a U.S. passport that allows the bearer to visit that country.

IMPORTANT: TRAVELERS SHOULD CHECK PASSPORT AND VISA REQUIREMENTS WITH THE CONSULAR OFFICIALS OF THE COUNTRIES TO BE VISITED WELL IN ADVANCE OF THEIR DEPARTURE DATES, SINCE SUCH INFORMATION IS SUBJECT TO CHANGE.

Passports

Persons who travel to a country where a U.S. passport is not required should have documentary evidence of their U.S. citizenship and identity to facilitate reentry into the United States. Countries that do not require a passport to enter or depart frequently require this evidence. Documentary evidence of U.S. citizenship may be an expired passport, a certified birth certificate, certificate of naturalization, certificate of citizenship, or report of birth abroad of a citizen of the United States. Documentary evidence of identity may be a valid driver's license or government identification provided they identify you by physical description or photograph.

Some Arab or African countries will not issue visas or allow entry if your passport gives evidence of travel to Israel or South Africa. If this applies to you, consult the nearest U.S. passport agency for guidance.

Visas

NECESSARY VISAS SHOULD BE OBTAINED BEFORE PROCEEDING ABROAD. Allow sufficient time for processing your visa application, especially if you apply by mail. Most foreign consular representatives are located in principal cities, particularly Chicago, New Orleans, New York, San Francisco, and Washington, D.C. In many instances, a traveler may be required to obtain visas from the consular office in the area of his or her residence. Addresses of foreign consular offices in the United States may be obtained by consulting the *Congressional Directory,* which is available in most libraries. **IT IS THE RESPONSIBILITY OF THE TRAVELER TO OBTAIN VISAS, WHERE REQUIRED, FROM THE APPROPRIATE EMBASSY OR NEAREST CONSULATE OF THE COUNTRY TO BE VISITED.** Further assistance may be obtained from travel agents and from visa information services such as World Wide Visas (800-527-1861) and International Visa Service (800-627-1112).

Immunizations

Under the International Health Regulations adopted by the World Health Organization, a country may require certificates of vaccination against yellow fever. A few countries still require a cholera immunization as well. Check with health-care providers or your records to ensure other immunizations (for example, tetanus and polio) are up-to-date. Prophylactic medication for malaria and certain other preventive measures are advisable for some travelers. No immunizations are required to return to the United States. Pertinent information is included in *Health Information for International Travel,* available from the U.S. Government Printing Office, Washington, D.C. 20402 for $5.00, or it may be obtained from your local health department or physician or by calling the Centers for Disease Control at 404-639-2572.

An increasing number of countries have established regulations regarding AIDS testing, particularly for long-term visitors. Check with the embassy or consulate of the country you plan to visit for the latest information on whether this is a requirement for entry.

Afghanistan: Passport and visa required. Tourist visa requires application forms, two photos and $10 fee. Business visa requires Afghan sponsor, two applications, two photos and $10 fee. Journalists must have letter stating purpose of visit, letter from employer, résumé, and published articles on Afghanistan. Visas must be approved by authorities in Afghanistan. Allow ample time for processing. For further information contact Embassy of the Republic of Afghanistan, 2341 Wyoming Avenue, NW, Washington, DC 20008 (202-234-3770-1).

Albania: Passport and visa required. Apply Albanian Mission, 131 Rue de la Pompe, Paris 16e France, or Via Asmara 9, Rome, Italy, or any other country that maintains diplomatic relations with Albania. (At the time of publication there was no Albanian Embassy or Consulate in the United States.)

Algeria: Passport and visa required. Obtain visa before arrival. Visa valid up to 90 days, requires two application forms, two photos, proof of onward/return transportation, sufficient funds, and $22 fee (money order or certified check). Company letter required for business visa. Visa not granted to passports showing Israeli or South African visas. Enclose prepaid self-addressed envelope for return of passport by registered, certified, or express mail. For currency regulations and other information, contact the Consular Section of the Embassy of the Democratic and Popular Republic of Algeria, 2137 Wyoming Avenue, NW, Washington, DC 20008 (202-265-2800).

Andorra: *See* **France.**

Angola: Passport and visa required. There is no U.S. representation in Angola at this time. Travel by U.S. citizens is not recommended. For additional information contact the Angolan Permanent Representative to the U.N., 747 Third Avenue, 18th Floor, New York, N.Y. 10017.

Antigua and Barbuda: Proof of U.S. citizenship required, return/onward ticket and/or proof of funds needed for tourist stay up to six months. AIDS test required for university students and others suspected of having HIV virus; U.S. test accepted. Check Embassy of Antigua and Barbuda, Intelsat Building, Suite 4M, 3400 International Drive, NW, Washington, DC 20008 (202-362-5122/5166/5211) for further information.

Argentina: Passport required. Visa not required for tourist stay up to three months. For official and other types of travel contact Argentine Embassy, 1600 New Hampshire Avenue, NW, Washington, DC 20009 (202-939-6400), or the nearest Consulate: CA (213-739-5959 and 415-982-3050), FL (305-373-1889), IL (312-263-7435), LA (504-523-2823), NY (212-603-0415), PR (809-754-6500), or TX (713-871-8935).

Armenia: Passport and visa required. For additional information contact Embassy of Russia, 1825 Phelps Place, NW, Washington, DC 20008 (202-939-8916), or the Russian Consulate: San Francisco (415-922-6642).

Aruba: Passport or proof of U.S. citizenship required. Visa not required to stay up to 14 days, extendable to 90 days after arrival. Proof of onward/return ticket or sufficient funds for stay may be required. Departure tax $9.50. For further information consult Embassy of the Netherlands (202-244-5300), or nearest Consulate General: CA (212-380-3440), IL (314-856-1429), NY (212-246-1429), or TX (713-622-8000).

Australia: Passport, visa, and onward/return transportation required. Transit visa not necessary for up to eight-hour stay at airport. Visitor visa valid one year for multiple entries up to six months, no charge, requires one application and one photo. Need company letter for business visa. Departure tax, $20 (Australian), paid at airport. Minors not accompanied by parent require notarized written parental consent from both parents. AIDS test required for permanent resident visa applicants age 15 and over; U.S. test accepted. Send prepaid envelope for return of passport by mail. Allow three weeks for processing. For further information contact the Embassy of Australia, 1601 Massachusetts Avenue, NW, Washington, DC 20036 (800-242-2878, 202-797-3000), or the nearest Consulate General: CA (213-280-0980 or 415-363-6160), HI (808-524-5050), IL (312-645-9440), NY (212-245-4000), or TX (713-629-9131).

Austria: Passport required. Visa not required for stay up to three months. For longer stays check with Embassy of Austria, 3524 International Court, NW, Washington, DC 20008 (202-895-6767), or nearest Consulate General: Los Angeles (213-444-9310), Chicago (312-222-1515), or New York (212-737-6400).

Azerbaijan: Passport and visa required. For additional information contact Embassy of Russia, 1825 Phelps Place, NW, Washington, DC 20008 (202-939-8916), or the Consulate General: San Francisco (415-922-6642).

Azores: *See* **Portugal.**

Bahamas: Proof of U.S. citizenship, photo ID and onward/return ticket required for stay up to eight months. Passport and residence/work permit needed for residence and business. Permit required for firearms and to import pets. Departure tax of $10 and security tax of $3 payable at airport. For further information call Embassy of the Commonwealth of the Bahamas, 2220 Massachusetts Avenue, NW, Washington, DC 20008 (202-319-2660), or nearest Consulate: Miami (305-373-6295) or New York (212-421-6420).

Bahrain: Passport and visa required. No tourist visas issued at this time. Transit visa available upon arrival for stay up to 72 hours, must have return/onward ticket. Business, work, or resident visas valid for three months, single-entry, require one application form, one photo, letter from company or No Objection Certificate (NOC) from Immigration Department in Bahrain and $30 fee ($20 for bearer of NOC). Yellow fever vaccination needed if arriving from infected area. Send SASE for return of passport by mail. Holders of passports bearing Israeli stamps will be delayed or denied entry. For departure tax and other information contact Embassy of the State of Bahrain, 3502 International Drive, NW, Washington, DC 20008 (202-342-0741/2); or the Permanent Mission to the United Nations, 2 United Nations Plaza, East 44th Street, New York, NY 10017 (212-223-6200).

Bangladesh: Passport and onward/return ticket required. Visa not required for tourist stay up to 14 days. Business visa requires two application forms, two photos, and company letter. Send SASE for return of passport by mail. For official/diplomatic travel, visa required and must be obtained in advance. Consult Embassy of the People's Republic of Bangladesh, 2201 Wisconsin Avenue, NW, Washington, DC 20007 (202-342-8373).

Barbados: If traveling directly from the United States to Barbados you may enter for up to three months with proof of U.S. citizenship, photo ID, and onward/return ticket. Passport required for longer visits and other types of travel. Business visas $25, single-entry and $30 multiple-entry (may require work permit). Departure tax of $25 is paid at airport. Check information with Embassy of Barbados, 2144 Wyoming Avenue, NW, Washington, DC 20008 (202-939-9200), or Consulate General in New York (212-867-8435).

Belgium: Passport required. Visa not required for business/tourist stay up to 90 days. Temporary residence permit required for longer stays. For residence authorization, consult Embassy of Belgium, 3330 Garfield Street, NW, Washington, DC 20008 (202-333-6900), or nearest Consulate General: Los Angeles (213-857-1244), Atlanta (404-659-2150), Chicago (312-263-6624), or New York (212-586-5110).

Belize: Passport, return/onward ticket, and sufficient funds required. Visa not required for stay up to one month. If visit exceeds one month, a stay permit must be obtained from the Immigration Authorities in Belize. AIDS test required for those staying more than three months; U.S. test accepted if within three months of visit. For longer stays and other information contact Embassy of Belize, Suite 2-J, 3400 International Drive, NW, Washington, DC 20008 (202-363-4505), or the Belize Mission in New York (212-599-0233).

Benin: Passport and visa required. Entry/transit visa for stay up to 90 days, requires $12 fee (no personal checks), two application forms, two photos, vaccination certificates for yellow fever and cholera, proof of return/onward transportation (guarantee from travel agency or photocopy of round-trip ticket), and letter of guarantee from employer. Send prepaid envelope for return of passport by certified or express mail. Apply at Embassy of the Republic of Benin, 2737 Cathedral Avenue, NW, Washington, DC 20008 (202-232-6656).

Bermuda: Proof of U.S. citizenship, photo ID, and onward/return ticket required for tourist stay up to 21 days. Departure tax $10 is paid at airport. For further information consult British Embassy (202-462-1340).

Bhutan: Passport and visa required. Visa requires $20 fee, two applications, and two photos. Tourist visas arranged by Tourism Department and issued at entry checkpoints in Bhutan. Apply two months in advance. For further information call the Consulate of the Kingdom of Bhutan in New York (212-826-1919).

Bolivia: Passport required. Visa not required for tourist stay up to 30 days. Business visa requires $50 fee and company letter with purpose of trip (no photo or application necessary). Send SASE for return of passport by mail. For official/diplomatic travel contact Embassy of Bolivia (Consular Section), 3014 Massachusetts Avenue, NW, Washington, DC 20008 (202-232-4828 or 483-4410) or nearest Consulate General: San Francisco (415-495-5173), Miami (305-358-3450), New York (212-687-0530), or Houston (713-780-8001). Check requirements for pets.

Botswana: Passport required. Visa not required for stay up to 90 days. For further information contact Embassy of the Republic of Botswana, Suite 7M, 3400 International Drive, NW, Washington, DC 20008 (202-244-4990/1), or nearest Honorary Consulate: Los Angeles (213-626-8484), San Francisco (415-346-4435), or Houston (713-622-1900).

Brazil: Passport and visa required. Visa must be obtained in advance. Multiple-entry visa valid up to 90 days (extendable), requires one application form, one photo, proof of onward/return transportation or notarized letter from bank as proof of sufficient funds for stay and yellow fever vaccination if arriving from infected area. No charge if you apply in person; $10 service fee if you apply by mail. Provide SASE for return of passport by mail. For travel with children or business visa contact Brazilian Embassy (Consular Section), 3009 Whitehaven Street, NW, Washington, DC 20008 (202-745-2828), or nearest Consulate: CA (213-282-3133), FL (305-377-1734), GA (404-659-0660), IL (312-372-2177), LA (504-588-9187), or NY (212-757-3080).

Brunei: Passport and visa required. Visa must be obtained in advance. Visa valid three months, requires $7.50 fee, one application form, two photos, letter stating purpose of visit, itinerary, onward/return ticket, and proof of sufficient funds. Yellow fever vaccination needed if arriving from infected area. Include prepaid envelope for return of passport by certified/registered mail. Allow at least one week for processing. For diplomatic/official travel and other visas, contact Embassy of the State of Brunei Darussalam, Suite 300, 2600 Virginia Avenue, NW, Washington, DC 20037 (202-342-0159), or Brunei Permanent Mission to the United Nations, 866 United Nations Plaza, Room 248, New York, NY 10017 (212-838-1600).

Bulgaria: Passport required. Tourist visa not required for stay up to 30 days. AIDS test required for those staying more than one month; U.S. test not accepted. For business visas and other information contact Embassy of the Republic of Bulgaria, 1621 22nd Street, NW, Washington, DC 20008 (202-387-7969 or 483-5885).

Burkina Faso: Passport and visa required. Single-entry visa valid three months for visit up to one month, extendable, requires $20 fee, two application forms, two photos, and yellow fever vaccination (cholera immunization recommended). Send passport by registered mail and include postage or prepaid envelope for return. Cash or money order only. For further information call Embassy of Burkina Faso, 2340 Massachusetts Avenue, NW, Washington, DC 20008 (202-332-5577), or Honorary Consulate in Decatur, GA (404-378-7278), Los Angeles, CA (213-824-5100), or New Orleans, LA (504-945-3152).

Burma: *See* **Myanmar**.

Burundi: Passport and visa required. Obtain visa before arrival to avoid long airport delay. Multientry visa valid for two months (must be used within two months of date of issue) requires $11 fee, three application forms, three photos, yellow fever and cholera immunizations, and return/onward ticket. Company letter needed for business travel. Send cash or U.S. postal money order only and SASE for return of passport by mail. For further information consult Embassy of the Republic of Burundi, Suite 212, 2233 Wisconsin Avenue, NW, Washington, DC 20007 (202-342-2574), or Permanent Mission of Burundi to the United Nations (212-687-1180).

Byelorussia: Passport and visa required. For additional information contact Embassy of Russia, 1825 Phelps Place, NW, Washington, DC 20008 (202-939-8916), or the Consulate General: San Francisco (415-922-6642).

Cambodia (formerly Kampuchea): The United States does not maintain diplomatic or consular relations with Cambodia and has no third country representing U.S. interests there. Travel by U.S. citizens is not recommended. Attention: U.S. citizens need a Treasury Department license in order to engage in any transactions related to travel to and within Cambodia. Before planning any travel to Cambodia, U.S. citizens should contact the Licensing Division, Office of Foreign Assets Control, Department of the Treasury, 1331 G Street, NW, Washington, DC 20220 (202-566-2701). Visa information must be obtained from a consulate in a country that maintains diplomatic relations with Cambodia.

Cameroon: Passport and visa required. Obtain visa before arrival to avoid difficulty at airport. Multiple-entry tourist visa for stay up to 90 days, requires $44.44 fee, two application forms, two photos, yellow fever and cholera immunizations, proof of onward/return transportation, and bank statement. If invited by family or friends, visa available for up to three months, may be extended one month. Invitation must be signed by authorities in Cameroon. Multiple-entry business visa, valid 12 months, requires company letter to guarantee financial and legal responsibility; include exact dates of travel. Enclose prepaid envelope for return of passport by registered, certified, or express mail. For additional information contact Embassy of the Republic of Cameroon, 2349 Massachusetts Avenue, NW, Washington, DC 20008 (202-265-8790 to 8794).

Canada: Proof of U.S. citizenship and photo ID required. Visa not required for tourists entering from the United States for a stay up to 180 days. U.S. citizens entering Canada from a third country must have a valid passport or official U.S. travel document. For student or business travel, check with the Canadian Embassy, 501 Pennsylvania Avenue, NW, Washington, DC 20001 (202-682-1740), or nearest Consulate General: CA (213-687-7432 and 415-541-7708), GA (404-577-6810), IL (312-427-1031), MA (617-262-3760), MI (313-567-2340), MN (612-336-4641), NY (212-586-2400), OH (216-771-1660), TX (214-922-9806), or WA (206-443-1777).

Cape Verde: Passport and visa required. Single-entry tourist visa (must be used within 120 days of issue), requires $12 fee, one application form, one photo, and yellow fever immunization if arriving from infected area. Include SASE for return of passport by mail. For further information contact the Embassy of the Republic of Cape Verde, 3415 Massachusetts Avenue, NW, Washington, DC 20007 (202-965-6820), or Consulate General, 535 Boylston Street, Boston, MA 02116 (617-353-0014).

Cayman Islands: *See* **West Indies, British.**

Central African Republic: Passport and visa required. Visa must be obtained before arrival. Multientry visa valid for one month requires $17.24 fee. Multientry visa valid for three months requires 34.48 fee. To obtain a visa you need 2 application forms, 2 photos, yellow fever immunization, onward/return ticket, and SASE for return of passport by mail. Company letter needed for business visa. For further information contact Embassy of Central African Republic, 1618 22nd Street, NW, Washington, DC 20008 (202-483-7800).

Chad: Passport and visa required. Transit visa valid for up to one week, onward ticket required. Single-entry visa valid two months for tourist/business stay up to 30 days (extendable), requires $12.25 fee, yellow fever and cholera vaccinations, three application forms, and three photos. For business visa need company letter stating purpose of trip. Send prepaid envelope for registered/certified return of passport. Apply Embassy of the Republic of Chad, 2002 R Street, NW, Washington, DC 20009 (202-462-4009), and check specific requirements.

Chile: Passport required. Visa not required for stay up to three months, may be extended. For official/diplomatic travel and other information consult Embassy of Chile, 1732 Massachusetts Avenue, NW, Washington, DC 20036 (202-785-3159), or nearest Consulate General: CA (213-624-6357 and 415-982-7662), FL (305-373-8623), PA (215-829-9520), NY (212-980-3366), or TX (713-621-5853).

China, People's Republic of: Passport and visa required. Transit visa required for any stop (even if you do not exit the plane or train) in China. Visitors must show hotel reservation and "letter of confirmation" from the China International Travel Service (CITS) or an invitation from an individual or institution in China. CITS tours may be booked through several different travel agencies and airlines in the United States and abroad, often advertised in newspapers and magazines. Visas for tour group members are usually obtained by the travel agent as part of the tour package. Visa requires $10 fee, two application forms, and two photos. Allow at least 10 days for processing. Medical examination required for those staying one year or longer. AIDS test required for those staying more than six months. For further information contact Chinese Embassy, 2300 Connecticut Avenue, NW, Washington, DC 20008 (202-328-2517), or nearest Consulate General: Chicago (312-346-0287), Houston (713-524-0780), Los Angeles (213-380-2508), New York (212-279-4275), or San Francisco (415-563-4885).

Colombia: Passport and proof of onward/return ticket required for stay up to 90 days. For information about longer stays, business, and official travel, contact Embassy of Colombia (Consulate), 1825 Connecticut Avenue, NW, Washington, DC 20009 (202-332-7476), or nearest Consulate General: CA (415-362-0080), FL (305-448-5558), IL (312-341-0658), LA (504-525-5580), NY (212-949-9898), PR (809-754-1675), or TX (713-527-8919).

Comoros Islands: Passport and onward/return ticket required. Visa for up to three weeks (extendable) issued at airport upon arrival. For further information consult Embassy of the Federal and Islamic Republic of Comoros, 336 East 45th Street, 2nd Floor, New York, NY 10017 (212-972-8010).

Congo: Passport and visa required. Single-entry visa fee $15 or multiple-entry $20, for tourist/business stay up to three months, requires yellow fever and cholera immunizations and onward/return ticket. First-time applicants need three application forms and three photos; returning visitors need only two. For business visa must have company letter stating reason for trip. Include SASE for return of passport by mail. Letter of introduction stating reason for trip, three applications, and three photos required. Apply Embassy of the People's Republic of the Congo, 4891 Colorado Avenue, NW, Washington, DC 20011 (202-726-5500/1).

Cook Islands: Passport and onward/return ticket required. Visa not needed for visit up to 31 days. For longer stays and further information contact Consulate for the Cook Islands, Kamehameha Schools, #16, Kapalama Heights, Honolulu, HI 96817 (808-847-6377).

Costa Rica: Valid passport required. Travelers are sometimes admitted with (original) certified U.S. birth certificate and photo ID for tourist stay up to 90 days. Tourist card issued upon arrival at airport. U.S. citizens must have onward/return ticket. For stays over 90 days, you must apply for an extension (within first week of visit) with Costa Rican Immigration and, after 90 days, obtain exit visa and possess a valid U.S. passport. Visitors staying over 90 days must have an AIDS test performed in Costa Rica. For travel with pets and other information contact Embassy of Costa Rica, 1825 Connecticut Avenue, NW, Suite 211, Washington, DC 20009 (202-328-6628 and 234-2495), or nearest Consulate General: CA (415-392-8488), FL (305-377-4242), IL (312-263-2772), LA (504-525-5445), NY (212-425-2620), or TX (713-785-1315).

Côte D'Ivoire (formerly Ivory Coast): Passport required. Visa not required for stay up to 90 days. Visa $33, requires four application forms, four photos, yellow fever vaccination, onward/return ticket, and financial guarantee. Include postage for return of passport by registered mail. For further information contact Embassy of the Republic of Cote D'Ivoire, 2424 Massachusetts Avenue, NW, Washington, DC 20008 (202-797-0300), or Honorary Consulates: CA (213-550-1288 and 415-391-0176) or AZ (602-257-0922).

Cuba: Passport and visa required. Tourist visa $26, business visa $36, valid for up to six months, requires one application and photo. Send cash or money order only and SASE for return of passport. Apply Cuban Interests Section, 2639 16th Street, NW, Washington, DC 20009 (202-797-8609 or 8518). AIDS test required for those staying longer than 90 days. **Attention:** U.S. citizens need a Treasury Department license in order to engage in any transactions related to travel to and within Cuba. Before planning any travel to Cuba, U.S. citizens should contact the Licensing Division, Office of Foreign Assets Control, Department of the Treasury, 1331 G Street, NW, Washington, DC 20220 (202-566-2701).

Curaçao: *See* **Netherlands Antilles.**

Cyprus: Passport required. Tourist/business visa issued upon arrival for stay up to three months. Departure tax of $8 paid at airport. AIDS test required for certain entertainers; U.S. test accepted. For other information consult Embassy of the Republic of Cyprus, 2211 R Street, NW, Washington, DC 20008 (202-462-5772), or nearest Consulate: San Francisco (415-893-1661), Chicago (312-677-9068), St. Louis (314-781-7040), or New York (212-686-6016).

Czech Republic: Passport required. Visa not required for stay up 30 days. For longer stays and other types of travel contact Embassy of the Czech Republic, 3900 Linnean Avenue, NW, Washington, DC 20008 (202-363-6315).

Denmark (including **Greenland**): Passport required. Tourist/business visa not required for stay up to three months. (Period begins when entering Scandinavian area: Finland, Iceland, Norway, Sweden.) Special rules apply for entry into the U.S.-operated defense area in Greenland. For further information contact the Royal Danish Embassy, 3200 Whitehaven Street, NW, Washington, DC 20008 (202-234-4300), or nearest Consulate General: CA (213-387-4277), Chicago (312-329-9644), or New York (212-223-4545).

Djibouti: Passport and visa required. Visas must be obtained before arrival. Single-entry visa valid for 30 days, extendable, requires $15 fee, two applications, two photos, yellow fever immunization, onward/return ticket, and sufficient funds. Company letter needed for business visa. Send prepaid envelope for return of passport by registered, certified, or express mail. Apply Embassy of the Republic of Djibouti, 1156 15th Street, NW, Suite 515, Washington, DC 20005 (202-331-0270), or the Djibouti Mission to the U.N., 866 United Nations Plaza, Suite 4011, New York, NY 10017 (212-753-3163).

Dominica: Proof of U.S. citizenship, photo ID, and return/onward ticket required for tourist stay up to six months. For longer stays and other information consult Consulate of the Commonwealth of Dominica, 820 2nd Avenue, Suite 900, New York, NY 10017 (212-599-8478).

Dominican Republic: Passport or proof of U.S. citizenship and tourist card or visa required. Tourist card for stay up to 60 days, available from Consulate or from airline serving the country, $10 fee. Visa issued by Consulate, valid up to five years, no charge. All persons are required to pay $20 departure fee. For business travel and other information call the Embassy of the Dominican Republic, 1715 22nd Street, NW, Washington, DC 20008 (202-332-6280), or nearest Consulate General: CA (213-858-7365), FL (305-358-3221), IL (312-772-6362), LA (504-522-1843), MA (617-482-8121), NY (212-768-2480), PA (215-923-3006), or PR (809-725-9550).

Ecuador: Passport and return/onward ticket required for stay up to three months. For additional information contact the Embassy of Ecuador, 2535 15th Street, NW, Washington, DC 20009 (202-234-7166), or nearest Consulate General: CA (213-628-3014 or 415-391-4148), FL (305-539-8214), IL (312-642-8579), LA (504-523-3229), MA (617-227-7200), NY (212-683-7555), or TX (214-747-6329).

Egypt: Passport and visa required. Transit visa for stay up to 48 hours available. Tourist visa, valid three months, requires $12 fee (cash or money order), one application form, and one photo. Visa may be issued at airport upon arrival for fee of $20. For business travel, need company letter stating purpose of trip. Enclose prepaid envelope for return of passport by certified mail. Proof of yellow fever immunization required if arriving from infected area. AIDS test required for workers and students staying over 30 days. Register with local authorities or at hotel within seven days of arrival. Company letter is required for business travel. Travelers must declare foreign currency on Form D upon arrival and show Form D and bank receipts upon departure. Individuals must present Form D and bank receipts upon departure. Maximum Egyptian currency allowed into and out of Egypt is LE20. For additional information consult Embassy of the Arab Republic of Egypt, 2310 Decatur Place, NW, Washington, DC 20008 (202-234-3903), or nearest Consulate General: CA (415-346-9700), IL (312-443-1190), NY (212-759-7120), or Houston (713-961-4915).

El Salvador: Passport and visa required. Visa, valid three months, requires $10 fee, one application form and one photo, letter from employment, and police clearance to show no criminal record (first-time applicants only). Personal checks not accepted. Apply Embassy of El Salvador, 2308 California Street, NW, Washington, DC 20008 (202-265-9671 or 331-4032), or nearest Consulate: CA (213-387-5776 or 415-781-7924), FL (305-371-8850), LA (504-522-4266), NY (212-889-3608), or TX (713-270-6239).

England: *See* **United Kingdom.**

Equatorial Guinea: Passport and visa required. Obtain visa in advance. Embassy of Equatorial Guinea was temporarily closed at the time this publication went to press. U.S. citizens wishing to travel there must apply for a visa in another country where Equatorial Guinea maintains an open embassy or consulate (Equatorial Guinea Embassy, 801 2nd Avenue, Suite 1403, New York, NY 10017).

Estonia: Passport required. Visas for entry or transit are issued at the Estonia border at time of entry. For further information check Embassy of the Republic of Estonia, 9 Rockefeller Plaza, Suite 1421, New York, NY 10017 (212-247-1450).

Ethiopia: Passport and visa required. Tourist/business visa valid for stay up to 30 days, fee $9.65 or transit visa for 48 hours, $4.85 requires one application, one photo, and yellow fever immunization. Business visa requires company letter and approval from Foreign Ministry in Addis Ababa (allow extra time for processing). Send $2 postage for return of passport or $15 for express mail service. Personal checks not accepted. For longer stays and other information contact Embassy of Ethiopia, 2134 Kalorama Road, NW, Washington, DC 20008 (202-234-2281/2).

Fiji: Passport, proof of sufficient funds, and onward/return ticket required. Visa issued upon arrival for stay up to 30 days and may be extended up to six months. For further information contact Embassy of Fiji, 2233 Wisconsin Avenue, NW, #240, Washington, DC 20007 (202-337-8320), or Mission to the U.N., One United Nations Plaza, 26th Floor, New York, NY 10017 (212-355-7316).

Finland: Passport required. Tourist/business visa not required for stay up to three months. (Period begins when entering Scandinavian area: Sweden, Norway, Denmark, Iceland.) Check Embassy of Finland, 3216 New Mexico Avenue, NW, Washington, DC 20016 (202-363-2430), or nearest Consulate General: Los Angeles (213-203-9903) or New York (212-573-6007).

France: Passport required to visit France, Andorra, Monaco, Corsica, and French Polynesia. All visas must be obtained in advance, with the following exceptions: Visa not required for tourist/business stay up to three months in France, Andorra, Monaco, and Corsica, and one month in French Polynesia. For official/diplomatic travel a visa is required and must be obtained in advance. For further information consult Embassy of France, 4101 Reservoir Road, NW, Washington, DC 20007 (202-944-6000/6015), or nearest Consulate: CA (213-653-3120 or 415-397-4330), FL (305-372-9798), HI (808-599-4458), IL (312-787-5359), LA (504-897-6381), MA (617-266-1680), MI (313-568-0990), NY (212-535-0100), PR (809-753-1700), or TX (713-528-2183).

French Guiana: Proof of U.S. citizenship and photo ID required for visit up to three months. For further information consult Embassy of France (202-944-6000).

French Polynesia: Includes Society Islands, French Southern and Antarctic Lands, Tuamotu, Gambier, French Austral, Marquesas, Kerguelen, Crozet, New Caledonia, Tahiti, Wallis, and Furtuna Islands. Passport required. Visa not required for visit up to one month. For longer stays and further information consult Embassy of France (202-944-6000).

Gabon: Passport and visa required. Visa applicants must obtain visa before arrival. Single-entry visa valid up to one month, requires two application forms, two photos, yellow fever vaccination, and $20 fee. Multiple-entry visa valid for two to four months, $50 (no personal checks accepted). Also need detailed travel arrangements, including flight numbers, arrival and departure dates, accommodations, and next destination. Business visa requires company letter stating purpose of trip and contacts in Gabon. Accompanying family must be included in letter. For longer stays and other information call Embassy of the Gabonese Republic, 2034 20th Street, NW, Washington, DC 20009 (202-797-1000).

Galápagos Islands: Passport and onward/return ticket required for visits up to three months. For further information consult Embassy of Ecuador (202-234-7166).

Gambia: Passport and visa required. Single-entry visa for stay up to three months, requires $12 fee, one application, one photo, and yellow fever immunization certificates. Multientry visa available, $24. For business visa, need company letter stating purpose of visit and itinerary. Allow at least two working days for processing. Include prepaid envelope for return of passport by mail. Apply Embassy of the Gambia, Suite 720, 1030 15th Street, NW, Washington, DC 20005 (202-842-1356 and 1359), or Permanent Mission of The Gambia to the U.N., 820 2nd Avenue, 9th Floor, New York, NY 10017 (212-949-6640).

Germany, Federal Republic of: Passport required. Tourist/business visa not required for stay up to three months. For longer stays, obtain temporary residence permit upon arrival. AIDS test required of applicants for Bavaria residence permits staying over 180 days; U.S. test not accepted. For further information contact Embassy of the FRG, 4645 Reservoir Road, NW, Washington, DC 20007 (202-298-4000), or nearest Consulate General: CA (415-775-1061), FL (305-358-0290), GA (404-659-4760), IL (312-263-0850), MA (617-536-4414), MI (313-962-6526), NY (212-308-8700), or TX (713-627-7770).

Ghana: Passport and visa required. Tourist visa required for stay up to 30 days (extendable). Requires $30 fee, one application form, four photos, onward/return ticket, financial guarantee, yellow fever and cholera immunizations. Allow three working days for processing. Include prepaid envelope for return of passport by certified mail. All foreign visitors who remain in Ghana for more than seven days must register with the Ghana Immigration Service within 48 hours of arrival. For additional information contact Embassy of Ghana, 3512 International Drive, NW, Washington, DC 20008 (202-686-4520), or Consulate General, 19 East 47th Street, New York, NY 10017 (212-832-1300).

Gibraltar: Passport required. Visa not required for tourist stay up to three months. For further information consult British Embassy (202-462-1340).

Gilbert Islands: *See* **Kiribati.**

Great Britain and Northern Ireland: *See* **United Kingdom.**

Greece: Passport required. Visa not required for tourist/business stay up to three months. If traveling on diplomatic/official passport, visa required and must be obtained in advance. AIDS test required for performing artists and students on Greek scholarships; U.S. test not accepted. For additional information consult Embassy of Greece, 2221 Massachusetts Avenue, NW, Washington, DC 20008 (202-232-8222), or nearest Consulate: CA (415-775-2102), GA (404-261-3313), IL (312-372-5356), LA (504-523-1167), MA (617-542-3240), or NY (212-988-5500).

Greenland: *See* **Denmark.**

Grenada: Passport is recommended, but tourists may enter with birth certificate and photo ID. Visa not required for tourist stay up to three months, may be extended to maximum of six months. For additional information consult Embassy of Grenada, 1701 New Hampshire Avenue, NW, Washington, DC 20009 (202-265-2561).

Guadeloupe: *See* **West Indies, French.**

Guatemala: Passport and visa, or tourist card and proof of citizenship required. Tourist card issued by Consulate or airline for $5, valid 30 days for single entry, requires proof of U.S. citizenship and photo ID. Visa available from Consulate, no charge, valid one year, multiple entries of 30 days each, requires passport, one application form, and one photo. Provide SASE for return of passport by mail. Length of stay for the visa and tourist card is determined by immigration authorities upon arrival. For travel by minors and other information contact Embassy of Guatemala, 2220 R Street, NW, Washington, DC 20008 (202-745-4952-4), or nearest Consulate: CA (213-482-7676 or 415-781-0118), FL (305-463-5857), LA (504-525-0013), NY (212-686-3837), or TX (713-953-9531).

Guiana, French: *See* **France.**

Guinea: Passport and visa required. Tourist/business visa for stay up to three months, requires three application forms, three photos, yellow fever immunization, and $25 fee (cash or money order only). Malaria suppressants are recommended. Departure tax $10 ($7 if traveling to another African country) payable at airport. For business visa need company letter stating purpose of trip and letter of invitation from company in Guinea. Provide SASE for return of passport by mail. Apply Embassy of the Republic of Guinea, 2112 Leroy Place, NW, Washington, DC 20008 (202-483-9420).

Guinea-Bissau: Passport and visa required. Visa must be obtained in advance. Visa valid up to 90 days, requires two application forms, two photos, yellow fever immunization, financial guarantee for the stay, and $12 fee. Include prepaid envelope for return of passport by express mail. Apply Embassy of Guinea-Bissau, 918 16th Street, NW, Mezzanine Suite, Washington, DC 20006 (202-872-4222).

Guyana: Passport and visa not required. Single-entry tourist/business visa for stay up to three months, no charge, requires three application forms and three photos. Business visa requires letter from company acknowledging responsibility and purpose of trip. For longer stays, multiple-entry visas, and other information consult Embassy of Guyana, 2490 Tracy Place, NW, Washington, DC 20008 (202-265-6900-03), or Consulate General, 866 U.N. Plaza, 3rd Floor, New York, NY 10017 (212-527-3155/6).

Haiti: Passport required. For further information consult Embassy of Haiti, 2311 Massachusetts Avenue, NW, Washington, DC 20008 (202-332-4090-2), or nearest Consulate: CA (415-957-1189), FL (305-859-2003), IL (312-337-1603), MA (617-723-5211), NY (212-697-9767), or PR (809-766-0758).

Holy See, Apostolic Nunciature of the: Passport required. Visa not required for tourist stay up to three months. For further information consult Apostolic Nunciature of the Holy See, 3339 Massachusetts Avenue, NW, Washington, DC 20008 (202-333-7121), or call Embassy of Italy (202-328-5500).

Honduras: Passport required. For additional information contact Embassy of Honduras (Consular Section), Suite 927, 1511 K Street, NW, Washington, DC 20005 (202-638-4348), or nearest Consulate: CA (213-623-2301 and 415-392-0076), FL (305-358-3477), IL (312-772-7090), LA (504-522-3118), NY (212-269-3611), or TX (713-622-4572).

Hong Kong: Passport and onward/return transportation by sea/air required. Visa not required for tourist stay up to 30 days, may be extended to three months. Confirmed hotel and flight reservations recommended during peak travel months. Departure tax $7 paid at airport. Visa required for work or study. For other types of travel consult British Embassy (202-462-1340).

Hungary: Passport required. Visa not required for stay up to 90 days. For business travel and other information check Embassy of the Republic of Hungary, 3910 Shoemaker Street, NW, Washington, DC 20008 (202-362-6730), or Consulate General, 8 East 75th Street, New York, NY 10021 (212-879-4127).

Iceland: Passport required. Visa not required for stay up to three months. (Period begins when entering Scandinavian area: Denmark, Finland, Norway, Sweden.) For additional information call Embassy of Iceland, 2022 Connecticut Avenue, NW, Washington, DC 20008 (202-265-6653-5), or Consulate General in New York (212-686-4100).

India: Passport and visa required. Obtain visa in advance. Tourist visa valid for stay up to one month, requires $5 fee, up to six months $25 fee, and up to 12 months $50 fee (no checks), one application form, two photos, onward/return ticket, and proof of sufficient funds. Visa must be obtained before arrival. Business visa requires $50 fee, two application forms, two photos, and company letter stating purpose of trip. Include prepaid envelope for return of passport by certified mail. Allow two weeks for processing. Yellow fever immunization needed if arriving from infected area. AIDS test required for all students and anyone over 18 staying more than one year; U.S. test sometimes accepted. Check requirements with Embassy of India, 2536 Massachusetts Avenue, NW, Washington, DC 20008 (202-939-9839/9869), or nearest Consulate General: Chicago (312-781-6280), New York (212-879-7800), or San Francisco (415-668-0683).

Indonesia: Passport and onward/return ticket required. Visa not required for tourist/business stay up to two months (nonextendable). For longer stays and additional information consult Embassy of the Republic of Indonesia, 2020 Massachusetts Avenue, NW, Washington, DC 20036 (202-775-5200), or nearest Consulate: CA (213-383-5126 or 415-474-9571), IL (312-938-0101), NY (212-879-0600), or TX (713-626-3291).

Iran: Passport and visa required. The United States does not maintain diplomatic or consular relations with Iran. Travel by U.S. citizens is not recommended. For visa information contact Embassy of Algeria, Iranian Interests Section, Washington, DC 20007 (202-965-4990).

Iraq: Passport and visa required. AIDS test required for stay over five days. The United States suspended diplomatic and consular operations in Iraq. Since February 1991, **U.S. passports are not valid** for travel in, to, or through Iraq without authorization from the Department of State. Application for exemptions to this restriction should be submitted in writing to Passport Services, U.S. Department of State, 1425 K Street, NW, Washington, DC 20524, Attn: CA/PPT/C, Room 300. **Attention:** U.S. citizens need a Treasury Department license in order to engage in any transactions related to travel to and within Iraq. Before planning any travel to Iraq, U.S. citizens should contact the Licensing Division, Office of Foreign Assets Control, Department of the Treasury, 1331 G Street, NW, Washington, DC 20220 (202-566-2701). For visa information contact a country that maintains diplomatic relations with Iraq.

Ireland: Passport required. Tourists are not required to obtain visas for stays under 90 days, but may be asked to show onward/return ticket. For further information consult Embassy of Ireland, 2234 Massachusetts Avenue, NW, Washington, DC 20008 (202-462-3939), or nearest Consulate General: CA (415-392-4214), IL (312-337-1868), MA (617-267-9330), or NY (212-319-2555).

Israel: Passport, onward/return ticket and proof of sufficient funds required. Tourist visa issued upon arrival valid for three months, may be renewed. Obtain visa in advance if traveling on official/diplomatic passport. Departure tax $11 payable at airport. Dual nationals should consult Embassy of Israel, 3514 International Drive, NW, Washington, DC 20008 (202-364-5500), or nearest Consulate General: CA (213-651-5700 and 415-398-8885), FL (305-358-8111), GA (404-875-7851), IL (312-565-3300), MA (617-542-0041), NY (212-351-5200), PA (215-546-5556), or TX (713-627-3780).

Italy: Passport required. Visa not required for tourist stay up to three months. For longer stays, employment, or study, obtain visa in advance. For additional information consult Embassy of Italy, Fuller Street, NW, Washington, DC 20009 (202-328-5500), or nearest Consulate General: CA (213-820-0622 or 415-931-4924), IL (312-467-1550), LA (504-524-2272), MA (617-542-0483), NY (212-737-9100), PA (215-592-7369), or TX (713-850-7520).

Ivory Coast: *See* **Côte d'Ivoire.**

Jamaica: If traveling directly from the United States, Puerto Rico, or the U.S. Virgin Islands, need return ticket, proof of U.S. citizenship, photo ID, and sufficient funds. Tourist card issued upon arrival for stay up to six months; must be returned to immigration authorities on departure. For business or study, visa must be obtained in advance, no charge. Departure tax $15 paid at airport. Check information with Embassy of Jamaica, Suite 355, 1850 K Street, NW, Washington, DC 20006 (202-452-0660), or nearest Consulate: CA (213-380-9471 or 415-886-6061), FL (305-374-8431), GA (404-593-1500), IL (312-663-0023), or NY (212-935-9000).

Japan: Passport and onward/return ticket required. Visa not required for tourist/business stay up to 90 days. For official/diplomatic travel visa required and must be obtained in advance, no charge. Departure tax $15.50 paid at airport. For specific information consult Embassy of Japan, 2520 Massachusetts Avenue, NW, Washington, DC 20008 (202-939-6800), or nearest Consulate: AK (907-279-8428), CA (213-624-8305 or 415-777-3533), GA (404-892-2700), Guam (646-1290), HI (808-536-2226), IL (312-280-0400), LA (504-529-2101), MA (617-973-9772), MO (816-471-0111), NY (212-371-8222), OR 9503-221-1811), TX (713-652-2977), or WA (206-682-9107).

Jordan: Passport and visa required. Multiple-entry visa valid up to five years, no charge, requires one application form, one photo, letter stating purpose of visit, and itinerary. Persons holding passports with Israeli visas cannot enter Jordan. Send SASE for return of passport by mail. For details check Embassy of the Hashemite Kingdom of Jordan, 3504 International Drive, NW, Washington, DC 20008 (202-966-2664).

Kazakhstan: Passport and visa required. For additional information contact Embassy of Russia, 1825 Phelps Place, NW, Washington, DC 20008 (202-939-8916), or the Consulate General: San Francisco (415-922-6642).

Kenya: Passport and visa required. Transit visa for stay up to seven days issued at airport, $6 fee. For other travel, visa must be obtained in advance. Single-entry visa for tourist/business stay up to six months, $10; requires one application form, two photos, and onward/return ticket. Yellow fever and cholera immunizations recommended. Multiple-entry visa for up to one year available, $50. Payment by money order, cashiers check, or company check only. Apply Embassy of Kenya, 2249 R Street, NW, Washington, DC 20008 (202-387-6101), or Consulate General: Los Angeles (213-274-6635) or New York (212-486-1300).

Kiribati (formerly Gilbert Islands): Passport and visa required. For additional information consult British Embassy (202-462-1340).

Korea, Democratic People's Republic of (North Korea): The United States does not maintain diplomatic or consular relations with North Korea and has no third country representing U.S. interests there. **Attention:** U.S. citizens need a Treasury Department license in order to engage in any transactions related to travel to and within North Korea. Before planning any travel to North Korea, U.S. citizens should contact the Licensing Division, Office of Foreign Assets Control, Department of the Treasury, 1331 G Street, NW, Washington, DC 20220 (202-566-2701). Visa information must be obtained from a consulate in a country that maintains diplomatic relations with North Korea.

Korea, Republic of (South Korea): Passport required. Visa not required for a tourist stay up to 15 days. For longer stays and other types of travel, visa must be obtained in advance. Tourist visa for longer stay requires one application form and one photo. Business visa requires application form, one photo, and company letter. Multiple-entry visa normally valid five years for visits up to 90 days, requires one application form, one photo, and affidavit of support. Fine imposed for overstaying visa and for long-term visa holders not registered within 60 days after entry. For further information check Embassy of the Republic of Korea (Consular Division), 2600 Virginia Avenue, NW, Suite 208, Washington, DC 20037 (202-939-5660/63), or nearest Consulate General: CA (213-385-9300 and 415-921-2251), GA (404-522-1611), IL (312-822-9485), MA (617-348-3660), NY (212-752-1700), TX (713-961-0186), or WA (206-441-1011).

Kuwait: Passport and visa required. AIDS test required for stay over six months; U.S. test accepted. For further information contact the Embassy of the State of Kuwait, 2940 Tilden Street, NW, Washington, DC 20008 (202-966-0702), or Consulate, 321 East 44th Street, New York, NY 10017 (212-973-4318).

Kyrgyzstan: Passport and visa required. For additional information contact Embassy of Russia, 1825 Phelps Place, NW, Washington, DC 20008 (202-939-8916), or the Consulate General: San Francisco (415-922-6642).

Laos: Passport and visa required. Visa requires $35 fee, three application forms, three photos, onward/return transportation, sufficient funds, cholera immunization, and SASE for return of passport by mail. Transit visas for stay up to seven days requires onward/return ticket and visa for next destination. Short-stay visa valid one month for single entry up to 15 days; nonimmigrant visa is available for stays up to 30 days. Send tourist visa applications for individuals and tour groups to tourism office in Vientiane or Embassy in Washington. Check information with Embassy of the Lao People's Democratic Republic, 2222 S Street, NW, Washington, DC 20008 (202-332-6416/7).

Latvia: Passport required. Tourist/business visas issued at point of entry. For further information contact Embassy of Latvia, 4325 17th Street, NW, Washington, DC 20011 (202-726-8213).

Lebanon: Passport and visa required. Since January 1987, **U.S. passports are not valid** for travel in, to, or through Lebanon without authorization from the Department of State. Application for exemptions to this restriction should be submitted in writing to Passport Services, U.S. Department of State, 1425 K Street, NW, Washington, DC 20524, Attn: CA/PPT/C, Room 300. For further information contact Embassy of Lebanon, 2560 28th St., NW, Washington, DC 20008 (202-939-6300), or nearest Consulate General: Los Angeles (213-467-1253), Detroit (313-567-0233), or New York (212-744-7905).

Leeward Islands: *See* **Virgin Islands, British.**

Lesotho: Passport required. Visa issued upon arrival for stay up to three months, may be extended. For longer stays and other types of travel, check Embassy of the Kingdom of Lesotho, 2511 Massachusetts Avenue, NW, Washington, DC 20008 (202-797-5533).

Liberia: Passport and visa required. Transit visitors with onward ticket can remain at airport up to 48 hours. Other travelers must obtain visas before arrival. Tourist/business entry visa valid three months, no fee, requires two application forms, two photos, cholera and yellow fever vaccinations, and medical certificate to confirm that traveler is in good health and free of any communicable disease. Company letter needed for business visa. Include SASE for return of passport by mail. Obtain exit permit from immigration authorities upon arrival, one photo required. For business requirements call Embassy of the Republic of Liberia, 5201 16th Street, NW, Washington, DC 20011 (202-723-0437 to 0440), or nearest Consulate: CA (213-277-7692), GA (404-753-4754), IL (312-643-8635), LA (504-523-7784), MI (313-342-3900), or NY (212-687-1025).

Libya: Passport and visa required. AIDS test required for those seeking residence permits; U.S. test accepted. Since December 1981, **U.S. passports are not valid** for travel in, to, or through Libya without authorization from the Department of State. Application for exemptions to this restriction should be submitted in writing to Passport Services, U.S. Department of State, 1425 K Street, NW, Washington, DC 20524, Attn: CA/PPT/C, Room 300. **Attention:** U.S. citizens need a Treasury Department license in order to engage in any transactions related to travel to and within Libya. Before planning any travel to Libya, U.S. citizens should contact the Licensing Division, Office of Foreign Assets Control, Department of the Treasury, 1331 G Street, NW, Washington, DC 20220 (202-566-2701). Application and inquiries for visas must be made through a country that maintains diplomatic relations with Libya.

Liechtenstein: Passport required. Visa not required for tourist/business stay up to three months. For further information consult the Swiss Embassy (202-745-7900).

Lithuania: Passport and visa required. Visa requires one application form and $25 fee. For further information contact Embassy of Lithuania, 2622 16th Street, NW, Washington, DC 20009 (202-234-5860).

Luxembourg: Passport required. Visa not required for tourist/business stay up to three months. For additional information contact Embassy of Luxembourg, 2200 Massachusetts Avenue, NW, Washington, DC 20008 (202-265-4171), or the nearest Consulate: CA (213-394-2532 and 415-788-0816), FL (305-373-1300), GA (404-952-1157), IL (312-726-0355), MO (816-474-4761), NY (212-370-9850), OH (513-422-4697), or TX (214-746-7200).

Macau: Passport required. Visa not required for visits up to 60 days. For further information consult nearest Portuguese Consulate: Washington, DC (202-332-3007), San Francisco (415-346-3400), New Bedford (508-997-6151), Newark (201-622-7300), New York (212-246-4580), Providence (401-272-2003), or Portuguese Consulate in Hong Kong (231-338).

Madagascar: Passport and visa required. Visa valid six months for single-entry up to one month, $22.50 or multiple entries, $44.15 (no personal checks). Requires four application forms, four photos, yellow fever and cholera immunizations, proof of onward/return transportation, and sufficient funds for stay. Include a prepaid envelope for return of passport by registered mail. Allow four months to process visa for longer stay. For additional information contact Embassy of the Democratic Republic of Madagascar, 2374 Massachusetts Avenue, NW, Washington, DC 20008 (202-265-5525/6), or nearest Consulate: New York (212-986-9491), Philadelphia (215-893-3067), or Palo Alto, CA (415-323-7113).

Malawi: Passport required. Visa not required for stay up to one year. Strict dress codes apply for anyone visiting Malawi. Women must wear dresses that cover the knees and may not wear slacks except in specifically designated areas. Men with long hair cannot enter the country. For further information about this and other requirements, contact the Embassy of Malawi, 2408 Massachusetts Avenue, NW, Washington, DC 20008 (202-797-1007), or Malawi Mission to the U.N., 600 Third Avenue, New York, NY 10016 (212-949-0180).

Malaysia (and the **Borneo States, Sarawak** and **Sabah):** Passport required. Visa not required for stay up to three months. Yellow fever and cholera immunizations necessary if arriving from infected areas. For entry of pets or other types of visits, consult Embassy of Malaysia, 2401 Massachusetts Avenue, NW, Washington, DC 20008 (202-328-2700), or nearest Consulate: Los Angeles (213-621-2991), Honolulu (808-525-8144), New York (212-490-2722), Portland (503-246-0707), or San Francisco (415-421-4627).

Maldives: Passport required. Tourist visa issued upon arrival, no charge. Visitors must have proof of onward/return transportation and sufficient funds (minimum of $10 per person per day of stay). Check with Embassy of Maldives in Sri Lanka for further information. The Embassy is located at 25 Melbourne Avenue, Colombo 4, Sri Lanka.

Mali: Passport and visa required. Visa must be obtained in advance. Tourist/business visa for stay up to one week, may be extended after arrival, requires $17 fee (cash or money order), two application forms, two photos, proof of onward/return transportation, and yellow fever immunization. For business travel, must have company letter stating purpose of trip. Send SASE for return of passport if applying by mail. Apply Embassy of the Republic of Mali, 2130 R Street, NW, Washington, DC 20008 (332-2249).

Malta: Passport required. Visa not required for stay up to three months (extendable—extension must be applied for prior to expiration of original visa). For additional information consult Embassy of Malta, 2017 Connecticut Avenue, NW, Washington, DC 20008 (202-462-3611/2), or nearest Consulate: CA (213-685-6365 and 415-468-4321), MA (617-742-1913), MI (313-525-9777), MO (816-833-0033), MN (612-228-0935), NY (212-725-2345), PA (412-262-8460), or TX (713-497-2100).

Marshall Islands, Republic of the: Proof of U.S. citizenship, sufficient funds for stay, and onward/return ticket required for stay up to 30 days. Entry permit not needed to bring in sea-going vessel. Obtain necessary forms from airline or shipping agent serving Marshall Islands. Departure fee $10 (those over age 60 exempt). Health certificate required if arriving from infected areas. AIDS test may be required for visits over 30 days; U.S. test accepted. Check information with Representative Office, Suite 1004, 1901 Pennsylvania Avenue, NW, Washington, DC 20006 (202-234-5414), or office in Honolulu (808-942-4422).

Martinique: *See* **West Indies, French.**

Mauritania: Passport and visa required. Obtain visa before arrival. Visa valid three months, requires $10 fee (money order only), two application forms, four photos, yellow fever and cholera immunizations, and proof of onward/return transportation. Business travelers must have proof of sufficient funds (bank statement) or letter from sponsoring company. Passports with Israeli or South African visas may be delayed or denied a visa. For further information contact Embassy of the Republic of Mauritania, 2129 Leroy Place, NW, Washington, DC 20008 (202-232-5700/01), or Permanent Mission to the U.N., 600 Third Avenue, 37th Floor, New York, NY 10016 (212-737-7780).

Mauritius: Passport, sufficient funds for stay, and onward/return ticket required. Visa not required for tourist/business stay up to three months. For travel on diplomatic/official passport, notify Embassy in advance of name, passport number, and purpose of visit. For further information consult Embassy of Mauritius, Suite 441, 4301 Connecticut Avenue, NW, Washington, DC 20008 (202-244-1491/2), or Honorary Consulate in Los Angeles (818-788-3720).

Mayotte Island: *See* **France.**

Mexico: Passport and visa not required of U.S. citizens for tourist/transit stay up to 90 days. Tourist card is required. Tourist card valid three months for single entry up to 180 days, no charge, requires proof of U.S. citizenship, photo ID, and proof of sufficient funds. Tourist cards may be obtained in advance from Consulate, Tourism Office, and most airlines serving Mexico upon arrival. Departure tax $10 is paid at airport. Notarized consent from parent(s) required for children travelling alone, with one parent, or in someone else's custody. (This permit is not necessary when a minor is in possession of a valid passport.) AIDS test required for permanent residence visas. For other types of travel and details, check Embassy of Mexico, 1019 19th Street, NW, Suite 810, Washington, DC 20036 (202-736-1000), or nearest Consulate General: CA (212-624-3261, 415-392-5554, and 619-231-8414), CO (303-333-1130), IL (312-855-1380), LA (504-522-3596), NY (212-689-0456), PR (809-764-0258), or TX (214-522-9741, 713-524-2300, 512-227-9145, and 915-533-3644).

Micronesia, Federated States of (Kosrae, Yap, Ponape, and Truk): Proof of citizenship and identity required for tourist visit up to one year. Departure fee $5. Entry permit may be needed for other types of travel; obtain forms from airline. Check requirements with Embassy of the Federated States of Micronesia, 1725 N Street, NW, Washington, DC 20036 (202-223-4383).

Miquelon Island: Proof of U.S. citizenship and photo ID required for visit up to three months. For further information consult Embassy of France (202-944-6000).

Moldova: Passport and visa required. For additional information contact Embassy of Russia, 1825 Phelps Place, NW, Washington, DC 20008 (202-939-8916), or the Consulate General: San Francisco (415-922-6642).

Monaco: Passport required. Visa not required for visit up to three months. For further information consult French Embassy (202-944-6000), or nearest Honorary Consulate of the Principality of Monaco: CA (213-655-8970 or 415-362-5050), IL (312-642-1242), LA (504-522-5700), NY (212-759-5227), or PR (809-721-4215).

Mongolia: Passport and visa required. Transit visa for stay up to 48 hours requires onward ticket, visa for next destination, and $20 fee. Tourist visa for up to 90 days requires confirmation from Mongolian Travel Agency (Zhuulchin) and $20 fee. Business visa requires letter from company stating purpose of trip and invitation from Mongolian organization and $20 fee. Submit one photo (no application form), itinerary, and prepaid envelope for return of passport by certified or special delivery mail. AIDS test required for students and anyone staying longer than three months; U.S. test accepted. For additional information contact Embassy of the People's Republic of Mongolia, 10201 Irongate Road, Potomac, MD 20854 (301-983-1962).

Morocco: Passport required. Visa not required for stay up to three months, extendable. For additional information consult Embassy of Morocco, 1601 21st Street, NW, Washington, DC 20009 (202-462-7979 to 7982), or Consulate General in New York (212-758-2625).

Mozambique: Passport and visa required. Visa must be obtained in advance. Entry visa valid 30 days from date of issuance, requires two application forms, two photos, immunization for yellow fever and cholera, $15 fee, and letter (from company or individual) giving detailed itinerary. Visitors must exchange $25 at point of entry and declare all foreign currency. Visitors must carry passport at all times during stay. Apply Embassy of the People's Republic of Mozambique, Suite 570, 1990 M Street, NW, Washington, DC 20036 (202-293-7146).

Myanmar (formerly Burma): Passport and visa required. Single-entry visas, for stay up to 14 days, require $16 fee for tourist visa and $30 fee for business visa, two application forms, three photos, and itinerary. Tourists must be part of a tour group. Business visa requires company letter and invitation from a Myanmarian company; extendable after arrival. Overland travel into and out of Myanmar is not permitted. Enclose prepaid envelope for return of passport by registered/certified mail. Allow two to three weeks for processing. Minimum of $100 must be changed for local currency upon arrival. For further information contact Embassy of the Union of Myanmar, 2300 S Street, NW, Washington, DC 20008 (202-332-9044-6), or the Permanent Mission of Myanmar to the U.N., 10 East 77th Street, New York, NY 10021 (212-535-1311).

Namibia: Passport, onward/return ticket, and proof of sufficient funds required. Visa not required for tourist or business stay up to 90 days. Consult Embassy of Namibia, 1605 New Hampshire Avenue, NW, Washington, DC 20009 (202-986-0540) for further information on entry requirements.

Nauru: Passport and visa required. Passengers must have onward/return ticket. For specific information contact Consulate of the Republic of Nauru in Guam, First Floor, ADA Professional Building, Marine Drive, Agana, Guam 96910.

Nepal: Passport and visa required. Tourist visa for stay up to 15 days issued at Kathmandu Airport upon arrival, extendable to 3 months, requires $20 fee (postal money order), one application form, and photo. For other types of travel obtain visa in advance. For additional information contact Royal Nepalese Embassy, 2131 Leroy Place, NW, Washington, DC 20008 (202-667-4550), or Consulate General in New York (212-370-4188).

Netherland Antilles (Islands include Bonaire, Curaçao, Saba, Statia, St. Martin [St. Maarten]): Passport or proof of U.S. citizenship required. Visa not required for stay up to 14 days, extendable to 90 days after arrival. Tourists may be asked to show onward/return ticket or proof of sufficient funds for stay. Departure tax $10 when leaving Bonaire and Curacao, $4 in Statia, $10 in St. Martin. For further information consult Embassy of the Netherlands (202-244-5300), or nearest Consulate General: CA (212-380-3440), IL (314-856-1429), NY (212-246-1429), or TX (713-622-8000).

Netherlands: Passport required. Visa not required for tourist/business visit up to 90 days. Tourists may be asked to show onward/return ticket or proof of sufficient funds for stay. For further information contact Embassy of the Netherlands, 4200 Linnean Avenue, NW, Washington, DC 20008 (202-244-5300), or nearest Consulate General: CA (213-380-3440), IL (312-856-0110), NY (212-246-1429), or TX (713-622-8000).

New Caledonia: *See* **French Polynesia.**

New Zealand: Passport required. Visa not required for tourist/business stay up to three months, must have onward/return ticket and visa for next destination. Proof of sufficient funds may also be required, either 1000 NZ dols (approx. 500 U.S. dols.), or with prearranged accommodations, 400 NZ dols/person/day. For additional information contact Embassy of New Zealand, 37 Observatory Circle, NW, Washington, DC 20008 (202-328-4800), or nearest Consulate General: Los Angeles (213-477-8241).

Nicaragua: Passport must be valid six months beyond duration of stay, onward/return ticket and sufficient funds ($200 minimum) required. Check further information with Embassy of Nicaragua, 1627 New Hampshire Avenue, NW, Washington, DC 20009 (202-939-6531 to 34).

Niger: Passport and visa required. Visa valid between 6 and 24 months (from date of issuance), depending on type/category of travelers. Requires three application forms, three photos, yellow fever and cholera vaccinations, proof of onward/return transportation, and letter of invitation. For further information contact Embassy of the Republic of Niger, 2204 R Street, NW, Washington, DC 20008 (202-483-4224).

Nigeria: Passport and visa required. Visa, no charge, valid for one entry within 12 months, requires one photo, yellow fever and cholera vaccinations, and for tourism a letter of invitation is required. Business visa requires letter from counterpart in Nigeria and letter of introduction from U.S. company. For further information contact Embassy of the Republic of Nigeria, 2201 M Street, NW, Washington, DC 20037 (202-822-1500 or 1522), or nearest Consulate General: San Francisco (415-552-0334), Atlanta (404-577-4800), or New York (212-715-7200).

Niue: Passport, onward/return ticket, and confirmed hotel accommodations required. Visa not required for stay up to 30 days. Visitors must have confirmed accommodations and onward/return transportation. For additional information consult Embassy of New Zealand (202-328-4800).

Norfolk Island: Passport and visa required. Visa issued upon arrival for visit of up to 30 days, extendable, requires confirmed accommodations and onward/return ticket. Also obtain Australian transit visa in advance for travel to Norfolk Island. For both visas consult Australian Embassy (202-797-3000).

Norway: Passport required. Visa not required for stay up to three months. (Period begins when entering Scandinavian area: Finland, Sweden, Denmark, Iceland.) For further information contact Royal Norwegian Embassy, 2720 34th Street, NW, Washington, DC 20008 (202-333-6000), or nearest Consulate General: CA (415-986-0766 to 7168 and 213-933-7717), MN (612-332-3338), NY (212-421-7333), or TX (713-521-2900).

Oman: Passport and visa required. Tourist/business visas for single-entry issued for stay up to three weeks. Requires $21 fee, one application form, two photos, and cholera immunization if arriving from infected area. Allow one week to 10 days for processing. Entry not granted to passports showing Israeli or Libyan visas. For transit and road travel check Embassy of the Sultanate of Oman, 2342 Massachusetts Avenue, NW, Washington, DC 20008 (202-387-1980-2).

Pakistan: Passport and visa required. Visa must be obtained before arrival. Tourist visa requires one application form, one photo, and proof of onward/return transportation. Validity depends on visit (minimum three months), multiple entries, no charge. Need letter from company for business visa. Include prepaid envelope for return of passport by registered mail. AIDS test required for stays over one year. For applications and inquiries in Washington area, contact Embassy of Pakistan, 2315 Massachusetts Avenue, NW, Washington, DC 20008

(202-939-6200). All other areas apply to Consulate General, 12 East 65th Street, New York, NY 10021 (212-879-5800).

Palau, The Republic of: Proof of U.S. citizenship onward/return ticket required for stay up to 30 days (extendable). Must apply for extension in Palau, $50 fee. Obtain forms for entry permit from airline or shipping agent serving Palau. For further information consult with Representative Office, 444 North Capitol Street, Suite 308, Washington, DC 20008 (202-624-7793).

Panama: Passport, tourist card or visa, and onward/return ticket required. Tourist card valid 30 days, available from airline serving Panama for $2.50 fee. For longer stays and official/diplomatic travel information contact Embassy of Panama, 2862 McGill Terrace, NW, Washington, DC 20008 (202-483-1407).

Papua New Guinea: Passport and onward/return ticket required. Visa not required (for tourists) if arriving via Jackson Airport, Port Moresby, for stay up to 30 days, no extensions. AIDS test required for work permit; U.S. test accepted. For longer stays and further information contact Embassy of Papua New Guinea, Suite 300, 1615 New Hampshire Avenue, NW, Washington, DC 20009 (202-745-3680).

Paraguay: Passport required. Visa not required for tourist/business stay up to 90 days (extendable). AIDS test required for resident visas. For additional information consult Embassy of Paraguay, 2400 Massachusetts Avenue, NW, Washington, DC 20008 (202-483-6960).

Peru: Passport required. Visa not required for tourist stay up to 90 days, extendable after arrival. Tourists may need onward/return ticket. For official/diplomatic passport and other travel, visa required and must be obtained in advance. Business visa requires company letter stating purpose of trip and $27 fee. For further information contact Embassy of Peru, 1700 Massachusetts Avenue, NW, Washington, DC 20036 (202-833-9860-9), or nearest Consulate: CA (213-651-0296 and 415-362-5185), FL (305-374-1407), IL (312-853-6173), NJ (201-278-2221), NY (212-644-2850), PR (809-763-0679), or TX (713-781-5000).

Philippines: Passport and onward/return ticket required. For entry by Manila International Airport, visa not required for transit/tourist stay up to 21 days. Visa required for longer stay, maximum of 59 days, one application form, one photo, no charge. Company letter needed for business visa. AIDS test required for permanent residency; U.S. test accepted. For entry at military bases and other types of visas, check Embassy of the Philippines, 1617 Massachusetts Avenue, NW, Washington, DC 20036 (202-483-1533), or nearest Consulate General: CA (213-387-5321 and 415-433-6666), HI (808-595-6316), IL (312-332-6458), NY (212-764-1330), TX (713-524-0234), or WA (206-441-1640).

Poland: Passport required. Visa not required for stay up to 90 days. Visitors must register at hotel or with local authorities within 48 hours after arrival. AIDS test required for student visas; U.S. test accepted. Apply Embassy of the Republic of Poland (Consular Division), 2224 Wyoming Avenue, NW, Washington, DC 20008 (202-232-4517 or 2501), or nearest Consulate General: Chicago, IL, 1530 Lakeshore Drive, 60610 (312-337-88166); Los Angeles, CA, 3460 Wilshire Boulevard, Suite 1200, 90010 (213-365-7900); or New York, NY, 233 Madison Avenue, 10016 (212-889-8360).

Portugal (Includes travel to the Azores and Madeira Islands): Passport required. Visa not required for visit up to 60 days (extendable). For travel with pets and other information consult nearest Consulate: DC (202-332-3007), CA (415-346-3400), MA (617-536-8740 and 508-997-6151), NJ (201-622-7300), NY (212-246-4580), or RI (401-272-2003).

Qatar: Passport and visa required. Single-entry visa $33; multiple-entry visa, valid three to six months for $60 fee or valid 12 months for $115 fee; transit visa $6. Visas require No Objection Certificate from Qatar Ministry of Interior, two application forms, two photos, and SASE for return of passport by mail. Business visa must be obtained through sponsor in Qatar. AIDS test required for work and student visas; U.S. test accepted if within three months of visit. For specific information contact Embassy of the State of Qatar, Suite 1180, 600 New Hampshire Avenue, NW, Washington, DC 20037 (202-338-0111).

Reunion: See *France*.

Romania: Passport and visa required. Transit and tourist visa may be obtained at border in Romania or from Embassy before departure. Single-entry transit visa valid 72 hours or tourist visa valid six months for stay up to 60 days, requires $30 fee (double-entry, $68), and letter stating reason for trip and itinerary. No application or photos needed. Provide SASE for return of passport by mail. Allow three weeks for processing (emergency visas may be granted in two to three days.) For dual nationals, family visits, and other information contact Embassy of Romania, 1607 23rd Street, NW, Washington, DC 20008 (202-232-4747-9).

Russia: Passport and visa required. For additional information contact Embassy of Russia, 1825 Phelps Place, NW, Washington, DC 20008 (202-939-8916), or the Consulate General: San Francisco (415-922-6642).

Rwanda: Passport and visa required. Multiple-entry visa for stay up to three months requires $15 fee, two application forms, two photos, and immunizations for yellow fever. Exact date of entry into Rwanda required with application. Include prepaid envelope or postage for return of passport by certified mail. Apply Embassy of the Republic of Rwanda, 1714 New Hampshire Avenue, NW, Washington, DC 20009 (202-232-2882).

Saint Kitts and Nevis: Proof of U.S. citizenship, photo ID and return/onward ticket required for stay up to six months. AIDS test required for work permit, residency, or student visas; U.S. test not accepted. For further information consult Embassy of St. Kitts and Nevis, 2501 M Street, NW, Washington, DC 20037 (202-833-3550), or Permanent Mission to the U.N., 414 East 75th Street, 5th Floor, New York, NY 10021 (212-535-1234).

Saint Lucia: Proof of U.S. citizenship, photo ID, and return/onward ticket required for stay up to six months. For additional information contact Embassy of Saint Lucia, 2100 M Street, NW, Suite 309, Washington, DC 20037 (202-463-7378/9), or Permanent Mission to the U.N., 820 Second Street, 9th Floor, New York, NY 10017 (212-697-9360).

St. Martin (St. Maarten): *See* **Netherlands Antilles** or **West Indies, French.**

St. Pierre: Proof of U.S. citizenship and photo ID required for visit up to three months. For specific information consult Embassy of France (202-944-6000).

Saint Vincent and the Grenadines: Proof of U.S. citizenship, photo ID, and return/onward ticket required for tourist stay up to six months. Proof of citizenship, return/onward ticket, and/or proof of sufficient funds necessary. Check Embassy of Saint Vincent and the Grenadines, 1717 Massachusetts Avenue, NW, Suite 102, Washington, DC 20036 (202-462-7806 or 7846), or Consulate, 801 Second Avenue, 21st Floor, New York, NY 10017 (212-687-4490) for further information.

San Marino: Passport required. Visa not required for tourist stay up to three months. For additional information contact the nearest Honorary Consulate of the Republic of San Marino: District of Columbia (1155 21st Street, NW, Suite 400, Washington, DC 20036, 202-223-3517), Detroit (313-528-1190), or New York (212-736-3911).

Sao Tome and Principe: Passport and visa required. Tourist/business visa for visit up to two weeks (extendable), no charge, requires two application forms, two photos, and yellow fever immunization. Company letter is required for a business visa. Enclose prepaid envelope or postage for return of passport by certified or special delivery mail. Apply Permanent Mission of Sao Tome and Principe, 801 Second Avenue, Suite 1504, New York, NY 10017 (212-697-4211).

Saudi Arabia: Passport and visa required. No tourist visa issued at this time. Transit visa valid 24 hours for stay in airport, need onward/return ticket. Business visa requires $15 fee (money order only), one application form, one photo, company letter stating purpose of visit, invitation from Foreign Ministry in Saudi Arabia, and SASE for return of passport by mail. Meningitis and cholera vaccinations are highly recommended. Medical report required for work permits; U.S. test accepted. For details and requirements for family visits, contact The Royal Embassy of Saudi Arabia, 601 New Hampshire Avenue, NW, Washington, DC 20037 (202-333-4595), or nearest Consulate General: Los Angeles (213-208-6566), New York (212-752-2740), or Houston (713-785-5577).

Scotland: *See* **United Kingdom.**

Senegal: Passport required. Visa not needed for stay up to 90 days. U.S. citizens need onward/return ticket and yellow fever vaccination. For further information contact Embassy of the Republic of Senegal, 2112 Wyoming Avenue, NW, Washington, DC 20008 (202-234-0540).

Seychelles: Passport, onward/return ticket, and proof of sufficient funds required. Visa issued upon arrival for stay up to one month, no charge, extendable up to one year. Consult Permanent Mission of Seychelles to the U.N., 820 Second Avenue, Suite 203, New York, NY 10017 (212-687-9766) for further information.

Sierra Leone: Passport and visa required. Single-entry visa valid three months, requires $12.50 fee (cash or money order), two application forms, two photos, return/onward ticket, and proof of financial support from bank or employer. Cholera and yellow fever immunizations required and malarial suppressants recommended. Adult travelers (over age 16) must exchange $100 minimum upon arrival and declare other foreign currency on an exchange control form (M), certified and stamped at the port of entry. For further information consult Embassy of Sierra Leone, 1701 19th Street, NW, Washington, DC 20009 (202-939-9261).

Singapore: Passport and onward/return ticket required. Visa not required for tourist/business stay up to two weeks, extendable to three months maximum. For additional information contact Embassy of Singapore, 1824 R Street, NW, Washington, DC 20009 (202-667-7555).

Slovakia: Passport required. Visa not required for stay up to 30 days. For longer stays and other types of travel, contact Embassy of the Slovak Republic, 3900 Linnean Ave., NW, Washington DC, 20008 (202-363-6315).

Solomon Islands: Passport, onward/return ticket, and proof of sufficient funds required. Visitors permit issued upon arrival for stay up to two months in one-year period. For further information consult British Embassy (202-462-1340).

Somalia: Passport and visa required. Visa for stay up to three months, requires four application forms, four photos, return/onward ticket, cholera and yellow fever immunizations, and $13 fee. Business visa requires company letter stating purpose of trip. Send check or money order and SASE for return of passport by mail. For further information contact Embassy of the Somali Democratic Republic, Suite 710, 600 New Hampshire Avenue, NW, Washington, DC 20037, or Consulate in New York (212-688-9410).

South Africa: Passport and visa required. Visa must be obtained in advance. Multiple-entry visa valid one year if passport remains valid, no charge, requires one application form (no photo), proof of onward/return transportation, visa for next destination, and yellow fever vaccination if arriving from infected area. Malarial suppressants also recommended. Enclose prepaid envelope or postage for return of passport by certified or express mail. Allow two to three weeks for processing. For business travel, a company letter is required. For more information contact Embassy of South Africa, Attn: Consular Office, 3201 New Mexico Avenue, NW, Washington, DC 20016, or nearest Consulate: (202-966-1650), CA (213-657-9200), IL (312-939-7929), NY (212-213-4880), or TX (713-850-0150).

Spain: Passport required. Visa not required for tourist stay up to six months. If traveling on diplomatic/official passport, visa required and must be obtained in advance. For additional information check with Embassy of Spain, 2700 15th Street, NW, Washington, DC 20009 (202-265-0190/1), or nearest Consulate General: CA (415-922-2995 and 213-658-6050), FL (305-446-5511), IL (312-782-4588), LA (504-525-4951), MA (617-536-2506), NY (212-355-4080), PR (809-758-6090), or TX (713-783-6200).

Sri Lanka: Passport, onward/return ticket, and proof of sufficient funds ($30 per day) required. Tourist visa not required for stay up to one month. For business or travel on official/diplomatic passport, visa required and must be obtained in advance. Business visa valid one month, requires one application form, two photos, and $5 fee. Include $6 postage for return of passport by registered mail. Yellow fever and cholera immunizations needed if arriving from infected area. For further information contact Embassy of the Democratic Socialist Republic of Sri Lanka, 2148 Wyoming Avenue, NW, Washington, DC 20008 (202-483-4025-8), or nearest Consulate: CA (805-323-8975 and 504-362-3232), HI (808-373-2040), or NJ (201-627-7855).

Sudan: Passport and visa required. Visa must be obtained in advance. Transit visa valid up to seven days, requires $6 fee (cash or money order), onward/return ticket, and visa for next destination, if appropriate. Tourist/business visa for single entry up to three months (extendable), requires $9 fee, one application form, one photo, proof of sufficient funds for stay, and SASE for return passport. Business visa requires company letter stating purpose of visit and invitation from Sudanese officials. Malarial suppressants and vaccinations for yellow fever, cholera, and meningitis recommended. Visas not granted to passports showing Israeli or South African visas. Allow four weeks for processing. Travelers must declare currency upon arrival and departure. Check additional currency regulations for stay longer than two months. Contact Embassy of the Republic of the Sudan, 2210 Massachusetts Avenue, NW, Washington, DC 20008 (202-338-8565 to 8570), or Consulate General, 210 East 49th Street, New York, NY 10017 (212-421-2680).

Suriname: Passport and visa required. Multiple-entry visa valid one year for stays up to two months (extendable), requires two application forms, two photos, and $17 fee. Business visa requires letter from sponsoring company. For return of passport by mail, send $5 for registered mail, $9.95 for Express Mail, or $15.50 for Federal Express. For additional information contact Embassy of the Republic of Suriname, Suite 108, 4301 Connecticut Avenue, NW, Washington, DC 20008 (202-244-7488 and 7490), or the Consulate: Miami (305-593-2163).

Swaziland: Passport required. Visa not required for stay up to 60 days. Temporary residence permit available in Mbabane for longer stay. Visitors must report to immigration authorities or police station within 48 hours unless lodging in a hotel. Yellow fever and cholera immunizations required if arriving from infected area and antimalarial treatment recommended. For further information consult Embassy of the Kingdom of Swaziland, 3400 International Drive, NW, Suite 3M, Washington, DC (202-362-6683).

Sweden: Valid passport required. Visa not required for stay up to three months. (Period begins when entering Scandinavian area: Finland, Norway, Denmark, Iceland.) For further information check Embassy of Sweden, Suite 1200, 600 New Hampshire Avenue, NW, Washington, DC 20037 (202-944-5600), or nearest Consulate General: Los Angeles (213-470-2555), Chicago (312-781-6262), or New York (212-751-5900).

Switzerland: Passport required. Visa not required for tourist/business stay up to three months. For further information contact Embassy of Switzerland, 2900 Cathedral Avenue, NW, Washington, DC 20008 (202-745-7900), or nearest Consulate General: CA (415-788-2272), GA (404-872-7874), IL (312-915-0061), NY (212-758-2560), or TX (713-650-0000).

Syria: Passport and visa required. Obtain visa in advance. Single-entry visa valid six months or double-entry for three months, $15; multiple-entry visa valid six months, $30. Submit two application forms, two photos (signed), and fee (payment must be money order only). Enclose prepaid envelope (with correct postage) for return of passport by mail. Any visitor over 12 must exchange $100 upon arrival in Syria. AIDS test required for students and others staying over one year; U.S. test sometimes accepted. For group visas and other information contact Embassy of the Syrian Arab Republic, 2215 Wyoming Avenue, NW, Washington, DC 20008 (202-232-6313).

Tahiti: *See* **West Indies, French.**

Taiwan: Passport and visa required. Visas for stay up to two months, no charge, requires one application form and two photos. AIDS test mandatory for anyone staying over three months; U.S. test sometimes accepted. For business travel or other information contact Coordination Council for North American Affairs (CCNAA), 4201 Wisconsin Avenue, NW, Washington, DC 20016-2137 (202-895-1800). Additional offices are in Atlanta, Boston, Chicago, Guam, Honolulu, Houston, Kansas City, Los Angeles, New York, San Francisco, and Seattle.

Tajikistan: Passport and visa required. For additional information contact Embassy of Russia, 1825 Phelps Place, NW, Washington, DC 20008 (202-939-8916), or the Consulate General: San Francisco (415-922-6642).

Tanzania: Passport and visa required. Obtain visa before departure. Visas for mainland Tanzania are valid for Zanzibar. Tourist visa (valid six months from date of issuance) for one entry up to 30 days, may be extended after arrival. Requires $10.50 fee (no personal checks). Enclose prepaid envelope for return of passport by certified or registered mail. Visitors must exchange at least $50 at point of entry. Yellow fever and cholera immunizations recommended (required if arriving from infected area) and malarial suppressants advised. Allow one month for processing. For business visa and other information consult Embassy of the United Republic of Tanzania, 2139 R Street, NW, Washington, DC 20008 (202-939-6125), or Tanzanian Permanent Mission to the U.N., 205 East 42nd Street, 13th Floor, New York, NY 10017 (212-972-9160).

Thailand: Passport and onward/return ticket required. Visa not needed for stay up to 15 days if arrive and depart from Don Muang Airport in Bangkok. For longer stays obtain visa in advance. Transit visa, for stay up to 30 days, $10 fee, or tourist visa for stay up to 60 days, $15 fee. For business visa valid up to 90 days, need $20 fee and company letter stating purpose of visit. Submit one application form, two photos, and postage for return of passport by mail. Apply Embassy of Thailand, 2300 Kalorama Road, NW, Washington, DC 20008 (202-234-5052 or 483-7200), or nearest Consulate General: CA (213-937-1894), IL (312-236-2447), or NY (212-754-1770).

Togo: Passport required. Visa not required for stay up to three months. Americans traveling in remote areas in Togo occasionally require visas. Yellow fever and cholera vaccinations are required. Check further information with Embassy of the Republic of Togo, 2208 Massachusetts Avenue, NW, Washington, DC 20008 (202-234-4212/3).

Tonga: Passport and onward/return ticket required. Visa not required for stay up to 30 days. For additional information consult the Consulate General of Tonga, 360 Post Street, Suite 604, San Francisco, CA 94108 (415-781-0365).

Trinidad and Tobago: Passport required. Visa not required for tourist/business stay up to two months. If traveling on official/diplomatic passport or for other travel, visa required and must be obtained in advance. Business visa requires passport and company letter. For further information consult Embassy of Trinidad and Tobago, 1708 Massachusetts Avenue, NW, Washington, DC 20036 (202-467-6490), or nearest Consulate in New York (212-682-7272).

Tunisia: Passport and onward/return ticket required. Visas not required for tourist/business stay up to four months. For further information consult Embassy of Tunisia, 1515 Massachusetts Avenue, NW, Washington, DC 20005 (202-862-1850), or nearest Consulate: San Francisco (415-922-9222) or New York (212-742-6585).

Turkey: Passport required. Visa not required for tourist/business stay up to three months. If traveling on official/diplomatic passport or for other travel, visa required and must be obtained in advance. For further information contact Embassy of the Republic of Turkey, 1714 Massachusetts Avenue, NW, Washington, DC 20036 (202-659-0742), or nearest Consulate: CA (213-937-0118), IL (312-263-0644), NY (212-949-0160), or TX (713-622-5849).

Turkmenistan: Passport and visa required. For additional information contact Embassy of Russia, 1825 Phelps Place, NW, Washington, DC 20008 (202-939-8916), or the Consulate General: San Francisco (415-922-6642).

Turks and Caicos: *See* **West Indies, British.**

Tuvalu: Passport and onward/return ticket and proof of sufficient funds required. Visitors permit issued upon arrival. For further information consult British Embassy (202-462-1340).

Uganda: Passport and visa required. Obtain visa before arrival. Visa, valid within three months to six months, $20 fee (money order), requires two application forms, two photos, and immunization certificates for yellow fever, cholera, typhoid and malaria suppressants are required as well. For business visa and other information contact Embassy of the Republic of Uganda, 5909 16th Street, NW, Washington, DC 20011 (202-726-7100-02), or Permanent Mission to the U.N. (212-949-0110).

Ukraine: Passport and visa required. For additional information contact Embassy of Russia, 1825 Phelps Place, NW, Washington, DC 20008 (202-939-8916), or the Consulate General in San Francisco (415-922-6642).

United Arab Emirates: Passport and visa required. Tourist visa must be obtained by relative/sponsor in UAE. Transit visa issued upon arrival at discretion of airport authorities for stay up to 15 days. Both visas require sponsor/relative to meet visitor at airport. Business visas issued only by Embassy, and require company letter and sponsor in UAE to send a letter or telex to Embassy confirming trip. Single-entry visa valid two months for stay up to 30 days, $18 fee. Multiple-entry visa (for business only), valid six months from date of issue for maximum stay of 30 days per entry, $225 fee, paid by cash, money order, or certified check. Submit one application form, one photo, and prepaid envelope for return of passport by certified/registered mail. AIDS test required for work or residence permits; testing must be performed upon arrival; U.S. test not accepted. For further information contact Embassy of the United Arab Emirates, Suite 740, 600 New Hampshire Avenue, NW, Washington, DC 20037 (202-338-6500).

United Kingdom (England, Northern Ireland, Scotland, and Wales): Passport required. Visa not required for stay up to six months. For additional information consult the Consular Section of the British Embassy, 19 Observatory Circle, NW, Washington, DC 20008 (202-896-0205), or nearest Consulate General: CA (213-385-7381 and 415-981-3030), GA (404-524-5856), IL (312-346-1810), MA (617-437-7160), NY (212-752-8400), OH (216-621-7674), or TX (214-637-3600).

Uruguay: Passport required. Visa not required for stay up to three months. For official/diplomatic passport, visa required and must be obtained in advance. For additional information consult Embassy of Uruguay, 1918 F Street, NW, Washington, DC 20008 (202-331-1313-6), or nearest Consulate for additional information: CA (213-394-5777), FL (305-358-9350), IL (312-236-3366), LA (504-525-8354), or NY (212-753-8191/2).

Uzbekistan: Passport and visa required. For additional information contact Embassy of Russia, 1825 Phelps Place, NW, Washington, DC 20008 (202-939-8916), or the Consulate General: San Francisco (415-922-6642).

Vanuatu: Passport and onward/return ticket required. Visa not required for stay up to 30 days. For further information consult the British Embassy (202-462-1340).

Vatican: *See* **Holy See.**

Venezuela: Passport and visa/tourist card required. Tourist card can be obtained from airlines serving Venezuela, no charge, valid 60 days, cannot be extended. Multiple-entry visa valid up to one year, extendable, available from any Venezuelan Consulate, requires $2 fee (money order or company check), one application form, one photo, onward/return ticket, proof of sufficient funds, and certification of employment. For business visa, need letter from company stating purpose of trip, responsibility for traveler, and name and address of companies to be visited in Venezuela. All travelers must pay departure tax ($18) at airport. Business travelers must present a Declaration of Income Tax in the Ministerio de Hacienda (Treasury Department). For additional information contact nearest Consulate: MD (111 Water Street, Suite 402, Baltimore 21202 (301-962-0362/3), CA (415-512-8340), FL (305-577-3834), IL (312-236-9655), LA (504-522-3284), MA (617-266-9355), NY (212-826-1660), PA (215-923-2905), PR (809-766-4250), or TX (713-961-5141).

Vietnam: The United States does not maintain diplomatic or consular relations with Vietnam and has no third country representing U.S. interests there. Travel is not recommended by U.S. citizens. **Attention:** U.S. citizens need a Treasury Department license in order to engage in any transactions related to travel to and within Vietnam. Before planning any travel to Vietnam, U.S. citizens should contact the Licensing Division, Office of Foreign Assets Control, Department of the Treasury, 1331 G Street, NW, Washington, DC 20220 (202-566-2701). Visa must be obtained from consulate in a country that maintains diplomatic relations with Vietnam.

Virgin Islands, British: Islands include Anegarda, Jost van Dyke, Tortola, and Virgin Gorda. Proof of U.S. citizenship, photo ID, onward/return ticket, and sufficient funds required for tourist stay up to three months. AIDS test required for residency or work; U.S. test accepted. Consult British Embassy for further information (202-462-1340).

Wales: *See* **United Kingdom.**

Western Samoa: Passport and onward/return ticket required. Visa not required for stay up to 30 days. For longer stays contact Embassy of Western Samoa, 115 15th Street, NW, Suite 510, Washington, DC 20005 (202-833-1743).

West Indies, British: Islands include Anguilla, Montserrat, Cayman Islands, Turks, and Caicos. Proof of U.S. citizenship, photo ID, onward/return ticket, and sufficient funds required for tourist stay up to three months. AIDS test required for residency or work; U.S. test accepted. Consult British Embassy for further information (202-462-1340).

West Indies, French: Islands include Guadeloupe, Isles des Saintes, La Desirade, Marie Galante, Saint Barthelemy, St. Martin, and Martinique. Passport and onward/return ticket required for visit up to three months. For further information consult Embassy of France (202-944-6000).

Yemen Arab Republic: Passport and visa required. Visa valid 30 days from date of issuance for single entry, requires one application form and two photos. For tourist visa need proof of onward/return transportation and employment and $10 fee. Visitors visa requires letter of invitation and $20 fee. Business visa requires $20, company letter stating purpose of trip, and approval by telex from Foreign Ministry in Yemen. Payment by money order only and include postage for return of passport by registered mail. Entry not granted to passports showing Israeli or South African visa. Yellow fever and cholera vaccinations and malaria suppressants recommended. Check information with Embassy of the Yemen Arab Republic, Suite 840, 600 New Hampshire Avenue, NW, Washington, DC 20037 (202-965-4760), or Yemen Mission to the U.N., 866 United Nations Plaza, Room 435, New York, NY 10017 (212-355-1730).

Yugoslavia: Passport required. Visa not required for tourist stay up to 30 days. If traveling on business a visa is required. Business visa valid one year, no charge and no photo, requires one application form. For business visa need company letter stating purpose and length of trip and name and address of company to be visited in Yugoslavia. Send prepaid envelope or postage for return of passport by certified mail. Apply Embassy of the Socialist Federal Republic of Yugoslavia, 2410 California Street, NW, Washington, DC 20008 (202-462-6566), or nearest Consulate: NY (212-838-2300), IL (312-332-0169), CA (415-776-4941), PA (412-471-6191), or OH (216-621-2093).

Zaire: Passport and visa required. Visa must be obtained before arrival. Transit visa for stay up to eight days, single-entry $8; double-entry $16. Tourist visa, valid one month $20; two months $40, and three months $50, requires three photos, three applications, yellow fever immunization, and onward/return ticket. Business visa valid six months, $60, need company letter accepting financial responsibility for traveler. No personal checks, send money order and enclose SASE for return of passport by mail. Apply Embassy of the Republic of Zaire, 1800 New Hampshire Avenue, NW, Washington, DC 20009 (202-234-7690/1), or Permanent Mission to the U.N., 747 Third Avenue, New York, NY 10017 (212-754-1966).

Zambia: Passport and visa required. Obtain visa in advance. Visa valid up to six months, requires $15 fee (cash only), two application forms, and two photos. Yellow fever and cholera immunizations recommended. Allow three weeks for processing. Apply Embassy of the Republic of Zambia, 2419 Massachusetts Avenue, NW, Washington, DC 20008 (202-265-9717-21).

Zanzibar: *See* **Tanzania.**

Zimbabwe: Passport, onward/return ticket, and proof of sufficient funds required. Visa not required. Visitors must declare currency upon arrival. For regulations check with Embassy of Zimbabwe, 1608 New Hampshire Avenue, NW, Washington, DC 20009 (202-332-7100).

Customs Information

At reentry into the United States, you must declare all articles in your possession that you have acquired abroad, stating their actual purchase price or, if they were not purchased, their market value in the country where you acquired them. You will fill out a declaration form before reaching customs to show to the federal inspectors.

If you were out of the country for 48 hours or more, you will be exempt from paying duty and federal tax on the first $400 worth of goods. Generally, values above that amount are subject to duty at a straight 10 percent. For example, if you bring in $600 worth of goods, you will pay about $20 in duty. If you are traveling with your family, remember that each family member is allowed the same $400 exemption.

The items brought into the United States must be for your own use or for personal gifts. You may not resell them for profit.

If you leave the United States with foreign-made goods already in your possession, be sure to register them, using their serial numbers, with the customs office *before* leaving or bring proof (sales slips, for example) with you that you bought them in the United States. If you lack proof of domestic purchase or registration, you may be charged duty upon reentry.

There are customs restrictions on bringing in certain plants, animals, medications, and foods, and children may not bring in alcohol. You can get a list of restricted items from the U.S. Department of Agriculture, Washington, DC 20205.

Further information may be obtained from your local office of the Treasury Department and from the U.S. Customs Service, P.O. Box 7407, Washington, DC 20004. The telephone number is 202-566-8195.

State Tourism Offices

Alabama Bureau of Tourism
532 South Perry Street
Montgomery, AL 36104
800-ALABAMA

Alaska Division of Tourism
Box E
Juneau, AK 99811
907-465-2010

Arizona Office of Tourism
1100 W. Washington Ave.
Phoenix, AZ 85007
602-542-8687

Arkansas Department of Parks and Tourism
One Capitol Mall
Little Rock, AR 72201
800-NATURAL

California Tourism Office
1121 L Street
Sacramento, CA 95814
916-322-1396

Colorado Tourism Board
1625 Broadway, Suite 1700
Box 38700
Denver, CO 80202
800-433-2656

Connecticut Department of Economic Development
865 Brook Street
Rocky Hill, CT 06067
800-282-6863

D.C. Convention and Visitors Association
1212 New York Avenue, NW
Washington, DC 20005
202-789-7000

Delaware Tourism Office
99 Kings Highway
Box 1401
Dover, DE 19903
800-441-8846

Florida Division of Tourism
126 Van Buren Street
Tallahassee, FL 32399-2000
904-487-1462

Georgia Department of Industry and Trade
Box 1776
Atlanta, GA 30301
800-847-4842

Hawaii Visitors Bureau
2270 Kalakaua Avenue
Honolulu, HI 96815
808-923-1811

Idaho Travel Council
Department of Commerce
700 West State Street
Boise, ID 83720
800-635-7820

Illinois Travel Information Center
c/o Department of Commerce and Community Affairs
620 East Adams Street
Springfield, IL 62701
217-782-7139

Indiana Department of Commerce Tourist Development Division
1 North Capitol Avenue, Suite 700
Indianapolis, IN 46204
800-289-ONIN

Iowa Development Commission Tourist Travel Division
600 East Grand Avenue
Des Moines, IA 50309
800-345-IOWA

Kansas Department of Travel and Tourism
400 West 8th Street, 5th Floor
Topeka, KS 66603
800-2-KANSAS

Kentucky Department of Travel Development
2200 Capitol Plaza Tower
Frankfort, KY 40601
800-225-TRIP

Louisiana Office of Tourism
Box 94291
Baton Rouge, LA 70804
800-33-GUMBO

Maine Publicity Bureau
97 Winthrop Street
Hallowell, ME 04347
207-289-6070

Maryland Office of Tourist Development
217 East Redwood Street
Baltimore, MD 21202
800-543-1036

Massachusetts Department of Commerce and Development Division of Tourism
100 Cambridge Street
Boston, MA 02202
617-727-3201

Michigan Department of Commerce Travel Bureau
Box 30226
Lansing, MI 48909
800-5432-YES

Minnesota Office of Tourism
375 Jackson Street
250 Skyway Level
St. Paul, MN 55101
800-657-3700

Mississippi Department of Economic Development
Division of Tourism
P.O. Box 22825
Jackson, MS 39205-3297
800-647-2290

Missouri Division of Tourism
Truman State Office Building
Box 1055
Jefferson City, MO 65102
314-751-4133

Montana Travel Promotion Division
1424 Ninth Avenue
Helena, MT 59620
800-541-1447

Nebraska Department of Economic Development
Division of Travel and Tourism
301 Centennial Mall South
Box 94666
Lincoln, NE 68509
800-228-4307

Nevada Commission on Tourism
Capitol Complex
Carson City, NV 89710
800-NEVADA-8

New Hampshire Office of Vacation Travel
Box 856
Concord, NH 03301
603-271-2666

New Jersey Office of Travel and Tourism
CN-826
Trenton, NJ 08625
800-JERSEY-7

New Mexico Tourism and Travel
Joseph Montoya Building
1100 St. Francis Drive
Santa Fe, NM 87503
800-545-2040

New York Division of Tourism
One Commerce Plaza
Albany, NY 12245
800-255-5697

North Carolina Travel and Tourism Division
430 North Salisbury Street
Raleigh, NC 27611
800-VISIT-NC

North Dakota Tourism Division
Liberty Memorial Building
Capitol Grounds
Bismarck, ND 58505
800-437-2077

Ohio Department of Development
Division of Travel and Tourism
Box 1001
Columbus, OH 43266
800-BUCKEYE

Oklahoma Tourism and Recreation Department
P.O. Box 60000
Oklahoma City, OK 73146
800-652-6552

Oregon Economic Development
Division of Tourism
775 Summer Street, NE
Salem, OR 97310
800-547-7842

Pennsylvania Bureau of Travel Development
453 Forum Building
Harrisburg, PA 17120
800-VISIT-PA

Rhode Island Tourism Division
7 Jackson Walkway
Providence, RI 02903
800-556-2484

South Carolina Department of Parks, Recreation, and Tourism
Box 71
Columbia, SC 29202
803-734-0235

South Dakota Division of Tourism
Capitol Lake Plaza
P.O. Box 1000
Pierre, SD 57501
800-843-1930

Tennessee Department of Tourism
Box 23170
Nashville, TN 37202
615-741-2158

Texas Travel and Information Division
Box 5064
Austin, TX 78763
512-483-3705

Utah Travel Council
Council Hall
Capitol Hill
Salt Lake City, UT 84114
801-538-1030

Vermont Travel Division
134 State Street
Montpelier, VT 05602
802-828-3236

Virginia Division of Tourism
1021 East Cary Street
Richmond, VA 23219
800-VISIT-VA

Washington Tourism Development
101 General Administration Building
Olympia, WA 98504
206-753-5630

West Virginia Division of Tourism and Parks
2101 Washington Street East
Charleston, WV 25305
800-CALL-WVA

Wisconsin Division of Tourism
123 West Washington Avenue
Box 7606
Madison, WI 53707
800-432-TRIP

Wyoming Division of Tourism
1-25 at College Drive
Cheyenne, WY 82002
800-225-5996

Government Tourist Information Centers

Aruba Tourism Authority
100 Harbor Boulevard
Weehawken, NJ 07087
201-330-0800

Australian Tourist Commission
489 Fifth Avenue
New York, NY 10017
800-445-4400

Austrian National Tourist Office
11601 Wilshire Boulevard
Los Angeles, CA 90025
213-477-3332

Bahamas Tourist Office
150 East 52nd Street
New York, NY 10022
212-758-2777

Balkan Holidays
41 East 42nd Street
New York, NY 10017
212-573-5330

Barbados Board of Tourism
800 Second Avenue
New York, NY 10017
212-986-6516

Belgian Tourist Office
745 Fifth Avenue
New York, NY 10151
212-758-8130

Bermuda Department of Tourism
310 Madison Avenue
New York, NY 10017
800-223-6106

Brazilian Consulate General
3810 Wilshire Boulevard
Los Angeles, CA 90010
213-382-3133

British Tourist Office
40 West 57th Street
New York, NY 10019
212-581-4700

Canadian Consulate
300 South Grand Avenue
Los Angeles, CA 90071
213-687-7432
See also **Quebec.**

Chilean National Tourist Board
510 West 6th Street
Los Angeles, CA 90014
213-627-4293

Chinese Tourist Board
60 East 42nd Street
New York, NY 10165
212-867-0271

Colombian Consulate
1825 Connecticut Avenue, NW
Washington, DC 20009
202-332-7476

Costa Rican Tourist Board
3540 Wilshire Boulevard
Los Angeles, CA 90010
213-382-8080

Travel **557**

Cyprus Consulate General
13 East 40th Street
New York, NY 10016
212-686-6016

CEDOK (Czech Republic and Slovakia)
10 East 40th Street
New York, NY 10016
212-689-9720

Denmark Tourist Board
655 3rd Avenue
New York, NY 10017
212-949-2333

Egyptian Tourist Authority
323 Geray Street
San Francisco, CA 94102
415-781-7676

French Government Tourist Office
610 Fifth Avenue
New York, NY 10020
212-757-1125

German National Tourist Office
122 East 42nd Street
New York, NY 10068
212-661-7200

Greek National Tourist Organization
645 Fifth Avenue
New York, NY 10022
212-421-5777

Grenada Department of Tourism
820 Second Avenue
New York, NY 10017
212-687-9554

Honduran Tourist Bureau
1138 Fremont Avenue
South Pasadena, CA 91030
213-682-3377

Hong Kong Tourist Association
590 Fifth Avenue
New York, NY 10036
212-869-5008

India Tourist Office
30 Rockefeller Plaza North
New York, NY 10112
212-586-4901

Indonesian Tourist Office
3457 Wilshire Boulevard
Los Angeles, CA 90010
213-387-2078

Ireland Tourist Board
757 Third Avenue
New York, NY 10017
212-418-0800

Israeli Government Tourist Office
350 Fifth Avenue
New York, NY 10018
212-560-0621

Italian Tourist Office
630 Fifth Avenue
New York, NY 10020
212-245-4961

Jamaican Tourist Board
801 Second Avenue
New York, NY 10017
212-688-7650

Japan National Tourist Office
360 Post Street
San Francisco, CA 94108
415-989-7140

Kenyan Tourist Office
424 Madison Avenue
New York, NY 10017
212-486-1300

Korean National Tourist Office
510 West 6th Street
Los Angeles, CA 90014
213-623-1226

Luxembourg National Tourist Office
801 Second Avenue
New York, NY 10017
212-370-9850

Macau Tourist Office
P.O. Box 1860
3133 Lake Hollywood Drive
Los Angeles, CA 90078
213-851-3402

Malaysian Tourist Centre
818 West 7th Street
Los Angeles, CA 90017
213-689-9702

Mexican Tourist Office
10100 Santa Monica Boulevard
Los Angeles, CA 90067
213-203-8151

Monaco Government Tourist Office
845 Third Avenue
New York, NY 10022
212-759-5227

Morocco National Tourist Office
20 East 46th Street
New York, NY 10017
212-557-2520

Netherlands Board of Tourism
355 Lexington Avenue
New York, NY 10017
212-370-7367

New Zealand Tourist Office
501 Santa Monica Boulevard
Santa Monica, CA 90401
800-388-5494

Norway Scandinavia Tourist Offices
655 Third Avenue
New York, NY 10017
212-949-2333

Panama Tourist Bureau
2355 Salzedo Street
Coral Gables, FL 33134
305-442-1892

Philippine Department of Tourism
3460 Wilshire Boulevard
Los Angeles, CA 90010
213-487-4525

Portuguese Tourism Office
590 Fifth Avenue
New York, NY 10036
212-354-4403

Puerto Rican Tourism Office
1290 Avenue of the Americas
New York, NY 10104
212-599-6262

Quebec Tourism
17 West 50th Street
New York, NY 10020
212-397-0220 or 800-363-7777

Romanian National Tourist Office
573 Third Avenue
New York, NY 10016
212-697-6971

Russian Travel Information Office (INTOURIST)
630 Fifth Avenue
New York, NY 10111
212-757-3884

Singapore Tourist Board
590 Fifth Avenue
New York, NY 10036
212-302-4861

South African Tourism Board
747 Third Avenue
New York, NY 10017
212-838-8841

Spanish National Tourism Office
665 Fifth Avenue
New York, NY 10022
212-759-8822

Sri Lankan Tourist Board
2148 Wyoming Avenue
Washington, DC 20008
202-483-4025

Swedish Tourist Board
655 Third Avenue
New York, NY 10017
212-949-2333

Swiss National Tourist Office
608 Fifth Avenue
New York, NY 10020
212-757-5944

Tahitian Tourist Board
12233 Olympic Boulevard
Los Angeles, CA 90064
212-207-1919

Taiwan Visitors Association
1 World Trade Center
New York, NY 10048
212-466-0691

Thailand Tourism Authority
3440 Wilshire Boulevard
Los Angeles, CA 90010
213-382-2353

Trinidad and Tobago Tourist Board
25 West 43rd Street
New York, NY 10036
212-719-0540

Tunisian Tourist Office
1515 Massachusetts Avenue, NW
Washington, DC 20005
202-862-1850

Turkish Tourism Office
821 United Nations Plaza
New York, NY 10017
212-687-2194

Venezuelan Tourist Bureau
1 World Trade Center
New York, NY 10048
212-432-9144

Virgin Islands Tourism Office
1270 Avenue of the Americas
New York, NY 10021
212-582-4520

BEST VACATION BETS

Sylvia McNair's book *Vacation Places Rated* assesses over 100 U.S. vacation areas, rating them on such features as urban activities, climate, access to recreational areas, population density, and "special attractions" like amusement parks and professional sports events. These are McNair's top 10 choices:

1. Walt Disney World, Buena Vista, Florida
2. Disneyland, Anaheim, California
3. Knott's Berry Farm, Buena Park, California
4. Universal City Studios Tour, Universal City, California
5. Sea World, Orlando, Florida
6. Sea World, San Diego, California
7. Kings Island, Kings Island, Ohio
8. Six Flags Magic Mountain, Valencia, California
9. Cedar Point, Sandusky, Ohio
10. Busch Gardens, Tampa, Florida

Theme Parks

Although the traditional American tourist attractions—from Mount Rushmore to the Grand Canyon to the Statue of Liberty to the Golden Gate—are still high on many travelers' itineraries, since the 1950s the greatest volume of visitors has been seen at "theme" amusement parks modeled on the pioneering, enormously successful Disneyland. U.S. amusement parks entertain over 170 million visitors a year. These are the top 10 according to *Amusement Business Magazine*.

1. Walt Disney World, Buena Vista, Florida
2. Disneyland, Anaheim, California
3. Knott's Berry Farm, Buena Park, California
4. Universal City Studios Tour, Universal City, California
5. Sea World, Orlando, Florida
6. Sea World, San Diego, California
7. Kings Island, Kings Island, Ohio
8. Six Flags Magic Mountain, Valencia, California
9. Cedar Point, Sandusky, Ohio
10. Busch Gardens, Tampa, Florida

Traveling Tips for the Disabled

Determination and good planning are the keys to enjoyable travel for the disabled. If you are disabled, check with your health insurance agent about vacation coverage. In addition, engage a travel agent who specializes in travel for the disabled. Here are some further tips.

Air Travel

Telephone the airline ahead of time about accommodations and possible extra charges. Virtually all major airports have some barrier-free facilities, and special arrangements can be made for disabled passengers.

Buses

Because of space limitations, bus lines generally are less accommodating than other carriers. However, many do have special seating and reduced rates.

Railroads

Trains normally have seating arrangements and toilet facilities for the disabled. Call ahead to arrange for seating and assistance.

Sea Travel

Travel by ship is possible, but it can be difficult, since ocean-going vessels are not designed for the handicapped. Generally they are not barrier-free.

Parks/Camping

Many domestic and international campsites provide accommodations for the disabled, and some European sites are even designated as "Handi-Camps." Information on facilities for the handicapped may be obtained from local chapters of the Easter Seal Society, and a national park guide for the handicapped is available from the National Park Service, U.S. Department of the Interior, Washington, DC 20240.

Hotels/Motels

Many hotel and motel chains have special facilities, as do some nonchain hotels and motels. Check with your travel agent.

Further Information

- Society for the Advancement of Travel for the Handicapped (SATH) (718-858-5483).
- Mobility International, for information about travel in the United Kingdom (01-403-5688).
- National Park Service, for information on U.S. highway rest areas for disabled travelers (202-208-6843).

TRAVELING WITH PETS

Although most travelers leave home without them, vacationing with pets is possible; if you plan carefully, taking your pet along can save on guilt, worry, and even money. It's easier to leave the goldfish in the care of friends, but the family dog can go with you almost anywhere. Information and suggestions to make this easier appear below.

Travel Checklist

Proper identification (name and address tag)
Certificate of good health signed by your veterinarian
Proof of up-to-date immunizations
Pet carrier
Pet toys
Blanket
First aid kit, including bandages, antiseptic, and medications (including tranquilizers) prescribed by your veterinarian
Food (and can opener, if needed)
Thermos of water
Plastic bowls
Leash and muzzle
Flea powder or flea collar
Grooming tools

Pretravel Suggestions

Introduce your pet to car travel with trial runs.
Allow your pet to become familiar with the pet carrier before your trip.
Do not feed your pet for several hours before the trip.
Exercise your pet right before leaving.

Travel Restrictions

Automobile: No restrictions.
Bus: Except for seeing-eye dogs, pets are prohibited on buses in interstate travel.
Train: Pets may be taken only in private compartments or in the baggage car.
Airplane: Pets can come on board in pet carriers or can remain in the baggage compartment. Restrictions vary, so inquire of individual airlines in advance.
National park: Pets are allowed on leashes except in bathing areas.
State and private park: Restrictions vary; check with the individual facility.
Hotel, motel, and campground: Most do accept pets; notify the owner ahead of time.

International Travel (including Hawaii)

Most countries require a recent certificate of good health and proof of immunizations. In addition, the following places may require a quarantine (at the owner's expense) for the number of days indicated. The number of days in quarantine may vary according to the type of pet and its state of health. Check individual embassies or consulates for specific requirements.

Hawaii	180	Norway	120
Hong Kong	180	Panama	180
Jamaica	180	Singapore	30
Jordan	42	Sweden	120
Korea	21	Trinidad and Tobago	180
Malta	180	United Kingdom	180
Mauritius	180		

Returning Home

Upon your return, a quarantine officer at customs will check documents and inspect your animal. The official may require confinement of any animal that you have purchased abroad; typically confinement is in your own home rather than in official quarantine. Pets purchased abroad also will require proof of immunization, certificates of good health, and payment of an import duty.

TRAVELERS' FIRST-AID KIT

Antiseptic lotion or ointment
Aspirin or acetaminophen
Cold and cough remedies
Gauze bandages and adhesive tape, elastic bandages
Heating pad
Ice pack
Identification bracelet
Insect repellent and insect bite medication
Medical information regarding condition, allergies, medications, blood type, and special needs
Milk of magnesia and diarrhea medication
   Moleskin for blisters and calluses
Physician's name, address, and telephone number
Prescription medications and refills
Sunscreen and sunburn relief lotion
Telephone numbers of emergency contacts
Thermometer
Throat lozenges
Vitamins

International Auto Registration Marks

Country	Code	Country	Code
Afghanistan	AFG	Guernsey	GBG
Albania	AL	Guyana	GUY
Alderney (Channel Islands)	GBA	Haiti	RH
Algeria	DZ	Hong Kong	HK
Andorra	AND	Hungary	H
Argentina	RA	Iceland	IS
Australia	AUS	India	IND
Austria	A	Indonesia	RI
Bahamas	BS	Iran	IR
Bahrain	BRN	Iraq	IRQ
Bangladesh	BD	Ireland	IRL
Barbados	BDS	Isle of Man	GBM
Belgium	B	Israel	IL
Belize	BH	Italy	I
Benin	DY	Ivory Coast	CI
Botswana	RB	Jamaica	JA
Brazil	BR	Japan	J
Brunei	BRU	Jersey	GBJ
Bulgaria	BG	Jordan	JOR
Burundi	RU	Kenya	EAK
Cambodia	K	Kuwait	KWT
Canada	CDN	Laos	LAO
Central African Republic	RCA	Lebanon	RL
Chile	RCH	Lesotho	LS
Colombia	CO	Liberia	LB
Congo	RCB	Libya	LAR
Costa Rica	CR	Liechtenstein	FL
Cuba	C	Luxembourg	L
Cyprus	CY	Madagascar	RM
Czech Republic	CZ	Malawi	MW
Denmark	DK	Malaysia	MAL
Ecuador	EC	Mali	RMM
Egypt	ET	Malta	M
El Salvador	ES	Mauritania	RIM
Ethiopia	ETH	Mauritius	MS
Faroe Islands	FR	Mexico	MEX
Fiji	FJI	Monaco	MC
Finland	SF	Morocco	MA
France	F	Myanmar	BUR
Gambia	WAG	Netherlands	NL
Germany, Federal Republic of	FRG	Netherlands Antilles	NA
Ghana	GH	New Zealand	NZ
Gibraltar	GBZ	Nicaragua	NIC
Great Britain	GB	Niger	RN
Greece	GR	Nigeria	WAN
Grenada	WG	Norway	N
Guatemala	GCA	Pakistan	PAK

Panama	PA	Sri Lanka	CL
Papua New Guinea	PNG	Suriname	SME
Paraguay	PY	Swaziland	SD
Peru	PE	Sweden	S
Philippines	RP	Switzerland	CH
Poland	PL	Syria	SYR
Portugal	P	Taiwan	RC
Romania	RO	Tanzania	EAT
Rwanda	RWA	Thailand	T
St. Lucia	WL	Togo	TG
St. Vincent	WV	Trinidad and Tobago	TT
Samoa	WS	Tunisia	TN
San Marino	RSM	Turkey	TR
Senegal	SN	Uganda	EAU
Seychelles	SY	United States	USA
Sierre Leone	WAL	Uruguay	ROU
Singapore	SGP	Vatican City	SCV
Slovakia	Q	Venezuela	YV
Somalia	SP	Vietnam	VN
South Africa	ZA	Zaire	ZRE
South Korea	ROK	Zambia	Z
South Yemen	ADN	Zimbabwe	ZW
Spain	E		

Additional Sources of Information

AYH Handbook and Hostelers Manual: Europe. American Youth Hostels, 1987.

AYH Handbook and Hostelers Manual: United States. American Youth Hostels, 1987.

The Stephen Birnbaum Travel Guides. Houghton-Mifflin, 1976.

The Business Traveler's Handbook, Prentice-Hall, 1983.

Fielding Travel Books. William Morrow, 1948– .

Fodor's Guides. Fodor's Travel Publications, 1980– .

Frommer's Guides. Prentice-Hall, 1977– .

Grimes, Paul. *The New York Times Practical Traveler.* Times Books, 1985.

Kirk, Robert William. *You Can Travel Free.* Pelican, 1985.

Mobil Travel Guides, 6 vols. Prentice-Hall, 1992.

The Official Airline Guides. Dun and Bradstreet, 1988.

Rand McNally European Atlas. Rand McNally, 1992.

Rand McNally Road Atlas of Britain. William Collins, 1985.

Rand McNally Road Atlas: United States, Canada and Mexico. Rand McNally, 1992.

Simony, Maggy. *The Traveler's Reading Guide: Ready-Made Reading Lists for the Armchair Traveler,* rev. ed. Facts On File, 1987.

20

Household Tips

Washing Fabrics / 565
Wash-Water Temperatures / 567
Stain Removal / 568
Cooking Equivalents and Substitutions / 580
Cooking Times and Serving Sizes / 584
Refrigeration Food Storage / 589
How to Store Coffee / 589
Temperature of Food for Control of Bacteria / 590
Herbs and Spices / 591
Herbal Salt Substitutes / 591
Chemical Additives / 592
Alcoholic Drink Recipes / 600
Champagne Bottle Sizes / 605
Wines and Their Service / 606
Clothing Size Conversion Tables / 607
Standard Sizes Chart / 608
Additional Sources of Information / 610

Washing Fabrics

Washer Loads

Cottons and Linens

Fabrics must be of fast color and sturdy construction. Wash in very hot water with all-purpose detergent for a full washer cycle. Results are better if white fabrics are washed by themselves. Two large sheets or tablecloths and a variety of smaller articles wash more effectively than a load made up of all large articles.

A load may include:

cotton dresses	shirts	sheets	T-shirts
cotton nightwear	cotton slips	socks	towels
pillowcases	table linen		

Load size: For good washability, load washer about 3 pounds lighter than manufacturer's recommendation (6 pounds in a 9-pound washer).

Lightweight or Sheer Cottons

Wash in warm water, or cool water for dark colors, with an all-purpose detergent and a shortened washing cycle.

A load may include:

blouses	slips
dresses	negligees and robes

Load size: About 3 pounds lighter than manufacturer's recommendation.

Similarly Soiled Articles of Synthetic Fibers

Use warm or cool water, an all-purpose detergent, and a shortened cycle. Include white nylons in an all-white load only; they easily pick up color from other fabrics. If articles are badly soiled, a hot-water wash may be needed.

Load size: A 3- or 4-pound load of easy-care fabrics washes and dries with fewer wrinkles than a capacity load.

Heavy Work Clothes and Other Badly Soiled Laundry

Divide into loads according to color. Use hot water unless running colors or shrinkage is a problem. Use plenty of all-purpose detergent. Pretreat, soak, and use full washer cycle.

A load may include:

children's sturdy play clothes
coveralls, overalls, work pants
shop or laboratory coats

heavy socks
shirts, skirts, slacks, shorts

Load size: Light. Allow plenty of room for washer action.

Articles That May Run

Some dark-colored cottons, denims, socks, and jeans may be washed together if you do not mind some mixing of colors. Otherwise, sort out the fabrics that are likely to bleed color and wash them separately. Use cool wash water at full washer cycle or shorter if clothes are only lightly soiled.

Miscellaneous Items

These include bulky pieces, blankets, bedspreads, and throw rugs, which need to be washed separately because they fill the washer. Woolens, electric blankets, sweaters, and other items also may require special handling.

Soaking

Generally it pays to soak heavily soiled work and play clothes, dusty curtains and draperies, heavily soiled slipcovers, and certain stained articles to help loosen stains.

The most satisfactory way of soaking clothes is to agitate them in the washer for a few minutes in warm water with detergent. The addition of detergent helps hold the dirt suspended in the water. Use about half the amount of detergent needed for washing. Extract water and follow with a complete washing cycle.

If you have only a few items to soak, use a small container rather than the washer. Submerge clothes in a warm detergent solution and let them soak for 15 minutes. Soaking to remove stains may take longer. Stir the clothes around a bit, extract water, and add the garments to a normally soiled load of similar fabrics for the complete washing cycle. If soaked clothes are extremely dirty, wash them by themselves.

Water Temperature

Medium-hot water (approximately 120° F) is a good temperature for washing some bright or dark colors that do not actually run in the wash but that may fade in time from washing in hot water. This temperature also works well for washing lingerie that you do not want to put in very hot water.

The "warm" setting of an automatic washer usually controls the temperature at about 100° F. Most washers rinse with water at this temperature. In some cycles, and at the "cold" setting, cold water may be used.

Cold water (80° F or less) is recommended for lightly soiled items and fabrics and fibers that lose color, wrinkle, or shrink in hot water.

For more information on the right temperature for various washing jobs, consult the Wash-Water Temperatures guide below.

Rinsing

If you are not getting good rinsing in your washer, you may be overloading or adding too much detergent, or the extraction of the wash water may not be as effective as it should be. See that the spinning mechanism of the washer is in perfect working order.

Fabric Softeners

Fabric softeners, which generally are added to rinse water, make textiles soft and fluffy. They also reduce the static electricity that builds up on some fabrics when they rub against each other and minimize wrinkles and deep creases.

Softener is added to the final rinse water in proportion to the weight of clothes rather than the amount of rinse water. Use softener each time you want fabrics softened; the effect is lost in the next washing. An overdose of softener may decrease the absorbency of fabrics. Some fabric softeners come in disposable sheets that are added to the dryer.

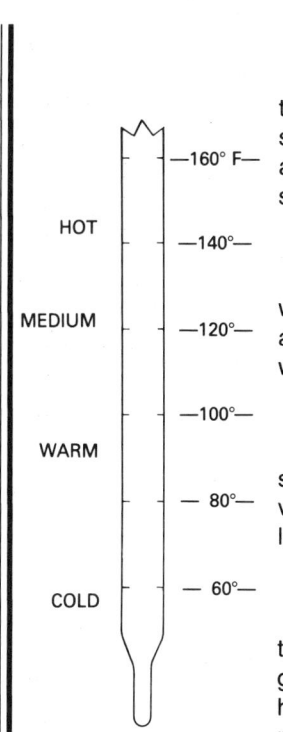

WASH-WATER TEMPERATURES

HOT — 160° F — Very hot; water fills only from "hot" line of water heater, with temperature control set for "hot." Provides most soil removal and sanitizing; ideal for white cottons and linens and heavily soiled articles of washfast colors. Wrinkles synthetic fabrics; may cause some colors to run.

— 140° —

MEDIUM — 120° — Hot, mixed with some cold water. Fills automatically, on washers with "medium" water control. Lightly soiled loads usually wash clean. Provides no sanitizing; somewhat superior to warm water in soil removal.

— 100° —

WARM — 80° — Temperature of "warm" setting in automatics. Suitable for silk and washable woolens, comfortable for hand washing. Provides no sanitizing; protects colors. Wrinkles synthetic fabrics less than hot water.

COLD — 60° — Temperature of unheated water supply. For lightly soiled or thoroughly pretreated laundry. For use with plenty of liquid detergent, a cold-water detergent, or a granular detergent dissolved in hot water before adding. Gives least cleaning, no sanitizing, minimum wrinkling of synthetic fabrics; may not remove wear wrinkles.

Stain Removal

Many common stains fall into one of three categories—greasy, nongreasy, and combination. These stains can be removed by following the appropriate method for each given below. When necessary, separate directions are given for washable and nonwashable articles. Directions for nonwashables are for articles made of fabrics that are not damaged by the application of small amounts of water.

Greasy Stains

Washable Articles

Regular washing, either by hand or by machine, removes some greasy stains. Some stains can be removed by rubbing soap or detergent into the stain and then rinsing with warm water. On some wash-and-wear or permanent-press fabrics, it may be necessary to rub soap or detergent thoroughly into the stain and allow it to stand for several hours, or overnight, before rinsing. Often, however, a grease solvent is necessary; this is effective even after an article has been washed. Sponge the stain thoroughly with the grease solvent and dry. Repeat if necessary. It often takes extra time to remove greasy stains from a fabric with a special finish.

A yellow stain may remain after a solvent treatment if the stain has been set by age or heat. To remove a yellow stain, use a chlorine or peroxygen bleach. If it is safe for the fabric, a strong sodium perborate treatment is usually the most effective.

Nonwashable Articles

Sponge stains well with grease solvent and dry. Repeat if necessary. It may take extra time to remove greasy stains from fabrics with a special finish.

A yellow stain may remain after a solvent treatment if the stain has been set by age or heat. To remove a yellow stain, use a chlorine or peroxygen bleach. If safe for the fabric, a strong sodium perborate treatment is usually the most effective.

Nongreasy Stains

Many fresh stains can be removed by simple treatments. Stains set by heat or age may be difficult or impossible to remove.

Washable Articles

Sometimes, regular laundry methods will remove nongreasy stains; in other cases, laundering will actually set the stains. Sponge the stain with cool water or soak it in cool water for 30 minutes or longer; some stains require an overnight soak. If the stain persists after sponging or soaking, work a soap or detergent into it, then rinse. If the stain remains after detergent treatment, use a chlorine or peroxygen bleach.

Nonwashable Articles

Sponge the stain with cool water. If it remains, rub soap or detergent on the stain and work it into the fabric. Rinse. A final sponging with alcohol helps to remove the soap or detergent and to dry the fabric more quickly. Test alcohol on the fabric first to be sure it does not affect the dye. Dilute the alcohol with two parts of water before using it on acetate. If the stain remains after rinsing, use a chlorine or peroxygen bleach.

Combination Stains

Combination stains are caused by materials that contain both greasy and nongreasy substances.

Washable Articles

Sponge the stain with cool water or soak in cool water for 30 minutes or longer. If the stain persists, work soap or detergent into it, then rinse thoroughly. Allow the article to dry. If a greasy stain remains, sponge with a grease solvent. Allow the article to dry. Repeat if necessary. If a colored stain remains after the fabric dries, use a chlorine or peroxygen bleach.

Nonwashable Articles

Sponge the stain with cool water. If it remains, rub soap or detergent on the stain and work it into the fabric. Rinse the spot well with water. Allow the article to dry. If a greasy stain remains, sponge with a grease solvent. Allow to dry. Repeat if necessary. If a colored stain remains after fabric dries, use a chlorine or peroxygen bleach.

Specific Stains

Acids

If an acid is spilled on a fabric, rinse the area with water immediately. Then apply ammonia to the stain. Rinse again with water. Strong acids, such as sulfuric (used in batteries) and hydrochloric (used for cleaning brick), may damage or destroy some fibers before the acid can be rinsed out. The amount of damage depends on the kind of fiber and acid and on the concentration and temperature of the acid solution. Often, however, thorough rinsing before the acid dries on the fabric will prevent serious damage. Diluted solutions of weak acids, such as acetic (vinegar), will not damage fibers.

Both weak and strong acids may change the color of some dyes. The use of ammonia after rinsing with water neutralizes any acid left in the fabric and sometimes restores colors that have changed.

Adhesive Tape

Scrape gummy matter from stains carefully with a dull table knife; avoid damaging fabric. Sponge with a grease solvent.

Alcoholic Beverages

Follow directions for nongreasy stains. An alternate method, if alcohol does not affect the color of the fabric, is to sponge the stain with rubbing alcohol. Dilute alcohol with two parts of water before using on acetate. If a stain remains, use a chlorine or peroxygen bleach.

The alcohol in alcoholic beverages will cause bleeding of some dyes, which results in loss of color or formation of a dye ring around the edge of the stain. When either change occurs, the original appearance of the fabric cannot be restored.

Alkalis

If an alkali is spilled on a fabric, rinse the area with water immediately. Then apply vinegar to the stain. Rinse again with water. Strong alkalis, such as lye, may damage or destroy some fibers before they can be rinsed out. The amount of damage depends on the kind of fiber and alkali and on the concentration and temperature of the alkali solution. In many cases, however, prompt rinsing will prevent serious damage. Silk and wool are the fibers most easily damaged by alkalis. Diluted solutions of such weak alkalis as ammonia will not damage fibers. Both strong and weak alkalis may change the color of some dyes. The use of vinegar after rinsing with water neutralizes any alkali left in the fabric and sometimes restores colors that have changed.

Antiperspirants and Deodorants

Wash or sponge the stain thoroughly with soap or detergent and warm water. Rinse. If the stain is not removed, use a chlorine or peroxygen bleach. Antiperspirants that contain such substances as aluminum chloride are acid; they may cause fabric damage and change the color of some dyes. Fabric color may be restored by sponging with ammonia. Dilute ammonia with an equal volume of water for use on wool or silk. Rinse.

Blood

Follow directions for nongreasy stains, with one variation. If the stain is not removed by soap or detergent, put a few drops of ammonia on it and repeat the treatment with detergent. Rinse. Follow with a bleach treatment if necessary. Blood stains that have been set by heat will be difficult to remove.

Bluing

Follow directions for nongreasy stains.

Butter and Margarine

Follow directions for greasy stains.

Candy and Syrup

For chocolate candy and syrup, follow directions for combination stains. For other candy and syrup, follow directions for nongreasy stains.

Carbon Paper

Work soap or detergent into the stain; rinse well. If the stain is not removed, put a few drops of ammonia on it and repeat the treatment; rinse well. Repeat again if necessary.

Catsup and Chili

Follow directions for nongreasy stains.

Chewing Gum

Scrape gum off without damaging fabric. The gum can be scraped off more easily if it is first hardened by rubbing it with ice. If a stain remains, sponge thoroughly with a grease solvent.

Chlorine

Use one of the following treatments to remove yellow chlorine bleach stains from fabrics with resin finishes, or to prevent such stains from appearing. Always treat the fabric before ironing it. On some fabrics, the yellow stains form before ironing; on others, after ironing. In either case, ironing before the chlorine is removed weakens the fibers.

Yellow stains caused by the use of chlorine bleach on wool and silk cannot be removed. White or faded spots caused by use of chlorine bleach on colored fabrics cannot be restored to the original color.

Treatment for any fabric. Rinse fabric thoroughly with water. Then soak for 30 minutes or longer in a solution containing one teaspoon of sodium thiosulfate to each quart of warm water. Rinse thoroughly. To strengthen the treatment, make the sodium thiosulfate solution as hot as is safe for the fabric.

Treatment for white or colorfast fabrics. Rinse the fabric thoroughly with water. Then use a color remover, following the directions given on the package for removing stains.

Chocolate

Follow directions for combination stains.

Cocoa

Follow directions for nongreasy stains.

Coffee and Tea

With cream. Follow directions for combination stains.
Without cream. Follow directions for nongreasy stains.
Alternatively, for both types of stains, and if safe for the fabric, pour boiling water through the spot from a height of 1 to 3 feet.

Correction Fluid

Sponge the stain with acetone or amyl acetate. Use amyl acetate on acetate, Arnel®, Dynel®, and Verel®; use acetone on other fabrics.

Cosmetics

(eye shadow, lipstick, liquid makeup, mascara, pancake makeup, powder, blush)
Washable articles. Apply undiluted liquid detergent to the stain, or dampen the stain and rub in soap or detergent until thick suds are formed. Work in until the outline of the stain is gone; then rinse well. Repeat if necessary. It may help to dry the fabric between treatments.
Nonwashable articles. Sponge with a grease solvent until no more color is removed. If the stain is not removed, use the method given for washable articles.

Crayon

Follow directions for cosmetics.

Cream

Follow directions for combination stains.

Dyes

Follow directions for nongreasy stains; if bleach is needed, use chlorine bleach or color remover. A long soak in sudsy water often is effective on fresh dye stains.

Egg

Follow directions for nongreasy stains.

Fish Slime, Mucus, Vomit

Follow directions for nongreasy stains or treat the stain with lukewarm solution of salt and water—¼ cup salt to each quart of water. Sponge the stain with solution or soak the stain in it. Rinse well.

Flowers

See **Grass, Flowers, and Foliage.**

Food Coloring

Follow directions for nongreasy stains.

Fruit, Fruit Juices

Follow directions for nongreasy stains or, if it is safe for the fabric, pour boiling water through the spot from a height of 1 to 3 feet. When any fruit juice is spilled on a fabric, it is a good idea to sponge the spot immediately with cool water. Some fruit juices, citrus among them, are invisible on the fabric after they dry but turn yellow on aging or heating. This yellow stain may be difficult to remove.

Furniture Polish

Follow directions for greasy stains or, if the polish contains wood stain, follow directions given for paint.

Glue and Mucilage

Airplane glue, household cement. Follow directions for correction fluid.

Casein glue. Follow directions for nongreasy stains.

Plastic glue. Wash the stain with soap or detergent and water before the glue hardens; some types of glues cannot be removed after they have hardened.

To remove some dried plastic glue stains, immerse the stain in a hot 10-percent acetic acid solution or hot vinegar. Keep acid or vinegar at or near the boiling point until the stain is removed. This may take 15 minutes or longer. Rinse with water.

Other types of glues and mucilage. Follow directions for nongreasy stains, but soak the stain in hot water instead of cool.

Grass, Flowers, and Foliage

Washable articles. Work soap or detergent into the stain, then rinse. If it is safe for the dye, sponge the stain with alcohol. Dilute the alcohol with two parts of water for use on acetate. If the stain remains, use a chlorine or peroxygen bleach.

Nonwashable articles. Use the methods for washable articles, but try alcohol first if it is safe for the dye.

Gravy, Meat Juice

Follow directions for combination stains.

Grease (car grease, lard)

Follow directions for greasy stains.

Gum

See **Chewing Gum.**

Ice Cream

Follow directions for combination stains.

Ink, Ballpoint

Sponge the stain repeatedly with acetone or amyl acetate, or spray it with hair spray. This will remove fresh stains. Old stains may also require bleaching. Washing removes some types of ballpoint ink stains but sets other types. To see if the stain will wash out, mark a scrap of similar material with the ink and wash it.

Ink, Black (India ink)

Treat the stain as soon as possible. These stains are very hard to remove if dry.

Washable articles. Force water through the stain until all loose pigment is removed; otherwise, the stain will spread when treated. Wash with soap or detergent, several times if necessary. Then soak the stain in warm suds containing 1 to 4 tablespoons of ammonia to a quart of water. Dried stains may need to be soaked overnight. An alternative method is to force water through the stain until all loose pigment is removed, wet the spot with ammonia, and then work soap or detergent into it. Rinse. Repeat if necessary.

Nonwashable articles. Force water through stain until all loose pigment is removed; otherwise, the stain will spread when you treat it. Sponge stain with a solution of water and ammonia (1 tablespoon of ammonia per 1 cup of water). Rinse with water. If stain remains, moisten it with ammonia, then work soap or detergent into it. Rinse. Repeat if necessary. If ammonia changes the color of the fabric, sponge first with water, then moisten with vinegar. Rinse well.

Ink, Drawing (colors other than black)

Follow directions for nongreasy stains. If bleach is needed, use a color remover if it is safe for the dye. If a color remover is not safe, try other bleaches.

Ink, Writing

Washable articles. Follow directions for nongreasy stains. Because writing inks vary greatly in composition, it may be necessary to try more than one kind of bleach. Try a chlorine bleach on all fabrics for which it is safe. For other fabrics, try peroxygen bleach. A few types of inks require treatment with color removers. A strong bleach treatment may be needed. However, a strong bleach may leave a faded spot on some colored fabrics. If a yellow stain remains after bleaching, treat it as a rust stain.

Nonwashable articles. If possible, use a blotter (for small stains) or absorbent powder to remove excess ink before it soaks into the fabric. Then follow directions for washable articles.

Iodine

Washable articles. Three methods for removing iodine stains are given below. If the method you try first does not remove the stain, try another.

Water—Soak in cool water until the stain is removed; some stains require soaking overnight. If the stain remains, rub it with soap or detergent and wash it in warm suds. If the stain is not removed, soak the fabric in a solution containing 1 tablespoon of sodium thiosulfate to each pint of warm water, or sprinkle the crystals on the dampened stain. Rinse well as soon as the stain is removed.

Steam—Moisten the stain with water; then hold it in the steam from a boiling tea kettle.

Alcohol—If alcohol is safe for the dye, cover the stain with a pad of cotton soaked in it. If necessary, keep the pad wet for several hours. Dilute with two parts water for use on acetate.

Nonwashable articles. Try the steam or alcohol methods given above.

Lacquer

Follow directions for correction fluid.

Margarine

Follow directions for greasy stains.

Mayonnaise and Salad Dressing

Follow directions for combination stains.

Medicines

Gummy, tarry, and with an oily base. Follow directions for grease stains.

In sugar syrup or in water. Wash the stain out with water.

Dissolved in alcohol (tinctures). Sponge the stain with alcohol. Dilute with two parts of water for use on acetate.

With iron. Follow directions for rust.

With dyes. Follow directions for dyes.

Mercurochrome and Merthiolate

Washable articles. Soak overnight in a warm soap or detergent solution that contains 4 tablespoons of ammonia to each quart of water.

Nonwashable articles. If safe for the dye, sponge with alcohol as long as any of the stain is removed. Dilute the alcohol with two parts of water for use on acetate. If the stain remains, place a pad of cotton saturated with alcohol on it. Keep the pad wet until the stain is removed; this may take an hour or more. If alcohol is not safe for the dye, wet the stain with liquid detergent. Add a drop of ammonia with a medicine dropper. Rinse with water, and repeat if necessary.

Metals

To remove stains caused by tarnished brass, copper, tin, and other metals, use vinegar, lemon juice, acetic acid, or oxalic acid. The two acids, because they are stronger, will remove stains that cannot be removed by vinegar or lemon juice. As soon as the stain is removed, rinse well with water. Do not use chlorine or peroxygen bleaches. These bleaches may cause damage because the metal in the stain hastens their action.

Mildew

Washable articles. Treat mildew spots while they are fresh, before the mold growth has a chance to weaken the fabric. Wash the mildewed article thoroughly, and dry it in the sun. If the stain remains, treat it with a chlorine or peroxygen bleach.

Nonwashable articles. Send the article to a dry cleaner promptly.

Milk

Follow directions for nongreasy stains.

Mud

Let the stain dry, then brush well. If the stain remains, follow directions for nongreasy stains. Stains from iron-rich clays not removed by this method should be treated as rust stains.

Mustard

Washable articles. Rub soap or detergent into the dampened stain; rinse. If the stain is not removed, soak the article in a hot detergent solution for several hours, or overnight if necessary. If the stain remains, use a bleach.

Nonwashable articles. If alcohol is safe for the dye, sponge the stain with it. Dilute the alcohol with two parts of water for use on acetate. If alcohol cannot be used, or if it does not remove the stain completely, follow the treatment for washable articles but omit the soaking.

Nail Polish

Follow directions for correction fluid. Nail polish removers also can be used to remove stains. Before using nail polish remover on acetate, Arnel®, Dynel®, or Verel®, test it on a scrap of material to make sure it will not damage the fabric.

Oil (fish-liver oil, linseed oil, machine oil, mineral oil, vegetable oil)

Follow directions for greasy stains.

Paint, Varnish

Treat stains promptly, as they are always harder—and sometimes impossible—to remove after they have dried on fabric. Because there are so many different kinds of paints and varnishes, no one method will remove all stains. Read the label on the container; if a certain solvent is recommended as a thinner, it may be more effective in removing stains than the solvents recommended.

Washable articles. To remove fresh stains, rub soap or detergent into the stain and wash. If the stain has dried or is only partially removed by washing, sponge it with turpentine until no more paint or varnish is removed (for aluminum paint stains, dry-cleaning may be more effective than turpentine). While the stain is still wet with the solvent, work soap or detergent into it, put the article in hot water, and soak it overnight. Thorough washing will remove most types of paint stains. If the stain remains, repeat the treatment.

Nonwashable articles. Sponge fresh stains with turpentine until no more paint is removed (for aluminum paint stains, dry-cleaning may be more effective than turpentine). If the stain remains, put a drop of liquid detergent on it and work it into the fabric with the edge of the bowl of a spoon. Alternately, sponge the stain with turpentine and treat with detergent as many times as necessary. If alcohol is safe for the dye, sponge the stain with it to remove turpentine and detergent. Dilute the alcohol with two parts of water for use on acetate. If alcohol is not safe for the dye, sponge the stain first with warm soap or detergent solution, then with water.

Pencil

A soft eraser will remove pencil marks from some fabrics. If the marks cannot be erased, follow directions for carbon paper.

Perfume

Follow directions for alcoholic beverages.

Perspiration

Wash or sponge the stain thoroughly with soap or detergent and warm water. Work carefully, because some fabrics are weakened by perspiration; silk is the fiber most easily damaged. If perspiration has changed the color of the fabric, try to restore it by treating it with ammonia or vinegar. Apply ammonia to fresh stains and vinegar to old stains; rinse with water.

If an oily stain remains, follow directions for greasy stains. Remove any yellow discoloration with a chlorine or peroxygen bleach. If it is safe for fabric, the strong sodium perborate treatment recommended for greasy-stain removal is often the most effective for these stains.

Plastic

To remove stains caused by plastic hangers or buttons that have softened and adhered to the fabric, dry-cleaning is the safest and most effective method.

Rust

Oxalic-acid method. PRECAUTION: OXALIC ACID IS POISONOUS IF SWALLOWED. Moisten the stain with oxalic acid solution (1 tablespoon of oxalic acid crystals in 1 cup warm water). If the stain is not removed by a single treatment, heat the solution and repeat. If the stain is stubborn, place oxalic acid crystals directly on it. Moisten the stain with water as hot as is safe for the fabric and allow it to stand a few minutes, or dip it in hot water. Repeat if necessary. Do not use this method on nylon. Rinse the article thoroughly. If it is allowed to dry in the fabric, oxalic acid will cause damage.

Cream-of-tartar method. If the treatment is safe for the fabric, boil the stained article in a solution containing 4 teaspoons of cream of tartar to each pint of water. Boil until the stain is removed. Rinse thoroughly.

Lemon-juice method. Spread the stained portion over a pan of boiling water and squeeze lemon juice on it; or sprinkle salt on the stain, squeeze lemon juice on it, and spread the fabric in the sun to dry. Rinse thoroughly. Repeat if necessary.

Color removers can be used to remove rust stains from white fabrics.

Sauces, Soups

Follow directions for combination stains.

Scorch Stains

If the article is washable, follow the directions for nongreasy stains. To remove light scorch stains from an article that is nonwashable, apply hydrogen peroxide. The strong treatment may be needed to remove the stains. Repeat if necessary. Severe scorch stains cannot be removed, however, because the fabric already has been damaged.

Shellac

Using alcohol, sponge or soak the stain. Dilute the alcohol with two parts water for use on acetate. If alcohol bleeds the dye, try turpentine.

Shoe Polish

Because there are many different kinds of shoe polish, no one method will remove all stains. It may be necessary to try more than one of the methods given below.

1. Follow directions for cosmetics.
2. Sponge the stain with alcohol if it is safe for the dye in the fabric. Dilute the alcohol with two parts water for use on acetate.
3. Sponge the stain with grease solvent or turpentine. If turpentine is used, remove it by sponging with a warm soap or detergent solution or with alcohol.

If the stain is not removed by any of these methods, use a chlorine or peroxygen bleach. If safe for the fabric, the strong sodium perborate treatment recommended for greasy-stain removal is often the most effective.

Silver Nitrate

Dampen the stain with water. Then put a few drops of tincture of iodine on the stain. Let it stand for a few minutes. Then treat it as an iodine stain. Unless a stain on silk or wool is treated when fresh, a yellow or brown discoloration will remain.

Soft Drinks

Follow directions for nongreasy stains. When any soft drink is spilled on a fabric, sponge the spot immediately with cool water. Some soft drinks are invisible after they dry but turn yellow on aging or heating. The yellow stain may be difficult to remove.

Soot, Smoke

Follow directions for cosmetics.

Syrup

See **Candy and Syrup.**

Tar

Follow directions for greasy stains. If the stain is not removed by this method, sponge it with turpentine.

Tea

See **Coffee and Tea.**

Tobacco

Follow directions for grass.

Typewriter Ribbon

Follow directions for carbon paper.

Unknown Origin

If the stain appears greasy, treat it as a greasy stain; otherwise, treat it as a nongreasy stain.

Urine

To remove stains caused by normal urine, follow directions for nongreasy stains. If the color of the fabric has been changed, sponge the stain with ammonia. If this treatment does not restore the color, sponging with acetic acid or vinegar may help. If the stain is not removed by one or both of these methods, see directions for medicines and yellowing.

Vegetables

Follow directions for nongreasy stains.

Walnuts, Black

These stains are very difficult to remove.
Washable articles. If the treatment is safe for fabric, boil washable articles in soap or

detergent solution. This will remove fresh stains. If the stain is not removed, use a strong chlorine or sodium perborate bleach treatment. If the stain remains, treat it as a rust stain.

Nonwashable articles. These stains cannot be removed at home. Send the article to a dry cleaner.

Wax (floor, furniture, car)

Follow directions for greasy stains.

Yellowing; Brown Stains

To remove storage stains—or unknown yellow or yellow-brown stains—from fabrics, use as many of the following treatments as necessary, if safe for the fabric, in the order given.

1. Wash.
2. Use a mild treatment of a chlorine or peroxygen bleach.
3. Use the oxalic-acid method for treating rust stains.
4. Use a strong treatment of a chlorine or peroxygen bleach.

Cooking Equivalents and Substitutions

Common Kitchen Measures

pinch (a few grains) = less than 1/8 teaspoon
3 teaspoons = 1 tablespoon
2 tablespoons = 1 fluid ounce
4 tablespoons = 1/4 cup
5 tablespoons + 1 teaspoon = 1/3 cup
16 tablespoons = 1 cup
1 cup = 1/2 pint or 8 fluid ounces

2 cups = 1 pint
2 pints = 1 quart
4 quarts = 1 gallon
2 dry pints = 1 dry quart
8 dry quarts = 1 peck
4 pecks = 1 bushel

Cooking Measurement Abbreviations

Measure	Abbreviation	Measure	Abbreviation
teaspoon	tsp.	gram	g
tablespoon	tbsp.	milligram	mg
ounce	oz.	kilogram	kg
fluid ounce	fl. oz.	liter	l
pint	pt.	milliliter	ml
pound	lb.	degrees Fahrenheit	°F
quart	qt.	degrees Celsius	°C

Metric Cooking Measure Equivalents

Customary	Metric
1 teaspoon	4.9 milliliters
1 tablespoon	14.8 milliliters
1 ounce (dry)	28.35 grams
1 fluid ounce	29.57 milliliters
1 cup	236.6 milliliters
1 pint	473.2 milliliters
1 quart	946.4 milliliters
0.9 quart (dry)	1 liter
1.06 quarts (liquid)	1 liter
1 pound	454 grams
2.2 pounds	1 kilogram
32° Fahrenheit (freezing point)	0° Celsius
212° Fahrenheit (boiling point)	100° Celsius

Food Weights and Measures

Bread

1-pound loaf	12 to 16 slices
1 slice	½ cup soft or ¼ cup dry bread crumbs

Dairy

1 pound cheese	4 to 5 cups, shredded
1 pound cottage cheese	2 cups
3 ounces cream cheese	6 tablespoons
8 ounces cream cheese	1 cup
1 pound butter	2 cups (4 sticks)
1 quart milk	4 cups
1 pound instant nonfat dry milk	5 quarts liquid skim milk
13-ounce can evaporated milk	1⅔ cups
½ pint cream	1 cup
1 cup heavy cream	2 cups, whipped

Eggs

3 to 4	1 cup
8 to 10 whites	1 cup
12 to 14 yolks	1 cup
1 yolk	2 tablespoons

Flour

1 pound all-purpose flour	4 cups, sifted
1 pound cake flour	4¾ to 5 cups, sifted
1 pound whole-wheat flour	3½ to 3¾ cups, unsifted
1 pound cornmeal	3 cups

Fruit

juice of 1 medium lemon	2 to 3 tablespoons
juice of 1 medium orange	$1/3$ to $1/2$ cup
granted rind of medium orange	1 tablespoon
1 apple	1 cup, sliced
1 pound apples	3 cups, pared and sliced
3 to 4 bananas (1 pound)	$1^{3}/_{4}$ cups, mashed
1 pound cherries	2 cups, pitted
1 pound cranberries	2 cups
1 pound grapes	$2^{1}/_{2}$ cups, seeded
1 pound raisins	$2^{1}/_{2}$ cups
1 pound cut candied fruit	3 cups
1 pound finely cut dates	$1^{1}/_{2}$ cups

Meat and poultry

1 pound ground cooked meat	5 cups
1 pound diced cooked meat	5 cups
$3^{1}/_{2}$-pound chicken	3 cups diced, cooked

Nuts

1 pound almonds in shell	$1^{1}/_{4}$ cups, shelled
1 pound pecans in shell	2 cups, chopped
1 pound walnuts in shell	$1^{1}/_{2}$ to $1^{3}/_{4}$ cups, chopped
$1/4$ pound chopped nuts	about 1 cup

Sweeteners and flavorings

1 pound confectioners' sugar	$3^{1}/_{2}$ cups
1 pound brown sugar	$2^{1}/_{4}$ to $2^{1}/_{2}$ cups, firmly packed
1 pound granulated sugar	2 cups
1 pound honey, molasses, or syrup	$1^{1}/_{3}$ cups
1 pound cocoa	4 cups
1 ounce unsweetened chocolate	1 square
6-ounce package chocolate chips	1 cup

Vegetables

1 whole bay leaf	$1/4$ teaspoon, crushed
1 pound split peas	$2^{1}/_{2}$ cups
1 large green pepper	1 cup, diced
$1/4$ pound sliced mushrooms ($1^{1}/_{4}$ cups)	$1/4$ to $1/2$ cup, cooked
1 medium onion	$1/2$ cup, chopped
1 pound potatoes (3 medium)	$2^{1}/_{2}$ cups, sliced
1 pound green beans (3 cups)	$2^{1}/_{2}$ cups, cooked
1 pound cabbage	$2^{1}/_{2}$ cups, cooked
1 pound carrots	$2^{1}/_{2}$ cups, diced, or 2 cups, cooked
1 medium bunch celery	$4^{1}/_{2}$ cups, chopped
1 pound tomatoes (3 medium)	$1^{1}/_{2}$ cups, cooked

Food Substitutions

Ingredient	Substitution
Baking powder (1 teaspoon)	1/4 teaspoon baking soda + 1/2 teaspoon cream of tartar
Baking powder (1 1/4 teaspoons)	1/2 teaspoon baking soda + 2 tablespoons vinegar
Black pepper	White pepper or paprika
Bouillon (1 cup)	1 bouillon cube dissolved in 1 cup hot water
Bread crumbs (1 cup)	3/4 cup cracker crumbs
Butter (1 cup)	1 cup margarine *or*
	1 cup vegetable shortening *or*
	7/8 cup lard
Buttermilk or sour milk (1 cup)	1 cup yogurt *or*
	1 cup whole milk + 1 tablespoon lemon juice *or*
	1 tablespoon vinegar *or*
	1 3/4 teaspoons cream of tartar
Carrots	Parsnips or baby white turnips
Chocolate:	
semisweet (1 2/3 ounces)	1 ounce unsweetened chocolate + 4 teaspoons sugar
unsweetened (1 ounce— 1 square)	3 tablespoons cocoa powder + 1 tablespoon shortening
Cream, heavy (1 cup)	7/8 cup buttermilk or yogurt + 3 tablespoons butter
Croutons	Cubes of crustless white bread sautéed in butter
Curry powder	Turmeric plus cardamom, ginger powder, and cumin
Dry mustard	Prepared mustard
Egg, for thickening or baking	2 egg yolks
Flour:	
all-purpose, for thickening	1 1/2 teaspoons cornstarch *or*
	1 1/2 teaspoons arrowroot *or*
	1 tablespoon quick-cooking tapioca
all-purpose, for bread baking	Up to 1/2 cup bran, whole-wheat flour, or cornmeal + enough all-purpose flour to fill cup
cake (1 cup sifted)	1 cup minus 2 tablespoons all-purpose flour
Fresh herbs (1 tablespoon)	1/3 to 1/2 teaspoon dried herbs
Honey (1 cup)	1 1/4 cups sugar + 1/4 cup liquid
Lemon juice	Vinegar *or* lime juice *or* white wine
Mayonnaise, homemade (1/2 cup)	1/2 cup commercial mayonnaise + 1/2 teaspoon lemon juice and 1/2 teaspoon prepared mustard
Olive oil	Vegetable oil
Onion, chopped (1 cup)	1 tablespoon instant minced onion, reconstituted
Parsley	Chervil
Scallions	Green or white onions, or onion powder to taste
Shallots	2 parts onion + 1 part garlic
Sugar, granulated (1 tablespoon)	1 tablespoon maple sugar
(1 cup)	1 3/4 cups confectioners' sugar *or*
	1 cup molasses + 1/2 teaspoon baking soda
Tomato sauce (2 cups)	3/4 cup tomato paste + 1 cup water
Wine vinegar	Cider vinegar with a little red wine *or* white distilled vinegar with a little white wine
Yeast, active dry (1 tablespoon— 1 package)	1 3/5-ounce cake yeast

Kosher Substitutions

According to Jewish dietary laws, certain food items, such as pork products, shellfish, and some cuts of beef, are not allowed to be eaten. Also, meat and dairy products are not to be eaten at the same time. Below is a list of ingredients that may be problematic in preparing a kosher dish. On the right are acceptable replacements for these items.

Ingredient	Substitution
Butter	In pastry: all-vegetable margarine or vegetable shortening
	To sauté vegetables: all-vegetable margarine
	To fry meat or poultry: equal parts rendered chicken fat and oil; oil; equal parts oil and all-vegetable margarine
Ham or bacon	Used as flavoring: an equal quantity of anchovies, mushrooms, or pungent vegetables
Milk or cream	In chicken stew, soup, or sauce: for each ½ cup, ½ cup chicken stock mixed with 1 egg yolk and 1 teaspoon cornstarch
	In pancakes: an equal quantity of water, 1 tablespoon oil for each cup of flour, and twice as many eggs
Shellfish	An equal amount of firm fish that has both fins and scales

Cooking Times and Serving Sizes

Oven Temperatures

175° to 225° F	Warm
250° to 275° F	Very slow
300° to 325° F	Slow
350° to 375° F	Moderate
400° to 425° F	Hot
450° to 475° F	Very hot

Cooking Times for Meat, Poultry, Fish

To Roast Beef (325 ° F)

Cut	Weight in pounds	Minutes per pound	Internal temperature (F)
Standing rib	4 to 8		
rare		20 to 25	140°
medium		25 to 30	160°
well-done		30 to 35	170°

Rolled rib	5 to 7		
rare		30 to 35	140°
medium		35 to 40	160°
well-done		40 to 45	170°
Rib eye	4 to 6		
rare		20	140°
medium		22	160°
well-done		24	170°
Sirloin tip	3½ to 4	35 to 40	160°
Tenderloin (roast at 425°)			
whole	4 to 6	10	140°
half	2 to 3	20	140°

To Broil Steak (2 inches from preheated oven broiler)

1-inch-thick sirloin, porterhouse, T-bone, or rib
    rare   5 minutes each side
    medium   7 minutes each side
    well-done 10 minutes each side

1½-inch-thick sirloin, porterhouse, T-bone, or rib
    rare   6 minutes each side
    medium   8 minutes each side
    well-done 12 minutes each side

For filet mignon, decrease the cooking time by 1 minute on each side. When grilling steak over hot charcoals, have the grill 3 inches from the fire and cook the meat 1 minute less on each side.

To Roast Veal (325° F)

Cut	Weight in pounds	Minutes per pound	Internal temperature (F)
Leg	5 to 8	25 to 30	170°
Loin	4 to 6	30 to 35	170°
Rib (rack)	3 to 5	35 to 40	170°
Rolled rump	3 to 5	40 to 45	170°
Rolled shoulder	4 to 6	40 to 45	170°

To Roast Lamb (325° F)

Cut	Weight in pounds	Minutes per pound	Internal temperature (F)
Leg	5 to 8	30 to 35	175° to 180°
Shoulder	4 to 6	30 to 35	175° to 180°
Cushion shoulder	3 to 5	30 to 35	175° to 180°
Rib (rack)	4 to 5	40 to 45	175° to 180°
Rolled shoulder	3 to 5	40 to 45	175° to 180°
Crown roast	4 to 6	40 to 45	175° to 180°

To Broil Lamb

Broil 1-inch chops or patties about 6 minutes on each side, 1½-inch chops 9 minutes on each side, and 2-inch chops 11 minutes on each side.

To Roast Pork (350° F)

To prevent trichinosis, pork must always be cooked to the well-done stage with no traces of pink showing. A meat thermometer will show 185° when the pork is cooked through.

Cut	Weight in pounds	Minutes per pound	Internal temperature (F)
Loin, center	3 to 5	40	185°
Loin, half	5 to 7	45	185°
Loin, rolled	3 to 5	50	185°
Sirloin	3 to 4	50	185°
Crown	4 to 6	45	185°
Picnic shoulder	5 to 8	40	185°
Rolled shoulder	3 to 5	45	185°
Fresh ham (leg)			
whole	10 to 14	30	185°
half	5 to 7	40	185°
Spareribs	3	30	185°

To Broil Pork

Chops (¾ to 1 inch thick), shoulder steaks (½ to ¾ inch thick), and patties (1 inch thick) should be broiled about 11 minutes on each side.

To Roast Ham and Other Cured Pork (325° F)

Cut	Weight in pounds	Minutes per pound	Internal temperature (F)
Whole ham	10 to 14		
uncooked		20	160°
fully cooked		10	130°
Half ham	5 to 7		
uncooked		25	160°
fully cooked		15	130°
Picnic shoulder	5 to 8	30	170°
Rolled shoulder	2 to 4	40	170°

For all boneless meat, allow ⅓ to ½ pound per serving; if the meat contains bone, estimate ½ to ¾ pound per serving.

To Roast Chicken (375° F)

Chickens weighing between 2 and 4 pounds can be roasted for 30 minutes per pound. Add 15 minutes to the total roasting time if the chicken is stuffed. When the chicken is done, a meat thermometer inserted in the thickest part of the thigh will read 190° F; a thermometer inserted in the stuffing will read 165° F. Estimate 1/2 pound per serving.

To Roast Turkey (325° F)

Ready-to-cook weight in pounds	Total number of hours
4 to 8	3 to 4
8 to 12	4 to 4 1/2
12 to 16	4 1/2 to 5
16 to 20	6 to 7 1/2
20 to 24	7 1/2 to 9

Turkey is done when a meat thermometer inserted in the thickest part of the thigh reads 185° F, or when a thermometer inserted in the stuffing reads 165° F. Plan on 1/2 pound per serving.

To Roast Duck or Goose (325° F)

Roast duck or goose about 30 minutes per pound. Estimate 1 pound per serving.

To Cook Fish

Fish can be cooked at either a very high temperature for a short time or a low temperature for a longer period. Following are general guidelines:

Baked: 10 minutes at 500° F
Broiled: 15 minutes
Deep-fried: 2 minutes at 370° F
Pan-fried: 10 minutes
Poached or steamed: 10 minutes per pound

Allow 3/4 to 1 pound of whole fish per serving, 1/2 pound per serving of dressed fish, fillets, and steaks.

To Cook Shellfish

There are many ways to cook shellfish. Here are just a few.

Starting with boiling water, drop in seafood and let it simmer as follows: shrimp, 5 minutes; crab, 20 minutes; lobster, 20 to 40 minutes.
Clams can be steamed until their shells just open.
Shrimp, scallops, clams, and oysters can be deep-fried at 370° F for about 3 minutes.

Allow the following quantities per serving:

1 quart unshelled soft-shell clams
1 to 2 crabs
1 small lobster or 1 pound unshelled lobster
6 to 8 oysters
²/₃ cup or ¹/₃ pound shelled scallops
¹/₄ pound unshelled shrimp

Cooking Times for Fresh Vegetables

Vegetable	Amount per Serving	Cooking Time (in minutes)*
Artichoke	1 whole	30 to 40
Asparagus	5 to 7 stalks	10 to 15
Beans (green and wax)	¹/₃ pound	5 to 10
Beans (lima)	³/₄ pound	20 to 25
Beets	¹/₃ pound	35 to 45, whole
Broccoli	¹/₂ pound	10 to 15
Brussels sprouts	¹/₃ pound	5 to 10
Cabbage	¹/₃ pound	5
Carrots	¹/₃ pound	10 to 15
Cauliflower	¹/₃ pound	20 to 25, whole; 10 to 15, flowerets
Corn	1 to 2 ears	5
Eggplant	¹/₄ medium, sliced, broiled or sautéed	5 to 10
Mushrooms	¹/₄ pound, caps or sliced, sautéed	5
Onions	¹/₃ pound	20 to 30, whole
Peas	¹/₂ pound	5 to 10
Peppers (green)	1 medium, sliced sautéed	3 to 5
Potatoes	1 medium	20 to 25, sliced; 1¹/₂ hours, baked, 350° F
	3 small new	20 to 25, whole
Potatoes (sweet) or yams	1 medium, sliced	30 to 35
Spinach	¹/₂ pound	5
Squash (summer) or zucchini	¹/₂ pound, sliced, boiled or sautéed	5 to 10
Tomatoes	¹/₂ pound, sliced	5 to 10 (without water)
Turnips	¹/₃ pound, cubed	25 to 30

* Boiled or steamed unless otherwise noted.

Cooking Time for Fresh Fruit

To cook any of the fruits below, prepare the fruit according to the directions and add to the proper amount of boiling water. Add sugar and cook for the appropriate time.

Fruit	Amount[1]	How to Prepare	Amount of Boiling Water (cups)	Amount of Sugar (cups)	Cooking Time After Adding Fruit (in minutes)
Apples	8 medium	Pare and slice	1/2	1/4	8 to 10 (slices); 12 to 15 (sauce)
Apricots	15	Halve; pit and peel if desired	1/2	3/4	5
Cherries	1 quart	Remove pits	1	2/3	5
Cranberries	1 pound	Sort	1 or 2, as desired[2]	2	5
Peaches	6 medium	Pare, pit, and halve or slice	3/4	3/4	5
Pears	6 medium	Pare, core, and halve or slice	2/3	1/3	10 (soft varieties); 20 to 25 (firm varieties)
Plums	8 large	Halve, pit	1/2	2/3	5
Rhubarb	1 1/2 pounds	Slice	3/4	2/3	2 to 5

[1] Makes 6 servings, about 1/2 cup each.
[2] Cranberries make 6 servings with 1 cup water; 8 servings with 2 cups water.

REFRIGERATION FOOD STORAGE

Food	Maximum Recommended Storage Time
Beef	3–5 days
Butter	2 weeks
Canned goods	1 year
Cereal	2–3 months
Cheese	1–3 weeks
Eggs	1–2 weeks
Fish	1 day
Frankfurters	1 week
Ground meat	1–2 days
Milk	1 week
Pasta	2 years
Poultry	1–2 days
Rice	2 years

HOW TO STORE COFFEE

Bean form:
    room temperature   4 to 5 weeks
    freeze   5 to 6 months
        (grind amount needed only)
    refrigerator   avoid
Ground:
    room temperature   7 to 10 days
    freezer   5 to 6 weeks
    refrigerator   up to 3 weeks

TEMPERATURE OF FOOD FOR CONTROL OF BACTERIA

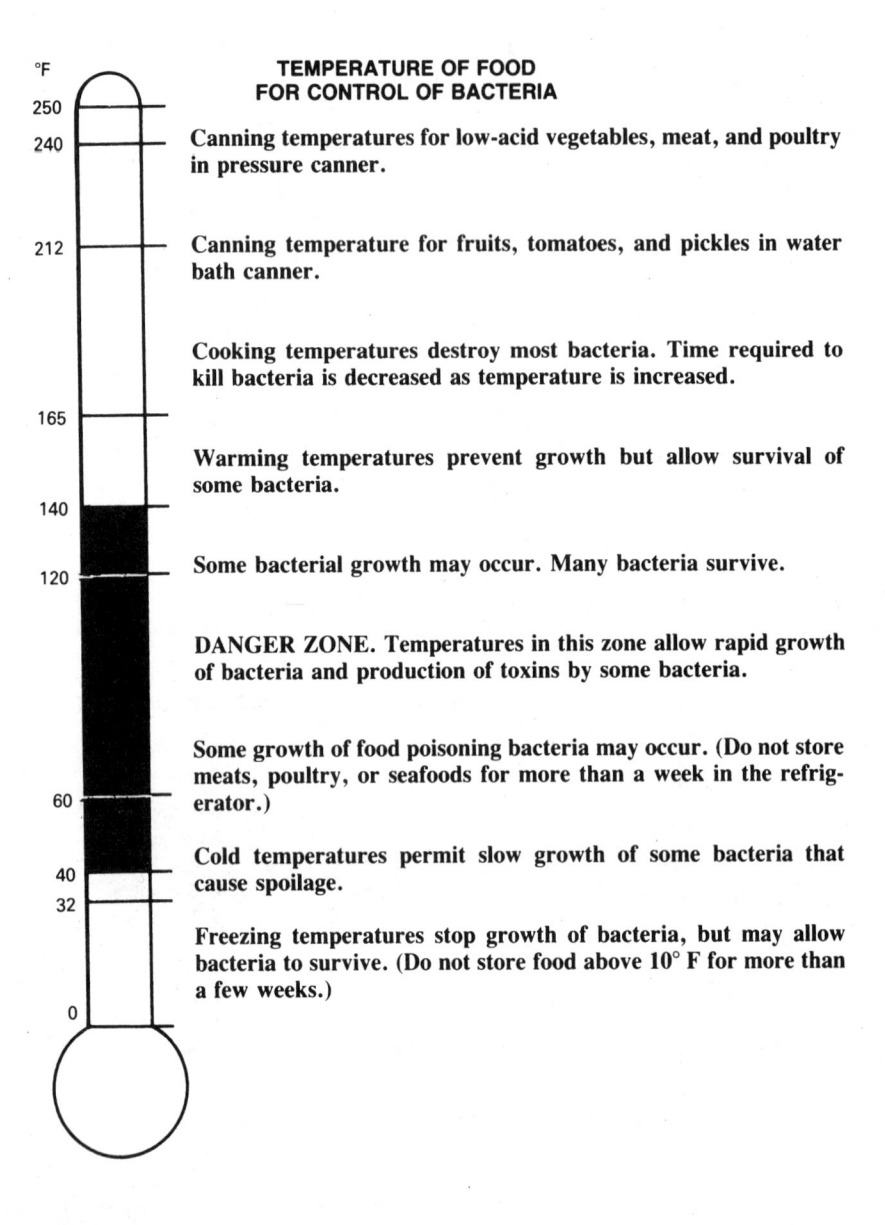

°F

250

240 — Canning temperatures for low-acid vegetables, meat, and poultry in pressure canner.

212 — Canning temperature for fruits, tomatoes, and pickles in water bath canner.

Cooking temperatures destroy most bacteria. Time required to kill bacteria is decreased as temperature is increased.

165 —

Warming temperatures prevent growth but allow survival of some bacteria.

140 —

120 — Some bacterial growth may occur. Many bacteria survive.

DANGER ZONE. Temperatures in this zone allow rapid growth of bacteria and production of toxins by some bacteria.

Some growth of food poisoning bacteria may occur. (Do not store meats, poultry, or seafoods for more than a week in the refrigerator.)

60 —

40 — Cold temperatures permit slow growth of some bacteria that cause spoilage.

32 —

Freezing temperatures stop growth of bacteria, but may allow bacteria to survive. (Do not store food above 10° F for more than a few weeks.)

0

Herbs and Spices

Herbs can provide creative, flavorful alternatives to salt for seasoning foods. Through the skillful use of herbs and spices, you can create imaginative flavors and turn simple foods into gourmet delights.

Herbs and spices differ only in that herbs grow in temperate areas while spices grow in tropical regions. Many people like to grow their own herbs in order to have a fresh supply throughout the growing season. Professional cooks also prefer fresh herbs. But fresh herbs are less concentrated, and two to three times as much of them should be used if a recipe calls for dried herbs.

Here are some tips for cooking with herbs and spices.

- In general, the weaker the flavor of the main staple item, the lower the level of added seasoning required to achieve a satisfactory balance of flavor in the end product.
- Dried herbs are stronger than fresh, and powdered herbs are stronger than crumbled. A useful formula is $1/4$ teaspoon powdered herb = $3/4$ to 1 teaspoon crumbled-2 teaspoons fresh.
- Leaves should be finely chopped because the more cut surface exposed, the more flavor will be absorbed.
- A mortar and pestle can be kept in the kitchen to powder-dry herbs when necessary.
- Scissors are often the best utensil for cutting fresh herbs.
- Be conservative with amounts until you are familiar with the strength of an herb. The aromatic oils can be too strong if a great deal is used.
- The flavoring of herbs is lost by extended cooking. Add herbs to soups or stews about 45 minutes before completing the cooking. For cold foods such as dips, cheeses, vegetables, and dressings, herbs should be added several hours, or even overnight, before using.
- For casseroles and hot sauces, add finely chopped fresh or dried herbs directly to the mixture.
- To become familiar with the specific flavor of an herb, try mixing it with butter and/or cream cheese, letting it set for at least an hour, and then spreading it on a plain cracker.
- Dried herbs should be stored in plastic bags, boxes, or tins rather than cardboard containers; they should be out of direct sunlight and away from the stove.

HERBAL SALT SUBSTITUTES

These can be placed in shakers and used instead of salt.

Basic salt substitute	Use 2 teaspoons garlic powder and 1 teaspoon each of basil, oregano, and powdered lemon rind (or dehydrated lemon juice). Put ingredients into a blender and mix well. Store in a glass container and add rice to prevent caking.
Tangy salt substitute	Mix well 3 teaspoons basil, 2 teaspoons each of savory (summer is best), celery seed, ground cumin seed, sage, and marjoram, and 1 teaspoon lemon thyme. Powder with a mortar and pestle.
Spicy seasoning	Mix in a blender 1 teaspoon each of cloves, pepper, and coriander seed (crushed), 2 teaspoons paprika, and 1 tablespoon rosemary. Store in an airtight container.

Selecting Herbs and Spices to Go with Foods

What Goes with What

Beef:	bay leaf, chives, cloves, cumin, garlic, hot pepper, marjoram, rosemary, savory
Bread:	allspice, caraway, cardamom, curry powder, marjoram, oregano, poppy seed, rosemary, thyme
Cakes:	allspice, cardamom, ginger
Cheese:	anise, basil, chervil, chives, curry, dill, fennel, garlic, marjoram, oregano, parsley, sage, thyme
Fish:	sweet basil, chervil, dill, fennel, French tarragon, garlic, parsley, thyme
Fruit:	anise, cinnamon, coriander, cloves, ginger, lemon verbena, mint, rose geranium, sweet cicely
Lamb:	garlic, marjoram, oregano, rosemary, thyme
Pork:	coriander, cumin, garlic, ginger, hot pepper, pepper sage, savory, thyme
Poultry:	garlic, oregano, rosemary, sage, savory
Salads:	anise, basil, chives, dill, French tarragon, garlic chives, marjoram, mint, oregano, parsley, savory, sorrel, tarragon (many are best used fresh or added to salad dressing; otherwise, use herb vinegars for extra flavor)
Sauces:	allspice, basil, cardamom, chili powder, chives, cumin, curry, fennel, ginger, marjoram, oregano, parsley, rosemary
Soups:	bay leaf, chervil, French tarragon, marjoram, parsley, savory, rosemary
Stews:	allspice, basil, cardamom, chili powder, curry, dill, ginger, parsley, sage
Vegetables:	basil, chervil, chives, dill, French tarragon, marjoram, mint, parsley, pepper, thyme

Chemical Additives

The information on the following pages comes from the Center for Science in the Public Interest and is available from the organization as a color chart entitled "Chemical Cuisine." The address is 1875 Connecticut Ave., NW, Suite 300, Washington, DC 20009-5728.

Following each entry is a letter that corresponds to one of the three categories below.

(A) Avoid. The additive is unsafe in the amounts normally consumed or is poorly tested.
(C) Caution. The additive may be unsafe, is poorly tested, or is used in foods that people tend to eat too much of.
(S) Safe. The additive appears to be safe.

Definitions of additive terms

Antioxidants retard the oxidation of unsaturated fats and oils, colorings, and flavorings. Oxidation leads to rancidity, flavor changes, and loss of color. Most of these effects are caused by the reaction of oxygen in the air with fats.

Chelating agents trap trace amounts of metal atoms that would otherwise cause food to discolor or go rancid.

Emulsifiers keep oil and water mixed together.

Flavor enhancers contribute little or no flavor of their own, but accentuate the natural flavor of foods. They are most often used when very little of a natural ingredient is present.

Thickening agents are natural or chemically modified carbohydrates that absorb some of the water that is present in food, thereby making the food thicker. Thickening agents "stabilize" factory-made foods by keeping the complex mixtures of oils, water, acids, and solids well mixed.

ALGINATE; PROPYLENE GLYCOL ALGINATE
Thickening agent, foam stabilizer
Ice cream, cheese, candy, yogurt

Alginate, an apparently safe derivative of seaweed (kelp), maintains the desired texture in dairy products, canned frosting, and other factory-made foods. Propylene glycol alginate, a chemically modified algin, thickens acidic foods (soda pop, salad dressing) and stabilizes the foam in beer. (S)

ALPHA TOCOPHEROL (vitamin E)
Antioxidant, nutrient
Vegetable oil

Vitamin E is abundant in whole wheat, rice germ, and vegetable oils. It is destroyed by the refining and bleaching of flour. Vitamin E prevents oils from turning rancid. (S)

ARTIFICIAL COLORINGS

Most artificial colorings are synthetic chemicals that do not occur in nature. Though some are safer than others, colorings are not listed by name on labels. Colorings are used almost solely in foods of low nutritional value (candy, soda pop, gelatin desserts, etc.). Several dyes have caused allergic reactions (Yellow No. 5) or promoted cancer, and there is evidence that colorings may cause hyperactivity in some sensitive children. The use of coloring usually indicates that fruit or other natural ingredients have not been used. (A)

ARTIFICIAL FLAVORINGS
Soft drinks, candy, breakfast cereals, gelatin desserts, other food items

Hundreds of chemicals are used to mimic natural flavors; many may be used in a single flavoring, as in cherry soda pop. Most flavoring chemicals also occur in nature and are probably safe, but they may cause hyperactivity in some children. (A)

ASCORBIC ACID (vitamin C); ERYTHORBIC ACID
Antioxidant, nutrient, color stabilizer
Oily foods, cereals, soft drinks, cured meats

Ascorbic acid helps maintain the red color of cured meats and prevents the formation of nitrosamines (*see also* SODIUM NITRITE). It helps prevent loss of color and flavor by reacting with unwanted oxygen. It is used as a nutrient additive in drinks and breakfast cereals. Sodium ascorbate is a more soluble form of ascorbic acid. Erythorbic acid (sodium erythorbate) serves the same functions as ascorbic acid but has no value as a vitamin. (S)

ASPARTAME
Artificial sweetener
Drink mixes, gelatin desserts, other foods

Aspartame, made up of two amino acids, was thought to be the perfect artificial sweetener, but questions have arisen about the quality of the cancer tests done on it. In addition, some individuals have reported severe adverse behavioral effects after drinking diet soda. People with PKU (phenylketonuria) should avoid it. (C)

BETA CAROTENE
Coloring; nutrient
Margarine, shortening, non-dairy whiteners, butter

Beta carotene is used as an artificial coloring and a nutrient supplement. The body converts it to vitamin A, which is part of the light-detection mechanism of the eye. (S)

BROMINATED VEGETABLE OIL (BVO)
Emulsifier, clouding agent
Soft drinks

BVO keeps flavor oils in suspension and gives a cloudy appearance to citrus-flavored soft drinks. The residues of BVO found in body fat are cause for concern. Safer substitutes are available. (A)

BUTYLATED HYDROXYANISOLE (BHA)
Antioxidant
Cereals, chewing gum, potato chips, vegetable oil

BHT retards rancidity in fats, oils, and oil-containing foods. While most studies indicate it is safe, a 1982 Japanese study demonstrated that it causes cancer in rats. This synthetic chemical often can be replaced by safer chemicals. (A)

BUTYLATED HYDROXYTOLUENE (BHT)
Antioxidant
Cereals, chewing gum, potato chips, oils, other edibles

BHT retards rancidity in oils. It both increased and decreased the risk of cancer in various animal studies. Residues of BHT occur in human fat. BHT is unnecessary or is easily replaced by safe substitutes. (A)

CAFFEINE
Stimulant
Coffee, tea, cocoa (natural), soft drinks (additive)

Caffeine may cause miscarriages or birth defects and should be avoided by pregnant women. It also keeps many people from sleeping. New evidence indicates that caffeine may cause fibrocystic breast disease in some women. (A)

CALCIUM (OR SODIUM) PROPIONATE
Preservative
Bread, rolls, pies, cakes

Calcium propionate prevents mold growth on bread and rolls. The calcium is a beneficial mineral; the propionate is safe. Sodium propionate is used in pies and cakes, because calcium alters the action of chemical leavening agents. (S)

CALCIUM (OR SODIUM) STEAROLYL LACTYLATE
Dough conditioner, whipping agent
Bread dough, cake fillings, artificial whipped cream, processed egg whites

This additive strengthens bread dough so it can be used in breadmaking machinery for more uniform grain and greater volume. It acts as a whipping agent in dried, liquid, or frozen egg whites and artificial whipped cream. Sodium stearoyl fumarate serves the same purpose. (S)

CARRAGEENAN
Thickening and stabilizing agent
Ice cream, jelly, chocolate milk, infant formula

Carrageenan is obtained from seaweed. Large amounts of carrageenan have harmed test animals' colons; the small amounts in food are probably safe. Better tests are needed. (C)

CASEIN; SODIUM CASEINATE
Thickening and whitening agent
Ice cream, ice milk, sherbet, coffee creamers

Casein, the principal protein in milk, is a nutritious protein that contains adequate amounts of all the essential amino acids. (S)

CITRIC ACID; SODIUM CITRATE
Acid flavoring, chelating agent
Ice cream, sherbet, fruit drinks, candy, carbonated beverages, instant potatoes

Citric acid is versatile, widely used, cheap, and safe. It is an important metabolite in virtually all living organisms and is especially abundant in citrus fruits and berries. It is used as a strong acid, a tart flavoring, and an antioxidant. Sodium citrate, also safe, is a buffer that controls the acidity of gelatin desserts, jam, ice cream, candy, and other foods. (S)

CORN SYRUP
Sweetener, thickener
Candy, toppings, syrups, snack foods, imitation dairy foods

Corn syrup is a sweet, thick liquid made by treating cornstarch with acids or enzymes. It may be dried and used as corn syrup solids in coffee whiteners and other dry products. Corn syrup contains no nutritional value other than calories, promotes tooth decay, and is used mainly in low-nutrition foods. (C)

DEXTROSE (GLUCOSE, CORN SUGAR)
Sweetener, coloring agent
Bread, caramel, soda pop, cookies, other foods

Dextrose is an important chemical in every living organism. A sugar, it is a source of sweetness in fruits and honey. Added to foods as a sweetener, it represents empty calories and contributes to tooth decay. Dextrose turns brown when heated and contributes to the color of bread crust and toast. (C)

DIGLYCERIDES See MONOGLYCERIDES AND DIGLYCERIDES.

ETHYLENEDIAMINE TETRAACETIC ACID (EDTA)
Chelating agent
Salad dressing, margarine, sandwich spreads, mayonnaise, processed fruits and vegetables, canned shellfish, soft drinks

Modern food-manufacturing technology, which involves metal rollers, blenders, and containers, results in trace amounts of metal contamination in food. EDTA traps metal impurities, which would otherwise promote rancidity and the breakdown of artificial colors. (S)

FERROUS GLUCONATE
Coloring, nutrient
Black olives, vitamin pills

Used by the olive industry to generate a uniform jet-black color and in pills as a source of iron, this substance is safe. (S)

FUMARIC ACID
Tartness agent
Powdered drinks, pudding, pie fillings, gelatin desserts

A solid at room temperature, inexpensive, and highly acidic, fumaric acid is the ideal source of tartness and acidity in dry food products. However, it dissolves slowly in cold water, a drawback cured by adding dioctyl sodium sulfosuccinate (DSS), a poorly tested, detergentlike additive. (S)

GELATIN
Thickening and gelling agent
Powdered dessert mix, yogurt, ice cream, cheese spreads, beverages

Gelatin is a protein obtained from animal bones, hooves, and other parts. It has little nutritional value, because it contains little or none of several essential amino acids. (S)

GLYCERIN (GLYCEROL)
Maintainer of water content
Marshmallows, candy, fudge, baked goods

Glycerin forms the backbone of fat and oil molecules and is quite safe. The body uses it as a source of energy or as a starting material in making more complex molecules. (S)

GUMS (ARABIC, FURCELLERAN, GHATTI, GUAR, KARAYA, LOCUST BEAN, TRAGACANTH)
Thickening agents, stabilizers
Beverages, ice cream, frozen puddings, salad dressings, dough, cottage cheese, candy, drink mixes

Gums derive from natural sources (bushes, trees, or seaweed) and are poorly tested. They are used to thicken foods, prevent sugar crystals from forming in candy, stabilize beer foam (arabic), form gel in pudding (furcelleran), encapsulate flavor oils in powdered drink mixes, and keep oil and water mixed in salad dressings. Tragacanth sometimes causes severe allergic reactions. (S)

HEPTYL PARABEN
Preservative
Beer, noncarbonated soft drinks

Heptyl paraben—short for the heptyl ester of parahydroxybenzoic acid—is a preservative. Studies suggest that this chemical is safe, but, like other additives in alcoholic beverages, it has never been tested in the presence of alcohol. (C)

HYDROGENATED VEGETABLE OIL
Source of oil or fat
Margarine, processed foods

Vegetable oil, usually a liquid, can be made into a semisolid by treating it with hydrogen. Hydrogenation reduces the levels of polyunsaturated oils. Many people eat too much oil and fat of all kinds, natural and hydrogenated. High-fat diets promote obesity, heart disease, and possibly cancer. (C)

HYDROLYZED VEGETABLE PROTEIN (HVP)
Flavor enhancer
Instant soups, frankfurters, sauce mixes, beef stew

HVP consists of vegetable (usually soybean) protein that has been chemically broken down into the amino acids of which it is composed. HVP is used to bring out the natural flavor of food. (S)

INVERT SUGAR
Sweetener
Candy, soft drinks, many other foods

Invert sugar, an even mixture of dextrose and fructose, two sugars, is sweeter and more soluble than sucrose (table sugar). Invert sugar forms when sucrose is split in two by an enzyme or acid. It contributes to tooth decay. (C)

LACTIC ACID
Acidity regulator
Spanish olives, cheese, frozen desserts, carbonated beverages

This safe acid occurs in almost all living organisms. It inhibits spoilage in Spanish-type olives, balances the acidity in cheese-making, and adds tartness to frozen desserts, carbonated fruit-flavored drinks, and other goods. (S)

LACTOSE
Sweetener
Whipped topping mix, breakfast pastry

Lactose is a carbohydrate found only in milk. One-sixth as sweet as table sugar, it is added to food as a slightly sweet source of carbohydrate. Milk turns sour when bacteria convert lactose to lactic acid. Many non-Caucasians have trouble digesting lactose. (S)

LECITHIN
Emulsifier, antioxidant
Baked goods, margarine, chocolate, ice cream

A common constituent of animal and plant tissues, lecithin is a source of the nutrient choline. It keeps soil and water from separating, retards rancidity, reduces spattering in a frying pan, and leads to fluffier cakes. Major sources are egg yolks and soybeans. (S)

MANNITOL
Sweetener, other uses
Chewing gum, low-calorie foods

Not quite as sweet as sugar and poorly absorbed by the body, mannitol contributes only half as many calories as sugar. Used as the "dust" on chewing gum, it prevents gum from absorbing moisture and becoming sticky. (S)

MONOGLYCERIDES and DIGLYCERIDES
Emulsifiers
Baked goods, margarine, candy, peanut butter

These substances make bread softer, improve the stability of margarine, and make caramel less sticky. They prevent staleness and keep the oil in peanut butter from separating. Monoglycerides and diglycerides are safe, though most foods they are used in are high in refined flour, sugar, or fat. (S)

MONOSODIUM GLUTAMATE (MSG)
Flavor enhancer
Soup, seafood, poultry, cheese, sauces, stews, other foods

This amino acid brings out the flavor of protein-containing foods. Large amounts of MSG fed to infant mice destroyed nerve cells in the brain. Public pressure forced baby food companies to stop using MSG. MSG causes "Chinese restaurant syndrome," a burning sensation in the back of the neck and forearms, tightness of the chest, and headache, in some people. (C)

PHOSPHORIC ACID; PHOSPHATES
Acidulant, chelating agent, buffer, emulsifier, nutrient, discoloration inhibitor
Baked goods, cheese, powered foods, cured meats, soft drinks, breakfast cereals, dehydrated potatoes

Phosphoric acid acidifies and flavors cola beverages. Phosphate salts are used in hundreds of processed foods for many purposes. Calcium and iron phosphates act as mineral supplements. Sodium aluminum phosphate is a leavening agent. Calcium and ammonium phosphates serve as food for yeast in bread. Sodium acid pyrophosphate prevents discoloration. Phosphates are not toxic, but their widespread use has led to dietary imbalances that may contribute to osteoporosis. (C)

POLYSORBATE 60
Emulsifier
Baked goods, frozen desserts, imitation dairy products

Polysorbate 60 is short for polyoxyethylene-(20)-sorbitan monostearate. Along with its close relatives, polysorbate 65 and 80, it works the same way that monoglycerides and diglycerides do, but smaller amounts are needed. They keep baked goods from going stale, deep dill oil dissolved in bottled dill pickles, help coffee whiteners dissolve in coffee, and prevent oil from separating out of artificial whipped cream. (S)

PROPYL GALLATE
Antioxidant
Vegetable oils, meat products, potato sticks, chicken soup base, chewing gum

This substance retards the spoilage of fats and oils and is often used with BHA and BHT because of the synergistic effect these additives have. The best long-term feeding study on this additive was peppered with suggestions but not proof of cancer. (A)

QUININE
Flavoring
Tonic water, quinine water, bitter lemon

This drug can cure malaria and is used as a bitter flavoring in a few soft drinks. There is a slight chance that quinine may cause birth defects, so pregnant women should avoid quinine-containing beverages and drugs. Quinine has been very poorly tested. (A)

SACCHARIN
Synthetic sweetener
Diet products

Saccharin is 350 times sweeter than sugar. Studies have not shown that saccharin helps people lose weight. In 1977 the FDA proposed that saccharin be banned because of repeated evidence that it causes cancer. It is gradually being replaced by aspartame. (A)

SALT (SODIUM CHLORIDE)
Flavoring
Most processed foods

Salt is used liberally in many processed foods. Other additives contribute additional sodium. A diet high in sodium may cause high blood pressure, which increases the risk of heart attack and stroke. (A)

SODIUM BENZOATE
Preservative
Fruit juices, carbonated drinks, pickles, preserves

Manufacturers have used sodium benzoate for over 70 years to prevent the growth of microorganisms in acidic foods. (S)

SODIUM CARBO-XYMETHYL-CELLU-LOSE (CMC)
Thickening and stabilizing agent
Ice cream, beer, pie fillings, icings, diet foods, candy

CMC is made by reacting cellulose with a derivative of acetic acid. Studies indicate that it is safe. (S)

SODIUM NITRITE; SODIUM NITRATE
Preservative, coloring, flavoring
Bacon, ham, frankfurters, luncheon meats, smoked fish, corned beef

Nitrite can lead to the formation of small amounts of potent cancer-causing chemicals (nitrosamines), particularly in fried bacon. Nitrite is tolerated in foods because it can prevent the growth of bacteria that cause botulism poisoning. Nitrite also stabilizes the red color in cured meats and gives a characteristic flavor. Companies should find safer methods of preventing botulism. Sodium nitrate is used in dry-cured meats because it slowly breaks down into nitrite. (A)

SORBIC ACID; POTASSIUM SORBATE
Prevents growth of mold
Cheese, syrup, jelly, cakes, wines, dry fruits

These additives occur naturally in many plants and are safe under normal circumstances. (S)

SORBITAN MONOSTEARATE
Emulsifier
Cakes, candy, frozen puddings, icings

Like monoglycerides, diglycerides, and polysorbates, this additive keeps oil and water mixed. In chocolate candy, it prevents the discoloration that normally occurs when the candy is warmed up and then cooled down. (S)

SORBITOL
Sweetener, thickening agent, maintainer of moisture
Dietetic drinks and foods, candy, shredded coconut, chewing gum

Sorbitol occurs naturally in fruits and berries and is a close relative of the sugars; however, it is half as sweet as sugar. It is used in noncariogenic chewing gum because oral bacteria do not metabolize it well. Large amounts of sorbitol (2 ounces for adults) have a laxative effect, but otherwise it is safe. Diabetics use sorbitol because it is absorbed slowly and does not cause blood sugar to increase rapidly. (S)

STARCH; MODIFIED STARCH
Thickening agent
Soups, gravies, baby foods

Starch, the major component of flour, potatoes, and corn, is used as a thickening agent. However, it does not dissolve in cold water. Chemists have solved this problem by reacting starch with various chemicals. These modified starches are added to some foods to improve their consistencies and to keep the solids suspended. Starch and modified starches make foods look thicker and richer than they really are. (S)

SUGAR (SUCROSE)
Sweetener
Table sugar, sweetened foods

Sucrose, ordinary table sugar, occurs naturally in fruit, sugar cane, and sugar beets. Americans each consume about 65 pounds of refined sugar per year. Sugar, corn syrup, and other refined sweeteners make up about one-eighth of the average diet, but they contain no vitamins, minerals, or protein. (A)

SULFUR DIOXIDE; SODIUM BISULFITE
Preservative, bleach
Dried fruits, wines, processed potatoes

Sulfiting agents prevent discoloration (in dried fruits, some "fresh" shrimp, and some dried, fried, and frozen potatoes) and bacterial growth (in wines). They also destroy vitamin B_1 and can cause severe reactions in asthmatics. This additive has caused at least seven deaths. (A)

VANILLIN; ETHYL VANILLIN
Substitute for vanilla
Ice cream, baked goods, beverages, chocolate, candy, gelatin desserts

Vanilla flavoring is derived from a bean, but vanillin, the major flavor component of vanilla, is cheaper to produce in a factory. A derivative, ethyl vanillin, comes closer to matching the taste of real vanilla. Both chemicals are safe. (S)

Outlawed Additives

Name	Year Outlawed	Use
Cobalt sulfate	1966	Beer foam stabilizer
Cyclamate	1970	Artificial sweetener
Dulcin	1950	Artificial sweetener
Green No. 1	1966	Coloring agent
Orange B	1978	Coloring agent
Red No. 2	1976	Coloring agent
Safrole	1960	Root beer flavoring
Violet No. 1	1973	Coloring agent

Alcoholic Drink Recipes

Except where otherwise indicated, *shake* means to shake with cracked ice and then strain into a glass; *stir* means to stir over ice in the glass; and *straight up* means served without ice.

Alexander

Shake 1 oz. brandy, 1 oz. crème de cacao, and 1 oz. cream.

Bacardi Cocktail

Shake 1½ oz. Bacardi® rum, the juice of ½ lime, and ½ teaspoon grenadine.

B & B

Stir ½ oz. benedictine and ½ oz. brandy (or cognac); B & B may also be served straight up.

Black Russian

Stir 1½ oz. vodka and ¾ oz. Kahlua.®

Black Velvet

Pour equal parts Guinness® stout and champagne over ice in a tall glass.

Bloody Mary

Shake or stir 1½ oz. vodka, 3 oz. tomato juice, the juice of ½ lemon, a dash each of Worcestershire® and Tabasco® sauce, and a pinch each of salt, pepper, and celery salt.

Bronx Cocktail

Shake 1 oz. gin, ½ oz. dry vermouth, ½ oz. sweet vermouth, and ½ oz. orange juice.

Bullshot

Substitute consommé for tomato juice and follow the directions for Bloody Mary.

Champagne Cocktail

Mix 1 lump sugar, 2 dashes angostura bitters, and 1 oz. brandy; top with chilled champagne.

Cuba Libre (Rum and Coke®)

Over ice in a tall glass, pour 1 oz. light rum and the juice of ½ lime; top with cola.

Daiquiri

Shake 1½ oz. light rum, the juice of 1 lime, and 1 teaspoon powdered sugar (often served with the addition of crushed fruit or fruit juice as strawberry daiquiri, peach daiquiri, etc.; blended with crushed ice, it becomes a frozen daiquiri).

Gibson

A martini with the addition of a pearl onion instead of the traditional olive.

Gimlet

Shake 1 oz. gin and 1 oz. Rose's® lime juice or the juice of 1 lime.

Gin and Tonic

Pour 2 oz. gin over ice in a tall glass; top with tonic water.

Gin Fizz

Shake 2 oz. gin, the juice of ½ lemon, and 1 teaspoon powdered sugar; top with soda water in a tall glass.

Grasshopper

Shake ½ oz. crème de menthe, ½ oz. white crème de cacao, and ½ oz. cream.

Harvey Wallbanger

Add 1 oz. Galliano® to a Screwdriver.

Jack Rose

Shake 1½ oz. apple brandy, the juice of ½ lime, and 1 teaspoon grenadine.

Kir

To a glass of chilled white wine, add 1 teaspoon crème de cassis.

Mai Tai

Shake 2 oz. rum, 1 oz. curaçao, the juice of ½ lime, ½ oz. grenadine, ½ oz. almond-flavored syrup, and ½ teaspoon powdered sugar; serve over crushed ice.

Manhattan

Stir with cracked ice 1½ oz. whiskey, ¾ oz. sweet vermouth, and a dash of angostura bitters; serve over ice or straight up with a maraschino cherry.

Margarita

Shake 1½ oz. tequila, ½ oz. Cointreau® or triple sec, and the juice of ½ lime; serve in a chilled, salt-rimmed glass.

Martini

Stir gin and dry vermouth; strain into a chilled glass. The original ratio of gin to vermouth was 2:1, but contemporary tastes tend toward "drier" ratios of 3:1, 5:1, and even 7:1. Serve straight up with an olive or, less traditionally, over ice or with a lemon twist. Made with a pearl onion, it is called a Gibson; with vodka, a vodka martini or Vodkatini.

Mint Julep

Mix in a tall glass 1 lump sugar, 1 tablespoon water, and 4 sprigs of mint; fill the glass with crushed ice; add 2 oz. bourbon, and serve with straws, without stirring.

Old-Fashioned

Mix in a short glass ½ lump sugar, 2 dashes angostura bitters, and 1 dash water; stir in ice cubes and 2 oz. whiskey.

Orange Blossom

Shake 1 oz. gin and 1 oz. orange juice.

Pimm's Cup

Over ice in a tall glass, pour 1 oz. Pimm's No. 1 Cup®; top with lemonade, 7-Up®, or ginger ale.

Piña Colada

Over crushed ice in a tall glass, pour ½ oz. light rum, ½ oz. dark rum, 1 oz. each of orange, lime, and pineapple juice, and 1 dash of grenadine; top with coconut milk.

Pink Gin

Add 1 dash angostura bitters to 2 oz. gin. Pink Gin may be served straight up or with water or soda and ice.

Planter's Punch

Over crushed ice in a tall glass, pour 2 oz. soda water, the juice of 2 limes, and 2 teaspoons powdered sugar; stir to frost glass; add 2 dashes angostura bitters and 2 oz. rum.

Rickey

Over cracked ice, pour 2 oz. gin and the juice of ½ lime; top with soda water. This traditional gin rickey is often modified by substituting other spirits; hence, Scotch rickey, Irish rickey, etc.

Rob Roy

Using Scotch whiskey, follow the directions for a Manhattan.

Rusty Nail

Stir 2 oz. Scotch whiskey with 1 oz. Drambuie.®

Salty Dog

Stir 2 oz. gin, 2 oz. grapefruit juice, and ¼ teaspoon salt.

Sangre

A Bloody Mary made with tequila instead of vodka.

Screwdriver

Over ice in a tall glass, pour 2 oz. vodka; top with orange juice.

7 & 7

Over ice, pour 1½ oz. Seagram's® whiskey; top with 7-Up.®

Sidecar

Shake 1 oz. brandy, ½ oz. Cointreau® or triple sec, and the juice of ½ lemon.

Singapore Sling

Shake 2 oz. gin, ½ oz. cherry brandy, the juice of ½ lemon, and 1 teaspoon powdered sugar; pour over ice cubes in a tall glass and top with soda water.

Stinger

Shake or stir 1 oz. brandy and 1 oz. white crème de menthe.

Tequila Sunrise

Shake or stir in a tall glass 1½ oz. tequila and 3 oz. orange juice; add 1 oz. grenadine; do not stir.

Toddy

Dissolve 1 lump sugar in a little water in a short glass; add 2 oz. spirits (brandy, gin, rum, or whiskey) and top with water (with boiling water, the drink is a hot toddy).

Tom Collins

Shake 2 oz. gin, the juice of $1/2$ lemon, and 1 teaspoon powdered sugar; pour over ice cubes in a tall glass and top with soda water (made with vodka in place of gin, this is a Vodka Collins).

Whiskey Sour

Shake 2 oz. whiskey, the juice of $1/2$ lemon, and $1/2$ teaspoon powdered sugar.

White Lady

Shake $1 1/2$ oz. gin, 1 teaspoon powdered sugar, 1 teaspoon cream, and 1 egg white.

Zombie

Blend with cracked ice 3 oz. rum, $1/2$ oz. apricot brandy, 1 oz. pineapple juice, the juice of 1 lime and 1 orange, and 1 teaspoon powdered sugar. Strain into a tall frosted glass; float $1/2$ oz. rum (151 proof) on top before serving with straws.

Mixing Drinks

Always be sure of your ingredients and measure them accurately. A jigger is $1 1/2$ ounces, a pony $3/4$ ounce, a bar spoon $1/2$ teaspoon, and a dash 7 to 10 drops.

Ice should always be the first ingredient that goes into the glass. Use new ice for every drink and do not let drinks stand too long before serving. The best bartenders chill cocktail glasses in the refrigerator before serving.

Drinks containing fruit juices, eggs, or other dissimilar ingredients should always be shaken fast and vigorously. The ingredients will mix more readily and completely in a shaker or an electric blender. Never shake drinks mixed with carbonated water or ginger ale. Stir them smoothly and not too vigorously for about half a minute. This will keep the drink sparkling and prevent a flat taste. It also will chill the drink properly and thoroughly.

When a drink calls for fruit juice, use fresh juice if possible. The juice is put into the mixing glass with the proper amount of sugar or other sweetener before the liquor.

Fine granulated sugar can be used for sweetening in most cases. Many people prefer simple syrup, which can easily be made by dissolving $1/2$ pound of fine granulated sugar in $3/4$ cup of boiling water. One teaspoon of simple syrup is equivalent to one of sugar.

For drinks requiring a twist of lemon, orange, or lime, use a piece of peel about $1 1/2$ inches long and $1/4$ inch wide. Twist this over the drink to extract a bit of oil, and then drop in the peel.

Liquor Needed for Drinks Served

Liquor is commonly sold in 750-milliliter and 1-liter bottles. A 750-milliliter bottle is equivalent to 25.4 fluid ounces. One liter is equivalent to 33.8 fluid ounces.

Number of People	Number of Drinks (for cocktails)	Amount Needed
4	10 to 16	1 750-ml bottle
6	15 to 22	2 750-ml bottles
8	18 to 24	2 750-ml bottles
12	20 to 40	3 750-ml bottles
20	40 to 65	3 one-liter bottles

Number of People	*(for buffet or dinner)*	Amount Needed
4	8 cocktails	1 750-ml bottle
	8 glasses of wine	2 one-liter bottles
	4 liqueurs	1 750-ml bottle
	10 highballs	1 750-ml bottle
6	12 cocktails	1 750-ml bottle
	12 glasses of wine	3 one-liter bottles
	8 liqueurs	1 750-ml bottle
	16 highballs	2 750-ml bottles
8	16 cocktails	1 750-ml bottle
	16 glasses of wine	3 one-liter bottles
	16 liqueurs	1 750-ml bottle
	18 highballs	2 750-ml bottles
20	40 cocktails	3 750-ml bottles
	40 glasses of wine	7 one-liter bottles
	25 liqueurs	2 750-ml bottles
	50 highballs	3 one-liter bottles

Number of People	*(for after-dinner party)*	Amount Needed
4	12 to 16	1 750-ml bottle
6	18 to 26	2 750-ml bottles
8	20 to 34	2 750-ml bottles
12	25 to 45	3 750-ml bottles
20	45 to 75	3 one-liter bottles plus one 750-ml bottle

CHAMPAGNE BOTTLE SIZES

Name	Capacity	Bottles
Bottle	.75 liter	1
Magnum	1.5 liters	2
Jeroboam	3 liters	4
Rehoboam	4.5 liters	6
Methuselah	6 liters	8
Salmanazar	9 liters	12
Balthazar	12 liters	16
Nebuchadnezzar	15 liters	20

Wines and Their Service

Red table wines should be served cool or at room temperature. Room temperature means about 65 to 68° F, so some cooling may be necessary. Red wines go well with all foods with the possible exception of seafood. White table wines, rosé wines, and all sparkling wines, both red and white, should be served well chilled. Dry wines should not be served with sweet dishes.

So that corks stay moist and tight, store wines on their side. If the cork is removed an hour or two before serving, red wines will expand a bit and give off a delightful scent. Smell the cork to see if it is sour-smelling; if so, the wine has started to turn to vinegar and should not be served; it can, however, be kept for cooking.

Many good wines will contain a small amount of sediment. This is harmless and will settle on the bottom of the bottle if it is stood upright for about two hours before serving. When serving champagne, hold the bottle at a slight angle for a few seconds after the cork is removed. This will reduce the amount of frothing and will maintain a maximum amount of sparkle.

Wineglasses should be placed to the right of the water goblet; they are arranged according to their use, the first wineglass being closest to the water goblet. If more than one wine is served, the glasses used first are removed when the course is through.

The person serving should fill his or her own glass one-quarter full and then taste the wine to check the quality and flavor. Then the other glasses should be filled half to three-quarters full, but never to the very top. Wine is poured as soon as a course is served. The person pouring should not lift the glasses from the table.

When more than one wine is served, remember that light wine comes before heavy or full wine, dry white wine precedes sweet red wine, and dry red wine is served before white sweet wine. The "correct" wine is always the one you like best; however, certain wines complement certain foods. The following wine and food list is a guide to what people generally like. One's own taste should be the final judge.

Canapés, crackers, olives, cheese dips, other hors d'oeurves: sherry, vermouth, or champagne.
Soups: sherry or Madeira.
Seafood: Chablis, Rhine wine, Moselle, dry sauterne, white Burgundy.
Fowl: Rhine wine, dry sauterne, champagne, Bordeaux, white or red Burgundy (with game).
Meats: claret, red Burgundy, rosé (with cold cuts).
Cheese or nuts: port, sherry, red Burgundy, muscatel, zinfandel, Barbera.
Desserts: sweet sauterne, champagne, port, muscatel, Tokay.
After dinner: brandy, Cointreau, benedictine, crème de menthe.

Clothing Size Conversion Tables

Women

Blouses and sweaters

U.S.	32	34	36	38	40	42	44
British	34	36	38	40	42	44	46
Continental	40	42	44	46	48	50	52

Coats and dresses

U.S.	8	10	12	14	16	18	20
British	30	32	34	36	38	40	42
Continental	36	38	40	42	44	46	48

Shoes

U.S.	5–5$\frac{1}{2}$	6–6$\frac{1}{2}$	7–7$\frac{1}{2}$	8–8$\frac{1}{2}$	9
British	3$\frac{1}{2}$–4	4$\frac{1}{2}$–5	5$\frac{1}{2}$–6	6$\frac{1}{2}$–7	7$\frac{1}{2}$
Continental	36	37	38	39	40

Stockings

U.S. and British	8	8$\frac{1}{2}$	9	9$\frac{1}{2}$	10	10$\frac{1}{2}$
Continental	0	1	2	3	4	5

Men

Hats

U.S.	6$\frac{5}{8}$	6$\frac{3}{4}$	6$\frac{7}{8}$	7	7$\frac{1}{8}$	7$\frac{1}{4}$	7$\frac{3}{8}$	7$\frac{1}{2}$
British	6$\frac{1}{2}$	6$\frac{5}{8}$	6$\frac{3}{4}$	6$\frac{7}{8}$	7	7$\frac{1}{8}$	7$\frac{1}{4}$	7$\frac{3}{8}$
Continental	53	54	55	56	57	58	59	60

Shirts

U.S. and British	14	14$\frac{1}{2}$	15	15$\frac{1}{2}$	16	16$\frac{1}{2}$	17
Continental	36	37	38	39	41	42	43

Shoes

U.S.	7	7$\frac{1}{2}$	8	8$\frac{1}{2}$	9	9$\frac{1}{2}$	10	10$\frac{1}{2}$	11
British	6$\frac{1}{2}$	7	7$\frac{1}{2}$	8	8$\frac{1}{2}$	9	9$\frac{1}{2}$	10	10$\frac{1}{2}$
Continental	39	40	41	42	43	43	44	44	45

Socks

U.S. and British	9½	10	10½	11	11½	12	12½
Continental	39	40	41	42	43	44	45

Suits and coats

U.S. and British	34	36	38	40	42	44	46
Continental	44	46	48	50	52	54	56

Standard Sizes Chart

Interior Materials

Walls	Thicknesses (in inches)	Lengths (in feet unless otherwise indicated)	Widths (in feet unless otherwise indicated)
Decorative hardboard (embossed surface)	¼	4 to 16	4
Fiberboard (burlap or cork-surfaced)	15/32	8, 10, 12, 14	4
Gypsum board (plain or vinyl-surfaced)	¼, ⅜, ½	6 to 16	2, 4
Hardboard (tempered or untempered)	⅜, 3/16, ¼, 5/16	6 to 16	4
Hardwood plywood (prefinished)	5/32, 3/16, ¼, 7/16	7, 8	4
Hardwood plywood (veneered paneling)	⅛ to ¾	7, 8, 9, 10	4
Particle-core plywood	¾, 7/16	7, 8, 9, 10	4
Plastic-surfaced hardboard	⅛, 3/16, ¼	6, 7, 8, 10	16", 4
Prefinished hardboard	⅛, 3/16, ¼	6 to 16	16", 4
Textured plywood (rough-sawn, brushed, grooved)	⅜, ⅝	8, 9, 10	4
Unfinished plywood	¾ to 1⅞	8, 9, 10	4
Vinyl-surfaced plywood	3/16, ¼, 5/16	7, 8	4
Wood-grained hardboard	3/16, ¼	7, 8, 9, 10	4

Ceilings

Acoustical panels	½, ¾, 1	2, 8, 10, 12, 14	2, 4
Acoustical tiles	½	12"	12"
Decorative acoustical tile (embossed, textured, etc.)	½	12", 2, 4	12", 2
Fiberglass acoustical panels	2	8, 10½, 12½, 14, 16	4
Plastic-surfaced hardboard blocks	¼	16"	16"
Wood-grained planks	½	4	5 3/16", 6 ⅜", 8 3/16"

Floors	Widths (in inches)	Depths (in inches)	Heights (in inches unless otherwise indicated)
Asphalt (or asphalt-asbestos) tile	1/8, 3/16	9"	9"
Ceramic-tile sheets	1/8, 1/4	12"	12"
Indoor-outdoor carpet		as desired	3, 6, 9, 12, 15
Indoor-outdoor carpet tile		9", 12"	9", 12"
Sheet vinyl		as desired	6, 9, 12
Vinyl and vinyl-asbestos tile	0.50 to 1/8	9", 12", 18", 36"	4", 9", 12", 18", 36"
Wood parquet blocks	5/16, 7/16	9", 10"	9", 10"
Wood strips	3/8	2"	1 to 8

Bathroom fixtures			
Bathtubs	4'6", 5', 5'6"	2', 2'6", 2'7", 2'8"	1'2", 1'3", 1'4"
Compact corner tubs	3'2", 3'6", 4'	3'3", 3'10", 4'1 1/2"	12"
One-piece fiberglass recessed shower units	3', 4', 5'	3'	6'1 1/2"
One-piece fiberglass tub/shower units	5'	2'8 7/8"	6'1 1/2"
Shower stalls	2'6" to 3'6"	2'6" to 3'6"	6'3" to 6'5"
Sinks	19" to 30"	16" to 20"	2'7" (counter height)
Toilets (tank size)	18" to 23 1/2"	25" to 30"	18 1/2" to 40"

Kitchen Equipment			
Built-in ovens (set in cabinet)	23 3/4 to 36	23 1/2	29 3/4
Built-in ranges (set in countertop)	12 to 42	19 to 22	34 to 36
Dishwashers	24	24 1/4 to 30	34 to 36
Double sinks (set in counters)	32	20	2'7"
Drop-in ranges and ovens (recessed into base cabinets)	30	24 to 27 1/4	34 to 36
Free-standing ranges and ovens	20 to 42	24 3/4 to 26 5/8	35 to 36
Freezers (chest)	46 1/2 to 72	29, 32	36, 37
Freezers (upright)	24 to 32	26 to 32	57 to 71
Ranges and eye-level ovens	30	27 1/8 to 28 3/4	59 1/8, 64 1/8
Refrigerators	28 to 35	25 to 30	61 to 36
Single sinks (set in counters)	24, 30	21	2'7"
Slide-in ranges and ovens (set between base cabinets)	20 to 36	24 to 26 7/8	34 to 36
Triple sinks (set in counters)	42, 45	21, 22	2'7"

Exterior Materials

Siding	Thicknesses (in inches)	Lengths (in feet unless otherwise indicated)	Widths
Aluminum (horizontal)		9'4½", 10, 12½, 16	8", 10"
Hardboard lap (horizontal)	³/₈, ⁷/₁₆	12, 16	6", 8", 9", 10", 12"
Hardboard panels (vertical)	¼, ⁵/₁₆, ³/₈, ⁷/₁₆	6, 7, 8, 9, 10, 16	4'
Plywood panels (vertical—rough-sawn, brushed, grooved)	³/₈, ½, ⁵/₈	8, 9, 10, 12	4'
Prefinished steel (horizontal)		12'6"	8", 9½"
Vinyl lap (horizontal)		12½"	8", 12"
Vinyl V-grooved (vertical)		10	10"
Wood lap (horizontal)	½, ⁵/₈, ¾	3 to 20	6", 8", 10", 12"

Doors and windows	Thicknesses (in inches)	Heights	Widths
Bifold, 2-door units	1⅛, 1⅜	6'8"	2', 2'8", 3'
Bifold, 4-door units	1⅛, 1⅜	6'8"	3', 4', 5', 6'
Flush (hollow, solid)	1⅜, 1¾, 2¼	6'8", 7'	6"
Louvered	1⅛, 1⅜	6'6", 6'8", 7'	1'3" to 3'
Panel	1⅜, 1¾	6'8", 7'	1'2" to 3'4"
Sash (with one or more glass panels)	1⅜, 1¾	6'8", 7'	2' to 3'6"
Sliding glass, 2-panel units		6'8"	5', 6', 6'2¼", 8', 8'¼"
Sliding glass, 3-panel units		6'8"	9', 9¾", 12', 12'¾"
Steel entry (single, double, sidelight)	1¾	6'8"	2'8", 3'

Additional Sources of Information

Organizations and Services

Energy Conservation Center
Public Service Electric and Gas Company
P.O. Box 1258
Newark, NY 07101
800-854-4444

Specialists can provide information on specific energy needs such as weatherization, appliance efficiency and rebates, and home energy audit publications. The center receives calls weekdays between 9 A.M. and 5 P.M., EST.

Genova Plumbers Hotline
7034 East Court Street
Davison, MI 48423
800-521-7488

The staff can suggest solutions to plumbing problems involving gutters and plastic fittings as well as more technical problems. The hotline operates weekdays between 8 A.M. and 5 P.M., EST.

Major Appliance Consumer Action Panel (MACAP)
20 North Wacker Drive
Chicago, IL 60606
800-621-0477
312-984-5858 (in Illinois, Alaska, and Hawaii)

MACAP will respond to written inquiries about problems with major appliances. Call for further instructions. It is open weekdays from 8:30 A.M. to 5 P.M., CST.

Shopsmith, Inc.
6530 Poe Avenue
Dayton, OH 45414
800-543-7586

Shopsmith will answer questions related to woodworking. If they cannot answer your question, they will research the information and call back. Call weekdays between 9 A.M. and midnight and Saturdays between 9 A.M. and 6 P.M., EST.

Soap and Detergent Association
475 Park Avenue South
New York, NY 10016
212-725-1262

This association will answer questions on all aspects of soaps and detergents. They also have free publications. Call Monday through Friday from 9 A.M. to 4:45 P.M., EST.

Books

Brody, Jane. *Jane Brody's Good Food Book.* Bantam, 1987.
Canning, Freezing and Drying. Lane, 1981.
Claiborne, Craig. *The New York Times Cookbook,* rev. ed. HarperCollins, 1990.
Cunningham, Marion, ed. *Fannie Farmer Cookbook,* Knopf, 1990.
The Family Circle Good Cook's Book. Simon & Schuster, 1993.
Heinerman, John. *The Complete Book of Spices.* Keats, 1983.
Lichine, Alexis. *Alexis Lichine's New Encyclopedia of Wines & Spirits,* 5th ed. Knopf, 1987.
McGowan, John, and Roger DuBern. *Good Housekeeping Book of Home Maintenance,* Hearst, 1985.
Mr. Boston Official Bartender's Guide. Warner, 1987.

Netzer, Corinne T. *The Brand-Name Calorie Counter.* Dell, 1986.

Pinkham, Mary Ellen. *Mary Ellen's Best of Helpful Kitchen Hints,* Warner, 1980.

The Stanley Complete Step-by-Step Book of Home Repair and Improvement. Simon & Schuster, 1993.

Reader's Digest How to Do Just About Anything: A Money-Saving A to Z Guide to Over 1200 Practical Problems. Reader's Digest, 1986.

Rombauer, Irma S., and Marion R. Becker. *Joy of Cooking.* Bobbs-Merrill, 1978.

Rombauer, Irma S., and Marion R. Becker. *Joy of Cooking, Volume 2.* New American Library, 1989.

Root, Waverley. *Food: An Authoritative Visual History and Dictionary of the Foods of the World.* Simon & Schuster, 1980.

Root, Waverley, ed. *Herbs and Spices: A Guide to Culinary Seasoning.* McGraw-Hill, 1985.

Simon, André L. *A Concise Encyclopedia of Gastronomy.* Overlook, 1983.

Time/Life Complete Home Repair Manual. Prentice-Hall, 1987.

21

The Outdoors

Poisonous Cultivated and Wild Plants / *614*

Frost Dates for Spring / *616*

Frost Dates for Autumn / *617*

Germination Tables / *618*

Ground Covers / *619*

Vines for Special Uses / 619

Botanical Names of Plants / *620*

National Park Directory / *624*

National Wildlife Refuges / *629*

Cloud Nomenclature / *643*

Earthquakes / 646

Lunar and Solar Eclipses / *646*

Constellations / *650*

Additional Sources of Information / *651*

Poisonous Cultivated and Wild Plants

The following chart lists 50 poisonous plants. It tells which portions, or areas, of the plant are toxic, describes symptoms of the illnesses they cause, and indicates which plants are or may be fatal.

Plants	Toxic Portions	Symptoms of Illness; Degree of Toxicity
Autumn crocus	Bulbs	Nausea, vomiting, diarrhea; may be fatal.
Azalea	All parts	Nausea, vomiting, depression, breathing difficulty, prostration, coma; fatal.
Belladonna	Young plants, seeds	Nausea, twitching muscles, paralysis; fatal.
Bittersweet	Leaves, seeds, roots	Vomiting, diarrhea, chills, convulsions, coma.
Bleeding heart (Dutchman's-breeches)	Foliage, roots	Nervous symptoms, convulsions.
Buttercups	All parts	Digestive system injury.
Caladium	All parts	Intense burning and irritation of the tongue and mouth; can be fatal if the base of the tongue swells, blocking air passage of the throat.
Castorbean	Seeds, foliage	Burning in mouth, convulsions; fatal.
Cherry	Twigs, foliage	Gasping, excitement, prostration.
Daffodil	Bulbs	Nausea, vomiting, diarrhea; may be fatal.
Daphne	Berries (red or yellow)	Severe burns to mouth and digestive tract followed by coma; fatal.
Delphinium	Young plants, seeds	Nausea, twitching muscles, paralysis; fatal.
Dumbcane (Dieffenbachia)	All parts	Intense burning and irritation of the tongue and mouth; fatal if the base of the tongue swells, blocking air passage of the throat.
Elderberry	Roots	Nausea and digestive upset.
Elephant ear	All parts	Intense burning and irritation of the tongue and mouth; fatal if the base of the tongue swells, blocking air passage of the throat.
English holly	Berries	Severe gastroenteritis.
English ivy	Leaves, berries	Stomach pains, labored breathing, possible coma.
Foxglove	Leaves, seeds, flowers	Irregular heartbeat and pulse, usually accompanied by digestive upset and mental confusion; may be fatal.
Goldenchain	All parts, especially seeds	Excitement, staggering convulsions, coma; may be fatal.
Horse chestnut	All parts	Nausea, twitching muscles, sometimes paralysis.
Hyacinth	Bulbs	Nausea, vomiting, diarrhea; may be fatal.
Hydrangea	Buds, leaves, branches	Severe digestive upset, gasping, convulsions; may be fatal.
Iris	Freshly underground portions	Severe but not usually serious digestive upset.

Plants	Toxic Portions	Symptoms of Illness; Degree of Toxicity
Jack-in-the-pulpit	All parts, especially roots	Intense irritation and burning of the tongue and mouth.
Jimson weed (thorn apple; datura)	All parts	Abnormal thirst, distortion of vision, delirium, incoherence, coma; may be fatal.
Larkspur	Young plants, seeds	Nausea, twitching muscles, paralysis; fatal.
Laurel	All parts	Nausea, vomiting, depression, breathing difficulty, prostration, coma; fatal.
Lily of the valley	Leaves, flowers	Irregular heartbeat and pulse usually accompanied by digestive upset and mental confusion; may be fatal.
Mayapple	Unripe apples, leaves, and roots	Diarrhea, severe digestive upset.
Mistletoe	All parts, especially berries	Fatal
Monkshood	All parts, especially roots	Digestive upset and nervous excitement; juice in plant parts is fatal.
Morning glory	Seeds	Large amounts cause severe mental disturbances; fatal.
Mushrooms, wild	All parts of many varieties	Fatal.
Narcissus	Bulbs	Nausea, vomiting, diarrhea; may be fatal.
Nightshade	All parts, especially unripe berries	Intense digestive disturbances and nervous symptoms; often fatal.
Oak	Foliage, acorns	Gradual kidney failure.
Oleander	All parts	Severe digestive upset, heart trouble, contact dermatitis; fatal.
Philodendron	All parts	Intense burning and irritation of the tongue and mouth; fatal if the base of the tongue swells, blocking air passage of the throat.
Poinsettia	All parts	Severe digestive upset; fatal.
Poison hemlock	All parts	Stomach pains, vomiting, paralysis of the central nervous system; may be fatal.
Poison ivy and oak	All parts	Intense itching, watery blisters, red rash.
Poppy	Foliage, roots	Nervous symptoms, convulsions.
Potato	Foliage, green parts of vegetable	Intense digestive disturbances, nervous symptoms.
Privet	Berries, leaves	Mild to severe digestive disturbances; may be fatal.
Rhododendron	All parts	Nausea, vomiting, depression, breathing difficulty, prostration, coma; fatal.
Rhubarb	Leaf blade	Kidney disorder, convulsions, coma; fatal.
Rosary pea	Seeds, foliage	Burning in mouth, convulsions; fatal.
Snowdrop	Bulbs	Vomiting, nervous excitement.
Tomato	Vines	Digestive upset, nervous disorders.
Wisteria	Seeds, pods	Mild to severe digestive disturbances.

Frost Dates for Spring

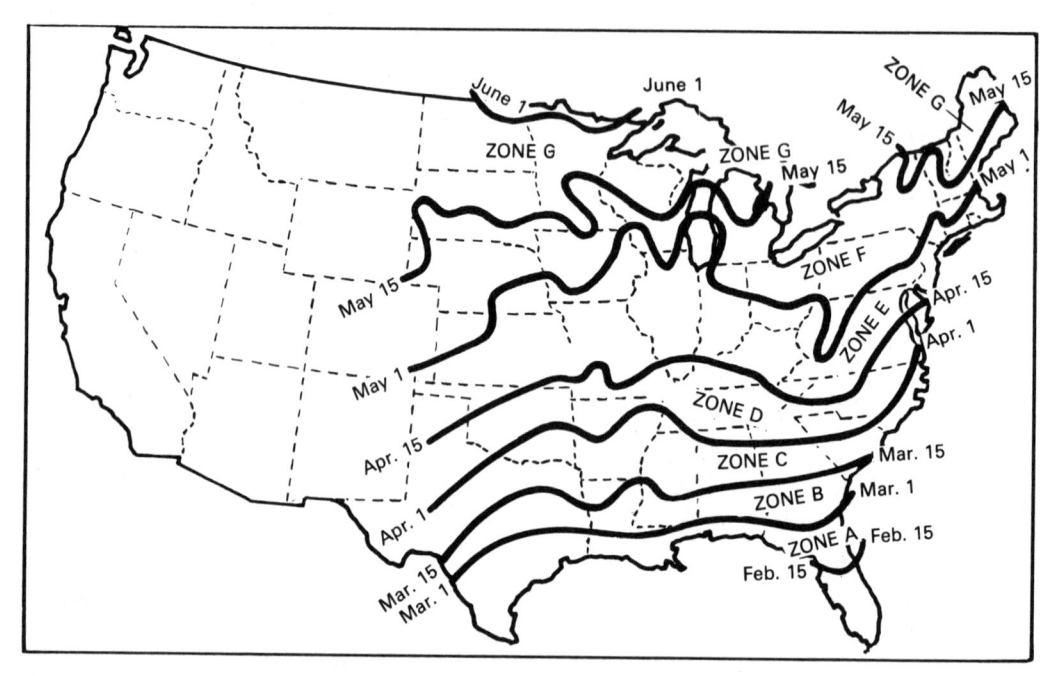

A zone map of the United States based on the average dates of the latest killing frost in spring east of the Rocky Mountains. Source: United States Department of Agriculture.

Frost Dates for Autumn

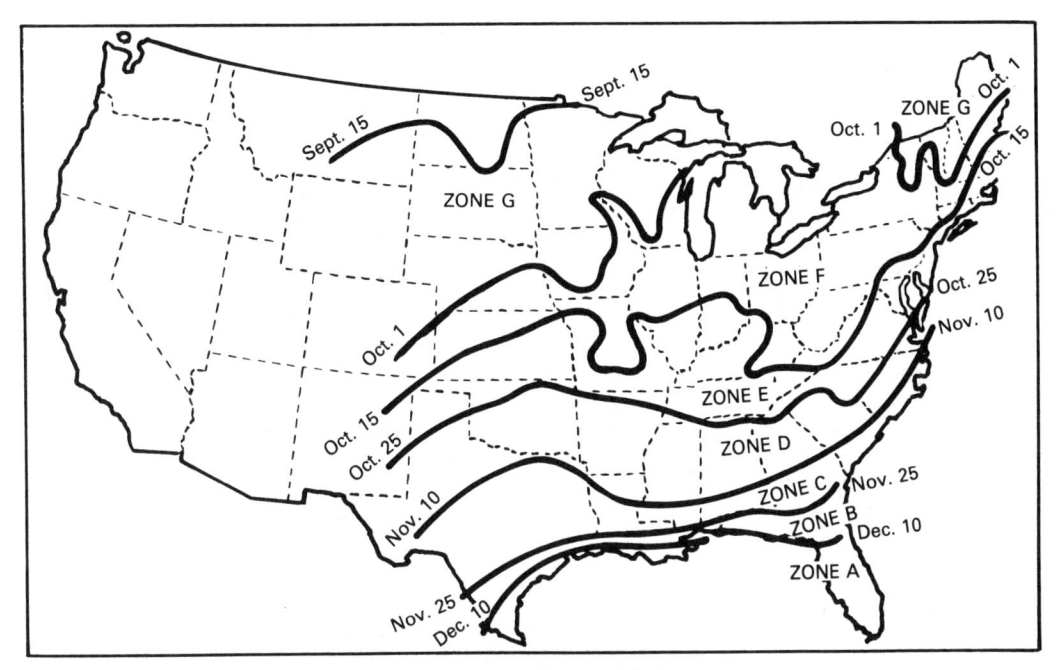

A zone map of the central and eastern part of the United States based on the average dates of the first killing frost in autumn. **Source: United States Department of Agriculture.**

Germination Tables

Annual Flowers

	Approximate number of days until germination		Approximate number of days until germination
Acrolinium	8–10	Four-o'clock	12–15
Ageratum	7–11	Gaillardia	12–15
Alyssum, sweet	10–13	Gomphrena	20–25
Browallia	18–20	Helichrysum	5–10
Cacalia	8–12	Larkspur	15–20
Calendula	10–12	Lupine	25–30
California poppy	5–10	Marigold	5–8
Candytuft	6–9	Nicotiana	20–25
Canterbury bell	12–15	Petunia	18–20
Celosia (coxcomb)	20–25	Phlox Drummondi	20–25
		Pinks	5–8
Centaurea (ragged robin)	5–20	Portulaca	18–20
		Scabiosa	18–20
Chrysanthemum	6–8	Snapdragon	20–25
Cosmos	5–15	Sweetpea	15–20
Cynoglossum	11–15	Verbena	8–10
Flax	13–16	Zinnia	5–8

Vegetable Garden Plants

	Approximate number of days until germination		Approximate number of days until germination
Asparagus	21–28	Kohlrabi	6–8
Beans, bush	6–10	Lettuce	6–10
Beans, bush lima	6–10	Muskmelon	6–10
Beans, pole	6–10	Mustard	4–5
Beans, pole lima	7–12	Okra	15–20
Beets	7–10	Onion	8–12
Broccoli	6–10	Parsley	18–24
Brussels sprouts	6–10	Parsnip	12–18
Cabbage	6–10	Peas	6–10
Cabbage, Chinese	6–10	Pepper	10–14
Carrots	10–15	Pumpkin	6–10
Cauliflower	6–10	Radish	4–6
Celery	12–20	Rhubarb	12–14
Chard, Swiss	7–10	Rutabaga	4–7
Collards	6–10	Spinach	6–12
Corn, sweet	7–12	Squash, bush	6–10
Cress, garden	4–5	Squash, vine	6–10
Cucumber	6–8	Tomato	6–10
Eggplant	10–15	Turnip	4–7
Endive	8–12	Watermelon	8–12

Ground Covers

Botanical Name	Common Name
Sun	
Antennaria neodioica (1, 6)	Pussytoes
Arctostaphylas uva-ursi (1, 2, 3, 6)	Bearberry
Cotoneaster apiculata (1)	Cranberry cotoneaster
Cotoneaster dammeri and *cultivars* (1)	Bearberry cotoneaster
Euonymus colorata (3, 4, 6)	Purpleleaf wintercreeper
Juniperus horizontalis and *cultivars* (6)	Creeping juniper
Juniperus procumbens nana (4, 6)	Japanese juniper
Lonicera japonica halliana (3, 4, 6)	Hall's honeysuckle
Pachistima canbyi (1, 2, 6)	Pachistima
Potentilla tridentata (1, 2, 6)	Wineleaf cinquefoil
Potentilla verna nana (1, 5)	Cinquefoil
Sedum species (5, 6)	Stonecrop
Waldsteinia ternata (1, 3, 6)	Barren strawberry
Shade	
Ajuga reptans and *cultivars* (3, 4)	Carpet bugle
Convallaria majalis (4, 5)	Lily of the valley
Euonymus fortunei varieties (3, 4, 6)	Wintercreeper
Hedera helix and *cultivars* (4, 6)	English ivy
Hosta species (5)	Plantain lily
Liriope spicata (6)	Lily turn
Pachysandra terminalis (2, 6)	Japanese spurge
Vinca minor and *cultivars* (3, 6)	Periwinkle or myrtle

1. Requires well-drained soil
2. Requires acid soil
3. Good in sun or shade
4. Confine; may grow out of bounds
5. Herbaceous
6. Foliage retention in winter

VINES FOR SPECIAL USES

Botanical name	Common name
akebia quinata (1, 2, 3, 4)	Five-leaf akebia
Clematis species and *hybrids* (1, 2, 3, 4)	Virgin's-bower
Euonymus fortunei (2, 3)	Wintercreeper
Hedera helix and *cultivars* (2)	English ivy
Hydrangea petiolaris (1, 2)	Climbing hydrangea
Parthenocissus tricuspidata (2)	Boston ivy
Wisteria floribunda (1, 2, 3, 4)	Japanese wisteria

1. Flowering
2. Wall cover
3. Screening
4. Trellis

Botanical Names of Plants

Common name	Botanical name	Common Name	Botanical name
Acacia, giraffe	*Acacia giraffae*	Bryony, white	*Bryonia alba*
Adder's-tongue	*Erythronium sibiricum*	Buckwheat	*Fagopyrum sagittatum*
	Ophioglossum vulgatum islandicum	Buttercup, creeping	*Ranunculus repens*
Alder, European	*Alnus glutinosa*	Cabbage	*Brassica oleracea*
hazel	*A. rugosa*		*B. oleracea capitata*
red	*A. ruba*	Kerguelen	*Pringlea antiscorbutica*
Alfalfa	*Medicago sativa*	Cacao	*Theobroma cacao*
Almond	*Prunus amygdalus*	Calotrope, fantan	*Calotropis procera*
Aloe	*Aloe* sp.	Capeberry, South African	*Myrica cordifolia*
Amaryllis	*Amaryllis* sp.	Carpotroche	*Carpotroche brasiliensis*
Angelica	*Angelica polyclada*	Carrot	*Daucus carota*
garden	*A. archangelica*	Cashew	*Anacardium occidentale*
Apple	*Malus pumila*	Castor bean	*Ricinus communis*
	M. sylvestris	Catalpa, Chinese	*Catalpa ovata*
Apricot	*Prunus armeniaca*	northern	*C. speciosa*
Arborvitae, eastern	*Thuja occidentalis*	Cedar	*Cedrus* sp.
giant	*T. plicata*	California incense	*Libocedrus decurrens*
Arum, East Asian	*Pinellia ternata*	Celery, garden	*Apium graveolens dulce*
Ash, European	*Fraxinus excelsior*	wild	*A. graveolens*
green	*F. pennsylvanica*	Chaulmoogra tree	*Gynocardia odorata*
white	*F. americana*	common	*Hydnocarpus anthelmintica*
Asparagus, garden	*Asparagus officinalis*		
Aspen, European	*Populus tremula*	wight	*H. wightiana*
quaking	*P. tremuloides*	Cherry, black	*Prunus serotina*
Aster	*Aster* sp.	mazzard	*P. avium*
Attalea	*Attalea funifera*	pin	*P. pennsylvanica*
Avocado, American	*Persea americana*	Chestnut, Chinese	*Castanea mollissima*
		common horse-	*Aesculus hippocastanum*
Balloon vine	*Cardiospermum halicacabum*	Chickpea, gram	*Cicer arietinum*
		Chinaberry	*Melia azedarach*
Balsam, garden	*Impatiens balsamina*	Chrysanthemum, corn	*Chrysanthemum segetum*
Barley	*Hordeum vulgare*	Pyrenees	*C. maximum*
Bean, broad	*Vicia faba*	Cinchona, ledgerbark	*Cinchona ledgeriana*
kidney	*Phaseolus vulgaris*	Clarkia, rose	*Clarkia elegans*
sieva	*P. lunatus*	Clover, alsike	*Trifolium hybridum*
Beech, American	*Fagus grandifolia*	burdock	*T. lappaceum*
European	*F. sylvatica*	crimson	*T. incarnatum*
Beet, common	*Beta vulgaris*	Egyptian	*T. alexandrinum*
Birch, European white	*Betula pendula*	Persian	*T. resupinatum*
paper	*B. papyrifera*	red	*T. pratense*
sweet	*B. lenta*	strawberry	*T. fragiferum*
white	*B. populifolia*	subterranean	*T. subterraneum*
yellow	*B. lutea*	uckling	*T. dubium*
Blackberry	*Rubus* sp.	yellow sweet	*Melilotus officinalis*
Bladderpod	*Lesquerella densipila*	white	*Trifolium repens*
Blood-lily, Katharine	*Haemanthus katharinae*	white sweet	*Melilotus alba*
Blueberry, highbush	*Vaccinium corymbosum*	Clubmoss, common	*Lycopodium clavatum*
Brake, sword	*Pteris ensiformis*	Cocklebur, oriental	*Xanthium orientale*

Common name	Botanical name	Common Name	Botanical name
Coconut	Cocos nucifera	filmy	Hymenophyllum atrovirens
Coffee, Arabian	Coffea arabica	grape	Botrychium virginianum
Coneflower, pinewoods	Rudbeckia bicolor	holly	Crytomium falcatum
Coreopsis, goldenwave	Coreopsis drummondii	lady	Athyrium filix-femina
lance	C. lanceolata	maidenhair	Adiantum pedatum
plains	C. tinctoria	pine	Anemia adiantifolia
Corn	Zea mays	royal	Osmunda regalis
Cornflower	Centaurea cyanus	tropical	Gleichenia flabellata
Coronilla, crownvetch	Coronilla varia	water	Azolla pinnata
Cosmos	Cosmos sp.	wood	Thelypteris normalis
Cotton, Levant	Gossypium herbaceum	Fescue, alta	Festuca elatior arundinacea
Sea Island	G. barbadense	meadow	
upland	G. hirsutum	red	F. elatior
Coventry bells	Campanula trachelium	Fig	Ficus carica
Cowpea	Vigna glabra	Filbert	Corylus sp.
yard-long	V. sesquipedalis	Fir, cascades	Abies amabilis
common	V. sinensis	grand	A. grandis
Crotalaria	Crotalaria vitellina	noble	A. procera
Croton, purging	Croton tiglium	red	A. magnifica
Cucumber	Cucumis sativus	white	A. concolor
Currant, European black	Ribes nigrum	Flax, common	Linum usitatissimum
red	R. sativum	Forget-me-not	Myosotis sp.
Cypress, Arizona	Cupressus arizonica	Foxglove, common	Digitalis purpurea
bald	Taxodium distichum	Grecian	D. lanata
		Frenchweed	Thlaspi arvense
Dahlia	Dahlia sp.		
Dandelion	Taraxacum officinale	Ginkgo	Ginkgo biloba
Daphne	Daphne sp.	Gladiolus, common horticultural	Gladiolus hortulanus
Date	Phoenix dactylifera		
Davallia, Fiji	Davallia fejeensis	Gooseberry, Chinese	Actinidia chinensis
Desert willow	Chilopsis linearis	Gourd, snake	Trichosanthes sp.
Dock, curly	Rumex crispus	Grape, European	Vitis vinifera
Dogbane	Apocynum sp.	fox	V. labrusca
Dogwood, cornelian cherry	Cornus mas	roundleaf	
flowering	C. florida	Grass, Bermuda	Cynodon dactylon
Dollar plant	Lunaria annua	buffalo	Buchloe dactyloides
Douglas fir	Pseudotsuga menziesii	Canada blue-	Pao compressa
common	P. taxifolia	canary	Phalaris canariensis
		cocksfoot orchard	Dactylis glomerata
Eggplant	Solanum melongena	colonial bent-	Argostis tenuis
garden	S. melongena esculentum	common carpet-	Axonopus affinis
Elm, American	Ulmus americana	crested wheat-	Asgropyron cristatum
Endive	Cichorium endivia	dallis	Paspalum dilatatum
Erysimum, plains	Erysimum asperum	desert wheat-	Agropyron desertorum
Eucalyptus	Eucalyptus sp.	Italian rye-	Lolium multiflorum
Euphorbia, snow-on-the-mountain	Euphorbia marginata	Johnson	Sorghum halepense
		Kentucky, blue-	Poa pratensis
		perennial rye-	Lolium perenne
False-cypress, Lawson's	Chamaecyparis lawsoniana	quack	Agropyron repens
nootka	C. nootkatensis	reed canary	Phalaris arundinacea
Fern, common staghorn	Platycerium bifurcatum	Sudan	Sorghum vulgare sudanense
common sword	Nephrolepis exaltata		

Common name	Botanical name	Common Name	Botanical name
Hackberry, common	*Celtis occidentalis*	silver	*A. saccharinum*
Hart's-tongue	*Phyllitis scolopendrium*	sugar	*A. saccharum*
Hemlock, eastern	*Tsuga canadensis*	Marattia	*Marattia salicina*
western	*T. heterophylla*	Marbleseed, western	*Onosmodium occidentale*
Hemp	*Cannabis sativa*	Marigold	*Tagetes* sp.
Hibiscus, kenaf	*Hibiscus cannabinus*	winter cape	*Dimorphoteca aurantiaca*
Hickory, shagbark	*Carya ovata*	Meadowrue, Sierra	*Thalictrum polycarpum*
Holly, American	*Ilex opaca*	Milkweed, common	*Asclepias syriaca*
English	*I. aquifolium*	Millet, pearl	*Pennisetum glaucum*
Hollyhock	*Althaea rosea*	Morning glory, common	*Ipomoea purpurea*
Horsetail, common	*Equisetum arvense*	orizaba	*I. orizabensis*
Hyssop, hedge	*Gratiola* sp.	Muskmelon	*Cucumis melo*
		Mustard, black	*Brassica nigra*
Indigo	*Indigofera* sp.	white	*B. hirta*
Iris, blue flag	*Iris versicolor*		
German	*I. germanica*	Nasturtium	*Tropaeolum* sp.
grass	*I. graminea*	Niger seed	*Guizotia abyssinica*
Ironweed, kinka oil	*Vernonia anthelmintica*		
		Oak, black	*Quercus velutina*
Jarcaranda	*Jacaranda* sp.	English	*Q. robur*
Jimsonweed	*Datura stramonium*	scarlet	*Q. coccinea*
Juniper, Savin	*Juniperus sabina*	southern red	*Q. falcata*
		white	*Q. alba*
Kale	*Brassica oleracea acephala*	Oat, common	*Avena sativa*
Kamala tree	*Mallotus philippinensis*	Okra	*Hibiscus esculentus*
Knotweed, prostrate	*Polygonum aviculare*	Olive	*Olea europaea sativa*
		common	*O. europaea*
Lamb's quarter	*Chenopodium album*	Oncoba, gorli	*Oncoba echinata*
Larch, western	*Larix occidentalis*	Onion, garden	*Allium cepa*
Larkspur, rocket	*Delphinium ajacis*	Orange, sweet	*Citrus sinensis*
Lemon	*Citrus limon*	trifoliate	*Poncirus trifoliata*
Lentil	*Lens culinaris*		
Lespedeza, common	*Lespedeza striata*	Palm, African oil	*Elaeis guineensis*
Korean	*L. stipulacea*	Pansy, wild	*viola tricolor*
wand	*L. intermedia*	Parinarium	*Parinarium* sp.
Lettuce	*Lactuca sativa*	Parsley	*Petroselinum crispum*
Licania	*Licania rigida*	common curly	*P. latifolium*
Lilac, common	*Syringa vulgaris*	Parsnip	*Pastinaca sativa*
Lily, regal	*Lilium regale*	Pea, field	*Pisum sativum arvense*
Linden, American	*Tilia americana*	garden	*P. sativum*
Litsea	*Litsea* sp.	sweet	*Lathyrus odoratus*
Locust, black	*Robinia pseudoacacia*	Peach	*Prunus persica*
Lotus, East Indian	*Nelumbo nucifea*	Peanut	*Arachis hypogaea*
Lupine	*Lupinus arcticus*	Pear	*Pyrun communis*
tree	*L. angustifolius*	Peavine, flat	*Lathyrus sylvestris*
		Pecan	*Carya illinoensis*
Macadamia, Queenslandnut	*Macadamia ternifolia*	Peony, fernleaf	*Paeonia tenuifolia*
Magnolia, great-leaved	*Magnolia macrophylla*	Pepper, bush red	*Capsicum frutescens*
southern	*M. grandiflora*	Pepperwort	*Marsilea minuta*
Malope	*Malope trifida*	Perilla, common	*Pefrilla frutescens*
Mango, common	*Mangifera indica*	Persimmon, common	*Diospyros virginiana*
Maple, red	*Acer rubrum*	Petunia	*Petunia* sp.

Common name	Botanical name	Common Name	Botanical name
Phlox, Drummond	*Phlox drummondii*	Rye	*Secale cereale*
Pine, Austrian	*Pinus nigra*		
eastern white	*P. strobus*	Safflower	*Carthamus tinctorius*
jack	*P. banksiana*	Sage, garden	*Salvia officinalis*
loblolly	*P. taeda*	scarlet	*S. splendens*
longleaf	*P. palustris*	Salsify, vegetable-oyster	*Tragopogon porrifolius*
ponderosa	*P. ponderosa*	Scammony, glorybind	*Convolvulus scammonia*
shore	*P. contorta*	Scarlet runner	*Phaseolus coccineus*
shortleaf	*P. echinata*	Sequoia, giant	*Sequoiadendron giganteum*
slash	*P. caribea*		*Sequoia gigantea*
sugar	*P. lambertiana*	Sesame, oriental	*Sesamum indicum*
western white	*P. monticola*	Snapdragon, common	*Antirrhinum majus*
Pineapple	*Ananas comosus*	Sorghum	*Sorghum bicolor*
Pink, clove	*Dianthus caryophyllus*	Soybean	*Glycine max*
Pistachio	*Pistacia* sp.	Spicebush, Japanese	*Lindera obtusiloba*
Plum, garden	*Prunus domestica*	Spiderwort	*Tradescantia paludosa*
Japanese	*P. salicina*	Virginia	*T. virginiana*
Podocarpus	*Podocarpus* sp.	Spikemoss	*Selaginella selaginoides*
Polypody, rock	*Polypodium virginianum*	Spinach	*Spinacia oleracea*
Pomegranate, common	*Punica granatum*	Spruce, Norway	*Picea abies*
Poplar, eastern	*Populus deltoides*	red	*P. rubens*
Mongolian	*P. suaveolens*	Sitka	*P. sitchensis*
yellow, or tulip tree	*Liriodendron tulipfera*	white	*P. glauca*
		Spurge, South American	*Sebastiania fruticosa*
Poppy, corn	*Papaver rhoeas*	Spurry, corn	*Spergula avensis*
opium	*P. somniferum*	Sterculia, hazel	*Sterculia foetida*
oriental	*P. orientale*	Stillingia	*Stillingia* sp.
Portulaca, common	*Portulaca grandiflora*	Stock, common	*Matthiola incana*
Potato	*Solanum tuberosum*	Strawberry, chiloe	*Fragaria chiloensis*
Primrose, evening	*Oenothera biennis*	pine	*F. ananassa*
Lemarck	*O. lamarckiana*	Strophanthus	*Strophanthus glaber*
Pumpkin	*Cucurbita pepo*	arrow poison	*S. sarmentosus*
Purslane, common	*Portulaca oleracea*	Sugarcane	*Saccharum officinarum*
Pycnanthus, akomu	*Pycnanthus kambo*	Sumac	*Rhus* sp.
		Sunflower, common	*Helianthus annuus*
Quillwort	*Isoetes braunii*	Sweetcane	*Saccharum spontaneum*
		Sweetgum, American	*Liquidambar styraciflua*
Radish, garden	*Raphanus sativus*	Sweet potato	*Ipomoea batatas*
Rape, bird	*Brassica campestris*	Sweet william	*Dianthus barbatus*
winter	*B. napus*		
Red cedar, eastern	*Juniperus virginiana*	Tallow wood	*Ximenia americana*
Redtop	*Agrostis alba*		*X. caffra*
Redwood	*Sequoia sempervirens*	Tara vine	*Taraktogenos kurzii*
Rhododendron, catawba	*Rhododendron catawbiense*	Tetradenia, Asian	*Tetradenia glauca*
		Timothy	*Phleum pratense*
Rhubarb, garden	*Rheum rhaponticum*	Tobacco	*Nicotiana glutinosa*
medicinal	*R. officinale*	common	*N. tabacum*
sorrel	*R. palmatum*	Tomato, common	*Lycopersicon esculentum*
Rice	*Oryza sativa*	Trefoil, bird's foot	*Lotus corniculatus*
Rose, cabbage	*Rosa centifolia*	Tulip	*Tulipa* sp.
Rubber, pará	*Hevea brasiliensis*	Tung oil tree	*Aleurites fordii*
Rutabaga	*Brassica napobrassica*	Tupelo, water	*Nyssa acquatica*

Common name	Botanical name	Common Name	Botanical name
Turnip	*Brassica rapa*	Waterweed, Canadian	*Elodea canadensis*
		Wheat	*Triticum aestivum*
Vetch, common	*Vicia sativa*	Willow, basket	*Salix viminalis*
hairy	*V. villosa*	big catkin	*S. gracilistyla*
Hungarian	*V. pannonica*	black	*S. nigra*
narrow leaf	*V. angustifolia*	pussy	*S. discolor*
one-flower	*V. articulata*	white	*S. alba*
purple	*V. benghalensis*		
tiny	*V. hirsuta*	Yellow trumpet, Florida	*Stenolobium stans*
wooly pod	*V. dasycarpa*	Yew, English	*Taxus baccata*
Violet, field	*Viola arvensis*	Pacific	*T. brevifolia*
		Yucca	*Yucca* sp.
Walnut, eastern black	*Juglans nigra*		
Waterlily	*Nymphaea alba*	Zinnia, oblong leaf	*Zinnia angustifolia*
Watermelon	*Citrullus vulgaris*		

National Park Directory

Acadia National Park
Bar Harbor, Maine
Area: 41,888 acres
Season: Year-round

Major attractions: Mountains (highest point on Atlantic Coast) showing marine erosion and glaciation; lakes; forests; marine life.
Activities: Camping, fishing, hiking, horseback riding, nature walks, picnicking, swimming, sea cruises.

Arches National Park
Moab, Utah
Area: 73,379 acres
Season: Year-round

Major attractions: Huge rock formations caused by erosion; mountains; Colorado River gorge.
Activities: Camping, fishing, canoeing, whitewater boating.

Badlands National Park
Interior, South Dakota
Area: 242,755 acres
Season: Year-round

Major attractions: Multicolored peaks and spires caused by erosion; fossil sites; wildlife; Pine Ridge Indian Reservation near site of Wounded Knee battleground.
Activities: Camping, fishing, hiking, picnicking.

Big Bend National Park
Big Bend National Park, Texas
Area: 801,163 acres
Season: Year-round

Major attractions: Mountains; canyons, desert; U.S. and Mexican flowers; trees; wildlife.
Activities: Camping, boating, fishing, hiking, horseback riding, picnicking, pack trips.

Biscayne National Park
Homestead, Florida
Area: 173,467 acres
Season: Year-round

Major attractions: Underwater coral reefs; marine life.
Activities: Boating, snorkeling, scuba diving.

Bryce Canyon National Park
Bryce Canyon, Utah
Area: 35,836 acres
Season: Year-round

Major attractions: Multicolored rock erosions.
Activities: Camping, fishing, hiking, boating, picnicking, museum tours.

Canyonlands National Park
Moab, Utah
Area: 337,570 acres
Season: Year-round

Major attractions: Rock formations; ancient cliff dwellings; Green River and Colorado River canyons.

Activities: Boating, whitewater trips, hiking, camping, fishing, horseback riding, picnicking.

Capitol Reef National Park
Torrey, Utah
Area: 241,905 acres
Season: Year-round

Major attractions: Colorful rock formations; desert plants and wildlife; pioneer exhibits.

Activities: Camping, hiking, fishing, four-wheel-drive trails.

Carlsbad Caverns National Park
Carlsbad, New Mexico
Area: 46,775 acres
Season: Year-round

Major attractions: Possibly world's largest cavern with spectacular underground formations; above-ground desert plants and rock formations.

Activities: Cavern tours, hiking, nature walks, picnicking.

Channel Islands National Park
Ventura, California
Area: 249,355 acres
Season: Year-round

Major attractions: Marine life and sea birds.

Activities: Hiking, boating, fishing, picnicking, scuba diving, snorkeling.

Chickasaw National Recreation Area
Sulphur, Oklahoma
Area: 9,521 acres
Season: Year-round

Major attractions: Mineral springs, wild animals; birds and plants.

Activities: Camping, fishing, hiking, nature walks, picnicking.

Crater Lake National Park
Crater Lake, Oregon
Area: 183,224 acres
Season: Year-round

Major attractions: Deepest lake in the United States (2,000 feet) in crater of extinct volcano; multicolored rocks; forests, mountain flowers, and wildlife.

Activities: Camping, hiking, fishing, boating, cross-country skiing.

Denali National Park and Preserve
Denali, Alaska
Area: 4,716,726 acres
Season: Year-round

Major attractions: Peaks of Alaska Range, including Mount McKinley (20,320 feet); rare wildlife and subarctic plant life; huge Denali fault; break in earth's crust.

Activities: Camping, dog-sledding, hiking, fishing.

Everglades National Park
Homestead, Florida
Area: 1,506,499 acres
Season: Year-round

Major attractions: Immense subtropical wilderness; mangrove swamps; wild animals and rare birds.

Activities: Boating, camping, fishing, guided tours, hiking, nature walks, picnicking.

Gates of the Arctic National Park and Preserve
Fairbanks, Alaska
Area: 7,523,888 acres
Season: Year-round

Major attractions: Snow-covered peaks of Brooks Range north of Arctic Circle; tundra wilderness; wildlife.

Activities: Hunting, fishing, camping, mountain climbing.

Glacier Bay National Park
Gustavus, Alaska
Area: 3,226,000 acres
Season: May to September

Major attractions: Great Mendenhall Glacier; iceberg formations from glaciers; dense coastal rain forests; wildlife; nearby, Mount Logan, highest point in Canada (19,850 feet).

Activities: Camping, hiking, hunting, fishing.

Glacier National Park
West Glacier, Montana
Area: 1,056,000 acres
Season: June through September

Major attractions: Rugged mountain peaks of Continental Divide; glaciers; numerous alpine lakes and streams; rare wildflowers; wildlife; ancient Blackfoot hunting grounds.

Activities: Hiking on old hunting and exploration trails, nature walks, horseback riding, camping, fishing.

Grand Canyon National Park
Grand Canyon, Arizona
Area: 1,218,376 acres
Season: Year-round

Major attractions: Mile-deep, 1.5-billion-year-old canyon of Colorado River, showing geologic features with fossil plants and animals; multicolored rocks; wide range of wild plants and animals; Havasupai Indian reservation.

Activities: Camping, hiking, horseback riding, boating, whitewater trips, nature walks, picnicking.

Grand Teton National Park
Moose, Wyoming
Area: 309,993 acres
Season: June to September

Major attractions: Mountains; trails of famous early explorers; perennial snow fields; wild plants, animals, and birds.

Activities: Camping, hiking, fishing, boating, horseback riding.

Great Smoky Mountains National Park
Gatlinburg, Tennessee
Area: 520,269 acres
Season: Year-round

Major attractions: Highest mountains in the eastern United States (6,500 feet); wide range of plants; wildlife;

Activities: Camping, fishing, hiking, nature walks, museums, horseback riding, picnicking.

Guadalupe Mountains National Park
Salt Flat, Texas
Area: 86,415 acres
Season: Year-round

Major attractions: Desert wilderness; limestone fossil reef; wildlife; highest point in Texas (8,749 feet).

Activities: Camping, hiking.

Haleakala National Park
Makawao, Maui, Hawaii
Area: 28,655 acres
Season: Year-round

Major attractions: Haleakala crater; scenic pools; rare wildlife; semitropical vegetation.

Activities: Hiking, nature walks, picnicking.

Hawaii Volcanoes National Park
Hawaii National Park, Hawaii
Area: 229,178 acres

Major attractions: Volcano activity; semitropical plants; birds.

Activities: Hiking, nature walks, camping,

Hot Springs National Park
Hot Springs, Arkansas
Area: 5,839 acres
Season: Year-round

Major attractions: Ancient hot springs for bathing with reputed therapeutic benefits.

Activities: Bathing, museum tours, hiking, nature trails, picnicking, camping.

Isle Royale National Park
Houghton, Michigan
Area: 571,790 acres
Season: April to October

Major attractions: Historic fisheries; hardwood and evergreen forests; pre-Columbian copper mines; wildlife.

Activities: Camping, hiking, fishing, kayaking, boating (no cars permitted on island).

Katmai National Park and Preserve
King Salmon, Alaska
Area: 3,700,000 acres
Season: May to September

Major attractions: Varied subarctic environment; Alagnak Wild River; Valley of 10,000 Smokes; wildlife.

Activities: Fishing, wildlife-watching; kayaking.

Kenai Fjords National Park
Seward, Alaska
Area: 670,000 acres
Season: May to September

Major attractions: Mountains; ice fields; fjord system; varied marine life.

Activities: Fishing, boating, mountain climbing, camping, hiking, bird watching (150 species).

Kings Canyon National Park
Three Rivers, California
Area: 460,331 acres
Season: May to October

Major attractions: High Sierra peaks; giant sequoia trees; mile-deep canyon; alpine lakes; glaciers and snowfields; wildlife.

Activities: Camping, hiking, horseback riding, fishing, cross-country skiing.

Kobuk Valley National Park
Kotzebue, Alaska
Area: 1,750,000 acres
Season: Year-round

Major attractions: Baird Mountain peaks; forests, tundra; great sand dunes; prehistoric archeological sites; arctic wildlife.

Activities: Hiking, boating, mountain climbing, fishing.

Lake Clark National Park and Preserve
Anchorage, Alaska
Area: 2,636,839 acres
Season: June to September

Major attractions: Aleutian Range peaks; Cook Inlet; live volcanoes; fossils; forests; wildlife.

Activities: Camping, fishing, boating, hiking, bird-watching, hunting.

Lassen Volcanic National Park
Mineral, California
Area: 106,372 acres
Season: June to October

Major attractions: Live volcano (intermittent eruptions from 1914 to 1921); hot springs.

Activities: Camping, hiking (150 miles of trails), boating, winter sports.

Mammoth Cave National Park
Mammoth Cave, Kentucky
Area: 52,419 acres
Season: Year-round

Major attractions: Large cavern (330 miles of passageways); underground river.

Activities: Boating, camping, fishing, hiking, nature walks, picnicking.

Mesa Verde National Park
Mesa Verde National Park, Colorado
Area: 51,333 acres
Season: May to October

Major attractions: Pre-Columbian cliff dwellings; lookout showing six mountain ranges in four states.

Activities: Camping, picnicking, hiking, cliff-dwelling tours.

Mount Rainier National Park
Ashford, Washington
Area: 235,613 acres
Season: June to November

Major attractions: Mountain terrain featuring glaciers, forests, and subalpine meadows.

Activities: Hiking, winter sports, camping, guided climbs to summit (14,410 feet) for experienced mountaineers.

North Cascades National Park
Sedro Woolley, Washington
Area: 504,781 acres
Season: April to October

Major attractions: Alpine wilderness area featuring mountains, lakes, forests, glaciers, wildlife.

Activities: Camping, fishing, hiking, boating, horseback riding.

Olympic National Park
Port Angeles, Washington
Area: 922,654 acres
Season: Year-round

Major attractions: Rain forests of giant evergreens; mountains; glaciers; wildlife; rocky beaches on peninsula between Pacific Ocean and Puget Sound.

Activities: Camping, fishing, hiking, bird-watching, horseback riding, boating.

Petrified Forest National Park
Petrified Forest National Park, Arizona
Area: 93,530 acres
Season: Year-round

Major attractions: World's largest display of petrified coniferous trees in six groups of logs now in the form of jasper and agate; prehistoric Indian rock carvings; painted desert of eroded layers of red and yellow sediment.

Activities: Hiking, nature walks, picnicking, camping.

Redwood National Park
Crescent City, California
Area: 110,132 acres
Season: Year-round

Major attractions: Redwood forests, including tallest known tree in the world; Pacific Ocean coastline.

Activities: Camping, hiking, fishing, white-water trips nearby.

Rocky Mountain National Park
Estes Park, Colorado
Area: 265,198 acres
Season: Year-round

Major attractions: Mountains; lakes; streams; forests; wildflower meadows; wild animals.

Activities: Camping, hiking, fishing, horseback riding, mountaineering classes, winter skiing.

Sequoia National Park
Three Rivers, California
Area: 402,482 acres
Season: Year-round

Major attractions: High Sierra peaks, including Mount Whitney (14,494 feet); sequoia forests; wildlife.

Activities: Camping, hiking, fishing, horseback riding, photographic trips.

Shenandoah National Park
Luray, Virginia
Area: 196,039 acres
Season: Year-round

Major attraction: Blue Ridge Mountains; hardwood forests; wildflowers.

Activities: Camping, hiking, horseback riding, nature walks, picnicking.

Theodore Roosevelt Memorial National Park
Medora, North Dakota
Area: 70,446 acres
Season: May to October

Major attractions: Little Missouri River badlands; site of former President Theodore Roosevelt's ranch; wildlife.

Activities: Hiking, camping, picnicking, float trips, bird-watching.

Virgin Islands National Park
St. John, U.S. Virgin Islands
Area: 14,689 acres
Season: Year-round

Major attractions: Tropical plant and animal life; marine life; sandy beaches; colonial plantations; early Carib relics.

Activities: Camping, fishing, hiking, nature walks, picnicking, swimming, diving.

Voyageurs National Park
International Falls, Minnesota
Area: 219,400 acres
Season: Year-round

Major attractions: Evergreen forests; ancient rock outcroppings; bogs; glacial lakes; wildlife.

Activities: Boating (access to interior is mainly by boat), camping, fishing, hiking, canoeing.

Wind Cave National Park
Hot Springs, South Dakota
Area: 28,060 acres
Season: Year-round

Major attractions: Limestone caverns; bison herds; wildlife.

Activities: Camping, hiking, nature walks, picnicking.

Wrangell-St. Elias National Park and Preserve
Glennallen, Alaska
Area: 8,945,000 acres
Season: Year-round

Major attractions: Largest U.S. national park; greatest concentration of peaks over 14,000 feet in North America; rugged coastline; boreal forests; alpine tundra; wildlife.

Activities: Mountain climbing, hunting, fishing, camping, boating.

Yellowstone National Park
Yellowstone National Park, Wyoming
Area: 2,219,791 acres
Season: Year-round

Major attractions: Oldest national park; spectacular wilderness; Old Faithful geyser; hot springs; lakes, streams, and waterfalls; wildlife; the Grand Canyon of the Yellowstone.

Activities: Camping, hiking, fishing, photography, horseback riding, boating, picnicking, winter ski touring.

Yosemite National Park
Yosemite National Park, California
Area: 761,170 acres
Season: June to October

Major attractions: Mountain peaks over 10,000 feet; spectacular granite domes and monoliths; highest waterfall in the United States; sequoia groves; wildlife.

Activities: Camping, hiking, horseback riding, fishing, downhill and cross-country skiing in winter.

Zion National Park
Springdale, Utah
Area: 146,597 acres
Season: June to October

Major attractions: Huge canyons and gorges carved by mountain rivers; colorful rock cliffs; wildlife.

Activities: Camping, hiking, horseback riding, boating.

National Wildlife Refuges Locations and Facilities

This is not a listing of the entire Refuge System, but of only those refuges that offer visitor opportunities. The address given is that of the office that administers the refuge; it does not necessarily reflect the location of the refuge.

Refuge conditions, regulations, and activities are varied and subject to change. Please check with the refuge manager regarding conditions, regulations, and facilities for the disabled before taking a trip to a refuge.

Refuge	Spring	Summer	Fall	Winter	Visitor center, contact station	Foot trails	Auto tour	Bicycling	Boating—nonmotorized	Boating—motorized	Environmental study area	Backcountry use	Hunting	Fishing	Camping	Picnicking	Swimming	Refuge leaflet	Species list	Food/lodging nearby
ALABAMA																				
Bon Secour, P.O. Box 1650, Gulf Shores, AL 36542	■					■														■
Choctaw, Box 808, Jackson, AL 36545			■	■																
Eufaula, Route 2, Box 97-B, Eufaula, AL 36027 (Alabama and Georgia)	■		■	■	■	■	■	■	■	■			■	■				■	■	■
Wheeler, Box 1643, Decatur, AL 35602			■	■	■	■	■	■	■	■	■		■	■				■	■	■
ALASKA																				
Alaska Maritime (Headquarters), 202 West Pioneer Avenue, Homer, AK 99603	■	■	■		■													■		■
Alaska Peninsula Unit		■																		
Aleutian Islands Unit, Box 5251, FPO Seattle, WA 98791	■								■	■	■	■	■	■	■	■				
Bering Sea Unit			■																	
Chukchi Sea Unit																				
Gulf of Alaska Unit																				
Alaska Peninsula, P.O. Box 277, King Salmon, AK 99613									■	■	■	■	■	■	■	■		■		
Becharof																				
Artic, 101 12th Avenue, Box 20, Fairbanks, AK 99701			■						■	■	■	■	■	■	■	■		■		
Innoko, P.O. Box 69, McGrath, AK 99627			■						■	■	■	■	■	■	■	■		■		
Izembek, Box 127, Cold Bay, AK 99571	■	■	■		■	■			■	■	■	■	■	■	■	■		■	■	■
Kanuti, 101 12th Avenue, Box 20, Fairbanks, AK 99701	■								■	■	■	■	■	■	■	■				
Kenai, P.O. Box 2139, Soldotna, AK 99669	■	■	■		■	■			■	■	■	■	■	■	■	■		■		■
Kodiak, 1390 Buskin River Road, Kodiak, AK 99615		■	■		■				■	■	■	■	■	■	■	■		■	■	■
Koyukuk, Box 287, Galena, AK 99741			■						■	■	■	■	■	■	■	■		■		
Nowitna, Box 287, Galena, AK 99741									■	■	■	■	■	■	■	■		■	■	
Selawik, Box 270 Kotzebue, AK 99752									■	■	■	■	■	■	■	■		■	■	

629

Refuge conditions, regulations, and activities are varied and subject to change. Please check with the refuge manager regarding conditions, regulations, and facilities for the disabled before taking a trip to a refuge.

Location	Spring	Summer	Fall	Winter	Visitor center, contact station	Foot trails	Auto tour	Bicycling	Boating—nonmotorized	Boating—motorized	Environmental study area	Backcountry use	Hunting	Fishing	Camping	Picnicking	Swimming	Refuge leaflet	Species list	Food/lodging nearby
Tetlin, Box 155, Tok, AK 99780	■	■	■		■													■		■
Togiak, P.O. Box 270, Dillingham, AK 99576		■	■															■		
Yukon Delta, P.O. Box 346, Bethel, AK 99559	■	■	■		■													■		■
Yukon Flats, 101 12th Avenue, Box 20, Fairbanks, AK 99701																		■		■
ARIZONA																				
Buenos Aires, P.O. Box 106, Sasabe, AZ 85633	■		■	■	■	■	■						■		■	■		■	■	■
Cabeza Prieta, Box 418, Ajo, AZ 85321	■		■	■	■							■	■		■			■	■	■
Cibola, Box AP, Blythe, CA 92225 (Arizona and California)			■	■	■		■	■	■	■			■	■				■	■	■
Havasu, Box A, Needles, CA 92363 (Arizona and California)					■				■	■			■	■	■	■	■	■	■	■
Imperial, Box 72217, Martinez Lake, AZ 85364 (Arizona and California)	■		■	■	■	■			■	■			■	■	■	■		■	■	■
Kofa, Box 6290, Yuma, AZ 85364	■		■	■		■						■	■		■			■	■	■
San Bernardino, RR# 1, Box 228R, Douglas, AZ 85607	■		■	■	■									■				■	■	■
ARKANSAS																				
Felsenthal, P.O. Box 67, Manila, AR 72442			■	■	■	■	■		■	■			■	■	■	■		■	■	■
Holla Bend, Box 1043, Russellville, AR 72801			■	■		■	■	■	■	■			■	■		■		■	■	■
Wapanocca, Box 279, Turrell, AR 72384	■		■	■		■	■		■				■	■				■	■	■
Big Lake, Box 67, Manila, AR 72442	■	■	■	■					■	■			■	■				■	■	■
Cache River																				■
White River, Box 308, 321 West 7th Street, De Witt, AR 72042			■	■	■	■			■	■			■	■	■	■		■	■	■
CALIFORNIA																				
Cibola (See Arizona)																				
Havasu (See Arizona)																				
Imperial (See Arizona)																				

Kern, Box 670, Delano, CA 93216
Klamath Basin Refuges, Route 1, Box 74, Tulelake CA 96134
   Clear Lake
   Lower Klamath (Oregon and California)
   Tule Lake
Modoc, Box 1610, Alturas, CA 96101
Sacramento Valley Refuges, Route 1, Box 311, Willows, CA 95988
   Colusa
   Delevan
   Sacramento
   Sutter
Salton Sea, P.O. Box 120, Calipatria, CA 92223
   Coachella Valley
   Tijuana Slough
San Francisco Bay, Box 524, Newark, CA 94560-0524
   Antioch Dunes
   Humboldt Bay
   Salinas River
   San Pablo Bay
San Luis, Box 2176, Los Banos, CA 93635
   Kesterson
   Merced

COLORADO
Alamosa, Box 1148, Alamosa, CO 81101
   Monte Vista
Arapaho, Box 457, Walden, CO 80480
Browns Park, 1318 Highway 318, Maybell, CO 81640

CONNECTICUT
Salt Meadow, Box 307, Charlestown, RI 02813
Stewart B. McKinney, 910 Lafayette Blvd., Rm. Bridgeport, CT 06604

DELAWARE
Bombay Hook, Route 1, Box 147, Smyrna, DE 19977
Prime Hook, Route 1, Box 195, Milton DE 19968

FLORIDA
Arthur R. Marshall Loxahatchee, Route 1, Box 278, Boynton Beach, FL 33437
Hobe Sound

Refuge	Spring	Summer	Fall	Winter	Visitor center, contact station	Foot trails	Auto tour	Bicycling	Boating—nonmotorized	Boating—motorized	Environmental study area	Backcountry use	Hunting	Fishing	Camping	Picnicking	Swimming	Refuge leaflet	Species list	Food/lodging nearby
Chassahowitzka, P.O. Box 4139, Homosassa, FL 32647	■	■	■	■		■			■	■	■		■	■					■	■
Cedar Keys	■	■	■	■					■	■				■				■	■	■
Crystal River				■																■
Egmont Key	■	■	■	■		■			■	■	■			■				■		■
Lower Suwannee	■		■					■	■	■	■		■	■						■
Passage Key	■		■	■															■	■
Pinellas	■		■	■																■
J. N. "Ding" Darling, 1 Wildlife Drive, Sanibel, FL 33957	■		■	■		■	■	■	■	■	■			■				■	■	■
Caloosahatchee	■		■	■																■
Island Bay	■		■	■					■	■										■
Matlacha Pass	■		■	■					■	■	■									■
Pine Island	■		■	■					■	■										■
Lake Woodruff, Box 488, DeLeon Springs, FL 32028			■	■		■		■	■		■		■	■				■		■
Merritt Island, Box 6504, Titusville, FL 32780			■	■	■	■	■		■	■	■		■	■				■	■	■
Pelican Island		■		■					■	■										■
National Key Deer, Box 510, Big Pine Key, FL 33043		■		■	■	■		■			■							■	■	■
Crocodile Lake		■		■																■
Great White Heron	■	■	■	■					■	■	■			■						■
Key West	■	■	■	■					■	■	■			■						■
St. Marks, Box 68, St. Marks, FL 32355	■		■	■	■	■		■	■	■	■		■	■				■	■	■
St. Vincent, Box 447, Apalachicola, FL 32320	■		■	■		■			■	■	■		■	■				■	■	■

GEORGIA

Eufaula (See Alabama)

Okefenokee, Rt. 2, Box 338, Folkston, GA 31537
Piedmont, Round Oak, GA 31038
Savannah Coastal Refuges, Box 8487, Savannah, GA 31402
- Blackbeard Island
- Harris Neck
- Savannah (Georgia and South Carolina)
- Tybee
- Wassaw
- Wolf Island

HAWAII

Hawaiian and Pacific Islands Refuges, P.O. Box 50167, Honolulu, HI 96850
- Hawaiian Islands
- James C. Campbell
- Kakahaia
- Kilauea Point, Box 87, Kilauea, Kauai, HI 96754
- Hanalei

IDAHO

Deer Flat, Box 448, Nampa, ID 83653-0448
Snake River Islands
Kootenai, HCR 60, Box 283, Bonners Ferry, ID 83805
Southeast Idaho Refuges, 250 S. Fourth Avenue, Pocatello, ID 83201
- Bear Lake, 370 Webster, P.O. Box 9, Montpelier, ID 83254
- Camas, HC 69, Box 1700, Hamer, ID 83425
- Grays Lake, HC 70, Box 4090, Wayan, ID 83285
- Minidoka, Route 4, P.O. Box 290, Rupert, ID 83350

ILLINOIS

Chautauqua, Route 2, Havana, IL 62644
Crab Orchard, Box J, Carterville, IL 62918
Mark Twain, 311 North 5th Street, Suite 100, Quincy, IL 62301
- Batchtown Division, Box 142, Brussels, IL 63013
- Calhoun Division, Box 142, Brussels, IL 62013
- Gardner Division, P.O. Box 88, Annada, MO 63330
- Gilbert Lake Division, Box 142, Brussels, IL 62013
- Keithsburg Division, Route 1, Wapello, IA 52653
Upper Mississippi River Wild Life and Fish Refuge (See Minnesota)
Savanna District, Post Office Building, Savanna, IL 61074

Refuge	Spring	Summer	Fall	Winter	Visitor center, contact station	Foot trails	Auto tour	Bicycling	Boating—nonmotorized	Boating—motorized	Environmental study area	Backcountry use	Hunting	Fishing	Camping	Picnicking	Swimming	Refuge leaflet	Species list	Food/lodging nearby
INDIANA																				
Muscatatuck, Box 189 A, Route 7, Seymour, IN 47274	■	■	■	■	■	■	■	■	■		■		■	■				■	■	■
IOWA																				
Des Soto, Route 1, Box 114, Missouri Valley, IA 51555 (Iowa and Nebraska)	■		■		■	■								■				■	■	■
Mark Twain (See Illinois)																				
Big Timber Division, Route 1, Wapello, IA 52653					■	■			■	■			■	■				■	■	■
Louisa Division, Route 1, Wapello, IA 52653					■	■			■	■			■	■				■	■	■
Union Slough, Route 1, Box 52, Titonka, IA 50480	■		■			■							■					■	■	■
Upper Mississippi River Wild Life and Fish Refuge (See Minnesota)																				
McGregor District, P.O. Box 460, McGregor, IA 52157	■	■	■		■				■	■			■	■	■	■		■	■	■
KANSAS																				
Flint Hills, Box 128, Hartford, KS 66854			■		■				■	■			■	■				■	■	■
Kirwin, Route 1, Box 103, Kirwin, KS 67644			■		■		■		■	■	■	■	■	■	■	■	■	■	■	■
Quivira, Route 3, Box 48A, Stafford, KS 67578	■		■		■	■	■				■		■	■				■	■	■
LOUISIANA																				
Bogue Chitto, 1010 Gause Boulevard, Building 936, Slidell, LA 70458	■		■	■					■	■			■	■				■	■	■
Catahoula, P.O. Drawer LL, Jena, LA 71342			■	■	■		■				■		■	■				■	■	■
D'Arbonne, Box 3065, Monroe, LA 71201	■		■	■		■			■	■	■		■	■				■	■	■
Upper Quachita	■		■	■					■	■			■	■					■	■
Delta-Breton, Venice, LA 70091	■			■					■	■			■	■				■	■	
Lacassine, Route 1, Box 186, Lake Arthur, LA 70549			■	■	■		■		■		■		■	■				■	■	■
Sabine, MRH 107, Hackberry, LA 70645	■		■	■	■	■	■		■	■	■		■	■				■	■	■
Tensas River, Route 2, Box 295, Tallulah, LA 71282	■		■	■	■	■	■		■	■	■		■	■				■	■	■

MAINE
Moosehorn, Box X, Calais, ME 04619
   Cross Island
   Franklin Island
Petit Manan, P.O. Box 279, Milbridge, ME 04658
Rachel Carson, Route 2, Box 751, Wells, ME 04090

MARYLAND
Blackwater, Route 1, Box 121, Cambridge, MD 21613
Eastern Neck, Route 2, Box 225, Rock Hall, MD 21661

MASSACHUSETTS
Great Meadows, Weir Hill Rd., Sudbury, MA 01776
   Oxbow
Parker River, Northern Boulevard, Plum Island, Newburyport, MA 01950
   Monomoy
   Nantucket

MICHIGAN
Seney, Seney, MI 49883
Shiawassee, 6975 Mower Road, Route 1, Saginaw, MI 48601

MINNESOTA
Agassiz, Middle River, MN 56737
Big Stone, 25 NW 2nd Street, Ortonville, MN 56278
Minnesota Valley, 4101 E. 80th Street, Bloomington, MN 55420
Minnesota Wetlands Complex, Route 1, Box 76, Fergus Falls, MN 56537
Detroit Lakes Wetland Management District, Route 3, Box 47D, Detroit Lakes, MN 56501
Fergus Falls, Wetland Management District, Route 1, Box 76, Fergus Falls, MN 56537
Litchfield Wetland Management District, 305 North Sibley, Litchfield, MN 55353
Morris Wetland Management District, Route 1, Box 208, Morris, MN 56267
Rice Lake, Route 2, Box 67, McGregor, MN 55760
Sherburne, Route 2, Zimmerman, MN 55398
Tamarac, Rural Route, Rochert, MN 56578
Upper Mississippi River Wildlife and Fish Refuge (Headquarters), 51 East 4th Street, Winona, MN 55987 (Illinois, Iowa, Minnesota, and Wisconsin)
   Winona District

635

Refuge	Spring	Summer	Fall	Winter	Visitor center, contact station	Foot trails	Auto tour	Bicycling	Boating—nonmotorized	Boating—motorized	Environmental study area	Backcountry use	Hunting	Fishing	Camping	Picnicking	Swimming	Refuge leaflet	Species list	Food/lodging nearby
MISSISSIPPI																				
Mississippi Sandhill Crane Complex, Box 699, Gautler, MS 39553	■	■	■	■	■	■												■	■	■
Noxubee, Route 1, Box 142, Brooksville, MS 39739	■	■	■	■	■	■	■						■	■				■	■	■
Yazoo, Route 1, Box 286, Hollandale, MS 38748	■	■	■	■	■	■	■						■	■				■	■	■
Hillside	■		■	■									■	■						■
Morgan Brake	■		■	■					■	■			■	■						■
Panther Swamp	■		■	■					■	■			■	■						■
MISSOURI																				
Mark Twain (See Illinois)																				
Clarence Cannon, Box 88, Annada, MO 63330	■		■	■	■	■	■				■							■	■	■
Mingo, Route 1, Box 103, Puxico, MO 63960	■		■	■	■	■	■	■	■				■	■				■	■	■
Squaw Creek, Box 101, Mound City, MO 64470	■		■	■	■	■	■							■				■	■	■
Swan Lake, Box 68, Sumner, MO 64681	■		■	■	■		■		■									■	■	■
MONTANA																				
Benton Lake, Box 450, Black Eagle, MT 59414	■		■		■		■						■					■	■	■
Bowdoin, Box J, Malta, MT 59538	■		■		■	■	■						■	■				■	■	■
Charles M. Russell, Box 110, Lewistown, MT 59457	■	■	■		■				■	■		■	■	■	■			■	■	■
Lee Metcalf, Box 257, Stevensville, MT 59870	■		■	■	■	■							■	■				■	■	■
Medicine Lake, HC 51, Box 2, Medicine Lake, MT 59247	■		■		■		■		■				■	■				■	■	■
National Bison Range, Moiese, MT 59824		■	■		■	■	■				■					■		■	■	■
Red Rock Lakes, Monida Star Route, Box 15, Lima, MT 59739		■	■		■				■				■	■	■			■	■	■
NEBRASKA																				
Crescent Lake, HC 68, Box 21, Ellsworth, NE 69340	■	■			■													■	■	■
Fort Niobrara, Hidden Timber Route, HC 41, Box 67, Valentine, NE 69201	■	■	■		■	■	■		■					■				■	■	■

Refuge conditions, regulations, and activities are varied and subject to change. Please check with the refuge manager regarding conditions, regulations, and facilities for the disabled before taking a trip to a refuge.

Location																			
Valentine						■					■		■		■		■	■	
Rainwater Basin Wetland Management District, Box 1786, Kearney, NE 68847			■	■		■							■		■			■	■

NEVADA

Desert National Wildlife Range, 1500 North Decatur Boulevard, Las Vegas, NV 89108			■			■								■					
Ash Meadows			■ ■									■		■				■ ■	
Pahranagat			■ ■			■ ■							■	■				■ ■	■
Ruby Lake, Ruby Valley, NV 89833			■ ■			■					■	■ ■ ■		■		■		■	
Sheldon, P.O. Box 111, Room 308, U.S. Post Office Building, Lakeview, OR 97630			■ ■								■	■ ■ ■	■	■					
Stillwater, Box 1236, 1510 Rio Vista Road, Fallon, NV 89408			■ ■			■		■			■ ■ ■	■ ■ ■	■	■ ■				■ ■	■
Fallon												■							

NEW HAMPSHIRE

Wapack, Weir Hill Road, Sudbury, MA 01776			■ ■ ■													■			

NEW JERSEY

Edwin B. Forsythe, Box 72, Oceanville, NJ 08231			■			■	■			■ ■ ■ ■ ■	■ ■	■ ■		■		■		■ ■	■
Brigantine			■			■					■ ■	■ ■		■		■		■ ■	■
Barnegat, Box 544, Barnegat, NJ 08005			■			■						■		■				■ ■	■
Great Swamp, Pleasant Plains Road, RD 1, Box 152, Basking Ridge, NJ 07920			■			■					■ ■			■				■ ■	■

NEW MEXICO

Bitter Lake, Box 7, Roswell, NM 88201			■			■				■ ■ ■	■ ■	■ ■ ■	■	■	■			■ ■	■
Bosque del Apache, Box 1246, Socorro, NM 87801			■ ■ ■			■ ■ ■				■ ■	■ ■	■ ■		■		■		■ ■ ■	■
Sevilleta, General Delivery, San Acacia, NM 87831			■							■		■		■					
Las Vegas, Route 1, Box 399, Las Vegas, NM 87701						■ ■ ■	■			■								■	■
Maxwell, Box 276, Maxwell, NM 87728			■ ■ ■			■ ■				■		■		■		■		■ ■ ■	■

NEW YORK

Iroquois, P.O. Box 517, Alabama, NY 14003			■ ■ ■ ■			■ ■ ■		■		■ ■	■ ■	■ ■		■		■		■ ■	■
Montezuma, 3395 Route 5/20 East, Seneca Falls, NY 13148			■			■ ■ ■				■	■ ■	■ ■		■		■		■ ■	■
Wertheim, P.O. Box 21, Shirley, NY 11967			■			■	■				■	■		■				■ ■	■
Morton			■			■					■			■				■	
Target Rock			■			■					■			■				■ ■	■

NORTH CAROLINA

Alligator River, P.O. Box 1969, Manteo, NC 27954			■ ■ ■ ■	■						■				■					
Currituck			■																
Pea Island			■ ■ ■			■				■		■		■				■ ■	■
Mackay Island, P.O. Box 31, Knotts Island, NC 27950 (North Carolina and Virginia)			■ ■			■				■	■ ■	■		■				■ ■	■
Mattamuskeet, Route 1, Box N-2, Swanquarter, NC 27885			■ ■			■				■	■	■ ■		■				■ ■	■

Refuge conditions, regulations, and activities are varied and subject to change. Please check with the refuge manager regarding conditions, regulations, and facilities for the disabled before taking a trip to a refuge.

	Recommended best wildlife viewing season(s)																			
	Spring	Summer	Fall	Winter	Visitor center, contact station	Foot trails	Auto tour	Bicycling	Boating—nonmotorized	Boating—motorized	Environmental study area	Backcountry use	Hunting	Fishing	Camping	Picnicking	Swimming	Refuge leaflet	Species list	Food/lodging nearby
Cedar Island	■		■	■										■				■	■	■
Pungo	■	■	■	■									■					■	■	■
Swanquarter	■	■	■	■									■	■				■	■	■
Pee Dee, Box 780, Wadesboro, NC 28170	■		■	■	■	■	■				■		■	■				■	■	■

NORTH DAKOTA

	Spring	Summer	Fall	Winter	VC	Foot	Auto	Bike	B-nm	B-m	ESA	BC	Hunt	Fish	Camp	Picnic	Swim	Leaflet	Species	Food
Arrowwood, Rural Route 1, Pingree, ND 58476	■		■		■	■	■		■		■		■	■				■	■	■
Long Lake, Moffit, ND 58560	■		■		■						■		■					■	■	■
Valley City Wetland Management District, Rural Route 1, Valley City, ND 58072	■	■	■															■	■	■
Audubon, Rural Route 1, Coleharbor, ND 58531	■		■		■	■	■		■	■			■	■				■	■	■
Lake Ilo, Dunn Center, ND 58626	■		■										■	■				■	■	■
Des Lacs, Box 578, Kenmare, ND 58746	■		■		■	■	■		■		■		■	■		■		■	■	■
Crosby Wetland Management District, Box 148, Crosby, ND 58730	■		■						■				■	■				■	■	■
Lostwood, Rural Route 2, Kenmare, ND 58746	■		■		■	■	■						■					■	■	■
Devils Lake Wetland Management District, Box 908, Devils Lake, ND 58301	■	■	■		■		■		■	■			■	■				■	■	■
Lake Alice	■	■	■												■					
Sullys Hill National Game Preserve, Ft. Totten, ND 58335	■	■	■		■	■	■				■					■		■	■	■
J. Clark Salyer, P.O. Box 66, Upham, ND 58789	■		■		■	■	■		■				■	■				■	■	■
Kulm Wetland Management District, Box E, Kulm, ND 58456	■		■										■	■				■	■	■
Tewaukon, Rural Route 1, Box 75, Cayuga, ND 58013	■		■		■		■		■		■		■	■		■		■	■	■
Upper Souris, Rural Route 1, Foxholm, ND 58738	■		■		■	■	■		■				■	■		■		■	■	■

OHIO

	Spring	Summer	Fall	Winter	VC	Foot	Auto	Bike	B-nm	B-m	ESA	BC	Hunt	Fish	Camp	Picnic	Swim	Leaflet	Species	Food
Ottawa, 14000 W. State, Route 2, Oak Harbor, OH 43449	■		■			■					■		■					■	■	■

OKLAHOMA
Little River, General Delivery, Broken Box, OK 74962
Salt Plains, Route 1, Box 76, Jet, OK 73749
Sequoyah, Route 1, Box 18A, Vian, OK 74962
Tishomingo, Route 1, Box 151, Tishomingo, OK 73460
Washita, Route 1, Box 68, Butler, OK 73625
  Optima
Wichita Mountains, Route 1, Box 448, Indiahoma, OK 73552
OREGON
Hart Mountain National Antelope Refuge, U.S. Post Office Building, Lakeview, OR 97630
Klamath Basin Refuges, Route 1, Box 74, Tulelake, CA 96134
  Bear Valley
  Klamath Forest
  Lower Klamath (Oregon and California)
  Upper Klamath
Malheur, Box 245, Princeton, OR 97720
Umatilla, P.O. Box 239, Umatilla, OR 97882 (Oregon and Washington)
  Cold Springs
  McKay Creek
Western Oregon Refuges, 26208 Finley Refuge Road, Corvallis, OR 97333
  Ankeny
  Bandon Marsh
  Baskett Slough
  Cape Meares
  William L. Finley
Willapa (See Washington)
Columbian White-tailed Deer (Oregon and Washington)
Lewis and Clark
PENNSYLVANIA
Erie, RD 1, Wood Duck Lane, Guy Mills, PA 16327
Tinicum National Environmental Center, Suite 104, Scott Plaza 2, Philadelphia, PA 19113
PUERTO RICO
Caribbean Islands, Box 510, Carr. 301, KM 5.4, Boqueron, PR 00622
  Buck Island (Virgin Islands)

Refuge conditions, regulations, and activities are varied and subject to change. Please check with the refuge manager regarding conditions, regulations, and facilities for the disabled before taking a trip to a refuge.

Refuge	Spring	Summer	Fall	Winter	Visitor center, contact station	Foot trails	Auto tour	Bicycling	Boating—nonmotorized	Boating—motorized	Environmental study area	Backcountry use	Hunting	Fishing	Camping	Picnicking	Swimming	Refuge leaflet	Species list	Food/lodging nearby
Cabo Rojo (Puerto Rico)	■	■				■					■							■		■
Culebra (Puerto Rico)	■	■									■									■
Desecheo (Puerto Rico)				■														■		
Green Cay (Virgin Islands)	■	■									■								■	■
Sandy Point (Virgin Islands)	■										■									■
RHODE ISLAND																				
Ninigret, Shoreline Plaza, Route 1A, Box 307, Charlestown, RI 02813	■																			
Block Island														■						
Sachuest Point	■		■	■	■	■												■	■	■
Trustom Pond	■		■	■	■	■					■							■	■	■
SOUTH CAROLINA																				
Cape Romain, 390 Bulls Island Road, Awendaw, SC 29429	■	■	■	■	■	■			■	■			■	■				■	■	■
Carolina Sandhills, Route 2, Box 330, McBee, SC 29101	■	■	■	■	■	■	■	■	■	■			■	■				■	■	■
Pinckney Island	■	■	■	■		■		■						■						■
Santee, Route 2, Box 66, Summerton, SC 29148	■	■	■	■	■	■	■	■	■	■			■	■				■	■	■
SOUTH DAKOTA																				
Lacreek HWC 3, Box 14, Martin, SC 57551*		■	■		■	■	■		■	■			■	■		■	■	■	■	
Lake Andes, Route 1, Box 77, Lake Andes, SD 57356		■	■		■	■	■		■	■			■	■		■		■	■	■
Karl E. Mundt				■														■		
Madison Wetland Management District, Box 48, Madison, SD 57042	■	■	■		■								■	■					■	■
Sand Lake, Rural Route 1, Box 25, Columbia, SD 57433	■	■	■		■	■	■		■	■			■	■		■		■	■	■
Waubay, Rural Route 1, Box 79, Waubay, SD 57273	■	■	■		■	■	■		■	■			■	■		■		■	■	■

TENNESSEE
- Cross Creeks, Route 1, Box 229, Dover, TN 37058
- Hatchie, Box 187, Brownsville, TN 38012
- Chickasaw
- Lower Hatchie
- Reelfoot, Route 2, Highway 157, Union City, TN 38261
- Lake Isom
- Tennessee, Box 849 Paris, TN 38242

TEXAS
- Anahuac, Box 278, Anahuac, TX 77514
- McFaddin
- Texas Point
- Aransas, Box 100, Austwell, TX 77950
- Attwater Prarie Chicken, Box 518, Eagle Lake, TX 77434
- Brazoria, Box 1088, Angleton, TX 77515
- Big Boggy
- San Bernard
- Buffalo Lake, Box 228, Umbarger, TX 79091
- Grulla (New Mexico and Texas)
- Muleshoe, Box 549, Muleshoe, TX 79347
- Hagerman, Route 3, Box 123, Sherman, TX 75090
- Laguna Atascosa, Box 450, Rio Hondo, TX 78583
- Santa Ana, Route 1, Box 202A, Alamo, TX 78516
- Rio Grande Valley

UTAH
- Bear River Migratory Bird Refuge, Box 459, Brigham City, UT 84302 (temp. closed)
- Fish Springs, P.O. Box 568, Dugway, UT 84022
- Ouray, 1680 West Highway 40, Room 1220, Vernal, UT 84078

VERMONT
- Missisquoi, Route 2, Swanton, VT 05488

VIRGINIA
- Back Bay, 4005 Sandpiper Road, P.O. Box 6286, Virginia Beach, VA 23462
- Chincoteague, Box 62, Chincoteague, VA 23336
- Eastern Shore of Virginia, RFD 1, Box 122B, Cape Charles, VA 23310
- Great Dismal Swamp, P.O. Box 349, Suffolk, VA 23434 (North Carolina and Virginia)
- Mason Neck, 14416 Jefferson Davis Highway, Suite 20-A, Lorton, VA 22191

Refuge conditions, regulations, and activities are varied and subject to change. Please check with the refuge manager regarding conditions, regulations, and facilities for the disabled before taking a trip to a refuge.

Refuge	Spring	Summer	Fall	Winter	Visitor center, contact station	Foot trails	Auto tour	Bicycling	Boating—nonmotorized	Boating—motorized	Environmental study area	Backcountry use	Hunting	Fishing	Camping	Picnicking	Swimming	Refuge leaflet	Species list	Food/lodging nearby
Presquile, Box 620, Hopewell, VA 23860	■		■	■		■							■					■	■	■
WASHINGTON																				
Columbia, 44 South 8th Avenue, P.O. Drawer F, Othello, WA 99344	■		■	■	■	■	■		■	■			■	■					■	■
Nisqually, 100 Brown Farm Road, Olympia, WA 98506	■		■	■	■	■					■								■	■
Dungeness, P.O. Box 698, Sequin, WA 98382	■		■	■		■								■					■	■
San Juan Islands, 100 Brown Farm Road, Olympia, WA 98506		■																		■
Ridgefield, 301 N. Third, P.O. Box 457, Ridgefield, WA 98642	■		■	■		■					■		■	■		■			■	■
Conboy Lake, P.O. Box 5, Glenwood, WA 98619	■					■					■		■	■					■	
Turnbull, Route 3, Box 385, Cheney, WA 99004	■					■	■	■			■			■				■	■	■
Umatilla, P.O. Box 239, Umatilla, OR 97882 (Oregon and Washington)			■	■	■				■	■		■	■	■	■				■	■
McNary, Box 308, Burbank, WA 99323			■	■	■	■					■		■	■				■	■	■
Toppenish, Route 1, Box 1300, Toppenish, WA 98948	■		■			■	■						■					■	■	■
Willapa, Ilwaco, WA 98624	■		■	■					■	■		■	■	■	■			■	■	■
Columbian White-tailed Deer (Oregon and Washington)																				
Lewis and Clark (See Oregon)																				
WISCONSIN																				
Horicon, West 4279 Headquarters Road, Mayville, WI 53050	■		■		■	■	■	■	■		■		■	■				■	■	■
Necedah, Star Route West, Box 386, Necedah, WI 54646	■	■	■		■	■	■	■			■		■	■				■	■	■
Upper Mississippi River Wild Life and Fish Refuge (See Minnesota)																				
La Crosse District, P.O. Box 415, La Crosse, WI 54601	■		■						■	■		■	■	■	■			■	■	■
Trempealeau, Route 1, Trempealeau, WI 54661	■		■			■	■	■	■		■		■	■				■	■	■
WYOMING																				
National Elk Refuge, Box C, Jackson, WY 83001				■	■						■		■	■				■	■	■
Seedskadee, P.O. Box 67, Green River, WY 82935	■		■						■	■			■	■	■			■		■

Cloud Nomenclature

For illustrations of cloud types, see page 645.

altocumulus (Ac) Similar to cirrocumulus, with patches of small clouds occasionally separated by thin breaks. Although altocumulus clouds also may be identified by a "mackerel sky" pattern, they are lower, at around 10,000 feet, and the clumps of white or gray water droplets or ice crystals are larger. The clouds may develop directly overhead, depending on the temperature of the atmosphere, and may produce a shower.

altostratus (As) Dull, drab gray or blue middle-level clouds that usually contain moisture in the form of water droplets. Altostratus clouds are often opaque, giving a "ground glass" view of the sun or moon behind them. They may be a source of virga, filaments of ice crystals or water droplets that fall toward Earth but evaporate before touching the ground.

cirrocumulus (Cc) Loosely packed sheets of small white cloud segments at altitudes of around 18,000 to 20,000 feet, forming a "mackerel sky" resembling scales on a fish. The clouds may consist of ice crystals or water droplets or both. The patchy appearance is caused by vertical air currents at the cloud level, indicating a lack of stability and a possible approaching storm.

cirrostratus (Cs) Translucent veils of white fibrous cloud that tend to occur at altitudes of around 20,000 feet or more. Cirrostratus clouds often cover the entire sky and may cause the appearance of halos or reflected images of the sun or moon. They may signal an approaching storm.

cirrus (Ci) Generally, the highest clouds, forming "mares' tails" at altitudes between 20,000 and 40,000 feet. The clouds may appear as delicate white filaments, featherlike tufts, or fibrous bands of ice crystals.

cumulonimbus (Cb) Thunderstorm clouds that may vary considerably in altitude from ominously dark lower portions below 5,000 feet to white anvil-shaped tops that may reach upward to 50,000 feet. They contain large amounts of moisture, some of which may be in the form of hail. The cumulonimbus cloud may appear alone or as part of a wall of advancing storm clouds.

cumulus (Cu) Low-level billowy clouds that are usually dark on the bottom while the top resembles a giant white cotton ball. A cumulus cloud may be relatively tall, extending from a base around 2,000 feet to a top near 10,000 feet above ground. It casts a dark shadow and may be a source of moisture but generally produces no more than a summer shower.

nimbostratus (Ns) Low, dark rain clouds with ragged tops that have bottoms only a few hundred feet above ground and may range upward to an altitude of 3,000 feet. They obscure the sun and are associated with continuous rain, sleet, or snow but are rarely accompanied by thunder or lightning.

stratocumulus (Sc) Dark, gray rolls of clouds that usually cover the entire sky at an altitude from 1,500 to 6,500 feet. The rounded segments may appear checkered or wavelike and there may or may not be breaks of blue sky between segments. Stratocumulus clouds contain moisture but are usually not rain producers.

stratus (St) Wispy foglike clouds that hover a few hundred feet above ground, sometimes obscuring hills or tall buildings. They may begin as ground fog and can be a source of drizzle.

Beaufort Scale of Wind Force

Beaufort no.	Knots (mph)	Description	Effect at sea	Effect ashore
0	Less than 1	Calm	Sea is like a mirror.	Smoke rises vertically.
1	1–3 (1–3)	Light air	Ripples with the appearance of a scale are formed but without foam crests.	Wind vanes are not moved, but wind direction is shown by smoke drift.
2	4–6 (4–7)	Light breeze	Small wavelets, still short but more pronounced, appear; crests have a glassy appearance but do not break.	Wind is felt on face; leaves rustle; ordinary vane is moved by wind.

Beaufort Scale of Wind Force (continued)

Beaufort no.	Knots (mph)	Description	Effect at sea	Effect ashore
3	7–10 (8–12)	Gentle breeze	Large wavelets appear. Crests begin to break. Foam is of glassy appearance, perhaps with scattered white horses.	Leaves and small twigs are in constant motion; wind extends light flag.
4	11–16 (13–18)	Moderate breeze	Small waves appear, becoming longer; there are fairly frequent white horses.	Dust and loose paper are raised; small branches are moved.
5	17–21 (19–24)	Fresh breeze	Moderate waves arise, taking a more pronounced long form; many white horses are formed (with chance of some spray).	Small trees in leaf begin to sway; crested wavelets form on inland waters.
6	22–27 (25–31)	Strong breeze	Large waves begin to form; the white foam crests are more extensive everywhere (probably with some spray).	Large branches are in motion; whistling is heard in telegraph wires; umbrellas are used with difficulty.
7	28–33 (32–38)	Moderate gale (high wind)	Sea heaps up and white foam from breaking waves begins to be blown in streaks along the direction of the wind. Spindrift begins.	Whole trees are in motion; inconvenience is felt in walking against the wind.
8	34–40 (39–46)	Fresh gale	Moderately high waves of greater length appear; edges of crests break into spindrift. The foam is blown in well-marked streaks along the direction of the wind.	Twigs are broken off trees, and the wind generally impedes progress.
9	41–47 (47–54)	Strong gale	High waves appear. Dense streaks of foam arise along the direction of the wind. Sea begins to roll. Spray may affect visibility.	Slight structural damage occurs (chimney pots and slate removed).
10	48–55 (55–63)	Storm	Very high waves with long overhanging crests appear. The resulting foam in great patches is blown in dense white streaks along the direction of the wind. On the whole, the surface of the sea takes on a white appearance. The rolling of the sea becomes heavy and shocklike. Visibility is affected.	It is seldom experienced inland. Trees are uprooted; considerable structural damage occurs.
11	56–63 (64–72)	Violent storm	Exceptionally high waves appear. (Small and medium-sized ships might for a long time be lost to view behind the waves.) The sea is completely covered with long white patches of foam lying along the direction of the wind. Everywhere the edges of the wave crests are blown into froth. Visibility is affected.	It is very rarely experienced and is accompanied by widespread damage.

Beaufort Scale of Wind Force (continued)

Beaufort no.	Knots (mph)	Description	Effect at sea	Effect ashore
12	Above 63 (72)	Hurricane	The air is filled with foam and spray. The sea is completely white with a driving spray; visibility is very seriously affected.	Devastation occurs.

CIRRUS

CIRROSTRATUS

CIRROCUMULUS

ALTOCUMULUS

ALTOSTRATUS

CUMULONIMBUS

CUMULUS

STRATOCUMULUS

NIMBOSTRATUS

STRATUS

EARTHQUAKES

Earthquakes are generally measured according to the Richter scale, a system developed by American geologist Charles Richter in 1935. The scale measures ground motion (in the form of seismic waves) on a seismograph.

For every whole number of the scale, there is a tenfold increase (or decrease) in ground motion. In terms of energy release, however, the increment is far greater: Each whole number represents approximately a 30-fold change in energy.

The largest earthquake ever recorded, in Japan in 1933, measured 8.9 on the Richter scale. The 1989 earthquake in northern California measured 7.1 on this scale.

A different scale, developed by Giuseppe Mercalli in 1902, describes the effects of earthquake shocks.

The two scales are compared below.

Richter scale		Mercalli scale	
2.5	Not felt by many but appears on seismometers	I	Felt only by a few under certain favorable conditions
3.5	Felt by many	III	Felt indoors, especially on upper floors of buildings, but not always recognized as an earthquake
4.5	Moderate local damage	VI	Felt by everyone; slight damage
6.0	Much destruction	VIII	Partial collapse in substantial buildings; slight damage in specially designed buildings; heavy damage in poorly built structures
7.0	Major earthquake	X	Most masonry and frame structures destroyed; ground badly cracked
8.0	Great earthquake	XI	Few structures remain standing, including bridges; large cracks in ground

Lunar and Solar Eclipses

An eclipse occurs when a celestial body, such as the Earth or moon, casts a shadow so that another celestial body seems to disappear. An eclipse of the moon (lunar eclipse) occurs when the sun, Earth, and moon are in a straight line so that the moon is in the shadow of Earth. As each of the celestial bodies is in constant motion with respect to the others, and the alignment of the bodies is not always perfect, an eclipse seldom lasts more than a few minutes. The eclipse may be total or partial.

Because a lunar eclipse results in the total surface of the moon being in the shadow of Earth, the eclipse is visible from any point on Earth. But the shadow of a solar eclipse is visible only along an arc-shaped path on a portion of Earth, and it moves at a speed of between 1,060 and 2,100 miles per hour, depending on the latitude of the shadow, the rotation of Earth, and the speed of the moon through its own orbit. An annular eclipse is one in which the moon's shadow allows the corona, or outer fringe, of the sun to reach Earth.

Because the sun, Earth, and moon travel in relatively predictable orbits, astronomers since the days of ancient Babylonia (700 B.C.) have been able to calculate the future dates on which the sun, Earth, and moon will once again be in alignment. Therefore, they can forecast the time and place of eclipses many years in advance. For example, at regular intervals of 18 years, 9 to 11 days (depending on leap years), and 8 hours (a period of one saros), the sun and moon will return to the same orbital node relative to Earth. During one saros, there are usually 41 total or partial solar eclipses and 29 lunar eclipses, or an average of about four eclipses a year. But each successive solar eclipse is observed about 120 degrees to the west of the previous phenomenon and can be expected to recur at the same longitude on Earth after a period equivalent to three times the length of one saros. Each solar eclipse may affect an area only about 100 miles wide and any given place on Earth can expect a total eclipse about once every 400 years.

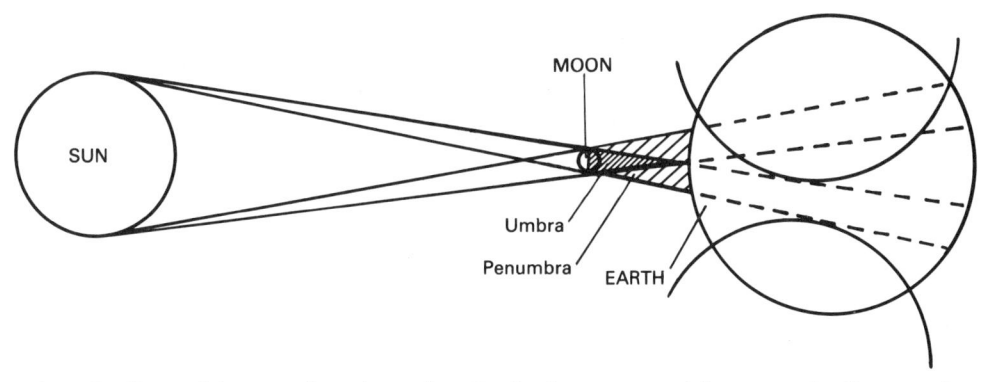

A total eclipse of the sun takes place when Earth, the moon, and the sun are in alignment in such a way that the umbra of the shadow of the moon reaches Earth (the umbra is the dark central part of the cone-shaped shadow projecting from the moon to Earth during this phenomenon). All the light of the sun is blocked or eclipsed because of the moon's position. The penumbra (the lighter shadow) shows a partial solar eclipse. The two arcs indicate positions of Earth where a total eclipse would not be possible.

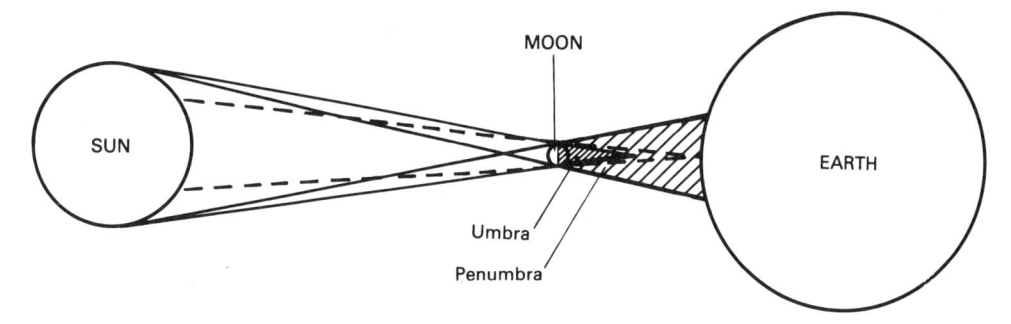

In an annular solar eclipse, the alignment is just the same as in a total solar eclipse, but the moon is too far away from Earth at the time for the umbra of the shadow to reach Earth. The circle of the moon is not large enough to block our seeing the sun, so a ring of light can be seen surrounding the moon's circle.

Total Eclipses of the Sun, 1900–2010

Date	Approximate duration (min:sec)	Maximum width (miles)	Course of central line
1900 May 28	2:10	58	Mexico, United States, Spain, North Africa
1901 May 18	6:17	149	Indian Ocean, Sumatra, Borneo, New Guinea
1903 September 21	2:02	157	Antarctica
1904 September 9	6:19	146	Pacific Ocean
1905 August 30	3:46	123	Canada, Spain, North Africa, Arabia
1907 January 14	2:24	119	Soviet Union, China
1908 January 3	4:20	93	Pacific Ocean
1908 December 23	0:12	6	South America, Atlantic Ocean, Indian Ocean
1909 June 17	0:24	32	Greenland, Soviet Union
1910 May 9	4:14	371	Antarctica
1911 April 28	4:58	120	Pacific Ocean
1912 April 17	0:02	1	Atlantic Ocean, Europe, Soviet Union
1912 October 10	2:02	54	Brazil, South Atlantic Ocean
1914 August 21	2:15	113	Greenland, Europe, Middle East
1916 February 3	2:36	69	Pacific Ocean, South America, Atlantic Ocean
1918 June 8	2:23	70	Pacific Ocean, United States
1919 May 29	6:50	153	South America, Atlantic Ocean, Africa
1921 October 1	1:52	189	Antarctica
1922 September 21	5:59	142	Indian Ocean, Australia
1923 September 10	3:37	106	Pacific Ocean, Central America
1925 January 24	2:32	130	Northeast United States, Atlantic Ocean
1926 January 14	4:11	92	Africa, Indian Ocean, Borneo
1927 June 29	0:50	48	England, Scandinavia, Arctic Ocean, Soviet Union
1928 May 19	...	...	(Umbra barely touched Antarctica)
1929 May 9	5:07	122	Indian Ocean, Malaya, Philippines
1930 April 28	0:01	1	Pacific Ocean, United States, Canada
1930 October 21	1:55	54	South Pacific Ocean
1932 August 31	1:45	104	Arctic Ocean, East Canada
1934 February 14	2:53	79	Borneo, Pacific Ocean
1936 June 19	2:31	83	Greece, Turkey, Soviet Union, Pacific Ocean
1937 June 8	7:04	156	Pacific Ocean, Peru
1938 May 29	4:04	420	South Atlantic Ocean
1939 October 12	1:32	276	Antarctica
1940 October 1	5:35	137	South America, Atlantic Ocean, Africa
1941 September 21	3:22	91	Soviet Union, China, Pacific Ocean
1943 February 4	2:39	146	Japan, Pacific Ocean, Alaska
1944 January 25	4:09	91	South America, Atlantic Ocean, Africa
1945 July 9	1:15	57	Canada, Greenland, Scandinavia, Soviet Union
1947 May 20	5:14	124	Argentina, Brazil, Central Africa
1948 November 1	1:56	53	Africa, Indian Ocean
1950 September 12	1:13	90	Arctic Ocean, Soviet Union, Pacific Ocean
1952 February 25	3:05	89	Africa, Arabia, Iran, Soviet Union
1954 June 30	2:35	96	United States, Canada, Scandinavia, Soviet Union
1955 June 20	7:08	159	Indian Ocean, Thailand, Pacific Ocean
1956 June 8	4:44	269	South Pacific Ocean
1957 October 23	...	...	(Umbra touched Antarctica)
1958 October 12	5:11	131	Pacific Ocean, Argentina
1959 October 2	3:01	76	Atlantic Ocean, Africa
1961 February 15	2:44	164	Europe, Soviet Union

Total Eclipses of the Sun, 1900–2010 (continued)

Date	Approximate duration (min:sec)	Maximum width (miles)	Course of central line
1962 February 5	4:08	92	Borneo, New Guinea, Pacific Ocean
1963 July 20	1:40	63	Pacific Ocean, Alaska, Canada
1965 May 30	5:16	124	New Zealand, Pacific Ocean
1966 November 12	1:57	53	South America, Atlantic Ocean
1967 November 2	...	...	(Umbra touched Antarctica)
1968 September 22	0:40	68	Soviet Union
1970 March 7	3:28	99	Pacific Ocean, Mexico, Eastern United States
1972 July 10	2:36	111	Soviet Union, North Canada
1973 June 30	7:04	160	Atlantic Ocean, Central Africa, Indian Ocean
1974 June 20	5:08	216	Indian Ocean, Australia
1976 October 23	4:46	125	Africa, Indian Ocean, Australia
1977 October 12	2:37	63	Pacific Ocean, Colombia, Venezuela
1979 February 26	2:52	195	Northwest United States, Canada, Greenland
1980 February 16	4:08	93	Africa, Indian Ocean, India, China
1981 July 31	2:03	68	Soviet Union, Pacific Ocean
1983 June 11	5:11	125	Indian Ocean, New Guinea
1984 November 22	1:59	53	New Guinea, South Pacific Ocean
1985 November 12	1:59	431	Antarctica
1986 October 3	0:01	1	North Atlantic Ocean
1987 March 29	0:08	3	South Atlantic Ocean, Central Africa
1988 March 18	3:46	109	Sumatra, Borneo, Philippines
1990 July 22	2:33	130	Soviet Union, Pacific Ocean
1991 July 11	6:54	161	Hawaii, Mexico, South America
1992 June 30	5:20	186	South Atlantic Ocean
1994 November 3	4:15	119	Bolivia, Brazil, South Atlantic Ocean
1995 October 24	2:10	49	India, Southeast Asia, Indonesia
1997 March 9	2:50	231	Arctic Ocean, Russia
1998 February 26	4:08	95	Pacific Ocean, Venezuela, Atlantic Ocean
1999 August 11	2:23	70	Central Europe, Middle East, India
2001 June 21	4:57	124	South Atlantic Ocean, Africa, Madagascar
2002 December 4	2:04	54	Southern Africa, Indian Ocean
2003 November 23	1:57	308	Antarctica
2005 April 8	0:42	17	South Pacific Ocean, Colombia, Venezuela
2006 March 29	4:07	114	Africa, Turkey, Georgia, Russia, Kazakhstan
2008 August 1	2:27	147	China, Russia, Kazakhstan
2009 July 22	6:39	161	India, China, Pacific Ocean
2010 July 11	5:20	161	Pacific Ocean, Chile

Constellations

Twelve Zodiacal Constellations

Aquarius, the Water-Bearer
Aries, the Ram
Cancer, the Crab
Capricornus, the Goat
Gemini, the Twins
Leo, the Lion
Libra, the Balance or Scales
Pisces, the Fishes
Sagittarius, the Archer
Scorpius, the Scorpion
Taurus, the Bull
Virgo, the Virgin

Twenty-Eight North of the Zodiac

Andromeda, the Chained Lady
Aquila, the Eagle
Auriga, the Charioteer
Boötes, the Herdsman
Camelopardalis, the Giraffe
Canes Venatici, the Hunting Dogs
Cassiopeia, the Lady in the Chair
Cepheus, the King
Coma Berenices, Berenice's Hair
Corona Borealis, the Northern Crown
Cygnus, the Swan
Delphinus, the Dolphin
Draco, the Dragon
Equuleus, the Colt
Hercules (Kneeling)
Lacerta, the Lizard
Leo Minor, the Lesser Lion
Lynx, the Lynx
Lyra, the Lyre
Ophiuchus, the Serpent Holder
Pegasus, the Winged Horse
Perseus, the Hero
Sagitta, the Arrow
Serpens, the Serpent
Triangulum, the Triangle
Ursa Major, the Greater Bear
Ursa Minor, the Lesser Bear
Vulpecula, the Fox

Forty-Eight South of the Zodiac

Antlia, the Air Pump
Apus, Bird of Paradise
Ara, the Altar
Caelum, the Engraver's Chisel
Canis Major, the Greater Dog
Canis Minor, the Lesser Dog
Carina, the Keel
Centaurus, the Centaur
Cetus, the Whale
Chamaeleon, the Chameleon
Circinus, the Pair of Compasses
Columba, (Noah's) Dove
Corona Australis, the Southern Crown
Corvus, the Crow
Crater, the Bowl
Crux, the (Southern) Cross
Dorado, the Gilthead or Swordfish
Eridanus, the River
Fornax, the Furnace
Grus, the Crane
Horologium, the Clock
Hydra, the Water-Serpent or Hydra (fem.)
Hydrus, the Water-Snake or Sea-Serpent (masc.)
Indus, the Indian
Lepus, the Hare
Lupus, the Wolf
Mensa, the Table Mountain
Microscopium, the Microscope
Monoceros, the Unicorn
Musca, the Fly
Norma, the Square or Rule
Octans, the Octant
Orion, the Hunter
Pavo, the Peacock

Phoenix, the Fabulous Bird
Pictor, the Painter's Easel
Piscis Austrinus, the Southern Fish
Puppis, the Stern
Pyxis, the (Ship's) Compass
Reticulum, the Net
Sculptor, the Sculptor's Shop
Scutum, the Shield
Sextans, the Sextant
Telescopium, the Telescope
Triangulum Australe, the Southern Triangle
Tucana, the Toucan
Vela, the Sails
Volans, the Flying Fish

Additional Sources of Information

Organizations and Services

American Astronomical Society
200 Florida Avenue, NW
Washington, DC 20009

American Horticultural Society
Mount Vernon, VA 22121

American Institute of Biological Scientists
730 11th Street, NW
Washington, DC 20001

American Meteorological Society
45 Beacon Street
Boston, MA 02108

American Museum of Natural History
Central Park West and 79th Street
New York, NY 10024

Appalachian Mountain Club
5 Joy Street
Boston, MA 02108

Bureau of Outdoor Recreation
Interior Building
18th and C Streets
Washington, DC 20240

Garden Club of America
598 Madison Avenue
New York, NY 10022

Men's Garden Clubs of America
5560 Merle Hay Road
Des Moines, IA 50323

National Oceanic and Atmospheric Administration
6010 Executive Boulevard
Rockville, MD 20852

National Parks and Conservation Association
1701 18th Street, NW
Washington, DC 20009

National Park Service
Interior Building
18th and C Streets, NW
Washington, DC 20240

National Recreation and Park Association
1601 North Kent Street
Arlington, VA 22209

National Weather Service Public Affairs
8060 13th Street
Silver Spring, MD 20910

National Wildlife Federation
1412 16th Street, NW
Washington, DC 20036

Sierra Club
530 Bush Street
San Francisco, CA 94108

U.S. Department of Interior
Interior Building
18th and C Streets, NW
Washington, DC 20240

U.S. Fish and Wildlife Service
Interior Building
18th and C Streets, NW
Washington, DC 20240

The Wilderness Society
1901 Pennsylvania Avenue, NW
Washington, DC 20006

Books

Alden, Peter. *Peterson's First Guide to Mammals.* Houghton Mifflin, 1987.

Asimov, Isaac. *Universe.* Walker & Co., 1980.

Audubon Society and Elbert L. Little, Jr. *Audubon Field Guide to North American Trees.* Knopf, 1980.

Berry, Richard. *Discover the Stars: Star Watching Using the Naked Eye, Binoculars or a Telescope.* Crown, 1987.

The Complete Guide to America's National Parks. National Park Foundation, latest edition.

Encyclopedia of Astronomy. McGraw-Hill, 1983.

Faust, Joan Lee, Ed. *The New York Times Garden Book.* Lyons and Burford, 1991.

Lambert, David, and Ralph Hardy. *Weather and Its Work.* Facts On File, 1988.

Muirden, James. *The Astronomer's Handbook: A Guide to Exploring the Heavens*, 3rd ed. Harper & Row, 1987.

Pasachoff, Jay M. *A Field Guide to Stars and the Planets*, 3rd ed. Houghton Mifflin, 1992.

Peterson, Roger T. *Peterson's First Guide to Birds.* Houghton Mifflin, 1986.

Peterson, Roger T. *Peterson's First Guide to Wildflowers.* Houghton Mifflin, 1986.

Rand McNally Cosmopolitan World Atlas, rev. ed. Rand McNally, 1987.

Rand McNally Road Atlas and Vacation Guide. Rand McNally, 1987.

Weather and Forecasting. Macmillan Field Guide Series, 1987.

Woodall's North American Campground Directory. Woodall, 1988.

22

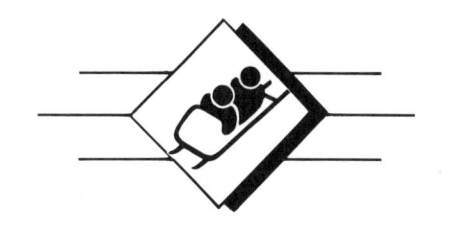

Sports and Games

Baseball / *654*

Basketball / *657*

Bowling / *660*

Football / *661*

Official Football Signals / *663*

Golf / *664*

Ice Hockey / *666*

Soccer / *668*

Tennis / *669*

Volleyball / *672*

Horse Racing / *673*

Auto Racing / *674*

Olympic Games / *675*

Board Games / *678*

The Most Landed-On Spaces on the Monopoly® Game Board / *681*

Card Games / *682*

Additional Sources of Information / *685*

Baseball

Baseball, named for the three bases and home plate that are parts of the playing field, has 9 or 10 players on each side. The offensive team sends to home plate one batter at a time, who with a wooden or metal bat attempts to hit a small cowhide-covered ball thrown from the pitcher to the catcher, two members of the defensive team. The defensive team also consists of four infielders and three outfielders. If the batter hits the ball on the ground, he must run toward first base; he is out if a defensive player throws the ball to a teammate standing on first base before the runner reaches the base. The batter is also out if the ball he hits is caught by a defensive player before it hits the ground, or if the batter fails in three attempts to strike the pitched ball or fails to hit three pitches determined by the umpire to be strikes. This last situation is called a strikeout. Outs may also be made by tagging a baserunner with the ball when the runner is between bases, or by stepping on second base, third base, or homeplate while holding the ball if the runner is forced to move to that base because the batter or another baserunner is moving to occupy the preceding base. The offensive team attempts to score runs by causing offensive baserunners to go around all four bases and cross home plate safely. This can be done by accumulating hits, balls hit between the two foul lines that go uncaught, allowing a batter to safely reach first base (a single), second base (a double), or third base (a triple), thus driving runners ahead of him to circle the bases. Batters can also reach base and move the runners ahead up a base by obtaining a walk, four pitches

BASEBALL FIELD
(1) pitcher; (2) catcher; (3) first baseman; (4) second baseman; (5) third baseman; (6) shortstop; (7) left fielder; (8) center fielder; (9) right fielder.

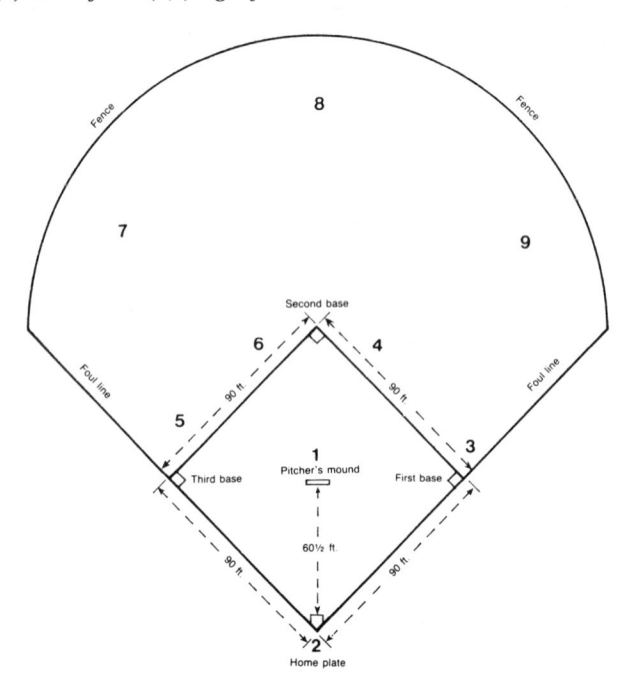

determined by the umpire not to be strikes that the batter does not swing at. Runs also can be scored with a home run, whereby a batter hits the ball over the outfield fence or far enough that he can circle the bases. The game is divided into nine innings, with three outs for each team in each inning. The batting, or offensive, team takes the field (defensive positions) after making three outs, when the opponents become batters. At the end of nine innings, the team that has accumulated the most runs is the winner.

U.S. and Canadian Major League Teams

American League

Eastern Division	Western Division
Baltimore Orioles	California Angels
Boston Red Sox	Chicago White Sox
Cleveland Indians	Kansas City Royals
Detroit Tigers	Minnesota Twins
Milwaukee Brewers	Oakland Athletics
New York Yankees	Seattle Mariners
Toronto Blue Jays	Texas Rangers

National League

Eastern Division	Western Division
Chicago Cubs	Atlanta Braves
Florida Marlins	Cincinnati Reds
Montreal Expos	Colorado Rockies
New York Mets	Houston Astros
Philadelphia Phillies	Los Angeles Dodgers
Pittsburgh Pirates	San Diego Padres
St. Louis Cardinals	San Francisco Giants

World Series

Every year since 1903 (with the exception of 1904), the winners of major league baseball's American League pennant have played the winners of the National League pennant in the World Series. In 1903, and again from 1919 to 1921, this was a best-of-nine-games series. From 1905 to 1918, and since 1922, this has been a best-of-seven-games series. The results since 1903 follow.

	Winner	League	Loser	League	Games
1903	Boston Red Sox	AL	Pittsburgh Pirates	NL	5–3
1904	No series				
1905	New York Giants	NL	Philadelphia Athletics	AL	4–1
1906	Chicago White Sox	AL	Chicago Cubs	NL	4–2
1907	Chicago Cubs	NL	Detroit Tigers	AL	4–0–1*
1908	Chicago Cubs	NL	Detroit Tigers	AL	4–1
1909	Pittsburgh Pirates	NL	Detroit Tigers	AL	4–3
1910	Philadelphia Athletics	AL	Chicago Cubs	NL	4–1
1911	Philadelphia Athletics	AL	New York Giants	NL	4–2

	Winner	League	Loser	League	Games
1912	Boston Red Sox	AL	New York Giants	NL	4–3–1*
1913	Philadelphia Athletics	AL	New York Giants	NL	4–1
1914	Boston Braves	NL	Philadelphia Athletics	AL	4–0
1915	Boston Red Sox	AL	Philadelphia Phillies	NL	4–1
1916	Boston Red Sox	AL	Brooklyn Dodgers	NL	4–1
1917	Chicago White Sox	AL	New York Giants	NL	4–2
1918	Boston Red Sox	AL	Chicago Cubs	NL	4–2
1919	Cincinnati Reds	NL	Chicago White Sox	AL	5–3
1920	Cleveland Indians	AL	Brooklyn Dodgers	NL	5–2
1921	New York Giants	NL	New York Yankees	AL	5–3
1922	New York Giants	NL	New York Yankees	AL	4–0
1923	New York Yankees	AL	New York Giants	NL	4–2
1924	Washington Senators	AL	New York Giants	NL	4–3
1925	Pittsburgh Pirates	NL	Washington Senators	AL	4–3
1926	St. Louis Cardinals	NL	New York Yankees	AL	4–3
1927	New York Yankees	AL	Pittsburgh Pirates	NL	4–0
1928	New York Yankees	AL	St. Louis Cardinals	NL	4–0
1929	Philadelphia Athletics	AL	Chicago Cubs	NL	4–1
1930	Philadelphia Athletics	AL	St. Louis Cardinals	NL	4–2
1931	St. Louis Cardinals	NL	Philadelphia Athletics	AL	4–3
1932	New York Yankees	AL	Chicago Cubs	NL	4–0
1933	New York Giants	NL	Washington Senators	AL	4–1
1934	St. Louis Cardinals	NL	Detroit Tigers	AL	4–3
1935	Detroit Tigers	AL	Chicago Cubs	NL	4–2
1936	New York Yankees	AL	New York Giants	NL	4–2
1937	New York Yankees	AL	New York Giants	NL	4–1
1938	New York Yankees	AL	Chicago Cubs	NL	4–0
1939	New York Yankees	AL	Cincinnati Reds	NL	4–0
1940	Cincinnati Reds	NL	Detroit Tigers	AL	4–3
1941	New York Yankees	AL	Brooklyn Dodgers	NL	4–1
1942	St. Louis Cardinals	NL	New York Yankees	AL	4–1
1943	New York Yankees	AL	St. Louis Cardinals	NL	4–1
1944	St. Louis Cardinals	NL	St. Louis Browns	AL	4–2
1945	Detroit Tigers	AL	Chicago Cubs	NL	4–3
1946	St. Louis Cardinals	NL	Boston Red Sox	AL	4–3
1947	New York Yankees	AL	Brooklyn Dodgers	NL	4–3
1948	Cleveland Indians	AL	Boston Braves	NL	4–2
1949	New York Yankees	AL	Brooklyn Dodgers	NL	4–1
1950	New York Yankees	AL	Philadelphia Phillies	NL	4–0
1951	New York Yankees	AL	New York Giants	NL	4–2
1952	New York Yankees	AL	Brooklyn Dodgers	NL	4–3
1953	New York Yankees	AL	Brooklyn Dodgers	NL	4–2
1954	New York Giants	NL	Cleveland Indians	AL	4–0
1955	Brooklyn Dodgers	NL	New York Yankees	AL	4–3
1956	New York Yankees	AL	Brooklyn Dodgers	NL	4–3
1957	Milwaukee Braves	NL	New York Yankees	AL	4–3
1958	New York Yankees	AL	Milwaukee Braves	NL	4–3
1959	Los Angeles Dodgers	NL	Chicago White Sox	AL	4–2

	Winner	League	Loser	League	Games
1960	Pittsburgh Pirates	NL	New York Yankees	AL	4–3
1961	New York Yankees	AL	Cincinnati Reds	NL	4–1
1962	New York Yankees	AL	San Francisco Giants	NL	4–3
1963	Los Angeles Dodgers	NL	New York Yankees	AL	4–0
1964	St. Louis Cardinals	NL	New York Yankees	AL	4–3
1965	Los Angeles Dodgers	NL	Minnesota Twins	AL	4–3
1966	Baltimore Orioles	AL	Los Angeles Dodgers	NL	4–0
1967	St. Louis Cardinals	NL	Boston Red Sox	AL	4–3
1968	Detroit Tigers	AL	St. Louis Cardinals	NL	4–3
1969	New York Mets	NL	Baltimore Orioles	AL	4–1
1970	Baltimore Orioles	AL	Cincinnati Reds	NL	4–1
1971	Pittsburgh Pirates	NL	Baltimore Orioles	AL	4–3
1972	Oakland Athletics	AL	Cincinnati Reds	NL	4–3
1973	Oakland Athletics	AL	New York Mets	NL	4–3
1974	Oakland Athletics	AL	Los Angeles Dodgers	NL	4–1
1975	Cincinnati Reds	NL	Boston Red Sox	AL	4–3
1976	Cincinnati Reds	NL	New York Yankees	AL	4–0
1977	New York Yankees	AL	Los Angeles Dodgers	NL	4–2
1978	New York Yankees	AL	Los Angeles Dodgers	NL	4–2
1979	Pittsburgh Pirates	NL	Baltimore Orioles	AL	4–3
1980	Philadelphia Phillies	NL	Kansas City Royals	AL	4–2
1981	Los Angeles Dodgers	NL	New York Yankees	AL	4–2
1982	St. Louis Cardinals	NL	Milwaukee Brewers	AL	4–3
1983	Baltimore Orioles	AL	Philadelphia Phillies	NL	4–1
1984	Detroit Tigers	AL	San Diego Padres	NL	4–1
1985	Kansas City Royals	AL	St. Louis Cardinals	NL	4–3
1986	New York Mets	NL	Boston Red Sox	AL	4–3
1987	Minnesota Twins	AL	St. Louis Cardinals	NL	4–3
1988	Los Angeles Dodgers	NL	Oakland Athletics	AL	4–1
1989	Oakland Athletics	AL	San Francisco Giants	NL	4–0
1990	Cincinnati Reds	NL	Oakland Athletics	AL	4–1
1991	Minnesota Twins	AL	Atlanta Braves	NL	4–3
1992	Toronto Blue Jays	AL	Atlanta Braves	NL	4–3

* The third figure represents a tied game. In 1907 the first game was tied 3–3 in 12 innings of play; in 1912 the second game was tied 6–6 in 11 innings.

Basketball

Basketball usually is played indoors on a rectangular wooden court by two teams, each with five players. At both ends of the court are suspended two goals, or baskets, consisting of a circular metal rim 10 feet above the floor attached to a square backboard made of wood, plastic, or fiberglass. A cord net is hung below the rim. The object is to shoot the ball so that it goes through the basket from above and to prevent your opponents from doing the same. Basketball uses a large rubber ball covered with leather.

Play begins with a jump ball. The official throws the ball upward at the center circle between two opposing players. The two players try to tip or slap the ball to a teammate and thus gain possession of the ball. Each team defends one goal. There is an offensive and defensive half of the court for each team, divided by the midcourt line. The ball can be advanced down the court by passing to a teammate, dribbling (bouncing the ball while walking or running), or shooting the ball at the basket. Running or walking while holding the ball is not permitted. If a shot goes in the basket, two points are awarded to the shooting team. If a shot is missed (usually hitting the rim or backboard), a defensive player may rebound the ball (catch it as it bounces away from the basket). He then may begin to advance the ball to the other end of the court in preparation for a shot by his team. An offensive player may also rebound a missed shot and shoot again. A shot made from beyond the three-point line (23 feet 9 inches from the center of the basket) scores three points instead of the usual two.

Holding, pushing, grabbing, and similar types of body contact are not permitted; these are called fouls. They may result in a foul shot or free throw, an unimpeded shot taken by the offended player from a line on the court 15 feet from the basket. A successful free throw scores one point.

Professional basketball games are divided into four 12-minute quarters; the team with more points at the end of that time wins the game.

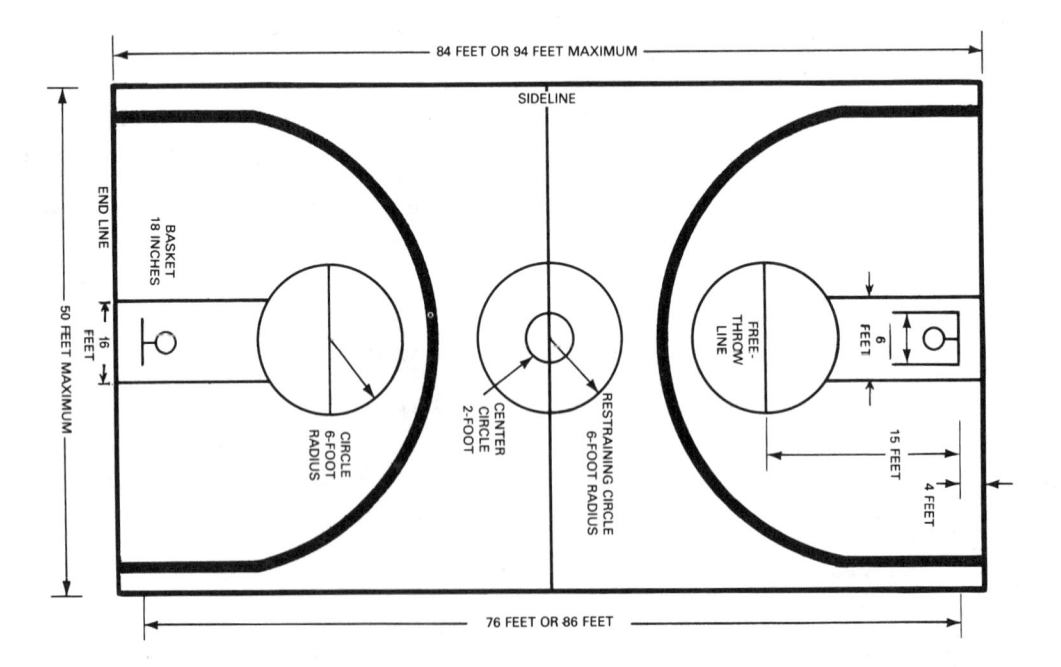

National Basketball Association (NBA)

Eastern Conference

Atlantic Division
Boston Celtics
Miami Heat
New Jersey Nets
New York Knicks
Philadelphia 76ers
Washington Bullets

Central Division
Atlanta Hawks
Charlotte Hornets
Chicago Bulls
Cleveland Cavaliers
Detroit Pistons
Indiana Pacers
Milwaukee Bucks

Western Conference

Midwest Division
Dallas Mavericks
Denver Nuggets
Houston Rockets
Minnesota Timberwolves
Orlando Magic
San Antonio Spurs
Utah Jazz

Pacific Division
Golden State Warriors
Los Angeles Clippers
Los Angeles Lakers
Phoenix Suns
Portland Trail Blazers
Sacramento Kings
Seattle SuperSonics

National Basketball Association Champions

Each year the Eastern conference champions meet the Western Conference champions in a seven-game series for the NBA championship. The playoffs and the championship series, played in the spring, mark the end of the basketball season that started the previous winter.

Year	Winners	Conference	Losers	Conference
1947	Philadelphia Warriors	E	Chicago Stags	W
1948	Baltimore Bullets	W	Philadelphia Warriors	E
1949	Minneapolis Lakers	W	Washington Capitols	E
1950	Minneapolis Lakers	W	Syracuse Nationals	E
1951	Rochester Royals	W	New York Knickerbockers	E
1952	Minneapolis Lakers	W	New York Knickerbockers	E
1953	Minneapolis Lakers	W	New York Knickerbockers	E
1954	Minneapolis Lakers	W	Syracuse Nationals	E
1955	Syracuse Nationals	E	Fort Wayne Pistons	W
1956	Philadelphia Warriors	E	Fort Wayne Pistons	W
1957	Boston Celtics	E	St. Louis Hawks	W
1958	St. Louis Hawks	W	Boston Celtics	E
1959	Boston Celtics	E	Minneapolis Lakers	W
1960	Boston Celtics	E	St. Louis Hawks	W

Year	Winners	Conference	Losers	Conference
1961	Boston Celtics	E	St. Louis Hawks	W
1962	Boston Celtics	E	Los Angeles Lakers	W
1963	Boston Celtics	E	Los Angeles Lakers	W
1964	Boston Celtics	E	San Francisco Warriors	W
1965	Boston Celtics	E	Los Angeles Lakers	W
1966	Boston Celtics	E	Los Angeles Lakers	W
1967	Philadelphia 76ers	E	San Francisco Warriors	W
1968	Boston Celtics	E	Los Angeles Lakers	W
1969	Boston Celtics	E	Los Angeles Lakers	W
1970	New York Knickerbockers	E	Los Angeles Lakers	W
1971	Milwaukee Bucks	W	Baltimore Bullets	E
1972	Los Angeles Lakers	W	New York Knickerbockers	E
1973	New York Knickerbockers	E	Los Angeles Lakers	W
1974	Boston Celtics	E	Milwaukee Bucks	W
1975	Golden State Warriors	W	Washington Bullets	E
1976	Boston Celtics	E	Phoenix Suns	W
1977	Portland Trail Blazers	W	Philadelphia 76ers	E
1978	Washington Bullets	E	Seattle Supersonics	W
1979	Seattle Supersonics	W	Washington Bullets	E
1980	Los Angeles Lakers	W	Philadelphia 76ers	E
1981	Boston Celtics	E	Houston Rockets	W
1982	Los Angeles Lakers	W	Philadelphia 76ers	E
1983	Philadelphia 76ers	E	Los Angeles Lakers	W
1984	Boston Celtics	E	Los Angeles Lakers	W
1985	Los Angeles Lakers	W	Boston Celtics	E
1986	Boston Celtics	E	Houston Rockets	W
1987	Los Angeles Lakers	W	Boston Celtics	E
1988	Los Angeles Lakers	W	Detroit Pistons	E
1989	Detroit Pistons	E	Los Angeles Lakers	W
1990	Detroit Pistons	E	Portland Trail Blazers	W
1991	Chicago Bulls	E	Los Angeles Lakers	W
1992	Chicago Bulls	E	Portland Trail Blazers	W
1993	Chicago Bulls	E	Phoenix Suns	W

Bowling

Bowling, or tenpins, is an indoor sport in which a player attempts to knock down 10 wooden pins that are arranged in a triangular formation. This is accomplished by rolling a ball down a wooden lane, or alley. The ball, which weighs at most about 16 pounds, is fitted with three holes for thumb and finger grips. Each game is divided into 10 frames, and the bowler is allowed a maximum of two rolls per frame, except for the last frame, where he is allowed three. If a player knocks down all 10 pins with one roll, it is called a strike; the second roll of the frame is not used, except for the tenth frame, where three strikes are possible. If a player knocks down all 10 pins using both rolls of the frame, it is called a spare. The number of pins knocked down by the end of the game determines the score, with spares scoring 10 plus the number of pins knocked down on the next roll and strikes scoring 10 plus the number of pins knocked down on the next two rolls. A perfect game of 12 consecutive strikes scores 300.

BOWLING ALLEY

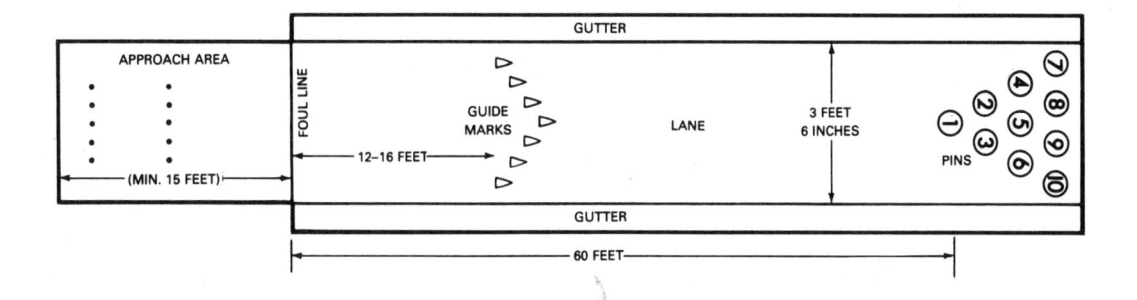

football

American football has 11 players on each team and is played on a large rectangular field. At each end of the field is an end zone, where the H-shaped goal posts are placed. The object is to gain possession of an inflated leather or pigskin ball and move it across the opponents' goal line by running or passing, thus scoring a touchdown, which is worth six points. Passing the ball is usually done by the quarterback. Points also are scored by kicking the ball through the goalposts. This opportunity is given automatically after a touchdown; the point is called a point after touchdown, or extra point. A field goal scores three points. The defensive team can score by downing an offensive player in his own end zone. This is called a safety and scores two points.

The offensive team must gain 10 yards in four tries, called downs, or give up possession of the ball. If 10 or more yards are gained, the offense has four more downs to advance the ball. If on the fourth down (or, rarely, before) it seems unlikely that the 10-yard minimum will be reached, the offense has the option of kicking the ball to the opponents. This is called a punt, and the defensive team, after catching the ball, goes on offense. The defensive team may also gain possession of the ball, and thus become the offense, by catching a ball passed by the quarterback and intended for a teammate (interception), or by recovering the ball after it has been dropped by an offensive player (fumble). The defense hinders the attempts of the offense to gain yardage by tackling the ball carrier and pulling him to the ground. Because blocking and tackling can be very rough, football players wear protective helmets and substantial padding.

The game is divided into four 15-minute periods; the team with the most points after the end of that time is the winner.

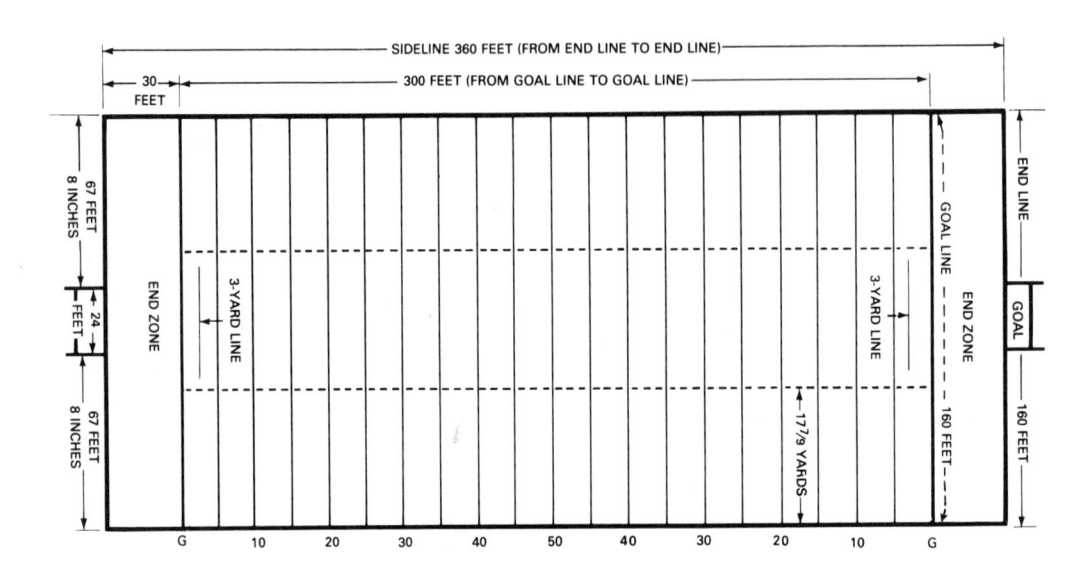

National Football League (NFL)

National Conference

Eastern Division	Central Division	Western Division
Dallas Cowboys	Chicago Bears	Atlanta Falcons
New York Giants	Detroit Lions	Los Angeles Rams
Philadelphia Eagles	Green Bay Packers	New Orleans Saints
Phoenix Cardinals	Minnesota Vikings	San Francisco 49ers
Washington Redskins	Tampa Bay Buccaneers	

American Conference

Eastern Division	Central Division	Western Division
Buffalo Bills	Cincinnati Bengals	Denver Broncos
Indianapolis Colts	Cleveland Browns	Kansas City Chiefs
Miami Dolphins	Houston Oilers	Los Angeles Raiders
New England Patriots	Pittsburgh Steelers	San Diego Chargers
New York Jets		Seattle Seahawks

OFFICIAL FOOTBALL SIGNALS

TOUCHDOWN, FIELD GOAL, or SUCCESSFUL TRY

ILLEGAL FORWARD PASS
If followed by raised hand flung downward: **International Grounding of Pass.**

FIRST DOWN

DEAD BALL or NEUTRAL ZONE ESTABLISHED
With raised fist closed: **Fourth Down.**

LOSS OF DOWN

ILLEGAL CHUCKING

NO TIME OUT or TIME IN WITH WHISTLE

DELAY OF GAME or EXCESS TIME OUT
If followed by forearms rotated over and over in front of body: **Illegal Formation.**

PERSONAL FOUL

HOLDING

ILLEGAL USE OF HANDS

PENALTY REFUSED, INCOMPLETE PASS, PLAY OVER, or MISSED GOAL

DOUBLE TOUCH

PASS JUGGLED INBOUNDS AND CAUGHT OUT OF BOUNDS

SAFETY

INTERFERENCE WITH FORWARD PASS OR FAIR CATCH

INVALID FAIR CATCH SIGNAL

INELIGIBLE RECEIVER or INELIGIBLE MEMBER OF KICKING TEAM DOWNFIELD

TIME OUT
If followed by placing one hand on top of cap: **Referee's Time Out**;
If followed by arm swung at side: **Touchback.**

OFFSIDE, ENCROACHING, or FREE KICK VIOLATION

ILLEGAL MOTION AT SNAP

CRAWLING, PUSHING, or HELPING RUNNER

UNSPORTSMANLIKE CONDUCT

ILLEGAL CUT

The Super Bowl

The Super Bowl, played in January, marks the end of the professional football season that began the previous fall. The first four Super Bowls were played between the champions of the National Football League and those of the American Football League. The two leagues then merged; the game has since been played between the National Football Conference champions and the American Football Conference champions. The winners and losers follow.

	Year	Winners	League	Losers	League	Score
I	1967	Green Bay Packers	NFL	Kansas City Chiefs	AFL	35–10
II	1968	Green Bay Packers	NFL	Oakland Raiders	AFL	33–14
III	1969	New York Jets	AFL	Baltimore Colts	NFL	16–7
IV	1970	Kansas City Chiefs	AFL	Minnesota Vikings	NFL	23–7
V	1971	Baltimore Colts	AFC	Dallas Cowboys	NFC	16–13
VI	1972	Dallas Cowboys	NFC	Miami Dolphins	AFC	24–3
VII	1973	Miami Dolphins	AFC	Washington Redskins	NFC	14–7
VIII	1974	Miami Dolphins	AFC	Minnesota Vikings	NFC	24–7
IX	1975	Pittsburgh Steelers	AFC	Minnesota Vikings	NFC	16–6
X	1976	Pittsburgh Steelers	AFC	Dallas Cowboys	NFC	21–17
XI	1977	Oakland Raiders	AFC	Minnesota Vikings	NFC	32–14
XII	1978	Dallas Cowboys	NFC	Denver Broncos	AFC	27–10
XIII	1979	Pittsburgh Steelers	AFC	Dallas Cowboys	NFC	35–31
XIV	1980	Pittsburgh Steelers	AFC	Los Angeles Rams	NFC	31–19
XV	1981	Oakland Raiders	AFC	Philadelphia Eagles	NFC	27–10
XVI	1982	San Francisco 49ers	NFC	Cincinnati Bengals	AFC	26–21
XVII	1983	Washington Redskins	NFC	Miami Dolphins	AFC	27–17
XVIII	1984	Los Angeles Raiders	AFC	Washington Redskins	NFC	38–9
XIX	1985	San Francisco 49ers	NFC	Miami Dolphins	AFC	38–16
XX	1986	Chicago Bears	NFC	New England Patriots	AFC	46–10
XXI	1987	New York Giants	NFC	Denver Broncos	AFC	39–20
XXII	1988	Washington Redskins	NFC	Denver Broncos	AFC	42–10
XXIII	1989	San Francisco 49ers	NFC	Cincinnati Bengals	AFC	20–16
XXIV	1990	San Francisco 49ers	NFC	Denver Broncos	AFC	55–10
XXV	1991	New York Giants	NFC	Buffalo Bills	AFC	20–19
XXVI	1992	Washington Redskins	NFC	Buffalo Bills	AFC	37–24
XXVII	1993	Dallas Cowboys	NFC	Buffalo Bills	AFC	52–17

Golf

Golf is an outdoor game in which players hit a small hard ball with specially designed clubs that consist of a metal shaft and a wooden or metal club head. The object is to strike the ball with the club so that the ball goes into a cup that is sunk in the ground and marked with a flag. A standard golf course is divided into 18 holes, each with a tee, where the initial stroke is made; a grass fairway; and a green, a smooth grass surface where the cup is located. Each player attempts to reach the green and hit the ball into the cup using as few strokes as possible. Obstacles—such as water, tall grass called rough, or traps filled with sand—may be found near the green or fairway. As many as 14 different types of clubs may be used depending on the length of shot required or the terrain. The distance from tee to cup varies greatly, but generally it is from 100 to 600 yards. The length and difficulty of the hole determine the par, the number of strokes that a good golfer would need to put the ball into the cup. After 18 holes, the player with the lowest number of strokes is the winner of that round. Golf tournaments are typically won by the player with the best (lowest) cumulative score after four rounds.

The Masters

Four major golf tournaments carry the most important titles in professional golf. They are the Masters, the Professional Golfer's Association Tournament (PGA), the U.S. Open, and the British Open. The Masters, played at the Augusta National Golf Club in Augusta, Georgia, is the most sought-after title in professional golf. The winners of the Masters Tournament follow.

Year	Winner	Score	Year	Winner	Score
1934	Horton Smith	284	1964	Arnold Palmer	276
1935	Gene Sarazen*	282	1965	Jack Nicklaus	271
1936	Horton Smith	285	1966	Jack Nicklaus*	288
1937	Byron Nelson	283	1967	Gay Brewer	280
1938	Henry Picard	285	1968	Bob Goalby	277
1939	Ralph Guldahl	279	1969	George Archer	281
1940	Jimmy Demaret	280	1970	Billy Casper*	279
1941	Craig Wood	280	1971	Charles Coody	279
1942	Byron Nelson*	280	1972	Jack Nicklaus	286
1943	No tournament held		1973	Tommy Aaron	283
1944	No tournament held		1974	Gary Player	278
1945	No tournament held		1975	Jack Nicklaus	276
1946	Herman Keiser	282	1976	Ray Floyd	271
1947	Jimmy Demaret	281	1977	Tom Watson	276
1948	Claude Harmon	279	1978	Gary Player	277
1949	Sam Snead	282	1979	Fuzzy Zoeller*	280
1950	Jimmy Demaret	283	1980	Severiano Ballesteros	275
1951	Ben Hogan	280	1981	Tom Watson	280
1952	Sam Snead	286	1982	Craig Stadler*	284
1953	Ben Hogan	274	1983	Severiano Ballesteros	280
1954	Sam Snead*	289	1984	Ben Crenshaw	277
1955	Cary Middlecoff	279	1985	Bernhard Langer	282
1956	Jack Burke	289	1986	Jack Nicklaus	279
1957	Doug Ford	283	1987	Larry Mize*	285
1958	Arnold Palmer	284	1988	Sandy Lyle	281
1959	Art Wall, Jr.	284	1989	Nick Faldo	283
1960	Arnold Palmer	282	1990	Nick Faldo	278
1961	Gary Player	280	1991	Ian Woosnam	277
1962	Arnold Palmer*	280	1992	Fred Couples	275
1963	Jack Nicklaus	286	1993	Bernhard Langer	277

* Won in a playoff.

Ice Hockey

Ice hockey is played on a rectangular rink that is surrounded by a wooden wall. At each end of the ice is placed a netted goal. Six skaters make up each team, including the goalie, whose job it is to protect the goal. By using wooden sticks, the players attempt to propel a rubber disc, called the puck, across the ice and into the opponents' goal. This scores a point.

The game begins with a faceoff in the center of the ice. The official drops the puck between two players, one from each team. Both teams try to gain control of the puck and to advance it toward the opponent's goal by skating with the puck, passing it to a teammate, or shooting it directly toward the goal. The defense tries to hinder this advance by deflecting or intercepting a pass or shot or by bodychecking an opposing player. This is physically blocking an opponent with a hip or shoulder.

There is a wide range of penalties for which the offending player may be removed from the ice for a stated number of minutes. During this time, the penalized team plays with one fewer player than its opponents, giving a power play to the fully manned team. Penalty times range from two minutes for minor violations to ejection from the game for the most serious fouls. Holding on to the puck or to an opponent, checking from behind, tripping, using the stick illegally, and fighting all normally result in penalties. The offensive player in control of the puck must cross his own blue line before any of his teammates. In moving down the ice and attacking the opponent's end, if an attacking player without the puck crosses that line first, he is offside. This is a violation, leading to a resetting of the puck and a new faceoff.

Hockey is a rough sport and players wear hip pads, shoulder pads, padded gloves, and helmets. The game consists of three 20-minute periods with rest periods in between. The team with more goals at the end of that time wins the game.

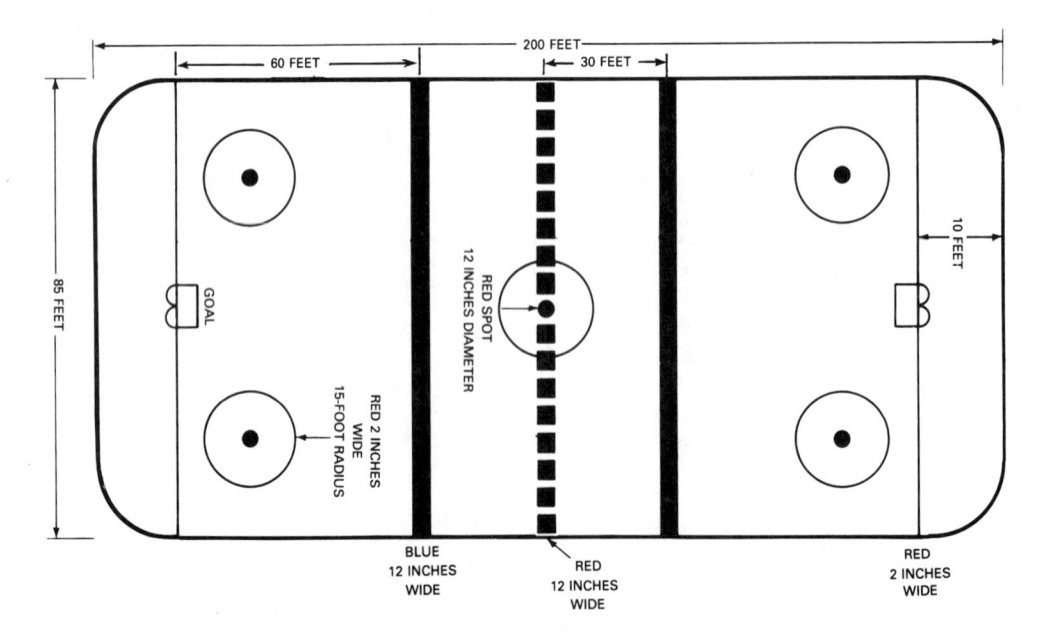

National Hockey League

Western Conference

Pacific Division

Anaheim Mighty Ducks
Calgary Flames
Edmonton Oilers
Los Angeles Kings
San Jose Sharks
Vancouver Canucks

Central Division

Chicago Blackhawks
Dallas Stars
Detroit Red Wings
St. Louis Blues
Toronto Maple Leafs
Winnipeg Jets

Eastern Conference

Northeast Division

Boston Bruins
Buffalo Sabres
Hartford Whalers
Montreal Canadiens
Ottawa Senators
Pittsburgh Penguins
Quebec Nordiques

Atlantic Division

New Jersey Devils
New York Islanders
New York Rangers
Philadelphia Flyers
Florida Panthers
Tampa Bay Lightning
Washington Capitals

The Stanley Cup

The Stanley Cup is awarded to the championship team following a best-of-seven-games series between professional ice hockey conference champions. Until 1910, amateurs and professionals were permitted to play on the same teams, but since 1910, the cup has been presented to entirely professional teams and since 1917 to the champions of the National Hockey League (NHL). Stanley Cup winners follow.

1894	Montreal A.A.A.
1895	Montreal Victorias
1896	Winnipeg Victorias
1897	Montreal Victorias
1898	Montreal Victorias
1899	Montreal Victorias
1900	Montreal Shamrocks
1901	Winnipeg Victorias
1902	Montreal A.A.A.
1903	Ottawa Silver Seven
1904	Ottawa Silver Seven
1905	Ottawa Silver Seven
1906	Montreal Wanderers
1907	Kenora Thistles (Jan.)
	Montreal Wanderers (March)
1908	Montreal Wanderers
1909	Ottawa Senators
1910	Montreal Wanderers
1911	Ottawa Senators
1912	Quebec Bulldogs
1913	Quebec Bulldogs
1914	Toronto Ontarios
1915	Vancouver Millionaires
1916	Montreal Canadiens
1917	Seattle Metropolitans
1918	Toronto Arenas
1919	Championship series unfinished
1920	Ottawa Senators
1921	Ottawa Senators
1922	Toronto St. Patricks
1923	Ottawa Senators
1924	Montreal Canadiens
1925	Victoria Cougars
1926	Montreal Maroons
1927	Ottawa Senators
1928	New York Rangers
1929	Boston Bruins
1930	Montreal Canadiens
1931	Montreal Canadiens
1932	Toronto Maple Leafs
1933	New York Rangers
1934	Chicago Black Hawks
1935	Montreal Maroons
1936	Detroit Red Wings
1937	Detroit Red Wings
1938	Chicago Black Hawks
1939	Boston Bruins
1940	New York Rangers
1941	Boston Bruins
1942	Toronto Maple Leafs
1943	Detroit Red Wings
1944	Montreal Canadiens
1945	Toronto Maple Leafs
1946	Montreal Canadiens
1947	Toronto Maple Leafs
1948	Toronto Maple Leafs
1949	Toronto Maple Leafs
1950	Detroit Red Wings
1951	Toronto Maple Leafs
1952	Detroit Red Wings
1953	Montreal Canadiens
1954	Detroit Red Wings
1955	Detroit Red Wings
1956	Montreal Canadiens
1957	Montreal Canadiens
1958	Montreal Canadiens
1959	Montreal Canadiens
1960	Montreal Canadiens
1961	Chicago Black Hawks
1962	Toronto Maple Leafs
1963	Toronto Maple Leafs
1964	Toronto Maple Leafs
1965	Montreal Canadiens
1966	Montreal Canadiens
1967	Toronto Maple Leafs
1968	Montreal Canadiens
1969	Montreal Canadiens
1970	Boston Bruins
1971	Montreal Canadiens
1972	Boston Bruins
1973	Montreal Canadiens
1974	Philadelphia Flyers
1975	Philadelphia Flyers
1976	Montreal Canadiens
1977	Montreal Canadiens
1978	Montreal Canadiens
1979	Montreal Canadiens
1980	New York Islanders
1981	New York Islanders
1982	New York Islanders
1983	New York Islanders
1984	Edmonton Oilers
1985	Edmonton Oilers
1986	Montreal Canadiens
1987	Edmonton Oilers
1988	Edmonton Oilers
1989	Calgary Flames
1990	Edmonton Oilers
1991	Pittsburgh Penguins
1992	Pittsburgh Penguins
1993	Montreal Canadiens

Soccer

Soccer, often referred to as "football" outside the United States, is played by two opposing teams of 11 players each on a rectangular field. At either end of the field is a goal, constructed of a pair of upright posts with a crossbar. The object of the game is for one set of players to force the ball into the goal defended by the opposing team.

At the beginning of a game, the choice of field ends and the opportunity to kick off are decided by a coin toss. Once play has started, players may not touch the ball with their hands with two exceptions: Goalkeepers within their areas may touch the ball with their hands, and when the ball goes out of bounds by crossing the touch lines, it is thrown back by hand. The team in possession of the ball is the offensive team. By kicking it or using their heads, members of the offensive team try to move the ball down the field until one of its members is in a position to shoot the ball into the goal of the opposing team.

The defending team may gain possession of the ball by intercepting passes or by tackling opposing players. A tackle can be either a use of the feet or a charge against an opponent's shoulder. The penalty for a violent or dangerous tackle is a direct free kick at the ball by the opposing side.

When the ball goes out of play by passing over the goal line beyond the goal posts, it is restarted by the opposing team to the one that sent it out of bounds. The defending team kicks the ball back into play from within that half of the goal area nearest to where it crossed the line; the offensive team kicks it back from the corner circle at the nearest corner flag. As with free kicks, generally, the ball may not be touched again by the kicker until it has been touched by another player. A goal may be scored from a direct corner kick.

When a goal is scored, the game is restarted with a kickoff by the team conceding the goal. A match consists of two 45-minute periods. At the end of the match, the team scoring the greater number of goals is the winner. If no goals are scored, or an equal number of goals is scored by both teams, the game is considered a draw.

The World Cup

The World Cup championship, the contest for international soccer supremacy, is played every four years at different locations throughout the world. The results since 1930 follow.

	Winner	*Loser*
1930	Uruguay	Argentina
1934	Italy	Czechoslovakia
1938	Italy	Hungary
1942	No competition	
1946	No competition	
1950	Uruguay	Brazil
1954	West Germany	Hungary
1958	Brazil	Sweden
1962	Brazil	Czechoslovakia

	Winner	*Loser*
1966	England	West Germany
1970	Brazil	Italy
1974	West Germany	Netherlands
1978	Argentina	Netherlands
1982	Italy	West Germany
1986	Argentina	West Germany
1990	West Germany	Argentina

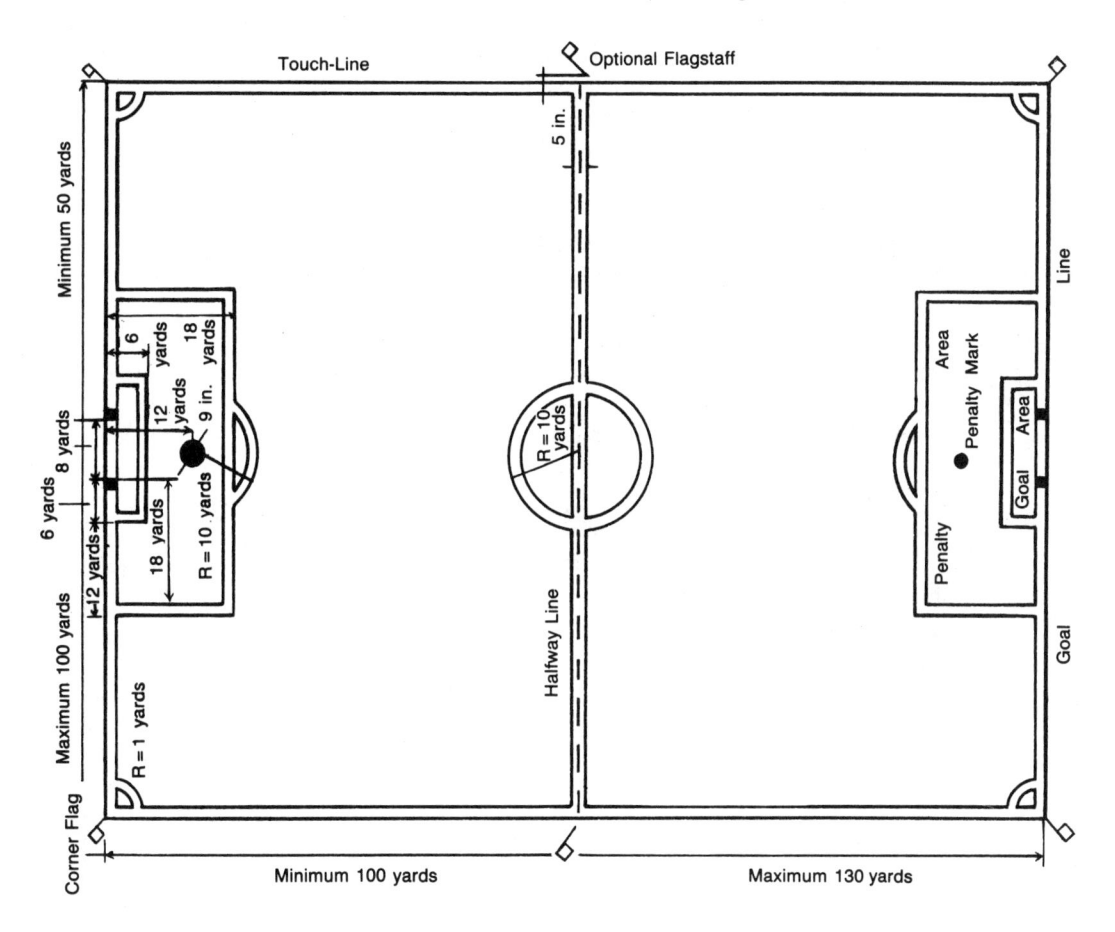

Tennis

Tennis is played either indoors or outdoors on a rectangular court, which may be grass, clay, or synthetic. A small felt-covered rubber ball is hit back and forth over a net with wooden or metal rackets, which are fitted with strings made of lamb's gut, nylon, or synthetic material.

The net, which is 3 feet above the court's surface at its midpoint, is stretched across the court. Tennis may be played either as singles, with one player on each side, or as doubles, with two players on each side. In doubles, the court is 9 feet wider than in singles, because of the addition of two doubles alleys.

To initiate play, the server stands behind the baseline and to the right of the center mark and hits the ball with the racket so that the ball lands in the diagonally opposite service court of the opponent. If this first serve does not land in this service area because it is hit too long or too wide, or hits the net, the server may try again with a second serve. If this second serve is not a legal serve, the receiver scores a point. At each point the serve alternates left to right, with the server always serving from behind the baseline to the diagonally opposite service court. The receiver attempts to return a legal serve by hitting the ball anywhere into the opponent's court, which includes the alleys in doubles. Play continues until one player (or one team, in doubles) fails to make a legal return. A point is then scored by the opponent.

Four points, designated as 15, 30, 40, and game, constitute a game; a player must win each game by at least two points. Thus, if after six points in any game each player has scored three, the score is 40–40 (this is called deuce). One player must then score two consecutive points to win the game; this player has the advantage after winning the first of these two points. Having the advantage, if the player wins the second consecutive point, he or she wins the game; but if the opponent wins that point, the score goes back to 40–40, or deuce. Play then continues until one player wins the game by scoring two consecutive points.

Each player (or team, in doubles) alternates by serving one game and receiving the next. The first to win six games wins a set, provided the margin of victory is two games or more. Thus, if the score reaches six games to four, the set is over, but at six to five, play continues. If the score reaches six to six, a tiebreaker is usually employed. A match consists of the best two out of three sets in women's play and usually the best three out of five in men's play.

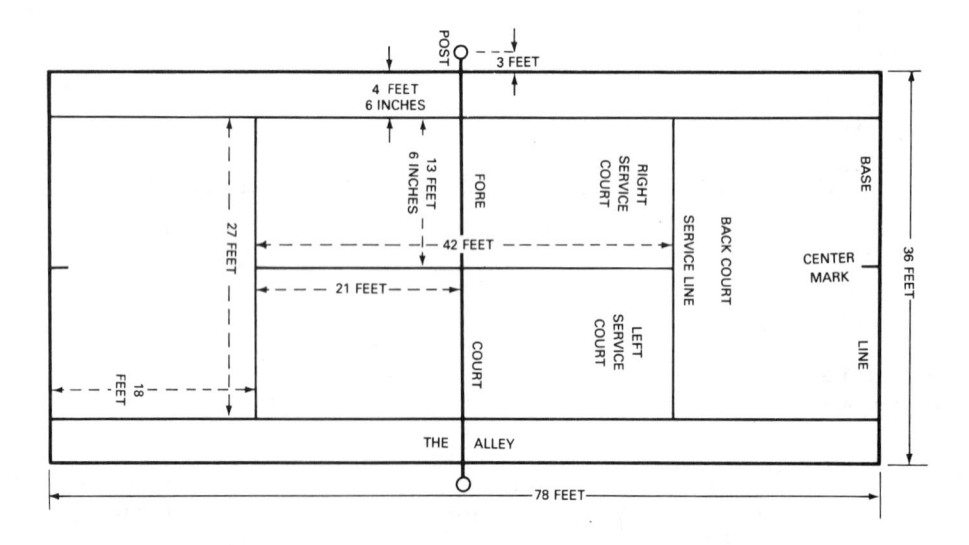

Wimbledon

There are four major championships in professional tennis that make up the Grand Slam: the French Open, the Australian Open, the U.S. Open, and the All-England Lawn Tennis Championships, better known as Wimbledon. Wimbledon is the oldest and most prestigious tournament of the four. The winners since 1877 follow.

Men's Singles Champions

Year	Champion	Year	Champion	Year	Champion
1877	Spencer W. Gore	1916	No tournament held	1955	Tony Trabert
1878	P. F. Hadow	1917	No tournament held	1956	Lew Hoad
1879	J. T. Hartley	1918	No tournament held	1957	Lew Hoad
1880	J. T. Hartley	1919	Gerald Patterson	1958	Ashley Cooper
1881	William Renshaw	1920	Bill Tilden	1959	Alex Olmedo
1882	William Renshaw	1921	Bill Tilden	1960	Neale Fraser
1883	William Renshaw	1922	Gerald Patterson	1961	Rod Laver
1884	William Renshaw	1923	William Johnston	1962	Rod Laver
1885	William Renshaw	1924	Jean Borotra	1963	Chuck McKinley
1886	William Renshaw	1925	Jean Rene Lacoste	1964	Roy Emerson
1887	Herbert Lawford	1926	Jean Borotra	1965	Roy Emerson
1888	Ernest Renshaw	1927	Henri Cochet	1966	Manuel Santana
1889	William Renshaw	1928	Jean Rene Lacoste	1967	John Newcombe
1890	Willoughby Hamilton	1929	Henri Cochet	1968	Rod Laver
1891	Wilfred Baddeley	1930	Bill Tilden	1969	Rod Laver
1892	Wilfred Baddeley	1931	Sidney Wood	1970	John Newcombe
1893	Joshua Pim	1932	Ellsworth Vines	1971	John Newcombe
1894	Joshua Pim	1933	Jack Crawford	1972	Stan Smith
1895	Wilfred Baddeley	1934	Fred Perry	1973	Jan Kodes
1896	Harold Mahoney	1935	Fred Perry	1974	Jimmy Connors
1897	Reginald Doherty	1936	Fred Perry	1975	Arthur Ashe
1898	Reginald Doherty	1937	Donald Budge	1976	Bjorn Borg
1899	Reginald Doherty	1938	Donald Budge	1977	Bjorn Borg
1900	Reginald Doherty	1939	Bobby Riggs	1978	Bjorn Borg
1901	Arthur Gore	1940	No tournament held	1979	Bjorn Borg
1902	H. Laurence Doherty	1941	No tournament held	1980	Bjorn Borg
1903	H. Laurence Doherty	1942	No tournament held	1981	John McEnroe
1904	H. Laurence Doherty	1943	No tournament held	1982	Jimmy Connors
1905	H. Laurence Doherty	1944	No tournament held	1983	John McEnroe
1906	H. Laurence Doherty	1945	No tournament held	1984	John McEnroe
1907	Norman Brookes	1946	Yvon Petra	1985	Boris Becker
1908	Arthur Gore	1947	Jack Kramer	1986	Boris Becker
1909	Arthur Gore	1948	Bob Falkenburg	1987	Pat Cash
1910	Anthony F. Wilding	1949	Ted Schroeder	1988	Stefan Edberg
1911	Anthony F. Wilding	1950	Budge Patty	1989	Boris Becker
1912	Anthony F. Wilding	1951	Dick Savitt	1990	Stefan Edberg
1913	Anthony F. Wilding	1952	Frank Sedgman	1991	Michael Stich
1914	Norman Brookes	1953	Vic Seixas	1992	Andre Agassi
1915	No tournament held	1954	Jaroslav Drobny		

Women's Singles Champions

1884	Maud Watson	1921	Suzanne Lenglen	1958	Althea Gibson
1885	Maud Watson	1922	Suzanne Lenglen	1959	Maria Bueno
1886	Blanche Bingley	1923	Suzanne Lenglen	1960	Maria Bueno
1887	Lottie Dod	1924	Kitty McKane	1961	Angela Mortimer
1888	Lottie Dod	1925	Suzanne Lenglen	1962	Karen Susman
1889	Blanche Bingley Hillyard	1926	Kitty McKane Godfree	1963	Margaret Smith
1890	L. Rice	1927	Helen Wills	1964	Maria Bueno
1891	Lottie Dod	1928	Helen Wills	1965	Margaret Smith
1892	Lottie Dod	1929	Helen Wills	1966	Billie Jean King
1893	Lottie Dod	1930	Helen Wills Moody	1967	Billie Jean King
1894	Blanche Bingley Hillyard	1931	Cilly Aussem	1968	Billie Jean King
1895	Charlotte Cooper	1932	Helen Wills Moody	1969	Ann Jones
1896	Charlotte Cooper	1933	Helen Wills Moody	1970	Margaret Smith Court
1897	Blanche Bingley Hillyard	1934	Dorothy Round	1971	Evonne Goolagong
1898	Charlotte Cooper	1935	Helen Wills Moody	1972	Billie Jean King
1899	Blanche Bingley Hillyard	1936	Helen Jacobs	1973	Billie Jean King
1900	Blanche Bingley Hillyard	1937	Dorothy Round	1974	Chris Evert
1901	Charlotte Cooper Sterry	1938	Helen Wills Moody	1975	Billie Jean King
1902	Muriel Robb	1939	Alice Marble	1976	Chris Evert
1903	Dorothea Douglass	1940	No tournament held	1977	Virginia Wade
1904	Dorothea Douglass	1941	No tournament held	1978	Martina Navratilova
1905	May Sutton	1942	No tournament held	1979	Martina Navratilova
1906	Dorothea Douglass	1943	No tournament held	1980	Evonne Goolagong
1907	May Sutton	1944	No tournament held	1981	Chris Evert Lloyd
1908	Charlotte Cooper Sterry	1945	No tournament held	1982	Martina Navratilova
1909	Dora Boothby	1946	Pauline Betz	1983	Martina Navratilova
1910	Dorothea Douglass Chambers	1947	Margaret Osborne	1984	Martina Navratilova
1911	Dorothea Douglass Chambers	1948	A. Louise Brough	1985	Martina Navratilova
1912	Ethel Larcombe	1949	A. Louise Brough	1986	Martina Navratilova
1913	Dorothea Douglass Chambers	1950	A. Louise Brough	1987	Martina Navratilova
1914	Dorothea Douglass Chambers	1951	Doris Hart	1988	Steffi Graf
1915	No tournament held	1952	Maureen Connolly	1989	Steffi Graf
1916	No tournament held	1953	Maureen Connolly	1990	Martina Navratilova
1917	No tournament held	1954	Maureen Connolly	1991	Steffi Graf
1918	No tournament held	1955	A. Louise Brough	1992	Steffi Graf
1919	Suzanne Lenglen	1956	Shirley Fry		
1920	Suzanne Lenglen	1957	Althea Gibson		

Volleyball

Volleyball is played either outdoors or indoors on a rectangular court, with six players to a side. An inflated ball is hit back and forth over a net; the players try to prevent the ball from hitting the court on their own side. The net's top is 8 feet above the floor (slightly lower in women's play). To initiate play the ball is served by hitting it with the hand or fist and thereby sending it over the net toward the opponent's court. After the serve, the ball may be hit with any part of the body. The ball may be hit a maximum of three times by each team, the third hit sending the ball over the net. Catching or holding the ball is not permitted.

If the receiving team allows the ball to hit the floor on its side, or hits the ball out of bounds, the serving team scores a point and serves again. If the serving team allows the ball to hit the floor, hits it out of bounds, or fails to make a legal serve, the serve is transferred to the opponents, but no point is scored. The first team to reach 15 points wins the game, provided the margin of victory is at least two points. In championship play, a match is won by winning three out of five games. (*See illustration of court below.*)

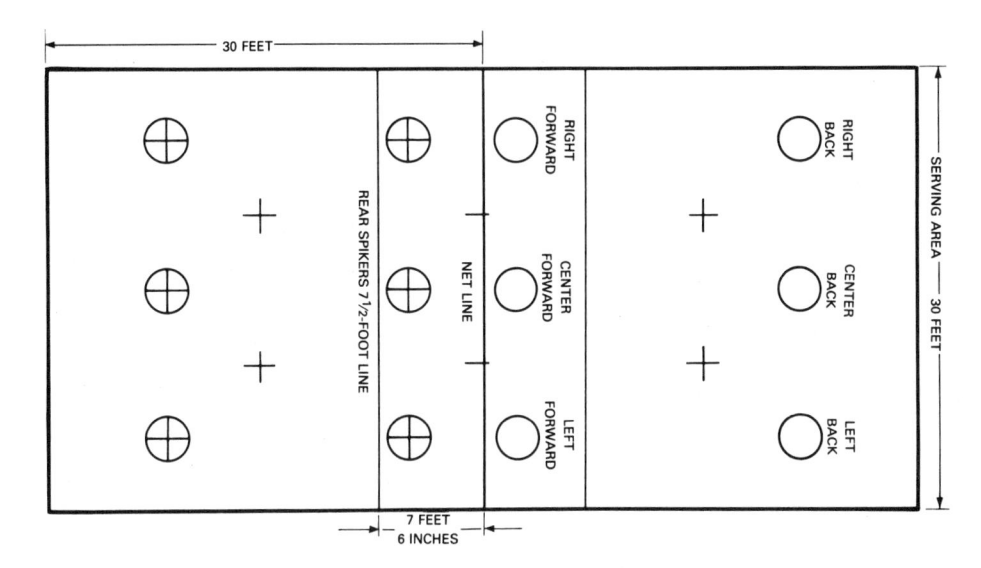

HORSE RACING

The Triple Crown

The best-known horse races in America are the Kentucky Derby, the Preakness, and the Belmont Stakes. These three races for three-year-olds make up horse racing's Triple Crown. Eleven horses have won all three events.

Year	Horse	Year	Horse
1919	Sir Barton	1946	Assault
1930	Gallant Fox	1948	Citation
1935	Omaha	1973	Secretariat
1937	War Admiral	1977	Seattle Slew
1941	Whirlaway	1978	Affirmed
1943	Count Fleet		

Winning Horses in the Kentucky Derby

(Held at Churchill Downs; 1 1/4 miles)

1875	Aristides	1880	Fonso	1885	Joe Cotton
1876	Vagrant	1881	Hindoo	1886	Ben Ali
1877	Baden Baden	1882	Apollo	1887	Montrose
1878	Day Star	1883	Leonatus	1888	Macbeth II
1879	Lord Murphy	1884	Buchanan	1889	Spokane

Year	Winner	Year	Winner	Year	Winner
1890	Riley	1925	Flying Ebony	1960	Venetian Way
1891	Kingman	1926	Bubbling Over	1961	Carry Back
1892	Azra	1927	Whiskery	1962	Decidedly
1893	Lookout	1928	Reigh Count	1963	Chateauguay
1894	Chant	1929	Clyde Van Dusen	1964	Northern Dancer
1895	Halma	1930	Gallant Fox	1965	Lucky Debonair
1896	Ben Brush	1931	Twenty Grand	1966	Kauai King
1897	Typhoon II	1932	Burgoo King	1967	Proud Clarion
1898	Plaudit	1933	Brokers Tip	1968	Forward Pass*
1899	Manuel	1934	Cavalcade	1969	Majestic Prince
1900	Lieutenant Gibson	1935	Omaha	1970	Dust Commander
1901	His Eminence	1936	Bold Venture	1971	Canonero II
1902	Alan-a-Dale	1937	War Admiral	1972	Riva Ridge
1903	Judge Himes	1938	Lawrin	1973	Secretariat
1904	Elwood	1939	Johnstown	1974	Cannonade
1905	Agile	1940	Gallahadion	1975	Foolish Pleasure
1906	Sir Huon	1941	Whirlaway	1976	Bold Forbes
1907	Pink Star	1942	Shut Out	1977	Seattle Slew
1908	Stone Street	1943	Count Fleet	1978	Affirmed
1909	Wintergreen	1944	Pensive	1979	Spectacular Bid
1910	Donau	1945	Hoop Jr.	1980	Genuine Risk
1911	Meridian	1946	Assault	1981	Pleasant Colony
1912	Worth	1947	Jet Pilot	1982	Gato del Sol
1913	Donerail	1948	Citation	1983	Sunny's Halo
1914	Old Rosebud	1949	Ponder	1984	Swale
1915	Regret	1950	Middleground	1985	Spend a Buck
1916	George Smith	1951	Count Turf	1986	Ferdinand
1917	Omar Khayyam	1952	Hill Gail	1987	Alysheba
1918	Exterminator	1953	Dark Star	1988	Winning Colors
1919	Sir Barton	1954	Determine	1989	Sunday Silence
1920	Paul Jones	1955	Swaps	1990	Unbridled
1921	Behave Yourself	1956	Needles	1991	Strike the Gold
1922	Morvich	1957	Iron Liege	1992	Lil E. Tee
1923	Zev	1958	Tim Tam	1993	Sea Hero
1924	Black Gold	1959	Tomy Lee		

* In 1968, Dancer's Image finished first but was disqualified.

AUTO RACING

Indianapolis 500 Winners

Year	Winner	Year	Winner	Year	Winner
1911	Ray Harroun	1924	L. L. Corum-Joe Boyer	1937	Wilbur Shaw
1912	Joe Dawson	1925	Peter DePaolo	1938	Floyd Roberts
1913	Jules Goux	1926	Frank Lockhart	1939	Wilbur Shaw
1914	Rene Thomas	1927	George Souders	1940	Wilbur Shaw
1915	Ralph DePalma	1928	Louis Meyer	1941	Floyd Davis-Mauri Rose
1916	Dario Resta	1929	Ray Keech	1942	No race held
1917	No race held	1930	Billy Arnold	1943	No race held
1918	No race held	1931	Louis Schneider	1944	No race held
1919	Howard Wilcox	1932	Fred Frame	1945	No race held
1920	Gaston Chevrolet	1933	Louis Meyer	1946	George Robson
1921	Tommy Milton	1934	Bill Cummings	1947	Mauri Rose
1922	Jimmy Murphy	1935	Kelly Petillo	1948	Mauri Rose
1923	Tommy Milton	1936	Louis Meyer	1949	Bill Holland

Year	Winner	Year	Winner	Year	Winner
1950	Johnnie Parsons	1965	Jim Clark	1980	Johnny Rutherford
1951	Lee Wallard	1966	Graham Hill	1981	Bobby Unser
1952	Troy Ruttman	1967	A. J. Foyt	1982	Gordon Johncock
1953	Bill Vukovich	1968	Bobby Unser	1983	Tom Sneva
1954	Bill Vukovich	1969	Mario Andretti	1984	Rick Mears
1955	Bob Sweikert	1970	Al Unser	1985	Danny Sullivan
1956	Pat Flaherty	1971	Al Unser	1986	Bobby Rahal
1957	Sam Hanks	1972	Mark Donohue	1987	Al Unser
1958	Jimmy Bryan	1973	Gordon Johncock	1988	Rick Mears
1959	Rodger Ward	1974	Johnny Rutherford	1989	Emerson Fittipaldi
1960	Jim Rathmann	1975	Bobby Unser	1990	Arie Luyendyk
1961	A. J. Foyt	1976	Johnny Rutherford	1991	Rick Mears
1962	Rodger Ward	1977	A. J. Foyt	1992	Al Unser Jr.
1963	Parnelli Jones	1978	Al Unser	1993	Emerson Fittipaldi
1964	A. J. Foyt	1979	Rick Mears		

Olympic Games

Summer Games

Year	Location
1896	Athens, Greece
1900	Paris, France
1904	St. Louis, Missouri
1908	London, England
1912	Stockholm, Sweden
1920	Antwerp, Belgium
1924	Paris, France
1928	Amsterdam, The Netherlands
1932	Los Angeles, California
1936	Berlin, Germany
1948	London, England
1952	Helsinki, Finland
1956	Melbourne, Australia
1960	Rome, Italy
1964	Tokyo, Japan
1968	Mexico City, Mexico
1972	Munich, West Germany
1976	Montreal, Canada
1980	Moscow, USSR
1984	Los Angeles, California
1988	Seoul, South Korea
1992	Barcelona, Spain
*1996	Atlanta, Georgia

Winter Games

Year	Location
1924	Chamonix, France
1928	St. Moritz, Switzerland
1932	Lake Placid, New York
1936	Garmisch-Partenkirchen, Germany
1948	St. Moritz, Switzerland
1952	Oslo, Norway
1956	Cortina, Italy
1960	Squaw Valley, California
1964	Innsbruck, Austria
1968	Grenoble, France
1972	Sapporo, Japan
1976	Innsbruck, Austria
1980	Lake Placid, New York
1984	Sarajevo, Yugoslavia
1988	Calgary, Canada
1992	Albertville, France
*1994	Lillehammer, Norway
1998	Nagano, Japan

* Beginning in 1994, winter and summer games will be played in alternating four-year cycles, winter games coming in 1994, 1998, and so on, and summer games being played in 1996, 2000, and so on.

1992 Olympic Events

Summer Games

Men

Baseball (team)
Boxing
Judo
Roller hockey
Soccer (team)
Water polo (team)
Weightlifting
Wrestling
   Freestyle
   Greco-Roman

Men's swimming

50 m, 100 m, 200 m, 400 m, 1500 m freestyle
100 m, 200 m backstroke
100 m, 200 m breaststroke
100 m, 200 m butterfly
200 m, 400 m individual medley
400 m, 800 m freestyle relay
400 m medley relay
Diving
   Springboard
   Platform

Men and Women

Archery
Badminton
Basketball (team)
Canoeing/Kayaking
Cycling
Equestrian*
Fencing
Field Hockey
Gymnastics
Handball (team)
Judo
Rowing
Shooting*
Table tennis
Tae Kwon Do
Tennis
Volleyball (team)
Yachting

Men's track and field

100 m, 200 m, 400 m dash
800 m, 1500 m, 5000 m, 10,000 m run
110 m, 400 m hurdles
3000 m steeplechase
20 m, 50 m walk
400 m relay (4 × 100)
1600 m relay (4 × 400)
Marathon
High jump
Long jump
Triple jump
Pole vault
Shot put
Discus throw
Javelin throw
Hammer throw
Decathlon
Modern pentathlon

Women's track and field

100 m, 200 m, 400 m dash
800 m, 1500 m, 3000 m, 10,000 m run
10 K walk
100 m, 400 m hurdles
400 m relay (4 × 100)
1600 m relay (4 × 400)
Marathon
High jump
Long jump
Shot put
Discus throw
Javelin throw
Heptathlon

* In equestrian events men and women competed against one another; in shooting they competed separately, as well as against one another.

Women's swimming

50 m, 100 m, 200 m, 400 m, 800 m freestyle
100 m, 200 m backstroke
100 m, 200 m breaststroke
100 m, 200 m butterfly
200 m, 400 m individual medley
400 m freestyle relay
400 m medley relay
Diving
  Springboard
  Platform
Synchronized swimming

Winter Games

Except for bobsledding and ice hockey, all winter sports at the 1992 Olympic games were divided into two classes, one for men and the other for women. Only men competed in bobsledding and ice hockey events. In paired figure skating and ice dancing, men and women performed together.

Biathlon   Men: 10 K, 20 K, 4 × 7.5 K relay
           Women: 7.5 K, 15 K, 3 × 7.5 K relay
2-man bobsledding
4-man bobsledding
Figure skating
Ice dancing
Ice hockey
Luge
Alpine skiing
  Downhill
  Slalom
  Giant slalom
  Super giant slalom
  Combined
Freestyle skiing
  Moguls
Cross country skiing
  Men: 10 K, 30 K, 50 K
    Pursuit method
    4 × 10 K relay
  Women:
    5 K, 15 K, 30 K
    Pursuit method
    4 × 5 K relay

Ski jumping
  90 m, 120 m (large hill), 120 m team
Nordic combined
  Individual
  Team
Speed skating
  Men: 500 m, 1000 m, 1500 m, 5 K, 10 K
  Women: 500 m, 1000 m, 1500 m, 3 K, 5 K
Speed skating (short track)
  Men: 1000 m, 5 K
  Women: 500 m, 3 K
Demonstration sports
  Freestyle skiing
    Ballet
    Aerials
  Speed skiing
  Curling

Board Games

Backgammon

Backgammon is a board game played by two players, each with 15 markers, or stones, which at the beginning of the game are placed in a standard initial configuration (see diagram) on the board. The board is divided into two tables, each with 12 triangular spaces, or points. Each player rolls two dice to determine the number of points moved by the stones, with black moving around the board in one direction and white moving in the opposite direction. The numbers on each die can be combined to move one stone the total amount indicated, or each die's value can be applied separately to single stones. If "doubles" are thrown (i.e., two 6s), the player can move twice as many points as are shown on the dice—in this case, four stones can move 6 spaces each, one can move 6 spaces and one 18 spaces, two can move 12 spaces each, or one stone can move 24 spaces. The object of the game is to be the first person to move his or her stones around the board and then off, called bearing off.

Any number of stones of the same color may stay on one point, but stones of the opposite color may not occupy the same point. A point occupied by two or more stones of the same color is said to be closed; it prevents the opponent from landing there. A point occupied by one marker (or none) is open. A single stone on any point is called a blot, and the opponent may land there with a hit. This sends the blot back to the beginning by placing it on the bar. It must enter the game again by rolling a number on one of the dice corresponding to an open point or to one occupied by stones of the same color before the owner may make another move.

Backgammon Starting Position

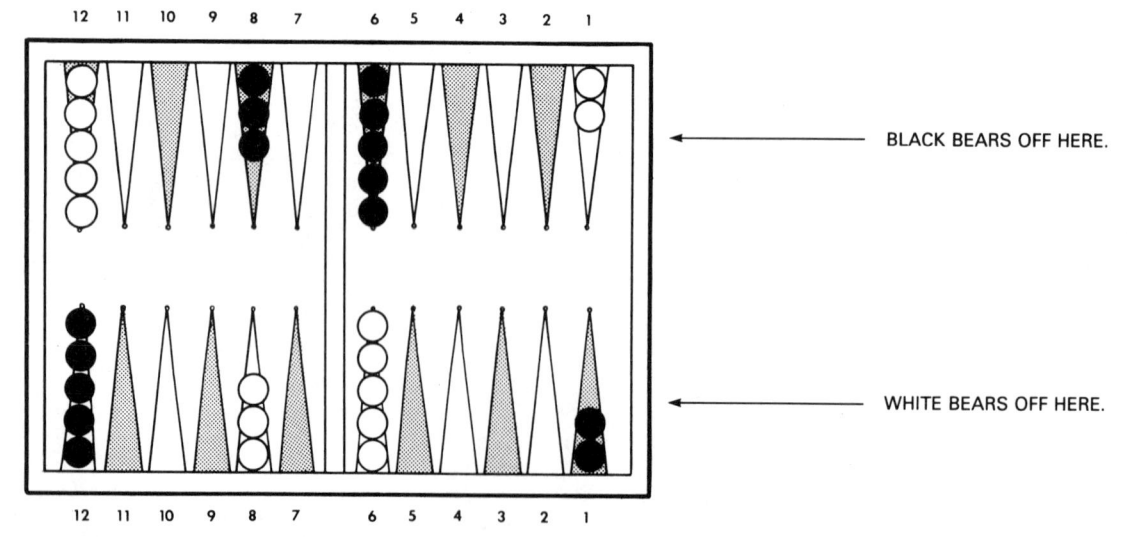

White moves counterclockwise from top to bottom.
Black moves clockwise from bottom to top.

Backgammon depends on the roll of the dice and is therefore partially a game of chance, but it can also involve complex strategy and tactics. The game may make use of the doubling cube, which is a die with a number on each face (2, 4, 8, 16, 32, 64). Using this cube, either player can at any point in the game double the stakes, whether they be points, as in tournament play, or money, as in the gambling version.

Checkers

Checkers is played by two players on a board with 64 squares alternating light and dark. Only the dark squares of the board are used. The board is eight squares wide and eight squares long. Each player uses 12 wooden discs called checkers, usually red for one player and black for the other. The pieces are set up on the dark squares of the first three ranks, four in each rank. Black moves first, and the players alternate turns by moving one checker forward diagonally toward the opposing player's checkers. The object is to jump over the opponent's pieces, which are then removed from play. A player wins when all the opponent's pieces have been removed. If a player manages to advance a piece to the last rank on the opposite end of the board, that piece becomes a king and thereby acquires the capability of moving backward as well as forward.

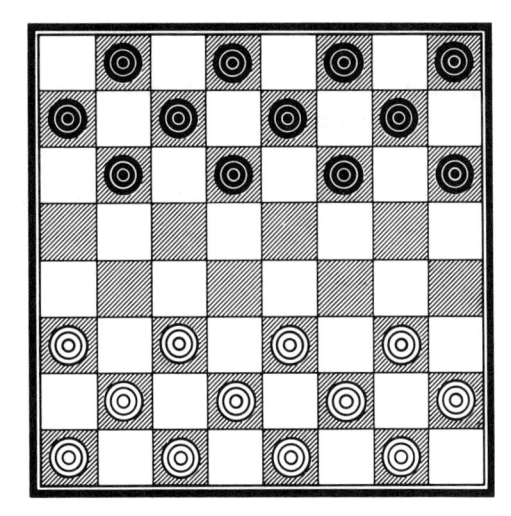

Checkers Starting Position

Chess

Chess is a game for two players, one of them directing the white pieces and one of them the black pieces. It is played on a board with 64 squares of alternating colors, black and white. The board is eight squares wide and eight long. Squares on the board are normally referred to by coordinates, using numbered ranks and lettered files. Each player has 16 pieces: eight pawns, two rooks, two knights, two bishops, a queen, and a king. To start the game, the pieces are set up using the 32 spaces of ranks 1 and 2 (for one color) and 7 and 8 (for the other color). Rooks occupy the outermost files (a and h), with knights placed next to them (b and g); next to them are the bishops (c and f). Toward the center of the board (d and e) the king and queen are placed, with the white queen on a white square and the black queen on a black square. The pawns are placed in front of these pieces, using ranks 2 and 7.

The object of the game is to capture the opponent's king by placing him in checkmate. In this position, the king is under attack by an opposing piece (check), and wherever the king moves, it remains under attack by that or another opposing piece. The attacking side thus wins the game. If a player feels that checkmate is unavoidable, he or she may give up, or resign. If neither white nor black is able to checkmate the opponent or force resignation, a draw may be agreed upon. If the king is not in check, and if a player can make no moves, or if all otherwise legal moves would expose his king to check, the game ends in a stalemate.

Any piece may capture, or take, an opponent's piece by landing on the square occupied by that piece. However, the king can not be captured and is instead put into check when attacked. If a piece is captured, it is removed from the board. If a pawn reaches the last rank (1 or 8), it is immediately "promoted" to a queen, rook, bishop, or knight at its owner's wish, without regard to the number of them the owner already has.

Each type of piece moves in a prescribed way. A rook moves forward or back, left or right as many squares in one direction as is desired. Knights move two squares in one direction (forward, back, left, or right) and one square at right angles to the first direction—or one square in one direction and two squares at right angles to the first move—resulting in an L-shaped move. The knight is the only piece that may jump over another piece. Bishops move diagonally any number of spaces in one direction. The queen moves forward, back, left, right, or diagonally any number of spaces in one direction. The king moves as the queen does, but one space at a time. Pawns move forward only, one space at a time, except for the first move, which may be two spaces. Pawns capture pieces by moving diagonally. There are only two instances in which pieces may move in other than these prescribed ways:

Chess Starting Position

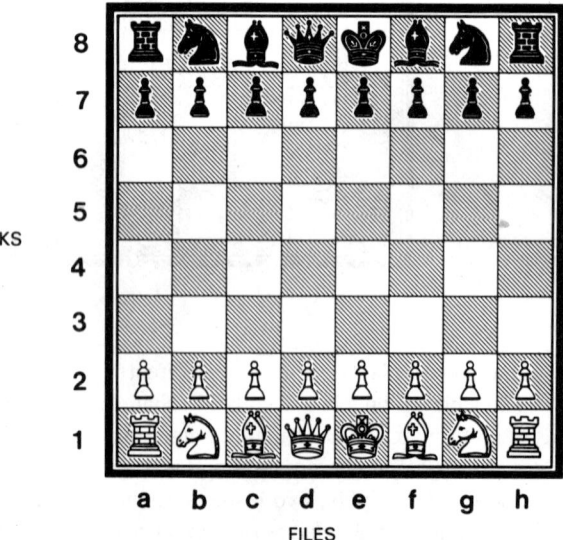

1. *Castling* is a two-part move involving the king and a rook. If neither of these pieces has moved previously, if there are no pieces placed between them, and if the king is not in check, or moving to or through a guarded square, the king may move two spaces toward the rook, and the rook may move to the far side next to the king.

2. If, by moving ahead two squares on an opening move, a black pawn becomes placed next to an opposing white pawn on the same rank, the white pawn may take the black pawn by moving diagonally to the square immediately behind it. This is called taking *en passant*, or capturing in passing. Of course, a black pawn may capture a white pawn in the same way.

Monopoly®

Monopoly® uses a board with 40 spaces around the perimeter. Players, starting with a fixed amount of money, roll two dice and, in turn, advance their tokens around the board the number spaces indicated by the dice. If a player lands on any of 22 properties, that player may buy it at a stated price. This money goes into the bank. The player then receives a deed for that property, which states the rent that an opposing player must pay the owner if he or she lands on it. The object of the game is to accumulate the properties and, by charging rent when an opponent lands there, to drive opposing players into bankruptcy. Properties are grouped by colors, with two or three to a group. If a player acquires all the properties within a single color, that player may develop those properties by purchasing houses and hotels. These dramatically increase the rent.

In addition to the color-coded properties, which are given street names, there are also four railroads and two utility companies that may be purchased. These also carry rents, but they may not be developed. If a player lands on any of six spaces, three called "Chance" and three "Community Chest," that player must pick up a card from two piles placed in the center of the board and follow its instructions. These involve monetary transactions either beneficial or harmful to the player. There is a neutral space called "Free Parking," a "Jail" space, two tax spaces, and a space called "Go." Play begins on the Go space and the players collect $200 each time they circle the board and pass it.

In informal play, Monopoly® may involve considerable negotiation and trading among players. The game ends when all but one player has gone bankrupt; the remaining player is the winner.

THE MOST LANDED-ON SPACES ON THE MONOPLY® GAME BOARD

According to Irvin R. Hertzel of Iowa State University, there are 10 spaces on the Monopoly® game board you can count on landing on more than the others. Using a computer, Hertzel, a mathematician, was able to figure out the overall probability of landing on each square. The following are the 10 most landed-on spaces.

1. Illinois Avenue
2. Go
3. B.&O. Railroad
4. Free Parking
5. Tennessee Avenue
6. New York Avenue
7. Reading Railroad
8. St. James Place
9. Water Works
10. Pennsylvania Railroad

Scrabble®

Scrabble® is a word game for two, three, or four players. The game uses a Scrabble® board with 225 spaces, 100 lettered tiles, and a tile rack for each player. Each player, starting with seven letters, attempts to form words on the board using letters from his or her own hand and from words on the board. Words may read from left to right or from top to bottom. Usually a new word uses one letter from a word already on the board, with which it interlocks at right angles, as in a crossword. Letters may be added to an existing word to form a new one.

Each player, after using some or all his or her tiles to form a word on the board, replenishes the playing hand from the pool of remaining tiles, which are face down. Thus each player always has seven tiles with which to form words, except toward the end of the game, when the pool runs out.

Each letter has a numerical value associated with it; this number is marked on the tile. Players score for each word formed, based on the value of each letter in the word. These are recorded using pencil and paper. Scores may be augmented by using certain premium spaces on the board. These special spaces result in doubling or tripling the values of single letters or complete words. When no player is able to form additional words, each player's score is tallied. Values of unplayed letters for each player are subtracted. The highest score wins the game.

Card Games

Blackjack

Blackjack is a gambling game using a standard 52-card deck. A counts as 1 or 11; K, Q, J, and 10 count as 10 each; all other cards count their face number. The object is to hold two or more cards totaling 21 or as close to 21 as possible without going over. Cards are dealt one at a time, clockwise, starting with the player at the dealer's left. Each player receives one down card and one face-up card. After this initial deal, each player may stand and refuse more cards or take additional cards face-up. For example, having been dealt a king down and a six up (totaling 16), if the player chooses to take an additional card and receives another six, that player is out with 22. An ace and a picture card or a 10 is called blackjack; it totals 21 and beats all other hands.

Various betting methods are used, but usually bets are made before and after the initial deal and after each subsequent deal. All players play against the dealer, and bets are settled depending on which hands are closest to but not over 21; if the dealer has the same count as a given player, the hand is considered a stand-off.

Bridge

Contract bridge uses a standard 52-card deck and is a game for four players, in partnerships of two. The teams are designated North–South and East–West. Cards in each suit rank A (high), K, Q, J, 10, 9, . . . 2 (low), and suits rank spades (high), hearts, diamonds, and clubs (low). Each player receives cards, dealt one at a time clockwise starting at the dealer's left.

Each player in turn gets a chance to make a bid, which is a statement of the intention to win more than six tricks. At the same time the player either declares a high-ranking suit (trump) or declares no trump. If a player chooses not to bid, he or she may pass. Bids go around the table in clockwise rotation, with each bid being higher than any preceding bid. A bid may be doubled by an opponent or redoubled by a partner. These double the scoring value of a bid if it is played. This bidding segment of the game is called the auction, and the highest bid becomes the contract. One member of the contracting team declares the trump and becomes the declarer. That person's partner spreads his or her hand face up on the table and becomes the dummy.

The object of the game is to win tricks in order to fulfill the contract or to defeat the opponent's attempt to fulfill it. The player to the declarer's left leads, and all players must follow suit if possible. A trick is won by the highest card of the suit led if no trump is played, or by the highest trump played.

When all 13 tricks have been taken, the result is scored. There is a complicated scoring system depending primarily on whether or not the contract was made and by how much. The two members of a partnership score their combined tricks as a single unit. Extra points may be scored in several ways. A bonus is scored if a doubled or redoubled bid is made. One of two types of slams is scored if the contracting team wins 12 tricks or all 13. Honors points are scored when a player receives certain cards in the deal (A, K, Q, J, 10 of trump, or the four aces if no trump has been declared).

When a side accumulates 100 or more points in trick scores, the game is over. The side that first wins two out of three games wins a rubber. After each rubber, partnerships may change and play may begin again.

Pinochle

Pinochle is played by two to four players and uses a 48-card deck, which includes two of each rank from 9 to A in all four suits. The rank of cards in each suit is A (high), 10, K, Q, J, 9. Cards are dealt three at a time, clockwise, starting to the dealer's left. In two-hand pinochle, both players receive 12 cards; in three-hand (auction pinochle), each receives 15; and in four-hand (partnership pinochle), each receives 12 cards. The remaining cards, if any, form the stock. After an ad hoc high-ranking suit, called trump, has been determined, the player to the left of the dealer leads by placing a card in the middle, followed by each player in rotation. Tricks are won by the high trump or by the higher card of the suit led if no trump is played. The winner of the trick leads for the next trick. Except in two-hand pinochle, a player must always follow the suit that is led, if possible.

Scoring is done by examining cards taken in tricks, with each ace counting 11, each ten 10, each king 4, each queen 3, and each jack 2. Nines do not score. Points can also be scored by winning the last trick. In addition, certain combinations of cards, called melds, have scoring value. These include the flush (A, 10, K, Q, J in the same suit), the marriage (K and Q in the same suit), groups of cards of the same rank (four aces, four kings, etc.), and two special melds, the nine of trump and the pinochle (queen of spades and jack of diamonds).

Points taken in tricks are added to those accumulated by melding. Usually the player or team that first reaches 1,000 points wins the game.

Poker

Poker is a popular card game using a standard 52-card deck, with cards ranking A (high), K, Q, J, 10, 9, . . . 2 (low). The ace can also rank low if used as part of A-2-3-4-5. Jokers are sometimes used as wild cards, which can stand for any card the holder chooses. There are hundreds of forms of poker, but invariably the cards are dealt clockwise, one at a time, starting with the player to the dealer's left. Usually each player receives five cards face down, but depending on the type of poker, more cards may be dealt, or some may be face up.

Poker is a gambling game using chips of different monetary value. Bets by players go into a pile of chips called the pot. The object is to win the pot, either by showing the best hand or by making a bet that no one is willing to match. The rank of poker hands without wild cards is as follows:

1. *Royal flush:* a sequence of ace, king, queen, jack, ten of the same suit
2. *Straight flush:* five cards in sequence in the same suit
3. *Four of a kind:* four cards of the same rank
4. *Full house:* three of a kind and a pair
5. *Flush:* five cards of the same suit
6. *Straight:* five cards in sequence, regardless of suit
7. *Three of a kind:* three cards of the same rank
8. *Two pair:* two cards of the same rank and two others of a different rank
9. *One pair:* two cards of the same rank
10. *High card:* five unmatched cards, one with the highest rank of the five

Rummy

Rummy uses a regular deck of 52 cards. The cards rank K (high), Q, J, 10, . . . 2, A (low). Cards are dealt one at a time, clockwise, starting at the dealer's left. The number of cards dealt to each player depends on the number of players in the game: with two players, 10 cards each; with three or four players, seven cards each; with five or six players, six cards each. The undealt remainder of the deck is placed face down, forming the stock. Its top card is turned up next to the stock, forming the discard pile. The object is to form groups (three or more cards of the same rank) or sequences (three or more cards of the same suit in sequence of rank). This is called melding.

One at a time and proceeding clockwise, players draw one card from the top of the stack or the top of the discard pile. If melding is possible, groups or sequences are placed face up in front of the player. A player may also lay off, or add to his or her own or an opponent's melds. A player's turn ends by placing one card face up on the discard pile. When one player melds all the cards remaining in a hand, that player goes out, thus ending that deal, which is then scored. The player going out scores his or her own melds plus the points left in the opponents' hands. The other players score just their own melds. Aces count as one; all picture cards count as 10; and the rest of the cards count as their face number. High score wins.

Except when going out, a player must discard one card after each play, whether or not that player has melded or laid off.

Solitaire

Solitaire, or Patience, refers to a group of card games played by one person. The most popular and best known of these games is Klondike. Using a standard 52-card deck, a tableau or layout is dealt in front of the player, consisting of seven piles of cards. The first pile on the far left has one card, the second pile two, and so on to the far right pile, which has seven cards. These cards are face down except for the top card in each pile. On these piles, descending sequences are built in alternating colors. For example, a red nine may be placed on a black ten. Entire sequences or individual cards may be moved from pile to pile, provided correct colors and sequences are maintained. If a down card in a pile is revealed, it is turned face up and may then become part of a sequence. When a pile is exhausted, a king may replace it.

When they become available, aces are placed above the original layout. The object is to build sequences in suit from the four aces (the foundations) up to the four kings, thus using all cards of the original layout as well as the remaining cards, which form the stock. From the stock, the player turns up one card at a time, forming a waste pile. The top card of the waste pile is available for play on the layout or foundations. The player goes through the stock only once and wins the game if he or she successfully places the entire deck on the foundations. Many players employ alternative, more liberal methods of dealing the stock.

Additional Sources of Information

Organizations and Services

General

Amateur Athletic Union of the U.S.
3400 West 86th Street
P.O. Box 68207
Indianapolis, IN 46268
317-872-2900

National Collegiate Athletic Association (NCAA)
6201 College Boulevard
Overland Park, KS 66211
913-339-1906

U.S. Olympic Committee
1750 East Boulder Street
Colorado Springs, CO 80909
719-632-5551

Baseball

American League
350 Park Avenue
New York, NY 10022
212-339-7600

Baseball Hall of Fame
Box 590
Cooperstown, NY 13326
607-547-9988

Major League Baseball Commissioner's Office
350 Park Avenue
New York, NY 10022
212-339-7800

National League
350 Park Avenue
New York, NY 10022
212-339-7700

Basketball

Naismith Memorial Basketball Hall of Fame
1150 West Columbus Avenue
Springfield, MA 01105
413-781-6500

National Basketball Association
645 Fifth Avenue
New York, NY 10022
212-826-7000

Football

National Football League
410 Park Avenue
New York, NY 10022
212-758-1500

Pro Football Hall of Fame
2121 George Halas Drive, NW
Canton, OH 44708
216-456-8207

Golf

Ladies Professional Golf Association (LPGA)
2570 Vousia Street
Daytona, FL 32114
904-254-8800

U.S. Golf Association
Liberty Corner Road
Far Hills, NJ 07931
908-234-2300

Professional Golfer's Association of America
100 Avenue of the Champions
Palm Beach Gardens, FL 33418
407-624-8400

U.S. Golf Association Hall of Fame
Golf House
Far Hills, NJ 07931
908-234-2300

Hockey

Hockey Hall of Fame
Exhibition Place
Toronto, ON M6K 3C3
Canada
416-595-1345

National Hockey League
1155 Metcalfe Street
Suite 960
Montreal, Quebec H3B 2W2
Canada
514-288-9220

Horse Racing

National Museum of Racing
Union Avenue
Saratoga Springs, NY 12866
518-584-0400

U.S. Trotting Association
750 Michigan Avenue
Columbus, OH 43215
614-224-2291

Thoroughbred Racing Association of North America
3000 Marcus Avenue
Lake Success, NY 11042
516-328-2660

Soccer

U.S. Soccer Federation
1811 South Prairie Avenue
Chicago, IL 60616
312-808-1300

Tennis

International Tennis Hall of Fame and Museum
194 Bellevue Avenue
Newport, RI 02840
401-849-3990

U.S. Tennis Association
1212 Avenue of the Americas
New York, NY 10036
212-302-3322

Track and Field

Intercollegiate Association of Amateur Athletes of America (IC4A)
P.O. Box 3
Centerville, MA 02632
508-771-5060

International Amateur Athletics Federation
3 Hans Crescent
Knightsbridge
London SW1X 0LN, England
(011)44-1-581-8771

The Athletics Congress
P.O. Box 120
Indianapolis, IN 46206
317-261-0500

U.S. Track and Field Hall of Fame
P.O. Box 120
Indianapolis, IN 46206
317-261-0483

Books

Ainslie, Tom. *Ainslie's Complete Guide to Thoroughbred Racing.* Simon & Schuster, 1988.

Collins, Bud, and Zander Hollander. *Bud Collins' Modern Encyclopedia of Tennis.* Doubleday, 1980.

Fischler, Shirley, and Stan Fischler. *The Complete Record of Professional Ice Hockey.* Macmillan, 1983.

Fisher, David, and Reginald Bragonier, Jr. *What's What in Sports: The Visual Glossary of the Sports World.* Hammond, 1984.

Frommer, Harvey. *Sports Lingo: A Dictionary of the Language of Sports.* Atheneum, 1983.

Hollander, Zander. *The Complete Handbook of Pro Basketball.* New American Library, annual.

Morrison, Ian. *Pictorial History of Golf.* Southmark, 1990.

Neft, David S. *Sports Encyclopedia: Baseball.* St. Martin's, 1991.

Neft, David S., and Richard M. Cohen. *The Football Encyclopedia.* St. Martin's, 1991.

Neft, David S., and Richard M. Cohen. *The Sports Encyclopedia: Pro Basketball,* 4th ed. St. Martin's, 1991.

Odd, Gilbert. *Encyclopedia of Boxing.* Book Sales, Inc., 1989.

The Oxford Companion to Sports and Games. Oxford University Press, 1974.

Reichler, Joseph L. *The Baseball Encyclopedia: The Complete and Official Record of Major League Baseball,* 7th ed. Macmillan, 1989.

Treat, Roger. *The Encyclopedia of Football,* 16th rev. ed. Doubleday, 1979.

Webster's Sports Dictionary, G & C Merriam, 1976.

23

Health

Anatomical Drawings with Parts of the Body Labeled / *689*

Height and Weight Charts for Adults and Children / *693*

Table of Approximate Dates of Childbirth / *696*

Life Expectancy Tables / *697*

Deaths and Death Rates / *699*

Home Remedies / *701*

Shelf Life of Medicine / *702*

Infectious Diseases and How They Are Spread / *703*

Combining Forms of Medical Terms / *704*

Breast Self-Examination (BSE) / *705*

Recommended Daily Dietary Allowances (RDAs) / *708*

Nutritive Values of Foods / *710*

Vitamin Food Chart / *732*

Vaccines / *736*

Activities and the Calories They Consume / *736*

Safe Alcohol Consumption / *737*

Additional Sources of Information / *739*

Health 689

Anatomical Drawings with Parts of the Body Labeled

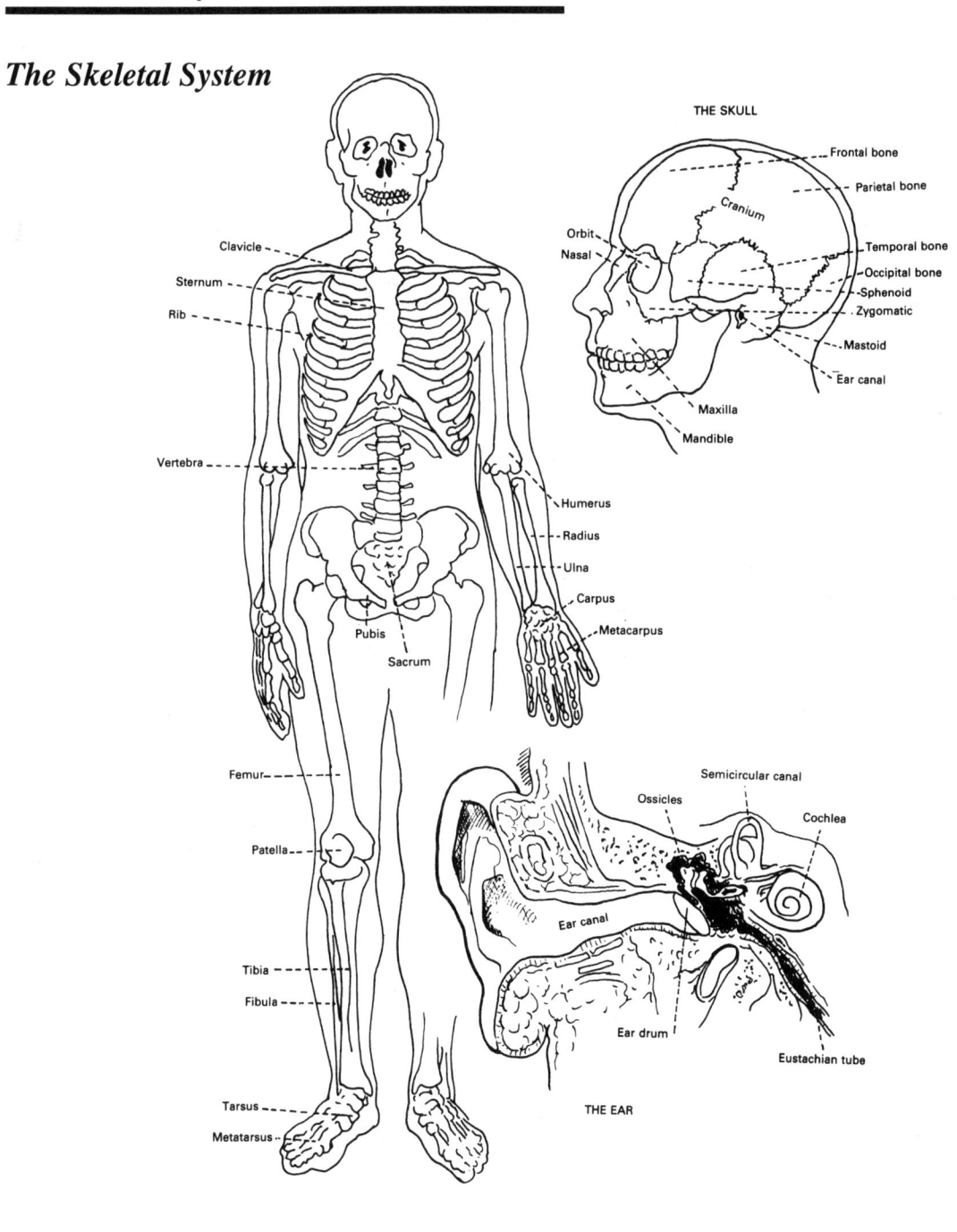

The Skeletal System

The Muscles

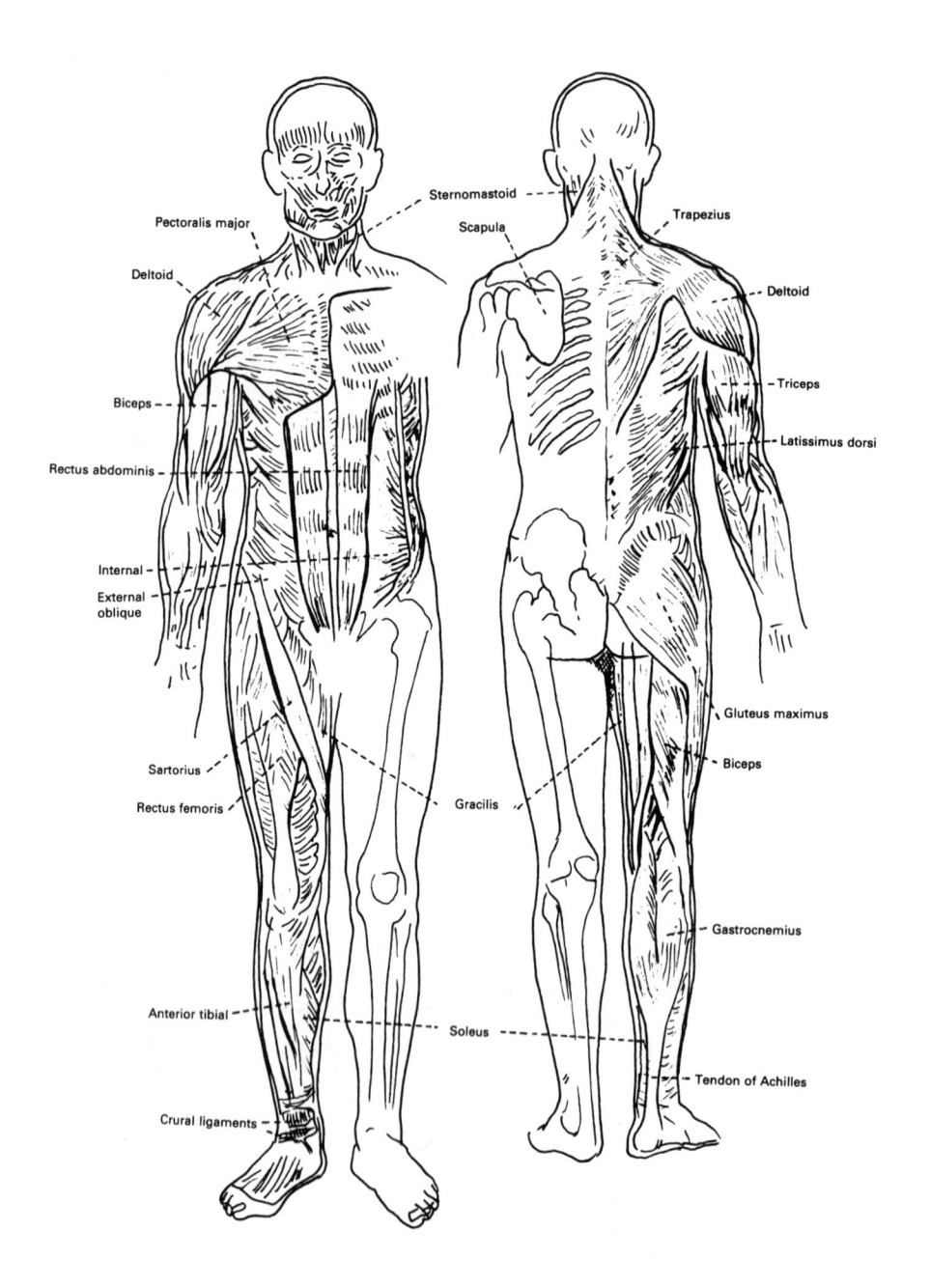

The Alimentary System

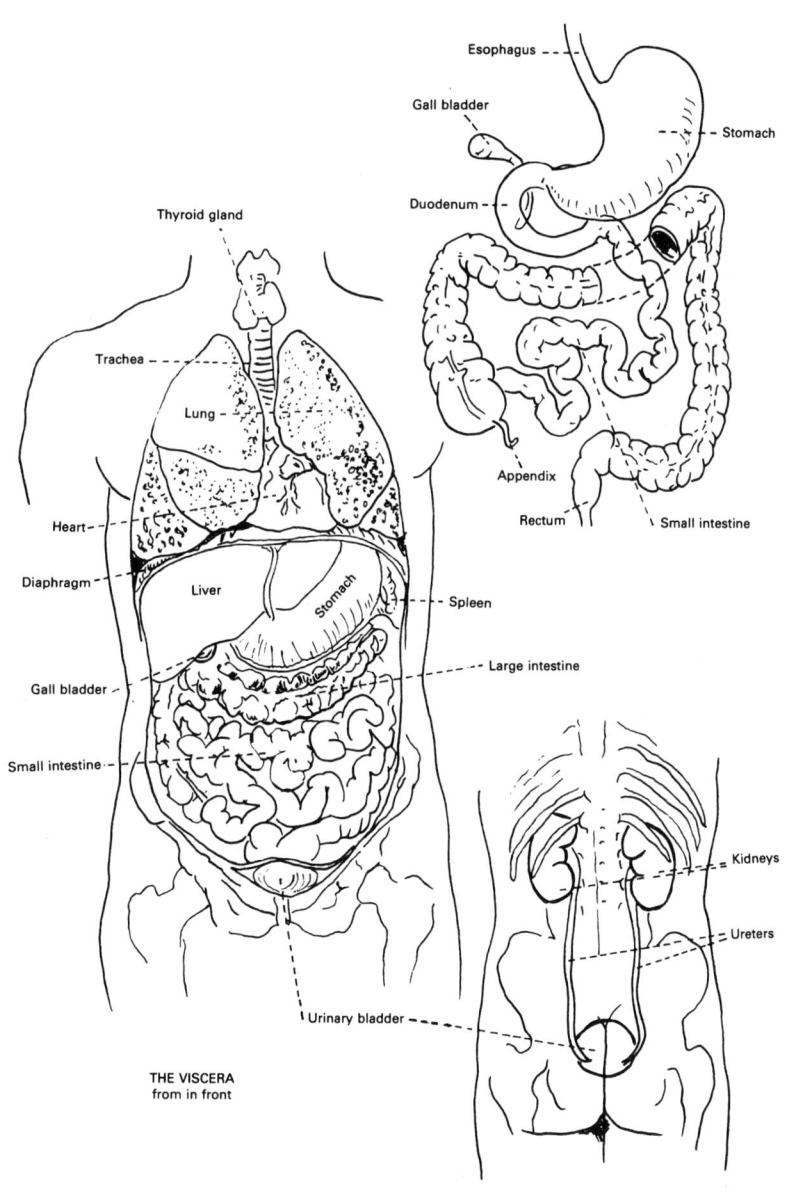

THE VISCERA
from in front

THE URINARY TRACT

The Brain and Spinal Cord

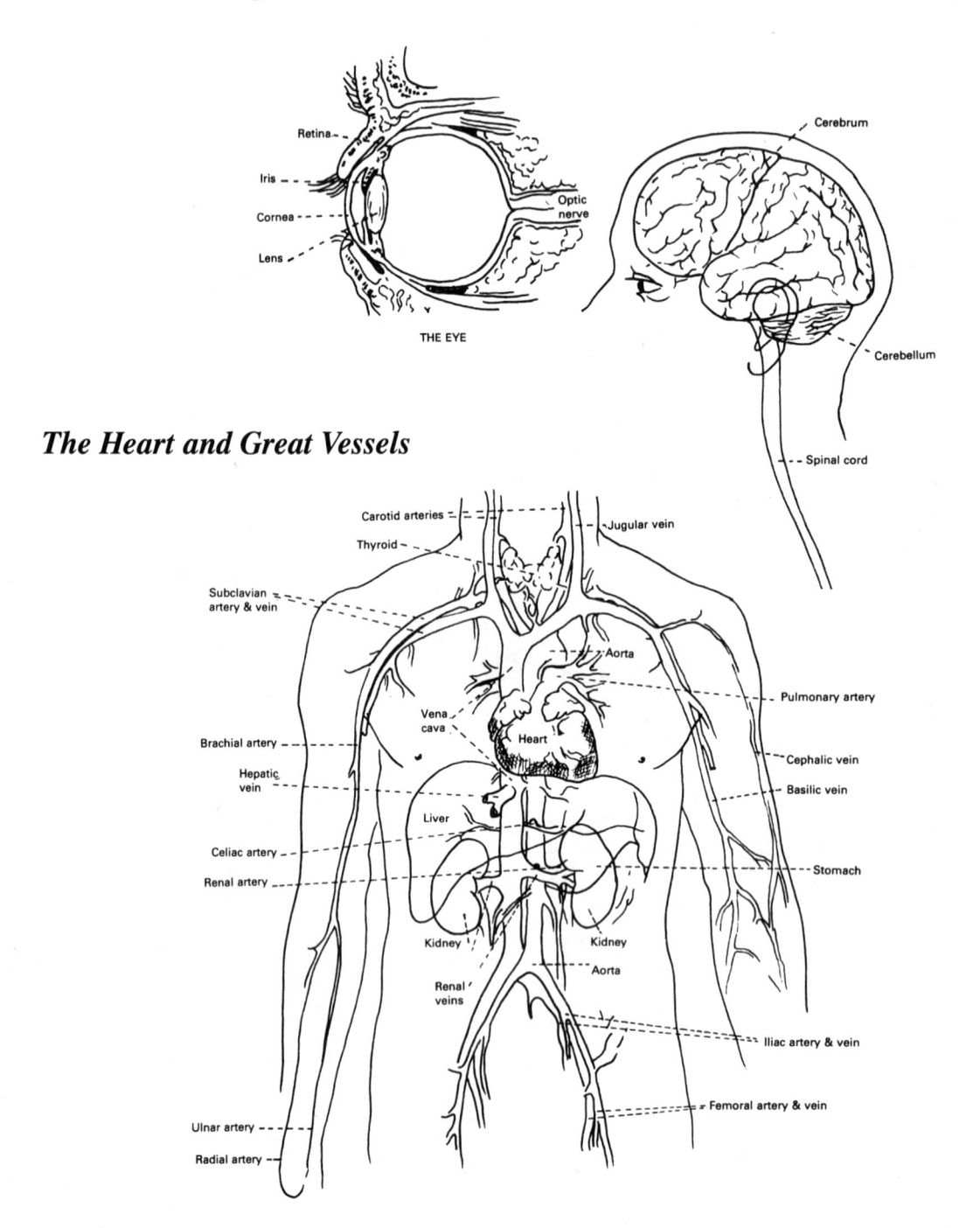

THE EYE

The Heart and Great Vessels

Height and Weight Charts for Adults and Children

Height and Weight Charts for Adults

Desirable Weights in Pounds for Persons 25 to 59 Years Old

Men

Height (in shoes)	Small frame	Medium frame	Large frame
5 ft. 2 in.	128–134	131–141	138–150
5 ft. 3 in.	130–136	133–143	140–153
5 ft. 4 in.	132–138	135–145	142–156
5 ft. 5 in.	134–140	137–148	144–160
5 ft. 6 in.	136–142	139–151	146–164
5 ft. 7 in.	138–145	142–154	149–168
5 ft. 8 in.	140–148	145–157	152–172
5 ft. 9 in.	142–151	148–160	155–176
5 ft. 10 in.	144–154	151–163	158–180
5 ft. 11 in.	146–157	154–166	161–184
6 ft.	149–160	157–170	164–188
6 ft. 1 in.	152–164	160–174	168–192
6 ft. 2 in.	155–168	164–178	172–197
6 ft. 3 in.	158–172	167–182	176–202
6 ft. 4 in.	162–176	171–187	181–207

Women

Height (in shoes)	Small frame	Medium frame	Large frame
4 ft. 10 in.	102–111	109–121	118–131
4 ft. 11 in.	103–113	111–123	120–134
5 ft.	104–115	113–126	122–137
5 ft. 1 in.	106–118	115–129	125–140
5 ft. 2 in.	108–121	118–132	128–143
5 ft. 3 in.	111–124	121–135	131–147
5 ft. 4 in.	114–127	124–138	134–151
5 ft. 5 in.	117–130	127–141	137–155
5 ft. 6 in.	120–133	130–144	140–159
5 ft. 7 in.	123–136	133–147	143–163
5 ft. 8 in.	126–139	136–150	146–167
5 ft. 9 in.	129–142	139–153	149–170
5 ft. 10 in.	132–145	142–156	152–173
5 ft. 11 in.	135–148	145–159	155–176
6 ft.	138–151	148–162	158–179

Height and Weight Charts for Children

Desirable Weights in Pounds for Boys and Girls 5 to 18 Years Old

Boys

Height (in inches)	5	6	7	8	9	10	11	12	13	14	15	16	17	18
38	34	34												
39	35	35												
40	36	36												
41	38	38	38											
42	39	39	39	39										
43	41	41	41	41										
44	44	44	44	44										
45	46	46	46	46	46									
46	47	48	48	48	48									
47	49	50	50	50	50	50								
48		52	53	53	53	53								
49		55	55	55	55	55	55							
50		57	58	58	58	58	58	58						
51			61	61	61	61	61	61	61					
52			63	64	64	64	64	64	64					
53			66	67	67	67	67	68	68					
54				70	70	70	70	71	71	72				
55				72	72	73	73	74	74	74				
56				75	76	77	77	77	78	78	80			
57					79	80	81	81	82	83	83			
58					83	84	84	85	85	86	87			
59						87	88	89	89	90	90	90		
60						91	92	92	93	94	95	96		
61							95	96	97	99	100	103	106	
62							100	101	102	103	104	107	111	116
63							105	106	107	108	110	113	118	123
64								109	111	113	115	117	121	126
65								114	117	118	120	122	127	131
66									119	122	125	128	132	136
67									124	128	130	134	136	139
68										134	134	137	141	143
69										137	139	143	146	149
70										143	144	145	148	151
71										148	150	151	152	154
72											153	155	156	158
73											157	160	162	164
74											160	164	168	170

Girls

Height (in inches)	Age												
	5	6	7	8	9	10	11	12	13	14	15	16	17	18
38	33	33												
39	34	34												
40	36	36	36											
41	37	37	37											
42	39	39	39											
43	41	41	41	41										
44	42	42	42	42										
45	45	45	45	45	45									
46	47	47	47	48	48									
47	49	50	50	50	50	50								
48		52	52	52	52	53	53							
49			54	55	55	56	56							
50			56	57	58	59	61	62						
51			59	60	61	61	63	65						
52			63	64	64	64	65	67						
53			66	67	67	68	68	69	71					
54				69	70	70	71	71	73					
55				72	74	74	74	75	77	78				
56					76	78	78	79	81	83				
57					80	82	82	82	84	88	92			
58						84	86	86	88	93	96	101		
59						87	90	90	92	96	100	103	104	
60						91	95	95	97	101	105	108	109	111
61							99	100	101	105	108	112	113	116
62							104	105	106	109	113	115	117	118
63								110	110	112	116	117	119	120
64								114	115	117	119	120	122	123
65								118	120	121	122	123	125	126
66									124	124	125	128	129	130
67									128	130	131	133	133	135
68									131	133	135	136	138	138
69										135	137	138	140	142
70										136	138	140	142	144
71										138	140	142	144	145

Table of Approximate Dates of Childbirth

Find the date of the last menstrual period in the top line (lightface type) of the pair of lines. The dark number (boldface type) in the line below will be the expected day of delivery.

January	1 2 3 4 5 6 7 8 9 10 11 12 13 14 15 16 17 18 19 20 21 22 23 24 25 26 27 28 29 30 31	
October	**8 9 10 11 12 13 14 15 16 17 18 19 20 21 22 23 24 25 26 27 28 29 30 31 (1 2 3 4 5 6 7**	**November**
February	1 2 3 4 5 6 7 8 9 10 11 12 13 14 15 16 17 18 19 20 21 22 23 24 25 26 27 28	
November	**8 9 10 11 12 13 14 15 16 17 18 19 20 21 22 23 24 25 26 27 28 29 30 31 (1 2 3 4 5**	**December**
March	1 2 3 4 5 6 7 8 9 10 11 12 13 14 15 16 17 18 19 20 21 22 23 24 25 26 27 28 29 30 31	
December	**6 7 8 9 10 11 12 13 14 15 16 17 18 19 20 21 22 23 24 25 26 27 28 29 30 31 (1 2 3 4 5**	**January**
April	1 2 3 4 5 6 7 8 9 10 11 12 13 14 15 16 17 18 19 20 21 22 23 24 25 26 27 28 29 30	
January	**6 7 8 9 10 11 12 13 14 15 16 17 18 19 20 21 22 23 24 25 26 27 28 29 30 31 (1 2 3 4**	**February**
May	1 2 3 4 5 6 7 8 9 10 11 12 13 14 15 16 17 18 19 20 21 22 23 24 25 26 27 28 29 30 31	
February	**5 6 7 8 9 10 11 12 13 14 15 16 17 18 19 20 21 22 23 24 25 26 27 28 29 30 31 (1 2 3 4 5 6 7**	**March**
June	1 2 3 4 5 6 7 8 9 10 11 12 13 14 15 16 17 18 19 20 21 22 23 24 25 26 27 28 29 30	
March	**8 9 10 11 12 13 14 15 16 17 18 19 20 21 22 23 24 25 26 27 28 29 30 31 (1 2 3 4 5 6**	**April**
July	1 2 3 4 5 6 7 8 9 10 11 12 13 14 15 16 17 18 19 20 21 22 23 24 25 26 27 28 29 30 31	
April	**7 8 9 10 11 12 13 14 15 16 17 18 19 20 21 22 23 24 25 26 27 28 29 30 31 (1 2 3 4 5 6 7**	**May**
August	1 2 3 4 5 6 7 8 9 10 11 12 13 14 15 16 17 18 19 20 21 22 23 24 25 26 27 28 29 30 31	
May	**8 9 10 11 12 13 14 15 16 17 18 19 20 21 22 23 24 25 26 27 28 29 30 31 (1 2 3 4 5 6 7**	**June**
September	1 2 3 4 5 6 7 8 9 10 11 12 13 14 15 16 17 18 19 20 21 22 23 24 25 26 27 28 29 30	
June	**8 9 10 11 12 13 14 15 16 17 18 19 20 21 22 23 24 25 26 27 28 29 30 31 (1 2 3 4 5 6 7**	**July**
October	1 2 3 4 5 6 7 8 9 10 11 12 13 14 15 16 17 18 19 20 21 22 23 24 25 26 27 28 29 30 31	
July	**8 9 10 11 12 13 14 15 16 17 18 19 20 21 22 23 24 25 26 27 28 29 30 31 (1 2 3 4 5 6 7**	**August**
November	1 2 3 4 5 6 7 8 9 10 11 12 13 14 15 16 17 18 19 20 21 22 23 24 25 26 27 28 29 30	
August	**8 9 10 11 12 13 14 15 16 17 18 19 20 21 22 23 24 25 26 27 28 29 30 31 (1 2 3 4 5 6**	**September**
December	1 2 3 4 5 6 7 8 9 10 11 12 13 14 15 16 17 18 19 20 21 22 23 24 25 26 27 28 29 30 31	
September	**7 8 9 10 11 12 13 14 15 16 17 18 19 20 21 22 23 24 25 26 27 28 29 30 31 (1 2 3 4 5 6 7**	**October**

Life Expectancy Tables

by Race, Sex, and Age

| Age (years) | Expectation of life in years ||||| Expected deaths per 1,000 alive at specified age[1] |||||
| | | White || All Other || | White || All Other ||
	Total	Male	Female	Male	Female	Total	Male	Female	Male	Female
At birth	75.3	72.7	79.2	64.8	73.5	9.86	9.08	7.15	20.04	17.17
1	75.0	72.3	78.8	65.2	73.8	0.69	0.69	0.53	1.18	0.91
2	74.1	71.4	77.8	64.2	72.9	0.52	0.50	0.41	0.91	0.75
3	73.1	70.4	76.9	63.3	71.9	0.40	0.38	0.32	0.72	0.61
4	72.1	69.5	75.9	62.3	71.0	0.33	0.32	0.27	0.59	0.49
5	71.7	68.5	74.9	61.4	70.0	0.29	0.29	0.23	0.51	0.40
6	70.2	67.5	73.9	60.4	69.0	0.26	0.27	0.21	0.45	0.32
7	69.2	66.5	73.0	59.4	68.0	0.24	0.26	0.19	0.40	0.27
8	68.2	65.5	72.0	58.5	67.1	0.21	0.23	0.17	0.34	0.23
9	67.2	64.5	71.0	57.5	66.1	0.18	0.20	0.15	0.28	0.22
10	66.2	63.6	70.0	56.5	65.1	0.16	0.17	0.13	0.24	0.23
11	65.2	62.6	69.0	55.5	64.1	0.17	0.17	0.13	0.24	0.25
12	64.3	61.6	68.0	54.5	63.1	0.22	0.24	0.16	0.34	0.27
13	63.3	60.6	67.0	53.5	62.1	0.32	0.39	0.22	0.55	0.30
14	62.3	59.6	66.0	52.6	61.2	0.47	0.59	0.30	0.83	0.33
15	61.3	58.6	65.1	51.6	60.2	0.63	0.82	0.39	1.16	0.37
16	60.4	57.7	64.1	50.7	59.2	0.79	1.03	0.48	1.47	0.42
17	59.4	56.8	63.1	49.8	58.2	0.91	1.21	0.53	1.78	0.48
18	58.5	55.8	62.1	48.8	57.3	0.99	1.31	0.55	2.07	0.54
19	57.5	54.9	61.2	47.9	56.3	1.03	1.37	0.53	2.33	0.63
20	56.6	54.0	60.2	47.1	55.3	1.06	1.42	0.50	2.61	0.70
21	55.6	53.0	59.2	46.2	54.4	1.10	1.47	0.48	2.89	0.79
22	54.7	52.1	58.3	45.3	53.4	1.13	1.51	0.47	3.10	0.88
23	53.8	51.2	57.3	44.4	52.4	1.15	1.53	0.47	3.23	0.95
24	52.8	50.3	56.3	43.6	51.5	1.17	1.55	0.49	3.28	1.03
25	51.9	49.4	55.3	42.7	50.6	1.18	1.55	0.49	3.28	1.10
26	50.9	48.4	54.4	41.9	49.6	1.20	1.56	0.52	3.38	1.18
27	50.0	47.5	53.4	41.0	48.7	1.23	1.58	0.54	3.50	1.28
28	49.1	46.6	52.4	40.2	47.7	1.27	1.62	0.56	3.69	1.39
29	48.1	45.7	51.5	39.3	46.8	1.32	1.67	0.59	3.94	1.51
30	47.2	44.7	50.5	38.5	45.9	1.38	1.73	0.62	4.20	1.65
31	46.2	43.8	49.5	37.6	44.9	1.45	1.79	0.66	4.47	1.78
32	45.3	42.9	48.6	36.8	44.0	1.51	1.86	0.70	4.78	1.91
33	44.4	42.0	47.6	36.0	43.1	1.59	1.93	0.73	5.14	2.02
34	43.5	41.0	46.6	35.1	42.2	1.66	2.02	0.76	5.53	2.13
35	42.5	40.1	45.7	34.3	41.3	1.75	2.11	0.80	5.96	2.25
36	41.6	39.2	44.7	33.5	40.4	1.85	2.22	0.85	6.39	2.37
37	40.7	38.3	43.7	32.7	39.5	1.94	2.32	0.91	6.79	2.53
38	39.8	37.4	42.8	32.0	38.6	2.04	2.42	0.99	7.11	2.71
39	38.8	36.5	41.8	31.2	37.7	2.14	2.52	1.09	7.40	2.92

Health 697

Life Expectancy Tables (continued)

by Race, Sex, and Age

Age (years)	Expectation of life in years					Expected deaths per 1,000 alive at specified age[1]				
		White		All Other			White		All Other	
	Total	Male	Female	Male	Female	Total	Male	Female	Male	Female
40	37.9	35.6	40.9	30.4	36.8	2.25	2.63	1.20	7.69	3.16
41	37.0	34.7	39.9	29.7	35.9	2.38	2.76	1.33	8.02	3.40
42	36.1	33.8	39.0	28.9	35.0	2.53	2.93	1.46	8.38	3.65
43	35.2	32.9	38.0	28.1	34.1	2.71	3.13	1.59	8.78	3.90
44	34.3	32.0	37.1	27.4	33.3	2.92	3.38	1.73	9.23	4.15
45	33.4	31.1	36.1	26.6	32.4	3.15	3.66	1.89	9.69	4.43
46	32.5	30.2	35.2	25.9	31.5	3.41	3.98	2.07	10.19	4.74
47	31.6	29.3	34.3	25.1	30.7	3.71	4.33	2.29	10.80	5.07
48	30.7	28.4	33.4	24.4	29.8	4.05	4.71	2.54	11.53	5.43
49	29.8	27.5	32.4	23.7	29.0	4.43	5.12	2.84	12.37	5.83
50	28.9	26.7	31.5	23.0	28.2	4.85	5.58	3.16	13.30	6.27
51	28.1	25.8	30.6	22.3	27.3	5.31	6.10	3.51	14.25	6.75
52	27.2	25.0	29.7	21.6	26.5	5.84	6.73	3.90	15.21	7.30
53	26.4	24.2	28.8	20.9	25.7	6.43	7.49	4.32	16.14	7.91
54	25.6	23.3	28.0	20.3	24.9	7.08	8.35	4.76	17.07	8.59
55	24.7	22.5	27.1	19.6	24.1	7.79	9.29	5.24	18.04	9.31
56	23.9	21.7	26.2	18.9	23.4	8.55	10.29	5.77	19.09	10.09
57	23.1	21.0	25.4	18.3	22.6	9.37	11.37	6.34	20.27	11.01
58	22.3	20.2	24.6	17.7	21.8	10.27	12.55	6.97	21.61	12.12
59	21.6	19.4	23.7	17.1	21.1	11.23	13.81	7.64	23.10	13.38
60	20.8	18.7	22.9	16.4	20.4	12.27	15.18	8.39	24.68	14.76
61	20.1	18.0	22.1	15.9	19.7	13.37	16.63	9.18	26.36	16.17
62	19.3	17.3	21.3	15.3	19.0	14.52	18.12	10.02	28.15	17.51
63	18.6	16.6	20.5	14.7	18.3	15.69	19.62	10.91	30.07	18.72
64	17.9	15.9	19.7	14.1	17.7	16.91	21.18	11.84	32.12	19.85
65	17.2	15.2	19.0	13.6	17.0	18.20	22.80	12.85	34.31	21.00
70	13.9	12.1	15.3	11.0	13.9	27.31	34.77	20.03	47.63	29.38
75	10.9	9.4	11.9	8.8	11.0	41.31	53.66	31.61	65.79	42.53
80	8.3	7.1	8.9	6.9	8.5	63.71	82.84	51.62	94.32	65.05
85 and over	6.2	5.3	6.5	5.6	6.7	1,000.00	1,000.00	1,000.00	1,000.00	1,000.00

The above figures are based on statistics published in the late 1980s.

[1] Based on the proportion of the cohort who are alive at the beginning of an indicated age interval who will die before reaching the end of that interval. For example, out of every 1,000 people alive and exactly 50 years old at the beginning of the period, between 4 and 5 (4.85) will die before reaching their 51st birthdays.

Deaths and Death Rates

Death Rates, 1970 to 1990, and Deaths, 1970 to 1985, from Selected Causes

Beginning in 1970, the table on the following pages excludes deaths of nonresidents of the United States. The standard population for this table is the total population of the United States enumerated in 1940. Beginning in 1979, deaths are classified according to the ninth revision of *International Classification of Diseases;* for earlier years, they are classified according to the revision in use at that time.

Cause of Death	Deaths (1,000)					Crude Death Rate Per 100,000 Population[2]				
	1970	1980	1985	1989	1990[1] prel.	1970	1980	1985	1989	1990[1] prel.
All causes	**1,921.0**	**1,989.8**	**2,086.4**	**2,150.5**	**2,162.0**	**945.3**	**878.3**	**873.9**	**866.3**	**861.9**
Major cardiovascular diseases	1,008.0	988.5	977.9	931.8	920.4	496.0	436.4	409.6	375.4	366.9
Diseases of the heart	735.5	761.1	771.2	733.9	725.0	362.0	336.0	323.0	295.6	289.0
Percent of total	38.3	38.3	37.0	34.1	33.5	38.3	38.3	37.0	34.1	33.5
Rheumatic fever and rheumatic heart disease	14.9	7.8	6.6	6.1	6.3	7.3	3.5	2.8	2.5	2.5
Hypertensive heart disease[3]	15.0	24.8	23.7	23.3	23.6	7.4	10.9	9.9	9.4	9.4
Ischemic heart disease	666.7	565.8	536.8	498.0	489.3	328.1	249.7	224.8	200.6	195.1
Other diseases of endocardium	6.7	7.2	9.5	12.2	12.3	3.3	3.2	4.0	4.9	4.9
All other forms of heart disease	32.3	155.5	194.6	193.5	15.9	68.7	81.5	78.2	77.1	
Hypertension[3]	8.3	7.8	7.8	8.8	9.2	4.1	3.5	3.2	3.5	3.7
Cerebrovascular diseases	207.2	170.2	153.1	145.6	145.3	101.9	75.1	64.1	58.6	57.9
Atherosclerosis	31.7	29.4	23.9	19.4	16.5	15.6	13.0	10.0	7.8	6.6
Other	25.3	20.0	22.0	24.3	24.4	12.5	8.8	9.2	9.8	9.7
Malignancies[4]	330.7	416.5	461.6	496.2	506.0	162.8	183.9	193.3	199.9	201.7
Percent of total	17.2	20.9	22.1	23.1	23.4	17.2	20.9	22.1	23.1	23.4
Of respiratory and intrathoracic organs	69.5	108.5	127.3	142.3	143.8	34.2	47.9	53.3	57.3	57.3
Of digestive organs and peritoneum	94.7	110.6	116.6	119.7	121.3	46.6	48.8	48.8	48.2	48.4
Of genital organs	41.2	46.4	49.7	55.0	58.0	20.3	20.5	20.8	22.1	23.1
Of breast	29.9	35.9	40.4	43.1	45.1	14.7	15.8	16.9	17.4	18.0
Of urinary organs	15.5	17.8	18.9	20.2	20.4	7.6	7.9	7.9	8.2	8.1
Leukemia	14.5	16.5	17.3	18.2	18.7	7.1	7.3	7.3	7.4	7.4
Accidents and adverse effects	114.6	105.7	93.5	95.0	93.6	56.4	46.7	39.1	38.3	37.3
Motor vehicle	54.6	53.2	45.9	47.6	47.9	26.9	23.5	19.2	19.2	19.1
All other	60.0	52.5	47.6	47.5	45.7	29.5	23.3	19.9	19.1	18.2
Chronic obstructive pulmonary diseases and allied conditions[5]	30.9	56.1	74.7	84.3	89.0	15.2	24.7	31.3	34.0	35.5
Bronchitis, chronic and unspecified	5.8	3.7	3.6	3.8	3.4	2.9	1.6	1.5	1.5	1.3
Emphysema	22.7	13.9	14.2	15.5	16.5	11.2	6.1	5.9	6.2	6.6
Asthma	2.3	2.9	3.9	4.9	4.6	1.1	1.3	1.6	2.0	1.8
Other	([6])	35.6	53.0	6.02	64.6	([6])	15.7	22.2	24.3	25.7
Pneumonia and influenza	62.7	54.6	67.6	76.6	78.6	30.9	24.1	28.3	30.8	31.3
Pneumonia	59.0	51.9	65.6	75.0	76.7	29.0	22.9	27.5	30.2	30.6
Influenza	3.7	2.7	2.1	1.6	1.9	1.8	1.2	0.9	0.6	0.8
Diabetes mellitus	38.3	34.9	37.0	46.8	48.8	18.9	15.4	15.5	18.9	19.5

Cause of Death	Deaths (1,000)					Crude Death Rate Per 100,000 Population[2]				
	1970	1980	1985	1989	1990[1] prel.	1970	1980	1985	1989	1990[1] prel.
Suicide	23.5	26.9	29.5	30.2	30.8	11.6	11.9	12.3	12.2	12.3
Chronic liver disease and cirrhosis	31.4	30.6	26.8	26.7	25.6	15.5	13.5	11.2	10.8	10.2
Other infective and parasitic diseases	6.9	5.1	8.1	29.2	32.2	3.4	2.2	3.4	11.8	12.8
Human immunodeficiency virus (HIV) infection (AIDS)	([7])	([7])	([7])	22.1	24.1	([7])	([7])	([7])	8.9	9.6
Homicide and legal intervention	16.8	24.3	19.9	22.9	25.7	8.3	10.7	8.3	9.2	10.2
Nephritis, nephrotic syndrome, and nephrosis	8.9	16.8	21.3	21.1	20.9	4.4	7.4	8.9	8.5	8.3
Septicemia	3.5	9.4	17.2	19.3	19.8	1.7	4.2	7.2	7.8	7.9
Certain conditions originating in the perinatal period	43.2	22.9	19.2	18.8	17.5	21.3	10.1	8.1	7.6	7.0
Congenital anomalies	16.8	13.9	12.8	12.9	13.4	8.3	6.2	5.4	5.2	5.3
Benign neoplasms[8]	4.8	6.2	6.7	6.7	7.0	2.4	2.7	2.8	2.7	2.8
Ulcer of stomach and duodenum	8.6	6.1	6.6	6.5	6.2	4.2	2.7	2.8	2.6	2.5
Hernia of abdominal cavity and intestinal obstruction[9]	7.2	5.4	5.4	5.5	5.6	3.6	2.4	2.2	2.2	2.2
Anemias	3.4	3.2	3.7	4.0	4.2	1.7	1.4	1.5	1.6	1.7
Cholelithiasis and other disorders of gall bladder	4.0	3.3	3.0	3.0	3.0	2.0	1.5	1.2	1.2	1.2
Nutritional deficiencies	2.5	2.4	2.9	3.0	3.1	1.2	1.0	1.2	1.2	1.2
Tuberculosis	5.2	2.0	1.8	2.0	1.8	2.6	0.9	0.7	0.8	0.7
Infections of kidney	8.2	2.7	2.0	1.4	1.1	4.0	1.2	0.8	0.6	0.4
Viral hepatitis	1.0	0.8	0.9	1.5	1.7	0.5	0.4	0.4	0.6	0.7
Meningitis	1.7	1.4	1.2	1.1	1.2	0.8	0.6	0.5	0.4	0.5
Acute bronchitis and bronchiolitis	1.3	0.6	0.6	0.6	0.6	0.6	0.3	0.3	0.3	0.2
Hyperplasia of prostate	2.2	0.8	0.5	0.4	0.3	1.1	0.3	0.2	0.2	0.1
Symptoms, signs, and ill-defined conditions	25.8	28.8	31.0	27.0	26.3	12.7	12.7	13.0	10.9	10.5
All other causes	108.8	120.0	153.0	171.5	174.1	53.5	53.0	64.4	69.1	69.4

[1]Based on a 10-percent sample of deaths. Includes deaths of nonresidents. [2]1970, 1980, and 1990 based on resident population enumerated as of Apr. 1; 1985 and 1989 estimated as of July 1. Estimates do not reflect revisions based on the 1990 Census of Population. [3]With or without renal disease. [4]Includes other types of malignancies not shown separately. [5]Prior to 1980, data are shown for bronchitis, emphysema, and asthma. [6]Included in "all other causes." Comparable data not available separately. [7]Data are included in several other categories. [8]Includes neoplasms of unspecified nature; beginning 1980 also includes carcinoma in situ. [9]Without mention of hernia.

Cause of Death	Crude death rate per 100,000 population[1]							Deaths (1,000)		
	1960	1970	1980	1984	1985	1989	1990	1970	1980	1985
Diabetes melitus	16.7	18.9	15.4	15.1	15.5	18.8	19.5	38.3	34.9	37.0
Suicide	10.6	11.6	11.9	12.4	12.3	12.6	12.3	23.5	26.9	29.5
Chronic liver disease and cirrhosis	11.3	15.5	13.5	11.6	11.2	10.6	10.2	31.4	30.6	26.8
Nephritis, nephrotic syndrome, and nephrosis	7.6	4.4	7.4	8.5	8.9	8.6	8.3	8.9	16.8	21.3
Homicide and legal intervention	4.7	8.3	10.7	8.4	8.3	9.3	10.2	16.8	24.3	19.9
Certain conditions originating in the perinatal period	37.4	21.3	10.1	8.0	8.1	7.0	7.5	43.2	22.9	19.2
Septicemia	1.1	1.7	4.2	6.4	7.2	7.7	7.9	3.5	9.4	17.2

Cause of Death	Crude death rate per 100,000 population[1]							Deaths (1,000)		
	1960	1970	1980	1984	1985	1989	1990	1970	1980	1985
Congenital anomalies	12.2	8.3	6.2	5.5	5.4	5.1	5.3	16.8	13.9	12.8
Other infective and parasitic diseases	4.3	3.4	2.2	2.9	3.4	3.1	4.2	6.9	5.1	8.1
Benign neoplasms[7]	2.7	2.4	2.7	2.7	2.8	na	na	4.8	6.2	6.7
Ulcer of stomach and duodenum	6.3	4.2	2.7	2.8	2.8	2.7	2.5	8.6	6.1	6.6
Hernia of abdominal cavity and intestinal obstruction[8]	5.1	3.6	2.4	2.2	2.2	2.2	2.2	7.2	5.4	5.4
Anemias	1.9	1.7	1.4	1.5	1.5	na	na	3.4	3.2	3.7
Cholelithiasis and other disorders of gallbladder	2.6	2.0	1.5	1.3	1.2	1.2	1.2	4.0	3.3	3.0
Nutritional deficiencies	([5])	1.2	1.0	1.1	1.2			2.5	2.4	2.9
Infections of kidney	4.3	4.0	1.2	0.9	0.8	0.5	0.4	8.2	2.7	2.0
Tuberculosis	6.1	2.6	0.9	0.7	0.7	0.7	0.7	5.2	2.0	1.8
Meningitis	1.3	0.8	0.6	0.5	0.5	0.4	0.5	1.7	1.4	1.2
Viral hepatitis	0.5	0.5	0.4	0.4	0.4	0.6	0.7	1.0	0.8	0.9
Hyperplasia of prostate	2.5	1.1	0.3	0.2	0.2	0.2	0.1	2.2	0.8	0.5
Acute bronchitis and bronchiolitis	0.7	0.6	0.3	0.2	0.3	0.2	0.2	1.3	0.6	0.6
Symptoms, signs, and ill-defined conditions	11.4	12.7	12.7	12.6	13.0	12.0	10.5	25.8	28.8	31.0
All other causes	39.7	53.3	53.0	59.6	64.4	69.4	69.4	108.8	120.0	153.0

x Not applicable.   *P=provisional   na=not available

[1] Based on resident population enumerated as of April 1 for 1960, 1970, and 1980 and estimated as of July 1 for other years.

[2] With or without renal disease. [3] Includes other types of malignancies not shown separately. [4] Prior to 1980, data are shown for bronchitis, emphysema, and asthma. [5] Included in "all other causes." Comparable data not available separately. [6] Excludes pneumonia of newborn. [7] Includes neoplasm of unspecified nature; beginning in 1980, also includes carcinoma in situ. [8] Without mention of hernia.

Source: U.S. National Center for Health Statistics, *Vital Statistics of the United States,* annual; and unpublished data.

Home Remedies

The following should not be considered medical advice and is presented for informational purposes only. Always consult a doctor for medical problems.

acetaminophen   A painkiller and fever reducer used as a popular alternative to aspirin. It is often equally as effective but has fewer of the side effects of aspirin, such as stomach irritation. Acetaminophen can also be safely used by those allergic to aspirin.

alcohol   A mild antiseptic or germ killer used topically.

ammonia   For fainting, used as "smelling salts" by holding an open container under the victim's nose so vapor can be inhaled. Ammonia can also be used as a counterirritant and to neutralize insect bites.

aspirin   A relatively safe, effective, and inexpensive painkiller and inflammation and fever reducer.

baking soda   Used to neutralize acid burns.

benzalkonium chloride   A detergent-type cleanser and disinfectant for treating wounds.

boric acid   A weak germ and fungus killer, used as dusting powder.

burned toast   Used as a substitute for activated charcoal. (*see* **universal antidote**).

calamine lotion Used for sunburn and minor thermal (heat) burns that do not result in blisters.

chloride of lime (bleaching powder) A disinfectant. Avoid direct contact with the wound.

coffee Used as a stimulant in shock cases if the victim is conscious and bleeding internally.

egg white Used as a demulcent to soothe the stomach and retard absorption of a poison.

epsom salts Dissolved in warm water, can be used in treating wounds and to make wet dressings for them.

flour Made into a thin paste, can be used as a demulcent to soothe the stomach and retard absorption of a poison.

hydrogen peroxide A germ killer when in direct contact with bacteria.

milk Used as a demulcent to soothe the stomach and retard absorption of a poison.

milk of magnesia Used as a substitute for magnesium oxide (*see* **universal antidote**). Milk of magnesia is also used in small doses as an antacid for stomach upset.

mineral oil Used as drops to treat thermal (heat) burns of the eye.

oil of cloves Used for temporary relief of a toothache.

olive oil Used as drops to treat thermal (heat) burns of the eye. Olive oil is also used as an emollient to soften skin.

petrolatum (Vaseline®) A skin softener and protective ointment used on wound dressings.

powdered mustard (dry mustard) Used as an emetic. Dissolve one to three teaspoonfuls in a glass of warm water.

salt *See* **table salt.**

soap suds (not detergents) Used as an emetic and as an antidote for poisoning by certain metal compounds, such as mercuric chloride. Soap and clean water can also be used to cleanse wounds.

starch, cooked Made into a thin paste as a demulcent to soothe the stomach and retard absorption of a poison.

table salt Used as an emetic. Dissolve two teaspoonfuls in a glass of warm water. (Clean sea water can be used if an emetic or a wound cleanser is needed for an accident near an ocean beach.)

tea Made strong, used as a substitute for tannic acid. Tea is also used as a stimulant in shock cases when appropriate.

universal antidote Recommended as an antidote for poisoning when the poison cannot be identified. The universal antidote is made by mixing $1/2$ ounce activated charcoal, $1/4$ ounce magnesium oxide or milk of magnesia, and $1/4$ ounce tannic acid in a glass of water.

Vaseline® *See* **petrolatum.**

vinegar (acetic acid) Used to neutralize alkali burns.

SHELF LIFE OF MEDICINE

Pharmacists generally do not mark containers with expiration dates, though the containers usually show the dates of the original prescriptions. If a prescription drug is more than one year old but is not in its original container clearly showing the expiration date, it should be replaced. First-aid creams in tubes usually have expiration dates marked on the tubes, but the dates are generally hard to see. After the components separate, the creams should not be used. Vitamins and minerals will keep for a long time if protected from heat, moisture, and light. A good rule of thumb about the shelf life of drugs is "When in doubt, throw it out." Below is a list of the shelf life of some common drugs.

Cold tablets	1–2 years
Laxatives	2–3 years
Minerals	6 years or more
Nonprescription painkiller tablets	1–4 years
Prescription antibiotics	2–3 years
Prescription antihypertension tablets	2–4 years
Travel sickness tablets	2 years
Vitamins	6 years or more

Infectious Diseases and How They Are Spread

Disease	Agent	Transmission
AIDS (acquired immune deficiency syndrome)	Virus	Contact of body fluid (semen, blood, vaginal secretions) with that of an infected person. Sexual contact and sharing of unclean paraphernalia for intravenous drugs are the most common means of transmission.
Blastomycosis	Fungus	Inhaling contaminated dust
Botulism	Bacteria	Consuming contaminated food
Chicken pox	Virus	Direct or indirect contact with infected person
Common cold	Virus	Direct or indirect contact with infected person
Diphtheria	Bacteria	Direct contact with infected person
Encephalitis	Virus	Mosquito bite
Gonorrhea	Bacteria	Sexual contact
Hepatitis	Virus	Direct or indirect contact with infected person
Herpes simplex	Virus	Direct contact with infected person
Histoplasmosis	Fungus	Inhaling contaminated dust
Hookworm	Nematode	Contact with contaminated soil
Infectious mononucleosis	Virus	Direct or indirect contact with infected person
Influenza	Virus	Direct or indirect contact with infected person
Lyme disease	Bacteria	Deer tick bite
Malaria	Protozoa	Mosquito bite
Measles	Virus	Direct or indirect contact with infected person
Mumps	Virus	Direct or indirect contact with infected person
Pertussis (whooping cough)	Bacteria	Direct or indirect contact with infected person
Poliomyelitis	Virus	Direct contact with infected person
Rubella (German measles)	Virus	Direct or indirect contact with infected person
Scarlet fever	Bacteria	Direct or indirect contact with infected person
Spotted fever	Rickettsia	Tick bite
Syphilis	Bacteria	Sexual contact
Tapeworm	Nematode	Consuming infected meat or fish
Toxoplasmosis	Protozoa	Consuming raw meat; contact with contaminated soil
Trichomoniasis	Protozoa	Sexual contact
Typhus	Rickettsia	Lice, flea, tick bite
Yellow fever	Virus	Mosquito bite

Combining Forms of Medical Terms

Prefix	Meaning of prefix	Example
a-, ab-, an-	away, lack of, without	astigmatism
acro-	extremity, end	acroparesthesia
adeno-	gland	adenous
adreno-	adrenal gland	adrenocortex
aero-	gas, air	aerophagia
allo-	different, another	allorhythmia
ambi-	both, both sides	ambidextrous
antero-	before, in front of	anterograde
anti-	against	antiseptic
arterio-	artery	arteriospasm
arthro-, arthr-	joint	arthritis
bacterio-	bacteria	bacteriological
blephari-	eyelash, eyelid	blepharitis
brady-	slow	bradycardia
broncho-	windpipe	bronchospasm
cardio-	heart, heart region	cardiovascular
cephalo-	head	cephalometry
cerebro-	brain	cerebrovascular
cervico-	neck	cervicobrachial
chole-	bile	cholecystis
chondro-	cartilage	chondroblastoma
chromo-	color	chromogen
chylo-	lymph	chylomicron
contra-	against, opposite	contraindication
costo-	rib	costochondral
cyst-	bladder, sac	cystitis
dacryo-	tears	dacryocystitis
derma-	skin	dermatitis
dextro-	right side	dextromanual
dys-	abnormal, bad, painful	dysentery
encephalo-, encephal-	brain	encephalitis
endo-	inside	endocardium
entero-	intestines	enterospasm
ep-, epi-	at, over, upon	epiglottis
ex-, exo-	out, outside	excrement
fibrino-	threadlike	fibrinogen
fibro-	fiber, fibrous	fibrocystic
galact-	milk	galactose
gastro-	stomach	gastroenteric
gloss-	tongue	glossitis
hemi-	half	hemiplegic
hepato-	liver	hepatocolic
hydro-	water	hydrocephalic
hyper-	above, beyond	hyperacidity
hypo-	below, less	hypoglycemia

Prefix	Meaning of prefix	Example
ileo-	end of small intestine	ileocolic
ilio-	flank, upper hip bone	iliopelvic
infra-	below, inferior	infraorbital
inter-	between	interdigital
intra-	within	intrauterine
kerat-	cornea, hard tissue	keratoid
laryngo-, larying-	voice box	laryngitis
leuko-, leuk-	white	leukocyte
mega-	abnormally large	megacolon
mela-	black	melanin
myelo-, myel-	marrow, nerve sheath	myelination
myo-	muscle	myospasm
neo-	new	neoplasm
nephro-, nephr-	kidney	nephritis
neuro-, neuri-, neur-	nerve	neuritis
osteo-	bone	osteoarthritis
peri-, pneumo-	around or about the lungs or air	pericardial pneumonia
sacro-	sacrum (triangular bone above tailbone)	sacroiliac
sero-	serum, blood	serofibrous
tachy-	rapid	tachycardia
thrombo-	blood clot	thrombosis
tracheo-	windpipe	tracheotomy
utero-	uterus, womb	uterotomy
vaso-	blood vessel	vasodilator
ventro-	belly, abdominal	ventroptosia
zymo-	enzyme, fermentation	zymocide

Breast Self-Examination (BSE)

It is important for you to know the signs of breast cancer, because most breast cancers are discovered by women themselves, not their doctors. If you discover any of the signs of breast cancer, see your doctor immediately. It is a frightening experience to find a lump or another possible cancer sign, but you should know that 8 of 10 lumps are *not* cancerous. Many women have naturally lumpy breasts. But your doctor should determine whether a lump or other sign is actually cancer or a harmless condition.

Ask for a Breast Exam

Don't be embarrassed. Asking your doctor or nurse for a breast examination as part of an office visit is one good way to learn what is normal for your breasts. But examination by a doctor is not enough—you, too, should examine your breasts monthly. Ask your doctor or nurse to teach you breast self-examination (BSE) to be sure you are practicing it correctly.

Practice Breast Self-Examination

Breast self-examination is an important key to early diagnosis. Along with regular examination by your physician, monthly BSE can give you peace of mind because it helps you know how your breasts normally feel.

Knowing the normal feel of your breasts makes it easier to notice any changes early, when treatment is most effective. To examine your breasts correctly, you should follow the six steps described.

1. Stand before a mirror. Inspect both breasts for anything unusual, such as any discharge from the nipples or puckering, dimpling, or scaling of the skin.

The next two steps are designed to emphasize any changes in the shape or contour of your breasts. As you do them, you should be able to feel your chest muscles tighten.

2. Watching closely in the mirror, clasp hands behind your head and press hands forward.

3. Next, press hands firmly on hips and bow slightly toward the mirror as you pull your shoulders and elbows forward.

Some women do the next part of the exam in the shower: Fingers glide over soapy skin, making it easy to concentrate on the texture underneath.

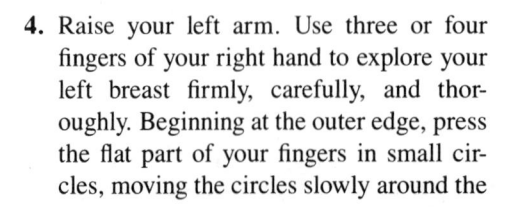

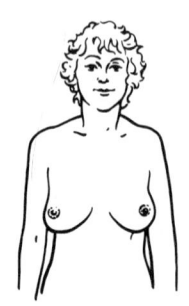

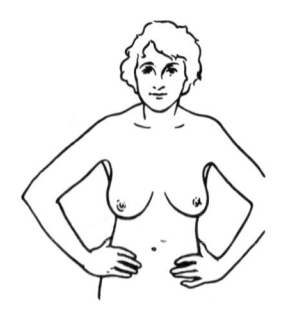

4. Raise your left arm. Use three or four fingers of your right hand to explore your left breast firmly, carefully, and thoroughly. Beginning at the outer edge, press the flat part of your fingers in small circles, moving the circles slowly around the

breast. Gradually work toward the nipple. Be sure to cover the entire breast. Pay special attention to the area between the breast and the armpit, including the armpit itself. Feel for any unusual lump or mass under the skin.

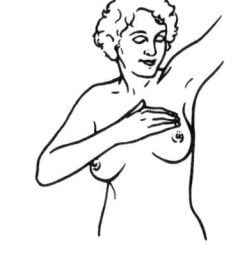

5. Gently squeeze the nipple and look for a discharge. Repeat the exam on your right breast.

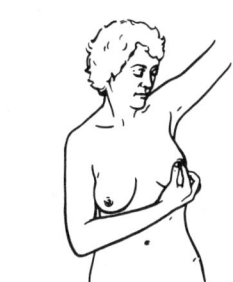

6. Repeat steps 4 and 5 lying down. Lie flat on your back with your left arm over your head and a pillow or folded towel under your left shoulder. This position flattens the breast and makes it easier to examine. Use the same circular motion described earlier. Repeat on your right breast.

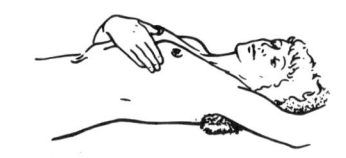

When to Examine Your Breasts

Every month! If you menstruate, the best time to practice BSE is two or three days after the end of your period, when your breasts are least likely to be tender or swollen. If you no longer menstruate, choose a day such as your birthdate to practice BSE. That way, you will remember to do it every month.

When to Get a Mammogram

The National Cancer Institute, the American College of Radiology, and the American Cancer Society recommend regular mammograms for women over 40, either annually, or once every two years, depending on a woman's age and medical history. Detection through mammography screening can lead to early treatment, adding years to the lives of women receiving such treatment.

Unfortunately, only a little more than a third of American women follow these guidelines. Of the 34 million women who do not get mammograms as recommended, about 4 million are expected to contract breast cancer at some point.

Consult your physician for more information about whether it is time for you to get a mammogram.

Recommended Daily Dietary Allowances (RDAs)

Recommended Daily Dietary Allowances (RDAs) of Proteins

	Age	Weight (in pounds)	Heights (in inches)	Grams of protein needed
Males	11–14	99	62	45
	15–18	145	69	59
	19–24	160	70	58
	25–50	174	70	63
	51+	170	68	63
Females	11–14	101	62	46
	15–18	120	64	44
	19–24	128	65	46
	25–50	138	64	50
	51+	143	63	50
Pregnant				65
Nursing				62–65

* In this and the following tables, heights and weights are medians of the U.S. population and are not meant to suggest ideal height-to-weight ratios.

Recommended Daily Dietary Allowances (RDAs) of Fat-Soluble Vitamins (in International Units)

	Age	Weight (in pounds)	(in inches)	Vitamin A	Vitamin D	Vitamin E
Males	11–14	99	62	1,000	10	10
	15–18	145	69	1,000	10	10
	19–24	160	70	1,000	10	10
	25–50	174	70	1,000	5	10
	51+	170	68	1,000	5	10
Females	11–14	101	62	800	10	8
	15–18	120	64	800	10	8
	19–24	128	65	800	10	8
	25–50	138	64	800	5	8
	51+	143	63	800	5	8
Pregnant				800	10	10
Nursing				1,200–1,300	10	11–12

Recommended Daily Dietary Allowances (RDAs) of Water-Soluble Vitamins (in Milligrams)

	Age	Pounds	Height (in inches)	Vitamin C	Folate	Niacin	Riboflavin	Thiamine	Vitamin B_6	Vitamin B_{12}
Males	11–14	99	62	50	150	17	1.5	1.3	1.7	2.0
	15–18	145	69	60	200	20	1.8	1.5	2.0	2.0
	19–24	160	70	60	200	19	1.7	1.5	2.0	2.0
	25–50	174	70	60	200	19	1.7	1.5	2.0	2.0
	51+	170	78	60	200	15	1.4	1.2	2.0	2.0
Females	11–14	101	62	50	150	15	1.3	1.1	1.4	2.0
	15–18	120	64	60	180	15	1.3	1.1	1.5	2.0
	19–24	128	65	60	180	15	1.3	1.1	1.6	2.0
	25–50	138	64	60	180	15	1.3	1.1	1.6	2.0
	51+	143	63	60	180	13	1.2	1.0	1.6	2.0
Pregnant				70	400	17	1.6	1.5	2.2	2.2
Nursing				90–95	260–280	20	1.7–1.8	1.6	2.1	2.6

Recommended Daily Dietary Allowances (RDAs) of Minerals (in Milligrams)

	Age	Pounds	Height (in inches)	Calcium	Phosphorus	Iodine	Iron	Magnesium	Zinc
Males	11–14	99	62	1.200	1.200	150	12	270	15
	15–18	145	69	1.200	1.200	150	12	400	15
	19–24	160	70	1.200	1.200	150	10	350	15
	25–50	174	70	800	800	150	10	350	15
	51+	170	68	800	800	150	10	350	15
Females	11–14	101	62	1.200	1.200	150	15	280	12
	15–18	120	64	1.200	1.200	150	15	300	12
	19–24	128	65	1.200	1.200	150	15	280	12
	25–50	138	64	800	800	150	15	280	12
	51+	143	63	800	800	150	10	280	12
Pregnant				1.200	1.200	175	*30	320	15
				1.200	1.200	200	15	355	16–19

* A pregnant woman often requires iron supplement tablets because of the difficulty of providing an adequate iron intake in an otherwise balanced diet.

Nutritive Values of Foods

Composition of Foods (100 grams, Edible Portion)

Food and description	Water (percent)	Food energy (calories)	Protein (grams)	Fat (grams)	Carbohydrate Total (grams)	Carbohydrate Fiber (grams)	Ash (grams)
Ale, *See* Beverages, alcoholic: Beer							
Almonds, roasted and salted	.7	627	18.6	57.7	19.5	2.6	3.5
Apple butter	51.6	58	.4	.8	46.8	1.1	.4
Apple juice, canned or bottled	87.8	47	.1	Trace	11.9	.1	.2
Apples, raw, fresh, not pared	84.4	58	.2	.6	14.5	1	.3
Apricots, raw	85.3	51	1.0	.2	12.8	.6	.7
Asparagus, cooked spears, boiled, drained	93.6	20	2.2	.2	3.6	.7	.4
Avocados, raw	74	167	2.1	16.4	6.3	1.6	1.2
Baby foods:							
Cereals:							
Barley, added nutrients	6.6	348	13.4	1.2	73.6	1.2	5.2
Oatmeal, added nutrients	7	375	16.5	5.5	66	1.5	5
Desserts, canned:							
Custard pudding	76.5	100	2.3	1.8	18.6	.2	.8
Fruit pudding	75.7	96	1.2	.9	21.6	.3	.6
Dinners, canned:							
Beef noodle	88.2	48	2.8	1.1	6.8	.3	1.1
Cereal, egg yolk, bacon	84.7	82	2.9	4.9	6.6	.1	.9
Beef with vegetables	81.6	87	7.4	3.7	6	.2	1.3
Chicken with vegetables	79.6	100	7.4	4.6	7.2	.2	1.2
Turkey with vegetables	81.3	86	6.7	3.2	7.6	.5	1.2
Veal with vegetables	85	63	7.1	1.6	5.1	.2	1.2
Fruits, canned:							
Applesauce	80.8	72	.2	.2	18.6	.5	.2
Bananas	77.5	84	.4	.2	21.6	.1	.3
Peaches	78.1	81	.6	.2	20.7	.5	.4
Pears	82.2	66	.3	.1	17.1	1	.3
Plums with tapioca	74.8	94	.4	.2	24.3	.3	.3
Prunes with tapioca	76.7	86	.3	.2	22.4	.3	.4
Meats, poultry, and eggs, canned:							
Beef, strained	80.3	99	14.7	4	(0)	(0)	1
Beef heart	81.1	93	13.5	3.8	.4	(0)	1.2
Chicken	77.2	127	13.7	7.6	(0)	(0)	1.5
Lamb, strained	79.3	107	14.6	4.9	(0)	(0)	1.2
Liver, strained	79.7	97	14.1	3.4	1.5	(0)	1.3
Pork, strained	77.7	118	15.4	5.8	(0)	(0)	1.1
Veal, strained	80.7	91	15.5	2.7	(0)	(0)	1.1
Vegetables, canned:							
Beans, green	92.5	22	1.4	.1	5.1	.8	.9
Beets, strained	89.2	37	1.4	.1	8.3	.6	1
Carrots	91.5	29	.7	.1	6.8	.6	.9
Peas, strained	85.5	54	4.2	.2	9.3	.8	.8
Spinach, creamed	88.1	43	2.3	.7	7.5	.4	1.4
Squash	92.1	25	.7	.1	6.2	.8	.9
Sweet potatoes	82.3	67	1.0	.2	15.5	.5	1
Tomato soup, strained	83.4	54	1.9	.1	13.5	.2	1.1

Calcium (milli-grams)	Phosphorus (milli-grams)	Iron (milli-grams)	Sodium (milli-grams)	Potassium (milli-grams)	Vitamin A (international grams)	Thiamine (milli-grams)	Riboflavin (milli-grams)	Niacin (milli-grams)	Ascorbic (milli-grams)
235	504	4.7	198	773	0	.05	.92	3.5	0
14	36	.7	2	252	0	.01	.02	1.2	2
0	9	.6	1	101	—	.01	.02	.1	1
7	10	.3	1	110	90	.03	.02	.1	4
17	23	.5	1	281	2,700	.03	.04	.6	10
21	50	.6	1	183	900	.16	.18	1.4	26
10	42	.6	4	604	290	.11	.20	1.6	14
736	821	53.2	452	413	0	3.71	1.20	32.2	0
757	734	48.2	437	374	0	2.58	1.05	21.3	0
64	62	.3	150	94	100	.02	.12	.1	1
27	34	.3	128	75	100	.03	.05	.1	3
12	29	.5	269	159	620	.02	.05	.5	2
29	60	.8	301	36	520	.05	.06	.4	—
13	84	1.2	304	113	1,100	.07	.17	1.6	2
22	85	.9	265	71	1,000	.09	.15	1.6	2
38	63	.6	348	122	1,000	.13	.13	1.8	2
11	71	.8	323	95	800	.08	.15	2	2
4	7	.4	6	64	40	.01	.02	.1	Trace
13	10	.2	29	118	70	.02	.02	.7	35
6	14	.3		80	500	.01	.02	.7	3
7	8	.2	4	62	30	.02	.02	.2	2
5	12	.4	38	44	250	.01	.02	.2	2
7	21	.9	33	120	400	.02	.06	.4	4
8	127	2	228	183	—	.01	.16	3.5	0
5	155	3.7	208	—	—	.6	.62	3.6	0
—	129	1.9	263	96	—	.02	.16	3.5	0
9	124	2.1	241	181	—	.02	.17	3.3	—
6	182	5.6	253	202	24,000	.05	2.00	7.6	10
8	130	1.5	223	178	—	.19	.20	2.7	—
10	145	1.7	226	214	—	.03	.20	4.3	—
33	25	1.1	213	93	400	.02	.06	.3	3
18	27	.7	212	228	20	.02	.03	.1	3
23	21	.5	169	181	13,000	.02	.03	.4	3
11	63	1.2	194	100	500	.08	.09	1.2	10
64	63	.6	272	142	5,000	.02	.13	.3	6
24	17	.4	292	138	2,400	.02	.04	.3	8
16	34	.4	187	180	4,900	.04	.03	.4	8
24	52	.4	294	200	1,000	.05	.12	.7	3

Food and description	Water (percent)	Food energy (calories)	Protein (grams)	Fat (grams)	Carbohydrate Total (grams)	Carbohydrate Fiber (grams)	Ash (grams)
Bacon, Canadian, broiled or fried, drained	49.9	277	27.6	17.5	.3	0	4.7
Bacon, cured:							
Canned	16.7	685	8.5	71.5	1.0	0	2.3
Broiled or fried, drained	8.1	611	30.4	52	3.2	0	6.3
Baking powders:							
Cream of tartar, with tartaric acid	1.0	78	.1	Trace	18.9	Trace	—
Sodium aluminum sulfate with monocalcium phosphate monohydrate	1.6	129	.1	Trace	31.2	Trace	—
Bamboo shoots, raw	91.0	27	2.6	.3	5.2	.7	.9
Bananas, raw, common	75.7	85	1.1	.2	22.2	.5	.8
Barley, pearled, light	11.1	349	8.2	1.0	78.8	.5	.9
Bass, striped, oven-fried	60.8	196	21.5	8.5	6.7	—	2.5
Beans, common:							
White, cooked	69	118	7.8	.6	21.2	1.5	1.4
Canned, solids and liquids, with pork and tomato sauce	70.7	122	6.1	2.6	19	1.4	1.6
Beans, lima, boiled, drained	71.1	111	7.6	.5	19.8	1.8	1
Beans, snap, green, boiled, drained	92.4	25	1.6	.2	5.4	1	.4
Bean sprouts, mung, boiled, drained	91	28	3.2	.2	5.2	.7	.4
Beef:							
Chuck, choice, braised or pot-roasted (81% lean, 19% fat)	49.4	327	26	23.9	0	0	.7
Corned, cooked, medium fat	43.9	372	22.9	30.4	0	0	2.9
Hamburger:							
Lean, cooked	60.0	219	27.4	11.3	0	0	1.3
Regular, cooked	54.2	286	24.2	0	0	0	1.3
Ribs, roasted (55% lean, 45% fat)	36.3	481	18.3	44.7	0	0	.7
T-bone steak, choice, broiled (56% lean, 44% fat)	36.4	473	19.5	43.2	0	0	.9
Beef greens, common, boiled, drained	93.6	18	1.7	.2	3.3	1.1	1.2
Beets, boiled, drained	90.1	32	1.1	.1	7.2	.8	.7
Beverages, alcoholic:							
Beer, alcohol 4.5% by volume (3.6% by weight)	92.1	42	.3	0	3.8	—	.2
Gin, rum, vodka, whiskey:							
80-proof (33.4% alcohol by weight)	66.6	231	—	—	Trace	—	—
86-proof (36.0% alcohol by weight)	64	249	—	—	Trace	—	—
90-proof (37.9% alcohol by weight)	62.1	262	—	—	Trace	—	—
94-proof (39.7% alcohol by weight)	60.3	275	—	—	Trace	—	—
100-proof (42.5% alcohol by weight)	57.5	295	—	—	Trace	—	—
Wines:							
Dessert, alcohol 18.8% by volume (15.3% by weight)	76.7	137	1	0	7.7	—	.2

Calcium (milli-grams)	Phosphorus (milli-grams)	Iron (milli-grams)	Sodium (milli-grams)	Potassium (milli-grams)	Vitamin A (international grams)	Thiamine (milli-grams)	Riboflavin (milli-grams)	Niacin (milli-grams)	Ascorbic (milli-grams)
19	218	4.1	2,555	432	(0)	.92	.17	5	—
15	92	1.4	—	—	(0)	.23	.10	1.5	—
14	224	3.3	1,021	236	(0)	.51	.34	5.2	—
0	0	0	7,300	3,800	(0)	(0)	(0)	(0)	(0)
1,932	2,904	—	10,953	150	(0)	(0)	(0)	(0)	(0)
13	59	.5	—	533	20	.15	.07	.6	4
8	26	.7	1	370	190	.05	.06	.7	10
16	189	2	3	160	(0)	.12	.05	3.1	(0)
—	—	—	—	—	—	—	—	—	—
50	148	2.7	7	416	0	.14	.07	.7	0
54	92	1.8	463	210	130	.08	.03	.6	2
47	121	2.5	1	422	280	.18	.10	1.3	17
50	37	.6	4	151	540	.07	.09	.5	12
17	48	.9	4	156	20	.09	.10	.7	6
11	140	3.3	60	370	40	.05	.20	4	—
9	93	2.9	1,740	150	—	.02	.18	1.5	0
12	230	3.5	48	558	20	.09	.23	6	—
11	194	3.2	47	450	40	.09	.21	5.4	—
8	153	2.4	60	370	90	.05	.14	3.4	—
8	166	2.6	60	370	80	.06	.16	4.1	—
99	25	1.9	76	332	5,100	.07	.15	.3	15
14	23	.5	43	208	20	.03	.04	.3	6
5	30	Trace	7	25	—	Trace	.03	.6	—
—	—	—	1	2	—	—	—	—	—
—	—	—	1	2	—	—	—	—	—
—	—	—	1	2	—	—	—	—	—
—	—	—	1	2	—	—	—	—	—
—	—	—	1	2	—	—	—	—	—
8	—	—	4	75	—	.01	.02	.2	—

Food and description	Water (percent)	Food energy (calories)	Protein (grams)	Fat (grams)	Carbohydrate Total (grams)	Carbohydrate Fiber (grams)	Ash (grams)
Table, alcohol 12.2% by volume (9.9% by weight)	85.6	85	.1	0	4.2	—	.2
Beverages, carbonated, nonalcoholic:							
Cola	90	39	(0)	(0)	10	(0)	—
Ginger ale	92	31	(0)	(0)	8	(0)	—
Root beer	89.5	41	(0)	(0)	10.5	(0)	—
Biscuits, baking powder, baked with enriched flour	27.4	369	7.4	17	45.8	.2	2.4
Blackberries, canned, solids and liquid, juice pack	85.8	54	.8	.8	12.1	2.7	.5
Blueberries, canned, solids and liquid, water pack	89.3	39	.5	.2	9.8	1	.2
Bouillon cubes or powder	4	120	20	3	5	—	68
Bran flakes (40% bran), added thiamine	3	303	10.2	1.8	80.6	3.6	4.4
Brazil nuts	4.6	654	14.3	66.9	10.9	3.1	3.3
Breads:							
White:							
Enriched, with 1% to 2% nonfat dry milk	35.8	269	8.7	3.2	50.4	.2	1.9
Toasted	25.3	314	10.1	3.7	58.7	.2	2.2
Whole-wheat, with 2% nonfat dry milk	36.4	243	10.5	3.0	47.7	1.6	2.4
Toasted	24.3	289	12.5	3.6	56.7	1.9	2.9
Broccoli spears, boiled, drained	91.3	26	3.1	.3	4.5	1.5	.8
Bulgur, dry, from hard red winter wheat	10	354	11.2	1.5	75.7	1.7	1.6
Buns. *See* Rolls and buns							
Butter	15.5	716	.6	81	.4	0	2.5
Buttermilk, fluid, cultured (from skim milk)	90.5	36	3.6	.1	5.1	0	.7
Cabbage, common:							
Raw	92.4	24	1.3	.2	5.4	.8	.7
Shredded, boiled, drained	93.9	20	1.1	.2	4.3	.8	.5
Cakes:							
Baked from home recipes:							
Angelfood	31.5	269	7.1	.2	60.2	0	1
Boston cream pie	34.5	302	5	9.4	49.9	0	1.2
Chocolate with chocolate icing	22	369	4.5	16.4	55.8	.3	1.3
Fruitcake, dark, with enriched flour	18.1	379	4.8	15.3	59.7	.6	2.1
White, without icing	24.2	375	4.6	16	54	.1	1.2
Candy:							
Chocolate:							
Bittersweet	1.8	477	7.9	39.7	46.8	1.8	2.3
Fudge	8.2	400	2.7	12.2	75	.2	1.8
Semisweet	1.1	507	4.2	35.7	57	1	1.2
Sweet	.9	528	4.4	35.1	57.9	.5	1.2
Hard	1.4	386	0	1.1	97.2	0	.3

Calcium (milligrams)	Phosphorus (milligrams)	Iron (milligrams)	Sodium (milligrams)	Potassium (milligrams)	Vitamin A (international grams)	Thiamine (milligrams)	Riboflavin (milligrams)	Niacin (milligrams)	Ascorbic (milligrams)
9	10	.4	5	92	—	Trace	.01	.1	—
—	—	—	—	—	(0)	(0)	(0)	(0)	(0)
—	—	—	—	—	(0)	(0)	(0)	(0)	(0)
—	—	—	—	—	(0)	(0)	(0)	(0)	(0)
121	175	1.6	626	117	Trace	.21	.21	1.8	Trace
25	17	.9	1	170	150	.02	.03	.3	10
10	9	.7	1	60	40	.01	.01	.2	7
—	—	—	24,000	100	—	—	—	—	—
71	495	4.4	925	—	(0)	.40	.17	6.2	(0)
186	693	3.4	1	715	Trace	.96	.12	1.6	—
70	87	2.4	507	85	Trace	.25	.17	2.3	Trace
81	101	2.8	590	99	Trace	.23	.20	2.7	Trace
99	228	2.3	527	273	Trace	.26	.12	2.8	Trace
118	271	2.7	627	325	Trace	.25	.15	3.4	Trace
88	62	.8	10	267	2,500	.09	.20	.8	90
29	338	3.7	—	229	(0)	.28	.14	4.5	(0)
20	16	0	987	23	3,300	—	—	—	0
121	95	Trace	130	140	Trace	.04	.18	.1	1
49	29	.4	20	233	130	.05	.05	.3	47
44	20	.3	14	163	130	.04	.04	.3	33
9	22	.2	283	88	0	.01	.14	.2	0
	101	.5	186	89	210	.03	.11	.2	Trace
70	131	1	235	154	160	.02	.10	.2	Trace
72	113	2.6	158	496	120	.13	.14	.8	Trace
63	91	.2	323	76	30	.01	.08	.2	Trace
58	284	5	3	615	40	.03	.17	1	0
77	84	1	190	147	Trace	.02	.09	.2	Trace
30	150	2.6	2	325	20	.01	.08	.5	0
90	142	1.4	33	269	19	.02	.14	.3	Trace
21	7	1.9	32	4	0	0	0	0	0

Food and description	Water (percent)	Food energy (calories)	Protein (grams)	Fat (grams)	Carbohydrate Total (grams)	Carbohydrate Fiber (grams)	Ash (grams)
Jelly beans	6.3	367	Trace	.5	93.1	Trace	.1
Marshmallows	17.3	319	2.0	Trace	80.4	0	.3
Peanut brittle	2	421	5.7	10.4	81	.5	.9
Carrots:							
Raw	88.2	42	1.1	.2	9.7	1	.8
Boiled, drained	91.2	31	.9	.2	7.1	1	.6
Cauliflower:							
Raw	91	27	2.7	.2	5.2	1	.9
Boiled, drained	92.8	22	2.3	.2	4.1	1	.6
Celery, raw	94.1	17	.9	.1	3.9	.6	1
Cheeses:							
Cheddar	37	398	25	32.2	2.1	0	3.7
Cottage, creamed	78.3	106	13.6	4.2	2.9	0	1
Cream	51	374	8	37.7	2.1	0	1.2
Parmesan	30	393	36	26	2.9	0	5.1
Pasteurized process, American	40	370	23.2	30	1.9	0	4.9
Cherries:							
Canned, sour, red, solids and liquid, water pack	88	43	.8	.2	10.7	.1	.3
Raw, sweet	80.4	70	1.3	.3	17.4	.4	.6
Chestnuts, fresh	52.8	194	2.9	1.5	42.1	1.1	1
Chewing gum	3.5	317	—	—	95.2	—	1.3
Chicken:							
Roasted light meat without skin	63.8	166	31.6	3.4	0	0	1.2
Roasted dark meat without skin	64.4	176	28	6.3	0	0	1.2
Chili con carne, canned:							
With beans	72.4	133	7.5	6.1	12.2	.6	1.8
Without beans	66.9	200	10.3	14.8	5.8	.2	2.2
Chocolate syrup, fudge type	25.4	330	5.1	13.7	54	.4	1.4
Clams, raw, soft, meat only	80.8	82	14	1.9	1.3	—	2
Cocoa, dry powder, high-fat, plain	3	299	16.8	23.7	48.3	4.3	5
Coconut meat:							
Dried, unsweetened	3.5	662	7.2	64.9	23	3.9	1.4
Fresh	50.9	346	3.5	35.3	9.4	4	.9
Cod, broiled	64.6	170	28.5	5.3	0	0	—
Coffee, instant, water-soluble solids:							
Beverage	98.1	1	Trace	Trace	Trace	Trace	.1
Dry powder	2.6	129	Trace	Trace	(35.)	Trace	9.7
Coleslaw, with mayonnaise	79	144	1.3	14	4.8	.7	.9
Cookies:							
Assorted, packaged, commercial	2.6	480	5.1	20.2	71	.1	1.1
Chocolate chip, home recipe, with enriched flour	3	516	5.4	30.1	60.1	.4	1.4
Oatmeal with raisins	2.8	451	6.2	15.4	73.5	.4	2.1
Corn, sweet, boiled, drained, white and yellow, kernels, cut off cob before cooking	76.5	83	3.2	1	18.8	.7	.5

Health 717

Calcium (milligrams)	Phosphorus (milligrams)	Iron (milligrams)	Sodium (milligrams)	Potassium (milligrams)	Vitamin A (international grams)	Thiamine (milligrams)	Riboflavin (milligrams)	Niacin (milligrams)	Ascorbic (milligrams)
12	4	1.1	12	1	0	0	Trace	Trace	0
18	6	1.6	39	6	0	0	Trace	Trace	0
35	95	2.3	31	151	0	.16	.03	3.4	0
37	36	.7	47	341	11,000	.06	.05	.6	8
33	31	.6	33	222	10,500	.05	.05	.5	6
25	56	1.1	13	295	60	.11	.10	.7	78
21	42	.7	9	206	60	.09	.08	.6	55
39	28	.3	126	341	240	.03	.03	.3	9
750	478	1.0	700	82	(1,130)	.03	.46	.1	(0)
94	152	.3	229	85	(170)	.03	.25	.1	(0)
62	95	.2	250	74	(1,540)	(.02)	.24	.1	(0)
1,140	781	.4	734	149	(1,060)	.02	.73	.2	(0)
697	771	.9	1,136	80	(1,220)	.02	.41	Trace	(0)
15	13	.3	2	130	680	.03	.02	.2	5
22	19	.4	2	191	110	.05	.06	.4	10
27	88	1.7	6	454	—	.22	.22	6	—
—	—	—	—	—	(0)	(0)	(0)	(0)	(0)
11	265	1.3	64	411	60	.04	.10	11.6	—
13	229	1.7	86	321	150	.07	.23	5.6	—
32	126	1.7	531	233	60	.03	.07	1.3	—
38	152	1.4	—	—	150	.02	.12	2.2	—
127	159	1.3	89	284	150	.04	.22	.4	Trace
—	183	3.4	36	235	—	—	—	—	—
133	648	10.7	6	1,522	30	.11	.46	2.4	0
26	187	3.3	—	585	0	.06	.04	.6	0
13	95	1.7	23	256	0	.05	.02	.5	3
31	274	1	110	407	180	.08	.11	3	—
2	4	.1	1	36	0	0	Trace	.3	0
179	383	5.6	72	3,256	0	0	.21	30.6	0
44	29	.4	120	199	160	.05	.05	.3	29
37	163	.7	365	67	80	.03	.05	.4	Trace
34	99	2.1	348	117	110	.11	.11	.9	Trace
21	102	2.9	162	370	50	.11	.08	.5	Trace
3	89	.6	Trace	165	400	.11	.10	1.3	7

Food and description	Water (percent)	Food energy (calories)	Protein (grams)	Fat (grams)	Carbohydrate Total (grams)	Carbohydrate Fiber (grams)	Ash (grams)
Cornbread, southern style, with whole-ground cornmeal	53.9	207	7.4	7.2	29.1	.5	2.4
Cornflour	12	368	7.8	2.6	76.8	.7	.8
Corn grits, degermed, enriched, cooked	87.1	51	1.2	.1	11	.1	.6
Cornstarch	12	362	.3	Trace	87.6	.1	.1
Crackers, saltines	4.3	433	9	12	71.5	.4	3.2
Cranberry sauce, sweetened, canned, strained	62.1	146	.1	.2	37.5	.2	.1
Cream:							
Half-and-half	79.7	134	3.2	11.7	4.6	0	.6
Heavy whipping	56.6	352	2.2	37.6	3.1	0	.4
Cress, garden, raw	89.4	32	2.6	.7	5.5	1.1	1.8
Cucumbers, raw, not pared	95.1	15	.9	.1	3.4	.6	.5
Dates, domestic, natural and dry	22.5	274	2.2	.5	72.9	2.3	1.9
Doughnuts:							
Cake-type, enriched flour	23.7	391	4.6	18.6	51.4	.1	1.7
Yeast-leavened, enriched flour	28.3	414	6.3	26.7	37.7	.2	1
Eggs, chicken:							
Fried	67.7	216	13.8	17.2	.3	0	1
Poached	73.3	163	12.7	11.6	.8	0	1.4
Scrambled	72.1	173	11.2	12.9	2.4	0	1.4
Endive, raw	93.1	20	1.7	.1	4.1	.9	1
Fats, cooking (vegetable fat)	0	884	0	100	0	0	0
Figs, dried, uncooked	23	274	4.3	1.3	69.1	5.6	2.3
Frankfurters. *See* Sausage							
Fruit cocktail, canned, solids and liquid, light syrup pack	83.6	60	.4	.1	15.7	.4	.2
Gelatin dessert, with water, plain	84.2	59	1.5	0	14.1	0	.2
Goose, domesticated, roasted	39.1	426	23.7	36.0	0	0	1.2
Grapefruit, raw, pulp, all varieties	88.4	41	.5	.1	10.6	.2	.4
Grape juice, canned or bottled	82.9	66	.2	Trace	16.6	Trace	.3
Haddock, dipped in egg, milk, and breadcrumbs, fried	66.3	165	19.6	6.4	5.8	—	1.9
Halibut, Atlantic and Pacific, broiled	66.6	171	25.2	7	0	0	1.7
Ham. *See* Pork							
Herring, pickled, Bismarck type	59.4	223	20.4	15.1	0	0	4
Hickory nuts	3.3	673	13.2	68.7	12.8	1.9	2
Horseradish, prepared	87.1	38	1.3	.2	9.6	.9	1.8
Ice cream and frozen custard:							
Regular, about 10% fat	63.2	193	4.5	10.6	20.8	0	.9
Rich, about 16% fat	62.8	222	2.6	16.1	18.0	0	.5
Ice cream cones	8.9	377	10	2.4	77.9	.2	.8
Jams and preserves	29	272	.6	.1	70	1.0	.3
Kale, boiled, drained, leaves and stems	91.2	28	3.2	.7	4	1.1	.9
Kidneys, beef, braised	53	252	33	12	.8	0	1.2
Leg of lamb, lean, roasted	61.6	192	28.6	7.7	0	0	2.1

Health 719

Calcium (milligrams)	Phosphorus (milligrams)	Iron (milligrams)	Sodium (milligrams)	Potassium (milligrams)	Vitamin A (international grams)	Thiamine (milligrams)	Riboflavin (milligrams)	Niacin (milligrams)	Ascorbic (milligrams)
120	211	1.1	628	157	150	.13	.19	.6	1
6	(164)	1.8	(1)	—	340	.20	.06	1.4	(0)
1	10	.3	—	11	60	.04	.03	.4	(0)
(0)	(0)	(0)	Trace	Trace	(0)	(0)	(0)	(0)	(0)
20	90	1.2	(1,100)	(120)	(0)	.01	.04	1	(0)
6	4	.2	1	30	20	.01	.01	Trace	2
108	85	Trace	46	129	480	.03	.16	.1	1
75	59	Trace	32	89	1,540	.02	.11	Trace	1
81	76	1.3	14	606	9,300	.08	.26	1	69
25	27	1.1	6	160	250	.03	.04	.2	11
59	63	3	1	648	50	.09	.10	2.2	0
40	190	1.4	501	90	80	.16	.16	1.2	Trace
38	76	1.5	234	80	60	.16	.17	1.3	0
60	222	2.4	338	140	1,420	.10	.30	.1	0
55	203	2.2	271	128	1,170	.08	.25	.1	0
80	189	1.7	257	146	1,080	.08	.28	.1	0
81	54	1.7	14	294	3,300	.07	.14	.5	10
0	0	0	0	0	—		0	0	0
126	77	3	34	640	80	.10	.10	.7	(0)
9	12	.4	5	164	140	.02	.01	.5	2
—	—	—	51	—	—	—	—	—	—
(11)	(240)	(2.1)	—	—	—	(.08)	(.24)	(8.1)	—
16	16	.4	1	135	80	.04	.02	.2	38
11	12	.3	2	116	—	.04	.02	.2	Trace
40	247	1.2	177	348	—	.04	.07	3.2	2
16	248	.8	134	525	680	.05	.07	8.3	—
—	—	—	—	—	—	—	—	—	—
Trace	360	2.4	—	—	—	—	—	—	—
61	32	.9	96	290	—	—	—	—	—
146	115	.1	63	181	440	.04	.21	.1	1
78	61	Trace	33	95	660	.02	.11	.1	1
156	198	.4	232	244	Trace	.05	.21	.5	Trace
20	9	1	12	88	10	.01	.03	.2	2
134	46	1.2	43	221	7,400	—	—	—	62
18	244	13.1	253	324	1,150	.51	4.82	10.7	—
12	237	2.2	290	290	—	.16	.30	6.1	—

Food and description	Water (percent)	Food energy (calories)	Protein (grams)	Fat (grams)	Carbohydrate Total (grams)	Carbohydrate Fiber (grams)	Ash (grams)
Lemonade concentrate, frozen, diluted with 4$^1/_3$ parts water, by volume	88.5	44	.1	Trace	11.4	Trace	Trace
Lemon juice, raw	91	25	.5	.2	8	Trace	.3
Lemon peel, candied	17.4	316	.4	.3	80.6	2.3	—
Lentils, whole, cooked	72	106	7.8	Trace	19.3	1.2	.9
Lettuce, raw, Boston, Bibb	95.1	14	1.2	.2	2.5	.5	1
Liver, beef, fried	56	229	26.4	10.6	5.3	0	1.7
Lobster, northern, canned or cooked	76.8	95	18.7	1.5	.3	—	2.7
Macadamia nuts	3	691	7.8	71.6	15.9	2.5	1.7
Macaroni, enriched, cooked (tender stage)	72	111	3.4	.4	23	.1	1.2
Mackerel, Atlantic, canned, solids and liquid	66	183	19.3	11.1	0	0	3.2
Mackerel, Pacific, canned, solids and liquid	66.4	180	21.1	10	0	0	2.5
Mangoes, raw	81.7	66	.7	.4	16.8	.9	.4
Margarine	15.5	720	.6	81	.4	0	2.5
Marmalade, citrus	29	257	.5	.1	70.1	.4	.3
Milk, cow's:							
Canned:							
Condensed (sweetened)	27.1	321	8.1	8.7	54.3	0	1.8
Evaporated (unsweetened)	73.8	137	7	7.9	9.7	0	1.6
Dry, skim, instant	4	359	35.8	.7	51.6	0	7.9
Fluid:							
Skim	90.5	36	3.6	.1	5.1	0	.7
Whole, 3.7% fat	87.4	65	3.5	3.5	4.9	0	.7
Milk, human, U.S. samples	85.2	77	1.1	4	9.5	0	.2
Molasses, cane, light	24	252	—	—	65	—	6.3
Mushrooms, canned, solids and liquid	93.1	17	1.9	.1	2.4	.6	1.6
Muskmelons:							
Cantaloupes	91.2	30	.7	.1	7.5	.3	.5
Honeydews	90.6	33	.8	.3	7.7	.6	.6
Mussels, Atlantic and Pacific, raw, meat and liquid	83.8	66	9.6	1.4	3.1	—	2.1
Mustard, prepared, yellow	80.2	75	4.7	4.4	6.4	1	4.3
Mustard greens, boiled, drained	92.6	23	2.2	.4	4	.9	.8
Nectarines, raw	81.8	64	.6	Trace	17.1	.4	.5
Noodles, egg, enriched, cooked	70.4	125	4.1	1.5	23.3	.1	.7
Oatmeal, cooked	86.5	55	2	1	9.7	.2	.8
Ocean perch, Atlantic (redfish), dipped in egg, milk, and breadcrumbs, fried	59	227	19	13.3	6.8	0	1.9
Okra, boiled, drained	91.1	29	2	.3	6	1	.6
Oleomargarine. See Margarine							
Olives:							
Green	78.2	116	1.4	12.7	1.3	1.3	6.4
Ripe, salt-cured, oil-coated, Greek-style	43.8	338	2.2	35.8	8.7	3.8	(9.5)

Calcium (milligrams)	Phosphorus (milligrams)	Iron (milligrams)	Sodium (milligrams)	Potassium (milligrams)	Vitamin A (international grams)	Thiamine (milligrams)	Riboflavin (milligrams)	Niacin (milligrams)	Ascorbic (milligrams)
1	1	Trace	Trace	16	Trace	Trace	.01	.1	7
7	10	.2	1	141	20	.03	.01	.1	46
—	—	—	—	—	—	—	—	—	—
25	119	2.1	—	249	20	.07	.06	.6	0
35	26	2	9	264	970	.06	.06	.3	8
11	476	8.8	184	380	53,400	.26	4.19	16.5	27
65	192	.8	210	180	—	.10	.07	—	—
48	161	2.0	—	264	0	.34	.11	1.3	0
8	50	.9	1	61	(0)	.14	.08	1.1	(0)
185	274	2.1	—	—	430	.06	.21	5.8	—
260	288	2.2	—	—	30	.03	8.8	—	
10	13	.4	7	189	4,800	.05	.05	1.1	35
20	16	0	987	23	3,300	—	—	—	0
35	9	.6	14	33	—	.02	.02	.1	6
262	206	.1	112	314	360	.08	.38	.2	1
252	205	.1	118	303	320	.04	.34	.2	1
1,293	1,005	.6	526	1,725	30	.35	1.78	.9	7
121	95	Trace	52	145	Trace	.04	.18	.1	1
118	93	Trace	50	144	140	.03	.17	.1	1
33	14	.1	16	51	240	.01	.04	.2	5
165	45	4.3	15	917	—	.07	.06	.2	—
6	68	.5	400	197	Trace	.02	.25	2.0	2
14	16	.4	12	251	3,400	.04	.03	.6	33
14	16	.4	12	251	40	.04	.03	.6	23
—	—	—	—	—	—	—	—	—	—
84	73	2	1,252	130	—	—	—	—	—
138	32	1.8	18	220	5,800	.08	.14	.6	48
4	24	.5	6	294	1,650	—	—	—	13
10	59	.9	2	44	70	.14	.08	1.2	(0)
9	57	.6	218	61	(0)	.08	.02	.1	(0)
33	226	1.3	153	284	—	.10	.11	1.8	—
92	41	.5	2	174	490	(.13)	(.18)	(.9)	20
61	17	1.6	2,400	55	300	—	—	—	—
—	29	—	3,288	—	—	—	—	—	—

Food and description	Water (percent)	Food energy (calories)	Protein (grams)	Fat (grams)	Carbohydrate Total (grams)	Carbohydrate Fiber (grams)	Ash (grams)
Onions, mature (dry):							
Boiled, drained	91.8	29	1.2	.1	6.5	.6	.4
Raw	89.1	38	1.5	.1	8.7	.6	.6
Onions, young green, raw, bulb and entire top	89.4	36	1.5	.2	8.2	(1.2)	.7
Opossum, roasted	57.3	221	30.2	10.2	0	0	2.3
Orange juice:							
Frozen concentrate, unsweetened:							
Diluted with 3 parts water, by volume	88.1	45	.7	.1	10.7	Trace	.4
Undiluted	58.2	158	2.3	.2	38	.2	1.3
Raw, all commercial varieties	88.3	45	.7	.2	10.4	.1	.4
Orange peel, candied	17.4	316	.4	.3	80.6	—	1.3
Oranges, all commercial varieties, peeled	86	49	1	.2	12.2	.5	.6
Oysters:							
Raw, meat only:							
Dipped in egg, milk, and breadcrumbs, fried	54.7	239	8.6	13.9	18.6	Trace	1.5
Eastern	84.6	66	8.4	1.8	3.4	—	1.8
Pacific and Western (Olympia)	79.1	91	10.6	2.2	6.4	—	1.7
Pancakes, home recipe, enriched flour	50.1	231	7.1	7	34.1	.1	1.7
Papayas, raw	58.7	39	.6	.1	10	.9	.6
Parsley, raw	85.1	44	3.6	.6	8.5	1.5	2.2
Parsnips, boiled, drained	82.2	66	1.5	.5	14.9	2	.9
Peaches:							
Canned, solids and liquid, heavy syrup pack	79.1	78	.4	.1	20.1	.4	.3
Raw	89.1	38	.6	.1	9.7	.6	.5
Peanut butter, with small amounts of added fat, salt	1.8	581	27.8	49.4	17.2	1.9	3.8
Peanuts:							
Raw, without skins	5.4	568	26.3	48.4	17.6	1.9	2.3
Roasted, salted	1.6	585	26.0	49.8	18.8	2.4	3.8
Pears:							
Canned, solids and liquid, heavy syrup pack	79.8	76	.2	.2	19.6	.6	.2
Raw, including skin	83.2	61	.7	.4	15.3	1.4	.4
Peas, green, immature:							
Boiled, drained	81.5	71	5.4	.4	12.1	2	.6
Canned:							
Alaska, regular pack, solids and liquids	82.6	66	3.5	.3	12.5	1.5	1.1
Low-sodium pack, solids and liquids	85.9	55	3.6	.3	9.8	1.3	.4
Peppers, sweet, immature, green, raw	93.4	22	1.2	.2	4.8	1.4	.4
Persimmons, native, raw	64.4	127	.8	.4	33.5	1.5	.9

Health **723**

Calcium (milligrams)	Phosphorus (milligrams)	Iron (milligrams)	Sodium (milligrams)	Potassium (milligrams)	Vitamin A (international grams)	Thiamine (milligrams)	Riboflavin (milligrams)	Niacin (milligrams)	Ascorbic (milligrams)
24	29	.4	7	110	40	.03	.03	.2	7
27	36	.5	10	157	40	.03	.04	.2	10
51	39	1	5	231	(2,000)	.05	.05	.4	32
—	—	—	—	—	—	.12	.38	—	—
9	16	.1	1	186	200	.09	.01	.3	45
33	55	.4	2	657	710	.30	.05	1.2	158
11	17	.2	1	200	200	.09	.03	.4	50
—	—	—	—	—	—	—	—	—	—
41	20	.4	1	200	200	.10	.04	.4	(50)
152	241	8.1	206	203	440	.17	.29	3.2	—
94	143	5.5	73	121	310	.14	.18	2.5	—
85	153	7.2	—	—	—	.12	—	1.3	30
101	139	1.3	425	123	120	.17	.22	1.3	Trace
20	16	.3	3	234	1,750	.04	.04	.3	56
203	63	6.2	45	727	8,500	.12	.26	1.2	172
45	62	.6	8	379	30	.07	.08	.1	10
4	12	.3	2	130	430	.01	.02	.6	3
9	19	.5	1	202	1,330	.02	.05	1	7
63	407	2	607	670	—	.13	.13	15.7	0
59	409	2	5	674	0	.99	.13	15.8	0
74	401	2.1	418	674	—	.32	.13	17.2	0
5	7	.2	1	84	Trace	.01	.02	.1	1
8	11	.3	2	130	20	.02	.04	.1	4
23	99	1.8	1	196	540	.28	.11	2.3	20
20	66	1.7	236	96	450	.09	.05	.9	
20	66	1.7	3	96	450	.09	.05	.9	9
9	22	.7	13	213	420	.08	.08	.5	128
27	26	2.5	1	310	—	—	—	—	66

Food and description	Water (percent)	Food energy (calories)	Protein (grams)	Fat (grams)	Carbohydrate Total (grams)	Carbohydrate Fiber (grams)	Ash (grams)
Pickles:							
Cucumber:							
Dill	93.3	11	.7	.2	2.2	.5	3.6
Fresh (as bread-and-butter pickles)	78.7	73	.9	.2	17.9	.5	2.3
Sour	94.8	10	.5	.2	2	.5	2.5
Pies:							
Baked, piecrust with unenriched flour:							
Apple	47.6	256	2.2	11.1	38.1	.4	1
Chocolate meringue	48.4	252	4.8	12	33.5	.2	1.2
Pecan	19.5	418	5.1	22.9	51.3	.5	1.2
Raisin	42.5	270	2.6	10.7	43	.3	1.2
Rhubarb	47.4	253	2.5	10.7	38.2	.6	1.2
Pimientos, canned, solids and liquid	92.4	27	.9	.5	5.8	.6	.4
Pineapple:							
Candied	18	316	.8	.4	80	.8	.8
Raw	85.3	52	.4	.2	13.7	.4	.4
Pineapple juice, canned, unsweetened	85.6	55	.4	.1	13.5	.1	.4
Pizza, with cheese, home recipe, sausage topping	50.6	234	7.8	9.3	29.6	.3	2.7
Plantain, raw	66.4	119	1.1	.4	31.2	.4	.9
Plums, raw, Damson	81.1	66	.5	Trace	17.8	.4	.6
Pollock, cooked, creamed (with flour, butter, milk)	74.7	128	13.9	5.9	4	—	1.5
Popcorn, popped, oil and salt added	3.1	456	9.8	21.8	59.1	1.7	6.2
Pork, fresh:							
Bacon:							
Fat class (25% lean, 75% fat)	26.4	631	7.1	66.6	0	0	.3
Thin class (40% lean, 60% fat)	34.3	545	9.4	56	0	0	.5
Composite of trimmed lean cuts (ham, loin, shoulder, spareribs):							
Medium-fat class (77% lean, 23% fat), roasted	45.2	373	22.6	30.6	0	0	1.6
Ham, roasted (72% lean, 28% fat)	43.7	394	21.9	33.3	0	0	1
Potato chips	1.8	568	5.3	39.8	50	(1.6)	3.1
Potatoes:							
Baked in skin	75.1	93	2.6	.1	21.1	.6	1.1
Boiled in skin	79.8	76	2.1	.1	17.1	.5	.9
French-fried	44.7	274	4.3	13.2	36	1	1.8
Potato salad, home recipe, with mayonnaise and French dressing, hard-cooked eggs, seasonings	72.4	145	3	9.2	13.4	.4	2
Pretzels	4.5	390	9.8	4.5	75.9	.3	5.3
Prunes, cooked, fruit and liquid, added sugar	50.7	180	1.2	.2	47.1	(.8)	.8
Puddings, starch base, home recipe							
Chocolate	65.8	148	3.1	4.7	25.7	.2	.7

Calcium (milli-grams)	Phosphorus (milli-grams)	Iron (milli-grams)	Sodium (milli-grams)	Potassium (milli-grams)	Vitamin A (international grams)	Thiamine (milli-grams)	Riboflavin (milli-grams)	Niacin (milli-grams)	Ascorbic (milli-grams)
26	21	1	1,428	200	100	Trace	.02	Trace	6
32	27	1.8	673	140	—	Trace	.03	Trace	9
17	15	3.2	1,353	—	100	Trace	.02	Trace	7
8	22	.3	301	80	30	.02	.02	.4	1
69	98	.7	256	139	190	.03	.12	.2	Trace
47	103	2.8	221	123	160	.16	.07	.3	Trace
18	40	.9	285	192	Trace	.03	.03	.3	1
64	26	.7	270	159	50	.02	.04	.3	3
7	17	1.5	—	—	2,300	.02	.06	.4	95
—	—	—	—	—	—	—	—	—	—
17	8	.5	1	146	70	.09	.03	.2	17
15	9	.3	1	149	50	.05	.02	.2	9
17	92	1.2	729	168	560	.09	.12	1.5	9
7	30	.7	5	385	—	.06	.04	.6	14
18	17	.5	2	299	(300)	.08	.03	.5	—
—	—	—	111	238	—	.03	.13	.7	Trace
8	216	2.1	1,940	—	—	—	.09	1.7	0
4	62	1.1	*	—	(0)	.35	.08	1.8	—
5	92	1.4	*	—	(0)	.46	.11	2.4	—
10	232	2.9	*	—	(0)	.50	.23	4.9	—
10	225	2.9	*	—	(0)	.49	.22	4.4	—
40	139	1.8	—	1,130	Trace	.21	.07	4.8	16
9	65	.7	—	503	Trace	.10	.04	1.7	20
7	53	.6	—	407	Trace	.90	.04	1.5	16
15	111	1.3	—	853	Trace	.13	.08	3.1	21
19	63	.8	480	296	180	.07	.06	.9	11
22	131	1.5	1,680	130	(0)	.02	.03	.7	(0)
31	37	1.5	4	329	760	.03	.07	.7	1
96	98	.5	56	171	150	.02	.14	.1	Trace

Food and description	Water (percent)	Food energy (calories)	Protein (grams)	Fat (grams)	Carbohydrate Total (grams)	Carbohydrate Fiber (grams)	Ash (grams)
Vanilla (blancmange)	76	111	3.5	3.9	15.9	Trace	.7
Pumpkin, canned	90.2	33	1	.3	7.9	1.3	.6
Raccoon, roasted	54.8	255	29.2	14.5	0	0	1.5
Radishes, raw, common	94.5	17	1	.1	3.6	.7	.8
Raisins, natural, uncooked	18	289	2.5	.2	77.4	.9	1.9
Raspberries, raw, black	80.8	73	1.5	1.4	15.7	5.1	.6
Rhubarb, cooked, added sugar	62.8	141	.5	.1	36	.6	.6
Rice, white, enriched, commercial, cooked	72.6	109	2	.1	24.2	.1	1.1
Rice products, breakfast:							
Flakes, added nutrients	3.2	390	5.9	.3	87.7	.6	2.9
Puffed or oven-popped, presweetened, honey, added nutrients	1.8	388	4.2	.7	90.6	.2	2.7
Rolls and buns, commercial, ready-to-serve							
Danish pastry	22	422	7.4	23.5	45.6	.1	1.5
Plain pan rolls, enriched	31.4	298	8.2	5.6	53	.2	1.8
Salad dressings, commercial:							
Blue and Roquefort cheese	32.2	504	4.8	52.3	7.4	.1	3.2
French, low fat	77.3	96	.4	4.3	15.6	.3	2.4
Italian	27.5	552	.2	60	6.9	Trace	5.4
Mayonnaise	15.1	718	1.1	79.9	2.2	Trace	1.7
Mayonnaise-type	40.6	435	1	42.3	14.4	—	1.7
Thousand Island	32	502	.8	50.2	15.4	.3	1.6
Salami, *See* Sausage							
Salmon, broiled or baked	63.4	182	27	7.4	0	0	1.6
Sauerkraut, canned, solids and liquid	92.8	18	1.0	.2	4.0	.7	2
Sausage, cold cuts, and luncheon meats:							
Brown-and-serve sausage, browned	39.9	422	16.5	37.8	2.8	0	3
Frankfurters, cooked	57.3	304	12.4	27.2	1.6	—	1.5
Liverwurst, smoked	52.6	319	14.8	27.4	2.3	0	2.9
Meatloaf	64.1	200	15.9	13.2	3.3	0	3.5
Polish-style sausage	53.7	304	15.7	25.8	1.2	0	3.6
Pork sausage, links or bulk, cooked	34.8	476	18.1	44.2	Trace	0	2.9
Salami, dry	29.8	450	23.8	38.1	1.2	0	7.1
Scrapple	61.3	215	8.8	13.6	14.6	.1	1.7
Vienna sausage, canned	63	240	14	19.8	.3	0	2.9
Scallops, bay and sea:							
Raw	79.8	81	15.3	.2	3.3	—	1.4
Steamed	73.1	112	23.2	1.4	—	—	—
Sesame seeds, dry, whole	5.4	563	18.6	49.1	21.6	6.3	5.3
Shad, baked with butter or margarine and bacon slices	64	201	23.2	11.3	0	0	1.4
Sherbet, orange	67	134	.9	1.2	30.8	0	.4
Shrimp:							
French-fried, dipped in egg, breadcrumbs, and flour, or butter	56.9	225	20.3	10.8	10	—	2

Calcium (milligrams)	Phosphorus (milligrams)	Iron (milligrams)	Sodium (milligrams)	Potassium (milligrams)	Vitamin A (international grams)	Thiamine (milligrams)	Riboflavin (milligrams)	Niacin (milligrams)	Ascorbic (milligrams)
117	91	Trace	65	138	160	.03	.16	.1	1
25	26	.4	2	240	6,400	.03	.05	.6	5
—	—	—	—	—	—	.59	.52	—	—
30	31	1	18	322	10	.03	.03	.3	26
62	101	3.5	27	763	20	.11	.08	.5	1
30	22	.9	1	199	Trace	(.03)	(.09)	(.9)	18
78	15	.6	2	203	80	(.02)	(.05)	(.3)	6
10	28	.9	374	28	(0)	.11	—	1	(0)
29	132	1.6	987	180	(0)	.35	.05	4.4	(0)
46	74	.9	706	—	(0)	.33	—	4.6	(0)
50	109	.9	366	112	310	.07	.15	.8	Trace
74	85	1.9	506	95	Trace	.28	.18	2.2	Trace
81	74	.2	1,094	37	210	.01	.10	.1	2
11	14	.4	787	79	—	—	—	—	—
10	4	.2	2,092	15	Trace	Trace	Trace	Trace	—
18	28	.5	597	34	280	.02	.04	Trace	—
14	26	.2	586	9	220	.01	.03	Trace	—
11	17	.6	700	113	320	.02	.03	.2	3
—	414	1.2	116	443	160	.16	.06	9.8	—
36	18	.5	747	140	50	.03	.04	.2	14
—	—	—	—	—	—	—	—	—	—
5	102	1.5	—	—	—	.15	.20	2.5	—
10	245	5.9	—	—	6,530	.17	1.44	8.2	—
9	178	1.8	—	—	—	.13	.22	2.5	—
9	176	2.4	—	—	(0)	.34	.19	3.1	—
7	162	2.4	958	269	(0)	.79	.34	3.7	—
14	283	3.6	—	—	—	.37	.25	5.3	—
5	64	1.2	—	—	—	.19	.09	1.8	—
8	153	2.1	—	—	—	.08	.13	2.6	—
26	208	1.8	255	396	—	—	.06	1.3	—
115	338	3	265	476	—	—	—	—	—
1,160	616	10.5	60	725	30	.98	.24	5.4	0
24	313	.6	79	377	30	.13	.26	8.6	—
16	13	Trace	10	22	60	.01	.03	Trace	2
72	191	2	186	229	—	.04	.08	2.7	—

		Food			Carbohydrate		
Food and description	Water (percent)	energy (calories)	Protein (grams)	Fat (grams)	Total (grams)	Fiber (grams)	Ash (grams)
Raw	78.2	91	18.1	.8	1.5	—	1.4
Syrups:							
Cane	26	263	0	0	68	0	1.5
Maple	33	252	—	—	65	—	.7
Sorghum	23	257	—	—	68	—	2.4
Table blends, chiefly light and dark corn syrup	24	290	0	0	75	0	.7
Soups, commercial, canned, prepared with equal volume of water:							
Bean with pork	84.4	67	3.2	2.3	8.7	.6	1.4
Beef noodle	93.2	28	1.6	1.1	2.9	Trace	1.2
Celery, cream of	92.3	36	.7	2.1	3.7	.2	1.2
Chicken, cream of	91.9	39	1.2	2.4	3.3	.1	1.2
Clam chowder, Manhattan type	91.9	33	1	5	.2	1.2	
Minestrone	89.5	43	2	1.4	5.8	.3	1.3
Mushroom, cream of	89.6	56	1	4	4.2	.1	1.2
Pea, split	85.4	59	3.5	1.3	8.4	.2	1.4
Tomato	90.5	36	.8	1	6.4	2	1.3
Vegetable beef	91.9	32	2.1	.9	3.9	.2	1.2
Vegetable with beef broth	91.7	32	1.1	.7	5.5	.3	1
Soybean flour, full-fat	8	421	36.7	20.2	30.4	2.4	4.6
Soybean milk, fluid	92.4	33	3.4	1.5	2.2	0	.5
Soybeans, cooked, dry mature seeds	71	130	11	5.7	10.8	1.6	1.5
Spaghetti, enriched:							
Cooked, firm (8–10 min.)	63.6	148	5	.5	30.1	.1	1.3
Cooked, tender (14–20 min.)	72	111	3.4	.4	23	.1	1.2
In tomato sauce with cheese, home recipe	77	104	3.5	3.5	14.8	.2	1.2
With meatballs, in tomato sauce, home recipe	70	134	7.5	4.7	15.6	.3	2.2
Spinach, boiled, drained	92	23	3	.3	3.6	.6	1.1
Squash:							
Summer:							
All varieties, boiled, drained	95.5	14	.9	.1	3.1	.6	.4
Winter: Butternut, baked	79.6	68	1.8	.1	17.5	1.8	1
Zucchini and Cocozelle, green	96	12	1.0	.1	2.5	.6	.4
Starch. See Cornstarch							
Strawberries, raw	89.9	37	.7	.5	8.4	1.3	.5
Sugar, beet or cane:							
Brown	2.1	373	0	0	96.4	0	1.5
Granulated	.5	385	0	0	99.5	0	Trace
Powdered	.5	385	0	0	99.5	0	Trace
Sunflower seed kernels, dry	4.8	580	24	47.3	19.9	3.8	4
Sweetbreads, beef, braised	49.6	320	25.9	23.2	0	0	1.3
Sweet potatoes, baked in skin	63.7	141	2.1	.5	32.5	.9	1.2
Swordfish, broiled, with butter or margarine	64.6	174	28	6	0	0	1.7

Calcium (milligrams)	Phosphorus (milligrams)	Iron (milligrams)	Sodium (milligrams)	Potassium (milligrams)	Vitamin A (international grams)	Thiamine (milligrams)	Riboflavin (milligrams)	Niacin (milligrams)	Ascorbic (milligrams)
63	166	1.6	140	220	—	.02	.03	3.2	—
60	29	3.6	—	425	0	.13	.06	.1	0
104	8	1.2	10	176	—	—	—	—	0
172	25	12.5	—	—	—	—	.10	.1	—
46	16	4.1	68	4	0	0	0	0	0
25	51	.9	403	158	260	.05	.03	.4	1
3	20	.4	382	32	20	.02	.03	.4	Trace
20	15	.2	398	45	80	.01	.02	Trace	Trace
10	14	.2	404	33	170	.01	.02	.2	Trace
14	19	.4	383	75	360	.01	.01	.4	—
15	24	.4	406	128	960	.03	.02	.4	—
17	21	.2	398	41	30	.01	.05	.3	Trace
12	16	.6	384	110	180	.10	.06	.6	Trace
6	14	.3	396	94	410	.02	.02	.5	5
5	20	.3	427	66	1,100	.02	.02	.4	—
8	16	.3	345	98	1,300	.02	.01	.5	—
199	558	8.4	1	1,660	110	.85	.31	2.1	0
21	48	.8	—	—	40	.08	.03	.2	0
73	179	2.7	2	540	30	.21	.09	.6	0
11	65	1.1	1	79	(0)	.18	.10	1.4	(0)
8	50	.9	1	61	(0)	.14	.08	1.1	(0)
32	54	.9	(382)	163	430	.10	.07	.9	5
50	95	1.5	407	268	640	.10	.12	1.6	9
93	38	2.2	50	324	8,100	.07	.14	.5	28
25	25	.4	1	141	390	.05	.08	.8	10
40	72	1	1	609	6,400	.05	.13	.7	8
25	25	.4	1	141	300	.05	.08	.8	9
21	21	11	1	164	60	.03	.07	.6	59
85	19	3.4	30	344	0	.01	.03	.2	0
0	0	.1	1	3	0	0	0	0	0
0	0	.1	1	3	0	0	0	0	0
120	837	7.1	30	920	50	1.96	.23	5.4	—
—	364	—	116	433	—	—	—	—	—
40	58	.9	12	300	8,100	.09	.07	.7	22
27	275	1.3	—	—	2,050	.04	.05	10.9	—

Food and description	Water (percent)	Food energy (calories)	Protein (grams)	Fat (grams)	Carbohydrate Total (grams)	Carbohydrate Fiber (grams)	Ash (grams)
Tapioca cream pudding	71.8	134	5	5.1	17.1	0	1
Tea, instant, beverage	99.4	2	—	Trace	.4	Trace	Trace
Tomatoes, ripe:							
Canned, solids and liquid	93.7	21	1	.2	4.3	.4	.8
Raw	93.5	22	1.1	.2	4.7	.5	.5
Tomato juice, canned or bottled	93.6	19	.9	.1	0	4.3	.2
Tongue, beef, medium-fat, braised	60.8	244	21.5	16.7	.4	0	.6
Tuna, canned:							
In oil, drained solids	60.6	197	28.8	8.2	0	0	2
In water, solids and liquid	70	127	28	.8	0	0	1.2
Turkey, all classes, total edible, roasted	55.4	263	27	16.4	0	0	1.2
Turnip greens, boiled, drained	93.2	20	2.2	.2	3.6	.7	.8
Turnips, boiled, drained	93.6	23	.8	.2	4.9	.9	.5
Walnuts, black	3.1	628	20.5	59.3	14.8	1.7	2.3
Watercress	93.3	19	2.2	.2	3	.7	1.2
Whale meat, raw	70.9	156	20.6	7.5	0	0	1
Wheat flour, whole (from hard wheats)	12	333	13.3	2	71	2.3	1.7
Whisky. See Beverages, alcoholic							
Wine. See Beverages, alcoholic							
Yogurt:							
Made from partially skimmed milk	89	50	3.4	1.7	5.2	0	.7
Made from whole milk	88	62	3	3.4	4.9	0	.7
Zucchini. See Squash							
Zwieback	5	423	10.7	8.8	74.3	.3	1.2

Calcium (milli- grams)	Phosphorus (milli- grams)	Iron (milli- grams)	Sodium (milli- grams)	Potassium (milli- grams)	Vitamin A (interna- tional grams)	Thiamine (milli- grams)	Riboflavin (milli- grams)	Niacin (milli- grams)	Ascorbic (milli- grams)
105	109	.4	156	135	290	.04	.18	.1	1
Trace	—	Trace	—	25	—	—	.01	Trace	—
6	19	.5	130	217	900	.05	.03	.7	17
13	27	.5	3	244	900	.06	.04	.7	23
7	18	.9	200	227	800	.05	.03	.8	16
7	117	2.2	61	164	—	.05	.29	3.5	—
(8)	234	1.9	—	—	80	.05	.12	11.9	—
16	190	1.6	41	279	—	—	.10	13.3	—
—	—	—	—	—	—	—	—	—	—
184	37	1.1	—	—	6,300	.15	.24	.6	69
35	24	.4	34	188	Trace	.04	.05	.3	22
Trace	570	6.0	3	460	300	.22	.11	.7	—
151	54	1.7	52	282	4,900	.08	.16	.9	79
12	144	—	78	22	1,860	.09	.08	—	6
41	372	3.3	3	370	(0)	.55	.12	4.3	(0)
120	94	Trace	51	143	70	.04	.18	.1	1
111	87	Trace	47	132	140	.03	.16	.1	1
13	69	.6	250	150	40	.05	.07	.9	(0)

* Average value per 100 g of pork of all cuts is 70 mg for raw meat and 65 mg for cooked meat.

Vitamin/Food Chart
(best food sources for each vitamin)

Vitamin	Chief functions	Results of deficiency	Characteristics	Good sources	Recommended daily allowances
Vitamin A Provitamin, carotene	Essential for maintaining the integrity of epithelial membranes; helps maintain resistance to infections; necessary for the formation of rhodopsin and prevention of night blindness	*Mild:* Retarded growth; increased susceptibility to infection; abnormal function of gastrointestinal, genitourinary, and respiratory tracts due to altered epithelial membranes; dry, shriveled, thickened skin, sometimes pustule formation; night blindness *Severe:* Xerophthalmia, a characteristic eye disease, and other local infections	Fat-soluble; not destroyed by ordinary cooking temperatures; destroyed by high temperatures when oxygen is present; marked capacity for storage in liver NOTE: Excessive intake of carotene, from which vitamin A is formed, may produce yellow discoloration of the skin (carotenemia).	Animal fats (butter, cheese, cream, egg yolk, whole milk; fish liver oil; liver; vegetables (green leafy, especially escarole, kale, and parsley, and yellow, especially carrots) *Artificial:* Concentrates in several forms; irradiated fish oils	Males *(11–51+ yrs.):* 1,000 mg retinol equivalents Females *(11–51+ yrs.):* 800 mg retinol equivalents In pregnancy: 1000 mg retinol equivalents In lactation: 1200 mg retinol equivalents Children: 400–700 mg retinol equivalents Infants: 400 mg retinol equivalents
Thiamine Vitamin B$_1$	Important role in carbohydrate metabolism; essential for maintenance of normal digestion and appetite; essential for normal functioning of nervous tissue	*Mild:* Loss of appetite; impaired digestion of starches and sugars; colitis, constipation, or diarrhea; emaciation *Severe:* Nervous disorders of various types; loss of coordinating power of muscles; beriberi; paralysis	Water-soluble; not readily destroyed by ordinary cooking temperature; destroyed by exposure to heat, alkali, or sulfites; not stored in body	Widely distributed in plant and animal tissues but seldom occurs in high concentration, except in brewer's yeast; other good sources are wholegrain cereals, peas, beans, peanuts, oranges, heart, liver, kidney, many vegetables and fruits, and nuts	Males *(11–51+ yrs.):* 1.2–1.5 mg Females *(11–51+ yrs.):* 1.0–1.1 mg In pregnancy: 1.4–1.6 mg In lactation: 1.5–1.7 mg

Thiamine (*cont.*)			*Artificial:* Concentrates from yeast; rice polishings; wheat germ	*Children:* 0.7–1.2 mg *Infants:* 0.3–0.5 mg
RIBOFLAVIN Vitamin B$_2$	Important in formation of certain enzymes and in cellular oxidation; normal growth; prevention of cheilosis and glossitis	Impaired growth; lassitude and weakness; cheilosis; glossitis, atrophy of skin; anemia; photophobia; cataracts	Water-soluble; alcohol-soluble; not destroyed by heat in cooking unless with alkali; unstable in light, especially in presence of alkali	Eggs, green vegetables, liver, kidney, lean meat, milk, wheat germ, dried yeast, enriched foods	*Males (11–51+ yrs.):* 1.4–1.7 mg *Females (11–51+ yrs.):* 1.2–1.3 mg *In pregnancy:* 1.6 mg
NIACIN Nicotinic acid Nicotinamide Antipellagra vitamin	As the component of two important enzymes, it is important in glycolysis, tissue respiration, and fat synthesis; nicotinic acid but not nicotinamide causes vasodilation and flushing; prevents pellagra	Pellagra; gastrointestinal disturbances; mental disturbances	Soluble in hot water and alcohol; not destroyed by heat, light, air, or alkali; not destroyed in ordinary cooking	Yeast, lean meat, fish, legumes, whole-grain cereals and peanuts, enriched foods	*Males 11–51+ yrs.):* 16–19 mg *Females (11–51+ yrs.):* 13–15mg *In pregnancy:* 17 mg *In lactation:* 20 mg *Children:* 9–16 mg *Infants:* 6–8 mg
VITAMIN B$_{12}$ Cyanoco-balamin	Produces remission in pernicious anemia; essential for normal development of red blood cells	Pernicious anemia	Soluble in water or alcohol; unstable in hot alkaline or acid solutions	Liver, kidney, dairy products; most of vitamin required by humans is synthesized by intestinal bacteria	*Males and females (11–51+ yrs.):* 3 mcg *In pregnancy:* 4 mcg *In lactation:* 5 mcg *Children:* 2–5 mcg *Infants:* 1–2 mcg

Vitamin/Food Chart (continued)

Vitamin	Chief functions	Results of deficiency	Characteristics	Good sources	Recommended daily allowances
VITAMIN C Ascorbic acid	Essential to formation of intracellular cement substances in a variety of tissues including skin, dentin, cartilage, and bone matrix; important in healing of wounds and fractures of bones; prevents scurvy; facilitates absorption of iron	*Mild:* Lowered resistance to infections; joint tenderness; susceptibility to dental caries, pyorrhea, and bleeding gums *Severe:* Hemorrhage; anemia; scurvy	Soluble in water; easily destroyed by oxidation and heat hastens the process; lost in cooking, particularly if water in which food was cooked is discarded; loss is greater if cooked in iron or copper utensils; quick-frozen foods lose little; stored in the body to a limited extent	Abundant in most fresh fruits and vegetables, especially citrus fruit and juices, tomatoes and oranges *Artificial:* Ascorbic acid; cevitamic acid	*Males (11–51+ yrs.):* 50–60 mg *Females (11–51+ yrs.):* 50–60 mg *In pregnancy:* 80 mg *In lactation:* 100 mg *Children:* 45 mg *Infants:* 35 mg The infant diet is likely to be deficient in vitamin C unless orange or tomato juice or another form is added.
VITAMIN D	Regulates absorption of calcium and phosphorus from the intestinal tract; antirachitic	*Mild:* Interferes with utilization of calcium and phosphorus in bone and teeth formation; irritability; weakness *Severe:* Rickets may be common in young children; osteomalacia in adults	Soluble in fats and organic solvents; relatively stable under refrigeration; stored in liver; often associated with vitamin A	Butter, egg yolks, fish liver oils, fish having fat distributed through the flesh, such as salmon, tuna fish, herring, and sardines, liver, oysters, yeast, and foods irradiated with ultraviolet light; formed in the skin by exposure to sunlight; artificially prepared forms exist	*Males and Females (11–51+ yrs.):* 200–400 IU;* after age 22, none except during pregnancy or lactation *In pregnancy:* 400–600 IU *In lactation:* 400–600 IU *Children:* 400 IU *Infants:* 400 IU

VITAMIN E Alpha tocopherol	Normal reproduction in rats; prevention of muscular dystrophy in rats	Red blood cell resistance to rupture is decreased	Fat soluble Stable to heat in absence of oxygen	Lettuce and other green, leafy vegetables, wheat germ oil, margarine, rice	*Males* *(11–51+ yrs.):* 8–10 mg α-tocopherol *Females* *(11–51+ yrs.):* 8 mg α-tocopherol *In pregnancy:* 10 mg α-tocopherol *In lactation:* 11 mg α-tocopherol *Children:* 10–15 IU* *Infants:* 5 IU*
VITAMIN B$_6$ Pyridoxine	Essential for metabolism of tryptophan; needed for utilization of certain other amino acids	Dermatitis around eyes and mouth; neuritis; anorexia; nausea and vomiting	Soluble in water and alcohol; rapidly inactivated in presence of heat, sunlight, or air	Blackstrap molasses, meat, cereal grains, wheat germ	*Males and Females* *(11–51+ yrs.):* 1.8–2.2 mg *In pregnancy:* 2.6 mg *In lactation:* 2.5 mg *Children:* 0.9–1.6 mg *Infants:* 0.3–0.6 mg
FOLACIN	Essential for normal functioning of hematopoietic system	Anemia	Slightly soluble in water; easily destroyed by heat in presence of acid; decreases when food is stored at room temperature NOTE: A large dose may prevent the appearance of anemia in a case of pernicious anemia but still permits neurological symptoms to develop.	Glandular meats, yeast, green, leafy vegetables	*Males and Females* *(11–51+ yrs.):* 0.4 mg *In pregnancy:* 800 mg *In lactation:* 500 mg *Children:* 100–300 mg *Infants:* 30–45 mg

* International Units

VACCINES

Vaccines are disease-specific immunizations. The period of effectiveness for common vaccines is shown below:

Vaccine	Immunization Period
Combination (diphtheria, tetanus toxoids, and whooping cough)	5–10 years
Diphtheria (antitoxin)	2–3 months
Diphtheria (toxoid)	5–10 years
Measles (attenuated virus)	Over 10 years
Measles (immune blood serum, gamma globulin, or placental extract)	A few weeks
Mumps (attenuated virus)	Probably life
Poliomyelitis (dead or attenuated virus)	Unknown
Rabies (attenuated virus)	Unknown
Rubella (attenuated virus)	Unknown
Tetanus (antitoxin)	A few weeks
Tetanus (toxoid)	5–10 years
Typhoid (dead germs)	2–3 years
Whooping cough (dead germs)	2–5 years

Activities and the Calories They Consume

For a person weighing approximately 150 pounds

Activity	Calories expended per hour
Rest and light activity	*50–200*
Lying down or sleeping	80
Sitting	100
Typing	110
Driving	120
Standing	140
Housework	180
Shining shoes	185
Moderate activity	*200–350*
Bicycling (5½ mph)	210
Walking (2½ mph)	210
Gardening	220
Canoeing (2½ mph)	230
Golf (foursome)	250
Lawn-mowing (power mower)	250
Fencing	300
Rowing a boat (2½ mph)	300

Activity	Calories expended per hour
Swimming (¼ mph)	300
Calisthenics	300
Walking (3¼ mph)	300
Badminton	350
Horseback riding (trotting)	350
Square dancing	350
Volleyball	350
Roller-skating	350
Stacking heavy objects (boxes, logs)	350
Vigorous activity	*over 350*
Baseball pitching	360
Ditch-digging (hand shovel)	400
Ice-skating (10 mph)	400
Chopping or sawing wood	400
Bowling (continuous)	400
Tennis	420
Water-skiing	480
Hill-climbing (100 feet per hour)	490
Basketball	500
Football	500
Skiing (10 mph)	600
Squash and handball	600
Bicycling (13 mph)	660
Rowing (machine)	720
Scull-rowing (race)	840
Running (10 mph)	900

Safe Alcohol Consumption

The effects of drinking alcoholic beverages depend in part on the amount of actual ethyl alcohol consumed and one's body weight. The level of alcohol in the blood is calculated in terms of milligrams (1 milligram = $1/_{28,350}$ of an ounce) of pure alcohol per deciliter (1 deciliter = 3.5 fluid ounces) of blood. This is usually expressed as mg/dl. Twelve ounces of beer, 4 ounces of wine, or a 1.5-ounce shot of 80-proof whiskey, gin, or vodka contain approximately the same amount of ethyl alcohol, 8 grams, or 8,000 mg.

Blood alcohol concentrations often are expressed as a percentage of blood, as .05 percent for 50 milligrams of alcohol per deciliters (dl) of blood. It is recommended that drinkers keep their blood alcohol concentration (BAC) below .04 percent.

Depending on body weight and other factors, it takes the average adult nearly one hour for his or her liver to metabolize (break down) 8 grams of alcohol. Alcohol tends to accumulate in the blood because it is absorbed faster than it is metabolized.

Alcohol is absorbed through the membranes of the mouth and esophagus, from the stomach, and from the intestines. The rate of absorption is affected by proteins, fats, and carbohydrates in the digestive tract, which can slow absorption; by carbonation in drink mixers, which increases absorption; by the amount of water added to dilute the alcoholic beverage or the water or soft drinks consumed between alcoholic beverages; and by the presence of congeners (chemicals such as methyl alcohol, tannins, and histamines) present in the type of alcoholic beverage being consumed. The health of the drinker is also important, as a healthy liver metabolizes alcohol more efficiently.

A blood level of 20 to 30 mg/dl (the equivalent of .02 to .03 percent, or one or two drinks for an average adult) causes central nervous system changes in behavior, coordination, and ability to think clearly. Because alcohol is an anesthetic, the drinker may not notice the changes in his or her own behavior.

At a blood level of 50 mg/dl (.05 percent), the drinker may experience sedation or a tranquilized feeling. Between 50 and 150 mg/dl (.05 to .15 percent), there is a definite loss of coordination.

A concentration of 80 to 100 mg/dl (.08 to .10 percent) is considered evidence of "legal intoxication" in many states, even though the alcohol level may be estimated by a breath test rather than actual blood analysis.

At blood levels between 150 and 200 mg/dl (.15 and .20 percent), a person is obviously intoxicated and may show signs of delirium.

At levels between 300 and 400 mg/dl (.30 and .40 percent), the drinker usually loses consciousness.

At an alcohol blood level above 500 mg/dl (.50 percent), the heart and respiration become so depressed that they cease to function, and death follows.

Drinking and Driving

It is unsafe to drink and drive; in addition, many states have very strict driving while intoxicated (DWI) laws. The following chart is intended as a general guideline of how long to wait after imbibing before driving a motor vehicle. The time varies, however, from person to person, and the best rule is "Don't drink and drive." In the following chart, one drink equals 1½ ounces of liquor (86 proof) or 4 ounces of wine or champagne or 12 ounces of beer.

Body Weight (pounds)	1 drink	2 drinks	3 drinks	4 drinks	5 drinks	6 drinks
100–119	0 hours	3 hours	6 hours	10 hours	13 hours	16 hours
120–139	0 hours	2 hours	5 hours	8 hours	10 hours	12 hours
140–159	0 hours	2 hours	4 hours	6 hours	8 hours	10 hours
160–179	0 hours	1 hour	3 hours	5 hours	7 hours	9 hours
180–199	0 hours	0 hours	2 hours	4 hours	6 hours	7 hours
200–219	0 hours	0 hours	2 hours	3 hours	5 hours	6 hours
Over 219	0 hours	0 hours	1 hours	3 hours	4 hours	6 hours

Additional Sources of Information

Organizations and Services

Alcoholics Anonymous World Services Office
468 Park Avenue South
New York, NY 10016

The American Academy of Allergy and Immunology
611 East Wells Street
Milwaukee, WI 53202

American Diabetes Association
149 Madison Avenue
New York, NY 10016

American Heart Association
New York City Affiliate
205 East 42nd Street
New York, NY 10017

American Lung Association
1740 Broadway
New York, NY 10019

American Medical Association
515 North State Street
Chicago, IL 60610

Cancer Information Clearinghouse
National Cancer Institute
9000 Rockville Pike
Building 31, Room 10A18
Bethesda, MD 20205

Cancer Information Service
National Cancer Institute
9000 Rockville Pike
Bethesda, MD 20205

Center for Science in the Public Interest
1501 16th Street, NW
Washington, DC 20036

Centers for Disease Control
1600 Clifton Road, NW
Atlanta, GA 30333

Health and Human Services Department
200 Independence Avenue, SW
Washington, DC 20201

National Institute of Child Health and Human Development
9000 Rockville Pike
Bethesda, MD 20892

National Institute on Drug Abuse Prevention
5600 Fishers Lane
Rockville, MD 20857

National Institutes of Health
9000 Rockville Pike
Bethesda, MD 20892

National Library of Medicine
8600 Rockville Pike
Bethesda, MD 20892

National Women's Health Network
1325 G Street, NW
Washington, DC 20036

The Nutrition Information Center
The New York Hospital–Cornell Medical Center
Memorial Sloan-Kettering Cancer Center
515 East 71st Street
Room 904
New York, NY 10021

The President's Council on Physical Fitness and Sports
450 Fifth Street, NW
Suite 7103
Washington, DC 20001

Smokenders
P.O. Box 3146
Glen Ellyn, IL 60138

U.S. Public Health Service
5600 Fishers Lane
Rockville, MD 20857

Books

Anderson, Kenneth. *Symptoms After 40*. Arbor House, 1987.

Blake, John Ballard, and Charles Roos. *Medical Reference Works*. Medical Library Association, 1967–75.

Boston Women's Health Book Collective. *The New Our Bodies, Ourselves*. Simon & Schuster, 1985.

Brace, Edward R., and Kenneth N. Anderson. *The New Pediatric Guide to Drugs & Vitamins*. Price Stern, 1987.

Brace, Edward R., and John P. Pacanowski. *Childhood Symptoms*. Revised Edition, 1992.

Brody, Jane. *Jane Brody's Nutrition Book*. Norton, 1981.

Brody, Jane. *Jane Brody's* The New York Times *Guide to Personal Health*. Times Books, 1983.

Directory of Medical Specialists. Marquis Who's Who, biannual.

Directory of Physicians in the United States. American Medical Association, biannual.

Friedman, Jo-Ann. *Home Health Care: A Guide for Patients and Their Families*. Norton, 1986.

Merck Manual of Diagnosis and Therapy, 15th ed. Merck, Sharp & Dohme, 1987.

Miller, Benjamin F., and Claire B. Keane. *Encyclopedia and Dictionary of Medicine, Nursing, and Allied Health*. Saunders, 1987.

Physician's Desk Reference. Medical Economics, annual.

Urdang Dictionary of Current Medical Terms. Wiley, 1981.

Wilson, Doris B., and Wilfred Wilson. *Human Anatomy*, 2nd ed. Oxford University Press, 1982.

Wolman, Benjamin B., ed. *International Encyclopedia of Psychiatry, Psychology, Psychoanalysis, and Neurology*, 12 vols. Aesculpius Publications, 1977.

24

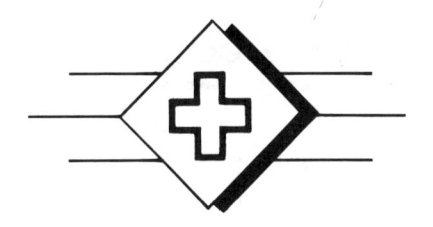

First Aid

Lifesaving Procedures / *742*

Mouth-to-Mouth Breathing / *743*

Pressure Points / *746*

Treatment for Health Emergencies / *749*

First-Aid Kits / *758*

Directory of Poison Control Centers / *759*

The Signs and Signals of Heart Attacks and Strokes / *763*

Additional Sources of Information / *763*

Lifesaving Procedures

The American Medical Association recommends that when a person is injured or becomes suddenly ill, priority be given to these objectives:

1. Maintain breathing
2. Maintain circulation
3. Prevent loss of blood
4. Prevent further injury
5. Prevent shock
6. Summon professional medical services

Maintaining Breathing and Circulation

When breathing stops, the victim has enough oxygen in the blood and other tissues to sustain life for only a very few minutes. Any delay in restoring the flow of oxygen to the brain and other body organs can result in death or permanent damage. Start artificial respiration and manual external cardiac massage immediately if the person is not breathing. Basic cardiopulmonary resuscitation (CPR)—mouth-to-mouth breathing and external cardiac massage—does not require equipment. It can be done by only one or two rescuers, but having more rescuers increases the chances for success.

If you are not directly involved in the rescue effort, you can help by calling a doctor, emergency medical services (EMS), or the police or fire department. But rescuers should not wait for professional support to arrive. Seconds count. Rescue may involve three related actions: opening an airway to the lungs, restoring breathing, and restoring circulation.

First, place the victim on his or her back on a hard, flat surface, such as the floor. If breathing has stopped because of poisonous gas or lack of oxygen, move the victim quickly to fresh air before beginning CPR.

Second, examine the victim closely for possible injuries or other obstacles that would interfere with CPR action. Check for a pulse in the carotid artery, on either side of the neck beneath the chin. Try to get the attention of the victim by talking, pinching, or tapping. If there is no response, assume that the person is unconscious. Look, listen, and feel for any signs of air moving in or out of the victim's lungs.

Mouth-to-Mouth Breathing

If there are no signs of breathing or there is no significant pulse, take the first step in artificial respiration by placing one hand under the victim's neck and the other on the forehead in order to tilt the head back. This extends the neck and helps prevent the tongue from dropping back into the throat, blocking the airway. If available, a plastic "stoma," or oropharyngeal airway device, should be inserted now. If none is available, turn the hand on the victim's forehead so that the thumb and index finger can pinch closed his or her nostrils. Your mouth should be placed over the victim's mouth so as to make an airtight seal.

Next, blow into the victim's mouth four times in succession, making each puff of increasing strength and volume. The victim's chest should expand. After the first set of puffs, remove your mouth and allow the victim's chest to fall. The mouth-to-mouth cycle of puffs should be repeated every five seconds (see "Mouth-to-Mouth Breathing," below).

If the victim's chest fails to expand, the problem may be an airway obstruction. Mouth-to-mouth respiration should be interrupted briefly to apply first aid for choking (see section on choking, pages 754-755).

MOUTH-TO-MOUTH BREATHING

If there are no signs of breathing, place one hand under the victim's neck and gently lift. At the same time, push with the other hand on the victim's forehead. This will move the tongue away from the back of the throat to open the airway.

While maintaining the backward head tilt position, place your cheek and ear close to the victim's mouth and nose. Look for the chest to rise and fall while you listen and feel for breathing. Check for about 5 seconds.

Next, while maintaining the backward head tilt, pinch the victim's nose with the hand that is on the victim's forehead to prevent leakage of air, open your mouth wide, take a deep breath, seal your mouth around the victim's mouth, and blow into the victim's mouth with four quick but full breaths. For an infant, give gentle puffs and blow through the mouth *and* nose and do not tilt the head back as far as for an adult.

If you do not get an air exchange when you blow, it may help to reposition the head and try again.

If there is still no breathing, give one breath every 5 seconds for an adult and one gentle puff every 3 seconds for an infant until breathing resumes.

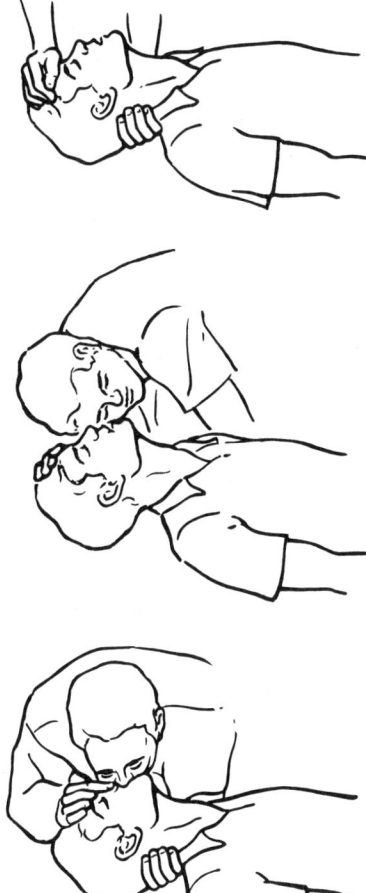

Cardiac Massage

Check the carotid artery pulse again. If there is no pulse, begin external cardiac massage by squeezing the heart between the sternum (breastbone) and the spinal column. To begin external cardiac massage, take a position facing the victim and uncover his or her chest. Find the bottom (xiphoid process) of the breastbone and place your index and middle fingers next to it to mark the location. Next, place the heel of your other hand on the sternum, just above the xiphoid process. Remove your first hand and place it on the second, interlocking the fingers. Holding your arms straight, rock back and forth from the hips and press downward so the sternum is depressed between one and two inches. Do not press on the xiphoid process and do not exert enough pressure to cause internal injuries to the liver or other organs in the area.

If possible, mouth-to-mouth breathing and external cardiac massage should be combined at a rate of 12 breath cycles and 60 chest compressions per minute. If at least two rescuers are available, one should perform mouth-to-mouth breathing while the other does chest compressions.

Check frequently for signs of a carotid artery pulse, a return of normal skin coloring, or signs of spontaneous breathing. Even if normal breathing returns, remain ready to resume CPR if necessary and until a doctor or other professional medical help arrives.

Mouth-to-Nose Breathing

When mouth-to-mouth breathing is not feasible, mouth-to-nose breathing can be performed in a similar manner by placing your mouth over the victim's nose and holding his or her lips closed between the thumb and forefinger.

For Small Children

If the victim is a small child, your mouth can be placed over both the nose and mouth. Be careful about extending the neck of an infant, because soft tissues in the neck may obstruct the upper airway if the head is tilted too far.

External cardiac massage for a small child should be done with the pressure of two thumbs or two fingers and compression should be limited to a depth of only one-half to one inch, depending on the size of the child.

For Drowning Victims

If drowning is the cause, do not wait until the victim can be transported to shore or placed on a flat surface to begin CPR. Mouth-to-mouth artificial respiration can be started while the victim is in a boat or is floating in the water. (See also section on drowning, page 757.)

Preventing Loss of Blood

Heavy bleeding, or hemorrhaging, is a life-threatening emergency. Bleeding from a large artery can result in death in less than five minutes. As with maintaining breathing and circulation, immediate action is needed. Notify a doctor, emergency medical service

(EMS), the police, or the fire department. If the victim can be moved safely and quickly, take him or her to a nearby hospital emergency room.

Covering the Wound

Unless there are injuries or other conditions that might interfere, keep the victim lying down with the bleeding part of the body raised higher than the rest of the body. If the bleeding is external, as from an open wound, place a clean cloth, handkerchief, pad, or similar object directly over the wound and press firmly, with both hands if necessary.

If blood soaks through the cloth, add more cloth and keep pressing, but do not take off the original pad or cloth until the bleeding is under control. Ice placed directly over the wound may help reduce the blood flow by causing constriction of the blood vessel that is the source of blood loss.

Apply firm pressure to the pressure point (see sidebar and section on pressure points, below), that can control blood flow to the wound. If possible, apply pressure to the pressure point with one hand while your other hand presses a pad over the wound. Do not apply a tourniquet unless there is no other way to stop the loss of blood. A tourniquet can result in the death of tissues to an arm, leg, hand, or foot and may lead to amputation.

General Care of the Victim

Heavy bleeding leads to symptoms of shock: thirst, cold and clammy skin, dizziness, and falling blood pressure. Keep the victim flat and covered with a blanket or coat. Also, maintain body temperature by making sure the victim is not lying on a cold or damp surface.

Unless the victim is unconscious or suffering from an abdominal wound, allow him or her to drink water or other beverages as needed; blood loss requires replacement of fluids. Do not give a wounded person alcoholic beverages, which would have the effect of increasing fluid depletion.

If the victim has suffered an open abdominal or chest wound and professional medical help is not immediately available, cover any protruding organs with a clean damp cloth held in place with a bandage or by hand pressure.

An open chest wound may result in a lung collapse unless the wound can be covered quickly with a gauze or cloth pad held in place by a firm bandage to prevent air from moving in or out of the lung. If a gauze pad is not available, make a pad from plastic sheeting, aluminum foil, or other clean material to form an airtight seal. If a bandage is not available, use a belt to hold the pad in place. Do not touch an open wound except as necessary to apply pressure or a pad or other dressing. Never try to explore a wound to locate fragments of metal, glass, or other debris that may have caused the injury.

Pressure Points

Fingers usually can be applied without worsening a victim's condition to control bleeding at a pressure point. There are a half-dozen pressure points where bleeding from an artery can be stopped or reduced by pressing the artery against a bone located next to it.

One of the main pressure points is in the area of the groin, where the femoral artery, supplying blood from the thigh to the foot, passes over one of the bones of the pelvis.

Bleeding in the upper arm may be controlled by pressing on an artery that passes over the top rib of the chest. Loss of blood for most of the rest of the arm can usually be stopped by compressing an artery that passes close to the upper arm bone at a point about halfway between the shoulder and elbow. A pressure point for bleeding from the neck, mouth, or throat area is near the base of the neck, where an artery passes alongside the trachea, or windpipe, just below the Adam's apple. Bleeding from the head between the level of the eye and the jawbone usually can be stopped by pressing on an artery that crosses the edge of the jawbone. For bleeding above the eye level, there is a pressure point in front of the upper portion of the ear.

PRESSURE POINTS

PRESSURE POINT FOR NECK, MOUTH, OR THROAT

To stop bleeding from the neck, mouth, or throat area, apply pressure at a point on the neck where an artery passes alongside the trachea, or windpipe. Place the thumb of the hand against the back of the victim's neck and the fingers on the neck just below the larynx, or Adam's apple. Then push the fingers against the artery.

STOP BLEEDING FROM TWO-THIRDS OF ARM

An artery supplying the lower arm passes close to the bone of the upper arm about halfway along the length of the upper arm. By applying pressure at that point, pressing the artery against the arm bone, bleeding from nearly any point beyond can be stopped.

PRESSURE POINT IN UPPER ARM

A pressure point for controlling the loss of blood in the area of the upper arm, shoulder, or armpit should be found where an artery passes over the outer surface of the top rib. Place the thumb in the position shown (the top rib is indicated in the drawing) and the fingers over the shoulder so they press against the area behind the collarbone. Apply pressure to the artery crossing the top rib.

BLEEDING BELOW EYE AND ABOVE JAWBONE

Bleeding from an artery supplying the area of the face below the level of the eye usually can be controlled by finding the pressure point that is located along the edge of the jawbone.

BLEEDING FROM HEAD ABOVE EYE LEVEL

For bleeding above the level of the eye, the rescuer should be able to find a pressure point where an artery passes over one of the skull bones in front of the upper portion of the ear, as shown in the drawing.

PRESSURE POINT FOR LEG

To stop bleeding from a leg or foot, apply pressure at a point in the area of the groin where the femoral artery passes over one of the bones of the pelvis, as shown in the drawing. If the blood flow slackens or stops, you can assume you have found the pressure point.

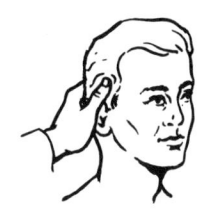

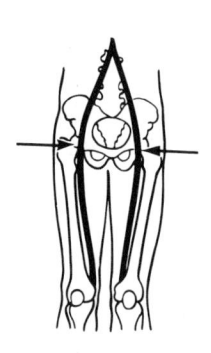

If at first you do not find the exact pressure point location, try again. The locations may vary somewhat with different body builds. You will know when you find the correct place, because bleeding will diminish or stop. As when a tourniquet is used, remember to release pressure at intervals to allow some blood to flow to deprived tissues. Do not continue compressing an artery if bleeding stops. If a tourniquet is applied, as when it may be necessary to stop the loss of blood from an arm or leg so seriously damaged it may have to be amputated, be sure to advise the doctor or EMS personnel who will eventually take charge. Better yet, attach a note or write a message with lipstick on the victim's forehead that a tourniquet has been used. Do not assume that a hospital emergency-room doctor or intern many miles away will be aware that a tourniquet, or any other special first-aid measures, may have been applied at the scene of the accident.

Preventing Further Injury

First aid in an emergency should be limited to no more than is necessary to save a life or prevent further injury. In most cases, do not move an injured person from an accident site before a doctor, emergency personnel, or police or fire personnel arrive. An exception is a situation, such as a building fire or potential explosion, in which the lives of the rescuers as well as the victims could be in danger. If there is an injury to the neck or spine, a victim should not be moved until a stretcher or other carrying device that provides firm support is available. Improper movement of the victim could cause a broken or dislocated bone that may damage an internal organ or pinch or sever a vital nerve trunk and result in death or permanent disability.

If the victim appears to have a head injury, movement should be delayed until a doctor has examined the person. Even then, any movement should be supervised by a physician. Do not move the head, or other body parts, if there is bleeding from the nose, mouth, or ears. If the victim is unconscious, you must assume that he or she has a head injury.

Never assume that an unconscious, disoriented, or apparently incoherent person is drunk. The victim may have suffered a head injury in a fall, a physical assault, or an accident. There are numerous causes of impaired consciousness, including brain hemorrhage, concussion, carbon monoxide poisoning, epilepsy, encephalitis, diabetic coma, hypoglycemia, heart trouble, psychiatric disorders, and barbiturates or other medications. Never give alcoholic beverages to an accident victim, and never offer fluids of any kind to a person who is unconscious or semiconscious or who has internal injuries.

Preventing Shock

Shock can be expected at any accident scene. It is a common, natural reaction to any severe physical or psychological injury. Generally, shock results from an automatic change in a person's blood circulation, as nature suddenly diverts blood to the vital organs in an effort to ensure the victim's survival. However, the natural reaction can also lead to death through circulatory collapse.

Shock prevention is next in priority to maintaining respiration and control of bleeding. Watch for—but do not wait for—the common shock signs: (1) a weak, rapid pulse, (2) skin that is cold and moist with "cold sweat," (3) dilated pupils or eyes that appear "vacant," (4) restless or abnormally anxious behavior, (5) nausea or thirst, (6) faintness and weakness. If the person becomes quiet and slips into unconsciousness, shock has already progressed beyond the first stages.

A usual first-aid measure for shock is to position the victim so the head is lower than the rest of the body, thus allowing gravity to pull blood toward the brain. An exception may be necessary if the victim has a head injury and cannot be moved.

Keep the victim warm and protected from the weather. However, do not provide too much warmth, which could lead to sweating with loss of vital body fluids and redirection of the blood flow from the vital organs to the surface of the body. Fluids may be given to a shock victim under certain circumstances—if the person is conscious, does not have internal injuries, and can swallow. Fluids can be vital for the survival of a victim who has suffered burns. It is better to give fluids in the early stages of shock, because fluids may not be absorbed from the digestive system later. If the accident site is some distance from the nearest hospital or doctor's office, small amounts of warm water or tea may be offered. But do not offer fluids if emergency service personnel or other professional help are nearby and the victim is likely to be anesthetized for surgery. If a physician is available, by telephone or otherwise, let the doctor make the final decision about fluids for accident victims.

Some persons at an accident scene may suffer only minor cuts and bruises but experience psychological shock. The signs and symptoms are the same as for victims with serious physical injuries. Time and personnel permitting, emotional shock cases should receive the same care for their shock symptoms as the severely injured. If those with psychological shock are allowed to slip into unconsciousness with possible circulatory failure, their condition will obviously complicate the overall rescue effort.

Treatment for Health Emergencies

Burns

Burns can be caused by contact with heat, chemicals, electricity, or radiation. One of the effects is "burn shock," in which body fluid is diverted from normal blood flow to the brain, heart, and other vital organs to the burned area of the body. Burn shock is the same as physical or psychological shock and can even follow severe sunburn. Small thermal burns, as may occur from fire, steam, or touching a hot object, usually result in pain, a reddened skin area, and blisters. In many cases, the burn can be treated with ice or cold water. Do not try to open a blister. It can be protected by a pad held in place with a loose bandage.

Never apply ointments or grease, including butter or margarine, baking soda, or other household substances, to a burned skin area.

A severe or extensive thermal burn requires professional care in a hospital. A doctor and/or emergency personnel should be summoned. While waiting for professional medical care, the victim should be made to lie down with the head and chest lower than the legs (shock position). Cover the burn area with a clean cloth to exclude air. Infection is a common complication if the skin is broken. If the victim is conscious and can swallow, provide adequate nonalcoholic liquids to drink. Because of burn shock, body tissues require fluid replacement.

First- and Second-Degree Burns

First-degree burns are marked by redness or other skin discoloration, pain, and swelling. An ordinary sunburn is typical of a first-degree burn. These burns generally are treated as small thermal burns and usually will heal with the application of cold water followed by a dry dressing.

Second-degree burns are often the result of exposure to flame, scalding liquids, or a very severe sunburn. The skin is usually reddish, mottled, and damaged, with signs of body fluid loss. These burns are treated as extensive thermal burns, requiring professional medical care.

Third-Degree Burns

Third-degree burns are marked by damage to tissues beneath the skin. The area may resemble a second-degree burn at first, but it quickly progresses to a whitish or charred coloration. Third-degree burns often result from contact with high-voltage electricity, steam, or boiling water, or from an accident in which the person is trapped in burning clothing. A third-degree burn is a true medical emergency. While ice or cold water may be used as a first-aid measure for first- or second-degree burns, nothing should be applied to a third-degree burn. Do not even remove clothing from burn areas. However, burn areas can be covered temporarily with sterile dressings, clean sheets, or even plastic garment bags. Do not put plastic materials over facial burns.

If the third-degree burn victim is conscious and not vomiting, small amounts of fluid should be offered. The recommended beverage is lukewarm water containing a teaspoon of salt and one-half teaspoon of baking soda per quart of liquid, to be sipped at a rate of one ounce every four or five minutes while waiting for professional medical help.

Chemical Burns

Chemical burns, either acid or alkali, are generally corrosive reactions that tend to affect the skin, eyes, and digestive tract. They usually result from spills, leaks, and splashes. A strong acid or alkali can cause permanent tissue damage. An alkali burn may be more serious than an acid burn because an acid usually is neutralized by contact with body tissues, whereas an alkali can continue causing damage until it is neutralized by another substance or washed away with copious amounts of water.

As a result, all chemical burns should be flooded—not merely rinsed—with water. It is usually important to remove contaminated clothing, which tends to absorb the chemical and hold it next to the skin, exacerbating the damage. Water flooding should continue while clothing is being removed. If possible, insert a hose under the clothing to inject water between the skin and the contaminated fabric.

Poisoning

A poison is anything that may be injurious to health or dangerous to life if it is swallowed, inhaled, or touched by the skin. Common sources of poisons include contaminated foods, carbon monoxide gas, cleaning products and solvents, certain household plants, pesticides, and medicines.

In any case of a swallowed poison, the container of food or other substance should be saved, with the label and any remaining contents, so that doctors or Poison Control Center personnel can recommend the most rapid and effective treatment.

First aid for most cases of swallowed poisons depends on the type of substance involved and the condition of the victim. Do not try to induce vomiting in any poisoning victim if he or she is unconscious or having convulsions.

Food Poisoning

Food poisoning may be caused by enterotoxins, or poisons produced by bacteria that may or may not still be in the food. Symptoms usually include nausea and vomiting, cramps, diarrhea, fever, and headache, which may begin minutes to hours after the food has been eaten.

First aid in most cases includes bed rest, preferably close to a bathroom, and avoidance of any food or beverage until vomiting has stopped. When vomiting has ended, the victim should be offered sweetened tea or soft drinks and strained broth or bouillon with a little salt added. It is important to replace the body fluids and electrolytes (minerals) lost in vomiting or diarrhea.

In addition to vomiting, cramps, or diarrhea, symptoms of poisoning may include loss of consciousness, confusion or disorientation, an unusual odor on the breath, pain or a burning sensation in the mouth or throat, and stains or discoloration in or about the mouth from the leaves or berries of poisonous plants.

If the symptoms are severe, with signs of shock or the presence of blood or mucus in the diarrhea, a doctor should be notified.

A potentially fatal form of food poisoning that does not always cause vomiting or diarrhea is botulism. It is caused by a bacteria-produced poison, usually found in home-canned or processed foods. Botulism attacks the nervous system. The victim may feel no symptoms for a day or two, then experience visual problems, dry mouth and swallowing difficulty, and constipation as the poison gradually paralyzes various organ systems. Immediate hospitalization is needed to prevent the spread of the paralyzing effects to the respiratory system.

Corrosive Poisons

Do not induce vomiting if the victim may have swallowed a corrosive substance, such as an acid or alkali, or has a burning pain in the mouth or throat. Examples of corrosive substances are toilet bowl cleaners, drain cleaners, lye, washing soda, and chlorine bleach.

- Do not attempt to "neutralize" swallowed acids or alkalis.
- Do not use activated charcoal for swallowed corrosive poisons.
- Do give the victim adequate amounts of milk or water.
- Do begin CPR if breathing stops.

Petroleum Distillates

For swallowed petroleum distillates, such as gasoline, kerosene, lighter fluid, paint thinner, or furniture polish, call the nearest Poison Control Center or hospital emergency room immediately for specific instructions. The exact type and amount of the poison may determine the treatment. Some products contain more than one kind of poison.

Symptoms may include coughing, choking, cyanosis (blue skin), breath-holding, a burning sensation in the stomach, lethargy, coma, convulsions, and spontaneous vomiting.

- Do not induce vomiting. There is a great risk that some of the vomited poison may enter the lungs; some hydrocarbon products are more than a hundred times as poisonous in the lungs as in the digestive tract.
- Do, if recommended by a doctor, give the person a glass of milk to dilute the poison and reduce stomach irritation.

Noncorrosive Poisons

Most medicines, such as aspirin, may be noncorrosive poisons. Generally, the doctor may recommend that you try to induce vomiting if the person has swallowed a noncorrosive poison that is not a petroleum distillate product. If you do not know whether the swallowed substance is corrosive or noncorrosive—or even if it is actually poisonous—call a Poison Control Center.

To induce vomiting, use syrup of ipecac (1 tablespoon for a child; 2 tablespoons for an adult) when it is available. The syrup of ipecac should be followed with one or more 8-ounce glasses of water.

If the person does not vomit within 15 minutes after one dose of syrup of ipecac, repeat the dose.

If syrup of ipecac is not available, use soapy water or a handwashing liquid detergent dissolved in water, or place the handle of a spoon or your finger at the back of the victim's throat. If the victim is a child, hold the child with the head lower than the hips while you induce vomiting. This position will reduce the chance of vomit entering the lungs.

Save a sample of the vomit so it can be analyzed in a medical laboratory.

Inhaled Poisons

A common type of inhaled poison is carbon monoxide gas, as produced by a car or truck engine in a confined area or by a faulty furnace or fireplace. The first symptoms are usually headache, yawning, breathing difficulty, dilated pupils, dizziness, faintness, ringing in the ears (tinnitus), nausea, and heart palpitations, followed by loss of consciousness. A distinctive sign is a cherry-red coloring of the mucous membranes. Persons with a light complexion may show a similar bright red coloring of the skin.

First aid requires fresh air and oxygen. Give mouth-to-mouth resuscitation until an emergency medical unit can arrive to provide 100-percent oxygen by mask. Do not give any stimulants, but keep the victim warm and as quiet as possible.

In rescuing a person from an inhaled poison, such as smoke or carbon monoxide, protect yourself against becoming a victim of the same dangerous situation. Be sure that oxygen is available by opening doors or windows of an enclosed space. If possible, carry an independent air supply if you must enter a confined or overheated area to rescue a victim of inhaled poisons. When a second rescuer is present, tie a rope around your waist and give the other end to the second rescuer, who can pull you to safety if you also are overcome by poisonous fumes.

Plant Poisons

The major contact poison plants in North America are poison ivy, poison oak, and poison sumac. They are usually identified by their clusters of three shiny leaflets. Signs and symptoms of contact with these plants include itching skin and blisters. These are effects of a poisonous resin in the leaves. Some first-aid relief can be had by diluting and washing away the resin with a strong laundry soap and water. Follow-up treatments can include mild wet dressings or starch or oatmeal baths to relieve the itching. Do not break the blisters. If there is oozing and crusting of the blisters, exposing them to dry air may give some relief. More serious adverse effects can result from chewing the leaves of poison ivy or inhaling the smoke of plants being burned. Swallowing or inhaling the resin causes painful swelling of the lining of the throat, accompanied by fever and weakness. The symptoms may require professional medical treatment.

Insect Bites

Bites or stings of ants, bees, hornets, wasps, yellow jackets, mosquitoes, and other insects usually result in the injection of substances under the skin of the person attacked. The body's reaction may vary from mild itching to a severe form of shock, depending on the venom or other foreign protein injected and the sensitivity of the person to the substance. Some hypersensitive persons can experience an extreme allergic reaction, known as *anaphylactic shock*, marked by breathing difficulty or circulatory failure within a few minutes after a bite or sting. Such individuals require special prescription drugs that should be carried when they expect to be near stinging or biting insects.

For most people who experience insect bites and stings, first aid may require only the application of ice or a cold compress to slow the rate of venom absorption. If the insect leaves its stinger in the skin, remove it with care, as the venom sac usually is still attached and should not be squeezed.

Ticks and other insects that may cling to the skin may require application of a petroleum product or similar irritant in order to remove them. In addition to local pain, swelling, and irritation, bites of ticks and other insects can result in serious infections requiring hospitalization.

Snake Bites

Most snake bites should be treated like those of any wild animal. If the bite is from a poisonous snake, the symptoms may vary according to the type of snake and its venom. But most poisonous snake bites will be followed immediately by an intense pain and a feeling of numbness in the bite area. The bite of a pit viper, such as a rattlesnake, cottonmouth, or copperhead, is often identified by fang punctures about one-half inch apart. It may also produce swelling. Other snake bites may or may not leave fang marks. A coral snake-bite wound may show a chewing action of the snake's jaws.

In general, a snake-bite victim should remain still. Any body movement will tend to increase the spread of venom. If the bite is in an arm or leg, the limb should be immobilized and kept lower than the level of the heart. If a hospital or other medical facility is less than 30 to 40 minutes away, the victim should be delivered there for professional care as quickly as possible. Other first-aid measures are suggested only for cases in which a doctor or hospital is not easily available.

A constriction band should be tied around the arm or leg a few inches above the bite and between the bite and the heart. The bite may be washed with soap and water and covered with a sterile dressing. Ice or a cold compress can be applied, but not directly over the bite. As in any other serious injury, the victim should be monitored closely for signs of shock. In some cases, an incision can be made in the bite area for removal of some of the venom by suction. However, incision and suction should be performed only if a doctor is not available and immediately after the bite has been inflicted. The person making the incision should be aware that when cutting into an arm or leg, there is a high risk of causing permanent damage to nerves, blood vessels, muscles, or other tissue.

Animal Bites

Animal bites, whether by a pet or a wild animal, can cause a puncture wound, laceration, or an avulsion, in which part of the flesh is torn away. First aid should be directed toward control of bleeding and protecting the wound from infection until it can be examined by a doctor. Unless the wound is extremely painful or bleeding profusely, clean it with soap and water and cover it with a sterile dressing before taking the victim to a doctor's office or hospital emergency room.

Many animal bites require a tetanus shot and, if the animal is identified as being rabid, additional protection against rabies. In most communities, local health authorities require notification of any serious animal bite.

Electric Shock

Severe electric shock can be caused by contact with ordinary electric lines in a home, office, or factory, as well as by high-voltage lines or a lightning bolt. An electric charge can have a number of effects on the body, including muscular contractions or seizures, paralysis of the lungs, abnormal heart function, bone fractures, thermal burns, and changes in blood chemistry.

Saving a person from further injury or death by electrocution should be done carefully so that the rescuer does not also become a victim. The electric shock victim first must be safely separated from contact with the electricity by turning the electricity off or by removing a wire or electric appliance with an insulated tool, such as a dry stick. In some cases, it may be easier to throw a loop of rope or cloth about the victim's arm or leg and drag him or her away from the source of electricity. If the victim is alive but unconscious, summon a doctor or emergency medical personnel. If breathing has stopped or there is no pulse, begin CPR immediately while awaiting the arrival of medical professionals.

Choking

Obstruction of the airways leading to the lungs can be caused by food, candy, chewing gum, or other objects accidentally inhaled. If air is unable to reach the lungs, the body's oxygen supply can become exhausted in a few minutes, resulting in death.

NOTE: A person whose windpipe (trachea) is blocked cannot talk but must make those around aware that he or she is choking, using sign language or any other means so that first aid can be given immediately.

There are two accepted ways of giving first aid to a choking person.

First Aid   **755**

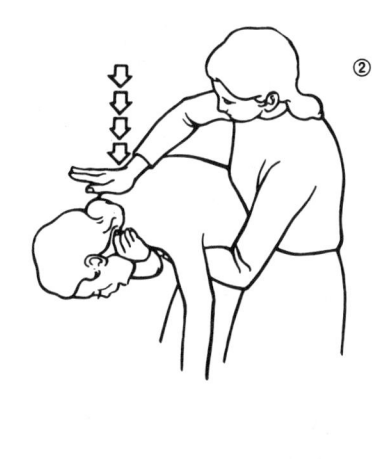

1. The Heimlich maneuver, which consists of a series of thrusts to the upper abdomen. Stand behind the victim and put your arms around his or her upper abdomen so that your hands can be clasped in a fist at the bottom of the victim's breastbone. Then quickly push your fist upward into the victim's chest, putting pressure on the lungs so that any air in them will be squeezed backward up into the windpipe, pushing the obstruction into the mouth. The Heimlich maneuver may have to be repeated six or more times to dislodge a foreign body in the throat. If the victim is pregnant, or very obese, the rescue pressure should be directed through the chest rather than the abdomen.
2. Firm blows over the spinal column between the shoulder blades. Stand behind the choking person and help him or her lean over, using one hand on the victim's chest to lend support. Then hit high on the back with the heel of your hand. Four or more back blows may be needed to dislodge the object in the windpipe.

Frostbite

The most common cold-weather injury is frostbite. Severe cold can constrict the blood vessels, thereby reducing the normal flow of warm blood to the exposed tissues. The symptoms usually include a very cold feeling in the exposed skin area followed by a loss of feeling. The skin may appear flushed or red at first, but later it becomes white or a grayish yellow. Because of the loss of feeling, the victim is often unaware of the danger of frostbite.

The victim should be taken into a warm environment and all tight or wet clothing in the affected body area should be removed. The frostbitten area should be immersed in warm—but not extremely hot—water (experts recommend a water temperature of around 105°F).

You can offer the victim hot coffee, tea, cocoa, or soup, but smoking should be avoided because it has an effect similar to that of cold, causing constriction of blood vessels. Do not rub the frostbitten tissues. If bleeding, swelling from fluid accumulation, or other complications develop after the exposed areas have thawed, notify a doctor immediately.

Abrasions

A minor break in the skin, such as may be caused by scraping or rubbing against a rough surface, should be washed with soap and water and treated with mild antiseptic, such as hydrogen peroxide. Then cover the abrasion with a sterile gauze dressing held in place with a bandage. If signs of infection appear, consult a doctor.

Black Eyes and Bruises

Black eyes and bruises are actually a type of closed wound in which blood from a damaged vessel in the soft tissues has leaked into a space beneath the skin. Apply ice or a cold compress to reduce the swelling and control the further loss of blood under the skin. In most cases, the pool of blood will be reabsorbed and the skin color will return to normal.

Boils and Blisters

A *boil* is a tender, often painful, pus-filled swelling of the skin. A boil is also known as a *furuncle*, and a group of furuncles is a *carbuncle*. Boils should be treated quickly and carefully to prevent the spread of a more serious infection and the formation of a scar. A boil around the nose or face can be particularly serious and should be treated with antibiotics by a doctor. Most other boils should be treated with moist heat to cause spontaneous rupture and drainage. The pus contains staphylococcus bacteria and should not be allowed to spread the infection.

Blisters are fluid-filled skin eruptions that may be caused by allergy, injury, sunburn, insect bites, infection, or drug reaction. Correcting the cause is important if the cause is an infection, allergy, or drug reaction. Most ordinary blisters can be treated with a mild antiseptic and a protective dressing. Do not puncture a blister. If the blister is accidentally broken, treat it as a wound.

Concussions

A concussion can result from a head injury and may be accompanied by a brief or longer period of unconsciousness. The victim may experience headache, blurred vision, or other signs of nervous system damage and may lapse into a coma. The victim, even if conscious, should be treated as an unconscious person. Keep the person quiet and warm, watch for signs of shock, and help maintain breathing if necessary while awaiting arrival of a doctor or emergency medical personnel.

Convulsions

A convulsion, or seizure, involves a disturbance of the nervous system that affects the muscles of movement. The person experiencing a convulsion may have uncontrollable twitching of the muscles, or the muscles may become rigidly contracted. There are many possible causes and types of such seizures. In general, however, first aid should be aimed at protecting the victim from self-injury. Place a firm but soft object, such as a folded handkerchief, in the mouth to protect the tongue. Do not try to protect the tongue with a hard object that may damage the teeth and do not insert your fingers between the jaws of the victim. Clothing about the neck should be loosened. Place pillows, cushions, or rolled blankets about the head and body. Meanwhile, summon a doctor or EMS.

Drowning

Drowning is a form of asphyxiation due to an inability of the victim to get oxygen into the lungs. It may also be complicated by inhalation of fluid into the lungs. First aid for a drowning victim requires CPR procedures (described on page 743–744) to maintain breathing and circulation. Do not waste time trying to squeeze water out of the lungs, particularly if the accident occurred in fresh water. If the victim has been in sea water, try to keep the body positioned with the head and chest lower than the abdomen and legs to assist fluid drainage from the lungs.

Heat Cramps, Heat Exhaustion, Heat Stroke

Prolonged exposure to high temperatures can lead to several life-threatening health problems. The most serious effects are heat exhaustion and heat stroke. *Heat cramps* are usually in the form of painful muscle spasms caused by excessive sweating and loss of body salt. The skin may be hot and dry or cool and clammy. In most cases, heat cramps can be treated with food and liquid containing sodium chloride (ordinary table salt).

Heat exhaustion, or heat prostration, is due to loss of body fluid. It is marked by nausea, weakness, excessive sweating, and faintness. The skin is pale and clammy, the pulse is weak, and the victim may show signs of shock. The loss of body fluid results in loss of blood volume and, in turn, a deficiency of oxygenated blood reaching the brain. Have the victim lie flat with the head down and give him or her small sips of cool, slightly salted liquids every few minutes. Do not give the victim too much fluid too rapidly.

Heat stroke, or sunstroke, is the most serious type of heat injury. It may begin suddenly with headache, dizziness, and fatigue. The skin is hot, dry, and flushed and the pulse is extremely rapid. The victim can develop a very high fever of around 105°F, experience convulsions, or become unconscious. Unless first aid is given immediately, the person may suffer circulatory collapse and die. Cool the body by wrapping the victim in wet clothing or bedding. Use snow or ice, if available, or immerse the person in cool water while awaiting the arrival of an emergency medical crew or a physician. Check the victim's temperature every 10 minutes to make sure the body temperature does not fall too rapidly. Hypothermia, or excessively cold body temperature, could complicate the condition.

Nosebleeds

Nosebleeds are usually caused by rupture of the numerous capillaries in the soft tissues near the tip of the nose. A nosebleed may be started by an injury, high blood pressure, physical activity, or sudden change in atmospheric pressure, as may occur in traveling from sea level to a mountaintop. First aid requires keeping the victim quiet and in a seated position with the head leaning forward. Apply pressure to the outside of the bleeding nostril, or insert gauze pads in one or both nostrils and squeeze the outside of the nose toward the midline. Also, apply ice or a cold compress to the nose and surrounding areas of the face. If the nose continues to bleed, notify a doctor.

FIRST-AID KITS

Many people are confused about the meanings of terms, such as bandages and dressings, used by health professionals. A *bandage* is a strip of muslin, gauze, or other material used to hold a compress or dressing in place. A *roller bandage* is a long strip of cloth that can be used as a dressing or compress as well as a bandage. A *triangular bandage* is one cut from a square of cloth along a diagonal line.

A *compress* is a square of fabric, generally of flannel or wool, used to apply heat, cold, or medications to the skin. A *dressing* can be anything placed over an open wound to control bleeding, absorb blood or secretions, and prevent infectious agents from entering the body through the wound. The best kind of dressing is a piece of sterile gauze, but in an emergency, any clean material may become a dressing—even sheet plastic or a newspaper. However, fluffy materials, such as cotton wool, should not be used because the loose fibers will stick to body tissues. Dressings are held in place by bandages.

An ideal family first aid kit should contain the following:

12	4-by-4-inch sterile dressings in sealed envelopes
12	2-by-2-inch sterile dressings in sealed envelopes
2	15-foot roller bandages, 1 inch wide
2	15-foot roller bandages, 2 inches wide
1	roll of adhesive tape
4	triangular bandages with safety pins
1	clean bedsheet
2	small bath towels
2	large bath towels
1	pair of blunt-nose scissors
1	pair of tweezers
1	pair of needle-nose pliers
1	eyedropper
1	set of measuring spoons
12	wooden tongue blades (for finger splints)
12	wood splints, 12–18 inches long
1	bar of antiseptic soap
1	package of salt
1	package of baking soda
1	package of aspirin tablets
1	package of antihistamine tablets
1	package of anti-motion sickness tablets
1	large package of adhesive bandages, assorted sizes
1	package of paper cups

Directory of Poison Control Centers

Following is a list of poison control centers and state offices that can refer you to local poison control centers. Also, check your local phone directory for nearby centers.

Alabama

Regional Poison Control Center
The Children's Hospital of Alabama
205-939-9201
205-933-4050
800-292-6678 (Alabama only)

Alaska

Anchorage Poison Center
Providence Hospital Pharmacy
907-261-3193
800-478-3193 (Alaska only)

Arizona

Arizona Poison and Drug Information Center
Arizona Health Sciences Center
602-626-6016
800-362-0101 (Arizona only)

Samaritan Regional Poison Center
Good Samaritan Regional Medical Center
602-253-3334

California

Fresno Regional Poison Control Center
Fresno Community Hospital and Medical Center
209-445-1222
800-346-5922

San Diego Regional Poison Center
UCSD Medical Center
619-543-6000
800-876-4766 (in 619 area code only)

San Francisco Bay Area Regional Poison Control Center
San Francisco General Hospital
415-476-6600

Santa Clara Valley Medical Center Regional Poison Center
408-299-5112
800-662-9886 (California only)

University of California, Davis, Medical Center
Regional Poison Control Center
916-734-3692
800-342-9293 (Northern California only)

UCI Regional Poison Center
UCI Medical Center
714-634-5988
800-544-4404 (Southern California only)

Colorado

Rocky Mountain Poison and Drug Center
303-629-1123

Connecticut

University of Connecticut Health Center
203-674-3456

Delaware

Wilmington Medical Center Delaware Division
302-655-3389

District of Columbia

National Capital Poison Center
Georgetown University Hospital
202-625-3333

Florida

The Florida Poison Information Center
Tampa General Hospital
813-253-4444
800-282-3171 (Florida only)

Georgia

Georgia Poison Center
Grady Memorial Hospital
404-589-4400
800-282-5846 (Georgia only)

Hawaii

Hawaii Poison Center
808-941-4411
800-362-3585 (outer islands only)

Idaho

Idaho Poison Center
208-378-2707
800-632-8000 (Idaho only)

Illinois

Rush Poison Control Center
Rush Presbyterian St. Luke's Medical Center
1-800-942-5969

Central and Southern Illinois Regional Poison Center
St. John's Hospital
217-753-3330
800-252-2022 (Illinois only)

Indiana

Indiana Poison Center
317-929-2323
800-382-9097 (Indiana only)

Iowa

Poison Information Center
515-241-6254
800-362-2327 (Iowa only)

Kansas

Stormont Vail Regional Medical Center
913-354-6106

Kentucky

Kentucky Regional Poison Center
Kosair Children's Hospital
502-629-7275
800-722-5725 (Kentucky only)

Louisiana

Louisiana Poison Control Center
800-256-9822

Maine

Maine Poison Control Center
207-871-2950

Maryland

Maryland Poison Center
410-528-7701
800-492-2414 (Maryland only; for DC suburbs, see *District of Columbia*)

Massachusetts

Massachusetts Poison Control System
617-232-2120
800-682-9211

Michigan

Blodgett Regional Poison Center
800-632-2727 (Michigan only)

Poison Control Center
Children's Hospital of Michigan
313-745-5711

Minnesota

Hennepin Regional Poison Center
Hennepin County Medical Center
612-347-3141
Petline: 612-337-7387

Minnesota Regional Poison Center
St. Paul-Ramsey Medical Center
612-221-2113

Mississippi

University Medical Center
601-354-7660

Missouri

Cardinal Glennon Children's Hospital Regional Poison Center
314-772-5200
800-366-8888

Montana

Department of Health and Environmental Sciences
Montana Poison Control System
408-444-2544
800-525-5042

Nebraska

The Poison Center
402-390-5555
800-955-9119 (Nebraska only)

Nevada

Washoe Medical Center
702-328-4129

New Hampshire

New Hampshire Poison Information Center
Dartmouth Hitchcock Medical Center
800-562-8236 (New Hampshire only)

New Jersey

New Jersey Poison Information and Education System
800-962-1253

New Mexico

New Mexico Poison and Drug Information Center
University of New Mexico
505-843-2551
800-432-6866 (New Mexico only)

New York

Department of Health
518-474-3785

North Carolina

Duke University Medical Center
800-672-1697 (North Carolina only)

North Dakota

North Dakota Poison Control Center
701-234-5575
800-732-2200 (North Dakota only)

Ohio

Central Ohio Poison Center
614-228-1323
614-461-2012
800-682-7625

Cincinnati Drug & Poison Information Center and Regional Poison Control System
513-558-5111
800-872-5111 (Ohio only)

Oklahoma

Oklahoma Poison Control Center
Oklahoma Children's Memorial Hospital
405-271-5454
800-522-4611 (Oklahoma only)

Oregon

Oregon Poison Center
Oregon Health Sciences University
503-494-8968
800-452-7165 (Oregon only)

Pennsylvania

Central Pennsylvania Poison Center
University Hospital
800-521-6110

Pittsburgh Poison Center
412-681-6669

The Poison Control Center (greater Philadelphia metropolitan area)
215-386-2100

Rhode Island

Rhode Island Poison Center
401-277-5727

South Carolina

Palmetto Poison Center
College of Pharmacy
University of South Carolina
803-765-7359
800-922-1117 (South Carolina only)

South Dakota

McKennan Poison Control
605-336-3894
800-952-0123 (South Dakota only)

Tennessee

Middle Tennessee Regional Poison Center
615-322-6435
800-288-9999
800-999-0789 (Johnson City area)

Texas

North Texas Poison Center
214-590-5000
800-441-0040 (Texas WATS)

Utah

Intermountain Regional Poison Control Center
801-581-2151
800-456-7707 (Utah only)

Vermont

Vermont Poison Center
Medical Center Hospital of Vermont
802-658-3456

Virginia

Blue Ridge Poison Center
804-925-5543
800-451-1428

National Capital Poison Center
(northern Virginia only)
Georgetown University Hospital
202-625-3333

Washington

Seattle Poison Center
Children's Hospital and Medical Center
206-526-2121
800-732-6985 (Washington only)

West Virginia

West Virginia Poison Center
304-348-4211
800-642-3625 (West Virginia only)

Wisconsin

Poison Center
University Hospital
608-262-3702

Wyoming

The Poison Center
402-390-5555

THE SIGNS AND SIGNALS OF HEART ATTACKS AND STROKES

Heart Attack Warning Signs

- Uncomfortable pressure, fullness, squeezing, or pain in the center of the chest lasting two minutes or more
- Spreading of pain to shoulders, neck, or arms
- Severe pain, dizziness, fainting, sweating, nausea, or shortness of breath

Not all of these signals are always present. Don't wait! Get help immediately.

Stroke Warning Signs

- Sudden, temporary weakness or numbness of the face, arm, and leg on one side of the body
- Temporary loss of speech, or trouble speaking or understanding speech
- Temporary dimness or loss of vision, particularly in one eye
- Unexplained dizziness, unsteadiness, or sudden falls

Many major strokes are preceded by "little strokes," warning signals like the above experienced days, weeks, or months before the more severe event.

In Case of Emergency

- If you are having chest discomfort that lasts for two minutes or more, call the emergency medical services (EMS) in your area.
- If you can get to a hospital faster by car, have someone drive you.

Before an Emergency

- Find out which hospitals in your area offer 24-hour emergency cardiac care.
- Select in advance the facility nearest your home and office, and tell your family and friends so that they will know what to do.
- Keep a list of emergency rescue service numbers next to your telephone and in a prominent place in your pocket, wallet, or purse.

Additional Sources of Information

Organizations and Services

American College of Emergency Physicians
1125 Executive Circle
Irving, TX 75259

American Medical Association
515 North State Street
Chicago, IL 60610

American National Red Cross
17th and D Streets, NW
Washington, DC 20006

National Association of Emergency Medical Technicians
9140 Ward Parkway
Kansas City, MO 64114

Books

American National Red Cross Standard First Aid and Personal Safety. Doubleday, 1989.
Brown, Andrew J. *First Aid: Principles and Practices.* Macmillan, 1987.
Consumer Guide editors and Charles Mosher. *Emergency First Aid.* Fawcett, 1980.
Emergency Family First Aid Guide. Simon & Schuster, 1978.
Henderson, John. *Emergency Medical Guide.* McGraw-Hill, 1978.

25

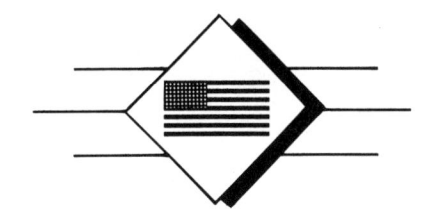

The United States

United States Map / *767*

Population / *768*

Immigration Statistics / *771*

Economic Statistics / *777*

Federal Government Finances
and Employment / *782*

State Government / *788*

Territories and Commonwealths / 789

State Flowers, Birds, Mottos, and Nicknames / 790

State Name Origins / 792

Admission of the 13 Original States / 794

Secession of American States / 794

Readmission of American States / 794

The Declaration of Independence / *795*

The Constitution of the United States
of America / *799*

The Emancipation Proclamation / *814*

The Monroe Doctrine / *816*

The Pledge of Allegiance / *816*

The U.S. Flag / *817*

Presidents of the United States / *819*

The Sequence of Presidential Succession / 822
The Electoral College / 822
Vice-Presidents of the United States / *823*
Weather Charts / *824*
Important Dates in American History / *829*
Government Benefits / *840*
Crime Rates / *844*
Government Structure / 848–849
How a Bill Becomes Law / *850*
Additional Sources of Information / *851*

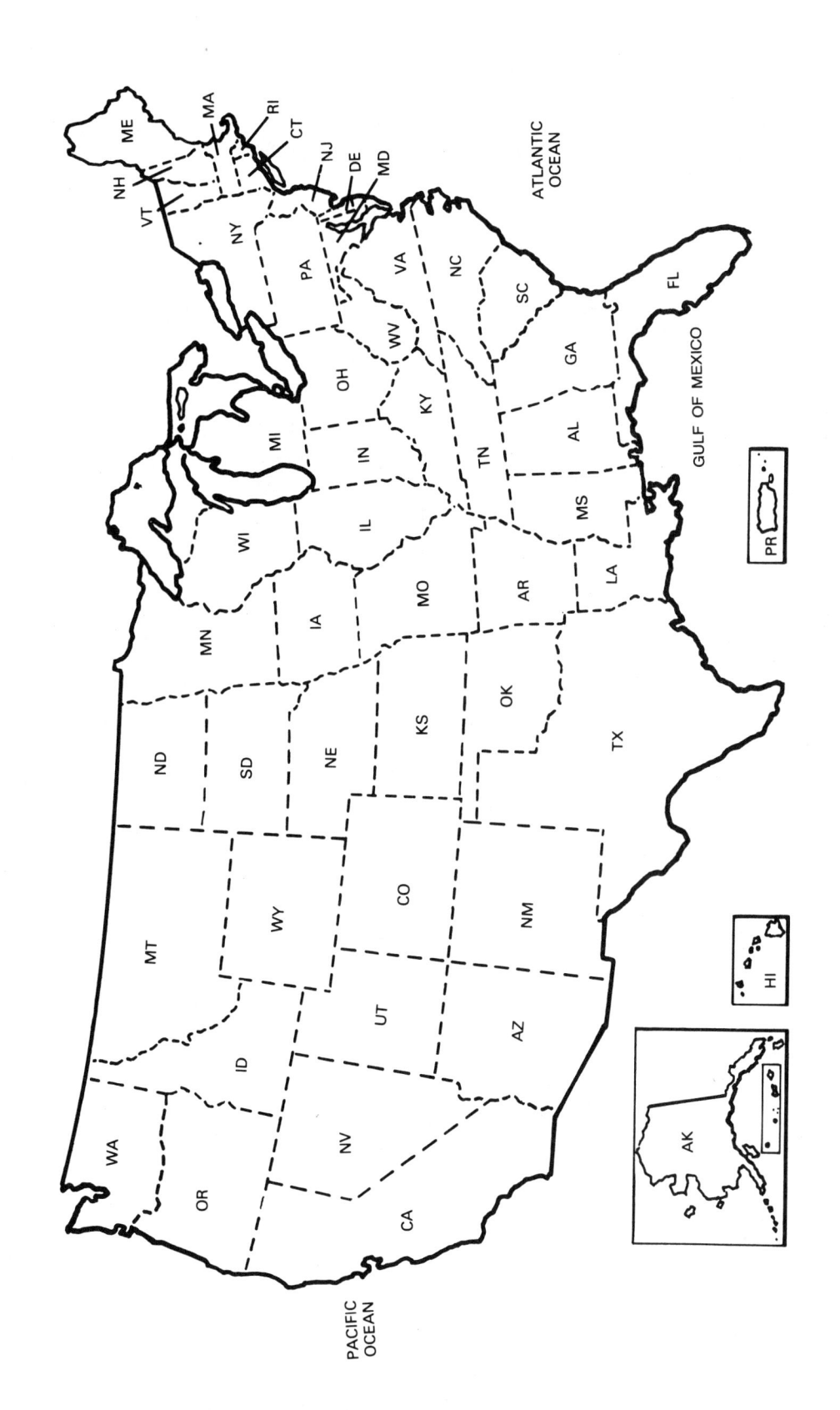

United States Map

Population

The United States boasts a heterogenous population, which, according to the 1990 census, has risen 9.8 percent, from 226.5 million to 248.7 million, since the previous census was taken in 1980. The tables in this section were drawn primarily from the Department of Commerce, Bureau of the Census, and reflect the most accurate profiles available of the population by race, sex, age, and region.

Resident Population, by Age, Race, and Hispanic Origin: 1990 [In thousands, except percent.]

Year and Sex	Total, all years	Under 5 years	5–9 years	10–14 years	15–19 years	20–24 years	25–29 years	30–34 years
ALL RACES[1]								
1990	248,710	18,354	18,099	17,114	17,754	19,020	21,313	21,863
Male	121,239	9,392	9,263	8,767	9,103	9,676	10,696	10,877
Female	127,470	8,962	8,837	8,347	8,651	9,345	10,617	10.986
WHITE								
1990	199,686	13,649	13,616	12,854	13,343	14,524	16,639	17,352
Male	97,476	7,004	6,991	6,607	6,846	7,388	8,385	8,700
Female	102,210	6,645	6,626	6,247	6,497	7,136	8,254	8,652
BLACK								
1990	29,986	2,786	2,671	2,602	2,658	2,579	2,708	2,682
Male	14,170	1,408	1,350	1,314	1,342	1,259	1,286	1,251
Female	15,816	1,377	1,321	1,287	1,316	1,320	1,422	1,431
NATIVE AMERICAN, ESKIMO, ALEUT								
1990	1,959	202	199	188	181	166	176	171
Male	967	103	101	96	93	85	87	83
Female	992	99	98	92	87	81	88	88
ASIAN, PACIFIC ISLANDER								
1990	7,274	590	596	552	604	632	691	726
Male	3,558	301	302	281	312	326	343	350
Female	3,716	288	294	270	291	306	348	376
HISPANIC ORIGIN								
1990	22,354	2,388	2,194	2,002	2,054	2,304	2,341	2,062
Male	11,388	1,218	1,119	1,023	1,084	1,262	1,250	1,074
Female	10,966	1,169	1,075	978	970	1,043	1,091	988
PERCENT								
Total, 1990[1]	100.0	7.4	7.3	6.9	7.1	7.6	8.6	8.8
White	100.0	6.8	6.8	6.4	6.7	7.3	8.3	8.7
Black	100.0	9.3	8.9	8.7	8.9	8.6	9.0	8.9
Native American, Eskimo, Aleut	100.0	10.3	10.2	9.6	9.2	8.5	9.0	8.7
Asian, Pacific Islander	100.0	8.1	8.2	7.6	8.3	8.7	9.5	10.0
Hispanic origin	100.0	10.7	9.8	9.0	9.2	10.3	10.5	9.2

[1] Includes other races, not shown separately.

35–39 years	40–44 years	45–49 years	50–54 years	55–59 years	60–64 years	65–74 years	75 years and over	5–13 years	14–17 years	18–24 years
19,963	17,616	13,873	11,351	10,532	10,616	18,107	13,135	31,970	13,280	26,738
9,902	8,692	6,811	5,515	5,034	4,947	7,942	4,624	16,367	6,824	13,616
10.061	8,924	7,062	5,836	5,497	5,669	10,165	8,512	15,603	6,455	13,122
16,082	14,506	11,586	9,505	8,968	9,211	16,026	11,826	24,036	9,942	20,358
8,054	7,227	5,737	4,657	4,331	4,335	7,069	4,146	12,346	5,120	10,366
8,027	7,279	5,849	4,847	4,638	4,876	8,857	7,680	11,690	4,823	9,992
2,337	1,876	1,406	1,179	1,033	962	1,503	1,005	4,784	2,014	3,712
1,083	866	642	532	457	414	618	348	2,418	1,023	1,825
1,254	1,010	763	647	576	547	886	657	2,367	991	1,887
150	126	97	77	62	51	72	42	352	143	238
73	61	47	37	29	24	32	16	179	73	123
76	65	50	40	32	27	40	26	173	70	116
670	572	406	312	251	219	301	154	1,040	454	890
317	267	195	152	114	94	134	71	528	234	459
353	305	210	160	137	124	167	83	512	219	431
1,661	1,204	954	756	639	554	723	438	3,813	1,557	3,184
846	640	468	364	302	255	315	166	1,946	807	1,735
815	644	486	392	337	299	408	272	1,867	750	1,449
8.0	7.1	5.6	4.6	4.2	4.3	7.3	5.3	12.9	5.3	10.8
8.1	7.3	5.8	4.8	4.5	4.6	8.0	5.9	12.0	5.0	10.2
7.8	6.3	4.7	3.9	3.4	3.2	5.0	3.4	16.0	6.7	12.4
7.7	6.4	5.0	3.9	3.2	2.6	3.7	2.1	18.0	7.3	12.2
9.2	7.9	5.6	4.3	3.5	3.0	4.1	2.1	14.3	6.2	12.2
7.4	5.7	4.3	3.4	2.9	2.5	3.2	2.0	17.1	7.0	14.2

State Populations

State	Population (in thousands)	Rank
Alabama	4,089	22
Alaska	570	48
Arizona	3,750	23
Arkansas	2,372	33
California	30,380	1
Colorado	3,377	26
Connecticut	3,291	27
Delaware	680	46
District of Columbia	598	(X)
Florida	13,277	4
Georgia	6,623	11
Hawaii	1,135	40
Idaho	1,039	42
Illinois	11,543	6
Indiana	5,610	14
Iowa	2,795	30
Kansas	2,495	32
Kentucky	3,713	24
Louisiana	4,252	21
Maine	1,235	39
Maryland	4,860	19
Massachusetts	5,996	13
Michigan	9,368	8
Minnesota	4,432	20
Mississippi	2,592	31
Missouri	5,158	15
Montana	808	44
Nebraska	1,593	36
Nevada	1,284	38
New Hampshire	1,105	41
New Jersey	7,760	9
New Mexico	1,548	37
New York	18,058	2
North Carolina	6,737	10
North Dakota	635	47
Ohio	10,939	7
Oklahoma	3,175	28
Oregon	2,922	29
Pennsylvania	11,961	5
Rhode Island	1,004	43
South Carolina	3,560	25
South Dakota	703	45
Tennessee	4,953	18
Texas	17,349	3
Utah	1,770	35
Vermont	567	49
Virginia	6,286	12
Washington	5,018	16
West Virginia	1,801	34
Wisconsin	4,955	17
Wyoming	460	50

Immigration Statistics

Immigration, 1820–1990

[In thousands, except rate. For fiscal years ending in year shown, except as noted.]

Period	Total Number	Rate[1]	Period or year	Total Number	Rate[1]	Year	Total Number	Rate
1820 to 1990	**56,994**	**3.4**	1911 to 1920	5,736	5.7	1981	597	2.6
1820 to 1830[2]	152	1.2	1921 to 1930	4,107	3.5	1982	594	2.6
1831 to 1840[3]	599	3.9	1931 to 1940	528	0.4	1983	560	2.4
1841 to 1850[4]	1,713	8.4	1941 to 1950	1,035	0.7	1984	544	2.3
1851 to 1860[4]	2,598	9.3	1951 to 1960	2,515	1.5	1985	570	2.4
1861 to 1870[5]	2,315	6.4	1961 to 1970	3,322	1.7	1986	602	2.5
1871 to 1880	2,812	6.2	1971 to 1980	4,493	2.1	1987	602	2.5
1881 to 1890	5,247	9.2	1981 to 1990	7,338	3.1	1988	643	2.6
1891 to 1900	3,688	5.3	1970	373	1.8	1989[6]	1,091	4.4
1901 to 1910	8,795	10.4	1980	531	2.3	1990[6]	1,536	6.1

[1] Annual rate per 1,000 U.S. population. Rate computed by dividing sum of annual immigration totals by sum of annual U.S. population totals for same number of years. [2] Oct. 1, 1819, to Sept. 30, 1830. [3] Oct. 1, 1830, to Dec. 31, 1840. [4] Calendar years. [5] Jan. 1, 1861, to June 30, 1870. [6] Includes persons who were granted permanent residence under the legalization program of the Immigration Reform and Control Act of 1986.

Immigrants, by Country of Birth: 1961 to 1990

[In thousands. For fiscal years ending in year shown.]

COUNTRY OF BIRTH	1961–70, total	1971–80, total	1981–89, total	1990	COUNTRY OF BIRTH	1961–70, total	1971–80, total	1981–89, total	1990
All countries	3,321.7	4,493.3	5,801.6	1,536.5	Thailand	5.0	44.1	55.5	8.9
Europe[1]	1,238.6	801.3	593.2	112.4	Turkey	6.8	18.6	18.4	2.5
Czechoslovakia	21.4	10.2	10.1	1.4	Vietnam	4.6	179.7	352.6	48.8
France	34.3	17.8	20.3	2.8	North America[1]	1,351.1	1,645.0	2,167.4	957.6
Germany	200.0	66.0	62.6	7.5	Canada	286.7	114.8	102.4	16.8
Greece	90.2	93.7	26.4	2.7	Mexico	443.3	637.2	974.2	679.1
Hungary	17.3	11.6	8.1	1.7	Caribbean[1]	519.5	759.8	777.3	115.4
Ireland	42.4	14.1	22.5	10.3	Barbados	9.4	20.9	15.7	1.7
Italy	206.7	130.1	29.6	3.3	Cuba	256.8	276.8	148.6	10.6
Netherlands	27.8	10.7	10.5	1.4	Dominican Republic	94.1	148.0	209.6	42.2
Poland	73.3	43.6	76.9	20.5	Haiti	37.5	58.7	119.9	20.3
Portugal	79.3	104.5	36.0	4.0	Jamaica	71.0	142.0	188.8	25.0
Romania	14.9	17.5	34.3	4.6	Trinidad and Tobago	24.6	61.8	32.8	6.7
Soviet Union	15.7	43.2	58.5	25.5	Central America[1]	97.7	132.4	312.5	146.2
Spain	30.5	30.0	13.9	1.9	Costa Rica	17.4	12.1	12.7	2.8
Sweden	16.7	6.3	9.0	1.2	El Salvador	15.0	34.4	134.4	80.2
Switzerland	16.3	6.6	6.2	0.8	Guatemala	15.4	25.6	55.6	32.3
United Kingdom	230.5	123.5	126.2	15.9	Honduras	15.5	17.2	37.5	12.0
Yugoslavia	46.2	42.1	16.4	2.8	Nicaragua	10.1	13.0	32.5	11.6
Asia[1]	445.3	1,633.8	2,478.8	338.6	Panama	18.4	22.7	25.6	3.4
Afghanistan	0.4	2.0	23.4	3.2	South America[1]	228.3	284.4	370.1	85.8
Cambodia	1.2	8.4	111.4	5.2	Argentina	42.1	25.1	20.3	5.4
China: Mainland	[2]96.7	[2]202.5	[2]341.8	31.8	Brazil	20.5	13.7	19.5	4.2
Taiwan	([2])	([2])	([2])	15.2	Chile	11.5	17.6	19.4	4.0
Hong Kong	25.6	47.5	53.6	9.4	Colombia	70.3	77.6	100.2	24.2
India	31.2	176.8	231.2	30.7	Ecuador	37.0	50.2	43.5	12.5
Iran	10.4	46.2	129.8	25.0	Guyana	7.1	47.5	84.0	11.4
Iraq	6.4	23.4	17.8	1.8	Peru	18.6	29.1	48.7	15.7
Israel	12.9	26.6	31.6	4.7	Venezuela	8.5	7.1	14.8	3.1
Japan	38.5	47.9	37.5	5.7	Africa[1]	39.3	91.5	156.4	35.9
Jordan	14.0	29.6	28.2	4.4	Egypt	17.2	25.5	27.3	4.1
Korea	35.8	272.0	306.5	32.3	Nigeria	1.5	8.8	26.5	8.8
Laos	0.1	22.6	135.2	10.4	South Africa	4.5	11.5	13.7	2.0
Lebanon	7.5	33.8	36.0	5.6	Australia	9.9	14.3	12.1	1.8
Pakistan	4.9	31.2	51.6	9.7	Other countries[3]	9.2	23.0	23.5	4.5
Philippines	101.5	360.2	431.5	63.8					
Syria	4.6	13.3	17.6	3.0					

[1] Includes countries not shown separately. [2] Data for Taiwan included with China: Mainland. [3] Includes New Zealand and unknown countries.

Immigrants Admitted, by Class of Admission: 1980–1990

Class of admission	1980	1985	1986	1987	1988	1989	1990
Immigrants, total	530,639	570,009	601,708	601,516	643,025	[1]1,090,924	[1]1,536,483
Numerically limited	289,479	264,208	266,968	271,135	264,148	280,275	298,306
New arrivals	239,590	226,505	228,522	239,941	234,586	252,401	273,416
Adjustments	49,889	37,703	38,446	31,194	29,562	27,874	24,890
Exempt from numerical limitation	241,160	305,801	334,740	330,381	378,877	[1]810,649	[1]1,238,177
New arrivals	99,765	129,860	147,588	147,054	143,299	150,030	162,313
Adjustments	141,395	175,941	187,152	183,327	235,578	[1]660,619	[1]1,075,864
Numerically limited, total	289,479	264,208	266,968	271,135	264,148	280,275	298,306
Unmarried sons/daughters of U.S. citizens and their children (1st preference)	5,668	9,319	10,910	11,382	12,107	13,259	15,861
Spouses, unmarried sons/daughters of alien residents, and their children (2d pref.)	110,269	114,997	110,926	110,758	102,777	112,771	107,686
Professional or highly skilled immigrants (3d preference)[2]	18,583	24,905	26,823	26,921	26,680	26,798	26,546
Married sons/daughters of U.S. citizens (4th preference)	10,752	18,460	20,702	20,703	21,940	26,975	26,751
Brothers or sisters of U.S. citizens (5th preference)[2]	90,167	70,481	70,401	68,966	63,948	64,087	64,252
Needed skilled or unskilled workers (6th preference)[2]	25,786	25,990	26,802	26,952	26,927	25,957	27,183
Conditional entries by refugees[3]	12,222	(X)	(X)	(X)	(X)	(X)	(X)
Nonpreference	–	7	–	3,040	6,029	7,068	20,371
Recaptured Cuban numbers	15,913	(X)	(X)	(X)	(X)	(X)	(X)
Natives of under represented countries, PL. 100-658	(X)	(X)	(X)	(X)	(X)	(X)	8,790
Other	119	49	404	2,413	3,740	3,360	866
Exempt from numerical limitations	241,160	305,801	334,740	330,381	378,877	[1]810,649	[1]1,238,177
Immediate relatives	157,743	204,368	223,468	218,575	219,340	217,514	231,680
Spouses of U.S. citizens	96,854	129,790	137,597	132,452	130,977	125,744	125,426
Children of U.S. citizens	27,207	35,592	40,639	40,940	40,863	41,276	46,065
Orphans	5,139	9,286	9,945	10,097	9,120	7,948	7,088
Parents of U.S. citizens	33,682	38,986	45,232	45,183	47,500	50,494	60,189
Refugee and asylee adjustments	75,835	95,040	104,383	91,840	81,719	84,288	97,364
Cuban Refugee Act, Nov. 1966	6,021	14,288	30,152	26,869	10,993	5,206	5,730
Indochinese Refugee Act, Oct. 1977	22,497	166	136	83	42	40	33
Refugee-Parolee Act, Oct. 1978	46,058	3,766	1,720	866	437	381	153
Asylees, Refugee Act of 1980	1,250	5,000	5,000	5,000	5,445	5,145	4,937

Immigrants Admitted, by Class of Admission: 1980–1990 (continued)

Class of admission	1980	1985	1986	1987	1988	1989	1990
Refugees, Refugee Act of 1980	(X)	71,820	67,375	59,022	64,801	73,516	86,511
Other refugees	9	–	–	–	1	–	–
Special immigrants	3,142	2,551	2,992	3,646	5,120	4,986	4,463
Ministers of religion[2]	1,529	1,853	2,060	2,041	2,207	2,595	2,786
Employees of U.S. Government abroad[2]	1,354	479	773	1,112	2,047	1,713	1,234
Foreign medical graduates, Act of Dec. 1981[2]	(X)	87	48	28	7	11	2
Other special immigrants[2]	259	132	111	465	859	667	441
Aliens adjusted[4]	254	105	95	12,834	69,069	13,459	8,360
Children born abroad to resident aliens or subsequent to issuance of visa	4,059	3,508	3,554	3,269	3,082		
Others not subject to numerical limitation	127	229	248	217	547	[5]8,782	[5]13,308

– Represents zero. X Not applicable
[1] Includes 478,814 (for 1989) and 880,372 (for 1990) persons who were granted permanent residence under the legalization program of the Immigration Reform and Control Act (IRCA) of 1986. [2] Includes spouses and children. [3] In 1980, conditional entries were a 7th preference class. [4] Under sections 244 and 249, Immigration and Naturalization Act. Includes Cuban/Haitian entrants under the Act of November 1986. [5] Includes Amerasians under Public Law 100-202. Amerasians are aliens born in Vietnam between January 1, 1962 and January 1, 1976 who were fathered by U.S. citizens.
– U.S. Immigration and Naturalization Service

Immigrants Admitted as Permanent Residents Under Refugee Acts, by Country of Birth: 1961–1990

[For fiscal years ending in year shown; covers immigrants who were allowed to enter the United States under 1953 Refugee Relief Act and later acts; Hungarian parolees under July 1958 Act; refugee-escapee parolees under July 1960 Act; conditional entries by refugees under Oct. 1965 Act; Cuban parolees under Nov. 1966 Act; beginning 1978, Indochina refugees under Act of Oct. 1977; beginning 1980, refugee-parolees under the Act of Oct. 1978, and asylees under the Act of March 1980; and beginning 1981 refugees under the Act of March 1980]

Country of birth	1961–1970, total	1971–1980, total	1981–1989, total	1990	Country of birth	1961–1970, total	1971–1980, total	1981–1989, total	1990
Total	212,843	539,447	916,256	97,364	Iran	58	364	38,124	8,649
					Iraq	119	6,851	7,399	141
Europe	**55,235**	**71,858**	**122,401**	**33,111**	Korea	1,316	65	118	2
Austria	233	185	340	84	Laos	–	21,690	133,140	9,824
Bulgaria	1,799	1,238	1,019	178	Malaysia	9	192	1,218	59
Czechoslovakia	5,709	3,646	7,321	883	Philippines	100	216	3,113	290
Germany	665	143	697	154	Syria	383	1,336	1,752	393
Greece	586	478	1,093	315	Thailand	13	1,241	26,182	4,077
Hungary	4,044	4,358	4,074	868	Turkey	1,489	1,193	1,620	276
Italy	1,198	346	308	86	Vietnam	7	150,266	303,916	20,537
Netherlands	3,134	8	10	4	Other Asia	1,307	1,538	2,658	365
Poland	3,197	5,882	29,986	3,903	**North America**	**132,068**	**252,633**	**111,930**	**9,910**
Portugal	1,361	21	19	2	Cuba	131,557	251,514	105,699	7,668
Romania	7,158	6,812	26,612	3,186	El Salvador	1	45	1,138	245
Soviet Union	871	31,309	49,120	23,186	Nicaragua	3	36	3,896	1,694
Spain	4,114	5,317	652	84	Other N. America	507	1,038	1,197	303
Yugoslavia	18,299	11,297	301	23	**South America**	**123**	**1,244**	**1,712**	**264**
Other Europe	2,867	818	849	155	Chile	4	420	511	20
Asia	**19,895**	**210,683**	**660,225**	**51,867**	Other S. America	119	824	1,201	244
Afghanistan	–	542	20,802	2,144	**Africa**	**5,486**	**2,991**	**19,937**	**2,212**
Cambodia	–	7,739	109,345	4,719	Egypt	5,396	1,473	357	69
China[1]	5,308	13,760	7,595	333	Ethiopia	2	1,307	16,860	1,682
Hong Kong	2,128	3,468	1,886	30	Other Africa	88	211	2,720	461
Indonesia	7,658	222	1,357	28	**Other**	**36**	**38**	**51**	**–**

– Represents zero. [1] Covers Mainland and Taiwan.

No. 11. Immigrants Admitted, by Leading Country of Birth and Metropolitan Area of Intended Residence: 1990

Metropolitan Area of Intended Residence	Total[1]	Mexico	El Salvador	Philippines	Vietnam[2]	Dominican Republic	Guatemala	Korea	China: Mainland	India
Total[3]	1,536,483	679,068	80,173	63,756	48,662	42,195	32,303	32,301	31,815	30,667
Los Angeles-Long Beach, CA	374,773	231,267	42,172	11,644	4,745	86	18,446	6,059	3,525	1,440
New York, NY	164,330	6,436	2,853	4,750	1,155	25,430	1,895	3,586	9,030	3,530
Chicago, IL	73,107	41,848	631	2,655	742	70	1,839	1,238	802	3,024
Anaheim-Santa Ana, CA	65,367	44,414	2,026	1,407	4,950	13	1,060	1,219	459	667
Houston, TX	58,208	34,973	9,285	677	2,014	48	988	263	473	854
Miami-Hialeah, FL	37,677	1,273	706	292	56	1,342	650	64	157	139
San Diego, CA	37,208	25,540	226	3,539	1,575	13	190	205	278	114
Riverside-San Bernardino, CA	35,616	27,159	998	1,224	505	2	581	373	136	269
Washington, DC-MD-VA	32,705	1,056	4,956	1,228	2,188	277	620	1,940	802	1,465
San Francisco, CA	29,144	7,060	2,871	3,574	1,459	6	686	358	3,782	248
Dallas, TX	28,533	19,391	1,595	270	1,015	15	377	391	248	523
San Jose, CA	26,250	10,766	654	2,440	3,881	14	148	516	963	816

No. 11. Immigrants Admitted (*continued*)

Metropolitan Area of Intended Residence	Total[1]	Mexico	El Salvador	Philippines	Vietnam[2]	Dominican Republic	Guatemala	Korea	China: Mainland	India
Oakland, CA	20,894	6,884	643	2,678	1,040	5	157	401	1,506	769
Boston-Lawrence-Salem-Lowell-Brockton, MA	20,776	215	698	246	1,435	2,093	494	241	1,115	501
Newark, NJ	16,089	127	521	883	197	538	235	195	226	813
Nassau-Suffolk, NY	14,823	262	2,643	424	94	829	365	389	394	807
Phoenix, AZ	14,714	10,726	206	211	692	5	198	146	176	130
El Paso, TX	14,476	14,009	25	33	5	1	15	59	18	20
Bergen-Passaic, NJ	13,144	665	275	724	15	1,480	85	727	161	790
Philadelphia, PA-NJ	11,440	382	64	577	1,228	126	37	909	439	931
Fresno, CA	11,193	8,066	175	156	74	—	55	28	75	280
McAllen-Edinburg-Mission, TX	9,937	9,719	29	10	—	2	27	7	2	1
Jersey City, NJ	9,921	155	636	889	61	1,153	173	160	156	612
Fort Lauderdale-Hollywood-Pompano Beach, FL	9,906	349	112	127	87	111	67	58	92	145
Fort Worth-Arlington, TX	9,736	6,805	182	82	635	5	56	82	68	200
Oxnard-Ventura, CA	9,508	7,251	195	548	80	3	124	103	54	93
Sacramento, CA	8,933	3,378	137	602	604	4	43	222	307	172
San Antonio, TX	8,668	7,304	103	139	99	13	95	104	47	43
Atlanta, GA	8,079	1,363	180	151	923	31	52	430	132	319
Seattle, WA	7,335	573	61	1,025	1,083	2	26	542	403	153
Bakersfield, CA	7,246	6,094	194	344	10	—	63	39	17	83
Detroit, MI	7,199	309	14	398	146	12	10	280	172	552
Honolulu, HI	6,706	44	6	3,051	537	—	—	678	511	16
Salinas-Seaside-Monterey, CA	6,695	5,570	119	292	66	1	13	106	33	24
Middlesex-Somerset-Hunterdon, NJ	6,414	177	68	433	46	636	51	205	222	1,093
San Juan, PR	6,181	41	22	11	1	5,171	7	4	55	5
Brownsville-Harlingen, TX	6,175	5,883	75	38	—	—	22	1	6	1
Visalia-Tulare-Porterville, CA	5,925	4,846	62	175	3	—	20	11	10	56
Denver, CO	5,509	2,967	36	148	364	3	32	202	110	77
Santa Barbara-Santa Maria-Lompoc, CA	5,489	4,483	43	178	28	1	127	49	24	27
Stockton, CA	5,463	2,886	33	490	292	—	16	16	64	87
Minneapolis-St. Paul, MN-WI	5,439	193	15	156	559	6	15	246	106	145
Austin, TX	5,044	3,496	183	37	195	1	27	70	60	53
West Palm Beach-Boca Raton-Delray Beach, FL	5,012	599	67	75	40	42	58	25	36	86
Las Vegas, NV	4,986	2,607	250	413	132	7	67	148	105	33
Tampa-St. Petersburg-Clearwater, FL	4,721	913	36	166	418	37	35	88	40	91
Bridgeport-Stamford-Norwalk-Danbury, CT	4,507	111	62	77	146	123	92	44	69	207
Portland, OR	4,493	1,071	39	147	654	1	33	283	190	50
Santa Cruz, CA	4,396	3,963	31	69	15	3	7	8	44	11
Tucson, AZ	4,232	3,338	34	50	159	—	19	36	41	23
Modesto, CA	4,062	2,869	36	62	34	2	22	26	20	98
Baltimore, MD	3,732	99	38	223	108	21	13	544	122	221
Merced, CA	3,696	2,755	37	47	1	—	8	9	10	118
Hartford-New Britain-Middletown-Bristol, CT	3,673	35	17	55	223	47	11	66	68	151
Lake County, IL	3,587	2,429	98	157	4	—	45	94	24	126
Providence-Pawtucket-Woonsocket, RI	3,566	75	35	88	33	539	259	36	73	45
Vallejo-Fairfield-Napa, CA	3,510	1,756	99	983	61	1	22	45	24	80
Orlando, FL	3,445	318	49	134	259	92	22	69	30	99
Aurora-Elgin, IL	3,085	2,601	15	37	15	4	17	25	4	51
Albuquerque, NM	2,878	2,264	27	35	154	1	34	38	27	35
Oklahoma City, OK	2,741	1,391	5	55	364	1	39	78	31	51
Laredo, TX	2,557	2,498	11	1	—	—	19	1	—	5

— Represents zero. [1] Includes other countries, not shown separately. [2] Data for immigrants admitted under the legalization program are not available separately for Vietnam and thus not included in this column. [3] Includes other metropolitan areas, not shown separately.

Economic Statistics

Federal Receipts, by Source: 1980–1992
[In millions of dollars. For fiscal years ending in year shown.]

Source	1980	1985	1989	1990	1991	1992, est.	Percent Distribution 1980	Percent Distribution 1992, est.
Total receipts[1]	517,112	734,057	990,691	1,031,308	1,054,264	1,075,706	100.0	100.0
Individual income taxes	244,069	334,531	445,690	466,884	467,827	478,749	47.2	44.5
Corporation income taxes	64,600	61,331	103,291	93,507	98,086	89,031	12.5	8.3
Social insurance	157,803	265,163	359,416	380,047	396,016	410,863	30.5	38.2
Employment taxes and contributions	138,748	234,646	332,859	353,891	370,526	383,663	26.8	35.7
Old-age and survivors insurance	96,581	169,822	240,595	255,031	265,503	271,784	18.7	25.3
Disability insurance	16,628	16,348	23,071	26,625	28,382	29,138	3.2	2.7
Hospital insurance	23,217	44,871	65,396	68,556	72,842	79,007	4.5	7.3
Railroad retirement/pension fund	2,323	2,213	2,391	2,292	2,371	2,329	0.4	0.2
Railroad social security equivalent account	—	1,391	1,407	1,387	1,428	1,405	—	0.1
Unemployment insurance	15,336	25,758	22,011	21,635	20,922	22,547	3.0	2.1
Other retirement contributions	3,719	4,759	4,546	4,522	4,568	4,653	0.7	0.4
Excise taxes	24,329	35,992	34,386	35,345	42,402	46,098	4.7	4.3
Federal funds	15,563	19,097	13,147	15,591	18,275	21,170	3.0	2.0
Alcohol	5,601	5,562	5,661	5,695	7,364	8,219	1.1	0.8
Tobacco	2,443	4,779	4,378	4,081	4,706	4,897	0.5	0.5
Windfall profits	6,934	6,348	—	—	—	—	1.3	—
Ozone depletion	—	—	—	360	562	662	—	0.1
Other taxes	585	261	317	2,460	2,549	4,343	0.1	0.4
Trust funds[1]	8,766	16,894	21,239	19,754	24,127	24,928	1.7	2.3
Highways	6,620	13,015	15,628	13,867	16,979	17,387	1.3	1.6
Airport and airway	1,874	2,851	3,664	3,700	4,910	5,193	0.4	0.5
Black lung disability	272	581	563	665	652	627	0.1	0.1
Hazardous substance response	—	273	883	818	810	825	—	0.1
Aquatic resources	—	126	187	218	260	278	—	—
Leaking underground storage	—	—	168	122	123	145	—	—
Vaccine injury compensations	—	—	99	159	81	120	—	—
Oil spill liability	—	—	—	143	254	283	—	—
Estate and gift taxes	6,389	6,422	8,745	11,500	11,138	12,063	1.2	1.1
Customs duties	7,174	12,079	16,334	16,707	15,949	17,260	1.4	1.6
Federal Reserve deposits	11,767	17,059	19,604	24,319	19,158	18,507	2.3	1.7

— Represents or rounds to zero. [1] Totals reflect interfund and intragovernmental transactions and/or other functions, not shown separately.

Personal Income Per Capita—States: 1980–1991
(In current dollars)

Region, Division, and State	1980	1985	1989	1990	1991[1]	Income rank 1980	Income rank 1991[1]
United States	9,919	13,942	17,738	18,696	19,082	(X)	(X)
Alabama	7,704	10,830	14,058	14,998	15,567	47	41
Alaska	13,835	18,405	20,585	21,646	21,932	1	6
Arizona	9,172	12,866	15,366	16,006	16,401	32	35
Arkansas	7,465	10,672	13,296	14,176	14,753	49	47
California	11,603	15,981	19,734	20,689	20,952	3	8
Colorado	10,598	14,805	17,815	18,860	19,440	13	14
Connecticut	12,112	18,083	24,422	25,395	25,881	2	1
Delaware	10,249	14,726	19,282	20,095	20,349	14	11
District of Columbia	12,322	17,499	22,083	23,603	24,439	(X)	(X)
Florida	9,764	13,954	17,851	18,539	18,880	24	18
Georgia	8,348	12,643	16,223	17,045	17,364	38	29
Hawaii	10,617	14,030	18,659	20,361		11	7
Idaho	8,569	10,933	14,276	15,250	15,401	36	44
Illinois	10,837	14,908	19,335	20,433	20,824	7	10
Indiana	9,245	12,516	16,124	16,921	17,217	31	32
Iowa	9,537	12,797	16,307	17,301	17,505	26	28
Kansas	9,941	13,930	16,962	18,104	18,511	17	21
Kentucky	8,022	10,852	14,021	14,992	15,539	43	42
Louisiana	8,682	11,495	13,338	14,528	15,143	34	45
Maine	8,218	11,913	16,455	17,183	17,306	39	30
Maryland	10,790	15,895	20,856	21,857	22,080	8	5
Massachusetts	10,612	16,145	21,853	22,555	22,897	12	3
Michigan	10,165	14,018	17,650	18,378	18,679	15	20
Minnesota	10,062	14,165	17,852	18,731	19,107	16	17
Mississippi	6,926	9,340	12,077	12,830	13,343	50	50
Missouri	9,298	13,344	16,687	17,479	17,842	29	25
Montana	8,924	11,056	14,520	15,304	16,043	33	39
Nebraska	9,274	13,129	16,382	17,490	17,852	30	24
Nevada	11,421	14,510	18,380	19,049	19,175	5	15
New Hampshire	9,788	15,389	20,334	20,773	20,951	23	9
New Jersey	11,573	17,622	23,628	24,881	25,372	4	2
New Mexico	8,169	11,288	13,452	14,254	14,844	41	46
New York	10,721	15,751	20,881	22,129	22,456	10	4
North Carolina	7,999	11,669	15,422	16,266	16,642	44	34
North Dakota	8,538	12,085	14,116	15,355	16,088	37	38
Ohio	9,723	13,224	16,646	17,568	17,916	25	23
Oklahoma	9,393	12,298	14,501	15,451	15,827	28	40
Oregon	9,866	12,702	16,258	17,182	17,592	19	27
Pennsylvania	9,891	13,661	17,608	18,679	19,128	18	16
Rhode Island	9,518	13,746	18,089	18,809	18,840	27	19
South Carolina	7,589	10,831	13,969	15,141	15,420	48	43
South Dakota	8,217	11,182	14,492	15,890	16,392	40	36
Tennessee	8,030	11,374	15,009	15,868	16,325	42	37
Texas	9,798	13,562	15,682	16,717	17,305	22	31
Utah	7,952	10,658	13,056	13,985	14,529	45	48
Vermont	8,577	12,490	16,895	17,506	17,747	35	26
Virginia	9,827	14,438	18,891	19,701	19,976	21	12

Personal Income Per Capita—States: 1980–1991 (continued)

Region, Division, and State	1980	1985	1989	1990	1991[1]	Income rank 1980	Income rank 1991[1]
Washington	10,725	14,096	17,790	18,777	19,442	9	13
West Virginia	7,915	10,227	12,751	13,744	14,174	46	49
Wisconsin	9,845	13,247	16,724	17,590	18,046	20	22
Wyoming	11,339	13,081	14,921	16,283	17,118	6	33
Northeast	10,603	15,567	20,661	21,736	22,111	(X)	(X)
New England	10,542	15,852	21,371	22,111	22,425	(X)	(X)
Middle Atlantic	10,624	15,470	20,412	21,604	22,001	(X)	(X)
Midwest	9,919	13,655	17,305	18,227	18,586	(X)	(X)
East North Central	10,077	13,771	17,541	18,444	18,799	(X)	(X)
West North Central	9,534	13,379	16,744	17,711	18,079	(X)	(X)
South	8,944	12,680	15,965	16,892	17,329	(X)	(X)
South Atlantic	9,171	13,320	17,273	18,126	18,449	(X)	(X)
East South Central	7,752	10,749	14,017	14,909	15,429	(X)	(X)
West South Central	9,326	12,802	14,956	16,000	16,571	(X)	(X)
West	10,843	14,750	18,271	19,226	19,598	(X)	(X)
Mountain	9,445	12,755	15,563	16,428	16,907	(X)	(X)
Pacific	11,343	15,474	19,223	20,200	20,541	(X)	(X)

X Not applicable. [1] Preliminary.

Household Type, by Median Income and Income Level: 1990

Item	All households	Family Households Total	Married couple	Male householder, wife absent	Female householder, husband absent	Nonfamily Households Total[1]	Single-person household Male householder	Single-person household Female householder
Median Income (dollars)								
All households	29,943	35,707	39,996	31,552	18,069	17,690	19,964	12,548
White	31,231	37,219	40,433	32,869	20,867	18,449	20,900	13,094
Black	18,676	21,899	33,893	24,048	12,537	11,789	13,126	7,674
Hispanic[2]	22,330	24,552	28,584	25,456	12,603	14,274	13,716	8,933
Number (1000)								
All households	94,312	66,322	52,147	2,907	11,268	27,990	9,450	14,141
Under $5,000	4,901	2,241	674	101	1,466	2,660	806	1,771
$5,000 to $9,999	9,184	3,712	1,700	189	1,823	5,471	1,378	3,918
$10,000 to $14,999	8,925	4,841	3,102	233	1,506	4,084	1,349	2,365
$15,000 to $19,999	8,296	5,176	3,626	293	1,257	3,120	1,200	1,578
$20,000 to $24,999	8,427	5,601	4,175	298	1,128	2,826	1,066	1,318
$25,000 to $34,999	14,864	10,808	8,564	531	1,713	4,057	1,599	1,691
$35,000 to $49,999	16,469	13,394	11,442	616	1,337	3,075	1,143	973
$50,000 and over	23,246	20,546	18,864	647	1,037	2,699	909	529

[1] Includes other nonfamily households not shown separately. [2] Hispanic persons may be of any race.

Money Income of Households—Percent Distribution, by Income Level and Selected Characteristics: 1990

Characteristic	Number of households (1,000)	Under $5,000	$5,000-$9,999	$10,000-$14,999	$15,000-$24,000	$25,000-$34,999	$35,000-$49,999	$50,000-$74,999	$75,000 and over	Median income (dollars)
Total[1]	94,312	5.2	9.7	9.5	17.7	15.8	17.5	14.9	9.7	29,943
Age of householder:										
15 to 24 years	4,882	13.3	14.2	14.7	24.3	16.6	11.2	4.6	1.1	18,002
25 to 34 years	20,323	5.0	6.9	8.2	19.8	19.3	20.9	14.2	5.8	30,359
35 to 44 years	21,304	3.3	4.5	5.8	14.0	16.5	21.7	21.4	12.8	38,561
45 to 54 years	14,751	3.3	5.0	5.3	12.4	14.1	19.5	21.6	18.7	41,922
55 to 64 years	12,524	5.5	7.9	8.4	16.7	15.1	17.8	16.1	12.5	32,365
65 years and over	20,527	6.6	21.4	17.0	22.5	12.9	9.5	5.7	4.4	16,855
White	80,968	4.0	8.8	9.2	17.7	16.1	18.0	15.8	10.4	31,231
Black	10,671	14.1	16.7	11.6	19.1	13.5	13.1	8.1	3.8	18,676
Hispanic[2]	6,220	7.5	13.7	12.9	21.1	16.5	14.8	9.1	4.3	22,330
Northeast	19,271	4.4	10.1	8.4	15.3	14.6	17.7	17.0	12.5	32,676
Midwest	23,223	5.1	10.0	9.6	17.7	15.8	18.0	15.2	8.6	29,897
South	32,312	6.6	10.2	10.4	19.2	16.0	16.7	13.0	7.9	26,942
West	19,506	3.8	8.4	8.8	17.6	16.5	17.8	15.7	11.5	31,761
Size of household:										
One person	23,590	10.9	22.5	15.7	21.9	13.9	9.0	4.2	1.9	15,344
Two persons	30,181	3.5	6.0	9.3	19.8	17.3	18.8	15.3	10.0	31,358
Three persons	16,082	4.0	5.6	6.4	14.8	16.4	20.6	19.6	12.7	36,765
Four persons	14,556	2.7	4.6	4.8	12.4	14.9	22.9	22.5	15.3	41,473
Five persons	6,206	2.3	5.0	6.3	12.8	16.2	21.2	21.4	14.8	39,275

Money Income of Households—Percent Distribution, by Income Level and Selected Characteristics: 1990 *(continued)*

Characteristic	Number of households (1,000)	Under $5,000	$5,000-$9,999	$10,000-$14,999	$15,000-$24,000	$25,000-$34,999	$35,000-$49,999	$50,000-$74,999	$75,000 and over	Median income (dollars)
Six persons	2,237	2.4	5.5	7.3	15.7	14.6	20.8	19.2	14.4	38,159
Seven persons or more	1,459	2.7	5.8	7.4	18.1	14.6	18.2	19.0	14.1	36,108
Family households	66,322	3.4	5.6	7.3	16.3	16.3	20.2	18.5	12.5	35,707
Married-couple families	52,147	1.3	3.3	5.9	15.0	16.4	21.9	21.3	14.9	39,996
Male householder, wife absent	2,907	3.5	6.5	8.0	20.3	18.3	21.2	15.3	6.9	31,552
Female householder, husband absent	11,268	13.0	16.2	13.4	21.2	15.2	11.9	6.7	2.5	18,069
Nonfamily households	27,990	9.5	19.5	14.6	21.2	14.5	11.0	6.4	3.3	17,690
Male householder	12,150	7.0	12.1	13.1	22.4	16.9	14.2	9.2	5.2	22,489
Female householder	15,840	11.4	25.3	15.7	20.3	12.7	8.6	4.2	1.8	14,099
Education attainment of householder:[3]										
Elementary school, 8 years or less	10,146	12.2	25.1	16.8	22.0	11.4	7.4	3.8	1.3	13,523
High school	42,120	5.5	11.0	11.2	20.4	17.7	18.0	12.1	4.7	25,953
1 to 3 years	10,077	9.4	18.0	14.3	22.7	14.7	12.0	6.6	2.3	18,191
4 years	32,043	4.2	8.8	10.3	19.7	17.9	19.9	13.8	5.5	28,744
College	37,163	1.9	3.5	4.8	12.6	15.3	20.5	22.5	18.9	43,112
1 to 3 years	16,451	2.8	5.3	6.7	16.5	17.3	21.7	20.2	9.4	35,724
4 years or more	20,712	1.3	2.0	3.3	9.5	13.7	19.5	24.3	26.4	50,549
Tenure:										
Owner occupied	60,395	2.7	6.5	7.7	15.5	15.5	19.6	19.0	13.5	36,298
Renter occupied	32,218	9.4	15.4	12.5	21.7	16.3	14.0	7.7	3.1	20,722
Occupier paid no cash rent	1,698	14.0	18.5	15.1	20.9	14.3	8.8	6.3	2.2	15,868

[1] Includes other races not shown separately. [2] Hispanic persons may be of any race. [3] 25 years old and over.
Source: U.S. Bureau of the Census, *Current Population Reports*, series P-60, No. 174; and unpublished data.

Federal Government Finances and Employment

Federal Outlays, by Detailed Function: 1980 to 1992
[In millions of dollars. For fiscal years ending in year shown; outlays stated in terms of checks issued or cash payments. See headnote, table 492]

Function	1980	1985	1989	1990	1991	1992, est.	Percent Distribution 1980	Percent Distribution 1992, est.
Total outlays	590,920	946,316	1,144,069	1,251,778	1,323,011	1,475,439	100.00	100.00
On-budget	*476,591*	*769,509*	*933,258*	*1,026,713*	*1,081,324*	*1,223,909*	*80.65*	*82.95*
Off-budget	*114,329*	*176,807*	*210,911*	*225,065*	*241,687*	*251,530*	*19.35*	*17.05*
National defense	133,995	252,748	303,559	299,331	273,292	307,304	22.68	20.83
Dept. of Defense—Military	130,912	245,154	294,880	289,755	262,389	294,039	22.15	19.93
Military personnel	40,897	67,842	80,676	75,622	83,439	79,289	6.92	5.37
Operation and maintenance	44,788	72,371	87,001	88,340	101,769	97,828	7.58	6.63
Procurement	29,021	70,381	81,620	80,972	82,028	73,952	4.91	5.01
R and D, test, and evaluation	13,127	27,103	37,002	37,458	34,589	36,145	2.22	2.45
Military construction	2,450	4,260	5,275	5,080	3,497	4,541	0.41	0.31
Family housing	1,680	2,642	3,257	3,501	3,296	3,404	0.28	0.23
Other	−1,050	553	50	−1,218	−46,229	−521	−0.18	−0.04
Atomic energy defense activities	2,878	7,098	8,119	8,988	10,004	11,685	0.49	0.79
Defense related activities	206	495	560	587	899	980	0.03	0.07
International affairs	12,714	16,176	9,573	13,764	15,851	17,811	2.15	1.21
International development and humanitarian assistance	3,626	5,409	4,836	5,498	5,141	6,154	0.61	0.42
Conduct of foreign affairs	1,366	2,043	2,886	3,050	3,282	3,560	0.23	0.24
Foreign information and exchange activities	534	805	1,106	1,103	1,253	1,343	0.09	0.09
International financial programs activities	2,425	−1,471	−722	−4,539	−3,648	−1,029	—	−0
International security assistance	4,763	9,391	1,467	8,652	9,823	7,783	0.81	0.53
Income security	86,540	128,200	136,031	147,277	170,846	198,093	14.64	13.43
General retirement and disability insurance	5,083	5,617	5,650	5,148	4,945	5,538	0.86	0.38
Federal employee retirement and disability	26,594	38,591	49,151	51,981	56,106	57,718	4.50	3.91
Housing assistance	5,632	25,263	14,715	15,891	17,200	19,438	0.95	1.32
Food and nutrition assistance	14,016	18,540	21,192	23,964	28,481	33,561	2.37	2.27
Other income security	17,163	22,715	29,706	31,404	37,030	45,145	2.90	3.06
Unemployment compensation	18,051	17,475	15,616	18,889	27,084	36,693	3.05	2.49
Health	23,169	33,542	48,390	57,716	71,183	94,593	3.92	6.41
Health care services	18,003	26,984	39,164	47,642	60,723	82,810	3.05	5.61
Health research	3,442	4,908	7,325	8,611	8,899	10,058	0.58	0.68
Consumer and occupational health and safety	1,006	1,182	1,356	1,462	1,560	1,724	0.17	0.12

						1992,	1980	1992, est.
Function	1980	1985	1989	1990	1991	est.		
Medicare	32,090	65,822	84,964	98,102	104,489	118,638	5.43	8.04
Social Security	118,547	188,623	232,542	248,623	269,015	286,732	20.06	19.43
On-budget	675	5,189	5,069	3,625	2,619	6,078	0.11	0.41
Off-budget	117,872	183,434	227,473	244,998	266,395	280,654	19.95	0.00
Veterans benefits and services	21,185	26,292	30,066	29,112	31,349	33,819	3.59	2.29
Income security for veterans	11,686	14,714	16,544	15,241	16,961	17,193	1.98	1.17
Educ., training, and rehab	2,342	1,059	459	278	427	696	0.40	0.05
Hospital and medical care	6,515	9,547	11,343	12,134	12,889	13,727	1.10	0.93
Housing for veterans	(Z)	214	878	517	85	1,153	0.00	0.08
Other	665	758	843	943	987	1,050	0.11	0.07
Education, training, employment, and social services	31,843	29,342	36,674	38,497	42,809	45,025	5.39	3.05
Elementary, secondary, and vocational education	6,893	7,598	9,150	9,918	11,372	13,052	1.17	0.88
Higher education	6,723	8,156	10,584	11,107	11,961	11,140	1.14	0.76
Research and general educ. aids	1,212	1,229	1,509	1,577	1,773	1,966	0.21	0.13
Training and employment	10,345	4,972	5,292	5,361	5,388	5,792	1.75	0.39
Other labor services	551	678	786	810	788	871	0.09	0.06
Social services	6,119	6,710	9,354	9,723	11,526	12,204	1.04	0.83
Commerce and housing credit	9,390	4,229	29,211	67,142	75,639	87,149	1.59	5.91
Mortgage credit	5,887	3,054	4,978	3,845	5,362	3,201	1.00	0.22
Postal Service	1,246	1,351	127	2,116	1,828	1,335	0.21	0.09
Deposit insurance	−285	−2,198	21,996	58,081	66,394	80,185	−0.05	5.43
Other commerce	2,542	2,022	2,019	3,100	2,054	2,427	0.43	0.16
Transportation	21,329	25,838	27,608	29,485	31,099	34,031	3.61	2.31
Ground transportation	15,274	17,606	17,946	18,954	19,545	21,086	2.58	1.43
Air transportation	3,723	4,895	6,622	7,234	8,184	9,042	0.63	0.61
Water transportation	2,229	3,201	2,916	3,151	3,148	3,633	0.38	0.25
Other transportation	104	137	124	146	223	270	0.02	0.02
Natural resources and environment	13,858	13,357	16,182	17,067	18,552	20,231	2.35	1.37
Water resources	4,223	4,122	4,271	4,401	4,366	4,729	0.71	0.32
Conservation and land management	1,043	1,481	3,324	3,553	4,047	4,374	0.18	0.30
Recreational resources	1,677	1,621	1,817	1,876	2,137	2,474	0.28	0.17
Pollution control and abatement	5,510	4,465	4,878	5,156	5,853	6,131	0.93	0.42
Other natural resources	1,405	1,668	1,890	2,080	2,148	2,522	0.24	0.17
Energy	10,156	5,685	3,702	2,428	1,662	4,026	1.72	0.27
Supply	8,367	2,615	2,226	1,062	1,170	3,000	1.42	0.20
Conservation	569	491	333	365	386	463	0.10	0.03
Emergency preparedness	342	1,838	621	442	−235	336	0.06	0.02
Information, policy, and regs	878	740	521	559	340	226	0.15	0.02
Community/regional develop	11,252	7,680	5,362	8,498	6,811	7,533	1.90	0.51
Community development	4,907	4,598	3,693	3,530	3,543	3,911	0.83	0.27
Area and regional development	4,303	3,117	1,894	2,868	2,743	3,144	0.73	0.21

Percent Distribution

Federal Outlays, by Detailed Function: 1980 to 1992 (*continued*)[In millions of dollars.]

Function	1980	1985	1989	1990	1991	1992, est.	Percent Distribution 1980	Percent Distribution 1992, est.
Disaster relief and insurance	2,043	(Z)	−226	2,100	525	478	0.35	0.03
Agriculture	8,839	25,565	16,919	11,958	15,183	17,219	1.50	1.17
Farm income stabilization	7,441	23,751	14,817	9,761	12,924	14,670	1.26	0.99
Research and services	1,398	1,813	2,102	2,197	2,259	2,550	0.24	0.17
Net interest	52,538	129,504	169,266	184,221	194,541	198,820	8.89	13.48
On-budget	*54,877*	*133,622*	*180,661*	*200,212*	*214,763*	*222,673*	*9.29*	*15.09*
Off-budget	*−2,339*	*−4,118*	*−11,395*	*−15,991*	*−20,222*	*−23,853*	*0.39*	*−1.62*
Interest on the public debt	74,808	178,898	240,963	264,820	286,004	292,992	12.66	19.86
Other interest	−10,224	−23,438	−19,755	−18,191	−20,266	−16,948	−1.73	−1.15
General science, space, and technology	5,832	8,627	12,838	14,444	16,111	16,373	0.99	1.11
Gen. science and basic research	1,381	2,019	2,642	2,835	3,154	3,612	0.23	0.24
General government	13,028	11,588	9,017	10,734	11,661	12,838	2.20	0.87
Legislative functions	1,038	1,355	1,652	1,763	1,916	2,230	0.18	0.15
Exec. direction and manag't	97	113	129	160	190	197	0.02	0.01
Central fiscal operations	2,612	3,492	5,517	6,004	6,097	6,790	0.44	0.46
General property and records management	327	96	−396	31	657	704	0.06	0.05
General purpose financial assistance	8,582	6,353	2,061	2,161	2,100	2,158	1.45	0.15
Other general government	569	521	814	800	1,280	1,505	0.10	0.10
Deductions, offsetting receipts	−351	−506	−893	−361	−718	−914	−0.06	−0.06
Administration of justice	4,584	6,270	9,474	9,995	12,276	14,061	0.78	0.95
Federal law enforcement	2,239	3,520	4,719	4,648	5,661	6,422	0.38	0.44
Federal litigative and judicial	1,347	2,064	3,255	3,579	4,352	5,029	0.23	0.34
Federal correctional activities	342	537	1,044	1,291	1,600	1,901	0.06	0.13
Criminal justice assistance	656	150	455	477	663	709	0.11	0.05
Undistributed offsetting receipts	−19,942	−32,698	−37,212	−36,615	−39,356	−38,761	−3.37	−2.63
On-budget	*−18,738*	*−30,189*	*−32,354*	*−31,048*	*−33,553*	*−32,665*	*−3.17*	*−2.21*
Off-budget	*−1,204*	*−2,509*	*−4,858*	*−5,567*	*−5,804*	*−6,095*	*−0.20*	*−0.41*
Employer share, employee retirement	*−15,842*	*−27,157*	*−34,283*	*−33,611*	*−36,206*	*−36,478*	*−2.68*	*−2.47*
Rents and royalties[1]	*−4,101*	*−5,542*	*−2,929*	*−3,004*	*−3,150*	*−2,282*	*−0.69*	*−0.15*

— Represents zero. Z Less than $500,000. [1] On Outer Continental Shelf.

Federal Deficit—Receipts, Outlays and Surplus or Deficit: 1970 to 1992

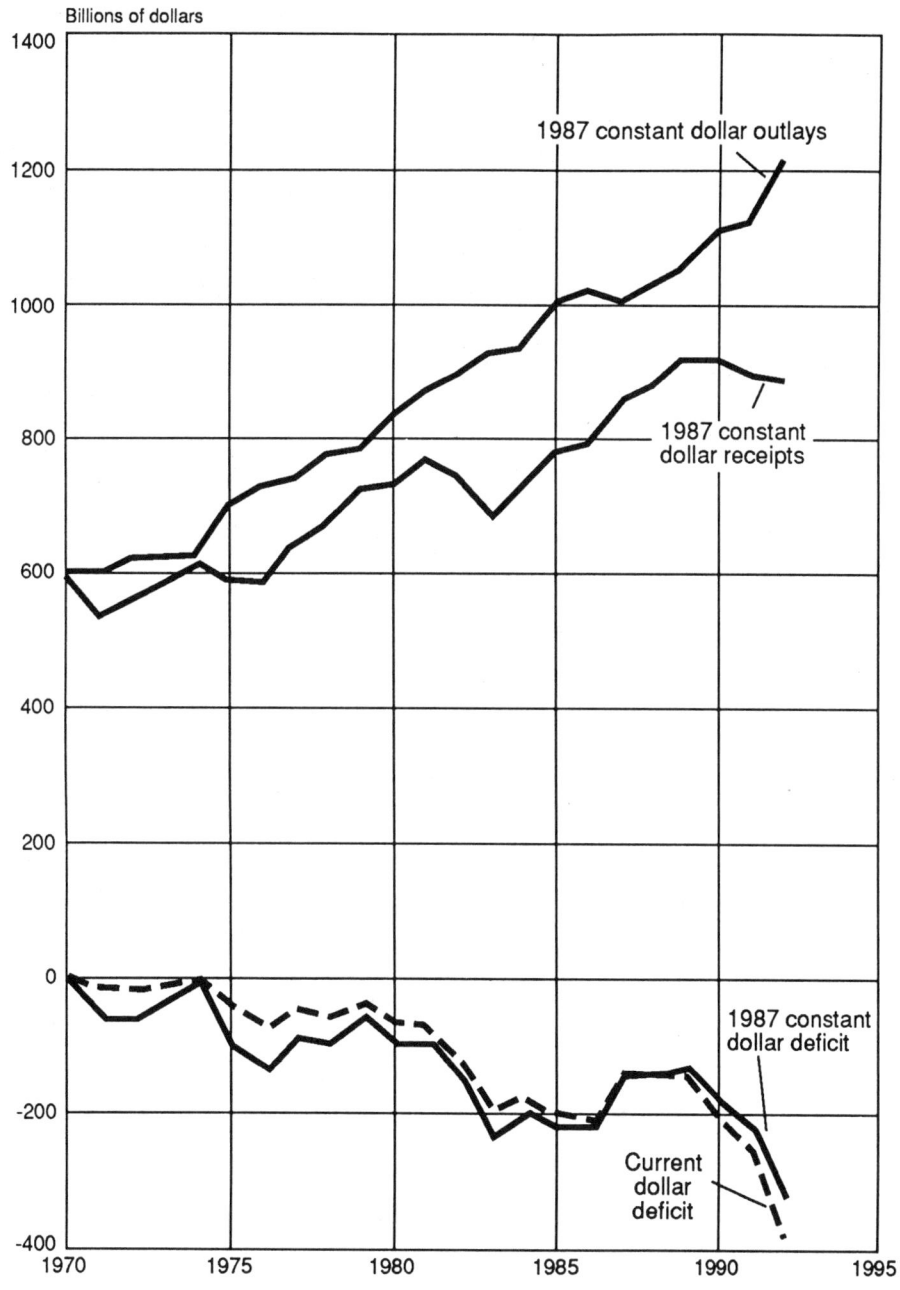

Billions of dollars

Note: Data for 1992 is projected.

Federal Budget—Summary: 1945–92

[In millions of dollars, except percent. For fiscal years ending in year shown. The Balanced Budget and Emergency Deficit Control Act of 1985 put all the previously off-budget Federal entities into the budget and moved Social Security off-budget. Minus sign (−) indicates deficit or decrease.]

Year	Receipts	Outlays[1] Total	Human resources	National defense	Percent of GNP[2]	Surplus or deficit(-)
1945	45,159	92,712	1,859	82,965	43.6	−48,720
1950	39,443	42,562	14,221	13,724	16.0	−4,702
1955	65,451	68,444	14,908	42,729	17.7	−4,091
1960	92,492	91,191	26,184	48,130	18.2	510
1965	116,817	118,228	36,576	50,620	17.6	−1,605
1966	130,835	134,532	43,257	58,111	18.2	−3,068
1967	148,822	157,464	51,272	71,417	19.8	−12,620
1968	152,973	178,134	59,375	81,926	21.0	−27,742
1969	186,882	183,640	66,410	82,497	19.8	−507
1970	192,807	195,649	75,349	81,692	19.8	−8,694
1971	187,139	210,172	91,901	78,872	19.9	−26,052
1972	207,309	230,681	107,211	79,174	20.0	−26,423
1973	230,799	245,707	119,522	76,681	19.2	−15,403
1974	263,224	269,359	135,783	79,347	19.0	−7,971
1975	279,090	332,332	173,245	86,509	21.8	−55,260
1976	298,060	371,779	203,594	89,619	21.9	−70,499
1976[5]	81,232	95,973	52,065	22,269	21.4	−13,336
1977	355,559	409,203	221,895	97,241	21.2	−49,745
1978	399,561	458,729	242,329	104,495	21.1	−54,902
1979	463,302	503,464	267,574	116,342	20.6	−38,178
1980	517,112	590,920	313,374	133,995	22.1	−72,689
1981	599,272	678,249	362,022	157,513	22.7	−73,916
1982	617,766	745,755	388,681	185,309	23.8	−120,003
1983	600,562	808,380	426,003	209,903	24.3	−207,977
1984	666,457	851,846	432,042	227,413	23.0	−185,586
1985	734,057	946,391	471,822	252,748	23.8	−221,623
1986	769,091	990,336	481,594	273,375	23.5	−237,898
1987	854,143	1,003,911	502,196	281,999	22.5	−169,257
1988	908,954	1,064,140	533,404	290,361	22.1	−192,897
1989	990,691	1,144,169	568,668	303,559	22.1	−206,132
1990	1,031,308	1,251,778	619,327	299,331	22.9	−220,470
1991	1,054,264	1,323,011	689,691	273,292	23.5	−268,746
1992, est.	1,075,706	1,475,439	776,900	307,304	25.2	−399,510

NA Not available. X Not applicable. [1] Includes off-budget receipts, outlays, and interfund transactions. [2] Gross national product as of fiscal year; for calendar year GNP, see table 701. [3] See text, section 10 for discussion of debt concept. [4] Change from previous year. For explanation of average annual percent change, see Guide to Tabular Presentation. [5] Represents transition quarter, July–Sept.

The United States

Total	Gross Federal Debt[3] Held by Federal Gov't Account	The public	Federal Reserve System	As percent of GNP[2]	Annual Percent Change[4] Receipts	Outlays	Gross Federal debt[3]	Outlays, off-budget
260,123	24,941	235,182	21,792	122.5	3.2	1.5	27.5	0.1
256,853	37,830	219,023	18,331	96.3	0.1	9.6	1.7	0.5
274,366	47,751	226,616	23,607	71.0	−6.0	−3.4	1.3	4.0
290,525	53,686	236,840	26,523	57.3	16.7	0.1	1.1	10.9
322,318	61,540	260,778	39,100	47.9	3.7	−0.3	2.0	16.5
328,498	64,784	263,714	42,169	44.5	12.0	13.8	1.9	19.7
340,445	73,819	266,626	46,719	42.8	13.7	17.0	3.6	20.4
368,685	79,140	289,545	52,230	43.4	2.8	13.1	8.3	22.3
365,769	87,661	278,108	54,095	39.4	22.2	3.1	−0.8	25.2
380,921	97,723	283,198	57,714	38.5	3.2	6.5	4.1	27.6
408,176	105,140	303,037	65,518	38.7	2.9	7.4	7.2	32.8
435,936	113,559	322,377	71,426	37.8	10.8	9.8	6.8	36.9
466,291	125,381	340,910	75,181	36.4	11.3	6.5	7.0	45.6
483,893	140,194	343,699	80,648	34.2	14.0	9.6	3.8	52.1
541,925	147,225	394,700	84,993	35.6	6.0	23.4	12.0	60.4
628,970	151,566	477,404	94,714	37.0	6.8	11.9	16.1	69.6
643,561	148,052	495,509	96,702	35.9	(X)	(X)	(X)	19.4
706,398	157,295	549,103	105,004	36.5	19.3	10.1	12.3	80.7
776,602	169,477	607,125	115,480	35.8	12.4	12.1	9.9	89.7
828,923	189,162	639,761	115,594	33.9	16.0	9.8	6.7	100.0
908,503	199,212	709,291	120,846	34.0	11.6	17.4	9.6	114.3
994,298	209,507	784,791	124,466	33.3	15.9	14.8	9.4	135.2
1,136,798	217,560	919,238	134,497	36.2	3.1	10.0	14.3	151.4
1,371,164	240,114	1,131,049	155,527	41.3	−2.8	8.4	20.6	147.1
1,564,110	264,159	1,299,951	155,122	42.4	11.0	5.4	14.1	165.8
1,816,974	317,612	1,499,362	169,806	46.0	10.1	11.1	16.2	176.8
2,120,082	383,919	1,736,163	190,855	50.7	4.8	4.6	16.7	183.5
2,345,578	457,444	1,888,134	212,040	53.0	11.1	1.4	10.6	193.8
2,600,760	550,507	2,050,252	229,218	54.4	6.4	6.0	10.9	202.7
2,867,538	677,214	2,190,324	220,088	55.9	9.0	7.5	10.3	210.9
3,206,347	795,906	2,410,441	234,410	58.7	4.1	9.4	11.8	225.1
3,598,993	911,751	2,687,242	258,591	64.0	2.2	5.7	12.2	241.7
4,077,510	1,000,227	3,077,283	(NA)	69.5	2.0	11.5	13.3	251.5

State Government

All states (except Nebraska) have a lawmaking body, in most cases called a *legislature* or *general assembly,* that is divided into two houses. (Nebraska's state government is unicameral, or single-chambered, and all its officials are called senators.) In most states, the upper house is called the Senate and the lower house is called the House of Representatives. State senators usually are elected every four years, while representatives or assembly members are elected every two years. State legislatures generally meet biennially, though a few meet annually.

The list below shows the name of each of the 50 states along with the year it became a state, the official abbreviation used by the United States Postal Service, the capital, and the name of the lawmaking body.

State Facts

State	Date Entered Union	Postal Abbreviation	Capital	Name of Lawmaking Body
Alabama	1819	AL	Montgomery	Legislature
Alaska	1959	AK	Juneau	Legislature
Arizona	1912	AZ	Phoenix	Legislature
Arkansas	1836	AR	Little Rock	General Assembly
California	1850	CA	Sacramento	Legislature[1]
Colorado	1876	CO	Denver	General Assembly
Connecticut	1788	CT	Hartford	General Assembly
Delaware	1787	DE	Dover	General Assembly
Florida	1845	FL	Tallahassee	Legislature
Georgia	1788	GA	Atlanta	General Assembly
Hawaii	1959	HI	Honolulu	Legislature
Idaho	1890	ID	Boise	Legislature
Illinois	1818	IL	Springfield	General Assembly
Indiana	1816	IN	Indianapolis	General Assembly
Iowa	1846	IA	Des Moines	General Assembly
Kansas	1861	KS	Topeka	Legislature
Kentucky	1792	KY	Frankfort	General Assembly
Louisiana	1812	LA	Baton Rouge	Legislature
Maine	1820	ME	Augusta	Legislature
Maryland	1788	MD	Annapolis	General Assembly[2]
Massachusetts	1788	MA	Boston	General Court
Michigan	1837	MI	Lansing	Legislature
Minnesota	1858	MN	St. Paul	Legislature
Mississippi	1817	MS	Jackson	Legislature
Missouri	1821	MO	Jefferson City	General Assembly
Montana	1889	MT	Helena	Legislative Assembly
Nebraska	1867	NE	Lincoln	Legislature
Nevada	1864	NV	Carson City	Legislature[1]

State	Date Entered Union	Postal Abbreviation	Capital	Name of Lawmaking Body
New Hampshire	1788	NH	Concord	General Court
New Jersey	1787	NJ	Trenton	Legislature[3]
New Mexico	1912	NM	Santa Fe	Legislature
New York	1788	NY	Albany	Legislature[1]
North Carolina	1789	NC	Raleigh	General Assembly
North Dakota	1889	ND	Bismarck	Legislative Assembly
Ohio	1803	OH	Columbus	General Assembly
Oklahoma	1907	OK	Oklahoma City	Legislature
Oregon	1859	OR	Salem	Legislative Assembly
Pennsylvania	1787	PA	Harrisburg	General Assembly
Rhode Island	1790	RI	Providence	General Assembly
South Carolina	1788	SC	Columbia	General Assembly
South Dakota	1889	SD	Pierre	Legislature
Tennessee	1796	TN	Nashville	General Assembly
Texas	1845	TX	Austin	Legislature
Utah	1896	UT	Salt Lake City	Legislature
Vermont	1791	VT	Montpelier	General Assembly
Virginia	1788	VA	Richmond	General Assembly[2]
Washington	1889	WA	Olympia	Legislature
West Virginia	1863	WV	Charleston	Legislature[2]
Wisconsin	1848	WI	Madison	Legislature[1]
Wyoming	1890	WY	Cheyenne	Legislature

[1] The lower house is called the Assembly.
[2] The lower house is called the House of Delegates.
[3] The lower house is called the General Assembly.

TERRITORIES AND COMMONWEALTHS

Name	Date Acquired	Abbreviation	Capital	Legislature
American Samoa	1899	AS	Pago Pago	Legislature
Federated States of Micronesia	1947	FM	Pohnpei	Legislature
Guam	1950	GU	Agana	Legislature*
Marshall Islands	1947	MH	Majuro	Parliament and Council of Local Chiefs
Midway Islands	1867	—		Administered by U.S. Navy
Northern Mariana Islands	1947	MP	Saipan	Legislature
Palau	1947	PW	Koror	Legislature
Puerto Rico	1898	PR	San Juan	Legislative Assembly
Virgin Islands	1927	VI	Charlotte Amalie	Legislature*
Wake Island	1899	—	Administered by U.S. Air Force	

* Legislatures are unicameral.

State Flowers, Birds, Mottos, and Nicknames

State	Flower	Bird	Motto	Nickname
Alabama	Camellia	Yellowhammer	We dare defend our rights	Heart of Dixie; Camellia State
Alaska	Forget-me-not	Willow ptarmigan	North to the future	The Last Frontier
Arizona	Saguaro	Cactus wren	*Diat Deus* (God enriches)	Grand Canyon State
Arkansas	Apple blossom	Mockingbird	*Regnat populus* (The people rule)	Land of Opportunity
California	Golden poppy	California valley quail	*Eureka* (I have found it)	Golden State
Colorado	Blue columbine	Lark bunting	*Nil sine numine* (Nothing without providence)	Centennial State
Connecticut	Mountain laurel	American robin	*Qui transtulit sustinet* (He who transplanted still sustains)	Constitution State; Nutmeg State
Delaware	Peach blossom	Blue hen chicken	Liberty and independence	First State; Diamond State
District of Columbia	American Beauty rose	Wood thrush	*Justitia Omnibus* (Justice for all)	Capital City
Florida	Orange blossom	Mockingbird	In God we trust	Sunshine State
Georgia	Cherokee rose	Brown thrasher	Wisdom, justice, and moderation	Empire State of the South; Peach State
Hawaii	Hibiscus	Nene goose	The life of the land is perpetuated in righteousness	Aloha State
Idaho	Syringa	Mountain bluebird	*Esto perpetua* (It is perpetual)	Gem State
Illinois	Native violet	Cardinal	State sovereignty—national union	Prairie State, Land of Lincoln
Indiana	Peony	Cardinal	Crossroads of America	Hoosier State
Iowa	Wild rose	Goldfinch	Our liberties we prize and our rights we will maintain	Hawkeye State
Kansas	Sunflower	Western meadowlark	*Ad astra per aspera* (To the stars through difficulties)	Sunflower State
Kentucky	Goldenrod	Kentucky cardinal	United we stand, divided we fall	Bluegrass State
Louisiana	Magnolia	Eastern brown pelican	Union, justice and confidence	Pelican State
Maine	Pine cone and tassel	Chickadee	*Dirigo* (I direct)	Pine Tree State
Maryland	Black-eyed Susan	Baltimore oriole	..... *Fatti maschii, parole femine* (Manly deeds, womanly words)	Old Line State; Free State

State	Flower	Bird	Motto	Nickname
Massachusetts	Mayflower	Chickadee	*Ense petit placidam sub libertate quietem* (By the sword we seek peace, but peace only under liberty)	Bay State; Colony State
Michigan	Apple blossom	Robin	*Si quaeris peninsulam amoenam circumspice* (If you seek a pleasant peninsula, look about you)	Great Lake State; Wolverine State
Minnesota	Showy lady slipper	Common loon	*L'Etoile du nord* (Star of the north)	North Star State; Gopher State
Mississippi	Magnolia	Mockingbird	*Virtute et armis* (By valor and arms)	Magnolia State
Missouri	Hawthorn	Bluebird	*Salus populi suprema lex esto* (The welfare of the people shall be the supreme law)	Show-Me State
Montana	Bitterroot	Western meadowlark	*Oro y plata* (Gold and silver)	Treasure State
Nebraska	Goldenrod	Meadowlark	Equality before the law	Cornhusker State
Nevada	Sagebrush	Mountain bluebird	All for our country	Sagebrush State; Battle-Born State
New Hampshire	Purple lilac	Purple finch	Live free or die	Granite State
New Jersey	Purple violet	Eastern goldfinch	Liberty and prosperity	Garden State
New Mexico	Yucca	Roadrunner	*Crescit eundo* (It grows as it goes)	Land of Enchantment
New York	Rose (any color)	Bluebird	*Excelsior* (Ever upward)	Empire State
North Carolina	Dogwood	Cardinal	*Esse quam videri* (To be rather than to seem)	Tar Heel State; Old North State
North Dakota	Wild prairie rose	Western meadowlark	Liberty and union, now and forever, one and inseparable	Peace Garden State
Ohio	Scarlet carnation	Cardinal	With God, all things are possible	Buckeye State
Oklahoma	Mistletoe	Scissor-tailed flycatcher	*Labor omnia vincit* (Labor conquers all things)	Sooner State
Oregon	Oregon grape	Western meadowlark	The union	Beaver State
Pennsylvania	Mountain laurel	Ruffed grouse	Virtue, liberty and independence	Keystone State
Rhode Island	Violet	Rhode Island hen	Hope	Little Rhody; Ocean State
South Carolina	Carolina jessamine	Carolina wren	*Dum spiro spero* (While I breathe, I hope)	Palmetto State
South Dakota	Pasqueflower	Pheasant	Under God, the people rule	Coyote State; Sunshine State
Tennessee	Iris	Mockingbird	Agriculture and commerce	Volunteer State

State	Flower	Bird	Motto	Nickname
Texas	Bluebonnet	Mockingbird	Friendship	Lone Star State
Utah	Sego Lily	Seagull	Industry	Beehive State
Vermont	Red clover	Thrush	Freedom and unity	Green Mountain State
Virginia	Flowering dogwood	Cardinal	*Sic semper tyrannis* (Thus always to tyrants)	Old Dominion
Washington	Rhododendron	Willow goldfinch	*Alki* (By and by)	Evergreen State
West Virginia	Big rhododendron	Cardinal	*Montani semper liberi* (Mountaineers are always free)	Mountain State
Wisconsin	Wood violet	Robin	Forward	Badger State
Wyoming	Indian paintbrush	Meadowlark	Equal rights	Equality State

United States Territories and Commonwealths

	Flower	Bird	Motto
American Samoa	Paogo (Ula-fala)		*Samoa Muamua le Atua* (In Samoa, God is first)
Guam	Puti tai nobio (bougainvillea)	Toto (fruit dove)	Where America's day begins
Puerto Rico	Maga	Reinita	*Joannes est nomen eius* (John is his name)
Virgin Islands	Yellow elder or yellow trumpet	Yellow breast	

State Name Origins

Alabama Originally the name for "tribal town," the territory of Alabama was later the home of the Alabama, or Alibamon, Indians of the Creek confederacy.

Alaska The Russians adopted the word meaning "great lands" or "land that is not an island" from the Aleutian word *alakshak*.

Arizona The Spanish coined the name either from the Pima Indian word meaning "little spring place" or from the Aztec *arizuma*, meaning "silver-bearing."

Arkansas Once the territory of the Siouan Quapaw (downstream people), *Arkansas* is the French derivative of this Indian name.

California The name of a fictitious earthly paradise in *Las Serged de Esplandian*, a sixteenth-century Spanish romance. It is believed that Spanish conquistadors named this state.

Colorado A Spanish word for "red." The name *Colorado* first referred to the Colorado River.

Connecticut The Algonquin and Mohican Indian word for "long river place."

Delaware This version of the name of Lord De La Warr, a governor of Virginia, was first used to name the Delaware River and later adopted by the Europeans to rename the local Indians, originally called the Lenni-Lenape.

District of Columbia Named for Christopher Columbus in 1791.

Florida In his search for the "Fountain of Youth," Ponce de Leon named this region "flowery Easter" or "feast of flowers" on Easter Sunday, 1513.

Georgia Named for King George II of England, who granted James Oglethorpe a charter to found the colony of Georgia in 1732.

Hawaii Commonly believed to be an English adaptation of the native word for "homeland," *hawaiki* or *owhyhee*.

Idaho A name coined by the state meaning "gem of the mountains" or "light on the mountains." Originally the name *Idaho* was to be used for the Pike's Peak mining territory in Colorado, and later for the mining territory of the Pacific Northwest. Others believe the name derives from the Kiowa Apache word for the Comanche.

Illinois From the French version of the Algonquin word meaning "men" or "soldiers," *Illini*.

Indiana English-speaking settlers named the territory to mean "land of the Indians."

Iowa From the Siouan *Ouaouia*, meaning "one who puts to sleep."

Kansas Derived from the Siouan *Kansa* or *Kaw*, meaning "people of the south wind," who lived south of the settlements of the northern Great Plains.

Kentucky Originally the term for the Kentucky Plains in Clark County, *Kentucky* is believed to derive from the Indian word meaning "dark and bloody ground," "meadow land," or "land of tomorrow."

Louisiana Present-day Louisiana is just a fraction of the territory that was named for the French king Louis XIV by Sieur de La Salle.

Maine Originally a French territory, *Maine* was the ancient French word for "province." It is also believed that it refers to the mainland, as distinct from the many islands off the state's coast.

Maryland Named for Queen Henrietta Maria, wife of Charles I of England.

Massachusetts The name of the Indian tribe that lived near Milton, Massachusetts, meaning "large hill place."

Michigan Believed to be from the Chippewa word *micigama*, meaning "great water," after Lake Michigan, although Alouet defined it in 1672 as designating a clearing.

Minnesota Named from the Sioux description of the Minnesota River, "sky-tinted water" or "muddy water."

Mississippi Most likely derived from the Chippewa words *mici* (great) and *zibi* (river), it was first written by La Salle's lieutenant Henri de Tonti as "Michi Sepe."

Missouri The Siouan word meaning "muddy water."

Montana Derived from the Latin word meaning "mountainous."

Nebraska From the Omaha or Oto word for "flat water" or "spreading water," describing the Platte and Nebraska rivers.

Nevada Spanish word meaning "snow-clad."

New Hampshire Captain John Mason named this colony for his home county in England in 1629.

New Jersey Named after the Isle of Jersey in England by John Berkeley and Sir George Carteret.

New Mexico Named by the Spanish for the territory north and west of the Rio Grande.

New York Originally named New Netherland, New York was later named after the Duke of York and Albany, who received a patent to the region from his brother Charles II of England and captured it from the Dutch in 1644.

North Carolina From the Latin name *Carolus*, meaning "Charles." The colony was originally given to Sir Robert Heath by Charles I and was to be called Province of Carolana. Carolana was divided into North and South Carolina in 1710.

North Dakota From the Sioux word meaning "friend" or "ally."

Ohio From an Iroquois Indian word variously meaning "great," "fine," or "good river."

Oklahoma The Choctaw Indian word meaning "red man," which was coined by the Reverend Allen Wright, a Choctaw speaking Indian.

Oregon Though its exact origin is unclear, one theory maintains that it may have been a variation on the name of the Wisconsin River, which was called *Ouaricon-sint* on a French map dated 1715. Later, the English explorer Major Robert Rogers named a river "called by the Indians Ouragon" in his request to seek a Northwest Passage from the Great Lakes. Another theory derives the word from the Algonquin *wauregan*, meaning "beautiful water."

Pennsylvania Named after the colony's founder, the Quaker William Penn. The literal translation is "Penn's woods."

Rhode Island Possibly named by Giovanni de Verrazano, who charted an island about the size of an island of the same name in the Mediterranean. Another theory suggests Rhode Island was named Roode Eylandt by Dutch explorer Adrian Block because of its red clay.

South Carolina *See* **North Carolina.**

South Dakota *See* **North Dakota.**

Tennessee The state of Franklin, or Frankland, from 1784 to 1788, it was finally named after the Cherokee villages called *tanasi* on the Little Tennessee River.

Texas Also written *texias, tejas*, and *teysas, Texas* is a variation on the Caddo Indian word for "friend" or "ally."

Utah Meaning "upper" or "higher," *Utah* is derived from a name used by the Navajos (Utes) to designate a Shoshone tribe.

Vermont It is believed Samuel de Champlain coined the name from the French words *vert* (green) and *mont* (mountain). Later, Dr. Thomas Young proposed this name when the state was formed in 1777.

Virginia Named for the Virgin Queen of England, Queen Elizabeth I, by Sir Walter Raleigh, who first visited its shores in 1584.

Washington Originally named the Territory of Columbia, it was changed to *Washington* in honor of the first U.S. president because of the already existing District of Columbia.

West Virginia Named when this area refused to secede from the Union in 1863.

Wisconsin A Chippewa word that was spelled *Ouisconsin* and *Mesconsing* by early explorers. Wisconsin was formally named by Congress when it became a state.

Wyoming The Algonquin word meaning "large prairie place," the name was adopted from Wyoming Valley, Pennsylvania, the site of an Indian massacre. It was widely known from Thomas Campbell's poem "Gertrude of Wyoming."

ADMISSION OF THE 13 ORIGINAL STATES

State	Date of Admission
1. Delaware	December 7, 1787
2. Pennsylvania	December 12, 1787
3. New Jersey	December 18, 1787
4. Georgia	January 2, 1788
5. Connecticut	January 9, 1788
6. Massachusetts	February 6, 1788
7. Maryland	April 28, 1788
8. South Carolina	May 23, 1788
9. New Hampshire	June 21, 1788
10. Virginia	June 25, 1788
11. New York	July 26, 1788
12. North Carolina	November 21, 1789
13. Rhode Island	May 29, 1790

SECESSION OF AMERICAN STATES

State	Secession Date
1. South Carolina	December 20, 1860
2. Mississippi	January 9, 1861
3. Florida	January 10, 1861
4. Alabama	January 11, 1861
5. Georgia	January 19, 1861
6. Louisiana	January 26, 1861
7. Texas	February 1, 1861
8. Virginia	April 17, 1861
9. Arkansas	May 6, 1861
10. North Carolina	May 20, 1861
11. Tennessee	June 8, 1861

READMISSION OF AMERICAN STATES

State	Date of Readmission
1. Tennessee	July 24, 1866
2. Arkansas	June 22, 1868
3. Alabama	June 25, 1868
4. Florida	June 25, 1868
5. Georgia	June 25, 1868*
6. Louisiana	June 25, 1868
7. North Carolina	June 25, 1868
8. South Carolina	June 25, 1868
9. Virginia	January 26, 1870
10. Mississippi	February 23, 1870
11. Texas	March 30, 1870

* readmitted a second time July 15, 1870

The Declaration of Independence

IN CONGRESS, JULY 4, 1776

The Unanimous Declaration of the Thirteen United States of America

When in the course of human events, it becomes necessary for one people to dissolve the political bands which have connected them with another, and to assume among the powers of the earth, the separate and equal station to which the laws of Nature and of Nature's God entitle them, a decent respect to the opinions of mankind requires that they should declare the causes which impel them to the separation.

We hold these truths to be self-evident, that all men are created equal, that they are endowed by their Creator with certain unalienable rights, that among these are life, liberty and the pursuit of happiness. That to secure these rights, governments are instituted among men, deriving their just powers from the consent of the governed,—That whenever any form of government becomes destructive of these ends, it is the right of the people to alter or to abolish it, and to institute new government, laying its foundation on such principles and organizing its powers in such form, as to them shall seem most likely to effect their safety and happiness. Prudence, indeed, will dictate that governments long established should not be changed for light and transient causes; and accordingly all experience hath shown, that mankind are more disposed to suffer, while evils are sufferable, than to right themselves by abolishing the forms to which they are accustomed. But when a long train of abuses and usurpations, pursuing invariably the same object evinces a design to reduce them under absolute despotism, it is their right, it is their duty, to throw off such government, and to provide new guards for their future security.—Such has been the patient sufferance of these Colonies; and such is now the necessity which constrains them to alter their former systems of government. The history of the present King of Great Britain is a history of repeated injuries and usurpations, all having in direct object the establishment of an absolute tyranny over these States. To prove this, let facts be submitted to a candid world.

He has refused his assent to laws, the most wholesome and necessary for the public good.

He has forbidden his Governors to pass laws of immediate and pressing importance, unless suspended in their operation till his assent should be obtained; and when so suspended, he has utterly neglected to attend to them.

He has refused to pass other laws for the accommodation of large districts of people, unless those people would relinquish the right of representation in the legislature, a right inestimable to them and formidable to tyrants only.

He has called together legislative bodies at places unusual, uncomfortable, and distant from the depository of their public records, for the sole purpose of fatiguing them into compliance with his measures.

He has dissolved Representative Houses repeatedly, for opposing with manly firmness his invasions on the rights of the people.

He has refused for a long time, after such dissolutions, to cause others to be elected; whereby the legislative powers, incapable of annihilation, have returned to the people at large for their exercise; the State remaining in the mean time exposed to all the dangers of invasion from without, and convulsions within.

He has endeavoured to prevent the population of these States; for that purpose obstructing the laws for naturalization of foreigners; refusing to pass others to encourage their migrations hither, and raising the conditions of new appropriations of lands.

He has obstructed the administration of justice, by refusing his assent to laws for establishing judiciary powers.

He has made judges dependent on his will alone, for the tenure of their offices, and the amount and payment of their salaries.

He has erected a multitude of new offices, and sent hither swarms of officers to harass our people, and eat out their substance.

He has kept among us, in times of peace, standing armies without the consent of our legislatures.

He has affected to render the military independent of and superior to the civil power.

He has combined with others to subject us to a jurisdiction foreign to our constitution, and unacknowledged by our laws; giving his assent to their acts of pretended legislation:

For quartering large bodies of armed troops among us:

For protecting them, by a mock trial, from punishment for any murders which they should commit on the inhabitants of these States:

For cutting off our trade with all parts of the world:

For imposing taxes on us without our consent:

For depriving us in many cases, of the benefits of trial by jury:

For transporting us beyond seas to be tried for pretended offenses:

For abolishing the free system of English laws in a neighbouring province, establishing therein an arbitrary government, and enlarging its boundaries so as to render it at once an example and fit instrument for introducing the same absolute rule into these colonies:

For taking away our charters, abolishing our most valuable laws, and altering fundamentally the forms of our governments:

For suspending our own legislatures, and declaring themselves invested with power to legislate for us in all cases whatsoever.

He has abdicated government here, by declaring us out of his protection and waging war against us.

He has plundered our seas, ravaged our coasts, burnt our towns, and destroyed the lives of our people.

He is at this time transporting large armies of foreign mercenaries to complete the works of death, desolation and tyranny, already begun with circumstances of cruelty and perfidy scarcely paralleled in the most barbarous ages, and totally unworthy of the head of a civilized nation.

He has constrained our fellow citizens taken captive on the high seas to bear arms against their country, to become the executioners of their friends and brethren, or to fall themselves by their hands.

He has excited domestic insurrections amongst us, and has endeavoured to bring on the inhabitants of our frontiers, the merciless Indian savages, whose known rule of warfare is an undistinguished destruction of all ages, sexes and conditions.

In every stage of these oppressions we have petitioned for redress in the most humble terms: Our repeated petitions have been answered only by repeated injury. A prince, whose character is thus marked by every act which may define a tyrant, is unfit to be the ruler of a free people.

Nor have we been wanting in attentions to our British brethren. We have warned them from time to time of attempts by their legislature to extend an unwarrantable jurisdiction over us. We have reminded them of the circumstances of our emigration and settlement here. We have appealed to their native justice and magnanimity, and we have conjured them by the ties of our common kindred to disavow these usurpations, which, would inevitably interrupt our connections and correspondence. They too have been deaf to the voice of justice and of consanguinity. We must, therefore, acquiesce in the necessity which denounces our separation, and hold them, as we hold the rest of mankind, enemies in war, in peace friends.

WE, THEREFORE, the Representatives of the United States of America, in General Congress, Assembled, appealing to the Supreme Judge of the world for the rectitude of out intentions, do, in the name, and by authority of the good people of these Colonies, solemnly publish and declare, That these United Colonies are, and of right ought to be FREE AND INDEPENDENT STATES; that they are absolved from all allegiance to the British Crown, and that all political connection between them and the State of Great Britain, is and ought to be totally dissolved; and that as free and independent States, they have full power to levy war, conclude peace, contract alliances, establish commerce, and to do all other acts and things which independent States may of right do. And for the support of this Declaration, with a firm reliance on the protection of Divine Providence, we mutually pledge to each other our lives, our fortunes and our sacred honor.

JOHN HANCOCK.

New Hampshire

JOSIAH BARTLETT
WM. WHIPPLE

MATTHEW THORNTON

Massachusetts Bay

SAML ADAMS
JOHN ADAMS

ROBT TREAT PAINE
ELBRIDGE GERRY

Rhode Island

STEP. HOPKINS

WILLIAM ELLERY

Connecticut

ROGER SHERMAN
SAML HUNTINGTON

WM. WILLIAMS
OLIVER WOLCOTT

New York

WM. FLOYD
PHIL. LIVINGSTON

FRANS. LEWIS
LEWIS MORRIS

New Jersey

Richd. Stockton
Jno Witherspoon
Fras. Hopkinson

John Hart
Abra Clark

Pennsylvania

Robt Morris
Benjamin Rush
Benja. Franklin
John Morton
Geo. Clymer

Jas. Smith
Geo. Taylor
James Wilson
Geo. Ross

Delaware

Caesar Rodney
Geo Read

Tho M'Kean

Maryland

Samuel Chase
Wm. Paca
Thos. Stone

Charles Carroll
of Carrollton

Virginia

George Wythe
Richard Henry Lee
Th Jefferson
Benja. Harrison

Thos. Nelson jr.
Francis Lightfoot Lee
Carter Braxton

North Carolina

Wm Hooper
Joseph Hewes

John Penn

South Carolina

Edward Rutledge
Thos. Heyward Junr.

Thomas Lynch Junr.
Arthur Middleton

Georgia

Button Gwinnett
Lyman Hall

Geo Walton.

The Constitution of the United States of America

PREAMBLE

WE THE PEOPLE of the United States, in order to form a more perfect Union, establish justice, insure domestic tranquility, provide for the common defense, promote the general welfare, and secure the blessings of liberty to ourselves and our posterity, do ordain and establish this Constitution for the United States of America.

ARTICLE I

SECTION 1. All legislative powers herein granted shall be vested in a Congress of the United States, which shall consist of a Senate and House of Representatives.

SECTION 2. The House of Representatives shall be composed of members chosen every second year by the people of the several States, and the electors in each State shall have the qualifications requisite for electors of the most numerous branch of the State Legislature.

No person shall be a Representative who shall not have attained to the age of twenty-five years, and been seven years a citizen of the United States, and who shall not, when elected, be an inhabitant of that State in which he shall be chosen.

Representatives and direct taxes shall be apportioned among the several States which may be included within this Union, according to their respective numbers, which shall be determined by adding to the whole number of free persons, including those bound to service for a term of years, and excluding Indians not taxed, three-fifths of all other persons. The actual enumeration shall be made within three years after the first meeting of the Congress of the United States, and within every subsequent term of ten years, in such manner as they shall by law direct. The number of representatives shall not exceed one for every thirty thousand, but each State shall have at least one Representative; and until such enumeration shall be made, the State of New Hampshire shall be entitled to choose three, Massachusetts eight, Rhode Island and Providence Plantations one, Connecticut five, New York six, New Jersey four, Pennsylvania eight, Delaware one, Maryland six, Virginia ten, North Carolina five, South Carolina five, and Georgia three.

When vacancies happen in the representation from any State, the executive authority thereof shall issue writs of election to fill such vacancies.

The House of Representatives shall choose their Speaker and other officers; and shall have the sole power of impeachment.

SECTION 3. The Senate of the United States shall be composed of two Senators from each State, chosen by the legislature thereof, for six years and each Senator shall have one vote.

Immediately after they shall be assembled in consequence of the first election, they shall be divided as equally as may be into three classes. The seats of the Senators of the first class shall be vacated at the expiration of the second year, of the second class at the expiration of the fourth year, and of the third class at the expiration of the sixth year, so that one-third may be chosen every second year; and if vacancies happen by resignation, or otherwise, during the recess of the legislature of any State, the executive thereof may make temporary appointments until the next meeting of the legislature, which shall then fill such vacancies.

No person shall be a Senator who shall not have attained to the age of thirty years, and been nine years a citizen of the United States, and who shall not, when elected, be an inhabitant of that State for which he shall be chosen.

The Vice President of the United States shall be President of the Senate, but shall have no vote, unless they be equally divided.

The Senate shall choose their other officers, and also a President pro tempore, in the absence of the Vice President, or when he shall exercise the office of President of the United States.

The Senate shall have the sole power to try all impeachments. When sitting for that purpose, they shall be on oath or affirmation. When the President of the United States is tried, the Chief Justice shall preside: and no person shall be convicted without the concurrence of two thirds of the members present.

Judgment in cases of impeachment shall not extend further than to removal from office, and disqualification to hold and enjoy any office of honor, trust or profit under the United States: but the party convicted shall nevertheless be liable and subject to indictment, trial, judgment and punishment, according to law.

SECTION 4. The times, places and manner of holding elections for Senators and Representatives, shall be prescribed in each State by the legislature thereof; but the Congress may at any time by law make or alter such regulations, except as to the places of choosing Senators.

The Congress shall assemble at least once in every year, and such meeting shall be on the first Monday in December, unless they shall by law appoint a different day.

SECTION 5. Each House shall be the judge of the elections, returns and qualifications of its own members, and a majority of each shall constitute a quorum to do business; but a smaller number may adjourn from day to day, and may be authorized to compel the attendance of absent members, in such manner, and under such penalties as each House may provide.

Each House may determine the rules of its proceedings, punish its members for disorderly behaviour, and, with the concurrence of two-thirds, expel a member.

Each House shall keep a journal of its proceedings, and from time to time publish the same, excepting such parts as may in their judgment require secrecy; and the yeas and the nays of the members of either house on any question shall, at the desire of one-fifth of those present, be entered on the journal.

Neither House, during the session of Congress, shall, without the consent of the other, adjourn for more than three days, nor to any other place than that in which the two Houses shall be sitting.

SECTION 6. The Senators and Representatives shall receive a compensation for their services, to be ascertained by law, and paid out of the Treasury of the United States. They shall in all cases, except treason, felony and breach of the peace, be privileged from arrest during their attendance at the session of their respective Houses, and in going to and returning from the same; and for any speech or debate in either House, they shall not be questioned in any other place.

No Senator or Representative shall, during the time for which he was elected, be appointed to any civil office under the authority of the United States, which shall have been created, or the emoluments whereof shall have been increased during such time; and no person holding any office under the United States, shall be a member of either House during his continuance in office.

SECTION 7. All bills for raising revenue shall originate in the House of Representatives; but the Senate may propose or concur with amendments as on other bills.

Every bill which shall have passed the House of Representatives and the Senate, shall, before it becomes a law, be presented to the President of the United States; if he approves he shall sign it, but if not he shall return it, with his objections to that House in which it shall have originated, who shall enter the objections at large on their journal, and proceed to reconsider it. If after such reconsideration two thirds of that House shall agree to pass the bill, it shall be sent, together with the objections, to the other House, by which it shall likewise be reconsidered, and if approved by two thirds of that House, it shall become a law. But in all such cases the votes of both Houses shall be determined by yeas and nays, and the names of the persons voting for and against the bill shall be entered on the journal of each House respectively. If any bill shall not be returned by the President within ten days (Sundays excepted) after it shall have been presented to him, the same shall be a law, in like manner as if he had signed it, unless the Congress by their adjournment prevent its return, in which case it shall not be a law.

Every order, resolution, or vote to which the concurrence of the Senate and House of Representatives may be necessary (except on a question of adjournment) shall be presented to the President of the United States; and before the same shall take effect, shall be approved by him, or being disapproved by him, shall be repassed by two thirds of the Senate and House of Representatives, according to the rules and limitations prescribed in the case of a bill.

SECTION 8. The Congress shall have power to lay and collect taxes, duties, imposts and excises, to pay the debts and provide for the common defense and general welfare of the United States; but all duties, imposts and excises shall be uniform throughout the United States;

To borrow money on the credit of the United States;

To regulate commerce with foreign nations, and among the several States, and with the Indian tribes;

To establish a uniform rule of naturalization, and uniform laws on the subject of bankruptcies throughout the United States;

To coin money, regulate the value thereof, and of foreign coin, and fix the standard of weights and measures;

To provide for the punishment of counterfeiting the securities and current coin of the United States;

To establish post offices and post roads;

To promote the progress of science and useful arts, by securing for limited times to authors and inventors the exclusive right to their respective writings and discoveries;

To constitute tribunals inferior to the Supreme Court;

To define and punish piracies and felonies committed on the high seas, and offenses against the law of nations;

To declare war, grant letters of marque and reprisal, and make rules concerning captures on land and water;

To raise and support armies, but no appropriation of money to that use shall be for a longer term than two years;

To provide and maintain a navy;

To make rules for the government and regulation of the land and naval forces;

To provide for calling forth the militia to execute the laws of the Union, suppress insurrections and repel invasions;

To provide for organizing, arming, and disciplining the militia, and for governing such part of them as may be employed in the service of the United States, reserving to the States respectively, the appointment of the officers, and the authority of training the militia according to the discipline prescribed by Congress;

To exercise exclusive legislation in all cases whatsoever, over such district (not exceeding ten miles square) as may, by cession of particular States, and the acceptance of Congress, become the seat of the Government of the United States, and to exercise like authority over all places purchased by the consent of the legislature of the State in which the same shall be, for the erection of forts, magazines, arsenals, dock-yards, and other needful buildings;—And

To make all laws which shall be necessary and proper for carrying into execution the foregoing powers, and all other powers vested by this Constitution in the Government of the United States, or in any department or officer thereof.

SECTION 9. The migration or importation of such persons as any of the States now existing shall think proper to admit, shall not be prohibited by the Congress prior to the year one thousand eight hundred and eight, but a tax or duty may be imposed on such importation, not exceeding ten dollars for each person.

The privilege of the writ of habeas corpus shall not be suspended, unless when in cases of rebellion or invasion the public safety may require it.

No bill of attainder or ex post facto law shall be passed.

No capitation, or other direct, tax shall be laid, unless in proportion to the census or enumeration herein before directed to be taken.

No tax or duty shall be laid on articles exported from any State.

No preference shall be given by any regulation of commerce or revenue to the ports of one State over those of another: nor shall vessels bound to, or from, one State, be obliged to enter, clear, or pay duties in another.

No money shall be drawn from the Treasury, but in consequence of appropriations made by law; and a regular statement and account of the receipts and expenditures of all public money shall be published from time to time.

No title of nobility shall be granted by the United States: And no person holding any office of profit or trust under them, shall, without the consent of the Congress, accept of any present, emolument, office, or title, of any kind whatever, from any King, Prince, or foreign State.

SECTION 10. No State shall enter into any treaty, alliance, or confederation; grant letters of marque and reprisal; coin money; emit bills of credit; make any thing but gold and silver coin a tender in payment of debts; pass any bill of attainder, ex post facto law, or law impairing the obligation of contracts, or grant any title of nobility.

No State shall, without the consent of the Congress, lay any imposts or duties on imports or exports, except what may be absolutely necessary for executing its inspection laws: and the net produce of all duties and imposts, laid by any state on imports or exports, shall be for the use of the Treasury of the United States; and all such laws shall be subject to the revision and control of the Congress.

No State shall, without the consent of Congress, lay any duty of tonnage, keep troops, or ships of war in time of peace, enter into any agreement or compact with another State, or with a foreign power, or engage in war, unless actually invaded, or in such imminent danger as will not admit of delay.

ARTICLE II

SECTION 1. The executive power shall be vested in a President of the United States of America. He shall hold his office during the term of four years, and together with the Vice President, chosen for the same term, be elected, as follows:

Each State, shall appoint, in such manner as the legislature thereof may direct, a number of electors, equal to the whole number of Senators and Representatives to which the State may be entitled in the Congress; but no Senator or Representative, or person holding an office of trust or profit under the United States, shall be appointed an elector.

The electors shall meet in their respective States, and vote by ballot for two persons, of whom one at least shall not be an inhabitant of the same State with themselves. And they shall make a list of all the persons voted for, and of the number of votes for each; which list they shall sign and certify, and transmit sealed to the seat of the Government of the United States, directed to the President of the Senate. The President of the Senate shall, in the presence of the Senate and House of Representatives, open all the certificates, and the votes shall then be counted. The person having the greatest number of votes shall be the President, if such number be a majority of the whole number of electors appointed; and if there be more than one who have such majority, and have an equal number of votes, then the House of Representatives shall immediately choose by ballot one of them for President; and if no persons have a majority, then from the five highest on the list the said House shall in like manner choose the President. But in choosing the President, the votes shall be taken by States, the representation from each State having one vote; a quorum for this purpose shall consist of a member or members from two-thirds of the States, and a majority of all the States shall be necessary to a choice. In every case, after the choice of the President, the person having the greatest number of votes of the electors shall be the Vice President. But if there should remain two or more who have equal votes, the Senate shall choose from them by ballot the Vice President.

The Congress may determine the time of choosing the electors, and the day on which they shall give their votes; which day shall be the same throughout the United States.

No person except a natural born citizen, or a citizen of the United States, at the time of the adoption of this Constitution, shall be eligible to the office of President; neither shall any person be eligible to that office who shall not have attained to the age of thirty-five years, and been fourteen years a resident within the United States.

In case of the removal of the President from office, or of his death, resignation, or inability to discharge the powers and duties of the said office, the same shall devolve on the Vice President, and the Congress may by law provide for the case of removal, death, resignation, or inability, both of the President and Vice President, declaring what officer shall then act as President, and such officer shall act accordingly, until the disability be removed, or a President be elected.

The President shall, at stated times, receive for his services, a compensation, which shall neither be increased nor diminished during the period for which he shall have been elected, and he shall not receive within that period any other emolument from the United States, or any of them.

Before he enter on the execution of his office, he shall take the following oath or affirmation:—"I do solemnly swear (or affirm) that I will faithfully execute the office of President of the United States, and will to the best of my ability, preserve, protect and defend the Constitution of the United States."

SECTION 2. The President shall be Commander in Chief of the Army and Navy of the United States, and of the militia of the several States, when called into the actual service of the United States; he may require the opinion, in writing, of the principal officer in each of the executive departments, upon any subject relating to the duties of their respective offices, and he shall have power to grant reprieves and pardons for offenses against the United States, except in cases of impeachment.

He shall have power, by and with the advice and consent of the Senate, to make treaties, provided two-thirds of the Senators present concur; and he shall nominate, and by and with the advice and consent of the Senate, shall appoint ambassadors, other public ministers and consuls, Judges of the Supreme Court, and all other officers of the United States, whose appointments are not herein otherwise provided for, and which shall be established by law: but the Congress may by law vest the appointment of such inferior officers, as they think proper, in the President alone, in the courts of law, or in the heads of departments.

The President shall have power to fill up all vacancies that may happen during the recess of the Senate, by granting commissions which shall expire at the end of their next session.

SECTION 3. He shall from time to time give to the Congress information of the State of the Union, and recommend to their consideration such measures as he shall judge necessary and expedient; he may, on extraordinary occasions, convene both Houses, or either of them, and in case of disagreement between them, with respect to the time of adjournment, he may adjourn them to such time as he shall think proper; he shall receive ambassadors and other public ministers; he shall take care that the laws be faithfully executed, and shall commission all the officers of the United States.

SECTION 4. The President, Vice President and all civil officers of the United States, shall be removed from office on impeachment for, and conviction of, treason, bribery, or other high crimes and misdemeanors.

ARTICLE III

SECTION 1. The judicial power of the United States, shall be vested in one Supreme Court, and in such inferior courts as the Congress may from time to time ordain and establish. The judges, both of the Supreme and inferior Courts, shall hold their offices during good behaviour, and shall, at stated times, receive for their services, a compensation, which shall not be diminished during their continuance in office.

SECTION 2. The judicial power shall extend to all cases, in law and equity, arising under this Constitution, the laws of the United States, and treaties made, or which shall be made, under their authority;—to all cases affecting ambassadors, other public ministers and consuls;—to all cases of admiralty and maritime jurisdiction;—to controversies to which the United States shall be a party;—to controversies between two or more States;—between a State and citizens of another State;—between citizens of different States,—between citizens of the same State claiming lands under grants of different States, and between a State, or the citizens thereof, and foreign States, citizens or subjects.

In all cases affecting ambassadors, other public ministers and consuls, and those in which a State shall be a party, the Supreme Court shall have original jurisdiction. In all the other cases before mentioned, the Supreme Court shall have appellate jurisdiction, both as to law and fact, with such exceptions, and under such regulations as the Congress shall make.

The trial of all crimes, except in cases of impeachment, shall be by jury; and such trial shall be held in the State where the said crimes shall have been committed; but when not committed within any State, the trial shall be at such place or places as the Congress may by law have directed.

SECTION 3. Treason against the United States, shall consist only in levying war against them, or in adhering to their enemies, giving them aid and comfort. No person shall be convicted of treason unless on the testimony of two witnesses to the same overt act, or on confession in open court.

The Congress shall have power to declare the punishment of treason, but no attainder of treason shall work corruption of blood, or forfeiture except during the life of the person attainted.

ARTICLE IV

SECTION 1. Full faith and credit shall be given in each State to the public acts, records, and judicial proceedings of every other State. And the Congress may by general laws prescribe the manner in which such acts, records, and proceedings shall be proved, and the effect thereof.

SECTION 2. The citizens of each State shall be entitled to all privileges and immunities of citizens in the several States.

A person charged in any State with treason, felony, or other crime, who shall flee from justice, and be found in another State, shall on demand of the executive authority of the State from which he fled, be delivered up, to be removed to the State having jurisdiction of the crime.

No person held to service or labour in one State, under the laws thereof, escaping into another, shall, in consequence of any law or regulation therein, be discharged from such service or labour, but shall be delivered up on claim of the party to whom such service or labour may be due.

SECTION 3. New States may be admitted by the Congress into this Union; but no new State shall be formed or erected within the jurisdiction of any other State; nor any State be formed by the junction of two or more States, or parts of States, without the consent of the legislatures of the States concerned as well as of the Congress.

The Congress shall have power to dispose of and make all needful rules and regulations respecting the Territory or other property belonging to the United States; and nothing in this Constitution shall be so construed as to prejudice any claims of the United States, or of any particular State.

SECTION 4. The United States shall guarantee to every State in this Union a republican form of Government, and shall protect each of them against invasion; and on application of the legislature, or of the executive (when the legislature cannot be convened) against domestic violence.

ARTICLE V

The Congress, whenever two thirds of both Houses shall deem it necessary, shall propose amendments to this Constitution, or on the application of the legislatures of two thirds of the several States, shall call a convention for proposing amendments, which, in either case, shall be valid to all intents and purposes, as part of this Constitution, when ratified by the legislatures of three fourths of the several States, or by conventions in three fourths thereof, as the one or the other mode of ratification may be proposed by the Congress; provided that no amendment which may be made prior to the year one thousand eight hundred and eight shall in any manner affect the first and fourth clauses in the Ninth Section of the First Article; and that no State, without its consent, shall be deprived of its equal suffrage in the Senate.

ARTICLE VI

All debts contracted and engagements entered into, before the adoption of this Constitution, shall be as valid against the United States under this Constitution, as under the Confederation.

This Constitution, and the laws of the United States which shall be made in pursuance thereof; and all treaties made, or which shall be made, under the authority of the United States, shall be the supreme law of the land; and the judges in every State shall be bound thereby, any thing in the Constitution or laws of any State to the contrary notwithstanding.

The Senators and Representatives before mentioned, and the members of the several State legislatures, and all executive and judicial officers, both of the United States and of the several States, shall be bound by oath or affirmation, to support this Constitution; but no religious test shall ever be required as a qualification to any office or public trust under the United States.

ARTICLE VII

The ratification of the conventions of nine States shall be sufficient for the establishment of this Constitution between the States so ratifying the same.

Done in convention by the unanimous consent of the States present the seventeenth day of September in the year of our Lord one thousand seven hundred and eighty seven and of the independence of the United States of America the twelfth. In witness whereof we have hereunto subscribed our names,

GO. WASHINGTON—*Presid't.*
and deputy from Virginia

Attest WILLIAM JACKSON *Secretary*

New Hampshire

JOHN LANGDON   NICHOLAS GILMAN

Massachusetts

NATHANIEL GORHAM   RUFUS KING

Connecticut

WM. SAML. JOHNSON   ROGER SHERMAN

New York

ALEXANDER HAMILTON

New Jersey

WIL: LIVINGSTON   WM. PATERSON
DAVID BREARLEY   JONA: DAYTON

Pennsylvania

B. FRANKLIN   THOS. FITZSIMONS
THOMAS MIFFLIN   JARED INGERSOLL
ROBT MORRIS   JAMES WILSON
GEO. CLYMER   GOUV MORRIS

Delaware

GEO: READ   RICHARD BASSETT
GUNNING BEDFORDJUN   JACO: BROOM
JOHN DICKINSON

Maryland

JAMES MCHENRY   DANL CARROLL
DAN OF ST. THOS. JENIFER

Virginia

JOHN BLAIR—   JAMES MADISON JR.

North Carolina

WM. BLOUNT   HU WILLIAMSON
RICHD. DOBBS SPAIGHT

South Carolina

J. RUTLEDGE   CHARLES PINCKNEY
CHARLES COTESWORTH PINCKNEY   PIERCE BUTLER

Georgia

WILLIAM FEW   ABR BALDWIN

Amendments

(The first ten amendments to the Constitution are called the **Bill of Rights** and were adopted in 1791.)

ARTICLE I

Congress shall make no law respecting an establishment of religion, or prohibiting the free exercise thereof; or abridging the freedom of speech, or of the press; or the right of the people peaceably to assemble, and to petition the Government for a redress of grievances.

ARTICLE II

A well regulated militia, being necessary to the security of a free State, the right of the people to keep and bear arms, shall not be infringed.

ARTICLE III

No soldier shall, in time of peace be quartered in any house, without the consent of the owner, nor in time of war, but in a manner to be prescribed by law.

ARTICLE IV

The right of the people to be secure in their persons, houses, papers, and effects, against unreasonable searches and seizures, shall not be violated, and no warrants shall issue, but upon probable cause, supported by oath or affirmation, and particularly describing the place to be searched, and the persons or things to be seized.

ARTICLE V

No person shall be held to answer for a capital, or otherwise infamous crime, unless on a presentment or indictment of a Grand Jury, except in cases arising in the land or naval forces, or in the militia, when in actual service in time of war or public danger; nor shall any person be subject for the same offense to be twice put in jeopardy of life or limb; nor shall be compelled in any criminal case to be a witness against himself, nor be deprived of life, liberty, or property, without due process of law; nor shall private property be taken for public use, without just compensation.

ARTICLE VI

In all criminal prosecutions, the accused shall enjoy the right to a speedy and public trial, by an impartial jury of the State and district wherein the crime shall have been committed, which district shall have been previously ascertained by law, and to be informed of the nature and cause of the accusation; to be confronted with the witnesses against him; to have compulsory process for obtaining witnesses in his favor, and to have the assistance of counsel for his defense.

Article VII

In suits at common law, where the value in controversy shall exceed twenty dollars, the right of trial by jury shall be preserved, and no fact tried by a jury, shall be otherwise reexamined in any Court of the United States, than according to the rules of the common law.

Article VIII

Excessive bail shall not be required, nor excessive fines imposed, nor cruel and unusual punishments inflicted.

Article IX

The enumeration in the Constitution, of certain rights, shall not be construed to deny or disparage others retained by the people.

Article X

The powers not delegated to the United States by the Constitution, nor prohibited by it to the States, are reserved to the States respectively, or to the people.

Article XI

The judicial power of the United States shall not be construed to extend to any suit in law or equity, commenced or prosecuted against one of the United States by citizens of another State, or by citizens or subjects of any foreign State.

Article XII

The electors shall meet in their respective States, and vote by ballot for President and Vice President, one of whom, at least, shall not be an inhabitant of the same State with themselves; they shall name in their ballots the person voted for as President, and in distinct ballots the person voted for as Vice President, and they shall make distinct lists of all persons voted for as President, and of all persons voted for as Vice President, and of the number of votes for each, which lists they shall sign and certify, and transmit sealed to the seat of the government of the United States, directed to the President of the Senate;— The President of the Senate shall, in the presence of the Senate and House of Representatives, open all the certificates and the votes shall then be counted;—The person having the greatest number of votes for President, shall be the President, if such number be a majority of the whole number of electors appointed; and if no person have such majority, then from the persons having the highest numbers not exceeding three on the list of those voted for as President, the House of Representatives shall choose immediately, by ballot, the President. But in choosing the President, the votes shall be taken by States, the representation from each State having one vote; a quorum for this purpose shall consist of a member or members from two-thirds of the States, and a majority of all the States shall be necessary to a choice.

And if the House of Representatives shall not choose a President whenever the right of choice shall devolve upon them, before the fourth day of March next following, then the Vice President shall act as President, as in the case of the death or other constitutional disability of the President.—The person having the greatest number of votes as Vice President, shall be the Vice President, if such number be a majority of the whole number of electors appointed, and if no person have a majority, then from the two highest numbers on the list, the Senate shall choose the Vice President; a quorum for the purpose shall consist of two-thirds of the whole number of Senators, and a majority of the whole number shall be necessary to a choice. But no person constitutionally ineligible to the office of President shall be eligible to that of Vice President of the United States.

ARTICLE XIII

SECTION 1. Neither slavery nor involuntary servitude, except as a punishment for crime whereof the party shall have been duly convicted, shall exist within the United States, or any place subject to their jurisdiction.

SECTION 2. Congress shall have power to enforce this article by appropriate legislation.

ARTICLE XIV

SECTION 1. All persons born or naturalized in the United States, and subject to the jurisdiction thereof, are citizens of the United States and of the State wherein they reside. No State shall make or enforce any law which shall abridge the privileges or immunities of citizens of the United States; nor shall any State deprive any person of life, liberty, or property, without due process of law; nor deny to any person within its jurisdiction the equal protection of the laws.

SECTION 2. Representatives shall be apportioned among the several States according to their respective numbers, counting the whole number of persons in each State, excluding Indians not taxed. But when the right to vote at any election for the choice of electors for President and Vice President of the United States, Representatives in Congress, the executive and judicial officers of a State, or the members of the legislature thereof, is denied to any of the male inhabitants of such State, being twenty-one years of age, and citizens of the United States, or in any way abridged, except for participation in rebellion, or other crime, the basis of representation therein shall be reduced in the proportion which the number of such male citizens shall bear to the whole number of male citizens twenty-one years of age in such State.

SECTION 3. No person shall be a Senator or Representative in Congress, or elector of President and Vice President, or hold any office, civil or military, under the United States, or under any State, who, having previously taken an oath, as a member of Congress, or as an officer of the United States, or as a member of any State legislature, or as an executive or judicial officer of any State, to support the Constitution of the United States, shall have engaged in insurrection or rebellion against the same, or given aid or comfort to the enemies thereof. But Congress may by a vote of two-thirds of each house, remove such disability.

SECTION 4. The validity of the public debt of the United States, authorized by law, including debts incurred for payment of pensions and bounties for services in suppressing insurrection or rebellion, shall not be questioned. But neither the United States nor any State shall assume or pay any debt or obligation incurred in aid of insurrection or rebellion against the United States, or any claim for the loss or emancipation of any slave; but all such debts, obligations and claims shall be held illegal and void.

SECTION 5. The Congress shall have power to enforce, by appropriate legislation, the provisions of this article.

ARTICLE XV

SECTION 1. The right of citizens of the United States to vote shall not be denied or abridged by the United States or by any State on account of race, color, or previous condition of servitude.

SECTION 2. The Congress shall have power to enforce this article by appropriate legislation.

ARTICLE XVI

The Congress shall have power to lay and collect taxes on incomes, from whatever source derived, without apportionment among the several States, and without regard to any census or enumeration.

ARTICLE XVII

SECTION 1. The Senate of the United States shall be composed of two Senators from each State, elected by the people thereof, for six years; and each Senator shall have one vote. The electors in each State shall have the qualifications requisite for electors of the most numerous branch of the State legislatures.

SECTION 2. When vacancies happen in the representation of any State in the Senate, the executive authority of such State shall issue writs of election to fill such vacancies: *Provided,* That the legislature of any State may empower the executive thereof to make temporary appointments until the people fill the vacancies by election as the legislature may direct.

SECTION 3. This amendment shall not be so construed as to affect the election or term of any Senator chosen before it becomes valid as part of the Constitution.

ARTICLE XVIII

SECTION 1. After one year from the ratification of this article the manufacture, sale, or transportation of intoxicating liquors within, the importation thereof into, or the exportation thereof from the United States and all territory subject to the jurisdiction thereof for beverage purposes is hereby prohibited.

SECTION 2. The Congress and the several States shall have concurrent power to enforce this article by appropriate legislation.

SECTION 3. This article shall be inoperative unless it shall have been ratified as an amendment to the Constitution by the legislatures of the several States, as provided in the Constitution, within seven years from the date of the submission hereof to the States by the Congress.

Article XIX

Section 1. The right of citizens of the United States to vote shall not be denied or abridged by the United States or by any State on account of sex.

Section 2. Congress shall have power to enforce this article by appropriate legislation.

Article XX

Section 1. The terms of the President and Vice President shall end at noon on the 20th day of January, and the terms of Senators and Representatives at noon on the 3d day of January, of the years in which such terms would have ended if this article had not been ratified; and the terms of their successors shall then begin.

Section 2. The Congress shall assemble at least once in every year, and such meeting shall begin at noon on the 3d day of January, unless they shall by law appoint a different day.

Section 3. If, at the time fixed for the beginning of the term of the President, the President elect shall have died, the Vice President elect shall become President. If a President shall not have been chosen before the time fixed for the beginning of his term, or if the President elect shall have failed to qualify, then the Vice President elect shall act as President until a President shall have qualified; and the Congress may by law provide for the case wherein neither a President elect nor a Vice President elect shall have qualified, declaring who shall then act as President, or the manner in which one who is to act shall be selected, and such person shall act accordingly until a President or Vice President shall have qualified.

Section 4. The Congress may by law provide for the case of the death of any of the persons from whom the House of Representatives may choose a President whenever the right of choice shall have devolved upon them, and for the case of the death of any of the persons from whom the Senate may choose a Vice President whenever the right of choice shall have devolved upon them.

Section 5. Sections 1 and 2 shall take effect on the 15th day of October following the ratification of this article.

Section 6. This article shall be inoperative unless it shall have been ratified as an amendment to the Constitution by the legislatures of three-fourths of the several States within seven years from the date of its submission.

Article XXI

Section 1. The eighteenth article of amendment to the Constitution of the United States is hereby repealed.

Section 2. The transportation or importation into any State, Territory, or possession of the United States for delivery or use therein of intoxicating liquors, in violation of the laws thereof, is hereby prohibited.

Section 3. This article shall be inoperative unless it shall have been ratified as an amendment to the Constitution by conventions in the several States, as provided in the Constitution, within seven years from the date of the submission hereof to the States by the Congress.

Article XXII

Section 1. No person shall be elected to the office of the President more than twice, and no person who has held the office of President, or acted as President, for more than two years of a term to which some other person was elected President shall be elected to the office of the President more than once. But this article shall not apply to any person holding the office of President when this article was proposed by the Congress, and shall not prevent any person who may be holding the office of President, or acting as President, during the term within which this article becomes operative from holding the office of President or acting as President during the remainder of such term.

Section 2. This article shall be inoperative unless it shall have been ratified as an amendment to the Constitution by the legislatures of three-fourths of the several States within seven years from the date of its submission to the States by the Congress.

Article XXIII

Section 1. The District constituting the seat of Government of the United States shall appoint in such manner as the Congress may direct:

A number of electors of President and Vice President equal to the whole number of Senators and Representatives in Congress to which the District would be entitled if it were a State, but in no event more than the least populous State; they shall be in addition to those appointed by the States, but they shall be considered, for the purposes of the election of President and Vice President, to be electors appointed by a State; and they shall meet in the District and perform such duties as provided by the twelfth article of amendment.

Section 2. The Congress shall have power to enforce this article by appropriate legislation.

Article XXIV

Section 1. The right of citizens of the United States to vote in any primary or other election for President or Vice President, for electors for President or Vice President, or for Senator or Representative in Congress, shall not be denied or abridged by the United States or any State by reason of failure to pay any poll tax or other tax.

Section 2. The Congress shall have power to enforce this article by appropriate legislation.

Article XXV

Section 1. In case of the removal of the President from office or of his death or resignation, the Vice President shall become President.

Section 2. Whenever there is a vacancy in the office of the Vice President, the President shall nominate a Vice President who shall take office upon confirmation by a majority vote of both Houses of Congress.

Section 3. Whenever the President transmits to the President pro tempore of the Senate and the Speaker of the House of Representatives his written declaration that he is unable to discharge the powers and duties of his office, and until he transmits to them a written declaration to the contrary, such powers and duties shall be discharged by the Vice President as Acting President.

Section 4. Whenever the Vice President and a majority of either the principal officers of the executive departments or of such other body as Congress may by law provide, transmit to the President pro tempore of the Senate and the Speaker of the House of Representatives their written declaration that the President is unable to discharge the powers and duties of his office, the Vice President shall immediately assume the powers and duties of the office as Acting President.

Thereafter, when the President transmits to the President pro tempore of the Senate and the Speaker of the House of Representatives his written declaration that no inability exists, he shall resume the powers and duties of his office unless the Vice President and a majority of either the principal officers of the executive department or of such other body as Congress may by law provide, transmit within four days to the President pro tempore of the Senate and the Speaker of the House of Representatives their written declaration that the President is unable to discharge the powers and duties of his office. Thereupon Congress shall decide the issue, assembling within forty-eight hours for that purpose if not in session. If the Congress, within twenty-one days after receipt of the latter written declaration, or, if Congress is not in session, within twenty-one days after Congress is required to assemble, determines by two-thirds vote of both Houses that the President is unable to discharge the powers and duties of his office, the Vice President shall continue to discharge the same as Acting President; otherwise, the President shall resume the powers and duties of his office.

Article XXVI

Section 1. The right of citizens of the United States who are eighteen years of age or older, to vote shall not be denied or abridged by the United States or by any State on account of age.

Section 2. The Congress shall have power to enforce this article by appropriate legislation.

The Emancipation Proclamation

President Lincoln first issued the Emancipation Proclamation, freeing the slaves, on September 22, 1862. The final proclamation was issued on January 1, 1863, as follows:

By the President of the United
States of America:

A Proclamation.

Whereas on the 22d day of September, A.D. 1862, a proclamation was issued by the President of the United States, containing, among other things, the following, to wit:

"That on the 1st day of January, A.D. 1863, all persons held as slaves within any State or designated part of a State the people whereof shall then be in rebellion against the United States shall be then, thenceforward, and forever free; and the executive government of the United States, including the military and naval authority thereof, will recognize and maintain the freedom of such persons and will do no act or acts to repress such persons, or any of them, in any efforts they may make for their actual freedom.

"That the executive will on the 1st day of January aforesaid, by proclamation, designate the States and parts of States, if any, in which the people thereof, respectively, shall then be in rebellion against the United States; and the fact that any State or the people thereof shall on that day be in good faith represented in the Congress of the United States by members chosen thereto at elections wherein a majority of the qualified voters of such States shall have participated shall, in the absence of strong countervailing testimony, be deemed conclusive evidence that such State and the people thereof are not then in rebellion against the United States."

Now, therefore, I, Abraham Lincoln, President of the United States, by virtue of the power in me vested as Commander-in-Chief of the Army and Navy of the United States in time of actual armed rebellion against the authority and government of the United States, and as a fit and necessary war measure for suppressing said rebellion, do, on this 1st day of January, A.D. 1863, and in accordance with my purpose so to do, publicly proclaimed for the full period of one hundred days from the first day above mentioned, order and designate as the States and parts of States wherein the people thereof, respectively, are this day in rebellion against the United States the following, to wit:

Arkansas, Texas, Louisiana (except the parishes of St. Bernard, Plaquemines, Jefferson, St. John, St. Charles, St. James, Ascension, Assumption, Terrebonne, Lafourche, St. Mary, St. Martin, and Orleans, including the city of New Orleans), Mississippi, Alabama, Florida, Georgia, South Carolina, North Carolina, and Virginia (except the forty-eight counties designated as West Virginia, and also the counties of Berkeley, Accomac, Northampton, Elizabeth City, York, Princess Anne, and Norfolk, including the cities of Norfolk and Portsmouth), and which excepted parts are for the present left precisely as if this proclamation were not issued.

And by virtue of the power and for the purpose aforesaid, I do order and declare that all persons held as slaves within said designated States and parts of States are, and henceforward shall be, free; and that the Executive Government of the United States, including the military and naval authorities thereof, will recognize and maintain the freedom of said persons.

And I hereby enjoin upon the people so declared to be free to abstain from all violence, unless in necessary self-defense; and I recommend to them that, in all cases when allowed, they labor faithfully for reasonable wages.

And I further declare and make known that such persons of suitable condition will be received into the armed service of the United States to garrison forts, positions, stations, and other places, and to man vessels of all sorts in said service.

And upon this act, sincerely believe to be an act of justice, warranted by the Constitution upon military necessity, I invoke the considerate judgment of mankind and the gracious favor of Almighty God.

The Monroe Doctrine

In his message to Congress on December 2, 1823, President James Monroe established what has come to be known as the Monroe Doctrine, a statement of U.S. foreign policy that expresses opposition to the extension of European control or influence in the Western Hemisphere. Following is part of Monroe's message:

> In the discussions to which this interest has given rise, and in the arrangements by which they may terminate, the occasion has been deemed proper for asserting as a principle in which rights and interest of the United States are involved, that the American continents, by the free and independent condition which they have assumed and maintain, are henceforth not to be considered as subjects for future colonization by any European power. . . . We owe it, therefore, to candor and to the amicable relations existing between the United States and those powers to declare that we should consider any attempt on their part to extend their system to any portion of this hemisphere as dangerous to our peace and safety. With the existing colonies or dependencies of any European power we have not interfered and shall not interfere. But with the governments who have declared their independence and maintain it, and whose independence we have, on great consideration and on just principles, acknowledged, we could not view any interposition for the purpose of oppressing them or controlling in any other manner their destiny by any European power in any other light than as the manifestation of an unfriendly disposition toward the United States.

The Pledge of Allegiance

I pledge allegiance to the flag of the United States of America, and to the Republic for which it stands, one nation under God, indivisible, with liberty and justice for all.

The phrase "under God" was added to the pledge by an Act of Congress in 1954. The original pledge, written in 1892 by Francis Bellamy, contained the phrase "my flag."

The U.S. Flag

History

The "Stars and Stripes" as we know it today, with its blue field of 50 white stars and 13 red and white stripes representing the original 13 colonies, underwent several transformations.

The first flag raised in the United States was hoisted by John Cabot in 1497; it flew the banners of England and St. Mark. As settlers populated the colonies, each territory adopted its own flag. By 1707, each colony had its own flag, the forerunners of the individual state flags today. The first colonial flag representing all the colonies, however, was believed to have been raised on Prospect Hill in Boston at the Battle of Bunker Hill. The "Continental Colors" bore the cross of the British flag in the upper left corner with 13 alternating red and white stripes extending horizontally. In 1777 the first Continental Congress "Resolved, that the Flag of the United States be thirteen stripes alternate red and white, that the Union be thirteen stars white on a blue field, representing a constellation."

As the new Union grew, Congress voted in 1794 to add two stripes and two stars to represent the two new states of Vermont and Kentucky. This flag is believed to be the one nicknamed the "Star-Spangled Banner." By 1818 five more states had joined, and on April 4, Congress voted to keep the number of stripes at 13 and to add a star to the field for every new state, the stars for the new states being added the July 4th after each state's admission to the Union.

The table below shows the order in which states joined the Union and the number of revisions the flag went through before arriving at its current design.

The U.S. Flag: 1777–1960

Date Used	Number of Stars	Designs	States Represented
June 14, 1777	13	1	Original 13 colonies
May 1, 1795	15	2	Vermont, Kentucky
July 4, 1818	20	3	Tennessee, Ohio, Louisiana, Indiana, Mississippi
July 4, 1819	21	4	Illinois
July 4, 1820	23	5	Alabama, Maine
July 4, 1822	24	6	Missouri
July 4, 1836	25	7	Arkansas
July 4, 1837	26	8	Michigan
July 4, 1845	27	9	Florida
July 4, 1846	28	10	Texas
July 4, 1847	29	11	Iowa
July 4, 1848	30	12	Wisconsin
July 4, 1851	31	13	California
July 4, 1858	32	14	Minnesota
July 4, 1859	33	15	Oregon
July 4, 1861	34	16	Kansas
July 4, 1863	35	17	West Virginia

Date Used	Number of Stars	Designs	States Represented
July 4, 1865	36	18	Nevada
July 4, 1867	37	19	Nebraska
July 4, 1877	38	20	Colorado
July 4, 1890	43	21	North Dakota, South Dakota, Montana, Washington, Idaho
July 4, 1891	44	22	Wyoming
July 4, 1896	45	23	Utah
July 4, 1908	46	24	Oklahoma
July 4, 1912	48	25	New Mexico, Arizona
July 4, 1959	49	26	Alaska
July 4, 1960	50	27	Hawaii

Care and Use of the Flag

Wherever and whenever it is displayed, the first requirement for flying the flag is that it be flown with respect. To show respect and honor to the symbol of the United States, fly it only in good weather, on all holidays and special occasions, and on official buildings such as schools when they are in session, post offices, courthouses, and the like. The flag generally is flown only from sunrise to sunset and at full staff. If it is displayed at night, it should be lit. Fly the flag at half staff to commemorate the death of an official and until noon on Memorial Day.

The White House flag is flown only when the president is in residence and only from sunrise to sunset. At the Capitol building, the flag flies over the appropriate wing when the House or Senate is in session. The flag is flown all night long and is lit by lights from the Capitol dome. Other special national monuments also fly the flag at night, notably Fort McHenry National Monument in Baltimore, Maryland, where Francis Scott Key was inspired to write "The Star-Spangled Banner."

When handling the flag, never let it touch the ground. When it flies with other flags, it should appear prominently above them. The flag should be to its own right (to the left, viewed face-on) with its staff in front of the staff of the other flag when placed against a wall with another flag. In a group of flags, the U.S. flag should be at the center. (The flag of the United Nations and a navy chaplain's church pennant may be flown above the U.S. flag.)

Hoist the flag quickly and lower it ceremoniously to the tempo of "Taps." If the flag is hung from a rope attached to a building, the field of stars should face away from the building; when hung over a street, the Union side should face north or east.

On a platform, the flag may be hung flat against the wall behind and above the speaker with the field of stars to the audience's left. In a church, the flag on its staff should be to the right of the speaker's platform and other flags to the left of the platform. If the flag is flown anywhere else in the chancel or on a platform, it should be to the right of the audience as they face the platform.

Salute when the flag passes in a parade or review, is being raised or lowered, is present at the playing of the national anthem, or is present at the saying of the Pledge of Allegiance.

Civilians should salute the flag by standing at attention and placing their right hands over their hearts. Men should remove their hats and hold them over their left shoulders with their right hand. Military personnel in uniform should give the military salute. Noncitizens should stand at attention.

Presidents of the United States

President	Term	Years of Birth and Death	Party	Vice-President	Congresses
1. George Washington	4/30/1789–3/3/1797	1732–1799	F	John Adams	1, 2, 3, 4
2. John Adams	3/4/1797–3/3/1801	1735–1826	F	Thomas Jefferson	5, 6
3. Thomas Jefferson	3/4/1801–3/3/1805	1743–1826	D-R	Aaron Burr	7, 8
	3/4/1805–3/3/1809			George Clinton	9, 10
4. James Madison	3/4/1809–3/3/1813	1751–1836	D-R	George Clinton	11, 12
	3/4/1813–3/3/1817			Elbridge Gerry	13, 14
5. James Monroe	3/4/1817–3/3/1821	1758–1831	D-R	Daniel D. Tompkins	15, 16, 17, 18
	3/4/1821–3/3/1825				
6. John Quincy Adams	3/4/1825–3/3/1829	1767–1848	D-R	John C. Calhoun	19, 20
7. Andrew Jackson	3/4/1829–3/3/1833	1767–1845	D	John C. Calhoun	21, 22
	3/4/1833–3/3/1837			Martin Van Buren	23, 24
8. Martin Van Buren	3/4/1837–3/3/1841	1782–1862	D	Richard M. Johnson	25, 26
9. William Henry Harrison	3/4/1841–4/4/1841	1773–1841	W	John Tyler	27
10. John Tyler	4/6/1841–3/3/1845	1790–1862	W	—	27, 28
11. James K. Polk	3/4/1845–3/3/1849	1795–1849	D	George M. Dallas	29, 30
12. Zachary Taylor	3/4/1849–7/9/1850	1784–1850	W	Millard Fillmore	31
13. Millard Fillmore	7/10/1850–3/3/1853	1800–1874	W	—	31, 32
14. Franklin Pierce	3/4/1853–3/3/1857	1804–1869	D	William R. King	33, 34

President	Term	Years of Birth and Death	Party	Vice-President	Congresses
15. James Buchanan	3/4/1857–3/3/1861	1791–1868	D	John C. Breckinridge	35, 36
16. Abraham Lincoln	3/4/1861–3/3/1865	1809–1865	R	Hannibal Hamlin	37, 38
	3/4/1865–4/15/1865			Andrew Johnson	39
17. Andrew Johnson	4/15/1865–3/3/1869	1808–1875	NU	—	39, 40
18. Ulysses S. Grant	3/4/1869–3/3/1873	1822–1885	R	Schuyler Colfax	41, 42
	3/4/1873–3/3/1877			Henry Wilson	43, 44
19. Rutherford B. Hayes	3/4/1877–3/3/1881	1822–1893	R	William A. Wheeler	45, 46
20. James Garfield	3/4/1881–9/19/1881	1831–1881	R	Chester A. Arthur	47
21. Chester A. Arthur	9/20/1881–3/3/1885	1829–1886	R	—	47, 48
22. Grover Cleveland	3/4/1885–3/3/1889	1837–1908	D	Thomas A. Hendricks	49, 50
23. Benjamin Harrison	3/4/1889–3/3/1893	1833–1901	R	Levi P. Morton	51, 52
24. Grover Cleveland	3/4/1893–3/3/1897	1837–1908	D	Adlai E. Stevenson	53, 54
25. William McKinley	3/4/1897–3/3/1901	1843–1901	R	Garret A. Hobart	55, 56
	3/4/1901–9/14/1901			Theodore Roosevelt	57
26. Theodore Roosevelt	9/14/1901–3/3/1905	1858–1919	R	—	57, 58
	3/4/1905–3/3/1909			Charles W. Fairbanks	59, 60
27. William H. Taft	3/4/1909–3/3/1913	1857–1930	R	James S. Sherman	61, 62
28. Woodrow Wilson	3/4/1913–3/3/1921	1856–1924	D	Thomas R. Marshall	63, 64, 65, 66
29. Warren G. Harding	3/4/1921–8/2/1923	1865–1923	R	Calvin Coolidge	67, 68
30. Calvin Coolidge	8/3/1923–3/3/1925	1872–1933	R	—	68
	3/4/1925–3/3/1929			Charles G. Dawes	69, 70
31. Herbert C. Hoover	3/4/1929–3/3/1933	1874–1964	R	Charles Curtis	71, 72

President	Term	Years of Birth and Death	Party	Vice-President	Congresses
32. Franklin D. Roosevelt	3/4/1933–1/20/1941	1882–1945	D	John N. Garner	73, 74, 75, 76
	1/20/1941–1/20/1945			Henry A. Wallace	77, 78
	1/20/1945–4/12/1945			Harry S Truman	79
33. Harry S Truman	4/12/1945–1/20/1949	1884–1972	D	—	79, 80
	1/20/1949–1/20/1953			Alben W. Barkley	81, 82
34. Dwight D. Eisenhower	1/20/1953–1/20/1961	1890–1969	R	Richard M. Nixon	83, 84, 85, 86
35. John F. Kennedy	1/20/1961–11/22/1963	1917–1963	D	Lyndon B. Johnson	87, 88
36. Lyndon B. Johnson	11/22/1963–1/20/1965	1908–1973	D	—	88
	1/20/1965–1/20/1969			Hubert H. Humphrey	89, 90
37. Richard M. Nixon	1/20/1969–1/20/1973	1913–	R	Spiro T. Agnew	91, 92
	1/20/1973–8/9/1974			Spiro T. Agnew,* Gerald R. Ford	93
38. Gerald R. Ford	8/9/1974–1/20/1977	1913–	R	Nelson A. Rockefeller	93, 94
39. James (Jimmy) Carter	1/20/1977–1/20/1981	1924–	D	Walter F. Mondale	95, 96
40. Ronald Reagan	1/20/1981–1/20/1989	1911–	R	George Bush	97, 98, 99, 100
41. George Bush	1/20/1989–1/20/1993	1924–	R	J. Danforth Quayle	101, 102
42. William Clinton	1/20/1993–	1946–	D	Albert A. Gore, Jr.	103

F = Federalist; D-R = Democratic-Republican; D = Democrat; W = Whig; R = Republican; NU = National Union Party, a coalition of Republicans and War Democrats (Andrew Johnson was a Democrat).

* Spiro T. Agnew resigned on October 10, 1973. Gerald R. Ford was inaugurated December 6, 1973.

THE SEQUENCE OF PRESIDENTIAL SUCCESSION

1. Vice-President
2. Speaker of the House
3. President Pro Tempore of the Senate
4. Secretary of State
5. Secretary of the Treasury
6. Secretary of Defense
7. Attorney General
8. Secretary of the Interior
9. Secretary of Agriculture
10. Secretary of Commerce
11. Secretary of Labor
12. Secretary of Health and Human Services
13. Secretary of Housing and Urban Development
14. Secretary of Transportation
15. Secretary of Energy
16. Secretary of Education

Any successor to the presidency must meet the requirements for the office as established in the Constitution.

THE ELECTORAL COLLEGE

The president and vice-president of the United States are elected not by popular vote, but by the Electoral College, as stipulated in Article II, Section 1, of the U.S. Constitution. On Election Day, each state selects a number of electors equal to that of its U.S. senators and representatives; these electors are all affiliated with the party that has received the highest popular vote in the state. Including the District of Columbia's three electoral votes, the total is 538, with a majority of 270 votes needed to win. The votes are counted in a joint session of Congress on January 6. If no candidate for president has won a majority, the House selects one of the three leading candidates, with all members from a state voting in a bloc; if no vice-presidential candidate has a majority, the Senate, voting as individuals, choose one from the top two candidates.

In three presidential elections, the winners of the largest number of popular votes failed to win the presidency:

1824: None of the four candidates—William Crawford, Andrew Jackson, John Quincy Adams, and Henry Clay—received a majority of the electoral votes. The House of Representatives chose John Quincy Adams to be president. John C. Calhoun was chosen vice-president by the Electoral College.

1876: Democratic presidential nominee Samuel Tilden and vice-presidential nominee Thomas A. Hendricks led their Republican counterparts Rutherford B. Hayes and William A. Wheeler in popular votes (4,284,020 to 4,036,572) and electoral votes (184 to 65). But a controversy raged over 20 unassigned electoral votes. To resolve contradictions between two sets of election returns, one each from the Democrats and the Republicans, Congress established a commission of 10 congressmen and 5 Supreme Court justices, whose verdict could be overturned only if both the House and Senate disputed it. The commission, which consisted of eight Republicans and seven Democrats, gave the Republicans all of the disputed votes; while the House voted against the decision, the Senate upheld it, bringing Hayes and Wheeler into office.

1888: The Democratic nominees were Grover Cleveland and Allen G. Thurman; the Republican candidates were Benjamin Harrison and Levi P. Morton. While Cleveland led Harrison 5,540,050 to 5,444,337 in popular votes, Harrison was ahead in electoral votes, 233 to 168, and won the election.

Vice-Presidents of the United States

Vice-President	Years of Birth and Death	President	Party
1. John Adams	1735–1826	George Washington	F
2. Thomas Jefferson	1743–1826	John Adams	D-R
3. Aaron Burr	1756–1836	Thomas Jefferson	D-R
4. George Clinton	1739–1812	Thomas Jefferson	D-R
		James Madison	D-R
5. Elbridge Gerry	1744–1814	James Madison	D-R
6. Daniel D. Tompkins	1774–1825	James Monroe	D-R
7. John C. Calhoun	1782–1850	John Quincy Adams	D-R
		Andrew Jackson	
8. Martin Van Buren	1782–1862	Andrew Jackson	D
9. Richard M. Johnson	1780–1850	Martin Van Buren	D
10. John Tyler	1790–1862	William Henry Harrison	W
11. George M. Dallas	1792–1864	James K. Polk	D
12. Millard Fillmore	1800–1874	Zachary Taylor	W
13. William R. King	1786–1853	Franklin Pierce	D
14. John C. Breckinridge	1821–1875	James Buchanan	D
15. Hannibal Hamlin	1809–1891	Abraham Lincoln	R
16. Andrew Johnson	1808–1875	Abraham Lincoln	NU
17. Schuyler Colfax	1823–1885	Ulysses S. Grant	R
18. Henry Wilson	1812–1875	Ulysses S. Grant	R
19. William A. Wheeler	1819–1887	Rutherford B. Hayes	R
20. Chester A. Arthur	1829–1886	James Garfield	R

	Vice-President	Years of Birth and Death	President	Party
21.	Thomas A. Hendricks	1819–1885	Grover Cleveland	D
22.	Levi P. Morton	1824–1920	Benjamin Harrison	R
23.	Adlai E. Stevenson	1835–1914	Grover Cleveland	D
24.	Garret A. Hobart	1844–1899	William McKinley	R
25.	Theodore Roosevelt	1858–1919	William McKinley	R
26.	Charles W. Fairbanks	1852–1918	Theodore Roosevelt	R
27.	James S. Sherman	1855–1912	William H. Taft	R
28.	Thomas R. Marshall	1854–1925	Woodrow Wilson	D
29.	Calvin Coolidge	1872–1933	Warren G. Harding	R
30.	Charles G. Dawes	1865–1951	Calvin Coolidge	R
31.	Charles Curtis	1860–1936	Herbert C. Hoover	R
32.	John N. Garner	1868–1967	Franklin D. Roosevelt	D
33.	Henry A. Wallace	1888–1965	Franklin D. Roosevelt	D
34.	Harry S Truman	1884–1972	Franklin D. Roosevelt	D
35.	Alben W. Barkley	1877–1956	Harry S Truman	D
36.	Richard M. Nixon	1913–	Dwight D. Eisenhower	R
37.	Lyndon B. Johnson	1908–1973	John F. Kennedy	D
38.	Hubert H. Humphrey	1911–1978	Lyndon B. Johnson	D
39.	Spiro T. Agnew	1918–	Richard M. Nixon	R
40.	Gerald R. Ford	1913–	Richard M. Nixon	R
41.	Nelson A. Rockefeller	1908–1979	Gerald R. Ford	R
42.	Walter F. Mondale	1928–	James (Jimmy) Carter	D
43.	George Bush	1924–	Ronald Reagan	R
44.	J. Danforth Quayle	1947–	George Bush	R
45.	Albert A. Gore, Jr.	1948–	Bill Clinton	D

Weather Charts

Average Precipitation for Selected States and Cities (in inches)

State	City	Jan/Feb	Mar/Apr	May/Jun	Jul/Aug	Sep/Oct	Nov/Dec
Alabama	Mobile	5.1	5.4	5.4	6.9	4.4	4.7
Alaska	Juneau	4.1	3.0	3.3	4.7	7.3	4.7
Arizona	Phoenix	0.7	0.6	0.1	0.9	0.8	0.8
California	Los Angeles	2.5	1.4	0.1	0.1	0.3	1.7
	San Francisco	3.8	2.2	0.1	0.04	0.7	3.0
Colorado	Denver	0.6	1.5	2.1	1.7	1.1	0.8
Connecticut	Hartford	3.3	3.7	3.9	3.4	3.7	4.0
Delaware	Wilmington	3.0	3.4	3.7	3.8	3.2	3.4
District of Columbia	Washington	2.7	2.9	3.5	3.9	3.2	3.1
Florida	Jacksonville	3.6	3.2	4.6	6.8	5.0	2.5
	Miami	2.0	2.6	7.7	6.6	6.6	2.2

Average Precipitation for Selected States and Cities (*continued*)
(in inches)

State	City	Jan/Feb	Mar/Apr	May/Jun	Jul/Aug	Sep/Oct	Nov/Dec
Georgia	Atlanta	4.8	5.0	3.9	4.3	3.2	4.1
Hawaii	Honolulu	2.9	1.9	0.8	0.5	1.5	3.4
Idaho	Boise	1.3	1.3	0.9	0.4	0.8	1.4
Illinois	Chicago	1.4	3.2	3.6	3.9	3.1	2.7
Indiana	Indianapolis	2.4	3.4	3.7	4.0	2.8	3.3
Iowa	Des Moines	1.0	2.8	4.1	4.0	3.1	1.6
Kansas	Dodge City	0.5	1.7	3.2	2.8	1.6	0.7
Kentucky	Louisville	3.1	4.4	4.0	4.0	2.9	3.7
Louisiana	New Orleans	5.5	4.7	5.2	6.1	4.3	5.1
Maine	Portland	3.4	3.9	3.5	3.0	3.5	4.7
Massachusetts	Boston	3.6	3.6	3.2	3.0	3.2	4.1
Michigan	Detroit	1.8	2.8	3.3	3.3	2.5	2.7
Minnesota	Duluth	1.0	2.1	3.4	3.8	3.2	1.5
	Minneapolis	0.9	2.2	3.7	3.6	2.5	1.3
Mississippi	Jackson	5.0	5.7	4.1	4.1	3.4	5.4
Missouri	Kansas City	1.1	2.8	4.9	4.2	4.1	1.8
	St. Louis	2.0	3.5	3.8	3.4	2.9	3.2
Montana	Helena	0.6	0.9	1.9	1.1	0.8	0.6
Nebraska	Omaha	0.8	2.4	4.2	3.4	3.0	1.3
Nevada	Reno	1.0	0.5	0.6	0.3	0.4	0.9
New Jersey	Atlantic City	3.3	3.6	3.0	4.0	2.9	3.5
New Mexico	Albuquerque	0.5	0.5	0.6	1.5	0.9	0.5
New York	Albany	2.3	3.0	3.5	3.3	2.9	3.1
	Buffalo	2.5	2.8	3.3	3.6	3.3	3.8
	New York	3.3	4.0	4.0	4.2	3.7	4.2
North Carolina	Raleigh	3.6	3.2	3.8	4.0	3.0	3.1
North Dakota	Bismarck	0.4	1.2	2.5	1.9	1.2	0.5
Ohio	Cleveland	2.1	3.0	3.6	3.5	3.0	3.1
	Columbus	2.2	3.2	4.0	4.0	2.6	3.0
Oklahoma	Oklahoma City	1.3	2.7	4.8	2.6	3.5	1.7
Oregon	Portland	4.6	3.0	1.8	0.9	2.2	5.7
Pennsylvania	Philadelphia	3.0	3.5	3.7	4.0	3.0	3.4
	Pittsburgh	2.5	3.3	3.7	3.5	2.7	2.9
Rhode Island	Providence	3.7	4.1	3.5	3.4	3.6	4.4
South Carolina	Charleston	3.4	3.5	5.5	6.9	3.9	2.7
South Dakota	Huron	0.6	1.6	3.0	2.2	1.4	0.6
Tennessee	Memphis	4.0	5.4	4.3	3.6	3.3	5.4
	Nashville	3.7	4.6	4.2	3.7	3.0	4.4
Texas	Dallas-Ft. Worth	2.0	3.1	3.9	2.3	3.5	2.1
	Houston	3.1	3.1	5.1	3.5	4.6	3.6
Utah	Salt Lake City	1.2	2.0	1.4	0.8	1.4	1.3
Vermont	Burlington	1.7	2.5	3.3	3.9	3.1	2.8
Virginia	Norfolk	3.6	3.4	3.8	4.0	3.5	3.0
	Richmond	3.2	3.3	3.7	4.7	3.4	3.2
Washington	Seattle-Tacoma	4.7	2.9	1.6	1.0	2.6	5.9
Wisconsin	Milwaukee	1.5	3.1	3.0	3.5	2.9	2.4
Wyoming	Lander	0.6	1.4	2.1	0.6	1.1	0.7

Normal Daily Mean Temperature—Selected Cities
(In Fahrenheit degrees. Airport data except as noted. Based on standard 30-year period, 1961 through 1990).

STATE	STATION	Jan.	Feb.	Mar.	Apr.	May	June	July	Aug.	Sept.	Oct.	Nov.	Dec.	Annual avg.
Alabama	Mobile	49.9	53.2	60.5	67.8	74.5	80.4	82.3	81.8	77.9	68.4	59.8	53.0	67.5
Alaska	Juneau	24.2	28.4	32.7	39.7	47.0	53.0	56.0	55.0	49.4	42.2	32.0	27.1	40.6
Arizona	Phoenix	53.6	57.7	62.2	69.9	78.8	88.2	93.5	91.5	85.6	74.5	61.9	54.1	72.6
Arkansas	Little Rock	39.1	43.6	53.1	62.1	70.2	78.4	81.9	80.6	74.1	63.0	52.1	42.8	61.8
California	Los Angeles	56.8	57.6	58.0	60.1	62.7	65.7	69.1	70.5	69.9	66.8	61.6	56.9	63.0
	Sacramento	45.2	50.7	53.6	58.3	65.3	71.6	75.7	75.1	71.5	64.2	53.3	45.3	60.8
	San Diego	57.4	58.6	59.6	62.0	64.1	66.8	71.0	72.6	71.4	67.7	62.0	57.4	64.2
	San Francisco	48.7	52.2	53.3	55.6	58.1	61.5	62.7	63.7	64.5	61.0	54.8	49.4	57.1
Colorado	Denver	29.7	33.4	39.0	48.2	57.2	66.9	73.5	71.4	62.3	51.4	39.0	31.0	50.3
Connecticut	Hartford	24.6	27.5	37.5	48.7	59.8	68.5	73.7	71.6	63.3	52.2	41.9	29.5	49.9
Delaware	Wilmington	30.6	33.4	42.7	52.2	62.5	71.5	76.4	75.0	68.0	56.2	46.3	35.8	54.2
District of Columbia	Washington	34.6	37.5	47.2	56.5	66.4	75.6	80.0	78.5	71.3	59.7	49.8	39.4	58.0
Florida	Jacksonville	52.4	55.2	61.1	67.0	73.4	79.1	81.6	81.2	78.1	69.8	61.9	55.1	68.0
	Miami	67.2	68.5	71.7	75.2	78.7	81.4	82.6	82.8	81.9	78.3	73.6	69.1	75.9
Georgia	Atlanta	41.0	44.8	53.5	61.5	69.2	76.0	78.8	78.1	72.7	62.3	53.1	44.5	61.3
Hawaii	Honolulu	72.9	73.0	74.4	75.8	77.5	79.4	80.5	81.4	81.0	79.6	77.2	74.1	77.2
Idaho	Boise	29.0	35.9	42.4	49.1	57.5	66.5	74.0	72.5	62.6	51.8	39.9	30.1	50.9
Illinois	Chicago	21.0	25.4	37.2	48.6	58.9	68.6	73.2	71.7	64.4	52.8	40.0	26.6	49.0
	Peoria	21.6	26.3	39.0	51.4	61.9	71.5	75.5	73.1	66.1	54.0	41.2	27.0	50.7
Indiana	Indianapolis	25.5	29.6	41.4	52.4	62.8	71.9	75.4	73.2	66.6	54.7	43.0	30.9	52.3
Iowa	Des Moines	19.4	24.7	37.3	50.9	62.3	71.8	76.6	73.9	65.1	53.5	39.0	24.4	49.9
Kansas	Wichita	29.5	34.8	45.4	56.4	65.6	75.7	81.4	79.3	70.3	58.6	44.7	33.0	56.2
Kentucky	Louisville	31.7	35.7	46.3	56.3	65.3	73.2	77.2	75.8	69.5	57.6	47.1	36.9	56.1
Louisiana	New Orleans	51.3	54.3	61.6	68.5	74.8	80.0	81.9	81.5	78.1	69.1	61.1	54.5	68.1
Maine	Portland	20.8	23.3	33.0	43.3	53.3	62.4	68.6	67.3	59.1	48.5	38.7	26.5	45.4
Maryland	Baltimore	31.8	34.8	44.1	53.4	63.4	72.5	77.0	75.6	68.5	56.6	46.8	36.7	55.1
Massachusetts	Boston	28.6	30.3	38.6	48.1	58.2	67.7	73.5	71.9	64.8	54.8	45.3	33.6	51.3
Michigan	Detroit	22.9	25.4	35.7	47.3	58.4	67.6	72.3	70.5	63.2	51.2	40.2	28.3	48.6
	Sault Ste. Marie	12.9	14.0	24.0	38.2	50.5	58.0	63.8	62.6	55.1	45.3	33.0	19.0	39.7
Minnesota	Duluth	7.0	12.3	24.4	38.6	50.8	59.8	66.1	63.7	54.2	43.7	28.4	12.8	38.5
	Minneapolis-St. Paul	11.8	17.9	31.0	46.4	58.5	68.2	73.6	70.5	60.5	48.8	33.2	17.9	44.9
Mississippi	Jackson	44.1	47.9	56.7	64.6	72.0	78.8	81.5	80.9	75.9	64.7	55.8	47.8	64.2
Missouri	Kansas City	25.7	31.2	42.7	54.5	64.1	73.2	78.5	76.1	67.5	56.6	43.1	30.4	53.6
	St. Louis	29.3	33.9	45.1	56.7	66.1	75.4	79.8	77.6	70.2	58.4	46.2	33.9	56.1
Montana	Great Falls	21.2	27.4	33.3	43.6	53.1	61.6	68.2	66.9	56.6	47.5	33.9	23.9	44.8
Nebraska	Omaha	21.1	26.9	38.6	51.9	62.4	72.1	76.9	74.1	65.1	53.4	39.0	25.1	50.6
Nevada	Reno	32.9	38.0	42.8	48.6	56.5	65.1	71.6	69.6	60.4	50.8	40.3	32.7	50.8
New Hampshire	Concord	18.6	21.8	32.4	43.9	55.2	64.2	69.5	67.3	58.8	47.8	37.1	24.3	45.1
New Jersey	Atlantic City	30.9	33.0	41.5	50.0	60.4	69.4	74.7	73.4	66.1	54.9	45.8	35.8	53.0
New Mexico	Albuquerque	34.2	40.0	46.9	55.2	64.2	74.2	78.5	75.9	68.6	57.0	44.3	35.3	56.2
New York	Albany	20.6	23.5	34.3	46.4	57.6	66.9	71.8	69.6	61.3	50.2	39.7	26.5	47.4
	Buffalo	23.6	24.5	33.8	45.2	56.6	65.9	71.1	69.0	61.9	51.1	40.5	29.1	47.7
	New York [1]	31.5	33.6	42.4	52.5	62.7	71.6	76.8	75.5	68.2	57.5	47.6	36.6	54.7
North Carolina	Charlotte	39.3	42.5	50.9	59.4	67.4	75.7	79.3	78.3	72.4	61.3	52.1	42.6	60.1
	Raleigh	38.9	42.0	50.4	59.0	67.0	74.3	78.1	77.1	71.1	60.1	51.2	42.6	59.3
North Dakota	Bismarck	9.2	15.7	28.2	43.0	55.0	64.4	70.4	68.3	57.0	45.7	28.6	14.0	41.6
Ohio	Cincinnati	28.1	31.8	43.0	53.2	62.9	71.0	75.1	73.5	67.3	55.1	44.3	33.5	53.2
	Cleveland	24.8	27.2	37.3	47.6	58.0	67.6	71.9	70.4	63.9	52.8	42.6	30.9	49.6
	Columbus	26.4	29.6	40.9	51.0	61.2	69.2	73.2	71.5	65.5	53.7	42.9	31.9	51.4
Oklahoma	Oklahoma City	35.9	40.9	50.3	60.4	68.4	76.7	82.0	81.1	73.0	62.0	49.6	39.3	60.0
Oregon	Portland	39.6	43.6	47.3	51.0	57.1	63.0	67.9	68.2	63.3	54.5	46.1	40.2	53.6
Pennsylvania	Philadelphia	30.4	33.0	42.4	52.4	62.9	71.8	76.7	75.5	68.2	56.4	46.4	35.8	54.3
	Pittsburgh	26.1	28.7	39.4	49.6	59.5	67.9	72.1	70.5	63.9	52.4	42.3	31.5	50.3
Rhode Island	Providence	27.9	29.7	37.4	47.4	57.3	66.9	72.7	71.3	64.1	53.6	44.0	32.8	50.4
South Carolina	Columbia	43.8	46.8	55.2	63.0	70.9	77.4	80.8	79.7	74.2	63.3	54.6	46.9	63.1
South Dakota	Sioux Falls	13.8	19.7	32.5	46.9	58.4	68.3	74.3	71.4	60.9	48.6	33.0	18.3	45.5
Tennessee	Memphis	39.7	44.2	53.1	62.9	71.2	79.1	82.6	81.0	74.2	63.1	52.5	43.7	62.3
	Nashville	36.2	40.4	50.2	59.2	67.7	75.6	79.3	78.1	71.8	60.4	50.0	40.5	59.1
Texas	Dallas-Fort Worth	43.4	47.9	56.7	65.5	72.8	81.0	85.3	84.9	77.4	67.2	56.2	46.9	65.4
	El Paso	42.8	48.1	55.1	63.4	71.8	80.4	82.3	80.1	74.4	64.0	52.4	44.1	63.2

Normal Daily Mean Temperature—Selected Cities (*continued*)
(**In Fahrenheit degrees.** Airport data except as noted. Based on standard 30-year period, 1961 through 1990).

STATE	STATION	Jan.	Feb.	Mar.	Apr.	May	June	July	Aug.	Sept.	Oct.	Nov.	Dec.	Annual avg.
	Houston	50.4	53.9	60.6	68.3	74.5	80.4	82.6	82.3	78.2	69.6	61.0	53.5	67.9
Utah	Salt Lake City	27.9	34.1	41.8	49.7	58.8	69.1	77.9	75.6	65.2	53.2	40.8	29.7	52.0
Vermont	Burlington	16.3	18.2	30.7	43.9	56.3	65.2	70.5	67.9	58.9	47.8	36.8	23.0	44.6
Virginia	Norfolk	39.1	41.0	48.6	57.0	66.1	74.1	78.2	77.2	71.9	61.2	52.5	43.8	59.2
	Richmond	35.7	38.7	48.0	57.3	66.0	73.9	78.0	76.8	70.0	58.6	49.6	40.1	57.7
Washington	Seattle-Tacoma	40.1	43.5	45.6	49.2	55.1	60.9	65.2	65.6	60.6	52.8	45.3	40.5	52.0
	Spokane	27.1	33.3	38.7	45.9	53.9	62.0	68.8	68.4	58.9	47.3	35.1	27.8	47.3
West Virginia	Charleston	32.1	35.5	45.9	54.8	63.5	71.4	75.1	73.9	67.7	56.2	46.8	37.0	55.0
Wisconsin	Milwaukee	18.9	23.0	33.3	44.4	54.6	65.0	70.9	69.3	61.7	50.3	37.7	24.4	46.1
Wyoming	Cheyenne	26.5	29.3	33.6	42.5	52.0	61.3	68.4	66.4	57.4	47.0	35.2	27.8	45.6

[1] City office data.

Sunshine, Average Wind Speed, Mean Number of Days Minimum Temperature Below 32 Degrees Fahrenheit, and Average Relative Humidity—Selected Cities
[Airport data, except as noted. For period of record through 1990, except as noted. M = morning. A = afternoon]

STATE	STATION	AVERAGE PERCENTAGE OF POSSIBLE SUNSHINE Length of record (yr.)	Annual	AVERAGE WIND SPEED (m.p.h.) Length of record (yr.)	Annual	Jan.	July	MINIMUM TEMPERATURE 32 DEGREES OR LESS Length of record (yr.)	Mean number (days)	AVG REL HUM Length of record (yr.)	Annual M	Annual A	Jan. M	Jan. A	July M	July A
Alabama	Mobile	[1]40	[1]59	42	9.0	10.4	7.0	28	23	28	86	57	81	61	89	60
Alaska	Juneau	33	30	45	8.3	8.3	7.5	46	142	24	84	73	80	77	83	70
Arizona	Phoenix	95	86	45	6.3	5.3	7.2	30	8	30	51	23	66	32	45	20
Arkansas	Little Rock	32	62	48	7.8	8.6	6.7	30	60	30	84	57	80	61	88	56
California	Los Angeles	32	73	42	7.5	6.7	7.8	31	(Z)	31	79	64	69	59	86	68
	Sacramento	42	78	41	7.9	7.2	9.0	40	17	30	82	46	90	70	76	28
	San Diego	50	68	50	6.9	5.9	7.4	30	(Z)	30	76	62	70	56	82	66
	San Francisco	38	66	63	10.6	7.2	13.6	31	2	31	84	61	86	66	86	59
Colorado	Denver	41	70	42	8.7	8.7	8.3	30	157	30	67	40	63	49	68	34
Connecticut	Hartford	36	57	36	8.5	9.0	7.5	31	135	31	76	52	71	56	78	51
Delaware	Wilmington	(NA)	(NA)	42	9.1	9.8	7.8	43	100	43	78	55	75	60	79	54
District of Columbia	Washington	42	56	42	9.4	10.0	8.2	30	71	30	74	53	69	55	76	53
Florida	Jacksonville	39	63	41	8.0	8.2	7.1	49	15	54	88	56	87	57	88	58
	Miami	14	73	41	9.3	9.5	7.9	26	(Z)	26	84	61	84	59	84	63
Georgia	Atlanta	55	61	52	9.1	10.5	7.6	30	54	30	82	56	78	59	88	60
Hawaii	Honolulu	38	69	41	11.4	9.7	13.3	21	—	21	72	56	81	62	67	51
Idaho	Boise	48	64	51	8.8	8.0	8.4	51	124	51	69	43	80	70	54	22
Illinois	Chicago	10	55	32	10.3	11.6	8.2	32	133	32	80	60	76	67	82	57
	Peoria	47	57	47	10.0	11.2	7.8	31	129	31	83	61	79	68	86	59
Indiana	Indianapolis	46	55	42	9.6	10.9	7.4	31	118	31	83	62	80	70	87	60
Iowa	Des Moines	40	59	41	10.9	11.7	9.0	29	135	29	79	60	75	67	82	57
Kansas	Wichita	37	65	37	12.3	12.2	11.3	37	111	37	80	55	79	62	78	48
Kentucky	Louisville	43	56	43	8.4	9.7	6.7	30	89	30	81	58	76	64	85	58
Louisiana	New Orleans	17	60	42	8.2	9.4	6.1	44	13	42	87	63	85	66	91	66
Maine	Portland	50	57	50	8.8	9.2	7.6	50	157	50	79	59	76	61	80	59
Maryland	Baltimore	40	57	40	9.2	9.7	8.0	40	97	37	77	54	71	57	81	53
Massachusetts	Boston	55	58	33	12.5	13.9	11.0	26	98	26	72	58	67	57	74	57
Michigan	Detroit	25	53	32	10.4	12.0	8.5	32	136	32	81	60	80	69	82	53
	Sault Ste. Marie	49	47	49	9.3	9.8	7.8	49	181	49	85	67	81	75	89	61
Minnesota	Duluth	40	52	41	11.1	11.6	9.4	29	185	29	81	63	76	70	85	59

Sunshine, Average Wind Speed, Mean Number of Days Minimum Temperature Below 32 Degrees Fahrenheit, and Average Relative Humidity—Selected Cities (*continued*)

STATE	STATION	AVG % POSSIBLE SUNSHINE Length of record (yr.)	Annual	AVG WIND SPEED Length of record (yr.)	Annual	Jan.	July	MIN TEMP 32° OR LESS Length of record (yr.)	Mean number (days)	HUMIDITY Length of record (yr.)	Annual M	A	Jan. M	A	July M	A
	Minneapolis-St. Paul	52	58	52	10.6	10.5	9.4	31	156	31	78	59	74	67	80	54
Mississippi......	Jackson..........	26	60	27	7.4	8.6	5.9	27	50	27	91	58	87	64	93	59
Missouri........	Kansas City......	18	62	18	10.8	11.5	9.4	18	110	18	81	60	76	63	84	57
	St. Louis	31	57	41	9.7	10.6	8.0	30	100	30	83	59	81	65	85	56
Montana........	Great Falls.......	46	61	49	12.8	15.3	10.1	29	157	29	66	45	66	60	65	29
Nebraska	Omaha..........	54	60	54	10.6	10.9	8.9	26	141	26	81	59	78	65	84	57
Nevada	Reno............	42	79	48	6.6	5.6	7.0	27	174	27	70	32	79	51	63	18
New Hampshire	Concord.........	49	54	48	6.7	7.2	5.7	25	173	25	81	54	75	58	84	52
New Jersey......	Atlantic City	30	56	32	10.1	11.0	8.5	26	110	26	81	56	77	58	83	57
New Mexico.....	Albuquerque	51	76	3	11.8	11.7	10.6	30	119	30	60	29	70	40	60	27
New York	Albany..........	52	52	52	8.9	9.8	7.4	25	149	25	80	57	77	63	81	55
	Buffalo..........	47	49	51	12.0	14.3	10.3	30	133	30	80	63	79	72	78	55
	New York........	104	58	58	9.4	10.7	7.6	77	80	61	72	56	68	60	75	55
North Carolina...	Charlotte	40	63	41	7.5	7.9	6.6	30	67	30	83	54	78	55	87	57
	Raleigh..........	36	59	41	7.8	8.5	6.7	26	78	26	85	54	78	55	89	58
North Dakota....	Bismarck	51	59	51	10.2	10.0	9.2	31	186	31	80	56	74	68	83	47
Ohio	Cincinnati	7	52	43	9.1	10.7	7.1	28	108	28	28	81	59	78	67	85
	Cleveland	47	49	49	10.6	12.3	8.6	30	124	30	79	62	77	69	81	57
	Columbus........	39	49	41	8.5	10.1	6.6	31	119	31	80	59	76	67	84	56
Oklahoma.......	Oklahoma City ...	36	68	42	12.4	12.8	10.9	25	77	25	79	54	77	59	80	49
Oregon	Portland	41	48	42	7.9	9.9	7.6	50	43	50	86	60	86	76	82	45
Pennsylvania	Philadelphia......	48	56	50	9.5	10.3	8.1	31	97	31	76	55	73	59	79	54
	Pittsburgh	38	46	38	9.1	10.7	7.2	31	123	30	78	57	75	65	83	54
Rhode Island	Providence.......	37	58	37	10.6	11.2	9.5	27	119	27	75	55	70	56	77	56
South Carolina...	Columbia........	37	64	42	6.9	7.2	6.3	24	61	24	87	51	82	54	89	54
South Dakota....	Sioux Falls.......	³48	³63	42	11.1	11.1	9.8	27	168	27	81	60	76	67	82	53
Tennessee.......	Memphis	35	64	42	8.9	10.1	7.5	49	57	51	81	57	78	63	84	57
	Nashville	48	56	49	8.0	9.2	6.5	25	76	25	84	57	79	63	89	57
Texas	Dallas-Ft. Worth ...	12	64	37	10.8	11.2	9.6	27	40	27	82	56	79	59	80	48
	El Paso..........	48	83	48	8.9	8.4	8.3	30	65	30	57	27	65	34	62	29
	Houston	21	56	21	7.9	8.3	7.0	21	21	21	90	59	85	63	92	58
Utah	Salt Lake City	52	66	61	8.9	7.7	9.6	31	125	31	67	43	79	69	52	22
Vermont	Burlington	47	49	47	8.9	9.7	7.9	26	156	25	77	59	71	63	78	53
Virginia	Norfolk..........	26	61	42	10.7	11.5	9.0	42	54	42	78	57	74	58	82	59
	Richmond	40	62	42	7.7	8.1	6.8	61	85	56	83	53	80	57	85	56
Washington	Seattle-Tacoma	24	46	42	9.0	9.8	8.3	31	31	31	83	62	81	74	82	49
	Spokane.........	42	54	43	8.9	8.8	8.6	31	139	31	77	52	85	78	64	27
West Virginia....	Charleston	⁴47	⁴40	43	6.3	7.5	5.0	43	100	43	83	56	77	62	90	60
Wisconsin	Milwaukee	50	54	50	11.6	12.7	9.7	30	141	30	81	64	76	68	82	61
Wyoming	Cheyenne........	51	65	33	13.0	15.4	10.3	31	171	31	65	44	57	50	70	38

— Represents zero.   Z Less than one-half a day.   [1] Recording site is in Montgomery, AL.   [2] City office data.   [3] Recording site is in Rapid City, SD.   [4] Recording site is Elkins, WV.

Important Dates in American History

Date	Event
1492	Columbus sails to Caribbean Islands.
1497	John Cabot explores North America from Canada to Delaware.
1513	Juan Ponce de Leon explores Florida.
1524	Giovanni da Verrazano leads French expedition along the coast from Carolina to Nova Scotia, entering New York harbor.
1565	St. Augustine, Florida, is founded.
1579	Francis Drake claims California for Britain.
1586	St. Augustine is destroyed by Francis Drake.
1587	Virginia Dare is the first baby born in America to English parents.
1607	The first European settlement in America is established at Jamestown, Virginia.
1609	Henry Hudson explores New York harbor and the Hudson River to Albany; Samuel de Champlain explores Lake Champlain in upstate New York; Spaniards settle Santa Fe, New Mexico.
1619	The first black slaves land at Jamestown, Virginia; the House of Burgesses, the first representative assembly in America, is established in Virginia.
1620	Pilgrims land in Plymouth, Massachusetts; the Mayflower Compact is drafted and signed.
1623	The Dutch found New Netherlands (later New York).
1626	Peter Minuit buys Manhattan Island from Native Americans.
1630	The Massachusetts Bay Colony is founded.
1631	Roger Williams, pioneer of religious tolerance, arrives in America.
1634	Maryland is founded as a Catholic colony.
1635	New Hampshire is founded by Captain John Mason; the first public school, the Boston Latin School, is established.
1636	Harvard, the first college in America, is founded; Roger Williams founds Providence, Rhode Island.
1639	The first constitution in America is written, the Fundamental Orders of Connecticut.
1647	Margaret Brent is the first woman to claim the right to vote.
1648	The first labor organization in the United States is authorized in the Massachusetts Bay Colony.
1652	Rhode Island enacts first American law declaring slavery illegal.
1654	The first Jews arrive in New Amsterdam.
1663	The Colony of New Jersey is founded by Sir William Berkeley and Sir George Carteret; the Carolinas are founded.
1664	The English capture New Netherlands.
1682	William Penn founds Pennsylvania.
1688	The first formal protest against slavery is made, by Pennsylvania Quakers.
1692	Nineteen persons (mostly women) are executed for "witchcraft" in Salem, Massachusetts.
1712	A slave revolt in New York leads to the execution of 21 blacks; six commit suicide.
1731	The first circulating library is founded, in Philadelphia.
1732	Georgia is founded by James Oglethorpe and others; Benjamin Franklin publishes the first *Poor Richard's Almanac*.
1741	The second slave uprising takes place in New York; 13 are hanged, 13 burned, and 71 deported.
1749	Black slavery is legalized in Georgia.
1754	The French and Indian War begins (called the Seven Years' War in Europe).
1758	The first Indian reservation is established.
1763	The French and Indian War ends.
1764	The Sugar Act places duties on lumber, foodstuffs, molasses, and rum in the colonies.
1765	Passage of the Stamp Act by Britain leads to the Declaration of Rights, signed by nine colonies opposed to taxation without representation.

Date	Event
1766	Britain repeals the Stamp Act.
1767	The Townshend Acts levy taxes on glass, painter's lead, paper, and tea.
1770	Five colonists are killed in the Boston Massacre.
1773	The Boston Tea Party takes place.
1774	The Intolerable Acts passed by Parliament curtail Massachusetts' self-rule and bar the use of Boston Harbor until tea is paid for; the first Continental Congress, an advisory council, is organized in response to British Parliament's Intolerable Acts.
1775	The American Revolution begins with the battles of Lexington and Concord.
1776	France and Spain each donate 1 million livres in arms to Americans; the Declaration of Independence is drafted and signed; Nathan Hale is executed by the British as a spy; the first fraternity, Phi Beta Kappa, is founded at the College of William and Mary; the Journeymen Printers' Strike is the first in the United States.
1777	The Continental Congress adopts a flag with stars and stripes; Washington defeats Lord Cornwallis at the battle of Princeton; Major General John Burgoyne captures Fort Ticonderoga, but Americans defeat him at Saratoga; the Federalist Papers, arguing for the ratification of the Constitution, begin publication.
1778	France agrees to assist the United States and sends a fleet; the British evacuate Philadelphia.
1779	George Washington orders a military campaign against the Iroquois.
1780	Benedict Arnold is discovered to be a traitor and escapes to the British.
1781	Colonial and French armies defeat the British at Yorktown, the last major battle of the Revolutionary War; the Articles of Confederation, the first written U.S. constitution, is ratified.
1783	The Revolutionary War ends with a treaty.
1784	The first daily newspaper, *Pennsylvania Packet and General Advertiser*, is published in Philadelphia.
1787	The Constitutional Convention begins in Philadelphia; Delaware ratifies the Constitution, thus becoming the first state admitted to the Union.
1788	New Hampshire is the ninth state to ratify the Constitution, thereby putting it into effect.
1789	George Washington is chosen the first president; John Adams, vice-president; Thomas Jefferson, secretary of state; and Alexander Hamilton, secretary of the treasury.
1790	Congress meets in Philadelphia, the temporary capital, and votes to found a new capital on the Potomac River; the United States signs the first treaty with the Iroquois.
1791	The Bill of Rights goes into effect; Vermont is the first state to enter the Union after the original 13 colonies.
1793	The invention of the cotton gin by Eli Whitney revives slavery in the South; the First Fugitive Slave Act is passed, making it a crime to harbor an escaped slave or to interfere with a slave's arrest.
1794	Suppression by the U.S. militia of the Whiskey Rebellion, in which farmers protest the liquor tax of 1791, established the authority of the new federal government.
1800	The seat of government moves from Philadelphia to Washington, D.C.; Congress passes a land act encouraging the purchase of property at low prices.
1801	Tripoli declares war on the United States.
1803	The Supreme Court declares an act of Congress unconstitutional in *Marbury v. Madison*; the United States buys the Louisiana Territory from Napoleon, doubling its land holdings.
1804	President Jefferson orders the Lewis and Clark expedition to explore the northwest; Vice-President Aaron Burr and Alexander Hamilton duel; Hamilton dies the next day.
1805	Conflict with Tripoli ends.
1807	Robert Fulton makes the first steamboat trip.
1808	The importation of slaves is outlawed (about 250,000 slaves are illegally imported between 1808 and 1860).
1811	While Shawnee Chief Tecumseh is away making alliances with other tribal leaders, Indiana Governor William Henry Harrison and 1,000 men destroy his settlement in the Battle of Tippecanoe, thwarting plans for an Indian confederacy.

Date	Event
1812	The War of 1812 begins.
1814	The War of 1812 ends with the Treaty of Ghent.
1816	The first savings bank is established, the Provident Institute for Savings, in Boston.
1817	The First Seminole War begins in the Spanish territory of Florida, with raids by U.S. troops on Seminole Indians reputedly harboring runaway slaves.
1818	The Connecticut state legislature is the first in the United States to eliminate the property requirement for voting.
1819	Florida is ceded to the United States by Spain.
1820	The Missouri Compromise dictates that Missouri be admitted to the Union as a slave state and Maine as a free state, and prohibits slavery in parts of the Louisiana Purchase.
1821	Troy Female Seminary, the first women's college in the United States, is founded by Emma Willard.
1823	President James Monroe, in the Monroe Doctrine, declares to Congress that the Western Hemisphere is to be off-limits to European colonization.
1825	The Erie Canal is opened, cutting travel time from New York City to Buffalo and the Great Lakes by one-third.
1827	*Freedom's Journal*, the first black U.S. newspaper, is published.
1828	The first U.S. passenger railroad, Baltimore & Ohio, begins service; the first Native American newspaper, *Cherokee Phoenix*, begins publication.
1829	The first school for the blind is incorporated in the United States.
1830	President Jackson signs the Indian Removal Act.
1831	Nat Turner leads a slave rebellion in Virginia.
1832	The first meeting of the New England Anti-Slavery Society is held; Oberlin College, Ohio, becomes the first college to establish coeducation.
1836	Texans are besieged at the Alamo in San Antonio; Texas declares independence from Mexico.
1837	The panic of 1837 begins a seven-year depression.
1838	Cherokees begin the Trail of Tears, their 1,200-mile forced march to Oklahoma.
1841	Oberlin College, Ohio, becomes the first college to confer degrees on women; the first wagon train leaves from Independence, Missouri, for California.
1843	Sojourner Truth, former slave, begins an abolitionist lecture tour.
1844	The first telegraph message is sent from Washington to Baltimore by Samuel F. B. Morse; Margaret Fuller becomes the first female journalist to work for a major U.S. newspaper, the *New York Tribune*.
1846	The United States declares war on Mexico; as a result, the United States obtains Texas, California, Arizona, New Mexico, Nevada, Utah, and part of Colorado; a treaty with Great Britain gives the United States the Oregon Territory to the 49th parallel; Henry David Thoreau is jailed for tax resistance.
1847	The first postage stamp is issued; Michigan becomes the first state to abolish capital punishment; Frederick Douglass founds the abolitionist newspaper *North Star*.
1848	The United States signs the Treaty of Guadalupe Hidalgo with Mexico, ending the Mexican War and increasing U.S. territory; the first women's rights convention is held in Seneca Falls, New York; gold is discovered in California.
1849	Eighty thousand gold prospectors flood California.
1850	Senator Henry Clay's Compromise of 1850 admits California to the Union as a nonslave state, while Utah and New Mexico enter with no decision on slavery.
1852	*Uncle Tom's Cabin*, by Harriet Beecher Stowe, is published.
1853	The American Labor Union is founded.
1854	The Republican party is formed in opposition to the Kansas-Nebraska Act, which left the issue of slavery to a vote by settlers.
1857	The Dred Scott decision by the Supreme Court upholds slavery.
1858	The Lincoln–Douglas debates are held in Illinois.
1859	John Brown, abolitionist, captures the U.S. arsenal at Harper's Ferry, West Virginia; Brown is hanged for treason.

Date	Event
1860	A nationwide shoemakers' strike wins workers higher wages; the National Labor Union is founded.
1861	The American Miners Association, the first national coal miners' union, is founded; the Civil War begins when Confederates fire on Fort Sumter, South Carolina; the first transcontinental telegraph line is completed.
1862	Slavery is abolished in Washington, D.C.; the Homestead Act grants land to settlers.
1863	Harriet Tubman frees 750 slaves in a raid; President Lincoln delivers the Gettysburg Address and issues the Emancipation Proclamation; draft riots in New York City kill approximately a thousand.
1864	Black prisoners of war are massacred by Confederate soldiers at Fort Pillow, Tennessee; General Sherman marches through Georgia, capturing Atlanta; the *New Orleans Tribune*, a black-run daily newspaper, begins publication; 133 Cheyenne and Arapahoe are killed by Colorado cavalry volunteers at Sand Creek.
1865	The Confederacy surrenders at Appomattox, Virginia, ending the Civil War; the first state civil rights law is passed, in Massachusetts; the Thirteenth Amendment abolishes slavery; the Ku Klux Klan is formed in Pulaski, Tennessee; President Lincoln is assassinated.
1868	Impeachment proceedings begin against President Andrew Johnson; the Fourteenth Amendment is ratified, guaranteeing due process to all but Native Americans; a U.S.–Sioux treaty is signed at Fort Laramie, Wyoming.
1869	The first national black labor group, the Colored National Labor Convention, meets in Washington, D.C.; the Central Pacific and Union Pacific railroads are linked at Promontory, Utah, forming the first transcontinental railroad; Elizabeth Cady Stanton and Susan B. Anthony establish the National Women's Suffrage Association to press for women's voting rights; Wyoming territory is the first to grant suffrage to women.
1870	The first woman candidate for U.S. president, Victoria Claflin Woodhull, announces she will run; the first sorority, Kappa Alpha Theta, is established at De Pauw University.
1871	The Great Chicago Fire takes place.
1872	Susan B. Anthony is arrested for voting; the Amnesty Act restores rights to Southern citizens except for 500 Confederate leaders; Yellowstone, the first U.S. national park, opens in Wyoming.
1873	The first illustrated daily newspaper, *New York Daily Graphic*, is established.
1875	The Civil Rights Act gives equal rights to blacks in public accommodations and jury duty.
1876	General Custer is defeated at the battle of the Little Bighorn.
1877	The United States violates its treaty with the Dakota Sioux by seizing the Black Hills; Chief Joseph surrenders with a starving remnant of Nez-Percé people.
1879	F. W. Woolworth opens his first 5 & 10 store.
1881	Sitting Bull surrenders; President Garfield is shot and killed; Booker T. Washington founds Tuskegee Institute for blacks; Spelman College opens in Atlanta to educate black women.
1881	The Supreme Court rules that Native Americans are aliens; the Civil Rights Act of 1875 is invalidated by the Supreme Court; the Brooklyn Bridge opens.
1884	Eleanor Roosevelt is born.
1885	The first skyscraper is built in Chicago.
1886	The Haymarket Square massacre takes place in Chicago as a bomb explodes and protesters demanding an eight-hour day are arrested; Geronimo surrenders to Arizona Territory leaders; the American Federation of Labor (AFL) is founded.
1887	Crazy Horse is assassinated while in custody.
1888	The Great Blizzard in the East causes 400 deaths.
1889	Jane Addams founds Hull-House, an immigrant settlement house and center for social reform, in Chicago.
1890	The United Mine Workers is formed; Sitting Bull is killed by police at Standing Rock Reservation, South Dakota; 200 Sioux are massacred by troops at Wounded Knee, South Dakota; The Sherman Antitrust Act is passed by Congress to fight business monopolies; William Kemmler is the first criminal to be executed by electrocution, at Auburn Prison, New York; Ellis Island becomes a port of entry for immigrants. *How the*

Date	Event
	Other Half Lives, by social reformer Jacob Riis, is published.
1893	Financial panic lasting for four years begins.
1894	Led by Eugene V. Debs, members of the American Railway Union hold a massive strike against the Pullman Palace Car Company.
1896	The Supreme Court's *Plessy v. Ferguson* decision upholds the "separate but equal" doctrine.
1898	The United States declares war on Spain; U.S. troops invade Puerto Rico to liberate it from Spain; Admiral Dewey captures Manila; feminist theorist Charlotte Perkins Gilman's *Women and Economics*, is published.
1899	Philippine insurrection against U.S. rule begins; *The Awakening*, an early feminist novel by Kate Chopin, is published; the Open Door Policy makes China an international market and preserves its integrity as a nation.
1900	The International Ladies Garment Workers Union is founded; prohibitionist Carry Nation leads the first bottle-smashing raid, in Wichita, Kansas.
1901	William McKinley is killed by anarchist Leon Czolgosz; J. P. Morgan incorporates the U.S. Steel Corporation, the first billion-dollar company.
1902	The last Philippine resistance to U.S. intervention ends.
1903	Panama declares its independence from Colombia, with U.S. support, and signs the Panama Canal Treaty; Orville and Wilbur Wright make the first flights in a mechanically propelled plane; Mary Harris "Mother" Jones leads a week-long march of child mill workers from Pennsylvania to President Theodore Roosevelt's New York City home.
1904	Civil rights leader Mary McLeod Bethune founds Daytona Literary and Industrial School for Training Negro Girls, in Florida.
1905	The Niagara Movement, later to become the NAACP, is founded.
1906	The San Francisco earthquake and fire occurs.
1907	Charles Curtis of Kansas becomes the first Native American U.S. senator.
1908	The United States bars Japanese immigration; women demonstrate in New York City, demanding an end to sweatshops and child labor; the Federal

Date	Event
	Bureau of Investigation (FBI) is established; the first Ford Model T is sold.
1909	The National Association for the Advancement of Colored People (NAACP) is founded; Native American leader Geronimo dies.
1911	The Triangle Shirt Waist Company fire in New York City kills 146 sweatshop workers, mostly women, and leads to demands for better working conditions.
1912	The "Bread and Roses" strike by 10,000 textile workers begins in Lawrence, Massachusetts; folk singer Woody Guthrie is born.
1913	Ratification of the Sixteenth Amendment authorizes income tax; the Federal Reserve System is adopted; the Seventeenth Amendment is ratified, providing for popular election of the U.S. Senate; the first important U.S. exhibition of modern art is held at the New York City Armory.
1914	The Colorado National Guard burns a striking miner's camp and kills 13 children and 7 adults in the Ludlow Massacre.
1915	The Women's International League for Peace and Freedom is founded; 25,000 women march in New York City demanding suffrage; Haiti becomes a U.S. protectorate after U.S. troops land there.
1916	The National Women's Party is founded; the first public birth control clinic opens, in Brooklyn, New York; Jeannette Rankin of Montana becomes the first woman elected to the House of Representatives; Margaret Sanger is arrested for operating a birth control clinic; the United States buys the Virgin Islands from Denmark; a military government is established in the Dominican Republic as the country is occupied by U.S. Marines.
1917	Women picket the White House for the right to vote; Puerto Rico becomes a U.S. territory; the United States declares war on Germany, entering World War I; a wartime draft is enacted; Emma Goldman is sentenced to two years for aiding draft resisters.
1918	The Sedition Act becomes law; World War I ends.
1919	The Supreme Court holds that freedom of speech does not apply to draft resistance; the Communist Party of America is founded; Congress overrides President Wilson's veto of Prohibition legislation.

Date	Event
1920	Five thousand alleged subversives are arrested nationwide in "Palmer raids"; the sale of alcoholic beverages is banned under the Eighteenth Amendment; women win the right to vote with ratification of the Nineteenth Amendment; the League of Women Voters is founded; the first transcontinental airmail route is established between New York City and San Francisco.
1921	Immigration is curtailed by quotas set by Congress; the Ku Klux Klan begins a revival of violence against blacks in the North, South, and Midwest; major powers meet at the Limitation of Armaments Conference to reduce naval construction, outlaw poison gas, restrict submarine attacks on merchantmen, and discuss the integrity of China; Margaret Sanger establishes the American Birth Control League, the predecessor to Planned Parenthood.
1922	Rebecca L. Felton, from Georgia, is appointed the first woman U.S. senator.
1923	Under presidential pressure, U.S. Steel institutes the eight-hour day, setting a landmark precedent.
1924	The Supreme Court upholds the involuntary sterilization of mentally retarded persons; Native Americans are declared citizens by Congress; the first U.S. gay rights organization, the Society for Human Rights, is founded in Chicago.
1925	Nellie Taylor Ross, the first woman governor in the United States, is sworn in, in Wyoming; John T. Scopes is convicted of teaching the theory of evolution; Tennessee bans the teaching of evolution.
1927	Charles Lindbergh makes the first intercontinental flight; *The Jazz Singer*, the first sound film, is released.
1928	Amelia Earhart is the first woman to fly across the Atlantic.
1929	The stock market crashes, beginning the Great Depression.
1931	The Scottsboro Boys trial begins in Alabama; the Empire State Building opens in New York City.
1932	Hattie Caraway, of Tennessee, is the first woman elected to the U.S. Senate.
1933	President Franklin Roosevelt closes all U.S. banks; during the "100 days," a special session of Congress, important New Deal legislation is passed, including the establishment of the National Recovery Administration and the Tennessee Valley Authority (TVA); Frances Perkins, Secretary of Labor, becomes the first woman Cabinet member; the Twenty-first Amendment, ending Prohibition, is passed.
1935	The Works Projects Administration (WPA) is established; the National Labor Relations Act, recognizing workers' right to organize and bargain collectively, passes; President Roosevelt signs the Social Security Act.
1936	Black track star Jesse Owens wins four gold medals at the Berlin Olympics, embarrassing Hitler.
1937	Amelia Earhart and her co-pilot disappear over the Pacific.
1938	The national minimum wage is enacted; the "War of the Worlds" broadcast by Orson Welles causes nationwide fear that Martians have invaded Earth.
1939	Sit-down strikes are outlawed by the Supreme Court; World War II begins with the German invasion of Poland.
1940	The Alien Registration Act (Smith Act) is passed; Congress approves the first peacetime draft.
1941	The Ford Motor Company signs its first contract with the United Auto Workers; the Japanese attack Pearl Harbor, bringing the United States into World War II.
1942	President Roosevelt issues an executive order to intern 120,000 Japanese-Americans on the West Coast; the Manhattan Project begins developing the atomic bomb; 492 die in a fire at Boston's Coconut Grove nightclub.
1943	President Roosevelt bars all war contractors from racial discrimination; a race riot in Detroit leaves 34 dead.
1944	Allies stage the D-Day invasion of Normandy; Congress passes the G.I. Bill of Rights, providing veterans' benefits.
1945	The Yalta conference, attended by Roosevelt, Churchill, and Stalin, brings Russia into World War II against Japan; Roosevelt dies; Truman becomes President; Nazi Germany and Japan are defeated, ending World War II in Europe and the Pacific; U.S. troops liberate the concentration

Date	Event
	camp at Dachau; the first atomic bomb is exploded, at Alamogordo, New Mexico; the United States drops atomic bombs on Hiroshima and Nagasaki; Congress passes the Communist Control Act; the United Nations Charter is adopted.
1946	The Atomic Energy Commission is formed; the Philippines is given independence.
1947	The cold war begins; aid is given to Greece and Turkey under the Truman Doctrine; Jackie Robinson, the first black major league baseball player, appears in his first game with the Brooklyn Dodgers; the Marshall Plan for European recovery is announced; the Department of Defense is created; the Central Intelligence Agency (CIA) and the National Security Council are established under the National Security Act; the House of Representatives cites the Hollywood Ten, accused of subversion, for contempt of Congress.
1948	Twelve Communist party leaders are indicted by the United States on grounds that they advocated the overthrow of the government; Alger Hiss, denying that he transmitted confidential government documents to spies, is indicted for perjury.
1949	The North Atlantic Treaty Organization (NATO) is formed by the United States, Canada, and 10 European nations.
1950	The United States recalls all consular personnel from the People's Republic of China; Truman orders the development of the hydrogen bomb; Senator Joseph McCarthy accuses State Department employees of Communist party affiliation; two of the Hollywood Ten are imprisoned for refusing to cooperate with the House Un-American Activities Committee; the Korean conflict begins; the United States sends 35 military advisors and agrees to give military and economic aid to South Vietnam.
1951	Julius and Ethel Rosenberg and Morton Sobel are convicted of espionage conspiracy; the Mattachine Society, an early gay rights organization, is formed in California; atomic energy is first used to generate electricity in the United States; Korean cease-fire talks begin.

Date	Event
1952	The United States explodes the world's first hydrogen bomb; the Immigration and Naturalization Act is passed, lifting the last racial and ethnic barriers to naturalization.
1953	President Truman announces development of the hydrogen bomb; Julius and Ethel Rosenberg are executed; Vice-President Richard Nixon gives his "Checkers" speech; the Korean conflict ends.
1954	Seven thousand square miles of the Pacific are irradiated by a Bikini Island hydrogen bomb test, which contaminates Japanese fishermen; the U.S. Air Force begins flying French reinforcements to Indochina; the *Brown v. Board of Education* ruling by the Supreme Court outlaws segregation in public schools; the Senate censures Joseph McCarthy; the Southeast Asia Treaty Organization (SEATO) is formed, comprising the United States, Great Britain, France, Australia, New Zealand, the Philippines, Pakistan, and Thailand.
1955	Rosa Parks refuses to give up her bus seat to a white person and begins the Montgomery, Alabama, bus boycott; the AFL and CIO merge, electing George Meany the first president; the United States agrees to help train the South Vietnamese army.
1956	Passage of the Federal Aid Highway Act inaugurates the first interstate highway system.
1957	Elizabeth Eckford is blocked from becoming the first black student at Little Rock Central High School; nine black students enroll at Little Rock High School with the help of federal troops; Congress approves the first bill protecting blacks' right to vote since the Reconstruction era.
1958	The United States launches its first satellite into orbit.
1959	Alaska and Hawaii become the forty-ninth and fiftieth states, respectively.
1960	More than 70,000 black and white students participate in sit-ins to protest a Greensboro, North Carolina, incident in which four blacks were denied service at a lunch counter.
1961	The United States breaks diplomatic ties with Cuba; the Bay of Pigs invasion of Cuba is

Date	Event
	thwarted; "freedom riders" test segregation laws in the Deep South; the Student Non-Violent Coordinating Committee (SNCC) voter registration drive begins in the South; the FBI launches its Socialist Worker Disruption Program; Alan B. Shepard, Jr. travels on the first U.S. manned space flight.
1962	The United States announces resumption of atmospheric nuclear testing after test-ban negotiations fail; James Meredith becomes the first black to enroll at the University of Mississippi; President Kennedy orders a blockade of Cuba, which begins the Cuban Missile Crisis; John H. Glenn, Jr., becomes the first American to orbit in space; *Silent Spring*, by Rachel Carson, is published, launching the environmental movement.
1963	The Supreme Court rules that states must provide free legal counsel for indigents; the Supreme Court bars mandatory Bible readings in public schools; Martin Luther King, Jr., leads a civil rights march on Washington, D.C.; a White House–Kremlin "hot line" is installed; the War Resisters League organizes its first demonstration against U.S. involvement in Vietnam; President Kennedy is assassinated; Congress passes the first Clean Air Act.
1964	The Twenty-fourth Amendment eliminates the poll tax in federal elections; a Civil Rights Act is passed by Congress; Congress passes the Gulf of Tonkin Resolution, giving President Lyndon Johnson power to wage war in Indochina; Martin Luther King, Jr., receives the Nobel Peace Prize; Panama suspends relations with the United States, which offers to negotiate a new Canal treaty; students at the University of California, Berkeley, protest limitations on their rights of free speech and assembly; Malcolm X disassociates himself from the separatist Nation of Islam and founds the Organization of Afro-American Unity.
1965	Malcolm X, black leader, is assassinated; 49 people are arrested during protests at Chase Manhattan Bank against loans to South Africa; Martin Luther King, Jr., leads a march on Selma, Alabama; a massive electric power failure blacks out most of the Northeast for the night of November

Date	Event
	9–10; the Supreme Court holds that the "right of privacy" covers the use of contraceptives.
1966	Federal courts outlaw the last poll tax; the National Organization for Women (NOW) is founded; Medicare begins to pay the health-care expenses of U.S. citizens age 65 and older.
1967	Two hundred thousand people march against the Vietnam War in New York City; Thurgood Marshall becomes the first black Supreme Court justice; six days of racial rioting in Newark, New Jersey, leave 23 dead; week-long racial rioting in Detroit leaves 43 dead; J. Edgar Hoover, director of the FBI, authorizes activities against black nationalist groups.
1968	Four black student demonstrators are killed by police in Orangeburg, South Carolina; 500 unarmed Vietnamese are killed by U.S. troops in the My Lai massacre; Martin Luther King, Jr., is assassinated; Robert F. Kennedy is assassinated hours after his California primary victory; the American Indian Movement is founded; a coalition of women's groups interrupts the Miss America Pageant in the first mass demonstration of the modern women's movement; the United States ends the bombing of North Vietnam; Representative Shirley Chisholm, from New York, becomes the first black woman elected to Congress.
1969	The Stonewall rebellion, at a bar in New York City, starts the modern gay rights movement; the Woodstock festival in upstate New York draws 300,000 for "three days of peace and music"; the Chicago Seven conspiracy trial begins, in which seven defendants are accused of inciting a riot at the 1968 Democratic National Convention; 2 million people nationwide demonstrate against U.S. involvement in Vietnam; 78 Native Americans seize Alcatraz Island, demanding it be made into a cultural center; Black Panthers Fred Hampton and Mark Clark are murdered by Chicago police; the United States begins peace talks with Vietnam, as troop withdrawal starts; Neil Armstrong becomes the first man to walk on the moon.
1970	Chicano activists gather in Crystal City, Texas, to found La Raza Unida Party; U.S. postal workers hold their first strike; the Ohio National Guard

Date	Event
	kills four students in a Vietnam War protest at Kent State University; Mississippi police kill two black students at Jackson State University; the United Farm Workers begins a lettuce boycott; the Environmental Protection Agency (EPA) is established; Congress passes the Occupational Safety and Health Act; the Chicago Seven are found not guilty, though five are convicted of crossing state lines with intent to incite riots; the first two U.S. women generals are named by President Nixon; the first Earth Day celebration takes place.
1971	Five hundred thousand people demonstrate in Washington, D.C., against the Vietnam War and 14,000 are arrested; Native Americans leave Alcatraz Island after holding it for 19 months; the Twenty-sixth Amendment is ratified, lowering the national voting age from 21 to 18; 43 are killed in an uprising at Attica state prison in New York.
1972	The Watergate break-in, which leads to the resignation of President Nixon, takes place; Nixon makes an unprecedented visit to China; the Senate approves a constitutional amendment barring discrimination against women because of their sex and sends the measure to the states to ratify; the Supreme Court rules the death penalty unconstitutional, and, in a unanimous decision, upholds the use of busing for school integration.
1973	A peace treaty is signed with Vietnam in Paris; President Nixon signs the Endangered Species Act; Oglala Sioux occupy Wounded Knee, South Dakota, and declare an independent Oglala Sioux nation; Spiro T. Agnew resigns as vice-president, and Gerald Ford becomes the first appointed vice-president; Nixon fires Archibald Cox, special prosecutor in the Watergate case, and William Ruckelshaus in the "Saturday Night Massacre"; Attorney General Elliot Richardson resigns; five of seven defendants in the Watergate trial plead guilty, and two are convicted; in the *Roe v. Wade* decision the Supreme Court rules that a state may not prevent a woman from having an abortion during the first six months of pregnancy; Congress overrides Nixon's veto of the War Powers Act, which curbs a president's power to commit armed forces to hostilities abroad without congressional approval.

Date	Event
1974	The Organization of Petroleum Exporting Countries (OPEC) lifts the oil embargo; the House Judiciary Committee votes Articles of Impeachment against President Nixon, and Nixon resigns; President Ford pardons former President Nixon.
1975	North Vietnamese troops enter Saigon; the Mohawk tribe reclaims part of its homeland in New York State; former Attorney General John N. Mitchell and ex-presidential advisers H. R. Haldeman and John D. Ehrlichman are found guilty in the Watergate trial; Congress votes $405 million in aid for South Vietnamese refugees; Vice President Rockefeller's blue-ribbon panel uncovers illegal CIA operations, including records on 300,000 persons and groups and infiltration by agents into black, antiwar, and political movements.
1976	The death penalty is ruled by the Supreme Court to be a constitutionally acceptable form of punishment; the nation celebrates its Bicentennial.
1977	President Carter pardons 10,000 Vietnam draft resisters; the Department of Energy is established; the National Women's Conference convenes in Houston.
1978	The "longest walk," by 300 Native Americans, begins, to protect treaty rights; gay activist and City Council member Harvey Milk and Mayor George Moscone are assassinated in San Francisco; the Senate votes to give the Panama Canal to Panama. The Middle East "Framework for Peace" is signed by Egypt and Israel after a Camp David conference led by President Carter.
1979	The Three Mile Island nuclear power plant has a near meltdown; 110,000 demonstrate in Washington, D.C., against nuclear power; Iranian students seize the U.S. embassy in Teheran.
1980	President Carter announces an embargo on the sale of grain and high technology to the Soviet Union because of its invasion of Afghanistan; the U.S. Olympic Committee votes not to participate in the Olympic Games in Moscow.
1981	Iran releases 52 American hostages held 444 days; John Hinckley, Jr., shoots President Reagan and three others; 100,000 protest U.S. interven-

Date	Event
	tion in El Salvador; Sandra Day O'Connor is appointed the first woman Supreme Court justice; 11,500 air traffic controllers strike and are fired by President Reagan; the first reusable spacecraft, the shuttle *Columbia*, completes its two-day mission.
1982	The ERA lapses without ratification; the Vietnam War Memorial is dedicated in Washington; Anne M. Gorsuch becomes the first Cabinet-level administrator to be cited for contempt of Congress, for refusing to turn over documents from the Environmental Protection Agency.
1983	Five thousand U.S. Marines and Army Rangers invade the island of Grenada; Congress applies the War Powers Act, demanding that troops leave Grenada; Federal District Judge Jack Tanner orders Washington State to pay female employees according to "comparable worth"; Dr. Sally K. Ride becomes the first American woman astronaut to travel in space; the Supreme Court holds that the Internal Revenue Service can deny tax exemptions to private schools that practice racial discrimination.
1984	Dr. Kathryn D. Sullivan becomes the first woman astronaut to walk in space; Geraldine A. Ferraro is the first woman candidate on a major party ticket to run for Vice President; the CIA acknowledges that it mined Nicaraguan harbors, touching off a controversy in Congress; veterans of the Vietnam War reach an out-of-court settlement with seven chemical companies in their class-action suit relating to the use of Agent Orange; a Salt Lake City federal judge rules that the United States had been negligent in its aboveground testing of nuclear weapons in Nevada from 1951 to 1962; the Senate votes to impose economic sanctions on South Africa in protest against apartheid; Palestinian Liberation Organization (PLO) hijackers seize an Italian cruise ship with Americans aboard, killing one; the United States and the Soviet Union meet at their first summit conference in six years; Congress passes the Gramm-Rudman Act in an attempt to curb the federal deficit.
1985	The United States and the Soviet Union agree to resume negotiations on reducing nuclear arms and the space weapons race. Soviet leader Chernenko

Date	Event
	dies and is succeeded by Mikhail Gorbachev; the Supreme Court bars public school teachers from positions in parochial schools; a summit meeting agreement is reached by Reagan and Gorbachev on stepping up arms control talks and cultural ties.
1986	The first official observance of the birthday of Martin Luther King, Jr. takes place; the space shuttle *Challenger* explodes moments after liftoff, killing all crew members, including a civilian, Christa McAuliffe; the United States bombs Tripoli and Benghazi, Libya, in retaliation against terrorist attacks; the antiviral drug azidothymidine (AZT) is found to improve the health of some AIDS patients; U.S. officials announce that AIDS cases and deaths will increase tenfold in the next five years; Congress passes antidrug legislation; the United States imposes more economic sanctions against South Africa; President Reagan walks out on arms talks with Soviet leader Mikhail Gorbachev in Iceland because of a disagreement over the development of the U.S. "Star Wars" program.
1987	The Iran–contra affair dominates public attention when it is revealed that arms were traded for hostages and money was funneled to Swiss bank accounts and used to finance the contras in Nicaragua; insider trading is revealed on Wall Street during the bull market; the United States violates the SALT II treaty with the Soviet Union; President Reagan appoints a commission to study the AIDS crisis and backs AIDS education; a clean-water act is passed over a presidential veto; the United States imposes duties on Japanese imports to curb the trade deficit; in a landmark case, surrogate mother Mary Beth Whitehead is denied custody of "Baby M"; the drug AZT is approved for fighting AIDS; animal forms are granted patent rights; U.S. ships are involved in a conflict in the Persian Gulf; Robert Bork is nominated by President Reagan to the Supreme Court but withdraws in the face of strong opposition; the Federal Communications Commission (FCC) drops the Fairness Doctrine, which allowed equal time on radio and television for controversial issues; "Black Monday" marks the end of the bull market, when Wall Street experiences its three biggest one-day point losses ever.

Date	Event
1988	Panamanian General Noriega is indicted on drug bribery charges, disrupting U.S.–Panama relations; Supreme Court Justice Anthony Kennedy is confirmed; the U.S.–Canada Trade Agreement approves lower barriers to trade; the space shuttle *Discovery* is launched successfully after delays caused by the 1986 tragedy; the United States agrees after a 13-year hiatus to meet with the Palestine Liberation Organization.
1989	In the largest spill in U.S. history, the *Exxon Valdez* strikes a reef in Prince William Sound, dumping 11 million gallons of oil on the Alaska shoreline; the federal Resolution Trust Corporation is created to liquidate the assets of failed savings and loan associations; Ronald Brown is elected chair of the Democratic National Committee, becoming the first black to lead a major political party; Oliver North is convicted by a jury for his involvement in the Iran–contra affair; the Supreme Court upholds the right to burn the U.S. flag and hands down the Webster decision, upholding a Missouri law prohibiting public employees from performing most abortions; President Bush declares the "war on drugs"; an earthquake in northern California leaves 60 dead and several thousand injured.
1990	Iraq annexes Kuwait, prompting the United States to send a large military force to the Persian Gulf; Washington, D.C., mayor Marion Barry is arrested and convicted on drug charges; Cincinnati museum director Dennis Barrie is indicted on obscenity charges for exhibiting photographs by Robert Mapplethorpe; Congress approves the Americans with Disabilities Act, prohibiting discrimination against people with physical or mental disabilities; Charles Keating, owner of a failed savings and loan, is indicted on 42 counts of criminal fraud; 87 die in a fire at the Happy Land social club in New York City.
1991	The United States attacks Iraq in a monthlong air assault culminating in a 100-hour ground war, causing about 100,000 Iraqi casualties and forcing Iraq to retreat from Kuwait; Clarence Thomas is appointed to the Supreme Court despite allegations of his sexual harassment of a colleague; the "October Surprise" theory, purporting that the 1980 Reagan campaign made a secret deal with Iran to keep the U.S. embassy hostages in captivity until after the election, gains wide exposure; basketball star Magic Johnson announces he has tested positive for the AIDS virus.
1992	The United States denies political asylum to thousands of Haitian refugees; Robert Alton Harris is put to death in California's first execution in 25 years, becoming the focus of a national debate over the death penalty; a California jury acquits four white Los Angeles police officers in the beating of black motorist Rodney King, after the beating was videotaped and broadcast around the world; that verdict provokes rioting in Los Angeles and other U.S. cities; the House of Representatives is engulfed in scandal regarding overdrafts of accounts at the House bank; President Bush draws international criticism at the U.N. Conference on Environment and Development (known as the "Earth Summit") for refusing to support a treaty intended to protect endangered species; President Bush and Russian President Boris Yeltsin hold the first U.S.–Russia Summit and agree on new strategic arms reductions goals; the Supreme Court upholds the underlying principle of *Roe v. Wade* while also permitting states to enact some restrictions on a woman's right to obtain an abortion, as long as they do not pose an "undue burden"; Panamanian General Noriega is convicted on racketeering, drug trafficking, and money laundering charges; the United States, Mexico, and Canada conclude negotiations on the North American Free Trade Agreement; Hurricane Andrew causes devastation in Florida and Louisiana; the United States sends forces into Somalia to guarantee the delivery of humanitarian aid to the famine-ridden country.
1993	Janet Reno sworn in as first female Attorney General; Cult leader David Koresh and many followers die in a Texas compound fire; President Clinton touches off controversy with his attempt to end the ban on homosexuals in the military; Federal trial finds two Los Angeles police officers guilty of violating civil rights of black motorist Rodney King; suspect arrested in bombing that killed six at the World Trade Center in New York City.

Government Benefits

The federal government provides financial assistance to U.S. citizens through a number of its agencies. You will find most government offices listed in the phone book under "U.S. Government." To name just a few of the agencies that offer aid to U.S. citizens, the Department of Education oversees student financial assistance, the Department of Health and Human Services provides for Medicare/Medicaid, the Department of Housing and Urban Development offers federal funds for low-income housing, and the Small Business Administration offers loans to small businesses. In this section, the benefits most Americans can receive from Social Security and Medicare hospital and medical insurance are outlined.

Social Security Benefits

Under the Old-Age, Survivors, and Disability Insurance program, commonly known as Social Security, working Americans who retire after age 62 or become disabled are entitled to receive cash benefits. Spouses and dependents are also eligible for limited benefits. Employees have an amount deducted from their wages each payday based on their average indexed monthly earnings (AIME); in 1991, the rate was 7.65 percent on earnings up to $53,400. Workers retiring at 65 receive full benefits as calculated from their AIME, while those retiring at ages 62 to 64 can collect immediately but are subject to reduced payment rates. Increases in Social Security benefit amounts are based on the Consumer Price Index. In December 1990, monthly payments for retired workers averaged $603, while the average disabled worker received $587.

To be fully insured and receive *retirement benefits*, a worker must have earned as many credits of coverage as the number of calendar years between age 21 (or since 1950) and retirement. In 1991, for every $540 in wages, a worker earned one credit of coverage, for up to four credits annually. Workers who have earned credit during at least 20 of the last 40 calendar quarters are eligible for *disability benefits*. (Disabled workers under age 31 must have worked during one-half the quarters after age 21, and a minimum of six quarters, to be eligible for benefits.) Blind persons qualify simply by being fully insured—that is, by having earned a number of credits equal to the number of years they have worked. *Survivor benefits*, payable to the spouse and dependents of deceased workers, are available if the worker earned six quarters of coverage during the last 13 calendar quarters.

Retirement Benefits

At age 62, retiring workers become eligible to collect Social Security payments. Those who begin collecting at this age, however, are permanently eligible for only 80 percent of the maximum possible payment, called the primary insurance amount (PIA); in general, workers retiring before age 65 have their benefits reduced by five-ninths of 1 percent for each month they receive benefits before reaching that age.

Spouses of workers who receive Social Security retirement or disability benefits may get a spouse's insurance benefit of half of the worker's PIA when the spouse reaches 65. As with the worker's benefits, spouses may begin getting reduced payments at age 62. Payments are also available for divorced spouses provided they were married to the worker for at least 10 years.

Disability Benefits

If a worker is unable to work because he or she is severely disabled, Social Security offers a monthly disability payment. The worker receives the payments until he or she is able to work again. If the worker is still disabled by age 65, the payments become those for a retired worker.

If a fully insured worker retires or is disabled, his or her spouse and children under 18 are entitled to half of the unreduced benefit. Benefits usually stop after children reach 18, though payments can continue until age 19 provided the child is enrolled in an elementary or secondary school full time.

Survivor Benefits

Benefits are available to spouses of deceased fully insured workers under one or more of the following conditions:

1. If the spouse is age 65 or over, he or she receives the full amount of the deceased's PIA; at age 60, he or she can start receiving payments at a reduced rate. (Widowed spouses of workers who had retired before age 65 are eligible for the reduced rate the worker would have received.)

If a spouse of a deceased worker becomes disabled before or within seven years after the worker's death, the last month in which he or she received mother's or father's insurance benefits (payments for dependent children), or the last month he or she previously received surviving spouse's benefits, the widow or widower is eligible for benefits of 71.5 percent of the worker's PIA.

2. As with children of disabled or retired workers, surviving children receive benefits until they are 18 or 19 if they are enrolled in school full time. Benefits for such children are three-quarters of the amount the worker would have received had he or she lived to collect full benefits.

3. The spouse of a deceased worker receives an additional 75 percent of the PIA—in what is called a "mother's or father's benefit"—if he or she cares for a child of the worker under age 16; these payments stop when the child reaches that age. Unless the spouse remarries, payments resume when he or she reaches age 60, as described above.

4. Dependent parents age 62 or over may receive benefits if they relied on the deceased worker for at least one-half of their support. Each parent receives 75 percent of the deceased's PIA; if only one parent survives, he or she gets $82^1/_2$ percent of the PIA.

5. A cash payment of $255 is made to a spouse who lived with the deceased worker or to a spouse or child eligible for immediate monthly survivor benefits.

Self-Employed and Household Workers

Self-employed persons are eligible for the same Social Security benefits and earn credits at the same rate as other workers. However, they must pay into the program at a higher rate (15.3 percent in 1991) and file taxes quarterly.

Household workers—maids, cooks, laundry workers, nursemaids, baby-sitters, chauffeurs, etc.—also are covered provided they are paid $50 or more in cash per quarter by at least one employer. Carfare can be applied if it is paid in cash, but room and board cannot be claimed. Whether the job is regular, full time, or part time, household workers can receive this benefit by showing their Social Security cards to their employers. The employer deducts the Social Security tax from the worker's pay and sends the total amount to the federal government.

Farm Owners and Workers

Self-employed farmers pay contributions to Social Security at the same rate as other self-employed persons. They can report two-thirds of their gross earnings if their earnings are $2,400 or less. Those whose gross income is $2,400 or more, and whose net income is $1,600 or less, can report $1,600. Cash or crop shares from a tenant or share farmer can be counted only if the farmer participated materially in the production or management.

A worker's earnings from farm work count toward benefits if the employer pays him or her at least $150 in cash in a given year, or if the employer spends $2,500 or more a year for agricultural labor.

Medicare

Medicare provides hospital and medical insurance for Social Security and Railroad Retirement beneficiaries 65 and over. Its hospital insurance program paid out about $63 billion in 1990, while its medical insurance program gave $41 billion in benefits. It also provides for those persons who are entitled to receive Social Security disability benefits for two years and to those with end-stage renal disease. Persons age 65 and over not otherwise eligible for hospital benefits may receive them by paying a special monthly premium on a voluntary basis. All persons over age 65 may receive supplemental medical insurance by paying a monthly premium.

Hospital Insurance

Those eligible for hospital insurance are covered for the following:

1. All medically necessary inpatient hospital care, once the patient has paid a deductible.
2. Up to 150 days of care in a skilled-nursing facility (nursing home) each year (except for coinsurance for first eight days).
3. Visits by home-care workers.
4. Hospice care for terminal illness.

Medical Insurance

Medical insurance is available to anyone over age 65 who agrees to pay a monthly premium ($24.80 in 1988), which is subsidized by a government contribution. The premium is usually deducted from Social Security payments. People may enroll in the program in a seven-month period beginning three months before their 65th birthday; those enrolling later must pay higher premiums.

Except for doctors' charges for X-ray or clinical laboratory services for hospital-bed patients, which are paid in full by individuals, members of this program pay 20 percent (after the first $75) of the total amount required for the following services:

1. Hospital, office, or home physicians' and surgeons' fees.
2. Diagnostic tests, surgical dressings, and splints; rental or purchase of medical equipment; the services of a physical therapist at home or in the office; outpatient physical therapy received from a hospital or an extended-care facility for those who have used up their hospital insurance coverage.
3. Physical therapy furnished under the supervision of a practicing hospital, clinic, skilled-nursing facility, or agency.
4. Certain services by podiatrists.
5. All outpatient services of a participating hospital (including diagnostic tests).
6. Services of licensed chiropractors who meet government standards, but only for manual manipulation treatment of the spine and treatment of subluxation of the spine proven by X-ray.
7. Supplies related to colostomies.

Home health services are covered 100 percent when medically necessary.

Monthly Payments for Selected Families

Beneficiary Family	Career Earnings Level/Average (45% of average)	Low Earnings ($9,801)[1]	Maximum Earnings ($53,400)
Primary Insurance amount (worker retiring at 65)	$ 751.10	$461.20	$1,022.90
Maximum family benefit (worker retiring at 65)	1,367.90	692.20	1,790.60
Disability maximum family benefit (worker disabled at 55; in 1991)*	1,126.80	640.90	1,562.80
Disabled worker: (worker disabled at 55)			
Worker alone	751.00	461.00	1,041.00
Worker, spouse, and 1 child	1,125.00	639.00	1,561.00
Retired worker claiming benefits at age 62:			
Worker alone[2]	600.00	368.00	810.00
Worker with spouse claiming benefits at—			
Age 65 or over	975.00	598.00	1,321.00
Age 62[2]	900.00	552.00	1,219.00
Widow or widower claiming benefits at—			
Age 65 or over[3]	751.00	461.00	1,022.00
Age 60	537.00	329.00	731.00
Disabled widow or widower claiming benefits at age 50–59[4]	537.00	329.00	731.00
1 surviving child	563.00	345.00	767.00
Widow or widower age 65 or over and 1 child[5]	1,314.00	692.00	1,789.00
Widowed mother or father and 1 child[5]	1,126.00	690.00	1,534.00
Widowed mother or father and 2 children[5]	1,365.00	690.00	1,788.00

* Assumes work beginning at age 22. (1) Estimate. (2) Assumes maximum reduction. (3) A widow(er)'s benefit amount is limited to the amount the spouse would have been receiving if still living but not less than 82.5 percent of the PIA. (4) Effective January 1984, disabled widow(er)s claiming benefit at ages 50–59 will receive benefit equal to 71.5 percent of the PIA (based on 1983 Social Security Amendment provision). (5) Based on worker dying at age 65.

Crime Rates

Crimes and Crime Rates, by Type: 1980–90
[Data refer to offenses known to the police.]

Item and year	Total	Violent crime Total	Murder[1]	Forcible rape	Robbery	Aggravated assault	Property crime Total	Burglary	Larceny—theft	Motor vehicle theft
Number of offenses (1,000):										
1980	13,408	1,345	23.0	83.0	566	673	12,064	3,795	7,137	1,132
1981	13,424	1,362	22.5	82.5	593	664	12,062	3,780	7,194	1,088
1982	12,974	1,322	21.0	78.8	553	669	11,652	3,447	7,143	1,062
1983	12,109	1,258	19.3	78.9	507	653	10,851	3,130	6,713	1,008
1984	11,882	1,273	18.7	84.2	485	685	10,609	2,984	6,592	1,032
1985	12,431	1,329	19.0	88.7	498	723	11,103	3,073	6,926	1,103
1986	13,212	1,489	20.6	91.5	543	834	11,723	3,241	7,257	1,224
1987	13,509	1,484	20.1	91.1	518	855	12,025	3,236	7,500	1,289
1988	13,923	1,566	20.7	92.5	543	910	12,357	3,218	7,706	1,433
1989	14,251	1,646	21.5	94.5	578	952	12,605	3,168	7,872	1,565
1990	14,476	1,820	23.4	102.6	639	1,055	12,656	3,074	7,946	1,636
Percent change, number of offenses:										
1980 to 1990	8.0	35.3	1.7	23.6	12.9	56.8	4.9	−19.0	11.3	44.5
1985 to 1990	16.5	36.9	23.2	15.7	28.3	45.9	14.0	0.0	14.7	48.3
1989 to 1990	1.6	10.6	8.8	8.6	10.6	10.8	0.4	−3.0	0.9	4.5
Rate per 100,000 population:										
1980	5,950	597	10.2	36.8	251	299	5,353	1,684	3,167	502
1981	5,858	594	9.8	36.0	259	290	5,264	1,650	3,140	475
1982	5,604	571	9.1	34.0	239	289	5,033	1,489	3,085	459
1983	5,175	538	8.3	33.7	217	279	4,637	1,338	2,869	431
1984	5,031	539	7.9	35.7	205	290	4,492	1,264	2,791	437
1985	5,207	557	7.9	37.1	209	303	4,651	1,287	2,901	462
1986	5,480	618	8.6	37.9	225	346	4,863	1,345	3,010	508
1987	5,550	610	8.3	37.4	213	351	4,940	1,330	3,081	529
1988	5,664	637	8.4	37.6	221	370	5,027	1,309	3,135	583
1989	5,741	663	8.7	38.1	233	383	5,078	1,276	3,171	630
1990	5,820	732	9.4	41.2	257	424	5,089	1,236	3,195	658
Percent change, rate per 100,000 population:										
1980 to 1990	−2.2	22.6	−7.8	12.0	2.4	41.8	−4.9	−26.6	0.9	31.3
1985 to 1990	11.8	31.4	19.0	11.1	23.0	39.9	9.4	−4.0	10.1	42.4
1989 to 1990	1.4	10.4	8.0	8.1	10.3	10.7	0.2	−3.1	0.8	4.4

[1] Includes nonnegligent manslaughter.

Crimes and Crime Rates, by Type and Area: 1989 and 1990

[In thousands, except rate. Rate per 100,000 population; Estimated totals based on reports from city and rural law enforcement agencies representing 96 percent of the national population.]

Type of crime	1989 MSA's[1] Total	1989 MSA's[1] Rate	1989 Other cities Total	1989 Other cities Rate	1989 Rural areas Total	1989 Rural areas Rate	1990 MSA's[1] Total	1990 MSA's[1] Rate	1990 Other cities Total	1990 Other cities Rate	1990 Rural areas Total	1990 Rural areas Rate
Total	12,430	6,496	1,149	5,034	673	1,974	12,605	6,547	1,188	5,303	683	2,022
Violent crime	1,492	780	90	394	64	189	1,648	856	102	458	70	207
Murder and nonnegligent manslaughter	19	10	1	5	2	5	20	11	1	5	2	6
Forcible rape	81	42	6	27	7	21	88	46	7	33	8	22
Robbery	560	293	13	58	5	16	620	322	14	63	5	16
Aggravated assault	832	435	69	304	50	147	920	478	80	357	55	163
Property crime	10,938	5,716	1,059	4,640	608	1,785	10,957	5,691	1,085	4,845	613	1,815
Burglary	2,702	1,412	237	1,040	229	673	2,611	1,356	236	1,053	227	671
Larceny-theft	6,762	3,534	771	3,380	339	995	6,803	3,533	797	3,559	346	1,024
Motor vehicle theft	1,474	771	50	221	40	117	1,543	801	52	232	41	121

[1] Metropolitan Statistical Areas.

Crime Rates by State, 1985–90, and by Type, 1990

[Offenses known to the police per 100,000 population.]

Region, division, and state	1985, total	1989, total	1990 Total	Violent crime Total	Violent crime Murder[1]	Violent crime Forcible rape	Violent crime Robbery	Violent crime Aggravated assault	Property crime Total	Property crime Burglary	Property crime Larceny—theft	Property crime Motor vehicle theft
United States	5,207	5,741	5,820	732	9.4	41	257	424	5,088	1,236	3,195	658
Northeast	4,627	5,072	5,193	757	8.6	29	353	366	4,437	1,020	2,598	818
New England	4,487	4,854	4,996	536	3.9	30	172	330	4,460	1,094	2,645	721
Maine	3,672	3,584	3,698	143	2.4	20	25	96	3,555	823	2,555	177
New Hampshire	3,252	3,596	3,645	132	1.9	35	27	68	3,514	735	2,534	244
Vermont	3,888	4,089	4,341	127	2.3	26	12	87	4,124	1,087	2,918	208
Massachusetts	4,758	5,136	5,298	736	4.0	34	217	481	4,562	1,113	2,525	924
Rhode Island	4,723	5,225	5,353	432	4.8	25	122	280	4,921	1,271	2,695	954
Connecticut	4,705	5,270	5,387	554	5.1	28	235	286	4,833	1,228	2,874	731
Middle Atlantic	4,675	5,147	5,263	834	10.2	29	416	379	4,429	995	2,582	852
New York	5,589	6,293	6,364	1,181	14.5	30	625	512	5,183	1,161	2,979	1,043
New Jersey	5,094	5,269	5,447	648	5.6	30	301	311	4,800	1,017	2,843	940
Pennsylvania	3,037	3,360	3,476	431	6.7	26	176	222	3,045	729	1,811	506
Midwest	4,674	4,949	5,102	594	7.0	43	199	346	4,508	983	3,024	501
East North Central	4,939	5,150	5,322	662	8.1	47	234	373	4,660	1,008	3,086	566
Ohio	4,187	4,733	4,843	506	6.1	47	189	265	4,337	983	2,864	491
Indiana	3,914	4,440	4,683	474	6.2	38	101	328	4,209	943	2,827	439
Illinois[3]	5,384	5,639	5,935	967	10.3	39	394	524	4,968	1,063	3,262	643
Michigan	6,366	5,968	5,995	790	10.4	78	234	468	5,204	1,143	3,347	714
Wisconsin	4,017	4,165	4,395	265	4.6	21	113	127	4,130	751	2,963	416

Crime Rates by State, 1985–90, and by Type, 1990 (*continued*)
[Offenses known to the police per 100,000 population.]

Region, division, and state	1985, total	1989, total	1990 Total	Violent crime Total	Murder[1]	Forcible rape	Robbery	Aggravated assault	Property crime Total	Burglary	Larceny—theft	Motor vehicle theft
West North Central	**4,046**	**4,473**	**4,579**	**432**	**4.4**	**31**	**114**	**282**	**4,147**	**925**	**2,876**	**346**
Minnesota	4,134	4,383	4,539	306	2.7	34	93	177	4,233	907	2,960	366
Iowa	3,943	4,081	4,101	300	1.9	18	39	240	3,801	808	2,823	170
Missouri	4,366	5,127	5,121	715	8.8	32	216	458	4,405	1,066	2,800	539
North Dakota	2,679	2,561	2,922	74	0.8	18	8	47	2,848	427	2,289	133
South Dakota	2,641	2,685	2,909	163	2.0	34	12	114	2,747	527	2,109	110
Nebraska	3,695	4,092	4,213	330	2.7	30	51	246	3,883	724	2,981	178
Kansas	4,375	4,983	5,193	448	4.0	40	118	286	4,745	1,167	3,244	335
South	**5,256**	**6,205**	**6,334**	**766**	**11.8**	**45**	**237**	**472**	**5,567**	**1,498**	**3,471**	**598**
South Atlantic	**5,375**	**6,425**	**6,546**	**857**	**11.4**	**45**	**277**	**523**	**5,689**	**1,525**	**3,589**	**576**
Delaware	4,961	4,865	5,360	655	5.0	88	165	397	4,705	970	3,291	444
Maryland	5,373	5,563	5,830	919	11.5	46	364	498	4,912	1,120	3,083	709
District of Columbia[2]	8,007	10,293	10,774	2,458	77.8	50	1,214	1,117	8,316	1,983	4,997	1,336
Virginia	3,779	4,211	4,441	351	8.8	31	123	188	4,090	731	3,031	327
West Virginia	2,253	2,363	2,503	169	5.7	24	38	102	2,334	657	1,523	154
North Carolina	4,121	5,254	5,486	624	10.7	34	152	426	4,862	1,530	3,048	284
South Carolina	4,841	5,619	6,045	977	11.2	54	152	759	5,069	1,380	3,302	386
Georgia	5,110	7,073	6,764	756	11.8	54	263	427	6,007	1,619	3,714	674
Florida	7,574	8,804	8,811	1,244	10.7	52	417	764	7,566	2,171	4,570	826
East South Central	**3,651**	**4,085**	**4,389**	**557**	**10.2**	**39**	**131**	**376**	**3,833**	**1,098**	**2,374**	**360**
Kentucky	2,947	3,317	3,299	390	7.2	29	69	285	2,909	767	1,943	199
Tennessee	4,167	4,514	5,051	670	10.5	50	191	419	4,381	1,264	2,545	572
Alabama	3,942	4,628	4,915	709	11.6	33	144	521	4,207	1,103	2,755	348
Mississippi	3,266	3,515	3,869	340	12.2	44	86	198	3,529	1,251	2,070	208
West South Central	**5,991**	**7,064**	**7,092**	**738**	**13.5**	**49**	**233**	**443**	**6,354**	**1,682**	**3,902**	**770**
Arkansas	3,585	4,556	4,867	532	10.3	43	113	365	4,335	1,211	2,834	289
Louisiana	5,564	6,241	6,487	898	17.2	42	270	569	5,588	1,438	3,549	602
Oklahoma	5,425	5,503	5,599	547	8.0	47	122	370	5,051	1,447	3,002	602
Texas	6,569	7,927	7,827	761	14.1	52	261	435	7,065	1,852	4,305	909
West	**6,405**	**6,550**	**6,405**	**808**	**9.1**	**45**	**263**	**491**	**5,597**	**1,304**	**3,515**	**778**
Mountain	**6,183**	**6,250**	**6,268**	**517**	**6.0**	**42**	**109**	**360**	**5,751**	**1,286**	**3,979**	**486**
Montana	4,549	3,998	4,502	159	4.9	24	22	108	4,343	709	3,391	243
Idaho	3,908	3,931	4,057	276	2.7	27	15	231	3,781	813	2,803	165
Wyoming	4,015	3,889	4,211	301	4.9	30	16	251	3,909	631	3,129	149
Colorado	6,919	6,039	6,054	526	4.2	46	91	385	5,528	1,209	3,891	428
New Mexico	6,486	6,574	6,684	780	9.2	59	115	606	5,904	1,739	3,828	337
Arizona	7,116	8,060	7,889	652	7.7	41	161	443	7,236	1,670	4,703	863
Utah	5,317	5,682	5,660	284	3.0	38	57	186	5,376	881	4,258	238
Nevada	6,575	6,272	6,064	601	9.7	62	238	291	5,463	1,367	3,503	593
Pacific	**6,486**	**6,656**	**6,452**	**910**	**10.2**	**46**	**317**	**536**	**5,543**	**1,310**	**3,352**	**880**
Washington	6,529	6,594	6,223	502	4.9	64	130	303	5,721	1,263	4,011	447
Oregon	6,730	6,161	5,646	507	3.8	47	144	312	5,139	1,135	3,545	459
California	6,518	6,763	6,604	1,045	11.9	43	377	614	5,558	1,345	3,198	1,016
Alaska	5,877	4,780	5,153	525	7.5	73	77	367	4,628	894	3,168	565
Hawaii	5,201	6,270	6,107	281	4.0	32	91	153	5,826	1,228	4,217	381

[1] Includes nonnegligent manslaughter. [2] Includes offenses reported by the police at the National Zoo. [3] Forcible rape figures for 1989 and 1990 were estimated using the national rate of forcible rapes when grouped by like agencies as figures submitted were not in accordance with national Uniform Crime Reporting program guidelines.

Crime Rates, by Type—Selected Large Cities: 1990
[Offenses known to the police per 100,000 population.]

City ranked by population size, 1990[1]	Crime index, total	Violent crime Total	Murder	Forcible rape	Robbery	Aggravated assault	Property crime Total	Burglary	Larceny—theft	Motor vehicle theft
New York, NY	9,699	2,384	31	43	1,370	941	7,316	1,638	3,668	2,009
Los Angeles, CA	9,225	2,405	28	58	1,036	1,283	6,821	1,477	3,519	1,825
Chicago, IL	([1])	([1])	31	([1])	1,335	1,477	8,220	1,803	4,670	1,747
Houston, TX	11,338	1,388	35	82	792	479	9,950	2,636	4,808	2,506
Philadelphia, PA	7,192	1,349	32	46	808	463	5,843	1,523	2,689	1,632
San Diego, CA	9,145	1,085	12	40	390	643	8,061	1,503	4,375	2,183
Detroit, MI	12,192	2,699	57	161	1,266	1,216	9,493	2,536	4,002	2,955
Dallas, TX	15,520	2,438	44	134	1,049	1,211	13,082	3,275	7,372	2,435
Phoenix, AZ	10,756	1,085	13	52	344	675	9,672	2,510	5,381	1,782
San Antonio, TX	12,477	612	22	46	306	238	11,865	2,780	7,495	1,590
San Jose, CA	4,869	601	5	53	132	411	4,269	735	2,996	538
Baltimore, MD	10,596	2,438	41	93	1,288	1,015	8,158	2,004	4,807	1,347
Indianapolis, IN	6,749	1,287	12	112	340	824	5,462	1,629	2,833	1,000
San Francisco, CA	9,662	1,711	14	58	974	665	7,951	1,467	4,915	1,569
Jacksonville, FL	10,463	1,830	28	111	622	1,070	8,633	2,753	4,931	949
Columbus, OH	9,907	1,110	14	102	560	434	8,798	2,343	5,117	1,338
Milwaukee, WI	9,299	1,000	25	79	660	237	8,299	1,482	4,709	2,108
Memphis, TN	9,872	1,488	32	136	680	640	8,384	2,544	3,763	2,078
Washington, DC	10,774	2,458	78	50	1,214	1,117	8,316	1,983	4,997	1,336
Boston, MA	11,851	2,379	25	94	1,049	1,212	9,472	1,783	5,162	2,527

[1] The rates for forcible rape, violent crime, and crime index are not shown because the forcible rape figures were not in accordance with national Uniform Crime Reporting guidelines.

Victimization Rates for Crimes Against Persons: 1973–90
[**Rates per 1,000 persons, 12 years old and over.** Includes attempted crimes. Data based on National Crime Survey; totals exclude personal larceny]

YEAR	Total[1]	White	Black	Hispanic[2]	MALE White	MALE Black	MALE Hispanic[2]	FEMALE White	FEMALE Black	FEMALE Hispanic[2]	VICTIM OFFENDER RELATIONSHIP Stranger	VICTIM OFFENDER RELATIONSHIP Nonstranger
1973	33	32	42	36	43	53	53	21	32	22	22	11
1980	33	32	41	40	43	53	54	22	31	27	21	12
1981	35	33	50	39	44	61	53	23	40	26	23	12
1982	34	33	44	40	42	57	49	25	33	32	22	12
1983	31	30	41	38	39	50	48	21	33	29	18	13
1984	31	30	41	35	38	51	45	22	33	26	17	14
1985	30	29	38	30	38	47	33	21	31	27	18	12
1986	28	28	33	27	35	39	39	21	29	15	16	12
1987	29	28	42	39	36	52	44	20	34	35	17	13
1988	30	28	40	35	34	47	(NA)	22	35	(NA)	18	12
1989	29	28	36	39	35	50	50	22	25	28	18	12
1990	30	28	40	37	36	53	50	21	28	25	18	12

NA Not available. [1] Includes races not shown separately. [2] Hispanic persons may be of any race.

Households Touched by Crime, 1981 and 1990, and by Characteristic, 1990

[A household is considered "touched by crime" if during the year it experienced a burglary, auto theft or household theft or if a household member was raped, robbed, or assaulted, or a victim of personal theft, no matter where the crime occurred. Data based on the National Crime Survey.]

TYPE OF CRIME	1981 Number (1,000)	1981 Percent touched	1989, pref. Number (1,000)	Total[1]	White	Black	Urban	Sub-urban	Rural
Total[2]	24,863	30.0	22,652	23.7	23.1	27.8	29.6	22.7	16.9
Violent crime	4,850	5.9	4,478	4.7	4.6	5.4	6.1	4.2	3.6
Rape	165	0.2	104	0.1	0.1	0.1	0.2	0.1	0.1
Robbery	1,117	1.3	967	1.0	0.8	2.2	1.8	0.7	0.4
Assault	3,890	4.7	3,591	3.8	3.8	3.6	4.4	3.5	3.2
Theft	17,705	21.4	15,905	16.7	16.6	17.0	20.3	16.5	11.6
Burglary	6,101	7.4	4,557	4.8	4.3	7.9	6.7	3.9	3.7
Motor vehicle theft	1,285	1.6	1,825	1.9	1.7	3.2	2.9	1.8	0.7

[1] Includes other races not shown sepatately. [2] Types of crime will not add to "total" since each household may report as many crime categories as experienced.

GOVERNMENT STRUCTURE

The chart on page 849 shows the structure of the U.S. government and its departments and agencies as of June 2, 1990. As the chart shows, the Constitution set forth the organization of the government, which operates on a system of checks and balances. The three branches of government, the legislative, executive, and judicial, each have the power to check the others. The legislative branch, the Congress, has the power to propose and make laws; the executive branch contains the office of the president, who has the ultimate power to enforce the law and oversee the government; and the judicial branch explains the law by ruling on the constitutionality of laws and trying cases.

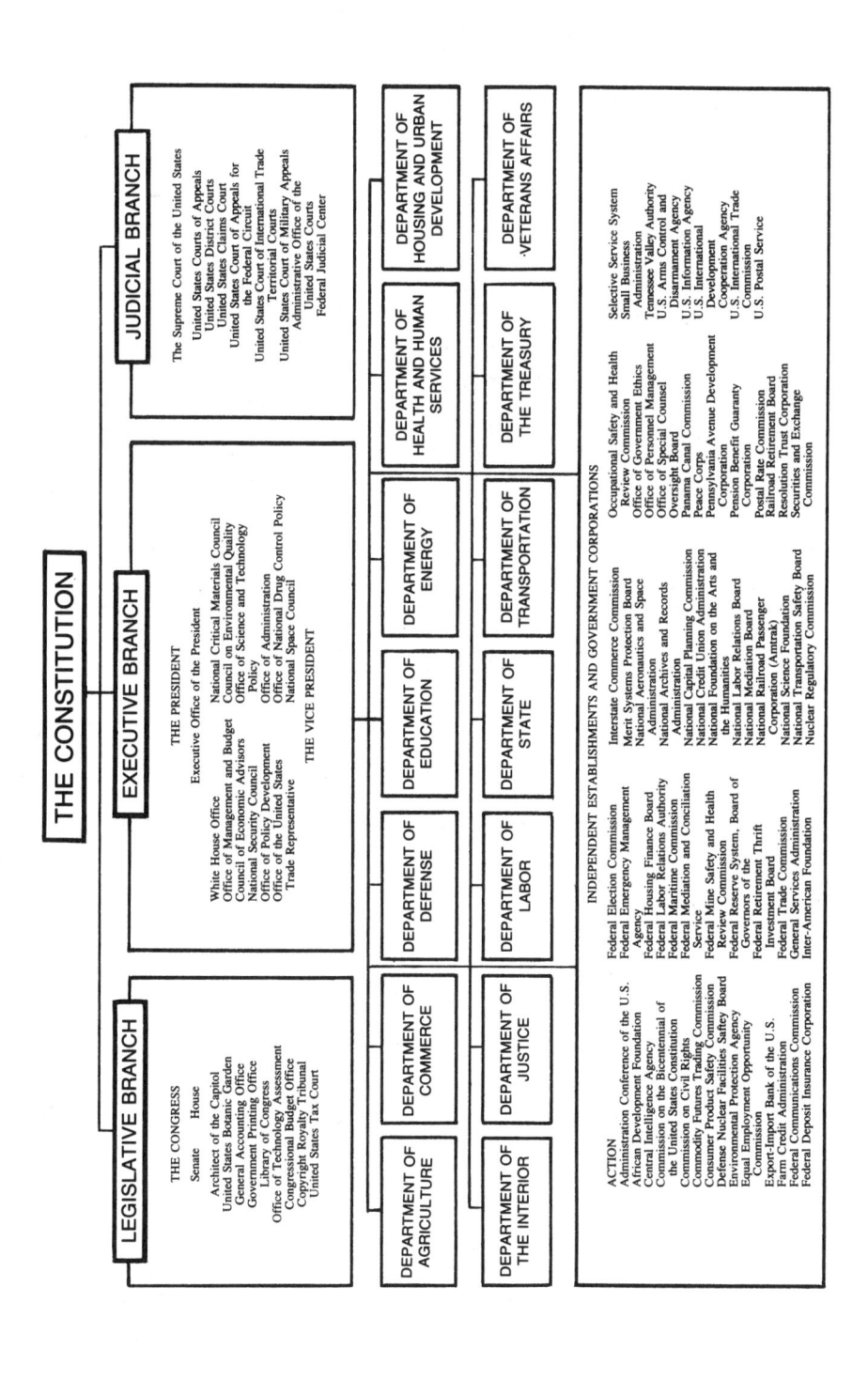

The United States

THE CONSTITUTION

LEGISLATIVE BRANCH

THE CONGRESS
Senate   House
Architect of the Capitol
United States Botanic Garden
General Accounting Office
Government Printing Office
Library of Congress
Office of Technology Assessment
Congressional Budget Office
Copyright Royalty Tribunal
United States Tax Court

EXECUTIVE BRANCH

THE PRESIDENT
Executive Office of the President

White House Office
Office of Management and Budget
Council of Economic Advisors
National Security Council
Office of Policy Development
Office of the United States
Trade Representative

National Critical Materials Council
Council on Environmental Quality
Office of Science and Technology Policy
Office of Administration
Office of National Drug Control Policy
National Space Council

THE VICE PRESIDENT

JUDICIAL BRANCH

The Supreme Court of the United States
United States Courts of Appeals
United States District Courts
United States Claims Court
United States Court of Appeals for the Federal Circuit
United States Court of International Trade
Territorial Courts
United States Court of Military Appeals
Administrative Office of the United States Courts
Federal Judicial Center

DEPARTMENT OF AGRICULTURE

DEPARTMENT OF COMMERCE

DEPARTMENT OF DEFENSE

DEPARTMENT OF EDUCATION

DEPARTMENT OF ENERGY

DEPARTMENT OF HEALTH AND HUMAN SERVICES

DEPARTMENT OF HOUSING AND URBAN DEVELOPMENT

DEPARTMENT OF THE INTERIOR

DEPARTMENT OF JUSTICE

DEPARTMENT OF LABOR

DEPARTMENT OF STATE

DEPARTMENT OF TRANSPORTATION

DEPARTMENT OF THE TREASURY

DEPARTMENT OF VETERANS AFFAIRS

INDEPENDENT ESTABLISHMENTS AND GOVERNMENT CORPORATIONS

ACTION
Administration Conference of the U.S.
African Development Foundation
Central Intelligence Agency
Commission on the Bicentennial of the United States Constitution
Commission on Civil Rights
Commodity Futures Trading Commission
Consumer Product Safety Commission
Defense Nuclear Facilities Safety Board
Environmental Protection Agency
Equal Employment Opportunity Commission
Export-Import Bank of the U.S.
Farm Credit Administration
Federal Communications Commission
Federal Deposit Insurance Corporation
Federal Election Commission
Federal Emergency Management Agency
Federal Housing Finance Board
Federal Labor Relations Authority
Federal Maritime Commission
Federal Mediation and Conciliation Service
Federal Mine Safety and Health Review Commission
Federal Reserve System, Board of Governors of the
Federal Retirement Thrift Investment Board
Federal Trade Commission
General Services Administration
Inter-American Foundation
Interstate Commerce Commission
Merit Systems Protection Board
National Aeronautics and Space Administration
National Archives and Records Administration
National Capital Planning Commission
National Credit Union Administration
National Foundation on the Arts and the Humanities
National Labor Relations Board
National Mediation Board
National Railroad Passenger Corporation (Amtrak)
National Science Foundation
National Transportation Safety Board
Nuclear Regulatory Commission
Occupational Safety and Health Review Commission
Office of Government Ethics
Office of Personnel Management
Office of Special Counsel
Oversight Board
Panama Canal Commission
Peace Corps
Pennsylvania Avenue Development Corporation
Pension Benefit Guaranty Corporation
Postal Rate Commission
Railroad Retirement Board
Resolution Trust Corporation
Securities and Exchange Commission
Selective Service System
Small Business Administration
Tennessee Valley Authority
U.S. Arms Control and Disarmament Agency
U.S. Information Agency
U.S. International Development Cooperation Agency
U.S. International Trade Commission
U.S. Postal Service

How a Bill Becomes Law

First Reading

To become law, a bill is introduced by a senator or representative in the Senate or Congress and is assigned a number or title by the clerk of the House. The bill is then assigned to the committee of the Senate or House that is responsible for the particular area the bill relates to (for example, a bill providing aid to farmers would go to the Committee on Agriculture). The committee debates the bill, listens to the opinions of interested people and members of the Congress, and sometimes offers amendments to the bill. The bill is then voted on by the committee and, if passed, is sent back to the clerk of the House. If the bill is unacceptable to the committee when they receive it, they may table it, killing consideration of the bill. This process is called the first reading of the bill.

Second and Third Readings

In the second reading, the clerk of the House reads the bill to the House, which then debates it and suggests amendments. At the third reading, after the bill is debated, a vote is called for and the title of the bill is read before the vote.

Passage

If the bill passes, it is sent to the other house, where it is again debated, amendments are added, and a vote is taken. If it passes with amendments, a joint congressional committee (composed of members of both the House and Senate) tries to reach a compromise between the two versions of the bill. If the bill is not passed by the second house, it dies.

Presidential Action

When the bill is passed, it is sent to the president. If he signs it, it becomes law. If he holds on to the bill for 10 days (not including Sundays), it automatically becomes law without his signature, unless Congress has adjourned during that time, in which case the bill is automatically killed in a process known as a *pocket veto*. If the president disapproves of the bill, he vetoes it, sending it back to the house that originally produced it, together with his objections.

Once back in the house, the bill is debated again in light of the president's comments and a roll-call vote is taken. To remain an active bill, it must receive at least a two-thirds vote from that house. If it does not, it is defeated. If the bill does get the support of two thirds of that house, it is sent to the other house, where it again must receive a vote of two thirds to override a presidential veto.

Additional Sources of Information

Andriot, Donna, Jay Andriot, and Laurie Andriot. *Guide to U.S. Government Statistics.* Documents Index, 1987.

Barone, Michael, and Grant Ujifusa, eds. *The Almanac of American Politics.* National Journal, 1987.

Baydo, Gerald. *A Synoptic History of America's Past.* Random House, 1981.

Congress and the Nation. Congressional Quarterly, published every four years.

Congressional Quarterly Almanac. Congressional Quarterly, annual.

Congressional Quarterly Weekly. Congressional Quarterly, weekly.

Consumer's Resource Handbook. U.S. Office of Consumer Affairs, latest edition.

Cordasco, Francesco. *Immigrant Children in American Schools.* A. M. Kelly, 1976.

Flags of America. National Flag Foundation, 1985.

Foner, Eric, and John A. Garraty, eds. *The Reader's Companion to American History.* Houghton Mifflin, 1991.

Garwood, Alfred N. *Almanac of the Fifty States.* Information Publication, 1987.

Hatch, Jane M. *The American Book of Days.* 3rd ed. H. W. Wilson, 1978.

Hornsby, Alton. *Chronology of African-American History.* Gale Research, Inc., 1991.

Kane, Joseph Nathan, and Gerard L. Alexander. *Nicknames and Sobriquets of U.S. Cities and States.* Scarecrow Press, 1979.

Lesko, Matthew. *Information U.S.A.* Viking, 1986.

Ornstein, Norman, ed. *Vital Statistics on Congress.* American Enterprise Institute for Public Policy Research, 1992.

Schlesinger, Arthur M., Jr., ed. *The Almanac of American History.* Putnam, 1984.

Shearer, Benjamin F., and Barbara S. Shearer. *State Names, Seals, Flags and Symbols.* Greenwood, 1987.

Statistical Abstract of the United States. U.S. Bureau of the Census, annual.

Urdang, Laurence, ed. *The Timetables of American History.* Simon & Schuster, 1983.

26

The World

Countries of the World / *853*

Great Events in World History / *871*

World Exploration and Discovery / *878*

Major World Cities / *884*

The United Nations / *891*

International Organizations / *893*

International Conversions / *895*

Foreign Dialing Codes / *896*

Seven Wonders of the Ancient World / *898*

The Six Wives of Henry VIII / *900*

Royal Rulers of Europe and Asia / *898*

Additional Sources of Information / *901*

Countries of the World

Afghanistan
Area: 647,500 km² (249,999 sq. mi.)
Capital: Kabul
Government: In transition
Population: 16,450,304
Languages: Pushtu, Afghan Persian, Turkic
Religions: Sunni Muslim, Shi'a Muslim

Albania
Area: 28,750 km² (11,100 sq. mi.)
Capital: Tirana
Government: In transition
Population: 3,335,044
Languages: Albanian, Greek
Religions: Muslim, Greek Orthodox, Roman Catholic

Algeria
Area: 2,381,740 km² (919,590 sq. mi.)
Capital: Algiers
Government: Republic
Population: 26,022,188
Languages: Arabic, French, Berber dialects
Religion: Sunni Muslim

Andorra
Area: 450 km² (174 sq. mi.)
Capital: Andorra la Vella
Government: Coprincipality of France and Spain
Population: 53,197
Languages: Catalan, French, Castilian
Religion: Roman Catholic

Angola
Area: 1,246,700 km² (481,351 sq. mi.)
Capital: Luanda
Government: In transition
Population: 8,668,281
Languages: Portuguese, Bantu dialects
Religions: Indigenous beliefs, Roman Catholic, Protestant

Anguilla
Area: 91 km² (35 sq. mi.)
Capital: The Valley
Government: Dependent territory of United Kingdom
Population: 6,922
Language: English
Religions: Anglican, Methodist

Antigua and Barbuda
Area: 440 km² (170 sq. mi.)
Capital: Saint John's
Government: Parliamentary democracy affiliated with United Kingdom
Population: 63,917
Languages: English, local dialects
Religions: Anglican, Methodist, Roman Catholic

Argentina
Area: 2,766,890 km² (1,068,296 sq. mi.)
Capital: Buenos Aires
Government: Republic
Population: 32,663,983
Languages: Spanish, English, Italian, German, French
Religions: Roman Catholic, Protestant, Jewish

Armenia
Area: 29,283 km² (11,306 sq. mi.)
Capital: Yerevan
Government: In transition
Population: 3,305,000
Languages: Armenian, Russian
Religion: Armenian Apolistic

Aruba
Area: 193 km² (75 sq. mi.)
Capital: Oranjestad
Government: Independent territory of Netherlands
Population: 64,052
Languages: Dutch, Papiamento, Spanish, English
Religions: Roman Catholic, Protestant

Australia
Area: 7,686,850 km² (2,967,893 sq. mi.)
Capital: Canberra
Government: Federal parliamentary state affiliated with Great Britain
Population: 17,288,044
Languages: English, native languages
Religions: Anglican, Roman Catholic, other Protestant faiths

Austria
Area: 83,850 km² (32,374 sq. mi.)
Capital: Vienna
Government: Federal republic
Population: 7,665,804
Language: German
Religions: Roman Catholic, Protestant

Azerbaijan
Area: 86,506 km² (33,400 sq. mi.)
Capital: Baku
Government: In transition
Population: 7,145,600
Languages: Azeri, Russian
Religions: Muslim

The Bahamas
Area: 13,940 km² (5,382 sq. mi.)
Capital: Nassau
Government: Independent commonwealth affiliated with United Kingdom
Population: 252,110
Languages: English, Creole
Religions: Baptist, Anglican, Roman Catholic, other Protestant

Bahrain
Area: 620 km² (239 sq. mi.)
Capital: Manama
Government: Monarchy
Population: 536,974
Languages: Arabic, English, Farsi, Urdu
Religions: Shi'a Muslim, Sunni Muslim

Bangladesh
Area: 144,000 km² (55,598 sq. mi.)
Capital: Dhaka
Government: Republic
Population: 116,601,424
Languages: Bangla, English
Religions: Muslim, Hindu

Barbados
Area: 460 km² (166 sq. mi.)
Capital: Bridgetown
Government: Parliamentary democracy affiliated with United Kingdom
Population: 254,626
Language: English
Religions: Anglican, Pentecostal, Methodist, Roman Catholic

Barbuda
See **Antigua and Barbuda.**

Belarus
Area: 207,718 km² (80,200 sq. mi.)
Capital: Minsk
Government: In transition
Population: 10,200,000
Languages: Byelorussian, Russian
Religions: Russian Orthodox, Baptist

Belgium
Area: 30,520 km² (11,784 sq. mi.)
Capital: Brussels
Government: Constitutional monarchy
Population: 9,921,910
Languages: Flemish, French
Religions: Roman Catholic, Protestant

Belize
Area: 22,960 km² (8,865 sq. mi.)
Capital: Belmopan
Government: Parliamentary democracy affiliated with United Kingdom
Population: 228,069
Languages: English, Spanish, Maya, Garifuna
Religions: Roman Catholic, Anglican, Methodist

Benin
Area: 112,620 km² (43,483 sq. mi.)
Capital: Porto-Novo
Government: Multiparty democracy
Population: 4,831,823
Languages: French, Fon, Yoruba, tribal dialects
Religions: Indigenous beliefs, Muslim, Christian

Bermuda
Area: 50 km² (19 sq. mi.)
Capital: Hamilton
Government: Dependent territory of United Kingdom
Population: 58,433
Language: English
Religions: Anglican, Roman Catholic, African Methodist

Bhutan
Area: 47,000 km² (18,147 sq. mi.)
Capital: Thimphu
Government: Monarchy
Population: 1,598,216
Languages: Dzongkha, other Tibetan dialects, Nepalese dialects
Religions: Lamaistic Buddhist, Hindu

Bolivia
Area: 1,098,580 km² (424,162 sq. mi.)
Capitals: La Paz and Sucre
Government: Republic
Population: 7,156,591
Languages: Spanish, Quechua, Aymara
Religions: Roman Catholic, Protestant

Bosnia and Herzegovina
Area: 51,129 km² (19,741 sq. mi.)
Capital: Sarajevo
Government: Republic
Population: 4,116,000
Languages: Serbian, Croatian
Religions: Muslim, Serbian Orthodox, Roman Catholic

Botswana
Area: 600,370 km² (231,803 sq. mi.)
Capital: Gaborone
Government: Parliamentary republic
Population: 1,258,392
Languages: English, Setswana
Religions: Indigenous beliefs, Christian

Brazil
Area: 8,511,970 km² (3,286,472 sq. mi.)
Capital: Brasília
Government: Federal republic
Population: 155,356,073
Languages: Portuguese, Spanish, English, French
Religion: Roman Catholic

British Virgin Islands
Area: 150 km² (58 sq. mi.)
Capital: Road Town
Government: Dependent territory of United Kingdom
Population: 12,396
Language: English
Religions: Methodist, Anglican, other Protestant faiths, Roman Catholic

Brunei
Area: 5,770 km² (2,228 sq. mi.)
Capital: Bandar Seri Begawan
Government: Constitutional sultanate
Population: 397,777
Languages: Malay, English, Chinese
Religions: Muslim, Buddhist, Christian, indigenous beliefs

Bulgaria
Area: 110,910 km² (42,822 sq. mi.)
Capital: Sofia
Government: In transition
Population: 8,910,622
Language: Bulgarian
Religions: Bulgarian Orthodox, Muslim, Jewish, Roman Catholic

Burkina Faso
Area: 274,200 km² (105,869 sq. mi.)
Capital: Ouagadougou
Government: Military
Population: 9,359,889
Languages: French, Sudanic tribal dialects
Religions: Indigenous beliefs, Muslim, Christian

Burma
See **Myanmar.**

Burundi
Area: 27,830 km² (10,745 sq. mi.)
Capital: Bujumbura
Government: Republic
Population: 5,831,233
Languages: Kirundi, French, Swahili
Religions: Roman Catholic, Indigenous beliefs, Protestant, Muslim

Cambodia
Area: 181,040 km² (69,900 sq. mi.)
Capital: Phnom Penh
Government: Disputed between National Government of Cambodia and the State of Cambodia
Population: 7,146,386
Languages: Khmer, French
Religions: Theravada Buddhist

Cameroon
Area: 475,440 km² (183,567 sq. mi.)
Capital: Yaoundé
Government: Unitary republic
Population: 11,390,374
Languages: English, French, African languages
Religions: Indigenous beliefs, Christian, Muslim

Canada
Area: 9,976,140 km² (3,851,788 sq. mi.)
Capital: Ottawa
Government: Confederation affiliated with United Kingdom
Population: 26,835,036
Languages: English, French
Religions: Roman Catholic, United Church, Anglican

Cape Verde
Area: 4,030 km² (1,556 sq. mi.)
Capital: Praia
Government: Republic
Population: 386,501
Languages: Portuguese, Crioulo
Religions: Roman Catholic and indigenous beliefs

Cayman Islands
Area: 260 km² (100 sq. mi.)
Capital: George Town
Government: Dependent territory of United Kingdom
Population: 27,489
Language: English
Religions: United Church, Anglican, Baptist, Roman Catholic

Central African Republic
Area: 622,980 km² (240,533 sq. mi.)
Capital: Bangui
Government: Military republic
Population: 2,952,382
Languages: French, Sangho, Arabic, Hunsa, Swahili
Religions: Christian (with animist beliefs), indigenous beliefs, Muslim

Chad
Area: 1,284,000 km² (495,752 sq. mi.)
Capital: N'Djamena
Government: Republic
Population: 5,122,467
Languages: French, Arabic, Sara, Sango
Religions: Muslim, Christian, indigenous beliefs/animism

Chile
Area: 756,950 km² (292,258 sq. mi.)
Capital: Santiago
Government: Republic
Population: 13,286,620
Language: Spanish
Religions: Roman Catholic, Protestant, Jewish

China
Area: 9,596,960 km² (3,705,386 sq. mi.)
Capital: Beijing
Government: Communist
Population: 1,151,486,981
Languages: Mandarin, Yue, Wu, Minbei, Minnan, Xiang, Gan, Hakka dialects, minority languages
Religions: Officially atheist; Confucianist, Taoist, Buddhist, Muslim, Christian

Christmas Island
Area: 135 km² (52 sq. mi.)
Capital: The Settlement
Government: Territory of Australia
Population: 2,278
Language: English
Religions: Buddhist, Muslim, Christian

Colombia
Area: 1,138,910 km² (439,733 sq. mi.)
Capital: Bogotá
Government: Republic
Population: 33,777,550
Language: Spanish
Religion: Roman Catholic

Comoros
Area: 2,170 km² (838 sq. mi.)
Capital: Moroni
Government: Independent republic
Population: 476,678
Languages: Arabic, French
Religions: Sunni Muslim, Roman Catholic

Congo
Area: 342,000 km² (132,046 sq. mi.)
Capital: Brazzaville
Government: Republic
Population: 2,309,444
Languages: French, Lingala, Kikongo
Religions: Christian, animist, Muslim

Cook Islands
Area: 240 km² (93 sq. mi.)
Capital: Avarua
Government: Self-governing in association with New Zealand
Population: 17,882
Language: English
Religion: Cook Islands Christian Church

Costa Rica
Area: 51,100 km² (19,730 sq. mi.)
Capital: San José
Government: Democratic republic
Population: 3,111,403
Languages: Spanish, English
Religion: Roman Catholic

Croatia
Area: 56,524 km² (21,824 sq. mi.)
Capital: Zagreb
Government: Republic
Population: 4,756,000
Language: Croatian
Religion: Roman Catholic

Cuba
Area: 110,860 km² (42,803 sq. mi.)
Capital: Havana
Government: Communist
Population: 10,732,037
Language: Spanish
Religion: Roman Catholic

Cyprus
Area: 9,250 km² (3,571 sq. mi.)
Capital: Nicosia
Government: Republic; northern part administered by Turkey
Population: 709,343
Languages: Greek, Turkish, English
Religions: Greek Orthodox, Muslim, Armenian, Maronite

The Czech Republic
Area: 78,864 km² (30,342 sq. mi.)
Capital: Prague
Government: Parliamentary democracy
Population: 10,298,731
Language: Czech
Religions: Roman Catholic, Czech Brethren

Denmark
Area: 43,070 km² (16,629 sq. mi.)
Capital: Copenhagen
Government: Constitutional monarchy
Population: 5,132,626
Languages: Danish, Faroese, Greenlandic, German
Religions: Evangelical Lutheran, other Protestant faiths, Roman Catholic

Djibouti
Area: 22,000 km² (8,494 sq. mi.)
Capital: Djibouti
Government: Republic
Population: 346,311
Languages: French, Arabic, Somali, Afar
Religions: Muslim, Christian

Dominica
Area: 750 km² (290 sq. mi.)
Capital: Roseau
Government: Parliamentary democracy
Population: 86,285
Languages: English, French patois
Religions: Roman Catholic, Methodist, Pentecostal, Seventh-Day Adventist, Baptist

Dominican Republic
Area: 48,730 km² (18,815 sq. mi.)
Capital: Santo Domingo
Government: Republic
Population: 7,384,837
Language: Spanish
Religion: Roman Catholic

Ecuador
Area: 283,560 km² (109,483 sq. mi.)
Capital: Quito
Government: Republic
Population: 10,751,648
Languages: Spanish, Indian languages (especially Quechua)
Religion: Roman Catholic

Egypt
Area: 1,001,450 km² (386,660 sq. mi.)
Capital: Cairo
Government: Republic
Population: 54,451,588
Languages: Arabic, English, French
Religions: Muslim, Coptic Christian

El Salvador
Area: 21,040 km² (8,124 sq. mi.)
Capital: San Salvador
Government: Republic
Population: 5,418,736
Languages: Spanish, Nahua
Religions: Roman Catholic, Protestant Evangelical

Equatorial Guinea
Area: 28,050 km² (10,830 sq. mi.)
Capital: Malabo
Government: Republic
Population: 378,729
Languages: Spanish, Pigdin English, Fang, Bubi, Ibo
Religions: Christian, pagan

Estonia
Area: 45,100 km² (17,413 sq. mi.)
Capital: Tallinn
Government: Republic
Population: 1,573,000
Language: Estonian
Religion: Lutheran

Ethiopia
Area: 1,221,900 km² (471,776 sq. mi.)
Capital: Addis Ababa
Government: One-party republic
Population: 53,191,127
Languages: Amharic, Tigrinya, Orominga, Guaraginga, Somali, Arabic, English
Religions: Muslim, Ethiopian Orthodox, animist

Falkland Islands
Area: 12,170 km² (4,699 sq. mi.)
Capital: Stanley
Government: Dependent territory of United Kingdom
Population: 1,968
Language: English
Religions: Anglican, Roman Catholic

Faroe Islands
Area: 1,400 km² (541 sq. mi.)
Capital: Tórshavn
Government: Self-governing overseas administrative division of Denmark
Population: 48,151
Languages: Faroese, Danish
Religion: Evangelical Lutheran

Fiji
Area: 18,270 km² (7,054 sq. mi.)
Capital: Suva
Government: Military republic
Population: 744,006
Languages: English, Fijian, Hindustani
Religions: Christian, Hindu, Muslim

Finland
Area: 337,030 km² (130,127 sq. mi.)
Capital: Helsinki
Government: Republic
Population: 4,991,131
Languages: Finnish, Swedish, Lapp, Russian
Religions: Evangelical Lutheran, Greek Orthodox

France
Area: 547,030 km² (211,208 sq. mi.)
Capital: Paris
Government: Republic
Population: 56,595,587
Languages: French, regional dialects
Religions: Roman Catholic, Protestant, Jewish, Muslim

French Guiana
Area: 91,000 km² (35,135 sq. mi.)
Capital: Cayenne
Government: Overseas department of France
Population: 101,603
Language: French
Religion: Roman Catholic

French Polynesia
Area: 4,000 km² (1,544 sq. mi.)
Capital: Papeete
Government: Overseas territory of France
Population: 195,046
Languages: French, Tahitian
Religions: Protestant, Roman Catholic

Gabon
Area: 267,670 km² (103,347 sq. mi.)
Capital: Libreville
Government: Republic
Population: 1,079,980
Languages: French, Fang, Myene, Bateke, Bapounou/Eschira, Bandjabi
Religions: Christian, animist, Muslim

The Gambia
Area: 11,300 km² (4,363 sq. mi.)
Capital: Banjul
Government: Republic
Population: 874,553
Languages: English, Mandinka, Wolof, Fula, local dialects
Religions: Muslim, Christian, indigenous beliefs

Georgia
Area: 69,699 km² (26,911 sq. mi.)
Capital: Tbilisi
Government: In transition
Population: 5,549,000
Languages: Georgian, Russian
Religions: Georgian Orthodox

Germany
Area: 356,910 km² (137,803 sq. mi.)
Capital: Berlin
Government: Federal republic
Population: 79,548,498
Language: German
Religions: Protestant, Roman Catholic

Ghana
Area: 238,540 km² (92,100 sq. mi.)
Capital: Accra
Government: Military
Population: 15,616,934
Languages: English, Akan, Moshi-Dagomba, Ewe, Ga-Adangbe
Religions: Indigenous beliefs, Muslim, Christian

Gibraltar
Area: 6.5 km² (2.5 sq. mi.)
Capital: Gibraltar
Government: Dependent territory of United Kingdom
Population: 29,613
Languages: English, Spanish, Italian, Portuguese, Russian
Religions: Roman Catholic, Anglican, Muslim, Jewish

Greece
Area: 131,940 km² (50,942 sq. mi.)
Capital: Athens
Government: Presidential parliamentary
Population: 10,042,956
Language: Greek
Religions: Greek Orthodox, Muslim

Greenland
Area: 2,175,600 km² (839,999 sq. mi.)
Capital: Nuuk (Godthåb)
Government: Self-governing overseas administrative division of Denmark
Population: 56,752
Languages: Eskimo dialects, Danish
Religion: Evangelical Lutheran

Grenada
Area: 340 km² (131 sq. mi.)
Capital: St. George's
Government: Parliamentary democracy affiliated with United Kingdom
Population: 83,812
Languages: English, French patois
Religions: Roman Catholic, Anglican, other Protestant faiths

Guadeloupe
Area: 1,780 km² (687 sq. mi.)
Capital: Basse-Terre
Government: Overseas department of France
Population: 344,897
Languages: French, Creole
Religions: Roman Catholic, Hindu, pagan African

Guatemala
Area: 108,890 km² (42,042 sq. mi.)
Capital: Guatemala City
Government: Republic
Population: 9,266,018
Languages: Spanish, Quiche, Cakchiquel, Kekchi, other Indian dialects
Religions: Roman Catholic, Protestant, traditional Mayan

Guernsey
Area: 194 km² (75 sq. mi.)
Capital: St. Peter Port
Government: British crown dependency
Population: 57,596
Languages: English, French, Norman-French
Religions: Anglican, Roman Catholic, other Protestant faiths

Guinea
Area: 245,860 km² (94,927 sq. mi.)
Capital: Conakry
Government: Republic
Population: 7,455,850
Languages: French, tribal languages
Religions: Muslim, Christian, indigenous beliefs

Guinea-Bissau
Area: 36,120 km² (13,948 sq. mi.)
Capital: Bissau
Government: Republic
Population: 1,023,544
Languages: Portuguese, Criolo, African languages
Religions: Indigenous beliefs, Muslim, Christian

Guyana
Area: 214,970 km² (83,000 sq. mi.)
Capital: Georgetown
Government: Republic
Population: 749,508
Languages: English, Amerindian dialects
Religions: Christian, Hindu, Muslim

Haiti
Area: 27,750 km² (10,714 sq. mi.)
Capital: Port-au-Prince
Government: Military republic
Population: 6,286,511
Languages: French, Creole
Religions: Roman Catholic/voodoo, Protestant

Honduras
Area: 112,090 km² (43,278 sq. mi.)
Capital: Tegucigalpa
Government: Republic
Population: 4,949,275
Languages: Spanish, Amerindian dialects
Religions: Roman Catholic, Protestant

Hong Kong
Area: 1,040 km² (402 sq. mi.)
Capital: Victoria
Government: Dependent territory of United Kingdom (until 1997)
Population: 5,855,800
Languages: Cantonese, English
Religions: Local religions, Christian

Hungary
Area: 93,030 km² (35,919 sq. mi.)
Capital: Budapest
Government: Republic
Population: 10,558,001
Language: Hungarian (Magyar)
Religions: Calvinist, Lutheran

Iceland
Area: 103,000 km² (39,768 sq. mi.)
Capital: Reykjavík
Government: Republic
Population: 259,742
Languages: Icelandic
Religions: Evangelical Lutheran, other Protestant faiths, Roman Catholic

India
Area: 3,287,590 km² (1,269,338 sq. mi.)
Capital: New Delhi
Government: Federal republic
Population: 866,351,738
Languages: Hindi, English, Bengali, Telugu, Marathi, Tamil, Urdu, Gujarati, Malayalan, Kannada, Oriya, Punjabi, Assamese, Kashmiri, Sindhi, Sanskrit, Hindustani
Religions: Hindu, Muslim, Christian, Sikh, Buddhist, Jains

Indonesia
Area: 1,904,570 km² (735,272 sq. mi.)
Capital: Jakarta
Government: Republic
Population: 193,560,494
Languages: Bahasa Indonesian, Javanese, English, Dutch
Religions: Muslim, Protestant, Roman Catholic, Hindu, Buddhist

Iran
Area: 1,648,000 km² (636,293 sq. mi.)
Capital: Teheran
Government: Theocratic republic
Population: 59,051,082
Languages: Farsi, Turk, Kurdish, Arabic, Luri, Baloch
Religions: Shi'a Muslim, Sunni Muslim, Zoroastrian, Jewish, Christian, Baha'i

Iraq
Area: 434,920 km² (167,923 sq. mi.)
Capital: Baghdad
Government: Republic
Population: 19,524,718
Languages: Arabic, Kurdish, Assyrian, Armenian
Religions: Shi'a Muslim, Sunni Muslim, Christian

Ireland
Area: 70,280 km² (27,135 sq. mi.)
Capital: Dublin
Government: Republic
Population: 3,489,165
Languages: Irish (Gaelic), English
Religions: Roman Catholic, Anglican

Israel
Area: (excluding occupied territories) 20,770 km² (8,019 sq. mi.)
Capital: Jerusalem
Government: Parliamentary democracy
Population: 4,264,605 (excluding occupied territories)
Languages: Hebrew, Arabic
Religions: Jewish, Muslim, Christian, Druze
See also **West Bank and Gaza Strip.**

Italy
Area: 301,230 km² (116,305 sq. mi.)
Capital: Rome
Government: Republic
Population: 57,772,375
Languages: Italian, German, French, Slovene
Religion: Roman Catholic

Ivory Coast
Area: 322,460 km² (124,502 sq. mi.)
Capital: Abidjan (also Yamoussoukro)
Government: Republic
Population: 12,977,909
Languages: French, Dioula, tribal languages
Religions: Indigenous beliefs, Muslim, Christian

Jamaica
Area: 10,990 km² (4,243 sq. mi.)
Capital: Kingston
Government: Parliamentary democracy affiliated with United Kingdom
Population: 2,489,353
Languages: English, Creole
Religions: Protestant, Roman Catholic, spiritualist cults

Japan
Area: 377,835 km² (145,882 sq. mi.)
Capital: Tokyo
Government: Constitutional monarchy
Population: 124,017,137
Language: Japanese
Religions: Shinto, Buddhist, Christian

Jersey
Area: 117 km² (45 sq. mi.)
Capital: Saint Helier
Government: British crown dependency
Population: 84,331
Languages: English, French, Norman-French
Religions: Anglican, other Protestant faiths, Roman Catholic

Jordan
Area: 91,880 km² (35,475 sq. mi.) (excluding West Bank)
Capital: Amman
Government: Constitutional monarchy
Population: 3,412,553 (excluding West Bank)
Languages: Arabic, English
Religions: Sunni Muslim, Christian

Kazakhstan
Area: 2,717,428 km² (1,049,200 sq. mi.)
Capital: Alma Alta
Government: In transition
Population: 16,538,000
Languages: Kazakh, Russian
Religion: Muslim

Kenya
Area: 582,650 km² (224,961 sq. mi.)
Capital: Nairobi
Government: One-party republic
Population: 25,241,978
Languages: English, Swahili, local languages
Religions: Protestant, Roman Catholic, indigenous beliefs, Muslim

Kiribati
Area: 710 km² (274 sq. mi.)
Capital: Tarawa
Government: Republic
Population: 71,137
Languages: English, Gilbertese
Religions: Roman Catholic, Protestant, Seventh-Day Adventist, Baha'i

Korea, North
Area: 120,540 km² (46,540 sq. mi.)
Capital: Pyongyang
Government: Communist
Population: 21,814,656
Language: Korean
Religions: Buddhist, Confucianist

Korea, South
Area: 98,480 km² (38,023 sq. mi.)
Capital: Seoul
Government: Republic
Population: 43,134,386
Language: Korean
Religions: Confucianist, Christian, Buddhist, Shamanist, Chondokyo

Kuwait
Area: 17,820 km² (6,880 sq. mi.)
Capital: Kuwait
Government: Nominal constitutional monarchy
Population: 2,204,400
Languages: Arabic, English
Religions: Sunni Muslim, Shi'a Muslim, Christian, Hindu, Parsi

Kyrgyzstan
Area: 198,509 km² (76,642 sq. mi.)
Capital: Frunze
Government: In transition
Population: 4,372,000
Languages: Kirghiz, Russian
Religions: Muslim

Laos
Area: 236,800 km² (91,428 sq. mi.)
Capital: Vientiane
Government: Communist
Population: 4,113,223
Languages: Lao, French, English
Religions: Buddhist, animist

Latvia
Area: 63,701 km² (24,595 sq. mi.)
Capital: Riga
Government: Republic
Population: 2,681,000
Languages: Latvian
Religions: Lutheran, Russian Orthodox, Catholic

Lebanon
Area: 10,400 km² (4,015 sq. mi.)
Capital: Beirut
Government: Republic
Population: 3,384,626
Languages: Arabic, French, Armenian, English
Religions: Muslim and Christian, each divided into sects (17 in all)

Lesotho
Area: 30,350 km² (11,718 sq. mi.)
Capital: Maseru
Government: Constitutional monarchy (military regime)
Population: 1,801,174
Languages: Sesotho, English, Zulu, Xhosa
Religions: Christian, indigenous beliefs

Liberia
Area: 111,370 km² (43,000 sq. mi.)
Capital: Monrovia
Government: Republic
Population: 2,730,446
Languages: English, Niger-Congo languages
Religions: Indigenous beliefs, Christian, Muslim

Libya
Area: 1,759,540 km2 (679,358 sq. mi.)
Capital: Tripoli
Government: Military dictatorship
Population: 4,350,742
Languages: Arabic, Italian, English
Religion: Sunni Muslim

Liechtenstein
Area: 160 km² (62 sq. mi.)
Capital: Vaduz
Government: Constitutional monarchy
Population: 28,476
Languages: German, Alemannic
Religions: Roman Catholic, Protestant

Lithuania
Area: 65,190 km² (25,170 sq. mi.)
Capital: Vilnius
Government: Republic
Population: 3,690,000
Languages: Lithuanian
Religions: Roman Catholic

Luxembourg
Area: 2,586 km² (998 sq. mi.)
Capital: Luxembourg
Government: Constitutional monarchy
Population: 388,017
Languages: Luxembourgish, German, French, English
Religions: Roman Catholic, Protestant, English

Macau
Area: 16 km² (6 sq. mi.)
Capital: Macau
Government: Overseas territory of Portugal until 1999
Population: 446,262
Languages: Portuguese, Cantonese
Religions: Buddhist, Roman Catholic

*†Macedonia
Area: 25,713 km² (9,928 sq. mi.)
Capital: Skopje
Government: Republic
Population: 2,033,964
Language: Macedonian
Religions: Eastern Orthodox, Muslim

Madagascar
Area: 587,040 km² (226,656 sq. mi.)
Capital: Antananarivo
Government: Republic
Population: 12,185,318
Languages: French, Malagasy
Religions: Indigenous beliefs, Christian, Muslim

Malawi
Area: 118,480 km² (45,745 sq. mi.)
Capital: Lilongwe
Government: One-party state
Population: 9,438,462
Languages: English, Chichewa, Tombuka
Religions: Protestant, Roman Catholic, Muslim, indigenous beliefs

Malaysia
Area: 329,750 km² (127,316 sq. mi.)
Capital: Kuala Lumpur
Government: Constitutional monarchy with hereditary rulers in peninsular states
Population: 17,981,698
Languages: Malay, English, Chinese dialects, Tamil, Hakka dialects, tribal languages
Religions: Muslim, Buddhist, Hindu, Confucianist, Christian

Maldives
Area: 300 km² (116 sq. mi.)
Capital: Male
Government: Republic
Population: 226,200
Languages: Divehi, English
Religion: Sunni Muslim

Mali
Area: 1,240,000 km² (478,764 sq. mi.)
Capital: Bamako
Government: Republic
Population: 8,338,542
Languages: French, Bambara
Religions: Muslim, indigenous beliefs, Christian

Malta
Area: 320 km² (124 sq. mi.)
Capital: Valletta
Government: Parliamentary democracy
Population: 356,427
Languages: Maltese, English
Religion: Roman Catholic

* These countries have not been recognized by the United States.

† The name Macedonia is in dispute.

Man, Isle of
Area: 588 km² (227 sq. mi.)
Capital: Douglas
Government: British crown dependency
Population: 64,075
Languages: English, Manx Gaelic
Religions: Anglican, other Protestant faiths, Roman Catholic

Martinique
Area: 1,100 km² (425 sq. mi.)
Capital: Fort-de-France
Government: Overseas department of France
Population: 345,180
Languages: French, Creole patois
Religions: Roman Catholic, Hindu, pagan African

Mauritania
Area: 1,030,700 km² (397,953 sq. mi.)
Capital: Nouakchott
Government: Military republic
Population: 1,995,755
Languages: Hasaniya Arabic, French, Toucouleur, Fula, Sarakole, Wolof
Religion: Muslim

Mauritius
Area: 1,860 km² (718 sq. mi.)
Capital: Port Louis
Government: Parliamentary democracy affiliated with United Kingdom
Population: 1,081,000
Languages: English, Creole, French, Hindi, Urdu, Hakka, Bojpoori
Religions: Hindu, Roman Catholic, Anglican, Muslim

Mayotte
Area: 375 km² (145 sq. mi.)
Capital: Dzaoudzi
Government: Territorial collectivity of France
Population: 75,027
Languages: Mahorian, French
Religions: Muslim, Christian

Mexico
Area: 1,972,550 km² (761,602 sq. mi.)
Capital: Mexico City
Government: Federal republic
Population: 90,007,304
Language: Spanish
Religions: Roman Catholic, Protestant

Moldova
Area: 33,701 km² (13,012 sq. mi.)
Capital: Kishinev
Government: In transition
Population: 4,341,000
Language: Romanian
Religions: Russian Orthodox, Seventh-Day Adventist

Monaco
Area: 1.9 km² (.7 sq. mi.)
Capital: Monaco
Government: Constitutional monarchy
Population: 29,712
Languages: French, English, Italian, Monegasque
Religion: Roman Catholic

Mongolia
Area: 1,565,000 km² (604,247 sq. mi.)
Capital: Ulaanbaatar
Government: In transition
Population: 2,247,068
Languages: Khalkha Mongol, Turkic, Russian, Chinese
Religions: Tibetan Buddhist, Muslim

Montserrat
Area: 100 km² (39 sq. mi.)
Capital: Plymouth
Government: Dependent territory of United Kingdom
Population: 12,504
Language: English
Religions: Anglican, other Protestant faiths, Roman Catholic

Morocco
Area: 446,550 km² (172,413 sq. mi.)
Capital: Rabat
Government: Constitutional monarchy
Population: 26,181,889
Languages: Arabic, French, Berber dialects
Religions: Muslim, Christian, Jewish

Mozambique
Area: 801,950 km² (309,633 sq. mi.)
Capital: Maputo
Government: Republic
Population: 15,113,282
Languages: Portuguese, indigenous languages
Religions: Indigenous beliefs, Christian, Muslim

Myanmar
Area: 676,550 km² (261,216 sq. mi.)
Capital: Yangon
Government: Military
Population: 42,112,082
Languages: Burmese, ethnic languages
Religions: Buddhist, Christian, Muslim, animist beliefs

Namibia
Area: 824,290 km² (318,258 sq. mi.)
Capital: Windhoek
Government: Republic
Population: 1,520,504
Languages: Afrikaans, German, English, indigenous languages
Religions: Christian, indigenous beliefs

Nauru
Area: 20 km² (8 sq. mi.)
Capital: Yaren
Government: Republic
Population: 9,333
Languages: Nauruan, English
Religions: Protestant, Roman Catholic

Nepal
Area: 140,800 km² (54,363 sq. mi.)
Capital: Kathmandu
Government: Constitutional monarchy
Population: 19,611,900
Languages: Nepali, local languages
Religions: Hindu, Buddhist, Muslim

Netherlands
Area: 37,310 km² (14,405 sq. mi.)
Capital: Amsterdam and The Hague
Government: Constitutional monarchy
Population: 15,022,393
Language: Dutch
Religions: Roman Catholic, Protestant

Netherlands Antilles
Area: 960 km² (371 sq. mi.)
Capital: Willemstad (on Curacao)
Government: Autonomous territory of Netherlands
Population: 183,872
Languages: Dutch, Papiamento, English, Spanish
Religions: Roman Catholic, Protestant, Jewish, Seventh-Day Adventist

New Caledonia
Area: 19,060 km² (7,359 sq. mi.)
Capital: Nouméa
Government: Overseas territory of France
Population: 171,559
Languages: French, Melanesian-Polynesian dialects
Religions: Roman Catholic, Protestant

New Zealand
Area: 268,680 km² (103,737 sq. mi.)
Capital: Wellington
Government: Parliamentary democracy affiliated with United Kingdom
Population: 3,308,973
Languages: English, Maori
Religions: Anglican, Presbyterian, Roman Catholic

Nicaragua
Area: 129,494 km² (49,998 sq. mi.)
Capital: Managua
Government: Republic
Population: 3,751,884
Languages: Spanish, English, Amerindian dialects
Religion: Roman Catholic

Niger
Area: 1,267,000 km² (489,189 sq. mi.)
Capital: Niamey
Government: Republic (under military control)
Population: 8,154,145
Languages: French, Hausa, Djerma
Religions: Muslim, indigenous beliefs, Christian

Nigeria
Area: 923,770 km² (356,668 sq. mi.)
Capital: Lagos
Government: Military
Population: 122,470,574
Languages: English, Hausa, Yoruba, Ibo, Fulani
Religions: Muslim, Christian, indigenous beliefs

Niue
Area: 260 km² (100 sq. mi.)
Capital: Alofi
Government: Self-governing territory affiliated with New Zealand
Population: 1,908
Languages: Polynesian (Tongan-Samoan dialect), English
Religions: Ekalesia Nieu, Mormon

Norfolk Island
Area: 40 km² (15.4 sq. mi.)
Capital: Kingston
Government: Territory of Australia
Population: 2,576
Languages: English, Norfolk
Religions: Anglican, other Protestant faiths, Roman Catholic, Seventh-Day Adventist

Norway
Area: 324,220 km² (125,181 sq. mi.)
Capital: Oslo
Government: Constitutional monarchy
Population: 4,273,442
Languages: Norwegian, Lapp, Finnish
Religions: Evangelical Lutheran, other Protestant faiths, Roman Catholic

Oman
Area: 212,460 km² (82,031 sq. mi.)
Capital: Muscat
Government: Absolute monarchy
Population: 1,534,011
Languages: Arabic, English, Baluchi, Urdu
Religions: Ibadhi Muslim, Sunni Muslim, Shi'a Muslim, Hindu

Pakistan
Area: 803,940 km² (310,401 sq. mi.)
Capital: Islamabad
Government: Federal republic
Population: 117,490,278
Languages: Urdu, English, Punjabi, Sindhi, Pushtu, Baluchi
Religions: Muslim, Christian, Hindu

Panama
Area: 78,200 km² (30,193 sq. mi.)
Capital: Panama
Government: Centralized republic
Population: 2,476,281
Languages: Spanish, English
Religions: Roman Catholic, Protestant

Papua New Guinea
Area: 461,690 km² (178,259 sq. mi.)
Capital: Port Moresby
Government: Parliamentary democracy affiliated with United Kingdom
Population: 3,913,186
Languages: Motu, local dialects, English
Religions: Roman Catholic, Protestant

Paraguay
Area: 406,750 km² (157,046 sq. mi.)
Capital: Asunción
Government: Republic
Population: 4,798,739
Languages: Spanish, Guarani
Religions: Roman Catholic, Mennonite, other Protestant faiths

Peru
Area: 1,285,220 km² (496,223 sq. mi.)
Capital: Lima
Government: Republic
Population: 22,361,785
Languages: Spanish, Quechua, Aymara
Religion: Roman Catholic

Philippines
Area: 300,000 km² (115,830 sq. mi.)
Capital: Manila
Government: Republic
Population: 65,758,788
Languages: Philipino (Tagalog), English
Religions: Roman Catholic, Muslim, Buddhist

Poland
Area: 312,680 km² (120,727 sq. mi.)
Capital: Warsaw
Government: Democratic state
Population: 37,799,638
Language: Polish
Religions: Roman Catholic, Russian Orthodox, Catholic

Portugal
Area: 92,080 km² (35,552 sq. mi.)
Capital: Lisbon
Government: Republic
Population: 10,387,617
Language: Portuguese
Religions: Roman Catholic, Protestant

Qatar
Area: 11,000 km² (4,247 sq. mi.)
Capital: Doha
Government: Traditional monarchy
Population: 518,478
Languages: Arabic, English
Religion: Muslim

Réunion
Area: 2,510 km² (969 sq. mi.)
Capital: Saint-Denis
Government: Overseas department of France
Population: 607,086
Languages: French, Creole
Religion: Roman Catholic

Romania
Area: 237,500 km² (91,699 sq. mi.)
Capital: Bucharest
Government: In transition
Population: 23,397,054
Languages: Romanian, Hungarian, German
Religions: Romanian Orthodox, Roman Catholic, Protestant, Greek Catholic

Russia
Area: 17,075,352 km² (6,592,800 sq. mi.)
Capital: Moscow
Government: In transition
Population: 147,386,000
Language: Russian
Religions: Russian Orthodox, Baptist, Jewish

Rwanda
Area: 26,340 km² (10,170 sq. mi.)
Capital: Kigali
Government: Republic (under military control)
Population: 7,902,644
Languages: Kinyarwanda, French, Kiswahili
Religions: Roman Catholic, Protestant, indigenous beliefs, Muslim

St. Helena
Area: 410 km² (158 sq. mi.)
Capital: Jamestown
Government: Dependent territory of the United Kingdom
Population: 6,695
Language: English
Religions: Anglican, other Protestant faiths, Roman Catholic

St. Kitts and Nevis
Area: 269 km² (104 sq. mi.)
Capital: Basseterre
Government: Constitutional monarchy affiliated with United Kingdom
Population: 40,293
Language: English
Religions: Anglican, other Protestant faiths, Roman Catholic

St. Lucia
Area: 620 km² (239 sq. mi.)
Capital: Castries
Government: Parliamentary democracy affiliated with United Kingdom
Population: 153,075
Languages: English, French patois
Religions: Roman Catholic, Protestant, Anglican

St. Pierre and Miquelan
Area: 242 km² (93 sq. mi.)
Capital: Saint-Pierre
Government: Territorial collectivity of France
Population: 6,356
Language: French
Religion: Roman Catholic

St. Vincent and the Grenadines
Area: 340 km² (131 sq. mi.)
Capital: Kingstown
Government: Constitutional monarchy affiliated with United Kingdom
Population: 114,221
Languages: English; French patois
Religions: Anglican, other Protestant faiths, Roman Catholic, Seventh-Day Adventist

San Marino
Area: 60 km² (23 sq. mi.)
Capital: San Marino
Government: Republic
Population: 23,264
Language: Italian
Religion: Roman Catholic

Sao Tome and Principe
Area: 960 km² (371 sq. mi.)
Capital: São Tomé and Principe
Government: Republic
Population: 128,499
Language: Portuguese
Religions: Roman Catholic, Evangelical Protestant, Seventh-Day Adventist

Saudi Arabia
Area: 2,149,690 km² (829,995 sq. mi.)
Capital: Riyadh
Government: Monarchy
Population: 17,869,558
Language: Arabic
Religion: Muslim

Senegal
Area: 196,190 km² (75,748 sq. mi.)
Capital: Dakar
Government: Republic
Population: 7,952,657
Languages: French, Wolof, Pulaar, Diola, Mandingo
Religions: Muslim, indigenous beliefs, Christian

Seychelles
Area: 455 km² (176 sq. mi.)
Capital: Victoria
Government: Republic
Population: 68,932
Languages: English, French, Creole
Religions: Roman Catholic, Anglican

Sierra Leone
Area: 71,740 km² (27,699 sq. mi.)
Capital: Freetown
Government: One-party republic
Population: 4,274,543
Languages: English, Mende, Krio, Temne
Religions: Muslim, indigenous beliefs, Christian

Singapore
Area: 633 km² (244 sq. mi.)
Capital: Singapore
Government: Republic
Population: 2,756,330
Languages: Chinese, Tamil, Malay, English
Religions: Buddhist, Muslim, Christian, Hindu, Sikh, Taoist Confucianist

Slovakia
Area: 49,035 km (18,928 sq. mi.)
Capital: Bratislava
Government: Parliamentary democracy
Population: 5,268,935
Language: Slovak
Religions: Roman Catholic, Greek Catholic, Protestant, Jewish, Orthodox

Slovenia
Area: 20,246 km² (7,817 sq. mi.)
Capital: Ljubljana
Government: Republic
Population: 2 million
Language: Slovene
Religions: Roman Catholic, Protestant

Solomon Islands
Area: 28,450 km² (10,985 sq. mi.)
Capital: Honiara
Government: Independent parliamentary state within British Commonwealth
Population: 347,115
Languages: Melanesian pigdin, English, local dialects
Religions: Anglican, Roman Catholic, other Protestant faiths

Somalia
Area: 637,660 km² (246,201 sq. mi.)
Capital: Mogadishu
Government: Republic
Population: 6,709,161
Languages: Somali, Arabic, Italian, English
Religion: Sunni Muslim

South Africa
Area: 1,221,040 km² (471,444 sq. mi.)
Capital: Pretoria, Cape Town
Government: Republic
Population: 40,600,518
Languages: Afrikaans, English, Zulu, Xhosa, Tswana
Religions: Christian, Hindu, Muslim

Spain
Area: 504,750 km² (194,884 sq. mi.)
Capital: Madrid
Government: Parliamentary monarchy
Population: 39,384,516
Languages: Castilian Spanish, Catalan, Galician, Basque
Religion: Roman Catholic

Sri Lanka
Area: 65,610 km² (25,332 sq. mi.)
Capital: Colombo
Government: Republic
Population: 17,423,736
Languages: Sinhala, Tamil, English
Religions: Buddhist, Hindu, Christian, Muslim

Sudan
Area: 2,505,810 km² (967,493 sq. mi.)
Capital: Khartoum
Government: Military
Population: 27,220,088
Languages: Arabic, Nubian, Ta Bedawie, Nilotic and Nilo-Hamitic dialects, Sudanic dialects, English
Religions: Sunni Muslim, indigenous beliefs, Christian

Suriname
Area: 163,270 km² (63,039 sq. mi.)
Capital: Paramaribo
Government: Military republic
Population: 402,385
Languages: Dutch, English, Sranan Tongo, Javanese
Religions: Hindu, Muslim, Roman Catholic, Protestant

Svalbard
Area: 62,049 km² (23,597 sq. mi.)
Capital: Longyearbyen
Government: Territory of Norway
Population: 3,942
Languages: Russian, Norwegian
Religion: Evangelical Lutheran

Swaziland
Area: 17,360 km2 (6,703 sq. mi.)
Capital: Mbabane
Government: Independent monarchy within British Commonwealth
Population: 859,336
Languages: English, siSwati
Religions: Christian, indigenous beliefs

Sweden
Area: 449,960 km² (173,729 sq. mi.)
Capital: Stockholm
Government: Constitutional monarchy
Population: 8,564,317
Languages: Swedish, Lapp, Finnish
Religions: Evangelical Lutheran, Roman Catholic

Switzerland
Area: 41,290 km² (15,942 sq. mi.)
Capital: Bern
Government: Federal republic
Population: 6,783,961
Languages: German, French, Italian, Romansch
Religions: Roman Catholic, Protestant, Jewish

Syria
Area: 185,180 km² (71,498 sq. mi.)
Capital: Damascus
Government: Military republic
Population: 12,965,996
Languages: Arabic, Kurdish, Armenian, Aramaic, Circassian, French
Religions: Sunni Muslim, Alawite, Druze, other Muslim sects, Christian

Taiwan
Area: 35,980 km² (13,892 sq. mi.)
Capital: Taipei
Government: Republic
Population: 20,658,702
Languages: Mandarin Chinese; Taiwanese and Hakka dialects
Religions: Buddhist, Confucianist, Taoist, Christian

Tajikistan
Area: 139,909 km² (54,019 sq. mi.)
Capital: Dushanbe
Government: In transition
Population: 5,112,000
Languages: Tadzhik, Russian
Religion: Muslim

Tanzania
Area: 945,090 km2 (364,899 sq. mi.)
Capital: Dar es Salaam
Government: One-party republic
Population: 26,869,175
Languages: Swahili, English
Religions: Christian, Muslim, indigenous beliefs

Thailand
Area: 514,000 km² (198,455 sq. mi.)
Capital: Bangkok
Government: Constitutional monarchy under martial law
Population: 56,814,069
Languages: Thai, English, local dialects
Religions: Buddhist, Muslim

Togo
Area: 56,790 km² (21,927 sq. mi.)
Capital: Lomé
Government: One-party republic
Population: 3,810,616
Languages: French, Ewe, Mina, Dagomba, Kabyè
Religions: Indigenous beliefs, Christian, Muslim

Tokelau
Area: 10 km² (4 sq. mi.)
Capital: None (various local government agencies)
Government: Territory of New Zealand
Population: 1,700
Languages: Tokelauan, English
Religions: Congregational Christian Church, Roman Catholic

Tonga
Area: 748 km² (289 sq. mi.)
Capital: Nuku'alofa
Government: Constitutional monarchy
Population: 102,272
Languages: Tongan, English
Religion: Christian

Trinidad and Tobago
Area: 5,130 km² (1,981 sq. mi.)
Capital: Port-of-Spain
Government: Parliamentary democracy
Population: 1,285,297
Languages: English, Hindi, French, Spanish
Religions: Roman Catholic, Hindu, Protestant, Muslim

Tunisia
Area: 163,610 km² (63,170 sq. mi.)
Capital: Tunis
Government: Republic
Population: 8,276,096
Languages: Arabic, French
Religions: Muslim, Christian, Jewish

Turkey
Area: 780,580 km² (301,382 sq. mi.)
Capital: Ankara
Government: Republican parliamentary democracy
Population: 58,580,993
Languages: Turkish, Kurdish, Arabic
Religions: Muslim (mostly Sunni), Christian, Jewish

Turkmenistan
Area: 488,000 km² (188,417 sq. mi.)
Capital: Ashkhabad
Government: In transition
Population: 3,621,700
Languages: Turkmen, Russian
Religion: Sunni Muslim

Turks and Caicos Islands
Area: 430 km² (166 sq. mi.)
Capital: Grand Turk (Cockburn Town)
Government: Dependent territory of United Kingdom
Population: 9,983
Language: English
Religions: Baptist, Methodist, Anglican, Seventh-Day Adventist

Tuvalu
Area: 26 km² (10 sq. mi.)
Capital: Funafuti
Government: Democracy affiliated with United Kingdom
Population: 9,317
Languages: Tuvaluan, English
Religion: Protestant

Uganda
Area: 236,040 km² (91,135 sq. mi.)
Capital: Kampala
Government: One-party republic
Population: 18,690,070
Languages: English, Luganda, Swahili, Bantu and Nilotic languages
Religions: Roman Catholic, Protestant, Muslim, indigenous beliefs

Ukraine
Area: 603,729 km² (233,100 sq. mi.)
Capital: Kiev
Government: In transition
Population: 51,704,000
Languages: Ukrainian, Russian
Religions: Russian Orthodox, Baptist, Roman Catholic, Jewish

United Arab Emirates
Area: 83,600 km² (32,278 sq. mi.)
Capital: Abu Dhabi
Government: Federation of seven emirates
Population: 2,389,759
Languages: Arabic, Farsi, English, Hindi, Urdu
Religions: Muslim, Christian, Hindu

United Kingdom
Area: 244,820 km² (94,525 sq. mi.)
Capital: London
Government: Constitutional monarchy
Population: 57,515,307
Languages: English, Welsh, Scottish Gaelic
Religions: Anglican, other Protestant faiths, Roman Catholic, Jewish

United States
Area: 9,372,610 km² (3,618,765 sq. mi.)
Capital: Washington, D.C.
Government: Federal Republic
Population: 252,502,000
Languages: English, Spanish
Religions: Protestant, Roman Catholic, Jewish

Uruguay
Area: 176,220 km² (68,039 sq. mi.)
Capital: Montevideo
Government: Republic
Population: 3,121,101
Language: Spanish
Religions: Roman Catholic, Protestant, Jewish

Uzbekistan
Area: 447,293 km² (172,700 sq. mi.)
Capital: Tashkent
Government: In transition
Population: 19,906,000
Languages: Uzbek, Russian
Religion: Muslim

Vanuatu
Area: 14,760 km² (5,699 sq. mi.)
Capital: Port-Vila
Government: Republic
Population: 170,319
Languages: English, French, Bislama
Religion: Christian

Vatican City
Area: 0.438 km² (108.7 acres)
Capital: Vatican City
Government: Independent papal state
Population: 738
Languages: Italian, Latin
Religion: Roman Catholic

Venezuela
Area: 912,050 km² (352,143 sq. mi.)
Capital: Caracas
Government: Republic
Population: 20,189,361
Languages: Spanish, Amerindian dialects
Religion: Roman Catholic

Vietnam
Area: 329,560 km² (127,243 sq. mi.)
Capital: Hanoi
Government: Communist
Population: 67,568,033
Languages: Vietnamese, French, Chinese, English, Khmer, tribal dialects
Religions: Buddhist, Confucianist, Taoist, Roman Catholic, indigenous beliefs, Muslim, Protestant

Wallis and Futuna
Area: 274 km² (106 sq. mi.)
Capital: Mata-Utu
Government: Overseas territory of France
Population: 16,590
Languages: French, Wallisian
Religion: Roman Catholic

West Bank and Gaza Strip
Area: 6,240 km² (2,410 sq. mi.)
Capital: None
Government: Israeli military rule
Population: 1,728,334 (excluding Israeli settlers)
Languages: Arabic, Hebrew, English
Religions: Muslim, Jewish, Christian

Western Sahara
Area: 2,860 km² (1,097 sq. mi.)
Capital: None
Government: Moroccan administrative protectorate
Population: 196,737
Languages: Hassaniya Arabic, Moroccan Arabic
Religion: Muslim

Western Samoa
Area: 2,860 km² (1,104 sq. mi.)
Capital: Apia
Government: Constitutional monarchy
Population: 190,346
Languages: Samoan, English
Religions: Congregational, Roman Catholic, other Protestant faiths

Yemen
Area: 527,970 km² (203,849 sq. mi.)
Capital: Sanaa
Government: Republic
Population: 10,062,633
Language: Arabic
Religions: Muslim, Christian, Hindu

*Yugoslavia, Federal Republic of
(consists of Serbia, the largest republic of preindependence Yugoslavia, and Montenegro, the smallest republic)
Area: 134,563 sq. km² (51,955 sq. mi.)
Capital: Belgrade
Government: Republic
Population: 10.5 million (1991 census)
Languages: Serbian, Hungarian (Vojvodina), Albanian (Kosovo), Montenegrin
Religions: Serbian Orthodox, Muslim, Roman Catholic

Zaire
Area: 2,345,410 km² (905,563 sq. mi.)
Capital: Kinshasa
Government: Republic
Population: 37,832,407
Languages: French, Lingala, Swahili, Kingwana, Kikongo, Tshiluba
Religions: Roman Catholic, Protestant, Kimbanguist, Muslim, indigenous beliefs

Zambia
Area: 752,610 km² (290,583 sq. mi.)
Capital: Lusaka
Government: Multiparty state
Population: 8,445,724
Languages: English, local languages and dialects
Religions: Christian, Muslim, Hindu, indigenous beliefs

Zimbabwe
Area: 390,580 km² (150,803 sq. mi.)
Capital: Harare
Government: Parliamentary democracy
Population: 10,720,459
Languages: English, Shona, Sindebele
Religions: Indigenous/Christian beliefs, Christian, indigenous beliefs, Muslim

* These countries have not been recognized by the United States.

Great Events in World History

1,600,000 B.C. Earliest human-like ancestors.

250,000 B.C. Earliest *Homo sapiens*.

70,000 B.C. Neanderthals use stone tools and fire.

40,000 B.C. Ice Age ends; Cro-Magnons migrate into Europe.

30,000 B.C. Neanderthals disappear.

28,000 B.C. Asians cross land bridge between Asia and America.

20,000 B.C. European cave art exists.

12,000 B.C. Dog domesticated from Asian wolf.

8000 B.C. Agriculture develops in Near East.

7000 B.C. Jericho settled and soon walled to protect from attack.

6500 B.C. Wheel invented by Sumerians.

6000 B.C. First true pottery made.

5000 B.C. Copper, first shapable metal, smelted in Persia.

4236 B.C. Earliest date on Egyptian calendar.

3760 B.C. Earliest date on Jewish calendar.

3600 B.C. Bronze made in southwestern Asia.

3100 B.C. Egypt united under first dynasty.

3000 B.C. Phoenicians migrate to eastern Mediterranean.

2780 B.C. First Egyptian pyramid built.

2700 B.C. Cheops builds Great Pyramid at Giza.

2697 B.C. Huang-ti becomes "Yellow Emperor" of China.

2640 B.C. Legendary Empress Si Ling-chi introduces silk production in China.

2340 B.C. Sargon establishes Semitic and Sumerian civilizations.

2150 B.C. Aryans invade Indus Valley.

2000 B.C. Bronze age begins in Europe.

1760 B.C. Shang dynasty is founded in China.

1750 B.C. Hammurabi, Babylonian king, issues code of laws.

1400 B.C. Iron Age begins in Asia.

1250 B.C. Exodus of Israelites from Egypt.

1193 B.C. Greeks destroy city of Troy.

1100 B.C. Pa-out-She, Chinese scholar, compiles first dictionary.

1050 B.C. Dorian tribes invade Peloponnesus.

1000 B.C. Hebrews establish Jerusalem as capital of Israel.

994 B.C. Teutons migrate to Rhine River area.

815 B.C. Carthage is founded by Phoenicians.

776 B.C. First Olympic Games are held in Greece.

753 B.C. Rome is founded.

580 B.C. King Nebuchadnezzar builds Hanging Gardens of Babylon.

563 B.C. Buddha is born.

559 B.C. Cyrus establishes Persian Empire.

551 B.C. Confucius is born.

508 B.C. Cleisthenes introduces democratic government in Athens.

460 B.C. Pericles establishes democracy in Athens.

450 B.C. Herodotus becomes known as father of history.

336 B.C. Alexander III, king of Macedonia, begins world conquest.

300 B.C. Meng-Tse spreads philosophy of Confucius in Orient.

236 B.C. Asoka, emperor of India, becomes Buddhist missionary.

218 B.C. Hannibal leads army from Spain over Alps to Italy.

215 B.C. Great Wall of China is built.

63 B.C. Cicero, orator, compiles record of Roman life.

55 B.C. Julius Caesar conquers Gaul, invades Britain.

27 B.C. Caesar Augustus becomes first Roman emperor.

5 B.C. Jesus Christ is born.

A.D. 30 Jesus is executed.

A.D. 32 Saul of Tarsus begins early Christian missionary work.

A.D. 64 Rome under Nero is partly destroyed by fire.

A.D. 79 Eruption of Vesuvius destroys Pompeii.

A.D. 132 Bar-Kokhba leads revolt against Rome and makes Israel independent.

A.D. 250 Mani founds Manichaeism, religion popular in Middle Ages.

A.D. 268 Goths invade Greece.

A.D. 312 Constantine becomes first Christian emperor of Rome.

A.D. 370 Asian Huns invade Europe.

A.D. 391 Augustine begins work as founder of Christian theology.

A.D. 406 Vandals invade Gaul; Romans leave Britain.

A.D. 410 Goths sack Rome.

A.D. 425 Angles, Saxons, and Jutes invade Britain.

A.D. 433 Attila the Hun begins reign.

A.D. 476 Goths depose Western Roman emperor, Romulas Augustus; Middle Ages begin.

A.D. 550 Justinian codifies Roman law in Corpus Juris Civilis.

A.D. 570 Muhammad is born at Mecca.

A.D. 620 Vikings invade Ireland.

A.D. 632 Muhammad dies.

A.D. 634 Muslims begin conquest of Near East and Africa.

A.D. 711 Moors invade Spain.

A.D. 768 Reign of Charlemagne begins.

A.D. 800 Charlemagne is crowned Holy Roman emperor.

A.D. 814 Arabic numerals are established.

A.D. 862 Viking Russ tribe seizes control of northern Russia.

A.D. 874 Vikings settle Iceland.

A.D. 900 Spain begins to drive out Moors.

A.D. 932 Printed books from woodblocks are developed in China.

A.D. 936 Otto I establishes Holy Roman Empire.

A.D. 981 Eric the Red begins settlement of Greenland.

A.D. 995 Fugiware Michiaga founds Japanese Golden Age.

A.D. 1000 Vikings begin exploration of North America.

1021 Muslim Druse sect is founded by Caliph al-Hakim.

1054 Byzantine Empire breaks with Holy Roman Church; Abdallah ben Yassim spreads Islamic culture in Africa.

1066 Normans, led by William the Conqueror, conquer Britain.

1096 First Crusade is launched to oust Muslims from Holy Land.

1148 Second Crusade begins.

1156 Civil wars are fought in Japan.

1161 Chinese use explosives in warfare.

1162 Thomas à Becket becomes archbishop of Canterbury.

1189 Last recorded Viking voyage to North America.

1190 Genghis Khan begins conquest of Asia.

1204 Crusaders capture and sack Constantinople.

1210 Mongols invade China; Francis of Assisi founds Franciscan religious order.

1215 England's Magna Carta is signed by King John.

1228 Sixth Crusade results in capture of Jerusalem.

1240 Mongols capture Moscow, destroy Kiev.

1259 Thomas Aquinas develops official Roman Catholic philosophy.

1260 Kublai Khan founds Yuan dynasty in China.

1264 Simon de Montfort founds House of Commons in Parliament.

1270 Gregorius Bar-Hebraeus writes a history of the world.

1271 Marco Polo leaves for China to visit Kublai Khan.

1274 Mongols attempt invasion of Japan but fail.

1291 Crusades end as Muslims rout Christians in Palestine.

1295 King Edward I summons first representative Parliament.

1336 Civil war lasting until 1392 begins in Japan.

1337 Hundred Years' War between England and France begins.

1347 Bubonic plague spreads from China to Cyprus.

1348 Black Death (plague) spreads to England.

1351 Plague reaches Russia; Europe's toll tops 25 million.

1363 Tamerlane begins conquest of Asia.

1368 Mongol dynasty ends in China; Ming dynasty begins.

1390 Turks conquer Asia Minor.

1402 Tamerlane conquers Ottoman Empire.

1419 Henry the Navigator begins period of African explorations.

1431 Jeanne d'Arc is burned as a witch at Rouen.

1453 Hundred Years' War ends; fall of Constantinople ends Byzantine Empire; Middle Ages end; Renaissance begins.

1454 Movable-type printing press is introduced.

1455 England's War of the Roses is fought.

1478 Spanish Inquisition is begun by Ferdinand and Isabella; period of exploration by Europeans begins.

1482 Portuguese colonize African Gold Coast.

1488 Bartholomew Diaz sails around Cape of Good Hope.

1492 Christopher Columbus discovers West Indies.

1497 John Cabot discovers Newfoundland.

1498 Vasco da Gama sails around Cape of Good Hope to India.

1500 Pedro Cabral discovers Brazil.

1502 Columbus discovers Nicaragua.

1505 Portuguese colonize Mozambique.

1507 First world map showing "America" is produced.

1513 Vasco Núñez de Balboa discovers the Pacific Ocean.

1517 Martin Luther's Reformation begins.

1521 Hernán Cortés conquers Aztecs and claims Mexico for Spain.

1522 Crew under Ferdinand Magellan circumnavigates the world.

1531 Francisco Pizarro begins conquest of Peru.

1534 Henry VIII is excommunicated and founds Church of England; John Calvin begins Reformation program in Switzerland; Ignatius Loyola founds Society of Jesus (Jesuits).

1541 Hernando de Soto discovers Mississippi River.

1547 Ivan IV becomes first czar of united Russia.

1557 Portuguese establish colony at Macao.

1558 Elizabeth I becomes queen of England.

1582 Gregorian calendar is introduced.

1588 Spanish Armada is defeated by English fleet.

1595 Dutch colonize Guinea Coast.

1600 English East India Company is chartered.

1602 Dutch East India Company is formed.

1604 Russia begins settlement in Siberia.

1606 Willem Jansz discovers Australia.

1607 English found North American colony of Virginia.

1610 Hudson Bay is discovered.

1618 Thirty Years' War begins as a conflict between Europe's Protestants and Catholics.

1620 English Pilgrims reach Cape Cod, found Plymouth Colony.

1626 Dutch found New Amsterdam (New York).

1637 Russian explorers reach Pacific coast of Siberia.

1642 French found Montreal in Canada; King Charles I battles Parliament in English Civil War.

1652 English and Dutch begin series of wars; Dutch East India Company founds settlement on the Cape of Good Hope.

1654 Portuguese take Brazil from Dutch.

1655 England takes Jamaica from Spain.

1661 English take control of Bombay in India.

1664 England takes New Amsterdam from Dutch; Manchu dynasty is founded in China.

1683 Turkish army overruns Vienna.

1686 English establish Dominion of New England.

1696 Peter the Great leads Russian modernization program.

1704 English seize Gibraltar from Spain.

1733 John Kay starts Industrial Revolution with flying sewing shuttle.

1759 England captures Quebec in war with France.

1763 Peace of Paris gives Canada to England.

1767 Townshend Acts tax American colony imports; Mason-Dixon line is established.

1770 Boston Massacre occurs; Townshend Acts are repealed except for the tax.

1773 Boston Tea Party occurs.

1774 First Continental Congress of American colonies is held.

1775 War of Independence begins in Massachusetts.

1776 Declaration of Independence is signed.

1781 English General Cornwallis surrenders at Yorktown.

1783 Treaty of Paris ends American War of Independence; India Act allows English control of India.

1788 First English convicts are transported to Australia; Sierra Leone is established as a refuge for blacks.

1789 George Washington is elected first U.S. president; U.S. Constitution takes effect; French Revolution begins.

1791 U.S. Bill of Rights takes effect.

1792 France is declared a republic; Denmark becomes the first country to ban slave trade.

1793 Maximilien Robespierre leads French reign of terror; Toussaint L'Ouverture leads revolt, ending French slavery in Haiti; first free settlers migrate to Australia.

1798 Napoleon Bonaparte invades Egypt, capturing Cairo; Thomas Malthus publishes essay on population explosion.

1803 Louisiana Purchase is completed.

1804 Lewis and Clark begin exploration of American Northwest; Bonaparte crowns himself Napoleon I, emperor of France.

1806 Napoleon dissolves Holy Roman Empire.

1807 England abolishes slave trade.

1809 David Ricardo develops modern concepts of finance.

1811 Simón Bolívar frees parts of South America from Spanish rule.

1812 War is fought between England and United States; Napoleon invades Russia, occupies Moscow.

1814 Napoleon is exiled to Elba.

1815 Napoleon is defeated at the Battle of Waterloo and exiled again.

1819 Florida is ceded by Spain to United States.

1820 Missouri Compromise on U.S. slave states becomes effective.

1821 José San Martin frees Chile and Argentina from Spanish control.

1823 Monroe Doctrine against foreign activity in America is adopted.

1833 England bans slavery and child labor in factories.

1836 Texas secedes from Mexico; battle of the Alamo is fought.

1846 War is fought between Mexico and United States; Irish potato famine occurs, with deaths reaching one million.

1848 Revolutions erupt throughout Europe; Marx and Engels produce *The Communist Manifesto*; Mexico cedes California and New Mexico to the United States.

1854 Crimean War is fought; Japan ends isolation, signs U.S. commercial treaty.

1860 Giuseppe Garibaldi begins nationalist movements in Europe.

1861 U.S. civil War begins; British establish colonial presence in what is now Nigeria.

1863 Emancipation Proclamation declares abolition of slavery in part of the United States.

1865 U.S. civil War ends; President Lincoln is assassinated.

1867 United States acquires Alaska from Russia; Dominion of Canada is established.

1868 Japan ends 700-year shogun rule, begins modernization.

1869 Suez Canal is completed.

1870 Franco-Prussian War is fought.

1883 Germany introduces health insurance.

1894 Sun Yat-sen begins move to end Manchu dynasty in China.

1898 War between Spain and United States is fought over Cuba; United States acquires Hawaiian Islands.

1900 Boxer Rebellion erupts in China, hundreds of Europeans are killed; England and Germany begin arms race.

1902 Boer War ends; England acquires South African states.

1903 Panama, aided by the United States, secedes from Colombia.

1904 Russo-Japanese War is fought; Japan acquires Korea and Manchuria.

1908 William d'Arcy discovers oil in Persian Gulf region.

1909 England introduces old-age pensions; assembly line production is introduced in Detroit.

1912 Chinese revolution ends Manchu dynasty and republic is formed; passenger ship *Titanic* sinks, with 1,513 lives lost; Balkan wars begin.

1914 World War I follows assassination of Austrian archduke; trench warfare begins, airplanes are used as weapons; Panama Canal opens.

1915 Poison gas is first used by Germany in warfare.

1916 Tanks are first used by England in warfare.

1917 United States joins Allies in European fighting; Bolsheviks led by Lenin seize power in Russia; Balfour Declaration urges Jewish state in Palestine.

1918 Russia withdraws from World War I fighting; Kaiser of Germany abdicates; Germany forms republic after revolt; armistice ends World War I.

1919 Treaty of Versailles causes heavy German economic losses; League of Nations is founded; Sinn Fein rebellion erupts in Ireland; Benito Mussolini introduces fascism in Italy; Gandhi begins passive resistance movement in India.

1920 Civil war is fought in Ireland; United States prohibits use of alcoholic beverages.

1921 Irish Free State is established.

1922 Union of Soviet Socialist Republics is established; fascists march on Rome; Mussolini is named prime minister of Italy; Palestine becomes British League of Nations protectorate.

1923 Adolf Hitler forms National Socialist Party in Germany; Turkey becomes a republic after revolt that ends sultanate.

1024 Joseph Stalin succeeds Lenin as leader of Soviet Union; new Chinese government is formed with communist members.

1927 Purge of communists leads to civil war in China.

1929 U.S. stock market crash triggers worldwide depression; fighting begins between Jews and Arabs in Palestine.

1931 Japanese organize puppet state in Manchuria; Spain becomes a republic, King Alfonso is deposed; British Empire status is changed to British Commonwealth.

1933 Adolf Hitler is named chancellor of Germany, and National Socialists (Nazis) purge opposition; Stalin purges opposition in Russia; United States ends prohibition experiment.

1934 Hitler assumes title of "Führer"; Mao Tse-tung starts "Long March" of Chinese communists.

1935 Italy invades Ethiopia; Hitler renounces Versailles Treaty and begins open rearmament; John Keynes publishes concept of government role in economy.

1936 Germany reoccupies Rhineland and forms "Axis" with Italy; General Franco begins Spanish Civil War; King Edward of England abdicates to marry American Wallis Simpson.

1937 Japanese invade China, capturing Peking and Shanghai; German aircraft bomb Spain in support of Franco.

1938 Germany annexes Austria and gains Czechoslovakia's Sudetenland in Munich Pact.

1939 Germany annexes Czechoslovakia; Franco captures Madrid, and Spanish Civil War ends; Italy invades Albania; Germany invades Poland, triggering World War II; Russo-Finnish War ends in defeat in Finland.

1940 Germany invades France, Belgium, Denmark, and Norway; Battle of Britain prevents German invasion of England; Japan joins Berlin-Rome Axis; Italy invades Greece and joins war against England and France.

1941 Germany invades Russia; Italy and Germany invade Egypt; Japanese attack U.S. bases in Hawaii; U.S. joins Allies in war against Axis powers.

1942 Japanese capture Philippines and much of Southeast Asia; Battle of Midway alters naval balance in Pacific; Germans begin retreat in North Africa.

1943 United States begins recapture of Japanese Pacific bases; Allies invade Sicily; Italians surrender; Germans surrender to Russians at Stalingrad.

1944 Allies invade Normandy; German retreat begins; Allies liberate Rome, Paris, and Brussels; U.S. forces defeat Japanese navy in Leyte Gulf.

1945 Yalta Conference is attended by United States, Great Britain, and Soviet Union; Germany surrenders; Mussolini is assassinated; Hitler commits suicide; atom bombs are dropped at Hiroshima and Nagasaki; Japan surrenders, ending World War II; Potsdam Conference discusses postwar settlements.

1946 League of nations is replaced by United Nations; Ho Chi Minh begins war against French in Indochina; German war crime trials are held in Nuremberg.

1947 Marshall Plan aids European war recovery; Arabs reject plan for separate Jewish and Arab states; independent states of India and Pakistan are formed.

1948 Nation of Israel is established; war begins between Israel and Arab League; Gandhi is assassinated by a Hindu extremist; communists gain control of Czechoslovakia; Korea is divided into North Korea and South Korea; Berlin is blockaded by Soviet Union.

1949 Mao Tse-tung's communists gain control of China; Nationalist Chinese move government to Taiwan; South Africa establishes apartheid policy; Germany is divided into East Germany and West Germany; North Atlantic Treaty Organization (NATO) is formed.

1950 North Korean troops invade South Korea.

1951 Chinese communists occupy Tibet.

1952 Jawaharlal Nehru is elected first prime minister of India.

1953 Group of doctors in USSR tried for allegedly killing Politburo members; Stalin dies; USSR announces development of hydrogen bomb; Vietnamese Viet Minh forces invade Laos.

1954 Viet Minh troops defeat French at Dien Bien Phu; Vietnam is divided into North Vietnam and South Vietnam; South-East Asia Treaty Organization (SEATO) is formed; French-Algerian War begins.

1955 European communist states sign Warsaw Pact; Argentine President Juan Perón is exiled.

1956 Soviets crush anti-Russian uprising in Hungary; Egypt nationalizes Suez Canal, British withdraw; Israel invades Egypt.

1957 Russia launches first artificial satellite, Sputnik I; Fidel Castro begins revolution in Cuba; European Common Market is formed.

1958 Egypt, Syria, and Yemen form United Arab Republic States; Charles de Gaulle is elected president of France; United States launches an artificial satellite, Explorer I.

1959 Fidel Castro overthrows Fulgencio Batista and becomes Cuban premier.

1960 Many European colonies in Africa gain independence.

1961 Bay of Pigs invasion of Cuba fails; Russian Yuri Gagarin is first man in space; communists build Berlin Wall; United States sends thousands of military advisers to Vietnam.

1962 Soviet missile crisis threatens in Cuba; Algeria votes for independence from France; Nelson Mandela imprisoned for anti-apartheid activities in South Africa.

1963 Russian Valentina Tereshkova is first woman in space; President Kennedy is assassinated; United States, Great Britain, and Soviet Union sign nuclear test ban treaty; North Vietnamese boats attack U.S. Navy in Gulf of Tonkin; President Lyndon Johnson orders attack on North Vietnam.

1965 U.S. Marines are sent to Vietnam; U.S. aircraft begin air strikes against North Vietnam.

1966 China undergoes "Cultural Revolution."

1967 Six-Day War between Israel and Arabs is fought; Israel occupies Jerusalem and West Bank of Jordan River.

1968 Martin Luther King, Jr., is assassinated; U.S. senator Robert Kennedy is assassinated; Soviets invade Czechoslovakia to crush uprising; Vietcong stage Tet offensive in South Vietnam; U.S. troop deployment in Vietnam passes 500,000; North Korea seizes U.S. Navy ship *Pueblo*.

1969 U.S. military begins withdrawal from Vietnam; U.S. astronauts land on the moon.

1970 U.S. troops invade Cambodia.

1971 Communist China replaces Taiwan in United Nations; Aswan High Dam completed in Egypt.

1972 President Nixon travels to China to renew relations; Great Britain takes over direct rule of Northern Ireland.

1973 Military coup in Chile overthrows Marxist government; Arabs attack Israel in October War; participants in Vietnam War sign peace agreements.

1974 Watergate scandal ends Nixon term in White House.

1975 Vietnam War ends with communist seizure of Saigon; communists take control of government of Cambodia; U.S. and Soviet spacecraft link up in space.

1978 United States votes to return Canal Zone to Panama in year 2000.

1979 Ayatollah Khomeini gains control of Iran; Shah of Iran leaves; Iranians seize U.S. Embassy in Tehran holding hostages; Soviet Union invades Afghanistan; Israel and Egypt sign peace treaty; Sandinistas force dictator Somoza to leave Nicaragua.

1980 War begins between Iran and Iraq; Solidarity trade union confronts communists in Poland.

1981 United States begins series of space shuttle flights; assassination attempt is made on President Ronald Reagan; assassination attempt is made on Pope John Paul II.

1982 Falklands War between Argentina and England is fought; Israel withdraws troops from Egypt's Sinai.

1983 Soviets shoot down South Korean airliner, and 269 are killed; Sally Ride is first U.S. woman in space; bomb kills 237 U.S. Marines in Beirut, Lebanon; U.S. forces invade island of Grenada.

1984 Marines withdraw from Beirut; Geraldine Ferraro is nominated as U.S. vice-president.

1985 Mikhail Gorbachev becomes leader of Soviet Union.

1986 U.S. space shuttle explodes in flight, killing crew; Corazon Aquino is elected president of Philippines; U.S. aircraft raid Libya in retaliation for terrorism; nuclear accident occurs at Soviet Chernobyl power station.

1987 Palestinian *intifada* uprising begins in Gaza and West Bank; Iran-contra aid scandal involves U.S. officials; Gorbachev introduces program of extensive economic and social reforms; United States and Soviet Union agree to reduce nuclear arms; U.S. Navy ship *Stark* is attacked in Persian Gulf.

1988 Cease-fire agreement is signed between Nicaraguan government and contra leaders; Iran accepts peace plan offer by Iraq; King Hussein abandons claim to West Bank territory and cedes authority to Palestine Liberation Organization; Palestine Liberation Organization recognizes Israel as a state and renounces terrorism; devastating earthquake in Armenia kills tens of thousands.

1989 Chinese military massacre protesters in Beijing's Tianamen Square; U.S. troops invade Panama, driving General Manuel Noriega into custody; Berlin Wall is opened; Soviet army withdraws from Afghanistan; playwright Vaclav Havel is elected president of Czechoslovakia; Romanian leader Nicolae Ceauşescu is overthrown and executed; opposition leader Patricio Aylwin is elected president of Chile, ending Pinochet military regime.

1990 Saddam Hussein's Iraqi army invades Kuwait, spurring international military buildup in the Persian Gulf; Germany is reunified; Soviet congress votes to begin popular elections for president; riots erupt in Britain over poll tax; Israeli police fire on Palestinians in Jerusalem, killing at least 17; Liberian president Samuel Doe is killed by rebels.

1991 U.S.–led multinational force attacks Iraq, freeing Kuwait; Soviet communists stage coup but are quickly rebuffed; Estonia, Lithuania, and Latvia declare full independence from USSR; the Soviet Union is dissolved, becoming the Commonwealth of Independent States; Haitian president Jean-Bertrand Aristide is exiled in a coup; Croatia and Slovenia declare independence from Yugoslavia; Communist government of Albania resigns; South Africa repeals the Population Registration Act, a fundamental apartheid law.

1992 The Russian Federation drops price controls; South African whites vote to end white minority rule through talks with the black majority; Croatia, Bosnia and Herzegovina, and Slovenia are recognized by the European Community and by the United States; delegates from 178 countries attend the U.N. Conference on Environment and Development ("Earth Summit"); Salvadoran government and leftist Farabundo Marti National Liberation Front sign peace treaty ending 12 years of civil war; Serbian nationalists lay siege to Sarajevo and begin campaign of "ethnic cleansing" of Muslims in Bosnia-Herzegovina; three nights of right-wing rioting against foreigners seeking asylum in Germany sets off wave of anti-foreigner violence and mass demonstrations against such violence; U.N. General Assembly ejects Yugoslavia for its support of Bosnian Serb militias; hundreds die in riots in India after Hindu extremists destroy a mosque in Ayodhya; U.N. authorizes U.S. troops to bring humanitarian aid to famine-stricken Somalia; Israel deports 400 Palestinians it believes to be members of militant Muslim groups.

1993 President Bush and Russian President Yeltsin sign START II accord to reduce nuclear arsenals; European Community's internal open market goes into effect; Czechoslovakia divides into two countries, the Czech Republic and Slovakia; U.S., France, and Britain conduct air raids on Iraq in response to Iraqi defiance of U.N.; Russian Congress of People's Deputies and President Yeltsin engage in struggle over whether executive or legislature should have more power; 200 killed by bombings in Bombay.

World Exploration and Discovery

40,000 B.C. Cro-Magnons migrate to Europe from Near East.

28,000 B.C. Humans migrate from Asia to Americas over land bridge.

5000 B.C. Sumerians migrate to Mesopotamia.

2300 B.C. Semites migrate from Arabia to Mesopotamia.

2000 B.C. Israelites migrate from Euphrates Valley to Canaan.

1000 B.C. Phoenician sailors explore Britain and western Africa.

700 B.C. Central Asian tribes migrate to Persia.

640 B.C. Greek explorer Colaeus reaches Gibraltar and Spain.

600 B.C. Egyptian pharaoh Necho circumnavigates Africa; Greek explorer Midacritus finds tin in England or Brittany.

510 B.C. Greek traveler Scylax explores Indus River, Red Sea, and Arabia.

500 B.C. Bantu tribes migrate through eastern Africa; Greek explorer Hekataios travels to Spain and North Africa; Carthaginian explorer Himlico visits French Atlantic Coast.

480 B.C. Carthaginian admiral Hanno explores west coast of Africa.

424 B.C. Greek traveler Herodotus visits North Africa, Italy, and Arabia.

400 B.C. Greek explorer Ctesias travels to Ganges River in India.

345 B.C. Greek explorer Pythias explores northwest European coastline.

327 B.C. Alexander the Great leads army to Indus Valley of India.

325 B.C. Greek admiral Nearchus attempts to circumnavigate Arabia.

302 B.C. Greek traveler Megasthenes visits India, Tibet, and Ceylon.

218 B.C. Hannibal leads army with elephants from Spain to Italy.

138 B.C. Decimus Brutus becomes first Roman to reach west coast of Spain.

128 B.C. Chinese explorer of central Asia has contact with Greeks.

112 B.C. Greek explorer Eudoxus sails to India and western Africa.

100 B.C. Greek explorer Hippalus finds direct ocean route to India.

55 B.C. Julius Caesar leads Roman army to Britain.

A.D. 20 King Juba of Morocco explores Canary Islands.

A.D. 80 Gnaeus Agricola explores Atlantic coast of Britain.

A.D. 100 Roman explorer Julius Maternus crosses Sahara to Sudan; Alexander, Greek trader, sails to Vietnam and Cambodia; Chinese explorer Kan Ying reaches Black Sea and turns back.

A.D. 370 Huns, nomadic Mongols, invade Europe and reach Gaul.

A.D. 400 Chinese monk Fa Hsien visits India, Ceylon, and Java.

A.D. 407 Northern European Goths and Vandals spread to Mediterranean.

A.D. 431 Gunavarman, prince of Kashmir, travels to Java and China.

A.D. 570 Brendan, Irish monk, reportedly discovers America.

A.D. 620 Vikings explore Ireland.

A.D. 645 Chinese monk Yuan Chuang travels overland to India and returns.

A.D. 861 Vikings discover Iceland.

A.D. 872 Iraqi traveler Ibn Wahab visits China.

A.D. 900 Mayans migrate from Central America to Yucatan Peninsula; Arab traveler Ibn Rosteh explores Malay Peninsula and Java.

A.D. 921 Arabian diplomat Ahmad Ibn Fodhlan explores Russia and Poland.

A.D. 950 Maori sailors discover New Zealand.

A.D. 980 Arabs migrate to east coast of Africa.

A.D. 981 Eric the Red discovers Greenland.

A.D. 986 Viking sailor Bjarne Herjulfsson sights North America.

A.D. 1000 Leif Ericsson explores Atlantic coast of North America.

1002 Thorwald Ericsson explores American coast below New England.

1007 Viking Thorfinn Karlsefni establishes North American colony.

1150 Polynesian Toi Kai Rakan opens settlement of New Zealand.

1165 Spanish rabbi Benjamin visits synagogues of Asia and Near East.

1245 Franciscan monk Giovanni Carpini travels to Mongol capital.

1271 Marco Polo begins 24-year journey to Orient and Near East.

1291 Vivaldi brothers try sailing Atlantic from Genoa to India; Italian explorer Malocello discovers Canary Islands.

1337 Josef Faquin circumnavigates known world of fourteenth century.

1350 Polynesian chief Marutuahu established colony in New Zealand.

1419 Portuguese King Henry begins African exploration.

1431 Portuguese explorer discovers Azores.

1440 Italian explorer Niccolò Conti travels in Indonesia and Malaya.

1446 Portuguese explorer Nuno Tristao is lost on second trip to Africa.

1455 Venetian sailor Cadamosto discovers Cape Verde Islands.

1482 Portuguese navigator Diego Cao explores Congo River; Portugal establishes African Gold Coast settlements.

1488 Portuguese explorer Bartholomeu Dias sails around Cape of Good Hope.

1492 Christopher Columbus discovers the West Indies; German navigator Martin Behaim shows Earth is spherical.

1493 Pope Alexander VI divides New World between Spain and Portugal.

1494 Bartolome Colon, brother of Columbus, explores Haiti.

1495 Francisco de Almeida establishes Portuguese naval bases in eastern Africa.

1497 Italian John Cabot discovers Newfoundland for England.

1498 Columbus discovers South America and Trinidad; Portuguese navigator Vasco da Gama finds sea route to India.

1499 Spanish explorer Vincent Yañez Pinzon discovers mouth of Amazon River.

1500 Portuguese explorer Pedro Cabral discovers Brazil.

1501 Amerigo Vespucci explores coast of Brazil; Spanish explorer Rodrigo Bastidas discovers Colombia.

1502 Columbus discovers Nicaragua; Spaniard Alonso de Ojeda explores Haiti, Guiana, and Venezuela.

1504 Portuguese explorer Pacheco Pereira visits India.

1505 Portuguese establish settlements in Mozambique; Portuguese nobleman Tristão da Cunha leads expedition to India.

1507 German maps by Martin Waldseemuller identify New World as "America."

1510 Afonso de Albuquerque establishes Portuguese base in India at Goa.

1512 Spanish priest Bartolomé Las Casas is missionary to Cuban Indians.

1513 Balboa, in Panama, discovers Pacific Ocean; Ponce de Leon explores Florida and West Indies; Portuguese reach Canton, China.

1514 Spanish explorer Francisco de Montejo travels to West Indies.

1516 Spanish explorer Juan Diaz de Solís discovers Rio de la Plata, Uruguay.

1517 Spanish explorer Fernandez de Cordoba discovers Mayan ruins.

1518 Pedro Alvarado explores Southeast Mexico for Spain; Spanish conquistador Juan de Grijalva discovers Aztec Empire.

1519 Hernán Cortés conquers Mexico for Spain.

1521 Ferdinand Magellan dies in an attempt to circumnavigate Earth.

1522 Spanish navigator Juan Sebastián Elcano is first to circumnavigate Earth.

1524 Italian explorer Giovanni da Verrazano discovers New York harbor; Francisco Pizarro explores the west coasts of Panama and Peru.

1526 Italian Sebastian Cabot explores Rio de la Plata, Uruguay.

1527 Cabeza de Vaca begins trek from Florida to Mexican west coast.

1528 Spanish explorer Panfilo de Narvaez dies near mouth of Mississippi.

1530 German adventurer Nikolaus Federmann explores Venezuela, Colombia, and the Andes.

1533 Spanish conquistador Francisco Pizarro conquers Peru; Spanish conquistador Sebastián de Benalcázar conquers Ecuador.

1535 Jacques Cartier explores Saint Lawrence River; Spanish explore Chile; Spanish explorer Antonio de Mendoza establishes city of Buenos Aires.

1536 Spaniard Jiménez de Quesada explores Colombia and Orinoco River; Spanish conquistador Domingo de Irala explores Parana and Paraguay rivers.

1540 Vásquez de Coronado explores Arizona and New Mexico; Spanish monk Andres Urdaneta explores Philippine Islands.

1541 Hernando de Soto discovers Mississippi River; Francisco de Orellana travels Amazon River from source in Peru to mouth; Gonzalo Pizarro crosses the Andes from Ecuador to the Amazon River.

1542 Portuguese explorer Mendes Pinto is first European in Japan.

1544 Spanish conquistadors explore coast of Oregon.

1553 English explorer Richard Chancellor establishes Russian trade route.

1554 English explorer Sir Hugh Willoughby dies seeking Northeast Passage.

1557 Portuguese establish Chinese base at Macao.

1562 French explorer Jan Ribault establishes colony in South Carolina.

1564 Miguel López de Legazpe claims Marianas and Philippines for Spain and founds Manila.

1569 Spanish explorer Alvaro Bazan crosses Chaco of South America.

1576 English explorer Sir Martin Frobisher searches for Northwest Passage.

1581 Cossack Timofeevich extends Russian territory into Siberia.

1582 Cossack Koltso aids Timofeevich in exploration of Siberia; Spanish explorer Berrio navigates Orinoco River.

1584 Sir Walter Raleigh explores Virginia and North Carolina.

1592 Explorer Cornelis de Houtman discovers Dutch route to East Indies.

1594 Dutch explorer Willem Barents searches for Northeast Passage.

1595 Dutch establish settlements on Guinea Coast.

1598 Van Neck leads second Dutch expedition to East Indies; English explorer Will Adams travels to Japan.

1602 Englishman Bartholomew Gosnold explores New England coast.

1603 Samuel de Champlain explores Saint Lawrence River as "route to China."

1607 Englishman John Smith helps establish Jamestown, Virginia.

1608 Champlain founds city of Quebec; John Smith explores Cape Cod and Chesapeake Bay.

1610 Henry Hudson discovers Hudson Bay and River; Dutch navigator Willem Schouten sails around Cape Horn.

1613 Dutch colonist Jan Coen establishes factories in Indonesia; English explorer William Baffin discovers Baffin Bay and Island.

1614 Dutch captain Christianssen establishes fort at Albany, New York.

1615 Champlain explores lakes Huron and Ontario.

1617 Dutch explorers Jakob LeMaire and Willem Schouten start trip around world.

1618 French explorer Imbert finds Timbuktu in Africa.

1620 English Pilgrims reach Cape Cod.

1626 French establish settlements in Madagascar; Dutch settle New Amsterdam in North America; French missionary Jean de Brébeuf explores Lake Huron region.

1631 English captain Thomas James explores James Bay in Canada.

1637 Russian explorers reach Pacific coast of Siberia.

1642 French explorer Sieur de Maisonneuve founds city of Montreal; Dutch explorer Abel Tasman discovers Van Dieman's Land (Tasmania).

1645 Capuchin monks explore Congo River.

1646 French missionary Isaac Jogues discovers Lake George.

1649 Cossack Dezhnev explores Siberia and Alaska for Russia; Cossack Stadukhin explores the Lena and Kolyma rivers in Siberia.

1652 Dutch colonist Jan van Riebeek founds Cape of Good Hope settlement.

1659 French fur trader Pierre Radisson explores Minnesota.

1670 French fur trader Perrot explores upper Mississippi region.

1673 French explorers Louis Joliet and Jacques Marquette navigate the length of the Mississippi.

1675 Belgian explorer Louis Hennepin discovers Niagara Falls and Mississippi source.

1679 Frenchman Daniel Duluth explores Minnesota and Great Lakes.

1681 Sieur de La Salle explores Mississippi and names delta area Louisiana; English buccaneer William Dampier explores South Pacific islands.

1682 Buero da Silva explores Central Mountains region of Brazil; Pieres de Campos explores rivers of South America.

1683 Dutch explorer Aerssen establishes colony of Surinam; German naturalist Kaempfer visits Java, Thailand, and Japan.

1685 French missionary Claude Allouez explores western Lake Superior.

1697 Cossack Atlasov explores Kamchatka Peninsula for Russia.

1699 William Dampier explores northwest coast of Australia.

1721 Norwegian missionary Hans Egede is first European in Greenland in 200 years.

1723 Russian adventurer Fedorov explores northwest coast of America.

1732 Gvozdev explores Bering Sea and Alaska coastline for Russia.

1741 Russian explorer Chrikov discovers some Aleutian Islands.

1744 Frenchman Charles La Condamine measures arc of meridian in Andes.

1745 Basov explores Aleutian Islands for Russia.

1770 English navigator James Cook explores east coast of Australia.

1772 English explorer Samuel Hearne is first European to reach Arctic Ocean; Frenchman Yves Kerguélen-Trémarec discovers Antarctic islands; James Cook searches for possible continent of Antarctica.

1776 Cook searches for possible Atlantic–Pacific maritime passage.

1784 Daniel Boone explores Appalachian and Ozark areas.

1789 Scottish fur trader Sir Alexander Mackenzie explores western Canada.

1790 Russian fur trader Aleksandr Baranov explores Alaska; American explorer Robert Gray discovers Columbia River.

1797 German adventurer Hornemann explores caravan routes of Sahara Desert.

1798 British explorer George Bass circumnavigates Tasmania.

1799 German explorer Alexander von Humboldt tours North and South America.

1802 English explorer Matthew Flinders circumnavigates Australia; Portuguese explorers cross Africa.

1804 Lewis and Clark begin exploration of Louisiana Purchase; Russian Lisyanskii explores Pacific from Hawaii to Alaska.

1805 Canadian Fraser explores Canada west of Rocky Mountains; Russian navigator Adam Krusenstern maps Sakhalin, discovers Amur's mouth.

1815 Russian navigator Otto Kotzebue discovers many Pacific islands.

1818 French explorer René Caillé crosses Sahara, reaching Timbuktu.

1819 English explorer Sir William Parry finds Northwest Passage in Arctic.

1820 American Nathaniel Palmer discovers Palmer Peninsula of Antarctica.

1821 Russian Fabian Bellinghausen leads South Pole expedition.

1825 British explorer Sir John Franklin surveys Canadian Arctic region.

1828 German physicist Georg Erman circumnavigates Earth, studying magnetic fields.

1829 English explorer Freemantle founds West Australia colony.

1830 British Lander brothers explore Niger River and delta.

1831 American Benjamin Bonneville explores Rocky Mountains and California; British explorer James Ross finds North Magnetic Pole.

1835 British colonist Bourke explores new areas of Australia; American pioneer Jim Bowie explores U.S. Southwest.

1837 American trapper Joseph Walker explores Sierra Mountains.

1840 Frenchman Dumont d'Urville discovers Antarctic islands.

1842 John Fremont begins exploration west of Rockies.

1843 British colonist Edward Eyre explores South and West Australia; Scottish explorer Sir James Ross proves Antarctica has ice barrier.

1846 German explorer Friedrich Leichhardt disappears crossing Australia.

1847 French naturalist Comte de Castelnau crosses South America west to east.

1848 American explorer Elisha Kane surveys Gulf of Mexico.

1850 English naval officer Sir Robert McClure discovers Northwest Passage.

1851 German explorer Heinrich Barth crosses Sahara Desert twice; American explorer Savage rediscovers Yosemite Valley.

1853 Englishman Sir Richard Burton is first non-Muslim to visit Mecca and Medina; American explorer Elisha Kane leads Arctic expedition.

1854 U.S. Commodore Matthew Perry ends isolation of Japan; German Schlagintweit brothers explore Central Asia; Portuguese explorer Silva Porto crosses South Africa, west to east.

1855 Russian adventurer Nevelskoi explores Amur and proves Sakhalin is an island.

1856 Scottish missionary David Livingstone explores Africa; English explorers Richard Burton and John Speke discovers Lake Tanganyika; English explorer Gregory crosses Australia east to west.

1857 British explorer John Speke discovers Lake Victoria.

1860 Irish explorer Robert Burke is first to cross Australia south to north; German explorer Karl Decken leads Kilimanjaro Mountain expedition; John Speke and James Grant prove Lake Victoria is source of Nile; American Isaac Hayes searches for "open sea" above Arctic Circle.

1863 Frenchman Louis Faidherbe explores Senegal and Niger River in Africa.

1864 Hermann Schlagintweit is first European to cross Kuenlun range.

1866 Doudart explores Mekong River route to source for France.

1871 Russian naturalist Aleksi Fedchenko explores Asian mountain ranges; British journalist Henry Stanley finds missing Livingstone; American Charles Hall is first to explore above 82 degrees north latitude.

1872 French colonist Francis Garnier searches for China–Tibet river route.

1874 John and Alexander Forrest survey western Australia.

1878 German Eduard Schnitzer (Emin Pasha) explores African lake country; English explorer Sir George Nares surveys Magellan Strait; Russian Grigori Potanin explores Gobi Desert of Mongolia.

1879 Swedish explorer Nils Nordenskjöld discovers Northeast Passage; Russian Nikolai Przhevalski is first to cross Tibet's Humboldt Mountains; Joseph Thompson explores Great Rift Valley of Africa.

1880 French colonist Pierre Brazza explores African river routes to sea.

1882 French explorer Pierre Bonvalot discovers ancient cities of Asia.

1883 French officer Foucauld explores Algerian oases and Morocco.

1885 Portuguese explorer Capelo crosses South Africa.

1888 Norwegian Fridtjof Nansen explores Greenland ice cap; French explorer Louis Binger leads African scientific expedition.

1889 German explorer Hans Meyer is first to scale Kilimanjaro peak; Austrian Oskar Baumann explores African rivers and lakes.

1891 German Erich von Drygalski explores West Greenland.

1892 Scottish oceanographer William Bruce explores Antarctic coastline; Englishman William Conway is first to scale 23,000-foot Himalayan peaks; American Robert Peary explores Greenland and proves it is an island.

1893 Swedish engineer Andre explores Arctic by balloon; German explorer Goetzen crosses Africa east to west.

1894 Englishwoman Mary Kingsley explores Ogowe River in Africa.

1895 French explorer Charles Bonin crosses Tibet and Mongolia; Englishman Frederick Jackson explores Franz Josef Land in Arctic.

1897 Gerlache de Gomery leads Belgian Antarctic expedition.

1899 Sweden's Sven Hedin finds sources of Bramaputra and Indus rivers.

1900 Norwegian Carsten Borchgrevink is early Antarctic explorer.

1906 Norwegian Roald Amundsen is first to navigate Northwest Passage.

1908 British explorer Sir Ernest Shackleton nearly reaches South Pole.

1909 American explorer Robert Peary is first to reach North Pole.

1910 Bavarian officer Wilhelm Filchner leads German Antarctic expedition.

1911 Norwegian explorer Roald Amundsen reaches South Pole; American explorer Bingham discovers Machu Picchu in Peru; British explorer Sir Douglas Mawson leads Antarctic expedition.

1912 British explorer Robert Scott reaches South Pole.

1913 Theodore Roosevelt explores central Brazilian rivers.

1926 Americans Floyd Bennett and Richard Byrd fly over North Pole; American Lincoln Ellsworth flies over North Pole; Italian engineer Umberto Nobile flies over North Pole, from Norway to Alaska.

1927 American Charles Lindbergh is first to fly solo across Atlantic Ocean.

1929 American explorer Richard Byrd is first to fly over South Pole; German Hugo Eckener makes round-the-world flight.

1931 Eckener flies over North Pole.

1932 British explorer St. John Philby crosses Arabia's Rub-al-Kali Desert; Jean Piccard explores stratosphere in balloon gondola.

1935 Lincoln Ellsworth flies over South Pole.

1937 Russian aviator Valeri Chkalov is first to fly from USSR to America over North Pole.

1947 Norwegian Thor Heyerdahl sails balsa raft from Peru to Polynesia.

1953 British mountaineer Sir Edmund Hillary and Tenzing Norgay of Nepal scale Mount Everest.

1956 Heyerdahl explores Easter Island and eastern Pacific.

1958 American explorer Anderson crosses North Pole in submarine.

1961 Russian cosmonaut Yuri Gagarin is first man to orbit Earth.

1962 John Glenn is first American to orbit Earth.

1969 American astronauts Neil Armstrong and "Buzz" Aldrin land on moon.

1975 Mars space probes, Viking 1 and 2, are launched by NASA.

1981 Space shuttle Columbia, the world's first reusable spacecraft, orbits Earth 36 times, carrying two astronauts, marking the beginning of the U.S. space shuttle program.

1986 Experimental airplane Voyager, using a single load of fuel, completes a flight around the world, setting a record for distance flown without refueling.

1992 U.S. Space shuttle Endeavor captures a stranded communications satellite and sends it back into orbit.

Major World Cities

An * indicates the population figure is for the metropolitan area.

City	Population
Addis Ababa, Ethiopia	1,739,130
Capital since 1896	
Ahmedabad, India	2,059,725
Founded in 1411	
Alexandria, Egypt	2,893,000
Founded by Alexander the Great, 332 B.C.	
Algiers, Algeria	1,523,000
Founded in tenth century on Roman site	
Amman, Jordan	900,000
Site of biblical city of Ammonites	
Amsterdam, The Netherlands	693,209
Founded in 1300	
Ankara, Turkey	2,541,899
Capital of Galacia around 300 B.C.	
Athens, Greece	885,737
Ancient Greek city-state in 700 B.C.	
Auckland, New Zealand	150,000
Founded 1840, original capital	
Baghdad, Iraq	1,984,142
Center of Islamic culture since 813	
Baku, Azerbaijan	1,741,000
Founded in ninth century	
Bandung, Indonesia	1,462,637
Founded in 1810	
Bangalore, India	2,628,593
Founded in sixteenth century	
Bangkok, Thailand	4,697,071
Capital since 1782	
Barcelona, Spain	1,667,699
Founded by Carthaginians around 300 B.C.	
Barranquilla, Colombia	917,486*
Inland seaport since 1935	
Beijing	5,531,460
Founded around 1122 B.C. as Peking; renamed in 1949	
Beirut, Lebanon	474,870
Site of ancient Phoenician settlement	
Belgrade, Serbia, Yugoslavia	1,087,915
Site of Singidunum, ancient Roman camp	
Belo Horizonte, Brazil	2,122,073
Cattle and cotton-trading center	
Berlin, Germany	3,022,000*
Founded in thirteenth century; capital of Germany 1871–1945, of United Germany since 1990	

City	Population
Birmingham, England	993,695
Market town since before thirteenth century	
Bogotá, Colombia	4,176,769*
Founded by conquistadors in 1538	
Bombay, India	8,243,405
Established in early Christian era	
Brisbane, Australia	1,215,300
Founded in 1824 as a penal colony	
Brussels, Belgium	139,678
Capital since 1530	
Bucharest, Romania	1,975,508
Capital since 1861	
Budapest, Hungary	2,109,173
Site of Aquincum, second-century Roman camp	
Buenos Aires, Argentina	11,125,554*
Settled by conquistadors in 1536	
Cairo, Egypt	6,052,836
Site of seventh-century Arab military camp	
Calcutta, India	3,305,006
Developed from 1690 English factory site	
Calgary, Alberta, Canada	706,000*
Originally (1875) Northwest Mounted Police post	
Cali, Colombia	1,369,331*
Founded by conquistadors in 1536	
Cape Town, South Africa	776,617
Founded in 1652 as Dutch naval base	
Caracas, Venezuela	1,246,677
Founded by conquistadors in 1567	
Casablanca, Morocco	2,408,600*
Site of ancient city of Anfa	
Chicago, Illinois	2,977,520
Originally portage site for fur traders	
Chittagong, Bangladesh	1,388,476*
Portuguese trading post in 1600s	
Chongqing, China	2,673,170
Former capital of Nationalist China	
Cologne, Germany	934,375
Site of Roman (A.D. 50) Colonia Agrippina	
Copenhagen, Denmark	469,706
Capital since 1443	
Córdoba, Argentina	1,134,086*
Founded in 1573; university founded 1613	
Damascus, Syria	1,343,000
City of Egyptians and Hittites before 1000 B.C.	
Delhi, India	4,884,234
Thirteenth-century capital of northern India	
Dhaka, Bangladesh	3,458,602*
Capital since 1971 secession from Pakistan	

City	Population
Dnepropetrovsk, Ukraine	1,182,000
Founded in 1787 at Cossack village site	
Donetsk, Ukraine	1,090,000
Founded in 1870, called Stalino until 1961	
Dresden, Germany	515,892
Originally (A.D. 922) a Slavonic settlement	
Dublin, Ireland	502,749
Originally a ninth-century Viking base	
Düsseldorf, Germany	567,372
Rhine River port since eleventh century	
Edmonton, Alberta, Canada	803,500*
Originally (1795) Hudson Bay trading post	
Essen, Germany	619,981
Ruhr Valley city founded in ninth century	
Frankfurt, Germany	623,724
Site of ancient Roman military camp	
Fukuoka, Japan	1,203,729
Thirteenth-century seaport on Hakata Bay	
Genoa, Italy	742,442
Roman settlement in third century B.C.	
Glasgow, Scotland	703,186
Founded by sixth-century missionaries	
Gorky, Russia	1,425,000
Founded in 1221; renamed for Maxim Gorky	
Guadalajara, Mexico	1,626,152
Originally founded in 1530	
Guangzhou, China	3,181,510
Inland seaport since third century B.C.	
Guatemala City, Guatemala	754,243
Founded as capital in 1776	
Guayaquil, Ecuador	1,572,615
Founded by conquistadors in 1535	
Hamburg, Germany	1,595,255
Founded in ninth century by Charlemagne	
Harbin, China	2,519,120
Village until linked by railroad in 1898	
Havana, Cuba	2,077,938
Founded in 1519 as Spanish navy base	
Ho Chi Minh City, Vietnam	2,700,938
Formerly Saigon, ancient Khmer village	
Hyderabad, India	2,093,488
Founded as Golconda; capital in 1589	
Hyderabad, Pakistan	751,529*
Founded in 1768 as capital of Sind	
Ibadan, Nigeria	847,000
Founded around 1830 as military camp	
Istanbul, Turkey	6,293,397
Until A.D. 300, Byzantium; until 1930, Constantinople	

City	Population
Jakarta, Indonesia	7,885,519
Founded in 1619 as Batavia; renamed 1971	
Jerusalem, Israel	493,000
Capital of ancient kingdoms of Israel and Judah	
Johannesburg, South Africa	632,369
Founded as gold-mining camp in 1886	
Kanpur, India	1,481,789
Village until ceded to British in 1801	
Karachi, Pakistan	5,180,562*
Founded in 1725 as Hindu trading center	
Kharkov, Ukraine	1,587,000
Founded in 1654 as outpost of Moscow	
Kiev, Ukraine	2,544,000
Russian "Mother of Cities," founded A.D. 882	
Kinshasa, Zaire	2,653,558
Founded in 1881 as Leopoldville; renamed 1966	
Kobe, Japan	1,447,547
Ancient fishing village until 1868	
Kuala Lumpur, Malaysia	919,610
Founded as tin-mining settlement in 1857	
Kuibyshev, Russia	1,280,000
Founded in 1586; temporary Russian capital in World War II	
Lagos, Nigeria	1,060,848
Former slave trading center; now the capital	
Lahore, Pakistan	2,952,689*
Capital of Mogul sultans in eleventh century	
La Paz, Bolivia	976,800
Founded in 1548; capital since 1898	
Leipzig, Germany	538,860
Founded in eleventh century; Bach was organist here	
Lima, Peru	6,233,800*
Site of oldest university of Americas (1551)	
Lisbon, Portugal	806,167
Ancient Phoenician, Carthaginian trading center	
Liverpool, England	469,642
Chartered in 1207 by King John	
Lodz, Poland	857,485
Founded in 1423; belonged to Russia until 1919	
London, England	6,735,353
Established in A.D. 43 as Roman town of Londinium	
Los Angeles, California	3,362,710
Founded in 1781 as capital of Spanish colony	
Madras, India	3,276,622
Founded in 1640 as British outpost	
Madrid, Spain	2,991,223
A Moorish fortress until 932	
Managua, Nicaragua	608,020
Established as capital in 1855 to end feud	

City	Population
Manila, Philippines	1,728,441
Founded by Spanish in 1571	
Marseilles, France	876,260
Originally Massilia, Ionian Greek colony, in 600 B.C.	
Mecca, Saudi Arabia	366,801
Birthplace of Muhammad in 570	
Medellín, Colombia	1,452,392*
Coffee, drugs, mining center founded 1675	
Melbourne, Australia	2,965,600
Founded 1835 by Tasmanian settlers	
Mexico City, Mexico	8,831,079
Aztec capital until captured by Cortés in 1521	
Milan, Italy	1,548,580
Ancient Celtic town captured by Romans in 222 B.C.	
Minsk, Byelorussia	1,543,000
Eleventh-century city on Moscow–Warsaw rail link	
Monterrey, Mexico	1,084,696
Founded in 1579; invaded by U.S. troops in 1846	
Montevideo, Uruguay	1,251,647
Settled by Spanish in 1726; capital since 1828	
Montreal, Quebec, Canada	3,021,300*
Site of Indian encampment, founded by French in 1642	
Moscow, Russia	8,818,000
Founded in 1147; became capital around 1340	
Munich, Germany	1,206,394
Founded in 1158; birthplace of Nazi movement, 1923	
Nagoya, Japan	2,147,667
Buddhist temple site in second century; now an industrial city	
Nanjing, China	2,091,400
Founded in 1368; twice capital in twentieth century	
Naples, Italy	1,207,750
Named Neapolis (New City) by Greek settlers around 600 B.C.	
New York City, New York	7,352,700
Founded in 1609 as New Amsterdam by Dutch; renamed 1664	
Novosibirsk, Russia	1,423,000
"Chicago of Siberia," founded in 1893 on Trans-Siberian Railway	
Odessa, Ukraine	1,141,000
Founded by Tartars in fourteenth century	
Osaka, Japan	2,644,691
Founded in sixteenth century as capital city	
Ottawa, Ontario, Canada	853,200*
Selected as capital in 1858 by Queen Victoria	
Palermo, Italy	714,246
Founded by Phoenicians in eighth century B.C.	
Paris, France	2,188,960
Grew from pre-Roman settlement named Lutetia Parisiorum	
Port-au-Prince, Haiti	461,464
Founded by sugar planters in 1749; capital since 1804	

City	Population
Pôrto Alegre, Brazil	1,275,483
Founded in 1742 by settlers from Azores	
Prague, Czech Republic	1,209,149
Grew from tenth-century trading center	
Pusan, South Korea	3,514,798
Originally a fishing village; opened to trade in 1443	
Pyongyang, North Korea	1,250,000
Existed as Heijo, Korean cultural center, in 1100 B.C.	
Quebec City, Quebec, Canada	615,400*
Site of Indian settlement visited by Cartier in 1535	
Quezon City, Philippines	1,546,019
Founded in 1940 as site of future capital	
Quito, Ecuador	1,137,705
Originally Quito Indian camp; captured by Incas in 1470	
Recife, Brazil	1,289,627
Settled by Portuguese in 1535	
Rio de Janeiro, Brazil	5,615,149
Founded by Portuguese in 1502; capital since 1889	
Riyadh, Saudi Arabia	666,840
One-time center of classic Arabic architecture	
Rome, Italy	2,828,692
According to legend, founded in 753 B.C. by Romulus	
Rosario, Argentina	1,071,384*
City in La Pampa region; founded in 1730	
Rotterdam, The Netherlands	575,266
North Sea port chartered in 1328	
St. Petersburg, Russia	4,948,000
Founded in 1703; named Leningrad from 1924 to 1991	
Salvador, Brazil	1,811,367
Founded in 1549 as Bahia	
Santiago, Chile	4,099,714
Founded in 1541 by conquistadors	
Santo Domingo, Dominican Republic	673,470
Oldest continuous European settlement in Americas, founded in 1496	
São Paulo, Brazil	10,099,086
Founded in 1554 by Jesuit missionaries on Indian campsite	
Sapporo, Japan	1,621,418
Founded in 1869 in government plan to develop Hokkaido Island	
Seoul, South Korea	9,639,110
Originally named Keijo, a Korean capital since 1392	
Seville, Spain	653,533
Originally Hispalis, a Phoenician trading center	
Shanghai, China	6,292,960
Existed as Hu-tsen in Sung dynasty, eleventh century	
Shenyang, China	3,944,240
Formerly Mukden, capital city of twelfth-century Tartars	
Singapore, Singapore	2,704,000
Originally Singhapura, destroyed in 1365; refounded in 1819	

City	Population
Sofia, Bulgaria	1,127,527
Founded as Sardica by second-century Romans; capital since 1879	
Stockholm, Sweden	666,810
Originally a fishing village, founded in thirteenth century	
Surabaja, Indonesia	2,027,913
Grew from seventeenth-century Javanese trading post	
Sverdlovsk, Russia	1,331,000
Founded in 1721 as Ekaterinburg (Catherine); renamed in 1924	
Sydney, Australia	3,531,000
First British settlement in Australia, 1788	
Taipei, Taiwan	2,270,983
Settled in eighteenth century by Chinese mainland immigrants	
Tashkent, Uzbekistan	2,124,000
Ancient central Asian city; existed in first century B.C.	
Tbilisi, Georgia	1,194,000
Also called Tiflis; settled in fourth century B.C.	
Tehran, Iran	6,042,584
Settled in thirteenth century by refugees from Mongol invasion	
Tianjin, China	5,152,180
Also called Tientsin, ancient trading center	
Tokyo, Japan	8,323,699
Founded in twelfth century as fortress for warlord	
Toronto, Ontario, Canada	3,666,600*
Originally Fort Rouille, 1749; York, 1793; renamed 1834	
Tripoli, Libya	551,477
Founded as Oea by Phoenicians in seventh century B.C.	
Tunis, Tunisia	596,654
Pre-Carthaginian city with access to Mediterranean	
Turin, Italy	1,059,505
Ancient Roman city of Augusta Taurinorum	
Valencia, Spain	718,750
Former city of Romans, Visigoths, Moors	
Vancouver, British Columbia, Canada	1,506,000
Originally settled in 1875 as Granville; renamed 1886	
Vienna, Austria	1,486,963
Capital of the Austro-Hungarian Empire 1278–1918; now capital of the Austrian republic	
Volgograd, Russia	988,000
Founded in 1589 as Tsaritsyn; later Stalingrad; renamed 1961	
Warsaw, Poland	1,673,688
Settled in eleventh century; capital since 1596	
Washington, D.C.	617,000
Founded in 1790 on site selected by George Washington	
Wellington, New Zealand	135,400
Founded in 1840; replaced Auckland as capital in 1865	
Yangon, Myanmar	2,513,023
Existed as fishing village in sixth century	
Yokohama, Japan	3,151,087
Feudal fishing village until opened to foreign trade in 1859	

The United Nations

The United Nations organization was established during World War II as an outgrowth of an agreement among 26 countries fighting the Germany–Italy–Japan Axis. It replaced the League of Nations as an instrument for the promotion of international peace and security.

The name was suggested by U.S. President Franklin D. Roosevelt in 1941 and was officially adopted the following year. The United Nations was formally organized on June 26, 1945, following an initial San Francisco conference to draft a charter.

The basic charter contains 19 chapters, divided into 111 articles, and provides for the support of a number of international organs and agencies. These include the General Assembly, Security Council, Secretariat, International Court of Justice, Trusteeship Council, Economic and Social Council, World Health Organization, Food and Agricultural Organization, International Bank for Reconstruction and Development, International Labor Organization, International Monetary Fund, International Civil Aviation Organization, International Telecommunications Union, Universal Postal Union, World Meteorological Organization, and Educational, Scientific, and Cultural Organization (UNESCO).

The United Nations System

Main committees
Standing and procedural committees
Other subsidiary organs

- Trusteeship Council
- Security Council
- General Assembly
- International Court of Justice
- Secretariat
- Economic and Social Council

Security Council related
- UNAVEM: United Nations Angola Verification Mission
- UNDOF: United Nations Disengagement Observer Force
- UNFICYP: United Nations Force in Cyprus
- UNIFIL: United Nations Interim Force in Lebanon
- UNIIMOG: United Nations Iran-Iraq Military Observer Group
- UNMOGIP: United Nations Military Observer Group in India and Pakistan
- UNTSO: United Nations Truce Supervision Organization
- Military Staff Committee

General Assembly related
- UNRWA: United Nations Relief and Works Agency for Palestine Refugees in the Near East
- UNCTAD: United Nations Conference on Trade and Development
- UNICEF: United Nations Children's Fund
- UNHCR: United Nations Office of High Commissioner for Refugees
- WFP: World Food Program
- UNITAR: United Nations Institute for Training and Research
- UNDP: United Nations Development Program
- UNEP: United Nations Environment Program
- UNU: United Nations University
- UNCHS (Habitat): United Nations Center for Human Settlements
- UNFPA: United Nations Population Fund
- UNSF: United Nations Special Fund
- WFC: World Food Council

Economic and Social Council
Regional Commissions
- ECA: Economic Commission for Africa
- ECE: Economic Commission for Europe
- ECLAC: Economic Commission for Latin America and the Caribbean
- ESCAP: Economic and Social Commission for Asia and the Pacific
- ESCWA: Economic and Social Commission for Western Asia

Functional Commissions
- Commission on Human Rights
- Commission on Narcotic Drugs
- Commission for Social Development
- Commission on the Status of Women
- Population Commission
- Statistical Commission

Sessional, standing, and ad hoc committees

Specialized agencies
- IAEA: International Atomic Energy Agency
- GATT: General Agreement on Tariffs and Trade
- ILO: International Labor Organization
- FAO: Food and Agriculture Organization of the United Nations
- UNESCO: United Nations Educational, Scientific, and Cultural Organization
- WHO: World Health Organization
- IMF: International Monetary Fund
- IDA: International Development Association
- IBRD: International Bank for Reconstruction and Development
- IFC: International Finance Corporation
- ICAO: International Civil Aviation Organization
- UPU: Universal Postal Union
- ITU: International Telecommunication Union
- WMO: World Meteorological Organization
- IMO: International Maritime Organization
- WIPO: World Intellectual Property Organization
- IFAD: International Fund for Agricultural Development
- UNIDO: United Nations Industrial Development Organization

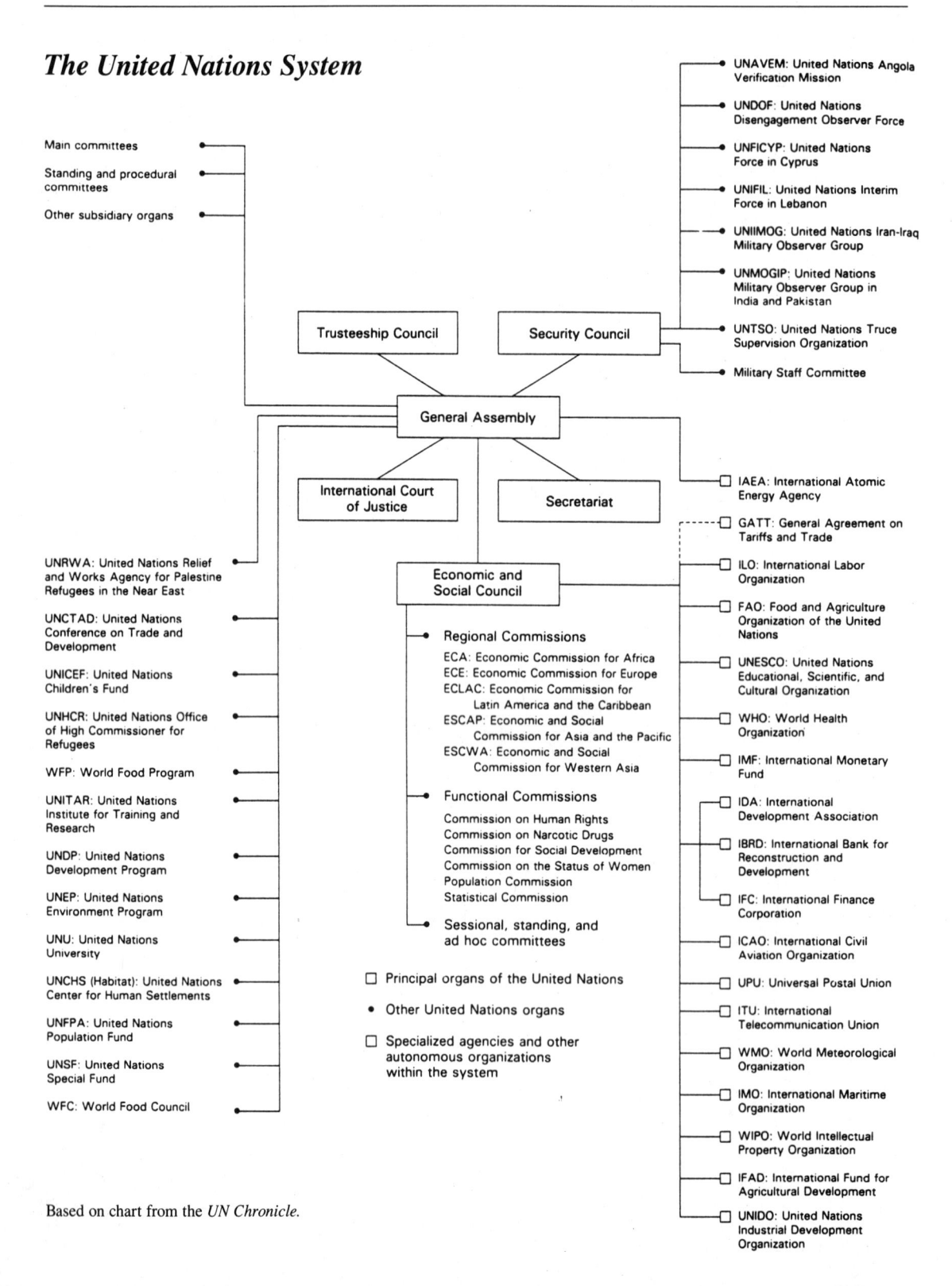

Legend:
- ☐ Principal organs of the United Nations
- ● Other United Nations organs
- ☐ Specialized agencies and other autonomous organizations within the system

Based on chart from the *UN Chronicle*.

International Organizations

A	AfDB	African Development Bank
	AL	Arab League (League of Arab States)
	ANZUS	ANZUS Council; treaty signed by Australia, New Zealand, and the United States
	APC	African Peanut (Groundnut) Council
	AsDB	Asian Development Bank
	ASEAN	Association of Southeast Asian Nations
B	BENELUX	Belgium, Netherlands, Luxembourg Economic Union
C	CACM	Central American Common Market
	CARICOM	Caribbean Common Market
	CCC	Customs Cooperation Council
	CDB	Caribbean Development Bank
	CE	Council of Europe
	CEAO	West African Economic Community
	CENTO	Central Treaty Organization
	CFA	African Financial Community
	CE	Council of Europe
	CP	Colombo Plan
E	EC	European Community
	ECA	Economic Commission for Africa (UN)
	ECE	Economic Commission for Europe (UN)
	ECLA	Economic Commission for Latin America (UN)
	ECOSOC	Economic and Social Council (UN)
	ECOWAS	Economic Community of West African States
	ECWA	Economic Commission for Western Asia (UN)
	EEC	European Economic Market
	EFTA	European Free Trade Association
	EIB	European Investment Bank
	ENTENTE	Political-Economic Association of Ivory Coast, Benin, Niger, Burkina Faso, and Togo
	ESCAP	Economic and Social Commission for Asia and the Pacific (UN)
	ESRO	European Space Research Organization
F	FAO	Food and Agriculture Organization (UN)
G	G-77	Group of 77
	GA	General Assembly (UN)
	GATT	General Agreement of Tariffs and Trade (UN)
	GCC	Gulf Cooperation Council
I	IADB	Inter-American Development Bank
	IAEA	International Atomic Energy Agency (UN)
	IBEC	International Bank for Economic Cooperation
	IBRD	International Bank for Reconstruction and Development ("World Bank," UN)
	ICAO	International Civil Aviation Organization (UN)
	ICJ	International Court of Justice (UN)
	IDA	International Development Association (IBRD affiliate, UN)
	IDB	Inter-American Development Bank

	IDB	Islamic Development Bank
	IEA	International Energy Agency (associated with OECD)
	IFAD	International Fund for Agricultural Development (UN)
	IFC	International Finance Corporation (IBRD affiliate, UN)
	IIB	International Investment Bank
	ILO	International Labor Organization (UN)
	IMF	International Monetary Fund (UN)
	IMO	International Maritime Organization (UN)
	INTELSAT	International Telecommunications Satellite Organization
	IOC	International Olympic Committee
	IOM	International Organization for Migration
	ITU	International Telecommunications Union (UN)
L	LAIA	Latin American Integration Association
N	NAM	Nonaligned Movement
	NATO	North Atlantic Treaty Organization
O	OAPEC	Organization of Arab Petroleum Exporting Countries
	OAS	Organization of American States
	OAU	Organization of African Unity
	ODECA	Organization of Central American States
	OECD	Organization for Economic Cooperation and Development
	OIC	Organization of the Islamic Conference
	OIEC	Organization for International Economic Cooperation
	OPEC	Organization of Petroleum Exporting Countries
P	PAHO	Pan American Health Organization
S	SAARC	South Asian Association for Regional Cooperation
	SADCC	Southern African Development Coordination Committee
	SC	Security Council (UN)
	SELA	Latin American Economic System
	SPC	South Pacific Commission
	SPF	South Pacific Forum
T	TC	Trusteeship Council (UN)
	TDB	Trade and Development Board (UN)
U	UDEAC	Economic and Customs Union of Central Africa
	UEAC	Union of Central African States
	UNCTAD	UN Conference on Trade and Development
	UNDP	UN Development Program
	UNESCO	UN Educational, Scientific, and Cultural Organization
	UNICEF	UN Children's Fund
	UNIDO	UN Industrial Development Organization
	UPU	Universal Postal Union (UN)
W	WEU	Western European Union
	WFC	World Food Council (UN)
	WFTU	World Federation of Trade Unions
	WHO	World Health Organization (UN)
	WIPO	World Intellectual Property Organization (UN)
	WMO	World Meteorological Organization (UN)
	WTO	World Tourism Organization

INTERNATIONAL CONVERSIONS

To convert from	To	Multiply by
Acres	Hectares	0.40468586
Acres	Kilometers, square	0.004046856
Acres	Meters, square	4046.856
Centimeters	Meters	0.01
Centimeters, square	Meters, square	0.0001
Degrees, Fahrenheit	Degrees, Celsius	subtract 32 and multiply by 5/9
Feet	Centimeters	30.48
Feet	Meters	0.3048
Feet	Kilometers	0.0003048
Feet, cubic	Liters	28.316847
Feet, cubic	Meters, cubic	0.028316847
Feet, square	Centimeters, square	929.0304
Feet, square	Meters, square	0.09390304

To convert from	To	Multiply by
Gallons, US liquid	Liters	3.785412
Gallons, US liquid	Meters, cubic	0.003785412
Grams	Ounces, troy	0.032151
Grams	Pounds, troy	0.002679
Hectares	Kilometers, square	0.01
Hectares	Meters, squares	10.000
Inches	Centimeters	2.54
Inches	Meters	0.0254
Inches, cubic	Milliliters	16.387064
Inches, cubic	Liters	0.016387064
Inches, cubic	Meters, cubic	0.000016387064
Inches, square	Centimeters, square	6.4516
Inches, square	Meters, square	0.00064516
Kilograms	Ounces, troy	32.15075

INTERNATIONAL CONVERSIONS

To convert from	To	Multiply by
Kilograms	Pounds, troy	2.679229
Kilograms	Tons, metric	0.001
Kilometers, square	Hectares	100
Kilometers, square	Miles, square	.3861
Liters	Milliliters	1000
Liters	Meters, cubic	0.001
Meters	Millimeters	1000
Meters	Centimeters	100
Meters	Kilometers	0.001
Meters, cubic	Liters	1000
Meters, cubic	Tons, register	0.353147
Miles, nautical	Kilometers	1.852
Miles, square	Hectares	258.99881
Miles, square	Kilometers, square	2.5899881
Miles, statute	Centimeters	160934.4

To convert from	To	Multiply by
Miles, Statute	Meters	1609.344
Miles, statute	Kilometers	1.609344
Ounces, avoirdupois	Grams	28,349523
Ounces, avoirdupois	Kilograms	0.028349523
Ounces, troy	Pounds, troy	0.083333
Ounces, troy	Grams	31.10348
Pints, U.S. liquid	Milliliters	473.176473
Pints, U.S. liquid	Liters	0.473176473
Pounds, avoirdupois	Grams	453.59237
Pounds, avoirdupois	Kilograms	0.45359237
Pounds, avoirdupois	Quintals	0.0045359237
Pounds, avoirdupois	Tons, metric	0.00045359237
Pounds, troy	Ounces, troy	12
Pounds, troy	Grams	373.2417216

Mathematical Conversions

To convert from	To	Multiply by
Quarts, dry	Liters	1.101221
Quarts, dry	Dekaliters	0.1101221
Quarts, liquid	Milliliters	946.352946
Quarts, liquid	Liters	0.946352946
Quintals	Tons, metric	0.1
Ton-miles, long	Ton-kilometers, metric	1.635169
Ton-miles, short	Ton-kilometric, metric	1.4359972
Tons, long	Kilograms	1016.047
Tons, long	Tons, metric	1.016047

To convert from	To	Multiply by
Tons, metric	Quintals	10
Tons, register	Meters, cubic	2.831685
Tons, short	Kilograms	907,185
Tons, short	Tons, metric	0.907185
Yards	Centimeters	91.44
Yards	Meters	0.9144
Yards, cubic	Liters	764,5549
Yards, cubic	Meters, cubic	0.7645549
Yards, square	Meters, square	0.836127

Foreign Dialing Codes

Note: For international telephone calls automatically routed through AT&T, dial "011," then dial the code for that country, the city code if one is indicated, and the subscriber telephone number to be reached. Other long-distance telephone services may have other procedures and should be consulted for their specific instructions.

Algeria	213
American Samoa	684
Andorra	33
(all points 628)	
Argentina	54
(Buenos Aires 1)	
Australia	61
(Melbourne 3)	
(Sydney 2)	
Austria	43
(Vienna 1)	
Bahrain	973
Belgium	32
(Brussels 2)	
(Ghent 91)	
Belize	501
Bolivia	591
(Santa Cruz 33)	
Brazil	55
(Brasília 61)	
(Rio de Janeiro 21)	
Cameroon	237
Chile	56
(Santiago 2)	
Colombia	57
(Bogot´1)	
Costa Rica	506
Cyprus	357
Czechoslovakia	42
(Prague 2)	
Denmark	45
(Aalborg 8)	
(Copenhagen 1 or 2)	
Ecuador	593
(Cuneca 7)	
(Quito 2)	
Egypt	20
(Alexandria 3)	
Port Said 66)	
El Salvador	503
England See United Kingdom.	
Ethiopia	251
(Addis Ababa 1)	
Fiji	697
Finland	358
(Helsinki 0)	
France	33
(Marseille 91)	
(Nice 93)	
(Paris 1)	
French Antilles	596
French Antilles-Guadeloupe	590
French Polynesia	689
Gabon	241
Germany	49
(Frankfurt 69)	
(Munich 89)	
(Berlin 30)	
(other areas of former East Germany 37)	
Greece	30
(Athens 1)	
(Rhodes 241)	
Guam	671
Guantanamo Bay U.S. naval base	53
(all points 99)	
Guatemala	502
(Guatemala City 2)	
(Antigua 9)	
Guyana	592
(Georgetown 2)	
Haiti	509
(Port-au-Prince)	
Honduras	504
Hong Kong	852
(Hong Kong 5)	
(Kowloon 3)	
Hungary	36
(Budapest 1)	
Iceland	354
(Akureyri 6)	
(Hahnarfjorour 1)	
India	91
(Bombay 22)	
(New Delhi 11)	
Indonesia	62
(Jakarta 21)	
Iran	98
(Teheran 21)	
Iraq	964
(Baghdad 1)	
Ireland	353
(Dublin 1)	
(Galway 91)	
Israel	972
(Haifa 4)	
(Jerusalem 2)	
(Tel Aviv 3)	
Italy	39
(Florence 55)	
(Rome 6)	
Venice 41)	
Ivory Coast	225
Japan	81
(Tokyo 3)	
(Yokohama 45)	
Jordan	962
(Amman 6)	
Kenya	254
Korea, South	82
(Pusan 51)	
(Seoul 2)	
Kuwait	965
Liberia	231
Libya	218
(Tripoli 21)	

Liechtenstein	41	Papua New Guinea	675	Switzerland	41
(all points 75)		Paraguay	595	(Geneva 22)	
Luxembourg	352	(Asuncion 21)		(Lucerne 41)	
Malawi	265	Peru	51	(Zurich 1)	
(Domasi 531)		(Arequipa 54)		Taiwan	886
Malaysia	60	(Lima 14)		(Tainan 6)	
(Kuala Lumpur 3)		Philippines	63	(Taipei 3)	
Mexico	52	(Manila 2)		Thailand	66
(Mexico City 5)		Poland	48	(Bangkok 2)	
(Tijuana 66)		(Warsaw 22)		Tunisia	216
Monaco	33	Portugal	351	(Tunis 1)	
(all points 93)		(Lisbon 1)		Turkey	90
Morocco	212	Qatar	974	(Istanbul 1)	
(Agadir 8)		Romania	40	(Izmir 51)	
Namibia	264	(Bucharest 0)		United Arab Emirates	971
(Olympia 61)		Saipan	670)	(Abu Dhabi 2)	
Netherlands	31	San Marino	39	(Al Ain 3)	
(Amsterdam 20)		(all points 541)		(Dubai 4)	
(The Hague 70)		Saudi Arabia	966	(Ras Al Khainah 77)	
Netherlands Antilles	599	(Riyadh 1)		(Sharjah 6)	
Netherlands Antilles-Aruba	297	Senegal	221	(Umm Al Quwain 6)	
(Aruba 8)		Singapore	65	United Kingdom	44
New Caledonia	687	South Africa	27	(Belfast 232)	
New Zealand	64	(Cape Town 21)		(Cardiff 222)	
(Auckland 9)		(Pretoria 12)		(Glasgow 41)	
(Wellington 4)		Spain	34	(London 71 or 81)	
Nicaragua	505	(Barcelona 3)		Uruguay	598
(Managua 2)		(Las Palmas, Canary Islands 28)		(Mercedes 532)	
Nigeria	234	(Madrid 1)		(Montevideo 2)	
(Lagos 1)		(Seville 54)		Vatican City	39
Norway	47	Sri Lanka	94	(all points 6)	
(Bergen 5)		(Kandy 8)		Venezuela	58
(Oslo 2)		Suriname	597	(Caracas 2)	
Oman	968	Sweden	46	(Maracaibo 61)	
Pakistan	92	(Göteborg 31)		Yemen Arab Republic	967
(Islamabad 51)		(Stockholm 8)		(Amran 2)	
Panama	507			Yugoslavia	38
				(Belgrade 11)	

Seven Wonders of the Ancient World

Artemision at Ephesus, the temple of the Greek goddess Artemis (also the Roman goddess Diana), was begun in 541 B.C. at Ephesus (now a site in Turkey) and completed 220 years later. The temple was 425 feet long and 220 feet wide with 127 marble columns, each 60 feet tall. The gates were made of cypress and the ceiling of cedar. The temple was destroyed by the Goths in A.D. 262.

The Colossus of Rhodes, a 100-foot-tall bronze statue of the sun god Helios, was erected between 292 and 280 B.C. in the harbor at Rhodes. According to legend, it appeared to stand astride the harbor but was actually on a promontory overlooking it. The statue was toppled by an earthquake around 224 B.C. and lay in ruins until A.D. 653, when the remains were sold as scrap metal.

The Hanging Gardens of Babylon, a series of five terraces of glazed brick, each 50 feet above the next, was erected by King Nebuchadnezzar for his wife, Amytis, in 562 B.C. The terraces, featuring rare and exotic plants, were connected by a winding stairway, a pumping device supplied water so the gardens could be irrigated by fountains.

The Mausoleum at Halicarnassus, a 140-foot-high white marble structure, was built in 352 B.C. at Halicarnassus (now a site in Turkey) in memory of King Mausolus of Caria. Its massive base contained the sarcophagus and supported 36 columns crowned with a stepped pyramid on which was constructed a marble chariot. It was destroyed for the use of stone to build a castle for the Knights of Saint John in 1402.

Olympian Zeus, a statue of the supreme god in Greek mythology, was executed in gold and ivory for the temple at Olympia. The figure of the seated Zeus was 40 feet tall and rested on a base that was 12 feet high. The portions of the statue representing the flesh of the god were covered with marble and his cloak was made of gold. Golden lions rested near his feet.

The Pyramids of Egypt were started by Khufu (Cheops) around 2700 B.C. as tombs for the ancient kings. The three largest and finest were erected during the Fourth dynasty at Gizeh, near Cairo. The largest of the group is the Khufu Pyramid, built of limestone blocks from a base 756 feet wide on each side and covering an area of 13 acres. It is 482 feet high. Smaller pyramids were built for wives and other members of the royal families.

The Tower of Pharos was a great lighthouse built on the island of Pharos, at Alexandria, Egypt, during the reign of Ptolemy Philadelphus, 285 B.C. Also called The Pharos, it was 500 feet tall with a ramp leading to the top. Light was produced with a fire and reflectors and could be seen from a distance of 42 miles.

Royal Rulers of Europe and Asia

Europe and Russia

Great Britain

William I the Conqueror	1066–1087
William II	1087–1100
Henry I	1100–1135
Stephen	1135–1154
Henry II	1154–1189
Richard I	1189–1199
John	1199–1216
Henry III	1216–1271
Edward I	1271–1307
Edward II	1307–1327
Edward III	1327–1377
Richard II	1377–1399
Henry IV	1399–1413
Henry V	1413–1422
Henry VI	1422–1461
Edward IV	1461–1483
Edward V	1483
Richard III	1483–1485
Henry VII	1485–1509
Henry VIII	1509–1547
Edward VI	1547–1553
Mary I	1553–1558
Elizabeth I	1558–1603
James I	1603–1625
Charles I	1625–1649
(Commonwealth period)	1649–1660
Charles II	1660–1685
James II	1685–1688
William III and Mary II	1689–1694
William III (alone)	1694–1702
Anne	1702–1714
George I	1714–1727
George II	1727–1760
George III	1760–1820
George IV	1820–1830
William IV	1830–1837
Victoria	1837–1901
Edward VII	1901–1910
George V	1910–1936
Edward VIII	1936
George VI	1936–1952
Elizabeth II	1952

France

Henri I	1031–1060
Philip I	1060–1108
Louis VI	1108–1137
Louis VII	1137–1180
Philip II	1180–1223
Louis VIII	1223–1226
Louis IX	1226–1270
Philip III	1270–1285
Philip IV	1285–1314
Louis X	1314–1316
John I	1316
Philip V	1316–1322
Charles IV	1322–1328
Philip VI	1328–1350
John II	1350–1364
Charles V	1364–1380
Charles VI	1380–1422
Charles VII	1422–1461
Louis XI	1461–1483
Charles VIII	1483–1498
Louis XII	1498–1515
François I	1515–1547
Henri II	1547–1559
François II	1559–1560
Charles IX	1560–1574
Henri III	1574–1589
Henri IV	1589–1610
Louis XIII	1610–1643
Louis XIV	1643–1715
Louis XV	1715–1774
Louis XVI	1774–1792
(First Republic)	1792–1804
Napoleon I	1804–1814

Louis XVIII	1814–1824
Charles X	1824–1830
Louis Philippe	1830–1848
(Second Republic)	1848–1852
Napoleon III	1852–1870

Germany

Frederick I	1710–1713
Frederick William I	1713–1740
Frederick II	1740–1786
Frederick William II	1786–1797
Frederick William III	1797–1840
Frederick William IV	1840–1861
William I	1861–1888
Frederick III	1888
William II	1888–1918

Russia

Ivan III	1462–1505
Vasilly III	1505–1533
Ivan IV	1533–1584
Theodore I	1584–1598
Boris Godunov	1598–1605
Theodore II	1605
Demetrius I	1605–1606
Basil IV	1606–1610
Wladyslaw (Polish Prince)	1620–1613
Mikhail Romanov	1613–1645
Alexia I	1645–1676
Theodore III	1676–1682
Ivan V and Peter I	1682–1689
Peter I (alone)	1689–1725
Catherine I	1725–1727
Peter II	1727–1730
Anna	1730–1740
Ivan VI	1740–1741
Elizabeth	1741–1762
Peter III	1762
Catherine II	1762–1796
Paul I	1796–1801
Alexander I	1801–1825
Nicholas I	1825–1855
Alexander II	1855–1881
Alexander III	1881–1894
Nicholas II	1894–1917

Asia

China

Yuan (Kublai Khan) dynasty	1260–1368
Ming dynasty	1368–1644
Manchu (Ch'ing) dynasty	1644–1912
Shun Chih	1644–1661
K'ang Hsi	1661–1722
Yung Cheng	1722–1735
Ch'ien Lung	1735–1796
Chia Ch'ing	1796–1820
Tao Kuang	1820–1851
Hsien Feng	1851–1861
T'ung Chi	1861–1875
Kuang Hsu	1875–1898
Tzu Hsi	1898–1908
P'u Yi	1908–1912

Japan

Tokugawa Shogun rule	1603–1868
(Meiji) Mutsuhito	1867–1912
Taishō (Yoshihito)	1912–1926
Shōwa (Hirohito)	1926–1989
Heisei (Akihito)	1989–

THE SIX WIVES OF HENRY VIII

Catherine of Aragon
Anne Boleyn
Jane Seymour
Anne of Cleves
Catherine Howard
Catherine Parr

Additional Sources of Information

Central Intelligence Agency, *The World Factbook*. U.S. Government Printing Office, annual.

Grun, Bernard. *The Timetables of History*. Touchstone, 1991.

The Harper Atlas of World History. Harper & Row, 1987.

Hoffman, Mark S. *The World Almanac and Book of Facts*. Pharos Books, annual.

Hulme, F. Edward. *Flags of the World: Their History, Blazonry and Associations*. Gordon Press, 1977.

Maps on File. Facts On File, 1987.

The New International World Atlas. Rand McNally, 1989.

Simony, Maggy. *The Traveler's Reading Guide: Ready-Made Reading Lists for the Armchair Traveler*, rev. ed. Facts On File, 1993.

Trager, James, ed. *The People's Chronology: A Year by Year Record of Human Events from Prehistory to the Present*. Holt, Rinehart and Winston, 1979.

Wetterau, Bruce. *Macmillan Concise Dictionary of World History*. Macmillan, 1986.

Wetterau, Bruce. *The New York Public Library Book of Chronologies*. Prentice Hall, 1990.

Organizations and Services

The Asia Foundation
465 California Street
San Francisco, CA 94108

Bureau of Public Affairs
U.S. Department of State
2201 C Street, NW
Washington, DC 20520

Carnegie Endowment for International Peace
2400 N Street, NW
Washington, DC 20037

Central Intelligency Agency
Public Affairs Director
McClean, VA 22050

European Community Press and Public Affairs
2100 M Street, NW
Washington, DC 20037

Middle East Institute
1761 N Street, NW
Washington, DC 20036

Organization of American States
17th Street and Constitution Avenue, NW
Washington, DC 20006

United Nations Headquarters
United Nations Plaza
New York, NY 10017

United Nations Information Center
1889 F Street, NW
Washington, DC 20006

United States Mission to the United Nations
799 United Nations Plaza
New York, NY 10017

Index

Aalto, Alvar, 195
Abacus, 196
Abaxial, 91
Abbreviations
   acronyms, 346–349
   common, 323–328
   cooking measures, 580
   geographic directional, 329
   street designators, 329–330
   titles that follow names, 392
   US Postal Service, 328–329
Abelard, Peter, 262
Aberration, 90
Abiogenesis, 91
Abrasions, 755
Absolutism, 270
Absorbing dynamometer, 95
Abstract dance, 162
Abstract impressionism, 180
Abutment, 95
Abyssal zone, 96
Academy Awards, 202–205
A cappella, 143
Accelerando, 143
Acceleration, 80, 95
Acceleration of gravity, 80
Accent (musical), 143
Accessory (legal), 424
Accompaniment (musical), 143
Accomplice, 424
Accrued interest, 448
Acetaminophen, 701
Achromatic, 95
Acid
   definition of, 93
   stain removal, 569
Acoustics, 95, 143
Acre, 25
Acronyms, 346–349
Acropolis, 196
Acrylic, 178
Actus reus, 424
Adagietto, 143
Adagio (dance), 163
Adagio (music), 143
Adagissimo, 143
Adam, Robert, 195
Adams, John, 819, 823
Adams, John Quincy, 819
Adaptation, 91
Additives, chemical, 592–599
Address (computer), 98
Adenosine triphosphate (ATP), 91
Adhesive tape, stain removal, 570
Adiabetic, 95
Adjective, 357, 359

Adjudication, 424
Adjustable rate mortgage, 445
Adler, Felix, 232
Ad libitum, 143
Adobe, 196
Adonis, 248
Adoption organizations, 519
Advent (holiday), 243
Adverb, 357, 360
Aeolus, 248
Aeschylus, 188
Aesthetics, 270
Affetuoso, 143
Affidavit, 424
Afghanistan
   statistics, 853
   visa requirements, 533
Age (geologic), 96
Agee, James, 207
Age of consent, 424
Aggregate, 95
Aging
   private organizations, 456
   state commissions and offices, 456–460
   see also Retirement
Agitato, 143
Agnew, Spiro, 824
Agnosticism, 270
Aiken, Conrad, 207
Ailey, Alvin, 156
Air (musical), 143
Air, en l', 162
Airlines
   codes and toll-free numbers, 526
   tips for disabled, 559
Air mileage, from New York City, 529
Airports, codes, 527
Aisle, 196
Alabama
   Better Business Bureaus, 463
   consumer protection office, 469
   crime rate, 846
   name origin, 792
   newspapers, 515
   poison control center, 759
   social services offices, 456, 494
   vital statistics, 770, 778, 788, 790
   weather, 824, 826, 827
   wildlife refuges, 629
   zoo, 68
Alaska
   Better Business Bureau, 463
   crime rate, 846
   name origin, 792
   newspapers, 515
   poison control center, 759

   social services offices, 456, 494
   vital statistics, 770, 778, 788, 790
   weather, 824, 826, 827
   wildlife refuges, 629–630
Albania
   statistics, 853
   visa requirements, 533
Albedo, 90
Albee, Edward, 183
Albéniz, Isaac, 138
Albers, Josef, 165
Alberta (Canada)
   Better Business Bureaus, 468
   library, 292
   museums, 301
   zoo, 75
Alberti, Leone Battista, 194
Alcohol
   definition, 94
   drink recipes, 600–604
   and driving, 738
   as home remedy, 701
   liquor needed for drinks served, 605
   mixing drinks, 604
   nutritive value of beverages, 712
   safe consumption, 737–738
   stain removal, 570
Alcoholism, organizations for, 461–462
Alcott, Louisa May, 207
Algeria
   dialing code, 896
   statistics, 853
   visa requirements, 533
Alginate, 593
ALGOL (language), 98
Algorithm, 98
Algren, Nelson, 207
Alibi, 424
Alimentary system, 691
Alkali
   definition of, 94
   stain removal, 570
Alla breve, 143
Allargando, 143
Allegory, 221
Allegretto, 144
Allegro, 144, 162
Allemande, 144
Allentando, 144
Alliteration, 221
Allongé, 162
All Saints' Day, 242
Allusion, 221
Alluvium, 96
Alonso, Alicia, 161
Alphabetization rules, 364–365

903

Alphabets
  Arabic, 49
  Braille, 49
  Greek, 50
  Hebrew, 50
  international radio, 48
  manual, 48
  recurrent letters of English, 346
  Russian, 51
Alpha tocopherol *see* Vitamin E
Alto, 144
Altocumulus cloud, 643
Altostratus cloud, 643
Altruism, 270
Ambulatory (aisle), 196
American Samoa
  consumer protection office, 493
  dialing code, 896
  social service offices, 460
  statistics, 792
AMEX, 448
Amicus curiae, 424
Amis, Kingsley, 214
Amish Mennonites, 234
Ammann, Jacob, 234
Ammonia, 701
Amnesty, 424
Amortization, 450
Ampere, 25, 81
Amphibian, 68
Amram, David, 128
Anachronism, 221
Anagram, 221
Analects (Confucius), 231, 246
Analog computer, 98
Analog-to-digital computer, 98
Analogy, 221
Analytical philosophy, 270
Analytic statement, 270
Anarchism, 270
Anatomical drawings, 689–692
Anaxagoras, 262
Anaximander, 262
Anaximenes, 262
Andante, 144
Andantino, 144
Andersen, Hans Christian, 214
Anderson, Sherwood, 207
Andorra
  dialing code, 896
  statistics, 853
Angelico, Fra, 173–174
Angola
  statistics, 853
  visa requirements, 533
Angst, 270
Anguilla, statistics, 853
Angular measures, 22
Animal kingdom, 55
Animals
  bites, 754
  extinct, 65–68
  first aid for, 60–65
  hoofed, 56, 58
  travel with pets, 560–561
  zoos, 68–74
  see also Invertebrates; Mammals; specific animals
Animato, 144
Anion, 94
Announcements, wedding, 372
Anode, 95
Anouilh, Jean, 186
Anselm, St., 262, 264
Answer (musical), 144
Antagonist, 221
Anthem, 144
Anthropology, general reference works, 304–305
Anthropomorphic soil, 97
Anthropomorphism, 221
Anthroposophy, 271
Anticlimax, 221
Antigua and Barbuda
  statistics, 853
  visa requirements, 533
Antihero, 222
Antioxidants, 592
Antiperspirants, stain removal, 570
Antithesis, 222
Aphrodite, 248
Apollo, 248
Apomecometer, 95
A posteriori knowledge, 271
Apostles, 257
Apostrophe, 363
Apothecaries' weights, 22
Apparel *see* Clothing
Appassionato, 144
Appeal (legal), 424
Appellate court, 425
Appendage, 91
Applied arts, 305
Appoggiatura, 144
Appraisal (real estate), 450
Appreciation (financial), 448
A priori knowledge, 271
Apse, 196
Aquatint, 178
Aquinas, St. Thomas, 262, 264, 266, 281
Arabesque (dance), 162
Arabesque (music), 144
Arabic alphabet, 49
Arcade, 196
Arch, 196
Architecture
  glossary of terms, 196–199
  illustrations of styles and elements, 200–201
  major architects, 190–196
    American, 190–192
    British, 192–193
    French, 193–194
    Italian, 194–195
    miscellaneous, 195–196
  see also specific architects
  reference works, 305–306
Architecture (computer), 98
Area
  equations and formulas, 79
  measures, 23, 24
Ares, 248
Argentina
  dialing code, 896
  statistics, 853
  visa requirements, 533
Argument, 271
Aria, 144
Arioso, 144
Aristophanes, 188
Aristotelianism, 271
Aristotle, 262, 269, 271, 278, 280
Arithmetic/logic unit, 98
Arizona
  Better Business Bureaus, 463
  consumer protection offices, 470
  crime rate, 846
  library, 284
  museum, 293
  name origin, 792
  newspapers, 515
  poison control centers, 759
  social service offices, 456
  vital statistics, 770, 778, 788
  weather, 824, 826, 827
  wildlife refuges, 630
  zoos, 68
Arkansas
  Better Business Bureau, 463
  consumer protection office, 471
  crime rate, 846
  name origin, 792
  newspapers, 515
  social services offices, 456, 494
  vital statistics, 770, 778, 788, 790
  weather, 826, 827
  wildlife refuges, 630
  zoo, 68
Armah, Ayi Kweh, 220
Armenia
  statistics, 853
  visa requirements, 533
Armstrong, Louis (Satchmo), 140
Arp, Jean (Hans), 170
Arpeggio, 144
Arpino, Gerald, 156
Arraignment, 425
Array (computer), 98
Art
  glossary of terms, 178–180
  movements and periods, 180–183
  painters and sculptors, 165–178
    American, 165–168
    Belgian, 170
    British, 168–169
    Dutch, 169–170
    Flemish, 170
    French, 170–173
    German, 173
    Italian, 173–176
    Mexican, 176
    miscellaneous, 177–178
    Spanish, 176–177
  see also specific painters and sculptors
  reference works, 305–306
Art deco, 180
Artemis, 248
Artemision at Ephesus, 898
Arthur, Chester, 820, 823

Article (language), 357
Art nouveau, 180
Aruba
  statistics, 853
  visa requirements, 533–534
Ascending (music), 144
Ascension Day, 242
Asceticism, 271
ASCII code, 98
Asclepius, 248
Ascorbic acid *see* Vitamin C
Ash Can School, 181
Ashlar, 196
Ashton, Sir Frederick, 158
Asimov, Isaac, 207
Aspartame, 593
Aspirin, 701
Assai, 144
Assault, 425
Assemblé, 162
Assembler (computer), 98
Assembly language, 98
Assessed valuation, 450
Asset
  current, 449
  definition of, 448
Associationism, 271
Association of ideas, 271
Assonance, 222
Assumable mortgage, 450
Assumption of the Blessed Virgin, 242
Astaire, Fred, 156
Astronomical unit (AU), 25
Astronomy
  glossary of terms, 90–91
  reference works, 306
  symbols, 33
A tempo, 144
Atheism, 271
Athena, 248
Atomic clock, 4
Atomism, 271
Atonal, 144
ATP *see* Adenosine triphosphate
Atrium, 196
Attachment (legal), 425
Attic, 196
Attitude (ballet), 162
Atwood, Margaret, 207
Aubade, 144
Auchincloss, Louis, 207
Auden, W.H., 207
Audubon, John James, 207
Augmentation, 144
Augustine of Hippo, St., 262
Austen, Jane, 214
Austin, Alfred, 225
Austin, Mary, 207
Australia
  dialing code, 896
  statistics, 853
  visa requirements, 534
Austria
  dialing code, 896
  statistics, 853
  visa requirements, 534
Authors *see* Literature; specific authors

Autobiography, 222
Automobiles
  drinking and driving, 738
  insurance, 440–441
  international registration marks, 562–563
Auto racing, 674–675
Auxiliary note, 144
Averroes, 262, 278
Avicenna, 262, 278
Avoirdupois weights, 22
Azerbaijan
  statistics, 854
  visa requirements, 534

Babism, 231
Baby foods, 710
Bach, Johann Sebastian, 134
Bach family (composers), 134
Backgammon, 678–679
Bacon, Francis (painter), 168
Bacon, Sir Francis (philosopher), 263, 269
Bacteria
  control of in food, 590
  definition of, 91
Bad faith, 271
Baha'i, 231
Bahamas
  statistics, 854
  visa requirements, 534
Bahrain
  dialing code, 896
  statistics, 854
  visa requirements, 534
Bail, 425
Baker v. Carr, 431
Baking soda, 701
Balancé, 162
Balance crane, 96
Balanchine, George, 156
Baldachin, 197
Baldwin, James, 207
Ballad, 144, 222
Ballet, 162
Ballet blanc, 162
Ballet d'action, 162
Ballo, 162
Ballon, 162
Balloon payment, 450
Ballroom dances, 162
Balzac, Honoré de, 214
Bangladesh
  statistics, 854
  visa requirements, 534
Baptistery, 197
Baptists, 234
Baraka, Imamu Amiri, 208
Barbados
  statistics, 854
  visa requirements, 534
Barber, Samuel, 128
Barbizon School, 181
Barbuda *see* Antigua and Barbuda
Baritone, 144
Barkley, Alben W., 824
Bar (lawyers'), 425
Bar line (musical), 144

Baroque architecture, 197
Baroque art, 181
Baroque music, 144
Barrier beach, 97
Barry, Philip, 183
Barth, John, 208
Barthelme, Donald, 208
Bartlett, John, 208
Bartók, Bela, 138
Baryshnikov, Mikhail, 160
Bas, en, 162
Base (chemical), 94
Baseball, 654–657, 685
Bashō, 220
BASIC (program), 98
Basic movement (dance), 162
Basie, William (Count), 140
Basilica, 197
Basketball, 657–660, 686
Bass (voice), 144
Basse danse, 162
Batch (computer), 98
Bathos, 222
Bathrooms, 609
Bathyal zone, 97
Bats (animals), 56
Baudelaire, Charles Pierre, 214
Baud rate, 98
Bauhaus School, 197
Baum, Lyman Frank, 208
Beach, Amy Marcy, 128
Bearing pile, 96
Bear market, 448
Beat (musical), 144
Beattie, Ann, 208
Beaufort wind force scale, 643–645
Beaumont, Francis, 184
Bebop/bop, 145
Beckett, Samuel, 186–187
Beckmann, Max, 173
Bed (sedimentary), 97
Beef *see* Meat
Beethoven, Ludwig van, 134
Behrens, Peter, 195
Beiderbecke, Bix, 140
Being (metaphysics), 271
Béjart, Maurice, 159
Bel canto, 145
Belgium
  dialing code, 896
  statistics, 854
  visa requirements, 534
Belize
  dialing code, 896
  statistics, 854
  visa requirements, 534
Belles-lettres, 222
Bellini, Vincenzo, 136
Bellini family (painters), 174
Belloc, Joseph, 214
Bellow, Saul, 208
Benchley, Robert, 208
Bench warrant, 425
Benefits, government, 840–843
  disability, 841
  farm owners and workers, 842
  hospital insurance, 842

Benefits, government (*continued*)
   medical insurance, 842–843
   Medicare, 842
   monthly payments for selected families, 843
   retirement, 840–841
   self-employed and household workers, 842
   Social Security, 840
   survivor, 841
Benét, Stephen Vincent, 208
Benét, William Rose, 208
Benin
   statistics, 854
   visa requirements, 535
Bentham, Jeremy, 263, 269, 278
Benzalkonium chloride, 701
Benzene ring, 94
Bequest, 425
Berceuse, 145
Berg, Alban, 130
Berkeley, George, 263
Berlage, Hendrik Petrus, 195
Berlioz, Hector, 132
Bermuda
   statistics, 854
   visa requirements, 535
Berne Convention for the Protection of Literary and Artistic Works, 422
Bernini, Giovanni Lorenzo, 174, 194
Bernstein, Leonard, 128
Beta carotene, 594
Beti, Mongo, 220
Betjeman, Sir John, 225
Better Business Bureaus
   Canada, 468–469
   US headquarters, 463
   US local, 463–468
BHA *see* Butylated hydroxyanisole
Bhagavad Gita, 246
BHT *see* Butylated hydroxytoluene
Bhutan
   statistics, 854
   visa requirements, 535
Bible, 246–247, 258
Bibliography, 222
Bid and asked price, 448
Bierce, Ambrose, 208
Big bang model, 90
Big Board, 448
Bill of particulars, 425
Bill of sale, 415
Binary (musical form), 145
Binary coded decimal, 98–99
Binary system, 98
Binder (real estate), 450
Binding over, 425
Bioethics, 271
Biography, 222
Biology
   glossary of terms, 91–93
   symbols, 33
   taxonomy, 55
Birds
   extinct, 66–67
   state, 790–792
Birthstones, 53

Bit (computer), 99
Bizet, Georges, 132
Black eye, 756
Black hole, 90
Blackjack (card game), 682
Bladder, 91
Blake, William, 169, 214
Blank verse, 222
Blasco Ibañez, Vicente, 214
Blastula, 91
Bleaching powder (chloride of lime), 702
Bleeding, preventing loss of blood, 744–747
Blisters, 756
Blitzstein, Marc, 128
Bloch, Ernest, 128
Block gauge, 96
Blok, Alexander, 214
Blood stain removal, 570
Blue chip stock, 448
Blue Cross-Blue Shield, 438
Board games, 678–682
Boccaccio, Giovanni, 214
Boccherini, Luigi, 136
Boccioni, Umberto, 174
Boethius, 263
Bohr theory, 95
Boilerplate language, 425
Boils, 756
Boito, Arrigo, 136
Bolero (dance), 145
Bolivia
   dialing code, 896
   statistics, 854
   visa requirements, 535
Böll, Heinrich, 214
Bolt (measure), 25
Bond
   definition of, 449
   funds, 447
   Treasury, 450
   zero-coupon, 450
Bond (chemical), 94
Bones, broken (animal), 60
Bonnard, Pierre, 170
Bontemps, Arna, 208
Book value, 449
Bootstrap (boot; computer), 99
Borges, Jorge Luis, 220
Boric acid, 701
Borodin, Aleksandr, 137
Borromini, Francesco, 194
Bosch, Hieronymus, 169
Bosnia and Herzegovina, statistics, 854
Boswell, James, 214
Botswana
   statistics, 855
   visa requirements, 535
Botticelli, Sandro, 174
Boulanger, Lili, 132
Boulez, Pierre, 132
Boundary map symbols, 37
Bournonville, Auguste, 161
Bourrée, pas de, 162
Bowers v. Hardwick, 432
Bowing (music), 145
Bowling, 660–661

Boyle, Kay, 208
Boyle's law, 95
Brace (musical), 145
Brackets (punctuation), 363
Bradbury, Ray, 208
Bradstreet, Anne, 208
Brahms, Johannes, 134
Braille
   alphabet/numbers, 49
   book information, 502
Brain, 692
Bramante, 194
Brancusi, Constantin, 177
Braque, Georges, 170
Brazil
   dialing code, 896
   statistics, 855
   visa requirements, 535
Breach of contract, 425
Bread, nutritive value, 714
Breaking and entering, 425
Breast self-examination, 705–707
Breathing, lifesaving procedures, 742–743
Brecht, Bertolt, 187–188
Breckinridge, John C., 823
Bridal showers, 372–373
Bridge (card game), 682–683
Bridges, Robert, 225
Brief (document), 425
Brisé, 162
British Columbia (Canada)
   Better Business Bureaus, 469
   library, 292
   museum, 301
   zoos, 75
British empiricism, 271
British idealism, 271
British thermal unit (Btu), 25, 81
Britten, Benjamin, 131
Brodsky, Joseph, 226
Broker (real estate), 450
Brominated vegetable oil, 594
Brontë, Charlotte, 214
Brontë, Emily, 214
Brooks, Gwendolyn, 208
Browning, Elizabeth Barrett, 215
Browning, Robert, 215
Brown v. Board of Education of Topeka, 431
Bruch, Max, 134
Bruckner, Anton, 130
Bruegel, Pieter (the Elder), 170
Bruhn, Erik, 161
Bruises, 756
Brunei
   statistics, 855
   visa requirements, 535
Brunelleschi, Filippo, 194
Btu *see* British thermal unit
Buber, Martin, 263
Buchanan, James, 820
Buchner, Georg, 188
Buck, Pearl, 208
Bud (biology), 91
Buddhism, 231
   symbols, 42

Budget
  federal *see* Federal budget
  personal, 436–437
Buffa, 145
Buffer (computer), 99
Buffo, 145
Bug (computer), 99
Bug (insect), 91
Bulfinch, Charles, 190
Bulgakov, Mikhail, 215
Bulgaria
  statistics, 855
  visa requirements, 535
Bull market, 449
Bundle (measure), 25
Burden of proof, 425
Burgess, Anthony, 215
Burglary, 425
Buridan's ass, 271
Burkina Faso
  statistics, 855
  visa requirements, 535
Burma *see* Myanmar
Burnham, Daniel Hudson, 190
Burns
  animal, 61
  chemical, 750
  scorch stains, 578
  treatment in emergency, 749–750
Burns, Robert, 215
Burr, Aaron, 823
Burroughs, Edgar Rice, 208
Burroughs, William S., 208
Burundi
  statistics, 855
  visa requirements, 535
Buses, tips for disabled, 559
Bush, George, 821, 824
Business
  appointments, 376–377
  entertainment, 377
  etiquette, 376–379
  gifts, 377
  letter writing, 378–379
  magazines, 511
  reference works, 307–308
  symbols, 40
  telephone calls, 378
Buttress, 197, 200
Butylated hydroxyanisole (BHA), 594
Butylated hydroxytoluene (BHT), 594
Byelorussia
  statistics, 855
  visa requirements, 536
Byrd, William, 131
Byron, Lord, 215
Byte, 99
Byzantine architecture, 197
Byzantine art, 181

Cable way, 96
Cabriole, 162
Cachuca, 163
Cacophony, 222
Cadence (language), 222
Cadence (music), 145
Cadenza, 145

Caesura, 222
Caffeine, 594
Cage, John, 128
Caisson, 96
Cake, nutritive value, 714
Cakewalk, 163
Calamine lotion, 702
Calcium propionate, 594
Calcium stearolyl lactylate, 594
Calder, Alexander, 165
Calderón de la Barca, Pedro, 189
Calendars
  lunar, 9
  perpetual, 11–14
Calhoun, John C., 823
Caliber, 25
California
  Better Business Bureaus, 463–464
  consumer protection offices, 471–473
  crime rate, 846
  libraries, 284
  museums, 293–294
  name origin, 792
  newspapers, 515–516
  poison control centers, 759
  social services offices, 457, 494
  vital statistics, 770, 778, 788, 790
  weather, 824, 826, 827
  wildlife refuges, 630–631
  zoos, 69
Calories, consumed by activities, 736–737
Calvino, Italo, 215
Calyx, 92
Camargo, Marie, 159
Camber, 96
Cambodia
  statistics, 855
  visa requirements, 536
Cambré, 163
Cambrian era, 85, 97
Cambridge Platonists, 271
Cameroon
  dialing code, 896
  statistics, 855
  visa requirements, 536
Campanile, 197
Camping, tips for disabled, 560
Camus, Albert, 215
Canada
  Better Business Bureaus, 468–469
  libraries, 292
  museums, 301–302
  statistics, 855
  visa requirements, 536
  zoos, 75
  see also specific provinces
Cancan, 163
Candlemas, 241
Candy, nutritive value, 714
Canetti, Elias, 215
Canon (musical composition), 145
Canonical hours, 252
Canova, Antonio, 174
Cantata, 145
Canticle, 145
Cantilever, 96, 197
Canzona, 145

Canzonet, 145
Capacity (legal), 425
Capek, Karel, 215
Cape Verde
  statistics, 855
  visa requirements, 536
Capital gain/loss, 449
Capitalization, 449
Capital stock, 449
Capote, Truman, 208
Capriccio, 145
Carat, 25
Caravaggio, Michelangelo Merisi da, 174
Carboniferous era, 85
Card games, 682–685
Cardiac massage, 744
Cardiopulmonary resuscitation (CPR), 742–744
Caricature, 178
Carnivore, 56, 92
Carracci family (painters), 174
Carrageenan, 594
Carroll, Lewis, 215
Cars *see* Automobiles
Carter, Betty, 140
Carter, Jimmy, 821
Cartesianism, 272
Cartoon, 178
Carving, 178
Case (measure), 25
Casein, 594
Cassatt, Mary, 165
Casting (sculpture), 178
Castle, Vernon, 156
Castrato, 145
Cataloging in publication data, 317
Catalyst, 94
Catch (musical), 145
Categorical imperative, 272
Cather, Willa, 208
Cathode, 95
Cathode ray tube, 99
Catholic Church *see* Roman Catholicism
Cation, 94
Cats, diseases, 61
Catullus, 215
Cause (philosophy), 272
Cavafy, C.P., 220
Cayman Islands, statistics, 856
CD-ROM, 99
CDs *see* Certificates of deposit
Cease and desist order, 425
Ceilings, standard sizes, 608
Cell, 92
Cellini, Benvenuto, 174
Central African Republic
  statistics, 856
  visa requirements, 536
Central processing unit, 99
Centrifugal force, 80
Cerrito, Fanny, 161
Certainty, 272
Certificate of notary, 397
Certificates of deposit (CDs), 447
Certiorari, 425
Cervantes Saavedra, Miguel de, 215
Cesaire, Aimé, 220

Cézanne, Paul, 171
Chaconne, 145
Chad
  statistics, 856
  visa requirements, 536
Chagall, Marc, 177
Chain of being, 272
Chamber music, 145
Chambers, Sir William, 192
Champagne bottle sizes, 605
Chandler, Raymond, 208
Channel (computer), 99
Chanson, 145
Chant, 145
Chaos, 248
Character (computer), 99
Chardin, Jean-Baptiste-Siméon, 171
Chassé, 163
Chat, pas de, 163
Chattel, 425
Chatterje, Bankim-Chandra, 220
Chaucer, Geoffrey, 215
Chávez, Carlos, 138
Chayefsky, Paddy, 183
Checkers, 679
Cheese, nutritive value, 716
Cheever, John, 209
Chekhov, Anton, 189, 215
Chelating agents, 592
Chemical additives, 592-599
Chemistry
  glossary of terms, 93-95
  symbols, 33-34
Cherubini, Maria Luigi, 136
Chess, 679-681
Chewing gum, stain removal, 571
Chiaroscuro, 178
Childbirth, table of approximate dates, 696
Children
  child abuse organizations, 462
  height and weight charts, 694-695
  museums for, 302-303
  organizations for disabled, 462
  organizations for runaways, 463
  resuscitation of, 744
Chile
  dialing code, 896
  statistics, 856
  visa requirements, 536
China
  Confucianism, 231-232
  royal rulers, 900
  statistics, 856
  Taoism, 239
  visa requirements, 536-537
Chirico, Giorgio de, 174
Chlorine, stain removal, 571
Chlorophyll, 92
Choir (church area), 197
Choking, 754-755
Chopin, Frédéric, 139
Chopin, Kate, 209
Chorale, 145
Chord (musical), 145
Choreography see Dance; specific choreographers
Christian, Charlie, 140

Christianity symbols, 42
Christie, Agatha, 215
Christmas, 15, 243
Christmas Island, statistics, 856
Chromatic scale (musical), 145
Chromosome, 92
Chronostratigraphy, 97
Church of Christ, 234
Church of England, 234
Church of Jesus Christ of Latter-Day Saints, 237
Cibber, Colley, 225
Circumference, 79
Circumstantial evidence, 425
Cirrocumulus cloud, 643
Cirrostratus cloud, 643
Cirrus cloud, 643
Ciseaux, 163
Cities
  crime rates, 847
  major world, 884-890
  map symbols, 37
Citric acid, 595
Class action, 425
Classical music see Music; specific composers
Classical revival, 197
Classicism, 181, 197
Clef, 146
Clemency, 425
Clementi, Muzio, 136
Clerestory, 197
Cleveland, Grover, 820
Climax (literary), 222
Clinton, Bill, 821
Clinton, George, 823
Clock (computer), 99
Clock (timepiece), 4
Cloister, 197
Closing (real estate), 450
Closure density, 90
Clothing, size conversion tables, 607-608
Cloud nomenclature, 643
Clymer, Reuben Swinburne, 239
COBOL (language), 99
Coda (ballet), 163
Coda (music), 146
Codicil, 425
Coffee, 594
  as home remedy, 702
  nutritive value, 716
  stain removal, 572
  storage, 589
Coleman, Ornette, 140-141
Coleridge, Samuel Taylor, 215
Colfax, Schuyler, 823
Collage, 178
Collateral, 449
Collette, 215
Colombia
  dialing code, 896
  statistics, 856
  visa requirements, 537
Colonnade, 197
Colon (punctuation), 362
Colorado
  Better Business Bureaus, 464

consumer protection offices, 473
crime rate, 846
library, 285
museum, 294
name origin, 792
newspapers, 516
poison control center, 759
social services offices, 457, 494
vital statistics, 770, 778, 788, 790
weather, 824, 826, 827
wildlife refuges, 631
zoos, 69
Color field painting, 181
Colors, 179
Colossus of Rhodes, 898
Coltrane, John, 141
Column, 197
Comedy, 222
Comma (music), 146
Comma (punctuation), 361-362
Command (computer), 99
Commission (real estate), 450
Common-law marriage, 426
Common time (music), 146
Commonwealths (US), 789, 792
Communications, reference works, 306-307
Community property, 426
Comoros Islands
  statistics, 856
  visa requirements, 537
Competency hearing, 426
Compiler (computer), 99
Complaint, 426
Complementary colors, 179
Composers see Music; specific composers
Composite Order, 197
Composition (art), 179
Compound (chemical), 94
Compound interval (music), 146
Compound time (music), 146
Computers
  data banks for research, 321
  glossary of terms, 98-102
Comte, Auguste, 263
Conceit (literary), 222
Conceptual art, 181
Conceptualism, 272
Concertmaster, 146
Concerto, 146
Concerto grosso, 146
Concert pitch, 146
Concussion, 756
Condominium, 450
Conduction (physics), 95
Confucianism, 231-232, 269
Confucius, 220
Congo
  statistics, 856
  visa requirements, 537
Congress (US), writing to senators and representatives, 522-523
Conjunction (language), 357
Connecticut
  Better Business Bureaus, 464
  consumer protection offices, 473-474
  crime rate, 845

Connecticut (*continued*)
   library, 285
   museums, 294
   name origin, 792
   newspapers, 516
   poison control center, 759
   social services offices, 457, 494
   vital statistics, 770, 778, 788, 790
   weather, 824, 826, 827
   wildlife refuges, 631
   zoos, 69
Connor, Ralph, 209
Conrad, Joseph, 215
Consent decree, 426
Console (computer), 99
Console (organ), 146
Consonance (musical), 146
Consort (chamber ensemble), 146
Conspiracy, 426
Con spirito, 146
Constable, John, 169
Constellations, 650–651
Constipation, animal, 61
Constitution (US), 799–807
   amendments, 808–814
Constructivism (art), 181
Consumerism
   magazines, 511
   state consumer protection offices, 469–493
Contempt of court, 426
Continental drift, 97
Continuo, 146
Contract
   definition, 426
   real estate, 450
   sample, 408–412
Contraction (dance), 163
Contralto, 146
Contredanse, 163
Control data, 99
Control unit (computer), 99
Convection, 95
Convertible securities, 449
Convulsions, 756
Cookies, nutritive value, 716
Cooking
   magazines, 512
   times and temperatures, 584–590
Cook Islands
   statistics, 856
   visa requirements, 537
Cool (jazz style), 146
Coolidge, Calvin, 820, 824
Cooper, James Fenimore, 209
Cooperative apartment, 450
Copland, Aaron, 128
Copyrights, 421–422
Corelli, Arcangelo, 136
Corigliano, John, 128
Corinthian Order, 197
Coriolis effect, 97
Corneille, Pierre, 187
Cornell, Joseph, 165
Cornice, 197
Corn sugar, 595
Corn syrup, 595

Corona, 90
Corot, Jean-Baptiste Camille, 171
Corps de ballet, 163
Corpus delicti, 426
Correction fluid, stain removal, 572
Correggio (Antonio Allegri), 174
Corroborating evidence, 426
Corrosives, 751
Cosmetics, stain removal, 572
Cosmogony, 272
Cosmology, 90, 272
Costa Rica
   dialing code, 896
   statistics, 856
   visa requirements, 537
Côte D'Ivoire
   dialing code, 896
   statistics, 860
   visa requirements, 537
Cottons, washing of, 565
Coulomb, 81
Coulomb's law, 80, 95
Counterexample, 272
Counterpoint (music), 146
Countersubject (music), 146
Countertenor, 146
Countries of the world, 853–870
   see also specific countries
Country dance, 163
Couperin, François, 132
Couplet, 146, 162
Coupon bond, 449
Courante, 146
Courbet, Gustave, 171
Coward, Noël, 184
Cowell, Henry Dixon, 128–129
CPR *see* Cardiopulmonary resuscitation
CPU *see* Central processing unit
Crane, Stephen, 209
Credit
   and personal finances, 441–442
   request for reason for adverse action, 417
Creep (geological), 97
Crescendo, 146
Cretaceous era, 84
Crime rates, 844–848
   households touched by crime, 848
   by state, 845–846
   by type, 844
   by type and area, 845
   by type and city, 847
   victimization rates, 847
Critical density, 90
Croatia, statistics, 856
Croisée, 163
Cronus, 248
Cross-examination, 426
Crossing (church area), 197
Crossword puzzle words, 330–337
CRT *see* Cathode ray tube
Cuba
   statistics, 856
   visa requirements, 537
Cubic measures, 21–22, 23
Cubism, 181
Cultural symbols, 38

cummings, e.e., 209
Cumulonimbus cloud, 643
Cumulus cloud, 643
Cunningham, Merce, 156
Currency *see* Money
Current assets, 449
Current liabilities, 449
Cursor, 99
Curtis, Charles, 824
Curved space, 90
Custody, 426
Customs information, 553
Cut time (music), 146
Cynics, 272
Cyprus
   dialing code, 896
   statistics, 857
   visa requirements, 537
Cyrenaics, 272
Czech Republic
   dialing code, 896
   statistics, 857
   visa requirements, 537
Czerny, Karl, 130

Da capo, 146
Dadaism, 181
Dairy, weights and measures, 581
Dalí, Salvador, 176
Dallapiccola, Luigi, 136
Dallas, George M., 823
Damages (legal), 426
d'Amboise, Jacques, 156
Dance
   dancers and choreographers, 156–161
      American, 156–158
      British, 158–159
      French, 159
      miscellaneous, 161
      Russian, 160–161
      see also specific dancers and choreographers
   glossary of terms, 162–165
Danger signs, 46
Danilova, Alexandra, 160
Danseur noble, 163
Dante Alighieri, 215
Dartmouth College v. Woodward, 431
Dash (punctuation), 362
Data acquisition system, 99
Database, 99
Data management system, 99
Daumier, Honoré, 171
David, Jacques-Louis, 171
Davies, Arthur Bowen, 165
Davies, Robertson, 209
da Vinci, Leonardo *see* Leonardo da Vinci
Davis, Miles, 141
Davis, Stuart, 165
Dawes, Charles G., 824
Day-Lewis, Cecil, 225
Daylight Saving Time, 7–8
Days, 2–3
Death/death rate charts, 699–701
Death penalty, 432
Debenture, 449
Debussy, Claude, 132

Decibel, 25
Decimals, 30, 78
Declaration of Independence, 795–798
Decree, 426
Decrescendo, 146
Deductive reasoning, 272
Deed (real estate), 450
Defamation, 426
Default judgment, 426
Defendant, 426
Defoe, Daniel, 216
Dégagé, 163
Degas, Edgar, 171
Deism, 272
Dekker, Thomas, 184–185
de Kooning, Willem, 165
Delacroix, Eugène, 171
Delaware
   Better Business Bureau, 464
   consumer protection offices, 474
   crime rate, 846
   museums, 294
   name origin, 792
   newspapers, 516
   poison control center, 759
   social services offices, 457, 494
   vital statistics, 770, 778, 788, 790
   weather, 824, 826, 827
   wildlife refuges, 631
Delibes, Léo, 133
Delius, Frederick, 131
della Robbia family (artists), 174
Dello Joio, Norman, 129
Demeter, 248
de Mille, Agnes, 156
Democritus, 263
Demographics, reference works, 315
Demuth, Charles, 165
Denmark
   dialing code, 896
   statistics, 857
   visa requirements, 538
Dennis Et Al. v. U.S., 431
Denouement, 222
Deodorants, stain removal, 570
Deontology, 272
Deoxyribonucleic acid (DNA), 92
Dependent clauses, 360
Deposition, 426
Descant, 146
Descartes, René, 263, 264, 269, 278
Descending (music), 146
Determinism, 272
Development (musical), 146
Développé, 163
Devonian era, 85
Dewey, John, 263, 278
Dewey Decimal System, 315–316
Dextrose, 595
Diacritical marks, 42
Diagenesis, 97
Diaghilev, Sergei Pavlovich, 160
Diagnostic routine (computer program), 99
Dialectic (philosophy), 272
Dialectical materialism, 272
Dialing codes, international, 896–897
Diarrhea, animal, 62

Diatonic scales, 147
Dickens, Charles, 216
Dickinson, Emily, 209
Diction, 222
Diderot, Denis, 263
Didion, Joan, 209
Diet *see* Food; Nutrition
Differential motion, 96
Digital computer, 99
Digitalization rate, 99
Diglycerides, 597
Dillard, Annie, 209
Diminished chord, 147
Diminished interval, 147
Diminuendo, 147
Diminution (music), 147
Dinesen, Isak, 216
Dinner parties *see* Parties
Diogenes, 263
Dionysus, 248
Directed verdict, 426
Disabled
   benefits, 841
   books for, 502
   disability insurance, 439
   operator services for, 501
   organizations for children, 462
   travel tips, 559–560
Discount, 449
Discovery *see* Exploration and discovery timetable
Discovery (legal), 426
Discretionary account, 449
Diseases *see* Medicine and health
Dis (Hades), 248
Disk (diskette), 99
Disk operating system, 99
Disorderly conduct, 426
Dissonance (musical), 147
Distress signals, 52
District attorney *see* Prosecutor
District of Columbia
   Better Business Bureau, 464
   consumer protection office, 474
   crime rate, 846
   library, 285
   museums, 294–295
   name origin, 792
   newspaper, 516
   poison control center, 759
   social services offices, 457, 494
   vital statistics, 770, 778, 790
   weather, 824, 826, 827
   zoo, 69
Divertimento, 147
Divertissement, 147
Dividend
   definition of, 449
   stock, 450
Divisi, 147
Djibouti
   statistics, 857
   visa requirements, 538
DNA *see* Deoxyribonucleic acid
Do (musical note), 147
Docket, 426
Doctorow, E.L., 209

Dog (animal), diseases of, 62
Dog (gripping device), 96
Doggerel, 222
Dolce, 147
Doldrums (region), 97
Dolente/doloroso, 147
Dolin, Anton, 158
Dome, 197
Domestic violence resources, 494–496
Dominant chord, 147
Dominica
   statistics, 857
   visa requirements, 538
Dominican Republic
   statistics, 857
   visa requirements, 538
Donatello, 174–175
Donizetti, Gaetano, 136
Donne, John, 216
Doors, standard sizes, 610
Doppio movimento, 147
Dorian mode, 147
Doric Order, 197
DOS *see* Disk operating system
Dos Passos, John, 209
Dostoyevsky, Fyodor, 216
Dot (music), 147
Double jeopardy, 426
Double stop (music), 147
Doubt, 274
Dove, Arthur Garfield, 165
Dow Jones average, 449
Dowland, John, 131
Downtime (computer), 99
Doxology, 147
Doyle, Sir Arthur Conan, 216
Drama
   playwrights, 183–190
      American, 183–184
      British, 184–186
      French, 186–187
      German, 187–188
      Greek, 188
      Irish, 188
      miscellaneous, 190
      Roman, 189
      Russian, 189
      Spanish, 189
      see also specific playwrights
   reference works, 315
Dred Scott v. Sanford, 431
Dreiser, Theodore, 209
Drinks, alcoholic *see* Alcohol
Drowning, 744, 757
Drug abuse organizations, 461–462
Drugs *see* Medications
Dryden, John, 216, 225
Drypoint, 179
Dualism, 274
Dubuffet, Jean, 171
Duchamp, Marcel, 171
Due process, 426
Duet, 147
Dufy, Raoul, 171
Dukas, Paul, 133
Dumas, Alexandre (père), 216
Duncan, Isadora, 156

Dunham, Katherine, 156
Duple, 147
Duration (music), 147
Dürer, Albrecht, 173
Durrell, Lawrence, 216
Duty, 274
Dvořák, Antonín, 139
Dynamic range, 99
Dynamics (music), 147

Eakins, Thomas, 166
Earth
   diagram, 87
   facts about, 88–89
Earthquakes, 646
Easement, 426
Easter Sunday, 15, 242
Écarté, 163
Eclipses, 646–649
Economics reference works, 307–308
Economic statistics (US), 777–781
   federal receipts, 777
   household type, by median income and income level, 779
   money income of households, 780–781
   personal income per capita, 778–779
Ecuador
   dialing code, 896
   statistics, 857
   visa requirements, 538
Edel, Leon, 209
Education reference works, 308
Effacé, 163
Eggs
   as home remedy, 702
   nutritive value, 718
   weights and measures, 581
Eglevsky, Andre, 160
Egocentric predicament, 274
Egoism, 274
Egypt
   dialing code, 896
   pyramids, 898
   statistics, 857
   visa requirements, 538
The Eight (painters), 181
Eighth note, 147
Eisenhower, Dwight D., 821
Elderly *see* Aging
Eleatics, 274
Electoral College, 822–823
Electrical power, formula for, 80
Electricity
   glossary of terms, 81
   symbols, 36–37
Electric shock, 754
Electrolyte, 94
Electromechanical brake, 96
Electromotive force, 95
Electron, 94
Elegy, 222
Elements
   alphabetical listing, 82–83
   definition, 94
   four basic, 275
Elgar, Sir Edward, 131
El Greco *see* Greco, El

Eliot, George, 216
Eliot, Thomas Stearns (T.S.), 185, 209
Ell (measure), 25
Ellington, Edward Kennedy (Duke), 141
Ellipsis, 361, 362
Ellison, Ralph, 209
El Salvador
   dialing code, 896
   statistics, 857
   visa requirements, 538
Elssler, Fanny, 161
Em (measure), 25
Emancipation, 426
Emancipation Proclamation, 814–815
Embryo, 92
Emerson, Ralph Waldo, 209
Eminent domain, 426
Empedocles, 263
Empirical knowledge, 274
Empiricism, 271, 274
Emulsifiers, 592
Encaustic, 179
Encyclopedists, 274
Endogenous factors, 92
Energy, definition, 95
Energy-matter relationship, 80
Engels, Friedrich, 263, 269
Engine, definition, 96
Engineering glossary, 95–96
Engineer's chain, 96
England *see* United Kingdom
Enlightenment, 274
English language
   American vs. British, 365–366
   commonly misused words, 367–368
   common phrases in other languages, 339
   parts of speech, 357
   punctuation, 360–363
   sentence components, 358–360
   see also Spelling
Engraving, 179
Enharmonic, 147
Ensor, James (Baron), 170
Entablature, 197
Entertainment
   business, 377
   magazines, 511
   see also Parties
Entrapment, 427
Entrechat, 163
Eocene era, 84
Eos, 248
Epaulement, 163
Epic, 222
Epictetus, 265
Epicureanism, 274
Epicurus, 265
Episcopal Church, 235
Episode (music), 147
Epistemology, 274
Epistolary novel, 222
Epsom salts, 702
Equal protection, 427
Equatorial Guinea
   statistics, 857
   visa requirements, 538
Equinox, 9, 97

Equity, 449, 450
Era, 97
Eris, 248
Ernst, Max, 173
Eros, 248
Error message, 99
Erythorbic acid, 593
Eschatology, 274
Escrow, 450
Essay, 222
Essence (philosophy), 274
Estate, 427
Estinto, 147
Estonia
   statistics, 857
   visa requirements, 538
Estuary, 97
Etching, 179
Ethical Culture, 232
Ethiopia
   dialing code, 896
   statistics, 857
   visa requirements, 538–539
Ethnology reference works, 304–305
Ethylenediamine tetracetic acid, 595
Ethyl vanillin, 599
Etiquette
   business, 376–379
   wedding, 371–376
Etude, 147
Euphony, 222
Euripides, 188
Eusden, Laurence, 225
Evans, Bill, 141
Evidence, 427
   circumstantial, 425
   corroborating, 426
   hearsay, 427
   preponderance of, 429
Evolution, 92
Exclamation point, 361
Exclusionary rule, 427
Ex-dividend, 449
Execute (computers), 100
Executor/executrix, 427
Exercise, calories consumed by, 736–737
Existentialism, 274
Expansion joint, 96
Exploration and discovery timetable, 878–883
Exposition (musical), 147
Expressionism, 181
Expression marks (music), 147
Eyewitness, 427

Fa (musical note), 148
Fable, 222
Facade, 198
Fairbanks, Charles W., 824
Fair hearing, 427
Fair use, 427
Falkland Islands, statistics, 858
Falla, Manuel de, 139
Fallacy, 273
False pretenses, 427
Falsetto, 148
Family planning organizations, 496–497

Fandango, 163
Fannie Mae, 450
Fantasia, 148
Farm owners/workers, benefits for, 842
Faroe Islands, statistics, 858
Farrell, Suzanne, 157
Fatalism, 274
Fates (mythology), 248
Faulkner, William, 209
Fauna, 92
Fauré, Gabriel, 133
Fauvism, 181
FDIC *see* Federal Deposit Insurance Corporation
Feast of the Epiphany, 241
Feast of the Immaculate Conception, 243
Federal budget, 785–787
Federal Deposit Insurance Corporation, 449
Federal government *see* Government
Federal Housing Administration, 451
Federal judicial system, 395
Fee, 427
Feininger, Lyonel, 166
Feld, Eliot, 157
Felony, 427
Felony murder, 427
Female, definition of, 92
Fermata, 148
Fermé, 163
Fermentation, 92
Ferrous gluconate, 595
Fertilization, 92
FHA *see* Federal Housing Administration
Fiction, 222
Fiduciary, 427, 449
Fielding, Henry, 216
Fifth (music), 148
Figuration (music), 148
Figure (art), 179
Fiji
 dialing code, 896
 statistics, 858
 visa requirements, 539
File (computer), 100
Fillmore, Millard, 819, 823
Film *see* Motion pictures
Finale (music), 148
Finance
 government, 782–784
 magazines, 511
 personal, 434–453
 see also Economic statistics (US); Federal budget
Finding (legal), 427
Finland
 dialing code, 896
 statistics, 858
 visa requirements, 539
First aid
 for animals, 60–65
 kits, 758
 lifesaving procedures, 742–749
 preventing further injury, 747–748
 preventing loss of blood, 744–747
 preventing shock, 748–749
 for travelers, 561

see also specific conditions, e.g., Frostbite
Fish, extinct, 67
Fitzgerald, Ella, 141
Fitzgerald, F. Scott, 209
Five Classics (Confucius), 246
Five positions (ballet), 163
Fjord, 97
Flag (US)
 care and use of, 818–819
 history, 817–818
Flamenco, 163
Flat (music), 148
Flaubert, Gustave, 216
Flavorings
 as additives, 592–593
 artificial, 593
 weights and measures, 582
Fletcher, John, 185
Floodplain, 97
Floors, standard sizes, 609
Floppy disk *see* Disk
Flora, 92
Florida
 Better Business Bureaus, 464
 consumer protection offices, 474–475
 crime rate, 846
 libraries, 285
 name origin, 792
 newspapers, 516
 poison control center, 759
 social services offices, 457, 494
 vital statistics, 770, 778, 788, 790
 weather, 824, 826, 827
 wildlife refuges, 631–632
 zoos, 70
Flour
 as home remedy, 702
 weights and measures, 581
Flowers
 birth month, 53
 funeral, 384
 germination tables, 618
 stain removal, 573
 state, 790–792
Fluid measures, 23, 24
Fokine, Michel, 160
Folacin, 735
Folk art, 181
Folklore reference works, 312
Fondu (ballet), 163
Fonteyn, Dame Margot, 158–159
Food
 kosher, 584
 poisoning, 750–751
 Recommended Daily Dietary Allowances, 708–709
 storage, 589
 substitutions, 583–584
 vitamin chart, 732–735
 weights and measures, 581–582
 see also Cooking; Nutrition
Foot (poetic), 222
Football, 661–664, 686
Force, 95
Ford, Gerald R., 821, 824
Foreign words and phrases, 339–345

Foreshortening, 179
Form (music), 148
Forms (Platonic), 274
Forster, E.M., 216
Forte, 148
Fortissimo, 148
FORTRAN (language), 100
Forum, 198
Forza, 148
Forzando, 148
Fouetté en tournant, 163
Four Horsemen of the Apocalypse, 247
Fourth (music), 148
Fox, George, 238
Fox-trot, 164
Fractions, 30, 78
Fragonard, Jean-Honoré, 171
France
 dialing code, 896
 royal rulers, 899–900
 statistics, 858
 visa requirements, 539
Franck, César, 133
Frankenthaler, Helen, 166
Franklin, Benjamin, 105, 209
Fraud, 427
Freddie Mae, 451
Freedom of Information Act, 420
Free verse, 222
Free will, 275
Freight ton, 25
French Antilles, dialing code, 896
French Guiana
 statistics, 858
 visa requirements, 539
French language, 339
French Polynesia
 dialing code, 896
 statistics, 858
 visa requirements, 539
Fresco, 179
Friedman, Jerome, 123
Frieze, 179, 198
Frisk *see* Stop and frisk
Frost, Robert, 210
Frostbite, 755
Frost dates, 616–617
Frost hollow, 97
Fruit
 cooking times, 588–589
 stain removal, 573
 weights and measures, 582
Fuentes, Carlos, 220
Fugue, 148
Fuller, Buckminster, 190
Fumaric acid, 595
Fundamental (music), 148
Funerals, 383–384
Funk music, 148
Furies (mythology), 248
Furman v. Georgia, 432
Futurism, 181

Gabo, Naum, 177
Gabon
 dialing code, 896
 statistics, 858

Gabon (*continued*)
  visa requirements, 539
Gainsborough, Thomas, 169
Galápagos Islands, visa requirements, 539
Galaxy, 90
Galileo, 4
Galop (dance), 148
Gambia
  statistics, 858
  visa requirements, 539
Games
  board, 678–682
  card, 682–685
  see also specific games
Garbage (computer), 100
García Lorca, Federico, 189, 216
García Márquez, Gabriel, 220
Gardening magazines, 513
Gardner, John, 210
Garfield, James, 820
Gargoyle, 198
Garner, John N., 824
Garnier, Jean Louis Charles, 193
Garnishment, 427
Gasket, 96
Gaudí y Cornet, Antonio, 195
Gauge, 25–26
Gauguin, Paul, 171
Gaza Strip, 870
Gelatin, 595
Gell-Mann, Murray, 123
Genealogy
  getting started in, 318–319
  organizations, 497
  reference works, 309
Generation (computer), 100
Generator (computer), 100
Genet, Jean, 187
Genitalia, 92
Genre (literary), 222
Genre painting, 179
Genus, 92
Geography
  glossary, 96–98
  reference works, 309
Geology
  definition, 97
  glossary, 96–98
  time chart, 84–85
Georgia (country), statistics, 858
Georgia (US state)
  Better Business Bureaus, 464
  consumer protection office, 475
  crime rate, 846
  library, 285
  name origin, 792
  newspapers, 516
  poison control center, 759
  social services offices, 457, 494
  vital statistics, 770, 778, 788, 790
  weather, 825, 826, 827
  wildlife refuges, 632–633
  zoo, 70
Georgian architecture, 198
Géricault, Théodore, 171
German language, 339

Germany
  dialing code, 896
  royal rulers, 900
  statistics, 858
  visa requirements, 539
Gerry, Elbridge, 823
Gershwin, George, 129
Gesso, 179
Ghana
  statistics, 858
  visa requirements, 539–540
Ghiberti, Lorenzo, 175
Giacometti, Alberto, 177
Gibbons, Orlando, 131
Gibraltar
  statistics, 858
  visa requirements, 540
Gide, André, 216
Gifts
  anniversary, 376
  business, 377
  declaration of form, 414
  wedding, 374–375
Gillespie, John Birks (Dizzy), 141
Gilt-edged security, 449
Ginnie Mae, 451
Ginsberg, Allen, 210
Giocoso, 148
Giorgione (da Castelfranco), 175
Giotto (di Bondone), 175, 194
Giraudoux, Jean, 187
Girder, 96
Glacier, 98
Glee (song), 148
Glinka, Mikhail, 137
Glissade, 164
Glissando, 148
Gluck, Christoph, 134–135
Glucose, 595
Glue, stain removal, 573
Glycerin, 596
Glycerol, 596
Goethe, Johann Wolfgang von, 216
Gogol, Nikolai, 216
Golden mean, 275
Golden rule, 275
Golding, William, 216
Goldsmith, Oliver, 185
Golf, 664–665, 686
Gombrowicz, Witold, 216
Good Friday, 242
Goodman, Benny, 141
Gordimer, Nadine, 220
Gore, Albert, 824
Gorgons, 248
Gorky, Arshile, 166
Gorky, Maxim, 189, 216
Gothic architecture, 198
Gothic art, 181
Gothic revival, 198
Gouache, 179
Gounod, Charles, 133
Government
  agencies and bureaus, 498–499
  benefits, 840–843
  departments, 849

federal financial outlays, by function, 782–784
federal information centers, 500–501
officials, forms of address, 387–389
state, 788–789
structure, 848–849
Goya y Lucientes, Francisco Jose de, 176
Grace note, 148
Graces (mythology), 248
Graduated payment mortgage, 445
Graham, Martha, 157
Grainger, Percy Aldridge, 139
Granados, Enrique, 139
Grandezza, 148
Grandfather clause, 427
Grand jury, 427
Grant, Ulysses S., 820
Grass, Günter, 217
Grass, stain removal, 573
Grave (music), 148
Graves, Michael, 190
Gravitational collapse, 90
Gravity inverse square law, 81
Grazioso, 148
Great Britain *see* United Kingdom
Greco, El, 176–177
Greece
  dialing code, 896
  statistics, 859
Greek alphabet, 50
Greek deities, 248–249
Greek prefixes, 349–352
Greek suffixes, 352–353
Greenland
  statistics, 859
  visa requirements, 538
Greenwich Mean Time, 3
Gregorian chant, 148
Gregory, Cynthia, 157
Grenada
  statistics, 859
  visa requirements, 540
Grid, 96
Grieg, Edvard, 139
Grimm brothers, 217
Gris, Juan, 177
Grisi, Carlotta, 161
Gropius, Walter, 190–191
Gross (measure), 26
Grosz, George, 173
Ground covers, 619
Grünewald, Mathias, 173
Guadeloupe, statistics, 859
Guam
  dialing code, 896
  social service offices, 460
  statistics, 792
Guantanamo Bay, dialing code, 896
Guardian, 427
Guatemala
  dialing code, 896
  statistics, 859
  visa requirements, 540
Guernsey, statistics, 859
GUI (computer system), 100
Guinea
  statistics, 859

Guinea (*continued*)
  visa requirements, 540
Guinea-Bissau
  statistics, 859
  visa requirements, 540
Gums, 596
Guyana
  dialing code, 896
  statistics, 859
  visa requirements, 540
Guzmán, Martin Luis, 220

Habeas corpus, 427
Haiku, 222
Haiti
  dialing code, 896
  statistics, 859
  visa requirements, 540
Half note, 148
Halls of fame, 521–522
Hals, Frans, 169
Hamlin, Hannibal, 823
Hammett, Dashiell, 210
Hamsun, Knut, 217
Hancock, Herbie, 141
Hand (measure), 26
Handel, George Frideric, 135
Handicapped *see* Disabled
Hanging Gardens of Babylon, 898
Hanson, Howard, 129
Hanukkah, 243
Haploid number, 92
Hard copy, 100
Harding, Warren G., 820
Hardouin Mansart, Jules, 194
Hardware (computer), 100
Hardy, Thomas, 217
Hargrave, Lawrence, 105
Harmonic tone, 149
Harmony, 149
Harrison, Benjamin, 820
Harrison, William Henry, 819
Hasek, Jaroslav, 217
Haut, en, 164
Hawaii
  Better Business Bureau, 465
  consumer protection offices, 475
  crime rate, 846
  library, 285
  museum, 295
  name origin, 793
  newspapers, 516
  poison control center, 760
  social service offices, 457
  vital statistics, 770, 778, 788, 790
  weather, 825, 826, 827
  wildlife refuges, 633
  zoos, 70
Hawkes, John, 210
Hawkins, Coleman, 141
Hawthorne, Nathaniel, 210
Haydn, Franz Joseph, 130
Hayes, Rutherford B., 820
Health *see* Medicine and health
Health insurance *see* Insurance, medical
Health Maintenance Organizations (HMOs), 438

Hearsay evidence, 427
Heart, 692
Heart attack, signs of, 763
Heat, definition, 95
Heat cramps/heat exhaustion/heat stroke, 757
Heating, glossary of terms, 81
Hebe, 248
Hebrew alphabet, 50
Hedonism, 275
Hegel, Georg, 265, 269, 281
Hegelianism, 275
Heidegger, Martin, 265
Height charts, 693–695
Heimlich maneuver, 755
Heinlein, Robert, 210
Helical gears, 96
Heller, Joseph, 210
Hellman, Lillian, 183, 210
Hemingway, Ernest, 210
Hemorrhage *see* Bleeding
Henderson, Fletcher, 141
Hendricks, Thomas A., 824
Henri, Robert, 166
Henry, O., 210
Henry VIII, 234, 235
  wives of, 900
Hephaestus, 248
Heptyl paraben, 596
Hera, 248
Heraclitus, 265
Herakles, 248
Heraldry reference works, 309
Herbaceous plant, 92
Herbivore, 92
Herbs, 591–592
Hermaphroditus, 248
Hermes, 248
Hero (literary), 222
Hersey, John, 210
Hertz, 26
Hesse, Hermann, 217
Hestia, 249
Hexadecimal, 100
High comedy, 222
High-level language (computer), 100
Highlight (art), 179
Highways *see* Roads
Hindemith, Paul, 135
Hinduism, 232
  symbols, 42
Hines, Earl (Fatha), 142
Historical novel, 222
Historic site symbols, 38
History
  exploration and discovery timetable, 878–883
  important US dates and events, 829–839
  important world dates and events, 871–877
  reference works, 310
HMOs *see* Health Maintenance Organizations
Hobart, Garret A., 824
Hobbes, Thomas, 265, 269
Hobson's choice, 275
Hockey *see* Ice hockey

Hoffmann, Josef Franz Maria, 195
Hofmann, Hans, 166
Hogarth, William, 169
Hogshead (measure), 26
Holbein, Hans (the Younger), 173
Holiday, Billie (Lady Day), 142
Holidays
  Canadian, 15–16
  foreign, 16–18
  religious, 241–243
  US, 15
Holm, Hanya, 157
Holocene era, 84
Holst, Gustav, 131
Holy Saturday, 242
Holy See *see* Vatican City
Home decoration magazines, 513
Home ownership *see* Real estate
Homeowners' insurance, 439–440
Homer, 217
Homer, Winslow, 166
Home remedies, 701–702
Homicide, 427
Homophonic, 149
Honduras
  dialing code, 896
  statistics, 859
  visa requirements, 540
Honegger, Arthur, 133
Hong Kong
  dialing code, 896
  statistics, 859
  visa requirements, 541
Hoover, Herbert, 820
Hopkins, Gerard Manley, 217
Hopper, Edward, 166
Hormone, 92
Horse racing, 673–674, 686
Horton, Lester, 157
Hospital insurance, 842
Hotels and motels
  tips for disabled, 560
  toll-free numbers, 526
Hotlines, 504–505
Hours, 2–3
Household workers, 842
Housekeeping (computer), 100
Howells, William Dean, 210
Hubble flow, 90
Hughes, Langston, 210
Hughes, Ted, 225
Hugo, Victor Marie, 187, 217
Humanism, 275
Hume, David, 265, 266, 278
Humperdinck, Engelbert, 135
Humphrey, Doris, 157
Humphrey, Hubert, 824
Hungary
  dialing code, 896
  statistics, 859
  visa requirements, 541
Hung jury, 427
Hunt, Richard Morris, 191
Hurston, Zora Neale, 210
Husserl, Edmund, 265, 278
Huygens, Christian, 4
Hybrid computer, 100

Hydrocarbon, 94
Hydrogenated vegetable oil, 596
Hydrogen peroxide, 702
Hydrographic map symbols, 38
Hydrolyzed vegetable protein, 596
Hydroxyl, 94
Hygeia, 249
Hymen (Greek god), 249
Hyperbole, 222
Hypnus, 249

Iamb, 222
Iambic pentameter, 222
Ibert, Jacques François Antoine, 133
Ibsen, Henrik, 190
Ice hockey, 666–667, 686
Iceland
    dialing code, 896
    statistics, 860
    visa requirements, 541
Icon (computer), 100
Idaho
    Better Business Bureaus, 465
    consumer protection office, 475
    crime rate, 846
    name origin, 793
    newspaper, 516
    poison control center, 760
    social services offices, 457, 494
    vital statistics, 770, 778, 788, 790
    weather, 825, 826, 827
    wildlife refuges, 633
Id al-Adha, 243
Idealism, 271, 275
Illinois
    Better Business Bureaus, 465
    consumer protection office, 476–477
    crime rate, 845
    libraries, 285–286
    museums, 295
    name origin, 793
    newspapers, 516
    poison control centers, 760
    social services offices, 457, 494
    vital statistics, 770, 778, 788, 790
    weather, 825, 826, 827
    wildlife refuges, 633
    zoos, 70
Imagery, 222
Imitation (music), 149
Immigration (US)
    admission, 775–776
    by class of admission, 773–774
    by country of birth, 772, 775–776
    metropolitan area of intended residence, 775–776
    statistics, 771–776
Immortality, 275
Immunity, 92
Immunity from prosecution, 427
Immunizations
    foreign requirements, 533–553
    vaccines, 736
Impanel, 427
Impasto, 179
Impeller, 96
Impresario, 149

Impressionism, 181
Impromptu, 149
Inbreeding, 93
In camera, 427
Incidental music, 149
Income see Economic statistics
Income fund, 449
Indeterminism, 275
Indexing (economic), 451
India
    dialing code, 896
    Hinduism, 232
    statistics, 860
    visa requirements, 541
Indiana
    Better Business Bureaus, 465
    consumer protection offices, 477
    crime rate, 845
    library, 286
    museums, 296
    name origin, 793
    newspapers, 516
    poison control center, 760
    social services offices, 457, 494
    vital statistics, 770, 778, 788, 790
    weather, 825, 826, 827
    wildlife refuge, 634
    zoos, 70
Indiana, Robert, 166
Indianapolis 500, 674–675
Indictment, 428
Individual Retirement Accounts (IRAs), 447, 448, 449
Indonesia
    dialing code, 896
    statistics, 860
    visa requirements, 541
Inductive reasoning, 275
Induration, 98
Infant, definition of, 428
Infectious diseases, 703
Information (legal), 428
Infringement, 428
Inge, William, 183
Ingres, Jean-Auguste, 171–172
Injunction, 428
Injury (legal), 428
Ink removal, 574
In loco parentis, 428
Innante ideas, 275
Inorganic chemistry, 94
Input (computer), 100
Input/output terminal, 100
Inquest, 428
In rem, 428
Insanity, definition of, 428
Insect bites, 753
Instruction (computer), 100
Instrumentalism, 275
Insurance
    auto, 440–441
    disability, 439
    life, 438–439
    medical, 437–438, 842–843
    property and liability, 439–440
Interest
    accrued, 448

definition of, 449, 451
tables of common, 435
Interface (computer), 100
Interjection (language), 357
Interlude (music), 149
Intermezzo, 149
International Date Line, 8
International organizations, 893–894
International style, 198
Interrupt (computer), 100
Interval (music), 149
Intestate, 428
Intonation (music), 149
Intuitionism, 275
Inventions time line, 105–125
Inversion (music), 149
Invertebrates, orders of, 59–60
Invert sugar, 596
Investments
    definition of, 449
    glossary of terms, 448–450
    and retirement, 446–447
Invitations
    party, 381
    wedding, 371–372, 380
Iodine, stain removal, 574–575
Ionesco, Eugene, 187
Ionian mode, 149
Ionic Order, 198
Iowa
    Better Business Bureaus, 465
    consumer protection office, 478
    crime rate, 846
    library, 286
    name origin, 793
    newspaper, 516
    poison control center, 760
    social service offices, 457
    vital statistics, 770, 778, 788, 790
    weather, 825, 826, 827
    wildlife refuges, 634
IRA see Individual Retirement Accounts
Iran
    dialing code, 896
    statistics, 860
    visa requirements, 541
Iraq
    dialing code, 896
    statistics, 860
    visa requirements, 541
Ireland
    dialing code, 896
    statistics, 860
    visa requirements, 541
Irony, 222
Irving, Washington, 210
Islam, 232–233
    symbols, 42
Isotope, 94
Israel
    dialing code, 896
    statistics, 860
    visa requirements, 541
Italian languagae, 339
Italy
    dialing code, 896
    statistics, 860

Italy (continued)
  visa requirements, 541
Ivanov, Lev, 160
Ives, Charles, 129
Ivory Coast see Côte D'Ivoire

Jackson, Andres, 819
Jackson, Shirley, 210
Jamaica
  statistics, 860
  visa requirements, 542
James, Henry, 210
James, William, 265, 278
Janáček, Leoš, 139
Japan
  dialing code, 896
  royal rulers, 900
  statistics, 860
  visa requirements, 542
Jarrell, Randall, 210
Jazz see Music; specific composers and performers
Jefferson, Thomas, 191, 819, 823
Jehovah's Witnesses, 237
Jenney, William Le Baron, 191
Jersey, statistics, 860
Jeté, 164
Jitterbug, 164
Joffrey, Robert, 157
Johns, Jasper, 166
Johnson, Andrew, 820, 823
Johnson, Lyndon B., 821, 824
Johnson, Philip Cortelyou, 191
Johnson, Richard M., 823
Johnson, Samuel, 217
Joint, 93
Jones, Inigo, 193
Jong, Erica, 210
Jonson, Ben, 185, 225
Jooss, Kurt, 161
Joplin, Scott, 142
Jordan
  dialing code, 896
  statistics, 861
  visa requirements, 542
Joule, 81
Joyce, James, 217
Joystick, 100
Judaism, 233
  symbols, 43
Judgment (legal), 428
Judicial system, federal, 395
  see also Supreme Court
Junk bond, 449
Jupiter (planet), 87–89
Jurassic period, 84
Jury, 428
  hung, 427
  polling, 429
Justice, 275

K (computer abbreviation), 100
Kabuki, 164
Kafka, Franz, 217
Kahlo, Frida, 176
Kahn, Louis Isadore, 191
Kandinsky, Wassily, 177

Kansas
  Better Business Bureaus, 465
  consumer protection offices, 478
  crime rate, 846
  library, 286
  museum, 296
  name origin, 793
  newspapers, 516
  poison control center, 760
  social services offices, 457, 495
  vital statistics, 770, 778, 788, 790
  weather, 825, 826, 827
  wildlife refuges, 634
  zoo, 70
Kant, Immanuel, 264, 265, 269
Karotype, 93
Karsavina, Tamara, 160
Kawabata, Yasunari, 220
Kazakhstan
  statistics, 861
  visa requirements, 542
Keats, John, 217
Kelly, Gene, 157
Kendall, Henry, 123
Kennedy, John F., 821
Kentucky
  Better Business Bureaus, 465
  consumer protection offices, 478
  crime rate, 846
  museum, 296
  name origin, 793
  newspapers, 516
  poison control center, 760
  social services offices, 458, 494
  vital statistics, 770, 778, 788, 790
  weather, 825, 826, 827
  zoo, 71
Kentucky Derby, 673–674
Kenya
  dialing code, 896
  statistics, 861
  visa requirements, 542
Keogh plan, 449
Kernel, 93
Kerouac, Jack, 210
Key (music), 149
Keyboard (computer), 100
Key signature, 149
Khachaturian, Aram, 137
Kidnapping, 428
Kierkegaard, Søren, 265
Kinetic energy, 81, 95
King, William R., 823
Kingdoms, scientific, 55
Kipling, Rudyard, 217
Kiribati
  statistics, 861
  visa requirements, 542
Kirstein, Lincoln, 157
Kitchen equipment, standard sizes, 609
Kite, 105
Klee, Paul, 177
Klimt, Gustav, 178
Kline, Franz, 166
Knot (measure), 26
Knox, John, 235
Kodály, Zoltán, 139

Kokoschka, Oskar, 178
Kollwitz, Käthe Schmidt, 173
Koran, 232, 246
Korea
  dialing code, 896
  statistics, 861
  visa requirements, 542
Kosinski, Jerzy, 211
Kuwait
  dialing code, 896
  statistics, 861
  visa requirements, 542
Kyd, Thomas, 185
Kyrgyzstan
  statistics, 861
  visa requirements, 542

La (musical note), 149
Label (computer), 100
Labrouste, Henri, 194
Lactic acid, 596
Lactose, 596
Landscape, 179
Language
  computer, 100
  foreign words and phrases, 339–345
  linguistic philosophy, 275
  linguistic reference works, 310
  philosophy of, 278
  see also specific languages
Language game, 275
Lantern, 198
Laos
  statistics, 861
  visa requirements, 543
Lao-tzu, 220, 239
Larceny, 428
Lardner, Ring, 211
Largo, 149
Larva, 93
Lasso, Orlando di (Roland de Lassus), 139
Latin prefixes, 353–354
Latin suffixes, 354
Latrobe, Benjamin Henry, 191
Latvia
  statistics, 861
  visa requirements, 543
Laundry
  stain removal, 568–580
  washing fabrics, 565–567
  wash–water temperatures, 567
Law
  bill's passage into, 850
  forms and contracts, 397–420
  legal terms, 424–430
  reference works, 310
  see also Judicial system, federal
Lawrence, D.H., 217
Laye, Camara, 220
Leaching, 98
Leacock, Stephen, 211
Leading question, 428
Leading tone, 149
Leaf, 93
League (measure), 26
Leases
  furnished house, 402–404

Leases (continued)
   'open" rental agreement, 405–407
   unfurnished apartment, 398–401
Lebanon
   statistics, 861
   visa requirements, 543
Lecithin, 597
Le Corbusier, 194
Ledoux, Claude, 194
Legal information *see* Judicial system, federal; Law
Legato, 149
Léger, Fernand, 172
Legislative process, 850
Leibniz, Gottfried Wilhelm, 265, 278
Length, 24, 29
Lent, 241
Lento, 149
Leonardo da Vinci, 107, 175, 195
Leoncavallo, Ruggiero, 136
Lesotho
   statistics, 861
   visa requirements, 543
Lessing, Doris, 217
Letter writing
   business, 378–379
   condolence, 384
   personal, 380–381
   to senators and representatives, 522–523
   thank-you notes, 375, 380
Lewis, H. Spencer, 239
Lewis, John A., 142
Lewis, Sinclair, 211
Liabilities (financial), 449
Liability insurance, 439–440
Libel *see* Defamation
Liberia
   dialing code, 896
   statistics, 861
   visa requirements, 543
Libraries, 284–292
Library of Congress, 285
   subject headings, 316–317
Libretto, 149
Libya
   dialing code, 896
   statistics, 862
   visa requirements, 543
Lichtenstein, Roy, 166
Liechtenstein
   dialing code, 897
   statistics, 862
   visa requirements, 543
Lien, 451
Lifar, Serge, 160
Life expectancy tables, 697–698
Life insurance, 438–439
Lighthouse of Pharos, 898
Light inverse square law, 81
Light pen, 100
Light-year, 26, 90
Limbourg brothers, 170
Lincoln, Abraham, 820
Linear measures, 21, 23
Linens, washing of, 565
Linguistics *see* Language
Linnaeus, Carolus, 55

Lipid, 93
Li Po, 220
Lippi family (painters), 175
Liquid measures *see* Fluid measures
Liquor *see* Alcohol
Listed stock, 449
Liszt, Franz, 139
Litany, 149
Literature
   Asian, African, and Latin American authors, 220–221
   definition, 222
   European authors, 214–219
   glossary of terms, 221–223
   holy books, 246–247
   Nobel Prize winners, 226–227
   pseudonyms of authors, 224–225
   Pulitzer Prize winners, 227–228
   reference works, 311
   US and Canadian authors, 207–213
   see also Poetry; specific authors
Lithography, 179
Lithuania
   statistics, 862
   visa requirements, 543
Little, R.W., 239
Living will, 418–419
Loans, 441–442
Locke, John, 266, 269, 278
Loggia, 198
Logic, 273, 276, 278
Logical positivism, 276, 281
London, Jack, 211
Longfellow, Henry Wadsworth, 211
Loos, Adolf, 196
Lorrain, Claude, 172
Louis, Morris, 166
Louisiana
   Better Business Bureaus, 465
   consumer protection offices, 478
   crime rate, 846
   name origin, 793
   newspapers, 517
   poison control center, 760
   social services offices, 458, 495
   vital statistics, 770, 778, 788, 790
   weather, 825, 826, 827
   wildlife refuges, 634
   zoos, 71
Low comedy, 222
Lowell, James Russell, 211
Lowry, Malcolm, 211
Lucretius, 266
Lully, Jean-Baptiste, 133
Lutheran Church, 235
Lutyens, Sir Edwin Landseer, 193
Luxembourg
   dialing code, 897
   statistics, 862
   visa requirements, 543

Macau
   statistics, 862
   visa requirements, 543–544
MacDowell, Edward, 129
Macedonia, statistics, 862
Machado de Assis, Joaquim Maria, 220

Machiavelli, Niccolò, 266, 269
Machine language, 100
Mackintosh, Charles Rennie, 196
Madagascar, statistics, 862
Madison, James, 819
Madrigal, 149
Maestoso, 149
Magazines
   arts and entertainment, 511
   business and finance, 511
   consumerism, 511
   cooking and dining, 512
   general interest, 512
   health and nutrition, 512
   home and gardening, 513
   men's, 513
   news, 513
   parenting, 513
   public, social, and political, 514
   science and mechanics, 514
   sports and outdoors, 514
   travel, 514
   women's, 514–515
Magistrate, 428
Magnetic memory, 100
Magnificat, 149
Magnum, 26
Magritte, René, 170
Mahfouz, Naguib, 220
Mahler, Gustav, 130
Mailer, Norman, 211
Maillol, Aristide, 172
Maimonides, 267
Maine
   Better Business Bureau, 465
   consumer protection offices, 478
   crime rate, 845
   name origin, 793
   newspapers, 517
   social services offices, 458, 495
   vital statistics, 770, 778, 788, 790
   weather, 825, 826, 827
   wildlife refuges, 635
Mainframe computer, 100
Major (music), 149
Majority, age of, 428
Major medical, 437–438
Major scale, 149
Makarova, Natalia, 160
Makemie, Francis, 236
Malamud, Bernard, 211
Malapropism, 222
Malawi
   dialing code, 897
   statistics, 862
   visa requirements, 544
Malaysia
   dialing code, 897
   statistics, 862
   visa requirements, 544
Maldives
   statistics, 862
   visa requirements, 544
Male, definition of, 93
Malevich, Kasimir, 178
Malfeasance, 428

918 *Index*

Mali
   statistics, 862
   visa requirements, 544
Malice aforethought, 428
Malory, Sir Thomas, 217
Malpractice, 428
Malraux, André, 217
Malta
   statistics, 862
   visa requirements, 544
Mamet, David, 183
Mammals
   definition, 93
   extinct, 67
   orders of, 56–58
   see also specific animals
Mammogram, 707
Man, Isle of, 863
Mandamus, 428
Mandelstam, Osip, 217
Manet, Edouard, 172
Manichaeanism, 276
Manitoba (Canada)
   Better Business Bureau, 469
   zoo, 75
Mann, Thomas, 217
Mannerism, 182
Mannitol, 597
Manslaughter, 428
Mantegna, Andrea, 175
Manzoni, Alessandro, 217
Mapp v. Ohio, 431
Maps
   Mercator projection, 98
   symbols, 37–38
Marbury v. Madison, 431
March (music), 150
Marcus Aurelius, 267
Margin (stock), 449
Market order, 449
Markova, Dame Alicia, 159
Marlowe, Christopher, 185
Mars (planet), 87–89
Marshall, Thomas R., 824
Marshall Islands visa requirements, 544
Martinique, statistics, 863
Martins, Peter, 157
Marvell, Andrew, 217
Marx, Karl, 267, 269, 281
Marxism, 276
Maryland
   Better Business Bureau, 465
   consumer protection offices, 479
   crime rate, 846
   libraries, 286
   museums, 296
   name origin, 793
   newspaper, 517
   poison control center, 760
   social services offices, 458, 495
   vital statistics, 770, 778, 788, 790
   weather, 826, 827
   wildlife refuges, 635
   zoos, 71
Mascagni, Pietro, 136
Masefield, John, 225
Mass (music), 150

Mass, measurement of, 23, 24
Massachusetts
   Better Business Bureau, 465
   consumer protection offices, 479–480
   crime rate, 845
   libraries, 286–287
   museums, 296–297
   name origin, 793
   newspapers, 517
   poison control center, 760
   social services offices, 458, 495
   vital statistics, 770, 778, 788, 791
   weather, 825, 826, 827
   wildlife refuges, 635
   zoos, 71
Massenet, Jules Emile Frédéric, 133
Massine, Léonide, 160
Mass number, 94
Mass/weight relationship, 81
Masters (golf), 665
Materialism, 276
Material witness *see* Witness
Mathematics
   area equations and formulas, 79–80
   basic rules and formulas, 78–80
   international conversions, 895
   philosophy of, 278
   symbols, 35–36
   volume equations and formulas, 79–80
   see also Decimals; Fractions; Triangles
Matisse, Henri, 172
Matter, 94
Matter era, 90
Maturity (bond/loan), 449
Maugham, Somerset, 217
Maundy Tuesday, 242
Maupassant, Henri Guy de, 218
Mauriac, François, 218
Mauritania
   statistics, 863
   visa requirements, 544
Mauritius
   statistics, 863
   visa requirements, 544
Mausoleum at Halicarnassus, 898
Mayotte, statistics, 863
Mazurka, 150, 164
McCarthy, Mary, 211
McCullers, Carson, 211
McCullock v. Maryland, 431
McKinley, William, 820
Mean sidereal day, 2
Mean solar day, 2
Measure (music), 150
Measures, 21–26
   angular, 22
   converting household, 28–29
   cooking equivalents, 580–581
   cubic (volume), 21–22
   food, 581–582
   glossary of special, 25–26
   historic, 29
   international conversions, 895
   linear, 21
   quick methods, 24–25
   square, 21
   see also Metric measurements

Meat
   cooking times, 584–586
   nutritive value, 712
   weights and measures, 582
Mechanical advantage, 96
Mechanics
   definition of, 95
   magazines, 514
Mechanism, 276
Mediant (music), 150
Medicare, 842
Medications
   home remedies, 701–702
   pharmacology symbols, 35
   shelf life, 702
   stain removal, 575
   see also specific drugs and medications
Medicine and health
   anatomical drawings, 689–692
   combining forms of medical terms, 704–705
   deaths and death rates, 699–701
   home remedies, 701–702
   hotlines, 503
   insurance, 842–843
   magazines, 512
   organizations, 502–503
   reference works, 311–312
   spread of infectious diseases, 703
   symbols, 35
   see also First aid; Immunizations; Medications
Melody, 150
Melville, Herman, 211
Memory (computer), 100
Men, magazines for, 513
Mencken, H.L., 211
Mendel's laws, 93
Mendelsohn, Erich, 196
Mendelssohn, Felix, 135
Mennonites *see* Amish Mennonites
Menotti, Gian Carlo, 129
Mens rea *see* Actus rea
Mensural music, 150
Mercator projection, 98
Mercurochrome, stain removal, 575
Mercury (planet), 87–89
Merthiolate, stain removal, 575
Message (computer), 101
Messiaen, Olivier Eugène Prosper Charles, 133
Metabolism, 93
Metaethics, 276
Metals, stain removal, 575–576
Metaphor, 222
Metaphysics, 276
Meter (music), 150
Meter (poetry), 223
Methodist Church, 235
Metis, 249
Metric measurements, 22–24
   cooking equivalents, 581
   international conversions, 895
   mile/kilometer conversions, 31
   prefixes, 40
Mexico
   dialing code, 897

Mexico (*continued*)
  statistics, 863
  visa requirements, 544–545
Meyerbeer, Giacomo, 135
Mezzo, 150
Mezzo-forte, 150
Mezzo-soprano, 150
Mi (musical note), 150
Michelangelo Buonarroti, 175, 195
Michener, James, 211
Michigan
  Better Business Bureaus, 466
  consumer protection offices, 480
  crime rate, 845
  libraries, 287
  museums, 297
  name origin, 793
  newspapers, 517
  poison control centers, 760
  social service offices, 458
  vital statistics, 770, 778, 788, 791
  weather, 825, 826, 827
  wildlife refuges, 635
  zoos, 71
Microcomputer, 101
Micronesia, visa requirements, 545
Microprocessor, 101
Middle C, 150
Middleton, Thomas, 185
Mies van der Rohe, Ludwig, 191
Mildew, stain removal, 576
Miletian School, 276
Mile-to-kilometer conversions, 31
Milhaud, Darius, 133
Military, forms of address, 390–391
Milk
  as home remedy, 702
  nutritive value, 720
Milk of magnesia, 702
Milky Way, 90
Mill, John Stuart, 267, 269, 278
Miller, Arthur, 183–184
Miller, Glenn, 142
Miller, Henry, 211
Miller, William, 235
Millet, Jean-François, 172
Mills, Robert, 191
Milton, John, 218
Minaret, 198
Mind-body problem, 276
Mineral kingdom, 55
Mineral oil, 702
Mingus, Charlie, 142
Minicomputer, 101
Minimalism, 182
Minnesota
  Better Business Bureau, 466
  consumer protection offices, 480
  crime rate, 846
  library, 287–288
  museums, 297
  name origin, 793
  newspapers, 517
  poison control centers, 760
  social services offices, 458, 495
  vital statistics, 770, 778, 788, 791
  weather, 825, 826, 827

wildlife refuges, 635
zoos, 71
Minor (music), 150
Minor scale, 150
Minuet, 150, 164
Miocene era, 84
Miquelon Island, visa requirements, 545
Miranda rule, 428
Miranda v. Arizona, 432
Miró, Joan, 177
Misdemeanor *see* Felony
Mishima, Yukio, 220
Mississippi
  Better Business Bureau, 466
  consumer protection offices, 480–481
  crime rate, 846
  name origin, 793
  newspaper, 517
  poison control center, 760
  social services offices, 458, 495
  vital statistics, 770, 778, 788, 791
  weather, 825, 826, 828
  wildlife refuges, 636
  zoo, 71
Missouri
  Better Business Bureaus, 466
  consumer protection offices, 481
  crime rate, 846
  libraries, 288
  museums, 297
  name origin, 793
  newspapers, 517
  poison control center, 760
  social services offices, 458
  vital statistics, 770, 778, 788, 791
  weather, 825, 826, 828
  wildlife refuges, 636
  zoos, 72
Mistrial, 428
Mitchell, Arthur, 157
Mitchell, Margaret, 211
Mitigating circumstances, 428
Mode (music), 150
Modeling (art), 179
Modem, 101
Modifiers (language), 359–360
Modigliani, Amedeo, 175
Modulation (music), 150
Module (architecture), 198
Moldova
  statistics, 863
  visa requirements, 545
Molière (Jean Baptiste Poquelin), 187
Molina, Tirso de, 189
Molto, 150
Momentum, 81, 95
Monaco
  dialing code, 897
  statistics, 863
Monad, 276
Mondale, Walter, 824
Mondrian, Piet, 169
Monet, Claude, 172
Money
  foreign currencies, 530–531
  symbols, 40
Money market fund, 449

Mongolia
  statistics, 863
  visa requirements, 545
Monism, 276
Monk, Thelonious, 142
Monochrome, 179
Monoglycerides, 597
Monophony, 150
Monopoly (game), 681
Monosodium glutamate, 597
Monotype, 179
Monroe, James, 819
Monroe Doctrine, 816
Montaigne, Michel de, 218
Montana
  consumer protection office, 481
  crime rate, 846
  name origin, 793
  newspapers, 517
  poison control center, 761
  social services offices, 458, 495
  vital statistics, 770, 778, 788, 791
  weather, 825, 826, 828
  wildlife refuges, 636
Montesquieu, Baron de, 267
Monteverdi, Claudio, 136
Montgomery, Lucy Maude, 211
Montserrat, statistics, 863
Moon
  eclipses of, 646–647
  phases of, 86
Moore, Douglas, 129
Moore, G.E., 267
Moore, Henry, 169
Moral turpitude, 429
Mordent, 150
More, Sir Thomas, 267
Morendo, 150
Morisot, Berthe, 172
Morley, Thomas, 131
Mormons *see* Church of Jesus Christ of
  Latter-Day Saints
Morocco
  dialing code, 897
  statistics, 863
  visa requirements, 545
Morpheus, 249
Morris dance, 164
Morrison, Toni, 211
Morse Code, 48
Mortgages, 443–445
  assumable, 450
  definition of, 451
Morton, Ferdinand (Jelly Roll), 142
Morton, Levi P., 824
Moses, 259
Moses, Grandma (Anna Mary Robertson), 166
Motels *see* Hotels and motels
Motherwell, Robert, 166
Motif (literature), 223
Motif (music), 150
Motion (music), 150
Motion pictures
  Academy Awards, 202–205
  reference works, 309
Mottos, state, 790–792

920 *Index*

Mouse (computer), 101
Mouth-to-mouth breathing, 742–743
Mouth-to-nose breathing, 744
Mozambique
   statistics, 863
   visa requirements, 545
Mozart, Wolfgang Amadeus, 130
MSG *see* Monosodium glutamate
Muhammad, 232
Muller v. Oregon, 431
Multiprogramming, 101
Munch, Edvard, 178
Municipal bond, 449
Munn v. Illinois, 431
Munro, Alice, 212
Mural, 179
Murasaki, Shikibu, 220
Murder, 429
   felony, 427
   homicide, 427
   manslaughter, 428
Murillo, Bartolomé, 177
Muscles, 690
Muses (mythology), 249
Museums
   Canada, 301–302
   children's, 302–303
   US, 293–301
Music
   classical, 146
   composers of classical, 128–140
      American, 128–130
      Austrian, 130–131
      British, 131–132
      French, 132–134
      German, 134–135
      Italian, 136–137
      miscellaneous, 138–140
      Russian, 137–138
   glossary of terms, 143–155
   jazz composers and performers, 140–143
   notes, 155
   reference works, 312
   symbols, 40–41
   symphony orchestra makeup, 151
   see also specific composers and performers
Mussorgsky, Modest, 137
Mustard
   as home remedy, 702
   stain removal, 576
Mutual fund, 447, 449
Myanmar
   statistics, 864
   visa requirements, 545
Mysticism, 276
Myth, definition of, 223
Myth of Er, 276
Mythology, reference works, 312

Nabis (painters), 182
Nabokov, Vladimir, 218
Nail polish, stain removal, 576
Naipaul, V.S., 221
Naive art, 182

Namibia
   dialing code, 897
   statistics, 864
   visa requirements, 545
Narthex, 198
Nash, John, 193
National Basketball Association (NBA), 659–660
National Football League (NFL), 662
National Hockey League (NHL), 667
Natsume Soseki, 221
Natural (music), 150
Natural feature map symbols, 38
Naturalism, 276
Naturalistic fallacy, 276
Natural law, 276
Natural rights, 276–277
Natural selection, 93
Nauru
   statistics, 864
   visa requirements, 545
Nave, 198
NBA *see* National Basketball Association
Nebraska
   Better Business Bureaus, 466
   consumer protection offices, 481
   crime rate, 846
   name origin, 793
   newspapers, 517
   poison control center, 761
   social services offices, 458, 495
   vital statistics, 770, 778, 788, 791
   weather, 825, 826, 828
   wildlife refuges, 636–637
   zoos, 72
Necessary and contingent truth, 277
Negligence, 429
Nemerov, Howard, 226
Nemesis, 249
Neoclassicism, 182
Neoplatonism, 277
Nepal
   statistics, 864
   visa requirements, 545–546
Neptune (planet), 87–89
Neruda, Pablo, 221
Netherlands
   dialing code, 897
   statistics, 864
   visa requirements, 546
Netherlands Antilles
   dialing code, 897
   statistics, 864
   visa requirements, 546
Networks, television, 520–521
Net worth, calculating, 451–452
Neuron, 93
Neutron star, 91
Nevada
   Better Business Bureaus, 466
   consumer protection offices, 481
   crime rate, 846
   name origin, 793
   newspapers, 517
   poison control center, 761
   social services offices, 458, 495
   vital statistics, 770, 778, 788, 791

   weather, 825, 826, 828
   wildlife refuges, 637
Nevelson, Louise, 167
New Caledonia
   dialing code, 897
   statistics, 864
Newfoundland Better Business Bureau, 469
New Hampshire
   Better Business Bureau, 466
   consumer protection office, 481
   crime rate, 845
   name origin, 793
   newspaper, 517
   poison control center, 761
   social services offices, 459, 495
   vital statistics, 770, 778, 789, 791
   weather, 826, 828
   wildlife refuge, 637
New Jersey
   Better Business Bureaus, 466
   consumer protection offices, 481–484
   crime rate, 845
   libraries, 288
   museum, 297
   name origin, 793
   newspapers, 517
   poison control center, 761
   social services offices, 459, 495
   vital statistics, 770, 778, 789, 791
   weather, 825, 826, 828
   wildlife refuges, 637
   zoos, 72
Newman, Barnett, 167
New Mexico
   Better Business Bureaus, 466
   consumer protection office, 484
   crime rate, 846
   museum, 298
   name origin, 793
   newspapers, 517
   poison control center, 761
   social services offices, 459, 495
   vital statistics, 770, 778, 789, 791
   weather, 825, 826, 828
   wildlife refuges, 637
   zoos, 72
News magazines, 513
Newspapers, 515–519
New Testament, 246, 258
Newton (unit of force), 81
Newton's second law, 81
New York
   Better Business Bureaus, 466
   consumer protection offices, 484–486
   crime rate, 845
   libraries, 288–289
   museums, 298–299
   name origin, 793
   newspapers, 517
   poison control center, 761
   social services offices, 459, 495
   vital statistics, 770, 778, 789, 791
   weather, 825, 826, 828
   wildlife refuges, 637
   zoos, 72
New Zealand
   dialing code, 897

New Zealand (*continued*)
  statistics, 864
  visa requirements, 546
Next of kin, 429
NFL *see* National Football League
NHL *see* National Hockey League
Niacin, 733
Nicaragua
  dialing code, 897
  statistics, 864
  visa requirements, 546
Nicknames, state, 790–792
Nicotinic acid *see* Niacin
Nielsen, Carl, 139
Niemeyer, Oscar, 196
Nietzsche, Friedrich Wilhelm, 267, 269, 278
Niger
  statistics, 864
  visa requirements, 546
Nigeria
  dialing code, 897
  statistics, 864
  visa requirements, 546
Nihilism, 277
Nijinska, Bronislava, 160
Nijinsky, Vaslav, 160
Nike (Greek goddess), 249
Nikolais, Alwin, 157
Nimbostratus cloud, 643
Niue
  statistics, 864
  visa requirements, 546
Nixon, Richard M., 821, 824
Nobel Prize, in literature, 226–227
Nobility
  British peerage, 391
  European and Asian rulers, 899–900
  forms of address, 390
Nocturne, 150
Noguchi, Isamu, 167
Nolo contendere, 429
Nominalism, 277
Nonfeasance *see* Malfeasance
Nonfiction, 223
Non sequitur, 277
Norfolk Island
  statistics, 864
  visa requirements, 546
Norman architecture, 198
North Carolina
  Better Business Bureaus, 466–467
  consumer protection office, 487
  crime rate, 846
  libraries, 289–290
  name origin, 793
  newspapers, 518
  poison control center, 761
  social services offices, 459, 495
  vital statistics, 770, 778, 789, 791
  weather, 825, 826, 828
  wildlife refuges, 637–678
North Dakota
  consumer protection offices, 487
  crime rate, 846
  name origin, 793
  newspaper, 518

poison control center, 761
social services offices, 459, 496
vital statistics, 770, 778, 789, 791
weather, 825, 826, 828
wildlife refuges, 638
zoo, 72
Northern Securities Co. v. U.S., 431
Norway
  dialing code, 897
  statistics, 865
  visa requirements, 546
Nosebleeds, 757
Notary certificate, 397
Notary public, 429
Notes, musical, 150, 155
Noun, 357, 359, 360
Nova Scotia Better Business Bureau, 469
Novel (fiction), 222, 223
Novella, 223
Noverre, Jean Georges, 159
Nucleus (cell), 93
Nureyev, Rudolf, 160
Nutrition
  food values, 710–731
  magazines, 512
  organizations, 502–503
  vitamin/food chart, 732–735
Nuts, weights and measures, 582
Nymphs (mythology), 249
Nyx, 249

Oates, Joyce Carol, 212
Obbligato, 150
Obelisk, 198
Object (part of speech), 359
Objectivism, 277
Obligation (ethics), 277
O'Casey, Sean, 188
Ockham's razor, 277
Octave, 151
Octet, 151
Odd lot, 449
Ode, 223
Odets, Clifford, 184
Offenbach, Jacques, 133
Offer (stock), 449
Off-line, 101
Ogive, 198
Ohio
  Better Business Bureaus, 467
  consumer protection offices, 487
  crime rate, 845
  libraries, 290
  museums, 299
  name origin, 793
  newspapers, 518
  poison control centers, 761
  social services offices, 459, 496
  vital statistics, 770, 778, 789, 791
  weather, 825, 826, 828
  wildlife refuge, 638
  zoos, 72–73
Ohm, 26, 81
Ohm's law, 81
Oil of cloves, 702
Oil painting, 179
O'Keeffe, Georgia, 167

Oklahoma
  Better Business Bureaus, 467
  consumer protection offices, 488
  crime rate, 846
  library, 290
  museum, 299
  name origin, 793
  newspapers, 518
  poison control center, 761
  social services offices, 459, 496
  vital statistics, 770, 778, 789, 791
  weather, 825, 826, 828
  wildlife refuges, 639
  zoos, 73
Oldenburg, Claes, 167
Old Testament, 246–247, 258
Oligocene era, 84
Olive oil, 702
Olympian Zeus, 898
Olympic Games, 675–677
Oman
  dialing code, 897
  statistics, 865
  visa requirements, 546
Omar Khayyam, 221
O'Neill, Eugene, 184
On the merits (court judgment), 429
Onomatopoeia, 223
Ontario (Canada)
  Better Business Bureaus, 469
  library, 292
  museums, 301–302
  zoo, 75
Ontology, 277
Op art, 182
Open court, 429
Opera, 151
Operating system (computer), 101
Operationalism, 277
Operetta, 151
Optical scanner, 101
Optimism, 277
Opus, 151
Oratorio, 151
Orchestra, 151
Order (architecture), 198
Ordinary Language Philosophy, 276
Ordovician era, 85
Oregon
  Better Business Bureau, 467
  consumer protection office, 488
  crime rate, 846
  museum, 299
  name origin, 793
  newspaper, 518
  poison control center, 761
  social services offices, 459, 496
  vital statistics, 770, 778, 789, 791
  weather, 825, 826, 828
  wildlife refuges, 639
  zoo, 73
Orff, Carl, 135
Organic chemistry, 94
Organizations, international, 893–894
Orozco, José Clemente, 176
Orthodox Eastern Church, 233
Orwell, George, 218

Osborne, John, 185
Osmosis, 93
Osseous, 93
Outdoor activities, magazines for, 514
Output (computer), 101
Ouvert (ballet), 164
Over-the-counter market, 449
Overture, 151
Ovid, 218
Oxidation, 94
Oxymoron, 223, 346

Paderewski, Ignace, 139
Pagoda, 198
Paine, Thomas, 212
Paint, stain removal, 576–577
Painting *see* Art; specific painters
Pakistan
   dialing code, 897
   statistics, 865
   visa requirements, 546
Palau, visa requirements, 547
Paleocene era, 84
Palestrina, Giovanni, 136
Palette, 179
Palindrome, 223, 349
Palladio, Andrea, 195
Palm Sunday, 242
Pan (Greek god), 249
Panama
   dialing code, 897
   statistics, 865
   visa requirements, 547
Pantheism, 277
Papua New Guinea
   dialing code, 897
   statistics, 865
   visa requirements, 547
Par (stock), 450
Parable, 223
Paradox, 223
Paraguay
   dialing code, 897
   statistics, 865
   visa requirements, 547
Parallel motion (music), 151
Parasites, animal, 62–63
Pardon (legal), 429
Parentheses, 363
Parents
   magazines, 513
   organizations for, 519
Parker, Charlie (Bird), 142
Parker, Dorothy, 212
Parks
   national park directory, 624–628
   tips for disabled, 560
Parmenides, 267
Parody, 223
Parole, 429
Parrish, Maxfield, 167
Parsec, 26
Part (music), 151
Par terre, 164
Parties, 381
   formal dinner, 381–383
      seating arrangements, 381–382

   tableware, 382–383
Partita (music), 151
Part song, 151
Pascal, Blaise, 267, 278
Pascal's wager, 277
Pas de deux, 164
Passbook savings accounts, 446–447
Passion music, 151
Passover, 242
Passport requirements, 532
Pastel, 180
Pasternak, Boris, 218
Pasticcio, 152
Pastorale, 152
Patents, 422–424
Pathetic fallacy, 223
Pathos, 223
Paton, Alan, 221
Pavane, 164
Pavlova, Anna, 161
Paxton, Sir Joseph, 193
Paz, Octavio, 221
Pediment, 198
Pei, I.M., 191
Penché, 164
Pencil, stain removal, 577
Pendentive, 198
Pendulums, 4
Pennsylvania
   Better Business Bureaus, 467
   consumer protection offices, 488–489
   crime rate, 845
   libraries, 290–291
   museums, 300
   name origin, 793
   newspapers, 518
   poison control centers, 761
   social services offices, 459, 496
   vital statistics, 770, 778, 789, 791
   weather, 825, 826, 828
   wildlife refuges, 639
   zoos, 73
Pentatonic scale, 152
Pentecost, 242
Pentecostal churches, 236
Per capita income, 778–779
Percent, 78
Percy, Walker, 212
Pergolesi, Giovanni Battista, 136
Period (punctuation), 360
Peripheral (computer), 101
Perjury, 429
Permian era, 85
Perrot, Jules, 159
Persephone, 249
Personalism, 277
Personification, 223
Perspective (art), 180
Perspiration, stain removal, 577
Perturbation, 91
Peru
   dialing code, 897
   statistics, 865
   visa requirements, 547
Pessimism, 277
Peter, St., 238, 250
Petipa, Marius, 161

Petit, Roland, 159
Petrarch, 218
Petrolatum (Vaseline), 702
Petroleum distillates, 752
Petronius, 218
Pets *see* Animals
pH, 94
Pharmacology symbols, 35
Phenomenalism, 277
Phenomenology, 278
Phenotype, 93
Phidias (Pheidias), 178
Philippines
   dialing code, 897
   statistics, 865
   visa requirements, 547
Philosopher king, 278
Philosophes, 278
Philosophy
   arguments against God's existence, 266
   famous quotes, 269
   glossary of terms, 270–272, 274–278
   logical argument, 273
   philosophers, 262–263, 265–270
   proofs for existence of God, 264
   reference works, 312–313
   see also specific philosophers
Philosophy of mind, 279
Philosophy of religion, 279
Philosophy of science, 279
Phosphates, 597
Phosphoric acid, 597
Photorealism, 182
Phrase (language), 360
Phrase (music), 152
Phyla, 55
Physicalism, 279
Physics
   basic formulas, 80–81
   glossary of terms, 95
   symbols, 34
Pi, 26
Pianissimo, 152
Piano (musical direction), 152
Piano quartet, 152
Piano quintet, 152
Pica, 26
Picasso, Pablo, 177
Pier (architecture), 199
Pierce, Franklin, 819
Piero della Francesca, 175
Pies, nutritive value, 724
Pilaster, 199
Pinochle (card game), 683
Pinter, Harold, 185
Pipe (measure), 26
Piqué, 164
Pirandello, Luigi, 190
Piranesi, Giovanni Battista, 195
Pirouette, 164
Pisano family (sculptors), 175
Pissarro, Camille, 172
Pistil, 93
Piston, Walter, 129
Pitch, 152
Pizzicato, 152
Plainsong, 152

Plaintiff, 429
Plants
 diagram, 87
 facts about, 88–89
 see also specific planets
Plant kingdom, 55
Plants
 botanical names, 620–624
 frost dates, 616–617
 germination tables, 618
 ground covers, 619
 poisonous, 614–615, 752–753
Plastic, stain removal, 577
Plath, Sylvia, 212
Plato, 267, 269, 278
Platonism, 279
Plato's cave, 279
Plautus, 189
Playwrights see Drama; specific playwrights
Plea, 429
Plea bargaining, 429
Pledged–account mortgage, 445
Pledge of Allegiance, 816
Pleistocene era, 84
Plessy v. Ferguson, 431
Plié, 164
Pliocene era, 84
Plisetskaya, Maya, 161
Plot (literary), 223
Plotinus, 267–268
Pluralism, 279
Plutarch, 218
Pluto (planet), 87–89
Plutus, 249
Poco (musical direction), 152
Poe, Edgar Allan, 212
Poetic license, 223
Poetry
 glossary of terms, 222–223
 poem defined, 223
 poet laureates, 225–226
 see also specific poets
Point (ballet), 164
Point (loan), 451
Point (measure), 26
Pointillism, 182
Poisoning, 750–753
 corrosives, 751
 directory of control centers, 759–762
 food, 750–751
 inhaled, 752
 noncorrosives, 752
 petroleum distillates, 752
 plant, 752–753
Poker (card game), 684
Poland
 dialing code, 897
 statistics, 865
 visa requirements, 547
Political philosophy, 279
Political science, reference works, 313
Polk, James, 819
Polka, 152, 164
Polling the jury, 429
Pollock, Jackson, 167
Polonaise, 152

Polychrome, 180
Polymer, 94
Polyphony, 152
Polyptych, 180
Polysorbate 60, 597
Pop art, 182
Pope, Alexander, 218
Popes, 238, 250–258
Population
 by state, 770
 demographic reference works, 315
 US, 768–769
 see also specific countries, subhead statistics
Pork, nutritive value, 724
Porpoises, 56
Port de bras, 164
Porter, Katherine Anne, 212
Portico, 199
Portugal
 dialing code, 897
 statistics, 865
 visa requirements, 547
Poseidon, 249
Positivism, 279
Postal Service (US), abbreviations, 328–329
Post and lintel construction, 199
Postimpressionism, 182
Postmodernism, 199
Potassium sorbate, 598
Potential energy, 81, 95
Poulenc, Francis, 133
Poultry
 cooking times, 587
 nutritive value, 716
 weights and measures, 582
Pound, Ezra, 212
Poussin, Nicolas, 172
Power (physics), 81, 95
Power of attorney, 417–418, 429
Pragmatism, 279
Pratt, E.J., 212
Praxiteles, 178
Precambrian era, 85
Prefixes
 Greek, 349–352
 Latin, 353–354
Preliminary hearing, 429
Prelude, 152
Premeditation, 429
Premier danseur, 164
Premium (stock), 450
Prendergast, Maurice Brazil, 167
Prepayment penalty, 451
Preponderance of evidence, 429
Preposition, 357
Pre-Raphaelite Brotherhood, 182
Presbyterian Church, 236
Presentment, 429
Presidents (US), 819–821
 and bill passage, 850
 succession sequence, 822
 see also specific presidents
Presocratics, 279
Pressure points, 745–747
Preventive detention, 429

Priapus, 249
Primary colors, 179
Primary memory, 101
Primates, 58
Prime meridian, 3
Principal (economic), 451
Principle of noncontradiction, 279
Principle of sufficient reason, 279
Principle of utility, 279
Privacy Act, 420
Probable cause, 429
Probate, 429
Probation, 429
Pro bono, 429
Process (writ), 429
Program music, 152
Progression (musical), 152
Prokofiev, Sergei, 137
Prologue, 223
Promenade, 164
Promissory note, 415
Pronoun, 357
Proofreaders' marks, 41
Propylene glycol alginate, 593
Propyl gallate, 597
Prose, 223
Prosecutor, 429
Protagonist, 223
Protective custody, 429
Protestantism, 234–236
Protozoa, 93
Proust, Marcel, 218
Psyche (Greek goddess), 249
Psychologism, 279
Public defender, 429
Puccini, Giacomo, 136
Puerto Rico
 Better Business Bureaus, 468
 consumer protection offices, 493
 social service offices, 460
 statistics, 792
 wildlife refuges, 639–640
Pugin, Augustus, 193
Pulitzer Prize
 fiction, 227–228
 general nonfiction, 228
Pulsar, 91
Pun, 223
Punctuation, 360–363
Purcell, Henry, 132
Purim, 241
Pushkin, Alexander, 218
Puts and calls, 450
Pye, Henry James, 225
Pynchon, Thomas, 212
Pyramid, 199
Pyramids of Egypt, 898
Pyridoxine see Vitamin B_6
Pythagoras, 268
Pythagoreans, 279
Pythagorean theorem, 80

Qatar
 dialing code, 897
 statistics, 865
 visa requirements, 547
QED, 279

Quadrille, 164
Quakers *see* Religious Society of Friends
Quarks, 91, 123
Quartet, 152
Quartz clocks, 4
Quasar, 91
Quayle, Dan, 824
Quebec (Canada)
    Better Business Bureaus, 469
    library, 292
    zoos, 75
Question mark, 361
Quinine, 598
Quintal, 26
Quintet, 152
Quire, 26
Quotation marks, 363

Rabelais, François, 218
Rabies, 63
Rachmaninoff, Sergei, 137
Racine, Jean, 187
Radiation era, 91
Radio
    alphabet, international, 48
    networks, 520–521
Ragtime, 152
Railroads
    map symbols, 37
    tips for disabled, 559
RAM (random access memory), 101
Ramadan, 243
Rambert, Dame Marie, 159
Rameau, Jean–Philippe, 134
Rand, Ayn, 212
Random access, 101
Rape, 430
Raphael (Santi or Sanzio), 175
Rationalism, 279, 280
Rauschenberg, Robert, 167
Ravel, Maurice, 134
RDAs *see* Recommended Daily Dietary Allowances
Re (musical note), 152
Reagan, Ronald, 821
Real estate, 443–445
    affordability, 443–444
    decision to buy, 443
    down payment, 444
    glossary of terms, 450–451
    going to contract, 445
    mortgage, 444–445
    old vs. new home, 444
    property and liability insurance, 439–440
Realism, 182, 280
Ream, 26
Reasonable doubt, 425
Receptor (biological), 93
Recitative, 152
Recommended Daily Dietary Allowances, 708–709
Recording for the Blind (RFB), 502
Red herring (stock), 450
Red shift, 91
Reduction (chemical), 94
Reel (dance), 164

Reference works
    anthropology and ethnology, 304–305
    applied arts, 305
    art and architecture, 305–306
    astronomy, 306
    communications, 306–307
    economics and business, 307–308
    education, 308
    film, 309
    genealogy and heraldry, 309
    general, 303–304
    geography and travel guides, 309
    history, 310
    law, 310
    linguistics, 310
    literature, 311
    medical science, 311–312
    music, 312
    mythology, folklore, and popular customs, 312
    philosophy, 312–313
    political science, 313
    recreation and sports, 313
    religion, 313–314
    science and technology, 314
    social science, 314
    sociology, 314
    statistics and demography, 315
    theater and performing arts, 315
Reformation Sunday, 242
Refrain, 152, 223
Refrigeratied food storage, 589
Regeneration, 93
Register (computer), 101
Register (musical), 152
Reinhardt, Ad, 167
Reinhardt, Django, 142
Relativism, 280
Release on one's own recognizance, 430
Relevé, 164
Relief (architecture), 199
Relief (art), 180
Religions
    forms of address for officials, 389–390
    Greek and Roman deities, 248–249
    historical timeline, 240–241
    holy books, 246–247
    reference works, 313–314
    symbols, 42–43
    US holidays, 241–243
    world's major, 231–239
    see also specific religions
Religious Society of Friends, 238
Rembrandt Harmenszoon van Rijn, 169
Remington, Frederic, 167
Renaissance, 182, 199
Renoir, Auguste, 172
Rental agreements *see* Leases
Rental cars, toll–free numbers, 526
Representatives (US), writing to, 522–523
Reptiles, extinct, 68
Requiem, 152
Resolution (musical), 152
Respighi, Ottorino, 136
Respiration *see* Breathing
Respiratory infections, animal, 64
Response time (computer), 101

Rest (musical), 152
Restraining order, 430
Résumés, 379–380
Retirement
    benefits, 840–841
    and investments, 446–447
    planning for, 447–448
Réunion, statistics, 865
Révérence, 164
Reverse mortgage, 445
Reynolds, Sir Joshua, 169
Rhea, 249
Rhetorical question, 223
Rhode Island
    Better Business Bureau, 467
    consumer protection offices, 489
    crime rate, 845
    name origin, 793
    newspaper, 518
    poison control center, 761
    social services offices, 459, 496
    vital statistics, 770, 778, 789, 791
    weather, 825, 826, 828
    wildlife refuges, 640
    zoo, 73
Rhyme, 223
Rhythm, 223
Ribera, Jusepe de, 177
Riboflavin, 733
Richardson, Henry Hobson, 191
Richler, Mordecai, 212
Rilke, Rainer Marie, 218
Rimbaud, Arthur, 218
Rimsky–Korsakov, Nicolai, 138
Rinforzando, 152
Ritardando, 152
Ritenuto, 152
Rivera, Diego, 176
Rivers, Larry, 167
Roads
    international signs, 46–47
    map symbols, 37
    travel symbols, 46–47
Robbery, 430
Robbins, Jerome, 158
Roberts, Sir Charles G.D., 212
Robinson, Bill (Bojangles), 158
Rockefeller, Nelson, 824
Rockwell, Norman, 167
Rococo, 182, 199
Rodin, Auguste, 172
Roe v. Wade, 432
ROM (read only memory), 101
Roman Catholicism, 238
    patron saints, 243–246
    popes, 238, 250–258
Romance (musical composition), 153
Roman deities, 248–249
Romanesque architecture, 199
Romanesque art, 182–183
Romania
    dialing code, 897
    statistics, 865
    visa requirements, 547
Roman numerals, 51
Romanticism, 183
Rondo, 153

Roosevelt, Franklin D., 821
Roosevelt, Theodore, 820, 824
Root (music), 153
Rosh Hashanah, 242
Rosicrucianism, 239
Ross, Sinclair, 185
Rossetti, Dante Gabriel, 169
Rossini, Gioacchino, 136–137
Rostand, Edmond, 187, 218
Roth, Philip, 212
Roth v. U.S., 431
Rothko, Mark, 167
Rouault, Georges, 172
Round (music), 153
Rousseau, Henri, 172
Rousseau, Jean Jacques, 268, 269
Rousseau, Théodore, 173
Rowe, Nicholas, 225
Royalty *see* Nobility
Rubens, Peter Paul, 170
Rubinstein, Anton, 138
Rummy (card game), 684
Rushdie, Salman, 221
Russell, Bertrand, 268, 269, 278
Russell, Charles T., 237
Russia
  royal rulers, 900
  statistics, 866
  visa requirements, 548
Russian alphabet, 51
Rust, stain removal, 577–578
Rwanda
  statistics, 866
  visa requirements, 548

Saarinen, Eero, 192
Saarinen, Eliel, 192
Saccharin, 598
St. Denis, Ruth, 158
St. Helena, statistics, 866
St. Kitts and Nevis
  statistics, 866
  visa requirements, 548
St. Lucia
  statistics, 866
  visa requirements, 548
St. Patrick's Day, 241
St. Pierre
  statistics, 866
  visa requirements, 548
Saints, 243–246
Saint-Saëns, Charles Camille, 134
St. Valentine's Day, 241
St. Vincent and the Grenadines
  statistics, 866
  visa requirements, 548
Salad dressings, nutritive value, 726
Salinger, J.D., 212
Sallé, Marie, 159
Salt, 598, 702
Samoa *see* American Samoa
Sandburg, Carl, 212
Sand, George, 218
San Marino
  dialing code, 897
  statistics, 866
  visa requirements, 548

Santayana, George, 268
Sao Tome and Principe
  statistics, 866
  visa requirements, 548
Sappho, 218
Sargent, John Singer, 167
Saroyan, William, 184, 212
Sartre, Jean-Paul, 187, 218, 268
Satie, Erik, 134
Satire, 223
Saturn (planet), 87–89
Satyrs (mythology), 249
Saudi Arabia
  dialing code, 897
  statistics, 866
  visa requirements, 548
Sausage, nutritive value, 726
Scale (musical), 153
Scarlatti, Alessandro, 137
Scarlatti, (Giuseppe) Domenico, 137
Scat singing, 153
Schenck v. U.S., 431
Scherzo, 153
Schiele, Egon, 178
Schoenberg, Arnold, 129
Scholasticism, 280
Schopenhauer, Arthur, 268
Schubert, Frans Seraph Peter, 131
Schuman, William, 129
Schumann, Clara, 135
Schumann, Robert, 135
Science
  magazines, 514
  reference works, 314
Scott, Sir Walter, 218
Scotus, John Duns, 268
Scrabble (game), 682
  words, 345
Scribain, Aleksandr, 138
Sculpture *see* Art; specific sculptors
Seabury, Samuel, 235
Seamaphore code, 47
Search and seizure, 430
Search warrant, 430
SEC *see* Securities and Exchange
    Commission
Second (musical interval), 153
Secondary colors, 179
Securities and Exchange Commission, 450
Security agreement, 415–417
Segal, George, 168
Selene, 249
Self-defense, 430
Self-employed, 842
Self-incrimination, 430
Sembene, Ousmane, 221
Semicolon, 362
Semitone, 153
Senators, writing to, 522–523
Seneca, 189, 269
Senegal
  dialing code, 897
  statistics, 866
  visa requirements, 548
Senghor, Léopold, 221
Senior citizens *see* Aging; Retirement
Sensationalism, 280

Sense data, 280
Sentences, 358
Septet, 153
Sequence (musical), 153
Sequester, 430
Serenade, 153
Serial processing, 101
Sessions, Roger, 129
Seurat, Georges, 173
Seventh (musical interval), 153
Seventh-Day Adventist Church, 236
Seven Wonders of the World, 898
Sexton, Anne, 212
Seychelles
  statistics, 866
  visa requirements, 548
Shadwell, Thomas, 225
Shahn, Ben, 168
Shakespeare, William, 185–186
Shared-appreciation mortgage, 445
Shavuot, 242
Shaw, George Bernard, 186
Shawn, Ted, 158
Sheeler, Charles, 168
Shellac, stain removal, 578
Shelley, Mary, 218
Shelley, Percy Bysshe, 218
Shellfish, cooking of, 587–588
Shepard, Sam, 184
Sheridan, Richard Brinsley, 186
Sherman, James S., 824
Sherwood, Robert, 184
Shinto, 239
  symbols, 43
Ships
  bell time signals, 52
  tips for disabled, 560
Shock
  animal, 64
  first aid for, 748–749
Shoe polish, stain removal, 578
Short story, 223
Shostakovich, Dmitri, 138
Show cause order, 430
Showers, bridal, 372–373
Shrove Tuesday, 241
Si (music), 153
Sibelius, Jean, 140
Sidereal time, 2, 91
Siding, standard sizes, 610
Sierra Leone
  statistics, 867
  visa requirements, 548
Signature (musical), 153
Sign language (manual alphabet), 48
Silurian era, 85
Silver nitrate, stain removal, 578
Simile, 223
Singapore
  dialing code, 897
  statistics, 867
  visa requirements, 549
Singer, Isaac Bashevis, 212
Siqueiros, David Alfaro, 176
Sirens (mythology), 249
Sixth (musical interval), 153
Skeletal system, 689

Skepticism, 280
Skin, animal disorders, 64
Skip (engineering), 96
Slander *see* Defamation
Slovakia
 statistics, 867
 visa requirements, 549
Slovenia, statistics, 867
Slur (music), 153
Smetana, Bedřich, 140
Smirke, Sir Robert, 193
Smith, Adam, 268
Smith, Bessie, 142
Smith, David, 168
Smith, Joseph, 237
Smyth, John, 234
Snake bites, 753–754
Soane, Sir John, 193
Soap suds, as home remedy, 702
Soccer, 668–669, 686
Social contract, 280
Social sciences, reference works, 314
Social Security benefits, 448, 840
Society of the Rose and Cross, 239
Sociology, reference works, 314
Socrates, 268, 269
Soda *see* Soft drinks
Sodium benzoate, 598
Sodium bisulfite, 599
Sodium carboxymethyl-cellulose, 598
Sodium caseinate, 594
Sodium chloride *see* Salt
Sodium citrate, 595
Sodium nitrate, 598
Sodium nitrite, 598
Soft drinks
 nutritive value, 714
 stain removal, 579
Software, 101
Sol (music), 153
Solar system, diagram of, 87
Soliloquy, 223
Solipsism, 280
Solitaire (card game), 685
Solo (music), 153
Solomon Islands
 statistics, 867
 visa requirements, 549
Solstice, 9
Solute, 94
Solvent, 94
Solzhenitsyn, Aleksandr, 218
Somalia
 statistics, 867
 visa requirements, 549
Sonata, 153
Sonatina, 153
Sonnet, 223
Sophists, 280
Sophocles, 188
Soprano, 153
Sorbic acid, 598
Sorbitan monostearate, 598
Sorbitol, 599
Sostenuto, 153
Sotto voce, 153
Soups, nutritive value, 728

South Africa
 dialing code, 897
 statistics, 867
 visa requirements, 549
South Carolina
 Better Business Bureaus, 467
 consumer protection offices, 489
 crime rate, 846
 library, 291
 name origin, 794
 newspapers, 518
 poison control center, 761
 social service offices, 459
 vital statistics, 770, 778, 789, 791
 weather, 825, 826, 828
 wildlife refuges, 640
 zoo, 73
South Dakota
 consumer protection office, 489
 crime rate, 846
 name origin, 794
 newspaper, 518
 poison control center, 762
 social services offices, 460, 496
 vital statistics, 770, 778, 789, 791
 weather, 825, 826, 828
 wildlife refuges, 640
 zoo, 73
Southey, Robert, 225
Soyinka, Wole, 221
Spain
 dialing code, 897
 statistics, 867
 visa requirements, 549
Spandrel, 199
Spanish language, 339
Speech, parts of, 357
Spelling
 commonly misspelled words, 338–339
 guidelines, 364
Spenser, Edmund, 218
Spices, 591–592
Spinoza, Benedict, 268
Spire, 199
Spiritism, 280
Spiritualism, 280
Spondee, 223
Spoonerism, 223
Sports
 magazines, 514
 Olympic Games, 675–677
 organizations and halls of fame, 521–522
 reference works, 313
 see also specific sports
Spotting (dance), 164
Sprains, animal, 64–65
Square dance, 165
Square measure, 21
Sri Lanka
 dialing code, 897
 statistics, 867
 visa requirements, 549
Staccato, 153
Staff (musical), 153
Stain removal
 greasy stains, 568

 nongreasy stains, 568–569
 specific stains, 569–580
Stamen, 93
Standard Oil Co. of New Jersey Et Al. v. U.S., 431
Stanley Cup (hockey), 667
Starch, 599, 702
Stars
 brightest, 89
 see also specific types, e.g., White star
State of nature, 280
States
 admission of 13 original, 794
 consumer protection offices, 469–493
 crime rates, 845–846
 flowers, birds, mottos, nicknames, 790–792
 government, 788–789
 name origins, 792–794
 population, 770
 secession and readmission, 794
 US Postal Service abbreviations, 328–329
 zip codes, 504–510
 see also specific states
Statistics, reference works, 315
Statute of limitations, 421, 430
Statutory rape, 430
Stay (court order), 430
Stein, Gertrude, 213
Steinbeck, John, 213
Stella, Frank, 168
Stenciling, 180
Stendahl, 219
Stevenson, Adlai E., 824
Stevenson, Robert Louis, 219
Still life, 180
Stimulus (biological), 93
Stock, 449
 definition of, 450
 funds, 447
 split, 450
Stoicism, 280
Stop and frisk, 430
Stoppard, Tom, 186
Storage capacity (computer), 101
Stowe, Harriet Beecher, 213
Strand, Mark, 226
Stratocumulus cloud, 643
Stratus cloud, 643
Strauss, Richard, 135
Strauss family (composers), 131
Stravinsky, Igor, 138
Streaming mode, 101
Stretto, 153
Strickland, William, 192
Strindberg, Johan Auguste, 190
Stroke, signs of, 763
Style (literary), 223
Styron, William, 213
Subdominant (music), 153
Subito, 154
Subject (music), 154
Subject (part of speech), 358
Subjectivism, 280
Submediant, 154
Subplot, 223

Subpoena, 430
Substance, 280
Subtonic, 154
Sudan
  statistics, 867
  visa requirements, 549
Suffixes
  Greek, 352–353
  Latin, 354
Sugar (sucrose), 599
Suite (musical), 154
Sukkoth, 242
Sulfur dioxide, 599
Sullivan, Louis Henry, 192
Sullivan, Sir Arthur, 132
Sully, Thomas, 168
Summary judgment, 430
Summons, 430
Sundial, 4
Super Bowl (football), 664
Supernaturalism, 280
Supernova, 2, 91
Supertonic, 154
Suprematism, 183
Supreme Court
  decisions, 431–432
  justices, 395–396
Suriname
  dialing code, 897
  statistics, 867
  visa requirements, 549
Surrealism, 183
Survivor benefits, 841
Svalbard, statistics, 867
Swaziland
  statistics, 868
  visa requirements, 550
Sweden
  dialing code, 897
  statistics, 868
  visa requirements, 550
Sweeteners
  artificial, 593, 598
  weights and measures, 582
  see also Sugar
Swift, Jonathan, 219
Swinburne, Algernon, 219
Switzerland
  dialing code, 897
  statistics, 868
  visa requirements, 550
Syllogism, 280
Symbiosis, 93
Symbol
  defined, 223
  travel, 46–47
  weather, 38–39
  see also specific fields, e.g., Astronomy
Symbolism (painting movement), 183
Symphonic poem, 154
Symphony, 154
Syncopation, 154
Synge, John Millington, 188
Synthetic statement, 281
Syria
  statistics, 868
  visa requirements, 550

Systematics see Taxonomy

Tableware, 382–383
Tabula rasa, 281
Tadzhikistan see Tajikistan
Taft, William H., 820
Taglioni, Marie, 161
Tagore, Rabindranath, 221
Taiwan
  dialing code, 897
  statistics, 868
  visa requirements, 550
Tajikistan
  statistics, 868
  visa requirements, 550
Tallchief, Maria, 158
Tallis, Thomas, 132
Talmud, 233, 247
Tamayo, Rufino, 176
Tango, 165
Tanizaki Jun'ichiro, 221
Tanzania
  statistics, 868
  visa requirements, 550
Taoism, 239
  symbols, 43
Tao-te-ching, 239, 247
Tartini, Giuseppe, 137
Tate, Nahum, 225
Tatlin, Vladimir, 178
Tatum, Art, 142
Tautology, 281
Taxonomy, 55
Tax shelter, 450
Taylor, Paul, 158
Taylor, Richard E., 123
Taylor, Zachary, 819
Tchaikovsky, Peter Ilyich, 138
Tea, 594
  as home remedy, 702
  stain removal, 572
Technology
  reference works, 314
  time line, 105–125
Teeth, animal disorders, 62
Teleological ethics, 281
Telephone dialing codes, international, 896–897
Television networks, 520–521
Tempera, 180
Temperature, 26–28
  cooking, 584–590
  see also Weather
Tempo, 154
Ten Commandments, 259
Tender offer, 450
Tennessee
  Better Business Bureaus, 467
  consumer protection office, 490
  crime rate, 846
  name origin, 794
  newspapers, 518
  poison control center, 762
  social service offices, 460
  vital statistics, 770, 778, 789, 791
  weather, 825, 826, 828
  wildlife refuges, 641

  zoos, 73
Tennis, 669–672, 687
Tennyson, Alfred Lord, 219, 225
Tenor, 154
Tense (verb), 359
Terminal (computer), 101
Ternary form, 154
Terrestrial, 93
Territories (US), 789, 792
Testament, 430
Texas
  Better Business Bureaus, 467–468
  consumer protection office, 490
  crime rate, 846
  libraries, 291
  museums, 300
  name origin, 794
  newspapers, 518
  poison control center, 762
  social services offices, 460, 496
  vital statistics, 770, 778, 789, 792
  weather, 825, 826, 828
  wildlife refuges, 641
  zoos, 74
Texture (art), 180
Texture (music), 154
Thackeray, William Makepeace, 219
Thailand
  dialing code, 897
  statistics, 868
  visa requirements, 550
Thales of Miletus, 269
Thanatos, 249
Tharp, Twyla, 158
Theater see Drama
Theme, 223
Theme and variation, 154
Theme parks, 559
Theodolite, 96
Thiamine, 732–733
Thickening agents, 593
Third (musical interval), 154
Thomas, Dylan, 219
Thomism, 281
Thomson, Virgil, 130
Thoreau, Henry David, 213
Ti (music), 154
Time, 3–14
  Daylight Saving, 7–8
  divisions of, 9–9
  glossary of periods of, 10
  international adjustments, 8
  International Date Line, 8
  ship's bell signals, 52
  zones, 5–7
  see also Calendars; Clocks
Time (music), 154
Time sharing, 101
Time signature, 154
Tintoretto (Jacopo Robusti), 175
Tipping, 452–453
Tissue (body), 93
Titans (mythology), 249
Titian (Tiziano Vecellio), 176
Title (real estate), 451
Titles
  abbreviations after names, 392

Titles (*continued*)
   forms of address, 387–391
Toccata, 154
Tocqueville, Alexis de, 219
Togo
   statistics, 868
   visa requirements, 550
Tokelau, statistics, 868
Tolstoy, Leo, 219
Tompkins, Daniel D., 823
Tonal center, 154
Tone (art), 180
Tonga
   statistics, 868
   visa requirements, 550
Tonic (music), 154
Torah, 233
Tort, 430
Toulouse–Lautrec, Henri de, 173
Tour en l'air, 165
Tourism *see* Travel
Tourneur, Cyril, 186
Townsmap symbols, 37
Tracery, 199
Track (computer), 101
Trains *see* Railroads
Transcendentalism, 281
Transept, 199
Transmigration of souls, 281
Transposition (music), 154
Travel
   best vacation bets, 558
   checklist, 525
   customs information, 553
   first-aid kit, 561
   government tourist information centers, 556–558
   guides, 309
   magazines, 514
   with pets, 560–561
   signs and symbols, 46–47
   state tourism offices, 553–556
   theme parks, 559
   tips for disabled, 559–560
   visa requirements, 532–553
   see also Airlines; Hotels and motels; Rental cars
Treasury bill, 447, 450
Treasury bond, 450
Treble clef, 154
Tremolo, 154
Triad (music), 154
Triangles, 80
Triassic period, 84
Trinidad and Tobago
   statistics, 868
   visa requirements, 550–551
Trio (music), 155
Triple Crown, 673
Triplet (music), 155
Triple time, 155
Trochee, 223
Trollope, Anthony, 219
Trompe l'oeil, 180
Tropism, 93
Troy weights, 22
Truman, Harry S, 821, 824

Ts'ao Hsueh-ch'in, 221
Tudor, Antony, 159
Tudor architecture, 199
Tunisia
   dialing code, 897
   statistics, 868
   visa requirements, 551
Turgenev, Ivan, 219
Turkey
   dialing code, 897
   statistics, 869
   visa requirements, 551
Turkmenistan
   statistics, 869
   visa requirements, 551
Turks and Caicos Islands, statistics, 869
Turn (music), 155
Turner, Joseph, 169
Turret, 199
Tuscan Order, 199
Tutti (music), 155
Tuvalu
   statistics, 869
   visa requirements, 551
Twain, Mark, 213
Twelve-tone music, 155
Tyche, 249
Tyler, Anne, 213
Tyler, John, 819, 823

Uccello, Paolo, 176
Uganda
   statistics, 869
   visa requirements, 551
Ukraine
   statistics, 869
   visa requirements, 551
Ulanova, Galina, 161
Unamuno, Miguel de, 269
Undset, Sigrid, 219
Unison (music), 155
Unitarian Universalist Association, 238
United Arab Emirates
   dialing code, 897
   statistics, 869
   visa requirements, 551
United Church of Christ, 236
United Kingdom
   dialing code, 897
   nobility, 391, 899
   statistics, 869
   visa requirements, 551
United Nations, 891–892
United States
   Constitution, 799–814
   crime rates, 844–848
   Declaration of Independence, 795–798
   economic statistics, 777–781
   Emancipation Proclamation, 814–815
   flag, 817–819
   immigration statistics, 771–776
   important dates and events, 829–839
   map of, 767
   Monroe Doctrine, 816
   Pledge of Allegiance, 816
   population, 768–770
   presidents, 819–821

   statistics, 869
   vice presidents, 823–824
   see also Government; States; specific states
Universal antidote, 702
Universals (philosophy), 281
University of California v. Bakke, 432
Upanishads, 232, 247
Updike, John, 213
Uranus (Greek god), 249
Uranus (planet), 87–89
Urban areas *see* Cities
Urine, stain removal, 579
Uruguay
   dialing code, 897
   statistics, 869
   visa requirements, 551
U.S. v. E.C. Knight Co., 431
Utah
   Better Business Bureau, 468
   consumer protection office, 490–491
   crime rate, 846
   library, 291
   name origin, 794
   newspapers, 518–519
   poison control center, 762
   social service offices, 460
   vital statistics, 770, 778, 789, 792
   weather, 825, 827, 828
   wildlife refuges, 641
   zoo, 74
Utilitarianism, 278, 281
Utopianism, 281
Uzbekistan
   statistics, 869
   visa requirements, 551

Vacations *see* Travel
Vaccines, 736
Vacuole, 93
Valence, 94
Valéry, Paul, 219
Valois, Dame Ninette de, 159
Values (painting), 180
Vanbrugh, Sir John, 193
Van Buren, Martin, 819, 823
Van der Weyden, Rogier, 170
Van Duyn, Mona, 226
Van Dyck, Sir Anthony, 170
Van Eyck, Jan, 170
Van Gogh, Vincent, 169–170
Vanillin, 599
Vanuatu
   statistics, 869
   visa requirements, 551
Varèse, Edgar, 130
Vargas Llosa, Mario, 221
Variation (dance), 165
Variation (music), 155
Varnish, stain removal, 576–577
Vatican City
   dialing code, 897
   statistics, 869
   visa requirements, 540
Vaughan, Sarah, 143
Vaughan Williams, Ralph, 132
Vault (architecture), 199, 200

Index 929

Veda, 232, 247
Vega Carpio, Lope de, 189
Vegetables
  cooking times, 588
  garden plants, 618
  weights and measures, 582
Velázquez, Diego, 177
Velocity, 81, 95
Venezuela
  dialing code, 897
  statistics, 870
  visa requirements, 551–552
Venturi, Robert, 192
Venus (planet), 87–89
Verb, 357, 358–359
Verdi, Giuseppe, 137
Verdict, 430
Vermeer, Jan, 170
Vermont
  consumer protection offices, 491
  crime rate, 845
  name origin, 794
  newspaper, 519
  poison control center, 762
  social services offices, 460, 496
  vital statistics, 770, 778, 789, 792
  weather, 825, 827, 828
  wildlife refuge, 641
Veronese, Paolo, 176
Verrocchio, Andrea del, 176
Verse, 223
Vessels (anatomical), 692
Vestris, Auguste, 159
Vestris, Gaetano, 159
Vice presidents (US), 823–824
Vienna Circle, 281
Vietnam
  statistics, 870
  visa requirements, 552
Villa-Lobos, Heitor, 140
Villella, Edward, 158
Vinegar, 702
Vines, 619
Virgil, 219
Virginia
  Better Business Bureaus, 468
  consumer protection offices, 491
  crime rate, 846
  library, 291
  museums, 300–301
  name origin, 794
  newspapers, 519
  poison control centers, 762
  social services offices, 460, 496
  vital statistics, 770, 778, 789, 792
  weather, 825, 827, 828
  wildlife refuges, 641–642
  zoo, 74
Virgin Islands
  consumer protection office, 493
  social service offices, 460
  statistics, 792, 855
  visa requirements, 552
Visa requirements, 532–553
  see also specific countries
Vitalism, 281
Vitamin A, 732

Vitamin B$_1$ *see* Thiamine
Vitamin B$_2$ *see* Riboflavin
Vitamin B$_6$, 735
Vitamin B$_{12}$, 733
Vitamin C, 593, 734
Vitamin D, 734
Vitamin E, 593, 735
Vitamin/food chart, 732–735
Vivace, 155
Vivaldi, Antonio, 137
Voice, 155
Voir dire, 430
Volleyball, 672–673
Volt, 81
Voltaire, 219, 269
Volume, 21–22, 23, 24, 79–80
Volute, 199
Vonnegut, Kurt, 213
Vuillard, Edouard, 173

Wagner, Otto, 196
Wagner, Richard, 135
Waiver, 430
Wakes, 383
Walker, Alice, 213
Wallace, Henry A., 824
Waller, Thomas (Fats), 143
Wallis and Futuna, statistics, 870
Walls, standard sizes, 608
Walter, Thomas Ustick, 192
Waltz, 155, 165
Warhol, Andy, 168
Warrant, 430
Warren, Robert Penn, 213, 226
Warton, Thomas, 225
Wash (painting), 180
Washing *see* Laundry
Washington
  Better Business Bureaus, 468
  consumer protection offices, 492
  crime rate, 846
  library, 292
  name origin, 794
  newspapers, 519
  poison control center, 762
  social services offices, 460, 496
  vital statistics, 770, 779, 789, 792
  weather, 825, 827, 828
  wildlife refuges, 642
  zoos, 74
Washington, George, 819
Washington (DC) *see* District of Columbia
Watercolor, 180
Watt, 81
Watteau, Jean-Antoine, 173
Wave equation, 81
Weather
  average temperatures, North America, 527–528
  average temperatures, worldwide, 528–529
  Beaufort wind force scale, 643–645
  charts for US cities and states, 824–828
  fronts, 39
  normal daily mean temperature for US cities, 826–827

  sunshine, wind speed, and humidity for US cities, 827–828
  symbols, 38–39
  see also specific states
Weber, Carl Maria von, 135
Webern, Anton von, 131
Webster, John, 186
Webster, Noah, 213
Webster v. Reproductive Health Services, 432
Weddings
  bachelor dinner, 373
  ceremony, 373–374
  division of expenses, 375
  gifts and thank-yous, 374–375
  invitations and announcements, 371–372, 380
  reception, 374
  showers, 372–373
Weidman, Charles, 158
Weight
  charts, 693–695
  formula, 81
  mass/weight relationship, 81
  physical definition, 95
Weights, 22–26
  avoirdupois, 22
  food, 581–582
  glossary of special, 25–26
  historic, 29
  troy and apothecaries', 22
Welty, Eudora, 213
Wesley, John, 235
West, Benjamin, 168
West Bank (Jordan River), 870
Western Sahara, statistics, 870
Western Samoa
  statistics, 870
  visa requirements, 552
West Indies, visa requirements, 552
West Virginia
  consumer protection offices, 492
  crime rate, 846
  name origin, 794
  newspapers, 519
  poison control center, 762
  social services offices, 460, 496
  vital statistics, 770, 779, 789, 792
  weather, 827, 828
Westwork, 199
Whales, 56
Wharton, Edith, 213
Wheeler, William A., 823
Whistler, James Abbott McNeill, 168
White, E.B., 213
White, Stanford, 192
Whitehead, Alfred North, 269, 278
Whitehead, William, 225
White star, 2, 91
Whitman, Walt, 213
Whole note, 155
Whole tone, 155
Wieniawski, Henri, 140
Wigman, Mary, 161
Wilbur, Richard, 226
Wilde, Oscar, 186, 219
Wilder, Thornton, 184

Wildlife refuges, 629–642
Will, 430
William of Ockham, 270
Williams, Mary Lou, 143
Williams, Tennessee, 184
Will to believe, 281
Will to power, 281
Wilson, Edmund, 213
Wilson, Henry, 823
Wilson, Woodrow, 820
Wimbledon (tennis), 671–672
Winchester disk drive, 101
Windows, standard sizes, 610
Wind speed symbols, 39
Wine
   nutritive value, 712–714
   service, 606
Wisconsin
   Better Business Bureaus, 468
   consumer protection offices, 492–493
   crime rate, 845
   libraries, 292
   museums, 301
   name origin, 794
   newspapers, 519
   poison control center, 762
   social services offices, 460, 496
   vital statistics, 770, 779, 789, 792
   weather, 825, 827, 828
   wildlife refuges, 642
   zoos, 74
Witness, 430
Wittgenstein, Ludwig, 270, 275
Wolfe, Thomas, 213
Wolfe, Tom, 213
Women, magazines for, 514–515
Wood, Grant, 168
Woodcut, 180

Woolf, Virginia, 219
Word (computer), 102
Wordsworth, William, 219, 225
Work (physics), 81, 85
World Cup (soccer), 668–669
World history *see* History
World Series (baseball), 655–657
Worms, 59–60
Wouk, Herman, 213
Wounds, animal, 65
Wraparound mortgage, 445
Wren, Sir Christopher, 193
Wright, Frank Lloyd, 192
Wright, Richard, 213
Writ, 430
Write (computer), 102
Write–protected disk, 102
Wrongful death, 430
Wyeth, Andrew, 168
Wyoming
   consumer protection office, 493
   crime rate, 846
   name origin, 794
   newspapers, 519
   poison control center, 762
   social services offices, 460, 496
   vital statistics, 770, 779, 789, 792
   weather, 825, 827, 828
   wildlife refuges, 642

X-Y digitizer, 102

Yeats, William Butler, 219
Yellow/brown stains, 580
Yemen
   dialing code, 897
   statistics, 870
   visa requirements, 552

Yield (financial), 450
Yom Kippur, 242
Young, Lester (Prez), 143
Young Hegelians, 281
Youskevitch, Igor, 161
Youthful offender, 430
Yugoslavia
   dialing code, 897
   statistics, 870
   visa requirements, 552

Zaire
   statistics, 870
   visa requirements, 552
Zambia
   statistics, 870
   visa requirements, 553
Zeno of Elea, 270
Zeno the Stoic, 270
Zero-coupon bonds, 450
Zeus, 249, 898
Ziggurat, 199
Zimbabwe
   statistics, 870
   visa requirements, 553
Zip codes, 504–510
Zodiac
   constellations, 650
   signs, 43–45
Zola, Emile, 219
Zoos
   Canadian, 75
   US, 68–74
Zurbarán, Francisco de, 177
Zweig, George, 123
Zwilich, Ellen Taaffe, 130
Zygote, 93